The
LINGUISTICS ENCYCLOPEDIA

The
LINGUISTICS
ENCYCLOPEDIA

Edited by
Kirsten Malmkjær

North American Consultant Editor
James M. Anderson

London and New York

First published 1991
by Routledge
11 New Fetter Lane, London EC4P 4EE

Simultaneously published in the USA and Canada
by Routledge
29 West 35th Street, New York, NY 10001

First published in paperback in 1995

Reprinted 1996

Routledge is an International Thomson Publishing company

Selection and editorial matter
© 1991 Kirsten Malmkjær
Individual entries © the authors

Printed and bound in Great Britain by Redwood Books,
Trowbridge, Wiltshire

British Library Cataloguing in Publication Data
A catalogue record for this book is available from the
British Library

Library of Congress Cataloguing in Publication Data
A catalogue record for this book is available from the
Library of Congress

ISBN 0–415–02942–2 (hbk)
ISBN 0–415–12566–9 (pbk)

For John Sinclair

Contents

List of subjects

Bold typeface indicates an entry. Other subjects listed are covered in some detail within entries. For key words not included here, please refer to the Index.

Preface

You are reading something, or listening to a lecture, or taking part in a conversation about language. You notice an unfamiliar term or realize that you don't know enough about what is being said to understand. At this point, you should seek out this encyclopedia. Strategies for the use of encyclopedias differ, but this one is designed to allow you to proceed in one of three ways:

1 You can consult the Index where you will find the term or subject in question appearing in its alphabetically determined place, with a page reference, or several, which will tell you where in the main body of the work it is defined, described and/or discussed.
2 If you are looking for a major field of linguistic study, you can consult the Subject List where the entries and other major subjects are listed in alphabetical order.
3 You can simply dive into the body of the work.

The entries are designed to be informative and easy of access. They do not provide as much information as you will find in a full book on any given topic, but they contain sufficient information to enable you to understand the basics, and to decide whether you need more. They end by listing some suggestions for further reading. The entries draw on many more works than those listed as further reading. These are mentioned in the text by author and year of publication, and a full reference can be found in the Bibliography at the end of the book.

Since linguistics does not come neatly divided into completely autonomous areas, almost all the entries contain cross-references to other entries. In spite of their interconnectedness, entries are kept separate for reasons of speed of reference and because it is usually possible to draw a line between the areas with which they deal. There is a division of labour within linguistics as within all other disciplines, and within its subdisciplines. In some cases, this division has been so prolific that it is hardly possible to cover all the sub-areas in one entry. For example, sociolinguistics is now such a wide field that I thought it best to treat its sub-areas separately. Similarly, there are so many varieties of syntactic theory, that a single entry on 'grammar' or 'syntax' seemed more likely to confuse than enlighten. Other areas, such as historical linguistics and psycholinguistics still seem sufficiently unified to be manageable as one.

This volume demonstrates the many-faceted face of linguistics. Its history begins longer ago than we know, along with its very subject matter, and will continue for as long as that subject matter remains. Having language is probably concomitant with wondering about language, and so, if there is one thing that sets linguistics apart from other disciplines, it is the fact that its subject matter must be used in the description. There is no metalanguage for language that is not translatable into language, and a metalanguage is, in any case, also a language.

According to some, language is literally all that there is. According to others, it reflects, more or less adequately, what there is. What seems certain is that we use it prolifically in creating and changing our momentary values and that in seeking to understand language, we are seeking to understand the cornerstone of the human mentality.

Kirsten Malmkjær
Cambridge, 1991

Key to contributors

T.A.	Tsutomu Akamatsu	R.F.I.	Robert F. Ilson
J.M.A.	James M. Anderson	C.-W.K	Chin-W. Kim
J.B.	Jacques Bourquin	G.N.L.	Geoffrey N. Leech
D.C.B.	David C. Brazil	D.G.L.	David G. Lockwood
E.K.B.	E. Keith Brown	M.J.McC.	Michael J. McCarthy
T.D.-E.	Tony Dudley-Evans	M.M.	Molly Mack
S.E.	Susan Edwards	M.K.C.MacM	Michael K.C. MacMahon
E.F.-J.	Eli Fischer-Jørgensen	K.M.	Kirsten Malmkjær
W.A.F.	William A. Foley	M.Nk	Mark Newbrook
R.F.	Roger Fowler	F.J.N.	Frederick J. Newmeyer
A.F.	Anthony Fox	M.Nn	Margaret Newton
M.A.G.	Michael A. Garman	A.M.R.	Allan M. Ramsay
C.H.	Christopher Hookway	W.S-Y.W.	William S-Y. Wang

The contributors

Tsutomu Akamatsu studied Modern Languages at Tokyo University of Foreign Studies, Phonetics at the University of London, and General Linguistics at the University of Paris. He earned his Ph.D. from the University of Leeds, where he is a lecturer in the Department of Linguistics and Phonetics. He is a member of the Société Internationale de Linguistique Fonctionnelle (SILF). He has published around fifty articles in linguistics journals, and his book *The Theory of Neutralization and the Archiphoneme in Functional Phonology* was published in 1988.

James M. Anderson holds a first degree in Spanish and received his Ph.D. in Linguistics from the University of Washington, Seattle, USA, in 1963. He taught Linguistics at the University of Calgary, Alberta, Canada, from 1968 and became a tenured professor there in 1970. He was appointed Professor Emeritus on his retirement in 1988. In addition to some forty articles and papers, his publications include *Structural Aspect of Language Change* (1973) and *Ancient Languages of the Hispanic Peninsula* (1988). He co-edited *Readings in Romance Linguistics* (1972). He was President of the Rocky Mountain Linguistics Society in 1982.

Jacques Bourquin, Docteur ès sciences, Docteur ès lettres, is Professor of French Linguistics at the University of Franche-Comté, Besançon, France. He has written a thesis entitled 'La dérivation suffixale (théorie et enseignement) au XIXe siècle', and several articles on the problem of reading, and on the epistemology of linguistics.

David C. Brazil was senior lecturer in English at the College of Further Education, Worcester, UK, from 1966 till 1975, when he became a Senior Research Fellow on the SSRC project 'Discourse Intonation' at the University of Birmingham, UK, led by Malcolm Coulthard. He received his Ph.D. from the University of Birmingham in 1978 and lectured there until his early retirement in 1986. Since then, he has been Visiting Professor at universities in Brazil and Japan. His main publications are *Discourse Intonation and Language Teaching* (1981), and *The Communicative Value of Intonation in English* (1985).

E. Keith Brown received his Ph.D. from the University of Edinburgh, UK, in 1972. He has lectured in Ghana and Edinburgh and has been Reader in Linguistics at the University of Essex, UK, since 1984. He has held visiting lectureships in Toronto, Stirling, and Cambridge, and his lecture tours have taken him to Germany, Poland, Bulgaria, Iran, and Japan. His major publications include (with J. E. Miller) *Syntax: A Linguistic Introduction to Sentence Structure* (1980) and *Syntax: Generative Grammar* (1982), and *Linguistics Today* (1984).

Tony Dudley-Evans is a lecturer in the English for Overseas Students Unit at the University of Birmingham, UK. He is co-editor of the *Nucleus* series and has co-authored a number of its volumes. *Writing Laboratory Reports* was published in 1985. He has written numerous articles on ESP-related themes; his current interests are Genre Analysis and its affiliation to the preparation of ESP materials, and Team Teaching.

Susan Edwards is a lecturer in the Department of Linguistic Science at the University of Reading and a qualified speech therapist.

Eli Fischer-Jørgensen was Professor of Phonetics at the University of Copenhagen from 1966 to 1981, and was appointed Professor Emeritus on her retirement. In addition to about seventy article publications on phonological problems, and several Danish language volumes, her publications include *Trends in Phonological Theory* (1975) and *25 Years' Phonological Comments* (1979). She was Chair of the Linguistics Circle of Copenhagen, 1968–72, and has served on the editorial boards of several journals devoted to Phonetics. In 1979 she presided over the ninth International Congress of the Phonetic Sciences, held in Copenhagen. She received honorary doctorates from the Universities of Åhus and Lund in 1978.

William A. Foley received his Ph.D. from the University of California, Berkeley. He taught for twelve years at the Australian National University, and now holds the Chair of Linguistics at the University of Sydney, Australia. He is especially interested in the languages of the islands of Melanesia, particularly the Papuan languages of New Guinea, about which he wrote a volume for the Cambridge University Press *Language Survey* series. His other interests include semantically and pragmatically based approaches to grammatical theory, and their application to the grammatical description of the languages of the Pacific.

Roger Fowler is Professor of English and Linguistics at the University of East Anglia, Norwich, UK. His numerous publications in the field of Critical Linguistics include *Literature as Social Discourse* (1981), *Linguistic Criticism* (1986) and, with R. Hodge, G. Kress and T. Trew, *Language and Control* (1979). Forthcoming books include *Language in the News*, a study of language and ideology in the British press.

Anthony Fox holds a Ph.D. from the University of Edinburgh. He is Senior Lecturer in the Department of Linguistics and Phonetics at the University of Leeds, UK. His research interests include Intonation and other suprasegmentals, Phonological Theory, and the linguistic study of German.

Michael A. Garman is a lecturer in the Department of Linguistic Science at the University of Reading, UK.

Christopher Hookway has been a Research Fellow of Peterhouse, Cambridge, UK. Since 1977 he has lectured in Philosophy at the University of Birmingham, UK. His publications include *Peirce*, (1985), and *Quine: Language, Experience and Reality*, (1988). He has edited *Minds, Machines and Evolution* (1984) and, with P. Pettit, *Action and Interpretation* (1978). His research interests are Epistemology, the Philosophy of Language, and American Philosophy.

Robert F. Ilson is an Honorary Research Fellow of University College London, UK, and Associate Director of the Survey of English Usage which is based there. He is Editor of the *International Journal of Lexicography* and the *Bulletin of the European Association for Lexicography*. He is Convenor of the Commission on Lexicography and Lexicology of the International Association for Applied Linguistics.

Chin-W. Kim received his Ph.D. in Linguistics from the University of California, Los Angeles, USA, in 1966. He is Professor of Linguistics, Speech and Hearing Sciences, and English as an International Language at the University of Illinois at Urbana-Champaign, USA. He contributed the entry 'Experimental Phonetics' in W.O. Dingwall (ed.) *Survey of Linguistic Science* (1978), and the entry 'Representation and derivation of tone' in D.L. Goyvaerts (ed.) *Phonology in the 80's* (1981). His fields of specialization are Phonetics, Phonology, and Korean Linguistics.

Geoffrey N. Leech is Professor of Linguistics and Modern English Language at the University of Lancaster, UK. He is co-author of *A Grammar of Contemporary English* and *A Comprehensive Grammar of the English Language*, both based on the Survey of English Usage based at University College London. He has also written books and articles in the areas of Stylistics, Semantics and Pragmatics, notably, *A Linguistic Guide to English Poetry* (1969), *Semantics: The Study of meaning* (2nd edn 1981), and *Principles of Pragmatics* (1983). In recent years, his research interests have focused on the computational analysis of English, using computer corpora: he began the LOB Corpus Project in 1970, and since 1983 has been co-director of UCREL.

David G. Lockwood received his Ph.D. from the University of Michigan (Ann Arbor), USA, in 1966. He has taught at Michigan State University since then, and has been a professor there since 1975. In addition to numerous articles, his publications include *Introduction to Stratificational Linguistics* (1972) and *Readings in Stratificational Linguistics* (1973), which he co-edited. His teaching specialities are Stratificational Grammar and Phonology, problem-oriented courses in Phonology, Morphology, Syntax and Historical Linguistics, Structure of Russian, and Comparative Slavic Linguistics.

Michael J. McCarthy is a lecturer in English Studies at the University of Nottingham, UK. He has published widely in the field of English Language Teaching, co-authoring *Vocabulary and Language Teaching* (1988). *Vocabulary* was published in 1990, and *Discourse Analysis for Language Teachers* is forthcoming. He holds a Ph.D. (Cantab.) in Spanish, and his current research interests are in ESP, Discourse Analysis, and Vocabulary.

Molly Mack received her Ph.D. in Linguistics from Brown University, USA. She is now an assistant professor in the Division of English as an International Language and in the Department of Linguistics at the University of Illinois at Urbana-Champaign, USA. Her research interests are in Speech Perception and Production, and the psycholinguistic and neurolinguistic aspects of Bilingualism. She also works as a consultant in Speech Research for the MIT Lincoln Laboratory, USA.

Michael K.C. MacMahon is a lecturer in the Department of English Language at the University of Glasgow, UK. He holds a Ph.D. on British neurolinguistics in the nineteenth century, and his publications have dealt with aspects of Phonetics, Dialectology and Neurolinguistics.

Kirsten Malmkjær was lecturer in Modern English Language and M.A. course tutor at the University of Birmingham, 1985–9, and is now a senior research associate in the Research Centre for English and Applied Linguistics, the University of Cambridge.

Mark Newbrook received his Ph.D. in Linguistics from the University of Reading, UK, in 1982. He has been lecturer in English Language at the National University of Singapore (1982–5), lecturer in Languages at the City Polytechnic of Hong Kong (1986–8), and lecturer in English at the Chinese University of Hong Kong from 1988. His leading publications include *Sociolinguistic Reflexes of Dialect Interference in West Wirral* (1986), *Aspects of the Syntax of Educated Singaporean English* (editor and main author) (1987), *Hong Kong English and Standard English: A Guide for Students and Teachers* (forthcoming).

Fredrick J. Newmeyer received a Ph.D. from the University of Illinois in 1969. He is a professor in the Department of Linguistics at the University of Washington, USA. He is Editor-in-Chief of *Linguistics: The Cambridge Survey*, and author of *English Aspectual Verbs* (1975), *Linguistic Theory in America* (1980), *Grammatical Theory: Its Limits and its Possibilities* (1983), and *Politics of Linguistics* (1986). His interests are Syntactic Theory and the History of Linguistics.

Margaret Newton holds the UK's first Ph.D. on Dyslexia. She is Director of the Aston House Consultancy and Dyslexia Trust in Worcester, UK, an independent charitable organization, which continues the clinical and research work in Dyslexia and the programme of dyslexia diagnosis, assessment and advice which Dr Newton and her colleagues began at the University of Aston in Birmingham, UK, in 1967. The team developed the diagnostic instruments known as the Aston Index and the Aston Portfolio of teaching techniques and prepared the Aston Videotapes on Dyslexia.

Allan M. Ramsay is a lecturer in Artificial Intelligence in the School of Cognitive Science at the University of Sussex, UK. He is co-author of *POP-11: A Practical Language for AI* (1985), *AI in Practice: Examples in POP-11* (1986), and *Formal Methods in AI* (forthcoming). His research interests include Syntactic Processing,

Formal Semantics, Applications of Logic and AI Planning Theory to Language.

William S.-Y. Wang received his Ph.D. from the University of Michigan, USA, in 1960. Since 1966 he has been professor of Linguistics at the University of California at Berkeley, USA, and Director of the Project on Linguistic Analysis. Since 1973, he has been Editor of the *Journal of Chinese Linguistics*.

Acknowledgements

The great majority of the work involved in editing this encyclopedia took place in the School of English at the University of Birmingham. My colleagues there were a constant source of inspiration, support and encouragement. My debt to them is implicit in a number of entries in this work, but I want to make explicit my gratitude to the following one-time or present members of the ELR team: Mona Baker, David Brazil, Deirdre Burton, Malcolm Coulthard, Flo Davies, Tony Dudley-Evans, Harold Fish, Ann and Martin Hewings, Michael Hoey, Diane Houghton, Tim Johns, Chris Kennedy, Philip King, Murray Knowles, Paul Lennon, Mike McCarthy, Charles Owen, and John Sinclair.

My present colleagues, Gillian Brown, Richard Rossner and John Williams, have been no less supportive, and have helped me to discover new perspectives on a number of topics. I am particularly grateful to John Williams for his advice on the entries on Psycholinguistics and Language Acquisition.

A number of students at Birmingham have been exposed in one way or another to versions or drafts of some of the entries. I should like to thank them all for their patience and reactions; in particular, I am grateful to Martha Shiro and Amy Tsui for their helpful comments.

It goes without saying that I am very grateful indeed to the contributors themselves, all of whom had busy schedules, but who were, in spite of this, always ready to read and re-read their entries during the editing stage. I should particularly like to thank Tsutomu Akamatsu, who worked tirelessly and with great kindness to help me from the planning stage and throughout the editing process. Tsutomu Akamatsu, James Anderson, David Crystal, Janet Dean Fodor, Michael Garman, Tim Johns, Chin-W. Kim, George Lakoff, Bertil Malmberg, Maggie-Jo St John, Bertil Sonesson, Peter Trudgill and George Yule provided valuable guidance in the choice of contributors.

I am grateful to Nigel Vincent, Geoffrey Horrocks and Dick Hudson for their comments on the entry on Lexical-Functional Grammar, to Bernard Comrie for advice on the entries on Language Typology and Language Universals, and to the North American Consultant Editor, James Anderson, and the two anonymous readers, for taking on the enormous task of reading and commenting on all the entries. I hope they will all find the end result improved. Of course, the faults which remain are my sole responsibility.

This encyclopedia was the brain child of Wendy Morris of Routledge. Without her encouragement and guidance, I could not have contemplated taking on such a major commitment. I am grateful to her, to Steve, Poul and Stuart, who also believed the book would see the light one day, and to Jonathan Price of Routledge for his help in the later stages of editing.

David, Tomas and Amy have lived with this project through all our life together, providing the most delightful distractions and keeping everything in perspective. I could not wish for a better context.

K.M.

PERMISSIONS

The three versions of the International Phonetic Alphabet (pp. 220–2) are reproduced by kind permission of the International Phonetic Association.

In the entry on Acoustic phonetics, Figures 9 and 14 (p. 6 and p. 9) are reprinted with permission of the publishers from *A Course in Phonetics*, 2nd edn, by Peter Ladefoged, © 1982 Harcourt Brace Jovanovich, Inc.

Figure 10 in ACOUSTIC PHONETICS (p. 7) is reprinted with permission of the Journal of the Acoustical Society of America. Tables 1 and 2 in DISCOURSE AND CONVERSATIONAL ANALYSIS, and the quotations on pp. 101–5 are reprinted from J.M. Sinclair and R.M. Coulthard (1975), *Towards an Analysis of Discourse: The English Used by Teachers and Pupils*, by permission of Oxford University Press.

Acoustic phonetics

Acoustic phonetics deals with the properties of sound as represented in variations of air pressure. A sound, whether its source is articulation of a word or an exploding cannon ball, disturbs the surrounding air molecules at equilibrium, much as a shove by a person in a crowded bus disturbs the standing passengers. The sensation of these air pressure variations as picked up by our hearing mechanisms and decoded in the brain constitutes what we call **sound** (see also AUDITORY PHONETICS). The question whether there was a sound when a tree fell in a jungle is therefore a moot one; there definitely were air-molecule variations generated by the fall of the tree, but unless there was an ear to register them, there was no sound.

The analogy between air molecules and bus passengers above is rather misleading, since the movements of the molecules are rapid and regular. Rapid in the sense that they **oscillate** at the rate of hundreds and thousands of times per second, and regular in the sense that the oscillation takes the form of a swing or a pendulum. That is, a disturbed air molecule oscillates much as a pushed pendulum swings back and forth.

Let us now compare air molecules to a pendulum. Due to gravity, a pushed pendulum will stop after travelling a certain distance, depending on the force of the push; will then begin to return to the original rest position, but instead of stopping

at this position, will pass it to the opposite direction due to inertia; will stop after travelling about the same distance as the initial displacement; again will try to return to the initial rest position; but will again pass this point to the other direction, etc., until the original energy completely dissipates and the pendulum comes to a full stop.

Imagine now that attached at the end of the pendulum is a pencil and that a strip of paper in contact with the pencil is being pulled at a uniform speed. One can imagine that the pendulum will draw a wavy line on the paper, a line that is very regular in its ups and downs. If we disregard for the moment the effect of gravity, each **cycle**, one complete back and forth movement of the pendulum, would be exactly the same as the next cycle. Now if we plot the position of the pendulum, the distance of displacement from the original rest position, against time, then we will have Figure 1, in which the y-ordinate represents the distance of displacement and the x-abscissa the time, both units representing arbitrary units. Since a wave form such as the one given in Figure 1 is generatable with the sine function in trigonometry, it is called a **sine wave** or a **sinusoidal wave**. Such a wave can tell us several things:

First, the shorter the time of duration of a cycle, the greater (the more frequent) the number

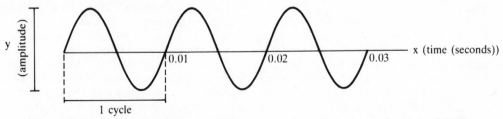

Figure 1 A sine wave whose cycle is one-hundredth of a second, thus having the frequency of 100 Hz

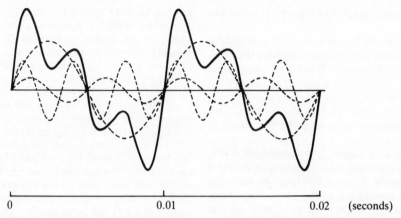

0   0.01   0.02   (seconds)

Figure 2 A complex wave formed with a combination of 100 Hz, 200 Hz, and 300 Hz component waves

of such cycles in a given unit of time. For example, a cycle having the duration of one hundredth of a second would have a frequency of 100 cycles per second (**cps**). This unit is now represented as **Hz** (named after a German physicist, Heinrich Hertz, 1857–94). A male speaking voice has on average 100–50 Hz, while a woman's voice is twice as high. The note A above the middle C is fixed at 440 Hz.

Secondly, since the y-axis represents the distance of displacement of a pendulum from the rest position, the higher the peak of the wave, the greater the displacement. This is called **amplitude**, and translates into the degree of loudness of a sound. The unit here is **dB** (decibel, in honour of Alexander Graham Bell, 1847–1922). A normal conversation has a value of of 50–60 dB, a whisper half this value, and rock music about twice the value (110–20 dB). However, since the dB scale is logarithmic, doubling a dB value represents sound intensity which is ten times greater.

In nature, sounds that generate the sinusoidal waves are not common. Well-designed tuning forks, whistles, sirens are some examples. Most sounds in nature have complex wave forms. This can be illustrated in the following way. Suppose that we add three waves together having the frequencies of 100 Hz, 200 Hz, and 300 Hz, with the amplitude of x, y, and z, respectively, as in

Figure 2. What would be the resulting wave form? If we liken the situation to three people pushing a pendulum in the same direction, the first person pushing it with the force z at every beat, the second person with the force y at every second beat, and the third person with the force x at every third beat, then the position of the pendulum at any given moment would be equal to the displacement which is the sum of the forces x, y, and z. This is also what happens when the simultaneous wave forms having different frequencies and amplitudes are added together. In Figure 2, the dark unbroken line is the resulting complex wave.

Again, there are a few things to be noted here. First, note that the recurrence of the complex wave is at the same frequency as the highest common factor of the component frequencies, i.e. 100 Hz. This is called **fundamental frequency**. Note secondly that the frequencies of the component waves are whole-number multiples of the fundamental frequency. They are called **harmonics** or **overtones**. An **octave** is a relation between two harmonics whose frequencies are either twice or one-half of the other.

There is another way to represent the frequency and amplitude of the component waves, more succinct and legible than Figure 2, namely by transposing them into a graph as in Figure 3. Since the component waves are represented in terms of lines, a graph like Figure 3 is called **line spectrum**.

Recall that the frequencies of the component waves in Figure 2 are all whole-number multiples of the lowest frequency. What if the component waves do not have such a property, that is, what if the frequencies are closer to one another, say, 90 Hz, 100 Hz, and 110 Hz? The complex wave that these component waves generate is shown in Figure 4.

Compared to Figure 2, the amplitude of the complex wave of Figure 4 decays rapidly. This is called **damping**. It turns out that the more the number of component waves whose frequencies are close to one another, the more rapid the rate of damping. Try now to represent such a wave in a line spectrum, a wave whose component waves have frequencies, say 91 Hz, 92 Hz, 93 Hz, etc. to 110 Hz. We can do this as in Figure 5.

What if we add more component waves between any two lines in Figure 5, say ten or twenty more? Try as we might by sharpening our pencils, it would be impossible to draw in all the components. It would be unnecessary also if we take the 'roof' formed by the lines as the envelope of the amplitude under which there is a component wave at that frequency with that amplitude, as in Figure 6. To contrast with the line spectrum in Figure 3, the spectrum in Figure 6b is called **envelope spectrum** or simply **spectrum**.

What is the significance of the difference in the two kinds of spectra, Figure 3 and Figure 6b? It turns out that, if we divide sound into two kinds, *melody* and *noise*, melody has the quality of the forms, i.e. it has regular, recurrent wave forms, while noise has the latter quality, i.e. irregular non-recurrent wave forms.

Before turning to speech acoustics, it is worth noting that every object, when struck, vibrates at a certain 'built-in' frequency. This frequency, called **natural resonance frequency**, is dependent

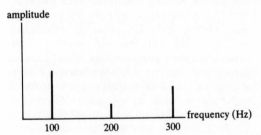

Figure 3 A line spectrum

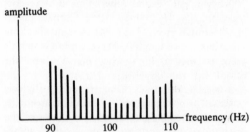

Figure 5 A line spectrum showing relative amplitudes and frequencies from 90, 91, 92 . . . to 110 Hz of the component waves

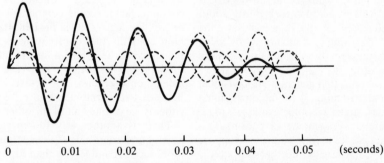

Figure 4 A 'decaying' complex wave formed with a combination of 90 Hz, 100 Hz, and 110 Hz component waves

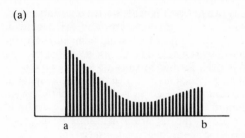

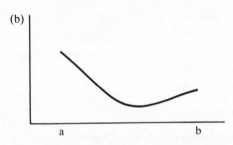

Figure 6 (a) A line spectrum with an infinite number of component waves whose frequencies range from a to b; (b) An envelope spectrum which is an equivalent of the line spectrum in Figure 6a

upon the object's size, density, material, etc. But in general, the larger the size, the lower the frequency (compare a tuba with a trumpet, a bass cello with a violin, or longer piano strings with shorter ones) and the more tense or compact the material, the higher the frequency (compare glass with carpet, and consider how one tunes a guitar or a violin).

ACOUSTICS OF SPEECH

VOWELS

A pair of vocal folds can be likened to a pair of hands or wood blocks clapping each other. As such, the sound it generates is, strictly speaking, a noise. This noise, however, is modified as it travels through the pharyngeal and oral (sometimes nasal) cavities, much as the sound generated by a vibrating reed in an oboe or a clarinet is modified. Thus what comes out of the mouth is not the same as the pure unmodified vocal tone. And to extend the analogy, just as the pitch of a

wind instrument is regulated by changing the effective length or size of the resonating tube with various stops, the quality of sounds passing through the supraglottal cavities is regulated by changing the cavity sizes with such 'stops' as the tongue, the velum, and the lips. It is immediately obvious that one cannot articulate the vowels [i], [ɑ], and [u] without varying the size of the oral cavity (see also ARTICULATORY PHONETICS). What does this mean acoustically?

For the sake of illustration, let us assume that a tube consisting of the joined oral and pharyngeal cavities is a resonating acoustic tube, much like an organ pipe. The most uniform 'pipe' or tube one can assume is the one formed when producing the neutral vowel [ə] (see Figure 7). Without going into much detail, the natural resonance frequency of such a tube can be calculated with the following formula:

$$f = (2n - 1)\ \frac{v}{4l}$$

Where f = frequency, v = velocity of sound, and l = length of the vocal tract

Since v is 340 m per second, and l is 17 cm in an average male, f is about 500 Hz when $n = 1$, 1,500 Hz when $n = 2$, 2,500 Hz when $n = 3$, etc. What

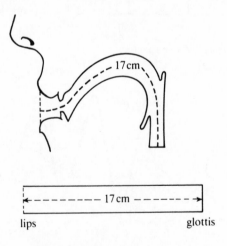

Figure 7 The vocal-tract shape and an idealized tube model of the tract for the most neutral vowel

this means is that, given a vocal tract which is about 17 cm long, forming the most neutral tract shape usually assumed for the schwa vowel [ə], the **white noise** (the vocal-fold excitation) at one end will be modified in such a way that there will be resonance peaks at every 1,000 Hz beginning at 500 Hz. These resonance peaks are called **formants**.

It is easy to imagine that a change in the size and shape of a resonating acoustic tube results in the change of resonance frequencies of the tube. For the purpose of speech acoustics, it is convenient to regard the vocal tract as consisting of two connected tubes, one front and the other back with the velic area as the joint. Viewed in

this way, vowel [i] has the narrow front (oral) tube and the wide back tube, while [ɑ] is its mirror image, i.e., [ɑ] has the wide front tube but the narrow back tube. On the other hand, [u] has the narrow area ('the bottle neck') in the middle (at the joint) and, with the lip rounding, at the very front as well. The vocal-tract shapes, the idealized tube shapes, and the resulting acoustic spectrum of these three vowels are as illustrated in Figure 8.

The formant frequencies of all other vowels would fall somewhere between or inside an approximate triangle formed by the three 'extreme' vowels. The frequencies of the first three formants of eight American English vowels

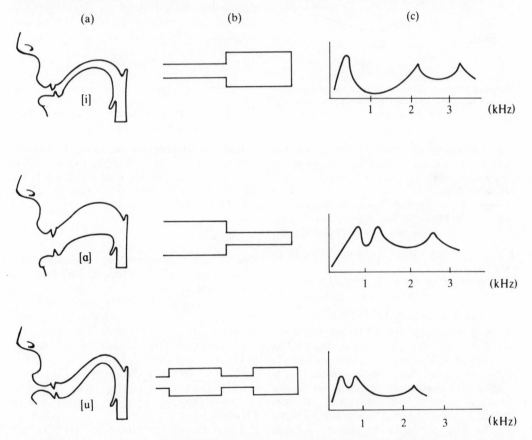

Figure 8 The vocal-tract shapes (a), their idealized tube shapes (b), and the spectra (c) of the three vowels [i], [ɑ], and [u]

Table 1 The frequencies of the first three formants in eight American English vowels

	[i]	[ɪ]	[ɛ]	[æ]	[a]	[ɔ]	[ʊ]	[u]
F1	280	400	550	690	710	590	450	310
F2	2250	1920	1770	1680	1100	880	1030	870
F3	2890	2560	2490	2490	2540	2540	2380	2250

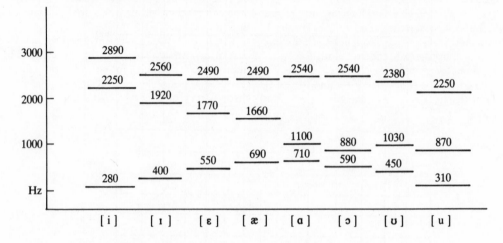

Figure 9 The frequencies of the first three formants in eight American English vowels

are given in Table 1:

Table 1 can be graphically represented as Figure 9 (adapted from Ladefoged, 1982, p. 176). A few things may be observed from this figure:

1 F1 rises progressively from [i] to [a], then drops to [u];
2 F2 decreases progressively from [i] to [u];
3 In general, F3 hovers around 2,500 Hz.

From this it is tempting to speculate that F1 is inversely correlated with the tongue height, or the size of the oral cavity, and that F2 is correlated with the tongue advancement, or the size of the pharyngeal cavity. While this is roughly true, Ladefoged feels that there is a better correlation between the degree of backness and the distance between the first two formants (i.e., F2–F1), since in this way, there is a better match between the traditional articulatory vowel chart and the formant chart with F1 plotted

against F2, as shown in Figure 10 (from Ladefoged, 1982, p. 179).

CONSONANTS

The acoustics of consonants is much more complicated than that of vowels, and here one can talk only in terms of generalities.

It is customary to divide consonants into **sonorants** (nasals, liquids, glides) and **obstruents** (plosives, fricatives, affricates). The former are characterized by vowel-like acoustic qualities by virtue of the fact that they have an unbroken and fairly unconstricted resonating tube. The vocal tract for nasals, for example, can be schematically represented as a reversed letter F shown in Figure 11.

The open nasal tract, functioning as a resonating acoustic tube, generates its own resonance frequencies, known as **nasal formants**, which

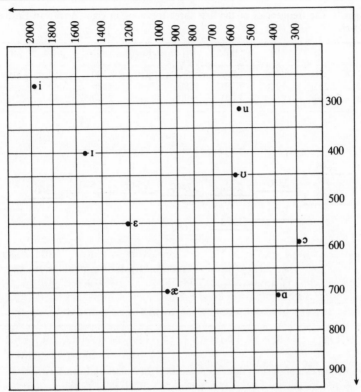

Figure 10 A formant chart showing the frequency of the first formant on the vertical axis plotted against the distance between the frequencies of the first and second formants on the horizontal axis for the eight American English vowels in Figure 9

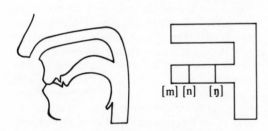

Figure 11 The vocal-tract shape and the idealized tube shape for nasal consonants [m], [n], and [ŋ]

are in general discontinuous with vowel formants. Different lengths of the middle tube, i.e. the oral tract, would be responsible for different nasals.

The acoustic structure of obstruents is radically different, for obstruents are characterized by either the complete obstruction of the airflow in the vocal tract or a narrow constriction impeding the airflow. The former creates a silence and the latter a turbulent airstream (a hissing noise). Silence means no sound. Then how is silence heard at all, and, furthermore, how are different silences, e.g. [p], [t], [k], distinguished from each other? The answer is that silence is heard and distinguished by its effect on the adjacent vowel, as illustrated in the following.

Assume a sequence [apa], and examine the behaviour of the lips. They are wide open for both [a]s, but completely closed for [p]. Though rapid, both the opening and closing of the lips is a

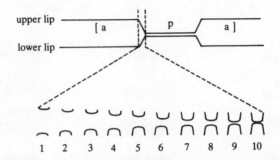

Figure 12 A schematic diagram of the closing of lips in [apa], its progression slowed down in ten steps

time-taking process, and if we slow it down, one can imagine the process shown in Figure 12.

Now, as we have seen, vowels have their own resonance frequencies, called formants. A closed tube, such as the one that a plosive assumes, can also be said to have its own resonance frequency, although it is inaudible because no energy escapes from the closed tube (for what it is worth,

it is $\frac{v}{2l}$). If we take the resonance frequency (i.e. formant) of the vowel to be x, and the resonance frequency of the plosive to be y, then the closing and opening of the lips can be seen to be, acoustically speaking, a transition from x to y and then from y to x. It is this formant transition towards and from the assumed value of the consonant's resonance frequency that is

responsible for the perception of plosives. This imagined place of origin of formant transitions is called **locus**. As for different places of plosives, the lengths of a closed tube for [p], [t], and [k] are different from each other; so would be the loci of these plosives; and so would be the transitional patterns. They are shown schematically in Figure 13. It can be seen that all formants rise rapidly from plosive to vowel in [pa], while higher formants fall in [ta], but converge in [ka].

A machine designed to analyse/decompose sound into its acoustic parameters, much as a prism splits light into its colour spectrum, is called a **spectrograph**, and its product is a **spectrogram**. A normal spectrogram shows frequency (ordinate) against time (abscissa), with relative intensity indicated by degrees of darkness of

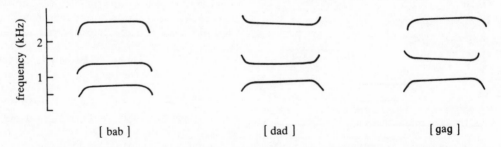

[bab]   [dad]   [gag]

Figure 13 A schematic spectrogram of the words [bab], [dad], and [gag], showing different patterns of transitions of upper formants for different places of articulation. Compare this with the real spectrogram in Figure 14

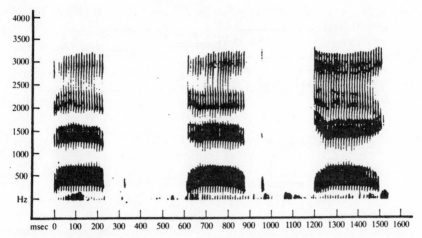

Figure 14 A spectrogram of the words [bab], [dad], and [gag].
Compare with Figure 13

spectrogram. A spectrogram of English words *bab*, *dad*, and *gag* is shown in Figure 14 (from Ladefoged, 1982, p. 182). Compare this with the schematic spectrogram of Figure 13.

In addition to the formant transitions, a noise in the spectrum generated by a turbulent airstream characterizes fricatives and affricates. This noise may vary in its frequency range, intensity, and duration depending upon the location and manner of the oral constriction. In general, sibilants are stronger in noise intensity than non-sibilants ([f], [θ], [h]: [h] being the weakest); affricates have a shorter noise duration than fricatives; and [s] is higher in its frequency range than [ʃ]. See the schematic spectrograms in Figure 15.

Acoustic phonetics developed in the 1940s with the advent of the age of electronics, and provided a foundation for the theory of distinctive features of Jakobson and Halle (Jakobson, Fant, and Halle, 1951) (see DISTINCTIVE FEATURES), which in turn formed the basis of

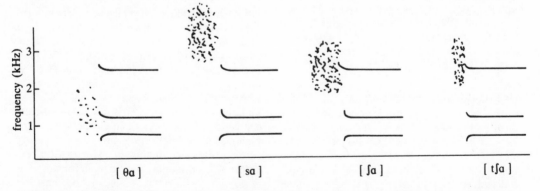

Figure 15 A schematic spectrogram showing different fricatives. Note that the difference between [θ] and sibilants is in the noise intensity; in the noise frequency between [s] and [ʃ]; and in the noise duration between [ʃ] and [tʃ]

generative phonology in the 1950s and 1960s (see GENERATIVE PHONOLOGY). Although this framework was overhauled by Chomsky and Halle (1968, especially Ch. 2), acoustic phonetics is still an indispensable tool both in instrumental phonetic research and in validation of aspects of phonological theories.

C.-W.K.

SUGGESTIONS FOR FURTHER READING

Fry, D.B. (1979), *The Physics of Speech*, Cambridge, Cambridge University Press.
Ladefoged, P. (1962), *Elements of Acoustic Phonetics*, Chicago, University of Chicago Press.
Ladefoged, P. (1982), *A Course in Phonetics*, 2nd edn, New York, Harcourt Brace Jovanovich.

Animals and language

Linguists' interest in animal communication systems has been largely fuelled by a desire to compare such systems with human language in order to show the differences between the two, and often, by implication, to show the superiority of human language over the communication systems of animals. One of the most famous attempts at setting up a system for carrying out such comparisons is that of Charles Hockett (1960; also Hockett and Altmann, 1968). For the purpose of the comparison, Hockett employs the notion of the **design feature**: a design feature is a property which is present in some communication systems and not in others; communication systems can then be classified into those that have a particular design feature and those that do not. Hockett lists sixteen such design features of human language, namely:

DF1 **Vocal–Auditory Channel**: it is in a sense coincidental that human language is realized through this channel; there are non-vocal sign systems for use by the deaf (see SIGN LANGUAGE), and if we found that apes, for instance, could use non-vocal sounds to engage in what we could conclusively show to be linguistic behaviour (see below), we would not disqualify this kind of communication on the grounds that it was not vocal–auditory.

DF2 **Broadcast Transmission and Directional Reception**: This is a consequence of the nature of sound.

DF3 **Rapid Fading**: again as a consequence of the nature of sound, human language does not 'hover in the air', but 'fades' rapidly.

DF4 **Interchangeability**: adult members of the speech community are interchangeably transmitters and receivers of the linguistic signal.

DF5 **Complete Feedback**: the speaker hears everything of what s/he says.

DF6 **Specialization**: Linguistic signals are specialized in the sense that their only true function is to convey the linguistic message. There is no isomorphism, for instance, between loudness of the signal and importance of the message – whether an important message is whispered or shouted does not, in principle, affect its importance. In Hockett's terms, 'the direct-energetic consequences of linguistic signals are biologically unimportant; only the triggering consequences are important'. He uses the example of a woman laying the table for dinner – a non-linguistic action. This action has the purpose of getting the table ready for dinner, but may also function to inform her husband that dinner will shortly be ready. In contrast, if the woman says to her husband *Dinner will shortly be ready*, then the *only* function this serves is to inform him that dinner will shortly be ready.

DF7 **Semanticity**: linguistic signs are connected to elements and features of the world.

DF8 **Arbitrariness**: there is no **iconicity**, or physical resemblance, between a linguistic sign and the element or feature of the world to which it is connected (except in the very rare instances of **onomatopoeia**: those linguistic signs which sound like what they represent, as in *tic-toc* for the sound a clock makes or *bow-wow* for the sound a dog makes; but even here languages differ – in Danish, the clock says *tik-tak* and the dog *vov-vov* – so some arbitrariness is still involved). An iconic system is more limited than an arbitrary one, because it can only refer to things and situations that can be imitated.

DF9 **Discreteness**: the messages a language is able to convey are not arranged along a continuum, but are discrete of each other. Had they been continuous, the system would have had to be iconic (compare bee-dancing, described below); a discrete system, however, can be either iconic or arbitrary.

DF10 **Displacement**: language can be used to talk about things that are remote in time and place from the interlocutors. A system without displacement could not be used to talk about the past or the future, to write fiction, to plan, speculate, or form hypotheses.

DF11 **Openness**: language allows for the making and interpretation of infinitely many new messages. Its grammatical patterning allows us to make new messages by blending old ones, analogizing from old ones, or transforming old ones. Second, in new contexts, old linguistic forms can take on new meanings, as when *hardware* was taken over for use in computer terminology, or as in the case of figurative language use.

DF12 **Tradition**: the conventions and (at least surface) structure of any one language are learned rather than inherited.

DF13 **Duality of Patterning**: every language has a pattern of minimal meaningless elements (phonemes) which combine with each other to form patterns of meaningful elements (morphemes). This duality goes right 'up' through the system; thus the morphemes combine with each other to form a further layer of meaningful patterning in the lexis, items of which form meaningful groups, etc.

DF14 **Prevarication**: the ability to lie. This feature is crucially dependent on displacement.

DF15 **Reflexiveness**: with language, we can communicate about language. In other words, language can function as its own **metalanguage**.

DF16 **Learnability**: a speaker of one human language can learn another.

Armed with this list, we can examine animal communication systems to see whether or not they possess all or some of the design features listed. In the discussion, I shall ignore the first three design features, since, as indicated above, they are incidental to human language.

It is only possible here to provide rough sketches of the communication systems of two non-human species, the stickleback and the honey bee. The communication systems of these two species are popular examples among linguists because of their respective simplicity and complexity.

Further details of the communicative and other behaviour of sticklebacks can be found in Tinbergen (1972). Male sticklebacks display a composite visual sign in the breeding season: their eyes go turquoise, their backs go green, and their undersides go bright red. Each male builds an algae tunnel nest and tries to get pregnant females to lay their eggs in it. The males are very aggressive towards each other during this time, but friendly toward pregnant females, who go a silvery grey colour. Tinbergen wished to discover whether the visual displays influenced the stickleback's behaviour during the breeding season, and, if so, to isolate those aspects of the visual display which caused the males to attack each other but to court the females. As it happened, the male sticklebacks were kept in tanks on the window ledge of Tinbergen's laboratory, and he noticed that whenever the mail van, which was bright red, passed the window the fish became very agitated and behaved very aggressively. He hypothesized, therefore, that it was the red colour of their underside which caused the male fish to attack each other, whereas the grey of the females attracted them. He tried and tested this hypothesis by presenting the male sticklebacks with wax models of various shapes and colours: they always reacted favourably to grey and with aggression to red; shape was unimportant.

So it seems that for male sticklebacks there are two meaningful signs: red and grey. Only having two signs in one's communication system need not be restrictive – think what can be done with the binary system. However, the effectiveness of the binary system arises largely from its Duality of Patterning, a feature noticeably lacking from the stickleback system. In fact, the only design features which the stickleback system seems to share with human language are Discreteness, Arbitrariness, and Semanticity: males and females signal differently, so there is no interchangeability. Presumably, the fish do not perceive the colour of their own undersides, so there is no Complete Feedback. The signals have a direct biological, as opposed to a purely communicative function, so there is no Specialization. The signal is linked to the bodily state of the fish in the here and now, so there is no Displacement. The fish do not appear to make new messages, so there is no Openness. The signalling is not learnt, but biologically determined, so there is no Tradition. The link with the state of the fish's body prevents Prevarication. The fish does not signal about the signal, so there is no Reflexiveness. As male and female stickleback cannot learn to use each other's signals, there seems to be no Learnability.

Compared to the communication system of sticklebacks, the worker honey bee's system appears to be at the pinnacle of sophistication; it was deciphered by the Austrian naturalist Karl von Frisch (1967). A simplified account of the system might go something like this: a bee that has located a food source will return to the hive and inform its colleagues of the discovery by dancing to them. If the food source is more than 50 metres away from the hive, the bee dances in a figure of eight, a dance which is called the **waggle-dance**. The length of the straight runs of this dance, up the long lines of the figure eight, called the **waggle-run**, is proportionate to the distance between the hive and the food source, and during the waggle-run, the dancer shakes its tail with a vigour which is in proportion to the richness of the food source. The frequency with which the bee dances also indicates distance: a bee returning from a food source 100 metres from the hive dances 10 times every 15 seconds, while a bee returning from 2 kilometres away dances only five times every 15 seconds. The direction of the food source is given by the orientation of the waggle-run. If the food source is less than 50 metres away from the hive, direction is not indicated, and the bee dances a **round dance**, which is livelier the richer the food source.

Bee dancing has Arbitrariness, Displacement, and Openness of the type that allows for infinitely many messages to be created, although not of the type that allows for making new messages of old – bees probably only ever dance about food, not about food as a symbol of anything else. As far as the workers are concerned, the system also has Interchangeability, and, in so far as the bee is aware of what it is doing, the system has Complete Feedback, Specialization, and Semanticity. It does not have Discreteness; bee dancing is a continuous system because of the proportionality of the signal to richness and distance of the food source. It is doubtful whether one would want to claim Tradition for it, and it has no Duality of Patterning. Nor do bees appear to engage in Prevarication, and there seems to be no Reflexiveness in the system. Finally, other bees do not learn to dance like the worker honey bee, so there is no Learnability.

The examples above illustrate how Hockett's method might be employed in the comparison of animal and human communication systems. However, there is some doubt about the usefulness of this approach; first, if one begins by defining language in terms of *human* language, it could be argued that other systems are put at a disadvantage from the start. In addition (Lieberman, 1977a, p. 6):

> Defining language in terms of the properties of human language is fruitless, because we do not know what they really are. Even if we knew the complete inventory of properties that characterize human language we probably would not want to limit the term 'language' to communication systems that had all of these properties. For example, it would be un-reasonable to state that a language that had all of the attributes of human language except relative clauses really was not a language. The operational definition of language is functional rather than taxonomic. It is a productive definition insofar as it encourages questions about what animals can do with their communication systems and the relation of these particular systems to human lan-guage.

As far as we know, the functions of animal communication systems are limited to the fol-lowing:

1 food – telling others that there is food, where it is, competing for it, begging for it when young;
2 alarm/warning;
3 territorial claims;
4 recognition and greeting;
5 reproduction;
6 grouping;
7 comforting;
8 indication of emotional state.

Humans habitually talk about numerous other subjects – arguably, language has many more, and much more complex functions, than animal communication systems *in so far as we under-stand the functions of the latter.*

In *The Descent of Man*, Darwin (1871) claimed that 'the difference in mind between man and higher animals, great as it is, certainly is one of degree and not kind'. He based this claim, partly, on the fact that the higher primates, in addition to communicating with each other by means of grunts and cries, have the same kind of gestural system as humans: staring is threatening, while keeping the head and gaze down is a sign of submission. These animals also gesticulate with their front legs, and use facial expressions similar to those of humans.

It is difficult to assess Darwin's claim: if it merely means that both humans and the higher primates have powers of cognition, then the claim is uninteresting and uncontroversial: all creatures can be said to have some powers of cognition which allow them to seek warmth or coolness, according to preference, and which ensure that they do not bump into things, and so on. However, if Darwin meant that humans and higher primates share certain mental states, then the claim has far-reaching consequences, not least in the field of animal ethics. For if there is only a difference in degree and not in kind between humans and the higher primates, it becomes even more difficult than it would otherwise be to argue that humans have a right to use higher primates for their own purposes. Furthermore, it is hard to say when a difference in degree becomes a difference in kind, so, progres-sing down the scale of living creatures (if the very notion of 'scale' makes sense in this context), what rights have humans over any creature?

I shall go no further into these difficult moral problems; however, it has sometimes been thought that the mark of difference in kind rather than degree is the ability of an animal to learn to use human language, and there is a fairly long tradition of attempting to teach human language to higher primates, in particular to chimpanzees. Most of these studies have involved chimpanzees reared in a human home or human-home-like environment, since it is in such an environment that most humans learn to speak. One early study, however, involved not a home-reared chimpanzee, but a performing one (Witmer, 1909; see Fouts and Rigby, 1977).

The chimpanzee in question, Peter, was em-ployed in Philadelphia's Keith Theatre. The psychologist Witmer met Peter when the latter was between four and six years old; Peter had received two and a half years of training for his theatrical work at this time. Witmer took Peter for intelligence tests at the Psychological Clinic in Philadelphia. It turned out that Peter could carry out simple reasoning tasks quite easily –

unlocking doors, opening boxes, and hammering nails in. He did not display any particular aptitude for writing. He could say *mama*, although unwillingly and with difficulty, having severe problems with vowels. However, it took him only a few minutes to learn to say /p/, and Witmer comments:

> If a child without language were brought to me and on the first trial had learned to articulate the sound 'p' as readily as Peter did, I should express the opinion that he could be taught most of the elements of articulate language within six months' time.

Witmer also noticed that although Peter could not speak, he understood words, and he thought that Peter would probably be able to learn to associate symbols with objects; several later experiments have confirmed that chimpanzees can indeed learn this associative connection, and one of these will be described below. Early on, however, the focus was on teaching chimpanzees to speak. Three more or less unsuccessful attempts at this involved the chimpanzees Joni, Gua, and Viki.

Joni was raised and observed by N. Kohts and her family between 1913 and 1916, when he was between one and a half and four years old. The study was not published until 1935, because Kohts was saving her notes on Joni for comparison with notes on the behaviour of her own child, Roody, between 1925 and 1929 when he was of the same age as Joni had been during the study involving him. Kohts did not specifically train Joni to speak, because she wanted to see if he would do so as relatively spontaneously as a human child does; but the only sounds he produced were those which young chimpanzees normally produce, from which Kohts concluded that his intellectual capacities were different in kind from those of humans.

Gua was a 7½ month-old chimpanzee adopted by W. and L. Kellogg, who had a son, Donald, of the same age as Gua. Gua and Donald lived in the same surroundings and were given the same treatment during the nine months of Gua's stay with the family. But while Donald made the normal babbling sounds of a human infant, Gua restricted herself to the barking, screeching, and crying noises of a young chimpanzee (Kellogg and Kellogg, 1967).

Keith and Catherine Hayes' experiment with the chimpanzee Viki met with more success, relatively speaking. The Hayes took Viki into their home when she was just a few days old and treated her as much as possible like a human child. Viki stayed with the Hayes for six years and learnt to articulate four words, *mama*, *papa*, *cup* and *up*, with difficulty, in a hoarse voice, and often in inappropriate contexts, so that it was unclear whether she understood their meanings (Hayes and Hayes, 1952).

By 1968, there was conclusive evidence that human speech is not, in fact, a suitable medium of communication for chimpanzees, for both behavioural and anatomical reasons (Lieberman, 1968; Gardner and Gardner, 1971). This means that there is no more justification for claiming that a chimpanzee cannot learn language because it cannot learn to speak, than one would have for claiming that a fish cannot learn to move because it cannot learn to walk – the fish simply has no legs, the chimpanzee simply does not have the appropriate voice box.

Since chimpanzees in the wild use a form of gestural communication system naturally, the Gardners, whose experiment with Washoe is probably the most famous chimpanzee language experiment of them all, chose to exploit this ability, and taught Washoe to communicate using American Sign Language (Ameslan), a language widely used in the United States by the deaf. It consists of gestures made by the arms, hands, and fingers, and the signs made are analogous to spoken words (see further SIGN LANGUAGE). Project Washoe ran from June 1966 until October 1970 at the University of Nevada in Reno. During this time Washoe learned to use over 130 signs correctly, both syntactically and contextually, and to transfer her use of old signs to new situations.

Washoe was between eight and fourteen months old when the Gardners bought her from a trader; they assumed that she was born in the wild and had lived with her natural mother for several months until she was captured. The

Gardners kept her in a caravan in their back garden, and anyone who came into contact with her used only Ameslan in her presence, both to communicate with her and with other humans, and since Washoe was never left alone except when she was asleep, she was the subject of a total immersion in Ameslan. She was taught by a mixture of a small amount of response shaping by reward, guidance by the tutors on how to form the signs, and observation of the tutors' signing behaviour; the Gardners claim that the latter method accounted for the vast majority of Washoe's learning. Her acquisition pattern was like that of a child (see LANGUAGE ACQUISITION). She began with manual babbling which was gradually replaced by true signing. She began to combine signs into sentences when she was between 18 and 24 months, during the 10th month of the experiment, and her early two-word combinations resembled those of children in subject matter. It appeared that a chimpanzee had finally learnt some rudimentary language.

Two other chimpanzee experiments tended to confirm this ability of chimpanzees. In one, a six-year-old chimpanzee, Sarah, was taught to communicate using pieces of plastic of different shapes and colours to stand for words. The system was invented and the experiment carried out by Premack and Premack (1972), who claimed that Sarah learnt a vocabulary of around 130 terms which she used correctly between 75 and 80 per cent of the time; her ability resembled that of a two year old child (1972, p. 99).

The second experiment involved teaching the chimpanzee, Lana, to read from a computer screen and to communicate with the computer. It took her six months to learn to read characters off the screen, to complete incomplete sentences, and to reject sentences that were grammatically incorrect. This experiment was held to confirm conclusively that chimpanzees can understand and use syntax (Rumbaugh et al., 1973).

However, doubt has since been cast on this conclusion by Herbert Terrace (1979), who worked with a chimpanzee called Nim Chimpsky. Nim was taught Ameslan like Washoe had been, but in controlled laboratory conditions. He appeared to display an acquisition pattern and

ability very similar to those of Washoe, but Terrace claims that careful study of the video recordings of Nim's behaviour, and of Washoe's, shows that neither animal is in fact using language like a human does (Yule, 1985, p. 29):

> The structure of Nim's longer 'utterances' was simply a repetition of simpler structures, not an expansion into more complex structures, as produced by human children. Moreover, in contrast to the human child, Nim only rarely used sign language to initiate interaction with his teachers. In general, he produced signs in response to their signing and tended to repeat signs they used.

In response, Gardner and Gardner (1978) and Gardner (1981) have argued that, whereas this might have been true of Nim, who was treated as a research animal and investigated by researchers who were not all fluent in Ameslan, it was not true of Washoe, who was home-reared (Yule, 1985, p. 30):

> In sharp contrast, the Gardners have stressed the need for a domestic environment. . . . Their most recent project involves a number of chimpanzees, Moja, Pili, Tatu and Dar, being raised together from birth in a domestic environment with a number of human companions who naturally use sign language. They report that these chimpanzees, beginning earlier than Washoe, are acquiring sign language much faster.

Controversy will probably continue to surround projects such as those described above, and it is doubtful whether it is possible to reach any firm conclusion on the exact degree to which chimpanzees can acquire human language, since opinions differ on the definition of language itself (see Lyons, 1981, 1.2; most introductory books on linguistics list some proposed definitions). However, according to Yule (1985, p. 31), Chomsky's (1972a) claim that 'acquisition of even the barest rudiments of language is quite beyond the capacities of an otherwise intelligent ape' does not stand up against evidence such as that derived from the chimpanzee experiments. Chimpanzees may never be able to discuss linguistic theory with us, but they clearly have at least a rudimentary linguistic ability.

K.M.

SUGGESTIONS FOR FURTHER READING

Linden, E. (1976), *Apes, Men and Language*,
Harmondsworth, Penguin.
Sebeok, T.A. (ed.) (1977), *How Animals Communicate*, Bloomington and London, Indiana University Press.
Sebeok, T.A. and Umiker-Sebeok, J. (eds.) (1980), *Speaking of Apes: A Critical Anthology of Two-way Communication with Man*, New York and London, Plenum Press.

Aphasia

Aphasia is the loss of normal language abilities as a result of some pathological condition. Taking each of the terms of this definition in turn, we may note, first, that a strict use of **aphasia** meaning 'total loss' v. **dysphasia** meaning 'partial loss' is sometimes followed, but that **aphasia** and, rather less commonly, **dysphasia** are most often used for any degree of loss. Second, 'normal' language abilities may vary with a number of factors, including chronological age and level of education, so that there is not a single norm for all. Most importantly, this raises the question of how far it is appropriate to talk of **developmental aphasia**, referring to the impaired development of language in childhood, v. **acquired aphasia**, where previously attained normal adult language abilities are lost. The difference between the two situations is at first sight considerable, and it is probably incumbent upon those who wish to acknowledge developmental aphasia as a concept to show that it takes forms which are essentially comparable to those found in acquired cases. At the other end of the human chronological scale, there is the increasingly recognized field of language in old age. The term **aphasia** is naturally applied here, as an extension of its use in acquired disorders, but there is an issue concerning what is normal for old age. Increasing difficulty in word finding, for example, associated with no obvious pathology, may not be appropriately brought under the heading of aphasia, if it is of a degree that is normal for a person's age. Here, as in most other areas of adult language abilities, the necessary normative linguistic studies have not been undertaken. Third, the term **language abilities** requires some interpretation. Traditional approaches within aphasiology have emphasized a fundamental distinction between 'speech' and 'language' abilities, and hence disorders, and it is worth noting that these terms still have clinical value even though the nature of the distinction is not, from a linguistic viewpoint, so fundamental as the tradition believed.

A clinician describing a patient as having speech and language difficulties is using these terms to denote articulatory and grammatical–semantic levels of disorder; but the strict adherence to this distinction by theoretical aphasiologists has led to problems in defining the boundary of **aphasia** (disorders of 'language' in the non-speech sense) as opposed to **dysarthria** (some weakness of the articulatory organs, arising from lesions throughout the central nervous system) (see LANGUAGE PATHOLOGY AND NEUROLINGUISTICS). Within this approach, the status of **dyspraxia** has proved difficult and controversial: it is thought to be characterized by impaired control v. implementation aspects of speech production.

At the other end of the language hierarchy, as

it were, a further boundary issue arises, as between types of 'semantic aphasia' and impairment of particular or general intellectual functions: terms such as **acalculia** (impaired manipulation of number concepts) imply that these stand outside aphasia, but they may also be attested in cases of aphasia, and, conceivably, form part of the aphasic disorder. The difficulty in such cases derives straightforwardly from our lack of knowledge concerning the boundary between meaning as expressed in language and non-linguistic knowledge systems.

A further issue arises when alternative media of language behaviour are considered, the most important being those involved in reading and writing: terms such as **agraphia** and **alexia** suggest that aphasia is restricted to spoken-language abilities, but most researchers and clinicians regard reading and writing performance as forming part of the total picture of an acquired language disorder.

Finally, the presence of some significant 'pathology' is a useful element in the definition, but it may be overridden in cases where it is felt that there is some frank impairment without detectable pathology; in such cases, the term **functional** as opposed to **organic** is used, e.g. where word-finding difficulties may be the only symptom of some condition perhaps brought on by psychological stress, or the normal process of aging.

The usually encountered causes, and resulting types, of brain damage in aphasia are: vascular disease, that is, problems in the blood supply – embolism, thrombosis or haemorrhage; tumour; trauma, i.e., external source of injury, as with gunshot wounds or road-traffic accidents; infection, leading to infarct – atrophied brain tissue – compression, rupture, and micro-organic invasion of brain cells. 'Cardio-vascular accidents' or CVA – frequently referred to as 'strokes' – are the single most common cause in most non-military situations, with thrombosis and embolism resulting in infarcts, and haemorrhage in compression of brain tissue.

Determining the precise extent and location of the damage is not at all easy in many cases. Differences of about 1 centimetre can be signi-

ficant for establishing an association with impairment to specific language functions, so the precision called for in establishing neurolinguistic correlations is of a high order. Further, typical infarcts may border on zones of softened cortical and subcortical tissue, whose functional integrity is hard to determine. Direct inspection of damaged areas is only available either during surgery or at autopsy – and the bulk of stroke cases in hospitals do not undergo surgery.

Indirect examination techniques include: bedside neurological-function examination, to determine, from the overall pattern of sensory-motor functions, where the lesion is likely to have occurred; instrumental investigations such as electroencephalography (EEG), and regional blood flow (rCBF), in which sensors are placed over the scalp in order to record patterns of activity in the brain; and more recent techniques of scanning, such as radionucleide (RN) and computerized axial tomography (CAT) scans. Scanning procedures are much more precise than the use of scalp sensors, but the scanning methods used have particular strengths and weaknesses in the sorts of damage they are positive to.

Because of the difficulties, expense and uncertainties of lesion-location attempts, most aphasic patients are classified into syndromes on the basis of clinical rather than neurological-location criteria. Thus while Broca's area (see LANGUAGE PATHOLOGY AND NEUROLINGUISTICS), is definable in neuroanatomical terms, most cases of **Broca's aphasia** that are seen outside research establishments are classified as such on the basis of their symptoms, rather than by site of lesion, which may never be known. That is, Broca's aphasia exists as a clinical entity, and it is in this sense that most of the major syndromes that we shall now consider are usually understood. The discussion of the following syndromes is fairly typical of recent aphasia test-battery performance data, and derives from Kertesz (1979).

Anomic aphasia or **Anomia**: the *symptom* of anomia, or general word-finding difficulty, is frequently found in other *syndromes*, where it is usually subclassified further, e.g. into word-production anomia, word-selection anomia, and different types of specific anomia, depending on which word-classes, e.g. verbs v. nouns, are most severely affected. As a syndrome, anomia is defined as the presence of the symptom in the marked absence of other aphasic symptoms. As such, it is frequently a syndrome that results from alleviation of symptoms present in some other syndrome – a sort of 'recovery syndrome'. It accounts for around one-third of a broad aphasic population, and is by far the mildest sort of aphasia. Anomic lesion sites tend to lie in the area of the lower parietal lobe, close to the junction with the temporal lobe (see LANGUAGE PATHO-LOGY AND NEUROLINGUISTICS for illustration).

Global aphasia: at the other end of the scale of severity, this syndrome accounts for around one-sixth of a general aphasic population, and is characterized by impairment of all testable language functions. Theoretically, it is possible for this broad-spectrum impairment to be either severe or mild; in practice, it is almost always severe, and global aphasia is typically the most disabling kind of aphasic syndrome. It is frequently found in acute cases of brain damage, and may be followed by uneven patterns of alleviation of certain symptoms, resulting in a case-history shift from this syndrome to another, non-global type. Global aphasia lesions tend to be distributed over the areas of the frontal, parietal, and temporal lobes that border the Rolandic and Sylvian fissures demarcating these areas.

Broca's aphasia: this may arise as global aphasia ameliorated in respect of comprehension abilities, or as a distinct syndrome from the outset. It has about the same incidence as global aphasia, but is less severe. Speech articulation is non-fluent and effortful, with many simplifications of consonant clusters and some substitutions. A component syndrome of **agrammatism** has been recognized, involving impairment of closed-class grammatical morphemes (see MORPHOLOGY), selective difficulties with verbs over nouns, and reduction in the variety of syntactic patterns; but it has also been suggested that an impaired ability to sequence phonologically unstressed elements with stressed ones may account for some of these agrammatic characteristics. Fluent control of

stereotypic utterances such as *Oh, I don't know!* may provide striking contrast with spontaneous productive attempts, and may also be employed by Broca's aphasics in ways that suggest that they know what they want to say but lack the means to structure their output appropriately. It is possible that their degree of intact comprehension abilities may be overestimated by the unwary. Comprehension is apparently better for concrete referential rather than abstract relational terms. Broca's lesions are generally found in the lower frontal lobe, just anterior to the Rolandic fissure that divides the frontal and parietal lobes.

Wernicke's aphasia: like Broca's aphasia, this is another classic syndrome, described by a pioneering nineteenth-century aphasiologist (see LANGUAGE PATHOLOGY AND NEUROLINGUISTICS), and it provides in many ways a complementary pattern to that of Broca's aphasia. Spontaneous speech production is fluent, though marked by numerous sound substitutions (**phonemic para-phasias**), word-form errors (**verbal paraphasias**) and nonce-forms (neologisms), and abnormal grammatical sequences (paragrammatisms). Identifiable words in the fluent output tend to be referentially vague, with much use of general proforms and stereotyped social phrases. There appears to be little self-monitoring ability – the patient is not aware that what s/he says is hard to interpret, and may not be able to stop when asked to. Comprehension of what others say is severely impaired. Lesion sites are generally in the upper surface of the temporal lobe, close to and often involving the auditory cortex, and sometimes extending to the parietal lobe.

Broca's and Wernicke's syndromes provide cardinal points for the delineation of four other types of aphasia, which all involve an impaired ability to transfer the results of processing in one area of the cortex to another.

In **conduction aphasia**, a subcortical lesion of restricted extent is supposed to be responsible for interfering with subcortical pathways, the arcuate fasciculus, running from Wernicke's area to Broca's area, i.e. carrying the results of semantic processing to the speech-output control area. This results in fluent speech output, with

Wernicke-type characteristics, together with relatively good comprehension, but severely impaired repetition abilities.

Transcortical motor aphasia is thought to involve an impaired connection between Broca's area and surrounding frontal-lobe association areas; as a result, spontaneous speech control is non-fluent and agrammatic, but connectors into Broca's area from the temporal–parietal auditory-comprehension areas are relatively spared, leading to better repetition abilities than are found in Broca's aphasia.

Transcortical sensory aphasia looks similar to Wernicke's aphasia in respect of fluent spontaneous output with many paraphasias and paragrammatisms; but here again the impairment seems to involve the connections between the auditory cortex and the surrounding association areas, leading to a situation which may be described as compulsive repetition, or **echolalia**. Note the contrast with Wernicke's aphasia, where the patient seems not to attend to what is said to her or him; in transcortical sensory aphasia what is said is faithfully retained and repeated, though without apparent comprehension.

Finally, **mixed transcortical aphasia** is defined as the simultaneous disconnection of both the speech-output control centre and the speech-perception centre from surrounding areas of cortex, so that these central production and perception abilities are effectively cut off from the interpretative processes of the rest of the cortex; for this reason, mixed transcortical aphasia is often referred to as the **isolation syndrome**.

It should be stressed that these are highly simplified and idealized thumbnail sketches of the major categories of acquired language disorders. They serve as cardinal points within some descriptive clinical framework, in relation to which the particular difficulties found with individual patients may be located. There is increasing awareness of the extent to which individual differences exist within broad classification categories such as Broca's and Wernicke's aphasia, and it may be that the days are passed when the approach to aphasiology in terms of syndromes can continue to yield benefits.

One alternative is to consider the presenting symptoms in more detail. In this connection, there is growing awareness in aphasiology of the need for, and of the potential of, more refined assessment of naturalistic language performance, as opposed to the highly constrained types of behaviours elicited in the standardized test batteries. Linguistic and psycholinguistic studies of normal adult conversational behaviour are important in this respect, including such aspects as turn-taking (see DISCOURSE AND CONVERSATIONAL ANALYSIS), eye-gaze, and non-verbal gestures (see KINESICS), as well as normal non-fluency – filled pauses, part- and whole-word repetitions, backtrackings, and false starts – and normal types and incidence of errors, including syntactic misformulations, incomplete utterances, and word-selection errors (see PSYCHOLINGUISTICS). These normative data, and the types of theories they support, provide an indispensable foundation for the appropriate assessment of aphasic conversational attempts.

The assessment of comprehension in naturalistic contexts is likewise of major importance; although it is possible for normal language users to understand words and constructions that are presented in isolation, and to compare aphasics' attempts on the same basis, there is reason to believe that this is essentially a metalinguistic skill that may bear little relation to the sorts of language demands that are made on the aphasic outside the assessment situation. In the typical situation of utterance, the specifically linguistic input, the acoustic signal, is accompanied by other types of auditory and visual input, deriving from the speaker and from the environment, and these inputs interact in complex ways. Furthermore, there is reason to believe that attentional factors play an important role in language understanding, and that these are difficult to engage in tasks and situations where language forms are being used in simulated rather than real acts of communication. Attempts have been made to devise 'communicative' assessment procedures, but much work remains to be done in refining these.

These sorts of pragmatic–linguistic considerations are consistent with developments in cognitive psychology also, such as 'spreading activation' theories of associative memory, and the concept of memory as distributed across various cognitive domains. Recent work in neuropsychology also emphasizes the role of right-hemisphere processing in functions for which the left hemisphere is dominant, and the distributed, interactive nature of processing within the hemispheres.

An age-old question in aphasia has been the extent to which aphasia is a unitary phenomenon. If we take this to mean that aphasia is a disorder that admits of no essential divisions, varying only in degrees of severity and modality of function, then it is a highly abstract concept, far removed from the observations on the specific dissociations of language functions in particular cases; but it has some value in emphasizing the holistic functioning of an impaired language capacity, in which compensatory strategies form part of a systemic response to specific functional impairment.

The case of written-language abilities represents a case in point. Naive localizationism (see LANGUAGE PATHOLOGY AND NEUROLINGUISTICS) led to the positing of **Exner's centre**, supposedly the seat of writing, and situated in the motor-association cortex of the left hemisphere. This relied on an uncritical acceptance of an insufficiently analysed notion of the various component skills that are involved in written-language production, representing the functional integration of many different areas of the brain.

Written-language abilities, including reading as well as writing, appear to be represented in the brain alongside spoken-language abilities in such a way that they may be impaired together, or differentially, under conditions that are not at all clear. What does seem to emerge from the available studies is that in some way written-language abilities are more vulnerable, since cases are so rarely found in which writing and reading are spared in comparison with spoken-language abilities. It may be that this is a puzzle that will be cleared up only with a better understanding of how brain cells actually support particular language functions.

S.E. and M.A.G.

SUGGESTIONS FOR FURTHER READING

Albert, M.L., Goodglass, H., Helm, N.A., Rubens, A.B., and Alexander M.P. (1981), *Clinical Aspects of Dysphasia*, Vienna, Springer.

Benson, D.F. (1979), *Aphasia, Alexia, and Agraphia*, New York, Churchill Livingstone.

Kertesz, A. (1979), *Aphasia and Associated Disorders*, New York, Grune and Stratton.

Lesser, R. (1978), *Linguistic Investigations of Aphasia*, London, Arnold.

Taylor Sarno, M., Newman, S., and Epstein, R. (1985), *Current Perspectives in Dysphasia*, Edinburgh, Churchill Livingstone.

Wyke, M.A. (1978), *Developmental Dysphasia*, London, Academic Press.

Articulatory phonetics

Articulatory phonetics, sometimes alternatively called **physiological phonetics**, is a sub-branch of phonetics concerned with the study of the articulation of speech sounds. **Speech sounds** are produced through various interactions of **speech organs** acting on either an **egressive** (i.e. outgoing) or an **ingressive** (i.e. incoming) airstream. Such articulation of speech sounds is peculiar to human beings (homo loquens 'speaking human') and is not shared by other animals.

The term **articulation** refers to the division of an egressive or ingressive airstream, with or without vocal vibration, into distinct sound entities through the above-mentioned interaction of speech organs. The concept of articulation in phonetics has evolved in such a way that present-day phoneticians use expressions like 'articulating such-and-such a speech sound' or 'the articulation of such-and-such a speech sound' as practically equivalent to 'pronouncing a speech sound as a distinct entity' and 'the pronunciation of a speech sound as a distinct entity', and the term 'articulation' will be used in this technical sense in what follows.

In articulatory phonetics a speech sound is primarily considered and presented as a discrete entity so that the replacement of one speech sound by another in an identical phonetic context is regarded as possible, at least in theory. However, phoneticians are also well aware that, in the vast majority of cases, speech sounds occur in sequential combination in connected speech, with the result that they partially blend into each other in such a way that the conception of speech sounds as discrete entities is unsatisfactory. Consequently, in articulatory phonetics, speech sounds are normally first presented as discrete entities showing how they are each articulated, and then as less than discrete entities showing how they articulatorily affect each other in the speech chain.

The human physiological organs which are employed for the articulation of speech sounds and which are hence called **speech organs** or **vocal organs** all have a more basically biological function than that of allowing for verbal communication by means of speech. Thus the teeth are used for chewing food; the tongue serves to push food around during chewing and then to carry it towards the food-passage into which it is swallowed; the lungs are used for breathing; the vocal folds function as a valve to prevent the accidental entry of foreign bodies into the wind-pipe; if foreign bodies are about to enter the wind-pipe, the vocal folds quickly close before being pushed open again by an egressive airstream which at the same time blows the foreign bodies upwards; in other words, what happens in

this case is a cough. The vocal folds also assist muscular effort of the arms and the abdomen; the vocal folds close to create a hermetic air-filled chamber below them, and this helps the muscles of the arms or the abdomen to be made rigid. The use of these biological organs for the purpose of articulating speech sounds is another property peculiar to human beings which is not shared by other animals.

In the articulation of speech sounds, the speech organs function as follows. A well-coordinated action of the **diaphragm** (the muscle separating the lungs from the stomach) and of the **intercostal muscles** situated between the ribs causes air to be drawn into, or be pushed out of, the **lungs** through the **trachea** or **wind-pipe**, which is a tube consisting of cartilaginous rings, the top of which forms the base of the larynx.

The **larynx**, the front of which is indirectly observable from outside and is popularly known as the Adam's apple, houses the two **vocal folds**, also known as **vocal lips**, **vocal bands**, or **vocal c(h)ords**. The whole of the larynx can be moved upward – in pronouncing an **ejective** sound like [p'] – or downward – in pronouncing an **implosive** sound like [ɓ] – (see THE INTERNATIONAL PHONETIC ALPHABET for information on phonetic symbols).

The vocal folds are fixed on the front–back axis in a horizontal direction, hinged together at the front end while being mobile sideways in two opposite directions at the back end where they are mounted on the arytenoid cartilages, which are also mobile. The vocal folds can thus be brought close together in such a way that their inner edges, which lightly touch each other, are set into vibration by an egressive or ingressive airstream as it rushes through between them. There is then said to be **vocal vibration** or **glottal vibration** or simply **voice**, and speech sounds articulated with vocal vibration are said to be **voiced** (e.g., [b z v]). The vocal folds can be made to approach each other in such a way that air passing through them causes **friction** without, however, causing vocal vibration; this happens in the case of [h]. Also, the vocal folds can be kept wide apart from each other (as in quiet breathing) so that air passes freely between them in either direction, causing neither glottal friction nor vocal vibration; speech sounds articulated with the vocal folds thus wide apart are said to be **voiceless** (e.g., [p s f]). Furthermore, the vocal folds can be brought tightly together to form a firm contact so that no air can pass through them either inwards or outwards: the only speech sound produced when this posture of the vocal folds is assumed and then released is the **glottal plosive**, also popularly known as the **glottal stop**, i.e. [ʔ]. The space between the vocal folds is known as the **glottis**, so that the above-mentioned four different postures of the vocal folds may be viewed as representing four different states of the glottis; they are among the most important in normal speech, though other states of the glottis are possible, including those for breathy or murmured speech and creaky or laryngealized speech.

The area in which the speech organs above the larynx are situated is generally referred to as the **vocal tract**. It consists of three cavities: **pharyngeal** or **pharyngal**, **nasal**, and **oral**. The pharyngeal cavity is also known as the **pharynx**. These three cavities function as **resonators** in that a tiny voiced sound originating from the vocal folds is amplified while passing through them. The shapes of the pharyngeal and oral cavities are variously changeable, while that of the nasal cavity is unalterable.

The pharyngeal cavity is bounded by the larynx at the bottom, by the pharyngeal wall at the back, by the root of the tongue at the front, and by the area of bifurcation into the nasal and oral cavities at the top. Apart from functioning as a resonator, the pharynx is responsible for producing **pharyngeal sounds** – to be exact, **pharyngeal fricatives** – with or without vocal vibration, i.e. [ʕ] or [ħ], in the articulation of which the root of the tongue is drawn backwards to narrow the pharynx.

The nasal cavity, which is larger than the pharyngeal or oral cavity, extends from the nostrils backwards and downwards to where the nasal cavity and the oral cavity meet. The nasal cavity can be closed off from the two other cavities or can remain open to them, depending on whether the movable **soft palate** or **velum** (see below) is raised, in which case there is said to be a **velic closure**, or lowered. Any speech sound articulated in such a way that the egressive airstream issues outwards through the nasal cavity is a **nasal sound** or a **nasalized sound**, as the case may be. On the one hand, a **nasal consonant** is produced if the air meets total obstruction at a given point in the oral cavity (e.g. [n]), or between the lips ([m]). On the other hand, a **nasalized vowel** such as [õ] is produced if the air is at the same time allowed to issue out freely through the oral cavity as well.

The oral cavity extends from where the front teeth lie to the end of the roof of the mouth at the top, and the end of the tongue at the bottom. The lips form the orifice to the oral cavity. It is in the oral cavity that further speech organs are situated, which will be examined below. Various interactions between these speech organs in the oral cavity, with or without the involvement of the lips, and with or without vocal vibration, and with or without the involvement of the nasal cavity, give rise to a number of different **manners** and **places of articulation** which are associated with a number of different speech sounds, oral or nasal.

Figure 1 shows the different speech organs found in the oral cavity, and the lips. The **lips** are obviously the easiest to observe from outside. They can be brought together to form a firm contact, or separated well apart from each other, or made to touch or approach each other lightly in such a way that audible friction may or may not occur as air passes between them. They can also be spread, or can assume a neutral un-rounded posture, or can be rounded.

The **teeth** are next easiest to observe, particularly the upper and lower front teeth. There are of course other teeth further towards the back, including the molars, which are also important in articulating some speech sounds.

What is sometimes called the **roof of the mouth** is what phoneticians refer to as the **teeth-ridge** and the **palate**. It consists of the following: (1) the front end (convex to the tongue) which is known as the **teeth-ridge** or the **alveolar ridge**; (2) the hard (concave) immovable part which is known as the **hard palate**; (3) the soft (also concave) mucous

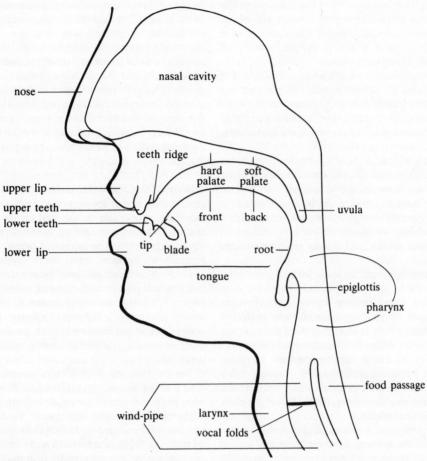

Figure 1 Speech organs

part capable of up-and-down movement known as the **soft palate** or **velum**; and (4) the pendent fleshy tip at the end of the soft palate, which is known as the **uvula**.

The **tongue** plays a prominent role in the articulation of speech sounds in the oral cavity. It is particularly versatile in the movements it is capable of making, in the speed with which it can move, and the shapes it is capable of assuming. For the purpose of describing various speech sounds articulated in the oral cavity, phoneticians conveniently divide the tongue into various parts in such a way that there is some

correlation between the division of the tongue and that of the roof of the mouth. Thus, as well as (1) the **tip** or **apex** of the tongue, we have (2) the **blade**, i.e. that part of the tongue which, when the tongue is lying at rest (this state of the tongue also applies to (3) and (4) below), faces the upper teeth-ridge, (3) the **front**, i.e. that part of the tongue which faces the hard palate, and (4) the **back**, i.e. that part of the tongue which faces the soft palate. Notice that the above-mentioned division of the tongue does not include what one might call the middle or the centre of the tongue which corresponds to the area consisting of the posterior part of the front of the tongue and the anterior part of the back of the tongue and whose recognition is implied in phoneticians' general practice of talking about central vowels or centralization of certain vowels.

Before speech sounds are articulated due to the intervention of various speech organs such as have been mentioned above, movement of an airstream is required; this airstream is then variously modified by speech organs into speech sounds.

There are three types of airstream mechanism. First, there is the **pulmonic airstream mechanism**. This is initiated by the lungs, and in normal speech the airstream is egressive, that is, the air is pushed out from the lungs. **Vowels** and many of the **consonants** require this type of airstream mechanism. Second, there is the **velaric airstream mechanism**. This is initiated by velar closure, i.e. the closure between the back part of the tongue and the soft palate, and the airstream is always ingressive. **Clicks** require this type of airstream mechanism. Third, there is the **glottalic airstream mechanism**. This is initiated by the glottis, which may be firmly or loosely closed, and the airstream is either egressive or ingressive. **Ejectives** (egressive) and **implosives** (ingressive) require this type of airstream mechanism, the firmly closed glottis for the former and the loosely closed glottis for the latter. Certain combinations of two of these types of airstream mechanism also occur.

In classifying speech sounds from the articulatory point of view, phoneticians frequently operate with the division between vowels and consonants. The so-called **semivowels**, e.g. [j w ɥ], are, articulatorily speaking, vowels.

Vowels are speech sounds in whose articulation (1) the highest part of the tongue which varies is located within a certain zone in the oral cavity which may be described as the **vowel area** (cf. the cardinal vowels discussed below) and (2) the egressive airstream from the lungs issues into the open air without meeting any closure or such constriction as would cause audible friction in the oral cavity as well as the pharyngeal cavity. Note that the occurrence of audible friction between the vocal folds, i.e. voice or vocal vibration, does not disqualify sounds as vowels

provided there occurs at the same time no closure or constriction in any of the above-mentioned cavities. Many phoneticians assume a vowel to be voiced by definition; others consider that some languages have voiceless vowels – indeed it is possible to argue that [h] in English is a voiceless vowel. The soft palate, when raised (cf. velic closure), prevents the airstream from entering the nasal cavity, and oral vowels are produced, e.g. [i]; but when lowered, the soft palate allows the airstream to enter the nasal cavity as well as the oral cavity, and nasalized vowels result, e.g. [õ].

In describing a vowel from the point of view of articulatory phonetics, many phoneticians customarily make use of a certain auditory-articulatory reference system in terms of which any vowel of any language may be described. The auditory–articulatory reference system in question is the **cardinal vowel system** devised by the English phonetician, Daniel Jones (1881–1967). The cardinal vowel system consists, as shown in Figure 2, of eight **primary** cardinal vowels, numbered from 1 to 8, and ten **secondary** cardinal vowels, numbered from 9 to 18; all of these eighteen cardinal vowels are oral vowels.

The primary cardinal vowels are posited in such a way that no. 1, [i], is articulated with the front of the tongue as high and front as possible consistently with its being a vowel – i.e., without becoming a consonant by producing audible friction; no. 5, [ɑ], is articulated with the back of the tongue as low and back as possible consistently with its being a vowel; nos 2, 3, and 4, [e ɛ a], are so articulated as to form an auditory equidistance between each two adjacent vowels from no. 1 to no. 5; nos 6, 7, and 8, [ɔ o u], are so articulated as to continue the auditory equidistance, with no. 8 being articulated with the back of the tongue as high and back as possible consistently with its being a vowel. Nos 1, 2, 3, 4, and 5 are articulated with the lips unrounded, and nos 6, 7, and 8 with the lips rounded.

The secondary cardinal vowels are posited in such a way that nos 9 to 16, [y ø œ Œ ɑ ʌ ɤ ɯ], correspond to the same points as nos 1 to 8, respectively, except for the posture of the lips in terms of rounded and unrounded, which is

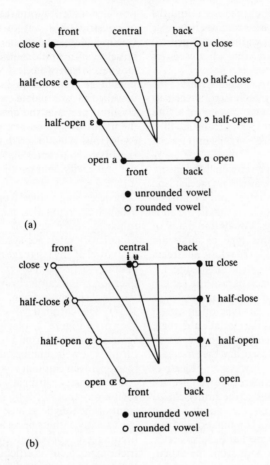

Figure 2 (a) Primary cardinal vowels (b) Secondary cardinal vowels

reversed. Nos 17 and 18, [i ʉ], are articulated with the central part of the tongue as high as possible consistently with their being vowels; the former is unrounded and the latter rounded. Thus, by connecting the highest points of the tongue in the articulation of all the cardinal vowels, we can conceive of what may be referred to as the **vowel area**.

Use of the cardinal vowel system enables phoneticians to specify a vowel of any given language with regard to the following: (1) the height of the part of the tongue which is the closest to the palate, the reference points being close, half-close, half-open, open; (2) the part of the tongue on the front–back axis which is the closest to the palate, the reference points being front, central, back; and (3) the posture of the lips, rounded or unrounded. In addition, phoneticians specify the posture, raised or lowered, of the soft palate, that is, whether the vowel is oral or nasalized.

Monophthongs are vowels in the articulation of which the tongue all but maintains its posture and position, thereby maintaining practically the same vowel quality throughout, e.g. the vowels in the English words *raw, too*, etc. On the other hand, **diphthongs** are vowels in the articulation of which the tongue starts with the position for one vowel quality and moves towards the position for another vowel within one syllable, e.g. the vowels in the English words *no*, *buy*, etc.

Consonants are speech sounds in the articulation of which the egressive or ingressive airstream encounters either a closure or a constriction which may or may not cause audible friction. Consonants may be classified according to the **manner of articulation** on the one hand and according to the **place of articulation** on the other. According to the various manners of articulation, consonants are classified into (1) plosives, (2) fricatives, (3) affricates, (4) approximants, (5) nasals, (6) rolls, (7) flaps, (8) ejectives, (9) implosives, and (10) clicks. Note that this classification is only one of different possible ones current among phoneticians.

1 A **plosive** is a sound in whose articulation the airstream meets a closure made by a firm contact between two speech organs, which prevents the airstream from issuing beyond the point of the closure. The closure is then quickly released, but since a complete, if brief, stopping of the airstream has taken place, the sound is considered to be **non-continuant**. Some examples of plosives are [p d ʔ]. The release of a plosive may be incomplete in certain sequences of plosives or of plosives followed by homorganic affricates (see below). In English, for example, [k] in *actor* is incompletely released, while in French [k] in *acteur* is completely released; similarly, [t] in *what change* in English and the second [t] in *toute table* in French are not released.

2 A **fricative** is a sound in whose articulation the airstream meets a narrowing between two speech organs and causes audible friction as it passes through this narrowing – a close approximation – in the vocal tract. Some examples of fricatives are [f z h], which are **central fricatives**, and [ɬ] which is a **lateral fricative**. In the articulation of a central fricative, the egressive air issues out along the median line in the oral cavity, while in that of a lateral fricative it issues out from one or both sides of the tongue.

3 An **affricate** is a sound in whose articulation the closure made by two speech organs for a plosive is slowly and partially released with the result that what is known in phonetics as a **homorganic fricative** immediately follows. In this sense, an affricate combines the characteristic of a plosive and that of a fricative; the term **homorganic** is used in phonetics to indicate that a certain consonant is articulated in the same place in the vocal tract as another consonant articulated in a different manner. Some examples of affricates are [tɹ dɹ tʃ dʒ], which are sequences of homorganically pronounced plosives and fricatives.

4 An **approximant** is a sound in whose articulation the airstream flows continuously, while two speech organs approach each other without touching, that is, the two speech organs are in **open approximation**. Consequently, there is no audible friction – the sound is **frictionless**. Approximants, which correspond to what the IPA (see THE INTERNATIONAL PHONETIC ALPHABET) formerly called **frictionless continuants and semivowels**, are by definition any speech sounds so articulated as to be just below **friction limit**, that is, just short of producing audible friction between two speech organs. Approximants are subdivided into **lateral approximants** and **median approximants**. Examples of lateral approximants include [l ɭ ʎ], in the case of which the two speech organs which are said to approach each other are the side(s) of the tongue and the side(s) of the teeth-ridge. Some examples of median approximants are [ʋ ɹ j w ʁ].

One particular type of speech sound which the IPA only partially recognizes but which should be fully recognized as median approximants are the speech sounds to which some refer as **spirants** and which are quite distinct from fricatives. The sounds correspond to the letters *b*, *d*, and *g* in, e.g., *haber*, *nada*, and *agua* in Spanish, in the articulation of which, in normal allegro speech, there occurs no audible friction. These spirants are often symbolized by ƀ, đ and ǥ respectively, although these symbols are not recognized by the IPA (see THE INTERNATIONAL PHONETIC ALPHABET). Note also that any close and 'closish' vowels, situated along or near the axis between the cardinal vowels nos 1 and 8 or nos 9 and 16 may justifiably be said to be approximants when they function as the so-called semivowels.

Approximants thus make up a category of heterogeneous speech sounds, including as they do certain of the vowels. There are divergent identifications of some approximants on the part of individual phoneticians.

5 A **nasal** is a sound in whose articulation the egressive airstream meets obstruction at a given point in the oral cavity and is channelled into the nasal cavity – the soft palate being lowered – through which it issues out. Some examples of nasals are [m n ŋ].

6 A **roll** or **trill** is a sound in whose articulation one speech organ strikes several times against the other rapidly, e.g. [r].

7 A **flap** or **tap** is a sound in whose articulation one speech organ strikes against the other just once, i.e. [ɾ].

8 An **ejective** is a sound in whose articulation a contact or constriction made by two speech organs at a given point in the oral cavity is released as the closed glottis is suddenly raised and pushes the compressed air in the mouth outwards, e.g. [p' s' ts'], and the air issues out as the oral closure is suddenly released. An ejective can thus be a **plosive**, a **fricative**, or an **affricate**.

9 An **implosive** is a sound in whose articulation a contact made by two speech organs in the oral cavity is released as air rushes in from outside. This is made possible by a sudden lowering of the loosely closed glottis, e.g. [ɓ], and the air then rushes further inwards as the oral closure is released. An implosive is thus a **plosive** as well.

10 A **click** is a sound in whose articulation a contact between two speech organs is made at a relatively forward part in the oral cavity at the same time as the closure made between the back of the tongue and the soft palate – velar closure – is released. As a result air rushes in as the back of the tongue slides backwards on the soft palate, e.g. [ǀ]. A click is a plosive as well.

Consonants may also be classified according to various **places of articulation**. The major places of articulation are as follows: (1) **bilabial**, i.e. both lips, as in [p]; (2) **labio-dental**, i.e. the lower lip and the upper front teeth, as in [f]; (3) **apico-dental**, i.e. the tip of the tongue and the upper front teeth, or the tip of the tongue placed between the upper and lower front teeth, as in [θ]; (4) **apico-alveolar**, i.e. the tip of the tongue and the teeth-ridge, as in [t]; (5) **blade-alveolar**, i.e. the blade of the tongue and the teeth-ridge, as in [s]; (6) **apico-post-alveolar**, i.e. the tip of the tongue and the back part of the teeth-ridge, as in [ɹ]; (7) **palatal**, i.e. the front of the tongue and the hard palate, as in [c]; (8) **alveolo-palatal**, i.e the front of the tongue, the hard palate, and the teeth-ridge, as in [ɕ]; (9) **palato-alveolar**, i.e. the tip and blade of the tongue, the back part of the teeth-ridge, and the hard palate, as in [ʃ]; (10) **retroflex**, i.e. the curled-up tip of the tongue and the hard palate, as in [ʂ]; (11) **velar**, i.e. the back of the tongue and the soft palate, as in [k]; (12) **uvular**, i.e. the uvula and the back of the tongue, as in [q]; (13) **pharyngeal**, i.e. the root of the tongue and the pharyngeal wall, as in [ʕ]; and (14) **glottal**, i.e. the vocal folds, as in [h].

Thus, for example, [p] is described as the voiceless bilabial plosive, [z] as the voiced blade-alveolar fricative, [tʃ] as the voiceless palato-alveolar affricate, [ŋ] as the voiced velar nasal, [ʎ] as the voiced palatal lateral approximant, [ʋ] as the voiced labio-dental approximant, [ɾ] as the voiced alveolar flap or tap, [r] as the voiced alveolar roll or trill, [p'] as the voiceless bilabial ejective, [ɓ] as the voiced bilabial implosive, and [ǀ] as the voiceless dental click.

It was mentioned above that speech sounds, when occurring in connected speech, i.e. in a flow of speech, partially blend into each other. Some phoneticians talk about **combinatory phonetics** in this connection. There are a number of such combinatory articulatory phenomena, but we shall concentrate on just one such phenomenon known as **assimilation**. Assimilation is said to occur when a speech sound undergoes a change in articulation in connected speech, becoming more like another immediately or otherwise adjacent sound. Thus, in English, for example, when [m] is replaced by [ɱ] before [f] or [v], as in *comfort* or *circumvent*, in an allegro pronunciation, its bilabiality changes into labio-dentality, and the pronunciation becomes ['kʌɱfət] or [ˌsəːkəɱ'vent]. In French, the voicelessness of [s] as in the word *tasse* is changed into voicedness, thus [s̬] (the diacritic mark ˬ signifying voicing), in normal pronunciation of e.g. *tasse de thé*, without [ş] being identical to [z] all the same: [taş də te] ≠ *[taz də te]. In English, the voice of [m] in, e.g., *mall* is either partially or completely lost in e.g. *small* under the influence of the voicelessness of [s] preceding it, producing [smɔ:l] (the diacritic mark ˳ signifies devoicing).

An assimilation in which the following sound affects the preceding sound, as in *comfort, circumvent, tasse de thé* is said to be regressive in nature and is therefore called **regressive assimilation**; an assimilation in which the preceding sound affects the following sound, as in *small*, is said to be progressive in nature and is therefore called **progressive assimilation**. Assimilation of these kinds relates to the question of what is called an **allophone** of a **phoneme** (see PHONEMICS) and to the question of a realization of a phoneme or an **archiphoneme** (see FUNCTIONAL PHONOLOGY).

What we have seen above concerns speech sounds to which phoneticians often refer as **segmental units** or **segmentals** for short, since they are phonetic units which occur sequentially. In languages there are also what phoneticians refer to as **suprasegmental units** or **suprasegmentals** which are associated in their occurrence with stretches of segmentals and therefore are coterminous with them. They may be in other cases associated in their occurrence with single segments but ultimately have implications on multiple segments. **Intonation** and **stress** are among the better known suprasegmentals (see INTONATION); another well-known segmental is **duration**: a segmental may be relatively long, i.e. a long sound (e.g. [i:] in *beet* [bi:t] in English; [t:] in *itta* [it:a] 'he/she/it/they went', in Japanese), or relatively short, i.e. a short sound (e.g. [ɪ] in *bit* [bɪt] in English; [t] in *ita* [ita] 'he/she/it/they was/were (here, there, etc.)', in Japanese).

Finally, **tones** which characterize **tone languages** are, physically speaking, comparable to intonation but are assigned to **morphemes**, i.e. to the smallest linguistic units endowed with meaning (see TONE LANGUAGES). Therefore, tones are, linguistically, comparable to phonemes and archiphonemes (see FUNCTIONAL PHONOLOGY), whose function it is to distinguish between morphemes, rather than to intonation. However, every language, be it tonal or not, has intonation.

T.A.

SUGGESTIONS FOR FURTHER READING

Abercrombie, D. (1967), *Elements of General Phonetics*, Edinburgh, Edinburgh University Press, chs 2, 4, 8, 9, and 10.

O'Connor, J.D. (1973), *Phonetics*, Harmondsworth, Penguin, ch. 2.

Ladefoged, P. (1982), *A Course in Phonetics*, 2nd edn, New York, Harcourt Brace Jovanovich, chs 1, 6, 7, 9, and 10.

Artificial Intelligence

ARTIFICIAL INTELLIGENCE

Any discussion of the relations between Artificial Intelligence (AI) and linguistics needs to start with a brief review of what AI actually is. This is no place to attempt a definition of AI, but we do need some rough guidelines.

Just about the only characterization of AI that would meet with universal acceptance is that it involves trying to make machines do tasks which are normally seen as requiring intelligence. There are countless refinements of this characterization: what sort of machines we want to consider; how we decide what tasks require intelligence; and so on. For the current discussion, the most important question concerns the *reasons why* we want to make machines do such tasks. Among all its other dichotomies, AI has always been split between people who want to make machines do tasks that require intelligence because they want more useful machines, and people who want to do it because they see it as a way of exploring how humans do such tasks. We will call the two approaches the **engineering approach** and the **cognitive-science approach** respectively.

The techniques required for the two approaches are not always very different. For many of the tasks that engineering AI wants solutions to, the only systems we know about that can perform them are humans, so that, at least initially, the obvious way to design them is to try to mimic what we know about humans. For many of the tasks that cognitive-science AI wants solutions to, the evidence on how humans do them is too hard to interpret to enable us to construct computational models, so the only approach is to try to design solutions from scratch and then see how well they fit what we know about humans. The main visible difference between the two approaches is in their criteria for success: an engineer would be delighted to have created something which outperformed a person; a cognitive scientist would regard it as a failure.

NATURAL-LANGUAGE PROCESSING V. COMPUTATIONAL LINGUISTICS

The distinction between the two approaches is as marked in AI work on language as in any other area. Language has been a major topic of AI research ever since people first thought that there might be some point in the discipline at all. As far as the engineering view of AI is concerned, the initial focus on language was on machine translation, since translation was viewed, with typical arrogance, as a mundane and easily mechanizable task. When it became apparent that this was not so, the focus switched to the use of language to enable people who were not explicitly trained in computer programming to make use of computers anyway – tasks such as interpreting and answering database queries, entering facts and

rules into expert systems, and so on.

Much of this work took the view that for constrained tasks of this kind, systems that could deal with **sublanguages** would suffice. It is possible to argue with this view. Conversing in a language which looks a bit like your native tongue but which differs from it in ways which are not made clear may be more difficult and irritating than having to learn an entirely new but very simple and explicit language. Whether or not users will be happier with a system that speaks a fragment of some natural language than with a formal language, it is clear that much work in engineering AI differs from work in traditional linguistics by virtue of the emphasis on sublanguages.

The cognitive-science view, on the other hand, is concerned with very much the same phenomena as traditional linguistics, and its theories are couched in very similar terms. The main divergences between this sort of AI work on language and work within other branches of linguistics concerns the degree of precision required, and the constraint that theories must pay attention to the possibility of being used in programs. I will show later that the need to see how to compute with your theory of language led to the comparative neglect of standard transformational approaches in AI, and thence to the emergence of competing theories of grammar which are now percolating back into linguistics as such.

As in all of AI, the two approaches feed off each other whilst retaining rather different flavours, and especially rather different criteria of success. The terms **natural language processing** (NLP) and **computational linguistics** (CL) are widely used for the engineering and cognitive-science viewpoints respectively. The discussion below will indicate, where possible, which way particular theories are best viewed, but it must be emphasized that they are highly interdependent: successful ideas from one are likely to influence work in the other; the failure of an idea in one is likely to lead to its rejection in the other.

HISTORY OF AI WORK ON NATURAL LANGUAGE

AI work on natural language is now as fragmented

as linguistics as a whole, though along different divisions. To understand the theories being used in AI, and to relate them to other work in linguistics, we need to see where they came from and how they fit into the overall framework. Therefore the discussion of particular concepts and theories will be preceded by a brief overview of the history of AI work in the field.

IN THE BEGINNING: MACHINE TRANSLATION

The earliest work on language within AI was concerned with machine translation (Weaver, 1955). The early approach to this task took the view that the only differences between languages were between their vocabularies and between the permitted word orders. Machine translation, then, was going to be just a matter of looking in a dictionary for appropriate words in the target language to translate the words in the source text, and then reorder the output so it fitted the word-order rules of the target language. The systems that resulted from this simple-minded approach appeared to be almost worse than useless, largely because of the degree of lexical ambiguity of a non-trivial subset of a natural language. Trying to deal with lexical ambiguity by including translations of each possible interpretation of each word led to the generation of text which contained so many options that it was virtually meaningless.

The superficial inadequacies of these systems, probably accompanied by overenthusiastic sales pitches by their developers, led in 1966 to a highly critical report from the American National Academy of Sciences and to a general loss of enthusiasm. Ironically, one of the earliest of these systems did remain funded, and eventually turned into what probably remains the most effective real machine-translation system, **SYSTRAN**. Furthermore, the 'transfer' approach to machine translation which underlies the massive EEC-funded EUROTRA project probably owes more to the early word-for-word approach than is usually made apparent.

SPEECH PROCESSING

Another group of early optimists, funded largely by the US advanced research-projects agency ARPA (later DARPA – Defense Advanced Research-Project Agency), attempted the task of producing systems capable of processing speech. Some of these systems more or less met their proclaimed targets of processing normal connected speech, over a restricted domain and with a 1,000 word vocabulary, with less than 10 per cent error. They do not, however, seem to have formed the basis on which a second generation of speech-processing systems would be built incorporating the lessons from the first round. It is not clear why this is so. It may be that the initial lessons were that the task was so much more complex than had been anticipated that no useful practical lessons had in fact been learned from the first round.

On this account, the main effect of this work was that AI workers were yet again made aware of the immense complexity of the task, realizing that little progress would be made until we had a more complete theoretical understanding of the various components of the linguistic system, and in particular an appropriate encoding of the acoustic signal. Certainly, subsequent reported work on speech seems to have concentrated on much more restricted tasks: recognition of spoken commands in 'hands busy' situations such as aircraft cockpits; automatic transcription of speech by 'talkwriters'; and so on. On the other hand, the reason for the apparent absence of large-scale follow-ups to the partial success of the ARPA projects may be that this work was deemed to be so successful that the Department of Defense took it over completely and classified it.

QUESTION ANSWERING

Other early workers attempted to build systems that could accumulate facts and answer questions about them. Most of these did very little analysis of the linguistic structure of the texts they were dealing with. The emphasis was on the sort of processing which goes on after the basic meaning has been extracted. Weizenbaum's (1966) **ELIZA** program, which simply permutes and echoes whatever the user types at it, is probably the best known of these systems. ELIZA does less work than probably any other well-known computer program, since all it does is recognize key words and patterns in the input and place them in predefined slots in output schemas (after suitable permutations, such as switching *you* to *me*).

The other programs of this period did little more syntactic processing, but did at least do some work on the patterns that they extracted. A reasonable example is Bobrow's (1968) program for solving algebra problems like the following:

> If the number of customers Tom gets is twice the square of 20 per cent of the number of advertisements he runs, and the number of advertisements he runs is 45, what is the number of customers Tom gets?

This appears to be in English, albeit rather stilted English. Bobrow's program processed it by doing simple pattern matching to get it into a form which was suitable for his equation-solving program. It is hard to say whether what Bobrow was doing was really language processing, or whether his achievement was more in the field of equation solving. It is clear that his program would have made no progress whatsoever with the following problem:

> If the number of customers Tom gets is twice the square of 20 per cent of the number of advertisements he runs, and he runs 45 advertisements, how many customers does he get?

The other pattern-matching programs of this time were equally frail in the face of the real complexity of natural language. It seems fair to say that the main progress made by these programs was in inference, not in language processing. The main lesson for language processing was that pattern matching was not enough: what was needed was proper linguistic theory.

LINGUISTIC THEORY

The apparent failure of the early work made AI researchers realize that they needed a more adequate theory of language. As is far too often the case with AI work, there was already a substantial body of research on the required

properties of language which had been ignored in the initial enthusiasm for writing programs. Towards the end of the 1960s, people actually went away and read the existing linguistic literature to find out what was known and what was believed, and what they might learn for their next generation of programs. Simultaneously, it was realized that NLP systems would need to draw on substantial amounts of general knowledge about the world in order to determine the meanings in context of words, phrases, and even entire discourses. Work in the late 1960s and early 1970s concentrated on finding computationally tractable versions of existing theories of grammar, and on developing schemes of meaning representation. These latter are required both to enable the integration of the specifically linguistic part of an NLP system with the sort of knowledge required for disambiguation and interpretation in context, and to actually link the NLP system to some other program which had information a user might want to access.

SYNTACTIC THEORY

It was rapidly found that the dominant theory of syntax at that time, the extended standard (EST) version of transformational grammar (TG) did not lend itself easily to computational treatment. There is a long gap between Friedman's (1969, 1971) system for experimenting with putative transformations to see whether they generate all and only the required forms and Stabler's (1987) attempt to combine unification grammar and government and binding theory, and during this time TG had virtually no direct representation within CL. The major threads in syntactic theory in CL for most of this time have been the following: (1) the use of adaptations of Fillmore's (1968) case grammar; (2) attempts to do without an explicit grammar at all; and (3) attempts to extend the power of phrase-structure grammar by incorporating mechanisms from programming languages.

Case grammar
Case grammar started out as an attempt to explain some apparent syntactic anomalies: why,

for instance, the sentences *John is cooking* and *Mary is cooking* can be collapséd to a single sentence *John and Mary are cooking*, whereas *John is cooking* and *The meat is cooking* cannot be collapsed to *John and the meat are cooking*; and why *She opened the door with a key* can be expanded to *The key opened the door* and *The door opened*, but not to *The key opened*. Within linguistics it remained an interesting, but essentially minor, theory (see CASE GRAMMAR). Within CL, and especially NLP, it became for a while more or less dominant.

The reason for this appears to be that the semantic roles that were invoked to explain the given phenomena mapped extremely directly onto the sorts of role that were already being discussed as the basis of techniques for meaning representation. The roles in case grammar could be interpreted directly as arcs in a **semantic network**, a graphical encoding of a set of relations between entities. Bruce (1975) provides an overview of a number of NLP systems employing some variant of case grammar. As the weakness of semantic-network representations becomes more apparent, it seems that case grammar is becoming less significant for AI, but its influence has not disappeared entirely.

Grammarless systems
It may seem odd to include a subsection on systems which do without grammar within a section called 'Syntactic Theory'. It would be unrealistic, however, to leave it out. To take the view that there *is* no syntactic level in language processing is to take a very strong view indeed as to what rules are required for the description of syntactic structure in NLP: none at all. The main proponents of this view, the **Yale School** based around Roger Schank, argue that whatever information is encoded in the organization of language can be extracted directly without building an intermediate representation.

It is not, in fact, all that easy to see what their claim really amounts to. Common sense tells us that they cannot entirely ignore the structure of the text they are processing, since if they did, then their systems would come up with identical interpretations for *The lion beat the unicorn all round the town* and *town lion unicorn round all the the the beat*. Which they do not, and just as well too: we would hardly be very impressed by an NLP system which could not tell the difference between these two. Furthermore, one of the core programs in the substantial suite they have developed is Riesbeck's (1978) **conceptual analyser**. This program makes explicit mention of syntactic categories like 'noun' and 'determiner' in order to segment the text and extract the relations between the concepts represented by the words in the text – exactly what we always regarded as the task of syntactic analysis. We could weaken their claim to say that by building the semantic representation by direct analysis of the relations of individual words in the input text they avoid constructing an unnecessary intermediate set of structures. This, however, fails to provide any serious contrast with theories like Montague grammar (Dowty *et al.*, 1981), generalized phrase-structure grammar (GPSG) (Gazdar *et al.*, 1985) and unification categorical grammar (UCG) (Klein, 1987). These theories contain extremely complex and specific rules about permissible configurations of structures, of the sort that the Yale School seems to avow. They also, however, contain very straightforward mappings between syntactic rules and rules for semantic interpretation, so that any structure built up using them can equally easily be seen as semantic and syntactic.

Phrase-structure grammar and programs
For most of the 1970s the main example of this third approach was Woods' (1970, 1973) **augmented transition network** (ATN) formalism, which incorporated virtually unchanged the basic operations of the programming language LISP. Many very successful systems were developed using this formalism, but it had comparatively little effect on linguistics as a whole because the choice of the operations from LISP seemed to have very little explanatory power. ATNs work quite well, but they do not seem to capture any significant properties of language.

More recent work which uses notions from the logic programming language PROLOG seems to have had a wider effect. This is presumably because of PROLOG's status as an attempt to mechanize the rules of logic, which are themselves attempts to capture the universal rules of valid inference. These grammars use the PROLOG operation of **unification**, a complex pattern-matching operation, to capture phenomena such as agreement, subcategorization, and long-distance dependency, rather than using the more standard programming operations of variable assignment and access.

The first such **unification grammar** was Pereira and Warren's (1980) **definite clause grammar (DCG)**. This was simply an attempt to capitalize on the facilities which came for free with PROLOG, without any very strongly held views on whether language was really like this or not. Since then, however, variants of unification seem to have taken over grammatical theory. Generalized phrase-structure grammar (Gazdar *et al.*, 1985), lexical-functional grammar (Bresnan and Kaplan, 1982), functional-unification grammar (Kay, 1985), restricted-logic grammar (Stabler, 1987) – the list seems to be growing daily. Unlike DCG, these later formalisms are generally defended in wider terms than their suitability for computer implementation, though at the same time they all respect the need to consider processing issues. This seemed, in the late 1980s, one of the most significant contributions of AI/NLP to general linguistic theory – a growing consensus on the general form of syntactic rules, which emerged initially from the AI literature but later came to be taken seriously within non-computational linguistics.

SYNTACTIC PROCESSING

As well as choosing an appropriate syntactic theory, it was necessary to construct programs which could apply the theory, either to analyse the structure of input texts or to generate well-formed output texts. The development of **parsing algorithms**, i.e. programs for doing syntactic analysis, became an area of intense activity. The debate initially concentrated on whether it was better to apply rules **top-down**, making guesses about the structure of the text and testing these by matching them against the words that were actually present, or **bottom-up**, inspecting the text and trying to find rules that would explain its structure. In each of these approaches, there are times when the system has to make a blind choice among different possible rules, since there is generally not enough information available to guide it directly to the right answer. The simplest way of dealing with this is to use **chronological backtracking**, in other words, whenever you make a choice, remember what the alternatives were and when you get stuck go back to the last choice-point which still has unexplored alternatives and try one of these.

It rapidly became apparent that, although this worked to some extent, systems that did this kind of naive backtracking tended to throw away useful things they had done as well as mistakes. To see this, consider the sentence *I can see the woman you were talking to coming up the path*. Most systems would realize that *see* often occurs as a simple transitive verb, so that the initial sequence *I can see the woman you were talking to* would be analysed as a complete sentence bracketed something like:

[[I]NP [can see [the woman you were talking to]NP]VP]S

The fact that there was some text left over would indicate that there was a mistake somewhere, and after further exploration an analysis more like the following might be made:

[[I]NP [can see [[the woman you were talking to]NP [coming up the path]VP]S]VP]S

It is hard to see how you could avoid having to explore the two alternatives. What should be avoidable is having to reanalyse the string *the woman you were talking to* as a NP simply because its initial analysis occurred during the exploration of a dead-end.

There were two major reactions to this problem. The first involved keeping a record of structures that had been successfully constructed, so that any attempts to repeat work that had already been done could be detected and the results of the previous round could be used immediately. This notion of a **well-formed substring table** (Earley, 1970) was later developed to include structures which were currently being constructed, as well as ones that had been completed, in Kay's (1986) **active chart**. The other approach to dealing with these problems was to try to write the rules of the grammar in such a way that mistaken hypotheses simply did not get explored. The grammar developed by Marcus (1980) was designed so that a parser using it would be able to delay making decisions about what to do next until it had the information it needed to make the right choice. Riesbeck (1978) designed a system which would directly extract the information embodied in the syntactic structure, rather than building an explicit representation of the structure and then trying to interpret its significance. This approach at least partly side-steps the issue of redoing work that has been done previously.

MEANING REPRESENTATION

AI has largely accepted from linguistics the view that language processing requires analysis at various levels. It has not, however, taken over the exact details of what each level is about. In particular, the AI view of semantics is very different from the linguistic treatment. It is inappropriate – and probably dangerous – at this point to try to give a characterization of the subject matter of semantics within linguistics (see SEMANTICS). But whatever it is, it is not the same as the need of AI systems to link the language they are processing to the other information they have access to, in order to respond appropriately.

We have already seen this in the discussion of early question-answering systems. Much of what purported to be language processing turned out there to be manipulations of the system's own knowledge: of how to solve algebra problems, or of the statistics of the last year's baseball games, or whatever. This is entirely appropriate. Probably the biggest single lesson linguistics will learn from AI is that you have to integrate the linguistic component of your model with the rest of its knowledge.

The easiest way to do this seems to be to have some form of internal **interlingua**, some representation language within which all the system's knowledge can be expressed. The nature of this interlingua depends on what the system actually knows. There have been three major proposals for representation languages: logic, programming languages, and semantic primitives. There are, of course, a wide variety of notations for these, and there is some degree of overlap, but the division does reflect genuinely different approaches to the question of internal representation.

Logic

Logic, in various guises, has long been used as a language for analysing the semantics of natural languages. It has also been widely recommended, for instance by Charniak and McDermott (1985), as a good general-purpose representation language for AI systems. It is therefore no surprise to see it being proposed as the language which NLP systems should use as the interlingua that connects them to the rest of the system of which they are a part.

There are two major traditions of using logic as the representation language in NLP systems. Firstly, the widely used **semantic network** representation can easily be seen as a way of implementing a subset of the first-order predicate calculus (FOPC) (see FORMAL LOGIC AND MODAL LOGIC) so as to facilitate certain types of inference. A semantic network is an implementation technique for recording a set of two-place relations between individuals as a labelled directed graph. As an example, we could represent some of the meaning of *John loves Mary* as the following set of relations:

agent(loving, John)
object(loving, Mary)

we could then represent these as a semantic network as follows:

```
               agent                    object
John ----------→ loving ←---------- Mary
```

N-place relations can be recorded by splitting them into collections of two-place relations. It is fairly easy to show that their expressive power is equivalent to that of a subset of FOPC, but the internal representation as a network of pointers can make it easier to perform such operations as finding out all the relations a particular individual enters into. Semantic networks frequently contain pointers which contain information about class hierarchies, since this is both useful and particularly amenable to processing within graphical representations.

Semantic networks have a long history within NLP. There has often been a connection between the use of case grammar as a grammatical formalism and semantic networks as a representation language. In particular, the relations that are represented in the network are often just the roles implied by the grammar. There is, however, no necessary link between the two theories. An alternative is to use the main verb of the sentence being interpreted as the label on an arc between its subject and object, though this can be awkward in the case of intransitive verbs, where there is no object to put at the far end of the arc, and in the case of bitransitive verbs or verbs with adjuncts, since there is no obvious place to put the extra items.

The other use of logic as a representation language has followed more directly from work within formal semantics (see FORMAL SEMANTICS). The semantic theories associated with grammatical theories like GPSG and UCG descend directly from work by logicians and philosophers of language on questions of logical relationships between sentences. The problems addressed within these theories range from questions of quantifier scope (why *Everyone has a mother* seems to say something about a relationship between each person and some particular other person who is their mother, whereas *Everyone likes a good story* seems to talk about a relationship between every person and every good story); through problems about propositional attitudes (how we characterize the truth conditions of a sentence such as *He knows I believe there is a cat in the garden*); to the need for a distinction between intensional and extensional readings of sentences (to explain why we can infer the existence of a unicorn from the truth of *John found a unicorn*, but not from *John looked for a unicorn*).

At various points this work has shown that FOPC is not in fact rich enough to express all the distinctions which can be made in natural language, and that more powerful formalisms such as modal logic and intensional logic may be needed. Progress in this area is rather hindered by the extreme computational intractability of these more powerful formalisms.

Procedural semantics
Just as with the inclusion of notions from programming languages into grammatical formalisms, the fact that the meaning representation is to be used by a computer has led a number of researchers to try to use a programming language as their representation language.

Winograd's (1972) program, **SHRDLU**, is perhaps the best-known example of this. Winograd realized that a hearer is not normally thought of just as a passive receiver of information. In any normal dialogue, the speaker expects the hearer to *do* something as a result of processing what they are told. If they are asked a question they are expected to answer it; if they are given an order they are expected to carry it out; if they are told a fact they are expected to remember it. Since the languages that are used to get computers to do things are programming languages, it seemed reasonable to require the interpretation to be expressed in a programming language, as a command to find the answer to a question, or to perform an action, or to assert something in a database, as appropriate.

Winograd used a special-purpose programming language called **MICRO-PLANNER** (Hewitt, 1971) for this **procedural semantics**. Norman *et al.* (1975) used the standard programming language **LISP** for their implementation of this idea. With the development of **PROLOG** as a language with alternative readings as either a version of FOPC or an executable programming language, the distinction between using logic and using procedural semantics has become rather blurred, as can be seen in for instance CHAT-80 (Warren and Pereira, 1982).

Semantic primitives
Any representation language has **primitives**, that is, terms which are basic, or taken as given, because it is not possible to define all the terms in

any vocabulary in terms of each other without introducing unexplained circularities. The choice of a programming language for the representation language provides one way out of the problem, since the semantics of this language as a programming language will define the semantics of the primitives. An alternative solution is to try to find some set of terms which can be taken as the real primitives of human thought, and try to base everything on these.

The major proponents of this notion are again the Yale School led by Roger Schank. Schank's theory of **conceptual dependency (CD)** is an attempt to find a minimal set of primitives which can be used for the interpretation of all natural-language texts. Schank motivates the development of his theory with the argument that any two sentences that would be judged by a native speaker to have the same meaning should have identical representations, and illustrates this by requiring that *John loves Mary* should have the same meaning as *Mary is loved by John*. CD is a brave attempt to find a manageable set of primitives which will support this argument. However, many linguists would not agree that any two sentences which differ in form can be identical in meaning.

The number of primitives in CD has fluctuated slightly as the theory has developed, but is remarkably stable when compared to the range of cases and roles that have been suggested in all the variants on case grammar. One reasonably representative version of the theory has eleven primitive actions, a set of roles such as **instrument** and **object** as in case grammar, and a notion of causal connection.

These actions have been widely reported (e.g. in Charniak and McDermott, 1985), and I will not go into details here. One thing I will note is that at first sight they seem remarkably biased towards human beings, with the action of **SPEAKing**, i.e. making a string of sounds of a language, having roughly the same status as **PTRANSing**, or moving an object from one place to another. Careful consideration, however, shows that if there is anything at all in the theory then this sort of claim is one of its more significant consequences. Furthermore, their analysis does seem

to work for a non-trivial subset of the language. The emphasis on human activities is perhaps less surprising when we realize that most of what humans talk about is things that humans do.

CD is not the only AI theory based on semantic primitives. Most others make weaker claims about the status of their primitives. Wilks' (1978) theory of **preference semantics**, for instance, used quite a large set of primitives (a hundred or more) as the basis for disambiguation of word senses in a translation program. This set of primitives is offered as a useful tool for this task, but very little is said about either their psychological reality or about whether or not they are a minimal set even for the task in hand. In many theories the presence of primitives is left unremarked: theories deriving from Montague semantics, for instance, simply permit the presence of uninterpreted elements of the vocabulary without any explanation at all.

BEYOND THE SENTENCE

NLP systems have always recognized that dealing with individual sentences was only part of the task. Processing larger texts requires research on at least two further topics: linguistic and structural properties of connected discourses; and the use of background knowledge.

Discourse processing
As soon as we move to connected discourses, we meet a collection of problems which simply did not present themselves when we were just considering isolated sentences. Some of them concern the problem of interpreting the individual sentences that make up the discourse, in particular the problem of determining referents for pronouns. Others concern the placing of each sentence in relation to the others: is it an elaboration, or an example, or a summary, or a change of topic (compare TEXT LINGUISTICS). Progress on these topics was fairly slow so long as people concentrated on systems for interpreting language. A few heuristics for pronoun dereferencing were developed, and there were some experiments on **story grammars** (e.g. Rumelhart, 1975), but generally not much was achieved. This

seems to be because it is possible to get at least some information out of a connected text even when its overall structure is not really understood, so that people were not really aware that there was a lot more there that they could have been getting.

The situation changed radically when serious attempts were made to get computers to *generate* connected texts. It soon became apparent that if you misuse cues about the structure of your text then human readers become confused. For instance, the use of pronouns in *John likes fish; he hates meat* and *Mary likes fish; Jane hates it* enables us to track the topic of the two texts – John in the first, fish in the second. Failure to use them, as in *John likes fish. John hates meat* and *Mary likes fish. Jane hates fish*, leads to confusion, since we have no clues to tell us what we are really being told about. Systems for comprehension of text which had no idea about topic and focus could cope with either example, so long as they had some vague heuristics about pronoun dereferencing. But systems which are to generate coherent text must have a more adequate understanding of what is going on. Work by Appelt (1985) and McKeown (1985) on language generation, and by Webber (1983) and Grosz and Sidner (1986) represents some progress in these areas.

This work also draws on the notion of language as rational, planned behaviour. This idea, which stems originally from suggestions by Wittgenstein (1953) and from Searle's (1969) work on speech acts (see SPEECH-ACT THEORY), was originally introduced into AI approaches to language by Allen and Perrault (1980) and Cohen and Perrault (1979). The idea here was to characterize complete utterances as actions which could be described in terms of their preconditions and effects. This characterization would enable connected texts and dialogues to be understood. Using existing AI theories of planning (Fikes and Nilsson, 1971), a speech act could be planned as just another act on the way to realizing the speaker's overall goal; and, perhaps more interestingly, such an act could be interpreted by trying to work out what goal the speaker could have that might be furthered by the act. There are many problems with this approach, not least the sheer difficulty of recognizing another's plan simply by reasoning forwards from their actions, but it certainly seems like a fruitful area for further research.

Background knowledge

In addition to needing an analysis of the functional structure of connected texts, we also clearly need to access substantial amounts of general knowledge. We need this both for interpreting texts in which a lot of background information is left unstated, and for generating texts which will leave out enough for a human reader to find them tolerable. Although it is again well known that we need such background knowledge, comparatively little work has been done on providing it. This must be at least partly because no-one has ever really had the resources to compile the sort of knowledge base that would be required for effective testing of theories about how to use it.

The only substantial attempt to do something about it comes again from the Yale School. Schank and Abelson (1977) developed the notion of a **script**, namely a summary of the events that constitute some stereotyped social situation. Scripts can be used in both the comprehension and generation of stories about such situations. Schank and Abelson argue that to tell a story for which both speaker and hearer have a shared script, all the speaker has to do is to provide the hearer with enough information to invoke the right script and instantiate its parameters, and then state those events in the current instance that *differ* from what is in the script.

There is a lot that seems right about this, not least that it explains the feeling of frustration that we experience when someone insists on spelling out all the details of a story when all we want is the bare bones plus anything unusual. Quite a number of programs based on it have been developed (Lehnert, 1978; Wilensky, 1978), showing that it is not just appealing but that it may also have practical applications. There is, however, still a substantial set of problems with it. Outstanding among these are the question of how we acquire and manage the many hundreds of thousands of scripts that we would need in order to cope with the range of stories that we do seem able to cope with, and the problems of mutual knowledge that arise when the speaker and hearer are trying to co-ordinate their view of the script that is currently in use. Schank (1982) makes an informal, if plausible, attempt to discuss the first of these problems; the second is a problem for all theories of how to organize connected discourse to reflect the social processes that underlie language use.

A.M.R.

SUGGESTIONS FOR FURTHER READING

Grosz, B.J., Sparck Jones, K., and Webber, B.L. (1986), *Readings in Natural Language Processing*, Los Altos, Morgan Kaufman.

Sparck Jones, K. and Wilks, Y. (1983), *Automatic Natural Language Parsing*, Chichester, Ellis Horwood.

Winograd, T. (1983), *Language as a Cognitive Process*, vol. 1: *Syntax*, Reading, MA, Addison Wesley.

Artificial languages

An **artificial language** is one which has been created for some specific purpose or reason, as opposed to a **natural language**, such as those spoken by most speech communities around the world, which is normally thought of as having evolved along with its speech community, and for which it is not possible to find some ultimate source of creation. The machine codes and various programming languages we use with computers (see ARTIFICIAL INTELLIGENCE) and the languages of logic (see FORMAL LOGIC AND MODAL LOGIC) are all artificial languages, but will not be dealt with in this entry which is devoted, rather, to those artificial languages which have been developed for general use in attempts to provide 'a neutral tongue acceptable to all' (Large, 1985, p. vii). The best-known such language is probably **Esperanto**, which was one hundred years old in 1987. In that year, the United Nations estimated that Esperanto was spoken by 8 million people, from 130 countries. There were around 38,000 items of literature in Esperanto in the Esperanto library at Holland Park, London, which is the largest in the world, and the Esperanto Parliamentary Group at

Westminster numbered 240 MPs. *The Linguist* (vol. 26, no. 1, Winter 1987, p. 8), lists the following further facts as evidence for the success of the language as an international medium of communication:

> Radio Peking broadcasts four half hour programmes in it each day, British Telecom recognise it as a clear language for telegrams, Dutch telephone booths have explanations for the Esperanto-speaking foreigner, it is available under the Duke of Edinburgh Award Scheme, and the Wales Tourist Board have begun issuing travel brochures in it. . . . Liverpool University has recently appointed a Lecturer in Esperanto, and the Dutch Government has given the computer firm BSO a grant of £3 million to develop a machine translation programme with Esperanto as the bridge, or intermediate language.

Before one rushes off to take lessons, however, it is worth knowing that there are around 300 million native speakers of varieties of English around the world, and that almost as many people use it as an additional language. In 1975,

English was the official language of twenty-one nations and one of the languages of government, education, broadcasting, and publication in a further sixteen countries (Bailey and Görlach, 1982, Preface).

Nevertheless, Esperanto is the most successful outcome of The Artificial Language Movement (Large, 1985), which began seriously in the seventeenth century with the efforts of Francis Bacon, among others, at developing a written language composed of **real characters**, symbols which represented concepts in a way that could be understood universally because they were pictorial, as he wrongly supposed that Chinese characters and Egyptian Hieroglyphics were (see WRITING SYSTEMS). Such a language would not only be universal, but would also reflect nature accurately, a major concern in that age of scientific endeavour, and it would be free of ambiguities, so that ideas could be expressed clearly in it. It would, however, require considerable powers of memory, since large numbers of characters would have to be remembered if the language was to be of general use, and interest in universal-language projects such as Bacon's (of which Large, 1985, gives a .comprehensive overview) faded during the eighteenth century.

The creation of a universal language came to be seen as a serious proposition again with the invention of **Volapük** in the late nineteenth century. Volapük was created by a German parish priest, Monsignor Johann Martin Schleyer (1832–1912), who was, according to Large (1985, p. 64), reputed to have 'some familiarity with more than 50 languages'. Schleyer thought that all natural languages were defective because their grammars were irrational and irregular, and his aim was to develop a language which would be simple to learn, grammatically regular, and in which thought could be clearly and adequately expressed. Its vocabulary consisted of **radicals** derived mainly from English words with some adaptation of words from German, French, Spanish, and Italian. The radicals were derived from the source words according to a number of rules. For instance, the letter *h* was excluded, and *r* almost totally eliminated because Schleyer thought that it was difficult to pronounce for

Chinese, old people and children; all radicals had to begin and end with a consonant; as far as possible, consonants and vowels should alternate in radicals. According to these rules, the English words *moon, knowledge, speak, world, tooth,* and *friend* become the Volapük radicals, *mun, nol, pük, vol, tut,* and *flen*. Nouns had four cases and two numbers, providing case and number endings as in the following example:

	Singular	Plural
Nominative	vol	vols
Genitive	vola	volas
Dative	vole	voles
Accusative	voli	volis

The compound *volapük* can thus be seen to be formed from the genitive of *vol* 'world' and *pük* 'speak' (meaning 'language').

It is possible to argue that Volapük has a masculine bias, in so far as the male term, for instance *blod* 'brother', is taken as the norm from which feminine variations are formed by means of the prefix *ji-*, thus *jiblod* 'sister'. Adjectives are formed by adding the suffix *-ik*. Verbs have one regular conjugation, and voice and tense are indicated by prefixes, while mood, person, and personal pronouns are indicated by suffixes. Word-building rules include using the suffix *-av* to indicate a science and the suffix *-al* to indicate spiritual or abstract concepts. Large (1985, p. 67) charts the growth of Volapük as follows:

The Volapük movement experienced a spectacular growth, spreading rapidly from Germany into Austria, France and the Low Countries, and thence to the far-flung corners of the globe. By 1889 there were some 283 societies or clubs scattered throughout the world as far away as Sydney and San Francisco, 1,600 holders of the Volapük diploma and an estimated one million Volapükists (at least according to their own estimates; one-fifth of this figure is a more realistic number). Over 300 textbooks on the language had been published and 25 journals were devoted to Volapük, seven being entirely published in the language. The First Volapük International Congress, held in Friedrichshafen in August

1884, was conducted in German ... as was the Second Congress in Munich (1887), but the Third International Congress, held in Paris in 1889, was completed exclusively in Volapük.

Subsequently, however, enthusiasm for the language as a possible universal medium of communication declined. The grammar, although regular, was complicated, offering several thousands of different forms of verbs, and because of the strict rules for deriving vocabulary from other languages, the words were often difficult or impossible to recognize, so the vocabulary simply had to be memorized. Therefore, the language was not one which non-experts or enthusiasts would find easy to appropriate, and attempts to simplify it were met with hostility by Schleyer. The controversy generated by the simplification issue within the movement led to its rapid decline so that by the time of Schleyer's death in 1912 the rival artificial language, **Esperanto**, had many more followers than Volapük, and had even won over large numbers of former Volapükists.

Esperanto was created by the Polish Jew and polyglot (Russian, French, German, Latin, Greek, English, Hebrew, Yiddish, and Polish, according to Large, 1985, p. 71), Ludwick Lazarus Zamenhof (1859–1917), who was by profession a medical doctor. His language was called **Lingvo Internacia** when first published in 1887, but this name was soon displaced by the author's pseudonym, Doctor Esperanto. Zamenhof thought that Volapük was too complicated to learn, and his familiarity with English convinced him that grammatical complexity such as that which Volapük displayed in spite of its regularity, was not a necessary feature of a universal language.

Esperanto has only sixteen grammatical rules (listed in Large, 1985, Appendix I) and its vocabulary is based largely on Romance languages and Latin. Like all living languages, Esperanto is able to adapt to changes in its environment, since it is highly receptive to new words, which, if they can be made to conform to Esperanto orthography, are simply taken over from their source; if they cannot easily be made to conform to Esperanto orthography or compounded from existing Esperanto roots, new

words will be created. All nouns end with *o*, adjectives with *a* and adverbs with *e*. Plurals end with *j* (/ɪ/). Use of affixes to common roots provides for further regularities of word formation, and ensures that families of words can be created from a relatively small stock of roots – 16,000 in the most comprehensive dictionary of Esperanto, *La Plena ilustrita vortaro*. From these roots ten times as many words can be formed. The Esperanto alphabet has twenty-three consonants and five vowels, each of which has one sound only, so that spelling and pronunciation are broadly phonological.

Zamenhof's aim in developing Esperanto was to provide an international language: 'one that could be adopted by all nations and be the common property of the whole world, without belonging in any way to any existing nationality' (quoted from Dr Esperanto, 1889, in Large, 1985, p. 72). Such a language would have to be easy to learn and must be a viable intermediary for international communication.

While many Esperantists feel that the language conforms to these requirements, it has been criticized for its use of circumflexed letters which makes writing and typing difficult, and because its words are not easily recognizable by those familiar with the natural-language words from which they are derived. The latter criticism is one which has been levelled at most artificial languages (see Large, 1985, chs 2–4), and is serious, since difficulty in recognizing roots will mean that they have to be learnt anew, and this, in turn, is a serious obstacle to universal spread of the language. It is also possible to argue that Esperanto is not, in fact, suitable as a truly universal language, because it is too Eurocentric to appeal to speakers of, for instance, Asian languages.

A less well-known artificial language which is still in fairly wide use is **Ido**, which resembles Esperanto in many ways (Large, 1985, p. 134):

The Idists organised their first World Congress in 1912, held in Vienna. The movement increased in strength during the inter-war period, only to be set back again by the Second World War. Today, it manages to maintain a tenuous foothold in several European countries, North America, and a few other scattered outposts. In Britain the International Language (Ido) Society of Great Britain promotes the language in various ways. It organises courses, particularly of the correspondence variety, publishes a journal, *Ido-Vivo*, three times per year and convenes annual meetings. Nevertheless, membership remains very small. Such national associations in turn are affiliated to La Uniono por la Linguo Internaciona (Ido), which publishes its own journal, *Progreso*, and organises international conferences.

Dissatisfaction with Ido led to the publication in 1922 of **Occidental** by Edgar von Wahl (or de Wahl). Occidental was conceived as a language for use in the western world alone. Its vocabulary is 'largely made up from "international" roots found in the chief Romance languages of Western Europe, or from Latin roots when no such common form could be found' (Large, 1985, p. 141).

The first artificial language to be published by a professional linguist was Otto Jespersen's **Novial**, which based its vocabulary largely on Ido and its grammar largely on Occidental. Novial became one of the six candidates for an international language which were considered by the **International Auxiliary Language Association (IALA)**, founded in 1924 with financial support from the Rockefeller Foundation and the Vanderbilt family. The other five languages receiving consideration were Esperanto, Esperanto II (a revised version of Esperanto), Ido, Occidental, and Latino sine flexione. By 1945, however, the IALA had come to the conclusion that rather than select one of these languages, the common base underlying them all should serve as the starting point for an auxiliary language whose vocabulary would be such that most educated speakers of a European language would be able to read it and understand its spoken form with no previous training (Large, 1985, p. 147):

> In order to identify this international vocabulary, the IALA looked at the chief members of the Anglo-Romanic group: English, French, Italian, and Spanish–Portuguese. If a word occurred in one of these four 'control languages' it was adopted at once. . . . If a word could not be found in at least three of the control languages, then German and Russian were also consulted.

The resultant language is known as **Interlingua** (Large, 1985, p. 150):

> The grammar of Interlingua is essentially romanic, and not unlike Edgar de Wahl's Occidental. It is intended to be as simple as possible whilst still remaining compatible with pan-occidental usage. Any grammatical feature which one of Interlingua's contributing languages has eliminated should not be included; neither should any grammatical feature be excluded which is to be found in all the contributing languages. . . . Interlingua has no genders, personal endings for verbs or declensions of nouns. It does include, however, a definite and indefinite article, a distinctive plural for nouns, and different endings to distinguish between different verbal tenses. . . . As regards pronunciation, it is virtually that of ecclesiastical Latin.

Interlingua is intended primarily for scientific communication, and within this field it made good progress for a time, but has now been superseded as an international language of science by English.

Other artificial languages invented in the twentieth century include **Eurolengo**, intended as a means of communication for use in business and tourism, and **Glosa**, which is intended to function as an international auxiliary language.

It is unlikely that any invented language will ever succeed as a universal means of communication. It requires special effort to learn a new language, and any such new language would be closer to some of the world's languages than to others. Those people most likely to need to communicate internationally are also quite likely to know one or more foreign languages, and when no common language is available to prospective communicators, translators and interpreters are used. Official international communication, in institutions like the United Nations, proceeds via translators and interpreters, and efforts are consequently being concentrated in areas which may be of help to translators and interpreters.

These efforts include the development of machine-translation systems like TITUS 4 which was first implemented in 1980. **TITUS 4** can translate texts between English, French, German, and Spanish, as long as the texts conform to the **controlled-syntax language** the system uses. This is not an artificial language as such, with its own vocabulary and syntactic rules, but is, rather, a simplified natural language. It comprises a subset of the vocabulary of the natural language and a subset of its syntactic rules, and it takes five or six days' full-time effort to master it. It is mainly used to produce abstracts for multilingual periodicals, but Streiff (1985, p. 191) expresses the hope that it may become 'a useful and reliable tool for export-market-oriented industry' which needs to publish technical brochures in several languages. Obviously, restricted languages for use in machine

translation could be developed for other sets of languages and to serve a number of fields and text genres, but international communication in the political arena is likely to remain too complex and multifaceted to proceed in restricted languages.

And since a number of natural languages, including English, already function as international means of communication, and given the availability of increasingly well-qualified translators and interpreters, it is probable that the pursuit of artificial languages will remain a minority occupation.

K.M.

SUGGESTIONS FOR FURTHER READING

Large, A. (1985), *The Artificial Language Movement*, Oxford, Basil Blackwell.

Auditory phonetics

DEFINITION

Auditory phonetics is that branch of phonetics concerned with the perception of speech sounds, i.e. with how they are heard. It thus entails the study of the relationships between speech stimuli and a listener's responses to such stimuli as mediated by mechanisms of the peripheral and central auditory systems, including certain cortical areas of the brain (see LANGUAGE PATHOLOGY AND NEUROLINGUISTICS). It is distinct from **articulatory phonetics** which involves the study of the ways in which speech sounds are produced by the vocal organs (see ARTICULATORY PHONETICS), and from **acoustic phonetics** which involves the analysis of the speech signal primarily by means of instrumentation (see ACOUSTIC PHONETICS). In fact, however, issues in auditory phonetics are often explored with reference to

articulatory and acoustic phonetics. Indeed, there may be no clear distinction made by some speech-perception researchers between aspects of acoustic and auditory phonetics due to the fact that the two fields are so closely related.

MECHANISMS INVOLVED IN SPEECH PERCEPTION

Auditory perception of the sounds of speech requires that a listener receive, integrate, and process highly complex acoustic stimuli which contain information ranging from relatively low to relatively high frequencies at varying intensities. Young adults can perceive sounds whose frequencies range from about 20 Hz (Hertz), i.e. 20 cycles per second, to about 20 kHz (kilo-Hertz), i.e. 20,000 cycles per second. However, this entire range is not utilized in the production of natural speech sounds; hence the effective perceptual range is much smaller. Likewise, the dynamic range of the human auditory system is extremely large – about 150 dB (decibels). That is, if the smallest amount of intensity required to detect a sound were represented as a unit of 1, the largest amount tolerable before the ear sustained damage would be 10^{15}. Needless to say, this full dynamic range is not utilized in normal speech perception.

Many of the principles concerning how acoustic stimuli are converted from sound-pressure waves into meaningful units of speech have been formulated and tested empirically since Helmholtz (1821–94) set forth his theories of hearing over a century ago (1863). Much of the data that has been obtained has come from psychometric, psycholinguistic, and neurolinguistic studies of humans and from physiological experiments

with animals. A description of the various scaling techniques and experimental procedures utilized in studies of auditory perception is beyond the scope of the present discussion, but the major findings which have been obtained by means of such techniques and procedures will be presented.

The fundamentals of auditory phonetics can best be understood by first viewing the role of the major physiological mechanisms involved in hearing with reference to the peripheral auditory system, including the ear and the auditory nerve, and the central nervous system, including certain areas of the brain. The combined role of these systems is to receive, transduce, encode, transmit, and process an acoustic signal. Although a detailed discussion of the acoustic properties of a signal would deal with, at least, frequency, intensity, duration, and phase, the focus of the

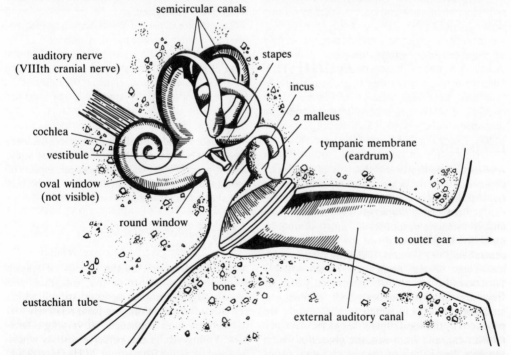

Figure 1 If the outer ear were depicted, it would appear at the far right of the figure. It would be the anterior portion of the ear, i.e. as it appears when viewed from the front. Note that, although the cochlea appears to be a discrete object, it is actually a coiled passage located within the bone of the skull. Ligaments of the ossicles are not shown.

present discussion will be on frequency – perhaps the most thoroughly studied parameter and the one most relevant to a discussion of auditory phonetics.

The **ear** is divided into three anatomically distinct components, namely the outer, middle, and inner ear, as represented in Figure 1.

The **outer ear** includes the **pinna** and the **external meatus** – the visible cartilaginous structures – and the **external auditory canal** which terminates at the **tympanic membrane** or **eardrum**. The outer ear 'collects' auditory signals which arrive as sound waves or changing acoustic pressures propagated through the surrounding medium, usually air. The outer ear also serves as protection for the delicate middle ear, provides some amplification and assists in sound localization, i.e. in determining where a sound originates.

The **middle ear** is bounded on one side by the tympanic membrane and on the other by a bony wall containing the **cochlea** of the inner ear. In addition to the **tympanic membrane**, the middle ear contains three **ossicles**; these are the **malleus**, **incus**, and **stapes**, a set of three tiny interconnected bones extending in a chain from the tympanic membrane to the **oval window** of the cochlea. The tympanic membrane vibrates in response to the sound waves impinging upon it; the ossicles greatly amplify these vibratory patterns by transferring pressure from a greater area, the tympanic membrane, to a much smaller one, the footplate of the stapes attached to the oval window of the cochlea.

The **inner ear** contains the **vestibule**, the **semicircular canals** – which primarily affect balance – and the **cochlea**, a small coiled passage of decreasing diameter. Running the length of the cochlea are the **scala tympani** and **scala vestibuli**, two fluid-filled canals which are separated from the fluid-filled **scala media** or **cochlear duct**. The vibratory patterns of sound-pressure waves are transferred into hydraulic pressure waves which travel through the scala vestibuli and scala tympani and from the base to the apex of the scala media.

One surface of the scala media contains a layer of fibres called the **basilar membrane**. This tapered membrane is narrow and taut at its base in the larger vestibular end of the cochlea, and wide and flaccid at its terminus or apex in the smaller apical portion of the cochlea. On one surface of the basilar membrane is the **organ of Corti** which contains thousands of inner and outer hair cells, each supporting a number of **cilia** or hairs. When the basilar membrane is displaced in response to the travelling waves propagating throughout it, the **tectorial membrane** near the outer edge of the organ of Corti also moves. It is believed that the shearing effect of the motion of these two membranes stimulates the cilia of the hair cells, thereby triggering a neural response in the auditory-receptor cells. These cells, in turn, relay electrochemical impulses to a fibre bundle called the **auditory nerve**, or the **VIIIth cranial nerve**. Information about the spatial representation of frequencies on the basilar membrane is preserved in the auditory nerve, which is thus said to have **tonotopic organization**.

The precise nature of the information received on the basilar membrane and encoded in the auditory nerve has been a matter of much investigation. The fact that the basilar membrane changes in width and rigidity throughout its length means that the amplitudes of pressure waves peak at specific **loci** or places on the membrane. Hence, the peak amplitudes of low-frequency sounds occur at the wider and more flaccid apex while the peak amplitudes of high-frequency sounds occur at the narrower and tauter base, which can, however, also respond to low-frequency stimulation. This was demonstrated in a series of experiments conducted by von Békésy in the 1930s and 1940s (see von Békésy, 1960).

This finding gave rise to one version of the **place** or **spatial theory of perception** in which the tonotopic organization of information on the basilar membrane is preserved in the auditory nerve. However, this theory does not adequately account for certain perceptual phenomena (Sachs and Young, 1979). It does not, for example, account for the perception of very low-frequency sounds or the existence of extremely small **j.n.d.**'s (just noticeable differences) obtained in **pure-tone experiments**, i.e. experiments which test listeners' ability to detect differences in the frequency of sounds whose wave forms are smooth and simple, rather than complex. In addition, it seems unable to account for the fact that the fundamental frequency of a complex tone can be perceived even if it is not present in the stimulus (Schouten, 1940). Moreover, it has been observed that, for frequencies of about 3–4 kHz or less, auditory-nerve fibres discharge at a rate proportional to the period of the stimulus. To explain such phenomena, researchers have proposed various versions of a **periodicity** or **temporal theory**. Such a theory is based upon the premise that temporal properties, such as the duration of a pitch period, are utilized to form the psychophysical percept of a stimulus. More recently, an **integrated theory, average localized synchronous response** (ALSR), has been proposed (Young and Sachs, 1979; Shamma, 1985). Such a theory maintains that information about the spatial tonotopic organization of the basilar membrane is retained, but synchronous rate information is viewed as the carrier of spectral information.

In addition, careful and highly controlled neurophysical experiments have been conducted to measure single-fibre discharge patterns in the auditory nerve of the cat (Kiang *et al.*, 1965). These studies have sometimes utilized speech-like stimuli and have demonstrated a relationship between the phonetic features of the stimuli and the fibre's **characteristic frequency**, i.e. that frequency requiring the least intensity in stimulation to increase the discharge rate of a neuron above its spontaneous rate of firing. For example, in response to two-formant vowel (see ACOUSTIC PHONETICS) stimuli, it has been found that activity is concentrated near the formant frequencies, suggesting that phonetic categories are based, at least in part, upon basic properties of the peripheral auditory system (Delgutte and Kiang, 1984). This finding has received support from non-invasive behaviourally based animal studies (Kuhl and Miller, 1975).

From the auditory nerve, auditory information begins its ascent to the cortex of the brain by way of a series of highly complex interconnections and routes from one 'relay station' or area to another. These interconnections and routes may be understood in general outline in the description below of the **afferent** or ascending pathway. In the description, the **nuclei** referred to are groups of nerve cell bodies. In addition to the afferent pathway, there is also an **efferent** or descending pathway, which will not be described here, which appears to have an inhibitory or moderating function.

A highly simplified description of the conduction path from auditory nerve to cortex is as follows: the auditory nerve of each ear contains about 30,000 nerve fibres which terminate in the **cochlear nucleus** of the lower brainstem. From the cochlear nucleus, some fibres ascend ipsilaterally (i.e. on the same side) to the **olivary complex**, then to the **inferior colliculus** of the midbrain via the **lateral lemniscus**. From here, fibres originate which proceed to the **medial geniculate body** of the **thalamus** and finally to the **ipsilateral auditory cortex** in the temporal lobe. Other fibres ascend contralaterally (i.e. on the opposite side) to the **accessory olive** and to the **superior olive**. They then follow a path similar, but not identical, to the one just described. In addition, other fibres originating at the cochlear nucleus proceed directly to the **contralateral dorsal nucleus**, while still others do so by way of the **ipsilateral accessory superior olive** (Harrison and Howe, 1974; Yost and Nielsen, 1977; Nauta and Fiertag, 1979).

At the **synapses**, where information is transmitted from neuron to neuron along the route described, there is increasing complexity as well as transformation of the signal. The 30,000 fibres of the two auditory nerves feed into about a million subcortical neurons in the auditory cortex (Worden, 1971; Warren, 1982). In addition, at each synapse, the input is transformed, i.e., it is recoded so that it can be understood at higher levels of the system. It is thus not entirely appropriate to consider the route which an auditory input follows as a pathway, or the synaptic junctions as simple relay stations.

The **auditory cortex**, like the auditory nerve, is characterized by tonotopic organization. Moreover, certain of its neurons exhibit differential sensitivity to certain types of stimuli. For example, some are responsive only to an increase in frequency while others are responsive only to a decrease. These findings are analogous to those obtained in studies of the mammalian visual system (Hubel and Wiesel, 1968) and they suggest that auditory-feature detectors subserve higher-order mechanisms of phonetic perception.

The auditory cortex alone cannot convert speech stimuli into meaningful units of language. Further processing must occur in an adjacent area in the temporal lobe known as **Wernicke's area**. This is graphically demonstrated by the fact that damage to this area usually results in deficits in speech perception. This language area is not present in both hemispheres and, for about 95 per cent of all right-handed adults, it and other language areas, e.g. **Broca's area**, are located only in the left hemisphere (see also APHASIA and LANGUAGE PATHOLOGY AND NEUROLINGUISTICS).

Since the early 1960s, a non-invasive perceptual technique known as **dichotic listening** has been widely employed to determine the relationship between the properties of speech sounds and the extent to which they are left- or right-lateralized in the brain. In a dichotic listening test, competing stimuli are presented simultaneously to both ears. Although the reliability and validity of this test have often been questioned, it seems that, for most right-handed subjects, right-ear accuracy is generally greater than left-ear accuracy for speech stimuli. It seems that the contralateral connections between the peripheral auditory and central nervous systems are stronger than the ipsilateral ones – at least when competing stimuli are presented – so that a right-ear advantage is interpreted as reflecting left-hemisphere dominance. This pattern has also been observed in electroencephalographic (EEG) studies and sodium amytal (Wada) tests, as well as in the examination of split-brain and aphasic (see APHASIA) subjects (Springer and Deutsch, 1985).

However, the finding of left-hemispheric dominance for speech has only emerged for certain types of speech stimuli. For example, while plosive consonants (see ARTICULATORY PHONETICS) yield a right-ear advantage in dichotic-listening tasks, vowels do not (Shank-weiler and Studdert-Kennedy, 1967). Moreover, suprasegmental information, such as fundamental frequency (F0), experienced subjectively as **pitch**, may or may not be mediated by the left hemisphere depending upon its linguistic status, that is, depending upon whether or not it carries linguistic information (Van Lancker and Fromkin, 1973; Blumstein and Cooper, 1974). This suggests that it is not necessarily the inherent properties of the stimuli which determine laterality effects, but the nature of the tasks to be performed with the stimuli as well as their status in the listener's linguistic system.

Clearly, the relationship between the acoustic/phonetic properties of speech and its processing in the brain is complex. In attempting to understand this relationship, it is also important to make a distinction between the auditory properties of speech, which are pre- or alinguistic, and the phonetic properties of speech, which are linguistic (Pisoni, 1973). The difference is not always readily apparent, and the task is further complicated by the fact that what may be perceived as auditory in one language may be perceived as phonetic in another. It is well known that languages often utilize different perceptually salient cues, and these differences have measurable behavioural consequences (Caramazza et al., 1973; Mack, 1982, 1984; Flege and Hillenbrand, 1986).

SELECTED ISSUES IN AUDITORY PHONETICS

One recurrent theme in auditory phonetics revolves around the question 'Is speech special?' In other words, is speech perception essentially akin to the perception of other acoustically complex stimuli or is it somehow unique? Several main sources of evidence are often invoked in discussions of this issue.

First, it is apparent that the frequencies used in producing speech are among those to which the human auditory system is most sensitive, and certain spectral and temporal features of speech stimuli correspond to those to which the mammalian auditory system is highly sensitive (Kiang, 1980; Stevens, 1981). This suggests that there is a close relationship between the sounds which humans are capable of producing and those which the auditory system most accurately perceives.

Moreover, experiments with prelinguistic infants have demonstrated that linguistic experience is not a necessary precondition for perception of some of the properties of speech, such as those involved in place and manner of articulation (Eimas *et al.*, 1971; Kuhl, 1979).

Other evidence is based upon what has been termed **categorical perception**. It has repeatedly been shown that a continuum of certain types of speech stimuli differing with respect to only one or two features is not perceived in a continuous manner. Categorical perception can be summarized in the simple phrase: 'Subjects can discriminate no better than they can label.' That is, if subjects are presented with a continuum in which all stimuli differ in some specific and equivalent way, and if those subjects are required to label each stimulus heard, they will divide the continuum into only those two or three categories, such as /d–t/ or /b–d–g/, over which the continuum ranges. If these subjects are also presented with pairs of stimuli from the same continuum in a discrimination task, they do not report that members of *all* acoustically dissimilar pairs are different, even though they actually are. Rather, subjects report as different only those pair members which fall, in the continuum, in that region in which their responses switch from one label to another in the labelling task. It has been argued that non-speech stimuli, such as colours and tones, are not perceived categorically; hence the special status of categorical perception of speech. It is important to note, however, that not all speech stimuli are perceived categorically. For example, **steady-state vowels** – vowels in which there are no abrupt changes in frequency at onset or offset – are not (Fry *et al.*, 1962).

Another source of evidence for the claim that speech is special may be found in **normalization**. The formant frequencies of speech give sounds their spectral identity and are a direct function of the size and shape of the vocal tract which produces them. Hence, the frequencies which specify an /e/ produced by a child are quite unlike those which specify an /e/ produced by an adult male (Peterson and Barney, 1952). None the less, both sounds are perceived as representations of the same phonetic unit. A process of normalization must take place if this perceptual equivalence is to occur.

It has been hypothesized that a listener 'derives' the size of the vocal tract which could have produced the sound by means of a calibration procedure in which certain vowels such as /ɪ/ or /u/ are used in the internal specification of the appropriate phonetic categories (Lieberman, 1984). If this type of normalization occurs, it does so extremely rapidly and without conscious mediation by the listener. Indeed, most individuals would probably be surprised to discover that the acoustic properties of a child's and an adult's speech production are quite dissimilar. Most would probably only be conscious of the fact that one sounded 'higher' than the other.

The above-cited topics – the match of the perceptual system to the production system, infant speech perception, categorical perception, and normalization – have often been interpreted as evidence that speech is special. But some linguists choose to view these as evidence that speech is *not* special, but rather that it is simply one highly elaborated system which is based upon a complex of productive and perceptual mechanisms which underlie other abilities, and even other sensory modalities, and which are thus not unique to speech.

Two other important issues involved in auditory perception are **segmentation** and **invariance**. Attempts to grapple with these issues have given rise to several major theories of relevance to auditory phonetics.

It is generally maintained that speech is highly encoded. That is, phonetic units in a word are not simply strung together, intact and in sequence, like beads on a string. The traditional view has been that speech sounds are **smeared** or time-compressed as a result, in part, of co-articulation. The encoded nature of the speech signal makes it a highly efficient and rapid form of communication, yet it also results in the production of phonetic segments which are, in context, at least somewhat different from the 'same' segments produced in isolation. How an encoded signal gives rise to a fully elaborated percept is still not entirely understood.

Closely related to the issue of segmentation is the notion of **invariance**, or, more properly, **non-invariance**. Various theories have been proposed in order to account for the fact that, although given phonetic segments may appear to be quite dissimilar acoustically, they are responded to perceptually and introspectively as if they are identical – or at least as if they are instantiations of the same phonetic unit. For example, the word-initial /d/ in *deed* is acoustically distinct from /d/ in *do*: in /dɪ/ the second-formant transition rises, while in /du/ it falls. Further, in /dɪ/ the second-formant transition may start at a frequency nearly 1,000 Hz higher than does the second-formant transition in /du/. Yet both syllable-initial consonants are considered to be the same unit, or, in traditional terminology, the same **phoneme** (see PHONEMICS). The size and salience of the invariant unit has been a matter of considerable debate, as has its level of abstractness and generalizability (Liberman *et al.*, 1952; Stevens and Blumstein, 1978; Kewley-Port, 1983; Mack and Blumstein, 1983).

Attempts to relate an acoustic signal to a listener's internal and presumably abstract representation of speech have given rise to various theories of speech perception.

One such theory, the **motor theory**, was developed in the 1960s. This theory related a listener's knowledge of his or her production to perception. That is, it was hypothesized that a listener interprets the afferent auditory signal in terms of the efferent motor commands required for its production (Liberman *et al.*, 1967). Essentially, the activity of the listener's own neuromuscular system serves as reference for perception.

A related theory, **analysis-by-synthesis**, was somewhat more complex (Stevens, 1960; Halle and Stevens, 1962). According to this approach, the auditory signal is analysed in terms of distinctive features, and rules for production are generated. Hypotheses about these rules are utilized to construct an internal 'synthesized' pattern of phonetic segments, which is compared to the acoustic input and is then either accepted or rejected.

A more recent theory, the **event approach**, is based upon a 'direct-realist perspective'. Here, the problems of segmentation and invariance are deemed more apparent than real. Speech is understood via the recognition of articulatory gestures underlying its production. It is not presumed that a 'distorted' acoustic stimulus is mapped onto an idealized abstract phonetic unit (Fowler, 1986).

And finally, the 1970s and 1980s witnessed a flourishing of perceptual models drawing heavily upon issues in artificial intelligence (Klatt, 1980; Reddy, 1980). In some cases, findings concerning human speech perception have guided computer-based models; in other cases, computers have been used as models and metaphors for human perception.

Not surprisingly, no single theory has been entirely successful in accounting for all aspects of speech perception in general or of auditory perception in particular. None the less, these theories have addressed, and often have answered, some important questions central to the study of auditory phonetics.

M.M.

SUGGESTIONS FOR FURTHER READING

Lieberman, P. and Blumstein, S.E. (1988), *Speech Physiology, Speech Perception, and Acoustic Phonetics*, Cambridge, Cambridge University Press.

Moore, B.C.J. (1982), *An Introduction to the Psychology of Hearing*, 2nd edn, London, Academic Press.

Warren, R.M. (1982), *Auditory Perception: A New Synthesis*, New York, Pergamon Press.

Augmented Transition Network (ATN) grammar

Augmented Transition Network (ATN) grammar is a technique and notation originally developed by Woods (1970) and, independently, by Thorne *et al.* (1968), and Dewer *et al.* (1969) for natural-language processing by computer (see ARTIFICIAL INTELLIGENCE). ATN was further developed by Woods (1973) and Kaplan (1972, 1973a, 1973b, 1975). Its conventionalized notation serves for a large family of syntactic analysers (Wanner and Maratsos, 1978, p. 120), and ATN became one of the most common methods of parsing natural language in computer systems during the 1980s. ATNs have served as the basis for psycholinguistic theories and experiments and are employed as components of lexical functional grammar (see LEXICAL FUNCTIONAL GRAMMAR) and other functional theories (see FUNCTIONAL UNIFICATION GRAMMAR).

An ATN is a particularly promising model of sentence comprehension, because, unlike earlier models which performed complete syntactic analyses, an ATN can make intermediate results available; and psycholinguistic research suggests that comprehension can be achieved on the basis of incomplete syntactic analysis (Wanner and Maratsos, 1978, p. 121) (see PSYCHOLINGUISTICS, pp. 368–9). Wanner and Maratsos (1978, p. 122) list three ATN operating characteristics which, among others, appear to correspond to operating characteristics of human comprehension: (1) an ATN processes sentences sequentially; (2) like a human parser, an ATN can use its 'linguistic knowledge' plus context to impose a phrase-structure analysis on an input sentence, and is not dependent on 'physical cues' like prosody or punctuation; (3) the processing procedures of an ATN naturally divide into tasks that correspond to linguistic units such as phrases and clauses.

An ATN can be described as a syntactic analyser which interacts with a perceptual analyser and a semantic analyser and shares with them a common lexicon and a common working memory. The **perceptual analyser** identifies linguistic input as a segmented string of words which is the input to the ATN. The ATN works its way through the string word by word producing, testing, and modifying hypotheses about syntactic categorization, phrase boundaries, and grammatical functions. The hypotheses are held in working memory where they can be accessed by the semantic and perceptual analysers.

The ATN has two main components: a recursive transition- network grammar and a processer. The **transition network grammar** stores representations of linguistic patterns and a set of context-sensitive operations which assign functions. The **processor** compares the stored patterns against current input and carries out the function-assigning operations (Wanner and Maratsos, 1978, pp. 123–4). It is called an **augmented** transition network, because it has, in addition to the features it shares with all recursive transition networks (see Winograd, 1983, Ch. 5), certain conditions and actions associated with the arcs (see below) of the network. **Conditions** restrict the circumstances under which an arc can be traversed, and **actions** perform feature-marking and structure-building operations (Winograd, 1983, p. 204).

An ATN consists of a set of labelled networks, each of which is composed of **states** which are represented as circles. Each state has a unique name which is written inside the circle. The states are connected by **arcs**, represented by arrows between the circles. The labels on the arcs specify conditions which must be met before a transition can be made between the states connected by the

Sentence Network

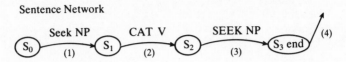

Noun–phrase Network

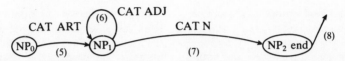

arc. The numbers on the arcs correspond to actions which must be performed when the arc is traversed. The actions are listed below the network. Wanner and Maratsos (1978, p. 124) present the elementary ATN grammar shown above.

Arc	Action
1	ASSIGN SUBJECT to current phrase
2	ASSIGN ACTION to current word
3	ASSIGN OBJECT to current phrase
4	ASSEMBLE CLAUSE
	SEND current clause
5	ASSIGN DET to current word
6	ASSIGN MOD to current word
7	ASSIGN HEAD to current word
8	ASSEMBLE NOUN PHRASE
	SEND current phrase

In principle, any number of independent networks are permitted. Keeping the networks independent makes the representation economical by avoiding redundancy. The noun phrase has essentially the same internal structure no matter where it occurs in the sentence, so the absence of a separate noun-phrase network would mean that exactly the same set of arcs would have to be specified in the sentence network to handle noun phrases before and after the verb. However, the economy of presentation is bought at the price of increased processing effort: the processor must be able to move about between the networks, so it needs to be able to store the identity of the arc that activates a particular network in order to be able to return to the correct arc when it has completed the network that had been activated by that arc. It also needs to be able to store partial

results of a network which it is instructed to leave so that it can resume analysis later. Finally, it needs to be able to transfer information between networks (Wanner and Maratsos, 1978, pp. 128–9).

Since the only way out of the initial state of the sentence network in the grammar presented above is via the arc labelled 'seek NP', a processor engaged in sentence analysis must immediately move to the noun-phrase network and determine whether the pattern of its input conforms to that of the noun-phrase network. If the first word of its current input is one which is labelled ART(icle) in the lexicon, the processor is able to move over the arc labelled CAT(egory) ART. That arc demands that the function label DET(erminer) be assigned to the current word. The association between the word and the function is stored in working memory, where it is kept available for possible further use in later stages of the process of analysis, and where it is accessible to other components of the comprehension system. At the next state, the processor must test the next input word to see whether it is labelled either ADJ(ective) or N(oun) in the lexicon, and so on, until a complete noun phrase has been assembled and sent.

Assembling involves packaging all the associations which have been made between words and function labels under the name NOUN PHRASE. **Sending** makes this package available to the sentence network as its current input. Since the SEEK NP instruction which the processor was given when in the initial state of the sentence network has been stored in memory, the processor can retrieve it, see that the instruction has been carried out, and proceed through the sentence network. When the processor comes to the end of the sentence network, it will assemble all the word-function associations made during the analysis and label the assembly a CLAUSE. If the input was *The old train left the station*, the package of associations can be represented as follows:

```
[CLAUSE
   SUBJECT  = [NOUN PHRASE
              DET   = the
              MOD   = old
              HEAD  = train
   ACTION   = left
   OBJECT   = [NOUN PHRASE
              DET   = the
              MOD   = station]]
```

(Wanner and Maratsos, 1978, pp. 125–7)

The recognition process involved in parsing with an ATN grammar is **active**: the input is not the sole determinant of the decisions made; rather, the decisions are a joint function of the input, the system's general information about linguistic patterns represented in the network, and its information about context found in the current path of analysis through the network.

The system can be made to cope with garden-path type ambiguity (see PSYCHOLINGUISTICS, pp. 370–1) by trying successive analyses of the problematic structure until one is found which the context allows. Thus, had the input sentence been *The old train the young*, the processor would have attempted the noun-phrase analysis of *the old train* first, but would have reached a dead end at state S_1, when the current word is *the* while the arc demands that the current word be a verb. In such a situation, the processor must backtrack over the input and arcs taken previously trying alternative arcs at each state. In the case of *The old train the young*, when the backtracking process reaches state NP_1 *old* can be recognized as a noun on arc 7, and the rest of the analysis follows straightforwardly (Wanner and Maratsos, 1978, p. 128). If such an approach is persistently adopted, a separate sequence of arcs is required for each sentence type that displays grammatical functions in different arrangements.

The ATN can, however, be given the power to alter a function label on any given element if subsequent context demands it, so that when faced with a sentence in the passive voice, for example, it may alter the label SUBJECT, which it has given to the initial noun phrase, to OBJECT after it has recognized passive voice. This recognition can be accomplished by adding CAT V arcs, which test for the presence of *be* and a past participle ending on the main verb.

Finally, an ATN can postpone a decision about the grammatical function of a problematic item by tagging it with HOLD. Elements in the HOLD list can be RETRIEVEd and assigned a function later in the analysis, when there is enough context to determine what the function should be (ibid. pp. 130–1). The HOLD list is particularly useful during the processing of relative clauses because it allows the ATN grammar to represent relative-clause patterns as systematic deformations of declarative-clause patterns. This strategy captures a grammatical generalization about the structural similarities between declarative and relative clauses (ibid., p. 137).

Wanner and Maratsos (1978, pp. 132–7) show how the grammar outlined above can be extended to handle restrictive, unreduced, non-extraposed relative clauses, that is, clauses which immediately follow and modify a head noun by limiting the range of possible entities it can refer to (**restrictive**), which are introduced by a relative pronoun (**unreduced**) and which are structurally identical to independent declarative clauses (**non-extraposed**) except that one element is missing. Wanner and Maratsos (1978, p. 132) give the following examples (head noun phrases in italics, the gap where an element is missing indicated by ____):

> ... *the girl* who ____ talked to the teacher about the problem ...
> ... *the teacher* whom the girl talked to ____ about the problem ...
> ... *the problem* that the girl talked to the teacher about ____ ...

As these examples demonstrate, the function fulfilled by the head noun is the same as the function which would have been fulfilled at the gap had the relative clause been an independent declarative clause:

> *The girl* talked to the teacher about the problem
> The girl talked to *the teacher* about the problem
> The girl talked to the teacher about *the problem*

Therefore, a listener must find the gap in the relative clause and decide what its function would have been in an independent declarative clause, in order to be able to determine what the function of the head noun is.

In the ATN framework, the gap-finding process is represented by the addition of three arcs to the basic NP network presented above. The first arc tests for the presence of a relative pronoun at the end of the head noun phrase. If a relative pronoun is found, the action associated with the arc places the head NP on the HOLD list, and the second new arc (marked SEEK S) instructs the processor to go to the sentence network and try to analyse the relative clause as if it were an independent declarative clause. The attempt will fail when the gap is reached, because there is no noun phrase to be found. However, the third new arc, a bypass arc (labelled RETRIEVE HOLD) allows the processor, if there is an item in the HOLD list, to retrieve that item, and once it is retrieved, the attempt to treat the relative clause as an independent clause will succeed (ibid., p. 134):

> When the ATN reaches the gap in the relative clause and SEEKs a noun phrase, the head NP will be on the HOLD list. Therefore, the bypass arc will RETRIEVE it from HOLD and restore it to working memory. The ordinary SEND action at the end of the noun phrase network will then return the head NP to the arc that initiated the SEEK NP, and that arc will automatically assign the head NP the same function label it would assign to a noun phrase that occurred at that point in an independent declarative clause.

The new noun-phrase network is represented below (the new arcs are arcs 9, 10, and 12; there is no alteration to the sentence network represented in the elementary grammar above) (ibid., p. 135):

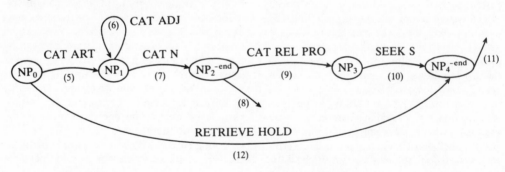

Arc	Action		
5	ASSIGN DET to current word	10	CHECK HOLD
6	ASSIGN MOD to current word		ASSIGN MOD to current clause
7	ASSIGN HEAD to current word	11	ASSEMBLE NOUN PHRASE
8	ASSIGN NOUN PHRASE		SEND current phrase
	SEND current phrase	12	(no action)
9	HOLD		

An interesting debate about the merits of ATNs as models of the human sentence-comprehension system relative to Frazier and Fodor's 'sausage-machine' approach (see PSYCHOLINGUISTICS, pp. 370–1) can be found in *Cognition* 6, nos 4 and 8, nos 2 and 4 (Frazier and Fodor, 1978; Fodor and Frazier, 1980; Wanner, 1980).

K.M.

SUGGESTIONS FOR FURTHER READING

Bates, M. (1978), 'The theory and practice of augmented transition network grammars', in L. Bolc (ed.), *Natural Language Comuni-cation with Computers*, (Lecture Notes on Computer Science, no. 63), Berlin, Springer.

Johnson, R. (1983), 'Parsing with transition networks', in M. King (ed.), *Parsing Natural Language*, London and New York, Academic Press, pp. 59–72.

Wanner, E. and Maratsos, M. (1978), 'An ATN approach to comprehension', in M. Halle, J. Bresnan, and G.A. Miller (eds), *Linguistic Theory and Psychological Reality*, Cambridge, MA, MIT Press, pp. 119–61.

Winograd, T. (1983), *Language as a Cognitive Process*, vol. 1: *Syntax*, Reading, MA, Addison Wesley.

Behaviourist linguistics

Behaviourism, the psychological theory behind behaviourist linguistics, was founded by J.B. Watson (1924). Its main tenet is that everything which some refer to as mental activity, including language use, can be explained in terms of **habits**, or patterns of **stimulus** and **response**, built up through **conditioning**. As these patterns of behaviour, an organism's **output**, and the conditioning through which they become formed, the **input** to the organism, are observable phenomena, behaviourism accorded well with the strong current of empiricism which swept the scientific communities in the USA and Britain early in the twentieth century.

In linguistics, one of the finest examples of the empiricist/behaviourist tradition is Leonard Bloomfield's book *Language* (1935; first published in 1933), although the most rigorous application of behaviourist theory to the study of language is probably *Verbal Behavior* published in 1957 by Burrhus Frederic Skinner, one of the most famous behaviourist psychologists of the twentieth century. This book was severely criticized by Chomsky (1959).

In *Language*, Bloomfield insists that a scientific theory of language must reject all data that are not directly observable or physically measurable. A scientific theory should be able to make predictions, but Bloomfield points out that (1935, p. 33):

> We could foretell a person's actions (for instance, whether a certain stimulus will lead him to speak, and, if so, the exact words he will utter) only if we knew the exact structure of his body at that moment, or, what comes to the same thing, if we knew the exact make-up of his organism at some early stage – say at birth or before – and then had a record of every change in that organism, including every stimulus that had ever affected the organism.

Language, according to Bloomfield, is a type of substitute for action. In his famous story, with translations into behaviourese of the main events, of Jack and Jill (pp. 22–7), in which Jill, being hungry ('that is, some of her muscles were contracting, and some fluids were being secreted, especially in her stomach'), asks Jack to fetch her an apple which she sees ('the light waves reflected from the red apple struck her eyes') on a tree, Bloomfield explains that Jill's hunger is a primary stimulus, S, which, had Jill been speechless, would have led to a response, R, consisting of her fetching the apple herself, had she been capable of so doing. Having language, however, Jill is able to make 'a few small movements in her throat and mouth, which produced a little noise'. This noise, Jill's words to Jack, is a substitute response, r, which now acts as a substitute stimulus, s, for Jack, who carries out the response R. So *Language enables one person to make a reaction (R) when another person has the stimulus (S)*', and instead of the simple sequence of events

$$S \longrightarrow R$$

we have the more complex

$$S \longrightarrow r \cdots\cdots\cdots s \longrightarrow R$$

and Jill gets her apple. But, again, this course of events depends on the entire life history of Jack and Jill (p. 23):

> If Jill were bashful or if she had had bad experiences of Jack, she might be hungry and see the apple and still say nothing; if Jack were ill disposed toward her, he might not fetch her the apple, even though she asked for it. The occurrence of speech (and, as we shall see, the wording of it) and the whole course of practical events before and after it, depend upon the entire life-history of the speaker and of the hearer.

The speech event has the meaning it has in virtue of its connection with the practical events with which it is connected. So (Bloomfield, 1935, p. 139):

> In order to give a scientifically accurate definition of meaning for every form of a language, we should have to have a scientifically accurate knowledge of everything in the speaker's world. The actual extent of human knowledge is very small, compared to this. We can define the meaning of a speech-form accurately when this meaning has to do with some matter of

which we possess scientific knowledge. We can define the meaning of minerals, for example, as when we know that the ordinary meaning of the English word *salt* is 'sodium chloride (NaCl)', and we can define the names of plants and animals by means of the technical terms of botany or zoology, but we have no precise way of defining words like love or hate, which concern situations that have not been accurately classified – and these latter are in the great majority.

Bloomfield therefore advocated leaving semantics, the study of meaning, well alone 'until human knowledge advances very far beyond its present state' (p. 140), advice which was heeded by both Zellig Harris and his pupil, Noam Chomsky – at least in the latter's early work; and Bloomfield and his followers concentrated instead on developing appropriate discovery procedures for the more easily observable aspects of language, such as its sounds and structures.

Skinner (1957), in contrast to Bloomfield, claims that it is possible to tackle linguistic meaning without recourse to the internal structure and life histories of speakers. His main aim is to provide what he calls a 'functional analysis' of verbal behaviour, by which he means an identification of the variables that control this behaviour, and a specification of how they interact to determine a particular verbal response. He describes these variables purely in terms of such notions as **stimulus**, **reinforcement**, **deprivation** and **response**, well-defined notions with which Skinner, in his twenty-years-long, distinguished career in behavioural psychology, had been able to make impressive progress in animal experimentation in laboratory conditions.

He makes four basic claims in *Verbal Behavior*:

1 Language behaviour can be accounted for in a way that is in principle no different from the behaviour of rats in laboratory conditions.
2 Language behaviour can be explained in terms of observable events, without reference to the internal structure of the organism.
3 This descriptive system is superior to others because its terms can be defined with reference to experimental operations.

4 So it is able to deal with semantics in a scientific way.

Skinner divides the responses of animals into two main categories:

1 **Respondents**, which are purely reflex responses to particular stimuli; things like shutting your eyes if a bright light is shone at them, or kicking if your knee is hit in a particular spot by a small hammer. Clearly, these are not central to learning theory, and Skinner's research is concentrated on the second category.

2 **Operants**, which is behaviour for which no particular obvious stimulation can initially be discovered, but which, it turns out, is susceptible to manipulation by the researcher.

A rat placed in a box will engage in **random operant behaviour**: it will run about in (what appears to the researcher to be) an unsystematic fashion, randomly pressing its nose against parts of the box. If the box contains a bar which, when pressed, releases a food pellet into a tray, then the chances are that the rat will sooner or later press this bar and obtain a food pellet during its random operant behaviour, and, if the rat is hungry, suffers **deprivation**, then it is likely to try pressing the bar again to obtain more food.

In Skinner's terms, the rat's pressing the bar is now becoming a conditioned **operant**, no longer random; the event consisting of the release of the food pellet is a **reinforcing event**, the food pellet itself being the **reinforcer**. The reinforcing event will increase the **strength** of the bar-pressing operant; the strength of an operant is measured in terms of the rate of response during extinction: that is, the researcher will have observed and estimated the average number of times during a certain interval that the rat would randomly press the bar before it was adjusted to release food; s/he will then estimate the average number of times that the rat will press the bar once the rat has been conditioned to expect food when pressing; next, s/he will adjust the bar so that food is no longer released when the bar is pressed; the strength of the operant is defined in terms of how long it takes the rat to revert to its preconditioned rate of bar-pressing. The rate of the bar-pressing operant is affected by another variable, **drive**, which is defined in terms of hours of deprivation – in the case of the rat and the food pellet, hours of food deprivation.

A box such as the one just described is often called a **Skinner box**. It can be constructed in such a way that a food pellet will only be released when a light is flashing; eventually, the rat will learn this, and only press the bar when the light is flashing. In this case, the flashing light is called the **occasion for the emission of the response**, the response is called a **discriminated operant**, and what the rat has learnt is called **stimulus discrimination**. If the box is so constructed that the rat only gets a food pellet after pressing for a specific length of time, then the rat will learn to press the bar for the required length of time, and what has been learnt in such a case is called **response differentiation**.

Skinner (1957) now goes about applying something very like this apparatus to human verbal behaviour, which he defines as *behaviour reinforced through the mediation of other persons*, listeners, whose responses mediate the responses of the speaker. The hearers' responses have been conditioned precisely in order to reinforce the behaviour of the speakers. Chomsky (1959) strongly objects to the implication here that parents teach their children to speak just so that the children can, in turn, reinforce the parents' speech.

Further, Skinner suggests that children learn by imitation, although, since there is no innate tendency to imitate (nothing being innate according to Skinner's brand of behaviourism), parents will initially respond in a reinforcing manner to random sound production on the child's part. Some of the sounds the child makes during random behaviour (not unlike the rat's random pressing of parts of the box) happen to sound like the sounds the parents make, and only these will be reinforced by the parents. Chomsky objects that children do not imitate the deep voices of their fathers, so that Skinner is using 'imitation' is a selective way, and that, in any case, he does not pay sufficient attention to the part played by the child in the language-acquisition process.

Skinner calls utterances **verbal operants**, and classifies them according to their relationship with discriminated stimulus, reinforcements, and other verbal responses.

A **mand** (question, command, request, threat, etc.) is a verbal operant in which the response is reinforced by a characteristic consequence and is therefore under the functional control of relevant conditions of deprivation or aversive stimulation. Chomsky suggests that this definition cannot account for cases more complex than those as simple as *Pass the salt*, when it might be appropriate to say that the speaker suffers salt deprivation. As soon as we come to utterances like *Give me the book*, *Take me for a ride*, *Let me fix it*, etc., it becomes highly questionable whether we can decide which kind of deprivation is at issue and what the required number of hours of deprivation might be.

Further, he points to the absurdity of the theory in its attempt to deal with threats in terms of the notion of aversive control. According to Skinner, if a person has a history of appropriate reinforcement, which means that if, in the past, a certain response was followed by the withdrawal of a threat of injury, or certain events have been followed by injury, then such events are **conditioned aversive stimuli**. A person would therefore have to have had a previous history of being killed before being likely to respond appropriately to a threat like *Your money or your life*. No-one has a past history of being killed. But an utterance will only be made if there is another person who mediates it. So no-one should ever be inclined to utter threats like *Your money or your life*. Yet people do. And, in general, speakers are not fortunate enough always to have their mands appropriately reinforced, that is, we do not invariably get what we want.

Skinner is aware of this problem, and sets up a second category of mand, the **magical mand**, which is meant to cover cases in which speakers simply describe whatever reinforcement would be appropriate to whatever state of deprivation or aversive stimulation they may be in. See below for Chomsky's comment on this type of mand.

Skinner's second main category of verbal operant is the **tact**, defined as a verbal operant in which a response of a given kind is evoked or strengthened by a particular object or event or property thereof. Some tacts are under the control of private stimuli. For instance *There was an elephant at the zoo* is a response to current stimuli which include events within the speaker, and this is clearly a problem for a theory which claims to avoid a Bloomfieldian position which takes account of speaker-internal events.

Responses to prior verbal stimuli are of two kinds: **echoic operants**, which cover cases of immediate imitation, and **intraverbal operants**, histories of pairings of verbal responses, which are meant to cover responses like *four* to the stimulus *two plus two*, and *Paris* to *the capital of France*, and also most of the facts of history and science, all translation and paraphrase, reports of things seen, heard, and remembered.

Finally, Skinner deals with syntax in terms of responses called **autoclitics**. A sentence is a set of key responses to objects (nouns), actions (verbs) and properties (adjectives and adverbs) on a skeletal frame. Chomsky's objection to this is that more is involved in making sentences than fitting words into frames. For example, *Struggling artists can be a nuisance* and *Marking papers can be a nuisance* fit the same frame, but have radically different sentence structures. Skinner's theory cannot account for such differences.

Chomsky's (1959) overall criticism of Skinner's application of his learning theory to human verbal behaviour is that while the notions described above are very well defined for experiments in the laboratory, it is difficult to apply them to real-life human behaviour.

First, the researcher in the laboratory can predict what a rat's response to a particular stimulation will be: that is, the stimulation is known by the researcher *before* the response is emitted. But in the case of a verbal response, a tact, such as *Dutch* to a painting, which Skinner claims to be under the control of subtle properties of the painting, such response prediction seems to be illusory. For, says Chomsky, suppose that someone says *Clashes with the wall-paper*, or *I thought you liked abstract art*, or *Never saw it before*, or *Hanging too low*, or whatever else; then

Skinner would have to explain that, in each case, the response was under the control of some different property of the painting – but which property could only be determined *after* the response was known. So the theory is no longer predictive.

Second, while the terms used for the rat experiments may have clear definitions, it is unclear that these hold when transferred to the verbal behaviour of humans. Skinner claims that proper nouns are controlled by a specific person or thing; this would mean that the likelihood that a speaker would utter the full name of some other person would be increased when s/he was faced with that person, and this is not necessarily the case. And it is certainly not the case that one goes around uttering one's own name all the time, yet this, again, would seem to be predicted by the theory. In fact, it looks as if, in this case, Skinner is merely using the term 'control' as a substitute for the traditional semantic terms 'refers to' or 'denotes'. So Skinner's claim to have surpassed traditional semantic theories does not seem to hold water.

Similarly, it seems that, in the case of Skinner's category of magical mands, where, according to Skinner, speakers describe the reinforcement appropriate to their state of deprivation, speakers are, in fact, simply asking for what they want. But, as Chomsky points out, no new objectivity is added to the description of verbal behaviour by replacing *X wants Y* with *X is deprived of Y*. All in all, Chomsky shows that the terms from experimental psychology do not retain their strict definitions in *Verbal Behavior*, but take on the full vagueness of ordinary language, and Skinner cannot be said to have justified his claims for the strictly behaviourist account of human language use.

K.M.

SUGGESTIONS FOR FURTHER READING

Bloomfield, L. (1933/5), *Language*, New York, Holt, Rinehart & Wilson (1933), London, George Allen & Unwin (1935).

Chomsky, N. (1959), Review of B.F. Skinner, *Verbal Behavior*, *Language*, 35, pp. 26–58, reprinted in Fodor and Katz (1964) and Jakobovits and Miron (1967).

Lyons, J. (1981), *Language and Linguistics: An Introduction*, Cambridge, Cambridge University Press, 7.4 and 8.2.

Bilingualism and multilingualism

Most of what is true of bilingualism holds also for multilingualism, and except where the context dictates otherwise, I shall refer to both states using the former term.

INDIVIDUAL BILINGUALISM

A **bilingual** (or **multilingual**) person is one whose linguistic ability in two (or more) languages is similar to that of a native speaker. It is estimated that half the population of the world is bilingual (Grosjean, 1982, p. vii).

It is as difficult to set up exact criteria for what is to count as bilingualism as it is to describe exactly all that a native speaker can do with her or his language. Besides, not all native speakers will have the same ability in all aspects of their language: specialist registers, for instance, are typically only accessible to specialists. Similarly, most bilinguals will not have access to all registers in both their languages, or to the same registers in both languages; for instance, if a native speaker of one language leaves her or his native country for another, and learns a new skill through the language of the new country of residence, s/he will typically be unable to converse fluently about this skill in her or his native language: typically, s/he will not have the required terminology at her or his disposal. A bilingual may thus have a different **preferred language** (Dodson, 1981) for different activities.

In addition, it is so difficult to say precisely where advanced foreign-language skill ends and bilingualism begins, that many scholars interpret bilingualism as a gradable phenomenon (see Baetens Beardsmore, 1986, Ch. 1, for various attempts at definition, and for definitions of many more types of bilingual than can be given here).

If a bilingual's ability in both languages is roughly equal, s/he is known as a **balanced bilingual** or **equilingual**; but such individuals are very rare. Often in situations of stress, pronunciation and inaccuracies in usage will show that an apparent equilingual is, in fact, less proficient in one language than another (Baetens-Beardsmore, 1986, p. 9). Still, a person who can pass as native in more than one language except in situations of stress might be said to be 'more' bilingual than a so-called **receptive** (as opposed to **productive**) bilingual, a person who can understand one of her or his languages without being able to speak or write it well. People who have not used their native language for a long time often find their ability in it reduced to this type, although they will typically regain fluency after a period of exposure to the native language. Such persons are known as **dormant** bilinguals (p. 16).

It is also possible to make distinctions between types of bilingual in terms of the process by which they have reached this status. A **natural** (Baetens-Beardsmore, 1986, p. 8) or **primary** (Houston, 1972) bilingual is a person whose ability in the languages is the result of a natural process of acquisition, such as upbringing in a bilingual home, or of finding herself or himself in a situation in which more than one language needs to be used, but who has not learnt either language formally as a foreign language. If formal instruction in a foreign language has been received, the bilingual is known as a **secondary** bilingual.

Finally, what one might refer to as a socio-psychological distinction may be drawn between **additive** bilingualism, in the case of which the bilingual feels enriched socially and cognitively by an additional language, and **subtractive** bilingualism, in the case of which the bilingual feels that the second language is a cause of some loss with respect to the first. The latter tends to be the case when there is tension between the cultures to which the two languages belong (Lambert, 1974; Baetens Beardsmore, 1986, pp. 22–3).

BILINGUAL CHILDREN

A child may become bilingual for a number of reasons. The language of the home may differ from that of the surrounding larger social group, or from that of the education system of the country of residence, in which case the child can hardly avoid becoming bilingual, and must succeed in the school language in order to benefit from the education system. Opinions vary about the best way for schools to introduce the language of the school to children whose home language differs from it, and the debate is typically related to the wider issues of the rights and position of minority groups in multiethnic societies (Tosi, 1982, p. 44).

Two main approaches predominate: (1) mother-tongue teaching, and (2) teaching in the school language exclusively with other languages introduced only as subjects, not as the media of instruction.

In **mother-tongue teaching**, children are first taught all their subjects in their mother tongue. The school language will be introduced gradually, and may then either take over completely, or both languages may continue to be used side by side. Only if both languages continue to be used as media of instruction do such programmes fall within Hamers and Blanc's definition of a bilingual education programme as (1989, p. 189): 'any system of school education in which, at a given moment in time and for a varying amount of time, simultaneously or consecutively, instruction is planned and given in at least two languages'.

The major argument in favour of mother-tongue teaching arises from research by Skutnabb-Kangas and Toukomaa (1976) into Finnish migrant children's levels of achievement in Swedish schools. Skutnabb-Kangas and Toukomaa found that these children under-achieved in literacy skills in both Finnish and Swedish if they had migrated earlier than the age of ten, whereas if migration had taken place after that age, the children achieved normally, ac-cording to both Swedish and Finnish norms. This suggests that for children who are not bilingual from birth, the mother tongue must be firmly established before the second language is introduced; otherwise, the children's competence in both languages will suffer. It should also be borne in mind when considering the question of mother-tongue teaching, that a child's language is closely associated with its cultural identity, and that it can be very disturbing for a child suddenly to have to switch to a new language at the same time as s/he is being introduced to the new cul-tural norms which inform the school system *and* to that system itself and to all the new infor-mation s/he is required to assimilate at school.

Mother-tongue teaching found favour in many places in the 1970s. In the USA, the 1968 Bilingual Education Act recognized the right of children from non-English-speaking back-grounds to be educated in their mother tongue during their early years at school while they gained proficiency in English (Thernstrom, 1980; J. Edwards, 1985), and a 1977 EEC Council directive which came into force in 1981 asked member states to ensure that their education systems enabled children of guest workers to retain their home culture and language while also learning the language of their host community (Hamers and Blanc, 1989, p. 192). In Britain, too, mother-tongue-teaching programmes were developed in areas with high concentrations of ethnic minorities, such as, for instance, Birmingham and Bradford (V.K. Edwards, 1984); indeed, it is only where large groups sharing a minority language exist that mother-tongue-teaching programmes can be instituted

in practice, for economic and other practical reasons: it is too expensive to employ teachers in all languages, and they are, in any case, not usually available.

In the 1980s, funding for mother-tongue teach-ing steadily decreased both in the USA and in Britain, while resources were diverted into pro-grammes to teach English as a second language (ESL). Minority groups were encouraged to provide education in the minority languages themselves (Kirp, 1983; Education For All, 1985), leaving the school system monolingual. These programmes aim to assimilate children into the mainstream culture and language as quickly as possible, through the exclusive use in the school of the mainstream language: children are required to cope with the school language from the start; all instruction is given in it, with, at best, a bilingual teacher or classroom assistant to assist in the initial stages, or with the help of extra language classes in ESL.

In order to preserve their children's ability in the home language, many parents faced with this type of situation choose to interact in the home language only, within the home, in the family group, and in the company of other speakers of the home language. This policy usually succeeds, and if there is a large, closely integrated com-munity speaking the minority language in question, the child may remain actively bilingual all its life. However, children of school age may refuse to interact in the home language, speak the language of the larger community between them-selves, and answer their parents in the majority language when addressed in the minority language (Tosi, 1982, pp. 59–60). This is often because the children do not want to be different from their peers.

On the other hand, parents who have decided to aim for total integration in the wider community for themselves and their children, and who have therefore not tried to maintain their own language or to teach it to their children, sometimes find that the children, usually once they become teenagers, feel cheated of part of their culture and of the language which they feel they should have inherited. Many such children seek to spend time in and to learn the language of their parents' country of origin later in life, perhaps attending institutions of higher education or becoming employed there.

If a child's parents have different mother tongues, they may decide to use both to communicate with the child from birth, typically on a one-parent–one-language basis, so that the child will be able to communicate with all members of its family in their respective languages. One of the earliest studies of a bilingual child brought up on the **one-parent–one-language** principle was Ronjat's (1913) study of his son Louis, who, after a period of mixing up his two languages, French and German, emerged as a fully fledged bilingual.

Subsequent studies (Leopold, 1970, 1978; Arnberg, 1979; Bain and Yu, 1980) report similar patterns of bilingualization. Leopold's daughter, Hildegard, used a mixture of her languages, English and German, regardless of whether her interlocutor spoke English or German, until she was two. From then on, she kept the languages increasingly sharply distinguished until at the age of four she was fully aware of using two separate languages (Leopold, 1970).

Volterra and Taschner (1978) describe this process in terms of a three-stage model. First, the child develops a vocabulary consisting of words from both languages, but only one word is used for one concept. This word may be from one of the child's languages, or it may be a compound of both languages' words for the concept in question (French *chaud* + English *hot* producing *shot*; see Grosjean, 1982, p. 184, for further examples). Next, the child distinguishes two vocabularies, but uses only one syntax. Finally, in the third stage, the child has two grammars, and it is only when the child has to change very quickly between the two languages that any interference between them occurs.

Other studies (Padilla and Liebman, 1975; Bergman, 1976; Meisel, 1989) indicate that some children seem able to keep their languages apart from the very beginning of language development.

As an alternative to the one-person–one-language method of bringing up a child bilingually, a **topic-related** strategy may be adopted: certain topics are always discussed in one language, other topics in the other language. Or, a **language-time** approach may be adopted (Schmidt-Mackey, 1977): for instance, one language may be used in the morning and another in the afternoon, or one language during the week and another during weekends.

The acquisition of several languages from birth, by whatever method, is called **simultaneous** acquisition (Grosjean, 1982, p. 179). The broad aspects of acquisition of more than one language are the same as those of acquisition of one language, that is, children growing up in a bilingual environment do not speak any later than children brought up monolingually; easier sounds appear before the more difficult fricatives and consonant clusters; words are overextended; utterances increase in length at the same rate; and simple syntactic structures appear before more complex ones (Padilla and Liebman, 1975; Doyle, Champagne, and Segalowitz, 1978; McLaughlin, 1978) (compare LANGUAGE ACQUISITION). The acquisition pattern for each language may, however, differ from the pattern followed by monolingual children acquiring each separate language, and is, as mentioned above, often characterized by mixing.

Another strategy sometimes adopted by parents from different language backgrounds is to allow the child to master one of the languages first, preventing any exposure to the second language until later (Zierer, 1977). If the second language is learnt after the age of three years, Grosjean (1982, p. 179) speaks of **successive** acquisition.

It is not possible to say which of these methods of promoting childhood bilingualism is the most successful *qua* method, and nor is the degree of bilingualism related to whether the languages are acquired simultaneously or successively (Grosjean, 1982, p. 179; pp. 192–3). In all cases where one of a bilingual child's languages is a minority language, that language is threatened when the child's contact with the majority language increases through schooling and other forms of social interaction, especially if the majority group treats the minority language as inferior.

The overriding factor which determines the

degree to which the minority language is retained seems to be not the method used to achieve bilingualism in the first place, but, rather, the degree to which the child perceives a need or good reason to retain the minority language (Grosjean, 1982, p. 175). If, for example, the minority-speaking parent, or grandparents and other family members with whom the child is frequently in contact do not speak the majority language, the child may see this as good reason for retaining the minority language. Even so, however, complete mastery of both languages will normally only be obtained and retained if the child belongs to a well-established, cohesive minority-language group, so that the minority language is used on social occasions to interact with a number of people, or if the child is able to spend lengthy periods on a regular basis in the country of the minority language. If good reason to use one of a bilingual's languages disappears, the language will fall out of use and appear to be forgotten (Leopold, 1970; Burling, 1978).

Leopold's (1970) study, however, indicates that an apparently forgotten language can be regained very quickly if the child again perceives good reason to use the language. His daughter was dominant in English until she was five, because at that time she lived in the USA, so that her exposure to English was far greater than her exposure to German. This affected her pronunciation of German, and she tended to use English syntax even when speaking German. However, when Hildegard was five, she spent six months in Germany, during which time German became her dominant language, affecting her pronunciation of English. Her English receded in general, although some English idioms and syntactic structures still influenced her German. When Hildegard returned to the USA her German began to recede again, but after six months during which the one-parent–one-language regime continued to be imposed, she had become truly bilingual, although dominant in English. English influenced her choice of lexis and some syntax in German, but her German pronunciation and morphology were no longer affected (Grosjean, 1982, pp. 180–1).

Parents sharing a language which is also the language of the country in which they live, may, of course, also decide to bring up their children bilingually, if they feel that this will benefit the children (see Saunders, 1982, 1988). Many people believe that children are better at learning second and subsequent languages than adults, but it is not clear that this is the case, except as far as pronunciation is concerned. However, children may, in general, be more willing to invest the time and effort involved than adults in general are (Singleton, 1983).

There is no firm evidence to suggest that being brought up bilingually causes an individual any kind of disturbance, and it is worth pointing out that in many parts of the world, bilingualism or multilingualism is the norm rather than the exception. There is no reason why parents who wish to bring up their children bilingually should not do so. However, there is no firm evidence, either, that being bilingual has any other benefits to the bilingual than that of being able to converse in two languages, and, in most cases, being familiar with two cultures. Bilinguals are no more intelligent, on average, than monolinguals (McLaughlin, 1978; Grosjean, 1982, p. 226).

MIXING

Bilinguals often engage in language mixing when communicating with another person who also speaks both languages. This may happen for a number of reasons; for instance, the bilingual may have forgotten the term for something in the language s/he is currently speaking, and use the other language's term instead; or the other language being spoken may not have a term for a particular concept the bilingual wants to refer to. In other cases, a word which is similar in both languages, or a name, may **trigger** a switch. A bilingual can obviously also choose to quote the speech of another person in the language the person was speaking, even when the bilingual is engaged is speaking another language. Language mixing can also be used to express emotion, close personal relationships and solidarity, and to exclude a third person from part of a conversation (Harding and Riley, 1986, pp. 57–60).

A distinction can be drawn between two types of linguistics mixing: (1) **code mixing** – the use of elements, most typically nouns, from one language in an utterance predominantly in another language; and (2) **code switching** – a change from one language to another in the same utterance or conversation (Hamers and Blanc, 1989, p. 35).

Kachru (1978) identifies three main varieties of code mixing in India. First, English may be mixed into a regional language. The resulting mixed code serves as a marker of high social prestige and is characteristic of the Indian educated middle class, whose members may use it between themselves, whereas they would speak the unmixed Indian regional language with servants. Second, philosophical, religious, or literary discourse may proceed in discourse in which Sanskrit or High Hindi is mixed with a regional language, as a mark of religious or caste identity. This variety may also be a mark of political conservatism. Finally, the Indian Law Courts mix Persian vocabulary with Indian, and Persianized code mixing may also serve as a marker of Muslim religious identity and of professional status (Hamers and Blanc, 1989, p. 153).

Code switching can take place at various points in an utterance: between sentences, clauses, phrases, and words. It is governed by different norms in different bilingual communities, but although the norms differ, and although the reasons for the switch are diverse, there is some evidence that the switching itself is guided by a number of constraints imposed by differences in structure between the languages involved. For instance, bilinguals tend to avoid switching intrasententially at a boundary between constituents which are ordered differently in the two languages, since this would result in a structure which would be ungrammatical in at least one of the languages (Poplack, Wheeler, and Westwood, 1989, pp. 132–3). Code switching is therefore more problematic when typologically different languages are involved than when the languages are typologically similar (ibid.) (see LANGUAGE TYPOLOGY).

THE PSYCHOLINGUISTICS OF BILINGUALISM

The main questions addressed in the psycholinguistics of bilingualism concern the representation, storage, organization, accessing, and processing of a bilingual's languages, and the degree to which the bilingual's languages are functionally dependent or independent.

The most promising account of how a bilingual's languages are stored and related is that given by Paradis (1978, 1980a, 1980b), according to whom the bilingual has one set of experiential and conceptual information, that is, one 'world-knowledge' store, and two language stores, one for each language, each connected to the world-knowledge store. In the language stores, conceptual features of the world knowledge are grouped together differently, so that, for instance, the English word *ball* is connected to conceptual features such as 'round' and 'bouncy', whereas the French word *balle* is connected, in addition, to the feature 'small' and the French word *ballon* is connected, in addition, instead, to the feature 'large'.

The ability of bilinguals to keep their languages apart or to mix them at will, as in code mixing and code switching (see above, pp. 61–2) is of special interest in psycholinguistic studies of bilingualism. It is an ability which seems to be lost in aphasic patients: Perecman (1989) reviews studies reporting aphasic patients using words from different languages in the same utterance, combining a stem from one language with a stem from another, blending syllables from different languages in a single word, using the intonation of one language with the vocabulary of another, using the syntax of one language with the vocabulary of another, replacing a word with a phonetically similar word from another language, responding in a language different from the language of address, and engaging in **spontaneous translation**: the immediate and unsolicited translation of an utterance, the patient's own, or that of another speaker, into another language. How is it, then, that a healthy bilingual is able to speak either language, to switch from one to the other at will, and to prevent themselves from producing a haphazard mixture?

Penfield's (1959) answer to this question is that there is an automatic switching system which ensures that when one language is being used – is switched on – any other language is kept switched off. However, as some bilinguals, such as simultaneous interpreters, are able to listen to one language while speaking another, a single switching system cannot be enough. Instead, Macnamara (1967) proposes that there is one system for production and another for perception. The bilingual has control of an output switch, which enables her or him to select a language for speaking or writing, whereas the input switch is automatically controlled by the input, the language being heard or read.

However, as Taylor (1976) has pointed out, and as the experience of many bilinguals confirms, it can often take a bilingual a few seconds to comprehend part of an utterance if the language spoken has suddenly been switched, a phenomenon which tends to contradict the automatic input-switch hypothesis. Nor can a switch model account for interference by one language on another, as occurs when, for instance, a bilingual inadvertently uses a word from the language s/he is not using at the time, something which most bilinguals have experienced themselves doing.

It can also be argued that there is no need to posit switches for turning the languages on or off at all. According to Paradis (1980c) a bilingual simply decides to use one language rather than another, just as s/he may decide to speak or to remain silent; and according to Obler and Albert (1978) the bilingual relies on a number of linguistic clues to which language is being used. It may thus be that both a bilingual's languages are 'on' all the time, although the one being used predominates.

The analysis of the speech of bilingual aphasics (see APHASIA) has been used extensively in attempts to answer questions concerning the organization in the brain and the processing of a bilingual's languages. This approach complements studies of healthy bilinguals' performance in dichotic-listening tasks and tachistoscope tests. Recent studies using these methods suggest that bilinguals process language mainly in the left hemisphere, just as monolinguals appear to do (Gordon, 1980; Soares and Grosjean, 1981).

Most bilingual aphasic patients recover all their languages at the same rate. Some patients, however, experience only **selective recovery**. Minkowski (1927), for instance, reports on a patient who never regained use of his mother tongue, Swiss German. He had learnt German, French, and some Italian at school and had, at the age of thirty moved to a French-speaking town where he became a professor of physics. After suffering a stroke, at the age of forty-four, the patient lost the use of all his languages and, although comprehension in all of them was soon restored, the patient had to relearn to speak. French, which had become the patient's predominant language, returned first, followed by standard German and some Italian.

Minkowski (1927) also reports a case of **successive restitution**: a patient who had become aphasic following a motor-cycle accident at the age of thirty-two first regained almost full use of German, then of his first language, Swiss German, and then, after at least sixteen months, of Italian and French.

Minkowski (1928) reports a case of yet another pattern of recovery, namely **antagonistic recovery** of an aphasic's languages. The patient first recovered French, but as other languages were recovered, French was gradually lost. In some cases, there is **alternate antagonism**: a language is recovered, then lost as another is recovered, but is recovered again with subsequent loss of the other language, and so on (Paradis, 1980b). Further examples of these and other patterns of language recovery in aphasics may be found in Paradis (1977). L'Hermitte et al. (1966) report a case of **mixed recovery** of French and English in a 46-year-old man whose languages interfered with one another in both speaking and writing.

Apparently, several factors influence the pattern of recovery of languages lost through aphasia. One is the degree of use of the languages just before injury occurs; another is the patient's psychological state before and after the injury, that is, if a patient has a particular emotional bond with one language, that language will tend to be recovered first. Third, the language used with the aphasic during therapy will obviously also influence the recovery process. It may also be the case that a language in which the bilingual was literate before the injury stands a better chance of being recovered than a language which s/he could only speak. In addition, the patient's age and the severity of the injury influence the recovery pattern.

However, as many aphasics who do not regain the ability to use all their languages are still able to comprehend them, and in view of the pheno-menon of alternate antagonism, Paradis (1977) suggests that the languages are not lost at all, but that the retrieval of the stored language is inhibited. He suggests (1981) that, while both languages may be stored identically in one single extended system, the elements of each language form separate subsystems within the extended system. Each of the subsets can be impaired individually, leading to the various types of non-parallel recovery just discussed, or the whole set may be inhibited, in which case parallel recovery will occur (Grosjean, 1982, pp. 240–67).

SOCIETAL BILINGUALISM

A **bilingual** or **multilingual society** is one in which two or more languages are used by large groups of the population, although not all members of each group need be bilingual. Canada, Belgium, and Finland, for example, are bilingual countries, and India, the Soviet Union, and many African and Asian countries are multilingual. If the languages spoken in a bilingual society have equal status in the official, cultural, and family life of the society, the situation is referred to as **horizontal** bilingualism, whereas **diagonal** bi-lingualism obtains when only one language has official 'standard' status (Pohl, 1965). Pohl includes diglossia (see DIGLOSSIA) as a third type of bilingualism, **vertical** bilingualism, but this involves dialects of the same language, rather than different languages. As Grosjean points out (1982, pp. 5–7), even countries such as Japan and Germany, which we might think of as mono-lingual, contain sizable minority groups speaking languages other than the official language; they are classified as monolingual, nevertheless, because the great majority of the inhabitants have the official language as their mother tongue, and none of the minority languages has official status.

In many African and Asian countries, political boundaries conflict with linguistic boundaries, largely as a result of colonization. After inde-pendence, such multilingual countries have typically chosen either one of the native languages or a language from outside the nation, normally that of the colonizers, for use as an official language. Thus Tanzania uses Swahili as the official language, while Ghana uses English and Senegal uses French.

The reason why Tanzania chose Swahili was not, as one might first imagine, that this was the native language of the majority of the popu-lation: quite the opposite is the case. Swahili was the mother tongue of only around 10 per cent of the population, but it was the medium of educa-tion in primary schools, was linked to the movement for independence, and was already in use as a **lingua franca** – a language known to, and used for communication between, groups who do not speak each other's language – in Tanzania, and also in Kenya and Uganda. It was thus a language known by a large proportion of the population – around 90 per cent are bilingual with Swahili as one of their languages – but, since it was the first language of so few, its choice as an official language would not be interpreted as favouritism towards any one group (Grosjean, 1982, p. 8). Tanzania is a diagonally bilingual country.

Canada is probably the best known example of a horizontally bilingual country. Others include Czechoslovakia, Cyprus, Ireland, Israel, and Finland; Belgium is officially trilingual with Flem-ish, French, and German. Official bilingualism may, as in Canada, operate throughout a country so that any person anywhere in that country can choose to be educated in and use either language for official business; or a country, such as Switzer-land, may be divided into areas in which only one of the languages is used in education and for official purposes.

In Canada, the Official Languages Act, passed in 1968–9, declared French and English official languages, and granted them equal status in all aspects of federal administration. Such a policy need not promote individual bilingualism; indeed, it can actively discourage it, because its aim is to ensure that speakers of either language have access to all official documents in their own language. Thus, in Canada, only 13 per cent of the population use both languages regularly; in Paraguay, by contrast, where Spanish is the official language in so far as it is used for official government business, while the Indian language Guarani is the national language used on public occasions and in the media, about 55 per cent of the population is bilingual (Grosjean, 1982, pp. 10–12).

In Canada, although it was intended that wherever at least 10 per cent of the population spoke whichever of the two languages was the minority language for the area, the federal government would fund bilingual education programmes, this part of the Act has not been fully implemented. One of the reasons for this is that while bilingual education may seem advantageous to speakers of the majority language, English (67 per cent), it may appear to threaten the French-speaking minority (26 per cent) with assimilation. To counter this threat, the government of Quebec province, in which French is the majority language, passed the Chartre de la Langue Française is 1977, which, contrary to federal policy, made French the only official language in the province. Clearly, the fact that Canada consists of a number of self-governing provinces has hampered the full implementation of federal policy; however, bilingualism appears to be growing among the school-age population in Canada (Grosjean, 1982, pp. 17–18).

K.M.

SUGGESTIONS FOR FURTHER READING

Grosjean, F. (1982), *Life with Two Languages: An Introduction to Bilingualism*, Cambridge, MA, and London, Harvard University Press.
Harding, E. and Riley, P. (1986), *The Bilingual Family: A Handbook for Parents*, Cambridge, Cambridge University Press.

Case grammar

Case grammar was developed in the late 1960s by Charles Fillmore (1966, 1968, 1969, 1971a, 1971b), who saw it as a 'substantive modification to the theory of transformational grammar' (Fillmore, 1968, p. 21), as represented by, for instance, Chomsky (1965). The latter model was unable to account for the functions of clause items as well as for their categories; it did not show, for instance, that expressions like *in the room*, *towards the moon*, *on the next day*, *in a careless way*, *with a sharp knife*, and *by my brother*, which are of the category prepositional phrase, simultaneously indicate the functions, location, direction, time, manner, instrument, and agent respectively. Fillmore suggested that this problem would be solved if the underlying syntactic structure of prepositional phrases were analysed as a sequence of a noun phrase and an associated prepositional case-marker, both dominated by a case symbol indicating the thematic role of that prepositional phrase (Newmeyer, 1986, p. 103), and that, in fact, every element of a clause which has a thematic role to play should be analysed in terms of case markers and case symbols.

The generative grammarians did not view case as present in the deep structure, but saw it, rather, as the inflectional realization of particular syntactic relationships, and these syntactic relationships were thought to be defined only in the surface structure (Fillmore, 1968, p. 14). In contrast to this view, Fillmore argues that the notion of case 'deserves a place in the base component of the grammar of every language', and that case relationships should be seen as primitive terms in the theory of base structure. Concepts such as 'subject' and 'object' would no longer need to pertain to base structure, but would be confined to the surface structure of some, but not necessarily all, languages (1968, pp. 2–3).

Fillmore's argument is based on two assumptions: (1) **the centrality of syntax** in the determination of case; and (2) **the importance of covert categories**. In traditional grammar (see TRADITIONAL GRAMMAR), **case** is morphologically identified, that is, cases are identified through the forms taken by nouns, and only then explained by reference to the functions of the nouns within larger constructions. Latin, for instance, has six cases: **nominative**, which indicates that the noun functions as subject in the clause; **vocative**, which is the form used to address someone; **accusative**, which indicates that the noun functions as object in the clause, but which must also be used after prepositions meaning 'to'; **genitive**, which indicates that the item referred to by the noun is the possessor of something; **dative**, which indicates that the noun functions as indirect object in the clause; and **ablative** which is used after prepositions meaning 'from'. The Latin noun *amicus*, 'friend', takes the following forms in the singular in the cases just mentioned: *amicus, amice, amicum, amici, amico, amico*.

Obviously, some of the rules governing the uses of the case system cannot be explained very clearly in functional terms; the use of one case after certain prepositions, and another after certain other prepositions seems a fairly arbitrary matter, and the notion of use to explain case in traditional grammar should be taken in a loose sense. Surface English bears little resemblance to the case systems of Latin, German, or Finnish, for example; in English the singular noun only alters its form in the genitive with the addition of *'s*, and the personal pronouns alone have *I–me–my*, etc. (see Palmer, 1971, p. 15 and pp. 96–7).

However, in a grammar which takes syntax as central, a **case relationship** will be defined with respect to the framework of the organization of the whole sentence from the start. Thus, the notion of case is intended to account for functional, semantic, deep-structure relations between the verb and the noun phrases associated with it, and not to account for surface-form changes in nouns. Indeed, as is often the case in English, there may not be any surface markers to indicate case, which is therefore a **covert category**, often only observable 'on the basis of selectional constraints and transformational possibilities' (Fillmore, 1968, p. 3); they form 'a specific finite set'; and 'observations made about them will turn out to have considerable cross-linguistic validity' (p. 5).

The term **case** is used to identify 'the underlying syntactic–semantic relationship' which is universal:

> the case notions comprise a set of universal, presumably innate concepts which identify certain types of judgements human beings are capable of making about the events that are going on around them, judgements about such matters as who did it, who it happened to, and what got changed.
>
> (Fillmore, 1968, p. 24)

The term **case form** identifies 'the expression of a case relationship in a particular language' (p. 21). The notions of subject and predicate and of the division between them should be seen as surface phenomena only; 'in its basic structure [the sentence] consists of a verb and one or more noun phrases, each associated with the verb in a particular case relationship' (p. 21). The various ways in which cases occur in simple sentences define sentence types and verb types of a language (p. 21).

According to Fillmore (1968), a sentence consists of a proposition, a tenseless set of verb–case relationships, and a modality constituent consisting of such items as negation, tense, mood, and aspect (Newmeyer, 1986, p. 105). Sentence (S) will therefore be re-written

Modality (M) + Proposition (P), and P will be rewritten as Proposition (P) + Verb (V) + one or more case categories (Fillmore, 1968, p. 24). The case categories, which Fillmore sees as belonging to a particular language but taken from a universal list of meaningful relationships in which items in clauses may stand to each other are listed as follows (pp. 24–5):

Agentive (A): the case of the typically animate perceived instigator of the action identified by the verb [*John opened the door*; *The door was opened by John*].

Instrumental (I): the case of the inanimate force or object causally involved in the action or state identified by the verb [*The key opened the door*; *John opened the door with the key*; *John used the key to open the door*].

Dative (D): the case of the animate being affected by the state or action identified by the verb [*John believed that he would win*; *We persuaded John that he would win*; *It was apparent to John that he would win*].

Factitive (F): the case of the object or being resulting from the action or state identified by the verb, or understood as a part of the meaning of the verb [Fillmore provides no example, but Platt (1971, p. 25) gives, for instance, *The man makes a wurley*].

Locative (L): the case which identifies the location or spatial orientation of the state or action identified by the verb [*Chicago is windy*; *It is windy in Chicago*].

Objective (O): the semantically most neutral case, the case of anything representable by a noun whose role in the action or state identified by the verb is identified by the semantic interpretation of the verb itself; conceivably the concept should be limited to things which are affected by the action or state identified by the verb. The term is not to be confused with the notion of direct object, nor with the name of the surface case synonymous with accusative [*The door opened*].

The examples provided make plain the mismatch between surface relations such as subject and object, and the deep-structure cases.

Fillmore (1968, pp. 26 and 81) suggests that another two cases may need to be added to the list given above. One of these, **benefactive**, would be concerned with the perceived beneficiary of a state or an action, while dative need not imply benefit to anyone. The other, the **comitative**, would account for cases in which a preposition seems to have a comitative function similar to *and*, as in the following example, which Fillmore quotes from Jespersen (1924, p. 90): *He and his wife are coming / He is coming with his wife.*

Verbs are selected according to their **case frames**, that is, 'the case environment the sentence provides' (Fillmore, 1968, p. 26). Thus (p. 27):

The verb *run*, for example, may be inserted into the frame [＿＿ A], . . . verbs like *remove* and *open* into [＿＿ O + A], verbs like *murder* and *terrorize* (that is, verbs requiring 'animate subject' and 'animate object') into [＿＿ D + A], verbs like *give* into [＿＿ O + D + A], and so on.

Nouns are marked for those features required by a particular case. Thus, any noun occurring in a phrase containing A and D must be [+ animate].

The case frames will be abbreviated as **frame features** in the lexical entries for verbs. For *open*, for example, which can occur in the case frames [＿＿ O] (*The door opened*), [＿＿ O + A] (*John opened the door*), [＿＿ O + I] (*The wind opened the door*), and [＿＿ O + I + A] (*John opened the door with a chisel*), the frame feature will be represented as +[＿＿ O(I)(A)], where the parentheses indicate optional elements. In cases like that of the verb *kill*, where either an I or an A or both may be specified, linked parentheses are used (p. 28): +[＿＿ D(I)A)].

The frame features impose a classification of the verbs of a language. These are, however, also distinguished from each other by their transformational properties (pp. 28–9):

The most important variables here include (*a*) the choice of a particular NP to become the surface subject, or the surface object, wherever these choices are not determined by a general rule; (*b*) the choice of prepositions to go with each case element, where these are determined by idiosyncratic properties of the verb rather than by a general rule; and (c) other special transformational features, such as, for verbs taking S complements, the choice of specific complementizers (*that, -ing, for, to*, and so forth) and the later transformational treatment of these elements.

Fillmore claims that the frame-feature and transformational-property information which is provided by a theory which takes case as a basic category of deep structure, guarantees a simplification of the lexical entries of transformational grammar.

With the list of cases go lists of roles fulfilled by the things referred to by the linguistic items in the various cases. One such list, organized hierarchically, is presented in Fillmore (1971a, p. 42):

(a) AGENT   (e) SOURCE
(b) EXPERIENCER   (f) GOAL
(c) INSTRUMENT   (g) LOCATION
(d) OBJECT   (h) TIME

The idea behind the hierarchy is that case information will allow predictions to be made about the surface structure of a sentence: if there is more than one noun phrase in a clause, then the one highest in the hierarchy will come first in the surface form of the clause, etc. This explains why *John opened the door* (AGENT, ACTION, OBJECT) is grammatical while *The door opened by John* (OBJECT, ACTION, AGENT) is not. Newmeyer (1986, pp. 104–5) mentions this type of syntactic benefit as a second kind of benefit. Fillmore claims that case grammar gains from taking case to be a primitive notion. A third claim is made for semantic benefit. Fillmore points out that the claim made in transformational-generative grammar, that deep structure is an adequate base for semantic interpretation, is false. Chomsky (1965) would deal with *the door* as, respectively, deep-structure subject and deep-structure object in the two sentences:

The door opened
John opened the door

Case grammar makes it clear that, in both cases, *the door* stands in the same semantic relation to

the verb, namely OBJECT: '*Open* is a verb which takes an obligatory OBJECT and an optional AGENT and/or INSTRUMENT' (Newmeyer, 1986, p. 104, paraphrasing Fillmore 1969, pp. 363–9).

As mentioned above, Fillmore (1968, pp. 30–1) claims that entering the cases associated with verbs in the lexicon would lead to considerable simplification of it, since many pairs, such as *like* and *please*, differ only in their subject selection while sharing the same case frames, +[___ O + E], in the case of *like* and *please*. However, transformationalists (Dougherty 1970; Chomsky, 1972b; Mellema, 1974) were quick, in their turn, to point to the problems involved in subject selection, the rules for which would seriously complicate the transformational component (see Newmeyer, 1986, pp. 105–6).

Fillmore (1977) lists a number of criticisms of case grammar, and his answers to them. For example, he points out that his own claim that the agent and dative cases are necessarily animate embodied a confusion of relational and categorial notions. It is not the case that, as Finke (1974) suggests, cases can be identified with items having specific properties, because (Fillmore, 1977, p. 66):

> even if some universe contained only one sort of object – say, human beings – the role-identifying function of the cases could still be maintained. One person could pick up another person, use that person's body for knocking down a third person . . . and so on. In a universe with only one sort of object, in short, the case relations of agent, instrument, patient, and experiencer could all be easily imagined.

Addressing the criticism made by Katz (1972) that Fillmore confuses the grammatical and the semantic sentence-constituent functions, where, according to Katz, the grammatical sentence-constituent functions include subject and object, while the semantic sentence-constituent functions include those which Fillmore calls cases, Fillmore (1977) suggests a new way of looking at the functional structure of sentences. He says that a message can be divided into those parts which are 'in perspective' and those that are 'out of perspective'. The theory of case should be concerned with the perspectival structuring of the message. The assignment by case frames of semantico-syntactic roles to participants in the situation represented by a sentence constrains the assignment of a **perspective** on the situation. For instance, any agent that is brought into perspective must be the subject of the sentence.

The theory of perspectival structuring relies on the idea that 'meanings are relativized to scenes' (Fillmore 1977, p. 59 and p. 73):

> The study of semantics is the study of the cognitive scenes that are created or activated by utterances. Whenever a speaker uses ANY of the verbs related to [a] commercial event, for example, the entire scene of the commercial event is brought into play – is 'activated' – but the particular word chosen imposes on this scene a particular perspective. Thus, anyone who hears and understands either of the sentences in (12) has in mind a scene involving all of the necessary aspects of the commercial event, but in which only certain parts of the event have been identified and included in the perspective. The buyer and the goods are mentioned in (12a), the buyer and the money in (12b). In each case, information about the other elements of the scene could have been included – via non-nuclear elements of the sentence as in (12c) and (12d):

(12) a. *I bought a dozen roses.*
      b. *I paid Harry five dollars.*
      c. *I bought a dozen roses from Harry for five dollars.*
      d. *I paid Harry five dollars for a dozen roses.*

Faced by criticism from Anderson (1971) and Mellema (1974), Fillmore accepts that there are some semantic generalizations which can only be formulated if the grammatical relations of subject and object are recognized at some level of representation in grammatical theory. For instance, whether a noun phrase be given a **holistic** or a **partitive** interpretation seems to depend on its grammatical status as object or subject, as exemplified in (1) *The garden was swarming with bees* (holistic: the *whole* garden is swarming with bees; *the garden* in subject position) and (2) *I loaded the truck with hay* (holistic: the *whole* truck is loaded; *the truck* in object position); versus (3) *Bees were swarming in the garden* (partitive: the garden is not necessarily full of bees) and (4) *I loaded hay onto the truck* (partitive: the truck may not be full of hay).

A major worry for case theory is that none of the linguists who have developed grammars in which the notion of case figures has been able to arrive at a principled way of defining the cases, or of deciding how many cases there are, or of deciding when two cases have something in common as opposed to being simply variants of one case (Cruse, 1973). For example, Huddleston (1970) points out that in *The wind opened the door, the wind* may be interpreted as having its own energy and hence as being agent, or as being merely a direct cause of the door opening, and hence as instrument, or as having a role which is distinct from both agent and instrument, called, perhaps, 'force'. On yet another view, a case feature 'cause' can be seen as a feature of both agent and instrument (Fillmore, 1977, p. 71). Fillmore thinks that this problem may be explained with reference to the notions of perspective and of meaning being relativized to scenes mentioned above. The wind is brought into perspective in the clause and is thus a **nuclear element**. And (pp. 79–80): 'perspectivizing corresponds, in English, to determining the structuring of a clause in terms of the nuclear grammatical relations'.

The obvious attractions of case grammar include the clear semantic relevance of notions such as agency, causation, location, advantage to someone, etc. These are easily identifiable across languages, and are held by many psychologists to play an important part in child language acquisition. However (Lyons, 1977a, pp. 87–8):

> case-grammar is no longer seen by the majority of linguists working within the general framework of transformational-generative grammar as a viable alternative to the standard theory. The reason is that when it comes to classifying the totality of the verbs in

a language in terms of the deep-structure cases that they govern, the semantic criteria which define these cases are all too often unclear or in conflict.

In spite of its failings, case grammar has been important in drawing the attention of an initially sceptical tradition of linguistic study to the importance of relating semantic cases or thematic roles to syntactic descriptions.

K.M.

SUGGESTIONS FOR FURTHER READING

Fillmore, C.J. (1968), 'The case for case', in E. Bach and R.T. Harms (eds), *Universals in Linguistic Theory*, New York, Holt, Rinehart & Winston, pp. 1–90.

Fillmore, C.J. (1977), 'The case for case reopened', in P. Cole and J.M. Sadock (eds), *Syntax and Semantics*, vol. 8: *Grammatical Relations*, New York, Academic Press.

Categorial grammar

The term **categorial grammar** was coined by Bar-Hillel (see Bar-Hillel, 1970, p. 372) to refer to a method of grammatical analysis initially developed by the Polish logicians Leśniewski and Ajdukiewicz (see Leśniewski, 1929; Ajdukiewicz, 1935; English translation in McCall, 1967, pp. 207–31) on the basis on Husserl's (1900/1913–21) 'pure grammar', a universal, rationalist (see RATIONALIST LINGUISTICS) grammar specifying the laws governing the combination of meaningful elements of languages.

According to Husserl, a sentence's meaningfulness depends on the possibility of seeing the sentence as an instance of the **sentence form** *This S is p*, where *S* is a **meaning category** standing for a 'nominal matter' and *p* is a meaning category standing for an 'adjectival matter'. The pure grammar has to do three things: (1) it must assign meaning categories to linguistic expressions on the basis of substitutability; (2) it must specify which combinations of meaning categories are possible; and (3) it must state the laws that govern the combination of meaning categories.

This outline system was formalized by Ajdukiewicz (1935), who postulates two **basic categories**, 'sentence' (s) and 'name' (n), and the notion of **functor** for derived categories. A

functor is an incomplete sign which needs to be completed by **variables**. For instance, in the sentence *Caesar conquered Gaul* (Frege, 1891), *conquered* is a functor which is incomplete until complemented by the arguments, the names *Caesar* and *Gaul*. Together, functor and name(s) yield the **value**, 'sentence' (s). The functor is the linguistic sign for a **function** in the mathematical sense, e.g. the function of squaring, $(\ )^2$, not in the sense in which the term is used in, for instance, functional grammar (see FUNCTIONAL GRAMMAR). It is not, however, confined to mathematical entities (Reichl, 1982, p. 46):

> The cataloguing rules of a library could also be considered a function. Here we have as the domain of the function the set of books and as range the set of sigla; to every book of the library as 'argument' the rule assigns a 'value', its shelfmark.

In being built on the mathematical notion of the function, categorial grammars differ crucially from phrase-structure grammars (Bach, 1988, p. 23): 'What corresponds in a categorial system to transformational kinds of rules in other theories are the operations that compose functions and change categories.'

In natural language, all the arguments for a function (a predicate expression) which yield a true sentence when combined with it are the linguistic expressions for the **extension** of the predicate. So the extension of *squints* is the class of squinting things. But when the function *squints* is applied to the names of individuals in the domain of discourse, some false sentences will also be generated, namely when a named individual to which the function is applied does not, in fact, squint. So the extension of *squints* determines the truth value of any sentence of the form 'x squints', and is therefore a function from individuals to truth values. The **intension** of *squints* is the property of squinting. Then (p. 47):

> If the extension of *squints* is some function f_1 (x) – where x ranges over individuals – with values in $\{T, F\}$, the extension of *runs* some function f_2 (x) and of *sleeps* some function f_3 (x) etc., then the extension of one-place predicate expressions in general can be viewed as a class of functions from individuals to truth-values, i.e. they have the general form ... $f(n)$ = s, i.e. a one-place predicate 'makes' (declarative) sentences – bearers of truth or falsehood – out of names.

We can thus see that categorial grammar, which has been developed in more recent works by Bar-Hillel (1970), Geach (1972), and Cresswell (1973), is based on the Aristotelean notion that (Geach, 1972, p. 483):

> the very simplest sort of sentence is a two-word sentence consisting of two heterogeneous parts – a name, and a predicative element (rhema). For example, 'petetai Sōkratēs', 'Socrates is flying'. This gives us an extremely simple example for application of our category theory:

petetai   Sōkratēs
s/n   n

The two-word Greek expression as a whole belongs to the category s of sentences; 'petetai' is a functor that takes a single name (of category n) 'Sōkratēs' as argument and yields as a result an expression of category s.

The idea is, then, that what is done with language can ultimately be reduced to picking out something and saying something about it, thereby producing a sentence. What is being picked out is referred to by a **name (N)**. That which is being said about N is expressed in the predicative element **(S/N)**, where S/N means something like 'that which, when combined with a name, yields a **sentence (S)**'.

Leśniewski and Ajdukewicz believed that S and N were the only basic categories necessary, since all others were derivable from them. Bar-Hillel, however, experimented for a time with additional fundamental categories and with new ways of combining them, until the arrival of Chomsky's phrase-structure grammars, at which point his work on categorial grammar ceased to be developmental, as he directed his efforts towards proving equivalences between phrase-structure and categorial grammars (see Bar-Hillel, 1970, p. 372).

Leśniewski, Ajdukiewicz, and Bar-Hillel all assume that S and N are **universal categories**, i.e. categories which are present in all languages. They also believe that each language contains a finite number of **basic categories**, with S and N among them, of course, but also possibly containing others, which may or may not be universal. In addition, they think that each language will contain a finite or infinite number of **functor** categories which can combine with each other or with the basic categories to form expressions belonging to any of the categories in the language (Bar-Hillel, 1970, p. 316).

As illustrated above with the case of S/N (intransitive verb), a functor is denoted by the symbol for the category with which it can combine (N), and by the symbol for the category which results from that combination (S). Categorial grammar was the first syntactic approach to adopt a policy of classifying modifiers according to the category of what they modify (McCawley, 1988, p. 192). The sign that indicates the functor is actually the sign for that **function** which will produce a given category when a given functor is completed by an **argument**. So the category to which *young* (an adjective) belongs, will be denoted by N/N, because when an adjective combines with (is completed by the argument) N it will produce another N, in this case, perhaps, the N *young boy* (Bar-Hillel, 1970, p. 332).

A simple categorial grammar of English, with dictionary expressions attached where appropriate, might look like this (adapted from Allwood *et al.* 1977, p. 135):

Basic categories	*Dictionary expressions*
S	none
N	*Amy, Tomas, Stuart, Poul....*

Derived categories	
S/S	*necessarily, possibly, not*
S/SS	*and, or, if – then, if and only if*
S/N	*runs, sleeps, sighs ...*
(S/N)(S/N)	*fast, carefully, slowly ...*
S/(S/N)	*someone, everyone*
(S/N)/N	*seeks ...*
N/N	*young, old, beautiful ...*

S/S here is the function whose functors are those linguistic expressions which form sentences from other sentences: if *S* is a sentence, then so is *necessarily/possibly/not S*. S/SS is the function whose functors are those linguistic expressions which combine sentences with sentences to form sentences: if S_1 and S_2 are both sentences, then so are S_1 *and/or* S_2 and *if/if and only if* S_1 *then* S_2. As we have seen above, the set of functors for S/N corresponds roughly to the set of intransitive verbs. (S/N)(S/N) is the function whose linguistic expressions are those which create intransitive verbs from intransitive verbs, or, more precisely, those which, when added to an S/N produce another S/N, that is, those which, when added to the category which combines with an N to form an S, still produce a member of the category which, when added to N, forms S. For example, just as *runs (S/N)* combines with, say, *Tomas (N)* to produce an S (*Tomas runs*), so does *runs fast ((S/N)(S/N))*, namely, *Tomas runs fast (S)*; etc.

In Bar-Hillel's (1970) notation, it is possible to distinguish **left-** from **right-concatenation**: i.e., it is possible to see whether, for example, an item joins another on the left or the right to form a category. Bar-Hillel indicates this by varying the direction of the oblique line; Lyons (1968) uses arrows.

Any category, such as S/N, which is not basic, such as S and N, is called a **derived** category, and, obviously, all derived categories will be functor categories. The possibilities of forming new derived categories in the grammar are endless, the general rule being (Allwood *et al.* 1977, p. 133):

If $C_1 \ldots C_n$ are categories then $C_1/C_2 \ldots C_n$ is a category

To philosophers, categorial grammar has long seemed attractive because it accords well with the so-called **Fregean Principle** that 'the meaning of the whole sentence is a function of the meaning of its parts' (Cresswell, 1973, p. 19), and because it seems to offer a way of showing isomorphism between semantics and syntax (Allwood *et al.* 1977, p. 136): 'The basic semantic types correspond to the two basic syntactic categories sentences and names.' Sentences correspond to truth values, names to entities. Lewis (1969/1983, pp. 189–232) uses a categorial grammar with a transformational component to derive a theory of meaning.

Oehrle *et al.* (1988, p. 8), however, note a relative lack of interest in categorial grammar among linguists until the 1980s. They suggest that this lack of interest derived from the view that natural language cannot be described with context-free grammars, and from most linguists' unfamiliarity with model-theoretic approaches to investigations of the relationship between syntax and interpretation. The papers in their collection are, however, symptomatic of (Bach, 1988, Introduction): 'a growing interest in categorial grammar as a framework for formulating empirical theories about natural language', particularly in theories based on Montague grammar (see MONTAGUE GRAMMAR). He notes that the influence of categorial grammar is being felt in theories of generalized phrase-structure grammar, and concludes (pp. 32–3):

The distinguishing characteristic of this work and its most interesting feature is the centrality which it accords to the notion of functions and arguments, an idea that has formed an important core of thinking about language for more than a century.

K.M.

SUGGESTIONS FOR FURTHER READING

Geach, P. (1972), 'A program for syntax', in D. Davidson and G. Harman (eds), *Semantics of Natural Language*, Dordrecht, Reidel, pp. 483–97.

Oehrle, R.T., Bach, E., and Wheeler, D. (eds) (1988), *Categorial Grammars and Natural Language Structures*, Dordrecht, Reidel.

Corpora

At its most general, a **corpus** (plural: *corpora*) may be defined as a body or collection of linguistic data for use in scholarship and research. Since the early 1960s, interest has increasingly focused on **computer corpora** or **machine-readable corpora**, which are the main subject of this article. In the first three sections I shall begin, however, by considering the place in linguistic research of corpora in general, whether machine-readable or not. In the remaining sections I shall consider why computer corpora have been compiled or collected; what are their functions and their limitations; what are their applications, more particularly, their use in natural-language processing (NLP). This article will illustrate the field of computer corpora only by reference to corpora of Modern English.

CORPORA IN A HISTORICAL PERSPECTIVE

In traditional linguistic scholarship, particularly on **dead languages** (languages which are no longer used as an everyday means of communication in a speech community), the corpus of available textual data, however limited or fragmentary, was the foundation on which scholarship was built. Later, particularly in the first half of the twentieth century, corpora assumed importance in the transcription and analysis of extant, but previously unwritten or unstudied, languages, such as the Amerindian languages studied by linguists such as Franz Boas (1911) and the generation of American linguists who succeeded him.

The urgent task of analysing and classifying the unwritten languages of the world has continued up to the present day. But this development was particularly important for setting the scene for the key role of the corpus in American structural linguistics in the work of Bloomfield (1933) and the post-Bloomfieldians (see Harris, 1951, pp. 12ff., and (POST-) BLOOMFIELDIAN AMERICAN STRUCTURAL GRAMMAR) for whom the corpus was not merely an indispensable practical tool, but the *sine qua non* of scientific description (see BEHAVIOURIST LINGUISTICS). This era saw a shift from the closed corpus of a dead language – necessarily the only first-hand source of data – to a closed and finite corpus of a **living language** (a language in use as the means of communication in a speech community), where the lack of access to unlimited textual data is a practical restriction, rather than a restriction of principle. Another shift is from the written textual data of a dead language to the spoken textual data of a living and heretofore unwritten language. If we associate the terms 'text' and 'corpus', as tradition dictates, with written sources, this tradition must give way to a contrasting emphasis, in the post-Bloomfieldian era, on the primacy of spoken texts and spoken corpora.

However, a complete reversal of the post-Bloomfieldians' reliance on corpora was effected by the revolution in linguistic thought inaugurated by Chomsky (see RATIONALIST LINGUISTICS). Chomsky saw the finite spoken corpus as an inadequate and degenerate observational basis for the description of the infinite generative capacity of natural languages, and speaker intuitions replaced the corpus as the sole reliable source of data about the language.

It was in this unfavourable climate of opinion that the compilation of a systematically organized computer corpus – the first of its kind – was undertaken in the USA. The **Brown University Corpus of American English** (known as **Brown Corpus**, and consisting of c. 1 million text words) was compiled under the direction of Francis and Kučera in 1961–4 (see Francis and Kučera, 1964; rev. 1971, 1979; also Francis, 1982). It contained 500 written text samples of c. 2,000 words each, drawn from a systematic range of publications in the USA during 1961. Since that time, machine-readable corpora have gradually established themselves as resources for varied research purposes.

THE JUSTIFICATION FOR CORPORA IN LINGUISTICS

It is necessary, in view of the influential Chomskyan rejection of corpus data, to consider in what ways corpora (whether computerized or not) contribute to linguistic research. The following are six arguments against the Chomskyan view.

1 The opposition between the all-sufficient corpus of the post-Bloomfieldian linguist and the all-sufficient intuitions of the generative linguist is a false opposition, overlooking considerations of reasonable intermediate positions. Recent corpus users have accepted that corpora, in supplying first-hand textual data, cannot be meaningfully analysed without the intuition and interpretative skill of the analyst, using knowledge *of* the language (*qua* native speaker or proficient non-native speaker) and knowledge *about* the language (*qua* linguist). In other words, corpus use is seen as a question of corpus *plus* intuition, rather than of corpus *or* intuition.

2 The generativist's reliance on the native speaker's intuition begs a question about the analysis of language by proficient non-native speakers. In so far as such analysts have unreliable intuitions about what is possible in a language, their need for corpus evidence is greater than that of a native speaker. It is thus no accident that corpus studies of English have flourished in countries where a tradition of English linguistics is particularly strong, but where English is not a native language: e.g. Belgium, The Netherlands, Norway, Sweden.

3 The distinction between competence and performance, a cornerstone of Chomsky's rationalist linguistics, has been increasingly challenged since the 1950s, especially through the development of branches of linguistics for which detailed evidence of performance is arguably essential, such as sociolinguistics, psycholinguistics, pragmatics, and discourse analysis. To these may be added developments in applied linguistics, where it has become clear that studies of how language *is used*, both by native speakers and by learners, are relevant inputs to the study of language *learning*.

4 The generative linguist's reliance on 'intuition' has required the postulation of an 'ideal native speaker/hearer' and in practice of an invariant variety of the language in question (see Chomsky 1965). But research in sociolinguistics has highlighted the variability of the competences of different native speakers belonging to different social groupings, and even the dialectal variability of a single native speaker's language. As soon as the non-uniformity of the language is accepted as normal, it is evident that native speakers' knowledge of their language, as a social or cultural phenomenon, is incomplete, whether considered in terms of dialect or in terms of register (e.g., British native speakers of English obviously have unreliable intuitions about American usage, or about scientific or legal usage in their own country). Hence corpus studies

which range over different varieties reveal facts which are not accessible from intuition alone. (Good examples have been provided by various corpus-based studies of the English modal auxiliaries, notably Coates, 1983: here corpus analysis reveals an unexpectedly wide range of variation between spoken and written English, and between British and American English.)

5 Studies of corpora also bring to the attention an abundance of examples which cannot be neatly accommodated by intuition-based generalizations or categories. These cannot be dismissed as performance errors (see Sampson, 1987, pp. 17–20): rather, they invite analysis in terms of non-deterministic theories of language, accommodating **prototypes** (Rosch and Mervis, 1975; Lakoff, 1982), **gradience** (Bolinger, 1961; Quirk *et al.*, 1985, p. 90), or **fuzzy** categories (Coates, 1983). From the viewpoint of such theories, it is the linguist's intuition which is suspect, since the linguist who relies on intuition is likely to find clear-cut, prototypical examples to support a given generalization, or, in contrast, to find unrealistic counterexamples for which a corpus would provide no authentic support. Thus intuition may be seen not as a clear mirror of competence, but a distorting mirror, when it is used as the only resource for the linguistic facts to be analysed.

6 We turn finally to an argument applicable specifically to computer corpora. The goal of natural-language processing (NLP) by computer must reasonably include the requirement that the text to be processed should not be preselected by linguistic criteria, but should be unrestricted, such that any sample of naturally occurring English should be capable of analysis. Although this ambitious goal is well beyond the capabilities of present NLP systems in such complex tasks as machine translation, it motivates the use of computer corpora in computational linguistics (see ARTIFICIAL INTELLIGENCE), and shows that this branch of linguistics, like others mentioned in (3) above, cannot neglect the detailed study of performance, in the form of authentic textual data.

LIMITATIONS OF CORPORA

On the other hand, corpora have clear limitations. The Brown Corpus (see p. 74 above) illustrates two kinds of limitation general to corpus linguistics.

First, there is a limitation of **size**. Even though the million words of the Brown Corpus seem, at first blush, impressive, they represent only a minute sample of the written texts published in the USA in 1961, let alone of a theoretically conceivable 'ideal corpus' of all texts, written and spoken, in (Modern) English.

The second limitation, already implied, is a limitation of language variety. In the defining criteria of the Brown Corpus, 'written English' proclaims a limitation of medium; 'American English' one of geographical provenance; and '1961' a third limitation of historical period. In addition to those limitations, the Brown Corpus, by the detailed principles of its selection, includes certain registers (journalism, for example) but excludes others (poetry, for example). Hence, any study of Modern English based on the Brown Corpus must be accompanied by a caveat that the results cannot be generalized, without hazard, to varieties of the language excluded from its terms of reference.

Similarly, the limitation of corpus size means that samples provided in the corpus may be statistically inadequate to permit generalization to other samples of the same kind. While the size of the Brown Corpus may be considered adequate to the study of common features (e.g. punctuation marks, some affixes, common grammatical constructions), it is manifestly inadequate as a resource for (for example) lexicography, since the corpus contains only c. 50,000 word types, of which c. 50 per cent occur only once in the corpus. (By contrast, the corpus used for the *Collins COBUILD English Language Dictionary*, editor-in-chief John Sinclair, consisted of over 20 million text words (COBUILD, 1987).)

To some extent, however, the generalizability of findings from one corpus to another is itself a matter of empirical study. The list of the fifty most common words in the Brown Corpus is replicated almost exactly in a corresponding corpus of British English, the **Lancaster–Oslo/**

Bergen Corpus (known as the **LOB Corpus**; see Hofland and Johansson, 1982). In this very limited respect, therefore, the two corpora are virtually equivalent samples. As more corpora representing different language varieties are compared, it will become evident how far a sample may be regarded as representative of the language as a whole, or of some variety of it. Carroll (1971) has implemented a statistical measure of representativeness *within* a corpus (a function of frequency and dispersion), and this may again, with caution, be extended to approximate measures of representativeness for the language as a whole.

WHY SHOULD A CORPUS BE MACHINE-READABLE?

The advantages of a machine-readable corpus over a corpus stored, in the traditional way, on paper derive from capabilities of (1) automatic processing and (2) automatic transmission.

1 **Automatic processing** subsumes operations which vary from the simple and obvious, such as sorting the words of a text into alphabetical order, to complex and specialized operations such as **parsing** (syntactic analysis). The computer's advantage over a human analyst is that it can perform such operations with great speed, as well as accurately and consistently. Thus the computer can, in practice, accomplish tasks of text manipulation which could scarcely be attempted by even large numbers of (trained) human beings.

2 **Automatic transmission** includes transferring a text either locally (e.g. from a computer's storage to an output device such as a VDU or a printer), or remotely to other installations – either via a direct electronic link or through the mediation of a portable storage device, such as a magnetic tape, a diskette, or a compact disk. Thus technically, a corpus can be 'published' in the sense of being copied and made available to a user, in any part of the world, who has access to the necessary computer resources. (A practical note: certain corpora can be obtained, under specified conditions, from the Norwegian Computing Centre for the Humanities, PO Box

53, N-5014 Bergen University, Norway; or from the Oxford Text Archive, Oxford University Computing Service, 13 Banbury Road, Oxford OX2 6NN, UK.) In the present era of inexpensive but powerful microcomputers and storage devices, the computer corpus is becoming a potential resource for a large body of users – not only for research, but for educational applications. Technical availability, however, does not mean availability in a legal or practical sense – see 'Availability Limitations' in the next section.

COMPUTER CORPORA OF MODERN ENGLISH: DATA CAPTURE AND AVAILABILITY

WHAT IS AVAILABLE?

Focusing on Modern English, we may now consider some of the existing computer corpora, in addition to the Brown Corpus, in order to gain an impression of the extent of linguistic coverage which has been achieved.

The **LOB Corpus** mentioned above (see Johansson *et al.*, 1978) is a corpus of printed British English compiled in order to match as closely as possible the Brown Corpus of American English. Its size and principles of selection are virtually the same as those of the Brown Corpus.

The **London–Lund Corpus** (Svartvik *et al.*, 1982) is a corpus of c. 500,000 words of spoken English, transcribed in detailed prosodic notation, and constituting spoken texts of the **Survey of English Usage Corpus** compiled at London University under the direction of Randolph Quirk (see Quirk, 1960; Quirk and Svartvik, 1979). The London–Lund Corpus was computerized at Lund University, Sweden, under the direction of Jan Svartvik. (The whole of the Survey of English Usage Corpus is now being computerized by Sidney Greenbaum and Geoffrey Kaye.)

The **Leuven Drama Corpus** consists of approximately 1 million words of British dramatic texts (see Geens *et al.*, 1975).

The **Birmingham Collection of English Text** is best described as an ongoing constellation of text corpora, compiled primarily for lexicographical purposes under the direction of John Sinclair (see Renouf, 1984). This compilation contains over 20 million words, including over a million words of spoken English, as well as more specialized corpora: for example, a corpus of English-language teaching texts.

The **Oxford Text Archive** is another large and growing collection of machine-readable texts. It includes texts of various languages and various historical periods, among which is a considerable quantity of Modern English texts.

This selected list only represents the tip of the iceberg, in that there exist more specialized corpora – e.g. corpora of children's language and texts for the use of children – and many corpora are currently in the process of compilation. In fact, since the Brown Corpus came into being in the early 1960s, possibilities of **data capture**, i.e. of obtaining texts in machine-readable form, have increased astronomically. The Brown and LOB Corpora had to be compiled by **manual data capture**: texts had to be laboriously keyboarded and corrected by a human operator using an input device such as a card punch or terminal. But in the 1970s and 1980s, the development of computer typesetting and word-processing has meant that vast quantities of machine-readable text have come into existence as a by-product of commercial text-processing technologies. This may be termed **automatic data capture**, another source of which is the use of **optical character recognizers** (**OCRs**): machines which can scan a printed or typewritten text and automatically convert it into machine-readable form. Of most use for corpus compilation is a **general-purpose OCR**, such as the **KDEM machine** which, with training by an operator, can recognize texts printed in a wide variety of fonts and type sizes. The KDEM machine has been used for compiling the Birmingham Collection of English Text and the Oxford Text Archive.

Automatic data capture means that, in principle, corpora of unlimited size can be created. The terms 'collection' and 'archive' in the names of the Birmingham and Oxford compilations signal a consequential move away from the idea of a fixed, closed corpus towards data capture as an open-ended, ongoing process.

AVAILABILITY LIMITATIONS

In three respects, however, the above account paints too optimistic a picture of the current outlook of computer corpus research. First, the technical problems of data capture for research are considerable – but must be ignored here.

Second, automatic data capture is limited to written text, and is likely to remain so for some time to come. Spoken texts must first be transcribed into written form, which means that there is a grave shortage of spoken, in comparison with written, corpus data.

Third, machine-readable texts are subject to copyright and other proprietary restrictions, which impose strong constraints on their availability for research. The Brown Corpus, the LOB Corpus, the London–Lund Corpus, and parts of the Oxford Text Archive can be made available for purposes of academic research only (i.e., not for commercial or industrial exploitation). Other corpora or text collections are subject to stronger restrictions, and of the many corpora which have been automatically compiled, most are available, if at all, only through negotiation with their compilers and/or copyright holders.

PRE-PROCESSED CORPORA

To put ourselves in the position of a linguist using a computer corpus, we may initially imagine someone who wishes to investigate the use of the English word *big* (say, as part of a comparison of *big* and *large*). The task of the computer in this case is most naturally seen as that of producing a list (perhaps a sample list) of occurrences of *big* in a given corpus, together with sufficient context to enable the researcher to interpret examples in terms of their syntactic, semantic, or pragmatic determinants. This is what is provided by a **concordance program** (e.g. the **Oxford Concordance Program**; see Hockey and Marriott, 1980). A **KWIC concordance** is a particularly convenient form of concordance listing, in which each token of the target word (*big*) is placed in the middle of a line of text, with the remainder of the line filled with its preceding and following context.

A set of characters at the beginning of the line specifies the **location** of the given occurrence in the corpus. A concordance program is one of the simplest yet most powerful devices for retrieving information from a corpus. But it also illustrates a limitation of any corpus stored in the normal orthographic form. If the word to be investigated had been (for example) *little*, the concordance would have listed all the occurrences of *little*, whether as an adverb, a determiner, a pronoun, or an adjective, so the investigator would have had to sort the occurrences manually in order to identify those instances of *little* relevant to a comparison with *big*. Another type of difficulty would have arisen if the investigator had wanted to study *come* and *go*: here several different concordance listings would have been necessary, to find all morphological forms (*comes*, *came*, etc.) of the same verb.

This illustrates a general problem: that information which is not stored in orthographic form in the 'raw' corpus cannot be retrieved in a simple or useful way. An answer to this problem is to build in further information, by producing linguistically analysed or annotated versions of the corpus. A valuable first stage in the **pre-processing** of a corpus is **grammatical tagging**: that is, the attachment of a grammatical **tag** or **word-class label** to each word it contains. The result is a grammatically tagged corpus.

The Brown, LOB, and London–Lund Corpora now exist in grammatically tagged versions. Although manual tagging is possible in principle, in practice the tagging of a sizable corpus is feasible only if done automatically, by a computer program or suite of programs known as a **tagging system**. This ensures not only speed but consistency of tagging practice. The tagging of the LOB Corpus (using a set of 133 grammatical tags) was undertaken by a system which achieved 96–7 per cent success (see Garside *et al.*, 1987, chs 3 and 4). Where it made mistakes, these had to be corrected by human **post-editors**.

Grammatical tagging is only part of a larger enterprise, the **syntactic analysis** (or **parsing**) of a

corpus. This is being undertaken at various centres, and although at present there exists no completely parsed version of any of the corpora mentioned above, substantial parts of the Brown, LOB, and London–Lund Corpora have been parsed (Ellegård, 1978; Altenberg, 1987; Garside and Leech, 1987). From a parsed corpus or subcorpus it is possible to retrieve information (for example, in the form of a structurally defined concordance) about more abstract grammatical categories which cannot be specified in terms of words or word-classes: for example, types of phrases or clauses.

There is no reason why the preprocessing of a corpus should be restricted to grammatical analysis. For example, tagging of semantic classes, e.g. speech-act verbs (see SPEECH-ACT THEORY), or adverbs of frequency, or discourse features e.g. pronoun anaphora (see TEXT LINGUISTICS) can be undertaken either manually or automatically. Tagging of a wide range of linguistic features in the LOB and London–Lund Corpora has been undertaken by Biber (forthcoming) in a large-scale investigation of stylistic variation in English.

DATA RESOURCES: FREQUENCY LISTS AND CONCORDANCES

A corpus can also be processed in order to produce derived databases, or data resources, of various kinds. The simplest example is the production of word-frequency lists (e.g. Kučera and Francis, 1967; Carroll *et al.*, 1971; Hofland and Johansson, 1982), sorted in either alphabetical or rank order. With a tagged corpus, it is possible to automate the production of frequency lists which are **lemmatized**: that is, where different grammatical forms of the same word (or **lemma**) are listed under one entry, as in a standard dictionary (Francis and Kučera, 1982, provides such lists for the Brown Corpus).

A KWIC concordance of a corpus is itself a derived data-resource which may be made available independently, either in machine-readable form, or in microfiche form. For example, KWIC concordances of tagged and untagged versions of the LOB Corpus are available from the

Norwegian Computing Centre (see p. 76 for the address).

As more preprocessing of corpora is undertaken, one can envisage the availability of further types of derived data-resources, e.g. concordances and frequency lists of grammatical structures. (For one such format, a **distributional lexicon**, see Beale, 1987.)

APPLICATIONS OF CORPUS-BASED RESEARCH

Apart from applications in linguistic research *per se*, the following practical applications may be mentioned.

LEXICOGRAPHY

Corpus-derived frequency lists and, more especially, concordances are establishing themselves as basic tools for the lexicographer. KWIC concordances of the Birmingham Collection, for example, were systematically used in the compilation of the *Collins COBUILD English Language Dictionary* (COBUILD, 1987). Lemmatized KWIC concordances and frequency lists offer the lexicographer further advantages, as do frequency lists of collocations.

LANGUAGE TEACHING

Applications to the educational sphere are likely to develop more rapidly in the future, since cheaper and more powerful hardware is coming within the range of educational budgets. The use of concordances as language-learning tools is currently a major interest in computer-assisted language learning (CALL; see Johns 1986). In language-teaching and -learning research, the development of specialized corpora of, say, technical and scientific Englishes (see Yang, 1985, pp. 94–5) will have obvious applications to English for specific purposes (ESP), while the potential value of corpora for interlanguage research (e.g. corpora of learners' English, corpora of learners' errors) awaits further development.

TRANSLATION

Another potential application awaiting development is the use of bilingual corpora as aids to (the teaching of) translation, or as tools for machine or machine-aided translation. Such corpora already exist: for example, a 60-million-word corpus of parallel English and French versions of the *Canadian Hansard* (proceedings of the Canadian Parliament) is being used experimentally in the development of a new kind of corpus-based automatic-translation technique.

SPEECH PROCESSING

Machine translation is one example of the application of corpora for what computer scientists term **natural language processing**. In addition to machine translation, a major research goal for NLP is **speech processing**, that is, the development of computer systems capable of outputting automatically produced speech from written input (**speech synthesis**), or converting speech input into written form (**speech recognition**).

Although speech synthesizers are commercially available already, their output is a crude imitation of natural speech, and in order to produce high-quality speech with appropriate features of connected speech (such as stress, vowel reduction, and intonation), an essential tool is a corpus of spoken texts, including a version with detailed prosodic transcription. Two projects on these lines are those described in Altenberg (1987) and Knowles and Lawrence (1987).

Speech *recognition* is more difficult, although again, crude systems which perform recognition on a restricted vocabulary are commercially available. Research is still a long way from the ultimate goal – a computer system which will accurately recognize continuous speech using unrestricted vocabulary. Current progress is manifested in the developmental IBM recognizer, **Tangora**, capable of recognizing speech in the form of pause-separated words with a 20,000 word vocabulary. The research on which this IBM recognizer is based (Bahl *et al.*, 1983; Jelinek, 1986) illustrates how far corpus-based NLP has progressed towards one practical application: a set of corpora currently of over 350 million words has been used in the development of sophisticated probabilistic techniques of text analysis.

The problem is that acoustic processing can accomplish with sufficient accuracy only part of the task of speech recognition: the ambiguities of the spoken signal mean that a speech recognizer must incorporate a **language model**, predicting the most likely sequence of words from a set of sequences of candidate words left undecided by acoustic analysis. Thus the speech recognizer must incorporate sufficient 'knowledge' of the language to enable the most likely sequence of candidate words to be chosen. This knowledge of the language must include, at a basic collocational level, the knowledge that, say, the sequence *a little extra effort* is more likely than *a tickle extra effort*, or that *deaf ears* is more likely than *deaf years*. At a linguistically more abstract level, it may incorporate likelihoods of word-class sequences (grammatical-tagging information), likelihoods of syntactic structures (parsing information), or likelihoods of semantic dependencies (semantic information). To obtain accurate statistical estimates, very large quantities of textual data have to be analysed automatically. It is evident that this research programme coincides in essentials with that of automatic corpus preprocessing as described on pages 77–78.

CONCLUSION

The research paradigm for speech recognition, as mentioned above, is probabilistic. This is likely to be the dominant feature of corpus-based NLP. The strength of the corpus-based methodology is that it trains a computer to deal with unrestricted text input. Although any corpus, however large, used as a source of data is finite, a probabilistic system can use this as a basis for prediction of the nature of unencountered text. The negative side of this approach is that the system is fallible: but a small degree of inaccuracy may be tolerable.

Returning to the discussion in the first section,

we may observe in the methodology described in the preceding sections (of which Jelinek is the leading exponent) an ironic resemblance to the pre-Chomskyan corpus-based paradigm of post-Bloomfieldian American linguistics. Whereas Chomsky, by emphasizing competence at the expense of performance, rejected the significance of probabilities, the Jelinek approach is unashamedly probabilistic, using a sophistication of the Markov process probabilistic model of language which was summarily rejected by Chomsky in the early pages of his *Syntactic Structures* (1957).

Such probabilistic methods, using the minimum degree of linguistic knowledge compatible with achieving a practical end, may be regarded as simplistic and psychologically unrealistic by adherents of mainstream linguistics. But their apparent success suggests that the computer's superhuman ability to process quantitatively very large bodies of text can compensate, to a considerable degree, for a lack of the more 'intelligent' levels of linguistic capability used in human language processing. At least, this research programme illustrates supremely the fact that computer corpora have promising applications totally unforeseen by their early compilers.

G.N.L.

SUGGESTIONS FOR FURTHER READING

Aarts J. and Maijs, W. (eds) (1984), *Corpus Linguistics: Recent Developments in the Use of Computer Corpora in English Language Research*, Amsterdam, Rodopi.

Garside, R., Leech, G., and Sampson, G. (eds) (1987), *The Computational Analysis of English: A Corpus-based Approach*, London, Longman.

Sinclair, J. McH. (ed.) (1987), *Looking Up: An Account of the COBUILD Project in Lexical Computing*, London and Glasgow, Collins.

Creoles and pidgins

GENERAL INTRODUCTION

There are at least six possible linguistic sources for the term *pidgin* (Mühlhäusler, 1986, p. 1; Romaine, 1988, pp. 12–13): (1) according to the *Oxford English Dictionary* (*OED*) and Collinson (1929, p. 20), *pidgin* is a Chinese corruption of the English *business*; (2) others consider it a Chinese corruption of the Portuguese word for business, *occupação*; (3) or derived from the Hebrew for exchange or trade or redemption, *pidjom*; (4) or it may derive from a South Seas pronunciation of English *beach*, namely *beachee*, because the language was typically used on the beach; (5) or it may derive from the South American Indian language, Yago, whose word for people is *pidian*; (6) according to Knowlton (1967, p. 228), Professor Hsü Ti-san of the University of Hong Kong has written in the margin of a page of a book on Chinese Pidgin English (Leland, 1924) that the term *pidgin* may be derived from the two Chinese characters, *pei* and *ts'in* meaning 'paying money'. Many expressions in pidgin and creole languages have more than one source, so it is possible that all of these accounts are true.

The term 'creole' was originally used to refer to a person of European descent who was born and raised in a tropical or semitropical colony, but its meaning was later extended to include anyone living in these areas, and finally to the languages spoken by them (Romaine, 1988, p. 38).

Each of the possible etymologies for the term *pidgin* accords in some measure with the traditional account of the reasons for the development of pidgin languages: if the members of two or more cultures which do not use the same language come into regular contact with each other over a prolonged period, usually as a result of trade or colonization, it is probable that the resultant language contact will lead to the development of a **pidgin** language by means of which the members of the cultures can communicate with each other but which is not the native language of either speech community. A pidgin language is thus a **lingua franca** which has no native speakers, which is often influenced by languages spoken by people who travelled and colonized extensively, such as English, French, Spanish, Portugese, and Dutch, and by the languages of the people with whom they interacted repeatedly. Such languages often developed near main shipping and trading routes (Trudgill, 1974a, p. 166 and 169–70):

> English-based pidgins were formerly found in North America, at both ends of the slave trade in Africa and the Caribbean, in New Zealand and in China. They are still found in Australia, West Africa, the Solomon Islands . . . and in New Guinea. . . . (Not all pidgin languages have arisen in this way, though. Kituba, which is derived from Kikongo, a Bantu language, is a pidgin widely used in western Zaïre and adjoining areas. And Fanagolo, which is based on Zulu, is a pidgin spoken in South Africa and adjoining countries, particularly in the mines. There are several other indigenous pidgins in Africa and elsewhere.)

(See further Holm, 1988, pp. xvi–xix, for comprehensive maps of areas using pidgin and creole languages.) Pidgins also arose when Africans who did not share a language were working together on plantations and chose to communicate using what they could glean of the colonizer/slave-owner's language, to which they added elements of their own native languages. For second and subsequent generations, these pidgins often became the mother tongue, a **creole**, that is (Holm, 1988, p. 6): 'a language which has a jargon or a pidgin in its ancestry; it is spoken natively by an entire speech community, often one whose ancestors were displaced geographically so that their ties with their original language and sociocultural identity were partly broken'.

Examples of creoles include Sranan, an English-based creole spoken in coastal areas of Surinam (Trudgill, 1974a, p. 170), and the English-based West Indian creoles used mainly by people of African origin in the Caribbean (Sutcliffe, 1984, p. 219). Non-English-based creoles derived from other European languages include French-based creoles spoken in, among other places, Haiti, Trinidad, Grenada, French Guiana, Mauritius, the Seychelles, and some parts of Louisiana. There are also creoles based on Portuguese and Spanish (Trudgill, 1974a, p. 170). A pidgin may become creolized at any stage of its development (see below, p. 88).

Milroy (1984, p. 11) suggests that an Anglo-Danish pidgin must have been used to some extent in trade and commerce in some parts of early medieval England, and that 'as the bilingual situation receded, the varieties that remained must have been effectively Anglo-Norse creoles'.

Some generally fairly limited, anecdotal accounts of creoles and pidgins were written by travellers, administrators, and missionaries as long ago as the early sixteenth century. Although some early reports were written with the explicit aim of teaching Europeans something about the structure of a pidgin or creole so that they could use it to communicate with its speakers (Romaine, 1988, p. 7), the serious study of creoles and pidgins began with Schuchardt's series of papers on creole studies, *Kreolische Studien*, published in the 1880s (Schuchardt 1882, 1883), and Schuchardt (1842–1927) is regarded by many as the founding father of pidgin and creole linguistics (Romaine, 1988, p. 4).

However, creoles and pidgins tended to be regarded as merely inferior, corrupt versions of donor languages (Romaine, 1988, p. 6), and the study of them did not gain generally perceived respectability until 1959 when the first international conference on creole language studies was held in Jamaica by a group of scholars who recognized themselves as **creolists** (DeCamp,

1971a) and the proceedings published (Le Page, 1961). Growing interest in the relationship between American Black English and pidgin and creole English also helped establish the discipline as a proper academic concern, and the publication in 1966 of the first undergraduate textbook on pidgins and creoles (Hall, 1966) greatly helped to secure its place (Holm, 1988, p. 55). A second conference was held in Jamaica in 1968 (Hymes, 1971), and since then conferences on pidgin and creole linguistics have been held regularly (Day, 1980; Valdman and Highfield, 1980; *York Papers in Linguistics*, 1983).

In the development of a pidgin language, the **superstrate language** typically provides most of the vocabulary. Typically, the superstrate language will be that of the socially, economically, and/or politically dominant group, and will be considered the language that is being pidginized, so that a pidgin is often referred to as, for instance, Pidgin English or Pidgin French. The other language or languages involved are referred to as the **substrate language(s)**. The pidgin tends to retain many of the grammatical features of the substrate language(s). In spite of the fact that pidgins thus arise as two or more languages are mixed so that speakers of any one of these languages may perceive the pidgin as a debased form of their own language – an attitude clearly expressed by the superstrate-language-speaking authors of many early studies – it is important to note that it is now generally agreed among scholars of pidgin languages that they have a structure of their own which is independent of both the substrate and superstrate languages involved in the original contact (Romaine, 1988, p. 13).

LINGUISTIC CHARACTERISTICS OF PIDGINS AND CREOLES

It is impossible to give a comprehensive overview of all the linguistic characteristics of creoles and pidgins here, but see Holm (1988) for a full account.

In general, languages in contact build on those sounds which they have in common. Therefore, phonemes that are common throughout the world's languages are more likely to occur in pidgin and creole languages than those phonemes that occur in only very few of the world's languages. Thus /d/ or /m/, for instance, are more common in pidgins and creoles than /ð/ and /θ/. However, the actual pronunciation, or phonetic realization, of the phonemes frequently varies according to speakers' first languages, and during the creolization process (see below, pp. 87–9) pronunciation will tend toward the pronunciation used by the group whose children are using the language natively rather than toward the superstrate language pronunciation. In addition, if contact with the substrate language(s) is maintained and/or superstrate contact is lost early in the development of a creole, it tends to contain phonemes only found in the substrate language. In addition, the sound systems of pidgins and creoles are subject to the general patterns of phonological change which can be found throughout the world's languages (Holm, 1988, p. 107).

Creoles often retain pronunciations which are no longer retained in the source language. For instance, (Holm, 1988, p. 75):

> Miskito Coast CE [Creole English] retains the /aɪ/ diphthong that was current in polite eighteenth-century British speech in words like *bail* 'boil' and *jain* 'join'; this sound became /ɔɪ/ in standard English after about 1800. This makes the creole word for 'lawyer' homophonous with standard English *liar* (but there is no confusion since the latter takes the dialectal form *liard* analogous to *criard* 'crier' and *stinkard* 'stinker' – cf. standard *drunkard*.

Since the early contact situations which produced pidgins revolved around trade, work, and administration, and since most of the items and concepts involved were European, and since the Europeans involved were more powerful socially, economically, and politically, the vocabulary of early pidgins was mainly based on European languages and was limited to that required for trade, administration, and giving orders. Consequently, pidgins have rather smaller vocabularies than natural languages, but this tends to be compensated for by **multifunctionality** (one word

to many syntactic uses), **polysemy** (one word to many meanings), and **circumlocution** (phrase instead of single word) (Holm, 1988, p. 73), so that the semantic system need not be impoverished – certainly not in the later stages of the development of the language (Hall, 1972, p. 143):

> the vocabularies of pidgins and creoles manifest extensive shifts in meaning. Many of these changes are the result of the inevitable broadening of reference involved in pidginization. If a given semantic field has to be covered by a few words rather than many, each word must of course signify a wider range of phenomena. Two pidgin examples out of many: CPE [Chinese Pidgin English] *spit* means 'eject matter from the mouth', by both spitting and vomiting; MPE [Melanesian Pidgin English/Tok Pisin] *gras* means 'anything that grows, blade-like, out of a surface', as in *gras bilong hed* 'hair', *gras bilong maus* 'moustache', *gras bilong fes* 'beard'.

As Romaine (1988, p. 36) points out, the restricted vocabularies of pidgins lead to a high degree of **transparency** in pidgin compounds, that is, the meaning of a compound can often be worked out on the basis of the meanings of the terms that make up the compound. However, **semantic broadening**, which takes place when a term takes on new meanings while still retaining its original meaning can create confusion for the uninitiated. Thus, in most English creoles, *tea* has broadened in meaning to refer to any hot drink, so that '*coffee-tea* is used throughout the Anglophone Caribbean, including Guyana where Berbice CD [Creole Dutch] speakers use the term *kofitei*. . . . In Lesser Antillean CF [Creole French] "hot cocoa" is *dite kako* (cf. F *du thé* "some tea")' (Holm, 1988, p. 101).

Any gaps in the vocabulary of a pidgin in the early stages of development, will be filled in through borrowing or circumlocution. Later, however, at the stage which Mühlhäusler (1986) refers to as **stable** (see below, p. 88), a pidgin will often have set formulae for describing new concepts. He cites the use in Hiri Motu, an Australian pidgin, of the formula O-V-*gauna* to express that something is a thing for doing something to an object, as in (1986, p. 171):

Hiri Motu	Gloss	Translation
kuku ania gauna	smoke eat thing	pipe
lahi gabua gauna	fire burn thing	match
traka abiaisi gauna	truck raise thing	jack
godo abia gauna	voice take thing	tape recorder

A stable pidgin can also use grammatical categories to distinguish between meanings, as in the case of the Tok Pisin aspect marker of completion, *pinis* (ibid.).

Pidgins and creoles tend to have little or no inflectional morphology (see MORPHOLOGY) (though see Holm, 1988, pp. 95–6, for some examples of inflection in creoles), and are often characterized by shifts in morpheme boundaries, so that an English word with plural inflection, for instance *ants*, becomes a morpheme with either plural or singular meaning. In French-based creoles, the article often becomes agglutinated, as in Haitian Creole French, where *moon* is *lalin*, from French *la lune* 'the moon' (Holm, 1988, p. 97). The general lack in pidgins of bound morphemes greatly facilitates change of or increase in the syntactic functions of words (Holm, 1988, p. 103):

> Category changes found in Miskito Coast Creole include nouns from adjectives ("He catch *crazy*" 'He became psychotic'), from adverbs ("*afterwards*" 'leftovers'), and from prepositions ("He come from *out*," i.e. 'from abroad'). Verbs can come from nouns ("He *advantage* her," i.e. 'took advantage of') as well as adjectives ("She *jealousing* him," i.e. 'making him jealous').

Romaine (1988, pp. 27–8) notes that agreement markers are dropped in pidgins if they are redundant:

> For example, in the following English sentence, plurality is indicated in the noun and its modifier as well as in verb agreement in the third person singular present tense: *Six men come* (*cf. One man comes*). The equivalent

utterances in Tok Pisin show no variation in the verb form or the noun: *Sikspela man i kam/ Wanpela man i kam*. Thus there is a tendency for each grammatical morpheme to be expressed only once in an utterance, and for that morpheme to be expressed by a single form.

Mühlhäusler (1986, pp. 158–9) points out that the pronoun system of a pidgin is typically reduced, as in Chinese Pidgin English which has three pronouns, first, second, and third person, but no number distinctions. Most pidgin pronoun systems are not marked for gender or case (Romaine, 1988, p. 27).

Creoles contain a large number of syntactic features which are not found in the European languages which supply much of their vocabularies. Most of them rely on free rather than inflectional morphemes to convey grammatical information, so that typically the verb phrase, for instance, uses particles to indicate tense and aspect, and although these often have the form of auxiliary verbs from the lexical-source language, semantically and syntactically they resemble the substrate language's preverbal tense and aspect markers. If there are no such markers, the simple form of the verb refers to whichever time is specified earlier in the discourse, or by the general context (Holm, 1988, pp. 144–50). Studies of creole verb phrases in general have demonstrated the structural similarities of creoles and their structural independence of their superstrate languages, but (Holm, 1988, p. 174):

> it was comparative studies of the creoles' various words for 'be' that unequivocally demonstrated that the creoles were not merely simplified forms of European languages. These studies showed that the creoles were in certain respects more complex than their lexical-source languages in that they made some grammatical and semantic distinctions not made in the European languages. . . . [They] often use quite different words for 'be' depending on whether the following element is a noun phrase, an adjective, or an indication of location.

In addition, a 'highlighter be' exists, the function of which is to bring the following words into focus rather like extra stress on a word in English or like introducing it with *it's* as in *It's Jane who lives here* (*not Elizabeth*) (Holm, 1988, p. 179).

Serial verbs, that is, a series of two or more verbs which are not joined by a conjunction such as *and* or by a complemetizer such as *to*, and which share a subject, are also a common feature of creoles. These often function as adverbs and prepositions in European languages, to indicate (1) directionality, as in Jamaican Creole English, *ron go lef im*, 'run go leave him', meaning 'run away from him'; or (2) instrumentality, as in Ndjuka, *a teke nefi koti a meti*, 'he took knife cut the meat', meaning 'he cut the meat with a knife'. In addition, serial 'give' can be used to mean 'to' or 'for', and serial 'say' can be used to mean 'that' when introducing a quotation or a *that*-sentence. Serial 'pass'/'surpass'/'exceed' can be used to indicate comparison. Similar construction types are found in many African languages (Holm, 1988, pp. 183–90).

THE ORIGIN OF PIDGINS

One of the most important theories to surface at the first conference on pidgin and creole linguistics in Jamaica in 1959 (see above, p. 82) was the idea that all or most pidgins or creoles could be traced back to one common source, a Portuguese-based pidgin developed in the fifteenth century in Africa, which was later **relexified**, translated word for word, into the pidgins with other European bases which gave rise to modern creoles. This theory is known as the theory of **monogenesis** (one origin) or **relexification**, and it originates in its modern form in Whinnom's (1956) observation of the strong similarities in terms of vocabulary and structure between Philippine Creole Spanish and Ternate (Indonesia) Creole Portuguese. He hypothesized that a seventeenth-century pidgin version of the latter, itself possibly an imitation of the Mediterranean lingua franca Sabir, had been transported to the Philippines.

Others noted that many of the features of Philippine Creole Spanish were also present in Caribbean creoles, in Chinese Pidgin English and in Tok Pisin, but that these had been relexified

(Taylor, 1959, 1960; Thompson, 1961; Stewart, 1962a; Whinnom, 1965; Voorhoeve, 1973). Stewart (1962a) pointed out that while speakers from opposite ends of the Caribbean were able to converse in their French-based creoles, neither would easily be able to converse with a French speaker. So whereas the similarity of vocabulary could account for some mutual intelligibility, it was in fact syntactic similarity which was the more important factor, and this syntactic similarity pointed to a common origin for the French-based creoles.

In contrast to the monogenesis theory, Hall (1962) argued that pidgins would arise spontaneously wherever and whenever a need for a language of minimal communication arose, and that these could then be creolized. This view is known as the theory of **polygenesis** (multiple origin), and it found support in DeCamp's (1971a, p. 24) argument that there are 'certain pidgins and creoles which clearly developed without any direct Portuguese influence'. In fact, few creolists would argue for a pure monogenesis theory, but most accept that a certain amount of relexification is an important element in the development of pidgins and creoles, particularly when closely related lexicons, such as Creole Spanish and Creole Portuguese are involved (Holm, 1988, pp. 51–2).

THE DEVELOPMENT OF PIDGINS AND CREOLES

A particularly interesting and provocative explanation for the development and characteristics of creoles has been offered by Bickerton (1974, 1977, 1979, 1981, 1984a). Bickerton argues (1984, p. 173; emphasis added) 'in favor of a **language bioprogram hypothesis** (henceforth **LBH**) that suggests that the infrastructure of language is specified at least as narrowly as Chomsky has claimed'. The arguments for LBH are drawn from Bickerton's observations about the way in which a creole language develops from a pidgin which is in an early stage of development (ibid.):

> The LBH claims that the innovative aspects of creole grammar are inventions on the part of

the first generation of children who have a pidgin as their linguistic input, rather than features transmitted from preexisting languages. The LBH claims, further, that such innovations show a degree of similarity, across wide variety in linguistic background, that is too great to be attributed to chance. Finally, the LBH claims that the most cogent explanation of this similarity is that it derives from the structure of a species-specific program for language, genetically coded and expressed, in ways still largely mysterious, in the structures and modes of operation of the human brain.

The data Bickerton uses to support his hypothesis shows early-stage pidgin to lack any consistent means of marking tense, aspect, and modality, to have no consistent system of anaphora, no complex sentences, no systematic way of distinguishing case relations, and variable word order (1984a, p. 175). Children faced with this type of input impose ways of realizing the missing features, but they do not borrow these realizations from the language which is dominant in their environment, nor from the substrate language(s), and Bickerton concludes that 'the LBH or some variant thereof seems inescapable . . . [and] the LBH carries profound implications for the study of language in general, and for the study of language acquisition and language origins in particular' (1984a, p. 184).

Bickerton claims (p. 178) that the evidence he cites shows the similarities in creoles to arise from 'a single substantive grammar consisting of a very restricted set of categories and processes, which . . . constitute part, or all, of the human species-specific capacity for syntax'. He leans towards the view that the single, substantive grammar does, in fact, constitute *all* of universal grammar, and he thinks that this view is supported by Slobin's (1977, 1982, 1984b) notion of a **basic child grammar**, a grammar which is generated by a set of innate operating principles which children use to analyse linguistic input (compare LANGUAGE ACQUISITION). But Bickerton (1984a, p. 185) claims that these operating procedures 'fall out from the bioprogram grammar': a child receiving only pidgin

input will simply not have enough data for the operating principles alone to work on. In addition, Slobin's work shows that young children consistently violate the rules of their input language, and these violations are consistent with the rules Bickerton proposes for the bioprogram *and* with surface forms found in creoles (ibid.).

Many commentators have argued against innateness as the *only*, or even the most useful, explanation for the kind of phenomena which Bickerton (and Chomsky and his followers) have observed (see LANGUAGE ACQUISITION). In this entry, I shall concentrate on the arguments of commentators who dispute the reliability of Bickerton's data.

Goodman (1984, p. 193) points out that Bickerton bases his argument entirely on data provided by a number of elderly Japanese, Korean, and Filipino immigrants who arrived in Hawaii between 1907 and 1930. At this time, however, it is probable that a pidgin had already developed for use between English seamen and native Hawaiians (Clark, 1979). This pidgin was historically linked both to other Pacific pidgin Englishes and to Chinese Pidgin English, with which it shared certain vocabulary and grammatical features. Consequently, it cannot be assumed that 'the pidgin as spoken by 20th-century immigrants from Japan, Korea and the Philippines is in any way characteristic of the incipient stage of Hawaiian Creole English' (Goodman, 1984, p. 193).

Goodman (p. 194) argues that 'many widespread features of creole languages can be accounted for on the basis of similar structures in either the target or the substratal languages coupled with certain universal processes of selection in the context of language contact'. In his response to these arguments, however, Bickerton (1984b) questions the data which Goodman draws on in suggesting that a pidgin already existed in Hawaii when the subjects of Bickerton's study arrived there.

Maratsos (1984, p. 200) suggests that, judging from Bickerton's data, the input the creole speakers were presented with was too impoverished for them to have developed the creole. The creole, he notices, contains features of English vocabulary and syntax not found in the pidgin, so the creole speakers must have had access to linguistic sources other than the pidgin, and some relexification is likely to have been involved. Again, Bickerton (1984b, p. 215) counter-questions Maratsos' data.

Lightfoot (1984, p. 198) and Woolford (1984, p. 211) both point out that it is, in fact, extremely difficult to establish exactly what input creole speakers in the past may have had from their pidgin and from other sources, and what grammars they arrived at. Furthermore, comparable evidence from early stages of the formation of other pidgins and creoles would be required in order to evaluate Bickerton's claims for Hawaii Creole English, but little evidence of this nature is available (Romaine, 1988, p. 309). Nevertheless, because of the implications for linguistics of Bickerton's hypothesis, if it is correct, his work has had a profound effect on the study of creoles (Holm, 1988, p. 65).

As mentioned above, the creoles that concern Bickerton have arisen from pidgins which are at an early stage of development. The idea of developmental stages through which pidgins and creoles pass – a kind of life-cycle of pidgins and creoles – was present in Schuchardt's work, but found prominence in Hall (1962), (Romaine, 1988, p. 115). It has been developed by Todd

(1974, pp. 53–69) who distinguishes four phases of the **creolization process**: (1) marginal contact; (2) period of nativization; (3) influence from the dominant language; (4) the post-creole continuum.

Mühlhäusler (1980, p. 22) points out that there are, in fact, two factors involved in the development of, and changes in, pidgins and creoles: (1) **development** or **expansion** from jargon, through stabilized pidgin and expanded pidgin, to creole, and (2) **restructuring** of either a stabilized pidgin or a creole, through post pidgin or post creole, to superimposed language. Restructuring occurs as a result of contact with other languages and does not affect the overall power of the linguistic system; therefore the varieties on this continuum are roughly equal in terms of linguistic complexity. On the developmental continuum, however, the varieties differ in terms of linguistic complexity and in terms of overall referential and non-referential power. He depicts the contrast as shown in Figure 1 (1986, p. 11).

The notion of a continuum was first borrowed from traditional dialectology (see DIALECTOLOGY) and applied to the gradation of varieties between creole and standard English in the Caribbean by DeCamp (1961), (Holm, 1988, p. 55). These varieties are known as **mesolects**. The languages on the left of the mesolects in Figure 1 are

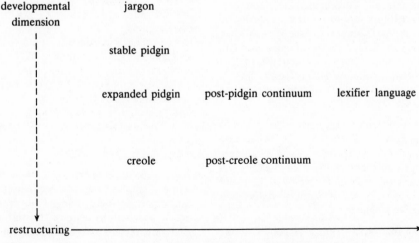

Figure 1 Factors involved in development and change in pidgins and creoles

called **basilects** and their related standard lexifier languages are called **acrolects**.

The early **jargon** phase is characterized by great variation in different speakers' versions of the jargon, a simple sound system, one- or two-word sentences and a very limited vocabulary (Romaine, 1988, p. 117), with some simple grammar to allow for longer utterances added later (Mühlhäusler, 1986, p. 52). The jargon is used only in restricted contexts such as trade and recruitment of labour.

In a **stable-pidgin** stage, speakers have arrived at a shared system of rules governing linguistic correctness, so that individual variation is diminished. The process of stabilization of a pidgin is generally characterized by **grammaticalization**, whereby autonomous words become grammatical markers. According to Mühlhäusler (1981), the stabilization stage in the pidgin or creole life-cycle is particularly important, because it is at this stage that the future shape of the language is determined.

An **expanded pidgin** has a complex grammar and a developing word-formation component, and the new constructions are added to the existing simpler grammar in an orderly fashion (Mühlhäusler, 1986, p. 177). It is spoken faster than its precursor, and is used in almost all areas of life (Romaine, 1988, p. 138). Expanded pidgins only arise in linguistically highly heterogeneous areas and typically accompany increased geographic mobility and intertribal contact due to colonial policies. Examples include West African Pidgin English, Tok Pisin (which also exists in creolized varieties), and recent varieties of Hiri Motu, Bislama, Solomon Island Pidgin, Sango, and some varieties of Torres Straits Broken (Mühlhäusler, 1986, p. 177):

> The importance of expanded pidgins to linguistic research is twofold. First, they illustrate the capacity of adults to drastically restructure existing linguistic systems; secondly, they call into question such dichotomies as first and second, primary and secondary, native and non-native language.

A creole may arise from a jargon, a stable pidgin, or an expanded pidgin. Since these differ

in the respects broadly outlined above, the degree of repair needed before they can function as adequate first languages for their speakers is also different. A **creolized jargon** will have undergone repair at all the linguistic levels, to bring about natural phonological, syntactic, semantic, and pragmatic systems. In the case of a **creolized stable pidgin**, pragmatic rules will have been arrived at, and the systems already at play in the stable pidgin will have been developed. A **creolized extended pidgin** differs from its basilect mainly in its stylistic and pragmatic potential (Romaine, 1988, p. 155).

According to Foley (1988), Tok Pisin has undergone two kinds of creolization: urban and rural. An urban environment in Papua New Guinea is highly diverse linguistically, so that the only language an urban child will typically have in common with its peers tends to be Tok Pisin. In rural parts of Papua New Guinea, particularly in the Sepik region, Tok Pisin has been perceived as a high-prestige language offering access to the outside world since at least as long ago as the 1930s (Mead, 1931), and parents are therefore very eager that their children, particularly boys, should use it. Foley (1988) suggests that this parental encouragement of the use of Tok Pisin, together with the fact that the native languages of many communities have very complex morphologies so that bilingual children find it easier to use Tok Pisin, has led to complete creolization of Tok Pisin and the disappearance of a number of the vernaculars.

Once a creole is in existence, it may, according to DeCamp (1971b) (1) continue almost without change, as appears to be the case for Haitian Creole; (2) become extinct; (3) evolve further into a normal language; (4) gradually merge with its acrolect through a process known as **decreolization**. During this process, a **creole continuum** of varieties between the creole and acrolect will emerge (Holm, 1988, p. 52):

> A creole continuum can evolve in situations in which a creole coexists with its lexical source language and there is social motivation for creole speakers to acquire the standard, so that the speech of individuals takes on features of the latter – or avoids features of the former

– to varying degrees. These varieties can be seen as forming a continuum from those farthest from the standard to those closest to it.

Mühlhäusler (1986, p. 237) defines a **post-pidgin** or **post-creole variety** as 'a pidgin or creole which, after a period of relative linguistic independence, has come under renewed vigorous influence from its original lexifier language, involving the restructuring and/or replacement of earlier lexicon and grammar in favour of patterns from the superimposed 'target' language'. American Black English is often considered a post-creole variety.

Romaine (1988, p. 188) points to the fact that, in Britain, many young Blacks of West Indian descent who spoke standard English in early childhood make a conscious effort to 'talk Black' when they reach their teens. She refers to this phenomenon as **recreolization**.

K.M.

SUGGESTIONS FOR FURTHER READING

Holm, J.A. (1988), *Pidgins and Creoles*, vol. I: *Theory and Structure*, Cambridge, Cambridge University Press.

Mühlhäusler, P. (1986), *Pidgin and Creole Linguistics*, Oxford, Basil Blackwell.

Romaine, S. (1988), *Pidgin and Creole Languages*, London and New York, Longman.

Critical linguistics

The term **critical linguistics** was first used in its currently accepted sense in 1979, as the title of the synoptic and programmatic concluding chapter of *Language and Control* by Fowler, Hodge, Kress, and Trew, a group of colleagues at that time working at the University of East Anglia, Norwich. The label is now used by increasing numbers of social scientists – particularly sociologists, political scientists, students of the media and sociolinguists – to designate analytic work on real texts of the kind advocated and illustrated in that book.

Critical linguistics is a socially directed application of linguistic analysis, using chiefly concepts and methods associated with the 'systemic–functional' linguistics developed by M.A.K. Halliday (see FUNCTIONALIST LINGUISTICS; SYSTEMIC GRAMMAR, and FUNCTIONAL GRAMMAR); its basic claims are that all linguistic usage encodes ideological patterns or discursive structures which *mediate* representations of the world in language; that different usages (e.g.

different sociolinguistic varieties or lexical choices or syntactic paraphrases) encode different ideologies, resulting from their different situations and purposes; and that by these means language works as a social practice: it is not, as traditional linguistics claims, a transparent medium for communication about an objective world, nor is it a reflection of a stable social structure, but it promulgates a set of versions of reality and thereby works as a constantly operative part of social processes.

Critical linguistics proposes that analysis using appropriate linguistic tools, and referring to relevant historical and social contexts, can bring ideology, normally hidden through the habitualization of discourse, to the surface for inspection. In this way, critical linguistics can shed light on social and political processes. Promising revelation through an analytic technique – indeed quite a simple set of tools – critical linguistics has been welcomed by a variety of workers concerned with discourse.

But it must also be conceded that the model is controversial. It is faulted by its critics within the academic institution of linguistics because it challenges some central established principles in the dominant schools of the subject; and by others, including people sympathetic to the aims of the venture, because it employs some notoriously difficult concepts such as 'ideology' and 'function' and is still in the process of clarifying them. And less rationally, critical linguistics is resisted in some quarters because its practitioners have made no bones about their socialist motives and have doggedly subjected the dominant discourses of authoritarianism, capitalism, and militarism to linguistic critique.

Note, however, that the words 'critical' and 'critique' do not essentially carry the negative connotations of carping and complaint that seem to inhabit their popular usage – 'You're always being critical . . . why can't you be constructive for once?' 'Critical' linguistics is simply a linguistics which seeks to understand the relationships between ideas and their social conditions of possible existence (see Connerton, 1976, 'Introduction').

To say that critical linguistics is 'an application of linguistic analysis' is to offer too superficial a characterization. Two qualifications need to be entered at this point. First, critical linguistics is not an automatic hermeneutic procedure which would allow one to identify linguistic structure (passive voice, say) and read off ideological or social significance from it. There is no invariant relationship between textual structure and its social meanings: the latter are dependent on the contexts in which the former occurs and the purposes for which it is used. Passives have quite different discourse functions in scientific writing and in newspaper headlines (and a variety of functions within each of these, particularly the latter). In fact, the critical linguist cannot have any idea of the discursive meaning of a piece of language unless s/he possesses rich and accurate intuitions and understanding of context, function and relevant social relations. Then the analysis will be plausible to the extent that this understanding of context is made explicit, and documented. It is necessary to insist that critical

linguistics is a *historical* discipline which requires high standards of documentation and argumentation. It has to be admitted that early work within this model tended to be cavalier about these historical requirements, choosing familiar types of contemporary texts and relying on the analyst's and her or his reader's intuitions to vouch for the suggested interpretation.

The second reason why we need to elaborate on 'an application of linguistic analysis' is that not any model of linguistic analysis will do the job: only a model with some very specific assumptions and procedures can be the basis for critical linguistics. This observation is perhaps surprising in view of the methodological pluralism of critical linguists. Believing, rightly, that any element of linguistic structure, from phonemes to semantic schemata, can carry ideological significance, practitioners have been happy to borrow 'modality' from Halliday, 'transformation' from Chomsky, 'speech act' from Searle, all in the course of one analysis. The point is that different models are good at describing different aspects of linguistic structure, and it would be absurd to spurn the insights that colleagues working in various frameworks have made available.

However, it must be understood that the meaning of any technical term (**metalanguage**) which has been derived elsewhere and appropriated for critical linguistics is to be construed in terms of the assumptions of the user, not those of the source. Critical linguists have been taken to task, for example, for talking about 'transformations' in their object texts, on the grounds that transformational-generative grammar (TG) is based on principles which are incompatible with those of the systemic-functional grammar, which is the main methodological source for critical linguists. But one does need to talk about syntactic relationships such as that between *Teachers reject pay deal* and *Pay deal rejected by teachers*; perhaps in discussing such variants we should avoid using the term *transformation*, but it is still inevitable that our discussion will be informed by the insights that have been gained in discussion of the constructions within TG. Nevertheless, a **transformation** in critical linguistics is a different idea from a trans-formation in TG (see TRANSFORMATIONAL-GENERATIVE GRAMMAR): for the former it is a relationship of variation between two syntactic constructions, the relationship to be understood in terms of the character of the discourse and of its contexts and purposes. A parallel appropria-tion and redefinition is called for whenever other terms are borrowed from models other than functional grammar.

Some basic assumptions of critical linguistics may now be listed. It will be evident that the major inspiration behind the model is the 'functional' linguistics of M.A.K. Halliday; and that the critical model is in several ways crucially at odds with mainstream linguistics both in its traditional and its contemporary modes. Other intellectual sources for critical linguistics, more prominent in recent years as scholars have worked to make the model less 'narrowly lin-guistic', more integrated with general theories of society and ideology, include French psycho-analytic, structuralist and poststructuralist theories for their accounts of discourse, intertextuality and the subject (see Kress, 1985b; Threadgold, 1986).

The **functional** approach: Halliday (1970, p. 142) claims that 'The particular form taken by the grammatical system of language is closely related to the social and personal needs that language is required to serve.' This is diametrically opposed to the Chomskyan assertion that linguistic form is a chance selection from the universal structural possibilities that are genetically present in and available to each infant. It is, of course, quite likely that what counts as a human lan-guage is formally constrained in the way Chomsky suggests, and that some structures may be universally present because of biological reasons. The theory of **natural semantics**, for example, gives plausible arguments to the effect that concepts like RED, CIRCLE, and UP are lexicalized in all languages studied, or can be easily learned through made-up words, because they reflect the natural biological characteristics of human beings (colour vision, vertical posture, etc.). But such explanations can account for only a minute portion of the vocabulary of a language.

If we think about a selection of other words, say *Aids, macho, interface, privatization*, it will be immediately clear that to say anything inter-esting about these words we need to refer to their social origins and uses. As for syntax, the interesting questions for the critical linguist concern the social functions of variation rather than the universal biological constraints on possible structures.

Halliday brings the functional theory closer to the details of language by proposing three **meta-functions**: the ideational, the interpersonal, and the textual. The **ideational function** is crucial to the theory of critical linguistics. This relates to traditional conceptions of language, since Halliday admits that it is about the expression of content. A disabling defect of conventional theories of representation was that 'content', the world being communicated about, was supposed to be a fixed objective reality represented neutrally through the transparent medium of language. Halliday, however (who refers to Whorf) (see MENTALIST LINGUISTICS), affirms that language 'lends structure to experience'. The ideational component, through structural mechanisms such as lexical categorization, transitivity, co-ordination, constitutes a structured grid through which a speaker's (that is to say a society's, a text's, a register's) view of the world is mediated. Ideational structure has a dialectical relationship with social structure (see below), both reflecting it and influencing it. This element of grammar has so far been the chief interest of critical linguists, who have found in it the linguistic key to the notion that a text, under social pressures, offers a mediated, partial, interpretation of the objective reality of which it claims to speak.

Ideational structure is, then, neither an auto-nomous structure within language (as, for example, the structure of the lexicon would be in generative linguistics), nor a predetermined reflection of a fixed reality, but an arbitrary, variable version of the world which can be understood only in relation to social contexts and purposes. Critical linguistics is still in the process of clarifying the nature of the concept and its contextual relations. The meanings in some sense pre-exist language, yet language is their primary mode of materialization and management. Think about *Aids*: the word is an acronymic label for a medical condition (acquired immune deficiency syndrome, caused by a virus transmitted through blood, semen, and vaginal fluid and thus easily transmitted during sexual intercourse) which existed before the label was devised. The acronym became very current in the 1980s – never out of the news – being a handy implement for managing public consciousness, the focus for discourses on morality, on education, on medical resources. Aids is not simply a physical condition in some individuals, it is also, helped by language, a concept in society, part of our way of perceiving and judging the contemporary situation.

Halliday's notion of **language as social semiotic** (see Halliday, 1978) – simultaneously socially derived and socially instrumental meanings – is one way of understanding these relationships; it is, for example, the model being investigated by recent Australian linguistic critics and semioticians such as Threadgold and Thibault, who find the original critical-linguistic model too closely preoccupied with linguistic structure. The East Anglians, as the authors of *Language and Control* and their associates have come to be called, foregrounded the term **ideology**: see Kress and Hodge (1979), or Trew's chapters in *Language and Control*, where he speaks cautiously of 'theory or ideology' and has in mind a Foucaultian conception of **discourse**.

The term *ideology* has too many misleading senses and reverberations to be discussed in detail here, but at least one should say that it is to be understood in a positive, not a negative, sense. By *ideology* critical linguists do not mean a set of ideas which are false, beliefs which betray a 'distorted consciousness' and are therefore politically undesirable. More pertinent is a neutral kind of definition which relates to the ways in which people order and justify their lives: 'the sum of the ways in which people both live and represent to themselves their relationship to the conditions of their existence' (Belsey, 1980, p. 42). Compare Kress' use of the much more manageable word 'discourse' (following

Foucault) in an effort to understand the social nature of meanings:

> Discourses are systematically-organised sets of statements which give expression to the meanings and values of an institution. Beyond that, they define, describe and delimit what it is possible to say and not possible to say . . . with respect to the area of concern of that institution, whether marginally or centrally.
>
> (Kress, 1985b, pp. 6–7)

A priority in critical linguistics is to agree on some ways of formally analysing or representing these 'sets of statements'. Available models exist in discourse analysis, structuralism, and psychology: for example, the 'general propositions' of Labov and Fanshel, Grice's 'conventional implicatures', Barthes' 'referential code', and most promisingly the various kinds of 'schemata', such as Minsky's 'frames', that have been proposed in cognitive psychology.

The form of the title of Kress' book (1985b), which because of our preconceptions may be perceived as cumbersome, is meant to capture another principle of critical linguistics: we must resist theorizing 'language' and 'society' as separate entities. The discourse of the institution of linguistics puts great pressure on us to do so, as can be seen from dichotomous book titles such as *Language and Society, Language and Social Context, Language and Social Behaviour*. Conventional sociolinguistics (Labov, Trudgill) presents 'language' and 'society' as two independent phenomena which can be separately described and quantified; variations in language (e.g. whether /r/ occurs or does not occur after a vowel and before a consonant, and with what frequency) can be observed to *correlate* with variations in society (e.g. socioeconomic class, sex, age).

But 'correlation', like 'reflection', is too weak an account of the relationship. Sociolinguistic variation is to be regarded as functional rather than merely fortuitous: this can already be seen in Labov's and Trudgill's own studies: hypercorrection and hypocorrection, for instance, do not simply reflect subjects' social situations, they express an intention to use language to change their situations. In such cases language can be seen as an intervention in social processes. Critical linguistics invites a view of language which makes 'intervention' a general principle: language is a **social practice**, one of the mechanisms through which society reproduces and regulates itself. Thus language is 'in' rather than 'alongside' society. It is the aim of critical linguistics to understand these dialectical processes, both as a theoretical understanding which involves a redefinition of linguistics, and also as a matter of practical analysis, the close reading of discourse within history.

R.F.

SUGGESTIONS FOR FURTHER READING

Chilton, P. (ed.) (1985) *Language and the Nuclear Arms Debate: Nukespeak Today*, London and Dover, NH, Frances Pinter.

Fowler, R., Hodge, R., Kress, G., and Trew, T. (1979), *Language and Control*, London, Routledge & Kegan Paul.

Kress, G. (1985), *Linguistic Processes in Sociocultural Practice*, Victoria, Deakin University Press.

Threadgold, T. (1986), 'Semiotics – ideology – language', in T. Threadgold, E.A. Grosz, G. Kress, and M.A.K. Halliday (eds), *Semiotics, Ideology, Language* (Sydney Studies in Society and Culture, 3), Sydney, Sydney Association for Studies in Society and Culture, pp. 15–60.

Dialectology

INTRODUCTION

Dialectology is the study of dialects – both descriptive and theoretical – and those engaged in this study are known as **dialectologists**. Interpreting the term dialect broadly to mean 'variety of language' (but see below), this means that it is concerned with analysing and describing related language varieties, particularly in respect of their salient differences and similarities. It is also concerned with developing theoretical frameworks for such analysis and description, and for arriving at generalizations and explanatory hypotheses about the nature of linguistic differentiation and variation.

Like most branches of linguistics, dialectology began to assume its modern form in the nineteenth century. It was, however, preceded by a long and widespread tradition of **folk-linguistics** – anecdotal and somewhat unsystematic discussion of regionalisms and variation in usage. This tradition has continued, with the result that

dialectology (in common with the study of grammar) has to deal with both theoretical and practical issues in respect of which folk-linguistic concepts and beliefs have had, and continue to have, considerable currency. It is therefore important to distinguish at the outset between the views and definitions adopted by academic dialectologists and those espoused by lay commentators.

Most crucially, the key term 'dialect' itself has various non-technical meanings. Some of these are mutually incompatible and most of them are also implicated in partisan, often negative, attitudes to non-standard speech; these meanings are usually rejected or seriously modified by dialectologists.

1 In popular usage, the term **dialect** usually refers to a geographical variety of a language, e.g., (the) Lancashire dialect (of English). Dialectologists, however, have increasingly used the term to refer to any user-defined variety, that is, any variety associated with speakers of a given

type, whether geographically or otherwise defined, e.g. members of a given social class, males/females, people of shared ethnic background, etc. One can thus speak of a 'middle-class dialect', etc., where 'dialect' must be distinguished from **register** (see FUNCTIONALIST LINGUISTICS). Further, the speech of any individual or homogeneous group can be characterized on many dimensions relating to different non-linguistic factors – different characterizations will be relevant for different purposes, and two or more dimensions may be combined in the characterization (e.g. 'middle-class Lancashire dialect').

The amount of emphasis placed on particular non-linguistic features of this kind has varied from period to period, and from school to school. **Generativist** work on language variation has, in addition, used the term *dialect* to refer to any variety or variety feature not shared by all speakers of a language, whether or not use of such a feature correlates with any non-linguistic factor; in cases where there is no such correlation, one may speak of **randomly distributed dialects**.

2 Forms of speech which are, or are believed to be, unwritten, unstandardized, and/or associated with groups lacking in prestige, formal education, etc., or culturally subordinated to other groups, are often described as **dialects**, by contrast with standardized, prestigious varieties (described as 'languages'). For instance, in popular usage, 'rural Yorkshire dialect' may be contrasted with 'the English language', and 'the dialects of Southern India' with 'the Tamil language'; linguists, however, would tend to make the distinction between the first terms in each pair and 'standard English' and 'classical or standard Tamil' respectively.

Most dialectologists hold that there is no correlation between linguistic type or structure and suitability for adoption as a standard, written, or prestigious variety, and regard this distinction as placing undue weight on these essentially accidental social properties of varieties; although they would accept that prolonged and marked differences of status can affect structure and, in particular, speakers' perceptions of the relevant varieties and their ability to intuit accurately about them. Dialecto-

logists would thus avoid using the terms 'dialect' and 'language' in this way, and would describe standard varieties as being dialects to the same degree as non-standard varieties, despite their differences in status.

3 Dialects are also often perceived as individually discrete units, collectively comprising the equally discrete languages of which they are dialects. This interpretation of the distinction is in fact incompatible with that outlined in (2) above – according to which languages and dialects are of necessity separate entities – but both are sometimes held simultaneously, often without any real synthesis; for instance, Chinese speakers, especially in South-East Asia, tend to think of Mandarin both as 'the Chinese language' and as one variety of it, although with a special status, and to think of the 'dialects', such as Hokkien, as dialects of Chinese, but also as separate from and inferior to Mandarin in its guise as Chinese.

In contrast, dialectologists would argue that neither dialects nor languages are really discrete. Dialects can be distinguished only in terms of differences in particular variable features, but these are liable to display differently situated boundaries (isoglosses; see below); in any event, close to a boundary, geographical or social, there is much fluctuation even within the usage of individual speakers. Furthermore, the transition between one language and its neighbour, particularly when they are genetically related languages (see HISTORICAL LINGUISTICS, pp. 212–16) or have been subject to prolonged contact, is, again, gradual, piecemeal and massively variable (e.g., Dutch and German). Attempts to use such criteria as mutual intelligibility in order to determine the location of the boundaries therefore founder on serious objections, both logical and factual. The distinction between dialect and language, and hence this kind of definition of dialect, cannot be sustained in any rigorous interpretation. Both terms are therefore used, increasingly, as shorthand expressions for any 'bundles' of variant forms which are sufficiently large/closely associated, and have roughly coinciding boundaries.

Other popular terms are also used differently

by dialectologists. The well-known term accent is generally used in the field in the strict sense of a variety differing relevantly from others only in phonological respects, not in grammar or lexis. There is some dispute as to just how 'phonological respects' should be defined for this purpose; thus some unpredictable phonological differences such as that between standard /brɪdʒ/ and Yorkshire dialect /brɪg/ would traditionally be regarded as accent differences only, but are now regarded, by some scholars, as so gross that they must count as differences in dialect. To take a clear case of accent: an American speaker who pronounces the *r* in *car*, and an English speaker who does not, differ in that respect only in accent, whereas the difference between *underpass* and *subway* is one of dialect proper. Similarly, the term **vernacular**, with a variety of popular meanings, has also been used in the literature in a more technical sense. For instance, *vernacular* may be used non-technically to refer to the current local language of a region as opposed to, e.g., classical or liturgical languages, or more generally to 'popular usage' of an informal, not to say uneducated, kind. It has been used in the field to refer to the most casual style of speech produced by speakers, or, more specifically, by the least standardized speakers.

REVIEW OF THE DEVELOPMENT OF THE SUBJECT OVER THE LAST CENTURY

Nineteenth-century dialectology was predominantly geographical – linguistic thought was not then socially oriented – and developed along with the related disciplines of phonetics and historical linguistics (descriptive and theoretical), most notably in Germany in the period after 1876. It rapidly spread to other areas, and in the United Kingdom the two major pioneering works appeared in 1889 (Ellis) and 1905 (Wright), the latter being associated with the English Dialect Society (see THE ENGLISH DIALECT SOCIETY) founded in 1873. Concern with the history of the relevant forms encouraged a general historical bias: interest in the origin in medieval languages of contemporary forms perceived in isolation, rather than in their contemporary patterning.

The description of current usage was in any case hampered by the absence of any structuralist theory, most obviously phoneme theory.

For various reasons to be outlined below, the subject was slow to assimilate structuralist ideas once these were developed, and this and the historical bias continued to affect the field until relatively recently. Treatment of phonology has suffered particularly badly from these constraints, though the focus on phonetic facts for their own sake has sometimes been regarded subsequently as more helpful than premature or theory-laden guesses at the underlying system.

Another early focus of interest, also now generally abandoned, was the search for **pure** dialect, i.e., the supposedly regular and systematic form of speech produced by those remote from standardizing influences. This was sought both with a view to recording it before it vanished in the face of modern developments in transport, education, media, etc., and in the belief that it was of greater theoretical interest than more mainstream usage, which was thought corrupt. The ensuing methodology involved the deliberate selection of **norms** – non-mobile, old, rural males, mostly uneducated – regardless of whether such speakers were really representative of their communities' current usage. As a result of changed attitudes to these and other issues, theoretical and methodological priorities are nowadays rather different, and older works – as well as being difficult to interpret – are widely perceived as unhelpful in approach and presentation, despite their undoubted usefulness in terms of tracing recent historical developments. This affects work researched as recently as the 1960s and some material published during the 1970s and early 1980s. A gradual shift of interest from phonology, lexis, and morphology to syntax – part of a general trend in linguistics – also reduces the relevance of older publications.

German scholars such as Georg Wenker and Ferdinand Wrede pioneered the concept of a dialect atlas in the 1870s (see also LANGUAGE SURVEYS). They developed extensive frameworks for **fieldwork** methodology and analysis, but were hindered by the sheer scale and time-consuming nature of such enterprises, and many of the results of their work were never published. The German method concentrated on indirect postal surveys, aimed at wide geographical coverage and at the elicitation, through amateur field-workers acting in a voluntary capacity, of dialect versions of standard lexical, grammatical, and phonological features.

Jules Gilliéron, who took on the task of surveying French dialects in 1897, employed the alternative direct approach, involving face-to-face interviews using a single, trained fieldworker; he thereby reduced the coverage severely, but obtained more complete and more reliable results in each locality. Major surveys of the Italian-speaking area of Europe and, later, of North American regions (Kenyon, 1930; Thomas, 1958; Kurath and McDavid, 1961 among many others; see Baugh and Cable, 1978, pp. 368–9, for an extensive list) were carried out by scholars trained in this tradition, although multiple fieldworkers gradually became the norm. The Survey of English Dialects, developed by Eugen Dieth and Harold Orton and run from Leeds University, UK, also used this method, and the form of questionnaire adopted in that study has been widely imitated in more traditional works on specific dialect areas.

Other surveys, such as the ongoing Linguistic Survey of Scotland, have employed both types of technique. Smaller-scale studies have continued to select approaches according to their own requirements and resources, and it is now generally accepted that each method has its advantages and drawbacks (e.g., indirect methods work much better for lexis, direct for phonology).

Atlases and more specific findings based on these surveys have often been used in support of positions adopted relative to contemporary theoretical issues. In particular, the early work was interpreted both by adherents and opponents of the **Neogrammarian Principle** (see HISTORICAL LINGUISTICS, pp.192–4) as supporting their respective views. This issue has now been largely superseded, but current disputes within variation theory (see below) are conducted using similar evidence. Much often depends on the method of presentation chosen;

where maps are used, for instance, a favourite device has been the isogloss, a line on the map supposedly dividing from each other areas where different variant forms occur. Isoglosses represent, of course, considerable idealizations, especially where non-geographical factors are not taken into account, and some of the debates on their significance depend heavily on the amount of information reduced to a single line in each case, and on the internal complexity of this information. The same applies to the statistical presentations of recent **urban dialectology** (Labov, 1966).

The rise of **structural linguistics** (see STRUCTURALIST LINGUISTICS) in the early twentieth century had relatively little impact on dialectology at first, owing to the ensuing separation of synchronic and diachronic studies, and dialectology's links with the diachronic side. As a result, emphasis on synchronic systems (phoneme inventory, etc.; see PHONEMICS) did not become usual in dialect studies until the 1950s. Studies commenced before this time are typically not informed by these notions, and at first they were much more current in American than in European dialectological circles (though see LANGUAGE SURVEYS on the **Linguistic Survey of Scotland**).

The rejuvenation of the subject proceeded at a rapid pace around 1960, and some structuralist tenets were themselves quickly challenged, in particular the tendency to dismiss **residual variability** in a dialect (that is, variability which still remains to be explained after a full analysis in terms of intralinguistic conditioning factors) as **free variation**. Whether this occurred across a community or within the speech of an individual, it was revealed to be highly structured and often predictable, to some extent, statistically at least, in terms of intralinguistic constraints and also the effects of non-linguistic factors.

Further changes were prompted by the criticisms made by sociologically aware commentators such as Pickford (1956). This led to a reappraisal of research methodology, including both informant selection and interview design and technique. After a series of publications in the field of structural dialectology in the mid–late

1950s (Weinreich, 1954; Moulton, 1960), the 1960s saw the development of a new tradition based on attempts to obtain more natural usage than that typical of questionnaire responses, on statistically sound sampling of the relevant populations, and on generativist formalism and concepts. William Labov pioneered this type of work in the USA, starting in the early 1960s.

Since then the new urban dialectology movement, which has concentrated largely on the hitherto neglected dialects of cities, has developed in many forms both in the USA and elsewhere, including the United Kingdom and the rest of Europe. Many of Labov's original ideas have been, in turn, seriously modified by himself and by others, though the early work in the tradition, including Peter Trudgill's (1974b) influential emulation of Labov's New York City study in Norwich, UK, did follow Labov closely. In the USA and to some extent elsewhere, formalization of the numerical aspects of variation has been pursued (Cedergren and Sankoff, 1974), and a rival tradition has developed under the influence of Bailey (1973) and Bickerton (1971), describing itself as the dynamic paradigm in contrast with Labov's **quantitative paradigm**.

This tradition differs sharply from Labovian ideas on such issues as the range of possible forms of dialect grammars, the scope of the variation to be found in rigorously defined combinations of environments such as one speaker in one style (the **inherent-variation debate**), and the relationship between variation and change. For instance, advocates of the dynamic paradigm have claimed, against Labov's position, that, if all relevant linguistic and non-linguistic factors are taken into account, there is *no* remaining variability (**inherent variation**) – unless change is actually in progress at the relevant point in the system – and that any such variability is in fact an effect, rather than a partial cause, of change. The studies conducted within the dynamic paradigm were, at least at first, mainly concerned with post-creole continua (see CREOLES AND PIDGINS), and it is possible to argue that in these situations the facts are typically very different: the dynamic paradigm, positing as it does a smaller range of possible patterns, is more successful in modelling

situations of this kind, where the structure of the variability present often seems to be simpler than in the areas studied by Labov and other adherents of his position.

Other studies, conducted in areas where the pattern of **norms** – forms perceived as suitable for emulation – is much more complex than in New York City, have produced results leading their authors to reject many of Labov's views, in particular his views on attitudinal factors and their consequences for informant behaviour. The best-known such studies have been carried out in northern Britain, most notably in Belfast by the Milroys (1980), who have also extended changes in methodology originally made by Labov himself: there has been a move away from formal interviews towards attempts to obtain still more natural usage, and a renewed interest in fieldwork technique (see FIELD METHODS) and in the concept of the vernacular. Another worker in northern Britain, Suzanne Romaine (1980), has been in the forefront of criticizing as oversimplified more general assumptions harboured in the Labovian tradition about the relative significance of various non-linguistic factors and the structure of variation. An attempt to remedy these problems had previously been made by those responsible for the Tyneside Linguistic Survey, a long-term project based in Newcastle, UK, and at one time headed by Barbara Strang; use of computers and a concern with the reliability of statistics and with the examination of a wide range of non-linguistic factors have marked this work. Despite these and other innovations, the debt of all workers in this field to Labov remains and is widely acknowledged.

Generative dialectology was another development of the 1960s; it is concerned neither with data collection nor with explanation of patterns of usage, but, rather, with providing formal descriptions of variation – mostly phonological – within some form of the generativist paradigm. The subject is closely linked with generative phonology (and syntax) and with applications of these techniques of analysis to historical phenomena, and, true to this tradition, it has displayed a tendency to posit recapitulation of historical developments in the minds of current speakers. For instance, the events of the **Great Vowel Shift** (see HISTORICAL LINGUISTICS), by which the long monophthongs of English shifted one 'notch' in tongue height in early modern times, are recapitulated in the derivation of the relevant words, as posited in this tradition – the **underlying representations** preserve preshift relationships.

In the best studies, the evidence for this sort of procedure has been synchronic and independent of the known history of the forms. Within its limited goals, generative dialectology has been successful – Newton's (1972) work on Modern Greek dialects stands out – but the interest of dialectologists as such seems to have moved elsewhere, and generative dialectology is increasingly practised by generativists themselves rather than within the field. Its failure to offer explanations has not endeared it to empiricist theoreticians.

Since the mid–late 1960s many young scholars have, however, found the new urban dialectological enterprise attractive, in part, perhaps, because it is openly concerned with widely spoken, modern varieties, rather than with obsolescent and obscure forms of speech, and because this leads it to findings of unprecedented practical relevance. Dialect differences, resulting misunderstandings, and sheer prejudice are important factors for the success and failure of educational systems and programmes, and views of all kinds are frequently espoused with great vigour, both by linguists and teachers and by members of the general public. It is clear that the vastly increased amount of information about the linguistic facts which is now available ought to form part of the basis for any discussion of these issues. Trudgill (1975) and others have used these facts to suggest that certain educational policies – those which can be seen to be based on folk-linguistic attitudes and which are hostile to non-standard usage – should be radically revised (see also LANGUAGE AND EDUCATION).

Another attraction of the field for young scholars lies in its theoretical orientation. There is a marked contrast with the heavily descriptive flavour of much earlier dialect study, the findings of which seem to many to be excessively concerned with minutiae lacking in general relevance – particularly in the area of lexis. As mentioned above, urban dialectologists have engaged in intense theoretical debate within their own field, and their work has also led to a renewal of theoretical activity within historical linguistics, itself now experiencing a considerable revival. However, the early adherence of the Labovian tradition to the dominant generativist paradigm of the time has been replaced by a more eclectic, often sceptical, approach to current synchronic linguistic theory, and to an increasingly voiced belief that the synchronic/diachronic distinction has itself been interpreted too rigorously.

In the early 1980s, moreover, the application to linguistics of findings in theoretical human geography has led to a fresh attack on specifically geographical aspects of variation and diffusion, and to the rediscovery of much fascinating data collected earlier. One of the best instances of this has been Trudgill's (1983) work on the diffusion of innovations from urban centres such as London, Chicago, and relatively small centres in Norway. Despite problems of methodology and interpretation (see above), comparison of older and newer findings is frequently highly illuminating, and even where only current data are available, techniques for the study of the diffusion of forms and ensuing patterns are being developed. In addition, purely descriptive studies, now more sophisticated in character than the earlier studies, continue to be undertaken.

M.Nk

SUGGESTIONS FOR FURTHER READING

Francis, W.N. (1983), *Dialectology*, London, Longman.

Petyt, K.M. (1980), *The Study of Dialect*, London, Deutsch.

Diglossia

The term **diglossia** was first introduced into English from French by Ferguson (1959; reprinted in Giglioli, 1972, to which page numbers mentioned here refer) to refer to 'one particular kind of standardization where two varieties of a language exist side by side throughout the community, with each having a definite role to play' (p. 232). Diglossia tends to be stable over several centuries. Ferguson illustrates from four speech communities in which this kind of standardization pertains, and whose languages are, respectively, Arabic, Modern Greek, Swiss German, and Haitian Creole (p. 233). Each of these languages has a **High (H)** and a **Low (L)** variant, with the possibility of different variants within the L variant, and H and L have specialized functions. H is used predominantly in sermons, letters, political speeches, lectures, in the media, and in poetry, L in more informal contexts, and it is important to use each variety in the appropriate circumstances. In addition, H usually has more prestige than L, although Trudgill (1974a) points out that in situations like that which pertained in Greece at the time when Trudgill was writing, where the two varieties Katharevousa (H) and Dhimotiki (L) had particular political orientations associated with them, the status of each tends to vary according to individuals' political points of view; the situations in which each may be employed, and which is taught in schools will also vary according to the politics of the ruling group at any one time. It is therefore useful to have some definition other than status of H and L, and Ferguson uses the notion of the **superposed variety** for this purpose. The superposed variety (H) is typically the variety which has been used in the literature of a community rather than as a spoken language among the majority of the populace (L), in a community where literacy has been the prerogative of the few for some time.

In the communities Ferguson studied, only the H form had received academic treatment inside the communities themselves; any study of the grammar, vocabulary, pronunciation, etc., of the L variety had been carried out by scholars foreign to the speech community in question; the grammars of the two varieties tended to be very different, while the bulk of the vocabulary was shared. However (Ferguson, 1959/Giglioli, 1972, p. 242):

> a striking feature of diglossia is the existence of many paired items, one H one L, referring to fairly common concepts frequently used in both H and L, where the range of meaning of the two items is roughly the same, and the use of one or the other immediately stamps the utterance or written sequence as H or L.

As literacy becomes widespread in a community, and communication between segments of it becomes more important, diglossia is sometimes perceived as problematic; in addition, there may be a desire in a community for a standard national language as, in Ferguson's words, 'an attribute of autonomy or sovereignty' (p. 247). At this point, **language planning** may take place in the community in question, which, in a diglossic situation, will typically mean that a choice will be made between the H or L variety as a standard, although sometimes a mixed variety may be chosen. Ferguson describes the sounder kinds of arguments that may be used for one or the other of these choices as follows (pp. 247–8):

> The proponents of H argue that H must be adopted because it connects the community with its glorious past or with the world community and because it is a naturally unifying factor as opposed to the divisive nature of the L dialects. . . . The proponents

of L argue that some variety of L must be adopted because it is closer to the real thinking and feeling of the people; it eases the educational problem since people have already acquired a basic knowledge of it in early childhood; and it is a more effective instrument of communication at all levels.

He also points to the fallacy committed by both sides, and by those who argue for a mixed variety, 'that a standard language can simply be legislated into place in a community', whereas, in fact (ibid.):

> H can succeed in establishing itself as a standard only if it is already serving as a standard language in some other community and the diglossia community, for reasons linguistic and non-linguistic, tends to merge with the other community. Otherwise H fades away and becomes a learned or liturgical language studied only by scholars or specialists and not used actively in the community. Some form of L or a mixed variety becomes standard.

If a speech community has a single communication centre, or if there are a number of such centres in one dialect area, then the L variety or varieties of the centre or centres will become the basis of the new standard.

Finally, Ferguson points to the value of studies of situations of diglossia in understanding processes of linguistic change, and to the interest they hold for social scientists.

K.M.

SUGGESTIONS FOR FURTHER READING

Ferguson, C.A. (1959), 'Diglossia', *Word*, 15: 325–40; reprinted in P.P. Giglioli (ed.) (1972), *Language and Social Context: Selected Readings*, Harmondsworth, Penguin, pp. 232–51.

Most books on **sociolinguistics** contain a section or sections on diglossia.

Discourse and conversational analysis

The term **discourse analysis** was first employed in 1952 by Zellig Harris as the name for 'a method for the analysis of connected speech (or writing)' (Harris, 1952, p. 1), that is, for 'continuing descriptive linguistics beyond the limits of a single sentence at a time', and for 'correlating "culture" and language' (p. 2).

Harris advocated the use of a distributional method which would discover which elements occurred next to each other, or in the same environment (p. 5). In this way, equivalence classes would be set up, and patterned combinations of the classes in the text would be discovered. In order to broaden the concept of equivalence, Harris employed the notion of the **grammatical transformation**, now well known

from the study of transformational-generative grammar (see TRANSFORMATIONAL-GENERATIVE GRAMMAR). This allowed him to say that, for instance, a sentence in the active voice, *Casals plays the cello*, is equivalent to *The cello is played by Casals*, which is in the passive voice, because for *every* sentence in the active voice, there is an equivalent sentence in the passive voice (1952, p. 19). Using transformations meant that the number of equivalence classes within a text was reduced to a manageable number. However, with Chomsky's appropriation of the notion of transformations as an intrasentential feature, and with the overwhelming dominance of linguistics by the transformational-generative movement which Chomsky came to lead, Harris' early attempt at dealing with longer stretches of text was not followed up, and the models of discourse analysis described below cannot be seen as direct developments of Harris's model.

Nevertheless, their interests are the same as Harris's. Thus J.B. Thompson (1984, p. 74) refers to discourse analysis as 'a rapidly expanding body of material which is concerned with the study of socially situated speech . . . united by an interest in extended sequences of speech and a sensitivity to social context'. Although the line between the study of speech and the study of written text is not hard and fast (see Hoey, 1983–4; and TEXT LINGUISTICS), I draw it here on practical grounds, and this entry is concerned with studies directed at spoken discourse.

There are two main directions within this area, one essentially linguistically based and influenced by the work of Michael Halliday, the other essentially sociologically based and influenced by the work of Harold Garfinkel. A third approach, which pays specific attention to the relationship between language and ideology, is described in the entry on **critical linguistics** in this volume. In addition, some models are based primarily on speech-act theory; see, for instance, Edmondson (1981). I shall refer to the first approach as **discourse analysis** and the second as **conversational analysis**. Discourse analysis is chiefly associated with John Sinclair, Malcolm Coulthard, and other members of the English Language Research group at the University of Birmingham. Conversational analysis is chiefly associated with Harvey Sacks, Emanuel Schegloff, and Gail Jefferson (Thompson, 1984, pp. 98–9).

The Birmingham model of discourse analysis was developed on the basis of 'a research project, *The English Used by Teachers and Pupils*, sponsored by the Social Science Research Council between September 1970 and August 1972, which set out to examine the linguistic aspects of teacher/pupil interaction' (Sinclair and Coulthard, 1975, p. 1). This project was thought to form a useful starting point for developing a model for the analysis of conversation which might be able to answer such questions as (ibid., p. 4):

how are successive utterances related; who controls the discourse; how does he do it; how, if at all, do other participants take control; how do the roles of speaker and listener pass from one participant to another; how are new topics introduced and old ones ended; what linguistic evidence is there for discourse units larger than the utterance?

These questions had proved difficult to answer by observing ordinary conversation, since this is (ibid., pp. 4–5):

the most sophisticated and least overtly rule-governed form of spoken discourse. . . . In normal conversation, for example, changes of topic are unpredictable. Participants are of equal status and have equal rights to determine the topic. . . . [In addition] a speaker can always sidestep and quarrel with a question instead of answering it, thus introducing a digression or a complete change of direction. . . . Thirdly, the ambiguity inherent in language means that people occasionally misunderstand each other; more often, and for a wide variety of reasons, people exploit the ambiguity and pretend to have misunderstood:

Father: Is that your coat on the floor again?
Son: Yes. (goes on reading)

It is clear that in this example, the son either does not grasp that his father's utterance is meant to function as a command for the son to pick up his coat, or he is exploiting the interrogative mood of his father's utterance, pretending to believe it to be meant as a straightforward question, to which the son provides a straightforward answer.

In a classroom with the teacher at the front of the class engaged in 'talk and chalk' teaching, these aspects of natural conversation would be likely to be minimized; the speech would follow more clearly definable patterns, the teacher would be in overall control, and attempts at communicating would be genuine, with little, and resolved, ambiguity. It would, however, be necessary to determine which aspects of the structure of classroom discourse were truly linguistic, and which were pedagogical (Sinclair and Coulthard, 1975, p. 19).

The descriptive system sought was to be **functional**, and should be able to answer questions about whether an utterance is intended to evoke a response, is itself a response, marks a boundary in the discourse, and so on. It should, furthermore, fulfil Sinclair's (1973) four criteria (Sinclair and Coulthard, 1975, pp. 15–16):

A. The descriptive apparatus should be finite, or else one is not saying anything at all, and may be merely creating the illusion of classification. . . .

B. The symbols or terms in the descriptive apparatus should be precisely relatable to their exponents in the data, or else it is not clear what one is saying. If we call some phenomenon a 'noun', or a 'repair strategy' or a 'retreat', we must establish exactly what constitutes the class with that label. The label itself is negligible – it is the criteria which matter. . . .

C. The whole of the data should be describable; the descriptive system should be comprehensive. This is not a difficult criterion to meet, because it is always possible to have a 'ragbag' category into which go all items not positively classified by other criteria. But the exercise of building it in is a valuable check on the rest of the description. For example, if we find that 95% of the text goes into the ragbag, we would reject the description as invalid for the text as a whole. If we feel uneasy about putting certain items together in the ragbag, this may well lead to insights later on.

D. There must be at least one impossible combination of symbols.

The initial data to be dealt with by the descriptive system consisted of tapes of six lessons based on the same material on hieroglyphs, and taught to groups of up to eight 10–11-year-old children by their own class teacher. It was decided to use a rank-scale model of description, because of its flexibility (Sinclair amd Coulthard, 1975, pp. 20–1):

The major advantage of describing new data with a rank scale is that no rank has any more importance than any other and thus if, as we did, one discovers new patterning it is a fairly simple process to create a new rank to handle it. . . .

The basic assumption of a rank scale is that a unit at a given rank . . . is made up of one or more units of the rank below . . . and combines with other units at the same rank to make one unit at the rank above . . . (Halliday 1961). The unit at the lowest rank has no structure [at the level of description at which the given rank scale operates]. . . . The unit at the highest rank is one which has a structure that can be expressed in terms of lower units, but does not itself form part of the structure of any higher unit [again, at the given level of linguistic description]. . . .

We assumed that when, from a linguistic point of view, classroom discourse became an unconstrained string of units, the organization would have become fundamentally pedagogic.

The final descriptive rank scale for the discourse level relates to the ranks for the pedagogic level and the grammatical level as in Table 1 (from Sinclair and Coulthard, 1975, p. 24):

Table 1 Rank scales for the pedagogic, grammatical, and discourse levels

Level of non-linguistic (pedagogic) organization	Level of discourse	Level of grammar
course period topic	lesson transaction exchange move act	sentence clause group word morpheme

However, the correspondences are only general, not one to one. Of the ranks at the level of discourse, **lesson** is obviously specific to classroom interaction and is replaced by other ranks in research using this model for the analysis of discourse in other situations (see below). The remaining ranks are, however, typically retained, although the type of unit at each rank tends to vary; for instance, the teaching exchange is specific to classroom and related discourse, but the **rank** of exchange itself is common to most types of discourse. The best way to understand the different ranks is by seeing how they were arrived at. This process is described by Sinclair and Coulthard (1975, pp. 21–3) as follows:

Initially we felt the need for only two ranks, *utterance* and *exchange*; utterance was defined as everything said by one speaker before another began to speak, exchange as two or more utterances. However, we quickly experienced difficulties with these categories. The following example has three utterances, but how many exchanges?

Teacher: Can you tell me why do you
           eat all that food?
           Yes.
Pupil: To keep you strong.
Teacher: To keep you strong. Yes. To
           keep you strong.
           Why do you want to be
           strong?   (Text G)

The obvious boundary occurs in the middle of the teacher's second utterance, which suggests that there is a unit smaller than utterance. Following Bellack [*et al.* (1966)] we called this a *move*, and wondered for a while whether moves combined to form utterances which in turn combined to form exchanges. However, the example above is not an isolated one; the vast majority of exchanges have their boundaries within utterances. Thus, although utterance had many points to recommend it as a unit of discourse, not least ease of definition, we reluctantly abandoned it. We now express the structure of exchanges in terms of moves. A typical exchange in the classroom consists of an *initiation* [I] by the teacher, followed by a *response* [R] from the pupil, followed by *feedback* [F], to the pupil's response from the teacher, as in the above example. . . .

While we were looking at exchanges, we noticed that a small set of words – 'right', 'well', 'good', 'O.K.', 'now', recurred frequently in the speech of all teachers. We realized that these words functioned to indicate boundaries in the lesson, the end of one stage and the beginning of the next. . . . We labelled them *frame.* . . . We then observed that frames, especially those at the beginning of a lesson, are frequently followed by a special kind of statement, the function of which is to tell the class what is going to happen. . . . These statements are not strictly part of the discourse, but rather metastatements about the discourse – we call them *focus.* . . . The boundary elements, frame and focus, were the first positive evidence of the existence of a unit above exchange, which we later labelled *transaction.* . . .

The highest unit of classroom discourse, consisting of one or more transactions, we call *lesson.* . . .

For several months we continued using these four ranks – move, exchange, transaction, lesson – but found that we were experiencing difficulty coding at the lowest rank. For example, to code the following as simply an initiation seemed inadequate.

Now I'm going to show you a word and I want you – anyone who can – to tell me if they can tell me what the word says. Now it's a bit difficult. It's upside down for some of you isn't it? Anyone think they know what it says?
(Hands raised)
Two people. Three people. Lets see what you think, Martin, what do you think it says?

We then realized that moves were structured and so we needed another rank with which we could describe their structure. This we called *act.*

By way of illustrating the layout which Sinclair and Coulthard (1975) used for presenting the results of their analysis, I shall analyse the quotation given above. Some of the conventions of the layout are (p. 61):

(a) Transaction boundaries are marked by a double line, exchange boundaries by a single line. . . .

(b) The page is divided into three columns for opening, answering, and follow-up moves. One reads down the first column until one reaches a horizontal line across the page, then reads down the second column to the line, then down the third column.

(c) Ideally the page would be divided into five columns to allow for framing and focusing moves, but restrictions on space have forced us to put these moves in the opening column. We indicate that they are not opening moves by removing the columns for answering and follow-up moves.

(d) An additional column . . . [on] the left-hand side . . . label[s] the exchange type. . . .

(h) Non-verbal surrogates of discourse acts are represented by NV.

(i) Diamond brackets are used to show that one element of structure is included within another. Thus 'I wonder what Andrew thinks about this one?' is el <n> [elicitation including a nomination].

I have assumed that Martin provides a responding move consisting of the act rep, and the teacher might provide a follow-up move consisting of the acts acc and e.

The acts are defined in terms of their function in the move, that is, in terms of what following acts they predict, *but also in terms of what actually*

Table 2

Exchange type	Opening move	Act	Answering move	Act	Follow-up move	Act
	Now FRAME	m				
Boundary	I'm going to show FOCUS you a word	ms				
	and I want you – anyone who can – to tell me if they can tell me what the word says.	S				
	Now it's a bit difficult. It's upside down for some of you, isn't it?	com				
Elicit	Anyone think they know what it says? NV Two people. Three people.	el b cu				
	Let's see what you think, Martin, what do you think it says?	el <n>	Martin's reply	rep	Teacher's follow-up	acc e

follows them. Thus the description is both forward and backward looking, that is, it is both **prospective** and **retrospective**. Acts are not defined in isolation, and an act which one might initially be inclined to label in one way might be reinterpreted as being of another type because of the act that follows it. In this way, the description is virtually completely based on the evidence available, and it is not necessary to hypothesize any more about the intentions of the interactants than what is obvious from the linguistic evidence and from the situation in which the discourse occurs. The importance of the situation and the interactants' understanding of it is similarly revealed by the discourse itself, and the grammarians traditional problem of the lack of a one-to-one correspondence between sentence form or mood – *declarative, interrogative, imperative* – and sentence function – *statement, question, command* – is resolvable by reference to situational features. Thus, in the classroom, an interrogative like 'What are you laughing at?' will not typically be interpreted as a question; the pupils' understanding of classroom conventions – laughing is not typically encouraged – tends to cause this interrogative to be understood as a command to stop laughing (or a reprimand for laughing).

The definitions of the acts used in the analysis above are shown below (see Sinclair and Coulthard, 1975, pp. 40–4, for a full list of definitions of all the acts, moves, exchanges, and transactions they employ).

Act		Definition
m	marker	Realized by a closed class of items – 'well' etc. (see above). Its function is to mark boundaries in the discourse.
el	elicitation	Realized by question. Its function is to request a linguistic response.
cu	cue	Realized by a closed class . . . 'hands up', 'don't call out', 'is John the only one'. Its sole function is to evoke an (appropriate) bid.
b	bid	Realized by a closed class of verbal and non-verbal items – 'Sir', 'Miss', teacher's name, raised hands, heavy breathing, finger clicking. Its function is to signal a desire to contribute to the discourse.
n	nomination	Realized by a closed class consisting of the names of all the pupils, 'you' . . . 'anybody', 'yes'. . . . The function of nomination is to call on or give permission to a pupil to contribute to the discourse.
com	comment	Realized by statement and tag question. . . . Its function is to exemplify, expand, justify, provide additional information. . . .
rep	reply	Realized by statement, question, moodless and non-verbal surrogates such as nods. Its function is to provide a linguistic response which is appropriate to the elicitation.
acc	accept	Realized by a closed class of items – 'yes', 'no', 'good'. . . . Its function is to indicate that the teacher has heard or seen and that the informative, reply or react was appropriate.
e	evaluate	Realized by statements and tag questions including words and phrases such as 'good', 'interesting', 'team point', commenting on the quality of the reply, react or initiation. . . .
ms	metastatement	Realized by a statement which refers to some future time when what is described will occur. Its function is to help pupils to see the structure of the lesson, to help them understand the purpose of the subsequent exchange, and see where they are going.

Similarly rigid definitions are provided for moves, exchanges, and transactions, and the essentially structure-orientated basis for the description should be obvious from the above.

While the basic theoretical assumptions underlying the original model have remained unchanged, there have been some modifications to the model itself, in particular the inclusion in the model of Brazil's work on intonation (see INTONATION). Most modifications, however, have been made by researchers applying the basic model to other types of discourse in which, for instance, the three-part structure of the exchange, I–R–F, of the classroom model was found to be inappropriate (Burton, 1980, 1981). Burton (1981) replaces the I–R–F structure of the exchange with a structure in terms of Opening, Supporting, and Challenging moves, and her study usefully draws on both the structural approach of Sinclair and Coulthard as described above, and on the work of conversational analysts, to be described below. She keeps to a rigorous structural description, but imports three concepts into the analysis, namely '(i) a notion of "discourse frame-work" based on a concept of reciprocal acts and cohesion; (ii) Keenan and Schiefflin's idea (1976) of 'Discourse Topic Steps' necessary for the establishment of a discourse topic; and (iii) an extension of Labov's (1970) preconditions for the interpretation of any utterance as a request for action' (p. 63). In the discourse framework, certain acts set up expectations of certain other acts. When this expectation is not fulfilled, a challenging move occurs. Keenan and Schiefflin's four discourse-topic steps are (Burton, 1981, p. 71):

1 The speaker must secure the attention of the hearer.
2 The speaker must articulate clearly.
3 The speaker must provide sufficient information for the listener to identify objects, persons, ideas included in the discourse topic.
4 The speaker must provide sufficient information for the listener to reconstruct the semantic relations obtaining between the referents in the discourse topic.

A hearer may challenge that any one of these steps has not been taken. Labov's preconditions are essentially similar to Searle's for speech acts (see SPEECH-ACT THEORY), and again, each precondition may be challenged.

In Burton's model, then, an Opening move is the first utterance of an exchange; a Supporting move is one which fulfils the expectations of the opening; a Challenging move is one which does not; a Bound-opening move expands on a topic once it has been established by adding detail; a Reopening move occurs when a speaker reasserts a topic despite the fact that another speaker has challenged it. This model is applied with great success to the analysis of drama texts in Burton (1980), and other applications and modifications of the model proposed by Sinclair and Coulthard (1975) may be found in Coulthard and Montgomery (1981), Mead (1985), and Coulthard (1985).

Taking seriously Sinclair's third criterion for the descriptive system (see above), analysts using the Birmingham model of discourse analysis are normally concerned to provide an analysis of the entire linguistic content of a given situation (Montgomery, 1977, 1981, adapts the model to deal with long stretches of monologue occurring as parts of dialogue or multiparty speech situations). In contrast, conversational analysts tend to concentrate on smaller, easily isolatable sequences consisting of just two, or a few speaker **turns**. They apply ethnomethodological strategies to conversation, that is, they see conversation as one of the social practices studied in ethnomethodology, the investigation of the ordered properties and ongoing achievements of everyday social practices (see Garfinkel, 1967).

The basic unit of conversational analysis is what Hymes (1967; all page references are to the 1986 revised reprint) calls the 'speech event'. Speech events take place in a 'speech community', the *social* unit of analysis, a **speech community** being defined as (p. 54) 'a community sharing rules for the conduct and interpretation of speech, and rules for the interpretation of at least one linguistic variety'. The knowledge of rules for the conduct and interpretation of speech is known as **communicative competence**, as opposed to the grammatical competence which consists of speakers' ability to interpret a linguistic variety (knowing the phonology, grammar, and semantics of a language or dialect).

The **speech events** taking place within a speech community are defined as (p. 56) 'activities, or aspects of activities, that are directly governed by rules or norms for the use of speech'. Such an event may consist of just a single speech act, or of several, and (ibid.):

> a speech act may be the whole of a speech event, and of a speech situation (say, a rite consisting of a single prayer, itself a single invocation). More often, however, one will find a difference in magnitude: a party (speech situation), a conversation during the party (speech event), a joke within the conversation (speech act). It is of speech events and speech acts that one writes formal rules for their occurrence and characteristics.

Speech-event analysis is founded on the assumption that 'members of all societies recognize certain communicative routines which they view as distinct wholes, separate from other types of discourse, characterized by special rules of speech and nonverbal behavior and often distinguishable by clearly recognizable opening and closing sequences' (Gumperz, 1986, p. 17).

Schegloff (1968/86; all references are to the 1986 reprint) focuses on opening sequences, discussing both their internal structure and the constraints they place on following sequences in the conversation. For instance, in the case of opening sequences in telephone conversations, there is a **distribution rule** for the first utterance, namely that the answerer speaks first. However, s/he does so in answer to a **summons** or **attention-getting device**, in this case the ringing of the telephone. Other summonses will occur in other situations, including (ibid., pp. 357–8):

(i) Terms of address (e.g., 'John?', 'Dr.', 'Mr Jones?', 'Waiter', etc.).

(ii) Courtesy phrases (e.g., 'Pardon me', when approaching a stranger to get his or her attention).

(iii) Physical devices (e.g., a tap on the shoulder, waves of a hand, raising of a hand by an audience member, etc.).

A summons is the first part of a two-part **sequence**, the **summons–answer sequence** (SA sequence). An answer is the second part, and it terminates the sequence. A is said to be conditionally relevant on the occurrence of S, i.e., it will be expected to occur straight away, i.e., S and A are in **immediate juxtaposition**. If A does not follow S immediately, S will typically be repeated (though not necessarily realized by the same lexical item or non- linguistic device – ringing a doorbell may be replaced by knocking on the door in a repeated summons). A is thus not just *absent* if it does not occur, it is *officially absent*; this distinguishes a sequence from a pair of items that just happen to occur in succession.

A variety of items can be used as **answer** to a summons, e.g., 'Yes?', 'What?', 'Uh huh?', turning of the eyes or body to face the person who has summoned, etc., and most of these either are or resemble questions in some respect. This has two consequences; first, that the summoner, who has elicited the question or question-like A, is obliged to talk again when the SA sequence is completed by the answer given by the summoned. Second, the summoned, having produced as A a question or question-like item is then obliged to listen for more to come when the SA sequence is completed. Thus, a SA sequence is always a preface to some further conversational or bodily activity, and never the final exchange of a conversation; that is, the SA sequence is **non-terminal**.

However, the summoner may not fulfil this obligation to speak again by beginning another SA sequence, so the SA sequence is **non-repeatable**. S/he must, instead, introduce the first **topic** (see below). SA sequences serve to establish the **availability** of the (at least) two interactants required for a conversation to take place. Availability is reaffirmed, or established as continuing, in conversations each time an interactant produces one of the **assent terms** of the society, such as 'mmhmm', 'yeah', etc. (these assent terms are among those few which may be used while another person is speaking without being heard as interruptions). Availability may in this way be **chained**. Schegloff (1968/86, p. 376) sums up the function of the SA sequence:

> sheerly by virtue of this two-part sequence, two parties have been brought together; each has acted; each by his action has produced and assumed further obligations; each is then available; and a pair of roles has been invoked and aligned.

The roles are those of **speaker** and **hearer** (pp. 379–80):

> SA sequences establish and align the roles of speaker and hearer, providing a summoner with evidence of the availability or unavailability of a hearer, and a prospective hearer with notice of a prospective speaker. The sequence constitutes a coordinated entry into the activity, allowing each party occasion to demonstrate his coordination with the other, a coordination that may then be sustained by the parties demonstrating continued speakership or hearership.

In telephone conversations, the SA sequence is typically followed by a greeting sequence; the telephone will ring (S); it will be answered (A) with, e.g., 'Hello'; the caller will say, e.g. 'Hello, this is . . .'; and the called will say, e.g., 'Oh, hi . . .' Greeting sequences can only occur at the beginning of conversations, and they allow all participants a turn at this point. They are not, however, used to open conversations among perfect strangers; strangers do not begin to talk without, e.g., an initiating courtesy phrase (see above) as S (see Coulthard, 1985, pp. 88–9).

A question–answer sequence (QA sequence) differs in a number of ways from a SA sequence. QA is less constraining than SA: a person who asks a question *may* speak again, but is not obliged to do so. And if s/he does speak again, s/he may ask another question. In addition, A need not follow immediately after Q. It may follow after a silence lasting some considerable time, but it may also follow after some intervening talk, as in (Schegloff, 1968/86, p. 365):

> Speaker 1: Have you seen Jim yet?
> Speaker 2: Oh is he in town?
> Speaker 1: Yeah, he got in yesterday.
> Speaker 2: No, I haven't seen him yet.

Sacks (1986) formulates two rules for two-party conversations, which cover Schegloff's just-mentioned points concerning QA sequences (Sacks 1986, p. 343):

> [1] If one party asks a question, when the question is complete, the other party properly speaks, and properly offers an answer to the question and says no more than that. . . .

> [2] A person who has asked a question can talk again, has, as we may put it, 'a reserved right to talk again', after the one to whom he has addressed the question speaks. *And*, in using the reserved right he can ask a question. I call this rule the 'chaining rule', and in combination with the first rule it provides for the occurrence of an indefinitely long conversation of the form Q–A–Q–A–Q–A–. . . .

A major aim of Sacks' article, and of a great deal of conversational analysis, is to relate its linguistic findings to power structures in societies and sections of them. Sacks shows how children, who do not have full rights to speak, will typically open a QA sequence with a Q which, in fact, demands another Q as answer; a child will typically initiate a conversation with a question like, 'Do you know what?', so that the other interactant will answer with another question like 'No, what?'. This means that the other interactant is given the role of questioner, so that the child has subtly created a situation in which s/he is given a right – even an obligation – to speak. Other researchers (Brown and Gilman, 1960; Ervin-Tripp, 1969) deal with terms of address and with the ways in which these are relatable to aspects of the social hierarchy, including, of course, power relations.

In this entry, I have so far concentrated on the more strictly linguistic aspects of sequences. Below I shall discuss two further important notions of conversational analysis, namely the notions, turn and topic.

Sequencing rules, such as those discussed above, are typically presented for what is known as **adjacency pairs** (Sacks *et al.*, 1974). Adjacency pairs are characterized as outlined above – they have two **pair parts**, a first and a second, with the second being conditionally relevant on the first.

As we have seen above, the adjacency pairs tend to define two roles for participants in a conversation, namely the roles of speaker and hearer or auditor. Duncan and Fiske (1977, p. 177) define these roles in terms of participant intentions as follows: 'A speaker is a participant who claims the speaking turn. An auditor is a participant who does not claim the speaking turn at a given moment.' Participants recognize and use a variety of cues, or **turn-taking strategies**, to indicate that they are ready to relinquish the turn, and to indicate that they wish to begin a turn (Capella and Street, 1985, p. 18):

> Turn-yielding clues include termination of gestures, completion of a grammatical clause, sociocentric sequences, prolonging the last syllable in a clause, change in pitch of the last word of a clause, and asking a question. Turn beginnings are frequently characterized by head shifts away from the speaker, gesturing, overloudness of speech and audible inhalation (Duncan 1972, 1983; Duncan and Niederehe 1974). Wiemann [1985] notes that these clues assume salience when placed at speaker 'transition-relevance' places and as a function of context.

In a **signalling approach** to turn taking such as the one just outlined, gaps in talk and simultaneous speech are seen as break-downs in the turn-taking system. In a **sequential-production approach** (Sacks, *et al.* 1974), on the other hand, these phenomena are considered regular features of conversation (Wiemann, 1985, p. 91), and turns are seen as constructed of (ibid., p. 92):

> unit-types, which in English include sentences, clauses, phrases and single words (Sacks *et al.* 1974, pp. 702–3, 720–2). Whether or not a particular construction functions as a unit-type at any given point in a conversation depends, to some extent at least, on the context at that point. At the end of a unit-type, a 'transition relevance place' occurs, at which point a change of speaker may, but need not, take place. . . . Potential 'next speakers' can legitimately interject themselves into the conversation by anticipating the completion

of a unit-type and moving with precise timing. If the timing is not quite precise enough, then a system-induced overlap results.

In a sequential production model, conversations and aspects of them such as turns and topics are thus considered to be mutually constructed by all the participants. During turns in a conversation, **topics** of conversation are introduced and dropped; Keenan and Schieffin's (1976) four discourse-topic steps were introduced above, and we saw that a hearer might challenge each of the steps necessary for what might be called 'topic-uptake' to take place. However, topics often 'drift', even when all the discourse-topic steps remain unchallenged (Coulthard, 1985, p. 81; emphasis added):

> The phenomenon of **topic drift** can be frustrating at times for conversationalists. Everyone has had the experience of failing to get in at the right time with a good story or experience, and then seeing it wasted because the opportunity never recurs.

Sacks (1967 MS, quoted in Coulthard, 1985, pp. 81–2) gives an example of a conversation in which the participants are competing for their chosen topics to become the topic of the conversation:

Roger:	Isn't the New Pike depressing?
Ken:	Hh. The Pike?
Roger:	Yeah! Oh the place is disgusting.
	⌈Any day of the week
Jim:	⌊I think that P.O.P is
	⌈depressing it's just –
Roger:	⌊But you go – you go – take –
Jim:	Those guys are losing money.
Roger:	But you go down – dow . down to the New Pike there's a buncha people oh :: and they're old and they're pretending they're having fun . but they're really not.
Ken:	How c'n you tell? Mm?
Roger:	They're – they're trying to make a living, but the place is on the decline, 's like a de⌈generate place
Jim:	⌊so's P.O.P
Roger:	Y'know?
Jim:	P.O.P. is just –

Roger: Yeah it's one of those pier joints
        y'know?
Jim: It's a flop! hehh.

In this conversation, Roger and Jim **skip-connect**, that is, they relate utterances back to their own last utterance rather than to the immediately preceding utterance (Coulthard, 1985, p. 82):

Each time one of them gets a turn he declines to talk about the previous speaker's topic and reasserts his own. Skip connecting is not an uncommon phenomenon, but apparently speakers only skip-connect over one utterance and thus, Ken's entry with what is a challenging question 'How c'n you tell' in fact preserves Roger's topic. Jim in his next turn is

forced to produce a normally connected utterance, but still is able to use it to assert P.O.P. as a possible topic, 'So's P.O.P.'

The conversation quoted above, of course, also demonstrates overlap of speaker turns, which fairly obviously does not lead to any breakdown in the conversation as a whole.

K.M.

SUGGESTIONS FOR FURTHER READING

Brown, G. and Yule, G. (1983), *Discourse Analysis*, Cambridge, Cambridge University Press.

Coulthard, M. (1985), *An Introduction to Discourse Analysis: New Edition*, London and New York, Longman.

Distinctive features

INTRODUCTION

Distinctive features have their origin in the theory of phonological oppositions developed by the Prague School (see Trubetzkoy, 1939). In this theory, words of a language are differentiated by oppositions between phonemes, and the phonemes themselves are kept apart by their **distinctive features** – phonetic properties such as 'voice', 'nasality', etc. These features are grouped phonetically into a variety of types, and the oppositions between the phonemes are also classified 'logically' in a number of different ways, according to the nature of the features concerned (see further FUNCTIONAL PHONOLOGY and PHONEMICS).

The theory of distinctive features was elaborated and radically transformed by Roman Jakobson (1896–1982), especially in the 1940s. For classical Prague School theory, features were merely dimensions along which oppositions between phonemes may be classified; Jakobson

made the features themselves, rather than indivisible phonemes, the basic units of phonology, and further developed the theory of their nature and role, attempting to make it simpler, more rigorous and more general.

THE ACOUSTIC CHARACTER OF FEATURES

Unlike the majority of phonological theories, which have taken articulatory parameters as the basis for phonetic description, Jakobson's theory characterizes features primarily in acoustic or auditory terms. The motivation for this is to be found in the act of communication which, according to Jakobson, depends on the possession of a common linguistic code by both speaker and hearer, and this can only be found in the sound which passes between them, rather than in the articulation of the speaker. Jakobson collaborated with the Swedish acoustic phonetician Gunnar Fant in the investigation of acoustic aspects of oppositions (cf. Jakobson *et al.* 1951), using the recently developed sound spectrograph, and was thus able to devise a set of acoustic or auditory labels for features, such as 'grave', 'strident', 'flat', etc., each defined primarily in terms of its acoustic properties, and only secondarily in terms of the articulatory mechanisms involved.

The use of acoustic features allows a number of generalizations which are more difficult to achieve in articulatory terms (see ARTICULATORY PHONETICS). The same set of features may be used for consonants and for vowels; for example, back and front vowels are distinguished by the same feature, 'grave' v. 'acute', as velar and palatal consonants. The same feature 'grave' may be used to group together labial and velar consonants on account of their 'dark' quality and oppose them to both dentals and palatals.

In later revisions of the set of features by Chomsky and Halle (1968), this original acoustic character of the features has been abandoned in favour of articulatory definition, which is felt to be more in keeping with the speaker-orientation of generative phonology (see GENERATIVE PHONOLOGY).

THE BINARY NATURE OF FEATURE OPPOSITIONS

An important and controversial aspect of Jakobson's theory is that feature oppositions are **binary**: they can only have two values, ' + ' or ' − ', representing the presence or the absence of the property in question. In Prague School theory, oppositions may be 'bilateral' or 'multilateral', according to whether there are two or more than two phonemes arranged along a single dimension, and they may also be 'privative' or 'gradual', according to whether the phonemes are distinguished by the presence versus the absence, or by more versus less of a feature. But by allowing only binary features with ' + ' or ' − ', Jakobson treats all oppositions as, in effect, 'bilateral' and 'privative'. This is justified by an appeal to the linguistic code; although it is true

that many phonetic distinctions are of a 'more-or-less' kind, the code itself allows only an 'either–or' classification. With oppositions the only relevant question is 'Does this phoneme have this feature or not?', to which the answer can only be 'yes' or 'no'. Thus 'the dichotomous scale is the pivotal principle of . . . linguistic structure. The code imposes it on the sound' (Jakobson *et al.* 1951, p. 9).

One consequence of this is that where more than two phonemes are arranged along a single phonetic parameter or classificatory dimension, more than one distinctive feature must be used. A system involving three vowel heights, 'high', 'mid', and 'low', for example, must be described in terms of the two oppositions: [+ compact] v. [− compact] and [+ diffuse] v. [− diffuse]; 'high' vowels are [− compact] and [+ diffuse], 'low' vowels are [+ compact] and [− diffuse], while 'mid' vowels are [− compact] and [− diffuse].

Binary values have remained a fundamental principle of distinctive features in more recent applications of the theory, though with some reservations. In terms of generative phonology, Chomsky and Halle (1968) note that features have two functions: a phonetic function, in which they serve to define physical properties, and a classificatory function, in which they represent distinctive oppositions. They suggest that features must be binary only in their classificatory function, while in their phonetic function they may be multivalued.

THE 'RELATIONAL' CHARACTER OF FEATURES

The feature values are 'relational', i.e. ' + ' is positive only in relation to ' − '. Each feature thus represents not an absolute property, but a relative one. This allows the same contrast to be located at different points on a scale. For example, in Danish there is a 'strong' versus 'weak' opposition which in initial position is found between a pair such as /t/ v. /d/, but which in final position is contained in the pair /d/ v. /ð/. Though the same sound may be found on different sides of the opposition in each case, it can be treated as the same opposition, since the first phoneme is 'stronger' *in relation to* the second in both cases. Despite this relational character, however, Jakobson maintains that distinctive features are actual phonetic properties of the sounds, and not merely abstract labels, since 'strength' in this sense is a definable phonetic property even if the terms of the opposition may be located at variable points along the scale. The feature itself remains invariant, the variation in its physical manifestation being non-distinctive.

THE UNIVERSAL CHARACTER OF FEATURES

A major aim for Jakobson is the identification of a universal set of features which may be drawn on by all languages, even though not all will necessarily be found in every language. Thus he establishes a set of only twelve features. This means that some of the features used must cover a wide phonetic range, a notorious example being [+ flat]; [+ flat] phonemes are characterized as having 'a downward shift or weakening of some of their upper frequency components' (Jakobson and Halle, 1956, p. 31), but in practice this feature is used to distinguish 'rounded' from 'unrounded', 'uvular' from 'velar', and *r* from *l*, as well as 'pharyngealized', 'velarized' and 'retroflex' sounds from sounds which lack these properties.

Many criticisms have been made of the original features and the way in which they were used. In their revision of Jakobson's feature framework Chomsky and Halle (1968) extend the set considerably, arguing that Jakobson was 'too radical' in attempting to account for the oppositions of all the languages of the world in terms of just twelve features. Their framework thus breaks down a number of Jakobson's features into several different oppositions as well as adding many more; they provide, for example, special features for clicks, which in Jakobson's framework were covered by other features. Other scholars (e.g. Ladefoged, 1971) have proposed further revisions of the set of features.

THE HIERARCHICAL STRUCTURE OF OPPOSITIONS

Not all features are of equal significance in the languages of the world; some features are dependent on others, in the sense that they can only occur in a language if certain other features are also present. This allows **implicational universals**, e.g. if a language has feature B it must also have feature A.

Jakobson supports this point with evidence from language acquisition and aphasia (see Jakobson, 1941). If a feature B can only occur in a language when another feature A is also present, then it follows that feature A must be acquired before feature B, and in aphasic conditions when control of oppositions is impaired, feature B will inevitably be lost before feature A. Thus, 'the development of the oral resonance features in child language presents a whole chain of successive acquisitions interlinked by laws of implication' (Jakobson and Halle, 1956, p. 41).

REDUNDANCY

The features utilized in specific languages are also not of equal significance; some are predictable from others. For example, in English all nasals are voiced, hence any phoneme which is [+ nasal] must also be [+ voice]. In the specification of phonemes, features which are predictable in this way, and which are therefore not distinctive, are termed **redundant**. In English, then, [+ voice] is redundant for [+ nasal] phonemes.

Redundancy of specific features is not universal, but depends on the system in question. For example, front unrounded vowels of the sort [i], and back rounded sounds of the sort [u], are found in English, German, and Turkish, but the status of the feature [+ flat], i.e. rounded, is different in each case. Rounding is redundant for both types of high vowels in English, since the rounding is predictable from the frontness or backness of the vowel. In German, where there are rounded as well as unrounded front vowels, rounding is predictable and therefore redundant only for the back vowels. In Turkish, which has both rounded and unrounded front and back vowels, rounding is redundant for neither front nor back vowels.

Table 1 gives two feature matrices for the English word *dog*, one (a) fully specified, the other (b) with redundant feature values marked by 0. Since there is no opposition between [+ flat] (rounded) and [− flat] (unrounded) consonants in English, and since [+ grave] (back) vowels are all rounded, the specification of the feature 'flat' is unnecessary. Similarly, all [+ nasal] consonants are [+ continuant], hence [− continuant] consonants must be [− nasal]; there are also no nasal vowels in English, hence [− nasal] is redundant for the vowel. All vowels are [+ continuant], and all non-tense phonemes are [+ voice], while neither vowels nor [− compact], [− continuant] consonants can be [+ strident]. All these restrictions are reflected in the 0 specifications in the matrix.

Table 1 Two feature matrices for *dog*

	(a)			(b)		
	/d/	/ɒ/	/g/	/d/	/ɒ/	/g/
vocalic	−	+	−	−	+	−
consonantal	+	−	+	+	−	+
compact	−	+	+	−	+	+
grave	−	+	−	−	+	+
flat	−	+	−	0	0	0
nasal	−	−	−	0	0	0
tense	−	−	−	−	−	−
continuant	−	+	−	−	0	−
strident	−	−	−	0	0	−
voice	+	+	+	0	0	0

Redundancy also applies in sequences. If a phoneme with feature A must always be followed by a phoneme with feature B, then the latter feature is predictable, and therefore redundant, for the second phoneme. For example, English has /spɪn/ but not */sbɪn/: voiced plosives are not permitted after /s/. Hence the feature [− voice] is redundant for /p/ in this context.

As a further illustration, consider the possible beginnings of English syllables. If phonemes are divided into major classes using the features [vocalic] and [consonantal], we obtain the four classes of Table 2.

Table 2

	Voc.	Cons.
V = vowel	+	−
C = 'true' consonant	−	+
L = 'liquid' (l, r)	+	+
H = 'glide' (h, w, j)	−	−

English syllables can only begin with: V, CV, LV, HV, CCV, CLV or CCLV. There are thus three constraints on sequences:

1 a [− vocalic] phoneme must be [+ consonantal] after C.
2 CC must be followed by a [+ vocalic] phoneme.
3 L must be followed by V.

Hence the sequence CCLV, which is fully specified for these features in Table 3a, can be represented as in 3b.

Table 3

	(a)				(b)			
	C	C	L	V	C	C	L	V
vocalic	−	−	+	+	−	−	0	0
consonantal	+	+	+	−	+	0	+	0

NATURAL CLASSES AND THE EVALUATION MEASURE

The assignment of features to individual phonemes is not arbitrary, but is intended to reflect **natural classes** of sounds. In terms of feature theory, a natural class is any group of phonemes which has fewer feature specifications than the total required for any one phoneme. Thus, as the class becomes more general, the number of features required decreases, e.g.:

/p/	[− compact], [+ grave],	[+ tense], [− continuant]
/p,t,k/		[+ tense], [− continuant]
/p,t,k,b,d,g/		[− continuant]

On the other hand, any set of phonemes which does not constitute a natural class, e.g. /p/, /s/, /a/, cannot be grouped together using a smaller number of features than is needed for any one of them.

This principle, together with that of redundancy, means that features are able to achieve generalizations which are not possible in the case of phonemes. The more general a description is, the smaller will be the number of features that are required. This allows the use of an evaluation measure, a **simplicity metric**, for descriptions, based on the number of features used.

In order to ensure that the description is also evaluated in terms of 'naturalness', Chomsky and Halle (1968) reintroduce the notion of **markedness**. Trubetzkoy (1939) used this concept; the **marked** term of an opposition was for him that phoneme which possessed the feature, as opposed to that which did not. Chomsky and Halle extend the notion so that the unmarked value of a feature can be ' + ' or ' − ', according to universal conventions. Thus, the phonological matrices include 'u' and 'm' as well as ' + ' and ' − ', and there are rules to interpret these as ' + ' or ' − ', as appropriate. For evaluation, only 'm' is taken into account, hence '0' is unnecessary. This proposal has not, however, been widely accepted.

THE PHONETIC CONTENT OF THE FEATURES

The set of features required and the phonetic characteristics ascribed to them have been, and continue to be, subject to change. Jakobson's original twelve features, with an approximate articulatory description in terms of International Phonetic Alphabet (IPA) categories, are:

vocalic/non-vocalic
(vowels and liquids v. consonants and glides)
consonantal/non-consonantal
(consonants and liquids v. vowels and glides)
compact/diffuse
(vowels: open v. close; consonants: back v. front)
grave/acute
(vowels: back v. front; consonants: labial and velar v. dental and palatal)
flat/plain
(rounded v. unrounded; uvular v. velar; r v. l; pharyngealized, velarized, and

retroflex v. plain)
sharp/plain
(palatalized v. non-palatalized)
nasal/oral
continuant/interrupted
(continuant v. stop)
tense/lax
(vowels: long v. short; consonants: fortis v. lenis)
checked/unchecked
(glottalized v. non-glottalized)
strident/mellow
(affricates and fricatives: alveolar v. dental, palato-alveolar v. palatal, labiodental v. bilabial).
voiced/voiceless

The feature framework of Chomsky and Halle is very complex, but the most important differences from Jakobson, apart from the use of articulatory rather than acoustic features, are:

1 Use of the feature **sonorant** v. **obstruent** in addition to vocalic and consonantal. Vowels, glides, nasals, and liquids are [+ sonorant]; the rest are [− sonorant].
2 Use of the features **anterior**, **coronal**, **high**, **back** and **low** in place of 'compact', 'grave', 'sharp', and some uses of 'flat'; other uses of flat are catered for by other features, e.g. **round**. For place of articulation, the main differences between the two frameworks are given in Table 4.

RECENT DEVELOPMENTS

In the 1970s, generative phonology (see GENERATIVE PHONOLOGY) was more concerned with rule systems than with features, and generally assumed Chomsky and Halle's framework with only minor modifications and additions. The rise in the 1980s of **non-linear** generative phonology, however, brought renewed interest in the nature of phonological representations and new developments in feature theory, particularly in the field of **feature geometry** (see Clements, 1985). In the approach of Jakobson or Chomsky and Halle, features are essentially independent properties of individual phonemes or segments;

Table 4

IPA category	Jakobson		Chomsky and Halle	
bilabial	grave	diffuse	anterior	////////
labio-dental	grave	diffuse	anterior	////////
dental	acute	diffuse	anterior	coronal
alveolar	acute	diffuse	anterior	coronal
palato–alveolar	acute	compact	////////	coronal
palatal	acute	compact	////////	high
velar	grave	compact	////////	high
uvular	grave	compact	back	////////
pharyngeal	grave	compact	back	low

in non-linear, and especially **autosegmental**, phonology, they are represented separately from segments, as independent 'tiers' linked to segmental 'timing slots'. It is claimed that these tiers are arranged hierarchically, so that individual feature tiers may be grouped together under, e.g., 'place' and 'manner' tiers, these being dominated by a 'supralaryngeal' tier. 'Supralaryngeal' and 'laryngeal' tiers are in turn dominated by a 'root' tier. Such an arrangement of feature tiers, which is justified by the fact that features behave as classes in phonological processes such as assimilation, can no longer be represented as a two-dimensional matrix.

A.F.

SUGGESTIONS FOR FURTHER READING

Baltaxe, C.A.M. (1978), *Foundations of Distinctive Feature Theory*, Baltimore, University Park Press.
Chomsky, N. and Halle, M. (1968), *The Sound Pattern of English*, New York, Harper & Row.
Jakobson, R. and Halle, M. (1956), *Fundamentals of Language*, The Hague, Mouton.

Dyslexia

The Greek term *dys-lexia* means 'a difficulty with words and linguistic processes'. Since the 1930s, it has increasingly been used to describe an extreme difficulty in acquiring the fundamental skills of written language in otherwise ordinarily functioning people. The difficulty leads to failure and underachievement in reading, spelling, and prose writing, in spite of ordinary educational opportunities. It is also marked by epiphenomena such as the disordering of letter and sound patterns; reversals and confusions in spoken and written language; poor fluency and sequencing abilities; short-term memory difficulties for symbolic series; disturbances in time judgements; directional and orientation confusions and the failure to develop asymmetric functions; disturbances in grapho-motor fluency; and a general inability to recognize linguistic patterns, e.g. syllables, rhyme, alliteration, linguistic rhythm, stress, and prosody. Money (1962, p. 16) describes these symptoms as 'a pattern of signs which appear in contiguity', and Miles (1983) describes the syndrome as a 'pattern of difficulties'.

Dyslexia was defined by the World Federation of Neurology, 1968, as 'a language disorder in children who, despite conventional classroom experience, fail to attain language skills of reading, writing and spelling commensurate with their intellectual abilities'. The United States Office of Education describes the difficulty as 'a disorder in one or more of the basic psychological processes involved in understanding or using language' (Newton, 1977). Newton (1977) writes: 'dyslexia appears to occur in all countries where universal literacy is sought by the use of a sequential, alphabetic/phonetic symbol-system of written language'. Tarnopol and Tarnopol (1976) found that forty-three developed countries recognized a specific learning phenomenon of 'reading' failure, and that they variously used the terms 'dyslexia', 'reading difficulties', or 'specific learning difficulties' to describe it. Estimates of the incidence of dyslexia vary from 4 per cent to 25 per cent of populations in societies where a phonetic alphabet is used, the variation probably depending upon the severity of the condition. However, it has been postulated in the 1980s that 10 per cent of children in the UK and USA can enter formal education with the pattern of difficulties described above. A brief definition of the term is 'A specific difficulty in acquiring literacy and fluency in alphabetic/phonetic scripts' (Newton *et al.*, 1985). The difficulty appears independent of intelligence, emotional state, socioeconomic status and cultural background.

Research from world sources indicates that the phenomenon, although manifested in **educational** failure, is linked to neurology and neuropsychology – involving differential specialization in the central nervous system itself, i.e. it is postulated that intrinsic developmental patterns of central-nervous-system functioning could be linked to literacy difficulties. Masland (1981) suggests that dyslexia may represent a difference in brain organization, and Newton (1984) refers to the phenomenon as 'differences in information-processing in the central nervous system'. These postulates of links between language and the brain have arisen from a long history of neurological and clinical observations.

These observations range from the first reference to a dominant hemisphere of the brain for language by Broca (1865), a French neurologist (see LANGUAGE PATHOLOGY AND NEUROLINGUISTICS), to the first use of the term **word blindness** by Kussmaul (1877), a German internist; the term 'dyslexia' was first used by Professor Berlin of Stuttgart in 1887 as an alternative to 'word blindness'. In 1892, Professor Déjérine of Paris found that in the brains of stroke patients with attendant dyslexia, the damage tended to be located in the posterior-temporal region in the left cerebral hemisphere, where the parietal and occipital lobes meet. The specialists mentioned above were in the main working with traumatized patients who suffered disturbances of spoken and written language. However, from 1895, James Hinshelwood, a Glasgow eye surgeon, published in *The Lancet* and *The British Medical Journal* a series of articles describing a similar disorder, but not apparently caused by brain injury. He described the phenomenon as

a *constitutional* defect occurring in children with otherwise normal and undamaged brains, characterized by a disability in learning to read so great that it is manifestly due to pathological conditions and where the attempts to teach the child by ordinary methods have failed. (Hinshelwood, 1917, p. 16)

Following upon Hinshelwood's seminal work in

this field, the notion of a developmental dyslexia was accepted by a number of medical and psychological authorities. These include the eminent American neurologist Samuel Orton, who, in 1937, described the underlying features of dyslexia as difficulties in acquiring series and in looking 'at random', associating the occurrence with unstable patterns of individual laterality. He related such patterns to hemispheric control of functions, and referred to the problem as one of 'lacking cerebral dominance'. The neurological conception of dyslexia may be summed up in Skydgaard's brief definition (1942): 'A primary constitutional reading disability which may occur electively', or at greater length in Critchley (1964, p. 5):

> Within the heterogeneous community of poor readers, there exists a specific syndrome wherein particular difficulty exists in learning the conventional meaning of a verbal symbol and of associating the sound with the symbol in appropriate fashion. Such cases are marked by their gravity and purity. They are 'grave' in that the difficulty transcends the more common backwardness in reading and the prognosis is more serious unless some special steps are taken in educational therapy. They are 'pure' in that the victims are free from mental defect, serious primary neurotic traits and all gross neurological deficits. This syndrome of developmental dyslexia is of constitutional and not of environmental origin and is often – perhaps even always – genetically determined. It is independent of the factor of intelligence and consequently may appear in children of normal IQ while standing out conspicuously in those who are in the above average brackets. The syndrome occurs more often in boys. The difficulty in learning to read is not due to peripheral visual anomalies but represents a higher level defect – an asymbolia. As an asymbolia, the problem in dyslexia lies in the normal 'flash' or global identification of a word as a whole, as a symbolic entity. Still further, the dyslexic also experiences a difficulty – though of a lesser degree – in synthesising the word itself out of its component letter units.

Since then, many eminent scientists have sought understanding in the patterns of links between sensory, motor, perceptual, linguistic, and directional mechanisms of the two hemispheres of the brain. It would appear from their studies that language, symbolic order, analytic, timing, and discrete skills are processed in the left hemisphere of the brain in most people, whereas global, visuo-spatial, and design skills have a pre-eminence in the right hemisphere in most people. The above localization of function would be the constellation for the right-dominant (right-handed) individual, whereas the left or ambi-lateral individual could have these skills subserved at random in either or both hemispheres. In relating such organizations of brain function to motor and language performance, Dimond and Beaumont (1974) report on the negative findings of the relationship between left-handedness and reading disabilities, and yet a positive relationship between reading disabilities and mixed lateral preference. He concludes that reading difficulties could be associated with indeterminate lateral preference, but not with clearly established left-preference. Zangwill (1971) refers to the complex organization between left-handers and right or left brain for language. Birch (1962) has postulated a theory of **hierarchical unevenness** in development, i.e. between auditory, visual, motor, perceptual, and linguistic mechanisms, causing inconsistency and confusion in language perception.

Cerebral dominance is viewed by some researchers more as a decision-processing system that is responsible for bringing order to our various mental activities and their final cognitive path. In this view, as expressed by Dimond and Beaumont (1974), the term refers to the cerebral control system that institutes order in a chaotic cognitive space. It involves itself in language, but at the same time it is a superordinate system that is independent of the natural-language mechanism *per se*. Similarly, Gazzaniga (1974, p. 413) writes: 'It is the orchestration of these processes in a finely tuned way that is the task of the dominant mechanism, and without it being formally established, serious cognitive dysfunction may result.' Other researchers have linked findings from cognitive psychology to the dyslexia phenomenon. Professor Miles and his team at Bangor University have postulated that lexical-encoding difficulties could be at the root of dyslexia; they compare access to **verbal-labelling strategies** between good and poor readers and spellers. The dyslexic population seem much poorer at using such linguistic facilitation (Miles and Paulides, 1981).

Following upon these neurological and neuropsychological observations on the nature of information processing in the central nervous system, other intriguing findings emerge. Clinical and psychological observation reveals that dyslectic persons are often superior in the so-called right-hemisphere skills, i.e. in skills which require basic aptitudes in spatial perception and integration. Dyslectic persons often succeed in the areas of art, architecture, engineering, photography, mechanics, technology, science, medicine, athletics, music, design, and craft. Some also succeed in mathematics, but there is also an overlap in percentages of cases between dyslexia and mathematical difficulties. The above would indicate probabilities of inherent differences in patterns of human central-nervous-system development. As a result of these differences, one could expect differential problems in acquisition of various human skills. The dyslexia phenomenon. therefore, could be regarded as the outcome of such eventualities of personal development.

In addition to these more ordinary variations of individual differences *vis à vis* written language, clinical observation also reveals a second group of potential dyslectic learners. This group is characterized by pre-, peri- and postnatal trauma and developmental anomalies which lead to the dyslectic pattern of difficulties, exacerbated by distractibility, hyperactivity, the 'clumsy-child syndrome', and the more organic motor and language difficulties. Children in this group often have visuo-spatial problems; grapho-motor difficulties resulting in poor handwriting; visual discrimination and sequencing anomalies; and perceptuo-motor difficulties. There can be overlap between the developmental, constitutional group and the so-called traumatized group, resulting in

a considerable number of children entering school at age five years with grave potential literacy problems.

Dr John Marshall of the Radcliffe Infirmary, Oxford, and Dr Max Coltheart of London University have made intensive studies of **acquired dyslexia** in brain-traumatized patients, and have sought to establish a rational taxonomy, grouping patients on the basis of their particularly outstanding characteristics (see Coltheart *et al.*, 1987). An information-processing model has been used as a basis for much of their work. Attempts have also been made to make analogous comparisons with developmental dyslexia. The term **deep dyslexia** is also used by such researchers to designate the nature of acquired dyslexia.

Since the mid-1940s, however, educationists, educational psychologists, and sociologists have been investigating the problem of school-learning failure in terms of psychogenic and environmental factors. Their standpoint has been that educational difficulties in the main derive from various combinations of extrinsic conditions – socioeconomic factors; emotional states and maladjustment due to trauma; inadequate standards and methods of teaching. Intrinsic causations, such as poor general underlying ability, i.e. 'intelligence', and/or general retardation of speech development, e.g. aphasic conditions (see APHASIA), have also been considered, as have physical handicaps such as defective sight and hearing. The terms **learning disabilities**, **specific learning disabilities**, and **reading disabilities** have been used to describe severe underfunctioning in reading, writing, and spelling. In the main. remedial techniques have been linked to diagnoses of the above factors. UK educational policy especially has, on the whole, favoured diagnosis of learning difficulties in the above psychogenic and environmental areas; and educational psychologists, educationists, etc., have been reluctant to ascribe underachievement in school to patterns of inherent difficulties related to the more neuropsychological aetiologies. The situation has been a contentious one; and the somewhat rigid stand often taken by educational specialists would appear to have frustrated attempts by many families, scientists,

psychologists, and neuropsychologists to provide help based upon appropriate understanding
and diagnosis.

From the early 1960s, however, in the UK, and
somewhat earlier in the USA and some mid-
European countries, a number of psychologists,
neuropsychologists, and neurologists began to
observe the pattern of difficulties described above.
While the terms **strephosymbolia**, **congenital-
alexia**, **legasthernia**, **word amblyopia**, **typholexia**,
amnesia visualis verbalis, **analphabetia partialis**,
bradylexia, and **script blindness** have been used
by various specialists and scientists in the field as
synonyms for dyslexia, the latter term has been
adopted by many as a scientific, neutral, and
definitive term for the observed phenomena –
pin-pointing the central issue of language involvement. The use of this term, with its emphasis
on developmental, linguistic, and symbolic factors
and constitutional issues, has resulted in a
continuing programme of research and clinical
observation, which has yielded new insights into
human learning, on the one hand, and probable
differences in learning, on the other. A central
feature has been the role of the left hemisphere of
the brain in perceptual, linguistic, ordering,
analytic, and sequencing mechanisms – all of
which, it is hypothesized, are needed for success
in encoding alphabetic/phonetic scripts, and for
the integration of such activities with other
essential right-hemisphere and inter-hemisphere
transmissions. The Harvard team in the USA is
especially renowned for its seminal work in this
field (see, for instance, Duffy *et al.*, 1980b;
Masland, 1981; Geschwind, 1982). Many
psychologists and a growing number of teachers
now acknowledge the usefulness of the word
dyslexia as a specific term to describe a specific
phenomenon.

Further clinical observation and research
appears to have established different kinds of
subgroups of difficulty within the total universe of
dyslexia. Because of the complex nature of
linguistic tasks, and the number of different
mechanisms involved, aspects of the pattern of
difficulties can differ with the individual. For
example, the phonological aspects of linguistic
ordering can be the problem for some, whereas

the visual route to reading, and/or grapho-motor
disturbances, can cause the confusion in others.
Indeed, some learners can experience difficulties
in all mechanisms, causing overwhelming confusions of the alphabetic/phonetic script in the
earliest days of school. In the ability to recognize
an individual's own pattern lies the most critical
issue of preparing and planning appropriate
remedial-teaching techniques.

Since the 1930s, effort has been directed internationally to the development of teaching techniques for dyslexic persons. The basic need is to
establish a kind of **mediational teaching** in which
the crucial elements of written language are
highlighted in such a way that a child who would
not automatically perceive them – and their
linkages – can do so. The responsibility of
teaching is to present the linguistic signal in such
a way that the child's own associative systems
can be used to make sense of the structures and
meaning of written language. Skilful teaching,
which can lead to effective learning, needs to be
based, therefore, upon the appropriate diagnosis
and assessment, leading to the identification of
individual needs. The key issue appears to be the
provision in all first and primary schools of
approved diagnostic and assessment measures
for the earliest recognition of a child's pattern of
learning, and the inclusion in teacher training of
such techniques; for example, does a child best
process information in a pictorial and spatial
manner? If so, the use of pictograms, visual-
recognition games, colour-coded materials, videotapes, computer-aided programs, and the
emphasis on pattern in visual discrimination can
all serve to provide the initial groundwork for
perceiving the nature of the task. If, however, a
child is better on the phonological route, teaching
proceeds through sound-patterns – rhymes,
doggerel, repetition, blending techniques, games,
and recitations, concentrating on simple, regular
consonant–vowel–consonant arrays. In both
systems, the teaching materials will be linked to a
child's own world of experience, its spoken
vocabulary, its love of story, jingles, and fun.
Research constantly shows that 'teaching to the
strength' is the most effective way forward. Once
a child is over the threshold of meaningful

perceptions helped by teaching based on this rule, then the business of linking the various sound–symbol–grapho-motor essentials can proceed. The phrase 'creating order in a chaotic cognitive space' can have real, practical meaning for the teacher.

Apart from the mediational aspects of teaching and its use of mnemonic systems to provide the necessary associative links, other essential techniques would include emphasis on rules and regularities, and the need for constant, repetitive reinforcement in a number of novel and interesting ways. Motivation becomes a prime factor in view of the very difficult nature of the task for the young learner; and effective teaching therefore relies upon the constant use of stimulating, lively and interesting material.

Remediation is one key area of understanding; but the other critical responsibility for education is the creation of opportunities for special aptitudes (as listed above) of dyslectic persons. Much research has centred around the stress-reaction patterns and acute anxieties which have been observed clinically over many years in dyslectic persons. The responsibility of education, therefore, would be to ensure good personal development, self-concept, self-confidence in the young learners by appropriate recognition of skills and abilities other than those of written language. The implications for curriculum development in secondary and tertiary education especially would lead to a 'positive approach to dyslexia', as described in a number of scientific and educational publications (see, for instance, *Bulletins of the Orton Society*, 1960, 1968, 1969 and 1970; Kershaw, 1974; and Newton *et al.*, 1985). Dyslexia difficulties can overwhelm the whole of education and life itself, if not appropriately recognized; and concomitant with the growth of scientific research and understanding in the dyslexia phenomenon since the 1930s, a number of lay independent pressure groups have arisen which

attempt to ameliorate the situation of the dyslectic learner. In the UK, these include the **British Dyslexia Association**, the **Dyslexia Institute**, the **Helen Arkell Dyslexia Centre**, and **Fairley House**, London. In the USA, the **ACLD** (**Association for Child Learning Difficulties**) and the **Orton Society** are two prestigious bodies whose activities have led to recognition and amelioration of dyslectic difficulties. Often beginning as parental pressure groups, these bodies have now established their own professional responsibilities, diagnoses, teaching, and teacher-training activities. Combined with the continuing efforts of universities, medical and paramedical authorities, and educational institutes, their efforts have resulted in increasing the understanding of dyslexia and the implications for statutory education and universal literacy.

In the UK, the 1981 Education Act makes a move forward in the recognition of and provision for this specific educational need. But as one perceives the overall scene in the late 1980s, concern must still be expressed for the many thousands of young people whose education and life opportunities will depend upon the findings of science, the open and professional attitudes of educationists, and the sponsorship and goodwill of governments in creating provision for their dyslectic pattern of difficulty.

M.Nn

SUGGESTIONS FOR FURTHER READING

Newton, M.J., Thompson, M.E., and Richards, I.L. (1979), *Readings in Dyslexia*, (Learning Development Aids Series), Wisbech, Cambs, Bemrose.

Pavlides, G. Th. and Miles, T.R. (1981), *Dyslexia Research and its Application to Education*, Chichester, John Wiley.

Thompson, M.E. (1984), *Developmental Dyslexia*, London, Edward Arnold.

Vellutino, F.R. (1979), *Dyslexia: Theory and Research*, London, MIT Press.

The English Dialect Society

In 1870 W.A. Wright called for the founding of an English Dialect Society (*Notes and Queries*, 1870; see Petyt, 1980, p. 76), and the Society got underway in 1873 with W.W. Skeat as its secretary and director. Between 1873 and 1896 it published many volumes on English dialects, including bibliographies, reprinted and original glossaries, and dialect monographs of varying length and type.

The Society's aim was to produce a definitive dialect grammar and dictionary, and in 1895 Joseph Wright, a self-taught academic from Yorkshire who became professor of Comparative Philology at Oxford, was appointed editor of both works. The Society was then disbanded, perceiving its task as having been completed. The dictionary was published in six volumes between 1898 and 1905 (Wright, 1898–1905), with the grammar forming part of volume VI and also appearing separately (Wright, 1905). The Society's influence continued in the form of regional dialect societies.

M.Nk

Field methods

In this article I will be discussing procedures used to collect information about the language of a traditional community, with a view to producing a grammar of that language. I will not be treating here the methods needed to gather material for a sociolinguistic study of language-internal variation (see LANGUAGE SURVEYS), nor those for investigating the acquisition of native language by children (see LANGUAGE ACQUISITION). The best source on the procedures of linguistic fieldwork remains Samarin (1967), but chapter 7 of Nida (1946) is also a very good summary and is strongly recommended. Much of the outline of elicitation procedures presented herein was learned from Nida.

The ideal way to study the language of a traditional community is *in situ*, living within the village, learning as much of the social customs of the people as possible. It is very important to understand something about the social contexts in which the language is used, for in many languages these will directly affect aspects of its structure. The only way these contexts can be learned and properly appreciated is by living in an environment where the language is used constantly, i.e. the village community. Further, it is very important, if the time available is sufficient, for the linguist actually to learn to speak the language. The best way to do this, of course, is to live in the village, where one is surrounded by the language in constant use. This is not to say that valuable work cannot be done without a speaking knowledge: many good descriptive studies have come from the pen of linguists who could not fluently speak the language under description. None the less, there will be many aspects of the language which may only be properly under-stood or, indeed, discovered, if the linguist possesses a speaking knowledge.

Living in the village may put the linguistic investigator under severe psychological and physical stress, often described as **culture shock**. S/he has to come to terms with possibly very different local concepts of proper social be-haviour, hygiene, and time than her or his own, and particular difficulty may arise from the fact that traditional people's conceptualization of privacy is often very different from that of European-based cultures. The 'goldfish bowl' existence that this implies for investigators, even when performing intimate functions, can be very stressful. Readable and thoroughly entertaining accounts of the rigours (and joys!) of fieldwork are provided in Bowen (1964) and Barley (1983). These are written by two anthropologists about their experiences in West Africa, but their de-scriptions are generalizable to fieldwork situations in traditional communities anywhere in the world. The best way to combat culture shock is with knowledge; understanding of the local people's conceptualizations of behaviour and the world will ultimately lead to apprecia-tion. In order to gain this knowledge and appreciation, a linguistic fieldworker needs to be something of an amateur anthropologist, using the same skills in gaining access to a people's cultural conceptualizations. Two very good manuals of anthropological techniques in field-work are Agar (1980) and Georges and Jones (1980).

Also before undertaking the project, the fieldworker must be very clear about what s/he intends to accomplish, for her/himself, but equally importantly, for the community whose language is to be studied. In most parts of the world where traditional communities exist today, the governments of the country concerned will require the fieldworker, typically a North American or European, to apply for a research visa. This visa application will necessarily entail a fairly detailed description of what the field-worker wishes to accomplish with the project, and on the basis of this, the government will either approve or reject the application. It is important that the fieldworker be aware of the political implications of all this. In many countries, traditional communities are at a severe social and economic disadvantage with respect to the modernizing elites of the central government, who, of course, give permission for the project to commence. The possible motives of these elites must always be borne in mind; they may view the fieldworker and the project as a useful tool for introducing modernizing ideologies and the breaking down of the conservatism of the traditional social order. If the fieldworker is to be a pawn of government policy, it is best to be aware of it and act accordingly.

Assuming the blessing of a central government with the best possible will towards the traditional community, the question then arises of the fieldworker's own responsibilities towards that community. S/he will be living with them, and they will be opening their lives and language to her/him, offering information about their cultural and linguistic conceptualizations, ideas which define them uniquely as human beings, as selves. On a personal level the fieldworker will form close friendships with people in the village, and it goes without saying that the kind of reciprocal social responsibilities that form the basis of true friendship in Australia, Europe, North America, and elsewhere will apply here as well. But beyond that, and on a professional level, the fieldworker must seek to help the local people in ways that they can understand and appreciate. What types of cultural or linguistic projects they would like done, s/he must en-deavour to accomplish.

On arriving in the village, the fieldworker can begin the proper task of learning the language. To do so, of course, will require one or more persons to serve as language teachers or **in-formants**. Social conditions will commonly constrain who can serve as an informant. For example, in many traditional communities it would be considered improper for the informant to be the opposite sex to the fieldworker. If the fieldworker is male, this can present special problems, for the men may commonly work away from the village during the day, in their gardens or the forest. He may then have to work with elderly, physically incapacitated men, but this is often a great boon, for elderly people usually possess the most detailed and accurate language information. On the other hand, constraints like this can be quite frustrating. It has been my experience in New Guinea that elderly women actually are the most knowledgeable about their native language, but because of cultural mores they are not possible informants for a male linguist. The best fieldworkers would seem to be a male and female team.

Even with such social constraints, it is quite likely that a range of people are available as potential informants. In selecting her/his primary informant(s) the fieldworker should look for someone who has a good command of the intermediate **contact language** (in very few areas today is monolingual fieldwork necessary, so I will ignore this possibility), is keen to teach the language and enthusiastic about the project, and has an outgoing, communicative personality. It is, of course, crucial that the informant be intelligent, but mental agility may not be immediately apparent to the culturally naive fieldworker because of the different ways this is expressed in various cultures. After a few weeks, however, the suitability and degree of mental alertness of the informant will become clear to the fieldworker, and if s/he is dissatisfied or if another obviously more qualified candidate presents her/himself, then a switch should be made, provided this will be an acceptable act in that culture. In some societies such a change would be a terrible social rebuff to the informant, and in such cases it is imperative that fieldworkers be sure about the suitability of someone as an informant before taking her/him on in the first place.

Having tied down an informant, the fieldworker is ready to initiate studying the language. By this point s/he has heard the language spoken around her/him, perhaps for several days, but is unlikely to have made much headway, for long unbroken chains of discourse are simply too difficult to process at the beginning. The first task the fieldworker faces is to master the sound system of the language, to learn the system of phonemes and allophones (see PHONEMICS). Only

with this solid foundation can s/he go on to control the morphology and the syntax.

The best way to learn the phonology is with simple words. The fieldworker should draw up a list of basic words, perhaps two to five hundred items, in the intermediate contact language of elicitation, in order to elicit the vernacular equivalents. The words should largely be nouns, with pronouns and a few basic adjectives, adverbs, and numerals included, because nouns are usually morphologically simpler than verbs and hence easier to record and analyse at the outset.

The nouns used should be those belonging to basic vocabulary, such as body parts, kin terms, household and local cultural objects, local animals and important plants, and geographical and natural objects. The fieldworker should say the word in the eliciting language, which will prompt the informant to provide the vernacular equivalent. The informant should say this twice, after which the fieldworker will attempt to repeat it. The informant will say if the attempt was correct or not. If correct, the fieldworker should then record the form in phonetic transcription in her/his field notebook. If incorrect, the informant should articulate it again, with the fieldworker then attempting to repeat it. This can go on two or three times, but in no case should the informant be expected to provide more than five repetitions. If the form is simply too difficult, go on to the next one and come back to it later. After transcribing about fifty words or so, the fieldworker should record these on tape for later, more detailed work. The fieldworker will pronounce the word in the eliciting language, after which the informant will say the vernacular equivalent two or three times with a two second pause between each repetition.

Following some basic mastery of the phonology, the fieldworker is ready to tackle the morphology. Some languages, such as those of South-East Asia, have little or no morphology, so what the fieldworker will actually get when trying to elicit morphology will be basic syntactic patterns of the noun and verb phrase. Both morphology and syntax ultimately need to be studied as they are used in actual spontaneous discourse in the language. Only in textual discourse will the natural morphological and syntactic patterns of the language emerge. However, at this stage, with just a basic knowledge of the phonology, the fieldworker is in no position to start transcribing complete narrative or conversational texts. S/he is simply too ignorant of the basic building blocks of the language to make any sense of the running discourse of texts. Hence, it is crucial at this stage that the fieldworker do some basic elicitation work in the morphological and syntactic patterns of the language in order to construct a picture of its fundamental units and constructions.

It is important to remember that data collected at this stage are highly constrained and may give a quite artificial view of the language. A description of a language should *never* be based principally on elicited data, for these may reflect the contrived situation of the eliciting session or even more likely the morphological and syntactic patterns of the contact language of elicitation. The primary data for a description must be the natural spontaneous data of narrative and conversational texts, collected in a variety of contexts.

Bearing in mind the contrived nature of elicited data, the fieldworker proceeds to study the morphology of the language. In most languages nouns are simpler morphologically than verbs, so it is judicious to begin with them. Nouns are typically inflected morphologically for number, gender, possession, and case, but case is predominantly a feature of clause-level grammar and will not show up contrastively in lists of nouns. A language need not have these inflectional categories (for example, Indonesian nouns lack all of them), or they may have others (noun classes in some Papuan languages or in Bantu languages), but these can be regarded as a good starting point.

The fieldworker should proceed to elicit basic noun stems in these inflectional categories. S/he already has the word for *eye* so s/he asks for *two eyes* (this will give the dual form if the language has a distinct dual category. S/he already has *house*, so asks for *many houses*. As always, the fieldworker should repeat what the informant has said to ensure that s/he has it correct, before writing it down. If one gets distinct inflectional forms for *man* versus *woman* and *boy* versus *girl* this suggests a gender

distinction operating in the language, and further elicitation exploring this will be warranted. Possessed nominals should be elicited using pronominal possessors: *my eye; your eye . . . my eyes, your eyes,* etc. One should try a couple of dozen or so basic words in different semantic categories for their possessed forms. If they all inflect according to the same pattern, the linguist can assume the language is regular. Differences in inflection among nouns indicate complications and most probably a system of noun classes.

Now the fieldworker is ready to turn to that more complex category – verbs. S/he should first elicit some verb forms in the simple present or present continuous, e.g. *she walks* or *she is walking*. The third-person singular form should be chosen for elicitation, as it is likely to cause the least confusion. First and second persons often get hopelessly garbled in translation, so that an elicited *I am hearing* as often as not comes back as *you are hearing*, and *vice versa*. The fieldworker should choose verbs denoting simple, easily perceived events like *walk, hit, run, jump, eat, sleep, stand, sing, talk,* etc. S/he should use a mixture of intransitive and transitive verbs to investigate whether these have significant differences, but should be aware that the native language may require the expression of an object with transitive verbs, so if a recurring partial seems to be associated with the elicited transitive verb forms, it is quite possibly just this.

Having got some basic verb forms, the fieldworker is now ready to fill out the paradigms. Verbs are commonly inflected for tense, aspect, mood, voice, and agreement for subject and object. Many languages lack some of these; for example, Thai marks its verbs only for aspect and mood (tense is not a category in Thai grammar), and even these are indicated by independent words, not bound morphemes. Other languages have additional verbal inflectional categories. Yimas, of New Guinea, inflects verbs for all five of those listed above as well as others, like direction or location of the action. Languages like Yimas have such morphologically complex verb forms, with so many inflectional categories and distinctions, that a fieldworker could never hope to discover all of them through early elicitation. Rather, many will crop up only when working with texts and will be the target of later, more informed elicitation. At this early stage the fieldworker is only concerned with getting an overview of the verbal morphology.

The fieldworker needs to get paradigms of both intransitive and transitive verbs in a few tenses. It is suggested that s/he elicit verbs in the simple present (*she walks/is walking*), past (*he walked*), and future tenses (*she will walk*). Many languages have much more complex tense systems than this (Yimas, for example, has seven distinct tenses), but the fieldworker is in no position at this stage to cope with the subtleties of meaning which the different forms may encode. Rather s/he should confined her/himself to the relatively straightforward system of present, past, and future, without assuming that all these may be true tense distinctions (future, for example, may be a mood). S/he should elicit paradigms for intransitive verbs (*I walk, you walk,* etc.) and transitive verbs (*I hit you, I hit him, I hit them . . . you hit me, you hit him, you hit us,* etc.) in all possible combinations of person and number for both subject and object, bearing in mind the common confusion and switch in first and second persons. The paradigms for intransitive and transitive verbs should be elicited in all three tenses and then in the negated forms for all three. The fieldworker may well notice systematic differences between the inflections for intransitive and transitive verbs; not uncommonly, for example, the agreement affix for the subject of an intransitive verb will be quite different from that of a transitive verb, as in so-called **ergative–absolutive** languages; Yimas is of this type.

With a basic idea of the morphology of the two principal parts of speech – nouns and verbs – the fieldworker is ready to undertake a preliminary study of the syntax. Simple clauses should be formed by combining a noun with an intransitive verb such as:

(1) The woman is cooking.
(2) The tree fell down.
(3) The child is sleeping.
(4) The old man will die.
(5) The boys will go tomorrow.
etc.

Similar sentences with two nouns and a transitive verb can be elicited:

(1) The woman is cooking meat.
(2) The man cut down the tree.
(3) The child sees the house.
(4) The old man will eat meat.
(5) The boys hit the ball.
etc.

Various combinations of nouns and verbs should be tried to see if these are linked to systematic structural differences in the clause. Different choices of verb may reveal case distinctions; for example, in some languages, the subject of *see* is in the dative case, but the subject of *hit* is in the nominative. Similar differences may show up in the case of the object. Also, different nouns with the same verbs may be responsible for different agreement affixes. This is because the nouns belong to different noun classes, and the verbal affixes vary for noun class: Yimas and the Bantu languages work this way. A syntactic-elicitation procedure like this will often provide information about word order of constituents within clauses, but this must be treated with suspicion. The word order of the clausal constituents of the elicited vernacular example may simply reflect that of the prompting language of elicitation, especially if the word order of the vernacular language is rather free. For example, a linguist studying a language of Indonesia using English as the eliciting language rather consistently got subject–verb–object (SVO) word order in the elicited examples and concluded that the language under investigation was also an SVO language. But as later studies have proved, the basic word order of the language is actually quite free and if any order is more basic, it is that with the verb in initial position, i.e. VSO or VOS.

If interference from the language of elicitation is a problem with clause-level syntax, it is much more of a problem with complex sentence constructions. Here the actual structure of the vernacular language can be disguised and highly distorted if the fieldworker relies heavily on elicited material for her/his description. Some constructions which are very common in everyday language usage may be rare or fail to show up at all in elicited material. For example, in Yimas, **serial-verb constructions** (see CREOLES AND PIDGINS) are extremely common, both in narrative texts and conversations; yet if one tries to elicit them using Tok Pisin equivalents, one is rarely successful. What one does get is a sentence consisting of conjoined clauses, essentially the structure of the Tok Pisin prompt. The prompted Yimas translation is a grammatical sentence in the language, but it is not the natural or spontaneous way of expressing it.

Thus, the proper materials for the study of complex sentences and other syntactic phenomena are texts. A **text** is a body of language behaviour generated continuously over a period by the informant and recognized as an integrated whole. The texts the fieldworker is initially concerned with are conversations and narratives. Other types of texts, such as songs, poems, and other forms of oral literature, are likely to be far too difficult at first, with many archaic and conventionalized forms, as well as those arising from poetic licence, and should only be approached at an advanced state of research, when the fieldworker's understanding of the grammar of the language is well developed.

Conversations, too, are likely to prove somewhat difficult because of their speed, the presence of multiple speakers, and reduced colloquial speech forms. However, they are a very important source of information on these phonologically reduced forms, as well as context-based uses of pronouns and deictics, so, difficult or not, they must be studied. It is prudent, though, to delay analysing conversations until a number of the more straightforward narrative texts have been transcribed and analysed.

Narrative texts are of two types: (1) personal experiences of the informant or her/his acquaintances; and (2) traditional myths and legends. The latter are the most popular form of texts with linguistic fieldworkers and are unquestionably a goldmine of information, but they are, in fact, more difficult to work with than the former, for their very status as myths sanctioned by tradition means that their form may be rather conventionalized and hence less indicative of the actual productive use of the language in everyday life.

Texts should be collected in the following way. A complete text is first recorded on tape. If a narrative, a translation by the informant in the contact elicitation language should also be recorded immediately following the vernacular version. This will prove useful later in analytical work. The text then needs to be transcribed. In the early stages of work it will be extremely difficult for the fieldworker to transcribe directly from the tape: her/his knowledge of the language is simply insufficient. Further, the informant is still present, so it is advantageous to make the best use of this. The most productive way to proceed is to play back a section of the recorded text (some five to ten seconds, at this stage) and get the informant to repeat that. It is important to check that the informant repeats what is on the tape (they often use this as an opportunity to edit their performance); one does not want the recorded and transcribed versions of the text to differ significantly, although it is wise to note down the changes the informant does try to make for later reference. The fieldworker then repeats what the informant has said and, if the informant says the repetition is correct, writes down this section of the text. If the repetition is incorrect, the whole procedure begins again. Once this section of the text has been correctly transcribed, the linguist can proceed to the next section, and so on, until the whole text is transcribed. By following this procedure with a number of texts, both narratives and conversations, a large corpus of material in the vernacular can be collected. Once the fieldworker's knowledge of, and fluency in, the language is up to it, s/he should be able to transcribe directly from the tape, without section-by-section repetitions by the informant.

A crucial step in field procedures is the analysis and expansion of textual material. Immediately after transcribing a complete text, the fieldworker should set to analysing it. In the early stages this will be difficult; word boundaries will be hard to ascertain, and many words and morphemes will be unknown. Isolatable words should be presented to the informant for glossing, but bound morphemes will not succumb to this treatment: the best the linguist can hope for is a glossing of the entire word containing the morpheme. However, with a gradually enlarging corpus, things will become clearer. Recurring morphological partials can be noted along with the translations of the words containing them. By collecting enough examples of these, it should be possible to establish the form and function of the bound morpheme. Commonly, important bound and free morphemes are not glossed by the informant, and the function of these can usually only be ascertained by carefully examining the contexts in which they occur.

A very important role of texts is in the basis for supplementary elicitation. Many morphemes and construction types will come to the fieldworker's attention for the first time in transcribed texts. S/he can use these examples as the basis to collect further data so that enough material is available to describe the morpheme or construction. For example, I first became aware of the existence of embedded nominalized complements in Yimas from their sporadic occurrences in texts. I used the examples from the texts, but substituted various components such as the nouns and verbs involved, to generate a corpus of complements more or less different in form. This allowed me to be more precise in my description of their forms and functions.

The foregoing might have given the impression that linguistic fieldwork consists largely of tedious drudgery, and I do not deny that it has its mechanical side. However, to describe a language from scratch, to sort out and put the pieces together, is a tremendously exciting intellectual exploration, like doing an immense crossword puzzle. And to live closely with a people still following a traditional lifestyle, who share their language and their lives with you, offers opportunities for personal growth (for the fieldworker and the village community!) and creative understanding that can hardly be matched in any other area.

W.A.F.

SUGGESTIONS FOR FURTHER READING

Nida, E. A. (1946), *Morphology: The Descriptive Analysis of Words*, Ann Arbor, University of Michigan Press, ch. 7.
Samarin, W. (1967), *Field Linguistics*, New York, Holt, Rinehart & Winston.

Finite-state (Markov process) grammar

Finite-state grammars are known within mathematics as **finite-state Markov processes**, and a model of this type is used by Hockett (1955) to model the 'single uniqueness' of human beings among other animals, namely 'the possession of speech' (p. 3). The model represents language in terms of block diagrams or control-flow charts as used in electrical engineering, and Hockett explains that 'in the present state of knowledge of neurophysiology, there is no guarantee that the units we posit do exist inside a human skin' (p. 4), so that the model is not physiological (ibid.):

Rather, it is a type of 'as if' mode, which can be explicated in the following two ways: (1) humans, as users of language, operate *as if* they contained apparatus functionally comparable to that we are about to describe; (2) an engineer, given not just the rough specifications presented below but also a vast amount of detailed statistical information of the kind we could work out if we had to, could build something from hardware which would speak, and understand speech, as humans do.

Hockett's model may thus be considered as a model of the human language faculty. It contains a **grammatic headquarters (GHQ)** which emits a flow of morphemes. This constitutes the input to the **phoneme source** the output of which is a flow of phonemes constructed according to a code. This latter flow is the input to the **speech transmitter**, which converts it to a **continuous speech signal**. Finally, a language user has a **speech receiver**, from whence speech signals follow a converse route back to the GHQ. It is the GHQ that is of interest here, since it is the seat of the finite-state grammar. Hockett imagines that (1955, p. 7):

> G.H.Q. can be in any of a very large number of different *states*. At any given moment it is necessarily in one of these states. Associated with each state is an array of probabilities for the emission of the various morphemes of the language . . . When some morpheme is actually emitted, G.H.Q. shifts to a new state. Which state the new one is depends, *in a determinate way* (not just probabilistically), on both the preceding state and on what morpheme has actually been emitted. . . . [A] specific combination of preceding state . . . and actually emitted morpheme . . . results always in the same next state.

Such a grammar is referred to by Chomsky (1957, p. 6) as a 'very simple communication theoretic model of language', according to which (p. 20) a speaker producing a sentence

> begins in the initial state, produces the first word of the sentence, thereby switching into a second state which limits the choice of the second word, etc. Each state through which he passes represents the grammatical restrictions that limit the choice of the next point in the utterance.

Chomsky (1957, p. 19) produces the following **state diagram**:

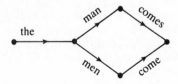

By adding **loops** to a grammar of this kind:

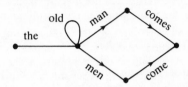

it can become able to produce an indefinite number of sentences, and will thus satisfy one of the requirements which grammars must meet: the requirement that the grammar generate an infinite number of sentences from the finite linguistic material the language provides. At the end of the sentence, the 'final state' will have been reached.

Another requirement that grammars of natural languages must meet is that they must be able to generate *all* of the possible sentences of the language, and Chomsky argues convincingly that no finite-state grammar will be able to meet this condition, since no natural language is a finite-state language. The finite-state model assumes that language is linear; it assumes that a sentence can be analysed as a string of items in immediate succession. Therefore, it is incapable of accounting for cases of **embedding**, that is, for cases in which one string of items 'breaks up' the regular succession of items within another string, as in *The woman who saw you was angry*, where the sentence *who saw you* breaks up the sentence *the woman was angry*. Chomsky provides the following examples (1957, p. 22):

(1) If S_1, then S_2
(2) Either S_3, or S_4
(3) The man who said that S_5 is arriving today

where 'S' stands for any declarative sentence. A finite-state grammar would have no way of accounting for the selection of one particular embedded sentence, or for the links of dependence which determine the selection of *then* rather than *or* in (1) and the selection of *or* rather than *then* in (2). So Hockett's claims that a finite-state grammar can be perceived as a model of the human speech capacity, and that one state predicts the following state, are not justified. Humans are able to generate structures containing embedded sentences, and there are many selections which are made by speakers of natural language which a finite-state grammar could not predict.

In the model's favour, however, it can be said that *spoken* language, at least, does reach hearers in a linear way with one word following the next in immediate succession, and Brazil (personal communication) thinks that a linear grammar of speech can be developed using insights gained from his study of intonation (Brazil, 1985; and see INTONATION).

It should also be pointed out (see Lyons, 1977a, p. 55) that the mathematical communication theory, **information theory**, which has developed since 1945 is highly sophisticated:

Chomsky did not prove, or claim to prove, that 'information theory' as such was irrelevant to the investigation of language, but merely that if it were applied on the assumption of 'word-by-word' and 'left to right' generation, it could not handle some of the constructions in English.

K.M.

SUGGESTIONS FOR FURTHER READING

Chomsky, N. (1957), *Syntactic Structures*, The Hague, Mouton, ch. 3.
Kimball, J.P. (1973), *The Formal Theory of Grammar*, Englewood Cliffs, NJ, Prentice Hall, ch. 2.
Lyons, J. (1977), *Chomsky*, revised edn, Glasgow, Fontana Collins, ch. 5.

Formal logic and modal logic

INTRODUCTION

Logic studies the structure of arguments, and is primarily concerned with testing arguments for correctness or **validity**. An argument is **valid** if the premises cannot be true without the conclusion also being true: the conclusion **follows from** the premises. Since the time of Aristotle, validity has been studied by listing patterns or **forms** of argument all of whose instances are valid. Thus, the form:

Premise	All *A* is *B*.
Premise	*C* is *A*,
Conclusion	so *C* is *B*.

is manifested in distinct arguments such as:

All men are mortal.
Socrates is a man,
so Socrates is mortal.

All Frenchmen are Europeans.

De Gaulle was a Frenchman,
so de Gaulle was European.

A third example clarifies the notion of validity:

All men are immortal.
Socrates is a man,
so Socrates is immortal.

Although the conclusion of this argument ('Socrates is immortal') is false, the argument is valid: one of the premises ('All men are immortal') is also false, but we can easily see that *if* both premises were true, the conclusion would have to be true as well.

There are good arguments which are not valid in this sense. Consider the argument:

All of the crows I have observed so far have been black.
I have no reason to think I have observed an unrepresentative sample of crows,
so all crows are black.

Both of the premises of this argument could be true while the conclusion was false. Such **inductive** arguments are central to the growth of scientific knowledge of the world. But **formal logic** is not concerned with inductive arguments; it is concerned with **deductive** validity, with arguments which meet the stricter standard of correctness described above (see Skyrms, 1975, for a survey of work in inductive logic).

Logically valid arguments are often described as **formally valid**: if an argument is valid, then any argument of the same form is valid. This means that logicians are not concerned with arguments which depend upon the meanings of particular descriptive terms, such as:

Peter is a bachelor, so Peter is unmarried.

Rather, they are concerned solely with arguments which are valid in virtue of their logical or grammatical structure; they are concerned with features of structure that are signalled by the presence of so-called **logical words**: **connectives**, like 'not', 'and', 'or', 'if . . . then . . . '; **quantifiers** like 'all', 'some', and so on. We can represent the **logical form** of an argument by replacing all the expressions in it other than logical words and particles by **variables**, as in the example in the opening paragraph. The logical form of the example in the present paragraph can be expressed:

a is F, so a is G.

We see that the argument is not logically valid because it shares this form with the blatantly invalid

John is a husband, so John is a woman.

To explain why Peter's being unmarried follows from his being a bachelor, we must appeal to the meanings of particular non-logical words like 'bachelor' and 'married'; it cannot be explained solely by reference to the functioning of logical words.

I have described logic as concerned with the validity of arguments. It is sometimes described as concerned with a particular body of truths, the **logical truths**. These are statements whose truth depends solely upon the presence of logical words in them. For example:

Either London is a city or it is not the case that London is a city.

This is claimed to be true by virtue of its logical form: any statement of the form

Either P or it is not the case that P.

is true and is an illustration of the **law of excluded middle**, i.e., there is no third intermediate possibility.

The two descriptions of logic are not in competition. Corresponding to any valid argument there is a **conditional statement**, i.e. an 'if . . . then . . . ' statement, which is a logical truth. For example:

If all men are mortal and Socrates is a man, then Socrates is mortal.

The Aristotelian approach to logic held sway until the late nineteenth century, when Gottlob Frege (1848–1925), Charles Peirce (1839–1914), and others developed new insights into the formal structure of arguments which illuminated complex inferences which had previously proved difficult to describe systematically. Philosophers normally hold that understanding a sentence requires at least some capacity to identify which of the arguments that the sentence can occur in are valid. Someone who did not see that 'Socrates is mortal' follows from the premises 'Socrates is a man' and 'All men are mortal' would put into question his or her understanding of those sentences. In that case, the formal structures revealed by logicians are relevant to the semantic analysis of language. It should be noted, however, that until recently, many logicians have believed that natural languages were logically incoherent and have not viewed their work as a contribution to natural-language semantics. The motivation for the revitalization of logic just referred to was the search for foundations for mathematics rather than the understanding of natural language. I shall describe the most important systems of modern logic, which reflect the insights of Frege, Peirce, Bertrand Russell (1872–1970), and their followers.

Logicians study validity in a variety of ways,

and, unfortunately, use a wide variety of more or less equivalent notations. It is important to distinguish syntactic from semantic approaches. The former studies proof, claiming that an argument is valid if a standard kind of proof can be found which derives the conclusion from the premises. It describes rules of inference that may be used in these proofs, and, sometimes, specifies axioms that may be introduced as additional premises in such proofs. This enables us to characterize an indefinite class of formally valid arguments through a finite list of rules and axioms. Semantic approaches to logic rest upon accounts of the truth conditions of sentences and the contributions that logical words make to them. An argument is shown to be valid when it is seen that it is not possible for the premises to be true while the conclusion is false (see FORMAL SEMANTICS). Semantic approaches often involve looking for **counterexamples**: arguments of the same form as the argument under examination which actually have true premises and a false conclusion (see, for example, Hodges, 1977, which develops the system of **truth trees** or **semantic tableaux** which provides rules for testing arguments in this way).

PROPOSITIONAL CALCULUS

The logical properties of **negation, conjunction, disjunction** and **implication** are studied within the **propositional** or **sentential calculus**. These notions are formally represented by **connectives** or **operators**, expressions which form complex sentences out of other sentences. 'And', for example, forms the complex sentence

Frege is a logician and Russell is a logician.

out of the two shorter sentences 'Frege is a logician' and 'Russell is a logician'. Logicians often speak of those sentence parts which can themselves be assessed as true or false as sentences: hence, the displayed sentence 'contains' the simpler sentences 'Frege is a logician' and 'Russell is a logician.' Similarly, 'It is not the case that . . . ' forms a complex sentence out of one simpler one. If A and B represent places that can be taken by complete sentences, a typical

notation for the propositional calculus is:

$\neg A$	It is not the case that A
$A \lor B$	A or B
$A \,\&\, B$	A and B
$A \to B$	If A then B

Complex sentences can be constructed in this way:

$$(A \lor \neg B) \to (C \,\&\, (B \to \neg D))$$

If either A or it is not the case that B, then both C and if B then it is not the case that D.

The propositional calculus studies the logical properties of sentences built up using these logical notions.

Logicians treat these connectives as **truth functional**. We can evaluate utterances of indicative sentences by establishing whether what was said was **true** or **false**: these are the two **truth values** recognized by standard systems of logic. In the use of natural language, the truth value of a sentence can depend upon the context of its utterance: this is most evident in context-sensitive aspects of language like tense and the use of personal pronouns. Classical systems of logic abstract from this relativity to context and assume that they are dealing with sentences which have determinate truth values which do not vary with context. This allows logical laws to be formulated more simply and does not impede the evaluation of arguments in practice. On pages 134–5 below, I shall indicate how logical systems can be enhanced to allow for context sensitivity.

When a sentence is constructed from other sentences using such expressions, the truth value of the resulting sentence depends only upon the truth values of the sentences from which it is made. Thus, whatever the meaning of the sentence negated in a sentence of the form $\neg A$, the resulting sentence is true if the original sentence is false, false if it is true. Similarly, a conjunction is true so long as each conjunct is true; and a disjunction is true so long as at least one disjunct is true. These relationships are expressed in **truth tables** (see Table 1). The two left-hand columns in Table 1 express the different possible combinations of truth values for A and B; and the other

Table 1 Truth tables

A	B	¬A	A & B	A ∨ B	A → B
t	t	f	t	t	t
t	f	f	f	t	f
f	t	t	f	t	t
f	f	t	f	f	t

columns indicate the truth values which the complex sentences have in those circumstances.

Systems of propositional calculus provide rules for the evaluation of arguments which reflect the meanings which the logical words receive according to this interpretation. A straightforward method of evaluation is to compute the truth values which the premises and the conclusion must have in each of the possible situations, and then inspect the result to determine whether there are any situations in which the premises are true and the conclusion is false. This method can become cumbersome when complex arguments are considered, and other methods, such as truth trees, can be easier to apply.

The propositional calculus serves as a core for the more complex systems we shall consider: most arguments involve kinds of logical complexity which the propositional calculus does not reveal. Some claim that it is oversimple in other ways too. They deny that logical words of natural languages are truth functional, or claim that to account for phenomena involving, for example, vagueness, we must admit that there are more then just two truth values, some statements having a third, intermediate, value between truth and falsity. Philosophers and logicians developed the notion of **implicature** partly to defend the logician's account of these logical words. They claim that phenomena which suggest that 'and' or 'not' are not truth functional reflect implicatures that attach to the expressions, rather than central logical properties (see PRAGMATICS). However, many philosophers would agree that this is insufficient to rescue the truth-functional analysis of 'if . . . then . . . ', with its implausible consequence that any indicative conditional sentence with a false antecedent is true. Such criticisms would not disturb those logicians who denied that they were contributing to natural-language semantics. They would hold it a virtue

of their system that their pristine simplicity avoids the awkward complexities of natural languages and provides a precise notation for scientific and mathematical purposes.

PREDICATE CALCULUS

Within the propositional calculus, we are concerned with arguments whose structure is laid bare by breaking sentences down into elements which are themselves complete sentences. Many arguments reflect aspects of logical structure which are not revealed through such analyses. The **predicate calculus** takes account of the logical significance of aspects of subsentential structure. It enables us to understand arguments whose validity turns on the significance of 'some' and 'all', such as:

> John is brave.
> If someone is brave, then everyone is happy.
> so John is happy.

Aristotelian logic, mentioned above, described some of the logical properties of **quantifiers** like 'some' and 'all'. However, it was inadequate, largely because it did not apply straightforwardly to arguments which involve **multiple quantification** – sentences which contain more than one interlocking quantifier. We need to understand why the following argument is valid, and also to see why the premise and conclusion differ in meaning:

> There is a logician who is admired by all philosophers.
> so Every philosopher admires some logician or other.

We shall now look at how sentences are analysed in the predicate calculus.

'John is brave' is composed of expressions of two sorts. 'John' is a **name** or **singular term**, and '( ) is brave' is a **predicate**. The predicate contains a gap which is filled by a singular term to form the sentence. 'Wittgenstein admired Frege' is similarly composed of predicates and singular terms. However, '( ) admired ( )' is a **two-place** or **dyadic** predicate or **relational expression**: it has two gaps which must be filled in order to obtain a complete sentence. There are also **triadic** predicates, such as '( ) gives ( ) to ( )', and there may even be expressions with more than three places. Following Frege, predicates are referred to as 'incomplete expressions', because they contain gaps that must be filled before a complete sentence is obtained. Predicates are normally represented by upper-case letters, and the names that complete them are often written after them, normally using lower-case letters. Thus, the examples in this paragraph could be written:

Bj.
Awf (or wAf).
Gabc

Combining this notation with that of the propositional calculus, we can symbolize

If Wittgenstein is a philosopher then Wittgenstein admires Frege.

thus

Pw → wAf.

We can introduce the logical behaviour of quantifiers by noticing that the sentence

All philosophers admire Frege.

can receive a rather clumsy paraphrase:

Everything is such that if it is a philosopher then it admires Frege.

Similarly,

Someone is brave.

can be paraphrased:

Something is such that it is brave.

In order to regiment such sentences, we must use the **variables** 'x', 'y', etc., to express the pronoun 'it', as well as the **constants** that we have already introduced.

Everything is such that ($Px \rightarrow Axf$)
Something is such that (Bx)

And the relation between these variables and the quantifiers is made explicit when we regiment 'Everything is such that' by '$\forall x$'; and 'Something is

such that' by ($\exists x$):

$$\forall x\, (Px \rightarrow Axf)$$
$$\exists x\, (Bx)$$

'$\forall$' is called the **universal quantifier**, '$\exists$' the **existential quantifier**. Our sample argument can then be expressed:

$$\exists x\, (Lx\ \&\ \forall y\, (Py \rightarrow Ayx)).$$
so $$\forall y\, (Py \rightarrow \exists x\, (Lx\ \&\ Ayx)).$$

The different variables 'keep track' of which quantifier 'binds' the variables in question.

Compare the two sentences:

Someone loves everyone.
Everyone is loved by someone.

These appear to have different meanings – although some readers may hear an ambiguity in the first. The notation of the predicate calculus helps us to see that the difference in question is a **scope distinction**. The former is naturally expressed:

$$\exists x\, \forall y\, (xLy).$$

and the latter is:

$$\forall y\, \exists x\, (xLy).$$

In the first case it is asserted that some individual has the property of loving everyone: the universal quantifier falls within the scope of the existential quantifier. In the second case, it is asserted that every individual has the property of being loved by at least one person: there is no suggestion, in this case, that it is the same person who loves every individual. The universal quantifier has **wide scope**, and the existential quantifier has **narrow scope**. The second statement follows logically from the first. But the first does not follow logically from the second.

Some car in the car park is not green.
It is not the case that some car in the car park is green.

reflects the scope difference between:

$$\exists x\, ((Cx\ \&\ Px)\ \&\ \neg Gx).$$
$$\neg \exists x\, ((Cx\ \&\ Px)\ \&\ Gx).$$

The former asserts that the car park contains at

least one non-green car; the second asserts simply that it does not contain any green cars. If the car park is empty, the first is false and the second is true. In the first sentence, the negation sign falls within the scope of the quantifier; in the second case, the scope relation is reversed.

TENSE LOGIC AND MODAL LOGIC

While the logic I have described above may be adequate for expressing the statements of mathematics and (a controversial claim) natural science, many of the statements of natural language have greater logical complexity. There are many extensions of this logical system which attempt to account for the validity of a wider range of arguments. **Tense logic** studies arguments which involve tensed statements. In order to simplify a highly complex subject, I shall discuss only propositional tense logic, which results from introducing tense into the propositional calculus. This is normally done by adding tense operators to the list of logical connectives. Syntactically, 'It was the case that' and 'It will be the case that' ('P' and 'F') are of the same category as negation. The following are well-formed expressions of tense logic:

PA.   It was the case that A.
⌐FPA. It is not the case that it will be the case that it was the case that A.

These operators are not truth functional: the present truth value of a sentence occupying the place marked by A tells us nothing about the truth value of either PA or FA. However, a number of fundamental logical principles of tense logic can be formulated which govern our tensed reasoning. For example, if a statement A is true, it follows that:

PFA.
FPA.

Moreover, if it will be the case that it will be the case that A, then it will be the case that A:

FFA→FA.

More complex examples can be found too. If

PA & PB.

it follows that:

$$(P(A \& B)) \lor (P (PA \& B)) \lor (P(A \& PB))$$

There is a variety of systems of tense logic, which offer interesting insights into the interplay of tense and quantification, and which augment these tense operators by studying the complex logical behaviour of temporal indexicals like 'now' (see McCarthur, 1976, Chs. 1–2).

Modal logic was the first extension of classical logic to be developed, initially through the work of C.I. Lewis (see Lewis, 1918). Like tense logic, it adds non-truth-functional operators to the simpler logical systems; in modal logic, these operators express the concepts of possibility and necessity. The concept of possibility is involved in assertions such as:

It is possible that it will rain tomorrow.
It might rain tomorrow.
It could rain tomorrow.

Necessity is involved in claims like:

Necessarily bachelors are unmarried.
A vixen must be a fox.

Other expressions express these modal notions too.

Just as tense logic formalizes temporal talk by introducing tense operators, so modal logic employs two operators, 'L' and 'M', which correspond to 'It is necessarily the case that' and 'It is possibly the case that' respectively. The sentences displayed above would be understood as having the forms 'M A' and 'L A' respectively. There is an enormous variety of systems of modal logic, and rather little consensus about which of them capture the logical behaviour of modal terms from ordinary English. Some of the problems concern the interplay of modal operators and quantifiers. Others arise out of kinds of sentences which are very rarely encountered in ordinary conversation – those which involve several modal operators, some falling within the scope of others. To take a simple example: if 'L' is a sentential operator like negation, then it seems that a sentence of the form 'LLLA' must be well formed. However, we have very few intuitions about the logical behaviour of sentences which assert that it is necessarily the case that it is necessarily the case that it is necessarily the case that vixens are foxes. Only philosophers concerned about the metaphysics of modality are likely to be interested in whether such statements are true and in what can be inferred from them.

Some principles of inference involving modal notions are uncontroversial. Logicians in general accept as valid the following inference patterns:

LA, so A.

For example: vixens are necessarily foxes, so vixens are foxes. If something is necessarily true then, *a fortiori*, it is true.

A, so MA.

For example: if it is true that it will rain tomorrow, then it is true that it might rain tomorrow; if today is Wednesday, then today might be Wednesday. In general, whatever is actually the case is possible. Moreover, there is little dispute that necessity and possibility are interdefinable. 'It is necessarily the case that A' means the same as 'It is not possible that it is not the case that A'; and 'It is possible that A' means the same as 'It is not necessarily the case that it is not the case that A.' Once one tries to move beyond these uncontroversial logical principles, however, the position is much more complex. There is a large number of distinct systems of modal logic, all of which have received close study by logicians. There is still controversy over which of these correctly capture the inferential properties of sentences about possibility and necessity expressed in English.

The extensions of the standard systems of logic are not exhausted by those alluded to here. **Deontic logic** is the logic of obligation and permission: it studies the logical behaviour of sentences involving words like 'ought' and 'may'. There is also a large body of work on the logic of subjective or counterfactual conditionals. Consider a claim such as:

If the door had been locked, the house would not have been burgled.

Although this is of a conditional form, the conditional in question is plainly not truth functional. If we substitute for the **antecedent** (the first clause in the conditional) another sentence with the same truth value, this can make a difference to the truth value of the whole sentence. For example:

If the window had been left open, the house would not have been burgled.

Like the statements studied in modal logic, such statements appear to be concerned with other possibilities. The first claim is concerned with what would have been the case had the possibility of our locking the door actually been realized (see Lewis, 1973).

Progress in both modal logic and the logic of these subjunctive conditionals has resulted in the development of **possible-world semantics** by Saul Kripke and a number of other logicians (see, for example, Kripke, 1963). This work, which is discussed in the article in this volume on FORMAL SEMANTICS, has led many philosophers and linguists to find in the work of formal logicians materials which can reveal the semantic structures of the sentences of a natural language.

C.H.

SUGGESTIONS FOR FURTHER READING

There are many introductory logic textbooks; the following illustrate contrasting approaches:

Hodges, W. (1977), *Logic*, Harmondsworth, Penguin.
Newton-Smith, W. (1985), *Logic*, London, Routledge & Kegan Paul.

Useful introductions to tense logic and modal logic are:

Chellas, B. (1980), *Modal Logic*, Cambridge, Cambridge University Press.
McCarthur, R. (1976), *Tense Logic*, Dordrecht, Reidel.
McCawley, J.D. (1981), *Everything that Linguists have Always Wanted to Know about Logic . . . But were Ashamed to Ask*, Oxford, Basil Blackwell. (Covers a lot of ground and relates it to the concerns of linguists.)

Formal semantics

INTRODUCTION

Inspired by the work of Alfred Tarski (1901–83) during the 1920s and 1930s, logicians have developed sophisticated semantic treatments of a wide variety of systems of formal logic (see FORMAL LOGIC AND MODAL LOGIC). Since the 1960s, as these semantic treatments have been extended to tense logic, modal logic, and a variety of other systems simulating more of the expressions employed in a natural language, many linguists and philosophers have seen the prospect of a systematic treatment of the semantics of natural languages. Richard Montague, David Lewis, Max Cresswell, Donald Davidson, and others have attempted to use these techniques to develop semantic theories for natural languages.

Underlying this work is the idea that the meanings of sentences are linked to their **truth conditions**; we understand a sentence when we know what would have to be the case for it to be true, and a semantic theory elaborates this knowledge. Moreover, the truth conditions of sentences are grounded in referential properties of the parts of those sentences in systematic ways. Tarski's contribution was to make use of techniques from set theory (see SET THEORY) in order to state what the primitive expressions of a language refer to, and in order to display the dependence of the truth conditions of the sentence as a whole upon these relations of reference.

Throughout, **true** is understood as a metalinguistic predicate. In general, the **object language** is the language under study: for example, our object language is English if we study the semantics of sentences of English. The **metalanguage** is the language we use to talk about the object language. 'True' belongs to the language we use in making our study, i.e., the metalanguage. Moreover, the primitive notion of truth is assumed to be **language-relative**, as in:

> 'Snow is white' is a true sentence of English.
> 'La neige est blanche' is a true sentence of French.

We shall use **TL** to stand for the predicate ' . . . is a true sentence of L'. The task is to construct a theory which enables us to specify the circumstances under which individual sentences of a given language are true. It will yield theorems of the form:

> S is TL if, and only if, p.

For example:

> 'La neige est blanche' is True(French) if, and only if, snow is white.

The interest of the theory lies in the way in which it derives these statements of truth conditions from claims about the semantic properties of the parts of sentences and about the semantic significance of the ways in which sentence parts are combined into grammatical wholes.

There are alternative approaches to the task of constructing such a semantic theory, and there is no space to consider all of the controversies that arise. In the space available, I shall develop a semantic theory for a formal language which mirrors some of the logical complexities of a natural language. The language will contain the connectives and quantifiers employed in the predicate calculus and also include some tense operators and modal operators (see FORMAL LOGIC AND MODAL LOGIC).

A SIMPLE LANGUAGE

First we consider a language L_1 which contains no quantifiers, tense operators, or modal operators. It contains three names, 'a', 'b' and 'c'; three

monadic (one-place) predicates, 'F', 'G', and 'H', and the **dyadic** (two-place) relational expression 'R' (see FORMAL LOGIC AND MODAL LOGIC). It also contains the standard logical connectives of propositional logic: '&', '⌐', 'v', and '→'.

The grammatical sentences of this language thus include the following:

> Fa, Hb, Ga, Gc, Rab, Gb & Rbb, Ha ∨ (Ha & ⌐Rbc).

We need to specify the truth conditions of all of these sentences together with the others that can be formulated within L_1.

We first specify the **referents** of the names, that is, we say who the bearers of the names are – which objects in the world the names stand for:

> (1a) ref(a) = Caesar
>   ref(b) = Brutus
>   ref(c) = Cassius

We then specify the **extensions** of the predicate expressions, that is, we say what property qualifies an object for having the predicate ascribed to it:

> (1b) ext (F) = {x: x is a Roman}
>   ext (G) = {x: x is a Greek}
>   ext (H) = {x: x is an emperor}
>   ext (R) = {<x,y>: x killed y}

We then state:

> (2)   If a sentence is of the form Pn, then it is TL if, and only if, ref(n) ∈ ext(P).

If a sentence is of the form Rnm, then it is TL if, and only if, < ref(n), ref(m)> ∈ ext(R).

(see SET THEORY for the meaning of ∈). It is easy to see that the following specifications of truth conditions follow from these statements:

> Fa is TL_1 if, and only if, Caesar is a Roman.
> Rbc is TL_1 if, and only if, Brutus killed Cassius.

and so on. We have constructed an elementary semantic theory for part of our elementary language.

It is easy to extend this to include sentential connectives:

> (3)   A sentence of the form A&B is TL_1 if, and only if, A is TL_1 and B is TL_1.
>
> A sentence of the form ⌐A is TL_1 if, and only if, A is not TL_1.

and so on. Relying upon such axioms, we can derive a statement of the TL_1 conditions of any sentence of our simple language.

The conditions listed under (1) specify semantic properties of subsentential expressions: names and predicates. Those under (2) explain the truth conditions of the simplest sentences in terms of the semantic properties of these subsentential expressions. Finally, those in (3) concern the semantic roles of expressions which are used to construct complex sentences out of these simple

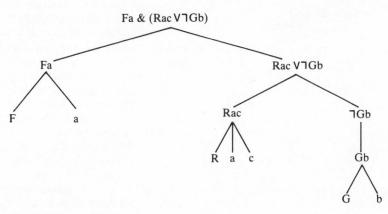

Figure 1

ones. I mentioned that L_1 was a rather simple language, and we can now notice an important aspect of this simplicity. Consider the sentence: 'Fa & (Rac ∨ Gb)'. We can represent the way in which this sentence is built out of its elements with a tree diagram (Figure 1).

The conditions in (1) state the semantic properties of expressions in the bottom nodes of the tree: those in (2) concern how the truth conditions of the next higher nodes are determined by these bottom semantic properties. All the higher nodes are explained by the conditions in (3). It is a feature of this language that, apart from the subsentential expressions at the bottom level, every expression of the tree has a **truth value**. It is true or false, and this is exploited in the conditions for explaining the truth conditions for complex sentences. We must now turn to a language which does not share this feature.

QUANTIFIERS

L_2 is obtained from L_1 by adding universal and existential quantifiers ('∀' and '∃') together with a stock of individual variables, 'x', 'y', 'z', etc., as in formal logic (see FORMAL LOGIC AND MODAL LOGIC). The grammatical sentences of L_2 include all the grammatical sentences of L_1 together with such expressions as:

$\exists x Fx$, $\exists x \forall y Rxy$, $\forall z(Hz \& \exists x Rzx)$.

The tree diagram in Figure 2 displays the structure

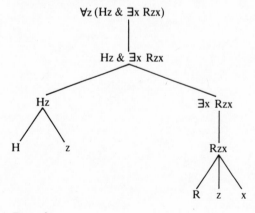

Figure 2

of the last of these. Such sentences are less straightforward than those discussed on page 137. First, it is unclear what the semantic properties of variables are: they do not refer to specific objects as names do. Second, the expressions 'Hz', 'Rzx' '∃x Rzx' and 'Hz & ∃x Rzx' contain **free variables**, variables which are not bound by quantifiers. It is hard to see how such expressions can be understood as having definite truth values. If that is the case, then we need a different vocabulary for explaining the semantic properties of some of the intermediate expressions in the tree. Furthermore, if these expressions do lack truth values, the condition we specified for '&', which was cast in terms of 'truth', cannot be correct: 'Hz & ∃x Rzx' is built out of such expressions and, indeed, is one itself.

First, we can specify a set D: this is the **domain** or **universe of discourse** – it contains everything that we are talking about when we use the language. The intuitive approach to quantification is clear. '∃xFx' is a true sentence of L_2 if at least one object in D belongs to the extension of 'F'; '∃x ∃y Rxy' is true so long as at least one pair of objects in D belongs to the extension of 'R'; '∀x Gx' is true if every object in D belongs to the extension of 'G'. The difficulties in the way of developing this idea emerge when we try to explain the truth conditions of sentences which involve more than one quantifier, such as '∃x ∀y Rxy', and those which contain connectives occurring within the scope of quantifiers, like '∀z(Hz & ∃x Rxz)'. The following is just one way to meet these difficulties. The strategy is to abandon the task of specifying truth conditions for sentences *directly*. Rather, we introduce a more primitive semantic notion of **satisfaction**, and then we define 'truth' in terms of satisfaction.

The problems to be faced here are largely technical, and it is not possible to go into the mathematical details here. However, it is possible to introduce some of the underlying concepts involved. Although variables do not refer to things as names or demonstrative expressions do, we can always (quite arbitrarily) allocate objects from the universe of discourse to the different variables. We shall call the result of doing this an **assignment** – it assigns values to all of the variables. It is evident that many different assignments could be constructed allocating different objects to the variables employed in the language.

We say that one of these assignments **satisfies** an open sentence if we should obtain a true sentence were we to replace the variables by names of the objects that the assignment allocates to them. For example, consider the open sentence

x is a city.

An assignment which allocated London to the variable '*x*' would satisfy this open sentence, since 'London is a city' is true. However, an assignment which allocated Brutus or the moon to this variable would not satisfy it. This close connection between satisfaction and truth should make it clear that an assignment will satisfy a **disjunctive** (*or*) sentence only if it satisfies at least one of the **disjuncts** (clauses held together by *or*). It will satisfy a **conjunctive** (*and*) sentence only if it satisfies both of the **conjuncts** (clauses held together by *and*).

We can then reformulate our statement of the truth conditions of simple quantified sentences. The existentially quantified sentence '∃*x* F*x*' is true so long as at least one assignment satisfies the open sentence 'F*x*'. If there is an assignment which allocates London to *x*, then at least one assignment satisfies '*x* is a city'; so 'Something is a city' is true. In similar vein, '∀*x* F*x*' is true if every assignment satisfies 'F*x*'. So far, this simply appears to be a complicated restatement of the truth conditions for quantified sentences described above. The importance of the approach through satisfaction, as well as the mathematical complexity, emerges when we turn to sentences involving more than one quantifier. Consider the sentence 'Someone admires every logician'. Its logical form can be expressed:

∃*x* ∀*y*(L*y*→*x*A*y*).

Under what circumstances would that be true?

As a first step, we can see that it is true so long as at least one assignment satisfies the open sentence:

∀*y*(L*y*→*x*A*y*).

But when does an assignment satisfy an open sentence containing a universal quantifier? We cannot say that every assignment must satisfy 'L*y*→*x*A*y*': that will be true only if *everybody* admires every logician, and so does not capture the truth conditions of the sentence that interests us. Rather, we have to say that an assignment satisfies our universally quantified open sentence so long as every assignment that agrees with it in what it allocates to '*x*' satisfies 'L*y*→*x*A*y*'. Our sentence is true so long as a large number of assignments satisfy 'L*y*→*x*A*y*' which have the following properties:

1 Each one allocates the same object to '*x*'.
2 Every member of the universe of discourse is assigned to '*y*' by at least one of them.

This provides only an illustration of the use that is made of the concept of satisfaction in formal semantics. More complete, and more rigorous treatments can be found in the works referred to in the suggestions for further reading. It illustrates how truth-conditional semantics can be extended beyond the fragment of a language where all of the subsentential expressions occurring in sentences have either truth values, references, or extensions.

TENSE AND MODALITY

I shall now briefly indicate how the semantic apparatus is extended to apply to L_2T and L_2TM: these are L_2 supplemented with tense operators and modal operators respectively (see FORMAL LOGIC AND MODAL LOGIC, pp. 134–5). L_2T contains the tense operators 'P' (it was the case that . . .) and 'F' (it will be the case that . . .). L_2M contains the modal operators 'L' (necessarily) and 'M' (possibly). In order to avoid forbidding complexity, we shall ignore problems that arise when we combine tense or modality with quantification. This means that we shall be able to consider the truth conditions of sentences without explaining these in terms of conditions of satisfaction.

Tensed language introduces the possibility that what is true when uttered at one time may be false when uttered at other times. Hence the truth predicate we need in our metalanguage if we are to describe the truth conditions of tensed sentences involves the idea of a sentence being true at a time:

'It is raining' is a true sentence of English at noon on 1 January 1991.

Similarly, we shall talk of expressions being satisfied by assignments at certain times and not at others. We can introduce a set T of moments: we order the members of T using the relational expression ' < ': '$t_1 < t_2$' means that t_1 (a member of T) is earlier than t_2. Unless time is in some way circular, this relation will be transitive, asymmetric, and irreflexive (see SET THEORY, pp. 404–5).

We shall also have to introduce more complexity into our extensions for predicates and relations. A car may be red at one time, and then be painted blue, so it does not unequivocally belong to the extension of 'red'. The extension of 'red' will be a set of ordered pairs, each pair consisting of an object and a time: $<a, t_3>$ will belong to the extension of 'red' if object a was red at time t_3. (Alternatively, we could retain a set of objects as the extension of 'red' and insist that a predicate will have a different extension at different times.) Similarly, the extension of the relation 'loves' will be a set of ordered triples, comprising two individuals and a time such that the first individual loved the second individual at that time.

The idea behind the semantics for tense is straightforward. 'PA' is true at a time if 'A' is true at some earlier time: 'FA' is true at a time if 'A' is true at a later time. More formally:

'PA' is true at t_n if, and only if, $\exists t_m (t_m < t_n$ & 'A' is true at t_m)

'FA' is true at t_n if, and only if, $\exists t_m (t_n < t_m$ & 'A' is true at t_m)

On this basis, we can account for the truth conditions of complex tensed sentences, especially when quantification is introduced.

The semantics for modality is analogous to that for tense. We can all conceive that the world might have been very different from the way it actually is: there are countless 'ways the world could have been'. Many sentences will have different truth values in these different **possible worlds**. Just as we have seen that the truth value of a sentence can vary from time to time, so it can vary from possible world to possible world. We make use of a set W of possible worlds, whose members, $w_1, w_2, \ldots w_n, \ldots$, include the actual world together with many others that are 'merely' possible. Just as tensed discourse led us to recognize that we should only talk of the truth value of a sentence at a time, so modal discourse leads us to relativize truth to a world:

S is a true sentence of L at t in w.

The intuitive idea is again straightforward. 'MA' is true in a world w if 'A' is true in at least one possible world, but not necessarily w itself. Once again we may have to adjust the semantic values of predicates: the extension of 'red' is extended into a set of ordered triples, which will serve as its **intension**. Each triple will consist in an object, a time and a world. $<o, t_n, w_n>$ belongs to the extension of 'red' if object o is red at time t_n in world w_n. Statements of truth conditions are again relativized:

'Fa' is true at t_n in w_n if, and only if, $<$ref(a), t_n, $w_n>$ belongs to the extension of 'F'.

'LA' is true at t_n in w_n if, and only if, 'A' is true at t_n in every world.
etc.

There is a large number of systems of modal logic and tense logic that have been described and studied in the literature. For example, systems of tense logic vary according to their conception of the members of the set of moments T, and of the relation between moments ' < '. Thus, there are systems which describe the structure of discrete time and others which assume that time is densely ordered; other systems allow for circular time or for the possibility that time branches. Modal logicians usually define a relation on the class of worlds which is analogous to ' < '. This is often called an **accessibility relation** or an **alternativeness relation**. If we express this relation 'R', then the truth conditions of sentences involving modal operators are expressed:

'LA' is true at t_n in w_n if, and only if, A is true at t_n in every world w_m such that w_nRw_m,

'MA' is true at t_n in w_n if, and only if, there is a world w_m such that w_nRw_m and 'A' is true in w_m.

This relation has no natural expression corresponding to the reading of '$<$' as 'earlier than'. However, examination of the structure of the class of world in this way has yielded insights into the understanding of sentences involving several iterated modal operators. Chellas (1980) or Hughes and Cresswell (1968) provide detailed introductions to the use of these techniques in studying the semantics of modal logics.

Many logicians have been occupied with extending this framework to account for a much larger fragment of English. The literature contains explorations of the semantics of adjectives and adverbs, the semantics of **subjunctive conditionals**, words like 'ought' and 'may', and sentences involving mental-state words such as 'believes' and 'desires'.

C.H.

SUGGESTIONS FOR FURTHER READING

Bridge, J. (1977), *Beginning Model Theory*, Oxford, Oxford University Press.

Lewis, D. (1983), 'General Semantics', in *Philosophical Papers*, vol. 1, Oxford, Oxford University Press.

McCawley, J.D. (1981), *Everything that Linguists have Always Wanted to Know about Logic: . . . But were Ashamed to Ask*, Oxford, Basil Blackwell.

Functional grammar

This article focuses mainly on functional grammar as developed by M.A.K. Halliday (see Halliday, 1985) and it should be read in conjunction with those on SCALE AND CATEGORY GRAMMAR and SYSTEMIC GRAMMAR. While Halliday's version of systemic grammar contains a functional component, and while the theory behind functional grammar is systemic, Halliday (1985) concentrates exclusively on the functional part of grammar 'that is, the interpretation of the grammatical patterns in terms of configurations of functions' (Foreword, p. x); these, according to Halliday, are particularly relevant to the analysis of text, where, by **text**, Halliday means 'everything that is said or written' (Introduction, p. xiv). The focus here is on language in use, and, indeed, Halliday (ibid.) defines a **functional grammar** as 'essentially a "natural" grammar, in the sense that everything in it can be explained, ultimately, by reference to how language is used'.

Halliday's functional grammar is not a formal grammar; indeed, he opposes the term 'functional' to the term 'formal'. In this respect, it differs from the **functional grammar** developed by S.C. Dik (1978), summarized in Dik (1980), and from Kay's (1984, 1985) functional unification grammar (see FUNCTIONAL UNIFICATION GRAMMAR). All three types of functional grammar, however, display some influence from Prague School linguistics, and Dik's description of 'a functional view of natural language' differs from Halliday's in terminology only, if at all (1980, p. 46):

A language is regarded in the first place as an instrument by means of which people can enter into communicative relations with one other [*sic*]. From this point of view language is primarily a pragmatic phenomenon – a symbolic instrument used for communicative purposes.

However, while Halliday's functional grammar

begins from the premise that language has certain functions for its users as a social group, so that it is primarily sociolinguistic in nature, Dik concentrates on speakers' competence, seing his grammar as (1980, p. 47) 'a theory of the grammatical component of communicative competence'. The notion of **communicative competence** derives from Hymes (1971a). It consists of **grammatical competence**, the speaker's ability to form and interpret sentences, and **pragmatic competence**, the ability to use expressions to achieve a desired communicative effect. Dik shares, in some measure, Chomsky's view of grammar as a part of cognitive psychology. Halliday makes no separation of grammatical and pragmatic competence; he sees grammar as a **meaning potential** shared by a language and its speakers.

Dik's functional grammar falls within the broad framework of transformational-generative grammar, but differs from it in that it does not allow underlying constituent order to differ from surface constituent order, and in that it does not allow constituents which are not present in surface structure to be posited at some point in the derivation (Moravcsik, 1980, p. 11). It begins a description of a linguistic expression with the construction of an **underlying predication** consisting of **terms**, which can be used to refer to items in the world, inserted in **predicate frames**, schemata which specify a predicate and an outline of the structures in which it can occur. Dik calls the set of terms and the set of predicate frames the **fund** of the language. A predicate frame for *walk* looks like this (Dik, 1980, p. 52):

$$walk_V \ (x_1: \text{animate}(x_1))_{Ag}$$

It says that *walk* is a verbal predicate (V) which takes one argument (x_1). The argument has the Agent function (Ag) and must be animate. In addition to predicate frames, the grammar has a lexicon consisting of **basic terms** such as *John*, which is specified as being a proper noun, animate, human, and male. It is hence an appropriate term for insertion into the predicate frame for *walk*, and this insertion will result in a predication. Non-simple terms can be formed by **term formation**. The predication is mapped onto

the form of the expression by means of rules which determine the form and the order of constituents.

It is not possible to deal in further detail with Dik's functional grammar here. It represents an interesting attempt at taking full account of the factors which guide speakers' use of language, their **performance**, within a framework of a formal grammatical system which was originally developed with competence alone in mind.

Halliday's functional grammar is based on the premise that language has two major functions, **metafunctions**, for its users; it is a means of reflecting on things, and a means of acting on things – though the only things it is possible to act on by means of a symbolic system such as language are humans (and some animals). Halliday calls these two functions the **ideational 'content' function** and the **interpersonal function**. Both these functions rely on a third, the **textual function**, which enables the other two to be realized, and which ensures that the language used is relevant. The textual function represents the language user's text forming potential.

Halliday's systemic theory, which, as mentioned above, underlies his functional grammar, 'is a theory of *meaning as choice*' (1985, p. xiv, my italics), and, for Halliday, grammar is always seen as meaningful (p. xvii):

> A language . . . is a system for making meanings: a semantic system, with other systems for encoding the meanings it produces. The term 'semantics' does not simply refer to the meanings of words; it is the entire system of meanings of a language, expressed by grammar as well as by vocabulary. In fact the meanings are encoded in 'wordings': grammatical sequences, or 'syntagms', consisting of items of both kinds – lexical items such as most verbs and nouns, grammatical items like *the* and *of* and *if*, as well as those of an in between type such as prepositions.

The ideational, interpersonal, and textual functions are therefore functional components of the semantic system that is language. The grammar enables all three of them to come into play at every point of every text: it receives meanings from each component and splices them together in the wordings, as Halliday shows through his analysis of the clause in English. The clause is chosen because it is the grammatical unit in which 'three distinct structures, each expressing one kind of semantic organization, are mapped onto one another to produce a single wording' (1985, p. 38; and p. 53):

> Ideational meaning is the representation of experience: our experience of the world that lies about us, and also inside us, the world of our imagination. It is meaning in the sense of 'content'. The ideational function of the **clause** is that of representing what in the broadest sense we can call 'processes': actions, events, processes of consciousness, and relations. . . .
>
> Interpersonal meaning is meaning as a form of action: the speaker or writer doing something to the listener or reader by means of language, The interpersonal function of the **clause** is that of exchanging roles in rhetorical interaction: statements, questions, offers and commands, together with accompanying modalities. . . .
>
> Textual meaning is relevance to the context: both the preceding (and following) text, and the context of situation. The textual function of the **clause** is that of constructing a message.

The message is constructed in the English clause in terms of theme and rheme. One element of the clause is given the special status of **theme** by being put first, and it then combines with the rest of the clause to constitute the message; other languages mark theme by other means; for instance, Japanese uses the suffix *-wa* to signify that whatever it follows is the theme (1985, p. 38). The theme is defined as 'the element which serves as the point of departure of the message; it is that with which the clause is concerned', and the rest of the message is referred to as the **rheme**; the theme is normally realized by nominal groups (examples (1), (2) and (3)) adverbial groups (5), or prepositional phrases (4).

Theme	Rheme
(1) Tomas	gave Sophie that Easter egg
(2) That Easter egg	was given to Sophie by Tomas
(3) Sophie	was given that Easter egg by Tomas
(4) At Easter	Tomas went to see Sophie and Katie
(5) Very soon	they were eating Easter eggs

Themes may, however, also be realized by clauses, as in the case of:

What Tomas gave to Sophie was an Easter egg.

However, in this case the clause *what Tomas gave to Sophie* functions as a nominal group in the whole clause; this phenomenon is referred to as **nominalization**. It is also possible to have cases of **predicated** theme having the form *it + be*, as in

It was an Easter egg that Tomas gave to Sophie.

The most usual themes in English are those realized by the grammatical subject of the clause, and these are are called **unmarked** themes; when the theme is something other than the subject, it is called **marked** theme (examples (4) and (5)).

In its interpersonal function, as an interactive event, an exchange between speakers, the clause in English is organized in terms of **mood**. Mood is the relationship between the grammatical subject of the clause and the finite element of the verbal group, with the remainder of the clause called the **residue**. So any **indicative** clause – a clause which has a subject and a finite element will have a mood structure. Subject and finite together make up the **proposition** of the clause, the part that can be affirmed, denied, questioned, and negotiated by speakers in other ways (wished about, hoped for, demanded, etc.). The grammatical subject of a declarative clause is recognizable as that element which is picked up in the pronoun of a **tag** (1985, p. 73):

> So in order to locate the Subject, add a tag (if one is not already present) and see which

element is taken up. For example, *that teapot was given to your aunt*: here the tag would be *wasn't it?* – we cannot add *wasn't she?*. On the other hand with *that teapot your aunt got from the duke* the tag would be *didn't she?*; we cannot say *didn't he?* or *wasn't it?*

It is that *by reference to which* the proposition is affirmed, denied, etc. The finite element further enhances the proposition as something to negotiate by (1) giving it a **primary tense** (past, present, future) and (2) a **modality**, an indication of the speaker's attitude in terms of certainty and obligation to what s/he is saying. Halliday represents the finite verbal operators as in Table 1 (1985, p. 75).

Table 1

Temporal operators

Past	Present	Future
did, was, had, used to	does, is, has	will, shall, would, should

Modal operators

Low	Median	High
can, may could, might	will, would, should, is to, was to	must, ought to, need, has to, had to

There are two moods within the indicative, realized through the ordering of subject and finite (1985, p. 74):

(a) The order Subject before Finite realizes 'declarative';
(b) The order Finite before Subject realized 'yes/no interrogative';
(c) In a 'WH-interrogative' the order is:
   (i) Subject before Finite if the WH-element is the Subject;
   (ii) Finite before Subject otherwise. . . .

(a) declarative

the duke	has	given that teapot away
Subject	Finite	
Mood		Residue

(b) yes/no interrogative

has	the duke	given that teapot away
Finite	Subject	
Mood		Residue

Examples of (c) would be:

(c.i)

who	gave	you that teapot
Subject	Finite	
Mood		Residue

(c.ii)

why	were	you	given that teapot
WH	Finite	Subject	
	Mood		
Residue			

In a third mood, the **imperative**, the subject is often missing, as in *Go away!* Halliday chooses to treat this absence as a case of **ellipsis** of the subject, that is, the subject is understood to be there, but is not explicitly mentioned; the hearer supplies it mentally. Sinclair (1972, p. 71) recognizes a fourth mood choice, **moodless**, made in clauses which have neither subject nor finite (which Sinclair treats as part of the predicator), as in the case of announcements (*Rotunda next stop*) and responses (*yes/no*).

The clause residue consists of three kinds of functional element: one (and only one) **predicator**, one or two **complements** and up to about seven **adjuncts**. The predicator is what there is of the verbal group in addition to the finite – if there is one; some clauses, known as **non-finite clauses**, have only a predicator 'for example *eating her curds and whey* (following *Little Miss Muffet sat on a tuffet*)' (Halliday, 1985, p. 78). It has four functions (ibid., p. 79):

(i) It specifies time reference **other than** reference to the time of the speech event, i.e. 'secondary' tense: past, present or future relative to the primary tense. . . . (ii) It specifies various other aspects and phases like seeming, trying, hoping. . . . (iii) It specifies the voice: active or passive. . . . (iv) It specifies the process (action, event, mental process, relation) that is predicated of the Subject. These can be exemplified from the verbal group *has been trying to be heard*, where the Predicator, *been trying to be heard*, expresses (i) a complex secondary tense, *been + ing*; (ii) a conative phase, *try + to*; (iii) passive voice, *be + -d*; (iv) the mental process *hear*.

The **complement** is anything that could have functioned as the subject in the clause, but which does not, including, thus, nominal groups realizing what other grammarians tend to refer to as direct and indirect objects, and also what Halliday refers to as **attributive** complement: for instance, *a famous politician* in *Dick Whittington became a famous politician*.

The **adjunct**(s) include those elements which do not have the potential of being used as subjects.

In its ideational function, as representation, the clause is structured in terms of processes, participants, and circumstances. These are specified through choices in the **transitivity system**. A **process** consists potentially of three components (1985, p. 101):

(i) the process itself;
(ii) participants in the process;
(iii) circumstances associated with the process.

Typically, these elements are realized as follows:

processes by verbal groups; participants by nominal groups; and circumstances by adverbial groups or prepositional phrases.

Halliday lists three principal types of process: **material processes**, processes of doing, have an obligatory **actor**, someone who does something, and an optional **goal**, 'one to which the process is extended' (1985, p. 103). When both are present, the clause is **transitive**; when only the actor is present it is **intransitive**. **Mental processes**, of feeling, thinking, and perceiving, have an obligatory **senser** and an obligatory **phenomenon**, although the phenomenon need not be present in the clause; it may only be there implicitly. **Relational processes** are processes of being, and there are six types of these in English (Table 2).

Any relational-process clause in the **attributive mode** contains two participants, **carrier** and **attribute**; one in the **identifying mode** contains **identified** and **identifier**. There are several further subdivisions of process and participant types (see Halliday, 1985, Ch. 5).

The principal circumstantial elements of clauses in English are (1985, p. 137): 'Extent and Location in time and space, including abstract space; Manner (means, quality and comparison); Cause (reason, purpose and behalf); Accompaniment; Matter; Role.' Again these are further subdivided.

Halliday (1971), in which choices in the transitivity system, in particular, are explored, is a fine illustration of the claim that functional grammar is particularly well suited to text analysis (see STYLISTICS).

Table 2

mode / type	(i) attributive	(ii) identifying
(1) intensive	Sarah is wise	Tom is the leader; the leader is Tom
(2) circumstantial	the fair is on Tuesday	tomorrow is the 10th; the 10th is tomorrow
(3) possessive	Peter has a piano	the piano is Peter's; Peter's is the piano

Source: Halliday 1985, p. 113

Halliday (1985) further explores grammatical functions above, below, and beyond the clause. Halliday (1978) relates both his grammatical theory and his theory of first-language acquisition (see LANGUAGE ACQUISITION) to an account of how language relates to the world in which it is used, thus producing one of the most comprehensive theories of language as a social phenomenon (see also CRITICAL LINGUISTCS).

K.M.

SUGGESTIONS FOR FURTHER READING

Dik, S.C. (1978), *Functional Grammar*, (North-Holland Linguistic Series; no. 37), Amsterdam, North-Holland.

Halliday, M.A.K. (1985), *An Introduction to Functional Grammar*, London, Edward Arnold.

Functional phonology

By **functional phonology** is normally meant the phonological theory predominantly associated with the Russian, Nikolaj Sergeyevich Trubetzkoy (1890–1938). This theory is also known as **Prague School phonology**, and there exists a fair amount of literature on it. Much less has been written in English about the functional-phonological theory developed by the Frenchman André Martinet (1908–) and his associates. Both streams of functional phonology are founded on linguistic functionalism (see FUNCTIONALIST LINGUISTICS) and have much in common.

Functionalists study phonic elements from the points of view of the various functions they fulfil in a given language. They identify and order these functions hierarchically. Some of the better-known functions are the following:

1 The **representative function**, whereby speakers inform listeners of whatever extralinguistic facts or states they are talking about. This corresponds to what the Austrian psychologist–linguist, Karl Bühler (1879–1963) – a member of the Prague Linguistic Circle – calls *Darstellungsfunktion*.

2 The **indexical** or expressive function (Bühler's *Kundgabefunktion* or *Ausdrucksfunktion*), whereby information is revealed to the listener about various aspects of the speaker. For example, British speakers who consistently use in their pronunciation of, e.g., *mate* a monophthongal vowel (e.g. [eː] which is very close to cardinal vowel no. 2 – see ARTICULATORY PHONETICS) instead of the corresponding diphthongal vowel ([ei]) thereby reveal that their geographical provenance is northern England or Scotland. A speaker of Chukchi of north-eastern Asia who pronounces [tʃ] reveals himself as an adult male while another Chukchi speaker who pronounces [ts] in its place shows herself/himself as an adult female or a child. The indexical function may further impart information about the speaker's socioeconomic status, occupation, degrees of formal education, etc.

3 The **appellative** or **conative function** (Bühler's *Appellfunktion*), which serves to provoke well-definable impressions or feelings in the listener. For example, an imperative tone in which a military order is given by a superior officer urges soldiers to undertake a certain action. Or, a specific intonation with which an utterance is made may have the effect of inducing the listener to carry out or not to carry out a certain act.

4 The **distinctive function**. This is a function which derives directly from the concept of opposition, and in the case of phonological analysis, from the concept of phonological opposition. It is the function by virtue of which linguistic forms are opposed to, or differentiated from, each other. The minimal linguistic form that is meaningful, or the minimal significant unit, is known as a **moneme**, which consists in the association between a **signifier** (vocal expression) and a **signified** (semantic content). For example, in English, *bet* and *bit* are monemes whose signifiers and signifieds are, respectively, /bet/ and 'bet', and /bɪt/ and 'bit'. Two further examples of monemes are *spell* and *smell*, whose signifiers and signifieds are, respectively, /s p–b e l/ (where /p–b/ is an **archiphoneme** – see below) and 'spell', and /smel/ and 'smell'. The members of the former pair are phonologically distinguished by virtue of the opposition between /e/ in *bet* and /ɪ/ in *bit*, and those of the latter pair by virtue of the opposition between /p–b/ and /m/. Conventionally, the letters enclosed by two diagonal lines stand for sequentially minimal distinctive units which may be phonemes (e.g. /b/ above) or archiphonemes (e.g. /p–b/ above). We say that a phoneme or an archiphoneme fulfils the distinctive function. Similarly, in a tone language (see TONE LANGUAGES), each of the tones fulfils the distinctive function, so that, for example, / ˉma/ 'mother' and / ′ma/ 'hemp' in Mandarin Chinese are phonologically differentiated from each other by virtue of the opposition between / ˉ/ (a high level tone) and / ′/ (a high rise from a mid-high level). Of course, a tone language also possesses phonemes and archiphonemes, so that, for example, / ˉma/ and / ˉta/ 'it, he, she' are differentiated from each other by virtue of the opposition between /m/ and /t/, while / ˉṣ i–y/ 'teacher' and / ˉṣu/ 'book' are distinguished from each other by virtue of the opposition between /i–y/ and /u/. Note that a phoneme, an archiphoneme, a tone or an architone has no meaning. The distinctive function is an indispensable phonological function in any given language.

5 The **contrastive function** (Martinet's *fonction contrastive*, Trubetzkoy's **kulminative Funktion**), which enables the listener to analyse a spoken chain into a series of significant units like monemes, words, phrases, etc. An accent in a language functions contrastively by bringing into prominence one, and only one, syllable in what is called an accentual unit. Since an accentual unit is in many languages (e.g., Polish, Spanish, Russian, Italian) what is commonly referred to as a word, the listener automatically analyses a spoken chain into a series of words. However, in such a language as German which allows cumulative compounding in word-formation, a compound word may consist of a number of elements, each of which bears an accent. To consider just one example, in the German word *Kleiderpflegeanstalt* 'valet service', each element (*Kleider-*, *-pflege-*, *-anstalt*) receives an accent, but with a hierarchy in the strength of the accent, so that the accent in *Kleider-* is the strongest, that in *-anstalt* less strong, and that in *-pflege-* the least strong. What is meant by the term **contrastive** is that the accented syllable contrasts with (stands out in relation to) the unaccented syllable(s) and thus characterizes the accentual unit as a whole.

6 The **demarcative** or **delimitative function**, which is fulfilled in such a way that the boundary between significant units is indicated. For example, in German, the phoneme sequence /nm/ reveals a boundary as existing between /n/ and /m/, since in this language no word either begins or ends with /nm/. The word *unmöglich* is a case in point, *un* being one significant unit (here a moneme) and *möglich* another significant unit (here a combination of monemes). In Tamil, to consider another language, an aspirated voiceless plosive occurs in word-initial position only. Consider, for example, *talai* [tʰ] 'head', *pontu* [-ḍ-] 'hole', *katu* [-ð-] 'ear'. The three different sounds are all realizations of one and the same phoneme /t̪/. The occurrence of the aspirated voiceless plosive in this language therefore indicates the boundary between the word which begins with it and the preceding word. Another example of a phonic feature functioning demarcatively is a fixed accent, i.e. an accent whose place in the accentual unit is always fixed in relation to (as the case may be) the beginning or end of the accentual unit. A fixed accent

functions not only contrastively but also demarcatively. An accent in Swahili always falls on
the last but one syllable of the accentual unit
which corresponds to a word, so that the occurrence of the accent shows that the following
word begins with the second syllable after the
accented syllable. Likewise, an accent in Finnish,
which is a fixed accent always falling on the initial
syllable of the accentual unit that corresponds to
a word, reveals that the word boundary occurs
between the accented syllable and the preceding
syllable. Of course, a free accent (i.e. one which is
not fixed) can only function contrastively and not
demarcatively as well.

7 The **expressive function**, whereby speakers
convey to listeners their state of mind (real or
feigned) without resorting to the use of an
additional moneme or monemes. For example,
a speaker of English may say 'That tree is
eNNNormous', overlengthening /n/ and employing an exaggerated high fall pitch over -nor-,
instead of saying 'That tree is absolutely enormous' or 'That tree is tremendously enormous',
employing the additional monemes *absolute* and
ly, or *tremendous* and *ly*. The specific
suprasegmental phonic elements just mentioned
fulfil the expressive function in that they indicate
the speakers' admiration, surprise, etc., at the
size of the tree in question. It should be noted in
this connection that intonation pre-eminently
fulfils the expressive function in which pitch
phenomena are exploited expressively, i.e.
speakers express definiteness or lack of definiteness, certainty or uncertainty, etc., in their
minds about what they predicate.

The above are some major functions of phonic
elements (there are other, minor, ones) that are
identified in various languages. They are all
recognized as major functions, but it is possible
to establish a hierarchy of functions in terms of
their relative importance from a functional point
of view. For example, Trubetzkoy (1969, p. 28)
says that the distinctive function is indispensable
and far more important than the culminative and
deliminative functions, which are expedient but
dispensable; all functionalists agree with him on
this point.

It has been pointed out (see paragraph 4
above) that the distinctive function derives directly from the concept of phonological opposition and that the distinctive function is
fulfilled by a phoneme, an archiphoneme, a tone
or an architone. As mentioned above, the
distinctive function is considered to be by far the
most important function, and in what follows we
shall be exclusively concerned with some aspects
of functional phonology which are relevant to
this function.

It is crucial to understand that, in functional
phonology, the concept of **phonological opposition** is primary, while the concept of the
phoneme is secondary; without a phonological
opposition, phonemes are inconceivable and
inadmissible; the concept of the phoneme derives
its validity from the fact that phonemes are
members of a phonological opposition. The
concept of phonological opposition is thus at the
centre of functional phonology.

A **phoneme** or an **archiphoneme** is a sum of
phonologically relevant features – relevant features for short – which themselves fulfil the
distinctive function. (Relevant features should
not be confused with distinctive features as
employed in generative phonology – see DISTINC-
TIVE FEATURES.) For example, the English
monemes *bark* and *mark*, or *park* and *mark*, are
distinguished from each other by virtue of the
opposition between /b/ and /m/, or between /p/
and /m/. Furthermore, /b/ and /m/, or /p/ and
/m/, are distinguished from each other because of
the opposition between the relevant features
'non-nasal' and 'nasal'. An opposition between
phonemes, between phonemes and archiphonemes, between archiphonemes, between relevant features, or between tones, is said to be a
phonological opposition. The inventory of the
distinctive units of a given language comprises
the phonemes and the archiphonemes, and the
tones as well in the case of a tone language. A
phoneme or an archiphoneme is realized by
sounds, generally referred to as **variants** or
realizations, each of which possesses the phonologically relevant phonic features which characterize the phoneme or the archiphoneme concerned, plus phonologically irrelevant features.

The same is true of realizations of a tone, except that these are pitches. Variants too are identified in terms of their functions, so that the functionalist talks about, for example, **combinatory variants** (variants associated with specific phonetic contexts in which they occur), **individual variants** (variants endowed with the indexical function), **stylistic variants** (variants indicative of different styles of speech), etc. These variants are also hierarchically identified according to their different functions in the phonology of a given language.

The **phonemes** and the **archiphonemes** of a given language are identified at the same time as mutually different sums of relevant features in terms of which they are definable, by means of the **commutation test**. In order to perform the commutation test, the functionalist chooses from within a corpus of data a certain number of **commutative series** which are associated with different phonetic contexts and each of which consists of a series of monemes, arranged in a parallel order, whose signifiers differ minimally from each other by the difference of a single segment at a corresponding point while the rest are identical.

Let us suppose that functionalists have at their disposal a corpus of English data. Let us also suppose that they have selected the following commutative series: commutative series 1, associated with the phonetic context [-ɪn], consisting of *pin, bin, tin, din, sin, zinn(ia), fin, vin(cible)*, etc.; commutative series 2, associated with the phonetic context [mæ-], consisting of *map, Mab, mat, mad, mass, Maz(da), maf(ia), mav(erick)*, etc.; commutative series 3, associated with the phonetic context [ʌ-ə], consisting of *upper, (r)ubber, utter, udder, (t)usser, (b)uzzer, (s)uffer, (c)over*, etc. More commutative series are, of course, available, but the three we have chosen will suffice to illustrate the commutation test here.

As functionalists go on to consider more and more different commutative series, a point of diminishing return is reached fairly soon. In commutative series 1 above, we can see that [p] is differentiated from [b], [t], [d], [s], [z], [f], [v], etc., and that in commutative series 2, [p] is differ-

entiated from [b], [t], [d], [s], [z], [f], [v], etc.: the phonetic differences between these segments are similarly minimal across the different commutative series. It will also be seen that, for example, [p] in commutative series 1 differs from [m] in the same series by the same phonetic difference that distinguishes [p] in commutative series 2 from [m] in that series, and furthermore, [p] in commutative series 3 from [m] in that series. The phonetic difference consists in the opposition between non-nasality (in [p]) and nasality (in [m]). Comparison between [p] and [t] in all three commutative series reveals bilabiality ascribable to [p] and apicality ascribable to [t].

Similarly, comparison between [p] and [b] in all three commutative series reveals voicelessness ascribable to [p] and voicedness ascribable to [b]. The latter phonetic difference needs some clarification, which will be provided below when the internal structure of a relevant feature is explained.

On the basis of this commutation test, functionalists identify, among other relevant features, the relevant features 'non-nasal', 'bilabial', and 'voiceless', the sum of which constitutes the phoneme /p/. Similarly, the sum of 'non-nasal', 'bilabial', and 'voiced' constitutes the phoneme /b/; the sum of 'non-nasal', 'apical', and 'voiceless' constitutes the phoneme /t/; the sum of 'non-nasal', 'apical', and 'voiced' constitutes the phoneme /d/; and so on. What have been referred to above as [p]s in the different commutative series are realizations of one and the same phoneme /p/. Likewise, other segments are realizations of other given phonemes.

If functionalists identify [b]s (correctly, [b̥]s, i.e. devoiced) in commutative series 1 and 2 as realizations of the same phoneme (/b/) whose realization is [b] (voiced) in commutative series 3, rather than as a realization of a different phoneme (/p/) whose realizations in all three commutative series are voiceless ([pʰ] or [p]), this is *not* because of phonetic similarity or orthography or functionalists' linguistic consciousness but because of the identical proportional relation of distinction that exists between [b]s and other segments in each of the different commutative series. The principle of the commutation test fundamentally and closely resembles that of the theory of the **micro-phoneme** and the **macro-phoneme** proposed in 1935 by the American linguist, William Freeman Twaddell (1906–82).

A **relevant feature** is identified in the course of the commutation test performed on a corpus of data obtained from a given language under phonological analysis. Unlike **distinctive features** with which generative phonology operates (see DISTINCTIVE FEATURES), there is no universal framework of relevant features set up *a priori* and applicable to any language. Furthermore, the **internal structure** of a relevant feature is a complex of multiple non-dissociable distinctive phonic features some of which may be present in some phonetic contexts while others may not be present in other phonetic contexts. Here lies a difference between a relevant feature on the one hand and a distinctive feature *à la* generative phonology on the other, since the latter refers to a single phonic feature. Yet another difference is that a relevant feature is not **binary**, while a distinctive feature in generative phonology always is. Thus, for example, the relevant features 'nasal' (as in /m/) and 'non-nasal' (as in /p/ and /b/) in English consonant phonemes which are opposed to each other are two different relevant features, and should never be confused with [+ nasal] and [− nasal] as used in generative phonology, where they are seen as deriving from the single distinctive feature, [nasal]. It goes without saying that, for example, the relevant features 'bilabial' (as in /p/), 'apical' (as in /t/), velar' as in /k/), etc., in English consonant phonemes which are opposed to each other are not binary.

We shall now look in some detail at the question of the **internal structure** of a relevant feature. For example, the relevant feature 'bi-labial' in English consists of not only the bilabial closure, but also all the other concomitant physiological phenomena occurring in the oral and pharyngeal cavities. To consider another example, the relevant feature 'voiced' (in, e.g., /b/) in English is a complex of glottal vibration, a relatively lax muscular tension in the supra-glottal vocal tract and all the other con-comitantly occurring physiological phenomena

when, e.g., /b/ is opposed to /p/, /d/ is opposed to /t/, /z/ is opposed to /s/, and so on. Glottal vibration is partially or entirely absent when /b/, /d/, /z/, etc., occur in postpausal or prepausal position (e.g., in *bark*, *cab*, etc.), but this does not change 'voiced' into 'voiceless' nor does it give primacy to the phonic feature **fortis** (i.e. relatively great muscular tension) which is opposed to the phonic feature **lenis**, over voicelessness, or even to the exclusion of voicelessness.

Such absence of a certain phonic feature is dictated by a particular phonetic context in which the relevant feature occurs, for the voicedness does occur in all those different phonic contexts that are favourable to voicing – say, in intervocalic position. A relevant feature in a given language is identified, in spite of any minor variation observed in terms of the presence or absence of some of its multiple non-dissociable distinctive phonic features, as a unitary entity which phonologically functions as a single global unit in opposition to another or other relevant features in the same language, which also functions or function phonologically as a single global unit or units. The term **non-dissociable** used in definitionally characterizing the relevant feature is therefore to be taken in this particular sense and not in the sense of 'constant'.

It may be the case that the common base of the member phonemes of a phonological opposition in a given language is *not* found in any other phoneme(s) of the same language. For example, in English, /m/ (defined as 'bilabial nasal'), /n/ ('apical nasal'), and /ŋ/ ('velar nasal') share the common base, 'nasal', which is not found in any other phoneme(s) of this language. In such a case, the phonemes are said to be **in an exclusive relation**; that is, the common base is **exclusive** to the phonemes in question. Some functionalists suggest the term **exclusive opposition** to designate conveniently this type of phonological opposition, whose member phonemes are in an exclusive relation. An exclusive opposition is of particular importance in functional phonology, as we shall see below.

On the other hand, it may be the case that the common base of the member phonemes of a phonological opposition in a given language *is* found in another or other phonemes of the same language. For example, again in English, /p/ ('voiceless bilabial non-nasal') and /t/ ('voiceless apical non-nasal') share the common base 'voiceless non-nasal' which is also found in /k/ ('voiceless velar non-nasal') of this language. In such a case, /p/ and /t/ are said to be in a **non-exclusive relation**, and some functionalists suggest the term **non-exclusive opposition** to designate conveniently this type of phonological opposition, whose member phonemes are in a non-exclusive relation.

The common base of the phonemes of an exclusive opposition (but not of a non-exclusive opposition) is the **archiphoneme**, which may be defined as the sum of the relevant features of the (two or more) phonemes of an exclusive opposition.

An exclusive opposition may or may not be a **neutralizable opposition**. However, a neutralizable opposition is bound to be an exclusive opposition; it is never a non-exclusive opposition. This brings us to the concept of **neutralization**, which may be illustrated as follows. In English, /m/–/n/–/ŋ/ (that is, the opposition between /m/, /n/, and /ŋ/) is operative in, say, moneme-final position (cf. *rum* v. *run* v. *rung*). It is, however, not operative e.g. moneme-medially before /k/ (cf. *anchor*) or /g/ (cf. *anger*), that is, there is no possibility of having /m/–/n/–/ŋ/ in such a position. According to functionalists, /m/–/n/–/ŋ/ which is operative in moneme-final position (the position of relevance for this phonological opposition) is neutralized in the position describable as 'moneme-medially before /k/ or /g/' (the position of neutralization for this phonological opposition). This neutralization results from the fact that the opposition between the relevant features 'bilabial' (in /m/), 'apical' (in /n/), and 'velar' (in /ŋ/), which is valid in moneme-final position, is cancelled (note, not 'neutralized') moneme-medially before /k/ or /g/. What is phonologically valid in the latter position is the common base of /m/, /n/, and /ŋ/, which is none other than the archiphoneme /m–n–ŋ/, definable as 'nasal'.

/m/–/n/–/ŋ/ in English is, then, said to be a neutralizable opposition which is operative in the position of relevance but is neutralized in the position of neutralization. Since the relevant feature 'nasal', which alone characterizes the archiphoneme /m–n–ŋ/, is not found in any other phoneme in English, the opposition /m/–/n/–/ŋ/ is, of course, an exclusive opposition. The phonic feature of velarity, which characterizes the realization (i.e. [ŋ] in ['æŋka] or ['æŋga]) of this archiphoneme, is not part of its phonological characteristics; rather, the occurrence of velarity in its realization is merely dictated by the fact that /k/ or /g/ which follows the archiphoneme is phonologically velar.

The concept of neutralization presented above is largely in line with Martinet and his associates' phonological analysis. In contrast, Trubetzkoyan phonological analysis is incapable of accounting for the neutralization of /m/–/n/–/ŋ/ moneme-medially before /k/ or /g/ in English, for Trubetzkoy always presents a phonological opposition as consisting of two, and not more than two, phonemes, and operates with other phonological concepts compatible with such a concept of phonological opposition. His presentation of various types of phonological opposition (bilateral, multilateral; proportional, isolated; privative, gradual, equipollent; constant, neutralizable) is always such that a phonological opposition is formed by two phonemes. (See Trubetzkoy, 1969, pp. 67–83, for a detailed explanation of these types of phonological opposition.)

In a case where a neutralizable opposition happens to be a phonological opposition consisting of two phonemes, Trubetzkoy accounts for its neutralization in the following way. For instance, in German, /t/–/d/, which is a bilateral opposition operative in, say, moneme-initial prevocalic position (cf. *Tank*, *Dank*), is neutralized in moneme-final position (cf. *und*, *freund*(*lich*)), where only the archiphoneme is valid and is 'represented' by the unmarked member of the opposition (/t/? [t]?). The phonetic or phonological status of the archiphoneme representative is a moot point over which there exists disagreement even among functionalists. As is evident from Trubetzkoy's use of the notion of the **mark** and the associated notions of **marked** and **unmarked**, a neutralizable opposition is supposed to be a privative opposition formed by the marked and the unmarked phonemes.

Martinet and the majority, if not all, of his associates give much the same account of the neutralization of such an exclusive opposition consisting of two phonemes, except that they generally do not resort to the concept of bilateral opposition and to the concept of the archiphoneme representative. It should be noted in passing that a few functionalists do not operate with the notions of the mark, marked, and unmarked in their account of any neutralization (see Akamatsu, 1988, ch. 11).

However, it is important to note that functionalists' concept of neutralization is an inevitable consequence of their prior belief in the concept of phonological opposition. It should be mentioned in this connection that some functionalists (see Vachek, 1966, p. 62; Buyssens, 1972a, 1972b) have abandoned the concept of the archiphoneme while claiming to operate with the concept of neutralization, a stance which has come under fire from other functionalists. The debate on this issue can be pursued through the writings of Akamatsu, Buyssens, and Vion in issues of *La Linguistique* from 1972 to 1977. It is also discussed in Davidsen-Nielsen (1978) and in Akamatsu (1988).

Finally, a few words are in order about the concepts of the **mark, marked**, and **unmarked**, and the concept of **correlation**. Most functionalists consider that one of the two phonemes of a privative opposition possesses the mark and hence is marked, while the other phoneme lacks it and hence is unmarked. Thus, with regard to /d/–/t/ in English, for example, /d/ is said to possess the mark, i.e. voice, and is marked, while /t/ is said to lack it and is hence unmarked. Some

functionalists disagree with this idea (see Akamatsu, 1988, ch. 11).

A **correlation** consists of a series of bilateral privative proportional oppositions and involves the concept of the mark. For example, a partial phonological system like

$$
\begin{array}{ccc}
p & t & k \\
b & d & g
\end{array}
$$

is a simple correlation wherein /p/ and /b/, /t/ and /d/, and /k/ and /g/ are said to be **correlative pairs**; /p/, /t/, and /k/ are said to be unmarked while /b/, /d/, and /g/ are said to be marked, the mark of correlation being voice. Furthermore, for example, a partial phonological system like

$$
\begin{array}{ccc}
p & t & k \\
b & d & g \\
m & n & \eta
\end{array}
$$

is a bundle of correlations wherein, in addition to the above-mentioned simple correlation with voice as the mark, there is a further correlation whose mark is nasality, which separates /p t k b d g/, on the one hand, and /m n ŋ/, on the other, from each other, so that the former group of phonemes is said to be unmarked and the latter marked.

T.A.

SUGGESTIONS FOR FURTHER READING

Martinet, A. (1964), *Elements of General Linguistics*, London, Faber & Faber, particularly chs 1–3.

Trubetzkoy, N.S. (1969), *Principles of Phonology*, Berkeley and Los Angeles, University of California Press, particularly chs 1, 3, 5, 6, and Part II.

Functional unification grammar

Functional unification grammar (Kay, 1984, 1985) seeks to accomplish the functionalist linguists' aim of describing language at all levels in terms of the functions it fulfils for its users (see FUNCTIONALIST LINGUISTICS and FUNCTIONAL GRAMMAR) by means of 'a clean, simple formalism' (1985, p. 253). Within the formalism, the notion of function which is employed is the mathematician's and logician's notion (see FORMAL LOGIC AND MODAL LOGIC), and the theory also draws heavily on set theory (see SET THEORY).

Functional unification grammar is a **competence grammar**; that is, a grammar written in a formalism that expresses linguistic universals, thought to constitute language users' linguistic knowledge. A separate **performance grammar** is derived from the competence grammar through a translation of its rules into a set of procedures similar to an augmented transition network grammar (see AUGMENTED TRANSITION NETWORK GRAMMAR).

The functions of functional unification grammar map attributes onto values, and its rules are formulated as **functional descriptions (FDs)**; that is, collections of attribute-value pairs. Each attribute-value pair is called a **descriptor**; in each descriptor, the attribute occurs to the left of the sign '=' and the value to the right. The set of possible attributes ranges from phonological to semantic properties. For example, for Finnish (Karttunen and Kay, 1985, p. 291), the following properties, among others, can occur as attributes:

Phonological: Emphasis
Morphological: Case, Number, Person, Tense, Voice
Semantic: Positive, Aspect, Quantity
Structural: Cat(egory), Pattern ($), Branching
Syntactic: Subject, Object, Adverb
Pragmatic: Topic, Contrast, New

Values can be either atomic designators (Yes, No, Nom, Sg, Past, NP, etc), or FDs. Typically, the values of syntactic and functional attributes are FDs.

The set of descriptors of an FD is written in square brackets. The order in which they occur is of no significance. The framework is similar to that of lexical-functional grammar (see LEXICAL-FUNCTIONAL GRAMMAR), except that functional unification grammar makes no use of phrase-structure rules to show constituent structure, so that the distinction between constituents and properties is blurred. A simple FD for the sentence *He saw her* is (Kay, 1985, p. 256):

$$
\begin{bmatrix}
\text{CAT} & = \text{S} \\
\text{SUBJ} & = \begin{bmatrix}
\text{CAT} & = \text{PRON} \\
\text{GENDER} & = \text{MASC} \\
\text{CASE} & = \text{NOM} \\
\text{NUMBER} & = \text{SING} \\
\text{PERSON} & = 3
\end{bmatrix} \\
\text{DOBJ} & = \begin{bmatrix}
\text{CAT} & = \text{PRON} \\
\text{GENDER} & = \text{FEM} \\
\text{CASE} & = \text{ACC} \\
\text{NUMBER} & = \text{SING}
\end{bmatrix} \\
\text{VERB} & = \text{SEE} \\
\text{TENSE} & = \text{PAST} \\
\text{VOICE} & = \text{ACTIVE}
\end{bmatrix}
$$

The FD above describes the 'surface form' of the sentence. If we reverse the values of SUBJ(ect) and D(irect)OBJ(ect), and if the value of VOICE is changed to PASSIVE, we get the grammatical FD for the sentence *She was seen by him*. In both cases, however, *he* is PROT(agonist) and *she* the GOAL. This 'deeper' or semantic structure can be captured by a semantic FD (ibid.):

$$
\begin{bmatrix}
\text{CAT} & = \text{S} \\[6pt]
\text{PROT} = &
\begin{bmatrix}
\text{CAT} & = \text{PRON} \\
\text{GENDER} & = \text{MASC} \\
\text{NUMBER} & = \text{SING} \\
\text{PERSON} & = 3
\end{bmatrix} \\[20pt]
\text{GOAL} = &
\begin{bmatrix}
\text{CAT} & = \text{PRON} \\
\text{GENDER} & = \text{FEM} \\
\text{NUMBER} & = \text{SING} \\
\text{PERSON} & = 3
\end{bmatrix} \\[20pt]
\text{VERB} & = \text{SEE} \\[6pt]
\text{TENSE} & = \text{PAST}
\end{bmatrix}
$$

Unification refers to an operation which merges the several FDs for a given linguistic entity into a single FD. The sign ' = ' is used for unification so that α = β stands for the result of unifying α and β. Unification of the two FDs shown above produces the FD below (Kay, 1985, p. 257).

Each string of atoms within square brackets is a **path**. At least one path identifies every value in an FD. Paths begin in the largest FD which encloses them. Attributes otherwise belong to the smallest enclosing FD. A pair consisting of a path in an FD and the value that the path leads to is a **feature** of the object described. If the value is a symbol, the pair is a **basic feature** of the FD, and any FD can be represented as a list of basic features. For example, the part of the list for the FD below dealing with the SUBJ/PROT is (Kay, 1985, pp. 259–61):

$$
\begin{aligned}
<\text{SUBJ CAT}> &= \text{PRON} \\
<\text{SUBJ GENDER}> &= \text{MASC} \\
<\text{SUBJ CASE}> &= \text{NOM} \\
<\text{SUBJ NUMBER}> &= 3 \\
<\text{PROT CAT}> &= \text{PRON} \\
<\text{PROT GENDER}> &= \text{MASC} \\
<\text{PROT CASE}> &= \text{NOM} \\
<\text{PROT NUMBER}> &= \text{SING} \\
<\text{PROT PERSON}> &= 3
\end{aligned}
$$

The unification operation is similar to the operation of forming unions of sets (see SET THEORY), except that unification cannot merge FDs which have different values for the same

He saw her.

$$
\begin{bmatrix}
\text{CAT} & = \text{S} \\[6pt]
\text{SUBJ} = \text{PROT} = &
\begin{bmatrix}
\text{CAT} & = \text{PRON} \\
\text{GENDER} & = \text{MASC} \\
\text{CASE} & = \text{NOM} \\
\text{NUMBER} & = \text{SING} \\
\text{PERSON} & = 3
\end{bmatrix} \\[24pt]
\text{DOBJ} = \text{GOAL} = &
\begin{bmatrix}
\text{CAT} & = \text{PRON} \\
\text{GENDER} & = \text{FEM} \\
\text{CASE} & = \text{ACC} \\
\text{NUMBER} & = \text{SING} \\
\text{PERSON} & = 3
\end{bmatrix} \\[24pt]
\text{VERB} & = \text{SEE} \\[6pt]
\text{TENSE} & = \text{PAST} \\[6pt]
\text{VOICE} & = \text{ACTIVE}
\end{bmatrix}
$$

attribute, and that in unification the merged FDs become identical (Karttunen and Zwicky, 1985, p. 17). FDs which have different values for the same attribute are called **incompatible**. Ambiguous sentences have two or more incompatible FDs. Incompatible FDs can, however, be combined in a **complex** FD which shows both the common and the differing parts of the incompatible FD. Thus the sentence *He likes writing books*, in which *writing* can either be a MOD(ifier) of *books*, or the second part of the verbal group *likes writing*, has two incompatible FDs which can be combined into a complex FD as follows (Kay, 1985, pp. 257–9):

He likes writing(−)books

$$
\begin{bmatrix}
\text{CAT} & = \text{S} \\
\text{SUBJ} & = \text{he} \\
\text{DOBJ} & = \begin{bmatrix}
\text{CAT} & = \text{NP} \\
\text{HEAD} & = \text{books} \\
\text{MOD} & = \begin{bmatrix} \text{CAT} = \text{PRESP} \\ \text{LEX} = \text{WRITE} \end{bmatrix}
\end{bmatrix} \\
\text{VERB} & = \text{LIKE} \\
\text{TENSE} & = \text{PRES} \\
\text{VOICE} & = \text{ACTIVE}
\end{bmatrix}
$$

He likes(−)writing books

$$
\begin{bmatrix}
\text{CAT} & = \text{S} \\
\text{SUBJ} & = \text{he} \\
\text{DOBJ} & = \begin{bmatrix}
\text{CAT} & = \text{NP} \\
\text{HEAD} = & \begin{bmatrix}
\text{CAT} & = \text{S} \\
\text{VERB} = & \begin{bmatrix} \text{CAT} & = \text{PRESP} \\ \text{LEX} & = \text{WRITE} \end{bmatrix} \\
\text{DOBJ} = & \begin{bmatrix} \text{CAT} & = \text{NP} \\ \text{HEAD} & = \text{books} \end{bmatrix}
\end{bmatrix}
\end{bmatrix} \\
\text{VERB} & = \text{LIKE} \\
\text{TENSE} & = \text{PRES} \\
\text{VOICE} & = \text{ACTIVE}
\end{bmatrix}
$$

He likes writing books

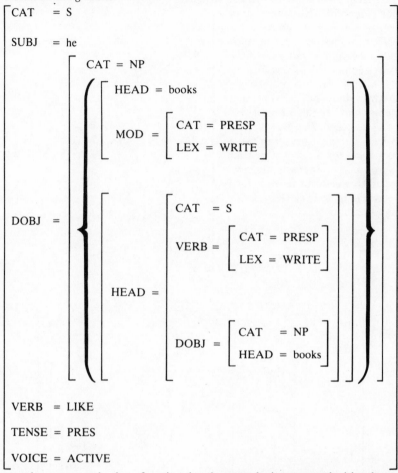

Constituency is presented in functional unification grammar in **C(onstituent) sets** and **Patterns** ($) (ibid. pp. 263–4):

$$
\begin{bmatrix}
\text{C-set} & = \text{(SUBJ VERB OBJ)} \\
\text{Pattern} & = \text{(SUBJ VERB OBJ)} \\
\text{CAT} & = \text{S} \\
\text{etc.}
\end{bmatrix}
$$

The value for $ can be interspersed with three dots, '. . .', to show that although the categories of the pattern must occur in the order shown, they may be interspersed with other material.

The whole grammar of a language can, in principle, be described in a complex FD, but it is often useful to retain its preunified modularity for parsing purposes, because it is then easier to identify specific structures. Karttunen and Kay (1985, pp. 293–7) provide two sections of a functional unification grammar for Finnish, one dealing mainly with verb inflection and subject-verb agreement and one dealing with Topic and Contrast.

An FD specifying a sentence to be uttered is the input to the sentence-generating device, which attempts to unify the FD for the sentence with the grammar. If the two descriptions are incompatible, there is no sentence in the language that meets the specification. If the unification is successful, the FD resulting from it will usually contain detail not contained in the input FD. If the FD which results from the unification has a constituent set, each constituent in turn is unified with the grammar until constituents which have no constituents of their own are produced. These are **terminals** which must match entries in the lexicon.

The parser gains access to the grammar via a set of functions which obtain rules with particular properties on demand. For example, if a string beginning with a determiner is to be matched to the grammar, the demand for an initial determiner is entered as the argument for the appropriate function which returns as values any rules which match the demand (Karttunen and Kay, 1985, p. 299). The rules have the form $F \to P_1 \ldots P_n$, where F is an FD and $P_1 \ldots P_n$ are paths which identify parts of F. A possible rule (p. 301) is illustrated below. It says (p. 301):

that any phrase whose description can be unified with the one given can be accommodated in the constituent structure in such a way as to dominate a pair of other constituents, the first of which is its subject and the second of which is its verb

and it provides for agreement in person and number between the subject and the verb.

The algorithm which produces rules from a functional unification grammar is a variant of the unification algorithm itself. It produces a result in disjunctive form providing a separate description for each possible phrase type. Each description can be turned into a rule by extracting its patterns and making them the right-hand sides of rules. Karttunen and Kay (1985, pp. 303–4) provide the following broad outline of the process by which an FD is reduced to disjunctive form (see also AUGMENTED TRANSITION NETWORK GRAMMAR):

The functional description has the structure of a tree with attribute-value pairs labeling terminal nodes and either 'and' or 'or' labeling the nonterminal nodes. Each term in the disjunctive normal form also has such a tree structure, but since all the nonterminals are labeled 'and', it would be possible to replace them all with a single nonterminal node. Each tree that represents one of these terms can be derived from the tree for the original expression by simply selecting certain arcs and nodes from it. The top node must be included. If a node labeled 'and' is included, then the arcs extending downward from it, and the nodes to which these lead, must also be included. If a node labeled 'or' is included, then exactly one of the arcs leading downward from it, and the node to which this leads, must be included. Arcs and nodes must be included only if they satisfy these requirements. It emerges that the terms of the resulting expression, and therefore the terms of the parsing grammar, differ from one another with respect to the choice of a downward arc from at least one 'or' node.

$$
\left[
\begin{array}{l}
\text{Cat} \quad = \text{S} \\[2ex]
\text{Subject} = [\text{Cat} = \text{NP}] \\[2ex]
\text{Verb} \quad = \left[
\begin{array}{l}
\text{Cat} \quad = \text{V} \\
\text{Number} = \langle \text{Subject Number} \rangle \\
\text{Person} \quad = \langle \text{Subject Person} \rangle
\end{array}
\right]
\end{array}
\right] \longrightarrow \langle \text{Subject} \rangle \langle \text{Verb} \rangle
$$

Functional unification grammar has proved particularly successful in machine parsing of natural language and has been applied in machine translation (see Nirenburg, 1987, pp. 211–14).

K.M.

SUGGESTIONS FOR FURTHER READING

Karttunen, L. and Kay, M. (1985), 'Parsing in a free word order language', in D.R. Dowty, L. Karttunen, and A.M. Zwicky (eds), *Natural Language Parsing: Psychological, Computational and Theoretical Perspectives*, Cambridge, Cambridge University Press, pp. 279–306.

Kay, M. (1985), 'Parsing in functional unification grammar', in D.R. Dowty, L. Karttunen, and A.M. Zwicky (eds), *Natural Language Parsing: Psychological, Computational, and Theoretical Perspectives*, Cambridge, Cambridge University Press, pp. 251–78.

Functionalist linguistics

Functionalism in linguistics arises from the concerns of Vilém Mathesius (1882–1945), a teacher at the Caroline University in Prague, who, in 1911, published an article, 'On the potentiality of the phenomena of language' (English translation in Vachek, 1964), in which he calls for a non-historical approach to the study of language (compare STRUCTURALIST LINGUISTICS). Some of the linguists who shared his concerns, including the Russian, Roman Osipovich Jakobson (1896–1982), and who became known as the **Prague School linguists**, met in Prague for regular discussions between 1926 and 1945, but the Prague School also included linguists not based in Czechoslovakia (Sampson, 1980, p. 103), such as the Russian, Nikolaj Sergeyevich Trubetzkoy (1890–1938) (see FUNCTIONAL PHONOLOGY). More recently, functionalism has come to be associated with the British linguist Michael Alexander Kirkwood Halliday (b. 1925) and his followers.

It was the belief of the Prague School linguists that 'the phonological, grammatical and semantic structures of a language are determined by the functions they have to perform in the societies in which they operate' (Lyons, 1981, p. 224), and the notions of **theme**, **rheme**, and **functional sentence perspective** which are still much in evidence in Halliday's work (see especially Halliday, 1985), originate in Mathesius' work (Sampson, 1980, p. 104).

J.R. Firth (1890–1960), who became the first professor of linguistics in England, took what was best in structuralism and functionalism and blended it with insights provided by the anthropologist Bronislaw Malinowski (1884–1942). Because both Firth and Malinowski were based in London, they and their followers, including Halliday and R.A. Hudson (b. 1939), are sometimes referred to as the **London School** (Sampson, 1980, ch. 9).

Malinowski carried out extensive fieldwork in the Trobriand Islands and argues that language is not a self-contained system – the extreme structuralist view – but is *entirely* dependent on the society in which it is used – in itself also an extreme view. He maintains that language is thus dependent on its society in two senses:

1 A language evolves in response to the specific demands of the society in which it is used.

2 Its use is entirely context-dependent: 'utterance and situation are bound up inextricably

with each other and the context of situation is indispensable for the understanding of the words' (1923).

He maintains (Sampson, 1980, p. 225):

that a European, suddenly plunged into a Trobriand community and given a word-by-word translation of the Trobrianders' utterances, would be no nearer understanding them than if the utterances remained untranslated – the utterances become comprehensible only in the context of the whole way of life of which they form part.

He distinguishes the immediate **context of utterance** from a general and generalizable **context of situation**, and argues that we must study meaning with reference to an analysis of the **functions** of language in any given culture. For example, in one Polynesian society Malinowski studied, he distinguished three major functions:

1 The **pragmatic function** – language as a form of action;
2 The **magical function** – language as a means of control over the environment;
3 The **narrative function** – language as a storehouse filled with useful and necessary information preserving historical accounts.

Malinowski is perhaps best known, however, for his notion of **phatic communion**. By this he means speech which serves the function of creating or maintaining 'bonds of sentiment' (Sampson, 1980, p. 224) between speakers (Malinowski, 1923, p. 315); English examples would include idle chat about the weather, and phrases like *How are you?*

In connection with the idea of context of situation and the idea of function as explanatory terms in linguistics, Firth points out that:

1 If the meaning of linguistic items is dependent on cultural context, we need to establish a set of categories which link linguistic material with cultural context. Thus, the following categories are necessary in any description of linguistic events (1957a, p. 182):

A The relevant features of participants: persons, personalities.

(i) The verbal action of the participants.
(ii) The non-verbal action of the participants.
B The relevant objects.
C The effect of the verbal action.

2 The notion that 'meaning is function in context' needs formal definition so that it can be used as a principle throughout the theory; both the smallest and the largest items must be describable in these terms.

To achieve this formal definition, Firth uses a Saussurean notion of system, though Firth's use of the term is more rigorous than Saussure's. Firth's **system** is an enumerated set of choices in a specific context. Any item will have two types of context: (1) the context of other possible choices in the system; and (2) the context in which the system itself occurs. The choices made in the systems will be functionally determined.

Halliday works within a highly explicit systemic theory which is clearly Firthian, but more fully elaborated, and the grammars written by scholars in the Hallidayan tradition are, therefore, often called **systemic grammars** (see SYSTEMIC GRAMMAR). When accounting for how language is used, for the choices speakers make, however, Halliday prefers to talk of **functional grammar**; as he puts it (1970, p. 141):

The nature of language is closely related to . . . the functions it has to serve. In the most concrete terms, these functions are specific to a culture: the use of language to organize fishing expeditions in the Trobriand Islands, described half a century ago by Malinowski, has no parallel in our own society. But underlying such specific instances of language use, are more general functions which are common to all cultures. We do not all go on fishing expeditions; however, we all use language as a means of organizing other people, and directing their behaviour.

This quotation shows both the influence from Malinowski, which reaches Halliday through Firth, and hints at how Halliday generalizes the notion of function in order that it may become more widely applicable as an explanatory term.

Halliday's theory of language is organized

around two very basic and common-sense observations which immediately set him apart from the other truly great twentieth-century linguist, Noam Chomsky (see RATIONALIST LINGUISTICS); namely, that language is part of the social semiotic; and that people talk to each other. Halliday's theory of language is part of an overall theory of social interaction, and from such a perspective it is obvious that a language must be seen as more than a set of sentences, as it is for Chomsky. Rather, language will be seen as a text, or discourse – the exchange of meanings in interpersonal contexts. The creativity of language is situated in this exchange. A Hallidayan grammar is therefore a grammar of meaningful choices rather than of formal rules.

By saying that language is part of the **social semiotic**, Halliday means that the whole of the culture is meaningful, is constructed out of a series of systems of signs. Language is one of these systems – a particularly important one, because most of the other systems are learnt through, and translatable into, language, and because it *reflects* aspects of the situations in which it occurs. It is one of Halliday's greatest achievements that he has been able to provide a systematic and coherent account of how particular situational aspects are reflected in the linguistic choices made by the participants in those situations, and the notion he invokes in this account is, again, the notion of the function.

As a social system, language is subject to two types of variation: variation according to *user*, and variation according to *use*. The first type of variation is in accent and dialect (see DIALECTOLOGY), and it does not, in principle, entail any variation in *meaning*. Different dialects, are, in principle, different ways of saying the same thing, and dialectal linguistic variation reflects the social order basically in terms of geography. Variation according to *use*, **register variation**, however, produces variation in meaning. A **register** is what you are speaking at a particular time, and is determined by what you and others – and which others – are doing there and then, that is, by the nature of the ongoing social activity. Register variation, therefore, reflects the social order in the special sense of the

variety of social processes. The notion of register is a notion required to relate the functions of language (see below) to those aspects of the situation in which it is being used which are the relevant aspects for us to include under the notion of **speech situation** or **context**.

According to Halliday, the relevant aspects of the situation are what he calls, respectively, **field**, **tenor**, and **mode**.

The **field of discourse** is *what is going on* – the social action, which has a meaning as such in the social system. Typically, it is a complex act in some ordered configuration, in which the text is playing some part. It includes 'subject matter' as one aspect of what is going on.

The **tenor of discourse** relates to *who is taking part* in the social action. It includes the role structure into which the participants in the discourse fit, that is, socially meaningful participant relationships, whether these are permanent attributes of the participants – mother–child – or whether they are role relationships that are specific to the situation – doctor–patient. Actual speech-roles are also included, and these may be created through the exchange of verbal meanings: through the exchange itself, it will become clear, for instance, who, at any particular time is **knower** and **non-knower** (Berry, 1981) with regard to any particular subject matter of the discourse.

The **mode of discourse** deals with the role that the text or language itself is playing in the situation at hand. It refers to the particular status that is assigned to the text within the situation and to its symbolic organization. A text will have a function in relation to the social action and the role structure (plea, reprimand, informing); it will be transmitted through some channel (writing, speech); and it will have a particular rhetorical mode (formal, casual).

It is now possible to determine the general principles governing the way in which these semiotic aspects of the situation are reflected in texts: each linguistically relevant situational component will tend to determine choices in one of the three semantic components which language comprises in virtue of being the system through which we talk to each other.

In virtue of being the means whereby we talk to each other, language has two major functions: it is a means of *reflecting on things*, that is, it has an **ideational function**; and it is a means of *acting* on things. But, of course, the only 'things' it is possible to act on symbolically – and language is a symbolic system – are *people* (and some animals, perhaps). So the second function of language is called the **interpersonal function**.

Finally, language has the function which enables the other two functions to operate, namely the function which represents the language user's text-forming potential; this is called the **textual function**, and 'it is through the options in this component that the speaker is enabled to make what he says operational in context, as distinct from being merely citational, like lists of words in a dictionary, or sentences in a grammar book' (Halliday, 1975, p. 17).

As indicated in the quotation just given, to each of the functions that language has for its users corresponds a component of the semantic system of language from which choices are made somewhat as follows:

The **field of discourse** – what is going on – will tend to determine choices in the **ideational component** of the language, among classes of things, qualities, quantities, times, places and in the transitivity system (see SYSTEMIC GRAMMAR).

The **tenor of discourse** – who is taking part – will tend to determine choices in the **interpersonal systems** of mood, modality, person, and key; in intensity, evaluation, and comment.

The **mode of discourse** – the part the text is playing – will tend to determine choices in the **textual component** of language, in the system of voice, among cohesive patterns, information structures, and in choice of theme. The concept of genre, too, is an aspect of what Halliday sees as mode.

But exactly *what* choices are made is subject to variation according to two further factors to which reference must be made in the explanation of the relationship between language and situation: namely, register and code.

By **register** is meant that concept of text variety which allows us to make sensible predictions about the kind of language which will occur in a given situation, that is, in association with a particular field, tenor, and mode. Register is (Halliday, 1978, p. 111): 'the configuration of semantic resources that the member of a culture typically associates with a situation type'. However, members of different (sub)cultures will differ in which text type they tend to associate with which situation type, and differences of this supralinguistic, sociosemiotic type are explained in terms of Bernstein's (1971) notion of the **code** (see LANGUAGE AND EDUCATION), which acts as a filter through which the culture is transmitted to a child.

It is important to remember that the interpersonal, ideational, and textual functions mentioned here are the **macrofunctions** of the semantic system of language; they are the functions which Halliday thinks of as universal. In addition, of course, language serves a number of **microfunctions** for its users, such as asking for things, making commands, etc., but the proper heading under which to consider these is that of speech-act theory (see SPEECH-ACT THEORY). Halliday also provides a functional account of how a child learns language, or, as he puts it, how a child's meaning potential develops (see LANGUAGE ACQUISITION) and of what a child understands a language to be, claiming that s/he arrives at this understanding of the nature of language through her or his growing awareness of the functions language can fulfil in her or his everyday life.

K.M.

SUGGESTIONS FOR FURTHER READING

Halliday, M.A.K. (1978), *Language as Social Semiotic*, London, Edward Arnold.

Sampson, G. (1980), *Schools of Linguistics: Competition and Evolution*, London, Hutchinson, Chs 5 and 9.

Generative grammar

A **generative grammar** of some language is the set of rules that defines the unlimited number of sentences of the language and associates each with an appropriate grammatical description. The concept is usually associated with linguistic models that have a mathematical structure and with a particular view of the abstract nature of linguistic study. It came to prominence in linguistic theory through the early work of Noam Chomsky and perhaps for this reason is often, though wrongly, associated exclusively with his school of linguistics. It is nevertheless appropriate to start with a quotation from Chomsky (1975b, p. 5):

> A language L is understood to be a set (in general infinite) of finite strings of symbols drawn from a finite 'alphabet.' Each such string is a sentence of L. . . . A grammar of L is a system of rules that specifies the set of sentences of L and assigns to each sentence a structural description. The structural description of a sentence S constitutes, in principle, a full account of the elements of S and their organization. . . . The notion 'grammar' is to be defined in general linguistic theory in such a way that, given a grammar G, the language generated by G and its structure are explicitly determined by general principles of linguistic theory.

The quotation raises a number of issues. The first and most general is that a language can be understood to consist of an infinite set of sentences and the grammar of that language to be the finite system of rules that describes the structure of any member of this infinite set of sentences. This view is closely related to the notion of a **competence grammar**: a grammar that models a speaker's knowledge of her or his language and reflects her or his **productive** or **creative** capacity to construct and understand infinitely many sentences of the language, including those that s/he has never previously encountered. I shall assume this position in what follows.

A second, more formal, issue is that the grammar of a particular language should be conceived of as a set of rules formalized in terms of some set of mathematical principles, which will not only account for, or **generate**, the strings of words that constitute the sentences of the language but will also assign to each sentence an appropriate grammatical description. The ability of a grammar simply to generate the sentences of the language is its **weak generative capacity**; its ability to associate each sentence with an appropriate grammatical description is its **strong generative capacity**.

A third issue concerns the universal nature of the principles that constrain possible grammars for any language, and hence define the bounds within which the grammar of any particular language will be cast. Here we shall be concerned with two interrelated questions. The first is a formal matter and concerns the nature of the constraints on the form of the rules of the grammar. A properly formal approach to this question would be formulated in mathematical terms: I will, however, limit myself to an informal outline of the issues involved and invite the reader interested in the formal issues to consult Gazdar (1987) and Wall (1972). The second is a substantive matter and concerns the nature of the linguistic principles that constrain the 'appropriate grammatical description' mentioned above. Since linguistic principles tend to vary from theory to theory, and indeed can change over time within one theory, it is perhaps hardly surprising that the establishment of the 'correct' grammar can be a matter of controversy.

To put some flesh on these observations, consider a simple example involving the analysis of a single sentence: *The cat sat on the mat.* We will make the simplifying assumption that words are the smallest unit that a grammar deals with, so, for example, although it is obvious that *sat*, as the past tense form of the verb SIT, is capable of further analysis, we will treat it as a unit of analysis. A more detailed account would need to discuss the grammar of the word. Given this simplification, the analysis shown in Figure 1 is largely uncontroversial, and we will suppose that this deliberately minimal account is the appropriate grammatical description mentioned above.

The analysis identifies the words as the smallest relevant units, and displays information about their **lexical categorization** (*the* is an Article, *mat* is a Noun, etc.). It also shows the **constituent structure** of the sentence, what are and what are not held to be proper subparts of the sentence, and assigns each constituent recognized to a particular **category** (*the cat* is a Noun Phrase, *on the mat* is a Prepositional Phrase, and so on). Implicitly it also denies categorial status to other possible groupings of words; *sat on*, for example, is not a constituent at all.

A simple grammar that will generate this sentence and its grammatical description is:

Syntax:

S	→ NP	VP
NP	→ Art	N
VP	→ V[1]	PP
PP	→ Prep	NP

Lexicon:

cat	N
mat	N
on	Prep
sat	V[1]
the	Art

(S = Sentence; NP = Noun Phrase; VP = Verb Phrase; Art = Article; N = Noun; V[1] = Verb of subclass [1]; PP = Prepositional Phrase; Prep = Preposition)

Simple though this grammar is, it is formulated in accordance with some general principles. The most general of these is that a grammar consists of a number of distinct **components**; in this case there are two: a **syntax**, which defines permissible constituent structures, and a **lexicon**, which lists the words in the language and the lexical class to which each belongs. The syntax rules are themselves constrained along the

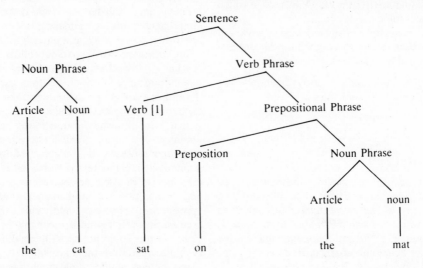

Figure 1

following lines:

1　All rules are of the form A → B C.
2　→is to be interpreted as 'has the constituents'.
3　A rule may contain only one category on the left hand side of →.
4　A rule may contain one or more categories (including further instances of the initial symbol 'S') on the right hand side of →.
5　Categories introduced on the right-hand side of → are ordered with respect to each other.
6　S is the **initial symbol**; i.e., the derivation of any sentence must start with this symbol.
7　When the left-hand side of a rule is a phrasal category, the right-hand side of the rule must contain the corresponding lexical category; e.g., an NP must have an N as one of its constituents (and may have other categories, Det, say).
8　The lexical categories N, V, P, Det, etc., are the **terminal vocabulary**; i.e., these symbols terminate a derivation and cannot themselves be further developed in the syntax.
9　The lexical categories may be augmented to indicate the membership of some subclass of the category; e.g., in the example, the category V is differentiated into V[1] (*lay, sat*), to distinguish it from V[2], V[3], etc., to which we will come.
10　The lexicon must be formulated in such a way that each word is assigned to one of the permissible lexical categories listed in 7.

The grammar can be easily extended. We could extend the lexicon:

a	Art
dog	N
under	Prep
lay	V[1]

We can add more rules to the syntax. For instance, *sat* and *lay* require to be followed by a PP: *The cat lay under the table*, but cannot be directly followed by an NP *the cat lay the mouse*, or by a sentence *the cat lay that the man chased the mouse*. They are characterized as V[1], i.e., verbs of subclass 1. By contrast, a verb like *caught* requires a following NP: *The cat caught*

the mouse but not *the cat caught under the table* or *the cat caught that the mouse lay under the table*. We will characterize these as V[2]. The verb *said* is different again: it requires a following sentence: *The man said that the cat caught the mouse* but not either *the man said the cat* or *the boy said under the table*. We will label it as a member of V[3]. To accommodate these different grammatical subclasses of verb we can add the following rules:

VP → V[2] NP
VP → V[3] S

This will entail additional vocabulary:

caught	V[2]
chased	V[2]
said	V[3]
thought	V[3]

This slightly enlarged grammar is capable of generating large numbers of sentences. It is true that they will exhibit a boringly limited range of syntactic structures and the difference between them will largely be lexical, but they will nevertheless be different. And with a modest number of additional rules of syntax and a few more lexical items, the number of distinct sentences the grammar will be capable of generating will become very substantial. Indeed, since the grammar contains the recursive rule VP → V[3] S, the formal power of the grammar is infinite.

This being the case, two things follow. The first is that the notion of **generative** must be understood to relate to the abstract capacity of the grammar to recognize a sentence as a member of the set of sentences it generates, rather than a capacity to physically produce any particular sentence, or indeed physically recognize some particular sentence as a member of the set of sentences it can generate. The second is that the grammar is in itself neutral as to production and recognition. A mathematical analogy is appropriate. Suppose we had a rule to generate even numbers. It should be clear that in a literal sense the rule could not actually produce all the even numbers: since there are infinitely many of them, the task would be never ending. It could, however, be the basis of an algorithm that could be used to produce an arbitrary even number as an example, or to check whether an arbitrary number is or is not an even number. In a comparable fashion we can construct an algorithm that will use a generative grammar in the construction of sentences together with their analyses, or the analysis of a particular sentence to see if it belongs to the set of sentences generated by the grammar. There are many ways of performing either task, so the set of rules which follow are merely exemplificatory. To produce sentences and assign them analyses of the kind shown in Figure 1 we could construct a **sentence generator** along the following lines:

1 Start with the initial symbol S.
2 Until all the category symbols are members of the terminal vocabulary (i.e. the lexical category symbols), repeat: for any category symbol that is not a member of the terminal vocabulary select a rule from the syntax which has this symbol as the left-hand constituent and develop whatever structure the rule specifies.
3 Develop each lexical category symbol with a word from the lexicon of the relevant category.
4 Stop when all the items are words.

To check whether a sentence is generated by the grammar and offer an analysis, we could construct a **parser** along these lines:

1 Identify the lexical category of each word.
2 Repeat: for any category symbol or sequence of category symbols select a rule of the grammar in which these occur as the right-hand constituents of a rule and show them as constituents of the symbol on the left-hand side of the rule.
3 Stop when all the category symbols are constituents of S.

Let us now relate this simple account to the issues with which we began. With respect to the first issue, the productive capacity of a grammar, even the simple grammar illustrated can account for large numbers of sentences, particularly since it contains the **recursive** rule VP → V[3] S, and the grammar can readily be extended. The second issue was concerned with the potential of an explicit rule system to derive the actual sentences of the language and to associate them with a grammatical description: given suitable generators and parsers our rules can do this. The final issue is more contentious. Our grammar is indeed couched in term of a set of principles of the sort that might be construed as universal principles of grammar design. Such principles can be formulated in mathematical terms. As to whether our grammar, as stated, also captures appropriate linguistic universals – this is clearly a matter that depends on what these are considered to be. The principles of constituent structure illustrated are not particularly controversial, but different theories may place other constraints.

E.K.B.

SUGGESTIONS FOR FURTHER READING

Chomsky, N. (1975), *The Logical Structure of Linguistic Theory*, New York, Plenum Press.

Gazdar, G. (1987), 'Generative grammar', in J. Lyons, R. Coates, M. Deuchar, and G. Gazdar (eds), *New Horizons in Linguistics*, vol. 2, Harmondsworth, Penguin, pp. 122–51.

Lyons, J. (1970), 'Generative syntax', in J. Lyons (ed.), *New Horizons in Linguistics*, Harmondsworth, Penguin.

Wall, R. (1972), *Introduction to Mathematical Linguistics*, Englewood Cliffs, NJ, Prentice Hall.

Generative phonology

INTRODUCTION

Generative phonology (GP) is the theory, or theories, of phonology adopted within the framework of generative grammar (see TRANS-FORMATIONAL-GENERATIVE GRAMMAR). Originating in the late 1950s, principally in work by Halle and Chomsky (Chomsky *et al.* 1956; Halle, 1959), it developed during the 1960s to reach a standard form in Chomsky and Halle's *The Sound Pattern of English* (1968) (*SPE*). Much of the work in the 1970s derived from *SPE* in an attempt to overcome the difficulties posed by this framework, and by the late 1970s the theory had fragmented into a number of competing models. The 1980s have seen more of a consensus, particularly with the development of **non-linear** phonology.

THE STANDARD MODEL

The *SPE* model of phonology adopts the framework of the 'standard theory' of generative grammar of Chomsky (1965), in which a central syntactic component enumerates abstract 'deep' structures which underlie the meaning, and which are related to actual 'surface' structures by means of transformations. Within this model, the role of the phonological component is to interpret such surface structures, assigning to them an appropriate pronunciation, and thus accounting for the speaker's competence in this area of the language.

The surface structures which constitute the input to the phonological rules are represented as a string of 'formatives' (morphemes) and a labelled syntactic bracketing. The phonological rules convert such a structure into a phonetic representation expressed in terms of a universal set of phonetic features.

In addition to phonological rules, we require a **lexicon**, a listing of those features of the formatives, including phonological attributes, which are not derivable by rule. Since formatives are subject to a variety of phonological processes in specific contexts, their lexical representation must be in the most general form from which the individual realizations can be derived. It will thus be morphophonemic (see MORPHOLOGY). For example, the German words *Rad* and *Rat*, both pronounced [raːt], will have different lexical representations, since inflected forms such as *Rades* [raːdəs] and *Rates* [raːtəs] are pronounced differently. In this case *Rad* can be given a lexical representation with a final /d/, since the [t] is derivable by general rule.

Although the segments of lexical representations are comparable to morphophonemes, Halle (1959, 1962) demonstrated that there is not necessarily any intermediate level, corresponding to the phoneme, between such representations and the phonetic representation. Thus in Russian there are pairs of voiced and voiceless 'obstruent' phonemes, i.e. plosives, affricates, and fricatives, and voiceless obstruents are regularly replaced by voiced ones when followed by a voiced obstruent; thus, [mok l, i] but [mog bi]. The same rule applies to /tʃ/ – [dotʃ 1, i] but [dodʒ bi dʃ bi] – though [dʒ] is not phonemically different from [tʃ]. This rule is a single process, but to incorporate a phonemic level would involve breaking it into two, since it would need to apply both to derive the phonemes and to derive the allophones. Hence the phoneme has no place in the GP framework; phonemic transcriptions are, according to Chomsky and Halle, merely 'regularized phonetic representations', while 'complementary distribution', the fundamental criterion of phonemic analysis, is 'devoid of any theoretical significance' (Chomsky, 1964a, p. 93).

Since the lexical representation is intended to

contain only non-predictable information, it will take the form of redundancy-free feature matrices in which predictable features are unspecified. Since, however, redundant features may be required for the operation of phonological rules, these features must be inserted by a set of conventions, **redundancy rules** or **morpheme-structure rules**, which express in indirect form the constraints on segment types and morpheme structures in the language concerned. These rules, together with rules to eliminate superfluous structure etc. are called **readjustment rules**, and they will apply before the application of the phonological rules proper.

The rules of the phonological component thus operate on fully specified feature matrices constituting the **phonological**, or **underlying**, representation. These rules are of the form:

$$A \rightarrow B/ C \underline{\qquad} D$$

where A is the feature matrix of the affected segment(s), and B the resulting matrix; C and D represent the context, _____ being the position of the affected segment(s) A. In the standard theory these rules are in part ordered so as to apply in a fixed sequence. Thus, from English /k/ we can derive [s] and [ʃ]: *electric* [k], *electricity* [s], and *electrician* [ʃ]; but since [ʃ] is also derived from [s] in, e.g., *racial*, cf. *race*, the [ʃ] of *electrician* is best derived by two ordered rules: /k/ → [s], [s] → [ʃ].

The application of rules may be constrained by grammatical factors. Thus the rules for English stress depend on whether the word is a noun or a verb: 'import v. im'port, while the realization of German /x/ as [x] or [ç] in words such as *Kuchen* [kuːxən] ('cake') and *Kuhchen* [kuːçən] ('little cow') depends on the morphological structure of the words, which can be represented as /kuːxən/ and /kuː + çən/ respectively. There is therefore no need for the phonemic 'separation of levels', nor for 'juncture phonemes' (see PHONEMICS).

A special case of the relationship between syntax and phonology is the **cyclical application of rules**, where some sets of rules may reapply to progressively larger morphological or syntactic domains. In the description of English stress, which takes up a large part of *SPE*, the different stress patterns of *blackboard eraser* and *black*

board-eraser follow the cyclical application of the stress rules. If these expressions have different structures, with different bracketing of constituents, then a cyclical procedure whereby rules apply within the brackets, after which the innermost brackets are deleted and the rules apply again, will achieve the desired results. On each cycle, primary stress is assigned, automatically reducing other levels by 1:

	[[[black] [board]] [eraser]]		
Cycle 1	[1]	[1]	[1]
Cycle 2	[1	2]	–
Cycle 3	[1	3	2]

	[[black] [[board] [eraser]]]		
Cycle 1	[1]	[1]	[1]
Cycle 2	–	[1	2]
Cycle 3	[2	1	3]

The rules are intended to capture significant generalizations, and a measure of this is the simplicity of the rules themselves. In a number of cases special formal devices are necessary to ensure that more general rules are also simpler. For example, assimilation is a very general process in which feature values of adjacent segments agree, but this would normally involve listing all combinations of features in the rules, e.g.:

$$\left[-\text{syll}\right] \longrightarrow \left\{ \begin{array}{l} \left[\begin{array}{c} +\text{ant} \\ -\text{cor} \end{array}\right] \Big/ \underline{\quad} \left[\begin{array}{c} +\text{ant} \\ -\text{cor} \end{array}\right] \\ \left[\begin{array}{c} +\text{ant} \\ +\text{cor} \end{array}\right] \Big/ \underline{\quad} \left[\begin{array}{c} +\text{ant} \\ +\text{cor} \end{array}\right] \end{array} \right\}$$

etc.

A simpler statement can be achieved by using 'Greek letter variables', e.g. [αanterior], where 'α' must have the same value ('+' or '–') for the two segments involved, e.g.

$$\left[-\text{syll}\right] \longrightarrow \left[\begin{array}{c} \alpha\text{ant} \\ \beta\text{cor} \end{array}\right] \Big/ \underline{\quad} \left[\begin{array}{c} \alpha\text{ant} \\ \beta\text{cor} \end{array}\right]$$

PROBLEMS AND SOLUTIONS

The SPE framework offered a new and often insightful way of describing phonological phenomena, and it was applied to a variety of languages. But it became clear that unconstrained application of the above principles can lead to excessively abstract phonological representations and insufficiently motivated rules. Consider the description of nasalization in French (Schane, 1968). French nasal vowels can be derived from non-nasal vowels followed by nasal consonants: /bɔn/ →[bɔ̃]; this process, involving a nasalization rule followed by a nasal consonant-deletion rule, applies in final position and before a consonant, but not before vowels – e.g. *ami* [ami] – or in the feminine – e.g. *bonne* [bɔn]. If we assume that feminine forms have an underlying /ə/, i.e. /bɔnə/, which prevents the application of the nasalization rules, followed by a further rule deleting the [ə], then the feminine is no longer an exception, and the rules can apply more generally.

Thus the application of rules can be manipulated by means of a suitably abstract phonological representation, in which segments are included whose sole purpose is to prevent or facilitate the application of rules. This procedure can easily be abused to give underlying forms which, though apparently well motivated in terms of formal adequacy, may be counterintuitive and quite spurious. For example, the rules of *SPE* predict that stress will not fall on the final syllable of an English verb if it contains a lax or short vowel followed by only a single consonant. The word *caress* [kə'res] appears to be an exception, but it can be made regular with a phonological representation containing a double final consonant, and with a rule of **degemination** to eliminate the superfluous consonant after the stress rules have applied. Similar considerations motivate representations such as /eklipse/ and /giraffe/. The problem is not that such representations are necessarily incorrect – though most generative phonologists assume that they are – but rather that the theory offers no way of distinguishing between legitimate and illegitimate abstractions in such representations.

Many different proposals have been made to solve these problems, and to reduce the arbitrariness and abstractness of phonological representations and rules. Chomsky and Halle themselves (*SPE*, Ch. 9) propose the use of **universal marking conventions** to maximize naturalness of segments. Under their proposal, feature values in lexical representations may be in terms of 'u' (unmarked) and 'm' (marked) instead of '+' and '−', these being 'interpreted as '+' or '−' according to universal principles. However, this approach has found little favour. Other proposals involve constraints on underlying representations or rules, but the problem with all such proposals is that they tend to be too strong, ruling out legitimate as well as illegitimate abstractions.

For example, to avoid underlying forms which are too remote from phonetic reality, we might propose that the underlying form of a formative should be identical with the alternant which appears in isolation. But this is clearly unsatisfactory, since the forms of German *Rat* and *Rad* cited above can only be predicted from the inflected stem. Or we might require the underlying form to be identical with one of its phonetic manifestations; however, none of the stems of, for example, the set of words *photograph*, *photography*, and *photographic* could serve as the underlying form of the others, since all have reduced vowels from which the full vowels of the others cannot be predicted. Similarly, constraints have been proposed on **absolute neutralisation**, in which an underlying contrast is posited which is never manifested on the surface, and on the use of phonological features, such as the double consonants of the above English examples, merely to 'trigger' or to inhibit the appropriate rules. But again, cases have been adduced where such devices seem justified. Thus all the proposals suffer from the drawback that they are often as arbitrary as the phenomena they purport to eliminate.

Another factor contributing to the power of generative phonology is **rule ordering.** Ordering relations among rules are either **intrinsic**, that is, dictated by the form of the rules themselves, or **extrinsic**, that is, specifically imposed on the grammar. The latter fall into a number of types. In view of the power that ordering gives to the grammar, some phonologists have sought to impose restrictions on permissible orderings, and some, e.g. Koutsoudas *et al.* (1974), argued for the complete prohibition of extrinsic ordering, requiring all rules to be either intrinsically ordered or to apply simultaneously.

By the late 1970s, some of these principles had been included in a range of alternative theories (see Dinnsen, 1979) which claimed to overcome the difficulties posed by the *SPE* framework, particularly by imposing a variety of constraints on phonological representations, rules or rule ordering. An important requirement made by a number of phonologists was that phonological descriptions must not only provide adequate descriptions, but must also be **natural**, and some theories explicitly adopted the label **natural phonology**. The theory of Stampe (1969, 1973; cf. Donegan and Stampe, 1979), for example, argues that speakers of all languages are susceptible to universal **natural processes**, for example rules of assimilation or word-final devoicing, which will thus form a part of the grammars of all languages, unless speakers learn to suppress them. The problem here is to determine which rules belong to this category. The theory of **natural generative phonology** of Vennemann and Hooper (see Hooper, 1976) is perhaps the most constrained of all, disallowing all non-intrinsic ordering and imposing further restrictions such as the **True Generalization Condition**, which prohibits the positing of any phonological rule which is apparently contradicted by surface forms. There could not, for example, be a rule voicing intervocalic consonants if voiceless consonants can occur intervocalically in phonetic forms of the language.

NON-LINEAR PHONOLOGY

Although these various alternative theories claimed to offer solutions to the problems of the *SPE* framework, and a number of them won a following, the 1980s saw the rise of a new trend, eclipsing most of the proposals and providing a set of more unified approaches. This new orientation addresses another weakness of *SPE* generative phonology: its linearity.

In the *SPE* framework, the phonological representation of a sentence takes the form of a linear sequence of segments and boundaries. The boundaries reflect a hierarchical syntactic structure, but the phonological segments themselves are in purely linear order. Although many phonological rules can be adequately stated in terms of such an order, a linear representation is less appropriate for **suprasegmental** features such as stress and tone. Two influential approaches which adopt a more structured, non-linear approach are autosegmental phonology and metrical phonology (see van der Hulst and Smith, 1982).

Autosegmental phonology (Goldsmith, 1976) began as a theory of tone. In the *SPE* framework, the purely segmental representations, which do not even recognize the syllable as a unit, imply that tones are specified as features of vowels. This becomes difficult, however, if, as in some approaches, **contour** tones, i.e. rises and falls, are regarded as sequences of pitch levels, since two successive features must be assigned to the same vowel. Furthermore, in many tone languages, particularly those of Africa, the number of tones is not always the same as the number of vowels, since more than one tone may occur on a given syllable, and tones may 'spread' to adjacent syllables (see TONE LANGUAGES). This is solved in the autosegmental framework by regarding the tones not as features of the vowels but as a separate, autonomous level, or **tier** of representation, related to the segments by rules of **association**, e.g.:

$$
\begin{array}{ccc}
\text{L} & \text{H} & \text{L} \\
| & | & \wedge \\
\end{array}
$$
u y a l i m a

A universal set of **well-formedness conditions** is proposed to determine the permissible associations, as well as rules which operate on the tonal tier itself. In more recent work, other phenomena, such as vowel harmony (Clements, 1976) and nasalization (e.g. Hyman, 1982), have been given a similar treatment.

Metrical phonology began as an interpretation of the stress rules of the *SPE* framework (see Liberman, 1975; Liberman and Prince, 1977), in which it was shown that the various stress levels could be derived from a hierarchically ordered arrangement of **strong** and **weak** nodes. Such a hierarchy results in a **metrical grid** from which the stress levels of individual syllables can be read off, e.g.:

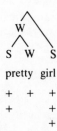

pretty girl

+   +   +

+   +

+

This theory, too, has been extended into other areas, such as syllable structure (Kahn, 1976), and even into tonal structure, which in some cases can be shown to involve hierarchical organization.

In both autosegmental and metrical phonology, a much richer phonological structure is postulated than that which underlies *SPE*, and this has been further developed so as to give a range of **suprasegmental** units such as **syllables**, **feet**, etc. (see Selkirk, 1980) or **tiers** such as **tonal tier**, **nasalization tier**, etc. The relationship and complementary nature of these theories have also been considered (Leben, 1982), and other hybrid theories have developed which combine features of both autosegmental and metrical principles, e.g. **CV-phonology** (Clements and Keyser, 1983). Other theories of generative phonology, e.g. **lexical phonology** (Mohanan,

1981), have also been considerably influenced by these non-linear frameworks (see Kiparsky, 1982; Pulleyblank, 1986).

The phonological representations assumed in these theories are very different from those of the *SPE* model, and there has been a shift of focus away from discussions of such issues as abstractness or rule ordering, and the appropriate formalisms, towards an exploration of the structural complexities of such representations. Nevertheless, many of the original principles of generative phonology, such as the postulation of an abstract underlying phonological structure related by rules to a phonetic representation, have not been abandoned.

A.F.

SUGGESTIONS FOR FURTHER READING

Chomsky, N. and M. Halle, (1968), *The Sound Pattern of English*, New York, Harper & Row.

Kenstowicz, M. and C. Kisseberth, (1979), *Generative Phonology: Description and Theory*, Orlando, FL, Academic Press.

Hogg, R. and C.B. McCully, (1987), *Metrical Phonology*, Cambridge, Cambridge University Press.

Goldsmith, J. (1989) *Autosegmental and Metrical Phonology*, Oxford, Basil Blackwell.

Mohanan, K.P. (1986), *The Theory of Lexical Phonology*, Dordrecht, Reidel.

Generative semantics

Generative semantics was an important framework for syntactic analysis within generative grammar in the late 1960s and early 1970s. This approach, whose leading figures were George Lakoff, James McCawley, Paul Postal, and John

R. Ross, at first posed a successful challenge to Chomsky's 'interpretive semantics' (see INTER-PRETIVE SEMANTICS): indeed, around 1970 probably the great majority of generative grammarians claimed allegiance to it. However,

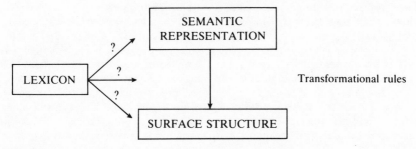

Figure 1

its relative importance had begun to decline by around 1973 or 1974, and today it has all but ceased to exist.

The leading idea of generative semantics is that there is no principled distinction between syntactic processes and semantic processes. This notion was accompanied by a number of subsidiary hypotheses: first, that the purely syntactic level of 'deep structure' posited in Chomsky's 1965 book *Aspects of the Theory of Syntax* (*Aspects*) (see TRANSFORMATIONAL-GENERATIVE GRAMMAR) cannot exist; second, that the initial representations of derivations are logical representations which are identical from language to language (the **universal-base hypothesis**); third, all aspects of meaning are representable in phrase-marker form. In other words, the derivation of a sentence is a direct transformational mapping from semantics to surface structure. Figure 1 represents the initial (1967) generative-semantic model.

In its initial stages, generative semantics did not question the major assumptions of Chomsky's *Aspects* theory; indeed, it attempted to carry them through to their logical conclusion. For example, Chomsky had written that 'the syntactic component of a grammar must specify, for each sentence, a *deep structure* that determines its semantic representation' (1965, p. 16). Since in the late 1960s little elaborative work was done to specify any interpretive mechanisms by which the deep structure might be mapped onto meaning, Lakoff and others took the word 'determines' in its most literal sense, and simply equated the two levels. Along the same lines, Chomsky's (tentative) hypothesis that

selectional restrictions were to be stated at deep structure also led to that level's being conflated with semantic representation. Since sentences such as (1a) and (1b), for example, share several selectional properties – the possible subjects of *sell* are identical to the possible objects of *from* and so on – it was reasoned that the two sentences had to share deep structures. But if such were the case, generative semanticists reasoned, then that deep structure would have to be so close to the semantic representation of the two sentences that it would be pointless to distinguish the two levels.

(1) (a) Mary sold the book to John.
     (b) John bought the book from Mary.

As Figure 1 indicates, the question of how and where lexical items entered the derivation was a topic of controversy in generative semantics. McCawley (1968) dealt with this problem by treating lexical entries themselves as structured composites of semantic material (the theory of **lexical decomposition**), and thus offered (2) as the entry for *kill*:

(2)

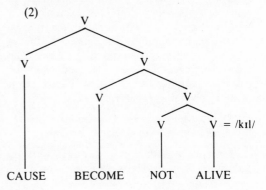

After the transformational rules had created a substructure in the derivation that matched the structure of a lexical entry, the phonological matrix of that entry would be insertable into the derivation. McCawley hesitantly suggested that lexical-insertion transformations might apply in a block after the application of the cyclic rules; however, generative semanticists never did agree on the locus of lexical insertion, nor even whether it occurred at some independently definable level at all.

Generative semanticists realized that their rejection of the level of deep structure would be little more than word-playing if the transformational mapping from semantic representation to surface structure turned out to be characterized by a major break before the application of the familiar cyclic rules – particularly if the natural location for the insertion of lexical items was precisely at this break. They therefore constructed a number of arguments to show that no such break existed. The most compelling were moulded after Morris Halle's classic argument against the structuralist phoneme (Halle, 1959) (see GENERATIVE PHONOLOGY). Paralleling Halle's style of argumentation, generative semanticists attempted to show that the existence of a level of deep structure distinct from semantic representation would demand that the same generalization be stated twice, once in the syntax and once in the semantics (see Postal, 1970).

Since a simple transformational mapping from semantics to the surface entails that no transformation can change meaning, any examples that tended to show that such rules were meaning changing presented a profound challenge to generative semantics. Yet such examples had long been known to exist: for example, passive sentences containing multiple quantifiers differ in meaning from their corresponding actives. The scope differences between (3a) and (3b), for example, seem to suggest that Passive is a meaning-changing transformation:

(3) (a) Many men read few books.
　　(b) Few books were read by many men.

The solution to this problem put forward by Lakoff (1971a) was to supplement the strict transformational derivation with another type of rule – a **global rule** – which has the ability to state generalizations between derivationally non-adjacent phrase markers. Examples (3a–b) were handled by a global rule that says that if one logical element has wider scope than another in semantic representation, then it must precede it in surface structure. This proposal had the virtue of allowing both the hypothesis that transformations are meaning preserving and the hypothesis that the deepest syntactic level is semantic representation to be technically maintained.

Soon many examples of other types of processes were found which could not be stated in strict transformational terms, but seemed instead to involve global relations. These involved presupposition, case asignment, and contractions, among other phenomena. For a comprehensive account of global rules, see Lakoff (1970).

In the late 1960s, the generative semanticists began to realize that as deep structure was pushed back, the inventory of syntactic categories became more and more reduced. And those remaining categories bore a close correspondence to the categories of symbolic logic (see FORMAL LOGIC AND MODAL LOGIC). The three categories whose existence generative semanticists were certain of in this period – sentence, noun phrase, and verb – seemed to correspond directly to the proposition, argument, and predicate of logic. Logical connectives were incorporated into the class of predicates, as were quantifiers. This was an exhilarating discovery for generative semanticists and indicated to them more than anything else that they were on the right track. For, now, the deepest level of representation had a 'natural' language-independent basis, rooted in what Boole (1854) had called 'The Laws of Thought'. What is more, syntactic work in languages other than English was leading to the same three basic categories for all languages. The universal base hypothesis, not surprisingly, was seen as one of the most attractive features of generative semantics.

The development of generative semantics in the early 1970s was marked by a continuous

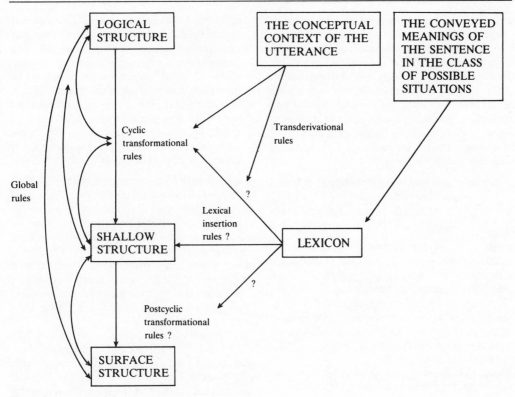

Figure 2

elaboration and enrichment of the theoretical devices that it employed in grammatical description. By 1972, George Lakoff's conception of grammatical organization appeared as in Figure 2 (an oversimplified diagram based on the discussion in Lakoff, 1974).

This elaboration was necessitated by the steady expansion of the type of phenomena that generative semanticists felt required a 'grammatical' treatment. As the scope of formal grammar expanded, so did the number of formal devices and their power. Arguments motivating such devices invariably took the following form:

(4) (a) Phenomenon P has in the past been considered to be simply 'pragmatic', that is, part of performance and hence not requiring treatment within formal grammar.

(b) But P is reflected both in morpheme distribution and in the 'grammaticality' judgements that speakers are able to provide.

(c) If anything is the task of the grammarian, it is the explanation of native-speaker judgements and the distribution of morphemes in a language. Therefore, P must be handled in the grammar.

(d) But the grammatical devices now available are insufficient for this task. Therefore, new devices of greater power must be added.

John R. Ross (1970) and Jerrold Sadock (1974) were the first to argue that what in the past had been considered to be 'pragmatic' phenomena were amenable to grammatical treatment.

Both linguists, for example, argued that the type of speech act (see SPEECH-ACT THEORY) which a sentence represents should be encoded directly in its semantic representation, i.e. its underlying syntactic structure. Analogously, George Lakoff (1971b) arrived at the conclusion that a speaker's beliefs about the world needed to be encoded into syntactic structure, on the basis of the attempt to account syntactically for judgements such as the following, which he explicitly regarded as 'grammaticality' judgements:

(5) (a) John told Mary that she was ugly and then she insulted him.
     (b) *John told Mary that she was beautiful and then she insulted him.

He also argued that in order to provide a full account of the possible antecedents of anaphoric expressions, even deductive reasoning had to enter into grammatical description (1971c). As Lakoff pointed out, the antecedent of *too* in (6), 'the mayor is honest', is not present in the logical structure of the sentence, but must be deduced from it and its associated presupposition, 'Republicans are honest':

(6) The mayor is a Republican and the used-car dealer is honest too.

The deduction, then, was to be performed in the grammar itself.

Finally, Lakoff (1973) concluded that the graded nature of speaker judgements falsifies the notion that sentences should be either generated, i.e. be considered 'grammatical', or not generated, i.e. be treated as 'ungrammatical'. Lakoff suggested instead that a mechanism be devised to assign grammaticality *to a certain degree*. The particulars of **fuzzy grammar**, as it was called, were explored primarily in a series of papers by John R. Ross (see especially Ross, 1973).

Not surprisingly, as the class of 'grammatical' phenomena increased, the competence–performance dichotomy became correspondingly cloudy. George Lakoff made it explicit that the domain of grammatical theory was no less than the domain of linguistics itself. Grammar, for Lakoff (1974, pp. 159–61), was to

specify the *conditions* under which sentences

can be *appropriately* used. . . . One thing that one might ask is whether there is anything that does *not* enter into rules of grammar. For example, there are certain concepts from the study of social interaction that are part of grammar, e.g. relative social status, politeness, formality, etc. Even such an abstract notion as *free goods* enters into rules of grammar. Free goods are things (including information) that everyone in a group has a right to. (Italics in original)

Since it is hard to imagine what might not affect the appropriateness of an utterance in actual discourse, the generative-semantic programme with great rapidity moved from the task of grammar construction to that of observing language in its external setting. By the mid 1970s, most generative semanticists had ceased proposing explicit grammatical rules altogether. The idea that any conceivable phenomenon might influence such rules made doing so a thorough impracticality.

As noted above, generative semantics had collapsed well before the end of the 1970s. To a great extent, this was because its opponents were able to show that its assumptions led to a too complicated account of the phenomenon under analysis. For example, interpretivists showed that the purported reduction by generative semantics of the inventory of syntactic categories to three was illusory. As they pointed out, there is a difference between nouns, verbs, adjectives, adverbs, quantifiers, prepositions, and so on in surface structure, regardless of what is needed at the most underlying level. Hence, generative semantics would need to posit special transformations to create derived categories, i.e. categories other than verb, sentence, and noun phrase. Along the same lines, generative semantics never really succeeded in accounting for the primary function of the renounced level of deep structure – the specification of morpheme order. As most syntacticians soon realized, the order of articles, adjectives, negatives, numerals, nouns, and noun complements within a noun phrase is not predictable, or even statable, on semantic grounds. How then *could* generative semantics state morpheme order? Only, it seemed, by supplementing the transformational rules with a close-to-the-surface filter that functioned to mimic the phrase-structure rules of a theory with the level of deep structure. Thus, despite its rhetorical abandonment of deep structure, generative semantics would end up slipping that level in through the back door.

The interpretive account of 'global' phenomena, as well, came to be preferred over the generative-semantic treatment. In general, the former involved coindexing mechanisms, such as traces, that codified one stage of a derivation for reference by a later stage. In one sense, such mechanisms were simply formalizations of the global rules they were intended to replace. Nevertheless, since they involved the most minimal extensions of already existing theoretical devices, solutions involving them, it seemed, could be achieved without increasing the power of the theory. Coindexing approaches came to be more and more favoured over global approaches since they enabled the phenomenon under investigation to be concretized and, in many cases, pointed the way to a principled solution.

Finally, by the end of the decade, virtually nobody accepted the generative-semantic attempt to handle all pragmatic phenomena grammatically. The mid and late 1970s saw an accelerating number of papers and books which cast into doubt the possibility of one homogeneous syntax–semantics–pragmatics and its consequent abandonment of the competence–performance distinction.

While the weight of the interpretivist counter-attack was a major component of the demise of generative semantics, it was not the deciding factor. It is not unfair, in fact, to say that generative semantics destroyed itself. Its internal dynamic led it irrevocably to content itself with mere descriptions of grammatical phenomena, instead of attempting explanations of them.

The dynamic that led generative semantics to abandon explanation flowed from its practice of regarding any speaker judgement and any fact about morpheme distribution as a *de facto* matter for grammatical analysis. Attributing the same theoretical weight to each and every fact about language had disastrous consequences.

Since the number of facts is, of course, absolutely overwhelming, simply *describing* the incredible complexities of language became the all-consuming task, with formal explanation postponed to some future date. To students entering theoretical linguistics in the mid 1970s, who were increasingly trained in the sciences, mathematics, and philosophy, the generative-semantic position on theory construction and formalization was anathema. It is hardly surprising that they found little of interest in this model.

At the same time that interpretivists were pointing out the syntactic limitations of generative semantics, that framework was co-opted from the opposite direction by sociolinguistics. Sociolinguists looked with amazement at the generative-semantic programme of attempting to treat societal phenomena in a framework originally designed to handle such sentence-level properties as morpheme order and vowel alternations. They found no difficulty in convincing those generative semanticists most committed to studying language in its social context to drop whatever lingering pretence they still might have of doing a grammatical analysis, and to approach the subject matter instead from the traditional perspective of the social sciences.

While generative semantics now no longer is regarded as a viable model of grammar, there are innumerable ways in which it has left its mark on its successors. Most importantly, its view that sentences must at one level have a representation in a formalism isomorphic to that of symbolic logic is now widely accepted by interpretivists, and in particular by Chomsky. It was generative semanticists who first undertook an intensive investigation of syntactic phenomena which defied formalization by means of transformational rules as they were then understood, and led to the plethora of mechanisms such as **indexing devices**, **traces**, and **filters**, which are now part of the interpretivists' theoretical store. Even the idea of lexical decomposition, for which generative semanticists were much scorned, has turned up in the semantic theories of several interpretivists. Furthermore, many proposals originally mooted by generative semanticists, such as the non-existence of extrinsic rule ordering, postcyclic lexical insertion, and treating anaphoric pronouns as bound variables, have since appeared in the interpretivist literature.

Finally, the important initial studies which generative semantics inspired on the logical and sublogical properties of lexical items, on speech acts, both direct and indirect, and on the more general pragmatic aspects of language are becoming more and more appreciated as linguistic theory is finally developing means to incorporate them. The wealth of information and interesting generalizations they contain have barely begun to be tapped by current researchers.

F.J.N.

SUGGESTIONS FOR FURTHER READING

Newmeyer, F. (1986), *Linguistic Theory in America*, 2nd edn, New York, Academic Press, especially chs 4 and 5.
McCawley, J. (1976), *Grammar and Meaning*, New York, Academic Press.

Genre analysis

Genre analysis is an important area within English for Specific Purposes (ESP) orientated studies (but see also STYLISTICS). The first use of the term in relation to ESP is Swales' (1981), who means by it 'a system of analysis that is able to reveal something of the patterns of organisation of a "genre" and the language used to express those patterns' (Dudley-Evans, 1987, p. 1).

A general definition of genre might explain that a **genre** is a text or discourse type which is recognized as such by its users by its characteristic features of style or form, which will be specifiable through stylistic and text-linguistic/discourse analysis, and/or by the particular function of texts belonging to the genre (see RHETORIC, STYLISTICS, TEXT LINGUISTICS and DISCOURSE AND CONVERSATIONAL ANALYSIS; see Miller, 1984, for a thorough discussion of the notion of genre). Swales' more specific definition of **genre** as (1981, p. 10): 'a more or less standardised communicative event with a goal or set of goals mutually understood by the participants in that event and occurring within a functional rather than a social or personal setting' can be understood as narrower, in so far as it creates a more 'technical' sense of genre, limiting its field of reference to those communicative events in the case of which it is possible to perceive a fairly specific function for the event; one would be hard put to say exactly what the function of some communicative events such as a lyric poem or a casual conversation might be. Indeed, Swales lists as 'classic attempts at genre analysis in Applied Linguistics literature' studies of doctor–patient interactions in casualty wards (Candlin *et al.*, 1978), of technical displays (Hutchinson, 1978), of dictated postoperative surgical reports (Pettinari, 1981), and of the investigation of qualifications in legal documents (Bhatia, 1981). Swales' own concern is with introductions to articles from pure, applied, and social sciences, and he considers the major aim of genre analysis to be (Dudley-Evans, 1987, p. 1): 'to gain insights into the nature of genre that will be useful in ESP materials writing and teaching'.

Another aim of genre analysis is to provide means of classifying both genres and subgenres. A genre often has several subgenres; for instance, the genre poetry numbers among its subgenres the sonnet, the epic poem, the lyric poem, and so on. Similarly, 'the research article genre is very broad, and can be broken down into a number of sub-genres such as the survey paper, the conference paper, research notes (a shorter form of the article reporting important results but with little comment) and the letter' (ibid. p. 2). In principle, it is possible to divide a genre into its subgenres, then the subgenres into subgenres of subgenres, and so on, in finer and finer detail, either by finer and finer specification of the context in which the genre occurs, or by specifying in finer and finer detail the linguistic features defining the genre (or both). The first approach has the potential to lead to the listing of genres like Crystal and Davy's (1969, p. 75) example *Washing powder advertising on television making use of a blue-eyed demonstrator*. The latter has the potential to lead to specifications of all the features of texts which differentiate them from other texts, i.e., each text would be quoted in full and would be called a genre. In practice, this problem is overcome by attending to those features of texts which a number of them share, instead of on those features which differentiate them from each other. However, research like that of Biber and Finegan (1986) has questioned whether even this approach is sound. They analysed a large corpus of texts including a variety of what would normally be considered different genres, for features such as question, first- and second-person pronoun, nominalization, passive, place and time adverbs and past and present tense. However, they found that there were often greater differences within genres than across them. Similarly, Carradine (1968), Dubois (1985), and Adams Smith (1986) call into question the idea that our intuitions about genres are supported by linguistic evidence alone; Adams Smith (1987) suggests that a more promising approach to genre analysis would correlate linguistic features of texts and features of human cognition (see further Adams Smith, 1987). These are valid theoretical points, and some work on genre analysis (Hewings and Henderson, 1987; Marshall, 1987) links it with schema-based approaches to the study of reading. Nevertheless, both types of study ('pure' genre analysis and schema theory linked studies) amply illustrate the usefulness of a linguistic

features based approach, and I describe one of each of the two types below, namely Dudley-Evans (1986) and Hewings and Henderson (1987). It is important to note, however, that the conventions governing writing in various genres change over time; this is amply illustrated in Dudley-Evans and Henderson's study of changes in economics articles over the last century (in progress), and in Bazerman's study of spectroscopic articles appearing in *Physical Review* between 1893 and 1980 (1984).

Learners can benefit from reading analyses and from carrying them out in at least two ways. On the one hand, their attention can be drawn to features such as signals of clause relations (see **coherence** under TEXT LINGUISTICS), to subtle linguistic markers indicating whether a writer is evaluating, commenting, or simply reporting, and to structural properties of the text; this type of awareness will help the learner to understand the text. On the other hand, the familiarity with a genre which learners gain from close analytical reading of examples of it will assist them in producing examples of the genre themselves.

Swales' (1981) pioneering study is based on the introductions to forty-eight articles, sixteen each from the pure, applied, and social sciences, proposing that these were structured around four **moves** (not to be confused with the **moves** used by Sinclair and Coulthard, 1975; see DISCOURSE AND CONVERSATIONAL ANALYSIS), namely: (1) establishing the field; (2) summarizing previous research; (3) preparing for present research; (4) introducing present research. However, after criticism by Bley-Vroman and Selinker (1984) and Crookes (1984), showing the difficulty of separating the two first moves, 'Swales (personal communication) now accepts that these two moves should be conflated to a single move, "Handling Previous Research" (HPR)' (Dudley-Evans, 1986, p. 131). Swales' model may therefore be presented as follows (adapted from Dudley-Evans, 1986, p. 130):

Move One: *Handling Previous Research*
              A: Asserting Importance of the
                  Topic
                  or

B: Stating Current Knowledge
    of the Topic

Move Two: *Preparing for Present Research*
    by
    A: Indicating a gap
        or
    B: Question Raising
        or
    C: Extending a finding

Move Three: *Introducing Present Research*
    by
    A: Giving the Purpose
        or
    B: Describing Present
        Research

These moves are largely lexically signalled (see below).

Although further research (Crookes, 1984; Cooper, 1985; Hopkins, 1985) has shown that Swales' moves are not present in all article introductions, and that the article introduction cannot properly be said to constitute a single genre, Swales' model 'is one that can be readily adapted for the analysis of other types ... and the procedures followed do have considerable potential for the analysis of other types of academic writing' (Dudley-Evans, 1986, p. 133). Some examples which illustrate this point are Dudley-Evans (1986) (see below), Adams Smith (1987), Jacoby (1987), Peng (1987), Marshall (1987), and Hewings and Henderson (1987) (see below).

Dudley-Evans (1986) analyses the introductions and discussion sections of seven dissertations written by native English-speaking students following an MSc course on 'The Conservation and Utilisation of Plant Genetic Resources'; his aim is 'to establish a model for the teaching of dissertation writing to overseas students taking the course' (ibid., p. 133). He identifies six moves in one of the dissertations, namely (ibid., p. 135):

Move 1: Introducing the Field
Move 2: Introducing the General Topic
         (within the Field)
Move 3: Introducing the Particular Topic
         (within the General Topic)

Move 4: Defining the Scope of the Particular
         Topic by
         (i) introducing research
              parameters
         (ii) summarising previous
              research
Move 5: Preparing for Present Research by
         (i) indicating a gap in previous
              research
         (ii) indicating a possible extension
              of previous research
Move 6: Introducing Present Research by
         (i)   stating the aim of the research
               or
         (ii) describing briefly the work
               carried out
         (iii) justifying the research

The other six dissertations follow this pattern, except that three of them omit move 1, and that the other three have one further move, 'Defining the Scope of the General Topic', between moves 2 and 3.

The most valuable signal for change from move 1 to 2 and 2 to 3 was found to be Hoey's (1983) Situation–Problem–Response–Evaluation pattern, (see TEXT LINGUISTICS), although paragraph structure and the readers' understanding of the subject matter also constitute important clues.

Move 4 is signalled by the following cyclical pattern (compare Dudley-Evans, 1986, pp. 138–9):

Headline (optional) which will include a statement introducing the research to be described, e.g., *In addition to x, y, z,* **there are other reasons why** . . .
Generalization Summarizing Previous Research, either outlining a given variable, or stating a problem involved in using a particular method, or describing the use of a method. This will be followed by
Description of Previous Research occasionally followed by
Evaluation of Previous Research

Moves 5 and 6 are signalled lexically, move 5 by the use of items such as *little* (**little** *consideration has been given to* . . .), *few, no* (*there have been* *few/no* investigations . . .), *limited, lack of, problems, difficulties* and *negative adverbs* (*are **not** available*), and move 6 by the following cycle (see ibid., pp. 140–1):

1 Statement of Aim
 or
 Description of Work Done

2 Justification of Work Done by
 (i) stating the possible benefit of the research
 (ii) referring to other related research
3 Limitations of Parameters (optional)
 eg., *Only two months were available for observation of the plants.*
 Hence it was impossible to observe the time of maturity.

The discussion sections were found to have three parts, of which the second is longest (Dudley-Evans, 1986, p. 141):

1 Introduction
2 Evaluation of Results
3 Conclusions and Future Work

In (2), the following moves occurred, of which, however, only the first was compulsory. Normally, the order outlined will be followed, but the structure of discussion sections is far less predictable than that of introductions (ibid., pp. 141–4, and personal communication):

1 **Information Move**, usually at the beginning, 'providing background information which the writer believes that the reader needs in order to understand fully the statement of the result that follows'.
2 **Statement of Results**, often referring to graphs and/or tables; commonly signalled by verbs like *reveal, find* and *show*.
3 **(Un)expected Outcome**, most often used when the result is unexpected; signalled by items like *surprising, unusual, awkward, difficult to explain* and . . . *was expected to produce better results.*
4 **Reference to Previous Research** (comparison), signalled with comparative adjectives.

5 **Explanation** of why the results were not as expected, or were different from those of previous research; signalled by modals, especially *may*.
6 **Problems with Results**, a rare move in which the writer comments on the validity of the results.
7 **Deduction**; a limited claim arising from a result or set of results; signalled by linkers such as *thus, therefore, clearly*, and a modal verb.
8 **Hypothesis**; a more general claim, typically placed under 3 above; signalled by modal expressions *it is **possible**, this **implies** that.*
9 **Reference to Previous Research** (support) in support of the hypothesis or deduction.
10 **Recommendation** for future work in the light of the results obtained; normally the dominant move in the third part of the discussion section (see above); signalled by modals like *should, could, would, must*, and verbs like *require*.
11 **Evaluation of Method** which is similar to a recommendation, but here the writer comments on the method with an implied recommendation for future research.

While Dudley-Evans mentions the importance of the reader's background knowledge in giving clues to structure, Hewings and Henderson (1987, p. 156) explicitly link 'work on "genre" in the field of text analysis, and the development of schema-based approaches to the study of reading'. Such approaches are based on the common-sense assumption that (Huckin, 1982) 'knowing something about a subject makes it easier to learn more about that subject: our prior knowledge serves as a framework which makes the new information more meaningful and easier to absorb'. In schema theory, this common-sense assumption is stated as follows (Hewings and Henderson, 1987, p. 167):

Schemata are abstract generic concepts constructed by the mind on the basis of patterns of experience (see Rumelhart, 1984). They are stored in long term memory and may be perceived as a framework we call up to help store new ideas and information. If appropriate schemata are already stored in the brain it is an easier matter to activate them than to try to establish new concepts and ideas on a sketchy or non-existent foundation.

Hewings' and Henderson's research arose in response to the difficulties faced by students following an introductory course in economics as part of a part-time social science degree programme. Because no formal qualifications were required for entry to the course, many students were unfamiliar with (had no schema for) academic writing and experienced comprehension difficulties when faced with it. However, since most were familiar with (had a schema for) the genre *textbook* from school, it was found relatively easy to highlight for the students their structural features, such as *chapters, contents list, index, summaries, questions for discussion, problems to be solved,* and *bibliography*, and to explain to them how each feature may be used to further and facilitate learning (ibid., pp. 167–8).

> Articles, on the other hand, proved more difficult. Various techniques were tried. Activities directed at skimming and scanning the text, looking for definitions and looking at tables and graphs, enabled students to say 'this text is about X', but it was no help to them in perceiving that the underlying purpose of these articles is fundamentally different from that of the textbook. . . . We, therefore, tried more directed methods.

The first method attempted was to concentrate on headings, but neither this nor the second method, the use of flow diagrams, proved efficient in improving the students' reading efficiency. A concentration on macrostructural elements, however, proved more effective. As in the case of Dudley-Evans' (1986) analysis of dissertations (see above), Hewings' and Henderson's analyses of bank review articles had highlighted a macro-structural pattern similar to Hoey's problem-solution pattern. They categorize this as **situation–policy–result–theory–conclusion** (Hewings and Henderson, 1987, p. 163), where the **situation** tends to encompass Hoey's 'situation' and 'problem', and **policy** can be seen as Hoey's

'solution'. **Result** and **theory** can both encompass Hoey's 'evaluation' (see TEXT LINGUISTICS). Hewings and Henderson report the use and the result of using this framework, alone or in conjunction with a lexical signalling approach, as follows (ibid., pp. 171–3):

> This framework was presented to students using an article with which they were already familiar. They were then asked to skim through another article, which they had also already studied, and make appropriate notes to correspond with the five sections. Students had to be discouraged from reading in detail and encouraged to look for the patterns within the text. The results of their 'notes' were discussed as a group. The macro-structure model itself was criticised, but more importantly, the students were able to discuss the article using a cohesive framework. They could see that the author was discussing a policy in terms of a situation and they were enabled to evaluate the author's arguments through perceiving this purpose . . .
>
> Another approach adopted, still using the macro-structure model was to combine it with lexical signals, particularly those given in headings . . . This type of activity again stimulates discussion and evaluation of what the writer is doing . . . The discussions generated encourage greater awareness of the overall structure.

The conclusion to their article appropriately highlights the connections between genre analysis, schema theory, and pedagogy (ibid., p. 173):

> Reading articles can be seen as demanding the creation of new sets of schemata, overlapping with those needed for textbooks, but generally of a more elaborate and evaluative nature. Development of appropriate schemata can be enhanced by viewing the texts to be read as belonging to different genre or sub-genre. The isolation of the features of the genre can then allow the creation of a pedagogic framework for the enhancement of reading efficiency and efficacy.

K.M.

SUGGESTIONS FOR FURTHER READING

ELR Journal (1987), vol. 1. *Genre Analysis and E.S.P.*, edited by Tony Dudley-Evans, Birmingham, English Language Research, The University of Birmingham.

Swales, J. (1990), *Genre Analysis: English in Academic and Research Settings*, Cambridge, Cambridge University Press.

Glossematics

INTRODUCTION

Glossematics is a structural linguistic theory developed in the 1930s by the two Danish linguists, Louis Hjelmslev (1899–1965) and Hans Jørgen Uldall (1907–57).

Hjelmslev had a broad background in comparative and general linguistics. He had studied under Holger Pedersen, whom he succeeded to the chair of comparative philology at the University of Copenhagen in 1937. In 1928 he published *Principes de grammaire générale*, which contains many of the ideas which were later developed further in his glossematic theory, above all the attempt to establish a general grammar in which the categories were defined formally on the basis of their syntagmatic relations (see STRUCTURALIST LINGUISTICS). In 1935 he published *La Catégorie des cas*, presenting a semantic analysis of the category of case.

Uldall had studied phonetics under Daniel Jones and anthropology under Franz Boas, and had felt a strong need for a new linguistic approach when trying to describe American Indian languages. He spent the years 1933–9 in Denmark, during which period he and Hjelmslev, in very close co-operation, developed the glossematic theory. In 1939 they were approaching a final version, but during the years of the war, which Uldall spent abroad working for the British Council, their co-operation was interrupted, and it was not until 1951–2 that they had an opportunity to work together again.

In the meantime, Hjelmslev had published an introduction to the theory, *Omkring sprogteoriens grundlæggelse* (1943a), which was published in English in 1953 under the title *Prolegomena to a Theory of Language*. In 1951–2, Uldall wrote the first part ('General theory') of what was planned to be their common work *Outline of Glossematics*, but this first part was not published until 1957. It contains a general introduction, largely in agreement with the *Prologemena*, but more comprehensible, and a description of a glossematic algebra, meant to be applicable not only to linguistics, but to the humanities in general. The plan had been that Hjelmslev should write the second part, containing the glossematic procedures with all rules and definitions.

However, during the long years of separation, Uldall had come to new conclusions on various points, whereas Hjelmslev on the whole had stuck to the old version of their theory. Some of the differences were due to the fact that Uldall was concerned with fieldwork (see FIELD METHODS), whereas Hjelmslev was more interested in the description of well-known languages. Moreover, he found the algebra constructed by Uldall unnecessarily complicated for the purposes of linguistics. Hjelmslev therefore found it difficult to proceed from Uldall's algebraic system and hesitated to write the second part (see Fischer-Jørgensen's Introduction to Uldall's *Outline*, 2nd edn, 1967). After a while, he decided to return to a simpler algebra used in earlier versions of the theory and to base the second part on the summary he had written in 1941 and revised in 1943. However, illness prevented him from fulfilling this plan. The summary was translated and edited by Francis Whitfield in 1975 under the title *Resumé of a Theory of Language*. This book consists of several hundred definitions and rules with no supporting examples.

An easier access to glossematics are Hjelmslev's many papers on various aspects of the theory, most of which are published in the two volumes of collected articles, *Essais linguistiques* (1959a) and *Essais linguistiques II* (1973b). The papers, 'Structural analysis of language' (1947) and 'A causerie on linguistic theory' (written in 1941) may be recommended as relatively easy introductions to the theory. But the most essential papers are 'Essai d'une théorie des morphèmes' (1938), describing the grammatical inflexional categories on the basis of glossematic functions, and 'La stratification du langage' (1954), which contains some revisions of the theory. However, the most important and widely read and commentated glossematic publication is *Omkring sprogteoriens grund-læggelse (OSG)* (1943a). (Page numbers refer to *OSG*, because the two editions (1953 and 1961) of the English translation have different page numbers, while both indicating the page numbers of *OSG*.) The shorter book, *Sproget* (1963), translated as *Language* (1970), is not a description of glossematic theory, but a general introduction to linguistics. Several of the chapters, however, show strong traces of glossematics. As short and easy introductions written by other linguists one may mention Martinet (1946), Malmberg (1964, pp. 140–57), Spang-Hanssen (1962), and Whitfield (1954).

GENERAL CHARACTER OF GLOSSE-MATIC THEORY

The goal of glossematics is to establish linguistics as an exact science on an **immanent** basis. In *OSG*, Hjelmslev states that it is in the nature of language to be a means to an end, and therefore to be overlooked. It is this peculiarity of language which has led scholars to describe it as 'a conglomerate of non-linguistic (e.g. physical, physiological, psychological, logical, socio-logical) phenomena', rather than as 'a self-sufficient totality, a structure *sui generis*'. This, however, is what the linguist should attempt to do (*OSG*, p. 7). Glossematics is 'a linguistic theory that will discover and formulate premisses of such a linguistics, establish its methods, and indicate its paths' (*OSG*, p. 8). 'Theory' in this connection does not mean a system of hypotheses but 'an arbitrary and at the same time appropriate system of premisses and definitions' (*OSG*, p. 14).

Behind the linguistic **process** (text), the linguist should seek a **system**, through which the process can be analysed as composed of a limited number of elements that constantly recur in various combinations (*OSG*, p. 10). For this purpose, it is necessary to establish a procedural method where each operation depends on those preceding it, and where everything is defined. The only concepts necessary to, but not defined within, the theory are a few, such as 'description', 'dependence', and 'presence', which are defined in epistemology. But before setting up the procedure, the linguistic theoretician must undertake a preliminary investigation of those objects which people agree to call languages, and attempt to find out which properties are common to such objects. These properties are then generalized as defining the objects to which the theory shall be applicable. For all objects of the nature premised in the definition, a general calculus is set up, in which all conceivable cases are foreseen, and which may therefore form the basis of language typology. The calculus itself is a purely deductive system independent of any experience. By virtue of this independence, the theory can be characterized as **arbitrary**, but by virtue of the premisses introduced on the basis of the preliminary experience it can be characterized as **appropriate** (*OSG*, p. 14). In his endeavour to establish linguistics as an exact science, Hjelmslev is inspired by formal logic, but his theory is not fully formalized, and he does not stick to logical functions but has chosen those functions which he found adequate for the description of language.

THE GLOSSEMATIC CONCEPT OF LANGUAGE

OSG is mainly concerned with the preconditions of the theory, i.e., with the features which, according to the preliminary investigations, characterize a **language**.

In his view of the nature of language, Hjelmslev is strongly influenced by Saussure (1916) (see STRUCTURALIST LINGUISTICS). Like Saussure, Hjelmslev considers language to be a sign structure, a **semiotic system**. Corresponding to Saussure's signifier and signified, Hjelmslev speaks of **sign expression** and **sign content**; and **expression** and **content** are described as the two **planes** of language (*OSG*, p. 44ff). It is a characteristic feature of glossematics that content and expression are regarded as completely parallel entities to be analysed by means of the same procedures, leading to analogous categories. At the same time, however, it is emphasized that the two planes are not conformal. A given sign content is not structured in the same way as the corresponding sign expression, and they cannot be divided into corresponding constituents or **figurae**, as Hjelmslev calls them. Whereas, e.g., the Latin sign expression *-us* in *dominus* can be analysed into the expression figurae *u* and *s*, the corresponding sign content is analysed into 'nominative', 'masculine', and 'singular', of which none corresponds specifically to *u* or *s*. In the same way the expression *ram* can be analysed into *r*, *a*, and *m*, and the corresponding content into 'he' and 'sheep', but *r*, *a*, and *m* do not correspond to any of these content elements.

From the point of view of its purpose, then, language is first and foremost a sign system; but from the point of view of its internal structure it is a system of figurae that can be used to construct signs. If there is conformity between content and expression, i.e. structural identity, there is no need to distinguish between the two planes. Hjelmslev calls such one-plane systems **symbolic systems** (for example, the game of chess); two-plane structures are called **semiotics**. A natural language is a semiotic into which all other semiotics can be translated, but the glossematic theory is meant to be applicable not only to (natural) languages but to all semiotic systems (*OSG*, pp. 90–7). It is worth pointing out that the terminology I have used above is that used in the English, Italian, and Spanish translations of *OSG*, and in the *Résumé*. In the Danish original, the terminology is different, and this terminology has been retained in the French and German translations, although the German gives references to the English terminology. Since this has caused a certain amount of confusion, the correspondences are presented here:

Version of OSG		Terminology
Original		
Danish	sprog	dagligsprog
French	langue	langue naturelle
German	Sprache	Alltagssprache
English and		
Résumé	semiotic	language
Italian	semiotica	lingua
Spanish	semiotica	lengua

Content and expression must be analysed separately, but with constant regard to the interplay between them, viz. the function between sign-expression and sign-content. Replacement of one sign-expression, e.g. *ram*, by another, e.g. *ewe*, normally results in another sign-content; conversely, the replacement of one sign-content, e.g. 'male sheep', by another, e.g. 'female sheep' brings about another sign-expression. Parts of signs (figurae) may be replaced in the same way, e.g. /a/ by /ɪ/ in the frame /r–m/, leading to the new sign-content 'edge', or 'male' by 'female' in the sign content 'male sheep' resulting in the new sign expression *ewe*. The smallest parts reached by the given procedure and whose replacement may bring about a change in the opposite plane are called **taxemes**. (In the expression plane, the level of taxemes corresponds roughly to that of phonemes.) For this replacement test, glossematics coined the term **commutation test**, which is now widely used. This test has, of course, also been applied by other linguists, e.g., the Prague School linguists, but it is characteristic of glossematics that it stresses the fact that the test may take its point of departure in any of the two planes, as illustrated in the examples above. By means of the commutation test, a limited number of commutable elements, **invariants**, is reached in both planes (*OSG*, pp. 66–7).

It happens that the commutation test gives a negative result in some well-defined positions for elements which have been found to be invariant in other positions. In this case, glossematics uses the traditional term **syncretism**. In Latin there is, for instance, syncretism between the content elements 'dative' and 'ablative' in masculine and neuter singular of the first declension, e.g. *domino*; and in German, there is syncretism between the expression taxemes /p t k/ and /b d g/ in final position – *Rad* and *Rat* are both pronounced [raːt] – whereas medially there is commutation – [raːdə], [raːtə] (in the Prague School, syncretism in the expression is called **neutralization**).

Syncretisms may be manifested in two ways: as **implications** or as **fusions**. When the manifestation is identical with one or more members entering into the syncretism, but not with all, it is called an **implication** – e.g. in German the syncretism /t/d/ is manifested by [t]. Otherwise it is called a **fusion** – e.g. in Danish there is syncretism between /p/ and /b/ in final position, manifested optionally by [p] or [b], or by something in between. **Latency** is seen as syncretism with zero – e.g. in French *petit* [pti], there is syncretism between /t/ and zero. When a syncretism is manifested by an implication, i.e. by one of its members, this member is called the **extensive** member of the opposition and the other is called the **intensive** member – thus in German /t/ is extensive and /d/ is intensive. This distinction is related to, but not identical with the Prague distinction between **unmarked** and **marked** members (see FUNCTIONAL PHONOLOGY).

Like Saussure, Hjelmslev also distinguishes between **form** and **substance**, and this distinction is basic in glossematics. But in contradistinction to Saussure, who sets up one form between two substances, sound and meaning, Hjelmslev operates with two forms, an expression form and a content form. Since the two planes are not conformal, each must be described on the basis of its own form. Form comprises all paradigmatic and syntagmatic functions (see STRUCTURALIST LINGUISTICS) and the terminal points of these functions, i.e. **elements** and **categories**.

In addition to form and substance, Hjelmslev introduces a third concept, **purport** (French *matière* – the Danish, rather misleading, term is *mening*, 'meaning'), which refers to sounds and meanings apart from the way in which they are formed linguistically, whereas substance designates linguistically formed purport. It may be formed differently by various sciences like physics or psychology. An example of purport in the content is the colour spectrum. It may be formed differently as content substance of the signs designating colours in different languages, i.e., the numbers of colours distinguished and the delimitations between them may be different. As an example of expression purport one may mention glottal closure or stricture, which may be substance for a consonant in one language and for a prosody or a boundary signal in other languages. (In *OSG*, 'substans' is sometimes used for 'mening', e.g. *OSG* pp. 69–70; this is corrected in the second edition of the English translation.)

The function between form and substance is called **manifestation**. A given form is said to be manifested by a given substance. Form is the primary object of the linguistic description, and differences between languages are mainly differences of form.

Form is also called **schema**, and in *OSG* **usage** is almost synonymous with substance. But sometimes, e.g. in the paper 'Langue et parole' (1943b), Hjelmslev draws a distinction between **schema, norm** and **usage**. In this case norm refers to the admissible manifestations, based on the mutual delimitation between the units, e.g. *r* as a vibrant distinguished from *l*, whereas usage refers to the manifestations actually used in the language, e.g. [r] as a tongue-tip vibrant. 'Norm' and 'usage' correspond to Coseriu's (1952) 'system' and 'norm' respectively; the phonemes of the Prague School, which are defined by distinctive features (see DISTINCTIVE FEATURES), belong to Hjelmslev's norm.

According to *OSG*, the **relation between form and substance** is a unilateral dependence, since substance presupposes form, but not *vice versa*. That substance presupposes form simply follows from the definition of substance as formed purport, but the claim that form does not presuppose substance is more problematic. It is evident that the calculus of possible languages can be a purely formal calculus and that it is possible to reconstruct a language, e.g. Proto-Indo-European, without attaching any substance to it (see HISTORICAL LINGUISTICS). But when concrete living languages are involved, it seems fairly obvious that both form and substance must be there. However, Hjelmslev argues that there may be several substances, e.g. speech and writing, attached to the same form, so that the form is independent of any specific substance. It is also said (e.g. in *OSG*, p. 71) that the description of substance presupposes the description of form but not *vice versa*. This is, however, not possible in the preliminary descriptions, but only in the glossematic procedure seen as a final control. In the paper 'La Stratification du langage' (1959a), it is stated explicitly that substance has to be taken into account in the operations of commutation and identification (see also Fischer-Jørgensen, 1967a).

'La Stratification du langage', which resulted from the discussions between Hjelmslev and Uldall in 1951–2, brings in certain revisions. First, content substance, content form, expression form and expression substance are called the four **strata of language**, and a distinction is made between **intrastratal** (**intrinsic**) and **interstratal** (**extrinsic**) functions. **Schema** covers the intrinsic functions in the two form strata, whereas **norm**, **usage**, and **speech act** cover interstratal (extrinsic) functions. Usage is no longer used synonymously with substance; the sign function is said to belong to usage – new signs may be formed at any moment – and figurae result from an intrastratal (intrinsic) analysis of each stratum. The sign function is, however, still considered to be a basic linguistic function. It is not quite clear what is meant by an intrinsic analysis of the substance strata. The paper seems to contain some concessions to Uldall's points of view in *Outline I*, written in 1952, views which have not been fully incorporated into Hjelmslev's own theory.

Secondly, a distinction is made between three **levels of substance**: the **apperceptive** level (Uldall's 'body of opinion'), the **sociobiological** level; and the **physical** level; and these three levels are ranked with the apperceptive level as primary. This represents progress compared to Hjelmslev's rather more physicalistic description of substance in *OSG*.

Substance plays a greater role in this paper than in *OSG*, although it appears clearly from *OSG* that Hjelmslev never meant to exclude substance from linguistics; he merely considers form to be its primary object. According to *OSG*, a detailed description of substance is undertaken in **metasemiology**, that is, a metasemiotic which has the linguist's descriptive language (also called a **semiology**) as its object language. In semiology, the ultimate irreducible variants of language, e.g. sounds, are minimal signs, and in metasemiology these units must be further analysed (see *OSG*, p. 108).

The description of style belongs to the so-called **connotative semiotics**.

On the whole, Hjelmslev sets up a comprehensive system of semiotics and metasemiotics (see *OSG*, pp. 101ff.; *Résumé*, 1975, p. XVIII; Rastier, 1985).

THE GLOSSEMATIC PROCEDURE

An important feature of glossematics is the claim that a formal description of a language must begin with an explicit analysis of texts by means of a constantly continued partition according to strict procedural rules. Such a continued partition is called a **deduction** (a somewhat uncommon use of this term). The functions registered in the analysis are of three types: **determination**, or unilateral presupposition; **interdependence**, or mutual presupposition; and **constellation**, or compatibility without any presupposition. These three functions have special names according to their occurrence in syntagmatics or paradigmatics (sequence or system). In syntagmatics, they are called **selection, solidarity** and **combination**, in paradigmatics, **specification, complementarity**, and **autonomy**, respectively. This very simple and general system of functions requires the different stages of the analysis to be kept apart, so that a particular function may be specified both by its type and by the stage to which it belongs. This procedure thus involves a hierarchical structure.

The analysis is guided by some general principles, of which the most important is the so-called **empirical principle** ('empirical' is used here in an unusual sense). This principle says that the description shall be free of contradiction (self-consistent), exhaustive, and as simple as possible, the first requirement taking precedence over the second, and the second over the third (*OSG*, p. 12). It is not quite clear whether Hjelmslev wants to apply the empirical principle both to the general calculus and to the description of actual languages. It is particularly in the interpretation of simplicity that glossematics differs from other forms of structural linguistics. According to glossematics, the simplest possible description is the one that leads to the smallest number of minimal elements, while the demand for exhaustiveness implies that as many categories and functions as possible must be registered. A principle of generalization (*OSG*, p. 63) prevents arbitrary reduction of the number of elements.

Before stating the functions in an actual case, it is necessary to undertake **catalysis**, that is, to interpolate an entity which is implied in the context. In German *guten Morgen!*, for example, a verb (i.e. a syncretism of all possible verbs) is catalyzed as a necessary prerequisite for the accusative (*OSG*, p. 84).

After the syntagmatic deduction is completed, a paradigmatic deduction is undertaken in which the language is articulated into categories. The paradigmatic deduction is followed by a synthesis. It is a characteristic feature of glossematics that analogous categories are set up for content and expression; Figure 1 gives an example of the parallelism.

It should be kept in mind that in glossematic terminology, **morphemes** are inflectional categories like case, person, etc., seen as content elements. **Verbal morphemes**, like tense, are considered to characterize the whole utterance, not just the verbal theme.

The definitions of the categories are based on

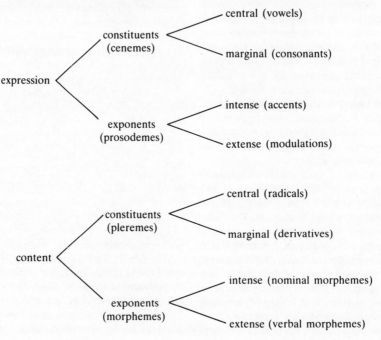

Figure 1

syntagmatic relations, the same definitions applying to content and expression. But for the categories exemplified in Figure 1, the definitions differ between earlier and more recent glossematic papers. In the recent version, **exponents** are defined as entering into a particular type of **government**, which establishes an utterance and is called **direction**, and **intense** and **extense** exponents are distinguished on the basis of their mutual relations (see Hjelmslev, 1951). A unit comprising both constituents and exponents is called a **syntagm**. The minimal syntagm within expression is the **syllable**, within content the **noun**.

The requirement that all categories should be defined by syntagmatic functions means that in the content analysis no separation is made between morphology and syntax. Both word classes, which according to glossematics are classes of content constituents or **pleremes**, and grammatical classes, classes of **morphemes**, are defined by their syntagmatic functions. The nominal and verbal morphemes are further divided into **homonexual** and **heteronexual** morphemes, according to relations within and across the boundaries of a **nexus** (roughly = a clause). Case, for instance, is a homonexual intense morpheme category, whereas mood is an extense morpheme category which can be either homo- or heteronexual (Hjelmslev, 1938).

Vowels and consonants are arranged in categories according to their possibilities of combination within the central and marginal parts of the syllable, respectively.

Since the principle of simplicity requires a minimal inventory of taxemes, a glossematic analysis often goes further in reduction of the inventory than other forms of analysis. Single sounds may be interpreted as clusters, e.g., long vowels as clusters of identical short vowels, Danish [p] as /b + h/, etc.; and formal syllable boundaries may be used to reduce the inventory, e.g. German [s] and [z] may be reduced to one taxeme by positing a syllable boundary after [s] in *reissen* [raisən] /rais-ən/ and before [z] in *reisen* [raizən] /rai-sən/ – by generalization from initial [z-] and final [-s] (e.g. *so* and *das*).

The inventory of sign expressions is also reduced as much as possible. This is accomplished by means of an **ideal notation**, in which syncretisms (including latencies) are resolved. Thus German *lieb–liebe* [li:p–li:bə] is in **actualized notation** /li:p/b–li:bə/, but in ideal notation /li:b–li:bə/, and French *petit–petite* [pti–ptit] is in ideal notation /pətit–pətitə/, where the stem is the same in masculine and feminine and the feminine ending is /ə/. The glossematic ideal notation is closely related to underlying forms in generative phonology (see GENERATIVE PHONOLOGY), but ordered rules are not used in glossematics.

Expression taxemes (vowels and consonants) are not analysed further into distinctive features, an analysis which is considered to belong to pure substance, but – both in content and in expression – taxemes within each category are arranged into dimensions in such a way that there is a minimal number of dimensional elements. These dimensional elements are called **glossemes**. The demand for a minimal number of glossemes being absolute, six taxemes are always arranged as 2×3, 10 as 2×5, etc. Since the number of dimensions is thus fixed irrespective of the language involved, this is called a **universal** analysis. But the placement of the taxemes within the system is language specific since it is governed by syncretisms, where such are found. If, for instance, a language has syncretism between p/b, t/d and k/g, with $\begin{smallmatrix}p\\b\end{smallmatrix}\ \begin{smallmatrix}t\\d\end{smallmatrix}\ \begin{smallmatrix}k\\g\end{smallmatrix}$ appearing in the position where the commutation is suspended (i.e. it is an implication), then $\begin{smallmatrix}p\\b\end{smallmatrix}\ \begin{smallmatrix}t\\d\end{smallmatrix}\ \begin{smallmatrix}k\\g\end{smallmatrix}$ will be placed in a two-dimensional array, /p t k/ as the extensive members, and /b d g/ as the corresponding intensive members. In cases where formal criteria are lacking, affinity to substance may be taken into account.

Members of grammatical categories like case (i.e. nominative, accusative, etc.) are subjected to a similar analysis. Hjelmslev's system of participative oppositions is described in his book on case (1935, pp. 111–26; but note that in this preglossematic work he starts from semantics, not from formal facts like syncretisms). Each dimension may contain from two to seven members, so the oppositions need not be binary.

A characteristic feature of glossematics is the

claim that the analysis of content should be continued below the sign level, not only in the case of grammatical endings like Latin -us, but also in the case of themes. Hjelmslev draws a parallel between the analysis of expression units like sl- and fl-, and content units like 'ram' and 'ewe', which may be analysed into 'he-sheep' and 'she-sheep' (OSG, pp. 62–5) by means of commutation. This is evidently feasible for small closed inventories like prepositions, modal verbs, restricted semantic categories of nouns like terms for family relations etc., but it seems an almost impossible task to reduce the whole inventory of nouns to a restricted number of content figurae, and Hjelmslev gives no further indications concerning the method of analysis. All his examples are analyses of signs (e.g. ram–ewe–bull–cow, or father–mother–brother–sister), but in the paper 'Stratification' (1954; reprinted 1959a), it is said that the analysis in figurae should be undertaken intrinsically in each stratum. This can, however, only be meant as a final control analysis of what has already been found by means of the commutation test, for commutation is an interstratal function operating with signs and parts of signs.

Another problem is the statement in 'Stratification' that the sign function belongs to usage and that it is always possible to form new signs. Thus, if the content form has to be different in different languages, it must be based on different possibilities of combination between the figurae and different types of relation between them within and beyond the sign, and it must be possible to distinguish between accidental gaps and systematic gaps in the sign inventory. There are thus many unsolved problems in this analysis (for discussions see, e.g., Fischer-Jørgensen 1967a; Rischel, 1976; Stati, 1985).

THE INFLUENCE OF GLOSSEMATICS

Applications of glossematics to actual languages are very rare. This is probably due partly to the rather forbidding terminology, which has been exemplified only sporadically above, and partly to the fact that, except for some fragments in scattered papers, the analytical procedure itself and the definitions were not published until 1975,

and only in the form of a condensed summary (the Résumé) without any examples. A few applications can, however, be mentioned, e.g. Alarcos Llorach's description of Spanish (1951), Børge Andersen's analysis of a Danish dialect (1959), and Una Canger's unpublished thesis on Mam. Knud Togeby's analysis of French (1951) is strongly influenced by glossematics, but also by American structuralism.

Glossematics has, however, been eagerly discussed, particularly in the Linguistic Circle of Copenhagen, and although there is no glossematic school as such, a whole generation of Danish linguists has been more or less influenced by Hjelmslev's general ideas about language and by his demand for a stringent method and definitions of the terms employed.

Outside Denmark glossematics was often discussed in the years following the publication of OSG, and particularly after the publication of Whitfield's English translation, e.g. by E. Coseriu (1954) and B. Malmberg (1964 and other publications). It has further had a strong influence on the theories of Sidney Lamb (1966) (see STRATIFICATIONAL SYNTAX) and S.K. Šaumjan (1962, English translation 1968). In the 1960s, the interest in glossematics was overshadowed by the success of transformational grammar, but from the end of the 1960s and, particularly, in the 1980s, there has been a renewed interest in glossematics, not only in the young generation of Danish linguists, but also outside Denmark, particularly in France and in southern Europe, especially Italy and Spain. Special volumes of the periodicals Langages (1967) and Il Protagora (1985) have been devoted to glossematics, and treatises concerned particularly with glossematics have been published (C. Caputo, 1986) or are in preparation.

This renewed interest is not in the first place concerned with the glossematic procedures or definitions of linguistic categories, which were the main subjects of discussion in the Linguistic Circle in Hjelmslev's lifetime (see, e.g., Recherches structurales 1949 and Bulletin du Cercle Linguistique de Copenhague 1941–65), but mainly with Hjelmslev's general ideas on content and expression, form and substance, and his system of semiotics and metasemiotics, i.e., with the epistemological implications of the theory. Moreover, Hjelmslev's demand for a structural analysis of the content has inspired the French school of semantics (see, e.g., Greimas, 1966), and the problem of levels in the substance described in 'La Stratification du langage' has also been taken up.

In this connection, a large number of translations of glossematic works into various languages have been undertaken. Thus glossematics is still a source of inspiration for linguists, semanticists, and philosophers.

E.F.-J.

SUGGESTIONS FOR FURTHER READING

Hjelmslev, L. (1973), 'A causerie on linguistic theory', in *Essais linguistiques II Travaux du Cercle Linguistique de Copenhague, vol. XIV*,

trans. C. Hendriksen, Copenhagen, Nordisk Sprog- og Kulturforlag, pp. 101–17.

Hjelmslev, L. (1947), 'Structural analysis of language', *Studia Linguistica*, pp. 69–78. Also in (1959) *Essais linguistiques II: Travaux du Cercle Linguistique de Copenhague, vol. XIV*, Copenhagen, Nordisk Sprog- og Kulturforlag, pp. 69–81.

Malmberg, B. (1964), *New Trends in Linguistics*, (Bibliotheca Linguistica, no. 1), Stockholm, Bibliotheca Linguistica.

Martinet, A. (1946), 'Au Sujet des fondements de la théorie linguistique de Louis Hjelmslev', *Bulletin de la Société de Linguistique de Paris*, 42(1): 19–42.

Whitfield, F.J. (1954), 'Glossematics', in A. Martinet and U. Weinreich (eds), *Linguistics Today: Publication on the Occasion of Columbia University Bicentennial*, New York, Linguistic Circle of New York, pp. 250–8.

Historical linguistics

INTRODUCTION

From a practical point of view, **historical linguists** map the world's languages, determine their relationships, and with the use of written documentation, fit extinct languages of the past into the jigsaw puzzle of the world's complex pattern of linguistic distribution.

From a theoretical perspective, the practitioner may be interested in the nature of linguistic change itself, that is, how and why languages change, and the underlying forces and processes which shape, mould and direct modifications. Of paramount concern is the notion of **language universals**, which shed light on the linguistic behaviour of the species. Such universals may reflect tendencies in language to change towards preferable types of sound

patterns, syllabic structures and even syntactic arrangements. Such universals may relate to physiological and cognitive parameters inherent in the organism in a form of marked and unmarked features of language. The historian must also identify the various influences that disrupt these tendencies with varying degrees of intensity related to the degree and nature of external contacts and internal conflicts.

Perhaps the greatest achievement of the forces at work in evolutionary biology has been the development of natural human language, and historical linguistic studies are important for our understanding of this complex behaviour. Only through such studies can we account for many of the social and cultural aspects of language and certain innate linguistic propensities of human kind. In its structural, social and biological complexity, and its relationships to other forms of communication, human language can only be fully understood when we know how it responds to internal and external stimuli.

HISTORICAL BACKGROUND

ANTIQUITY AND THE MIDDLE AGES

The foundations for historical linguistic studies in the west were laid down by the ancient Greeks, whose philosophical studies incorporated speculation on the nature of their language. The highest degree of sophistication was reached among the scholars of Alexandria during Hellenistic times. In **etymology** – in the ancient Greek sense 'the true meaning of the word' – they debated whether or not the names of things arose due to the natural attributes of the objects in question or were founded by convention, and a large part of the dialogue of Plato's *Cratylus* is devoted to this subject. The Greeks also discussed the nature of language in terms of a **pattern** (**analogy**) or its absence (**anomaly**), and formulated statements concerning the various **parts of speech** (see also TRADITIONAL GRAMMAR, RHETORIC and STYLISTICS).

The embryonic science of language initiated by the Greeks was passed on to the Romans, whose linguistic studies on Latin were in general the application of Greek thought, controversies and grammatical categories. Like the Greeks, the Romans were aware of word changes in both form and meaning from earlier texts but no significant headway was made in the study of etymology. Latin and Greek grammar were studied throughout the Middle Ages primarily from a pedagogical point of view.

THE RENAISSANCE

With the advent of the Renaissance, language studies underwent a change as both local and non-Indo-European languages came under linguistic scrutiny. As trade routes opened up to the east and explorers ranged the lands of the New World, data on exotic languages began to accumulate and stimulate the imagination. Once vernacular languages were deemed worthy of study and the world's diversity in linguistic structures was recognized, language studies turned to universal linguistic concepts and to the idea of **universal grammar** as expressed, for example, in the work of the **Port-Royal** grammarians of the seventeenth century (see PORT-ROYAL GRAMMAR). These concepts of French rationalists were somewhat at odds with the English empiricists, who fostered **descriptive phonetics** and the grammatical uniqueness of languages.

An important trend in the seventeenth century was the effort to compare and classify languages in accordance with their resemblances. The study of etymology also gained momentum but words were still derived from other languages haphazardly, by rearranging the letters, especially those of Hebrew, thought by many to have been the original language.

THE EIGHTEENTH CENTURY

Early in the eighteenth century, comparative and historical linguistics gained more consistency. For instance, J. Ludolf in 1702 stated that affinities between languages must be based on grammatical resemblances rather than vocabulary, and among vocabulary correspondences, the emphasis should be on simple words such as those which describe parts of the body. In a paper published in 1710, Leibnitz maintained that no known historical language is the source of the world's languages since they must be derived from a **proto-speech**. He also attempted to establish language classifications and toyed with the idea of a universal alphabet for all languages (see Robins, 1967).

During the eighteenth century, the gathering of information proceeded as specimens of more and more languages were added to the repertoire. Attention also turned to speculation on the **origin of language**, especially in the works of Hobbes, Rousseau, Burnett, Lord Mondboddo, Condillac, and Herder. The subject had been treated before as early as the ancient Egyptians but now it took on more substance in relation to supposed universals of language and its global diversity.

The fundamental historical study of language can be said to have begun in earnest at this time through efforts to compare and classify languages in accordance with their origins, hypothetical or otherwise. The crowning achievement in the latter part of the eighteenth century came with the discovery that the Sanskrit language of ancient India was related to the languages of Europe and to Latin and Greek.

SANSKRIT

The first known reference in the west to Sanskrit occurred at the end of the sixteenth century when F. Sassetti wrote home to his native Italy about the *lingua Sanscruta* and some of its resemblances to Italian. Others, too, such as B. Schulze and Père Coerdoux made similar observations on the resemblance of Sanskrit to Latin and European languages. The importance of these relationships came to the fore in 1786, however, when Sir William Jones, a judge in the English colonial administration, announced to the Royal Asiatic Society in Calcutta that Sanskrit, Greek, Latin, Gothic, and Celtic were seemingly from the same origin which perhaps no longer existed. In his words:

> The Sanskrit language, whatever be its antiquity, is of a wonderful structure; more perfect than the Greek, more copious than the Latin, and more exquisitely refined than either, yet bearing to both of them a stronger affinity, both in the roots of verbs and in the forms of grammar, than could possibly have been produced by accident; so strong indeed, that no philologer could examine them all three, without believing them to have sprung from some common source which, perhaps, no longer exists: there is a reason, though not quite so forcible, for supposing that both the Gothic and the Celtic, though blended with a very different idiom, had the same origin with the Sanskrit; and the Old Persian might be added to the same family.
>
> (in Lehmann, 1967, p. 15)

Interest in the discovery mounted, and early in the nineteenth century, Sanskrit was being studied in the west. Sanskrit philological studies were initiated in Germany by W. von Schlegel about the time the first Sanskrit grammar in English was published. The linguistic study of this language set in motion the comparison of Sanskrit with languages of Europe, forming the first period in the growth of historical linguistics and setting **comparative linguistics** on a firm footing. Meanwhile, systematic etymological studies helped clarify and cement the family ties of the Indo-European languages.

INDIAN LINGUISTIC TRADITION

Ancient Indian grammarians were centuries ahead of their European counterparts in language studies and from their best-known scholar, **Pāṇini**, whose studies, still extant, date back to the second half of the first millennium BC, we see brilliant independent linguistic scholarship in both theory and practice.

As far as is known, the inspiration for Sanskrit studies in India stemmed from the desire to preserve religious ritual and the orally transmitted texts of the earlier **Vedic** period (1200–1000 BC) from phonetic, grammatical, and semantic erosion. **Pāṇini's Sanskrit grammar**, the *Astadhyayi* or 'Eight Books' was a grammarian's grammar and not designed for pedagogical purposes. Phonetic description in this and other, later Indian works were not matched in the west until at least the seventeenth century. Nor were they equalled in grammatical analysis which involved ordered rules of word formation and extreme economy of statement. For example, a finished product such as *abhavat* 'he, she was' from a root form *bhu* 'to be', may be seen to pass through successive representation in an ordered sequence.

The identification of **roots** and **affixes** in ancient Sanskrit grammar inspired the concept of the morpheme in modern analysis, aided by the studies of Arabic and Hebrew, breaking away from the **Thrax–Priscian word and paradigm pedagogical model** of early Greek and Latin language studies.

THE IMPACT OF SANSKRIT ON THE WEST

The introduction of Sanskrit and its subsequent study in Europe was a prime inducement to **comparative–historical linguistics**. It came at an auspicious time: from Dante on, various but sporadic attempts had been made to shed light on relationships between languages and their historical developments and the time was right for more cohesive views of historical studies. It is generally accepted that the nineteenth century is the era *par excellence* of comparative–historical linguistics – a century in which most of the linguistic efforts were devoted to this subject, led, in the main, by German scholarship.

THE NINETEENTH CENTURY

A few of the best-known historical linguists of the early nineteenth century are the Dane, Rasmus Rask, and the Germans, Franz Bopp and Jacob Grimm. With these scholars comparative–historical linguistic studies of Indo-European languages had a definite beginning.

In his book *Über die Sprache und Weisheit der Inder* published in 1808, Friedrich von Schlegel (1772–1829) used the term *vergleichende Grammatik* 'comparative grammar' and in 1816, Bopp published a work comparing the verbal conjugations of Sanskrit, Persian, Latin, Greek, and German. After adding Celtic and Albanian, he called these the **Indo-European family of languages**. Bopp has often been considered the father of Indo-European linguistics.

Rask (1787–1832) wrote the first systematic grammars of Old Norse and of Old English and, in 1818, he published a comparative grammar outlining the **Scandinavian languages** and noting their relationships to one another. Through comparisons of word forms, he brought order into historical relationships matching a letter of one language to a letter in another, so that regularity of change could be observed.

Jacob Grimm (1785–1863), a contemporary of Bopp (1787–1832), restricted his studies to the **Germanic family**, paying special attention to **Gothic** due to its historical value of having been committed to writing in the fourth century. This endeavour allowed him to see more clearly than anyone before him the systematic nature of **sound change**. Within the framework of comparative Germanic, he made the first statements on the

nature of **umlaut** (see p. 198 below) and **ablaut**, or, as it is sometimes called **vowel gradation** (as found, for example, in German *sprechen*, *sprach*, *gesprochen*), and developed, more fully than Rask, the notion of *Lautverschiebung* or **sound shift**, which became the first law in linguistics and which has been referred to as **Grimm's Law**, or the **First Germanic Sound Shift**.

The work, published in 1822 and entitled *Deutsche Grammatik*, contained general statements about similarities between Germanic obstruents, i.e., plosives, affricates, and fricatives, and their equivalents in other languages. Using the old terms of Greek Grammar where $T = $ *tenuis* (p, t, k), $M = $ *media* (b, d, g) and $A = $ *aspirate* (f, θ, x), he noted

Proto Indo-European	=	Germanic
T		A
M		T
A		M

A modern tabulation of his conclusions would appear as:

Indo-European	>	Germanic
p		f
t		θ
k		x

Indo-European	>	Germanic
b		p
d		t
g		k

Indo-European	>	Germanic
bh		b
dh		d
gh		g

J.H. Bredsdorff (1790–1841), a disciple of Rask, tried to explain the causes of **language change** in 1821 (Bredsdorff 1821, 1886). He considered such factors as mishearing, misunderstanding, misrecollection, imperfection of speech organs, indolence, the tendency towards analogy, the desire to be distinct, the need of expressing new ideas, and influences from foreign languages.

Some of his ideas are still viable today. For instance, it is recognized that the tendency towards **analogy**, speakers' desire for uniformity, for regular patterns, causes language to become more rather than less regular in syntax and phonology. Colloquial speech, which popular, though rarely expert, opinion often classifies as **indolent**, can also eventually result in changes in pronunciation, spelling, grammatical patterning, and the semantic system. The influence from foreign languages is clearly observable when new words enter a language and become absorbed in its grammar and pronunciation system, as when *pizza* receives the English plural form *pizzas*, or when *weekend* is pronounced as beginning with /v/ in Danish and is given the plural ending *-er*. This often results in the ability of speakers of a language to express a new idea or name a new thing – pizzas were at one time unfamiliar in Britain, and Danish did not at one time have a word which could express the conceptualization of the weekend as a whole. Similarly, new inventions often result in the need for new terminology, as when the advent of computers led to the coinage of the term *software* by analogy with *hardware*, which was itself borrowed from another sphere, namely that of the traditional hardware store, selling things like nails, glue, string, and various tools.

In the mid nineteenth century, one of the most influential linguists, August Schleicher (1821–68), set about reconstructing the hypothetical parent language from which most European languages were derived – the **proto-language** (see pp. 209–11 below). He also devised the *Stammbaumtheorie* or **genealogical family-tree model** of the **Indo-European languages** (see pp. 212–16 below). He worked out a typological classification of languages based on the work of his predecessors in which he viewed languages as isolating, agglutinating, and inflectional (see LANGUAGE TYPOLOGY). On a more philosophical level, he brought to linguistics three important concepts mostly rejected today but which at the time stimulated much discussion and work in the discipline: namely, that language is a natural organism; that it evolves naturally in the Darwinian sense; and that language depends on the physiology and minds of people, that is, it has racial connotations. In short, he stimulated a

new and different approach to language study, namely a **biological approach**.

The work of Schleicher represents a culmination of the first phase of historical linguistics in the nineteenth century. In the second half of the century the discipline of linguistics became more cosmopolitan as scholars in countries other than Germany began seriously to investigate linguistic problems. Germany, however, remained the centre of linguistic attention throughout the century.

In 1863, Hermann Grassmann, a pioneer in internal reconstruction (see pp. 209–11 below), devised a phonetic law based on observations of the Indo-European languages, showing why correspondences established by Grimm did not always work. His **Law of the Aspirates** demonstrated that when an Indo-European word had two aspirated sounds (see ARTICULATORY PHONETICS) in the same syllable, one, usually the first, underwent de-aspiration. For example, Sanskrit *ba-bhú-va* 'he has become' < **bha-bhū-va* shows the reduplicated syllable of the root reduced through loss of aspiration (the asterisk indicates that the form is reconstructed).

This exception to Grimm's Law, where Sanskrit [b] corresponds to Germanic [b] and not to [bh], then, proved to be a law itself.

In 1875, still another phonetic law was proposed by Karl Verner (1846–96). This succeeded in accounting for other exceptions to Grimm's statements by showing that the place of the Indo-European accent was a factor in the regularity of the correspondences. For example, Indo-European [t] in [*pθtěr] > [ð] [faðar] in Germanic, not [θ] as might be expected. The accent later shifted in Germanic to the first syllable.

In his *Corsi di glottologia*, published in Florence in 1870, Gradziadio Ascoli (1829–1907) demonstrated by comparative methods that [k-] in certain places became [ʃ-] in Sanskrit. Compare the word for one hundred:

Latin	centum
Greek	hekaton
Old Irish	cet
Sanskrit	çata
Germanic	hundred

The discovery that [k] remains in some Indo-

European languages but became [ʃ] in Sanskrit ended the belief that Sanskrit was the oldest and closest language to the proto-form or parent language. Further investigation would reveal that this change [k > ʃ] occurred before a front vowel, in this case [e] which later merged with [a] in Sanskrit.

The formulation of sound laws which appeared to be systematic and regular to the extent that exceptions seemed to be laws themselves, gave rise to one of the most important and controversial theories in historical linguistics promulgated in the doctrine of the Neogrammarians or *Junggrammatiker*.

THE NEOGRAMMARIANS

Inspired in 1868 by the ideas of Wilhelm Scherer (1841–86) who, in his book on the history of the German language (Scherer, 1868), advocated fixed laws in sound change, the Neogrammarian movement soon dominated linguistic inquiry. To account for situations where phonetic laws were not upheld by the data, Scherer looked to **analogy** (see pp. 192–3 above) as the explanation for change. The chief representatives of the movement, Brugmann, Osthoff, Delbrück, Wackernagel, Paul, and Leskien, held that phonetic laws were similar to laws of nature of the physical sciences in their consistency of operation. In 1878, in the first volume of a journal edited by Brugmann (1849–1919) and Osthoff (1847–1909), *Morphologische Untersuchungen*, they delineated the Neogrammarian doctrine and the special designation *junggrammatische Richtung* 'Neogrammarian School of Thought'. The crux of their doctrine was, as Osthoff put it: 'sound-laws work with a blind necessity and all discrepancies to these laws were the workings of analogy'. Centred around the University of Leipzig, the Neogrammarians saw in sound change the application of laws of a mechanical nature opposed by the psychological process of the speakers towards regularization of forms resulting in analogically irregular sound changes.

The Neogrammarian doctrine did not go unopposed. For example, the psychologist,

Wilhelm Wundt (1832–1920), found fault with their views relating to psychological aspects of language. In addition, Hugo Schuchardt (1842–1927) of the University of Graz published an article in 1885 on the sound laws in which he considered language change to be due to a mixing process both within and outside language. Similarly, Ascoli (1829–1907) attributed much of the process of language change to a theory proposed by him called the Substratum Theory, in which languages were influenced by mixture of populations (see p. 200 below).

THE TWENTIETH CENTURY

The first decade of the twentieth century saw a shift away from German domination of linguistic science with the work of Ferdinand de Saussure (1857–1913) of the University of Geneva. His view of language as a system of arbitrary signs in opposition to one another, his distinction between language and speech, and his separation of descriptive linguistics and historical linguistics into two defined spheres of interest, earned him the reputation of one of the founders of structural linguistics (see STRUCTURALIST LINGUISTICS).

From this time on, the field of **descriptive linguistics** developed rapidly while historical linguistics and comparative studies lost their pre-eminence.

Today, among the disciplines that make up the broad field of linguistics (descriptive, historical, sociological, psychological, etc.) historical linguistics, from once being the embodiment of the discipline, has become another branch of the multivaried area of investigation. Twentieth–century advancements in historical–comparative language studies have been on the practical side, with the collection of data and reformulation of previous work. On the theoretical side, much has come from advancements in descriptive linguistics and other branches of the discipline. For example, from structural concepts such as the phoneme, and refinements in phonetics, to more stringent application of ordered rules and underlying structures, statistical methods and their relationship to language change and language universals.

PRINCIPLES, METHODS, OBJECTIVES AND DATA OF HISTORICAL LINGUISTICS

Certain principles in the field of historical linguistic enquiry are taken as axiomatic, for example:

All languages are in a continual process of change.

All languages are subject to the same kind of modifying influences.

Language change is regular and systematic, allowing for unhindered communication among speakers.

Linguistic and social factors are interrelated in language change.

Language systems tend toward as yet unspecified states of economy and redundancy.

A linguistic change or state not attested in known languages would be suspect if posited for an earlier stage through reconstruction. A phonological change, for example, of the type /b/ > /k/ between vowels runs counter to empirical linguistic facts. Similarly, no system of consonants in any known language consists entirely of voiced fricatives (see ARTICULATORY PHONETICS). Any reconstruction that ignored this observation and posited only voiced fricatives would be highly suspect.

The **diachronic study** of language may be approached by comparing one or more languages at different stages in their histories. **Synchronic** or **descriptive** studies underlie historical investigations inasmuch as an analysis of a language or a part thereof at period A can then be compared to a descriptive study at period B. For example, an investigation of English at the time of Chaucer, and another of Modern English would reveal a number of differences. Similarly, a descriptive statement of Latin and one of Modern French would disclose very different systems in phonology and morphosyntax. The **historical linguist** attempts to classify these differences and to explicate the manner and means by which they came about.

When the various historical facts of a language are discovered, the investigator might then establish general rules based on the data. These rules will demonstrate in more succinct form the manner in which the language changed and how it differs from other related languages.

Rules of change may be written in several ways: [t] > [d]/V__V states that the sound [t] becomes [d] in the environment between vowels. Such rules can also be stated in **feature specification**:

$$
\begin{bmatrix}
+\text{consonantal} \\
+\text{plosive} \\
+\text{coronal} \\
+\text{anterior} \\
-\text{voiced}
\end{bmatrix}
\rightarrow [+\text{voiced}]/[+\text{vocalic}]\_\_[+\text{vocalic}]
$$

As is often the case, an entire class of sounds, for example [p t k], behave in an identical manner and instead of different rules for each, one rule suffices:

$$
\begin{bmatrix}
+\text{consonantal} \\
+\text{plosive} \\
-\text{voiced}
\end{bmatrix}
\rightarrow [+\text{voiced}]/[+\text{vocalic}]\_\_[+\text{vocalic}]
$$

If we were to compare Latin and Italian, we would find such words as:

Latin	Italian	
noctem	notte	'night'
octo	otto	'eight'
lactem	latte	'milk'
factum	fatto	'fact'
lectum	letto	'bed'

In these examples and others that could be added, we discover that Latin [k] (e.g., in [noktem]) became Italian [t] in the environment before [t]. This assimilatory change is a general rule in Italian and can be stated as: [k] > [t]/____[t], or it can be stated in feature specifications. The rule helps account for the differences between Latin and Italian and between Italian and other Romance languages where a different set of rules apply to give, say, Spanish *noche* [nótʃe] and French *nuit* [nɥi].

Objectives of the practitioners of historical linguistics vary. Excluding here language changes resulting from evolutionary or maturation processes of developing neuroanatomical structures of Homo sapiens, some historical linguists are concerned with phonological, morphological, syntactic, and semantic changes that occur in languages over a given period of time, to acquire an understanding of the mechanisms underlying the modifications and to seek explanations for them. Answers to these questions also bear on the nature of the species and may be sought within cognitive and physiological parameters which govern the behaviour of the species.

Through historical studies some linguists may be more concerned with reconstruction and comparison of languages to arrive at historical relationships indicating common origins of languages which allow them to be grouped into families. The geographical distribution of families is of paramount importance in our understanding of migrations and settlement patterns over the surface of the earth.

Sociological aspects of language change encompassing questions of dialect, style, prestige, taboos, changes in social behaviour, technology, and even individual needs to be different, are also important considerations in the understanding of cultural associations and ultimately human behaviour.

The changes that languages undergo make up the data for historical linguistics which are themselves generally transmitted by and derived from written documentation or reconstructed from the languages in question if such records are not available.

In cases where the underlying language of the documentation is known, such as Old English, Latin, and Sanskrit, the investigator must try to determine the orthoepic features of the language through knowledge of the writing system employed, through commentary on the language by contemporary authors, by rhyme, and by the pronunciation of the descendent languages.

In dealing with primary written sources inscribed in an unknown language, the investigator must decipher the texts in order to gain a clear view of the underlying linguistic structure. The performance of this task must take into account the kind of writing system used, the direction of writing, and the phonetic basis underlying the orthographic signs. Morphemes and morpheme boundaries must be determined, syntactic features assessed and semantic properties determined.

PHILOLOGY

The forerunner of historical linguistics, **philological studies**, is concerned with language and culture. The term is generally used to denote the study of literary monuments or inscriptions to ascertain the cultural features of an ancient civilization. **Classical philology** continues the activities of the ancient Greeks and Alexandrians who delved into the already old texts of their ancestors. The philological tradition sank to a low ebb during the Middle Ages, but with the rediscovery of classical antiquity of the Renaissance, the discipline again prospered. Philological endeavours were given further impetus in the early nineteenth century as Sanskrit literature became available in the west. Historical linguistics was known as **comparative philology** until about the time of August Schleicher, who, because of his pure language work, preferred to be called a *glottiker*, that is, a **linguist**.

PHONOLOGICAL CHANGE

REGULARITY OF SOUND CHANGE

(For explanation of the phonetic terms in this and the following sections, see ARTICULATORY PHONETICS.)

The sounds of a language are affected over the course of time by modifications that tend to be regular and systematic in that the changes have a propensity to apply in the same manner to all relevant environments. The reflexes of the Latin vowel [a], for example, demonstrate this principle.

Latin [a] regularly became French [ɛ], as in the following words:

Latin	French	
marem	mer	[mɛʁ]
fabam	fève	[fɛv]
patrem	père	[pɛʁ]
labram	lèvre	[lɛvʁ]

This change of Latin [a] to French [ɛ] occurred when [a] was accented and free, that is, in an open syllable, as in [má-rem].

The accented Latin vowel [a] in an open syllable, but followed by a nasal, resulted in [ɛ̃]:

Latin	French	
manum	main	[mɛ̃]
panem	pain	[pɛ̃]
planum	plain	[plɛ̃]
famen	faim	[fɛ̃]

Cases where Latin [a] became French [a], while they may at first glance appear to have been exceptions to the above rule, were in fact the result of another regular sound change in which accented [a] behaved predictably in a closed environment, that is, in a closed syllable or one blocked by a consonant, as in [pár-te], [vák-ká], etc. Compare:

Latin	French	
partem	part	[paʁ]
vaccam	vache	[vaʃ]
carrum	char	[ʃaʁ]
cattum	chat	[ʃa]

When Latin [a] was closed by a nasal consonant, the result was a nasal [ã], as in:

Latin	French	
campu	champ	[ʃã]
grande	grand	[grã]
annu	an	[ã]
manicam (manca)	manche	[mãʃ]

Since the environment dictated the phonological change, the conditions of the modifications can be established along the following lines (where o = syllable boundary):

[a] >
- [ɛ]/ __ o con.
- [ɛ]/ __ o con. + nasal
- [a]/ __ con. o
- [ã]/ __ con. o + nasal

This general rule requires clarification based on further environmental factors that regularly affect the vowel [a]. For example:

alterum	autre	[otʁ]
valet	vaut	[vo]

where [a] plus [l] become [au] and subsequently reduces to [o].

Beginning in the period of Late Old French, the vowel [ɛ] (from [a]) underwent a further change to become [e] when the syllable became open through the loss of a final consonant, cf.

clavem	> clé	[kle]
pratum	> pré	[pre]

When [a] was unaccented, it underwent another set of changes which resulted in [ə] or [a] as in:

camisam	> chemise	[ʃəmiːz]
amicum	> ami	[ami]

The treatment of [a] in the above examples is intended to be indicative of the kind of regularity found in phonological change but is not meant to be exhaustive.

PHONOLOGICAL PROCESSES

The mechanisms by which phonological modifications occur entail changes in the features of a sound (e.g. voiceless, voiced, plosive, fricative) or the addition, loss or movement of sound segments. Many such changes are of an anticipatory nature whereby a modification takes place under the influence of a following sound. For example, the **assimilation** of [k] > [t]/ __ [t] in Latin *octo* [okto] to Italian *otto* is of this type, in which the feature velar is changed to dental before a following dental sound. Compare:

[k]	[t]
voiceless	voiceless
plosive	plosive
velar	dental

Other processes of this type include **nasalization** as in Latin *bonum* to Portugese *bom* [bõ], where a non-nasal vowel acquires the nasality of a following nasal consonant.

Often a velar consonant becomes a palatal consonant under the influence of a following front vowel that pulls the highest point of the tongue from the velar forward into the palatal zone as in Old English *kin* [kɪn] and Modern English *chin* [tʃɪn] or Latin *centum* [kentum] and Italian *cento* [tʃɛnto].

A specific kind of assimilation, referred to as **sonorization**, involves the voicing of voiceless consonants and appears to be motivated primarily by voiced surroundings. For example, voiceless [p], [t] and [k] become [b], [d] and [g] in the environment between vowels, as in the following examples:

Latin	> Spanish			
cupa	cuba ['kúba]	[p]	>	[b]
vita	vida ['bida]	[t]	>	[d]
amica	amiga [a'miga]	[k]	>	[g]

Assimilation may take place over syllable boundaries, as occurs through the process of **umlaut**, or, as it is sometimes called, **mutation**. The Proto-Germanic form [*musiz] gave Old English [mɪːs], (Modern English *mice*), when the vowel in the first syllable was drawn forward through the influence of the front vowel in the second syllable. Similarly, Latin *feci* gave rise to Spanish *hice* when the influence of the Latin vowel [i] raised [e] to [i] through assimilation. Final [i] subsequently lowered to [e]. Compare also Latin *veni* and Spanish *vine*.

The opposite of assimilation, **dissimilation**, modifies a segment so that it becomes less like another, often neighbouring segment, in the word. Dissimilation is less frequent than assimilation in the known histories of the world's languages. The conditioning factor may be juxtaposed to the sound which undergoes change or may operate at a distance. The first case is illustrated by Latin *luminosum* which became Spanish *lumbroso* where, after the loss of unaccented [i], the resultant cluster [mn] dissimilated to [mr] and subsequently became [mbr]. The nasal [n], by losing its nasal quality and changing to [r], became less like [m]. The second case is illustrated by Latin *arbor* which became Spanish *árbol* by changing [r] to [l] under the influence of the preceding [r].

The addition of a segment into a particular environment of the word, **epenthesis**, is essentially a form of anticipation of a following sound and may involve either consonants or vowels. The Old English word *glimsian* through the insertion of an epenthetic [p] in the environment [m__s] gave rise to Modern English *glimpse*. The inserted sound agrees with the preceding [m] in place of articulation (bilabial) and with the following [s] in manner of articulation (voiceless). Compare Old English *timr* and Modern English *timber*, Old English *ganra*, Modern *gander*.

Basque speakers borrowed a number of words from late Latin but lacked certain consonant clusters found in the lending language. Vowels were inserted in the borrowed words to make them more compatible to the Basque system of phonological distribution, which, for example, tended to avoid sequences of plosive plus [r]; compare:

Latin	Basque	
[krus]	[guruts]	'cross'
[libru]	[libiru]	'book'

The addition of a word-initial segment generally applied to facilitate the pronunciation of an initial consonant cluster is a process referred to as **prothesis**; for example,

Latin	Spanish
schola [skola]	escuela [eskwela]
stella [stela]	estrella [estreʎa]

Sounds are subject to deletion. The two most common processes of segment deletion are **apocope** and **syncope**, which are especially common in environments after accented syllables. In word-final position, apocope has been common in the history of many languages including French. Compare:

Latin	French
cane [kane]	chien [ʃjɛ̃]
caru [karu]	cher [ʃɛʁ]

Consonantal loss in word-final position is also common among many languages. Again, we see in French the deletion of consonants in forms such as Latin *pratu* > French *pré*.

Other word positions are also vulnerable to deletion of segments; Old and Middle English employed the cluster [kn-] as in *knight, knot, knee*. The [k] was lost in the transition period to Modern English.

The loss of a word-medial vowel, or syncope, occurs in English in words such as *vegetable* ['vɛdʒtəbl] where the unaccented second syllable lost the vocalic segment. The process does not commonly occur in English, however, but appears much more readily in the Romance languages.

Latin	Spanish	French
viride	verde	vert
lepore	liebre	lièvre
calidu	caldo	chaud

A change in the relative position of sounds, probably caused by a kind of anticipation, is referred to as **metathesis**. Adjacent sounds may be affected, as in the West Saxon dialect of Old English, where [ks] became [sk] in words such as *axian* > ask. Sounds separated by some phonetic distance may also undergo metathesis as: for example, popular Latin *mirac(u)lu* became Spanish *milagro* through the transposition of [l] and [r].

A number of other processes are often at work in language change. Stated briefly, some further changes that affect consonants are:

aspiration	[t] > [tʰ]
affrication	[t] > [ts]
labialization	[t] > [tʷ]
prenasalization	[t] > [nt]
glottalization	[t] > [t']
velarization	[t] > [ɫ]
rhotacization	[z] > [r]

or the opposite – de-aspiration, de-affrication, etc.

Further processes observed among vocalic segments are:

raising	[e] > [i]
lowering	[i] > [e]
fronting	[o] > [e]
backing	[e] > [o]
rounding	[i] > [u]
unrounding	[u] > [i]

lengthening	[a] > [aː]
shortening	[aː] > [a]
diphthongization	[e] > [ie]
monophthongization	[ie] > [e]

An entire syllable may undergo loss, a process called **haplology**, cf. Latin **stipipendium* > *stipendium*.

PHONETIC AND PHONOLOGICAL CHANGE

As we have seen, phonemes develop variants in accordance with environmental conditions and are the result of influences exercised through phonetic processes such as assimilation. We know, for example, that English vowels have nasalized variants preceding nasal consonants, as in the word *can't*, but not in other environments, compare *cat*, phonetically [kʰæ̃ːnt], [kʰæt]. These phonetic changes have no impact on the overall phonological system, since the variation is conditioned and predictable, affecting only the distribution of allophones (see PHONEMICS).

Sound changes that result in an increase or reduction in the number of phonemes in a language, or lead to the replacement of phonemes by others, are generally brought about by **splits** or **mergers**. A change in which several phonemes are replaced in a systematic way is called a **shift** which also may be partial or complete:

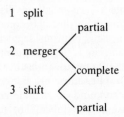

```
1  split
                            partial
2  merger  <
                            complete
3  shift   <
                            partial
```

If, in English, nasal consonants were to disappear, the form *can't* would be represented phonetically as [kʰæt] and would, in fact, contrast with *cat* as /kæ̃t/, /kæt/, with the distinguishing feature of nasal versus non-nasal vowel. What was once a phonetic feature of the language, through the loss of the nasal consonant, would then become a phonemic feature brought about by phonological split. Something similar to this occurred in French, where nasal and non-nasal vowels distinguish meaning:

Latin		French	
bonus	>	/bõ/ bon	'good'
bellus	>	/bo/ beau	'pretty, handsome'

At some stage in the history of English, allophonic conditioning led to the development of a velar nasal [ŋ] before a velar plosive through assimilation. In the course of Middle English, the voiced velar plosive disappeared in word-final position after the nasal consonant, as in the words *young* or *sing*. The velar nasal allophone of /n/, then, became a separate phoneme, as attested by such minimal pairs (see PHONEMICS) as

sin	/sin/
sing	/siŋ/

A phoneme may also split into multiple forms as attested in French, compare

Latin		French	
		k/__w	
/k/	>	s/__	$\begin{bmatrix} i \\ e \end{bmatrix}$
		s/__a	

in such words as

quando	>	quand	/kã/	'when'
centum	>	cent	/sã/	'hundred'
campus	>	champ	/ʃã/	'field'

Phonological split may also result in merger in which no new phonemes are created in the language. In some dialects of English, for example, /t/ split into [t] and [d] in certain environments and [d] merged with the phoneme /d/ already in the language. This was the case where *latter* /lætə/ became homophonous with *ladder* /lædə/ and *bitter* with *bidder*.

Mergers may be **partial** or **complete**. If merger is complete, there is a net reduction in the number of phonemes in the language. Such is the case in some varieties of Cockney, a non-standard dialect of London, where the two dental fricatives

/θ/ and /ð/ have merged completely with /f/ and /v/ respectively. Hence, *thin* /θɪn/ is pronounced /fɪn/ and *bathe* /beɪð/ is pronounced /beɪv/. Four phonemes were reduced to two:

$$/f/ \quad /θ/ \; > /f/$$
$$/v/ \quad /ð/ \; > /v/$$

In Black English pronunciation in the United States, /θ/ merges partially with /f/, i.e. /θ/ > /f/ in all positions except word initial. The form *with* is articulated as /wɪf/ but the word *thing* retains /θ/ as in /θɪŋ/ or /θæŋ/.

When a series of phonemes is systematically modified, such as /p/, /t/, /k/, > /b/, /d/, /g/ we may consider a shift to have occurred. A shift may be **partial**, inasmuch as all the allophones of the phoneme do not participate in it, or it may be **complete**, when they do. The modification of long vowels in Late Middle English known as the **Great Vowel Shift** (see p. 201 below) left no residue and appears to have been complete. The **First Germanic Consonant Shift**, in which /p/, /t/, /k/ > /f/, /θ/, /x/, however, left some of the voiceless plosives unaffected in specific environments, such as after /s/. Compare, for example, Latin *est* and German *ist* and see p. 192 above.

Phonological processes that lead to allophonic variation and subsequent new phonemes generally occur one step at a time. The change of Latin /k/ to French /ʃ/, for example, in words such as *cane* /kane/ to *chien* /ʃjẽ/, did not do so directly, but instead entailed two changes:

/k/ voiceless	> /tʃ/	voiceless	> /ʃ/ voiceless
plosive		plosive	*fricative*
velar		*palatal*	*palatal*

Phonological change usually takes place within the range of allophonic variation which varies by one feature. A phoneme /k/ might have allophones [tʃ] or [x] differing by one phonological feature, but not generally an allophone [ʃ] differing by two features. A change to /ʃ/ could be the result of either of the two allophones serving as intermediaries:

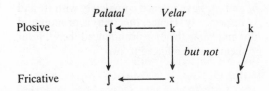

	Palatal	Velar	
Plosive	tʃ ←—— k		k
		but not	
Fricative	ʃ ←—— x		ʃ

NON-PHONOLOGICALLY MOTIVATED SOUND CHANGE

Many phonological changes are not conditioned by the surrounding environments but are motivated by other factors relating to external forces, such as substratum influences, internal forces inherent in the structural paradigmatic make-up of the language, and, as is often the case, by unknown factors whose influences, obscured by time, are no longer recoverable. The **First Germanic Consonant Shift**, for example, occurred at a time in which there were no written records for the Germanic languages and under unknown circumstances.

A major change in the history of English vowels took place at the end of the Middle English period (sixteenth century) in which the long tense vowels underwent a regular modification without the apparent assistance of an environmental stimulus. The modification is referred to as the **Great English Vowel Shift**.

Middle English	Early Modern English	
[miːs]	[mays]	'mice'
[muːs]	[maws]	'mouse'
[geːs]	[giːs]	'geese'
[goːs]	[guːs]	'goose'
[brɛːken]	[breːk]	'break'
[brɔːken]	[broːk]	'broke'
[naːm]	[neːm]	'name'

The vocalic movement upward in which the high vowels diphthongized can be shown schematically as:

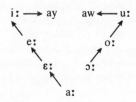

An upward pressure was also exerted on the back vowels of the Gallo-Roman language in about the ninth century during the evolution from Latin to French, and the high back vowel from Latin [uː] which had become [u] then shifted to [y].

Gallo–Roman Free Accented Vowels

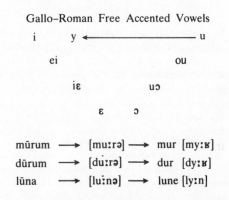

mūrum	→	[muːrə]	→	mur [myːʁ]
dūrum	→	[duːrə]	→	dur [dyːʁ]
lūna	→	[luːnə]	→	lune [lyːn]

Note [u] → [y] regardless of environmental position, where explanations other than those involving conditioned change must be sought. One plausible interpretation of the event, based on paradigmatic considerations, suggests that, with the reduction of Latin [au] → [ɔ] (*aurum* → *or* [ɔr]) which occurred prior to the change [u] → [y], the margin of tolerance, i.e. the physical space, between back vowels was not sufficient. The monophthongization of [au] consequently forced upward pressure on the back vowels and [u], the closest vowel, could go no closer and palatalized.

The plosive and fricative consonantal structure of Early Old French of the eleventh and twelfth centuries consisted of the phonetic inventory and relationships

		Labial	Dental	Pre-palatal	Palatal	Velar
Plosives	vl.	p	t	ts	tʃ	k
	vd	b	d	dz	dʒ	g
Fricatives	vl.	f	s			
	vd	v	z			

(vl. = voiceless; vd = voiced)

During the thirteenth century, the affricated palatal sounds ceased to be plosives and became fricatives:

ć	[ts]	→	s
ź	[dz]	→	z
č	[tʃ]	→	ʃ
ǧ	[dʒ]	→	ʒ

The result of these changes was a later Old French system of consonantal sounds as follows:

```
p   t   k
b   d   g
f   s   ʃ
v   z   ʒ
```

The rationale for these changes has been sought in a tendency to reduce the overcrowded palatal zone and a leaning towards symmetry by reducing the five orders (labials, dentals, etc.) to four in accordance with the four series of plosives and fricatives.

In other attempts to explain phonological modifications which fall outside the realm of conditioned change, the notion of **substratum influence** has often been invoked. Certain words in Spanish, for example, developed an [h] (which became ∅ in the modern language), where Latin had [f].

Latin	*Spanish*		
filium	hijo	[íxo]	'son'
fabam	haba	[áƀa]	'bean'
folia	hoja	[óxa]	'leaf'
feminam	hembra	[émbra]	'female'
fumum	humo	[úmo]	'smoke'

As the replacement of Latin [f] by [h] began in the north of the peninsula, where the Basque were in contact with Hispano-Roman speakers, and because Basque had no [f] sound, the notion has been put forward that Basque speakers, upon learning the Hispano-Roman language, substituted their closest sound. According to this view, this sound was [ph] which became [h]. Those words not affected (cf. Latin *florem* which became Spanish *flor*) are excused from the change on the basis of other criteria such as learned influences.

DIFFUSION OF LANGUAGE CHANGE

Besides the study of mechanisms and processes of language change, the historical linguist may also be concerned with how changes spread throughout a speech community. The vocabulary of a language may be modified by **lexical diffusion** in which a change begins in one or several words and gradually spreads throughout the relevant portions of the lexicon. One such ongoing change can be seen in words such as *present* which can be used as either a verb or a noun. At one time all such words were accented on the second syllable regardless of their status as noun or verb. In the period that gave rise to Modern English (sixteenth century) words such as *rebel, outlaw,* and *record* began to be pronounced with the accent on the first syllable when they were used as nouns. Over the next few centuries more and more words followed the same pattern, cf. *récess* and *recéss, áffix* and *affíx.* The diffusion process is still in progress, however, as indicated by the fact that many English speakers say *addréss* for both noun and verb and others use *áddress* as the noun and *addréss* for the verb. There are still many words that have as yet not been affected by the change, compare *repórt, mistáke* and *suppórt.*

Not all changes are processed through the gradual steps of lexical diffusion. Some changes affect all words in a given class at the same time. In some Andalusian dialects of Spanish, the phoneme /s/ has developed an allophone [h] in syllable-final position:

Standard pronunciation	*Andalusian*
[dos]	[doh]
[es]	[eh]
[mas]	[mah]

The change is regular and systematic, affecting all instances of syllable-final /s/ in the speech patterns of the individuals who adopt this dialect.

Along with linguistic diffusion of change throughout the lexicon of the language, the linguist may also take into account diffusion of change throughout the speech community. A given speech modification begins in the speech habits of one or several individuals and spreads (if it spreads at all) to an ever-increasing number of people. Whether or not diffusion occurs may depend on the relative prestige of the people who initiate the change and their influence on the speech population. If the prestige factor is high, there is a good chance that the innovation will be imitated by others. The loss of postvocalic /r/ in some eastern dialects of the United States was due to a change that originated in England and was brought to the New World by immigrants. Similarly, the adoption of the sound /θ/ in southern Spain, where no such sound existed, by speakers of the Andalusian dialect is due to their imitation of Castilian Spanish, the prestige dialect of Madrid and surroundings.

MORPHOLOGOCAL AND SYNTACTICAL CHANGE

EFFECTS OF SOUND CHANGE ON MORPHOLOGY

The effect of phonological change on aspects of morphology is evident in the restructuring of the plural forms in some English words:

	Germanic	Old English	Modern English	
Sing.	*mūs	mūs	[maʊs]	'mouse'
Pl.	*mūsi	mīs	[maɪs]	'mice'
Sing.	*fōt	fōt	[fʊt]	'foot'
Pl.	*fōti	fēt	[fiːt]	'feet'

In these and examples like them, the process of **umlaut** or **mutation** operated to change the stem vowel [uː] > [iː] and [oː] > [eː] through the fronting influence of a following close front [i] which then disappeared. Subsequently, [iː] > [ai] and [eː] > [iː] (see p. 198 above).

The influence of sound change on the morphological structures may also be seen in the Old English system of nominal forms whose suffixes marked case and gender. Compare the Old English masculine noun *hund* 'dog'.

Old English

	Singular	Plural
Nominative	hund	hund-as
Accusative	hund	hund-as
Genitive	hund-es	hund-a
Dative	hund-e	hund-um

Other nouns belonged to either masculine, feminine, or neuter types distinguished on the basis of case endings, e.g. feminine *gief* 'gift' declined along the lines of *gief-u* in the nominative singular, *gief-e* in the accusative singular, etc.

Through phonological change, the case and gender distinctions of Old English were lost. By the fifteenth century, the /m/ of the dative plural suffix had been effaced and unaccented vowels of the case endings had been reduced to /ə/.

Middle English

	Singular	Plural
Nominative	hund	hund-əs
Accusative	hund	hund-əs
Genitive	hund-əs	hund-ə
Dative	hund-ə	hund-ə

Previous distinctions between dative singular and dative plural, genitive singular and nominative plural, and so on, disappeared.

The distinction between singular and plural forms in Middle English was preserved by the continuance of the phoneme /s/, which survived also to mark the genitive singular forms. A genitive plural /s/ was added by analogy with the singular. The loss of case endings also obliterated the gender distinctions that were found among Old English forms. Sound change further modified the internal structure of morphemes such as *hund*, subject to the result of the Great Vowel Shift, which diphthongized /u/ to /au/ and resulted in:

Present-day English

Singular		Plural	
hound	/haund/	hounds	/haundz/
hound's	/haundz/	hounds'	/haundz/

Classical Latin contained six cases, which were reduced in the popular Latin speech of the Empire, and finally disappeared altogether in the Romance languages with the exception of Rumanian.

Increasing stress patterns in Popular Latin gradually neutralized the differences between long and short vowels by creating long vowels in accented syllables and short vowels in unaccented syllables regardless of the original arrangement.

With the concomitant loss of final -m in the accusative, the nominative, vocative, accusative, and ablative forms merged. The genitive and dative conformed to the rest of the pattern by analogy.

As in English, the loss of the case system brought on a more extensive and frequent use of prepositions and a more rigid word order to designate the relationships formerly employed by case functions.

	Classical Latin	Popular Latin	French
Sing.			
Nom.	porta	porta	la porte
Voc.	porta	porta	la porte
Acc.	portam	porta	la porte
Gen.	portae	de porta	de la porte
Dat.	portae	ad porta	à la porte
Abl.	portā	cum porta	avec la porte

WORD ORDER, PREPOSITIONS, AND ARTICLES

As long as relationships within a sentence were signalled by case endings, the meaning of the sentence was unambiguous. Compare the following Latin sentences:

Poeta puellam amat
Puellam poeta amat   'The poet loves the girl'
Poeta amat puellam
Puellam amat poeta

With the loss of case endings such as the accusative marker [m], subject and object would have become indistinguishable.

*Poeta puella amat
*Puella poeta amat

Fixed word order came into play, in which the subject preceded the verb and the object followed:

Poeta ama puella

This word order has persisted into the Romance languages, accompanied by the use of articles, and in Spanish by a preposition *a* to indicate personalized objects:

French: Le poète aime la jeune fille
Spanish: El poeta ama a la muchacha
Italian: Il poeta ama la ragazza

More extensive use of prepositions also became an important factor in signalling subject, object and verb relationships:

Latin: Puella rosam poetae in porta videt
French: La jeune fille voit la rose du poète à la porte
Spanish: La muchacha ve la rosa del poeta en la puerta.

The changing phonological conditions in the Latin of the Empire also had a profound effect on verbal forms. For example, compare Latin and French:

	Latin	Old French		French
Sing.				
1	cantō	chant(e)	[ʃãnt(ə)]	chante [ʃãt]
2	cantas	chantes	[ʃãntəs]	chantes [ʃãt]
3	cantat	chante	[ʃãntə]	chante [ʃãt]

The first person singular [o] was lost as were final consonants, and final unaccented vowels were weakened to [ə]. In the first person singular an analogical [e] was added by the fourteenth century.

The merger of verb forms in the French paradigm through phonological change necessitated some manner of differentiating them according to person and entailed the obligatory use of subject pronouns.

je chante
tu chantes
il chante

As the verb forms were clearly distinguishable in Latin by the endings, there was no need to employ subject pronouns except in special cases, as is still the case in languages such as Spanish and Italian; cf:

	Spanish	Italian
1	canto	canto
2	cantas	canti
3	canta	canta

Not unlike phonological change, morphological changes proceed on a regular and systematic basis. The Latin **synthetic future**, for example, *cantabō* 'I will sing', disappeared in all forms and was replaced by a new **periphrastic future** e.g. *cantare habeo* > *chanterai* [ʃãtre].

ANALOGICAL CHANGE

The effects of phonological change may be offset by analogical formations which regularize forms on the basis of others in the paradigm. An example in Old English is the word for *son*.

	Singular		Plural	
Nom.	sunu	'son'	suna	'sons'
Acc.	sunu		suna	
Dat.	suna		sunum	
Gen.	suna		suna	

The plural forms had no [s] but the word became *sons* by analogy with other words that did make the plural with *s*, such as *bāt* (nom. sing.) and *bātas* (nom. plur.) which became *boat* and *boats* respectively.

As discussed earlier, accented [á] in Latin became [ɛ] in French, as we see again in the following paradigm.

	Latin	Old French	French	
Sing.				
1	ámo	aim(e)	aime	[ɛm]
2	ámas	aimes	aimes	[ɛm]
3	ámat	aime	aime	[ɛm]
Pl.				
1	amámus	amons	aimons	[ɛmõ]
2	amátis	amez	aimez	[ɛme]
3	ámant	aiment	aiment	[ɛm]

These forms undergo regular phonological change into Old French, in which initial accented [a] became [ɛ] but remained as [a] in the first and second person plural, where it was in unaccented position. This led to an irregular paradigm. During the transition from Old French to Modern French, however, the paradigm was regularized through analogy with the singular and third person plural forms resulting in an irregular phonological development.

Similarly, an orthographic *e* (cf. also *chante*) was added to the first person singular to conform with the rest of the paradigm.

When phonological change threatens to eliminate a well-entrenched grammatical category such as, for instance, singular and plural in Indo-European languages, adjustments may occur that preserve the category; albeit in a new phonological form.

The loss of syllable- and word-final [s] in some dialects of Andalusian Spanish, for example, also swept away the earlier plural marker in [s]. For example, compare:

	Castilian		Andalusian (Eastern)	
	Singular	Plural	Singular	Plural
	libro	libros	libro	librɔ
	gato	gatos	gato	gatɔ
	madre	madres	madre	madrɛ
	bote	botes	bote	botɛ

In compensation for the loss of the plural indicator [s], the final vowel of the word opened (lowered a degree) to indicate plurality.

Morphological differentiation was also a factor in the modifications of the second person singular of the verb *to be* in the Romance languages. The distinction of second and third person in popular Latin was threatened by the loss of word-final /-t/; compare:

Latin	sum	
	es	> es
	est	> es(t)

The various Romance languages resorted to different strategies to maintain the distinction between the second and third persons singular. French distinguished them on the basis of pronouns which were obligatory in the language, Spanish borrowed a form from another part of the grammar no longer needed namely the disappearing synthetic future, and Italian resorted to analogy of the second person with that of the first person by adding /s-/. For example, compare:

French	Spanish	Italian
je suis	soy	sono
tu es [ɛ]	eres	sei
il est [ɛ]	es	è

Some syntactic changes appear to be unmotivated by modifications in the phonological or morphological component of the grammar. In Old and Middle English, an inversion rule relating to the formation of *yes/no* questions could apply to all verbs, for example, *They speak the truth* and *Speak they the truth?* During the sixteenth and seventeenth centuries, the rule changed to apply to a more limited set of verbs, those that function as auxiliaries. Disregarding the fact that the verbs *be* and *have* undergo an inversion even when they do not perform as auxiliaries and ignoring here the emergence of the auxiliary verb *do*, the change can be shown as follows:

Old
construction They speak   → Speak they?
          They can speak→ Can they speak?
New
construction They speak   → xxx
          They can speak→ Can they speak?

Historical linguistics has only in recent years begun to investigate syntactic change in a systematic manner in conjunction with syntactic developments in the field of synchronic studies.

LEXICAL AND SEMANTIC CHANGE

Besides changes in the grammar of language, modifications also occur in the vocabulary, both in the stock of words, **lexical change**, and in their meanings, **semantic change**. Words may be added or lost in conjunction with cultural changes. The many hundreds of words that once dealt with astrology when the art of divination based on the stars and their supposed influence on human affairs was more in vogue, have largely disappeared from the world's languages, while large numbers of new words related to technological developments are constantly revitalizing their vocabularies.

Some of the word-formation processes by which lexical changes occur in English are:

Process	*Examples*
compounding	sailboat, bigmouth
derivation	uglification, finalize
borrowings	yacht (Dutch), pogrom (Russian)
acronyms	UNESCO, RADAR
blends	smoke + fog > smog; motor + hotel > motel
abbreviations	*op. cit.*, *ibid.*, Ms
doublets	person, parson
back formations	(typewrite < typewriter; burgle < burglar)

echoic forms and inventions	miaow, moo, splash, ping
clipping	prof *for* professor, phone *for* telephone
proper names	sandwich < Earl of Sandwich (1718–92); boycott < Charles Boycott (1832–97)

Changes in the meanings of words constantly occur in all natural languages and revolve around three general principles: **semantic broadening**, that is, from the particular to the general, e.g. *holy day* > *holiday*, Old English *dogge*, a specific breed > *dog*; **semantic narrowing**, from the general to the particular, e.g. Old English *mete* 'food' > *meat*, a specific food, i.e. flesh, Old English *steorfan* 'to die' > *starve*; **shifts in meaning**, e.g. *lust* used to mean 'pleasure', *immoral* 'not customary', *silly* 'happy, blessed', *lewd* 'ignorant', and so on.

The etymological meaning of a word may help to determine its current meaning. English words such as television or telephone can be deduced from their earlier Greek and Latin meanings with respect to the components *tele* 'at a distance', *vision* 'see', *phone* 'sound'. Such is not always the case, however. Borrowed words as well as native forms may undergo semantic change so that etymological knowledge of a word may not be sufficient to assess its meaning. Compare the following:

English	*Latin*	
dilapidated	lapis	'stone'
eradicate	radix	'root'
sinister	sinister	'left'
virtue	vir	'man'

From the origin of *dilapidated* it might be thought that it referred only to stone structures, *eradicate* only to roots, *sinister* to left-handed people, and *virtue* only to men.

Words, then, do not have immutable meanings that exist apart from context. They tend to wander away from earlier meanings and their semantic values are not necessarily clear from historical knowledge of the word.

Changes in the material culture, sometimes called **referent change** have an effect on the meaning of a word as is the case of the English word *pen*, which once meant 'feather' from an even earlier *pet* 'to fly'. This name was appropriated when quills were used for writing but remained when pens were no longer feathers. Similarly, the word *paper* is no longer associated with the papyrus plant of its origin.

SOCIAL AND PSYCHOLOGICAL ASPECTS OF LANGUAGE CHANGE

Language change often comes about through the social phenomena of **taboos**, **metaphor**, and **folk etymologies**. The avoidance of particular words for social reasons seems to occur in all languages and **euphemisms** arise in their place. For instance, instead of *dies* one may use the expression *passes away*, which seems less severe and more sympathetic. Or, one *goes to the bathroom* instead of the *toilet*, but does not expect to take a bath; even dogs and cats may go to the bathroom in North America. Elderly people are *senior citizens* and the poor are *underprivileged*. Like all social phenomena, taboos change with time and viewpoint. In Victorian England the use of the word *leg* was considered indiscreet, even when referring to a piano.

Taboos may even cause the loss of a word, as in the classical Indo-European case of the word for 'bear'. A comparison of this word in various Indo-European languages yields:

Latin	*ursus*	Old Church Slavonic	*medvedi*
Greek	*arktos*	English	*bear*
Sanskrit	*ṛkṣah*	German	*Bär*

The presumed Indo-European ancestor of Latin, Greek, and Sanskrit was **arktos*. Avoidance of the term is thought to have occurred in the northern Indo-European regions, where the bear was prevalent, and another name, (employed, perhaps, not to offend it, was substituted in the form of **ber*- 'brown', that is, 'the brown one'. In Slavic the name invoked was *medv*- from Indo-European **madhu* 'honey' and **ed* 'to eat', that is 'honey eater'.

Taboo words may also account for seeming irregularities in phonological change. The name of the Spanish town of *Mérida*, for example, did not undergo the usual syncope of the post-tonic vowel as did other Spanish words of the *veride* > *verde* type, presumably because the result would have been *Merda* 'dung', a word that would have inspired little civic pride.

Unaccustomed morphological shapes in a given language are often replaced by more familiar ones through a process of **reinterpretation**. Loan words are readily subject to this process as they are often unfamiliar or unanalysable in the adopting language. Reinterpretation of forms is generally referred to as **folk etymology**. One example involves the Middle English word *schamfast*, which meant in Old English 'modest', that is 'firm in modesty'. To make the word more familiar, the form *fast* was changed to *face* and the word came to be *shamefaced*. Middle English *berfrey* 'tower', with nothing to do with bell, has become *bellfry* and associated with a *bell tower*. Words may change their shapes due to popular misanalysis, such as Middle English *napron* which was associated with *an apron* and became *apron*. Similarly, Middle English *nadder* became *adder*.

Among other characteristics of variation or style in language that may lead to semantic change (metonymy, synecdoche, hyperbole, emphasis, etc.), **metaphor**, a kind of semantic analogy, appears to be one of the most important aspects of linguistic behaviour. It involves a semantic transfer through a similarity in sense perceptions. Expressions already existent in the language are often usurped giving rise to new meanings for old words, for example, *a galaxy of beauties*, *skyscraper*. Transfer of meanings from one sensory faculty to another occur in such phrases as *loud colours*, *sweet music*, *cold reception*, and so on.

LINGUISTIC BORROWING

When a community of speakers incorporates some linguistic element into its language from another language, **linguistic borrowing** occurs. Such transferences are most common in the realm of vocabulary, where words may come and disappear with little consequence for the rest of the grammar. The borrowing language may incorporate some cultural item or idea and the name along with it from some external source; for example, Hungarian *goulash* and Mexican Spanish *enchilada* were taken into English through borrowings, and the words *llama* and *wigwam* were derived from American Indian languages.

When words are borrowed, they are generally made to conform to the sound patterns of the borrowing language. The German word *Bach* [bax] which contained a voiceless velar fricative [x], a sound lacking in most English dialects, was incorporated into English as [bɑːk]. English speakers adopted the pronunciation with [k] as the nearest equivalent to German [x]. In Turkish, a word may not begin with a sound [s] plus a plosive consonant. If such a word is borrowed, Turkish speakers added a prothetic [i] to break up the troublesome cluster. English *scotch* became Turkish [iskoʃ] and French *station* appears in Turkish as [istasjon]. Latin loan words in Basque encountered a similar kind of reconditioning: Latin *rege* became Basque *errege*, in that Basque words did not contain a word-initial [r-].

Only in relatively rare instances are sounds or sequences of sounds alien to the adopting language borrowed. The word-initial consonant cluster [kn-] does not occur in native English words, having been reduced to [n] in the past and persisting only in the orthography, but the word *knesset* 'parliament' from Hebrew has been taken over intact.

Borrowing is one of the primary forces behind changes in the lexicon of many languages. In English, its effects have been substantial, as is particularly evident in the extent to which the common language was influenced by Norman French, which brought hundreds of words into the language relating to every aspect of social and economic spheres, e.g.

> *Government and social order*: religion, sermon, prayer, faith, divine
> *Law*: justice, crime, judge, verdict, sentence
> *Arts*: art, music, painting, poet, grammar
> *Cuisine*: venison, salad, boil, supper, dinner

For the historical linguist, borrowings often supply evidence of cultural contacts where vocabulary items cannot be accounted for by other means. The ancient Greeks, for example, acquired a few words such as *basileus* 'king', and *plinthos* 'brick', non-Indo-European words from presumably a pre-Indo-European substratum language of the Hellenic Peninsula along with certain non-Indo-European suffixes such as -*enai* in *Athenai*.

Onomastic forms, especially those relating to **toponyms** such as names of rivers, towns, and regions, are especially resistant to change and are often taken over by a new culture from an older one. Compare, for example, *Thames, Dover* and *Cornwall*, incorporated into Old English from Celtic, and American and Canadian geographical names such as *Utah, Skookumchuck* and Lake *Minnewanka*.

A sampling of the broad range of sources that have contributed to the English lexicon are: *bandana* < Hindustani; *gimmick* < German; *igloo* < Inuktitut (Eskimo); *kamikaze* < Japanese; *ukulele* < Hawaiian; *zebra* < Bantu; *canyon* < Spanish; *henna* < Arabic; *dengue* < Swahili; *lilac* < Persian; *xylophone* < Greek; *rocket* < Italian; *nougat* < Provençal; *yen* < Chinese, and many others.

The social contexts in which linguistic borrowing occurs have often been referred to as the **substratum**, **adstratum**, and **superstratum**. When a community of speakers learns a new language which has been superimposed upon them as would have been the case when Latin was spread to the provinces of Spain or Gaul, and carry traces of their native language into the new language, we have what is commonly called **substratum influence**. The French numerical system partially reflecting multiples of twenty, for example, seems to have been retained from the Celtic languages spoken in Gaul prior to the Roman occupation, that is from the Celtic substratum. **Adstratum influence** refers to linguistic borrowing across cultural and linguistic boundaries as would be found, for example, between French and Spanish or French and Italian or German. Many words for items not found in the cultures of English colonists in

America were borrowed from the local Indians under adstratum conditions such as *chipmunk* and *opposum*. Influences emanating from the **superstratum** are those in which linguistic traits are carried over to the native or local language of a region as the speakers of a superimposed language give up their speech and adopt the vernacular already spoken in the area. Such would have been the case when the French invaders of England gradually acquired English, bringing into the English language a number of French terms.

The degree of borrowing from language to language or dialect to dialect is related to the perceived prestige of the lending speech. Romans, great admirers of the Greeks, borrowed many words from this source, while the German tribes in contact with the Romans took up many Latin words. English borrowed greatly from French after the Norman Conquest when the French aristocracy were the overlords of England.

While borrowing across linguistic boundaries is primarily a matter of vocabulary, other features of language may also be taken over by a borrowing language. It has been suggested that the employment of the preposition *of* plus a noun phrase to express possession in English, e.g., *the tail of the cat* versus *the cat's tail*, resulted from French influence: *la queue du chat*. In parts of France adjoining Germany the adjective has come to precede the noun, unlike normal French word order. This is due to German influence, e.g. *la voiture rouge* has become *la rouge voiture* cf. German *das rote Auto*.

Sometimes only the meaning of a foreign word or expression is borrowed and the word or words are translated in the borrowing. Such conditions are referred to as **loan translations**. The English expression *lightning war* is a borrowing from German *Blitzkrieg*. The word *telephone* was taken into German as a loan translation in the form of *Fernsprecher* combining the elements *fern* 'distant' and *Sprecher* 'speaker'.

LANGUAGE RECONSTRUCTION

The systematic comparison of two or more languages may lead to an understanding of the relationship between them and whether or not they descended from a common parent language. The most reliable criteria for this kind of genetic relationship is the existence of systematic phonetic congruencies coupled with semantic similarities. Since the relationship between form and meaning of words in any language is arbitrary, and since sound change is reflected regularly throughout the vocabulary of a given language, concordances between related languages, or lack of them, become discernible through comparisons. Languages that are genetically related show a number of **cognates**, that is, related words in different languages from a common source, with ordered differences.

When the existence of a relationship has been determined, the investigator may then wish to reconstruct the earlier form of the languages, or the common parent, referred to as the proto-language, in order to extend the knowledge of the language in question back in time, often even before written documentation. Reconstruction makes use of two broad strategies: (1) the phoneme that occurs in the largest number of cognate forms is the most likely candidate for reconstruction in the proto-language; (2) the changes from the proto-language into the observable data of the languages in question are only plausible in the sense that such changes can be observed in languages currently spoken.

A phoneme that occurs in the majority of the languages under consideration but nevertheless cannot be accounted for in the daughter language by a transition from the proto-language based on sound linguistic principles, should not be posited in the proto-form. For example, if a majority of languages had the sound [tʃ] and a minority contained [k] in both cases before the vowel [i], one would reconstruct the phoneme /k/ and not /tʃ/ by virtue of the fact that /k/ before /i/ has been often seen to become /tʃ/, while the reverse never seems to occur.

All things being equal, it may still not be reliable to use the statistical method. Given the following languages:

Sanskrit	bharami	bh-
Greek	phero	ph-
Gothic	baira	b-
English	bear	b-
Armenian	berem	b-

the predominance of [b-] suggests that it is the most likely candidate for the **proto-sound**. On the other hand, assuming that the simplest description is the best one and that phonological change occurs one step at a time, we might note that, given the various possibilities,

```
 *b(1)            *ph(2)           *bh(3)
 /  \             /  \             /  \
b    ph          b    bh          b    ph
```

changes (1) and (2) require at least two steps to derive one of the reflexes ([b] > [p] > [ph], [ph] > [p] > [b]) while change (3) requires only one step, that is, loss of aspiration and voiced to voiceless. The sound [bh-] appears to be the logical candidate for the proto-sound. Further inquiry would also show that Gothic and English reflect a common stage with [b-]. The predominance of [b-] in three of the five languages is then somewhat deceptive in terms of comparative reconstruction.

If we compare the words for *foot* in the Indo-European languages:

Latin	pēs
Greek	pous
Sanskrit	pad-
Old High German	fuoz
Old English	fōt
Church Slavonic	noga

we could disregard the form *noga* as being from another source (actually, it once meant 'claw') and consider either *[p] or *[f] as the initial proto-sound. As the Germanic branch of Indo-European has [f] where other languages have [p], we deduce a shift from [p] to [f] in Germanic and posit the proto-sound as *[p].

Through examination of the vocabulary of other related languages of the Indo-European family such as Umbrian *peři* 'foot', Lettish *peda* 'sole of foot', Church Slavonic *pesi* 'on foot' we could posit the proto-vowel as *[e].

Considerations in establishing the earlier form of the final consonant might come from the Latin genitive form *pedis*, from the Greek genitive πodos, Gothic and Old English *fō*t- among others. The proto-consonant in root-final position seems certain to have been a dental plosive ([t̪] or [d̪]). Noting that Germanic languages generally have [t] where other Indo-European languages (Latin, Greek, Sanskrit) have [d], compare Latin *decem*, Greek *deka*, Sanskrit *daça* and English *ten*, we might conclude that the proto-language had *[d], which became [t] in Germanic. The proto-word for *foot* can now be constituted as *[ped-], a non-attested hypothetical construct of the proto-language.

In reconstructing the phonological forms of an earlier language, the linguist will also be concerned with the possible motivating factors underlying the change as these will often give some insight into the direction of the modification and ultimately help to establish the proto-form. Among the following Romance words one can readily see the influence exerted by environmental conditions which led to modifications in some of the languages.

Spanish	Portugese	Italian	
agudo	agudo	acuto	'acute'
amigo	amigo	amico	'friend'

The appearance of voiced plosives [b, d, g] in Spanish and Portuguese, contrasted with their voiceless counterparts in Italian, suggests that the voiced surrounding (between vowels) gave rise to the voiced consonants and that Italian represents a more conservative or older stage of the language. There is no motivation for the process to have occurred the other way around with the voiced sounds becoming voiceless in voiced surroundings.

Some features of a proto-language are beyond recovery through reconstruction. The identification of proto-sounds or grammatical and syntactic characteristics of a parent unwritten language after complete loss through merger or other means in the descendant languages may simply not be reconstructable. Without written records of the period, we could not identify or reconstitute vowel quantity in proto-Romance

(Latin) speech. The phonological distinctiveness of vowel quantity in Latin is obvious from such words as *dīcō* 'I dedicate' and *dīcō* 'I say', but the modern descendant languages display no such oppositions in vowel quantity.

Similarly, the proto-language, Latin, had a system of **synthetic passive** forms, e.g. *amor, amaris, amatur*, etc., which left no trace in the Romance languages, where **analytic passives** developed as in Spanish *soy amado* and French *je suis aimé* 'I am loved', in conjunction with the Latin verb *esse* 'to be' and the past participle of the main verb. Without written records, such constructions in the proto-language would remain virtually undetected.

While the **comparative method** is the most powerful model for reconstruction, another – the **internal method** – may be utilized when comparative information is not available, or when the goal is to reconstruct earlier forms of a single language. The primary assumption underlying internal reconstruction is that many events in the history of a language leave discernible traces in its design. An examination of these traces can lead to a reconstruction of linguistic processes of change and thus to a reconstructed form of the language prior to events which changed it. By way of example, we can look at a few related forms in Spanish from the point of view of internal methods.

[nótʃe] noche 'night' [nokturnál] 'nocturnal'
[ótʃo] ocho 'eight' [oktagonál] 'octagonal'
[dítʃo] dicho 'said' [diktaθjón] 'dictation'

There is an alternation among these related words between [ʧ] ~ [kt] but no apparent motivation for a change such as [ʧ] > [kt], while, on the other hand [kt] > [ʧ] would not be unexpected. The [k] was pulled forward into the palatal zone by anticipation of [t] (assimilation) to become [j] and then the [t] was palatalized by the preceding [j], i.e. [kt] > [jt] > [ʧ].

We can now reconstruct the forms in [ʧ] as [kt].

*nókte
*ókto
*díkto

The undeciphered ancient Iberian language of Spain's Mediterranean coasts, known only from inscriptions and so far related to no other language, contains the following lexical forms:

baite   baikar
baiti   bainybar
baitolo   baiturane

Since the sequences *kar* and *-nybar* appear in other words, they are assumed to be separate morphemes, compare *balkar, antalskar*.

This suggests an alternation between *bait* and *bai*, in which the forms (allomorphs) occur as follows:

bai   +   consonant
bait   +   vowel

or

bai > bait/__vowel

We are now in a position to reconstruct *baikar* as an earlier form of **baitkar*, **baitnybar*, *baitturane*.

The reduction of the sequences **[-tk-] to [-k-], **[tn] > [n], [tt] > [t], is in accordance with the phonotactics of Iberian, which does not display sequences of plosive plus consonant as part of the language.

The results of this method of internal reconstruction are not verifiable, however, unless corroborating evidence can be found. In this case, we note that Basque has a form *bait* which, when combined with *-gare* becomes *baikare*, similarly, *bait-nago* > *bainago*, *bait-du* > *baitu* avoiding sequences alien to Basque and suggesting an affiliation between the two languages.

LINGUISTIC PALEONTOLOGY

The lack of cognate forms of a particular word in related languages may suggest that the earlier and common stage of the languages in question had no such word and linguistic differentiation occurred before such a word was needed to represent the relevant idea or cultural entity. For example, few words for metals are common to the Indo-European family of languages. This kind of information means to the practitioner of **linguistic paleontology** that words for these items were unknown in the proto-language, which, therefore, must have broken up during the period of pre-metal usage or Neolithic times. Conversely, the various cognates for names of trees such as 'beech' suggest that the word existed in the proto-speech and that the homeland of the speakers was located in the vicinity of these trees.

The lack of specific words in the parent language for grains and vegetables but many words for animals, both domestic and wild, alludes to a heavy reliance on meat. Words relating to the level of the family are abundant but those indicating a higher social order or political structure are not evident. Information of this kind may be used to reconstruct the cultural ambiance and the geographical location of the proto-speakers.

Pitfalls abound, however, in the study of linguistic paleontology; besides the fact that words may change their reference (a *robin* in England is not the same species as a *robin* in the United States), they are also readily borrowed from language to language. The word *tobacco*, common to the Romance languages, could easily lead to the false conclusion that the Romans smoked. The word itself appears to have spread from Spanish and Portuguese to the other Romance languages at a much later time.

GENETIC CLASSIFICATION OF LANGUAGE

A major result of historical and comparative linguistic investigation has been the mapping of the world's languages into families and subgroupings within these families. When a given language has been shown to belong within the folds of a particular grouping as defined by linguistic relationships indicating a common descent from an earlier proto-language, it is said to have been classified genetically. The most popular method for expressing genetic relationships is the family-tree diagram consisting of the parent language as the starting point and branches indicating the descended languages.

Genetic classification has shown that the vast majority of the languages currently spoken in Europe belong to one of four families: Indo-European, Uralic, Caucasian, and Basque.

INDO-EUROPEAN

The Indo-European family extended from Europe to India and in recent times has spread over much of the globe including, North America, South Africa, Australia, and New Zealand as well as a number of pockets around the world. It is the most thoroughly investigated and best-known family of languages today and is derived from a hypothetical parent called **Proto-Indo-European**, thought to have been spoken in the third millennium BC. Judging from the distribution of the various Indo-European languages, their migratory chronologies, and from archeological evidence (Kurgan Culture), the parent language is thought to have been spoken in the region of southeastern Europe.

The major groupings of the Indo-European family of languages are shown below. The **Germanic** branch of Indo-European has been divided into three subgroups: East Germanic languages are now extinct but the best known is Gothic, for which written texts exist from the fourth century AD. The North Germanic or Scandinavian branch includes Icelandic, Norwegian, Swedish, Danish, and Faroese. West Germanic contains German, Yiddish, Dutch, Flemish, Frisian, Afrikaans, and English. Afrikaans is a descendant of Dutch spoken by the early white settlers of South Africa, the Boers. Frisian is spoken along the northern coast of the Netherlands, the northwestern coast of Germany, and on the Frisian Islands. English is derived from the languages of the Angles, Saxons, and Jutes, Germanic tribes of northern Germany and southern Denmark

Proto-Indo-European

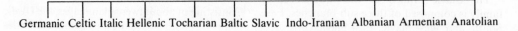

Germanic Celtic Italic Hellenic Tocharian Baltic Slavic Indo-Iranian Albanian Armenian Anatolian

who began settling in England in the fifth century, AD. Yiddish is an offshoot of German and in some estimations, basically a dialect of German.

The once widespread **Celtic** languages, extending from the British Isles to the Anatolian Peninsula are now generally extinct except for those surviving in the British Isles and Brittany. The continental Celtic languages are best known from Gaulish spoken in France, and Hispano-Celtic of Spain and Portugal which have bequeathed some documentation. The insular branch has been segmented into two groups – Brythonic and Goidelic – of which the former includes Welsh and Breton, and the latter Irish Gaelic and Scots Gaelic. Breton is an offshoot of now extinct Cornish, spoken in Cornwall up to the eighteenth century.

Prior to about the third century BC, linguistic relationships on the **Italic** peninsula are obscure, but clearly attested after this time as belonging to the Indo-European family are the two groups Oscan–Umbrian and Latin–Faliscan. Latin, in time, displaced the other languages on the peninsula and gave rise to the Romance group of languages.

Indo-European speakers entered the **Hellenic** peninsula apparently sometime early in the second millennium BC, and at a later time we can speak of two main groups: East Greek, called Attic–Ionic, the languages of Attica and much of Asia Minor, and West Greek. All modern Greek dialects except Tsakonian are descendants of Attic, the classical speech of Athens.

Tocharian was an Indo-European language recovered from manuscripts of the seventh and eighth centuries AD. It was once spoken in what is now Chinese Turkestan.

Lithuanian, Latvian (or Lettish), and the now extinct Old Prussian make up the **Baltic** languages, situated along the eastern coast of the Baltic Sea. Lithuanian contains an elaborate case system much like that established for the parent Indo-European language.

The **Slavic** branch of the Indo-European family is composed of three sub-branches: East, South, and West Slavic. East Slavic consists of Russian, Ukranian, and Byelorussian, the latter spoken in the western USSR around Minsk, while South Slavic is composed of Bulgarian, Serbo-Croatian, Slovene, and Macedonian, among others. The West Slavic branch includes Czech, Slovak, Polish, and Sorbian (Lusatian).

The **Indo-Iranian** branch was carried to India and Iran and consisted of two main branches: Indic and Iranian. The former appeared as Sanskrit, which subsequently evolved into the various Indo-European languages of India and Pakistan, such as Hindi, Urdu, Bengali, and Gujarati, while the latter evolved early into the Avestan and Old Persian dialects. Various Iranian languages are in use today and include Pastu, Persian, Kurdish and Ossetic, among others.

With an obscure line of descent from the proto-language, present-day **Albanian** is spoken in Albania and parts of Greece and Yugoslavia. Some see the language as an immediate descendant of the poorly known Illyrian, and others of the little-known Thracian languages. A third view posits an independent line from Proto-Indo-European.

Located in the Caucasus and northeastern Turkey, the **Armenian** language also continues a line of descent from the proto-language not yet agreed upon. Some scholars see it as a separate offshoot, others as related to the poorly understood Phrygian language of ancient south-east Europe.

Indo-European migrations into the **Anatolian** peninsula gave rise to Hittite and the related Luwian and Palaic languages. The little-known Lydian and Lycian are also thought to have been related to Hittite, the latter as a continuation of Luwian. All are extinct.

There are many other extinct languages such as Illyrian, Thrachian, Ligurian, Sicil, and Venetic, whose scanty documentation points to membership in the Indo-European family, but their affiliations are unclear.

URALIC

Consisting of about twenty languages, the Uralic family is spread out across the northern latitudes from Norway to Siberia. There are two major branches: Samoyedic and Finno-Ugric. The former is spoken in the USSR, the latter includes Hungarian, Finnish, Estonian, and Lappish. They are primarily agglutinating languages (see LANGUAGE TYPOLOGY) with an extensive system of cases. The proto-language may have been spoken in the northern Ural mountains about 6000 BC. The earliest texts are from the twelfth century, AD, a Hungarian funeral oration.

CAUCASIAN

Spoken in the region of the Caucasus mountains between the Black and the Caspian Seas, this family of about thirty-five languages may actually consist of two independent groups: North Caucasian and South Caucasian. The situation is still far from clear. The languages are characterized by glottalized consonants, complex consonant clusters, and few vowels. The earliest texts are in Georgian, a South Caucasian language, and date back to the fifth century AD.

ASIA

Language families indigenous to Asia are: Altaic, Sino-Tibetan, Austro-Asiatic, and Dravidian.

The thirty-five to forty-five languages of the **Altaic** family comprise three main branches: Turkic, Tungusic, and Mongolian, although some specialists include Japanese and Korean in this family. Geographically, these languages are found primarily in Turkey, the USSR, China, and Mongolia (and perhaps Japan and Korea). The family is characterized by agglutinating structures and some languages by vowel harmony. The earliest Turkish texts, the Lokhon inscriptions, date from the eighth century AD.

Second only to Indo-European in number of speakers, the **Sino-Tibetan** family contains about three hundred languages in two major branches: Tibeto-Burman and Sinitic (Chinese). The Sinitic branch encompasses northern and southern groups of languages. The principal language of the north is Mandarin and those of the south are Cantonese and Wu. Tibeto-Burman languages are found in Tibet, India, Bangladesh, and Burma. The region contains great linguistic diversity and, as yet, the overall linguistic picture is unclear. The languages are generally tonal (see TONE LANGUAGES).

The **Austro-Asiatic** family consists of about 150 languages, in two major groupings: Munda, which includes languages of central and northeast India; and the larger, Mon–Khmer group with Cambodian (Khmer), Vietnamese, and many others of Cambodia and Vietnam, Burma, and southern China. These languages are characterized by complex vowel systems, and some, e.g. Vietnamese, by tones. The Mon–Khmer branch may have been a unified language in the second millennium BC. The earliest texts date to the sixth century AD.

Found mainly in southern India, there are about twenty-three **Dravidian** languages. The most important, in terms of number of speakers, are Telegu, Tamil, Kannada, and Malayalam. Dravidian peoples appear to have been more widespread once but were displaced southward during the Indo-European incursions into northern India. The languages are commonly agglutinating and non-tonal with an order of retroflex consonants and word-initial stress.

AFRICA

The number of distinct languages spoken throughout Africa is estimated at about 1,000, all of which belong to one of the four language families: **Afro-Asiatic**, **Niger-Kordofanian**, **Nilo-Saharan**, and **Khoisan**.

Afro-Asiatic, often referred to by its older name of Hamitic–Semitic, is a group of languages spoken mainly across the northern half of the continent and throughout the Middle East, and consists of about 250 languages divided into six primary branches: Egyptian, now extinct except for the limited use of its descendant, Coptic, in religious rituals; Cushitic languages of Ethiopia, the Sudan, Somalia, and Kenya; Berber, once widespread across the northern regions of the continent but now primarily restricted to pockets of speakers in Morocco and Algeria; Chadic, spoken in the region of Lake Chad and distinguished from the other groups through the utilization of tones; Omotic, considered by some to be a branch of Cushitic; Semitic, the branch responsible in large part for the displacement of the Egyptian and Berber branches, spoken throughout the Middle East, across North Africa, and in Malta. The three best-known members of this branch are Arabic, Hebrew, and Amharic. Pharyngeal sounds and consonantal roots characterize many of the languages.

The **Niger–Kordofanian** language family covers much of the southern half of the African continent and embodies many more languages than Afro-Asiatic. Of the two main branches, Kordofanian and Niger–Congo, the latter consists of especially numerous sub-branches. The languages are typically tonal (except Swahili) and usually agglutinating in structure. Perhaps the best-known subgroup of Benue–Congo, itself a branch of Niger–Congo, is Bantu, which consists of over one hundred languages, including Swahili, Zulu, and Kikuyu.

Found primarily in east and central Africa, the **Nilo-Saharan** family contains several subgroups and about 120 languages. They are generally tonal and nouns are often inflected for case. This family is still relatively unexplored. Some of the languages are Masai (Kenya), Nubian (Sudan), and Kanuri (Nigeria).

Squeezed by Bantu expansion from the north and European expansion from the south, **Khoisan** speakers of approximately fifteen languages are now pretty well restricted to areas around the Kalahari desert. Hottentot is, perhaps, the most widely known of the Khoisan languages. This family, unlike any other, is characterized by clicks of various kinds which function as part of the consonantal system. A few neighbouring languages of the Bantu sub-branch, such as Zulu and Xhosa, have borrowed these clicks from the Khoisan languages. They are also characterized by tones and nasal vowels.

OCEANIA

It is estimated that throughout Oceania there are between 1,000 and 1,500 languages spoken today, which are believed to belong to one of three language families: **Indo-Pacific**, **Australian**, and **Austro-Tai**.

Of the estimated 700-plus languages of the **Indo-Pacific** family, nearly all of them are found on the island of New Guinea and some of the neighbouring islands. There appear to be at least fourteen branches, but classification is still in its infancy.

Approximately 200 **Australian** languages are each spoken by at least a few Aborigines and another sixty or so are extinct. Located predominantly in central Australia, north-central Arnhem Land, and northwestern Australia, they are characterized by simple vowel systems and case markings.

Spread out from Madagascar to Hawaii, the geographically enormous **Austro-Tai** family contains an estimated 550 languages in two major and remotely related subgroups: Kam-Tai and Austronesian, the latter also known as Malayo-Polynesian. There are about fifty languages of the former spoken in Thailand, Laos, Vietnam, and China, and about 500 of the latter, including Malagasy (Madagascar), Bahasa Indonesia/Malaysia (Malay), Tagalog, Fijian, Tahitian, Maori, and Hawaiian. The classification, however, remains controversial.

AMERICAN INDIAN LANGUAGES

While many relationships remain unclear with regard to Amerindian languages in the northern hemisphere, the following families have been identified, to which most of the languages belong: Eskimo–Aleut, Algonquian (north-east USA and Canada), Athapaskan (Alaska, western Canada and southwestern USA), Salish (Pacific northwest), Wakashan (Vancouver Island), Siouan (Great Plains), Uto-Aztecan (Mexico), Muskogean (southeastern USA), Iroquoian (eastern USA), Yuman (Baja California), Mayan (Mexico and Guatemala). It is estimated that nearly 400 distinct languages were spoken in North America in pre-Columbian times, 300 of these north of Mexico. Today, about 200 survive north of Mexico, but many of these are near extinction.

Along with Indo-Pacific languages, South American linguistic relationships are the least documented in the world, and estimates run from

1,000 to 2,000 languages, although only about 600 are actually recorded and 120 of these are extinct. Three major South American families which account for most of the known languages have been posited. They are: Andean–Equatorial, whose principal language is Quechua; Ge–Pano–Carib, extending from the Lesser Antilles to southern Argentina; and Macro-Chibchan, covering some of central America, much of northern South America, and parts of Brazil.

SOME LANGUAGE ISOLATES

In some cases, a single language has no known relationships with other languages and cannot be assigned to a family. When this occurs, the language in question is called an **isolate**. Some languages that have not been related to any other are Basque (spoken in northeastern Spain and southwestern France), Ainu (of northern Japan), Koutenay (British Columbia), Gilyak (Siberia), Taraskan (California), and Burushaski (spoken in Pakistan). There are also the extinct Sumerian, Iberian, Tartessian, and many other languages known only from inscriptional material.

                                    J.M.A.

SUGGESTIONS FOR FURTHER READING

Anderson, J.M. (1973), *Structural Aspects of Language Change*, London, Longman.
Antilla, R. (1972), *An Introduction to Historical and Comparative Linguistics*, New York, Macmillan.
Arlotto, A. (1972), *Introduction to Historical Linguistics*, Boston, University Press of America.
Bynon, T. (1977), *Historical Linguistics*, Cambridge, Cambridge University Press.
Lehmann, W.P. (1962), *Historical Linguistics: An Introduction*, New York, Holt, Rinehart & Winston.
Lehmann, W.P. (1967), *A Reader in Nineteenth Century Historical Indo-European Linguistics*, Bloomington and London, Indiana University Press.
Lockwood, W.B. (1972), *A Panorama of Indo-European Languages*, London, Hutchinson.
Robins, R.H. (1967), *A Short History of Linguistics*, London, Longman.
Ruhlen, M. (1975), *A Guide to the Languages of the World*, Language Universals Project, Stanford University.

Immediate Constituent analysis

What is referred to in this volume as **(Post-) Bloomfieldian American structural grammar** (see (POST-)BLOOMFIELDIAN AMERICAN STRUCTURAL GRAMMAR) is based on a 'bottom-up' approach to grammatical analysis – beginning with the smallest linguistic unit and showing how smaller units combine to form larger ones. **Immediate Constituent analysis** (henceforth **IC analysis**), however, begins with a sentence, say *Poor John ran away* (Bloomfield, 1935, p. 161), the immediate constituents of which are *poor John* and *ran away*, and works gradually down through its constituent parts until the smallest units that the grammar deals with, which will be the **ultimate constituents** of a sentence, are reached; it is a 'top-down' approach. Both approaches are solely concerned with the surface structures of language: that is, they deal only with the language that is physically manifest, whether written or spoken, and make no mention of underlying structures or categories of any kind. The constituents may be represented hierarchically in rectangular boxes (Allen and Widdowson, 1975, p. 55):

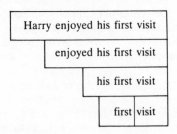

or in a Chinese box arrangement (W.N. Francis, 1958; Allen and Widdowson, 1975, p. 56):

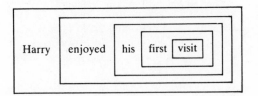

or lines between the constituents may be used (see Palmer, 1971, p. 124):

A ||| young |||| man || with ||| a |||| paper | follow- ||| ed || the |||| girl ||| with |||| a ||||| blue |||||| dress.

Alternatively, parentheses can be used, either, as in Palmer (1971, p. 125), within the sentence:

(((A) ((young) (man))) ((with) ((a) (paper)))) (((follow) (ed)) (((the) (girl)) ((with) ((a) ((blue) (dress))))))

or drawn below the sentence (E.A. Nida, 1968; Allen and Widdowson, 1975, pp. 55–6). According to Palmer (1971, p. 125), however, the best way to show IC structure is to use a **tree diagram** similar to the sort also employed by generative grammarians and transformational-generative grammarians (see GENERATIVE GRAMMAR and TRANSFORMATIONAL GENERATIVE GRAMMAR).

The main theoretical issue involved in IC analysis is, of course, the justification of the division of a sentence into one set of constituents rather than another set. Why, for instance, do we class *a young man* and *with a paper* as constituents rather than *a young; man with a;* and *paper*? The answer given by Bloomfield (1933/5), Harris (1951) and other proponents of IC analysis was that the elements which are given constituent status are those which may be replaced in their environment by others of the same pattern *or* by a shorter sequence of morphemes. The technical term used for this substitution test is **expansion**.

Thus, in Palmer's sentence above, it is clear that *a young man with a paper* can be replaced by a single morpheme, like *he*, for example, while *a young man with a paper followed*, in contrast, would fail the substitution test. *He* here would obviously not be a suitable substitute for that part of the item constituted by *followed*; it would, however, be suitable as a substitute for any item of the kind that we might call a **noun phrase**, of whatever length, that is, for any item conforming to a specific pattern. Similarly, *followed the girl with a blue dress* can be replaced by a two-morpheme item like, for instance, *sleeps*. A full analysis into ICs would give the tree shown below (Palmer, 1971, p. 125).

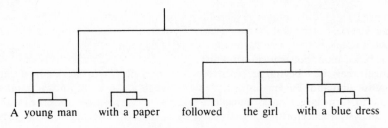

Cutting sentences into their constituents can show up and distinguish ambiguities, as in the case of (Palmer, 1971, p. 127) the ambiguous item *old men and women*, which may either refer to 'old men' and 'women of any age' or to 'old men' and 'old women'. The two different interpretations can be represented by two different tree structures:

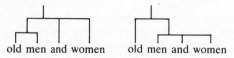

old men and women   old men and women

The type of expansion in the case of which the short item which can substitute for the longer item in the sentence is not actually part of that sentence item, is called **exocentric** expansion. Another type, called **endocentric**, is more easily understood literally as expansion, since it works by the addition of more and more items to a **headword** in a group; for instance, *old men* above is an expansion of *men*, and further expansions would be *happy old men*; *the happy old men*; *the three happy old men*; *the three happy old men in the corner*; etc.

As the headword here, *men* is an item of the type normally classed as a noun, it would be reasonable to call it, and any expansion of it, a **noun group**, **noun phrase** or **nominal group**, and labelling items in grammatical terms clearly adds an extra, highly informative dimension to the division of sentences into constituents. Mere division into constituents of the ambiguous item *time flies* will neither show nor account for the ambiguity:

time flies

A labelled analysis, in contrast, would show that in one sense *time* is a noun and *flies* is a verb, while in the other sense *time* is a verb and *flies* a noun. The second sense allows for the joke:

A: Time flies
B: I can't; they fly too fast

(Palmer, 1971, p. 132)

Labelled IC analysis is now commonly referred to as **phrase-structure grammar**; **scale and category grammar**, **tagmemics** and **stratificational grammar** are famous examples which go far beyond simple tree diagrams representing only sequential surface structure (see SCALE AND CATEGORY GRAMMAR, TAGMEMICS and STRATIFICATIONAL SYNTAX).

Pure IC, being developed by Bloomfield and his followers in the climate which then prevailed of strict empiricism, was meant to precede classification, but (Palmer, 1971, p. 128):

> In actual fact a great deal of IC cutting can be seen to be dependent upon prior assumptions about the grammatical status of the elements. . . . For instance, even when we start with a sentence such as *John worked* as the model for the analysis of *All the little children ran up the hill* we are assuming that both can be analysed in terms of the traditional categories of subject and predicate. This is implicit in the treatment of *All the little children* as an expansion of *John* and *ran up the hill* as an expansion of *worked*.

Of course, this fact does not prevent the notion of the immediate constituent from remaining very useful, and consequently much drawn on by contemporary grammarians; and IC as conceived by Bloomfield (1933/5), in spite of its shortcomings (see Palmer, 1971), presented a great advantage over the haphazard 'methodology' of traditional grammatical classification and parsing (see TRADITIONAL GRAMMAR).

K.M.

SUGGESTIONS FOR FURTHER READING

Palmer, F.R. (1971), *Grammar*, Harmondsworth, Penguin.

The International Phonetic Alphabet

The International Phonetic Alphabet is a means of symbolizing the segments and certain non-segmental features of any language or accent, using a set of symbols and diacritics drawn up by the **International Phonetic Association (IPA)**. It is one of a large number of phonetic alphabets that have been devised in Western Europe, but in terms of influence and prestige it is now the most highly regarded of them all. Hundreds of published works have employed it. It is used throughout the world by a variety of professionals concerned with different aspects of speech, including phoneticians, linguists, dialectologists, philologists, speech scientists, speech therapists, teachers of the deaf, language teachers, and devisers of orthographic systems.

Its origins lie in the alphabet (or rather alphabets) used by the forerunner of the IPA, the **Phonetic Teachers' Association**, founded in 1886 by the Frenchman Paul Passy (1859–1940). Since then, a number of slightly differing versions of the alphabet have been published at irregular intervals by the IPA.

Three versions of the alphabet can be found in current use: that 'revised to 1951', that 'revised to 1979' and that 'revised to 1989'. All are available in near-A4-size chart form (see the reproductions in Figures 1–3).

To understand the nature of the alphabet – which sounds are symbolized and in what manner – one needs to consult another of the Association's publications, *The Principles of the International Phonetic Association* (1949, with later reprints). The guiding principles for the symbolization of sounds are essentially, though not entirely, those that the Association drew up and publicized in August 1888.

The aim of the notation is to provide the means for making a phonemic transcription of speech, or, in the original words of the Association, 'there should be a separate letter for each distinctive sound; that is, for each sound which being used instead of another, in the same language, can change the meaning of a word' (Phonetic Teachers' Association, 1888). Thus, the distinction between English *thin* and *sin* can be indicated by the use of θ and s for the first segment in each word. It is often the case, however, that by the use of symbols, with or without diacritics, an allophonic as well as a phonemic (see PHONEMICS) notation can be produced. So, for example, the labio-dental nasal in some English pronunciations of the /m/ in *symphony* is symbolized allophonically as [ɱ] since the symbol exists to notate the phonemic difference between that sound and [m] in a language like Teke. Nevertheless, the phonemic principle has sometimes been set aside in order to allow the notation of discernible allophonic differences within a single phoneme. Thus, far greater use is made in practice of the ɱ symbol for notating the labio-dental nasal allophone of /m/ or /n/ in languages like English, Italian, and Spanish than for showing the phonemic contrast between /m/ and /ɱ/.

It is sometimes assumed that, since the alphabet is designated as *phonetic*, it should have the capacity to symbolize *any* human speech sound. This is not, nor has it ever been, the purpose of the alphabet. Its prime purpose is to handle the notation of *phonemes* in any one of the world's 3,000 or more languages. If such symbols (with or without diacritics) can also be used for an allophonic transcription (of whatever degree of phonetic narrowness), then this must be seen as a sort of bonus.

There are many sounds which are capable of being made, but for which there are no IPA symbols – labio-dental plosives or alveolar approximants, for example. In such cases, an *ad*

Figure 1 The International Phonetic Alphabet (revised to 1951)

CONSONANTS	Bi-labial	Labio-dental	Dental and Alveolar	Retroflex	Palato-alveolar	Alveolo-palatal	Palatal	Velar	Uvular	Pharyngal	Glottal
Plosive	p b		t d	ʈ ɖ			c ɟ	k g	q ɢ		ʔ
Nasal	m	ɱ	n	ɳ			ɲ	ŋ	ɴ		
Lateral Fricative			ɬ ɮ								
Lateral Non-fricative			l	ɭ			ʎ				
Rolled			r						ʀ		
Flapped			ɾ	ɽ					ʀ		
Fricative	ɸ β	f v	θ ð s z ʃ ʒ	ʂ ʐ	ʃ ʒ	ɕ ʑ	ç ʝ	x ɣ	χ ʁ	ħ ʕ	h ɦ
Frictionless Continuants and Semi-vowels	w ɥ	ʋ	ɹ				j (ɥ)	(w)	ʁ		

VOWELS

Close	(y ʉ u)	ʉ
Half-close	(ø o)	
Half-open	(œ ɔ)	
Open	(ɒ)	

	Front	Central	Back
	i y	ɨ u	ɯ u
	e ø	ɵ	ɤ o
	ɛ œ	ə	ʌ ɔ
	æ	ɐ	
	a ɶ		ɑ ɒ

(Secondary articulations are shown by symbols in brackets)

OTHER SOUNDS.—Palatalized consonants: ʃ, ʒ, etc.; palatalized ʃ, ʒ, ɕ, ʑ. Velarized or pharyngealized consonants: ɫ, d, z, etc. Ejective consonants (with simultaneous glottal stop): p', t', etc. Implosive voiced consonants: ɓ, ɗ, etc. ʄ fricative trill. σ, ℨ (labialized θ, ð, or s, z). ʪ, ʫ (labialized ʃ, ʒ). ɫ, ɾ, ɕ, ƕ (clicks, Zulu c, q, x). ɺ (a sound between r and l). ŋ Japanese syllabic nasal. ƻ (combination of x and ʃ). ʍ (voiceless w). ɹ, ɣ, ʁ (lowered varieties of i, y, u). ɐ (a vowel between ø and o).

Affricates are normally represented by groups of two consonants (ts, tʃ, dʒ, etc.), but, when necessary, ligatures are used (ʦ, ʧ, ʤ, etc.), or the marks ‿ or ͡ (ʦ or t͡s, etc.). ꞎ also denote synchronic articulation (m͡ŋ = simultaneous m and ŋ). c, ɟ may occasionally be used in place of tʃ, dʒ, and ʧ, ʤ for ts, dz. Aspirated plosives: ph, th, etc. r-coloured vowels: ɛɹ, aɹ, ɔɹ, etc., or ɛˑ, aˑ, ɔˑ, etc., or ɝ, ɚ, ɞ, etc.; r-coloured ə : əɹ or əˑ or ɔ or ɐ, ɔ˞.

LENGTH, STRESS, PITCH.— ꞉ (full length); ˑ (half length); ˈ (stress, placed at beginning of the stressed syllable); ˌ (secondary stress); ˉ (high level pitch); ˍ (low level); ´ (high rising); ˏ (low rising); ` (high falling); ˎ (low falling); ˆ (rise-fall); ˇ (fall-rise).

MODIFIERS.— ˜ nasality. ˳ breath (l̥ = breathed l). ˬ voice (ṣ = z). ˈ slight aspiration following p, t, etc. ˒ labialization (n̮ = labialized n). ˌ dental articulation (ṭ = dental t). ˴ palatalization (ẓ = ʒ). ˵ specially close vowel (ẹ = a very close e). ˶ specially open vowel (ẹ = a rather open e). ˬ tongue raised (e˔ or ẹ = ɇ). ˎ tongue lowered (e˕ or ẹ = ɛ). ˖ tongue advanced (u˖ or u̟ = ɯ). ˗ or ꞈ (tongue retracted (i˗ or i̠ = ɨ, t̠ = alveolar t). ˈ lips more rounded. ˈ lips more spread. Central vowels: ï (= i̵), ü (= ʉ), ë (= ə˖), ö (= ɵ), ö̈ (= ɵ), ɔ̈, ˸ (e.g. n̩) syllabic consonant. ˴ consonantal vowel. ʃˌ variety of ʃ resembling s, etc.

Figure 2   The International Phonetic Alphabet (revised to 1979)

C O N S O N A N T S		Bilabial	Labiodental	Dental, Alveolar, or Post-alveolar	Retroflex	Palato-alveolar	Palatal	Velar	Uvular	Labial-Palatal	Labial-Velar	Pharyngeal	Glottal
(pulmonic air-stream mechanism)	Nasal	m	ɱ	n	ɳ		ɲ	ŋ	ɴ				
	Plosive	p b		t d	ʈ ɖ		c ɟ	k ɡ	q ɢ		k͡p ɡ͡b		ʔ
	(Median) Fricative	ɸ β	f v	θ ð s z	ʂ ʐ	ʃ ʒ	ç ʝ	x ɣ	χ ʁ	ɥ	ʍ w	ħ ʕ	h ɦ
	(Median) Approximant		ʋ	ɹ	ɻ		j	ɰ		ɥ	w		
	Lateral Fricative			ɬ ɮ									
	Lateral (Approximant)			l	ɭ		ʎ						
	Trill			r					ʀ				
	Tap or Flap			ɾ	ɽ				ʀ				
C O N S O N A N T S (non-pulmonic air-stream)	Ejective	p'		t'				k'					
	Implosive	ɓ		ɗ				ɠ					
	(Median) Click	ʘ		ʇ	ʇ	ʗ							
	Lateral Click			ʖ									

DIACRITICS

̥ Voiceless n̥ d̥
̬ Voiced s̬ ţ
ʰ Aspirated tʰ
̤ Breathy-voiced b̤ a̤
̪ Dental t̪
̣ Labialized ṭ
ʲ Palatalized ṭ
ˠ Velarized or Pharyn-gealized ɫ, ɫ̢
̩ Syllabic n̩
̑ or ̯ Simultaneous sf (but see also under the heading Affricates)

\ or ˈ Raised e̍, ẹ, e̝ w
 or ˎ Lowered e̩, ẹ, e̞ ɣ
+ Advanced u̟+, ̣
 or ̠ Retracted i̠-, ̣, t̠
̈ Centralized ë
̃ Nasalized ã
˞ r-coloured a˞
etc.

ı = i
e = ə

˞ or ̣ Raised
i = ɪ
u = ʊ
ɜ = Variety of ə
ɹ = r-coloured ə

OTHER SYMBOLS

ɕ, ʑ Alveolo-palatal fricatives
ʄ, ʓ Palatalized ʃ, ʒ
ɹ̣ Alveolar fricative trill
ɺ Alveolar lateral flap
ɧ Simultaneous ʃ and x
ʥ Variety of ʃ resembling s, etc.

VOWELS

	Front	Back	Front	Back
	Unrounded		Rounded	
Close	i ɨ ʉ	ɯ u	y ʉ ʊ	u
Half-close	e ə	ɤ o	ø ɵ	o
Half-open	ɛ ɐ æ	ʌ ɔ	œ	ɔ
Open	a ɐ	ɑ	ɶ	ɒ

STRESS, TONE (PITCH)

ˈ stress, placed at begin-ning of stressed syllable:
ˌ secondary stress: ˉ high level pitch, high tone:
ˊ high rising: ˏ low level:
ˎ low rising: ˆ high falling:
ˇ rise-fall:

AFFRICATES can be written as digraphs, as ligatures, or with slur marks: thus ts, tʃ, dʒ: ʦ ʧ ʤ: c, ɟ may occasionally be used for tʃ, dʒ.

Figure 3 The International Phonetic Alphabet (revised to 1989)

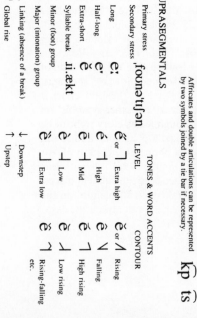

hoc method must be used by individual scholars for indicating such sounds. In due course, the IPA may decide to provide suitable symbols or diacritics.

It will be noticed that some 'boxes' on the charts contain no symbols. There are two possible reasons for this: one that the sound is a physiological impossiblity (e.g. a pharyngeal trill or a nasal lateral); the other that, as far as is known, such a sound, even though it may be pronounceable, is not used as a separate phoneme in any language.

Almost all the symbols and diacritics are assigned specific, unambiguous articulatory or phonatory values. Thus, in the word *cease*, the /s/ at the beginning and at the end of the syllable are the same, and must therefore be written in the same way. This principle may lead to difficulties, however, in interpreting correctly the actual phonetic quality of an allophone. For example, the glottal plosive [ʔ], used by many speakers of English as an allophone of /t/ in certain phonological contexts, might be interpreted as alveolar rather than glottal from its phonemic symbolization as /t/. The use of the bracketing conventions, / / for phonemes, [ ] for allophones, could assist in resolving any ambiguity.

Where the same symbol is used for more than one sound (e.g. ʀ for the uvular tap as well as the uvular trill, or j for the voiced palatal fricative and the equivalent approximant), the explanation lies either in the fact that no phonemic contrast exists between the sounds in question or in the opinion of the IPA the contrast is not sufficiently widespread in the world's languages to justify devising extra symbols.

The choice of symbols in the alphabet is based as far as possible on the set of 'ordinary letters of the roman alphabet', with 'as few new letters as possible' being used. A glance at the chart reveals that most of the symbols are either roman or adjustments of roman characters, for example by being inverted or reversed: ɹ is a turned r, ɔ a turned c; and so on. Symbols from other alphabets have been introduced, for example θ and χ from Greek, but the typeface has been cut so that it harmonizes visually with the roman

characters. Only when the roman alphabet has been exhausted have special, non-alphabetic characters been used, for example on the 1951 chart the symbol ɭ for the voiceless labialized palato-alveolar fricative, and ƀ, the alternative symbol for the voiceless alveolar affricate ts.

The alphabet may be written in two forms: either as handwritten approximations to the printed characters or in specially devised cursive forms. The *Principles* gives examples of some of the latter.

Typewriters are available, equipped with many of the IPA symbols and diacritics; for electric typewriters there are special 'golfball' typing heads. With the advent of computer typesetting, programs now exist so that a dot-matrix or laser-print output of the symbols and diacritics can be obtained.

Illustrations of the alphabet for connected texts can be found in the specimens of fifty languages included in the *Principles*. Some of the languages are transcribed in a phonemic form only, others in more of an allophonic than phonemic form.

The charts draw a distinction between consonants and vowels on the one hand and 'other sounds' or 'other symbols' on the other. A third section is devoted to non-segmental aspects of speech. This arrangement is intended to reflect the practical requirements of the user.

For the symbolization of consonants, the traditional articulatory phonetic parameters of **place of articulation**, **manner of articulation** and **state of the glottis** are employed. On the 1951 chart, there are eleven places, and on the 1979 chart ten single places and two double places (labial–palatal and labial–velar). Voiceless sounds are placed towards the left-hand side of the 'box', and voiced sounds towards the right. The place alveolo–palatal on the 1951 chart is relegated to the category of 'other symbols' on the 1979 chart, although it has every right to be considered alongside palato–alveolar and so on, since it is needed in a phonemic notation of, for example, Polish. On the 1951 chart, clear divisions are established between different places, regardless of the manner of articulation: on the 1979 chart, however, this is not always the case.

Certain differences of terminology, especially for manners of articulation are evident between the charts: cf. lateral non-fricative (1951) and lateral approximant (1979), rolled (1951) and trill (1979), frictionless continuant and semi-vowel (1951) and approximant (1979), etc. Non-pulmonic plosive sounds (ejectives, implosives, clicks), which had been located under 'other sounds' in 1951, have their own rightful position amongst the consonants in 1979. Other differences between the charts include the removal of certain symbols by 1979 (σ and 2 for example), a slightly different orientation of the vowel diagram, and the introduction (or, as it happens, reintroduction) of ɪ and ʊ as alternatives to i and o.

It is only in the symbolization of certain sounds that a consistent graphic principle can be noted. All the nasal symbols are constructed as variants of the letter 'n'; and all the retroflex symbols have a descender below the x-line which curls to the right. All the implosive symbols have a hook on top; and all ejectives have a ' following the symbol.

As indicated above, the great majority of the symbols and diacritics used in the alphabet are for notating the segments of speech. Even so, internationally agreed notations are still lacking for other aspects of speech, particularly non-segmental features such as phonation types, tempo, rhythm, and voice qualities. In view of the emphasis on segmental phonemic notation in the alphabet, however, such a gap is understandable.

A development of the alphabet is **International Phonetic Spelling**. Its purpose is to provide an orthographic representation of a language such that the pronunciation and the spelling system are brought into closer line with each other. An example, taken from the *Principles*, is the spelling of the English clause *weak forms must generally be ignored* as 'wiik formz məst jenərali bi ignord'. International Phonetic Spelling is, then, an alternative, but more phonemically realistic, roman-based reformed orthography. Examples of such an orthography for English, French, German and Sinhalese can be found in the *Principles*.

Another extension of the Association's alphabet is **World Orthography**, which, like International Phonetic Spelling, is a means of providing hitherto unwritten languages with a writing system. Its symbols are almost the same as those of the 1951 alphabet.

M.K.C.MacM.

SUGGESTION FOR FURTHER READING

Abercrombie, D. (1967), *Elements of General Phonetics*, Edinburgh, Edinburgh University Press, pp. 111–32.

MacMahon, M.K.C. (1986), 'The International Phonetic Association: the first 100 years', *Journal of the International Phonetic Association*, 16: 30–8.

Interpretive semantics

The label **interpretive semantics** describes any approach to generative grammar that assumes that rules of semantic interpretation apply to already generated syntactic structures. It was coined to contrast with **generative semantics** (see GENERATIVE SEMANTICS), which posits that semantic structures are directly generated, and then undergo a transformational mapping to surface structure. Confusingly, however, while 'generative semantics' is the name of a particular framework for grammatical analysis, 'interpretive semantics' is only the name for an approach to semantic rules *within* a set of historically related frameworks. Thus there has never been a comprehensive theoretical model of interpretive semantics as there has been of generative semantics.

After the collapse of generative semantics in the late 1970s, virtually all generative grammarians adopted the interpretive-semantic assumption that rules of interpretation apply to syntactic structures. Since the term no longer singles out one of a variety of distinct trends within the field, it has fallen into disuse.

Followers of interpretive semantics in the 1970s were commonly referred to simply as **interpretivists** as well as by the more cumbersome **interpretive semanticists**. A terminological shortening has been applied to the name for the approach itself: any theory that posited rules of semantic interpretation applying to syntactic structures is typically called an **interpretive theory**.

The earliest generative treatment of semantics, Katz and Fodor's 1963 paper, 'The structure of a semantic theory', was an interpretive one. The goals they set for such a theory were to underlie all subsequent interpretive approaches to semantics and, indeed, have characterized the majority position of generative grammarians in general with respect to meaning. Most importantly, Katz and Fodor drew a sharp line between those aspects of sentence interpretation deriving from linguistic knowledge and those deriving from beliefs about the world. That is, they asserted the theoretical distinction between **semantics** and **pragmatics** (see SEMANTICS and PRAGMATICS).

Katz and Fodor motivated this dichotomy by pointing to sentences such as *Our store sells horse shoes* and *Our store sells alligator shoes*. As they pointed out, in actual usage, these sentences are not taken ambiguously – the former is typically interpreted as ' . . . shoes for horses', the latter as ' . . . shoes from alligator skin'. However, they argued that it is not the job of a semantic theory to incorporate the purely cultural, possibly temporary, fact that shoes are made for horses, but not for alligators, and that shoes are made out of alligator skin, but not often out of horse

hide (and if they are, we call them 'leather shoes'). Semantic theory, then, would characterize both sentences as ambiguous – the only alternative, as they saw it, would be for such a theory to incorporate all of human culture and experience.

Katz and Fodor thus set the tone for subsequent work in interpretive semantics by assuming that the semantic component of the grammar has responsibility for accounting for the full range of possible interpretations of any sentence, regardless of how world knowledge might limit the number of interpretations actually assigned to an utterance by participants in a discourse.

Katz and Fodor also set a lower bound for their interpretive theory: namely, to describe and explain speakers' ability to (1) determine the number and content of the readings of a sentence; (2) detect semantic anomalies; (3) decide on paraphrase relations between sentences; and (4), more vaguely, mark 'every other semantic property that plays a role in this ability' (1963, p. 176).

The Katz–Fodor interpretive theory contains two components: the **dictionary**, later called the **lexicon**, and the **projection rules**. The former contains, for each lexical item, a characterization of the role it plays in semantic interpretation. The latter determines how the structured combinations of lexical items assign a meaning to the sentence as a whole.

The dictionary entry for each item consists of a **grammatical portion** indicating the **syntactic category** to which it belongs and a **semantic portion** containing **semantic markers, distinguishers**, and **selectional restrictions**. The semantic markers and distinguishers each represent some aspect of the meaning of the item, roughly corresponding to **systematic** and **incidental** aspects, respectively. For example, the entry for *bachelor* contains markers such as (Human), (Male), (Young), and distinguishers such as [Who has never married] and [Who has the first or lowest academic degree]. Thus a Katz–Fodor lexical entry very much resembles the product of a componential analysis (see SEMANTICS and LEXIS AND LEXICOLOGY).

The first step in the interpretation of a sentence

is the plugging in of the lexical items from the dictionary into the syntactically generated **phrase-marker** (see TRANSFORMATIONAL-GENERATIVE GRAMMAR). After insertion, **projection rules** apply upwards from the bottom of the tree, amalgamating the readings of adjacent nodes to specify the reading of the node which immediately dominates them.

Since any lexical item might have more than one reading, if the projection rules were to apply in an unconstrained fashion, the number of readings of a node would simply be the product of the number of readings of those nodes which it dominates. However, the selectional restrictions forming part of the dictionary entry for each lexical item serve to limit the amalgamatory possibilities. For example, the entry for the verb *hit* in the Katz–Fodor framework contains a selectional restriction limiting its occurrence to objects with the marker (Physical Object). The sentence *The man hits the colourful ball* would thus be interpreted as meaning ' . . . strikes the brightly coloured round object', but not as having the anomalous reading ' . . . strikes the gala dance', since *dance* does not contain the marker (Physical Object).

In the years following the appearance of Katz and Fodor's work, the attention of interpretivists turned from the question of the character of the semantic rules to that of the syntactic level most relevant to their application.

An attractive solution to this problem was put forward in Katz and Postal's book *An Integrated Theory of Linguistic Descriptions* (1964). Katz and Postal concluded that all information necessary for the application of the projection rules is present in the deep structure of the sentence, or, alternatively stated, that transformational rules do not affect meaning. This conclusion became known simply as the **Katz–Postal Hypothesis**.

The Katz–Postal Hypothesis received support on several grounds. First, rules such as **Passive** distort the underlying grammatical relations of the sentence relations that quite plausibly affect its semantic interpretation. Hence, it seemed logical that the projection rules should apply to a level of structure that exists before the applica-

tion of such rules, i.e. they should apply to deep structure. Second, it was typically the case that discontinuities were created by transformational rules (*look . . . up, have . . . en*, etc.) and never the case that a discontinuous underlying construction became continuous by the application of a transformation. Naturally, then, it made sense to interpret such constructions at an underlying level where their semantic unity is reflected by syntactic continuity. Finally, while there were many motivated examples of transformations which deleted elements contributing to the meaning of the sentence – the transformations forming imperatives and comparatives, for example – none had been proposed which inserted such elements. The rule which Chomsky (1957) had proposed to insert meaningless supportive *do* was typical in this respect. Again, this fact pointed to a deep structure interpretation.

The hypothesis that deep structure is the sole input to the semantic rules dominated interpretive semantics for the next five years, and was incorporated as an underlying principle by its offshoot, generative semantics. Yet there were lingering doubts throughout this period that transformational rules were without semantic effect. Chomsky expressed these doubts in a footnote in *Aspects of the Theory of Syntax* (1965, p. 224), where he reiterated the feeling that he had expressed in *Syntactic Structures* (1957) that *Everyone in the room knows at least two languages* and *At least two languages are known by everyone in the room* differ in meaning. Yet he considered that both interpretations might be 'latent' in each sentence. A couple of years later he gave his doubts even stronger voice, though he neither gave specific examples nor made specific proposals: 'In fact, I think that a reasonable explication of the term "semantic interpretation" would lead to the conclusion that surface structure also contributed in a restricted but important way to semantic interpretation, but I will say no more about the matter here' (1967, p. 407).

In the last few years of the 1960s there was a great outpouring of examples from Chomsky and his students which illustrated superficial levels of syntactic structure playing an important role in determining semantic interpretation. Taken as a whole, they seemed to indicate that any strong form of the Katz–Postal Hypothesis had to be false – everything needed for semantic interpretation was *not* present in the deep structure. And, while these facts might still allow one, legalistically, to maintain that transformations do not change meaning, the conclusion was inescapable that all of meaning is not determined before the application of the transformational rules. For example, Jackendoff (1969) cited the contrast between (1a) and (1b) as evidence that passivization has semantic effects:

(1) (a) Many arrows did not hit the target
    (b) The target was not hit by many arrows

The scope of *many* appears wider than that of *not* in (1a), but narrower in (1b). Jackendoff also argued that the rule proposed in Klima (1964) to handle simple negation, which places the negative before the finite verb, is also meaning-changing. As he observed, (2a) and (2b) are not paraphrases; the negative in (2a) has wider scope than the quantifier, but the reverse is true in (2b):

(2) (a) Not much shrapnel hit the soldier
    (b) Much shrapnel did not hit the soldier

In fact, it appeared to be *generally* the case that the scope of logical elements such as quantifiers and negatives is determined by their respective order in surface structure. Thus, the scope of the word *only* in (3a) is the subject, *John*, while in (3b) it may be the whole verb phrase, or just the verb, or just the object, or just one subconstituent of the object:

(3) (a) Only John reads books on politics
    (b) John only reads books on politics

Observations like these led Chomsky, Jackendoff, and others to propose rules taking surface structures as their input and deriving from those surface structures the representation of the scope of logical elements in the sentence. Nevertheless, it was clear that not *all* interpretation takes place on the surface. For example, in sentences (1a) and (1b), the semantic relation between *arrows, hit,* and *target* is the

same. Indeed, it appeared to be generally the case that the main propositional content of the sentence – the semantic relationship between the verb and its associated noun phrases and prepositional phrases – does not change under transformation. Hence, it made sense to continue to interpret this relationship at the level of deep structure.

By 1970, the term 'interpretive semantics' had come to be used most commonly to refer to the idea that interpretive rules apply to both deep and surface structures, rather than to deep structures alone. Nevertheless, Katz (1972) maintained only the latter approach to interpretive rules, and, therefore, quite understandably, he continued to use the term 'interpretive semantics' to refer to his approach.

Figure 1 depicts the model that was posited by the great majority of interpretivists in the early 1970s. The most comprehensive treatment of the interpretive semantic rules in the early 1970s was Ray Jackendoff's *Semantic Interpretation in Generative Grammar* (1972). For Jackendoff, as for interpretivists in general, there was no single formal object called a 'semantic representation'. Rather, different types of rules applying at different levels 'filled in' different aspects of the meaning. Jackendoff posited four distinct components of meaning, each of which was derived by a different set of interpretive rules:

(4) (a) Functional structure: the main propositional content of the sentence.
    (b) Modal structure: the specification of the scope of logical elements such as negation and quantifiers, and of the referential properties of noun phrases.
    (c) The table of coreference: the specification of which noun phrases in a sentence are understood as co-referential.
    (d) Focus and presupposition: The designation of what information in the sentence is understood as new and what is understood as old.

Functional structure is determined by **projection rules** applying to deep structure. Thus, the semantic relationship between *hit, arrows,*

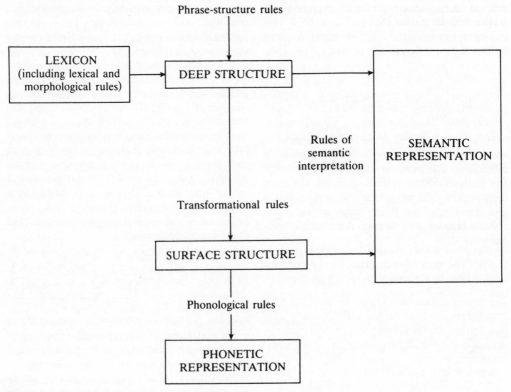

Figure 1

and *target* in (1a) and (1b) could be captured in part by rules such as (5a) and (5b), the former rule interpreting the deep-structure subject of both sentences as the semantic agent, and the latter rule interpreting the deep-structure object of both sentences as the semantic patient:

(5) (a) Interpret the animate deep-structure subject of a sentence as the semantic agent of the verb.
(b) Interpret the deep-structure direct object of a sentence as the semantic patient of the verb.

In **modal structure** are represented relationships such as those between *many* and *not* in (1a) and (1b). A rule such as (6) captures the generalization that the scope of the quantifier and the negative differs in these two sentences:

(6) If logical element A precedes logical element B in surface structure, then A is interpreted as having wider scope than B (where 'logical elements' include quantifiers, negatives, and some modal auxiliaries).

Jackendoff's third semantic component is the **table of coreference**. Indeed, by 1970 all interpretive semanticists agreed that **interpretive rules** state the conditions under which anaphoric elements such as pronouns are understood as being coreferential with their antecedents. This represented a major departure from the work of the preceding decade, in which it was assumed that pronouns replace full noun phrases under identity with another noun phrase by means of a transformational rule (see, for example, Lees and Klima 1963). In this earlier work, (7b) was derived from (7a) by means of a **pronominal-ization transformation** that replaced the second occurrence of *John* in (7a) by the pronoun *he* (the indices show coreference):

(7) (a) John₁ thinks that John₁ should win the prize
     (b) John₁ thinks that he₁ should win the prize

However, by the end of the 1960s, it came to be accepted that such an approach faces insuperable difficulties. The most serious problem involved the analysis of the famous class of sentences discovered by Emmon Bach and Stanley Peters and therefore called **Bach–Peters sentences**, involving **crossing co-reference**. An example from Bach (1970) is:

(8) [The man who deserves it₍ⱼ₎₁ will get [the prize he₁ desires]ⱼ

If pronominalization were to be handled by a transformation that turned a full noun phrase into a pronoun, then sentence (8) would require a deep structure with an infinite number of embeddings, since each pronoun lies within the antecedent of the other:

The man who deserves it will get the prize he desires

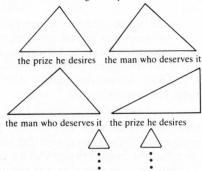

the prize he desires   the man who deserves it

the man who deserves it the prize he desires

Interpretivists concluded from Bach–Peters sentences that infinite deep structures could be avoided only if definite pronouns are present in the deep structure, which, in turn, implied the existence of an interpretive rule to assign co-referentiality between those base-generated pronouns and the appropriate noun phrases. Such a rule was posited to apply to the surface structure of the sentence.

Finally, surface structure was also deemed the locus of the interpretation of such discourse-based notions as **focus** and **presupposition**. In support of this idea, Chomsky (1971) noted that focusable phrases are *surface structure* phrases. This point can be illustrated by the question in (10) and its natural responses (11a–c). In each case, the focused element is in a phrase that did not even exist at the level of deep structure, but rather was formed by the application of a transformational rule. Therefore the interpretation of focus and presupposition must take place at surface structure:

(10) Is John certain to win?
(11) (a) No, he is certain to **lose**.
      (b) No, he's likely not to be **nominated**.
      (c) No, the election won't ever **happen**.

While the Jackendovian model outlined above is the best-known 1970s representative of interpretive semantics, it proved to have a rather short life-span. In particular, by the end of the decade most generative grammarians had come to conclude that no rules of interpretation at all apply to the deep structure of the sentence. Chomsky (1975a) noted that, given the **trace theory** of movement rules (Chomsky 1973), information about the functional structure of the sentence is encoded on the **indexed traces** and carried through the derivation to surface structure. Hence, functional structure as well could be determined at that level. On the other hand, Brame (1976), Bresnan (1978), and others challenged the very existence of transformational rules and thus, by extension, of a level of deep structure distinct from surface structures. Given such a conclusion, then necessarily all rules of semantic interpretation would apply to the surface.

The consensus by the end of the 1970s that semantic rules are interpretive rules applying to surface structure stripped the term 'interpretive semantics' of informational content. In its place labels began to be used that referred to the distinctive aspects of the various models of grammatical analysis. Thus, the Chomskyan wing of interpretivism was commonly known as the **extended standard theory (EST)** or **trace theory**, which itself by the 1980s had developed into the **government–binding theory**. The rival interpretivist wing is now represented by such transformationless models as **lexical-functional grammar** (Bresnan, 1982) (see LEXICAL-FUNCTIONAL GRAMMAR) and **generalized phrase-structure grammar** (Gazdar *et al.*, 1985).

F.J.N.

SUGGESTIONS FOR FURTHER READING

Chomsky, N. (1965), *Aspects of the Theory of Syntax*, Cambridge, MA, MIT Press.
Chomsky, N. (1972), *Studies on Semantics in Generative Grammar*, The Hague, Mouton.
Chomsky, N. (1977), *Essays on Form and Interpretation*, New York, North-Holland.
Newmeyer, F.J. (1986), *Linguistic Theory in America*, 2nd edn, New York, Academic Press, especially chs 4 and 6.

Intonation

Intonation is the term commonly given to variation in the pitch of a speaker's voice. In lay usage, it is often taken to include all such variation, and overall impressions of its effects are described variously in terms of characteristic 'tunes' or 'lilts', often with special reference to the speech of a particular individual or to that of a geographically defined group of speakers. As a technical term in linguistics, however, it usually has a more restricted application to those pitch phenomena which contribute to the meaning-defining resources of the language in question.

A distinction can be made between two types of language. In the **tone languages**, a group which includes, for instance, many of the languages in use in the Far East, the choice of one pitch treatment rather than another serves to differentiate particular lexical items (as well as sometimes serving a suprasegmental function, as described below). In the other group, which includes the modern European languages, it is said to have a **suprasegmental** function. This is to say that the lexical content of any utterance is held to be already determined by other means (i.e. by its segmental composition), so that intonation has to be thought of as adding meaning of some other kind to stretches of speech which are usually of greater extent than the single lexical item. Discovering what the stretches of speech are that are so affected, and developing a conceptual framework within which the peculiar contribution that intonation makes to meaning can be made explicit, are essential parts of the business of setting up systematic descriptions of the phenomenon.

It is fair to say that attempts to provide such descriptions of the intonation resources of particular languages have been rather less successful than have those which relate to other aspects of linguistic organization like syntax and segmental phonology. Certainly the descriptive models that have been proposed have commanded less widespread assent. One general reason for this is doubtless the comparative recency of serious analytical interest in speech compared with the many centuries of scholarly preoccupation with the written text. There are, however, two specific, and closely related problems that could be said to have got in the way of progress.

The first derives from what is, in reality, a pretheoretical definition of the phenomenon. The practice of starting with the nature of the speech signal as something susceptible to detailed physical analysis, and of proceeding on this basis to separate out pitch from other variables like **loudness** and **length** for individual attention has tended to obscure the fact that simultaneous variation on all these parameters probably plays a part in our perception of all the functional oppositions whereby differences in intonational meaning are created. Moreover, a strong tradition which has encouraged making an initial separation between what have been referred to as **levels of pitch** and **levels of stress** has made it difficult to appreciate the essential features of the unified system in which they both work.

The difficulty of knowing just what physical features of the data to take note of, and of appreciating how those features combine as realizations of perceived linguistic contrasts, is necessarily bound up with the second of the two problems. This is the difficulty of setting up a working hypothesis about just how intonation can be said to contribute to meaning. An essential early step is to find a way of discounting those innumerable phonetic variables which do not enter into a language user's perception of a meaningfully contrastive event, and this depends upon there being some, at least provisional, agreement as to what those events are. It is well recognized that progress in the field of segmental phonology depended upon prior agreement as to what was in contrast with what. The elaboration of the notion of the **phoneme**, as an abstract, meaning-discriminating entity, which might be represented in performance by a whole range of phonetically different events, provided a means of incorporating that agreement into descriptive models. In the field of intonation, however, there has been – and there still remains – disagreement of a quite fundamental kind about how the contribution that intonation makes to meaning should be conceptualized.

While the common-sense perception of the 'word' as a carrier of a readily identifiable 'meaning' provided a satisfactory start for setting up a working inventory of segmental phonemes,

there is no comparable basis for determining if, and how, one intonation pattern is in opposition to another. Pretheoretical judgements about the effects of intonation tend to be expressed in impressionistic terms, and commonly make reference to the attitudes, emotional nuances, or special emphases that are judged to be super-imposed upon what is being said.

A number of the descriptions that have been proposed have taken such judgements as their starting point and sought to systematize them. Among the better known are those of Kenneth Pike (1945) and O'Connor and Arnold (1961). When the orientation is towards the needs of the language learner, the approach can be said to have the merit of providing characterizations of meaning that are comparatively accessible, precisely because they are grounded in common-sense apprehensions of what is going on. A weakness, even in the pedagogical context, is that the judgements are inevitably made about the attitudinal implications of a particular intona-tion pattern, produced on a particular occasion, in association with a particular combination of grammatical and lexical features. The meaning label, presented as the characterization of an attitude, turns out on inspection to refer as much to the lexis of the utterance and – more import-antly – perhaps, to the particular circumstances in which the utterance is assumed to have occurred, as to intonation.

This focus upon the purely local meanings of intonation in unique contexts seems unlikely to be helpful to anyone who wants to get access to the comparatively abstract component of meaning which the actual intonation pattern contributes. An unfortunate consequence of the attitudinal approach can easily be the highly specific pairings of one utterance with one intonation pattern. No insight is provided into the nature of the finite system of oppositions on which both successful learning and a satisfactory theoretical perspective could be said to depend.

Attempts to integrate intonation into the various theoretical models that are currently in use have been strongly conditioned by the central position given to sentential grammar. Linguists of the American structuralist school hoped that intonation would provide criteria for determining the grammatical structure of sentences. More generally, the task of handling intonation has been seen, essentially, as one of extending the mechanisms that have been postulated to account for regularities in the syntax of the unspoken sentence to take in this extra feature.

The relationship between intonation and grammar has been viewed in a number of different ways. At a comparatively unsophisticated level, it is easy to show that, in some cases, a sentence which is capable of two different interpretations if presented on its own as a written specimen seems to lose its ambiguity when a particular intonation is supplied. On this basis it is possible to argue that intonation has a **grammatical function**, as the only perceptible differentiator of distinct grammatical structures. Not all intonational contrasts are easy to relate to grammatical differences, as these are usually understood, however. Neither can all sentences which are regarded as being structurally ambiguous be disambiguated by intonation. This apparently partial correspondence between the two features of the utterance has led some linguists to assign a **multifunctional** role to intonation, claiming that it sometimes indicates grammatical structure and sometimes does something else. Crystal's (1975) proposal, for instance, is that there is a continuum from what, in his terms, are the 'more linguistic' to the 'less linguistic' uses, where 'linguistic' seems to mean 'pertaining to sentence grammar'.

The concept of multifunctionalism is applied in a different way by Halliday (1967). The view of grammar as comprising three components, the **ideational**, the **interpersonal**, and the **textual component** (see FUNCTIONAL GRAMMAR and FUNCTIONALIST LINGUISTICS) provides a framework within which Halliday's rigorously defined theoretical position can be maintained. This is that all linguistic meaning is either lexical or grammatical. Except in some tone languages, therefore, meaning contrasts which are realized intonationally are to be treated as grammatical systems and integrated into the systemic network which relates all other contrasts to each other. The consequence of adopting this position is,

naturally, to extend the scope of grammar beyond its usually assigned limits.

Within the interpersonal component fall some of the features that others have regarded as attitudinal. Of considerable importance is the fact that engagement with textual matters, by opening up the focus of interest to take in matters beyond the bounds of the sentence, makes it possible to show that some intonational meaning must be explained by reference to the overall organization of the discourse. The concept of **delicacy** is invoked to determine just which occurrences of the proposed intonational features are to be incorporated into the description: they are those which can be integrated into the grammar in its present state. While this gives a coherence to the description which is lacking from the multifunctional view, it has to be said that, in spite of the considerable complexity of the expository apparatus, it remains selective with respect to which of the intonational features we find in naturally occurring speech it can account for.

Linguists working in the transformational-generative tradition have been strongly influenced by the work of Chomsky and Halle (1968) on the application of what are called **cyclical rules** to the distribution of stress (see GENERATIVE PHONOLOGY). The underlying contention of this work is that, if the syntactic rules that generate sentences are properly formulated, they will enable us to predict in advance the *normal* stress pattern of a sentence. The lexical items that are introduced into the sentence by the operation of transformational-generative type rules have each a rule-determined stress pattern. This pattern is then progressively modified in a way which can be consistently related to grammatical relationships holding among the components of the sentence.

There were problems in applying this approach as it was originally promulgated, and much attention was given to solving them, largely by revising the grammatical rule system on which the phonological end product was held to depend. The most consistent critic of this point of view, and, by implication, of the work that has taken it for a starting point, is Bolinger (1985);

for him, the relationship between grammar and intonation is 'casual' rather than 'causal'.

The concept of a **normal** or **neutral** intonation for any given sentence, which is crucial to the Chomsky and Halle approach, has had wide currency among linguists. Adopting it as part of a theory involves regarding such neutral realizations of the sentence as being in some generalizable sense in contrast with all other possible presentations.

Attempts to explicate the nature of this contrast have taken various forms. For some, versions which depart from the neutral form have some kind of added meaning: the neutral form is defined as the one which has no meaning not already present in the (unspoken) text. For others, the neutral form is the one which makes the least number of presuppositions. In less rigorously theoretical approaches, there is often an implication that the neutral version is statistically more likely to occur, or that it is the intonation pattern chosen when people read uncontextualized sentences aloud. There appears to be no evidence in support of either. Neither have we any reason to suppose that, by postulating a neutral–contrastive opposition in this way, we are any closer to achieving a detailed and workable characterization of intonational meaning.

A practical problem for the phonologist is the provision of transcription conventions which will make it possible to record intonation in written form. Early attempts, which sought to adapt the conventions of musical notation, overlooked the essentially phonemic nature of the phenomenon. The need to attend to a recurrent pattern of meaningful events rather than to all the incidental phonetic variation that accompanies it suggests that what is wanted is something of the same order of generality as a broad International Phonetic Script. The fact that no such analytical tool is in general use is obviously connected with the lack of consensus as to the function of intonation referred to above.

A well-canvassed discrepancy between an American predilection for 'levels' and a British preference for 'tunes' is only one aspect of the differences that exist concerning how the utterance should be segmented for the purposes of describing its intonation. There is a rough similarity between the categories referred to in the literature as **sense units**, **breath groups**, **tone groups** and **contours**, but the similarities are deceptive; and the various ways of further segmenting into **nucleus**, **head**, **tail**, **tonic**, **pre-tonic**, etc., compound the differences. The important point is that, whether this is explicit or not, each formulation amounts to a starting assumption about how the underlying meaning system is organized.

An approach which takes the setting up of a tenable working account of that system as the essential first step is that which has come to be referred to as **Discourse Intonation** (Brazil, 1985). In essence, the claim is that the communicative significance of intonation becomes accessible to investigation only when language is being used in the furtherance of some interactionally perceived purpose. The act of abstracting the sample sentence away from any context, and hence from any putative usefulness its production may have in the conduct of human affairs, isolates it from just those factors on which its intonational features depend. According to this, intonation is not to be regarded as a permanently attributable component of a sentence or of any other lexico-grammatical entity; it is rather one of the means whereby speakers both acknowledge and exploit the constantly changing state of understanding they share with a hearer or group of hearers. Its successful description depends, therefore, upon its being investigated in the context of a general theory of the organization of interactive discourse.

The stress patterns of words, as these are given, for instance, in dictionaries, provide a working template for the communicatively significant segment of discourse, the **tone unit**. Instead of being regarded as the elementary particles from which utterances are constructed, such citation forms are rather to be taken as the consequence of compressing all the features of the tone unit into a single word; in the atypical circumstances of speaking out a word merely to demonstrate its citation form, the word *is* the communicative unit.

In normal usage, however, the pattern is usually distributed over longer stretches of language. Thus, while the dictionary gives

> ²after'noon
> ¹evening

we commonly find, for instance,

> ²afternoons and ¹evenings
> ²evenings and after'noons
> ²saturday afternoons and ¹evenings

'Afternoon', with what is often referred to as secondary stress (indicated as ² in the above examples) followed by primary stress (indicated as ¹), and 'evening', with only primary stress, together represent the two subtypes of the tone unit. But instead of regarding these as exhibiting different degrees of 'stress', on a scale of difference which may have three, four, or more such levels, the description highlights their functional significance.

This results in a recognition both of their functional similarity and their functional difference. They are similar in that, as **prominent** syllables and represented in transcripts thus

> AFternoons and EVenings
> EVenings and afterNOONS
> SATurday afternoons and EVenings,

they have the identical effect of assigning **selective** status to the word they belong to. They are different in that the so-called primary stress carries the principal phonetic evidence for what is perceived as a meaningful choice of **pitch movement**, or **tone**. The meaning component deriving from this latter choice attaches not to the word but to the complete tone unit. The class of syllables labelled **prominent**, therefore, includes, as a subclass, those with which **tone choice** is associated, the **tonic** sylables. It is argued that to take the two kinds of event together as levels on a scale, and to include syllables which can be heard as having lesser degrees of 'stress', but which have no comparable function, is to obscure fundamental features of the way speech sound is organized to carry meaning.

The communicative value of **prominence** and **tone choice**, and of two other variables that are available in the tone unit, are all explicated by reference to the here-and-now state of speaker–hearer understanding. Co-operative behaviour is assumed on the part of both participants, so that speakers orientate towards a view of that state which they assume hearers share, and hearers, for their part, display a general willingness to go along with the assumption.

On this basis, an either/or distinction is made between words which, at the moment of utterance in the current interaction, represent a **selection** from a set of alternatives and are made **prominent**, and those for which the speaker assumes that there are currently no alternatives. The latter are made **non-prominent**. Thus, in a straightforward example, if meetings are known to take place on Saturdays, a response to

> when is the meeting?

might be

> on saturday afterNOON

But if meetings are known to take place in the afternoon, we might expect:

> on SATurday afternoon

Generalization from simple examples like these to take in all the consequences of speakers' choices in the **prominent/non-prominent option** requires elaboration, at some length, of the notion of **existential value**, which is central to the discourse approach to intonation.

The significance of choice of **tone** is likewise related to the special state of convergence which is taken to characterize the relationship between speaker and hearer at a particular moment in time. The central choice here is between a **proclaiming tone**, which ends low, and a **referring tone**, which ends high. At its most general, this choice is associated with a projected assumption as to which of two aspects of the relationship is foregrounded for the duration of the tone unit.

Proclaiming tones present the content of the tone unit as if in the context of separateness of viewpoint, while referring tones locate it presumptively in a shared world. A fairly concrete example would be:

i'm going to a MEETing // on SATurday afterNOON.

With referring tone in the first tone unit, and proclaiming tone in the second, the projected understanding would be that the hearer already knew that the speaker had a meeting to go to; what it was necessary to *tell* was when. If the tones were reversed, with proclaiming tone preceding referring tone, it would be a prior interest in what the speaker was going to do on Saturday afternoon that was taken for granted, and the fact that s/he was going to a meeting that was told. If both tone units were proclaimed, the speaker would be telling the hearer both what s/he was going to do and when s/he was going to do it.

Within each of the options, referring and proclaiming, there is a further choice of tone. A referring tone may be realized as either a **fall–rise** or a **rise**; a proclaiming tone as either a **fall** or a **rise–fall**. Choice in these sec-ondary systems depends upon the speaker's decision with respect to another aspect of the here-and-now state of the relationship. At any point in the progress of an interaction, it is possible to ascribe a **dominant** role to one of the participants. That is to say, one party or the other can be said to be exercising some kind of control over the way the interaction develops. On some occasions, like lessons, dominant status is assumed to be assigned by common consent for the duration of the interaction. On others, for instance during most social conversation, it is subject to constant negotiation and re-negotiation. The second version of each of the pairs of tones serves to underline the speaker's *pro tem* occupancy of dominant role. So the rising tone has the dual significance **referring + dominance**, and the rise–fall signifies **proclaiming + dominance**.

The set of meaningful variables associated with each consecutive tone unit is completed by two three-way choices, the most readily per-ceived phonetic correlate of which is **pitch level**. (Note that this is not to be confused with the **pitch movements**, or **glides**, which correlate with tone choice.) The reference points for the iden-tification of these variables are the prominent syllables, and the significance of each is once more explicated by reference to the immediate state of speaker–hearer understanding.

The first prominent syllable of each tone unit selects **high**, **mid** or **low key**. By selecting high key, the speaker can be said to attribute a certain expectation to the hearer and simultaneously to indicate that the content of the tone unit is contrary to that expectation. With low key, the expectation projected can be paraphrased roughly as that, in the light of what has gone before, the content of this tone unit will naturally follow. The mid-key choice attributes expecta-tions of neither kind to the hearer.

The relevant pitch levels are recognized, not by reference to any absolute standard, but on a relative basis within the immediately surround-ing discourse. The same is true of those which correlate with the other choice, **termination**. Provided there are two prominent syllables in the tone unit, pitch level at the second realizes **high**, **mid**, or **low termination**. If there is only one prominent syllable in the tone unit, key and termination are selected simultaneously. Termination is the means whereby a speaker indicates certain expectations of her/his own about how the hearer will react to the content of the tone unit. Its function is closely related to that of key in that the responses expected are distinguished by the respondent's choice of key. Thus high termination anticipates high key, mid termination anticipates mid key, while with low termination the speaker signals no particular expectation of this sort.

This last consideration provides a basis for recognizing a further phonological unit, of potentially greater extent than the tone unit, the **pitch sequence**. A pitch sequence is a concatenation of one or more tone units which ends in low termination. Both on its own, and in conjunction with special applications of the significance of key, the pitch sequence plays an important part in the larger-scale structuring of the discourse.

It will be noticed that the Discourse Model stops short of attempting to provide detailed phonetic prescriptions for the various meaning-ful features it postulates. This follows from the priority given to the meaning system. Useful investigation of just what hearers depend upon in their perception of one or other of those features is taken to be dependent upon prior recognition of how each fits into that system. It is to be expected that users will be tolerant of very considerable phonetic variation within the range that they will regard as realizations of the 'same' feature.

Variations in realization, which do not, however, affect the perception of oppositions within the system, seem likely to account for many of the so-called 'intonational' differences between dialects, and even among languages. The bulk of the systematic work carried out in intonation and related areas has concentrated upon English. There is a fairly common assumption, but a more-or-less unexamined one, that the intonation systems of different languages are radically different. Only by applying a method of analysis which relates intonational choices functionally to what use speakers are making of the language, can we hope to be in a position to compare like with like and to discover to what extent differences are differences of system and to what extent they are comparatively superficial matters of realization.

D.C.B.

SUGGESTIONS FOR FURTHER READING

Bolinger, D.L. (1985), *Intonation and its Parts: Melody in Spoken English*, London, Edward Arnold.

Brazil, D.C. (1985), *The Communicative Value of Intonation in English*, (Discourse Analysis Monograph, 8) English Language Research, University of Birmingham.

Crutenden, A. (1986), *Intonation*, Cambridge, Cambridge University Press.

Ladd, D.R. (1980), *The Structure of Intonational Meaning*, Bloomington, Indiana University Press.

Halliday, M.A.K. (1967), *Intonation and Grammar in British English*, The Hague, Mouton.

Kinesics

Kinesics is the technical term for what is normally known as **body language**, that is, the systematic use of facial expressions, gestures, and posture as components in speech situations. Although this visual system is important in so far as a large amount of information is often communicated by means of it, it is not usually held to fall within the scope of linguistics proper, which deals with specifically *linguistic* meaning, but rather to be part of the broader discipline of semiotics, which deals with signification in general (see SEMIOTICS). Nevertheless, it can be argued that it is not possible to provide adequate theories of naturally occurring conversation without paying attention to kinesics (Birdwhistell, 1970), and the felt need to video record, rather than simply sound record, conversations for study provides some support for this contention (see Gosling, 1981b).

In addition, kinesics is of interests to linguists in so far as the theory and methodology of it has been consistently influenced by linguistics (Birdwhistell, 1970, extract in Gumperz and Hymes, 1986, p. 385). Thus Birdwhistell (ibid.) acknowledges his debt to structural linguistics, particularly to the model provided by Trager and Smith (1951), while Gosling (1981a, 1981b) works within the framework of functional linguistics. Sapir (1927) refers to gestures as conforming to 'an elaborate and secret code that is written nowhere, known by none, and understood by all', and kineticists can be seen as attempting to unravel and write down this code.

Ekman and Friesen (1969) distinguish five major categories of kinesic behaviour (Gumperz and Hymes, 1986, p. 383; emphasis added):

(1) **emblems**, non-verbal acts which have a direct verbal translation, i.e., greetings, gestures of assent, etc.; (2) **illustrators**, movements tied to speech which serve to illustrate the spoken word; (3) **affective** displays such as facial signs indicating happiness, surprise, fear, etc.; (4) **regulators**, acts which maintain and regulate the act of speaking; (5) **adaptors**, signs originally linked to bodily needs, such as brow wiping, lip biting, etc.

Both Birdwhistell and Gosling wish to exclude the first three of these categories from study,

because, in Gosling's words, they are '*super-imposed* on the basic communicative gestures which realise discourse functions' (1981b, p. 171). Adaptors are excluded because they do not appear to be used in a systematic way during speech events, so it is the regulators which form the centre of kinesic research.

Structural kinesics is based on the notion of the **kinesic juncture** (Birdwhistell, 1970; reprinted in Gumperz and Hymes, 1986, p. 393):

The fact that streams of body behavior were segmented and connected by demonstrable behavioral shifts analogic to double cross, double bar and single bar junctures [see PHONEMICS] in the speech stream enhanced the research upon kinemorphology and freed kinesics from the atomistic amorphy of earlier studies dominated by 'gestures' and 'sign' language.

Birdwhistell provides the tentative table of kinemes of juncture shown below (ibid., p. 394).

Symbol	Term	Gross behavioral description
K#	Double cross	Inferior movement of body part followed by 'pause'. Terminates structural string.
K//	Double bar	Superior movement of body part followed by 'pause'. Terminates structural strings. . . .
K##	Triple cross	Major shift in body activity (relative to customary performance). Normally terminates strings marked by two or more K#s or K//s. However, in certain instances K## may mark termination of a single item kinetic construction, e.g., in auditor response, may exclude further discussion or initiate subject or activity change.
K =	Hold	A portion of the body actively involved in construction performance projects an arrested position while other junctural activity continues in other body areas.
K/	Single bar	Projected held position, followed by 'pause'. Considerable idiosyncratic variation in performance; 'pause' may be momentary lag in shift from body part to body part in kinemorphic presentation or may involve full stop and hold of entire body projection activity.
K.	Tie	A continuation of movement, thus far isolated only in displacement of primary stress.

In addition to the junctural kinemes, Birdwhistell isolates several stress kinemes which combine to form a set of suprasegmental kinemorphemes (ibid., p. 399). However, he points out that it is not possible to establish an absolute relationship between kinetic stresses and junctures and linguistic stress and intonation patterns.

Birdwhistell's study referred to above is based on a two-party conversation, and it is interesting that his observation of the links between intonation and kinetics, and between linguistic and kinetic junctures is confirmed in Gosling's (1981a, 1981b) analysis of a number of video-taped seminar discussions, that is, multiparty communicative events.

Gosling (1981b, p. 161) focuses on those 'recurrent features of non-vocal behaviour which . . . seem to be realisations of discourse function'. Kinetics is particularly important in the study of multiparty discourse, because in many discourse situations of this type, a speaker may address himself or herself to any one or more of the other participants at any one time, so it is impossible from a sound recording alone to establish ad-dressor–addressee relations (1981b, p. 162), and one loses important clues, such as the establishment of eye contact (ibid., p. 166), to how one speaker may select the next speaker, or to how an interactant may bid for a turn at speaking.

Gosling therefore argues that it would be useful to establish kinesics as a formal linguistics level which would include 'all those meaningful gestures or sequences of gestures which realise interactive functions in face-to-face communicative situations' (ibid., p. 163); it is the function of **discourse kinesics** to isolate and describe these (ibid., p. 170). They include some changes in body posture and posture change accompanied by intent gaze at present speaker, both of which appear to be signals of a desire to speak next; Gosling calls these **turn-claims** (ibid., p. 173). During a speaker's turn, Gosling suggests that the following gestures are typically used by the speaker (1981b, pp. 173–4):

(a) a movement of body posture towards a mid-upright position, with head fairly raised at the start, oriented towards previous speaker;

(b) some movement of the dominant hand at some stage, either immediately prior to, or fairly soon after the start of the 'turn'.

(c) If the 'turn' is of some length, and becomes positively expository in nature, rather than being an extended reaction, there is a tendency to the formation of a 'box' with both hands (possibly associated with neutralisation of gaze, or loss of eye contact). It also seems a fairly strong rule that dominant hand gesture precedes both-hands 'box' in any turn. Towards the end of a natural turn (i.e. one that is not interrupted), the 'box', if there is one, tends to disappear, and hands move towards an 'at rest' position.

(d) Associated with (a) above is the intake of breath, either before a phonation, or very soon afterwards.

Gosling also makes observations about the possible functions of gaze in addition to its function as bid for a speaking turn or as next-speaker nomination. For instance, a speaker who frequently redirects his or her gaze appears to be seeking **feedback**, and if a speaker establishes eye contact with another person who, however, does not take up the offer of a turn at speaking, then the present speaker seems to take this as a signal that s/he may continue to speak (1981b, p. 174).

Although it is clear that some useful statements can be made about kinesic behaviour, and although no-one would dispute the communicative import of such behaviour, kinesics is likely to remain a fairly peripheral area of linguistics, if it is included in that discipline at all, because of the great difficulties involved in providing fairly definitive statements about how non-vocal behaviour contributes to speech exchanges in a systematic way, and because it is difficult to perceive structure at the level of kinetic form.

K.M.

SUGGESTIONS FOR FURTHER READING

Abercrombie, D. (1968), 'Paralanguage', *British Journal of Disorders of Communication*, 3, pp. 55–9.

Birdwhistell, R.L. (1970), *Kinesics and Context: Essays on Body Motion Communication*, Philadelphia, University of Pennsylvania Press.

Gosling, J.N. (1981), *Discourse Kinesics* (English Language Research Monographs, 10), University of Birmingham.

Language acquisition

INTRODUCTION

Language acquisition or **first-language acquisition** is the term most commonly used to describe the process whereby children become speakers of their native language or languages, although some linguists prefer to use the term **language learning**, and Halliday (1975) refers to the process as one of **learning how to mean**.

According to Campbell and Wales (1970), the earliest recorded study of this process was carried out by the German biologist Tiedemann (1787) as part of a general study of child development, and other important early studies include Darwin (1877) and Taine (1877). However, 'it was in the superb, detailed study of the German physiologist Preyer (1882), who made detailed daily notes throughout the first three years of his son's development, that the study of child language found its true founding father' (Campbell and Wales, 1970, p. 243).

Preyer's study falls within the period which Ingram (1989, p. 7) calls **the period of diary studies (1876–1926)**. As the name suggests, the preferred data-collection method during this period was the **parental diary** in which a linguist or psychologist would record their own child's development. Few such studies were confined to the development of language alone; Preyer, for example, makes notes on many aspects of development in addition to the linguistic, including motor development and musical awareness (1882). The first published book to be devoted to the study of a child's language alone was C. and W. Stern's *Die Kindersprache* (1907) (not available in English), and it is from this work that the notion of **stages**

of language acquisition (see below) derives (Ingram, 1989, pp. 8–9). The diarists' main aim was to describe the child's language and other development, although some explanatory hypotheses were also drawn. These typically emphasized the child's 'genius' (Taine, 1877), an inbuilt language faculty which, according to Taine, enabled the child to adapt to the language which others presented it with, and which would, had no language been available already, have enabled a child to create one (p. 258).

Diaries continue to be used. However, with the rising popularity of behaviourist psychology (see also BEHAVIOURIST LINGUISTICS) after the First World War, **longitudinal** studies of individual children – studies charting the development of one child over a long period – came to be regarded as insufficient to establish what 'normal behaviour' amounted to. Different diaries described children at different intervals and concentrated on different features of the children's behaviour, so that it was impossible to draw clear comparisons between subjects. Instead, **large-sample studies** were favoured, studies of large numbers of children all of the same age, being observed for the same length of time engaged in the same kind of behaviour. Several such studies, concentrating on several age groups, would provide evidence of what was normal behaviour at each particular age, and the results of the studies were carefully quantified.

Behaviourism also prohibited as unscientific the drawing of conclusions about unobservables, such as inner mechanisms, in the explanation of behaviour, and only statements about the influence of the environment on the child's development were taken as scientifically valid. Environmental factors were therefore carefully controlled: all the children in a given study would come from similar socioeconomic backgrounds, and each study would use the same numbers of boys and girls.

Ingram (1989, pp. 11ff.) pinpoints the **period of large-sample studies** to 1926–57, the period beginning with M. Smith's (1926) study and ending with Templin's (1957) study. Studies carried out during this period concentrated mainly on vocabulary growth, mean sentence length, and pronunciation. **Mean sentence length** (Nice, 1925) was calculated by counting the number of words in each sentence a child produced and averaging them out. The results for these three areas for what was perceived as normal children (Smith, 1926; McCarthy, 1930; Wellman *et al.*, 1931) were compared with those for twins (Day, 1932; Davis, 1937), gifted children (Fisher, 1934), and lower-class children (Young, 1941).

The publication of Templin's study, the largest of the period, took place in the year which also saw the publication of Noam Chomsky's *Syntactic Structures* (1957) (see TRANSFORMATIONAL-GENERATIVE GRAMMAR), which heralded the end of the reliance on pure empiricism and be-haviourist psychology in linguistic studies (see RATIONALIST LINGUISTICS). Chomsky's work and that of his followers highlighted the rule-governed nature of language, and a major focus of attention of many linguists working on language acquisition since then has been the acquisition of syntactic rules. From a post-Chomskian vantage point, the large-sample studies seem linguistically naive in their neglect of syntax, and of the interaction between linguistic units (Ingram, 1989, p. 16):

> For example, data on what auxiliary verbs appear at what age do not tell us much about how rules that affect auxiliaries, such as Subject–Auxiliary Inversion are acquired; and norms of sound acquisition do not reveal much about how the individual child acquires a system of phonological rules.

In addition, early researchers did not usually have the benefit of sophisticated electronic recording equipment, so that the data may not be totally reliable. However, the need to establish norms, the need for careful selection of subjects and careful research design, and for measurement, still inform studies of language acquisition.

Ingram (1989, pp. 21ff.) refers to the period from 1957 onward as **the period of longitudinal language sampling**. In typical studies of this kind (Braine, 1963; Miller and Ervin, 1964; Bloom, 1970; Brown, 1973), at least three separate, carefully selected children – ones which are talkative and just beginning to use multiword utterances – are visited and recorded at regular intervals by the researcher(s). Braine (1963) supplemented this methodology with diaries kept by the mothers of the children. A sample of three children is considered the minimum required if any statement about general features of acquisition is to be made (Ingram, 1989, p. 21): 'if one is chosen, we do not know if the child is typical or not; if two, we do not know which of the two is typical and which is unusual; with three, we at least have a majority that can be used to make such a decision'.

Given Chomsky's (1965) distinction between **competence** and **performance** – between the underlying ability which allows linguistic behaviour to take place and the behaviour itself – researchers influenced by Chomsky's theory are not content simply to chart performance. Rather, the aim will be to arrive at statements concerning the state of the child's underlying linguistic competence at each stage of its development.

Wasow (1983) draws a distinction between research which aims primarily to chart performance, and research aimed primarily at using data in support of hypotheses concerning the nature of language, that is, research based on a prior linguistic theory. He calls the former research in **child language**, and the latter research in **language acquisition**. Linguists working in the Chomskian tradition have tended to be interested primarily in language acquisition, while psychologists have tended to be interested primarily in child language.

Ingram (1989, ch. 4), however, proposes a unified field of **child language acquisition** which studies children's language and examines it against the background of well-defined theories of grammar, using methods which can establish when a child's linguistic behaviour is rule-based. Such a discipline will be able to provide a theory of acquisition as well as a testing ground for theories of grammar (ibid, p. 64):

> The theory of acquisition will have two distinct components. One will be the set of principles that lead to the construction of the grammar, i.e., those that concern the child's grammar or linguistic competence. These principles will deal with how the child constructs a rule of grammar and changes it over time. The focus is on the nature of the child's rule system; it is concerned with *competence factors*. The second component looks at the psychological processes the child uses in learning the language. These are what we shall call *performance factors*. . . . In comprehension, performance factors deal with how the child establishes meaning in the language input, as well as the cognitive restrictions that temporarily retard development. In production, these factors describe the reasons why the child's spoken language may not reflect its linguistic competence. They also describe mechanisms the child may use to achieve the expression of their comprehension.

As examples of **competence factors**, Ingram mentions three principles – generalization, lexical and uniqueness – which will enter into the explanation of morphological acquisition. According to Dresher's (1981) **generalization principle**, learners will prefer a rule which requires few features to one which requires many. They will therefore prefer a rule which allows them to form the plural *foots* to one which compels them to form the plural *feet*, since the latter rule must contain, in addition to the instruction for forming the plural, the instruction that some plural forms are irregular. This principle explains why children often use regular inflections on irregular words, even though doing

so conflicts with what they hear adults doing.

To explain why they often do this *after* a period during which they have used irregular plurals correctly, Ingram (1985) proposes a **lexical principle**, according to which singular and plural forms are first learnt as separate words, while the realization that there is a plural morpheme, *-s* in English is only arrived at later.

Finally, we need to posit a **uniqueness principle** (Wexler and Culicover, 1980) to account for the fact that the child finally selects only the plural form that it hears used around it, *feet*, rather than supposing that there are two possible plurals, *foots* and *feet*.

Performance factors include, for example. Slobin's (1973, p. 412) **Principle A**: 'Pay attention to the ends of words', which might explain why it appears to be easier to acquire suffixes than prefixes. Ingram (1989, pp. 68–9) also proposes a principle instructing children to pay attention to stressed words and syllables, and suggests that factors of memory and planning might explain why children who appear to understand full sentences only produce, for instance, two-word utterances.

If the study of child language acquisition is to provide evidence for or against theories of adult grammar as well as insights into the child's progression towards it, the relationship between the child's grammar and that of the adult needs careful examination (Ingram, 1989, p. 70): 'Specifically, we want to develop a theory which defines the extent to which the child may change or *restructure* its language system.' Ingram (ibid., p. 73) proposes that the child's progression is subject to **the constructivist assumption** that 'the form of the child's grammar at any point of change which we shall call stage *n* will consist of everything at stage *n* plus the new feature(s) of stage *n* + *1*'. A principle will then be proposed to account for the change.

STAGES OF ACQUISITION

The establishment of **stages of acquisition** is probably the best-known outcome of research on children's language. Stages are normally outlined in introductory books in general linguistics, but they also appear, if only in very broad and relatively unspecific outline, in non-specialist literature such as booklets designed to inform new parents, most of whom will soon witness considerable interest being shown in their children's developing language by doctors, health visitors, and others concerned to establish whether a child is developing normally. These stages are, however, normally purely descriptive: parents and doctors etc. are not usually concerned with linguistic theory. However, the establishment of normal stages of development is important for speech therapists, who will be able to compare speech-impaired children with normal children, and to provide therapy aimed, ideally, to enable the speech-impaired child to reach parity with its peers (see SPEECH THERAPY).

Ingram (1989, ch. 3) discusses a number of possible meanings of the term 'stage', and describes the sets of stages proposed by Stern (1924), Nice (1925), and Brown (1973). He points out that (1989, p. 54) 'these general stages do little more than isolate co-occurring linguistic behaviors with a focus on the newest or most prominent'. Whilst such descriptive stages are important for parents and others interested in establishing that normal development is taking place, they are of limited theoretical importance for linguists, and Ingram (ibid.) proposes to limit the use of the term *stage* 'to those cases where we are referring to behaviors that are being explained in some way', namely by such principles as those referred to above. Obviously, the establishment of descriptive stages is only a first step towards reaching the explanatory stages.

While most parts of an infant's body need to grow and develop during its childhood, the inner ear is fully formed and fully grown at birth, and it is thought that infants in the womb are able to hear. Certainly, they are able within a few weeks of birth to discriminate human voices from other sounds, and by about two months they can distinguish angry from friendly voice qualities. Experiments have been devised using the **non-nutritive sucking technique** in which an infant is given a device to suck which measures the rate of sucking; a sound is played to the infant until the sucking rate stabilizes; the sound is changed; if the infant notices the sound change, the sucking rate will alter. Such experiments have shown that as early as at one month, infants are able to distinguish voiced from unvoiced sound segments (Eimas *et al.*, 1971), and by seven weeks they can distinguish intonation contours and places of articulation (Morse, 1972; Clark and Clark, 1977, pp. 376–7).

While this ability to discriminate human voice sound qualities does not, of course, amount to knowledge of human language – infants still need to learn which differences between sounds are meaningful in their language, which combinations of sounds are possible and which are not possible in their language, how to use intonation contours, and much besides – it does indicate that human infants are tuned in to human language from very early on in life. Nevertheless, the process of acquisition takes several years – indeed, according to Halliday (1975) it is perpetual, in so far as his phase III, the mastery of the adult language, goes on all through an individual's life.

The first year of a child's life may be referred to as **the period of prelinguistic development** (Ingram, 1989, pp. 83ff.), since children do not normally begin to produce words until they are a year old (though see below for Halliday's concept of a child language which appears before the child begins to use the adult language). The main reason for studying prelinguistic development as part of a theory of child language acquisition is to try to establish which links, if any, there are between the prelinguistic period and the period of linguistic development.

The only sounds a newborn baby makes, apart from possible sneezes, coughs, etc., are crying sounds. By three months old, the child will have added to these **cooing** sounds, composed of velar consonants and high vowels, while by six months, **babbling** sounds, composed of repeated syllables (*bababa, dadada, mamama,* etc.) have usually appeared. During the later babbling stage, from around nine to twelve months, intonation patterns and some imitation of others' speech are present, and the infant's sound production at this stage is often referred to as **sound play**. At this stage parents and other care-givers normally react to the child as if it were speaking – though many parents and care-givers in fact treat the child as if it were conversing much earlier.

Some people speak to babies and young children in a particular way known as **motherese**, **baby talk**, **care-taker speech**, or **care-giver speech**. For many English speakers, this is characterized by (Kaye, 1980) high pitch, a large range of frequencies, highly varied intonation, special words like *pussy* and *quack-quack*, short, grammatically simple utterances, repetition, and restriction of topics to those relevant to the child's world. However, it is by no means the case that all English-speaking adults speak in this way to babies and young children; many employ normal pitch, frequency range, intonation patterns, and vocabulary. It is probably true that most adults restrict topics when addressing babies and young children, but then, all topics of all conversations are geared to the occasion and to the interactants.

The changes in the child's vocalizations during the first year of its life are connected with gradual physiological changes in the child's speech apparatus, which does not begin to resemble its adult shape until the child is around six months old. Until then, the child's vocal tract resembles that of an adult chimpanzee (Lieberman, 1975). The vocal tract and pharynx (see ARTICULATORY PHONETICS) are shorter than the adult's, and the tract is wider in relation to its length. Since the baby has no teeth, the oral cavity is also flatter than the adult's (Goldstein, 1979). The tongue fills most of the oral cavity, and its movement is limited by this fact and by immaturity of its muscles. The infant has no cavity behind the back of the tongue, and its velum operates in such a way that breathing takes place primarily through the nose, not the mouth. This allows the baby to breathe while it is sucking, and causes its vocalizations to be highly nasalized and velarized.

Opinions vary on whether there is a connection between the babbling stage and the later acquisition of the adult sound system. According to the **continuity approach**, the babbling sounds are direct precursors of speech sounds proper, while according to the **discontinuity approach** there is no such direct relation (Clark and Clark, 1977, p. 389). Mowrer (1960) has argued in favour of the continuity hypothesis that babbling contains all the sounds found in all human languages, but that through selective reinforcement by parents and others this sound repertoire is narrowed down to just those sounds present in the language the child is to acquire. Careful observation, however, shows that many sounds found in human languages are not found in babbling, and that some of the sounds that are found in babbling are those with which a child may have problems when it starts to speak the adult language. Such findings cast doubt on the continuity hypothesis.

A pure discontinuity approach, however, fares little better than a pure continuity approach. One of its staunchest advocates is Jakobson (1968), according to whom there are two distinct sound production stages: the first is the babbling stage, during which the child makes a wide range of sounds which do not appear in any particular order and which do not, therefore, seem related to the child's subsequent development; during the second stage many of the sounds present in the first stage disappear either temporarily or permanently while the child is mastering the particular sound contrasts which are significant in the language it is acquiring. The problems with this approach are, first, that many children continue to babble for several months after the onset of speech (Menn, 1976); second, many of the sound sequences of later words seem to be preferred during the babbling stage – as if being rehearsed, perhaps (Oller *et al.*, 1976); finally, babbling seems often to carry intonation patterns of later speech, so that there seems to be continuity at at least the suprasegmental level (Halliday, 1975; Menn, 1976). Clark and Clark (1977, pp. 390–1) believe the following:

> Neither continuity nor discontinuity fully accounts for the facts. The relation between babbling and speech is probably an indirect one. For example, experience with babbling could be a necessary preliminary to gaining articulatory control of certain organs in the mouth and vocal tract. . . . If babbling simply

provided exercise for the vocal apparatus, there would be little reason to expect any connection between the sounds produced in babbling and those produced later on. . . . Still, there is at least some discontinuity. Mastery of some phonetic segments only begins when children start to use their first words.

The period between twelve and sixteen months, during which children normally begin to comprehend words and produce single-unit utterances, is usually referred to as the **one-word** stage. Benedict (1979) shows that the gap between comprehension and production is usually very great at this time: a child may be able to understand about a hundred words before it begins to produce words. At this stage, the child's utterances do not show any structural properties, and their meanings appear to be primarily functional (see the discussion of Halliday's study below).

At around 16–18 months, single-word utterances seem to begin to reflect semantic categories such as Agent, Action and Object (Ingram, 1989, pp. 242–3), though it is difficult to assign precise adult meanings to the child's utterances, even though the non-linguistic context often helps. For instance, while an adult may interpret /dəʊp/ 'boat' to mean 'look, a boat' or 'there's a boat'; /ɪtɒn/ 'it on' to mean 'put it on' or 'it is/has been put on' or 'I want it (put) on', it is questionable whether it is justifiable to assign such 'translations': how can we know whether the child has the exact concepts which the adult interpretations imply? What does seem obvious, however, is that the child at this stage is doing more than just naming objects, actions, etc., so many researchers prefer to call this stage the **holophrastic stage**.

Many children at the one-word and holophrastic stages have a tendency towards **overextension**: having learnt, perhaps, the word *ball* to refer to a ball, the child may use *ball* to refer to other round objects (Braunwald, 1978). The range of reference of a child's word is called its **associative complex**, and it is usually determined by such perceptual features as shape, size, sound, movement, taste, and texture (E. Clark, 1973). It

is likely that a child overextends because its vocabulary is limited; that is, if it is presented with a new object it will refer to it by a word it already knows for something which resembles the new object, just as adults tend to do (Ingram, 1989, p. 159). Some overextension is exclusively productive, that is, a child may be able to pick out the appropriate object in response to *motorcycle*, *bike*, *truck*, *plane*, but refer to them all as *car* in production (Rescorla, 1980, p. 230). This may be because the child has difficulty in retrieving the correct word (Thomson and Chapman, 1977; Rescorla, 1980).

The holophrastic period glides gradually into a stage during which it is possible to distinguish clearly two separate units produced in succession – /mɒmas pɛə/ 'Tomas' chair' – known as the **two-word stage**, normally lasting from around eighteen or twenty months until the child is two years old. During this time, the child's vocabulary grows rapidly. For instance, Smith's (1926) subjects' average productive vocabulary was 22 words at eighteen months, 118 words at twenty-one months, and 272 words at two years.

Many two-word utterances can be seen as instantiations of **pivot grammar** (Braine, 1963). According to the theory of pivot grammar, a child will notice that there is a small number of words which appear frequently and in fixed positions, usually before or after other words. On this basis, the child will construct a first theory of word classes, classifying the first kind of words as **pivot-class** words, and the second kind as **open-class** words. Different children will experience different words in each class, but Braine's subject, Andrew's, pivot grammar contained the two-word combinations in Table 1.

Braine claims that the child will notice that certain open-class words always come after a pivot, while other open-class words always come before a pivot, and that this information allows the child to begin to distinguish different word classes among the open-class words.

However, pivot grammar can only account for the utterances of a child who is at the very beginning of sentence use; even Braine's subject, Andrew, was, at this stage, also producing utterances consisting of a nominal plus an action

Table 1 A pivot grammar

Pivot-class word	Open-class word	Pivot-class word
all	broke; buttoned; clean; done; dressed; dry; fix; gone; messy; shut; through; wet.	
I	see; shut; sit.	
no	bed; down; fix; home; mama; more; pee; plug; water; wet.	
see	baby; pretty; train.	
more	car; cereal; cookie; fish; high; hot; juice; read; sing; toast; walk.	
hi	Calico; mama; papa.	
other	bib; bread; milk; pants; part; piece; pocket; shirt; shoe; side.	
	boot; light; pants; shirt; shoe; water.	off
	airplane; siren.	by
	mail; mama.	come

word, modifier, or personal–social word. It is clear that children soon move beyond such simple utterances as those which the pivot grammar above would allow for.

Other linguists, influenced by Chomsky's standard theory (1965), have attempted to account for children's early grammars by reference to **universal grammar**, a basic set of logical, hence at least partly semantic, relations thought to underlie all languages, which are innate in the child and which it thus brings to the language-learning process (Ingram, 1989, pp. 268–9). According to McNeill (1970), the major relations are those shown in Table 2 with the subcategorizations for the grammatical categories, and with examples (adapted from Ingram, 1989, p. 268):

Table 2 McNeill's (1970) universal logical relations with grammatical subcategorizations and examples

Relation	Subcategorization	Example
Predicate	[+VP, +NP__]	The dog *ate the apple*
Subject	[+NP, +__VP]	*The dog* ate the apple
Main verb	[+V, +__NP]	(The dog) *ate* the apple
Object	[+NP, +V__]	(The dog) ate *the apple*
Modifier	[+Det, +N__]	The dog (ate) *the* apple
Head	[+N, +Det__]	The *dog* (ate) the *apple*

The child has to discover how these relations are realized in the language it is acquiring, and it does so in a particular order; and, since the grammar is universal, the underlying relations and the order in which the child discovers them in its language is language-invariant: acquisition proceeds in the same way no matter what language the child is acquiring. According to McNeill, the reason the child develops a pivot grammar is not that it notices the frequency and position of the pivot words, but that it notices them as words which enter into relations with NP.

While McNeill's main aim was to account for children's use of language from the theoretical standpoint of Chomsky's (1965) standard theory, Bloom (1970) wished to begin with the child's language as data and use it to show that the relations existed. She proposed five tests for their existence:

1 **Sentence patterning**: if a construction such as *mommy sock* occurs in the same place as its head, in this case *sock*, without a change of meaning, then they are the same kind of constituent. So if *give sock* and *give mommy sock* both occur, then *sock* and *mommy sock* are constituents of the same type.

2 **Linear order**: Any construction ordered like an adult construction has the same grammatical relation as the adult construction. This test is fairly weak, since some relations, such as subject–object and possessive have the same order, and since adults tend to impose adult meanings on the child's utterances.

3 **Replacement sequences**: if a child replaces one sentence, say *mommy sock*, by an expansion of it, *mommy's sock*, uttering these in a row and in the same context, then the unexpanded sentence has the same structure as the expanded one.

4 **Replacement and deletion**: if a child deletes *Baby* in *Baby milk*, and utters *touch milk* (in a row and in the same context, as in (3) above), then this indicates that *Baby milk* was a subject–object construction meaning something like 'Baby touches the milk'.

5 **Non-linguistic context**; situational context, including the child's overt behaviour and aspects of the environment at the time of utterance, can often be used to infer the child's intended meaning.

Bloom and McNeil arrived at substantially the same conclusions by their varying routes (Ingram, 1989, pp. 276–9).

With the advent of case grammar (see CASE GRAMMAR) and generative semantics (see GENERATIVE SEMANTICS), linguists began to feel that theories such as those just outlined assigned too much structure and too little meaning to children's early utterances. Both Bowerman (1973) and Brown (1973) propose (Ingram, 1989, p. 284) 'that the primary development during this period is the acquisition of a basic set of semantic relations, which are the building blocks of later development'. Brown isolates eleven such relations, of two major subtypes: **operations of reference** (the first three in Table 3 below); and **semantic functions** (the rest) (adapted from Ingram, 1989, p. 284, on the basis of Brown, 1973, pp. 187–98).

Brown thinks that these particular relations reflect the knowledge the child has of the world at this stage, and that they are universal. Others have objected that these relations are too numerous for a child at the two-word stage (Braine, 1976; Howe, 1976). Howe (1976) also warns against assigning specific, adult meanings to child utterances, while Braine (1976) argues that children's early sentences express a small set of very specific meanings, peculiar to each individual child (compare the discussion of Halliday's theory below).

Proposals about how a child gets from the early semantic relations to a full-blown grammar include approaches which have become known as **semantic bootstrapping** (Macnamara, 1972, 1982; Grimshaw, 1981; Pinker, 1984): 'The child begins the acquisition of formal syntax by applying a set of procedures to the first semantic relations, resulting in essentially an immediate syntax' (Ingram, 1989, p. 303). First, the child acquires basic semantic notions, then it assigns syntactic properties to these (given here in parentheses): Name of person or thing (noun); Action or change of state (verb); Attribute (adjective); etc. (see Ingram, 1989, p. 319, for the full inventory).

Given these syntactic property assignments, the child constructs phrase structures like

Table 3 Brown's (1973) eleven basic semantic relations with definitions and examples

Relation	Definition and examples
1 Nomination	Naming a referent, without pointing, in response to questions like *what's that?*
2 Recurrence	Utterances like *more/another X*, where X is a referent already seen, or one of the same kind, or more of a mass already seen [usually already eaten (*Ed.*)]
3 Non-existence	The disappearance of something, e.g. *allgone egg*
4 Agent + Action	e.g. *Adam go; car go*
5 Action + Object	The object is usually something animate changing because of, or receiving the force of some action
6 Agent + Object	A direct relation without an intervening action, e.g. *Baby milk* meaning 'Baby touches the milk' (as discussed in relation to Bloom (1970) above)
7 Action + Location	The place of an action, e.g. *sit here*
8 Entity + Locative	Specifies the location of an entity, e.g. *doll chair* meaning that the doll is in the chair
9 Possessor + Possession	e.g. *doll chair* meaning that the chair belongs to the doll
10 Entity + Attribute	e.g. *yellow block*
11 Demonstrative and Entity	Nomination + pointing + use of demonstrative

Next, the child applies X-bar theory (see TRANSFORMATIONAL-GENERATIVE GRAMMAR), according to which each of the major lexical categories, such as N and V, is the head of a structure dominated by a phrasal node of the same category, in this case NP and VP. The child only applies X-bar if there is evidence for the higher category in the data. In the example we are working with, there is evidence for VP, but not for NP. Since VP is, in turn, dominated by S, the child can now construct the following tree:

Now the child assigns grammatical functions to the syntactic categories in the tree, i.e. Subject to N, and connects unattached branches to give

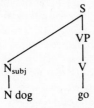

Further steps in the process include: (1) the creation and strengthening of phrase-structure rules; (2) adding new vocabulary with information about grammatical properties and strengthening existing entries; (3) collapsing of rules, when new rules are added to the phrase structure when it already has a rule which expands the same category. For example,

VP → PP and VP → NP

will be collapsed to

$$VP \rightarrow \begin{Bmatrix} PP \\ NP \end{Bmatrix}$$

(see further Ingram, 1989, pp. 316–30).

During the early stages of stringing more than two words together, many children's speech lacks grammatical inflections and function words, consisting of strings like *cat drink milk* (Yule, 1985, p. 141); this kind of language is known as **telegraphic speech** (Brown and Fraser, 1963). Even if children are presented with full sentences to imitate, they tend to repeat the sentences in telegraphic form.

Children normally begin to acquire grammatical morphemes at the age of around two years. The most famous study of the acquisition of grammatical morphemes is that of Berko (1958), who studied the acquisition by English-speaking children of plural -s, possessive -s, present tense -s, past-tense -ed, progressive -ing, agentive -er, comparative -er and -est, and compounds. Berko worked with children aged between four and seven years old, and she showed that five- and six-year-old children were able to add the appropriate grammatical suffixes to invented words when the words' grammatical class was clear from the context. Her experimental procedure has become known as the **wug procedure**, *wug* being one of the invented words used in the experiment.

This experiment and others like it may be used to argue for the hypothesis that children are 'tuned in', not only to the sounds of human language (see above) but also to its syntax, in the sense that they display 'a strong tendency . . . to analyse the formal aspects of the linguistic input' (Karmiloff-Smith, 1987, p. 369). Karmiloff-Smith (1979) shows that French children determine gender by attending to word endings from about the age of three, and Levy (1983) produces similar findings for Hebrew-speaking children. Karmiloff-Smith (1987, p. 370) argues that, since a child will get its message through without all the correct syntactic markers attached to it, the child must be showing analytical interest in adding them when it does so.

The order of acquisition of grammatical morphemes in English tends to be that -ing appears first, then the regular plural -s, then possessive -s and irregular past-tense forms, before the regular forms (Yule, 1985, pp. 143–4) (see the discussion of the generalization principle above). Yule (1985, pp. 144–5) isolates three stages for the acquisition of the most studied syntactic categories: question and negative formations. Stage I occurs between 18 and 26 months; stage II between 22 and 30 months; and stage III between 24 and 40 months. During stage I, children either simply begin any question with a *wh-* form such as *where* or *who*, or they use rising intonation. To form negatives, children at this stage simply begin the utterance with *no* or *not*. During stage II of question formation, intonation is still used, but more *wh-* forms become available. For negative formation, *don't* and *can't* begin to appear, and both these forms and *no* and *not* are placed in front of the verb instead of at the beginning of the utterance. In stage III, questions have the required inversion of subject and verb, although *wh-* forms do not always undergo the inversion: *Can I have a piece* versus *Why kitty can't stand up? Didn't* and *won't* appear for negatives during stage III, with *isn't* appearing very late (see Ingram, 1989, Ch. 9, for a far more detailed account, including reports of several studies of Subject–Aux Inversion).

Ingram (1989) discusses a number of proposed explanations for this acquisition pattern. According to **performance-factor approaches**, children have the adult rules available to them from the start, but are prevented by performance factors, such as limitations of memory, from applying them. According to **competence-factor approaches**, the child's speech reflects its grammar at the time, and the adult rules are acquired gradually, restricted at first to specific contexts and then increasingly generalized. Thus Kuczaj and Brannick (1979) propose that the child first learns to invert subject and verb for certain specific *wh-* words, and then gradually learns to do it for all *wh-* words.

Other areas of syntax which have received much attention include passives, relative clauses, and the use of pronouns to refer to noun phrases in the surrounding text.

Horgan (1978) shows that whereas children aged between two and four years recognize the passive form, they tend to misunderstand the relationship between the participants described by reversible passives such as *The cat was chased by the girl*; children tend to use this form to describe a picture of a cat chasing a girl. Horgan's

and other studies suggest that it takes several years for children to acquire full understanding of the range of application of the passive (Ingram, 1989, p. 471). According to Pinker (1984), children use their knowledge of oblique prepositional phrases such as *The cat was sitting by the fence* to generate what they first perceive as a parallel structure, e.g. *The cat was bitten by the dog* (Ingram, 1989, p. 472):

> This will eventually lead to a new phrase-structure rule which generates passives as well as oblique prepositional phrases. The difference between the two rules will be in the grammatical roles of the NPs. A last step will be the child's acquiring a second lexical entry for the passive form of the verb. For example, the child's lexicon will have 'bite' for active sentences and 'bitten' for passive ones. [compare LEXICAL-FUNCTIONAL GRAMMAR].

Children under five years of age use few relative clauses, preferring to string clauses together with *and* (Ingram, 1989, p. 476). Yule (1985, p. 144) provides a typical example from a two-year-old who repeated an adult's utterance *The owl who eats candy runs fast* as *Owl eat candy and he run fast*. As in the case of passives, it appears that four-year-old children have begun to acquire relative clauses, though they use them far less than adults do (Ingram, 1989, p. 483).

C. Chomsky (1969) provides evidence of 5- to 10-year-old children's abilities to process three types of constructions with pronominalization: (1) **blocked backward pronominalization**, as in *He found out that Mickey won the race*; (2) **backwards pronominalization**, as in *Before he went out, Pluto took a nap*; (3) **forward pronominalization**, as in *Pluto thinks he knows everything*. Each of the forty children in Chomsky's study was tested for their comprehension of five sentences of each type. The children were first introduced to two dolls called Mickey and Pluto. Then the test sentence and a question about it were presented to the child, e.g. *Pluto thinks that he knows everything. Pluto thinks that **who** knows everything?* Because the children had two dolls in their universe of discourse, the pronoun in sentences of types 2 and 3 could refer to either the doll named in the sentence or to the other doll, so Chomsky only took account of the children's performance with type 1 sentences. She took blocked backward pronominalization to be acquired by a child only if the child answered all five questions for this type of sentence correctly. Thirty-one of the children met this criterion, but all of them except three showed evidence of beginning acquisition. Chomsky concludes that the acquisition of pronominalization is maturationally determined, that is, independent of environmental factors and of intelligence and general cognitive development (Ingram, 1989, p. 489).

Later studies, for instance Ingram and Shaw (1981), in which a 100 children between three and eight years of age were studied, have shown four stages in the acquisition of pronominal reference, which show children to be moving from the exclusive use of linear order to a system which takes account of structural properties of sentences. The stages are (Ingram, 1989, p. 491):

stage 1: *Use of coreference*: a pronoun may refer to an NP in a clause which may either precede or follow it;

stage 2: *Use of linear order*: a pronoun may only refer to a preceding NP;

stage 3: *Use of dominance*: a pronoun may refer to a following NP if the appropriate structural conditions exist, i.e. children acquire backward pronominalization;

stage 4: *Use of dominance*: a pronoun cannot refer to a preceding NP under certain structural conditions, i.e. blocked forwards pronominalization is acquired.

The account given above of how children learn the language of their speech community has, of necessity, been limited in many ways, and the reader is encouraged to consult Ingram (1989) for a very thorough account of all of the issues and data involved. In particular, the present article pays very little attention to children's acquisition of the sound system of their language. Most people who come into contact with babies and young children find the acquisition process particularly rewarding and interesting to observe, and many people feel that

the child's linguistic environment is important to how the acquisition proceeds. That is, they believe that parents and other people can actively encourage and perhaps even speed up the process of acquisition.

The influence of the environment on language acquisition remains controversial within linguistics, although most researchers agree that the child's learning is affected in some measure by how and under which circumstances others talk to the child (Gleitman *et al.*, 1984). The controversy concerns the extent to which the child's innate language ability influences its learning of language. There are three main approaches to the question (Ingram, 1989, pp. 506–7):

The behaviorist wants to demonstrate . . . that the child's behavior can always be traced to adult variables. . . . A maturationist will minimize the influence of the environment: if a principle of grammar has not yet matured, then no amount of linguistic input will lead to its acquisition; if it has matured, then presumably some minimal exposure will be sufficient. . . . Lastly, a constructionist perspective falls between the two positions: readiness will be a factor, and thus the child will not acquire a form until the child's system is ready for it, but at the same time, the development of a structure will involve a set of interactions between the child's internal system and the linguistic environment.

Since the 1980s, constructionism has predominated, and it does seem to be the common-sense stance. However, it is very difficult to determine exactly what the effects of the environment are.

HALLIDAY'S ACCOUNT OF HOW A CHILD LEARNS TO MEAN

The remainder of this article will be devoted to Halliday's (1975) account of the process by which a child learns how to mean. This account differs from those discussed above in being specifically **socio-functional** in nature: language is seen as a system of meanings and of ways of expressing these meanings. The meanings are related to the functions language will serve for the child, and the meanings are learnt during interaction with other people.

Halliday's study of Nigel's language begins when Nigel is nine months old, a stage which most researchers would describe as prelinguistic. Halliday (1975, p. 14), however, takes a constant concomitance between sound and meaning, or expression and content, as qualification for a child sound to be part of a language, provided that it can be shown that this sound–expression pair 'can be interpreted by reference to a set of prior established functions' (ibid., p. 15). While adult language is usually thought to have three levels – sound, syntax, and meaning – the child language at this early stage is said by Halliday to have no syntax level: each element of the language is a content–expression pair (ibid., p. 12). Furthermore, the expressions at this stage bear no necessary relation to the expressions of the adult language, although there is **continuity** between child and adult language in Halliday's model, as we shall see below.

The prior established functions with reference to which the child's early utterances are interpreted are derived from Halliday's functional theory of language (see FUNCTIONAL GRAMMAR and FUNCTIONALIST LINGUISTICS) and from considerations of Bernstein's notion of critical socializing contexts (see LANGUAGE AND EDUCATION). The functions, with 'translations', are (see Halliday, 1975, pp. 18–21):

1 **Instrumental**; the *I want* function, by means of which the child satisfies its material needs.
2 **Regulatory**; the *do that* function, by means of which the child regulates the behaviour of others.
3 **Interactional**; the *me and you* function, by means of which the child interacts with others.
4 **Personal**; the *here I come* function, by means of which the child expresses its own uniqueness.
5 **Heuristic**; the *tell me why* function, through which the child learns about and explores the environment.
6 **Imaginative**; the *let's pretend* function, whereby the child creates an environment of its own.

7 **Informative**; the *I've got something to tell you* function of language as a means of conveying information. This function appears much later than the others, in Nigel's case at around twenty-two months of age.

Within each function there is a range of options in meaning at each particular stage of the learning process, and this range increases within each function as the child's language develops. At nine months old, Nigel had only two expressions which had constant meanings, one interactional, the other personal. But since there were no alternatives within each function, these expressions did not constitute a linguistic system. The first such system that Halliday accredits Nigel with derives from the time when he is $10\frac{1}{2}$ months old, when he employs the first four functions listed above, with alternatives in each. For instance, in the instrumental function Nigel has two options: a general demand, /nã/, which Halliday glosses as meaning 'give me that' and a more specific demand, /bø/, 'give me my toy bird'.

Halliday's phase I, the first stage in the process by which a child learns how to mean, then, begins at the time when a sound can be seen to be always associated with a meaning, in Nigel's case, at nine months. The child's language, at this stage is its own child language which bears no necessary relation to the adult system, and for which the source is largely unknown (1975, p. 24):

There is no obvious source for the great majority of the child's expressions, which appear simply as spontaneous creations of the glossogenic process. As far as the content of Nigel's early systems is concerned, the same observation might be made: the meanings are not, in general, derived from the adult language. No doubt, however, the adult language does exert an influence on the child's semantic system from a very early stage, since the child's utterances are interpreted by those around him in terms of their own semantic systems. In other words, whatever the child means, the message which gets across is one which makes sense and is translatable into the terms of the adult language. It is in this interpretation that the child's linguistic efforts are reinforced, and in this way the meanings that the child starts out with gradually come to be adapted to the meanings of the adult language.

Phase I ends when the child begins the transition into the adult language, in Nigel's case at 15–16½ months. The period of transition is Halliday's phase II, and it lasted in the case of Nigel until he was about 22½–24 months old and had mastered the adult multifunctional and multistratal linguistic *system*. The exploration of this system, that is, the mastery of the adult *language*, Halliday's phase III, lasts through the rest of the person's life.

The transition into the adult system is characterized by rapid growth in vocabulary, structure, and the ability to engage in dialogue, and, importantly, by 'a shift in the functional orientation' (Halliday, 1975, p. 41). It is necessary to show how the child's phase I functions, 'a set of simple, unintegrated *uses* of language' (ibid., p. 51), become integrated with the 'highly abstract, integrated networks of relations' which are describable in terms of the ideational, interpersonal, and textual functions of the adult language (see FUNCTIONALIST LINGUISTICS).

The adult system is structured around the distinction between the interpersonal and the ideational functions of language, the third function, the textual function, being an enabling function which allows for the realization of the other two. So, the question is (Halliday, 1975, p. 52): 'how does the child progress from the functional pattern of his Phase I linguistic system to the ideational/interpersonal system which is at the foundation of the adult language?'. The first clue to the answer to this question came from Nigel's intonation patterns (ibid., pp. 52–3):

Early in Phase II, Nigel introduced within one week . . . a systematic opposition between rising and falling tone; this he maintained throughout the remainder of Phase II with complete consistency. Expressed in Phase I terms, the rising tone was used on all utter-

ances that were instrumental or regulatory in function, the falling tone on all those that were personal or heuristic, while in the interactional function he used both tones but with a contrast between them. We can generalize this distinction by saying that Nigel used the rising tone for utterances demanding a response, and the falling tone for the others.

This distinction in intonation between utterances demanding a response and utterances which do not marks a distinction between **language as doing**, a **pragmatic** function, and **language as learning**, a **mathetic** function. And (ibid.):

This distinction between two broad generalized types of language use, the mathetic and the pragmatic, that Nigel expresses by means of the contrast between falling and rising tone, turns out to be the one that leads directly in to the abstract functional distinction of ideational and interpersonal that lies at the heart of the adult linguistic system. In order to reach Phase III, the child has to develop two major zones of meaning potential, one ideational, concerned with the representation of experience, the other interpersonal, concerned with the communication process as a form and as a channel of social action. These are clearly marked out in the grammar of the adult language. It seems likely that the ideational component of meaning arises, in general, from the use of language to learn, while the interpersonal arises from the use of language to act.

K.M.

SUGGESTIONS FOR FURTHER READING

Brown, R. (1973), *A First Language: the Early Stages*, Cambridge, MA, Harvard University Press.

Halliday, M.A.K. (1975), *Learning How To Mean: Explorations in the Development of Language*, London, Edward Arnold.

Ingram, D. (1989), *First Language Acquisition: Method, Description and Explanation*, Cambridge, Cambridge University Press.

Language and education

There is no doubt that an individual's linguistic abilities affect his or her chances of success in the formal education system of his or her culture, since much of what takes place in that system is linguistically realized. Nor is there any doubt, however, that the relationship between language and educational success is complex; Stubbs (1983, p. 15) lists a number of pertinent questions:

> How, for example, is language related to learning? How is a child's language related, if at all, to his success or failure at school? Does it make sense to call some children's language 'restricted'? What kind of language do teachers and pupils use in the classroom? Does a child's dialect bear any relation to his or her educational ability? What is the significance of the fact that over a hundred languages are spoken in Britain? Should special educational provision be made for the very high concentrations of speakers of immigrant languages in several areas of the country?

One sad but well-established fact has done much to raise such and similar questions: this is that a working-class (WC) child in Britain has less chance of doing well in the school system than a middle-class (MC) child. It is also a fact that there are, typically, certain differences in the children's language (Stubbs, 1983, p. 46). Faced with these two facts, it is tempting to draw the conclusion that the former is causally related to the latter. Two other possibilities, however, obtain (p. 47): possibly there is no causal connection between the two facts which may both be caused by something else – a possibility which will not be explored in this entry – or they may be related, but only indirectly.

People who believe in a direct causal connection between the two facts typically draw more or less directly on the work of Basil Bernstein (1971) and his notions of **restricted** and **elaborated** linguistic codes. The early version of this theory, which Bernstein later modified considerably, but which, according to Stubbs (1983, p. 49), is the version which is best known and which has been most influential on certain educationalists, posits a direct relation between social class and linguistic codes (ibid.):

> In the out-of-date version in which Bernstein's theories are most widely known, the argument runs thus. There are two different kinds of language, *restricted* and *elaborated* code, which are broadly related to the social class of speakers. MC speakers are said to use both codes, but some WC speakers are said to have access only to restricted code, and this is said to affect the way such speakers can express themselves and form concepts. This is claimed to be particularly important in education, since 'schools are predicated upon elaborated code'.

In other words, because elaborated code is used predominantly at school, and because the ability to use it is necessary for the formation of certain concepts which are important in the educational setting, a child with no access to elaborated code will be unable to succeed academically at school.

Elaborated code was said to be characterized by grammatical complexity and completeness, restricted code by grammatical simplicity and incompleteness and much use of brief imperatives and interrogatives; restricted code was also said to be logically simpler than elaborated code. This gross oversimplification of Bernstein's fully developed theory has been discredited indirectly by Labov (1969) (see below), but it led easily into the so-called **myth of linguistic deprivation** according to which speakers of non-standard English of any kind are deprived of appropriate linguistic stimulation in the home. The fault is thus seen to lie with the child who fails at school – the child fails because his or her language is inappropriate to the school situation, preventing him or her from forming the kinds of concepts necessary for academic success.

A less simplistic interpretation of Bernstein's work, however, suggests that the link between language and academic failure is indirect. Such an interpretation takes account of Bernstein's later version of the theory which includes considerations of contexts of socialization, of which there are four (reprint of extracts from Bernstein, 1970, in Giglioli, 1972, p. 170; emphasis added):

1 The **regulative** context – these are authority relationships where the child is made aware of the rules of the moral order and their various backings.
2 The **instructional** context, where the child learns about the objective nature of objects and persons, and acquires skills of various kinds.
3 The **imaginative** or **innovative** contexts, where the child is encouraged to experiment and re-create his world on his own terms, and in his own way.
4 The **interpersonal** context, where the child is made aware of affective states – his own, and others.

These are 'generalized situation types which have greatest significance for the child's socialization and for his interpretation of experience' (Halliday's foreword to Bernstein, 1973). Halliday goes on to explain the indirect causation theory thus:

What Bernstein's work suggests is that there may be differences in the relative orientation of different social groups towards the various functions of language in given contexts, and towards the different areas of meaning that may be explored within a given function. Now if this is so, then when these differences manifest themselves in the contexts that are critical for the socialization process they may have a profound effect on the child's social learning; and therefore on his response to education, because built into the educational

process are a number of assumptions and practices that reflect differentially not only the values but also the communication patterns and learning styles of different subcultures. As Bernstein has pointed out, not only does this tend to favour certain modes of learning over others, but it also creates for some children a continuity of cultures between home and school which it largely denies to others.

Such a view invites change in the school as much as in the pupils, and teaching programmes such as *The Wigan Language Project* (Mason, 1988) are designed to effect just such a reciprocal change.

Halliday (1973) suggests that of the child's seven models of language which arise from the functions that language has for the child (see LANGUAGE ACQUISITION), adults, including teachers, tend to have only the seventh, the **representational** model of language as a means of expressing propositions. Yet the **personal** function of language as a means of expressing one's own personality, and the **heuristic** function of language as a means of investigating reality and thus learning about things are obviously crucially important at school. The child has been using both functions naturally within its own meaning group in its own environment, but (ibid., p. 19) 'the ability to operate institutionally in the personal and heuristic modes is ... something that has to be learnt'.

Again, it is, then, possible to argue that some children enter school better equipped to operate institutionally with these two functions than other children because of the ways in which they have experienced language in the critical socializing contexts. Halliday advocates raising teachers' and other adults' awareness of what language is for the child. If the adult's focus is solely on the representational model of language, s/he will obviously be unlikely to be sensitive to the types of problems some children have in conforming to the educational institution's demands that the child employ the personal and heuristic functions in a particular way within it. Equally, if teaching materials are based solely on the representational model of language, they will fail to conform to what the child knows language to be, and the child will find it difficult to relate to such materials.

Labov's (1969, 1972b) studies of the language of Black and Puerto Rican children in New York supports the theory that the relationship between language and academic failure is indirect and that social context is a crucial factor in the explanation of the relationship (Stubbs, 1983, pp. 76–7):

> A major finding of sociolinguistics is that the *social context* is the most powerful determinant of verbal behaviour. Fieldwork with Black children (e.g. Labov, 1969) has shown that they produce vivid, complex language in unstructured situations with friends, but may appear monosyllabic and defensive in asymmetrical classroom or test situations where an adult has power over them. Philips (1972) has found exactly the same with American Indian children: that they are expressive outside the classroom, but silent, reticent and defensive inside it with their White teachers.

Such research indicates that it is something about the school situation which prevents some children from benefiting appropriately from the education which it offers them.

Labov also argues convincingly against the view that non-standard dialects are less 'logical' than standard dialects and that their speakers lack certain important concepts because their language denies them access to these concepts. Stubbs (1983, pp. 68–9) succinctly explicates Labov's arguments on this matter as follows:

> A criticism often raised against pupils' speech by teachers is that it is 'badly connected' and inexplicit. Teachers often feel this about Black English Vernacular (BEV) which has sentences like: 'he my brother' (SE [standard English]: 'he's my brother'. But there are many languages which do not use the verb *to be* in such sentences, for example Russian: 'on moj brat' (literally: 'he my brother'). . . . It would be ludicrous to argue that a Russian had a defective concept of existential relationships, just because of this detail in the grammar of his language. . . . A comparable example occurs with BEV forms like: 'He

come yesterday' (SE: 'he came yesterday'). Failure to mark explicitly the past tense in the verb does not indicate a failure to perceive past time. It merely means that in BEV *come* is in the same class as verbs like *put* and *hit* in SE (cf. 'I always *put* it there, I *put* it there yesterday').

> It is also easy to confuse logic and grammar. Many non-standard dialects of British and American English use double negatives such as: 'I don't know nothing' (SE: 'don't know anything'). It is sometimes said that such sentences are illogical on the grounds that if I *don't* know *nothing*, then I *do* know *something*. . . . Again, many languages use double negatives (e.g. French: 'je N'en sais RIEN'. Spanish: 'yo NO sabe [*sic.*] NADA'). Again, these languages may be foreign, but they are not illogical just because they often use two participles to negativize a sentence.

A child's accent and dialect may, however, also indirectly affect his or her academic success even in cases where educators do not consciously hold any views about the access to concept formation of dialect speakers, or about the logic of the dialects; teachers may consciously or subconsciously react in a negative way to non-standard language forms, and may tend to consider non-standard speakers less intelligent than standard speakers. This will tend to affect the way in which they deal with the various children, and there is a good chance that a child who is not expected to do well will realize this and conform to the teacher's expectation. It is also the case that (Stubbs, 1983, p. 86):

> Even if the teacher goes out of his way to accept the child's language as different but equally valuable, his own language is likely to be noticeably different from the child's in the direction of the standard, prestige variety. And the child will be aware that the teacher's form of language is the one supported by institutional authority. Children may then be caught in a double bind. They may recognize that to get ahead they must adopt the teacher's style of language, but to do this will separate them from their friends. A nonstandard dia-

lect may have low social prestige for schools, but serve the positive functions of displaying group loyalty for its speakers.

An obvious way to avoid imposing this dilemma on children would, of course, be for schools to stop giving institutional authority to the standard language. Schools could simply allow children to use any dialect and accent they wished in school. However, this solution is probably too simplistic, because it might result in more severe difficulties for the children later on; in society as a whole, dialect tolerance is minimal (Trudgill, 1979/83, pp. 66–7) suggests the following compromise:

the greatest dialect-related problem in the UK is the attitudes and prejudices many people hold toward nonstandard dialects. In the long term, it will probably be simpler to ease this problem by changing attitudes (as has already happened to some extent with accents) than by changing the linguistic habits of the majority of the population.

In the short run, however, we have to acknowledge the existence of these attitudes and attempt to help children to overcome them. Clearly many jobs and opportunities for upward social mobility will be denied to those who are not able to use standard English. To act on these motives in school with some degree of success, however, it is important to recognize that the teaching of higher status accents and of spoken standard English in school is almost certain to fail. Standard English is a dialect which is associated with a particular social group in British society and is therefore symbolic of it. Children will in most cases learn to speak this dialect only if they wish to become associated with this group and feel that they have a reasonable expectation of being able to do so. . . .

Writing, on the other hand, is a different matter. It is much easier to learn to write a new dialect than to learn to speak it, and in writing there is time for planning and checking back. Standard English, moreover, can be regarded as a dialect apart which is used in writing and whose use in written work does not necessarily commit one to allegiance to any particular social group.

In the 1980s, the question of how to deal with dialects in schools was largely overshadowed by that of how to accommodate those children whose home language is not English. The debate here centres on the notion of **mother-tongue teaching**: should a mother-tongue other than English be taught in schools or should the language of the school be exclusively English?

It is obvious that it is easier to come to a decision in favour of the former option in areas where there are large numbers of children sharing one non-English mother tongue than in areas with children speaking many different non-English mother tongues. For instance, in certain parts of Wales, Welsh is the medium of education, with English being introduced at some stage as a second language, in most schools because most of the children are Welsh speaking and because there is an active interest in the community in keeping the language, with its culture, alive (see Davies, 1981).

In most areas of Britain, however, schools still regard English as the medium of education; here, one or more other languages may be used as media of instruction early on because a child's learning process will obviously be severely hampered if it does not understand the language used in the school. In addition (Saifullah Kahn, 1980 p. 79):

It is also likely that this sudden switch to an environment that does not recognize and value the first language, its detachment from the home and the community life and the negative connotations related to minority status in the wider society, are bound to cause psychological stress, influence identity formation and thus affect educational achievement.

Furthermore, Skutnabb-Kangas and Toukomaa (1976) and Toukomaa and Skutnabb-Kangas (1977) have shown that Finnish-speaking children in Sweden learnt Swedish more efficiently when given the opportunity to develop their native Finnish language at the same time. Their research suggests that unless a child is proficient in its first language, it will not develop full proficiency in a second language. Although this research, and the considerations mentioned immediately above suggest the desirability of mother-tongue teaching, there are many other issues to be considered, for which see Saifullah Kahn, 1980.

K.M.

SUGGESTIONS FOR FURTHER READING

Stubbs, M. (1986), *Educational Linguistics*, Oxford, Basil Blackwell.

Stubbs, M. and H. Hillier, (eds) (1983), *Readings on Language, Schools and Classrooms*, London and New York, Methuen.

Trudgill, P.J. (1975), *Accent, Dialect and the School*, London, Edward Arnold.

Language and gender

In this entry, the term **gender** refers to the socially constructed categories **male** and **female**, and *not* to such grammatical categories as 'masculine', 'feminine', 'neuter'.

The study of language in relation to gender has two main foci. First, it has been observed by many linguists that men and women speak differently; secondly, it has been observed by many feminists and by some linguists that men and women are spoken about differently, and it is often claimed that the language is discriminatory against women. This entry will deal with both foci, although some linguists would claim that only the first is truly a linguistic issue. While it is undoubtedly the case that an entry could be written about each and every topic that language is used to refer to, it is also true that the question of how the language deals with men and women respectively has been a major topic in feminist debate; it is therefore fitting that the subject should be covered here (compare, also, the entries on METAPHOR and CRITICAL LINGUISTICS, both of which similarly suggest that the defining power of language is of major sociological importance).

DIFFERENCES IN MALE AND FEMALE LANGUAGE USE

Differences in male and female language use began to be noticed at least as early as the seventeenth century in the societies visited by missionaries and explorers, and the interest these differences caused often led to claims that in some societies men and women spoke completely different languages. This, however, is an over-statement; what tends to happen to varying degrees in various societies is that the gender of a speaker will determine or increase the likelihood of choices of certain phonological, morphological, syntactic, and lexical forms of a language while precluding or diminishing the likelihood of certain other choices (Coates, 1986, p. 35).

Coates (1986, pp. 35–40) and Smith (1985, pp. 3–6) provide surveys of a number of studies detailing **gender–exclusive** differences, that is, cases in which certain linguistic forms are used only by one sex. Gender-exclusive differences do not exist in European languages. However, there are in European languages certain forms which tend to be preferred by women and other forms which tend to be preferred by men; the differences which appear because of such tendencies are known as **gender-preferential** differences. The gender-exclusive/gender-preferential distinction probably reflects a distinction between societies in which gender roles are more strictly defined and societies in which they are less strictly defined (Coates, 1986, p. 40).

Early dialect studies provided little or no evidence of gender-preferentiality because early dialectologists tended to use elderly rural males as informants, so that little was known about how women spoke (see DIALECTOLOGY). However, with the advent of quantitative sociolinguistic studies (see LANGUAGE SURVEYS) which included female speakers, such as Trudgill's Norwich survey (1974b) and Labov's studies of language in New York (1971b, 1972a, 1972b), it began to appear that female speakers tend to use more **prestige forms** than males. The pattern revealed by Labov's New York City study (1972a), Trudgill's Norwich survey (1974b), Macaulay's (1977, 1978) study of Glasgow English, Newbrook's (1982) study of West Wirral, and Romaine's (1978) Edinburgh study, is summed up by Coates (following Coates, 1986, pp. 65–6):

1 In all styles, women tend to use fewer stigmatized forms than men.
2 In formal contexts, women seem to be more sensitive to prestige patterns than men.
3 Lower-middle-class women make major shifts in style; in the least formal style, they use a high proportion of the stigmatized variant, but in more formal styles, they correct their speech to correspond to that of the class above them.
4 Use of non-standard forms seems to be associated not only with working-class speakers, but also with *male* speakers.

Evidence of this kind seems to show that females are more sensitive to linguistic norms than males are, a conclusion strengthened by Trudgill's (1972, 1974b) self-evaluation test. Using tape-recordings, Trudgill played to his informants two or more pronunciations, more or less close to the **received pronunciation (RP)**, or standard, variant and to the non-standard Norwich variant respectively, and asked the informants to say which pronunciation was nearest their own. Then he compared the informants' answers with recordings of their own actual pronunciation. The test revealed that the females **over-reported** significantly while the males **under-reported**, i.e. female informants

thought their own pronunciation was closer to RP than it actually was, while male informants thought their own pronunciation was closer to the Norwich variant than it actually was. Assuming that what speakers *think* they do is what they would *like* to do, this shows that women want to use standard forms while men do not. For men, therefore, non-standard forms are prestigious, while for women, standard forms are prestigious. If it is further assumed that standard English has institutionalized prestige because it is the institutionalized norm, an assumption supported by research in social psychology (Coates, 1986, p. 75), then it is possible to argue further that standard English enjoys **overt prestige**, while non-standard forms enjoy **covert prestige**. Finally, it can be claimed 'that women are attracted by the norm of Standard English while men respond to the covert prestige of the vernacular' (Coates, 1986, p. 74).

At this point, it is appropriate to ask why this might be the case, and the typical explanation is that women, who occupy socially insecure positions, are seeking to appropriate some of the status attached to being an RP-speaker. This explanation is supported by Elyan *et al.*'s (1978) Lancashire study, which showed that women using RP were considered (Coates, 1986, p. 76):

more fluent, intelligent, self-confident, adventurous, independent and *feminine* than women with a regional accent. In addition, RP-accented women were also rated as being more *masculine* (judges had to rate each speaker for both masculinity and femininity on a nine-point scale). This may seem contradictory, but if masculinity and femininity are seen as two independent dimensions, then individuals have the choice of both characteristics.

In other words, a woman speaking RP may have greater access to traditionally male territories (jobs, activities . . .).

However, if it is accepted that, as much sociolinguistic research has shown, non-standard speech typically functions to maintain group identity, another explanation is possible: namely, that males tend to belong to close-knit groups while females tend not to. Males have greater access to membership of such groups than females, because they have greater access to work and to evening activities outside the home. Milroy's (1980) comparative study of Ballymacarrett, and the Clonard and the Hammer (parts of Belfast, Northern Ireland) supports this explanation (Coates, 1986, pp. 84–5):

> Ballymacarrett as a community differs from the other two: it suffers little from male unemployment. . . . The Hammer and the Clonard both had unemployment rates of around 35 per cent. . . . Men from these areas were forced to look for work outside the community, and also shared more in domestic tasks. . . . The women in these areas went out to work and, in the case of the young Clonard women, all worked together.

The young Clonard women used more non-standard forms than the young men. However, the study also showed that in the Hammer, where groups were less close-knit than they were in Ballymacarrett and Clonard (because of rehousing and unemployment), speakers – male and female – did not approximate more closely to standard English than speakers in the Clonard. Rather, there was 'a drift away from the focussed vernacular norms of more tight-knit groups' (Coates, 1986, p. 92). Group solidarity therefore seems more influential in activating group speech patterns than a desire to achieve a certain norm with covert or overt prestige, and it appears to be too simplistic to explain the different speech patterns of men and women by suggesting that men and women aim for different norms. The speech patterns in question appear, rather, to reflect the social fact that men generally have greater access to group membership than women.

In addition to differences in syntax, morphology, and pronunciation, men and women differ in terms of communicative strategies. When men and women converse, for instance, men tend to interrupt very frequently and are slow to provide supporting responses to women's speech turns (Zimmerman and West, 1975). Women, on the other hand, use more **facilitative tags** (Lakoff, 1975; Holmes, 1984) than men, that is, tags which

help a conversation to move along smoothly, and more *yes/no* questions (Fishman, 1980), which can, of course, also help to keep a conversation going.

Men also generally talk more than women (Bernard, 1972; Swacker, 1975; Eakins and Eakins, 1978). This clearly contradicts the popular belief that women talk more than men, and Spender (1980) explains that the reason that it *seems* to us that women speak more than men, even though studies show that it is the other way round, is that men are *expected* by the culture in general to talk, while women are expected to remain silent. When women do talk, therefore, it is more noticeable than when men talk.

When women talk to each other, the term **gossip** is often used to describe their activity, and in popular parlance this term is negatively loaded (it is rarely said of a group of men that they are gossiping). In anthropology and sociolinguistics, however, no negative connotations are attached to the term *gossip*, which is used to refer to 'informal communication between members of a social group' (Coates, 1986, p. 115). Gossip has the important function of maintaining the group's unity, morals, and values (D. Jones, 1980), and contains all the features which characterize women's way of interacting in conversation. It is a form of interaction which increases and reflects solidarity and support, and in which expressions intended to reflect or gain power for a speaker have no place.

These gender-related differences in speech patterns are acquired by children as they learn to speak (Coates, 1986, ch. 7), just as other gender stereotypes (how boys should behave and how girls should behave) and cultural values in general are learnt along with language (Halliday, 1978, p. 9).

THE DEFINITION THROUGH LANGUAGE OF GENDER ROLES

As a major vehicle for the transmission of cultural beliefs and values, language may profoundly affect female–male relations. The attitudes transmitted through language may either help to reinforce the *status quo*, or they may be a factor in changing it. It is possible to argue that the belief that standard English has been transmitting since the eighteenth century is that males are the species and women the subspecies, thus making it appear natural than males should be dominant. The main aspect of English usage normally mentioned in support of this argument is the use of *man* and *he* as **generic terms**, that is, as terms referring to the entire species – to all of human kind. The argument is as follows (see Miller and Swift, 1981, Chapters 1 and 2).

Use of *man* and the male pronouns as generics is usually justified on two grounds: (1) it is an ancient rule of English grammar; and (2) everybody knows that in generalizations, the male terms are meant to include females. Neither claim appears to stand up to scrutiny.

1 In Old English, *man* meant 'person' or 'human being', and was equally applicable to either sex. It is used in this way in *The Anglo-Saxon Chronicle*, where, for instance, Ercongota, the daughter of a seventh-century English king, is described as 'a wonderful man'. English at that time had *wer* for 'adult male' and *wif* for 'adult female'. The combined forms *wæpman* and *wifman* meant, respectively, 'adult male person' and 'adult female person'. Over time, *wifman* evolved into *woman*, and *wif* narrowed in meaning to 'wife'. *Man* narrowed in meaning in replacing *wer* and *wæpman*. The change in the meaning of *man* from broad to narrower, is similar to the way in which *deor* and *heafon* have narrowed from meaning 'animal' and 'sky' to meaning 'deer' and 'heaven' with the importation to English of the words *animal* and *sky*.

Later writers, like William Caxton, Shakespeare, and Chesterfield used *they* to refer to the species: 'Each of them should . . . make themself ready' (Caxton); 'God send everyone their heart's desire' (Shakespeare); 'If a person is born of a gloomy temper . . . they cannot help it' (Chesterfield).

However, early grammars of Modern English were written in the sixteenth and seventeenth centuries and were intended for boys from wealthy families to prepare them for the study of Latin. They used masculine gender pronouns, not because they could refer to both sexes, but because males dominated the world of education and literacy. No early grammar book has as one of its rules any that says that masculine pronouns include females when used in general reference, and the usage only became a general rule in 1746 when John Kirkly made it the twenty-first of eighty-eight grammatical rules, on the grounds that the male pronoun was more comprehensive than the female.

Later grammarians added to this feeling the notion that the use of *they* violated rules of number agreement – a consideration which, as we have seen above, did not concern Shakespeare, and one which appears to make the unwarranted assumption that number agreement is more important than gender agreement. Finally, in 1850, an Act of Parliament made it a law that 'words importing the masculine gender shall be deemed and taken to include females'. The second argument in favour of the use of male forms as generics states that we all know this to be the case.

2 However, the evidence appears to suggest that the terms in question are **false generics**. If they were true generic terms, there should be nothing odd about sentences like *Man breastfeeds his young; man suffers in childbirth; Diana Nyad became the first man to swim from the Bahamas to Florida*. Studies like that of Schneider and Hucker (1972) provide empirical evidence against *man* as a generic. They asked two groups of college students to select from magazines and newspapers, pictures to illustrate a sociology text book. One group were asked to find illustrations for headings like *Industrial man; Political man; Urban man*. The other group's headings were of the type *Industrial life; Political life; Urban life*. In a majority of cases, students of both sexes chose pictures of males to illustrate the titles including the term *man*, while choosing pictures including both sexes to illustrate the *life* titles. This shows that the term *man* is semantically loaded in favour of males, that is, it makes users think predominantly of males.

It is also odd, if we assume the generic status of the male forms, that *she* should nevertheless be used so often in generalizations about secretaries, nurses, primary-school teachers, baby-sitters, shoppers, child-minders, and cleaners, in fact, about just those workers who are most frequently female.

The effect of the use of the false generic is held to be that women are often being made invisible by the language, that is, the language has only a **negative semantic space** for women (Stanley, 1977); women are − MALE. As Graham (1975) argues, if you have a group C divided into two halves, A and B, then A and B can be equal members of C. But if you call the whole group A, one half A and the other half B, then the B half will be seen as deviant, the exception, the subspecies, the outsiders (Graham, 1975).

It is, furthermore, very easy to find evidence in support of the claim that when women are seen through language, they are seen in an unfavourable light (compare Spender 1980). Indeed, the term *woman* itself had negative connotations for most of the culture until the 1970s and retains these connotations in some groups in the early 1990s. The polite term, or **euphemism**, for a woman used to be, and in some circles it still is, *lady*, and there were (are) very clear rules for how a lady should behave and talk (see Robin Lakoff, 1975).

Some of these behavioural standards are reflected in linguistic usage; thus Stanley (1973) counts 220 English words for sexually promiscuous females and only twenty for sexually promiscuous males. This reveals some of the culture's general attitude to males and females; sexual vigour is seen as deviant in females; it is the male who is supposed to dominate in this field as in every other. The theory of maleness includes features such as courage, strength, toughness, vigour, rationality, while the theory of femaleness includes tenderness and emotionality. Consequently, it is not unusual to hear surprised statements to the effect that a female professional is able to combine her professional standing and ability with an undeniable femininity (it would be unlikely that anyone would remark on a man's ability to combine professionalism with masculinity). The language also still bears traces of the cultural norm of women as house*wives* and

men as workers outside the home; thus *working wife* and *working mother* are, to say the least, more likely to occur than *working husband* and *working father*.

Finally, it is easy to dig up linguistic evidence to support the argument that those qualities which are assigned to males are held in higher esteem than those assigned to females. Thus it can be complementary to call a girl a tomboy, but it can *never* be complementary to call a boy a sissy (derivative of *sister*).

All this demonstrates the ways in which males and females are stereotyped within the culture, and the way in which language use can highlight stereotypical features. For those in favour of altering the *status quo*, the question then arises as to the degree to which a change in language use can assist in this endeavour. The answer one gives will depend on how one views the relationship between language and culture in general, but it is unlikely that either of two possible extremist answers are correct. One such answer is that altering language use will achieve nothing, because any alternative terms will simply be infiltrated with the prejudices inherent in the old terms. At the other extreme, the answer would be that a change in language use alone would result in a change in the culture's beliefs about men and women respectively.

What cannot be doubted is that a heightened awareness of how language works for men and women as it is used by them and about them cannot but help aid an awareness of how they are viewed by the culture, including, of course, by themselves. It cannot be denied, either, that newsreaders and newspaper reporters in the 1990s are less likely to use male pronouns and more likely to use *they* as a singular term than they were in the 1960s. Refer to the entries on CRITICAL LINGUISTICS and METAPHOR for help in making up your own mind about the degree to which this may be a result of changes in attitude and of deliberate attempts to change language use.

K.M.

SUGGESTIONS FOR FURTHER READING

Coates, J. (1986), *Women, Men and Language*, London and New York, Longman.

Smith, P.M. (1985), *Language, the Sexes and Society*, Oxford, Basil Blackwell.

Language pathology and neurolinguistics

Language pathology is a convenient cover term for the study of all aspects of language disorders. As such, it includes the main disciplines involved, namely medical science (especially neuroanatomy and physiology) psychology (especially neuropsychology and cognitive psychology), linguistics, and education. It also covers all categories of disorder, including developmental as well as acquired disorders, disorders that are associated with other deficits such as hearing impairment or structural abnormality (such as cleft palate), or mental handicap, as well as those that are 'pure' language disorders. It comprises disorders that can be characterized at all levels of language structure and function, from articulatory and auditory speech-signal processing to problems of meaning, and it includes all modalities of language use, in production and comprehension, as represented through such media as speech, writing, and signing. Finally, it includes research and all aspects of intervention, from initial screening and diagnosis, through more extensive assessment procedures, to therapeutic management and remedial teaching.

Thus, many different professions are involved in the field of language pathology, including speech therapy (see SPEECH THERAPY), normal and special education, clinical and educational psychology, aphasiology (see below and APHASIA), pediatrics, ENT surgery and neurosurgery, audiology, and linguistics.

Within this field, certain historical factors have made a lasting impression. The **medical** approach was an early influence in the characterization of certain aspects of language disorder, particularly in the field of **aphasiology** which is concerned with acquired disorders associated with neurological damage. Within this approach people having language disorders are regarded as patients, and classification proceeds from the identification of symptoms to a diagnosis in terms of syndromes. **Syndromes** are symptom complexes which have a systematic internal relationship such that the presence of certain symptoms guarantees the presence or absence of certain others (see APHASIA).

A further characteristic of the medical approach is the categorization of language disorders in terms of their aetiology; thus, developmental disorders may be linked to difficulties noted with the mother's pregnancy, the delivery, or subsequent childhood illness, such as otitis media or 'glue ear', while acquired disorders may be linked to site of brain lesions, and the type of brain damage arising from either external sources – gunshot wounds yielding more focal destruction of brain tissue than 'closed head' injuries sustained in road traffic accidents, for example – or by diseases such as tumour or degenerative conditions such as Parkinsonism.

The **psychological** approach has also had considerable influence. The tendency here has been coloured by the dominant tradition, but it is possible to discern a consistent emphasis on language as possibly the most accessible, subtle, and complex form of overt human behaviour. Disorders in a complex system may provide valuable information on the properties of that system, both in the way that they arise – showing which parts of the system are vulnerable, and how far they may be selectively impaired – and in the sorts of compensatory processes that appear to take place.

A key feature of the behavioural approach has therefore been a concern with psychometric assessment of language functions in relation to other psychological capacities. The early assessments drew largely on intelligence tests, and focused attention on the link between language disorders and impaired psychological functions such as memory and perception. More modern aphasia test batteries such as the **Boston Diagnostic Aphasia Examination**, or the **Western Aphasia Battery** still contain components that derive from this tradition, such as the requirement to perform simple calculations, and the matching of shapes (see APHASIA).

The **linguistic** approach is of more recent origin, based on the methods of structural linguistics developed most completely in the 1930s to 1950s, and on the subsequent trends that derive directly or indirectly from the work of Chomsky. Jakobson is generally regarded as the first to apply the concepts of linguistics to the field of language disorders; he sought a connection between the linguistic characteristics of various disorders and the traditional lesion sites associated with them. In essence, this was the first exercise in what has since become known as **neurolinguistics** (see below). His work was not followed up, however, and what is now referred to as representative of the linguistic approach is a research tradition that has rather distinct origins and characteristics.

The **clinical linguistic** approach may generally be described as one which treats a presenting language disorder as a phenomenon which can be described in linguistic terms, independently of factors such as aetiology and general psychological functions – phonetic, phonological, morphological, syntactic, lexical, semantic, and pragmatic, to provide a fairly representative general inventory – and allows for the possibility that any particular case of a language disorder may involve a differential pattern of impairment across some or all of these levels. One implication of this view is the calling into question of the fundamental separation of 'speech' vs 'language'

in the taxonomy of disorders.

The clinical linguistic approach clearly has much to contribute to the appropriate description and interpretation of language disorders, but there is a general problem regarding the psychological reality of linguistic descriptions and models. For this reason, it is necessary to supplement the clinical linguistic approach by one which attempts to identify the psycholinguistic structures and processes involved in language behaviour, in impaired as well as in normal contexts. This leads us to consider the field of **neurolinguistics**. This term appears frequently to be used for what are, essentially, psycholinguistic studies of neurologically based language disorders. But there is what may be regarded as a more strict interpretation of the term, which we shall now briefly review.

Neurolinguistics is the study of the relationship between language and its neurological basis. It is convenient to distinguish three general orders of description in the study of language abilities: the linguistic, the psycholinguistic, and the neurolinguistic. The first may be represented by the general descriptive approach that recognizes such levels of organization as the phonetic, the phonological, the morphological, the syntactic, the lexical, and the semantic and pragmatic; techniques of description at these levels, when applied to the field of language pathology, constitute what we have referred to above as **clinical linguistics**. Alternatively, a rather more integrated system of linguistic description may be attempted, such as is found in the generative tradition (see TRANSFORMATIONAL-GENERATIVE GRAMMAR).

The second order of description is concerned with the evidence that reveals the nature of the linguistic structures and processes that are actually involved in the use of language; perceptual processes, information-processing strategies, memorial factors, and motor-control processes.

The third order of description is concerned with the nature of the neurological operations involved in these psycholinguistic processes; with the structure and function of the auditory system and its associated elements, and with the neural basis for articulatory gestures, and so on.

It is not very easy to understand the relationship between such distinct orders of description, partly because information in all three is still so incomplete. It would be premature to conclude that linguistic properties 'reduce' to, or can be explained by, psycholinguistic properties, and that these in turn can be accounted for in terms of the properties of the neurological substrata of language. For example, it has been observed, within the transformational-syntax tradition, that a number of constraints on the privilege of occurrence of certain syntactic elements may be expressed as a general constraint on movement of such elements – hence a constraint of **subjacency** is proposed to the effect that no constituent may be moved across more than one **bounding node**, a node which acts as a constituent boundary (e.g., NP; S) at a time. The psycholinguistic evidence for the role of subjacency in facilitating the operation of human parsing operations is a controversial matter, however; and the status of subjacency from a strict neurological perspective is currently difficult even to raise as an issue.

In what sense, then, can there be a neurolinguistics at present? There are two general answers to this question: the first lies in a general understanding of the neurological organization of language abilities – what might be called the **neurology of language**; the second is mainly found in the detailed study of language disorders where there is sufficient neurological evidence to allow for some interpretation of the linguistic and psycholinguistic characteristics of the disorder in neurological terms (see APHASIA).

An overview of the basic neurology of language may conveniently start with the articulatory system, which has four main components from the point of view of neurological involvement: (1) the **cortex** – the outer layer of so-called 'grey matter' in the brain – where initiating cells located primarily in the **motor strip** make connections with (2) long connecting fibres known as the **upper motor neurons**, which connect to control centres in the **basal ganglia**, **thalamus**, and **cerebellum**, and terminate in relay stations in the **brainstem** and **spinal cord**; (3) the **lower motor neurons** which carry signals from the relay stations out to the muscles of the head, neck and chest regions; and finally, (4) the muscles served by the lower motor neurons, and which are linked to a sensory feedback loop, to permit monitoring of motor control.

Starting with the first of these components, the relevant part of the cortex is located in the so-called **motor strip**, running anteriorly along the line of the fissures which serve to demarcate the **frontal lobe** in each hemisphere of the brain. Along this strip, the cells controlling muscles all over the body are organized systematically in such a fashion that those responsible for the lower limbs are located towards the top of the motor strip, while those innervating the muscles of the vocal tract are found at the bottom, close to the junction with the anterior part of the **temporal lobe**. The motor strip cells operate in conjunction with those of the immediately anterior portion of the frontal lobe, the **premotor cortex**, which is involved in certain controlling functions, and the **parietal lobe**, posterior to the frontal lobe, also contributes copiously to the upper motor neuron system that connects to the lower control centres.

The very rapid and precise movements of the speech organs require involvement not just of the motor cortex but sensory areas as well. The nervous system appears to function very broadly, therefore, in the control of speech output, through wide subcortical connections in each hemisphere. Each hemisphere is responsible for controlling the complete functioning of the oral tract musculature; thus both left and right sides of the tongue, for example, are controlled from each hemisphere. Such complex behaviour as speech requires consciously willed movements and semi-automatic and completely automatic control of sequences of movements, and it appears that all these aspects are represented in the signals carried by the upper motor neurons as they group together to pass down through the base of the brain. Some, the **cortico-bulbar neurons**, terminate in the brainstem, and others, the **cortico-spinal neurons**, pass down further into the spinal cord. Still other neurons connect to the basal ganglia and the thalamus; the cerebral cortex is thus able to influence this complex of structures, which in turn influences the brainstem and spinal cord relays.

As consciously willed movements become increasingly automatic, as in the development of speech patterns, they become part of the basal ganglia repertoire. There are both voluntary and postural inputs to the basal ganglia, allowing for the overriding of automatic sequences, and for the integration of information concerning the position of articulators relative to each other in the vocal tract. Part of the function of the cerebellum is bound up in the role of the thalamus and basal ganglia, to regulate postural reflexes and muscle tone – the resistance of muscles to movement.

The **reticular formation**, in the brainstem, is also involved in connections from the upper motor neurons, and appears to exert facilitating and inhibiting effects on certain types of slower-transmitting, or **gamma**, **neurons** whose function is to help to control the operation of the fast-transmitting, or **alpha**, **fibres** which are responsible for the movement of the main muscles. This control vs movement distinction is represented in both the upper and lower neuron systems. Most upper motor neurons diverge within the brainstem, carrying control from each hemisphere to each side of the oral tract.

The connection from the upper to the lower motor neurons marks the division between the **central** and **peripheral nervous systems**. Each lower motor neuron forms part of a **motor unit**, containing in addition the muscle that the lower motor alpha-neuron innervates, an associated muscle **spindle**, and a slow-transmitting gamma-neuron linked to the reticular formation and cerebellum via the upper/lower motor neuron relay. The spindle carries information on the state of the muscle – extended or contracted – which is used to regulate the innervation of the muscle via the fast-transmitting alpha-neuron. The lower motor neurons that are involved in movements of the oral tract connect from relays in the **pons** and **medulla** in the brainstem, and are known anatomically as **cranial nerves** – those conventionally numbered as V, VII, X, XI and XII being the most important – and the **thoratic nerves**, numbered from I to XII, connect from the spinal cord to control the muscles of the ribcage and the abdomen, and thus serve to initiate and regulate the pulmonary airstream mechanism.

If we now pass quickly over the speech signal that is created by the movement of articulators and carried by resultant movement of air particles, we can pick up the process of neurological involvement in speech audition at the point where mechanically boosted signals in the 2–6kHz speech frequency range are transported to neural impulses in the **organ of Corti**, lying along the **basilar membrane** in the inner ear (see also AUDITORY PHONETICS). The impulses take the form of very brief, all-or-none electrical activity, **action potentials**, travelling along the fibres of the **auditory nerve** from the **cochlea**. In ways that are still not completely understood, these action potentials carry frequency and amplitude information, as well as duration, to the **cochlea nuclei cells** in the medulla of the brainstem. These cells effectively extract critical features from the auditory nerve signal, by being selectively tuned to respond to different characteristics of the input.

Elsewhere in the medulla, important processing of temporal interactions occurs, which requires a contralateral blending of inputs from both ears. Some medullary neurons respond only to truly synchronous input from each ear, while others are tuned for critical intervals of asynchronous input. Such processing allows for accurate location of the speech signal source in space, and initiates appropriate orientation responses. Fibres from the medullary areas pass through the brainstem bilaterally, with links to the reticular formation and the cerebellum. The **reticular formation** is responsible for relaying sensory input and for readying the cortex as a whole for the arrival of this input. The **cerebellum**, while primarily associated with motor control, has a number of sensory inputs including the auditory, and, like the reticular formation, has rich connections with the cortex.

Further complex intermixing of binaural input takes place in the neurons of the **inferior colliculus** in the **midbrain**, some of which are specialized for **ipsilateral** or for **contralateral** input. The major output from here is to an area of the thalamus represented bilaterally as the **medial geniculate body**. This has two-way connections with the cells of the **auditory cortex**, and is thus rather more than simply a further relay station in the auditory system. One of the problems in defining the functions of cells higher up the system is the extent to which their operation is dependent on such higher brain processes as attention, emotion, memory, and so on. Likewise, the organization and function of cells in the auditory cortex is complex and difficult to determine. As in other sensory modalities, the relevant parts of the cortex are organized into a series of **projection fields**, or 'maps' of the relevant parts of the body, in this case the basilar membrane, with one field having primary function.

Thus far, we have not considered the way that language is organized within the brain itself, essentially between the auditory cortex and the motor speech cortex. Functionally, we can think of the cerebral cortex as consisting of four separate but interconnected areas, the frontal, the parietal, the temporal, and the occipital lobes, with each of these lobes being represented in the left and right hemispheres (see Figure 1).

Within this structure, the auditory cortex is located on the upper surface of the temporal lobe in each hemisphere, close to the junction between the temporal, parietal, and frontal lobes. This area is concerned, like the whole auditory system of which it forms a part, with all auditory processing, not just with speech. In most individuals, the left hemisphere is dominant, and this is linked to handedness – left-hemisphere dominance is particularly noticeable in right-handers. The implication of this for speech audition is that the auditory cortex in the left, i.e. normally dominant, hemisphere is more especially involved than the corresponding area on the right; and because the majority of nerve fibres travel to the auditory cortex contra-laterally, this leads to a typical **right-ear advantage** for speech, particularly for stop consonants (see ARTICULATORY PHONETICS) that are maximally distinct. This phenomenon has been viewed as evidence for a specialized speech-perception centre in the left hemisphere; but it is not clear that this specialization is strictly for speech sounds alone.

As far as speech production is concerned, we have noted the area of the cerebral cortex which is represented bilaterally at the base of the so-called motor strip, close to the junction of the frontal, parietal, and temporal lobes. This

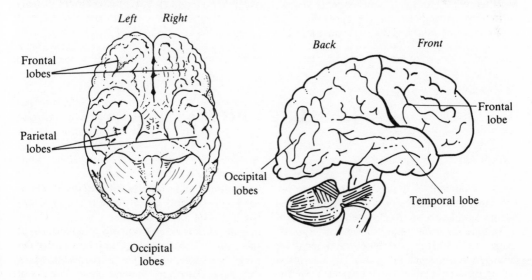

Figure 1

controls the musculature of the lips, tongue, velum, etc. (see ARTICULATORY PHONETICS) for both speech and non-speech activities such as blowing and swallowing. Again, the implication of cerebral dominance is that it is normally the left hemisphere that is most closely involved in speech functions, but the issue is not very clear. Generally, it appears that both hemispheres contribute to sensory feedback and motor control functions in speech as well as non-speech oral-tract activities; the motor nerve fibres are routed from the cortex to the oral tract in bilateral fashion. Nevertheless, dominance is a left-hemisphere characteristic for speech, and it appears that the reason for this may lie in an association between a specialized speech-control centre in the dominant hemisphere and the area of motor cortex devoted to the innervation of oral tract musculature. The function of such a specialized speech processor in production may be primarily bound up in the need for very rapid sequencing of the very precise articulatory movements in speech.

The evidence for hemispherically specialized speech control comes in the main from two remarkable sorts of surgical sources: silver electrode stimulation on the exposed brains of anesthetized but fully conscious patients in cases where precise mapping of the speech area is required prior to surgical intervention, and from so-called 'split brain' patients in whom the left and right hemispheres have been surgically sectioned, resulting in a situation where information that is made available only to the right hemisphere cannot be expressed in speech output, i.e. by the left hemisphere. Much information on the organization of language in the brain also comes from the study of brain-damaged patients, where, however, the evidence is frequently difficult to interpret as a result of problems in identifying the precise nature of the damage, and the effects of compensatory strategies (see APHASIA).

M.A.G.

SUGGESTIONS FOR FURTHER READING

Crystal, D. (1980), *An Introduction to Language Pathology*, London, Edward Arnold.

Espir, M.L.E. and Rose, F.C. (1983), *The Basic Neurology of Speech and Language*, 3rd edn, Oxford, Blackwell Scientific.

Perkins, W.H. and Kent, R.D. (1986), *Textbook of Functional Anatomy of Speech, Language and Hearing*, San Diego, College-Hill.

Walsh, K.W. (1978), *Neuropsychology: A Clinical Approach*, Edinburgh, Churchill Livingstone.

Whitaker, H. and H.A. Whitaker (1976), *Studies in Neurolinguistics*, vol. 1, New York, Academic Press.

Language surveys

The development of dialect studies during the late nineteenth century was greatly facilitated by the simultaneous development of a set of techniques for undertaking surveys of linguistic usage and of other variables associated with language (attitudinal etc.). During the intervening century, a large body of literature on the mechanics and requirements of language surveys has built up, and a large number of surveys have been carried out, some dialectological, some more general and in some cases macrolinguistic in character. The depth and scope of coverage of these surveys has varied greatly, in terms of the range of aspects of the language(s) with which they have dealt, in terms of the geographical and social constraints placed on selection of speakers for the survey, and in terms of the density of sampling across each population surveyed. Early works in this tradition dealt predominantly with geographical dialects, mainly rural, of familiar European languages – often using very small and unrepresentative samples of informants (see also DIALECTOLOGY).

More recently, one of the effects of the increasing sophistication of dialectologists with respect to sampling technique and general research methodology has been the growth of a tendency to aim at coverage of entire populations, without any prior decision as to which types of variety or speaker are most relevant. Furthermore, surveys of varieties traditionally perceived as entire languages, either singly or in geographically associated groupings, have become more common. These vary in level of sophistication from the often crude, general questions on language which form part of many government censuses etc., to highly detailed surveys of usage and other matters, both in immigrant communities in the west and, sometimes, across whole populations, including native speakers of indigenous languages. The main thrust of all these kinds of survey has typically been the investigation of actual usage, including bilingualism or bidialectism and the distribution of functions between the different languages or dialects spoken.

Much of this investigation, however, has of necessity been carried out through indirect channels such as informants' self-reports, which naturally vary considerably in reliability and completeness. In recognition of this, and because of the inherent interest of this sort of material, techniques have been developed – particularly within the Labovian tradition of urban dialectology – for studying informants' opinions and beliefs about their own and others' usage, and also for examining their subjective reactions to usage of various kinds, their impressions of the facts regarding distribution of functions etc. To some extent, it has been found possible to control certain aspects of the situation in which speech and/or comments on language are obtained, in particular formality, and thus to study the covariation of usage with such factors, as well as to obtain from actual data some evidence on the

accuracy or otherwise of informants' intuitions about their own usage. Devices such as reading passages and blank-filling tests are frequently used, in addition to conversational sections intended to produce approximations to normal speech. Some such techniques have, of course, long been employed out of necessity in more traditional studies where there has been insufficient time to obtain spontaneous instances of all phenomena being examined.

In their interest in both usage itself and attitudes/beliefs concerning it, workers in this area typically differ both from the **descriptivist** tradition, with its tenet enjoining concentration on usage alone, and from the **generativist** tradition, in which intuitions have been allocated a central place and status in argumentation, and in which the possibility of major discrepancy between intuitions and the usage to which they relate has seldom been a focus of attention. Theoretical considerations have, however, seldom exercised survey workers as much as problems in methodology; they have been concerned largely with description for its own sake, or with practical implications of their findings.

The features shared by most language surveys are those fairly obviously associated with sampling, data collection, and analysis. As a first step, the goals of the survey must be defined, i.e. what kind of material is desired (data *per se*, attitudes, etc.) and what is the purpose behind obtaining it – descriptive, theoretical, practical (e.g., remedial), etc. In the light of these considerations, the scope of the survey – the population to be sampled, the range and form of any questionnaire used, etc. – must be settled. Resources and theoretical/methodological persuasions will then yield a variety of decisions as to the means of approach to informants (direct, postal, etc.), the number of informants approached and the format used in selecting these, the number and background of field workers used, etc.

The main survey will often be preceded by a pilot study – a small-scale, often less rigorous study, aimed at determining the relative importance of potential linguistic or non-linguistic variables, or at testing other features or aspects of the survey in advance – and by examination of all available background material, both linguistic and demographic (size, density, origin, distribution and character of human population).

After the survey itself has been carried out, the material obtained will be analysed in accordance with whatever paradigm has been adopted, and conclusions will be drawn. In some cases, these latter may involve modification of the paradigm. Any practical recommendations arising from the conclusions will then emerge. It will be seen that there is considerable scope for variation in the detailed character of such surveys, and the range of formats may best be illustrated by consideration of the most important groups of surveys, of all types, undertaken over the last century or so.

THE GERMAN DIALECT SURVEY OF WENKER, WREDE, AND OTHERS (FROM 1876)

This pioneering survey was concerned strictly with rural non-standard dialects of German and coincided with the first studies of specific dialects, carried out in the same vein. Initially, the aims appear to have been purely descriptive, but the project was quickly drawn into controversies of a theoretical nature arising from the much-publicized pronouncements of the **Junggrammatiker** (e.g., the **Neogrammarian Principle** – see HISTORICAL LINGUISTICS, p. 194). Both adherents and opponents of the relevant tenets, which related to constraints on linguistic change, cited the findings in support of their divergent viewpoints.

Only actual data were collected – not evidence of beliefs, attitudes, etc. The survey began on a small scale in the Düsseldorf area, but was rapidly extended and eventually covered the entire European German Empire. Every village with a school was sampled; the method adopted was indirect, involving the mailing of a questionnaire to the schoolteacher at each location, with instructions about how it should be filled in. Approximately forty sentences were to be translated from standard German into the local dialect, and pronunciation was to be indicated using the regular orthography as best the teachers could. The intention was to obtain information

on the most specifically local forms, typically the most archaic; this reflects the nineteenth-century interest in supposedly pure speech (see also DIALECTOLOGY). However, the degree to which this was obtained is questionable, since teachers would vary a great deal in their ability to reproduce usage accurately, and the system adopted was obviously more suitable for syntax and morphology than for phonology. In addition, all nineteenth-century work on phonology was pre-structuralist, with only rare attempts at moving beyond surface phonetics to statements of systems.

Over 52,000 questionnaires were returned adequately completed, and after a few years the survey became based at the University of Marburg. The vast amount of data involved hindered the task of synthesis, and maps did not begin to appear until 1926, fifteen years after the death of Georg Wenker, the originator. Publication was sparse and the project was abandoned after eighty years in 1956. In 1939 48,000 copies of a second questionnaire were received, and the results, mainly concerning lexis, were published between 1953 and 1978 (F. Wrede and W. Mitzka, 1926–56, and W. Mitzka and L.E. Schmidt, 1953–78).

THE FRENCH DIALECT SURVEY OF GILLIÉRON AND EDMONT (FROM 1897)

In France, concern developed during the 1880s at the apparently imminent demise of local dialect in the face of the advance of standard French. Jules Gilliéron accepted the task of carrying out a survey of the relevant varieties, and, partly in view of the alleged urgency of his mission, adopted radically different techniques from those used in Germany – though he retained the German assumptions about the kind of speech/ speaker to be examined, and also the German interest in contemporary issues in historical linguistics. He employed the direct method, i.e., on-the-spot investigation by a field worker. In order to increase the level of consistency, he used only one, trained field worker – the amateur dialectologist Edmond Edmont.

These decisions necessarily reduced dramatically the geographical density of the coverage – only 683 locations in mainland France and Corsica were investigated over a period of some fifteen years; but the amount of linguistic detail obtained for each locality, the reliability and consistency of the material, and the speed of analysis and publication – carried out while the survey was progressing, using material posted back to Gilliéron – were all vastly superior to the corresponding features of the German survey. Edmont used one or two informants in each locality, predominantly males lacking in formal education, and worked with a large questionnaire which in its final form elicited 1,900 items from each informant. The resulting atlas appeared between 1902 and 1910 (J. Gilliéron and E. Edmont, 1902–10).

Two of Gilliéron's students, Karl Jaberg and Jakob Jud, later produced a similar but improved format for their atlas of the Italian-speaking area of Europe (1928–40), and Jud, together with their chief fieldworker Paul Scheuermeier – himself a successful innovator in fieldwork methodology – had a decisive influence on the early stages of American survey work (see below).

AMERICAN SURVEYS OF KURATH AND OTHERS (FROM 1931)

A large number of scholars began to work on a projected linguistic atlas of the United States and Canada in 1931. Owing to the huge area to be covered, it was necessary to treat each region as a self-contained unit, and the key role was that of overall co-ordinator; Hans Kurath, who took up this position, also directed the first regional survey – that dealing with New England. This proceeded rapidly, partly assisted by the smaller distances and denser settlement patterns in that area, and provided a model for other regions. The amount of variability was typically small by comparison with that to be found in Europe, owing to the relatively recent occupation of North America by English speakers, but, particularly in the east, large quantities of interesting material on folk-speech and other regionalized usage were collected. Prominent workers on the project have included Harold B. Allen, E. Bagby

Atwood and Guy S. Lowman.

By this time, tape-recorders were becoming more readily available, to some extent circumventing the problem of the role of the fieldworker in interpreting and recording the responses – a problem which had become increasingly obvious as awareness of the different character of broad and narrow transcriptions (see PHONEMICS) grew. Now decisions could at least be made later and at greater leisure on the evidence of a recording. Other aspects of the work also represented advances on the European studies; attempts, albeit somewhat haphazard and simplistic by later standards, were made to examine informants of different social and educational levels, and also of different age ranges, since the organizers realized that 'broad' dialect of the type traditionally studied in Europe was of lesser importance in a North American context.

The project has proceeded only slowly in recent decades, and following the publication of the New England work (H. Kurath et al., 1939–43) no major volumes on other areas appeared until 1961 (H. Kurath and R.I. McDavid, 1961). Under the influence of Allen the volumes dealing with the Upper Midwest appeared in 1973–6, but it is not clear when or if some of the remaining regional surveys will be completed.

THE SURVEY OF ENGLISH DIALECTS (SED) (DIETH, ORTON, AND OTHERS, FROM 1948)

Work on English dialects began in earnest at a relatively late date, though **The English Dialect Society** (1873–96) (see THE ENGLISH DIALECT SOCIETY) had sponsored various works on particular regions, including Joseph Wright's (1898–1905) dialect dictionary and accompanying dialect grammar. In the intervening period only regional dialect societies and various isolated academic investigations had been in existence, but after the Second World War Eugen Dieth, based in Zürich, Switzerland, suggested a general survey. Harold Orton, at Leeds, took up the role of organizer for England, and the **Linguistic Survey of Scotland** (see below) also began soon afterwards.

Despite Dieth's own enthusiasm for synchronic as opposed to purely historical issues, the form taken by the study as it developed was largely traditional. The focus was mainly on phonology and lexis, and in respect of the former the interest was predominantly diachronic, and the transcriptions used strictly phonetic (by intention) rather than phonemic. Furthermore, only informants of the standard European type – elderly uneducated males – were used, unless none was available. Some of the locations – though very few – were in this case urban, but the main focus was again on rural areas. An assortment of fieldworkers investigated 311 localities around 10–15 miles apart between 1948 and 1961.

Some tape-recordings were made, but little use was made of these in analysis, and attempts were accordingly made, as in North America, to standardize the training of field workers, though it is clear that this enterprise was not totally successful. The questionnaire was highly structured, with various different types of question, e.g. naming, completing, converting (i.e., obtaining a variant on a construction). This aspect of the survey was the focus of considerable attention, and many subsequent studies of particular dialects used questionnaires based on the SED model.

As usual, the rate of publication has been slow – an *Introduction* by Orton appeared in 1962, followed by four volumes of unprocessed responses sorted by regions (Orton *et al.*, 1962–71); there is a fairly clear bias towards northern areas in respect of accuracy and interest. After Orton's death in 1975, other workers continued the project and in 1978 a *Linguistic Atlas of England* appeared (Orton *et al.*, 1978), synthesizing some of the most important findings in map form (expense prohibited the display of all the data in this form). Many articles and a number of books (see in particular Wakelin, 1972) have also been based on SED data, and Leeds University continues as a centre of dialect studies under the aegis of Stanley Ellis. Attitudes to SED are at present ambivalent; the resurgence of interest in geographical issues and the desire for real-time material encourage use of the data, but for modern purposes it is often difficult to interpret

and it is sometimes plainly wrong or misleading.

THE LINGUISTIC SURVEY OF SCOTLAND (LSS) (FROM 1949)

The LSS differs from the studies described above in a number of ways: it is broader in scope within its geographical bounds, dealing with Gaelic as well as English, and with any form of usage, in either language, found in or just outside Scotland, rather than with 'broad' dialect alone (hence 'Linguistic' rather than 'Dialect' in its title); it is more eclectic in its methodology, using varying approaches to suit different kinds of data; it is an ongoing study rather than a once-for-all project – since 1965 it has been a department in the Faculty of Arts at its home base, the University of Edinburgh; from the outset its focus has been on synchronic and structuralist issues rather than on the traditionally popular diachronic matters, and its more specific concerns have continued to alter in accordance with changes in linguistics as a whole. Important workers have included J.C. Catford, Trevor Hill, James Y. Mather, Angus McIntosh, and Hans-Hennig Speitel.

The initial stages of the survey dealt with lexis, and were conducted by means of postal questionnaires (1951ff.) – over 2,600 copies were returned in a usable state by the local teachers who had been asked to supervise their completion by suitable informants. Fieldwork of a more direct nature commenced in 1955, and over 250 localities have been investigated in this way, using trained interviewers working from a standardized questionnaire aimed at eliciting phonological and morphological information. Wherever possible, the main points of phonological systems were to be determined on the spot rather than in later analysis, a policy not favoured in the American surveys owing to its time-consuming nature and the resulting strain placed on informants.

Serious publication did not begin until 1975, but the *Linguistic Atlas of Scotland* (Mather and Speitel, 1975ff.) has now appeared in three volumes. The Gaelic section of the survey has lagged behind, but work in this area, and also on Scots/Scottish English, is still in progress.

SURVEYS IN THE LABOVIAN TRADITION (1960S AND AFTER)

Labov's seminal work in New England and New York City (see DIALECTOLOGY) prompted a number of studies, varying considerably in scope and type but all influenced by the central tenets of Labov's position: the need to focus on statistically valid samples of the relevant populations; to work with a structured interview or other procedure designed to obtain speech at various levels of formality; to investigate intuitions and attitudes in addition to actual usage (not as a substitute for it). Some of these studies, such as the **Tyneside Linguistic Survey** (Barbara Strang, John Pellowe, etc.) have persisted over long periods without producing widely circulated results; others have been completed rapidly by one or a few investigators and quickly publicised.

Labov's own study of New York City, published in 1966, established many of the precedents for such surveys – around a hundred informants were used, selected through a stratified random sample – a random sample was taken from each of several 'strata' of the population, established on the basis of factors known to be relevant to its structure – and the interview elicited two conversational styles and also included a reading passage, a word list, linguistic exercises aimed at obtaining subjective reactions to variant forms, and more anecdotal discussion of this sort of issue. Labov himself later organized a longer-term study of the usage of New York Blacks, employing less formal contexts of observation (Labov, 1972b), and some subsequent work has emulated and extended this feature of his work (e.g. Milroy, 1980).

Even before these developments, however, the classical Labovian paradigm had been used by others, in particular Roger Shuy and his colleagues in their Detroit survey (Shuy et al., 1968). This large-scale project was one of the first to examine grammatical variation quantitatively, and also refined considerably the Labovian classification of variables as perceived and evaluated by speakers. In addition, the Detroit team pioneered the use of computers in processing and storing data – techniques which have been vastly extended more recently – and also pursued educational implications of their findings, another aspect of this kind of work which has repeatedly featured in later studies.

RECENT MACROLINGUISTIC SURVEYS

The previous section dealt with surveys produced within a framework developed by practitioners of the new discipline of sociolinguistics; but **sociolinguistics** is, of course, by no means confined to Labovian urban dialectology. A quite different, macrolinguistic type of study has also developed over the 1970s and 1980s, under the influence of sociolinguists. Studies of this latter kind seek, broadly speaking, to answer the question 'Who speaks what, about what subjects, where, when, to whom, etc.?' Some investigators have worked with second-hand data obtained from government censuses, etc., but more recently the need has been felt for more precise, theoretically sounder surveys carried out by experts.

One of the best-known such surveys is that carried out by the **Linguistic Minorities Project**, financed by the British Department of Education and Science. This project was concerned with the newer minority languages of the United Kingdom – those used by originally immigrant communities from Asia, the European Continent, and elsewhere. Earlier surveys (e.g., by the Inner London Education Authority in 1978 (ILEA, 1979)) had revealed the complexity of the linguistic situation in the schools of London and other British cities, and in addition had increased awareness of the educational consequences of failure to develop positive policies to deal with the many minority languages involved.

The Linguistic Minorities Project commenced operation in 1980 and has conducted questionnaire-based studies in several cities, dealing mainly with school-age subjects. The questionnaires have sought to establish: patterns of usage (fluency, frequency and domain of selection of each available language, etc.); nomenclature;

literacy; attitudes (including attitudes to the use of the languages in education and to their possible status as examination subjects); etc. As a result of the findings of these studies, various educational programmes have been instigated or altered in character, generally in the direction of providing more encouragement for and recognition of the home languages of students from immigrant/minority backgrounds.

Issues of this kind have also been examined in Wales (Council for the Welsh Language/Cyngor yr Iaith Gymraeg: 1978) and Canada (Cauldwell, 1982) where bilingualism is common and where the status and domain distribution of the two languages is very different. This sort of study is, however, in its infancy, and there is scope and

need for many other such studies and for programmes (educational, planning in the media, etc.) based on their results.

M.Nk

SUGGESTIONS FOR FURTHER READING

Ferguson, C.A. and Heath, S.B. (eds) (1981), *Language in the USA*, Cambridge, Cambridge University Press.
Francis, W.N. (1983), *Dialectology*, London, Longman.
Trudgill, P.J. (ed.) (1984), *Language in the British Isles*, Cambridge, Cambridge University Press (especially Part IV).

Language typology

Language typology is based on the assumption that

> the ways in which languages differ from each other are not entirely random, but show various types of dependencies among those properties of languages which are not invariant differences statable in terms of the 'type'. The construct of the 'type' is, as it were, interposed between the individual language in all its uniqueness and the unconditional or invariant features to be found in all languages (Greenberg, 1974, pp. 54–5).

The data provided by typological language studies show the limits within which languages can vary, and in so doing provide statements about the nature of language (Mallinson and Blake, 1981, p. 6). Each language is not necessarily assigned to one class only. For example, in Sapir's (1921) morphological typology, languages are arranged on a comparative scale in regard to some properties, and in Greenberg (1954) such

scales are made explicit by the provision of a metric with ten indices.

Since language typology is concerned with the ahistorical comparison of languages while genetic classification (see HISTORICAL LINGUISTICS, pp. 212–16) is historically determined, 'there is no contradiction in the fact that closely related languages might be separated in some particular typological classification, while languages only remotely or not at all related are classed together' (Greenberg, 1974, p. 56). Nor is there any reason why 'a typological characteristic should not itself involve an historic fact about the language as long as no assumption is made that the properties found in the language are themselves historically connected' (ibid.). For example, historicity is itself a criterion which distinguishes **natural** from **artificial languages** (see ARTIFICIAL LANGUAGES) such as Esperanto and Volapük (Stewart, 1962b).

Greenberg (1974, p. 13, n. 4) dates the first use of the word 'typology' in linguistic literature to the theses presented by the Prague linguists to the First Congress of Slavonic Philologists held in 1928. Until then, classification of languages was largely **genetic**, that is, it was based on the development of languages from older source languages (see HISTORICAL LINGUISTICS, pp. 209–16), and the only extensively used typology was morphological classification of languages as approximating towards **ideal types**: isolating, agglutinating/agglutinative, inflecting/flectional/fusional and polysynthetic/incorporating (although see Wundt, 1900).

An ideal **isolating language** is one in which there is a one-to-one correspondence between words and morphemes. Comrie (1989, p. 43) provides these examples from Vietnamese:

Khi tôi đến nhà bạn tôi,
when I come house friend I

chúng tôi bắt đầu làm bài
PLURAL *I seize head do lesson*

'When I came to my friend's house, we began to do lessons.'

In addition to Vietnamese, Chinese and several other South-East Asian languages are usually classified as close to isolating.

An **agglutinating** or **agglutinative language** is one which attaches separable affixes to roots (see MORPHOLOGY), so that there may be several morphemes in a word, but the boundaries between them are always clear. Each morpheme has a reasonably invariant shape, as the following example from Comrie (1989, p. 44) demonstrates. The example shows the declension of the Turkish noun *adam* 'man':

	Singular	*Plural*
Nominative	adam	adam-lar
Accusative	adam-ı	adam-lar-ı
Genitive	adam-ın	adam-lar-ın
Dative	adam-a	adam-lar-a
Locative	adam-da	adam-lar-da
Ablative	adam-dan	adam-lar-dan

Hungarian and Japanese are also usually classified as close to agglutinating.

An **inflecting, flectional**, or **fusional language** is one in which morphemes are represented by affixes, but in which it is difficult to assign morphemes precisely to the different parts of the affixes. For instance, in the Latin *Puellam bellam amo*, 'I love the beautiful girl', the *-am* ending on the noun and on the adjective marks the noun as feminine, singular, and accusative, and the *-o* ending on the verb represents first-person singular subject and present active indicative (Mallinson and Blake, pp. 20–1). Russian, Ancient Greek, and Sanskrit are also inflecting.

A **polysynthetic** or **incorporating language** makes great use of affixation and often incorporates what English would represent with nouns and adverbs in that element which resembles a verb. Ireland (1989, p. 108) provides the following example from Inuktitut (Baffin Island Eskimo):

Tavva   -guuq   ikpiarju(q) -ku(t)-
Then (suddenly) they say work-bag   by

-Luni- tigualaka   -mi
while she swept up (in one motion) LOC *(from)*

-uk   takanu-   nga ikijaq-
POSS   *that one there below her way out*

tuq- Luni qaja(q)r- mun
she   while kayak   towards

'Then suddenly, she swept up her work-bag from its place below her as she went out towards the kayak'.

Other Inuit (Eskimo) languages and some American Indian languages are also polysynthetic.

Few languages fall clearly into one of these categories, and linguists working in this tradition have provided increasingly complex classification systems. For instance, Sapir (1921) provides three parameters – grammatical concepts, grammatical processes, and firmness of affixation – with multiple values for each. According to Horne (1966), this gives rise to 2,870 language types, that is, about half as many types as there are languages, and if typology aims to order linguistic variety, then the value of such a system may be questioned. In addition, it is often difficult to establish word and morpheme boundaries, and even to arrive at a satisfactory definition of either phenomenon (see MORPHOLOGY), and these difficulties cause severe practical difficulties for morphological typology (see Comrie, 1989, pp. 46–52, for a thorough discussion).

The Prague School linguists were primarily interested in typologizing languages on the basis of their phonology. Phonological typology is based on the different ways in which languages organize sounds into phonological systems and syllable structures (Robins, 1989, p. 370). Perhaps the best-known distinction here is that between tone languages and non-tonal languages. This distinction is drawn according to the function in the different languages of voice pitch: briefly, in **tone languages** pitch helps distinguish one word from another, while in non-tonal languages pitch does not have this function. Within tone languages, distinctions may be made between those whose tones are of contrasting levels and those in which rising and falling pitch is part of the tone system itself. Tone languages can also be typologized on the basis of the number of tones they contain and on the basis of the uses to which the tones are put (see further TONE LANGUAGES).

Languages also differ phonologically in terms of the kinds of syllable structure they permit. Every known language contains CV syllables (syllables composed of a consonant, C, followed by a vowel, V), but languages like English and German permit a high degree of consonant clustering at the beginning and end of syllables, whereas Fijian and Hawaiian do not. A **consonant cluster** consists of several consonants in succession, e.g. German *Angst*, English *scream*; the Danish versions of these two clusters come together in the compound, *angstskrig*, 'scream of fear', with six consonants in pronunciation, which is /aŋstskRɪ/.

Since the middle of the twentieth century, typological research has mainly centred on syntax and has been closely linked with the study of language universals (see LANGUAGE UNIVERSALS). Some language universals are features present in all or an overwhelming majority of languages. Other universals are implicational: they state that *if* feature *x* is present in a language, then (it is highly likely that) feature *y* will also be present in that language. The interplay with typology can be seen in the selection of the features in terms of which universals are

defined. For instance, many of Greenberg's (1966b) universals (see LANGUAGE UNIVERSALS) imply a typological analysis in terms of the order of subject (S), object (O), and verb (V).

S, O, and V are, properly speaking, clause or sentence constituents, but typology involving them is normally referred to as **word-order typology**. Word-order typology also includes studies of the order of words or constituents within the noun phrase and of whether a language has prepositions or postpositions (see below).

The notion of a **basic word order** in terms of S, O, and V is common to a large number of studies in grammatical language typology: languages are typologized on the basis of the order in which S, O, and V typically occur in the simple sentences of the language. The most common basic word orders are SVO, as in English and French, and SOV, as in Japanese and Turkish. German has SVO in main clauses and SOV in subordinate clauses, and Robins (1989) classes it as an SVO language. VSO, as in Welsh, is the next most common, but all of the six logically possible configurations, SOV, SVO, VSO, VOS, OVS, OSV, are, in fact, found: Malagasy (West Indonesian language of Malagasy, previously Madagascar) has VOS, and Hixkaryana (Carib language of Northern Brazil) has OVS. There are also languages, such as Dyirbal (Australian language of northeastern Queensland), that do not appear to have any basic word order. This, however, merely means that typology in terms of word order is limited to those languages that have a basic word order, just as tone-language typology is limited to tone languages.

The relative frequencies of the six possible orders is (Tomlin, 1986, p. 3) SOV = SVO > VSO > VOS = OVS > OSV. Tomlin establishes this relative frequency on the basis of data from 1,063 languages, and explains it on the basis of interaction among three principles: the Theme First Principle, the Verb–Object Bonding principle, and the Animated First Principle.

The **Theme First Principle (TFP)** says that thematic information – information which is particularly salient to the development of the discourse – is likely to come first in simple main clauses. The **Verb–Object Bonding (VOB)** principle says that in general the O of a transitive clause is more tightly bound to the V than to S. The **Animated First Principle (AFP)** states that in basic transitive clauses, the NP which is most animated will precede others. The more of these principles which a constituent order allows to be realized, the more frequent the order. The principles are explained as arising from the processes and limitations of human information-processing ability (compare LANGUAGE UNIVERSALS, p. 283).

Word order within the noun phrase concerns the relative order of adjective (A), noun (N), genitive (G), and relative clause (Rel). For A and N there are, obviously, two possible configurations, AN (English; Turkish) and NA (French; Welsh). Languages with basic order NA are more tolerant of exceptions (French: *le petit prince* 'the little prince' as opposed to *le tapis vert* 'the carpet green') than AN languages: in English, for instance, *the carpet green* is distinctly odd, and such constructions are only found in set expressions like *princess royal* and *court martial* and in some poetry (and even there they seem archaic).

There are three possible configurations for N and Rel. In English, for instance, N precedes Rel: *the potato that the man gave to the woman*, while in Turkish, Rel precedes N (Comrie, 1989, p. 90):

adam-ın	kadın-a	ver -diğ
man GEN	*woman* DAT	*give* NOM SUF

-i	patates
his	*potato*

'man's to the woman giving his potato', that is 'the that-the-man-gave-to-the-woman potato'.

The third possibility is that Rel is **circumnominal**, that is, it surrounds N. Comrie (1989, p. 145) gives the following example from Bambara (a member of the Mande branch of the Niger–Congo languages, spoken in Senegal, Mali, and Burkina Faso (Upper Volta)):

tyɛ̀	be	[n	ye	so min	ye]	dyɔ
man the	PRESENT	*I*	PAST	*house*	*see*	*build*

'The man is building the house that I saw.'

The part in square brackets is the relative clause in this construction, but it is a construction which can stand alone, in which case it would mean 'I saw the house'. So in relative clauses in Bambara, N is expressed in the relative clause in the usual form for a noun of that grammatical relation within a clause, and there is no expression of it in the main clause. Bambara has SOV basic order, and the relative clause functions as Object in the main clause: 'The man is the house that I saw building.' It should be noted that there are languages which may not have any construction which could be called a relative clause at all (see Comrie, 1989, p. 144).

For G and N there are again two possible orders, GN and NG. English uses both: *the man's son / the son of the man*. French uses NG and Turkish GN.

Adpositional word-order typology is concerned with whether a language uses mainly **prepositions** (Pr) or **postpositions** (Po). English uses Pr: *for the man*; whereas Turkish uses Po: *adam için* 'the man for'. Pr and Po are adpositions (Ap), Pr being a pre-N adposition and Po a post-N adposition, hence we can typologize languages as ApN (English) or NAp (Turkish). Estonian uses both orders and most Australian languages have neither Pr nor Po (Comrie, 1989, p. 91).

Word-order typology is considered particularly important because although they are logically independent of each other, word-order parameters such as those discussed above seem to correlate. For example, NAp appears to correlate with SOV, while ApN appears to correlate with VSO; ApN correlates with NG, NAp with GN; VSO correlates with NA; SOV + NG correlates with NA (pp. 92–3).

Grammatical typology also uses grammatical categories such as case, gender, number, and tense as bases for classification.

Over time, languages may change in type (Greenberg, 1974, p. 64). For instance, languages without nasalized vowels may acquire them in the following way (ibid., p. 66): 'A previously oral vowel becomes nondistinctively nasalized by a preceding or following nasal consonant. The nasal consonant, the former conditioning factor, is lost and the oral and nasal vowels are now in contrast.'

Another powerful demonstration of this change of typology over time is found in the phenomenon of the *Sprachbund*. When languages are in close geographical proximity, and their speakers interact freely with each other, it sometimes happens that even if the languages are not genetically related, they come to share more features with each other than they share with other members of their language family. The study of this phenomenon is known as **areal typology**, and a group of languages which have become similar because of geographical proximity is known as a ***Sprachbund*** or **language union**.

Comrie (1989, pp. 204–5) suggests that the initial impetus to areal typology arose from the discovery that Modern Greek and Albanian (separate branches of Indo-European), Bulgarian and Macedonian (Slavonic), Rumanian (Romance) and other languages all spoken in the Balkan area, have a number of features in common which they do not share with other languages to which they are more closely related genetically. All the languages are Indo-European, but they belong to different branches (see HISTORICAL LINGUISTICS, pp. 212–13), and the other languages in these branches do not exhibit the features which the Balkan *Sprachbund* exhibits. These include a wide range of shared lexical items, as one would expect of languages in close geographical proximity. But each language also possesses all or some of the following features: (1) syncretism of genitive and dative case, that is, the same form is used to indicate both the possessor and indirect object in noun phrases; (2) postposed articles, that is, the definite article follows the noun; and (3) the loss of the infinitive, that is, each language translates *Give me something to drink* with the structure 'give (to-)me that I-drink', in which the place of the infinitive is taken by a finite subordinate clause introduced by a conjunction:

Rumanian	*Bulgarian*
dă-mi să beau	daj mi da pija

Albanian	*Modern Greek*
a-më të pi	dós mu na pjó

(Comrie, 1989, p. 206)

As Comrie (ibid., p. 209) goes on to point out, the phenomenon of typological change raises the question whether there are any constraints on language change. In fact, research reveals that there are a number of such constraints which are statable in the form of implicational universals such as (ibid., p. 210), 'a language will borrow non-nouns only if it also borrows nouns', 'a language will borrow affixes only if it also borrows lexical items from the same source'.

Main centres for research in language typology include Stanford University, the University of Southern California, the Department of Linguistics of the University of Cologne, Germany (Universalenprojekt), and the Leningrad section of the Linguistics Institute of the Academy of Sciences of the USSR (Structural Typology Group).

It is usually languages as such which are typologized, but the word **typology** may also be applied to analyses of grammatical or other properties of languages, for example to Bloomfield's (1933, pp. 194–6) division of syntactic constructions into endocentric and exocentric types (Greenberg, 1974, p. 14). An **endocentric** construction is one which is of the same form class as one of its constituents; for instance, *poor John* is of the same class, noun phrase, as *John*. An **exocentric** construction is one which is not of the same form class as any of its constituents; for instance, *John ran* is neither an NP nor a verb phrase, but a sentence.

K.M.

SUGGESTIONS FOR FURTHER READING

Comrie, B. (1989), *Language Universals and Linguistic Typology: Syntax and Morphology*, 2nd edn, Oxford, Basil Blackwell.

Greenberg, J.H. (1974), *Language Typology: A Historical and Analytic Overview*, The Hague, Mouton.

Language universals

INTRODUCTION

The study of **language universals** is based on the premise that 'underlying the endless and fascinating idiosyncrasies of the world's languages there are uniformities of universal scope. Amid infinite diversity, all languages are, as it were, cut from the same pattern' (Greenberg *et al.*, 1966, p. xv). The theory of language universals specifies which properties are necessary to human languages, which are possible, but not necessary, and which are impossible, so that (Comrie, 1989, pp. 33–4) 'over all, the study of language universals aims to establish limits on variation within human language'. Since the study of linguistic typology (see LANGUAGE TYPOLOGY) is concerned with studying this variation, there is a strong link between the two disciplines. For example, the study of language universals can help set the parameters for typological research: if it is discovered that all languages have vowels (a language universal: see below), then it will not be fruitful to make the presence versus absence of vowels a basis for the typological classification of languages (Comrie, 1989, p. 38).

There are two main approaches to the study of language universals, one influenced by the work of Joseph Greenberg, the second by the work of Noam Chomsky (Comrie, 1989, p. 2) The two approaches differ quite radically in terms of their attitude to evidence for and explanation of universals, and since the Chomskian approach is the simplest in both respects, I shall discuss it first.

THE CHOMSKIAN APPROACH TO UNIVERSALS

Linguists influenced by the work of Noam Chomsky distinguish two kinds of universal, formal and substantive universals (Chomsky, 1965). Some of these are features of all languages, while others represent a set of features from which each language selects a subset. For example, Jakobson's distinctive-feature theory (see DISTINCTIVE FEATURES) provides a list of 15–20 features, for which it is claimed that (Comrie, 1989, p. 15):

> the phonological system of any arbitrary language will make use of no distinctive feature not contained in the list, although it is not necessary that any individual language should make use of the whole set (thus English does not make use of the feature Checked).

A **formal universal** is one which determines the form of the grammar – the components, rule types, and the principles of rule interaction. A **substantive universal** refers to the content of the rules such as the categories and bar levels of X-bar theory (see TRANSFORMATIONAL-GENERATIVE GRAMMAR) (Hawkins, 1988b, p. 6).

One of the first universals to be established within this tradition, namely the universal 'all languages are structure dependent', is based on (Cook, 1988, p. 2): 'the principle of **structure-dependency**, which asserts that knowledge of language relies on the structural relationships in the sentence rather than on the sequence of items'. It is obvious that English speakers' ability to form *yes/no* questions, for instance, does not depend merely on knowledge that a word appearing at a certain place in a declarative clause must be moved to the front to form the interrogative. To form the question, *Will the letter arrive tomorrow?*, for example, one needs to move the third word of the declarative, *The letter **will** arrive tomorrow*, while to form the question, *Is this a dagger I see before me?*, one needs to move the second word of the declarative, *This **is** a dagger I see before me*. What is crucial in question formation is a knowledge of syntactic categories: to be able to form English questions, it is necessary to recognize the class of auxiliary verbs, and to know that items of this class are put first in questions.

But even this knowledge is not sufficient to explain English speakers' ability to form questions involving relative clauses. In *The man who is tall is John*, the related question is formed by moving the second auxiliary, while in *John is the man who is tall*, the related question is formed by moving the first auxiliary. Knowing how to form questions in sentences with relative clauses involves knowing that it is the auxiliary in the main clause that has to be moved, and this involves a knowledge of structure. Similarly, in forming passives, one needs to move a phrase, not just a word in a particular place in the sequence, and this again implies a knowledge of structure, since without such knowledge the identification of phrases would be impossible (see further TRANSFORMATIONAL-GENERATIVE GRAMMAR).

Universals established as transformational-generative grammar evolved include Chomsky's (1981, 1982) figurationality parameters (see TRANSFORMATIONAL-GENERATIVE GRAMMAR), for instance, the **head parameter**, which specifies the order of elements in a language. Any phrase will contain one element which is 'essential'. This element is called the **head** of the phrase (Cook, 1988, p. 7). For instance, in the verb phrase, *liked him very much*, *liked* is the head. The head in English appears on the left of the rest of the phrase, while in Japanese, for instance, it appears on the right. The innate, universal head parameter specifies that there are just these two possibilities, and that a language chooses one consistently, that is, 'a language has the heads on the same side in all its phrases' (ibid., p. 9). Parameters reduce the variation between languages to just a few possibilities.

The Chomskian tradition establishes its universals on the basis of careful, detailed analysis of one or a small number of languages. The surface structure of any language is explained with reference to certain highly abstract features which are shared by all languages because they are innate in humans (compare RATIONALIST LINGUISTICS). These constitute the **universal grammar** (Cook, 1988, pp. 1–2): 'a set of principles that apply to all languages and parameters that vary within clearly defined limits from one language to another'. Exactly what these innate universal features are is determined by grammatical analysis, but innateness serves within this tradition as the explanation for all the universals it establishes.

Innateness is chosen as an explanation because Chomskians see the study of language as a means of exploring the human mind. They explore language as a phenomenon internal to speakers, rather than as a social phenomenon. Innateness is justified as an explanation for universals on the grounds that the evidence children have available through the language they hear around them is insufficient for them to develop the complex, abstract grammar which underlies any language.

The evidence provided is very largely positive evidence, that is, evidence about what *does* occur in the language, as opposed to evidence about what does not occur. But no amount of positive evidence can serve as evidence of what is not permissible. Yet children end up using the language correctly and creatively, that is, they produce not only sentences which they have heard before, but also new sentences which, once the acquisition process is complete, are invariably grammatical. If people were not innately structured to produce only grammatical sentences, they might produce new sentences which were ungrammatical, since they have no externally derived evidence that such sentences cannot occur.

Of course, children who are in the process of acquiring language produce many sentences which are incorrect. However, even children whose acquisition process is not yet completed produce hardly any which violate the principles of Universal Grammar (Cook, 1988, pp. 64–5). Yet most of these principles are too abstract for a small child to have learnt them even if its parents and others with whom the child interacts were conscious of the principles, which typically they are not, and had tried to teach them to the child. It is very unlikely indeed that anyone ever tries to teach small children Chomsky's (1981) Binding Principles (Cook, 1988, p. 61); indeed it is most unlikely that the majority of language users have any notion that these principles are in operation.

Since Universal Grammar has to account for the acquisition of any language, its principles tend to be very abstract. And while the fact of their existence is predicted by the theory (Hoekstra and Kooij, 1988), syntactic analysis is required to establish what the universals are, so that the nature or existence of any one particular universal may be questioned if the accuracy of the syntactic analysis from which it is derived is questioned. Universals may be discarded, and new universals proposed as syntactic analysis develops. The firmest evidence for a universal which this tradition is interested in establishing is that syntactic analysis has revealed that a principle underlies an aspect of grammar, and that this principle is not one which a child could discover from any data available to it. Such a principle must be innate: it must be part of the Universal Grammar.

GREENBERG'S APPROACH TO UNIVERSALS

The universals isolated in the Greenberg tradition tend to be less abstract than those of Universal Grammar (see the previous section), and they are established on the basis of data from 'a large and representative sample of world languages' (Greenberg et al., 1966, p. xvi). The ideal base for the study of language universals is all potential human languages. However, many extinct languages were not recorded, or not recorded in sufficient detail to provide usable data, and there is obviously no evidence available from any languages which might evolve in the future. Research must therefore be limited to the study of languages which are available to present observation, even though it is logically possible that these may turn out, at some distant point in the future when quite different languages may have evolved, not to be at all representative of all of the possible kinds of language.

But even within this limit, it quite impractical to investigate and work with every single one of the world's languages, since it is estimated that there are around 4,000 of these, so that research awaiting evidence from them all would be unlikely ever to get off the ground. Obviously, a selection of languages must be made, and it must be made in such a way that biasing is, as far as possible, avoided. In particular, it is necessary to ensure that the languages chosen represent a range of genetic language families (see HISTORICAL LINGUISTICS, pp. 212–16), since languages of the same family share a number of traits simply because these have been inherited from the parent language and *not* because the traits are universals.

Ideally, the sample should consist of one language from each of 478 **language groups** isolated by Bell (1978). Each group contains a set of genetically related languages which are separated from their common ancestor by 3,500 years. In practice, however, samples are usually smaller, and those languages which have not been adequately described and whose speakers are not easily available to researchers are generally seriously under-represented. Indo-European languages, for instance, tend to be over-represented, while the languages of New Guinea and Amazonia are usually missing. Bias can also arise if a sample contains many languages from one geographical area, even if these represent different groups, because languages in geographical proximity tend to influence each other over time. Finally, bias may arise if languages of the same type (see LANGUAGE TYPOLOGY) predominate in a sample (Comrie, 1989, pp. 10–12).

Greenberg (1966b) works with a sample of thirty languages: Basque, Serbian, Welsh, Norwegian, Modern Greek, Italian, Finnish (European), Yoruba, Nubian, Swahili, Fulani, Masai, Songhai, Berber (African), Turkish, Hebrew, Burushaski, Hindi, Kannada, Japanese, Thai, Burmese, Malay (Asian), Maori, Loritja (Oceanic), Maya, Zapotec, Quechua, Chibcha, and Guaraní (American Indian). He proposes forty-five universals of the following three kinds.

I *Word-order universals*
(S = Subject; V = Verb; O = Object)

1 In declarative sentences with nominal subject and object, the dominant order is almost always one in which the subject precedes the object.

2 In languages with prepositions, the genitive almost always follows the governing noun, while in languages with postpositions it almost always precedes (Norwegian has both genitive orders).

3 Languages with dominant VSO order are almost always prepositional.

4 With overwhelmingly greater than chance frequency, languages with normal SOV order are postpositional.

5 If a language has dominant SOV order and the genitive follows the governing noun, then the adjective likewise follows the noun.

6 All languages with dominant VSO order have SVO as an alternative or as the only alternative basic order.

7 If, in a language with dominant SOV order, there is no alternative basic order, or only OSV as the alternative, then all adverbial modifiers of the verb likewise precede the verb.

II *Syntactic universals*

8 When a *yes/no* question is differentiated from the corresponding assertion by an intonational pattern, the distinctive intonational features of these patterns are reckoned from the end of the sentence rather than from the beginning.

9 With much more than chance frequency, when question particles or affixes are specified in position by reference to the sentence as a whole, if initial, such elements are found in prepositional languages, and, if final, in postpositional.

10 Question particles or affixes, when specified in position by reference to a particular word in the sentence, almost always follow that word. Such particles do not occur in languages with dominant order VSO.

11 Inversion of statement order so that verb precedes subject occurs only in languages where the question word or phrase is normally initial. This same inversion occurs in *yes/no* questions only if it also occurs in interrogative-word questions.

12 If a language has dominant order VSO in declarative sentences, it always puts interrogative words or phrases first in interrogative-word questions; if it has dominant order SOV in declarative sentences, there is never such an invariant rule.

13 If the nominal object always precedes the verb, then verb forms subordinate to the main verb also precede it.

14 In conditional statements, the conditional clause precedes the conclusion as the normal order in all languages.

15 In expressions of volition and purpose, a subordinate verbal form always follows the main verb as the normal order except in those languages in which the nominal object always precedes the verb.

16 In languages with dominant order VSO, an inflected auxiliary always precedes the main verb. In languages with dominant order SOV, an inflected auxiliary always follows the main verb.

17 With overwhelmingly more than chance frequency, languages with dominant order VSO have the adjective after the noun.

18 When the descriptive adjective precedes the noun, then the demonstrative and the numeral, with overwhelmingly more than chance frequency, do likewise.

19 When the general rule is that the descriptive adjective follows, there may be a minority of adjectives which usually precede, but when the general rule is that descriptive adjectives precede, there are no exceptions.

20 When any or all of the items (demonstrative, numeral, and descriptive adjective) precede the noun, they are always found in that order. If they follow, the order is either the same or its exact opposite.

21 If some or all adverbs follow the adjective they modify, then the language is one in

which the qualifying adjective follows the noun and the verb precedes its nominal object as the dominant order.

22 If, in comparisons of superiority, the only order, or one of the alternative orders, is standard–marker–adjective, then the language is postpositional. With overwhelmingly more than chance frequency, if the only order is adjective–marker–standard, the language is prepositional.

23 If in apposition the proper noun usually precedes the common noun, then the language is one in which the governing noun precedes its dependent genitive. With much better than chance frequency, if the common noun usually precedes the proper noun, the dependent genitive precedes its governing noun.

24 If the relative expression precedes the noun either as the only construction or as an alternative construction, either the language is postpositional, or the adjective precedes the noun or both.

25 If the pronominal object follows the verb, so does the nominal object.

III Morphological universals

26 If a language has discontinuous affixes, it always has either prefixing or suffixing or both.

27 If a language is exclusively suffixing, it is postpositional; if it is exclusively prefixing, it is prepositional.

28 If both the derivation and inflection follow the root, the derivation is always between the root and the inflection.

29 If a language has inflection, it always has derivation.

30 If the verb has categories of person–number or if it has categories of gender, it always has tense–mode categories.

31 If either the subject or object noun agrees with the verb in gender, then the adjective always agrees with the noun in gender.

32 Whenever the verb agrees with a nominal subject or nominal object in gender, it also agrees in number.

33 When number agreement between the noun and verb is suspended and the rule is based on order, the case is always one in which the verb precedes and the verb is in the singular.

34 No language has a trial number unless it has a dual. No language has a dual unless it has a plural.

35 There is no language in which the plural does not have some non-zero allomorphs, whereas there are languages in which the singular is expressed only by zero. The dual and trial are almost never expressed only by zero.

36 If a language has the category of gender, it always has the category of number.

37 A language never has more gender categories in non-singular numbers than in the singular.

38 Where there is a case system, the only case which ever has zero allomorphs is the one which includes among its meanings that of the subject of the intransitive verb.

39 Where morphemes of both number and case are present and both follow or precede the noun base, the expression of number almost always comes between the noun base and the expression of case.

40 When the adjective follows the noun, the adjective expresses all the inflectional categories of the noun. In such cases the noun may lack overt expression of one or all of these categories.

41 If in a language the verb follows both the nominal subject and nominal object as the dominant order, the language almost always has a case system.

42 All languages have pronominal categories involving at least three persons and two numbers.

43 If a language has gender categories in the noun, it has gender categories in the pronoun.

44 If a language has gender distinctions in the first person, it always has gender distinctions in the second or third person, or in both.

45 If there are gender distinctions in the plural of the pronoun, there are some gender distinctions in the singular also.

Although some universals, such as 'all languages have oral vowels' are **non-implicational** – they specify that a certain property is found in all languages without making reference to any other properties of language – it is evident from Greenberg's list that many other universals are **implicational** – they relate the presence of one property to the presence of some other property in such a way that *if* one property is present, then the other must also be present. Since for any two properties, *p* and *q*, it is logically possible that both may be present, that *p* may be present while *q* is not, that neither may be present, and that *q* may be present while *p* is not, we can see that an implicational universal delimits the logically possible combinations of linguistic properties: they specify that it is not the case that *p* can be present while *q* is not. It is only when all the other three possibilities are in fact manifest in some language(s), that there is any point in making an implicational universal claim. For instance, where *p* is 'nasalized vowels' and *q* is 'oral vowels', the claim 'if *p* then *q*' is empty, because, since all languages have oral vowels, the case where neither *p* nor *q* are manifest does not obtain. Therefore, the non-implicational universal 'all languages have oral vowels' together with the statement 'nasalized vowels are possible' render the implicational universal superfluous (Comrie, 1989, pp. 17–18).

Greenberg's list reproduced above also illustrates another parameter, in addition to the implicational/non-implicational parameter, along which universals may be classified, namely the distinction between **absolute universals**, which are exceptionless, and **universal tendencies**, to which there are exceptions (Comrie, 1989, p. 19):

> This distinction is independent of that between implicational and non-implicational universals, giving over all a fourfold classification. There are absolute non-implicational universals, such as: all languages have vowels. There are absolute implicational universals, such as: if a language has first/second person reflexives, then it has third person reflexives. There are non-implicational tendencies, such as: nearly all languages have nasal consonants (although some Salishan languages have no nasal con-

sonants). Finally, there are implicational tendencies, such as: if a language has SOV basic word order, it will probably have postpositions (but Persian, for instance, is SOV with prepositions).

In practice, given the constraints on research discussed above, it is often not possible to establish for certain whether a universal is absolute or just a strong tendency (ibid., p. 20).

Hawkins (1988b, p. 5) defines a **distributional** or **frequency universal** as one which states that languages of one type are more frequent than languages of another type. Distributional universals include 'the more similar the position of syntactic heads across phrasal categories, the more languages there are' and 'languages without self-embedded relative clauses are more frequent than those with' (Hawkins, 1988b, p. 5).

Linguists working in the Greenbergian tradition allow for variation in the explanation of the existence of the universals which they isolate: it is considered possible that some universals may require one type of explanation, while others may require explanation of another kind. For instance, some universals, such as the fact that all languages have at least three persons and two numbers may be explained from the point of view of discourse pragmatics: they facilitate communication because they allow speakers to make referential distinctions which make communication more efficient (Hawkins, 1988b, p. 11). Comrie (1989, p. 28) proposes a similar explanation of the fact that the existence of first- or second-person reflexive forms in a language implies the existence of third-person reflexive forms:

> For each of the first and second persons, there is hardly ever ambiguity in a given context whether different instances of the corresponding pronoun are coreferential or not: in a given sentence, all instances of *I* are coreferential, as are usually all instances of *we* and all instances of *you*. In the third person, however, there is potentially a vast number of referents. Some languages say *I hit myself* and some say *I hit me*, but it is not possible to have both interpreted literally with a semantic difference

of coreference. But if a language has both *he hit himself* and *he hit him* as possible sentences, then a semantically important distinction of coreference versus non-coreference can be made. Thus reflexivity is simply more important in the third person than in the first or second persons, and this is reflected in the implicational universal.

Other universals may be explained as resulting from constraints which one part of grammar imposes on other parts, or from constraints imposed by the level of meaning on the level of form. Keenan (1979; see also 1987) argues for a **Meaning–Form Dependency Principle (MFDP)**, also known as the **Functional Dependency Principle**, which explains why, if in a language there is morphological agreement between, say, nouns and adjectives in, for instance, number and gender, it is always the adjective that agrees with the noun. He argues that this agreement restriction in the morphology arises from a semantic restriction which tends to cause any function category, such as adjective, to change its interpretation to accord with that of its argument, for instance a noun, while the interpretation of the noun is typically invariant with different modifying adjectives. For instance, *flat* has a different interpretation in *flat tyre*; *flat beer*; and *flat road*, whereas *road* has the same interpretation in *flat road*; *dusty road* and *windy road* (Hawkins, 1988b, pp. 8–9). The MFDP thus explains (p. 9) 'a strong form of internal consistency within the grammar: a dependency in form . . . mirrors a dependency in meaning. That is, a universal morphological dependency follows from a semantic dependency'.

Some language universals may be explained by reference to the **processing demands** placed on language users by, for instance, memory constraints and by the relative ease or difficulty involved in processing certain structures in comprehension and production. For example, it is known that it is more difficult to process **centre-embedded relative clauses** (that is, relative clauses which come in the middle of the sentence) than it is to process **left-peripheral relative clauses** (relative clauses which come at the beginning of the sentence) or **right-peripheral relative clauses**

(relative clauses which come at the end of the sentence). This may be because centre embedding requires the processor to interrupt the processing of the main clause in order to process the embedded clause. Thus in *The man [that the boy kicked] ran away*, one has to interrupt the processing of *The man ran away* to process *that the boy kicked*. This becomes increasingly difficult if more than one clause is embedded. Consider: *The man [that the boy [that the dog [that the cat [that the mouse hated] scratched] bit] kicked] ran away.*

Languages tend to avoid centre embedding, even though it is, as we have seen, a possible construction in English. But the general tendency to avoid it, and the difficulty in processing it when it does occur might motivate the grammatical phenomenon of word correlation between verb position and relative-clause position (Comrie, 1989, p. 27):

> If a SOV language had postnominal relative clauses, then every single relative clause would be centre embedded, occurring between its head noun and the verb. . . . Likewise, if a VSO language had prenominal relative clauses, then every single relative clause would be centre-embedded. The attested correlation means that at least some noun phrases are left-peripheral (in SOV languages) or right peripheral (in VSO languages).

Certain properties of the human perceptual and cognitive apparatus are also relevant to the discussion of universals (Hawkins, 1988b, p. 15). For instance, Berlin and Kay (1969) have shown that if a language has a colour system at all, it will distinguish at least black and white. If it has three colours, the third will be red; if it has four, then the fourth will be either green or yellow; the fifth will be the other of green or yellow, the sixth will be blue, and the seventh brown. Kay and McDaniel (1978) point out that this universal feature can be explained by reference to the neural anatomy of the colour vision of humans.

As Hawkins (1988, p. 4) and Comrie (1989, p. 23) both point out, there is no reason why one should not embrace both the Chomskian and the Greenbergian approach and work toward a greater degree of precision in the kinds of explanation offered within each, since it is likely that natural languages are constrained by all of the phenomena mentioned. Each kind of explanation is likely to be able to provide elements which are necessary in a theory of universals, but it is unlikely that any one alone can produce a sufficient theory.

K.M.

SUGGESTIONS FOR FURTHER READING

Comrie, B. (1989), *Language Universals and Linguistic Typology: Syntax and Morphology*, 2nd edn, Oxford, Basil Blackwell.

Lexical-functional grammar

Lexical-functional Grammar (LFG) is a non-transformational, generative grammar developed by Joan Bresnan and Ronald Kaplan in the late 1970s (Bresnan, 1978, 1982; Bresnan and Kaplan, 1982; Kaplan and Bresnan, 1982). The main aim of LFGrammarians is to develop a grammar which does not conflict with the results of psycholinguistic research in language acquisition and processing (see PSYCHOLINGUISTICS), or with research on language in AI (see ARTIFICIAL INTELLIGENCE).

According to Chomsky's (1965) **competence hypothesis**, a model of language use will incorporate a generative grammar which expresses the users' knowledge of the language (p. 9). A grammar which expresses the users' knowledge of the language is said to be **psychologically real** or to have **psychological reality**. There can obviously be no doubt that language users have knowledge of the language they are using, but by the early 1970s it was becoming clear that transformational-generative grammars (see TRANSFORMATIONAL-GENERATIVE GRAMMAR) could not be successfully incorporated in psycholinguistic models of language comprehension and production (Fodor *et al.*, 1974; Levelt, 1974), that is, they might not be psychologically real.

Chomsky's response to challenges to the psychological reality of his evolving model of grammar has been to narrow down the notion of competence and to dismiss any discrepancies between his model of competence and psycholinguists' models of the knowledge speakers require to process language, as mere **performance factors**, factors which are only relevant to individual, here-and-now instances of actual communication. He holds such performance factors irrelevant to linguistic theory (Horrocks, 1987, pp. 225–7). In this way, the theory is protected, but the degree of overlap with evidence produced within other disciplines which study language is severely curtailed.

An alternative strategy when faced with evidence which runs counter to a theory is to consider aspects of the theory disproved by the evidence and to try to develop a new or adjusted theory which can account for the new evidence. Bresnan (1978) adopts this strategy, suggesting that a transformational characterization of linguistic knowledge might be wrong and that a competence grammar with an expanded lexical component and a contracted syntactic component might be a more promising candidate for incorporation in psycholinguistic theory. At around the same time, studies by Wanner and Maratsos (1978) and Kaplan (1972) showed that a competence grammar based on Augmented Transition Network grammars (ATN) see (AUGMENTED TRANSITION NETWORK GRAMMAR) could be computationally implemented and used to generate detailed and experimentally testable predictions (Bresnan and Kaplan, 1982, p. xx).

Proponents of LFG consider theoretical protectionism in the face of counterevidence unfortunate, because they think that the competence hypothesis requires linguists to explain how their formal models relate to the cognitive processes that derive and interpret them in actual language use, and because use must be part of the evidence for competence (Bresnan and Kaplan, 1982, pp. xxiii–xxiv):

> In attributing psychological reality to a grammar . . . we require more than that it provide us with a description of the abstract structure of the linguistic knowledge domain; we require evidence that the grammar corresponds to the speaker's *internal* description of that domain. Since we cannot directly observe this 'internal grammar', we must infer its properties indirectly from the evidence available to us (such as linguistic judgements, performance of verbal tasks in controlled experimental conditions, observation of the linguistic development of children, and the like). The data of linguistics are no more or less privileged for this inquiry than any other data.

Transformations presented a major difficulty for the enterprise of relating linguistic and psycholinguistic research, because if a theory incorporating transformations is to be seen as a model of speech processing, then difficulty in processing ought to increase in tandem with increase in the number of transformations involved in the derivation of a sentence. However, there is no evidence to support this **derivational theory of complexity** (Fodor *et al.*, 1974).

A major motivation for the incorporation of transformations was their success in showing systematic relationships between sentence types, such as actives and passives, without redundancy in the lexicon. The transformational rule for passivization moves the NP following V to the position in front of V, so that *Mary kissed John* becomes *John was kissed by Mary* (for a fuller statement see TRANSFORMATIONAL-GENERATIVE GRAMMAR). Without such a rule, it was held, it would be necessary to have two entries for *kiss* in the lexicon, one with an AGENT SUBJECT for active voice, and one with a THEME SUBJECT for the passive form.

In LFG, however, the lexicon is enriched so that its entries represent semantic predicate-argument structures independently of phrase-structure forms, while lexical rules capture redundancy. The **predicate-argument structure** shows how many arguments the predicate takes (see FORMAL LOGIC AND MODAL LOGIC) and their thematic roles. **Thematic roles** are 'abstractions over the finer-grained semantic structures of verbs' (Bresnan and Kanerva, 1989, p. 24) (compare FUNCTIONAL GRAMMAR). The entries for *kiss* as it is used in the two sentences about John and Mary express that in one the subject is the agent and the object is the patient, while in the other the subject is the patient and the *by*-object ($OBL(ique)_{AG(ent)}$) is the agent:

(1) kiss: kiss $\langle$ (SUBJ)   (OBJ) $\rangle$
                     AGENT   PATIENT

(2) kissed: kiss $\langle$ (OBL_{AG})   (SUBJ) $\rangle$
                     AGENT   PATIENT

The two lexical entries have the same predicate argument structure: kiss < AGENT PATIENT > , but differ in the grammatical functions which express the agent and patient arguments. The grammatical functions are held to be universal, but their phrase-structure realizations vary from language to language.

In order to capture the systematic relationship between the two lexical entries a lexical rule is proposed which changes SUBJ to an optional OBL_{AG} and OBJ to SUBJ:

(3) (SUBJ)→(OBL_{AG})/∅
     (OBJ)→(SUBJ)

For other languages there would be an identical

rule, except that the grammatical function names might be different (Bresnan and Kaplan, 1982, pp. xxv–xxvi).

The descriptive power of this lexical rule equals that of the passive transformation of Chomsky's (1965) standard theory and move alpha of his government–binding theory (1981). Both versions of Chomsky's theory (see TRANSFORMATIONAL-GENERATIVE GRAMMAR) represent both predicate-argument structures and the surface forms of sentences as syntactic phrase structures, so that the mapping between semantic arguments and surface forms must be expressed through operations on phrase structures. As (1) and (2) above show, LFG does not posit a one-to-one correspondence between semantic predicate-argument structure and grammatical functions (Chomsky's theta criterion: see TRANSFORMATIONAL-GENERATIVE GRAMMAR), and grammatical functions are not considered reducible to deep phrase-structure configurations. Rather, the phrase structure categories are considered to be universal, functional primitives bearing many-to-many relationships – and different relationships within different languages – to structural configurations. However, each mapping from predicate argument to grammatical function must assign a unique function to each predicate argument, and a unique predicate argument to each function which is associated with a predicate argument (some functions are not associated with a predicate argument; for example, an idiomatic object such as *tabs* in *keep tabs on* is a grammatical object which does not correspond to an argument in predicate–argument structure – see Bresnan, 1982, p. 46); this condition is called the **function–argument biuniqueness condition** (Bresnan, 1982, p. 5).

Since LFG does not require phrase-structure representations of predicate-argument relations, the structural component of the grammar is very simple. The entire transformational derivation is replaced by a single level of phrase structure which represents the surface form of a language. This is called the **constituent structure (c-structure)**. The sentence *Mary kissed John* has the c-structure:

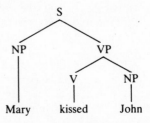

The c-structure is related to thematic-role structure by correlations between the grammatical functions associated with c-structure and the grammatical functions that are assigned to predicate-argument structure. Only lexical rules can alter the function–argument associations; syntactic rules must preserve them. Since active and passive verbs induce different grammatical relations, they must have different lexical entries. The requirement that syntactic rules preserve function–argument associations is called the **principle of direct syntactic encoding**. The correlations between c-structure grammatical functions and the grammatical functions assigned to predicate-argument structures are formally represented in **functional structures (f-structures)**. The f-structure for the c-structure given above is:

$$
\begin{bmatrix}
\text{SUBJ} & = & [\text{PRED} & = & \text{`MARY'}] \\
\text{TENSE} & = & \text{PAST} \\
\text{PRED} & = & \text{`KISS}\langle(\text{SUBJ})(\text{OBJ})\rangle \\
\text{OBJ} & = & [\text{PRED} & = & \text{`JOHN'}]
\end{bmatrix}
$$

F-structures are semantically interpreted while c-structures are phonologically interpreted. Because the grammatical relations of the predicates have already been lexically encoded, it is very easy to interpret f-structures. F-structures represent grammatical relations in a universal format which is independent of differences in surface form (Bresnan and Kaplan, 1982, pp. xxvi–xxix. So (Bresnan, 1982, p. 16):

in the lexical theory of passivization, grammatical functions are universal primitives which must be both lexically and syntactically encoded in each language. The lexical encodings map the grammatical functions onto thematic roles, or semantic predicate arguments, while the syntactic encodings map the grammatical functions onto surface syntactic and morphological structures. By formulating Passivization as a rule that changes the lexical encoding of universal grammatical functions, the lexical theory explains both its universal semantic effects . . . and its variable syntactic manifestations. . . . For these reasons, the lexical theory provides a more explanatory account of linguistic universals than structuralist theories such as transformational grammar.

Horrocks (1987, p. 243) demonstrates how LFG handles **nominalization**. In the sentence *The cat assaulted the mouse*, *assault* is a verb denoting a two-place predicate with agent and patient arguments assigned the grammatical roles, subject and object:

assault, V, 'ASSAULT ⟨(SUBJ) (OBJ)⟩'
AGENT   PATIENT

However, *assault* can also be used in noun phrases like *the cat's assault on the mouse*. The noun phrase has the same predicate argument structure as the sentence in which *assault* is a verb, a fact which is captured in the lexical entry for *assault* as a noun. Its arguments' grammatical roles differ, however (ibid.):

assault, N, 'ASSAULT⟨(SUBJ) (ON-OBJ)⟩'
AGENT   PATIENT

Nominalization is very common, and it is captured in the redundancy rule (ibid.):

derived nominalization: (OBJ)→(OF-OBJ)

The rule represents the most common form of nominalization in English, the form employing the preposition *of*. The lexical entry for *assault* would have to show that *on*, rather than *of*, is relevant to it. In general, exceptions to redundancy rules are dealt with in the relevant lexical entries. Lexical entries list only those syntactic functions which are peculiar to a particular lexical item and which ensure that sentences containing the item are well formed (grammatical) and semantically interpretable (meaningful).

Syntactic functions are classified according to the features $[\pm r]$ (thematically unrestricted or not) and $[\pm o]$ (objective or not) (Bresnan and Kanerva 1989, p. 24):

$$\begin{bmatrix} -r \\ -o \end{bmatrix} \text{SUBJ} \qquad \begin{bmatrix} +r \\ -o \end{bmatrix} \text{OBL}_\theta$$

$$\begin{bmatrix} -r \\ +o \end{bmatrix} \text{OBJ} \qquad \begin{bmatrix} +r \\ +o \end{bmatrix} \text{OBJ}_\theta$$

Thematically restricted functions are those whose thematic roles are fixed, such as oblique arguments and secondary objects. Subject and object, on the other hand, may correspond to virtually any thematic role, or they may be non-thematic. The $[o]$ feature takes account of the fact that there are certain object-like functions (adjuncts) that appear as arguments of transitive categories of predicators (verbs and prepositions) but not of the intransitive categories noun and adjective. OBL_θ is an abbreviation which covers multiple oblique functions, one for each instance of thematic role θ: OBL_{ao}, $\text{OBL}_{instr(ument)}$, and so on. The four-way classification provides the following 'natural classes' of syntactic functions (ibid., p. 25):

$[-r] = \text{SUBJ, OBJ}$ $[-o] = \text{SUBJ, OBL}_\theta$
$[+r] = \text{OBJ}_\theta \text{ OBL}_\theta$ $[+o] = \text{OBJ, OBJ}_\theta$

C-structures are derived by phrase-structure rules. Kaplan and Bresnan (1982, p. 176) provide the example in Figure 1 of the rewriting rules and the C-structure assigned by them to the sentence *A girl handed the baby a toy*. Its f-structure shows

S → NP VP
NP → DET N
VP → V NP NP

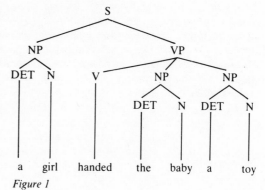

Figure 1

that *a girl* is the grammatical subject (SUBJ) of the sentence; *handed* denotes the semantic predicate (PRED); *the baby* is the grammatical object (OBJ); and *a toy* is the second grammatical object (OBJ2). This information is presented as a set of ordered pairs consisting of an **attribute**, the name of a grammatical function or feature (SUBJ, OBJ, NUMber, CASE, etc.), and the **value** of that attribute for this sentence (compare FUNCTIONAL UNIFICATION GRAMMAR). The values are of three primitive types and one non-primitive type (from Kaplan and Bresnan, 1982, p. 177):

Primitive
types:　(i) Simple symbols
　　　　(ii) Semantic forms that govern the process of semantic interpretation
　　　　(iii) Subsidiary f-structures, sets of ordered pairs representing complexes of internal functions
Non-
primitive: (iv) Sets of symbols, semantic forms, or f-structures.

The f-structure for the sentence we are working with is as follows, with TENSE having the simple symbol ((i) above) value PAST, and with type (iii) above in inner square brackets. The values of the PRED attribute are semantic forms ((ii) above). Semantic forms usually arise in the lexicon, in which case they are also known as **lexical forms**. Less commonly, semantic forms are produced by syntactic rules, for instance to represent unexpressed pronouns. Attributes are on the left and values are on the right (ibid.):

$$
\begin{bmatrix}
\text{SUBJ} & = & \begin{bmatrix} \text{SPEC} & = & \text{A} \\ \text{NUM} & = & \text{SG} \\ \text{PRED} & = & \text{`GIRL'} \end{bmatrix} \\
\text{TENSE} & = & \text{PAST} \\
\text{PRED} & = & \text{`HAND } \langle (\uparrow\text{SUBJ}) (\uparrow\text{OBJ2}) (\uparrow\text{OBJ}) \rangle \\
\text{OBJ} & = & \begin{bmatrix} \text{SPEC} & = & \text{THE} \\ \text{NUM} & = & \text{SG} \\ \text{PRED} & = & \text{`BABY'} \end{bmatrix} \\
\text{OBJ2} & = & \begin{bmatrix} \text{SPEC} & = & \text{A} \\ \text{NUM} & = & \text{SG} \\ \text{PRED} & = & \text{`TOY'} \end{bmatrix}
\end{bmatrix}
$$

The c-structures which are generated by the context-free c-structure grammar are augmented to produce a set of statements specifying various properties of the string's f-structure. Such a set is called the string's **functional description (f-description)**, and it serves as an intermediary between c-structure and f-structure. The statements in an f-description are derived from functional specifications associated with particular elements on the right-hand sides of c-structure rules and with particular categories in lexical entries.

The specifications consist of **templates** or **statement schemata**, which have the form of the statements to be derived from them except that they contain metavariables instead of f-structure variables. The metavariables are of two kinds: ↑ ↓ and ‖ ‖. These two types are associated with two types of grammatically significant tree relations: immediate domination and bounded domination (Kaplan and Bresnan, 1982, pp. 183–4). Here we shall deal only with immediate domination. The augmented rewriting rules are (ibid., p. 184):

S ⟶ NP   VP
      (↑SUBJ) = ↓   ↑ = ↓

NP ⟶ DET N

VP ⟶ V   NP   NP
              (↑OBJ) = ↓   (↑OBJ2) = ↓

The basic principle of these rules is that a function-assigning equation, such as (↑ OBJ) = ↓, should be associated with a non-head maximal projection, whereas the equation ↑ = ↓ should be assigned elsewhere. Each equation of the form (↑ G(rammatical) F(unction)) = ↓ is to be read 'my mother's functional structure's GF is equivalent to my functional structure', while each equation of the form ↑ = ↓ is to be read 'my mother's functional structure is equivalent to my functional structure' (Horrocks, 1987, p. 250), where a **mother** is the node in a tree that immediately dominates the node in question (called a **daughter**) (see TRANSFORMATIONAL-GENERATIVE GRAMMAR). S is the mother of NP and VP. The annotation to NP says that the subject of the

functional structure of the sentence is the same as the functional structure of the NP, i.e. the NP is the subject of the sentence, and the functional information associated with its constituents is the value of the SUBJ function in functional structure. The annotation to VP says that the functional structure of the sentence is the same as the functional structure of the VP. VP is the mother of V, so the annotation to V says that the functional structure of VP is the same as V's functional structure. Ultimately, therefore, the functional structure of the whole sentence is the same as the functional structure of the verb (Horrocks, 1987, p. 248).

The syntactic features and semantic content of lexical items are determined by schemata in lexical entries. The lexical entries for the vocabulary in our sentence are (Kaplan and Bresnan, 1982, p. 185):

a: DET,   (↑SPEC) = A
                 (↑NUM) = SG

girl: N,   (↑NUM) = SG
                 (↑PRED) = 'GIRL'

handed: V,   (↑TENSE) = PAST
                 (↑PRED) = 'HAND <
                 (↑SUBJ) (↑OBJ2) (↑OBJ)>'

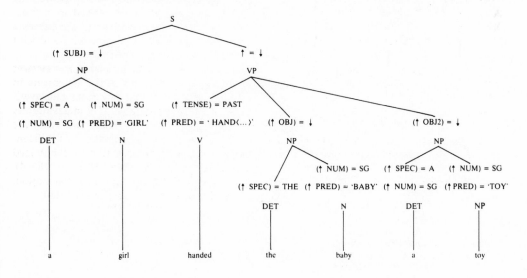

Figure 2

the: DET,   (↑SPEC) = THE
baby: N,   (↑NUM) = SG
                 (↑PRED) = 'BABY'
toy: N,   (↑NUM) = SG
                 (↑PRED) = 'TOY'

The rewriting rules together with the functional information provided in these lexical entries will assign the f-description in Figure 2 to the sentence (p. 186).

An f-description implies that certain relationships hold among the properties of the f-structure of the string in question, but some of these implications may not be fulfilled. For instance, an f-description may stipulate two distinct values for an attribute, or it may imply that an attribute name is an f-structure or a semantic form instead of a symbol. In such cases, a string will be ungrammatical, even if it has a well-formed c-structure (Kaplan and Bresnan, 1982, pp. 189–90). But a grammatical sentence must be assigned both a well-formed c-structure and a well-formed f-structure (Horrocks, 1987, p. 251), so the **functional well-formedness condition** allows for many types of ungrammaticality

(Kaplan and Bresnan, 1982, p. 190).

There are three conditions on functional well-formedness: uniqueness, completeness, and coherence. The **uniqueness** condition specifies that any given c-structure configuration or lexical item is assigned a unique value. It would be violated by strings like *The boys sings* and * *He will must leave*. The **completeness** condition specifies that the clause must contain a grammatical argument for each grammatical function assigned to an argument of the PRED of the clause. It would be violated by a string like *Fred hit*. The **coherence** condition specifies that every meaningful grammatical argument must occur in a clause whose PRED has a corresponding grammatical function assigned to one of its arguments. It would be violated by strings like *Sally hit Bill Fred* and *John jumped that the earth was flat*.

LFG can be presented schematically as in Figure 3 (Horrocks, 1987, p. 301). Pinker (1982) refers to a number of studies on child language acquisition which suggest that the rules which allow predicates to be combined with other predicates are stored with the individual pre-

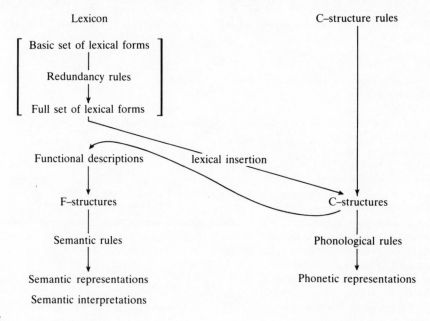

Figure 3

dicates, as presented in LFG. He proposes an acquisition model based on the assumption that the child is equipped to acquire LFG. Ford *et al.* (1982) show how syntactic closure phenomena are explained within LFG, and Ford (1982) produces findings which suggest that sentence production proceeds in successive stages during each of which a unit corresponding to a basic clause is constructed and then mapped onto the series of words which is uttered. The representations of meaningful relations provided in LFG are consistent with this suggestion.

K.M.

SUGGESTIONS FOR FURTHER READING

Bresnan, J.W. (ed.) (1982), *The Mental Representation of Grammatical Relations*, Cambridge, MA, and London, MIT Press, (particularly ch. 4 (Kaplan and Bresnan, 1982)).

Bresnan, J. and Kanerva, J.M. (1989), 'Locative inversion in Chichewa: a case study of factorization in grammar', *Linguistic Inquiry*, 20(1): 1–50.

Horrocks, G. (1987), *Generative Grammar*, London and New York, Longman.

Neidle, C. (1988), *The Role of Case in Russian Syntax*, Dordrecht, Kluwer (Appendix III).

Sells, P. (1985), *Lectures on Contemporary Syntactic Theories: An Introduction to Government–Binding Theory, Generalized Phrase Structure Grammar and Lexical-Functional Grammar*, Center for the Study of Language and Information, Stanford University, University of Chicago Press.

Lexicography

WHAT IS A DICTIONARY?

Lexicographers produce works of several types, e.g. **dictionaries**, **thesauruses**, and **glossaries**, but this article deals with their most typical product: dictionaries. A **lexicographic dictionary** is one which provides **lexically relevant information**, e.g. pronunciation and meaning, about **lexically relevant units**, e.g. words. These lexically relevant units are displayed in a **macrostructure** that is a succession of independent articles, **entries**, so ordered that any article may be found through an explicitly statable search procedure, an **algorithm**. The typical **dictionary algorithm**, alphabetical order, is based on the written form of the lexically relevant units rather than on their meaning, and the typical dictionary entry is **semasiological**, that is, going from name to notion. By contrast, the typical thesaurus entry is **onomasiological**, that is, going from notion to name.

LEXICALLY RELEVANT UNITS IN DICTIONARIES

The best-known type of lexically relevant unit is the lexical unit. A **lexical unit** is a constituent unit of the **lexical system**, the **vocabulary**, of a language; and the best-known type of lexical unit is the **word** (see MORPHOLOGY). A lexical unit, a **lexeme**, is a set of units of form, **morphemes**, that represents a set of units of content, **sememes**. The morphemic representation of a lexical unit is realized in writing by one or more sets of **graphical units** or **graphemes**, such as letters, and in speech by one or more sets of **phonological units** or **phonemes** (see PHONEMICS). The relation between form and content can best be understood as a **correspondence** or **mapping**. Table 1 shows what mappings can occur.

As shown in Table 1, *encyclop(a)edia* and *'controversy/con'troversy* are one lexical unit

Table 1 Form–content mappings

Mapping	Form	Content	Dictionary entries	Lexical units
One–one	*penicillin*/'peni'silin/	'drug x'	1	1
	encyclopaedia, encyclopedia	'reference book'	1	1
	controversy/'kontrəvəːsi, kən'trovəsi/	'dispute'	1	1
One–many	*crane*/'krein/	{ 'bird x' 'machine x'	1	1
	bank/'baŋk/	{ 'shore' 'financial institution' 'deposit or keep (money) in a bank	2 or 3	3
Many–one	*furze*/'fəːz/ *gorse*/'gɔːs/	'plant x'	2	2
Many–many	*toilet*/toilit/ *loo*/'luː/ *lavatory*/'lɑvatəri/	{ 'appliance x' 'site of appliance x'	3	6

apiece despite the variability of their morphemic representations in writing or in speech. In most dictionaries there would be a single entry for *controversy*, with two British English pronunciations, and a single entry for *encyclopaedia, encyclopedia*, here with two alphabetically adjacent spellings.

Since the macrostructure of dictionaries is based on the form of their lexically relevant units, most dictionaries would have a single entry each for *penicillin*, with one 'sense', and for the noun *crane*, with two 'senses'. About *bank*, however, dictionaries differ. Almost all would have separate entries for the **homographs** (see SEMANTICS) ¹*bank* 'shore' and ²*bank* 'financial institution' because of their different origins or **etymologies**: ¹*bank* came into Middle English from Scandinavian, while ²*bank* derives from French or Italian. As for the verb *bank*, some dictionaries would make it part of the entry for ²*bank* on etymological grounds; other dictionaries would make it yet a third homograph: ³*bank*.

Thus in most dictionaries today, the mapping of entries or articles onto lexically relevant units is usually either one–one, i.e. one entry to one unit as in the case of *penicillin, encyclop(a)edia, controversy, furze, gorse*, ¹*bank*, ²*bank*, ³*bank*, or one–many, i.e. one entry to many units, as in the case of *crane, lavatory, loo, toilet*. A many–one mapping would be exemplified by separate entries for *encyclopaedia* and *encyclopedia*. So most dictionaries are willing to bring together in a single entry a set of lexical units that differ in meaning but have a common etymology and at least one common morphemic representation, especially when their syntactic use, shown by their part of speech (see TRADITIONAL GRAMMAR), is the same.

However, certain modern French dictionaries, notably the Larousse *Dictionnaire du français contemporain* (*DFC*) and *Lexis*, impose additional restrictions on their entries. Each entry must have a single set of inflections and a single set of derivatives. A dictionary that applied this principle to English would have to make two homographs of the verb *shine:* ¹*shine* (*shined*) and ²*shine* (*shone*), and two homographs of the adjective *lame*, of which ¹*lame* 'crippled' would have the derivative *lameness* and ²*lame* 'inadequate' would have the derivatives *lameness* and *lamely*.

The lexical units discussed so far have had the form of single words. However, dictionaries usually enter other types of lexical unit as well. These include the following:

1 Units 'below' the word: **bound morphemes** that help to form inflections, derivatives, and compounds: *pre-, -ing, -ly, -ness, Eur-, -o-*.

2 units 'above' the word, such as:

   (a) units consisting of parts of more than one word, i.e., **blends** and **initialisms** like *smog* (*smoke* plus *fog*), *VIP, NATO*;

   (b) units including more than one complete word, i.e., **compounds** and **idioms** like *blackbird, bank on, give up, night owl, hammer and tongs, at all, kick the bucket.* For such **multiword combinations** to be considered true **multiword lexical units** the convention is that their meanings should be more than the sum of the meanings of their components. Thus *night owl* is a lexical unit but *nocturnal owl* is not, and *kick the bucket* is a lexical unit when it means 'die' but not when it means 'strike the pail with one's foot'.

An important class of lexical units, some single-word, some multiword, is the class of **proper names**, whether of real entities such as *Atlanta, Aristotle, Hood, Thomas*, or of fictional entities, such as *Atlantis, Ajax, Robin Hood*. It can be argued that proper names, though they are lexical units, are lexical units of no language in particular, or of all languages. However, the same argument could be advanced with respect to many technical terms like *penicillin*.

Many dictionaries, e.g. monolingual dictionaries for native speakers, strive to limit their entries to lexical units, including or excluding the proper names of real entities. Other dictionaries, e.g. monolingual learners' dictionaries and bilingual dictionaries, enter lexically relevant units that are not lexical units. Thus a dictionary might enter **routine formulas** like *Many happy returns!* because their use is pragmatically restricted. An English–French dictionary might enter *rural policeman*, which is not a lexical unit of English, because its French translation, *garde champêtre*, is a lexical unit of French. Similarly, it might enter the phrase *beat a drum*, which is not a lexical unit of English, in order to show that its French translation *battre du tambour*, though not itself a lexical unit of French, is nevertheless not a word-for-word equivalent of its English counterpart either – *a* in English would be *une* or *un* in French.

ORGANIZATION OF THE MACRO-STRUCTURE

For anyone consulting or producing a dictionary, there are three questions immediately relevant to its macrostructure: (1) Is the macrostructure single or multiple? (2) Which units are main entries and which are subentries? (3) What is the ordering of graphically similar units (**homologues**) and in particular graphically identical units (**homographs**)?

1 A dictionary may display all its lexically relevant units in a single A–Z list; alternatively, it may relegate certain types of unit (e.g. abbreviations, 'real' proper names) to appendices.

2 Dictionaries differ greatly in their main-entry policies. But here is a list of types of lexical unit going from those most likely to be main entries to those most likely to be subentries under one of their components: single morphemes (*furze, pre-*); blends (*smog*) and initialisms (*VIP, NATO*); noun compounds **written solid**, i.e. without a space between the parts of the compound (*blackbird*); noun compounds **written open**, i.e. with a space between the parts of the compound (*night owl, hammer and sickle*); verb compounds (phrasal verbs like *give up*); non-verb compounds and idioms (*at all, hammer and tongs, in front of*); verb idioms (*kick the bucket*). In general, English-language dictionaries have a far higher proportion of main entries than dictionaries of other languages.

One important class of possible subentries is derivatives whose meaning is that of the sum of their parts, such as *lameness* from *lame* and *pre-war* from *war*. By convention, such derivatives, unlike *nocturnal owl*, are regarded as lexical units despite their **semantic transparency**, that is, in spite of the fact that their meaning is easily understood on the basis of the meanings of the parts of which they are composed. Large dictionaries may make them main entries; many smaller dictionaries make them subentries to save space. However, such subentries are presented without explicit explanation of their meaning. Those formed by suffixation (*lameness*) are entered under their source (*lame*) as so-called **undefined run-ons**; those formed by prefixation (*pre-war*) are in English-language dictionaries typically listed in alphabetical order under the prefix, e.g. *pre-*; but in some dictionaries of other languages, e.g. those, like the Larousse *DFC* and *Lexis*, that homograph by derivational families, they appear out of alphabetical order under their sources, with cross-references to them from their proper alphabetical position in the macrostructure.

3 Graphically identical homologues (homographs, like ¹*bank n*, ²*bank n*, ³*bank v*) may be ordered historically – older before newer; by perceived frequency – more frequent before less frequent; or even by the alphabetical order of their part of speech – adjective before noun before verb. For graphically similar homologues, a variety of related algorithms may be used, such as lower-case before capital (*creole, Creole*), solid before spaced (*rundown, run down*), apostrophe before hyphen(s) (*o', -o-*) – or any of these rules may be reversed!

LEXICALLY RELEVANT INFORMATION

Dictionaries provide any or all of the following types of lexically relevant information about the lexically relevant units they enter:

1 Information about the etymology, or origin, of the unit.
2 Information about the form of the unit, including spelling(s) and pronunciation(s).
3 Syntactic categorization and subcategorization. In the first instance this information is given by a part-of-speech label (*noun, verb* etc.), but subcategorization can be supplied to any **delicacy** desired; that is, in finer and finer detail. Thus a lexical unit represented by the word-form *tell* may be categorized as *verb, verb transitive* (***tell** the truth*), or *verb ditransitive* (***tell** them the truth*).

4 Inflections. Thus, the entry for *tell* will show that its past and past participle are *told*.
5 Derivatives, especially if, like *lameness*, they are of the semantically transparent type that can qualify as undefined run-ons.
6 'Paradigmatic' information, such as **synonyms** (same meaning), **antonyms** (opposite meaning), **superordinates** (*crippled* is superordinate to one sense of *lame*), **converses** (like *buy* for *sell*), and even **paronyms** or **confusibles** (like *imply* for *infer*). A special case of synonymy is presented by pairs like *launchpad/launching pad* or *music box/musical box*, which differ only by the presence or absence of an affix.
7 Syntagmatic information; that is, information about the use of the item in forming sentences. Some syntagmatic information is conveyed by the syntactic categorization mentioned above. Additional information may also be provided about complementation (***tell** them to leave vs **saw** them leave*), collocation with specific words or types of words (***fond** of vs **fondness** for*; the association of *capsize* with boats or ships), and selectional restrictions (such as that the verb *frighten* requires a direct object that is 'animate': ***frightened** the child*, but not *****frightened** the stone*).
8 'Analogical' information about the lexical field of which a given lexical unit is a part. Subsuming and perhaps transcending paradigmatic and syntagmatic information, analogical information is given sparingly by English-language dictionaries and thesauruses, but much more extensively by French dictionaries – especially those produced by Robert. An English-language 'alphabetical and analogical' dictionary *à la* Robert might at its entry for *horse* provide cross-references to types of horse (*mare, pony*), its colours (*bay, roan*), its parts (*hock, pastern*), its gaits (*trot, canter*), and other 'horsy' words (*saddle, jockey, gymkhana*).
9 'Diasystematic' information, indicating whether or not something belongs to the unmarked standard core of the language that can be used at all times and in all places

and situations. According to Hausmann (1977, Ch. 8), lexically relevant units can receive – typically by means of labels or usage notes – any or all of the following types of diasystematic marking: **diachronic** (e.g. *archaic, neologism*); **diatopic** (e.g. *American English* for *elevator* 'lift', *British English* for *loo*); **diaintegrative** for foreign borrowings used in English (e.g. *German* for *Weltanschauung*); **diastratic** (e.g. *informal* for *loo*, *formal* for *perambulator*); **diaconnotative** (e.g. *from Webster's Ninth New Collegiate Dictionary* (*W9*), *often used disparagingly* for *dyke*); **diatechnical** (e.g. *law* for *tort, anatomy* for *clavicle*; **diafrequential** (e.g. *rare*); **dianormative** (e.g. *substandard for ain't*).

10 Explanation of use, meaning, and reference: see below.

The **domain** of the information provided by dictionaries may be a whole entry or part of an entry. Thus at an entry for the noun *crane*, the domain of both its spelling and its pronunciation is both lexical units it represents ('bird' and 'machine'). But at an entry for the verb *shine*, dictionaries must show that the domain of its inflection *shined* is restricted to the meaning 'polish', while *shone* prevails elsewhere. And an entry for *colour/color* should show that for all the lexical units it represents, the spelling *color* is American English and the spelling *colour* is British English: here the diatopic marking applies to spelling alone.

Finally, lexicographers and dictionary users alike should bear the following in mind.

1 Information may be given covertly as well as overtly. Thus the absence of a diasystematic label indicates that a lexical unit belongs to the common core of the language, and the absence of inflections in the entry for a unit may show that the unit has none, but may also imply that its inflections are regular (or can be inferred from the inflections of its components).

2 Information of the same type may be given in more than one way. Thus the transitivity of a verb may be shown by its part-of-speech label (*v.t.*), by the form of its definition, and/or by examples of its use, as well as by special codes as in learners' dictionaries.

3 Dictionary information can help with both understanding language ('decoding') and producing language ('encoding'). Some dictionaries, e.g. learners' monolingual dictionaries and the native-language to foreign-language parts of bilingual dictionaries, emphasize their encoding function more than others, e.g. monolingual dictionaries for native speakers.

DICTIONARY EXPLANATIONS

Dictionaries may offer explanations of the use, meaning, and reference of the lexically relevant units they enter. **Use** has to do with the syntactic and pragmatic functions of the unit; **meaning** with the relation of the unit to other lexically relevant units; and **reference** with the relation of the extralinguistic item named by the unit to other extralinguistic items.

Dictionaries use at least the following six explanatory techniques, alone or in combination.

1 **Illustration**. This includes pictures, tables, and diagrams.

2 **Exemplification**. Thus for the noun *vow* the example *You **made** a vow **to** uproot this injustice* shows collocation with *make* and complementation by a *to*-infinitive, as well as reinforcing the notion that a vow is a solemn promise.

3 **Expansion**. For example, *VIP* is expanded to '*Very Important Person*', *NATO* to '*North Atlantic Treaty Organisation*', or *smog* to '*smoke* plus *fog*'. Expansion is particularly appropriate for initialisms and blends, and functions as an etymology. When the ex- pansion is sufficiently informative, it also functions as a definition, as in the case of *VIP* and *smog*. In the case of *NATO*, however, expansion is not sufficiently informative to tell the dictionary user anything about the membership and purpose of NATO.

4 **Discussion**. Here this is used in more or less its everyday sense to mean a discursive and at most

semi-formalized technique that can present any of the types of information described on pages 294–5 above. A short discussion – a so-called **usage note** – can supplement or replace a label (e.g. 'often used disparagingly') or a definition. For example, at ^{1}*here adv*, *W9* explains the subentry *here goes* as follows: '– used interjectionally to express resolution or resignation esp. at the beginning of a difficult or unpleasant undertaking'. For lexical units serving as interjections or function words, discussion is often the explanatory technique of choice. A longer discussion in the form of a **synonym essay** or **usage essay** can present information too detailed to compress into examples and too loosely structured to be formalized as a definition.

5 **Definition**. This is a formalized paraphrase. The definition of a lexically relevant unit presupposes a delexicalization of the unit into its components; these components are then reassembled into another lexically relevant unit, and the content of this unit characterizes the meaning and reference of the **definiendum** – the item which is being defined – while its form instantiates the definiendum's use. For example, a lexical unit represented by *bachelor* might be delexicalized into the components 'male', 'adult', 'never been married', which are then reassembled into the lexically relevant noun phrase, 'man who has never been married'. The content of this definition characterizes the meaning and reference of the word *bachelor*, while the form of the definition – a countable noun phrase – instantiates the grammatical use of the word *bachelor* – a countable noun. Thus nouns are defined by noun phrases; verbs by verb phrases – which for transitive verbs may contain a slot for the direct object; adverbs, prepositions, adjectives, and even some bound morphemes (see MORPHOLOGY) by phrases or clauses that can function in the same way as the definiendum.

Such standard dictionary definitions may be classified into:

(a) **definitions by synonym**, in which all the information is compressed into a single lexical unit (e.g. *gorgeous*: 'striking');
(b) **analytical definitions**, in which primary syntactic, semantic, and referential information is provided by one part of the definition, the **genus**, and secondary information by the rest, the **differentiae** (e.g. *gorgeous*: 'strikingly beautiful', where *beautiful* is the genus and *strikingly* the differentia);
(c) **formulaic definitions**, in which primary semantic and referential information is provided by one part of the definition, while the rest provides primary syntactic information together with secondary semantic and referential information (e.g. *gorgeous*: 'of/having/that has striking beauty').

A single lexical unit may have more than one definition: these definitions may be linked by **parataxis** (apposition or asyndetic co-ordination, as in *gorgeous*: 'of striking beauty, stunning') or **hypotaxis** (subordination, as in *gorgeous*: 'of striking beauty; *specifically*, stunning').

Besides standard dictionary definitions, ordinary people, including lexicographers off duty, use definitions of other types, such as '*tired* is when you want to lie down'. Such **folk-definitions** are used in some dictionaries for young children. For example, *The Charlie Brown Dictionary* has *hog*: 'When a male pig grows, he becomes a *hog*.' Non-standard definitions are also used in the *Collins COBUILD English Language Dictionary* (COBUILD, 1987), which has *hog*: 'A *hog* is a male pig that has been castrated'.

Translation. The process of definition yields a definition as its product. At the level of a whole text, the process of translation likewise yields as its product a translation. But the translation of a lexically relevant unit need not yield a relexicalized translation of that unit. Sometimes, instead, it yields a definition, especially in the case of culture-specific items like *Scotch egg*, which Collins–Roberts explains as *œuf dur enrobé de chair à saucisse*; sometimes a discussion, as for pragmatically restricted routine formulae from a very different culture, and sometimes nothing at all, as when one language uses, for instance, a preposition (Spanish: *María vio* **a** *Clara*) in constructions in which another language uses none (English: *Maria saw Clara*).

Furthermore, the process of context-free lexical translation can produce translation equivalents either at the level of lexical units, or at the level of their morphemic representation. Thus there is a difference between the superficially similar English–French equations *penicillin:pénicilline*, where one English lexical unit has been translated into one French lexical unit, and *crane noun: grue*, where an English representation of two lexical units has been translated into a French representation of two analogous lexical units. The first case is a translation of an English one–one lexical mapping into a French one–one lexical mapping; the second, a translation of an English one–many lexical mapping into a French one–many lexical mapping. However, both equations can be regarded as one–one mappings of a single 'translation unit' of English onto a single French translation equivalent.

Other possible mappings of source-language translation units onto target-language translation equivalents are:

Mapping	E.t.u.	F.t.e.
one–many	*jacket* (garment)	(of woman's suit) *jaquette*; (of man's suit) *veston*
many–one	*bucket*; *pail*	*seau*
many–many	*furze*; *gorse*	*gênet(s) épineux*; *ajonc(s)*

E.t.u.: English translation unit(s)
F.t.e.: French translation equivalent(s)

In these last three cases, the translation units have been lexical units (of English), and their translated explanations have been translation equivalents (of French) – that is, lexical units, too. But, as we have seen, neither translation units nor their translated explanations need be lexical units. All permutations and combinations occur in bilingual dictionaries: lexical unit – lexical unit (*penicillin:pénicilline*); lexical unit – non-lexical unit (*Scotch egg:œuf dur enrobé* etc.); non-lexical unit – lexical unit (*rural policeman:*

garde champêtre); non-lexical unit – non-lexical unit (*beat a drum: battre du tambour*). Unfortunately, most bilingual dictionaries do not distinguish consistently between those translation units and translated explanations that are lexical units and those that are not.

The example '*jacket* (garment)' above shows that when bilingual dictionaries deal with a single morphemic representation of more than one lexical unit (e.g. *jacket noun 1*: 'garment x' *2*: 'skin of baked potato' . . .), they more and more use various devices to show which lexical unit they are translating, and the example '(of woman's suit) *jaquette*' shows that they use similar devices to distinguish the domains of their translations. Such orientating devices can utilize any of the types of lexically relevant information listed on pages 294–5.

Whatever explanatory technique or techniques they use, dictionaries must order their explanations when a single article treats of more than one lexical unit and therefore requires more than one explanation. Such lexical units, or 'senses', may be ordered historically, by perceived frequency, by markedness (unmarked before diasystematically marked) or semantically ('basic' before 'derived', 'literal' before 'figurative'). However, semantic ordering may coexist with any of the other ordering principles, in which case semantically related senses are grouped together, and each such 'sense group' is placed according to its age, its frequency, or its markedness. The ordering of senses may or may not follow the same principles as the ordering of homologues in the macrostructure. Thus some dictionaries that order senses by frequency nevertheless order homographs historically.

Subentries such as run-ons and idioms are either collected at one place in the article – typically near the end – or scattered throughout it, each subentry going near the sense to which it is felt to be most closely related.

LEXICOGRAPHIC EVIDENCE

Lexicographers need to decide which lexically relevant units should be entered in a dictionary and what information should be given about them, and like investigators in other fields they use evidence gained from three overlapping processes of investigation, namely **introspection**, **experiment**, and **observation**. Lexicographic observation may be of **primary sources**, i.e. authentic language in use (formerly written language only, but now sometimes recordings of spoken language also), or of **secondary sources**, i.e. existing dictionaries and grammars.

Moreover, introspection, observation, and experiment have come to be used not only to investigate language for lexicographic purposes, but also to investigate the use of dictionaries and, by market research, the wishes of dictionary users. Such investigations are undertaken not only to improve the form and content of dictionaries, but also for the commercial purpose of increasing their distribution.

THE SIGNIFICANCE OF DICTIONARIES

Dictionaries are important as repositories of information about language and about social attitudes – for instance, ethnic slurs have been marked diaconnotatively for far longer than sexual slurs; as texts with relatively explicit and formalized conventions; and as the oldest and most widespread self-instructional learning aid. They have long enjoyed the favour of the general public, and commend themselves to the attention of anyone interested in language – both for what they *say*, and for what they *are*.

R.F.I.

SUGGESTIONS FOR FURTHER READING

Benson, M., Benson, E. and Ilson, R.F. (1986), *Lexicographic Description of English*, Amsterdam and Philadelphia, John Benjamins.

Ilson, R.F. (ed.) (1985), *Dictionaries, Lexicography and Language Learning*, Oxford, Pergamon Press in association with the British Council.

Lexis and lexicology

INTRODUCTION

The study of **lexis** is the study of the vocabulary of languages in all its aspects: words and their meanings, how words relate to one another, how they may combine with one another, and the relationships between vocabulary and other areas of the description of languages, the phonology, morphology, and syntax.

LEXICAL SEMANTICS

Central to the study of lexis is the question of word meaning. If the word is an identifiable unit of a language then it must be possible to isolate a core, stable meaning that enables its consistent use by a vast number of users in many contexts over long periods of time. Linguists have attempted to see the meaning of a word in terms of the features that compose it – its **componential features** – and the process of analysis of those features as **lexical composition**. Most important in this respect is the work of Katz and Fodor (1963). According to them, words are decomposable into primitive meanings and these **primitives** can be represented by **markers**. In addition, **distinguishers**, specific characteristics of the referents of words, serve to differentiate between different word senses. The description of a word in a dictionary must cover the wide range of senses that words can have: the dictionary entry is a 'characterization of *every* sense that a lexical item can bear in *any* sentence' (ibid.). See SEMANTICS, pages 397–8, for a diagram and exposition of Katz and Fodor's descriptive apparatus as this is employed to deal with the term *bachelor*.

Another way of looking at the features of a word's meaning is **componential analysis** (CA). CA breaks the word down into a list of the components present in its meaning; thus *man* can be ascribed the features + HUMAN + ADULT + MALE (Leech, 1981, p. 90). Once again, the purpose of CA is to distinguish the meaning of a given word from that of any other word, but the features attached to a word will also identify it as belonging to a **field** or **domain** (Nida, 1975, p. 339) which it shares with other words having common components. *Father, mother, son, sister, aunt,* etc., are united in having the components of HUMAN and KINSHIP in common (ibid.). CA enables us to identify **synonyms**, i.e. words that have identical componential features, regardless of differences of register, and to identify anomalous combinations such as 'male woman' (Leech, 1967, p. 21) (compare, again, SEMANTICS, pp. 395–8 for more on componential analysis).

But CA and the kind of labelling proposed by Katz and Fodor are open to criticism. Most powerful among early criticisms to appear was that of Bolinger (1965b), who showed that the two categories of marker and distinguisher could easily be collapsed, rendering the distinction questionable: the distinction anyway did not correspond to any clear division in natural language (ibid.). Nor could such a theory easily cope with metaphor, or with the fact that much of natural-language meaning resides not only in words but in longer stretches of morphemes, or **frozen forms** (ibid.).

A further criticism of the decompositional approach to word meaning is its lack of **psychological validity**: discussion of the psychological reality of an abstract semantic level that the decompositional approach presupposes may be found in Fodor *et al.* (1975): see also Bolinger (1976) and Cuyckens (1982). Sampson (1979) argues for the indivisibility even of derived words, concluding that 'the "semantic atoms" of our language are the same as the items listed in an ordinary dictionary'.

Also important in the study of lexis is **semantic field theory**. Field theory holds that the meanings represented in the lexicon are interrelated, that they cluster together to form 'fields' of meaning, which in turn cluster into even larger fields until the entire language is encompassed. Thus *sprinting, trotting,* and *jogging* cluster into a field of running, which in turn clusters with many other verbs into a larger field of human motion, and so on to a field of motion in general. Lehrer (1969) sums up the central feature of field theory: 'that vocabulary is organized into lexical or conceptual fields, and the items within each field are tightly structured with respect to each other'. This view goes back to Trier in the 1930s (see Lyons, 1977b, p. 253; Lehrer, 1974, p. 17), and the notion that the entire vocabulary can be divided and subdivided into interlinked fields underpins such works as *Roget's Thesaurus.*

Field theory can be used to illustrate language change: the way semantic space is carved up and realized in lexical items changes constantly; it can also be used in contrastive analysis of different languages (see Lehrer, 1974) to illustrate how a given semantic area is subdivided similarly or differently in different languages. Languages often differ even in apparently quite basic lexical divisions, and fields such as temperature terms, kinship terms, colour terms, parts of the body, and divisions of the animal and vegetable worlds will divide the semantic space differently and reflect this in the vocabulary items covering those fields. Lehrer (1969 and 1978) offers seminal applications of field theory to cooking terms and makes interesting generalizations concerning the formal properties of words that share common fields.

But Lehrer (1974) and Lyons (1977b) both see shortcomings in field theory. For one thing, words are not always sharply separated from one another in fields, and Lehrer suggests that Berlin and Kay's (1969) view, that there are **focal points**, or **prototypes** (Rosch, 1973, 1977; Rosch *et al.,* 1976) within fields rather than clearly delineated boundaries between words, might capture better how lexical meaning is perceived. What is more, not all words are amenable to field analysis; even more fundamentally, perhaps, the relationship between actual words and the concepts they stand for – which can only be expressed in words – is not at all clear (Lehrer, 1974, p. 17). Lyons' criticism overlaps with Lehrer's: both see as a weakness in field theory the fact that it fails to take into account the contribution to meaning of *syntagmatic* features (see STRUCTURALIST LINGUISTICS), concentrating as it does solely on paradigmatic relations (Lehrer, 1969; Lyons, 1977b, p. 261). Thus we cannot say much about the meaning of *bark* without reference to *dog*, or the colour *auburn* without mention of its restricted collocation with *hair* rather than *bicycle* or *door*.

RELATIONS BETWEEN ITEMS

Field theory raises the question of how vocabulary items are related to one another in terms of meaning. Lexical semanticists have devoted much attention to formulating basic relations between words; chief among such efforts have been Ullmann (1962), Lehrer (1974), Nida (1975), Lyons (1977b), Leech (1981), and Cruse (1986). Leech and Lyons discuss basic or **primitive** semantic relations, principally **synonymy**, **antonymy** and **hyponymy**. Ullmann (1962, p. 141) discusses synonymy and concludes that it is very rare that words are 100 per cent interchangeable. Words may share identical componential features but may still be distinguished along a variety of dimensions of actual use. He quotes Collinson's (1939) set of nine principles whereby words may be distinguished; these include literary and nonliterary usage, neutrality versus marked evaluation, formal versus colloquial usage, etc. Taking usage into account conflicts with a purely componential view, which is only concerned with a word's inherent, abstract features.

Antonymy, or oppositeness, is also not an entirely straightforward matter. Leech (1981, p. 92) points out that possible 'opposites' to *woman* include *girl* and *man*. It is thus more correct to label woman as **incompatible** with *man*, *boy*, and *girl* within its field. Lyons also uses incompatibility, referring to the relationship between words in sets such as flower names or names of the days of the week (1977b, p. 288).

Further types of oppositeness distinguish between pairs such as *alive* and *dead* and *hot* and *cold*. The first pair are called by Lyons (1977b, p. 291) **ungradable**, the latter pair **gradable**: intermediate terms exist between *hot* and *cold*, namely *warm, cool*, etc. Leech calls such gradables **polar oppositions** (1981, p. 100). Opposite terms such as *big* and *small* may even have other **intensified** terms at the polar extremes which represent a more complex set: *enormous* occupying a position beyond *big*, *tiny* beyond *small*; while other terms occupy the territory in between: *middle-sized, average, medium*. In such cases it seems that terms like *big* and *small* have a focal or **core** status (see Carter, 1987). Gradable antonyms are relative in meaning, and their relativity is sociolinguistically determined (Lyons, 1977b, p. 274; Leech, 1981, p. 102).

Lyons (ibid.) prefers to keep the term *antonymy* for the gradable antonyms only and suggests **complementarity** as a description of the ungradables, **converseness** for the reversible relationship between terms such as *husband/wife*, *teacher/pupil*, where to say *A is B's husband* implies *B is A's wife*, and **directionality** for pairs such as *arrive/depart*, *come/go*. Directionality and converseness are given the more general heading **relative opposition** by Leech (1981, p. 102).

Hyponymy, the relation of inclusion, is dealt with by Lyons (1977b, pp. 291–5) and, with new insight, by Cruse (1975, 1986). Hyponymous relations can be expressed by taxonomic treediagrams, showing levels of generality and specificity and which words include which in their meaning. Thus a simple tree diagram for *car* showing its relations with its near neighbours might be:

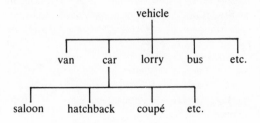

Vehicle is the **superordinate** term and *car* is a hyponym of it. *Van, car, lorry*, etc., are **co-hyponyms**. *Car* is then, in its turn, superordinate to *saloon, hatchback, coupé*, etc. Hyponymy, as is evident, is one of the major organizing principles of thesauruses. Not all taxonomic-type relations, however, are true examples of hyponymy: part-whole relations such as *finger/hand* may be termed **meronymy** and Lyons (1977b, pp. 293–301) points to a variety of types of **quasi-hyponymy**, which include sets such as *stroll/amble/plod* etc. under the superordinate *walk*, and *round/square/oblong* under *shape* (where *shape* is not of the same grammatical class as the quasi-hyponyms). Cruse (1975) argues that many quasi-hyponymic relations in natural language cannot be explained at all in terms of entailment and should be seen as purely conventional arrangements of phenomena in the world. Thus *watches, ties, cameras and other presents* has no permanent implication that *If it is a tie, it is therefore a present* (cf. *If it is a rose, it is therefore a flower*).

The discussion of relations between the items in sets that realize semantic fields does not necessarily imply that all items behave in the same way. If we consider the gradable antonyms it is clear that one term of the pair usually operates as the **unmarked** term, i.e. the question *How long will the meeting be?* is heard as a neutral question concerning duration: *How short will the meeting be?* will be heard as **marked**, or else can only function where 'brevity' is already given in the context. Likewise *How big is your house?* and *How wide is the room?* testify to the unmarked nature of *big* and *wide*. Among other incompatibles, one term can often double up as gender-marked – often, but not exclusively, male – and as gender-neutral. Lyons (1977b, p. 308) gives *dog* as an example, which can be used to refer to any dog, bitch, or puppy, but which can also be used to differentiate gender, as in the question *Is it a dog or a bitch? Tiger, fox* and *pig* are other examples. *Dog* can thus be said to be simultaneously superordinate to *bitch* and its co-hyponym.

SYNTAGMATIC FEATURES

So far, the discussion of lexical relations has proceeded firmly within the domain of semantics and the types of meanings carried by paradigmatic relations. But a parallel, vigorous line of study, dominated by British linguists, has concentrated its efforts during the mid–late twentieth century on syntagmatic aspects of lexis. The seeds of this variety of lexical studies are found in the work of J.R. Firth, and it is the notion of **collocation** that is Firth's principal contribution to the field.

In contrast with the decontextualized, **theoretical dictionary** (Leech, 1981, p. 207) which is the construct of decomposition, componential analysis, and semantic relations, Firth is concerned with an 'abstraction at the syntagmatic level . . . not directly concerned with the conceptual or idea approach to the meaning of words' (1957a, p. 196). He is concerned with the distribution of words in text, and how some occur predictably together more than others. One of the meanings of *night* is its collocation with *dark*, and *vice versa*: likewise, we can predict the restricted range of adjectives that commonly occur with *ass: silly, obstinate, stupid*, etc. (ibid.).

Much of the impetus to Firth's work on collocation is provided by his concern with literary stylistics, where it is frequently necessary to recognize certain collocations as **a-normal** (ibid.) in order to explain literary effect. Firth also gives a systematic classification of the collocational types with the verb *get* (1968, pp. 20–3) and sees these as 'a basis for the highly complex statement necessary to define the forms of *get* in a dictionary' (ibid.): this makes an interesting comparison with Katz and Fodor (1963), who were also preoccupied with the form an entry for a word in a dictionary might take (see above, pp. 298–9).

McIntosh (1961) continued Firth's work on collocation and used the term **range** to describe the **tolerance of compatibility** between words. The range of an item is the list of its potential collocates: thus *molten* has a range that includes

metal/lava/lead, etc., but not *postage*. The
sentence *The molten postage feather scores a
weather* violates the tolerance of compatibility of
the words within it: despite our willingness to
accommodate new and unusual collocations (e.g.
in literary works), we cannot contextualize such
an odd sentence. Yet range is not fossilized, and
part of the creative process of language change is
range extension, whereby a previously limited
range is broadened to accommodate new concepts, thus *ware* (whose range included *hard*,
table, and *house*) now includes in modern English
soft and *firm*, in computer jargon.

Firth's seminal ideas on collocation (1957a;
see also 1957b, pp. 11–13 and pp. 26–7) have
since been developed by, among others, Mitchell
(1958, 1971, 1975), Halliday (1966b), McIntosh
(1966), Sinclair (1966, 1987b), and Greenbaum
(1970). Central among these studies are
Halliday's and Sinclair's. Halliday (1966b) is
concerned with two concepts: collocation and
how this, in turn, defines membership of **lexical
sets**. Halliday's paper is entitled 'Lexis as a
linguistic level', and his purpose is to sketch out
'a lexical theory complementary to, but not part
of, grammatical theory'. Firth had already, to a
certain extent, separated lexical matters from
semantics and grammar (1957a, pp. 7–33);
Halliday was now concerned to make that
separation more complete. The many unresolved
issues of language patterning left over when
grammatical analysis, however thorough, was
complete, could either be relegated to semantics
or tackled at a **lexical level** of analysis, with the
aim of making lexical statements at a greater
level of generality than dictionaries do. As an
example of the **lexicality** of collocation, Halliday
compares the different collocability of *strong* and
powerful. The figure below shows the acceptability of *strong tea* but not of *strong car*, while
argument collocates with both. Moreover, the
relation is constant over a variety of grammatical
configurations: *He argued strongly against . . . ;
the strength of his argument*; *This car has more
power*; etc. So the lexical statement can operate
independently of grammatical restrictions.
Strong, strength, strongly, strengthen represent
the 'scatter' of the same **lexical item**.

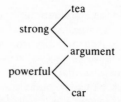

The lexical statement will not, however, remain independent but will ultimately be integrated with grammatical and other statements,
a truly Firthian position. That *strong* and
powerful, *qua* items, collocate with *argument*
entitles them to enter into the same set. Each will
also enter into different sets by virtue of their
non-overlapping collocations with *tea* and *car*,
respectively: item, set, and collocation are
mutually defining (ibid.).

Collocation and **set**, as terms in a lexical
description, are analogous to **structure** and
system in a grammatical theory (see SCALE AND
CATEGORY GRAMMAR and SYSTEMIC GRAMMAR):
the difference is that collocation is a relation of
probable co-occurrence of items, and sets are
open-ended (cf. the **closed** systems of grammar).
The **set** is a 'grouping of items with like privilege
of occurrence in collocation' (ibid.). Some items
in the language will not be amenable to lexical
statements of any real power or significance: *the*,
for example, is a **weak collocator**, combining,
potentially, with almost any common noun:
blond is a **strong collocator**, restricted to *hair* and
a few related words (*tresses, wig*, etc.). *The* is best
left to the grammarian to describe: it occupies
one end of the continuum running from grammatical to most lexical, while *blond* dwells at the
other end.

Words can thus predict their own environment
to a greater or lesser extent. Some items predict
the certain occurrence of others: when such
predictability is 100 per cent (e.g. *fro*
always predicts *to and*, and *kith* always
predicts *and kin*) we are justified in declaring the
whole of the fixed occurrence to be a single lexical
item.

The notion of collocation and lexical set can
also have a bearing on decisions concerning
polysemy and homonymy (see SEMANTICS, pp.
394–5). The occurrence of the word form *bank*

in two different collocational environments (*river, trees, steep*, cf. *money, deposit, cheque*) suggests that *bank* is best described as a homonym. Likewise, non-cognate word forms (e.g. *city* and *urban*) can be shown to have the same collocates, and therefore to belong to the same set.

The set can be demonstrated as a statistical reality: 2,000 occurrences of the word *sun* might be examined in terms of what occurs three words either side of it. These 12,000 collocates might show a significant frequency of *bright/hot/shine/light*, etc. A similar operation on 2,000 occurrences of *moon* might show *bright, shine*, and *light* to be statistically significant. These match with the collocates of *sun* and thus delineate *bright, shine*, and *light* as candidates for members of a set which *moon* and *sun* occur in. And so the process could repeat itself on masses of data, preferably some 20 million words of text, according to Halliday's reckoning.

Halliday's (1966b) work leans clearly towards data-based observations of lexical patterning, a field which Sinclair has since developed significantly. Sinclair (1966) also takes a Firthian approach to collocation and much of his argument agrees with Halliday, not least in his stressing that all text can be seen lexically as well as grammatically. Common function words are difficult to describe lexically and hardly attain the status of independent lexical items; the same is true of common verbs such as *take, make*, and *do*. Sinclair (1966) addressed some of the theoretical issues he later took up in the massive COBUILD project at the University of Birmingham where, under his direction, a vast corpus of 20 million words of text was stored on computer and analysed in depth (see also CORPORA). The most notable product of this research was the COBUILD (1987) dictionary, but many independent insights have emerged from the study of the corpus.

Chief among these new insights is the realization of the delicate relationship between sense and structure, that the different senses of an item are often paralleled by preferred structural configurations (see Sinclair, 1987a). It is also clear that the facts of lexical combinability often defy even native-speaker introspection, and, equally far-reaching, that much of natural language occurs in 'semi-preconstructed phrases that constitute single choices, even though they might appear to be analysable into segments' (Sinclair, 1987b). This last remark expands the concept of the lexicon from being a collection of words into a huge repository of meaning, many of whose items span several words or whole phrases and clauses; such findings confirm Bolinger's views on the nature of the lexicon (1965b, 1976).

Two other names central to the British approach to lexis are Mitchell (1958, 1966, 1971, 1975) and Greenbaum (1970). Mitchell was essentially concerned with all kinds of syntagmatic delimitation (see Cruse, 1986, ch. 2) and his work represents a unique blend of levels of analysis, a syntactico-lexical approach similar to that of Sinclair in the COBUILD project. Mitchell (1971) is of prime importance; he examines the delicate interrelation of syntax and lexis: configurations containing the same lexical morphemes do not necessarily mean the same when rearranged or inflected, for instance, the *hard* in *hard work* means something different from *hard* in *hardworking*. Equally *goings-on* means something different from that which is *on-going*. Syntagmatic bonds between lexical items are also responsible for the unproductive characteristics of fixed collocations, or **bound collocations** as Cruse (1986, p. 41) calls them, and the lack of productivity of idioms. Mitchell (1971) notes as a characteristic of idioms the frequent grammatical generalizability of their structure (e.g. tournures such as *kick the bucket, see the light, hit the sack, bite the bullet*); Greenbaum (1970) also focuses on collocation 'in certain syntactic relationships' and concludes that limited, homogeneous grammatical classes – in his case verb intensifiers – yield the most useful analytic results. The approach that treats collocation as a purely independent level Greenbaum calls **item-orientated**; an approach taking syntax and semantics into account is **integrated** (ibid.).

MULTIWORD LEXICAL ITEMS

The neo-Firthian tradition, with its emphasis on syntagmatic aspects of lexis, has run parallel to, and cross-fertilized, traditional studies of idioms and other fixed stretches of language that constitute single, indivisible meanings and which display degrees of semantic transparency or opacity and degrees of syntactic productivity. **Idioms**, in the sense of fixed strings whose meanings are not retrievable from their parts have been described by Weinreich (1969), Makkai (1972, 1978), and Strässler (1982), who gives good coverage of little-known Soviet work. Additionally, a wide variety of other types of multiword lexical units (Zgusta, 1967) have come under scrutiny, such as **binominals** (Malkiel, 1959), **conversational formulae** (Coulmas, 1981), and **restricted collocations** (Cowie, 1981). Bolinger (1976) and Sinclair (1987b) are also central to any study of multiword units, both of them arguing for the need to see idiomaticity and **analyticity** – the amenability of linguistic phenomena to be broken down into ever smaller analytic units – as equally important to language study. This idiomatic view of the lexicon shifts the emphasis irrevocably from seeing the word as the unit of the lexicon to the adoption of more eclectic units.

LEXIS IN A TRANSFORMATIONAL FRAMEWORK

In the simplest version of a transformational grammar, three components are present (Radford, 1981, p. 118): **categorical rules**, a **lexicon** or dictionary, and a **lexical-insertion rule**, which attaches actual lexical items to lexical category nodes, a later stage in the operation of sentence production, once the syntax has been worked out. The lexicon and categorical component are the **base** of the grammar (Chomsky, 1977). However, to guarantee that deviant sentences will not be produced, a **lexical entry** – what appears in the dictionary – has to specify additional information such as transitivity restrictions, complementation patterns, etc., as well as the basic morphological, semantic, and

phonological information which enable it to be used appropriately in the surface structure of a sentence.

Semantic information about a word generates **selection restrictions**, for instance, that certain verbs may only combine with animate objects (see Chomsky, 1965, pp. 106–11), as well as contributing to the word's **formal structure** (Bresnan, 1978), a more abstract representation of logical relationships. In Chomsky's (1965, p. 85) account of a transformational grammar, the item *boy* gets an entry reminiscent, but with syntactic additions, of the componential-feature analysis of lexical semantics: *boy* [+ N + Count + Common + Animate + Human]. The nature and type of information attached to a lexical entry, and the dividing lines between lexical 'idiosyncrasies' and the transformational component of the grammar have been the subject of much debate (Chomsky, 1970a; Jackendoff, 1975). For a general survey see Newmeyer (1980, pp. 112–20), who traces the debate within the genesis of generative semantics).

Although Chomsky's primary definition of the lexicon as an 'unordered list of all lexical formatives' (1965, p. 84) may seem to relegate lexis to an unstructured domain within language, the same work acknowledges the systematic semantic structuring of lexis along the lines of field theory (see above, pp. 299–300); indeed words are held to have **field properties** that unite them (1965, p. 160). Overall, the status of the lexicon within transformational-generative linguistics has shifted and grown over the years (e.g. Bresnan, 1978) and seems likely to continue to occupy its more central position within this and other branches of language study (compare LEXICAL-FUNCTIONAL GRAMMAR).

LEXIS AND DISCOURSE ANALYSIS

A growing area of interest has been the relationship between lexical choice and the organization of discourse. Halliday and Hasan's (1976) description of cohesion in English includes a chapter on the lexical cohesion observable in texts over clause and sentence boundaries (see TEXT LINGUISTICS, p. 464). Textual content may be repeated in identical lexical form or may be reiterated by use of synonymy, hyponymy, or selections from the class of general nouns. Additionally, collocation occurs over sentence boundaries and creates chains of mutually collocating words in texts. Hasan (1984) revised the 1976 model, rejecting collocation as non-structural and adding antonymy and meronymy to the structural devices for reiteration. She also examined devices for creating localized or **instantial** lexical relations realized in individual texts.

Work has also concentrated on the role of a large number of text-organizing words which duplicate the work of conjunctions and sentence connectors in the signalling of textual relations between clauses and sentences and in the creation of larger patterns of discourse. Words such as *reason*, *means*, *result*, and *effect* overtly indicate logical relations between clauses, such as temporality, causality, etc. Of importance here is work by Winter (1977) (see TEXT LINGUISTICS, pp. 465–6).

In the study of spoken discourse, much interesting research has focused on marker words which occur widely in large spoken corpora (e.g. Tottie and Backlund, 1986) and on the fixed formulae found in conversation (Coulmas, 1979). McCarthy (1987, 1988) has reported on types of lexical cohesion, or **relexicalization**, in conversation, and has argued for its intimate relationships with phonological features. His work owes much to Brazil (1985), who redefines the concept of paradigmatic lexical choice within the real-time constraints of discourse production.

M.J.McC.

SUGGESTIONS FOR FURTHER READING

Bazell, C.E., Catford, J.C., Halliday, M.A.K., and Robins, R.H. (eds) (1966), *In Memory of J.R. Firth*, London, Longman. (In particular the papers by Halliday, Sinclair, and Mitchell.)

Cruse, D.A. (1986), *Lexical Semantics*, Cambridge, Cambridge University Press.

Lehrer, A. (1974), *Semantic Fields and Lexical Structure*, Amsterdam, North-Holland.

Mentalist linguistics

Broadly speaking, any linguistic theory which makes claims about a relationship between language and the mind may be referred to as mentalist; this would include most theories of language, excluding only the most strictly behaviouristic theories such as those of Bloomfield and Skinner (see BEHAVIOURIST LINGUISTICS). Normally, a linguistic theory such as that of Noam Chomsky would certainly be referred to as mentalist, since one of Chomsky's claims is that the structure of language in some way mirrors the structure of the human mind. In this work, however, Chomsky's theory is covered under RATIONALIST LINGUISTICS because of its emphasis on innateness which need not be a corollary of a mentalistic theory. In this entry, I shall concentrate on the kind of linguistic theory advanced early in the twentieth century by the American linguists Edward Sapir (1884–1939) and Benjamin Lee Whorf (1897–1941), in particular on what has become known as the **Sapir–Whorf Hypothesis**.

At the turn of the century in the United States, many linguists were concerned to construct records of the American Indian languages before they disappeared as the Indians became more and more strongly influenced by white American society. Early on, these languages had been investigated by linguists from Europe who had tended to impose on them grammatical descriptions based on the categories appropriate to their own Indo-European language, but in 1911 this strategy was sharply criticized by Franz Boas (1858–1942) in his *Handbook of American Indian Languages*. Boas states in the preface that it is the task of the linguist to discover, for each language under study, its own particular grammatical structure, and to develop descriptive categories appropriate to it. For instance, many languages do not display the kinds of distinction which European linguists might tend to take for granted, such as the singular/plural and past/present distinctions, but may instead display distinctions between categories quite new to European linguists. For example, some Siouan languages distinguish in the article system between categories like

> Animate moving
> Animate at rest
> Animate long
> Inanimate high
> Inanimate collective objects.

Research into such phenomena greatly increased after the publication of Boas' *Handbook*, and many such differences between languages were subsequently discovered. For example, Hockett (1958) describes the tense system of Hopi as divided into three:

1 Timeless truths: *Mountains are high*.
2 Known or presumed known happenings: *I saw him yesterday*.
3 Events still in the realm of uncertainty: *He is coming tomorrow*.

So whereas in English, the speaker's attitude in terms of certainty or uncertainty about the propositional content of utterances is indicated in the modal system by means of the modal auxiliaries (*can, may, will, shall, should, ought, need*, etc.), in Hopi, the tense of the verb itself carries this information. In the same vein, Hockett says of Menomini that it has a five-way modality contrast:

1 Certainty
/pɪʔw/:   *he comes,*
            he is coming
            he came

2 Rumour
/pɪʔwen/: *he is said to be coming*
            it is said that he came

3 Interrogative
/pɪʔ/:   *is he coming?*
            did he come?

4 Positive, contrary to expectations
/pɪasah/:   *so he is coming after all*

5 Negative, contrary to expectations:
/pɪapah/:   *but he was going to come!*

Hopi also has three words which function where English only has one binder, *that*. Consider:

(1) I see that it is new
(2) I see that it is red
(3) I hear that it is new
(4) I hear that it is red

In Hopi, (1) has one word for *that*, (2) another, and (3) and (4) yet another; this is because three different types of 'representation to consciousness' are involved. In (1), the newness of the object is inferred by the speaker from a number of visual clues and from the speaker's past experience; in (2), the redness of the object is directly received in consciousness through the speaker's vision; in (3) and (4), the redness and newness are both perceived directly via the speaker's faculty of hearing (Trudgill, 1974a, pp. 25–6).

It seems clear, then, that languages, through their grammatical structure, as well as, more obviously, through their lexis, do not all 'interpret' the world and experience in the same way. The **mentalist** claim is that a person's native language sets up a series of categories which act as a pair of grid spectacles through which s/he views the world; it categorizes experience for the speakers of the language. This claim is, in a nutshell, what has become known as the Sapir–Whorf Hypothesis, also known as the doctrine of **cultural relativism/relativity** or **ontological** relativity/relativism. Some measure of influence of this theory can be perceived in all linguistic programmes which make claims about the influence of language on people's perception of an aspect of 'reality'. It has also provided much ground for discussion in the Philosophy of Language (see PHILOSOPHY OF LANGUAGE).

It should be pointed out that both Sapir and Whorf were important figures in the history of linguistics, quite apart from their contribution to the development of the Sapir–Whorf Hypothesis. Sapir became the first really well-known sociolinguist. He went to Columbia University in 1900 where he was taught by Boas, and made a field trip to study the Wishram Indians in 1905; from that time on, much of his work in linguistics was concerned with American Indian languages and cultures. He stressed the interrelationship between the study of culture and the study of language, insisting that one cannot be studied in isolation from the other, and insisting also that language is a universal human property, that no tribe has ever been found without a language, that language is an essentially perfect means of expression among every known people, and that there are no primitive languages. He met Whorf briefly in 1928, 1929, and 1930 at various scientific societies' meetings, but they did not really get to know each other until 1931 when Sapir went to Yale University as Sterling Professor of Anthropology and Linguistics and Whorf enrolled in the first course he gave there on American Indian Linguistics.

Whorf was not initially trained as a linguist, but as a chemical engineer at MIT, from whence he graduated in 1918. In 1919 he was selected as a trainee fire-prevention engineer by a fire insurance company, and, after graduating from the company school, began work as a fire-prevention inspector of properties insured by the company. He writes an interesting account of how this work sparked off his interest in linguistic meaning and in the way linguistic expressions can affect behaviour ('The relation of habitual thought and behavior to language', 1939):

> In the course of my professional work for a fire insurance company . . . I undertook the task of analyzing many hundreds of reports of circumstances surrounding the start of fires, and in some cases, of explosions. . . . In due course it became evident that not only a physical situation *qua* physics, but the meaning of that situation to people, was sometimes a factor, through the behavior of the people, in the start of the fire. And this factor of meaning was clearest when it was a LINGUISTIC MEANING, residing in the name or the linguistic description commonly applied to the situation. Thus, around a storage of what are called 'gasoline drums', behavior will tend to a certain type, that is, great care will be exercised; while around a storage of what are called 'empty gasoline drums', it will tend to be different – careless, with little repression of smoking or of tossing cigarette stubs about. Yet the 'empty' drums are perhaps more dangerous, since they contain explosive vapor.

Whorf began to study Aztec in 1926 but is best known for his work on Hopi. He made contact with a native speaker of Hopi who lived in New York, and then in 1932 Sapir obtained a small research grant for him which enabled him to carry out some field work. This resulted in the development of his notion that the strange grammar of Hopi might be evidence of a particular way of perceiving the world; the Hopi might live by different metaphors and myths from those by which we live, and their language might be evidence of this. Whorf took this message, that linguistic studies can show us much about how a people think and about what they believe, and used it to popularize linguistics. It is a message which has retained its appeal, as evidenced, for instance, in the form of Lakoff and Johnson's enormously popular (in academic terms) book *Metaphors We Live By* (1980).

Whorf's most famous example of what Sapir (see Mandelbaum, 1949, p. 158) calls 'the relativity of the form of thought' comes from his article 'An American Indian model of the universe', written in about 1936. Here he claims that 'the metaphysics underlying our language and thinking and modern culture' imposes the two cosmic forms, time and space, on the universe. We see space as static, three dimensional and infinite, and time as subject to the three-fold division into past present, and future. Hopi, in contrast, imposes on the universe two cosmic forms, **manifested** and **manifesting/ unmanifest**, or, they might be called the **objective** and the **subjective**. The manifested, or objective, comprises all that is, or has been, accessible to the senses, with no attempt to distinguish past from present, but excluding future. The subjective, or manifesting, or unmanifest comprises future *and* everything that we call mental – everything that appears in the minds of people, animals, plants, and things.

This type of phenomenon led Whorf to comment, equally famously, that (1940; reprinted in Carroll, 1956, p. 214)

> No individual is free to describe nature with absolute impartiality, but is constrained to certain modes of interpretation. . . . All observers are not led by the same physical evidence to the same picture of the universe, *unless their linguistic backgrounds are similar, or can in some way be calibrated.* (emphasis mine)

By 'calibration', Whorf means something very like translation, and the translatability criterion has become central in modern theories of meaning (see PHILOSOPHY OF LANGUAGE). Whorf appears to be saying that unless the languages of two cultures can be translated into each other, we must assume that the world views of the two cultures differ dramatically. Sapir omits the possibility of translation altogether in statements like the following: 'No two languages are ever sufficiently similar to be considered as repres-

enting the same social reality. The worlds in which different societies live are distinct worlds, not merely the same world with different labels attached.'

This hypothesis will be further discussed in PHILOSOPHY OF LANGUAGE. Suffice it to say here that the notion that translation is quite impossible between some languages tends to be contradicted by the research carried out by Sapir and Whorf themselves; presumably, since they are able to explain the differences between the languages under study and our own, and explain them, moreover, in our own language, translation, in some sense, has been possible. And clearly, if the hypothesis is to be useful to the areas of study I mentioned above, there must be some common ground from which differences in linguistic usage can be considered by the researcher.

K.M.

SUGGESTIONS FOR FURTHER READING

Carroll, J.B. (ed.) (1956), *Language, Thought and Reality: Selected Writings of Benjamin Lee Whorf*, Cambridge, MA, MIT Press.

Lyons, J. (1981), *Language and Linguistics: An Introduction*, Cambridge, Cambridge University Press, ch. 10.

Mandelbaum, D.G. (ed.) (1949), *Selected Writings of Edward Sapir in Language, Culture and Personality*, Berkeley and Los Angeles, University of California Press, and London, Cambridge University Press.

Metaphor

Eco (1984, p. 87) insists that metaphor 'defies every encyclopedic entry'. Nevertheless, metaphor merits such an entry because, although sometimes seen as merely one among the different

tropes (see STYLISTICS) available to a language user, it may equally be seen as a fundamental principle of all language use. It has even been claimed (Lakoff and Johnson, 1980, p. 3) that 'our ordinary conceptual system, in terms of which we both think and act, is fundamentally metaphorical in nature'. It should be pointed out, however, that even researchers taking a view of metaphor very much opposed to this would agree about the importance to linguistic theory of the phenomenon of metaphor. Thus Sadock (1979), according to whom metaphor falls outside linguistics proper because it has non-linguistic parallels while linguistics should be confined to the study of the uniquely linguistic aspects of human communication (p. 46), believes, in spite of this, that an understanding of metaphor is important for linguists because 'figurative language is one of the most productive sources of linguistic change' and 'Most lexical items [are] dead metaphors' (p. 48).

Lakoff and Johnson's book presents the most extreme form of **constructivism**, one of the two broad categories into which theories of metaphor may fall, the other being **non-constructivism** (Ortony, 1979b, p. 2). According to constructivism, 'the objective world is not directly accessible, but is constructed on the basis of the constraining influences of human knowledge and language'; on this view, metaphor may be seen as instrumental in *creating* reality, and the distinction between literal and figurative, including metaphorical, language tends to break down. Constructivists tend, in fact, not to distinguish metaphors from other tropes, and to take what Ortony (1979b, p. 4) terms a **macroscopic** view of metaphor: it is held that metaphors at sentence level are symptomatic of underlying systems of metaphor, or metaphoric models. These systems, or models, may be expressed in a sentence-level metaphor, for instance *Argument is war* (Lakoff and Johnson, 1980, p. 4). This underlying metaphor, or **metaphorical concept**, as Lakoff and Johnson call it, gives rise to expressions like *Your claims are indefensible*; *He shot down all of my arguments*; etc, from which the researcher can 'read off' the underlying metaphor.

According to non-constructivism, reality exists independently of human knowledge and language and can be 'precisely described through the medium of language' (Ortony, 1979b, p. 1). The language used for describing reality precisely is literal language which is clearly distinguishable from tropes, such as metaphors, which are, at best, ornamental, at worst, misleading. Non-constructivist writers on metaphor tend to take a **microscopic** view (ibid., p. 4), studying individual, sentence-level metaphors each of which they see as independent of others, rather than as part of any metaphorical system.

The identification and classification of metaphors have been the subjects of much discussion. According to many writers, for instance Beardsley (1967) and Searle (1979), the criterion for indentifying a metaphor is that, taken literally, the metaphorical utterance would be plainly false. Black (1979), however, points out that (p. 35):

> An obvious objection is that this test, so far as it fits, will apply equally to such other tropes as oxymoron or hyperbole, so that it would at best certify the presence of some figurative statement, but not necessarily a metaphor. A more serious objection is that authentic metaphors need not manifest the invoked controversion, though many of them do. Suppose I counter the conversational remark, 'As we know, man is a wolf ... ' by saying, 'Oh, no, man is not a wolf but an ostrich.' In context, 'Man is not a wolf' is as metaphorical as its opposite, yet it clearly fails the controversion test. The point is easy to generalize: The negation of any metaphorical statement can itself be a metaphorical statement and hence possibly true if taken literally. Nor need the examples be confined to such negatives. When we say, 'He does indeed live in a glass house,' of a man who actually lives in a house made of glass, nothing prevents us from using the sentence to make a metaphorical statement.

Black is of the opinion that there is no infallible test for discriminating the metaphorical from the literal; he claims, rather unhelpfully, it may be thought (ibid., pp. 35–6), that we recognize a metaphor because, on the one hand, we know what it is to be a metaphor, and, on the other hand, we judge that a metaphorical reading is preferable to a literal reading.

The broadest division of metaphors is that

which distinguishes **dead** from **live** metaphors. A dead metaphor is an expression like *leg of a table/chair*, which is in very common use and in the case of which we no longer think of the use of *leg* as metaphorical. Idioms such as *kick the bucket* can, in the case of many, be presumed to have begun life as metaphors (see Sadock, 1979, p. 48). A live metaphor is one which is new, or relatively new, or which has not become part of everyday linguistic usage, so that we know when hearing it that a metaphor has been used. Of this division, Black (1979, p. 26) says that it 'is no more helpful than, say, treating a corpse as a special case of a person: a so-called dead metaphor is not a metaphor at all, but merely an expression that no longer has a pregnant metaphorical use'. Instead, he proposes to distinguish, among live metaphors, to which he refers as **active**, between **strong** and **weak** metaphors. This distinction depends on two aspects of metaphors, namely their **emphasis** and their **resonance** (ibid., pp. 26–7):

> A metaphorical utterance is *emphatic* . . . to the degree that its producer will allow no variation upon or substitution for the words used. . . . Emphatic metaphors are intended to be dwelt upon for the sake of their unstated implications. . . . Some metaphors, even famous ones, barely lend themselves to implicative elaboration, while others, perhaps less interesting, prove relatively rich in background implications. For want of a better label, I shall call metaphorical utterances that support a high degree of implicative elaboration *resonant*.

A strong metaphor is one which is both emphatic and resonant.

Within the two broad categories of theory described above, a number of explicit theories of metaphor are discernible. One of the oldest of these is the Aristotelean **comparison view**, according to which a metaphor is an implicit **simile**, an implicit statement of comparison. Thus 'my love is like a red, red rose' is a simile: the presence in it of *like* marks it explicitly as a comparison between my love and a red red rose; however, 'my love is a red red rose' is a metaphor differing from the simile in that the comparison is left implicit. Richards (1936) called the subject of the metaphor (in this case, *my love*) the **topic** or **tenor**, and that in terms of which the tenor was being described (in this case *a red red rose*) the **vehicle**. The basis on which topic and vehicle could be thus put together he called the **ground.** So, on a comparison theory of metaphor, the similarity between the two terms in the metaphor would provide the **ground** for the comparison. The comparison view of metaphor is a special case of what is known as the **substitution** view, according to which a metaphor can be interchanged with a literal utterance; this view will always be open to the objection that if a literal statement could have been used just as well as the metaphor, it is difficult to explain why anyone should wish to use a metaphor at all. It is at this point that it is usually claimed that the metaphor is used for solely ornamental reasons.

According to Richards' own **tensive** theory of metaphor, the success of a metaphor depends on the **tension** or apparent incompatibility between topic and vehicle – an incompatibility which a successful metaphor shows to be only apparent. Richard's tensive view remains an aspect of Black's **interaction** view, but is most clearly developed by Sternberg *et al.* (1979).

The interaction view of metaphor may be summarized as follows (from Black, 1979, pp. 28–9):

1 A metaphorical statement has two distinct subjects, the primary and the secondary subject.
2 The secondary subject is to be regarded as a system rather than an individual thing.
3 The metaphorical utterance works by projecting upon the primary subject a set of associated implications, comprised in the implicative complex, that are predicable of the secondary subject.
4 The maker of a metaphorical statement selects, emphasizes, suppresses, and organizes features of the primary subject by applying to it statements isomorphic with the members of the secondary subject's implicative complex.
5 In the context of a particular metaphorical

statement, the two subjects interact in the following ways: (a) the presence of the primary subject incites the hearer to select some of the secondary subject's properties; and (b) invites him or her to construct a parallel implication-complex that can fit the primary subject; and (c) reciprocally induces parallel changes in the secondary subject.

At times, the metaphor will change the relationships between the primary and secondary subjects, and, in so doing, it will generate new knowledge and insight (ibid., p. 37); as such, metaphors are creative, they are **cognitive instruments** 'indispensable for perceiving connections that, once perceived, are *then* truly present. . . . Some metaphors enable us to see aspects of reality that the metaphor's production helps to constitute' (ibid., p. 39). A metaphor can show us how things are in the same way as do 'charts and maps, graphs and pictorial diagrams, photographs and realistic paintings, and above all models' (ibid., p. 41). All of these devices are correct or incorrect representations, or appropriate or inappropriate, rather than plainly true or false. Boyd (1979) takes this idea further, claiming that metaphors can *constitute* scientific theories.

It follows from a view such as Black's that metaphors can highlight certain aspects of a phenomenon while hiding others. For example, the metaphor of argument as war creates a focus on the conflict of opinions involved, while hiding another aspect, namely the fact that the parties to the argument are both giving some of their time, a valuable commodity, and might even be doing so in order to reach an agreement, that is, for a co-operative purpose (Lakoff and Johnson, 1980, ch. 3).

Searle (1979, p. 100) takes interaction theories to task for failing to distinguish between sentence and utterance meaning, having himself described metaphor as a case in which speaker meaning and sentence meaning come apart but are related to each other in a principled way (ibid., p. 93). Metaphor is always a property of the utterance meaning, never of the sentence meaning; rather, a sentence can be *used* to utter a metaphor (or to make a literal statement, or an ironical statement

or an indirect speech act; see SPEECH-ACT THEORY) (ibid., p. 96). The user of a sentence to make a metaphor *says metaphorically* that S is P, but means *S is R* (ibid., p. 113), that is, the metaphor can be given a literal paraphrase, albeit, possibly, a poor one. In spite of the extensive list of strategies and principles for determining that a metaphor has been uttered which Searle provides, he can be accused of failing to show how a hearer, having decided that a sentence is not being used literally, because, taken literally, it would be false, is then able to decide that the sentence is being used metaphorically rather than ironically or as an indirect speech act (Morgan, 1979, pp. 143–4). Morgan's own suggestion is that the purpose of making a metaphor is to convey emotionality and that hearers/readers recognize this (ibid., p. 149).

Cohen (1979, pp. 65–6) challenges Searle's view that metaphors are properties of utterance meaning rather than of sentence meaning on the grounds that whereas speech acts – properly described as an aspect of utterance rather than sentence meaning – are overridden in indirect speech, metaphors are not: thus both *The boy next door is a ball of fire* and *Tom said that the boy next door is a ball of fire* can only be understood by someone who understands the metaphor; the metaphor is therefore still a feature of the indirect speech. But in the case of *I am sorry* and *Tom said that he was sorry* only the former retains its status of apology; so a speech act is not retained when passing from direct to indirect speech:

> Arguably, therefore, metaphorical meaning inheres in sentences, not just in speech acts. . . . This point is a very serious difficulty for anyone, like Searle . . . who wants to construe metaphor solely in terms of speaker's meaning – the meaning of the utterance rather than of the sentence uttered.

According to Rumelhart (1979) the distinction between literal and figurative language, and consequently between utterance and sentence meaning is in itself suspect. He argues (pp. 80–1) that the processes of comprehension of non-literal speech form the basis of our linguistic competence. This can be seen by considering the way in which a child learns its first language (ibid., pp. 79–80):

> Presumably, a child learns a lexical item with respect to some particular domain of reference that in no way exhausts the set of situations to which the word can be correctly applied. In this domain of original use, some of the features of the situation presumably are relevant, and others presumably are not. Normally speaking, the process of language comprehension and production for a young child not fully familiar with the conventional range of application of a term must proceed through a process of fitting the aspects of the current situation into the closest lexical concept already available. Often this will conform with the conventional application of the term and it will therefore appear that the child is using the bit of language 'literally'. Just as often, the child will apply the concepts in a nonstandard way and appear to generate 'nonliteral' or 'metaphorical' speech. Thus, for example, if the term 'open' is learned in the context of (say) a child's mouth being open, and then it is applied to a door or a window, the child will appear merely to be demon-

strating an understanding of the term. On the other hand, if the child uses the term 'open' to mean 'turn on' (as with a television set or a light) the child will be perceived as having produced a metaphor. Yet the process of applying words to situations is much the same in the two cases – namely that of finding the best word or concept to communicate the idea in mind. For the child the production of literal and nonliteral speech may involve *exactly* the same processes.

There is much else that could be said about metaphors. However, the above should give an indication of the complexity of the issue, as will the recommended further reading which contains papers by linguists, philosophers, psychologists, sociologists, and educationalists, all of whom clearly feel that metaphor is a topic worthy of careful consideration.

K.M.

SUGGESTIONS FOR FURTHER READING

Ortony, A. (ed.) (1979), *Metaphor and Thought*, Cambridge, Cambridge University Press.

Montague grammar

Richard Montague was an American logician who taught in the philosophy department at UCLA. Between 1955 and his death in 1970, he published a series of papers in which he advocated, and began to execute, a programme for research in linguistics which has become increasingly influential since his death. His collected papers were published in 1974 as *Formal Philosophy*, under the editorship of Richmond Thomason. Montague's programme is sometimes referred to as **Montague semantics**, rather than 'grammar', because, unlike many systems of

grammar, Montague's programme does not contain a phonological component or a morphological component. Montague's central concern is to show that there is a one-to-one correspondence between syntactic rules which determine how a sentence is built up out of smaller syntactic parts, and semantic rules that determine how the meaning of a sentence is built up out of the meanings of its parts.

The distinctive features of Montague's programme are clear from 'English as a Formal Language' (Montague, 1974, ch. 6). He says there that he rejects 'the contention that an important theoretical difference exists between formal and natural languages', but he does not regard 'as successful the formal treatments of natural languages attempted by certain contemporary linguists'. Here, he rejects the approaches of Chomsky and his followers because they fail to acknowledge that 'the construction of a theory of truth' is 'the basic goal of serious syntax and semantics'.

His approach to language relies upon techniques drawn from formal and modal logic (see FORMAL LOGIC AND MODAL LOGIC), and his target is to construct a formal semantics (see FORMAL SEMANTICS) for a substantial fragment of a natural language like English. His objection to MIT linguists was that their syntactic categories were not motivated by the need to provide a formal semantics for the language under study. In papers like 'English as a formal language', he attempted to do syntax and semantics for a stilted and restricted fragment of English using the syntactic and semantic notions familiar from logicians' study of formal languages. This paper is much more accessible than the forbiddingly technical prose of the later papers for which he is best known: 'Universal grammar' and 'The proper treatment of quantification in ordinary English' (chs 7 and 8 in Montague, 1974).

The most distinctive feature of this later work is that Montague avoids the logician's normal practice of attempting to describe a natural language using syntactic categories designed for the description of artificial languages. Montague develops his own system of formal semantics employing categories such as **noun, noun phrase, adverb**, etc., which are not normally employed by logically minded philosophers of language.

This produces valuable insights into the logical structure of English sentences which are reflected in his work on quantified phrases.

Consider a sentence such as *Every horse gallops*. Montague describes 'gallops' as an intransitive verb. Ignoring complexities of time and world (see FORMAL SEMANTICS) we can take this to refer to a class of objects – viz. to all those things that gallop. 'Horse' is a common noun, which also refers to such a class. The need for distinct categories of expressions which refer to classes of objects emerges from the fact that only 'horse' can combine with 'every' to form a noun phrase, 'every horse'. The semantics assigns to 'every horse' a class which contains every class which includes among its members every horse. If the class associated with 'gallops' is one of these, then the sentence is true.

Montague's work engages with a variety of semantic phenomena which cannot be captured with the traditional categories of formal semantics. The books listed below describe these and also indicate the progress made by later scholars in developing Montague's ideas.

C.H.

SUGGESTIONS FOR FURTHER READING

Cresswell, M.J. (1973), *Logic and Languages*, London, Methuen.

Dowty, D.R., R.E. Wall, and S. Peters (1981), *Introduction to Montague Semantics*, Dordrecht, Reidel.

Montague, R. (1974), *Formal Philosophy*, edited and with an introduction by Richmond H. Thomason, New Haven, Yale University Press.

Morphology

BACKGROUND AND BASIC TERMS

While syntax is concerned with how words arrange themselves into constructions, **morphology** is concerned with *the forms of words themselves*. The term has been used by linguists for over a century, although opinions have varied as to precise definitions of the subject-area and scope. Interest in classifying language families across the world in the nineteenth century (see HISTORICAL LINGUISTICS, pp. 212–16) led to the study of how languages were differently structured both in broad and narrower ways, from the general laws of structure to the study of significant elements such as prefixes and inflections (see Farrar, 1870, p. 160; Lloyd, 1896). In the twentieth century the field has narrowed to the study of the internal structure of words, but definitions still vary in detail (see Bloomfield, 1933, p. 207; Nida, 1946, p. 1; Matthews, 1974, p. 3, as important main sources, and for an overview, Molino, 1985).

Most linguists agree that morphology is the study of the *meaningful* parts of words, but there have broadly been two ways of looking at the overall role played by these meaningful parts of words in language. One way has been to play down the status of the word itself and to look at the role of its parts in the overall syntax; the other has been to focus on the word as a central unit.

Whichever way is chosen, all linguists agree that within words, meaningful elements can be perceived. Thus in the English word *watched*, two bits of meaning are present: WATCH plus PAST TENSE. WATCH, and PAST TENSE are generally called **morphemes**. In the word *pens* two morphemes PEN and PLURAL are present. A word such as *unhelpful* has three morphemes: NEGATIVE + HELP + ADJECTIVE. But terms such as NEGATIVE, PLURAL, and ADJECTIVE are abstract; they are not real forms. The real forms that represent them (*in-*, *-s* and *-ful*) are therefore usually called **morphs** (see Hockett, 1947). We can represent the examples thus:

Words	Morphs	Morphemes
watched	watch-ed	WATCH + PAST
pens	pen-s	PEN + PLURAL
unhelpful	un-help-ful	NEGATIVE + HELP + ADJECTIVE

In theories where the word is an important unit, morphology therefore becomes the description of 'morphemes and their patterns of occurrence within the word' (Allerton, 1979, p. 47). In the American structuralist tradition interest lay more in the morpheme as the basic unit in syntax rather than in its role within the word; Harris (1946), for example, recognized only 'morphemes and sequences of morphemes' and eschewed the word as a unit of description. While this sidesteps the problem of defining the word, the morpheme itself has also presented difficulties of definition and identification. Bloomfield (1926) describes the morpheme as 'a recurrent (meaningful) form which cannot in turn be analyzed into smaller recurrent (meaningful) forms. Hence any unanalyzable word or formative is a morpheme'. The problem is: what is *meaningful*?

What is more, recurrent forms in themselves are also problematic. Nida (1946, p. 79) said that morphemes are recognized by 'different partial resemblances between expressions', which enables us to identify a common morpheme PAST in *sailed*, *landed* and *watched*, and a common morpheme SAIL in *sails*, *sailing*, *sailor*, *sail* and *sailed*. PAST and SAIL are both 'meaningful' and are established by noting the recurrent pieces of word forms (Robins, 1980, p. 155), in this case the morphs written as *-ed* and *sail*. However, the following examples from English show that there are serious problems with this approach (after Allerton, 1979, pp. 49–50):

(1) disarrange, disorganize,
(2) discern, discuss,
(3) dismay, disgruntle,
(4) disappoint, disclose.

Group 1 are clearly *morpheme + morpheme* words (they contain recurrent *and* meaningful parts). Group 2 cannot be analysed into parts and so represent single morphemes. Group 3 seem to have some sense of 'disturbance of a state' in their *dis-* element, but the parts *-may* and *-gruntle* can then only be labelled as **unique morphemes** in that they do not reoccur elsewhere. Group 4 looks superficially like group 1, but the parts *-appoint* and *-close* bear no meaningful relation to the morphemes APPOINT and CLOSE which appear elsewhere as separate words. Group 4 therefore contains **pseudo-morphemes**.

Bloomfield (1933, p. 244) had also noted what he called **phonetic–semantic resemblances** between recurrent parts of words which occur in very limited sets and yet do not seem to have any specifiable meaning nor any meaning at all beyond the limited set, for example:

/ð/   in *this, that, then, there*
/n/   in *not, neither, no, never*
/fl /   in *flash, flicker, flame, flare*
/sn / in *sniff, snort, snore, snot*

Firth (1930/64, p. 184) called such words **phonaesthemes**. Marchand (1969, ch. 7), who examines this phenomenon in great detail, calls it **phonetic symbolism**.

Other problems in labelling morphemes include variations of meaning within a single recurrent form (Bazell, 1949), which is evident in the English element *-er* in *leader* ('one who leads'), *recorder* (not 'one who records' in the phrase *to play the recorder*; see Allerton, 1979, p. 226), and

meaningfully related forms that have no phonetic resemblance (e.g. *go/went, city/urban*). The problems are basically those of trying to relate forms and meanings, and morphologists have never fully resolved them. Bolinger (1948) calls the morpheme 'scarcely easier to pin down than a word' and sees one of the main problems as being the separation of **etymology** which is rightly the study of how present-day words came to be formed in the past, and the description of the structure of words. Thus **diachronic morphology** will be interested in the elements that originally built words such as *disease* and *away*, words which to the vast majority of present-day English speakers would consist of a single morpheme each.

Bolinger, and after him Haas (1960), also recognized the difficulty of trying to identify morphemes on purely formal (distributional) grounds: for how does one separate the *cat* in *pussycat* from *cat* in *cattle*, or the *re-* in *recall* and *religion*? Bolinger's solution is that the morpheme be rather pragmatically defined as what the majority of speakers can recognize as one, or as the smallest element that can enter into *new* combinations (i.e. that an element must be **productive**). This enables us to dispense with 'meaning' and concentrate on 'a measurable fact, the recurring appearance in new environments' (Bolinger, 1965a, p. 187; see also Marchand, 1969, pp. 2ff.). This approach certainly clears away niggling difficulties such as any apparent relationship between the word *stand* and its purely formal recurrence in *understand* and *withstand* (which form their past like *stand* but have no obvious present-day connection and are not part of a productive set) (see Makkai, 1978); it also rules out the *cran* of *cranberry* from having the status of a morpheme. But problems remain: a cranberry *is* opposed in meaning to a strawberry or a loganberry, and so the elements preceding *-berry* certainly have some 'significance'.

One solution is to see morphemes as only having true significance in relation to the words they appear in and so to make the word absolutely central to morphology. Such an approach is seen in Aronoff (1976, p. 10). Whatever the case, there do seem to be strong arguments for separating **synchronic** from **diachronic** studies (see STRUCTURALIST LINGUISTICS), for without such a separation, the difficulties become insurmountable. To rescue the morpheme as a manageable unit it is also clear that neither form nor meaning alone are entirely reliable but must be wed in a compromise. The arbitrariness of meaning will persist in providing inconsistencies such as *selection* (act of selecting/things selected) compared with *election* (act of electing/*people elected) (Matthews, 1974, pp. 50–1), but linguists continue to seek statements that will express underlying meanings for apparently unrelated forms (e.g. Bybee, 1985, p. 4; Booij, 1986). It will generally be the case, though, that morphemes will be identified by an accumulation of formal and semantic criteria. Such criteria can be seen in operation in Nida's (1946) principle for identifying morphemes (see also Olu Tomori, 1977, pp. 25ff., for a summary and discussion).

However, the morpheme will often be recognized by semantic and distributional criteria without its form being identical. A clear example is the formation of plurals in English. If we compare the final elements in *hands* [z], *cats* [s], and *matches* [ɪz], we can observe a common meaning (PLURAL), a common distribution (distinct from that of the present-tense *-s* of verbs, such as *sees*, *writes*, etc.) and phonological resemblances. So, just as the sound [ɫ] in *bottle* does not contrast in *meaning* anywhere in English with the sound [l] in *lamp*, nor does [hændz] ever contrast with a word [hændɪz]; and just as we talk of the **phoneme** /l/ being realized by two **allophones** (see PHONEMICS), so the **morpheme** PLURAL is realized by different **allomorphs** (/-z/, /-s/, and /-ɪz/). Similarly, the English PAST morpheme has its allomorphs in the different realizations of *-ed* in *hooked* /t/, *raised* /d/, and *landed* /ɪd/.

Another way of looking at allomorphs is to say that the allomorphs of the English morpheme PLURAL alternate between /s/, /z/, and /ɪz/ and that these are three different **alternants** (see Matthews, 1974, pp. 85ff.). Alternation is usually studied in terms of the type of **conditioning** that brings it about. For instance, the English PLURAL allomorphs mentioned are **phonologically conditioned**: they follow the same rules as the allomorphs of present-tense third-person singular *-s* and the *'s* possessive (Bloomfield, 1933, p. 211). Whether a past participle ends in *-en* or *-ed*, however, is not determined by phonology and is thus said to be **grammatically** or **morphologically conditioned**.

But the notion of allomorphs and alternation raises a further problem. *Sheep* can be singular or plural, and *put* is the present, past, or past participle of the verb. To overcome this difficulty, some linguists have proposed the existence of a **zero morph** (written ∅). Then, in the case of English plurals, ∅ would be one allomorph of the morpheme PLURAL, alternating with /s/, /z/, and /ɪz/. Likewise ∅ would be an allomorph of PAST, alternating with /t/, /d/, and /ɪd/. Nida (1946, p. 3) justifies this approach by saying that the absence of an ending in verbs like *hit* and *cut* is 'structurally as distinctive as the presence of one', but other linguists have seriously challenged the viability of ∅ as a linguistic element. Haas (1960) calls zero allomorphs 'ghostly components' and Matthews (1974, p. 117) says incisively 'one cannot examine one's data and determine the "distribution" of "zero"'.

Not only this, but ∅ does not solve the problem of the existence of other plurals such as *man/men* and *foot/feet*, or past tenses such as *drink/drank* and *sing/sang*. An alternative, therefore, is to talk of **morphological processes**, whereby the individual elements (e.g. MAN + PLURAL) interact to form a unified product, *men*, and are in no way obliged to represent the segments as a **sequence** of morphemes (Matthews, 1974, pp. 122–3). This approach enables the analyst to dispense with the notion of allomorphs and to dispense with ∅: HIT + PAST simply interact to give the unified form *hit*, while SING + PAST interact to produce *sang*.

Morphemes and the morphs that represent them are, however, clearly of different types. In the word *repainted*, the morph *paint* can stand alone as a word and is therefore a **free morph**; *re-* and *-ed* cannot stand alone and are therefore **bound morphs**. Another distinction is often made between (1) morphs such as *head*, *line*, *-ist* and *de-*, which can be used in the creation of new words (e.g. *headline, communist, depopulate*), which are called **lexical morphs**, and (2) those which simply represent grammatical categories such as person, tense, number, definiteness, etc., which are called **grammatical morphs**.

Lexical morphs which are *not* of the kind *-ist* and *de-* but which form the 'core' of a word (Olu Tomori, 1977, p. 32), such as *help* in *unhelpful* or *build* in *rebuild* are known as **roots**. The root is that part of the word which is left when all the **affixes**, that is, all the morphs that have been added to it, whether before or after it (such as *de-, er-, -ist, -ing, -ed*, etc.) are taken away. The root is central to the building of new words. Not all roots can stand as free words, however: in the series *dentist, dental, dentures*, there is certainly a root to which various morphs are added to produce nouns and adjectives, but there is no free morph *dent* which represents the morpheme OF THE TEETH. So some roots are **bound** (*econom-*, as in *economist, economy, economic* is another example). Allerton (1979, p. 213) sums up this complex relationship between free and bound, lexical and grammatical morphemes, and roots and affixes. Affixes are divided into **prefixes**, occurring at the beginnings of words, and **suffixes**, occurring at the end of words. **Infixes**, morphs inserted within other morphs, also exist in some languages.

Not all linguists agree precisely on the definition of the term **root** (Matthews, 1974, pp. 39–40, has a different view; Malkiel, 1978, prefers to talk of **primitives**), but for most purposes it may be conveniently thought of as the core or unanalysable centre of a word.

THE SCOPE OF MORPHOLOGY

The different approaches to identifying morphemes and to the relationships between morphemes and words are reflections of different major trends in linguistics during the twentieth century, but most linguists are in agreement on the type of phenomena morphology is concerned with. A sample of English words will illustrate these areas:

(5) locates, locating, located
(6) location, locative, dislocate
(7) earache, workload, time-bomb

In group 5, the suffixes realize morphemes such as PRESENT, PAST, PRESENT PARTICIPLE, etc. but do not change the nature of *locate* as a verb; morphemes such as PRESENT, PAST, PLURAL, THIRD PERSON, and so on, are called **inflectional morphemes**. **Inflection** is a major category of morphology (see Matthews, 1972). Group 6 adds bound morphs to *locate* which change its word class and enable us to **derive** new words (an adjective, a noun and a verb with opposite meaning). The process of adding bound morphs to create new words of the same or different word classes (see below, pp. 318–19) is called **derivation.** Group 7 shows examples of words which are made by combining two free roots (e.g. *ear + ache*). This is called **composition** or **compounding** and *earache, workload*, and *time-bomb* are **compounds**. Groups 6 and 7 are different from 5, then, in that they enable new words to be formed; they are examples of **word-formation**, and the scope of morphology may be represented in the following way (see Bauer, 1983, p. 34):

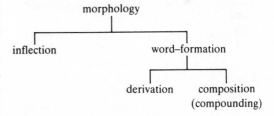

INFLECTION

Bloomfield (1933, p. 222) referred to inflection as the outer layer of the morphology of word forms and derivation as the inner layer. A simple example to illustrate what he meant by this is that the natural morphemic segmentation of the word-form *stewardesses* is as in (8), not as in (9) below:

(8) stewardess + es
(9) *steward + esses

In other words, inflections are added when all derivational and compositional processes are already complete. The plural forms of *motorbike* and *painter* are *motorbikes* and *painters*, not **motorsbike* and **paintser*. Inflections such as tense, number, person, etc. will be attached to ready-made **stems**. Stems are the forms to which inflections may be added, but which may already have derivational affixes. Examples of stems are *repaint* (which can yield *repaints, repainted*, etc.) and *computerize* (which can give *computerized, computerizing* etc.). Again, not all linguists agree on the use of these terms. The various terms can be related by the following example of some possible forms of the root *paint*:

root	*paint*
affixes	*(re-)*paint(*-ed*)
stem	*repaint*(-ed)
morphs	*re-paint-ed*
morphemes	AGAIN-PAINT-PAST

Inflectional categories such as tense, voice, and number play an important role in syntax and are called **morphosyntactic categories**, since they affect both the words around them and the words within which they occur (see Matthews, 1974, p. 66). Inflectional morphemes are very productive: the third-person singular present tense *-s* can be attached to any new English verb; the same cannot necessarily be said about derivational affixes (we can say *rework* and *dismissive* but not **rebe* or **wantive*, for example). Inflectional morphemes are semantically more regular than derivational ones; meaning will remain constant across a wide distributional range. Inflections create full conjugations and declensions for verbs and nouns; unlike derivations they usually do not produce 'gaps': whereas the past inflectional morph *-ed* can be attached to any of the verbs *arrive, dispose, approve*, and *improve* in English, only the first three form nouns with the *-al* suffix.

WORD FORMATION

There is broad, but not complete, agreement as to how the field of word-formation should be divided up. Marchand (1969, p. 2) distinguishes

between (1) formation involving 'full linguistic signs', i.e. compounding, prefixation, suffixation, derivation by the zero morph, and backformation (see below, pp. 319–20), and (2) formations not involving full linguistic signs, which include expressive symbolism (e.g. Firth's **phonaesthemes**, see p. 315), blending, clipping, and word manufacturing (see p. 320 for definitions of these terms). Adams (1973, ch. 10) adds acronyms to clippings, and both Adams (1973) and Bauer (1983) separate off the class of 'neo-classical compounds' (items such as *television* and *astronaut*), whereas Marchand (1969) subsumes many of the initial morphs of neo-classical formations under the general heading of prefixes. While there are undoubtedly hazy border areas, the general distinction between derivation and composition (compounding) holds good.

DERIVATION

Derivation is the reverse of the coin of inflection. Like inflection, it consists in adding to a root or stem an affix or affixes (the root is also sometimes called the **unmarked base form** and the affixed form the **marked form**; see Adams, 1973, p. 12). But while new inflections occur only very slowly over time, new derivational affixes seem to occur from time to time, principally in that speakers use elements of words that are not established as affixes in a way that makes them like established, productive ones (e.g. English *sputnik, beatnik, refusenik; alcoholic, workaholic, radioholic*; see Adams, 1973, p. 139, for further examples). Matthews (1984) gives a good summary of the arguments concerned in the separation of inflection from derivation.

Derivational affixes produce new words; their function is not to express morphosyntactic categories but to make new words. They are somewhat erratic in meaning and distribution: the suffix *-al* that creates nouns from verbs such as *arrive* and *dispose* forms adjectives from the nouns *brute* and *option*. What is more, whereas *nasal* means 'of the nose', *brutal* means 'like a brute' and *optional* means that something '*is* an option'. Derivational affixes vary in their productivity: English nouns ending in *-hood* are few and new ones are unlikely, as are adjectives with the negative prefix *ig-* (e.g. *ignoble*) or the suffix *-ose* (*jocose, verbose*) (see Kastovsky, 1986), but the *-ist* in *communist* is fully productive, as is the *-ize* verb-forming morph (*computerize, centralize*).

Within derivation, the distinction is often made between **class-maintaining** and **class-changing processes**. Class-changing produces a new word in a different word-class (e.g. *computer* (noun) – *computerize* (verb)), while class-maintaining produces a new word but does not change the class (e.g. *child* (noun) – *childhood* (noun)) (but see Bauer, 1983, pp. 31–2, for arguments against the distinction). Equally important is the phenomenon of **conversion** where a word changes word-class without any affixation, e.g. *a hoover* (noun) – *to hoover* (verb); *a service* (noun) – *to service* (verb) (see also Bolinger and Sears, 1981, p. 65); Malkiel (1978) calls this **internal derivation**.

COMPOSITION (COMPOUNDING)

Marchand (1969, p. 11) talks of compounding as occurring when two or more words combine into a morphological unit, and Adams (1979, p. 30) refers to the combination 'of two free forms, or words that have an otherwise independent existence'. Examples of compounds are *blackmail*, *bathroom*, *skyscraper*, and *gearbox*. They function to all intents and purposes like single words: if the room where I have my bath is old it is an *old bathroom*, not a *bath old room. Like single words they will be spoken with only one primary stress, and any inflectional suffixes will occur at the end of the whole unit (*bathrooms*, not *bathsroom). They occupy full, single grammatical slots in sentences, unlike idioms, which can be a whole clause (Bolinger and Sears, 1981, p. 62). Compounds may contain more than two free roots (e.g. *wastepaper basket*) and in some languages (e.g. Germanic ones) may contain in excess of half a dozen free roots (see Scalise, 1984, p. 34, for examples). Compounds may be formed with elements from any word-class but, in English at least, noun + noun compounds are the most common and are very

productive; verb + verb compounds are few in English.

The following are examples of noun compounds in English according to the form-classes of their components, following Bauer (1983) (for other approaches to classification see ibid., p. 202):

noun + noun	bookshelf	football
verb + noun	pickpocket	killjoy
noun + verb	nosebleed	moonshine
adjective + noun	software	slowcoach
particle + noun	in-crowd	aftertaste
verb + particle	clawback	dropout
phrase compounds	gin-and-tonic	forget-me-not

These all function as nouns. Similar constructions can function as verbs. Some combinations are rare, for example, verb + verb functioning overall as a verb: *to freeze-dry* is a recent occurrence, but the same type (verb + verb) functioning as an adjective seems more productive: Bauer (1983, pp. 211–12) gives *go-go* (*dancer*), *stop-go* (*economics*), and *pass-fail* (*test*) as recent instances.

Compounds are often divided into four semantic types: **endocentric**, **exocentric**, **appositional**, and **dvandva** (see Bauer, 1983, pp. 30–1). Where the second element is the grammatical headword and the first a modifier, as in *wristwatch* (where *wrist* modifies *watch*), the compound is **endocentric**. Endocentric compounds are **hyponyms** (see SEMANTICS, p. 393) of the headword. Where hyponymy of this kind does not exist, as in *scapegoat*, which is a kind of person, not a kind of goat, the compound is **exocentric** (the term **bahuvrihi** is also used for this type). Where the hyponymy is **bidirectional**, as in *sofa-bed*, which is a kind of sofa and/or a kind of bed, or *clock-radio*, which is a kind of clock and/or a kind of radio, these are known as **appositional compounds**. Where compound elements name separate entities neither of which is a hyponym of the other and either of which might seem to be the grammatical headword, then these are **dvandva** or **copulative compounds**, as in names such as *Slater-Walker*, *Austin-Rover*, or *Alsace-Lorraine*.

The type of compounds referred to as **neo-**

classical compounds take elements, usually from Greek or Latin, and make words in a way that often resembles derivation but which needs to be kept distinct, for often such elements can combine with each other without any other root being present, and are therefore acting like roots themselves. It is for this reason that they may be considered as similar to compounds. Examples are *anglophile* (cf. *hibernophile*, *francophile*, etc.), *telephone* (*television*, *telegram*), *astronaut* (*cosmonaut*), *biocrat*. *Anglophile* belongs to a medial *-o* type which includes *sphero-cylindrical*, *socio-political*, *physico-chemical*, etc. (see Adams, 1973, p. 132).

OTHER WORD-FORMATION TYPES

Backformation occurs when a suffix (or a morph perceived as a suffix) is removed from a complex word; *lecher – to lech*, or *liaison – to liaise* are recent English examples; Malkiel (1978) has interesting examples from old Provençal and modern French. Malkiel (ibid.) also gives examples of **clipping**, which can involve deletion of initial morphemes or final word-segments: *lab(oratory)*, *(aero)plane*, *(tele)phone*, etc. are examples. **Blends** are another interesting type of formation, where normally initial and terminal segments of two words are joined together to create a new word, for example, *brunch* (*breakfast + lunch*). Recent English examples include *selectorate* (*selectors + electorate*), *chunnel* (*channel + tunnel*), *fantabulous* (*fantastic + fabulous*). Cannon (1986) who provides the best description of blends sees them as popular but often short-lived.

Acronyms, words formed from the initial letters of a fixed phrase or title, are also popular and often equally short-lived. Recent English examples are *quango* (quasi-autonomous non-governmental organization), *misty* (more ideologically sound than you); established acronyms include *NATO*, *SALT* (strategic arms limitation talks) and *radar*. **Word manufacture**, the invention of completely new morphs, is rare in comparison to the kinds of word-formation described above. One example often cited is *kodak*. Equally, some words appear whose origin

is unknown or unclear (the OED attests *gazump* from the 1920s onwards with no etymological information) and literary works often contain one-off inventions (see Bauer, 1983, p. 239, for some examples).

Word-formation processes are variably productive but constantly in operation to expand the lexicon as new meanings emerge, social and technological change takes place, and individuals create new forms. Recently, the advent of computers has given English items like *software* and *firmware*, and an extended meaning of *hardware*, plus a host of other terms. A survey, in the London *Observer* newspaper in 1987, of the professional jargon of young City professionals included compounds such as *Chinese wall*, *concert party*, *dawn raid*, *marzipan set*, and *white knight*, all with specific meanings within the world of financial dealing, as well as clever acronyms such as *oink* (one income, no kids) and *dinky* (dual income, no kids yet) (*Observer*, 23 March 1987, p. 51).

MORPHOPHONOLOGY (OR MORPHO-NOLOGY, OR MORPHOPHONEMICS)

Morphophonology in its broadest sense is the study of the phonological structure of morphemes (the permitted combinations of phonemes within morphemes in any given language; see Vachek, 1933), the phonemic variation which morphemes undergo in combination with one another (e.g. *hoof* → *hooves* in English), and the study of alternation series (e.g. recurrent changes in phonemes before certain suffixes in English: *electric* → *electricity*, *plastic* → *plasticity*; *malice* → *malicious*, *pretence* → *pretentious*; see Trubetzkoy, 1931). Such changes are from one **phoneme** to another, not just between allophones (see also Trubetzkoy, 1929).

The study of such changes is carried out within a morphological framework. Swadesh (1934) points out that the /f/ in *leaf* and the /f/ in *cuff* are phonemically the same but morphologically distinct in that their plurals are formed in /v/ and /f/ respectively. This latter fact can be represented by a morphophonemic symbol /F/, which would represent /v/ before /z/ plural and /f/ elsewhere

(Harris, 1942; see also Lass, 1984, pp. 57–8).

The broad areas covered by morphophonemics in Trubetzkoy's terms have been successively narrowed and rebroadened in linguistics over the years (see Kilbury, 1976, for a detailed survey). Hockett (1947) concentrates on 'differences in the phonemic shape of alternants of morphemes' in his definition of morphophonemics, rather than on the phonemic structure of morphemes themselves. Wells (1949) takes a similar line. Hockett (1950) later returns to a broader definition which 'subsumes every phase of the phonemic shape of morphemes', and later still gives morphophonemics a central place in the description of language (1958, p. 137). One of the problems in studying the phonemic composition of alternants is the separation of those alternants whose phonemes differ purely because of phonological rules, those which differ purely on lexicogrammatical grounds and those which might be seen as most narrowly morphophonologically determined (see Matthews, 1974, p. 213, for a critique of these distinctions).

Central to the study of alternation is the notion of **sandhi**, which comes from a Sanskrit word meaning 'joining' (see Andersen, 1986, pp. 1–8, for a general definition). Sandhi rules attempt to account for the phonological modification of forms joined to one another. A distinction is usually drawn between **external sandhi**, which occurs across word-boundaries, and **internal sandhi**, which occurs within word-boundaries (see Matthews, 1974, p. 111). Matthews gives an example of a sandhi rule for ancient Greek: 'any voiced consonant is unvoiced when an s (or other voiceless consonant) follows it'; this rule is realized in, for example, the forms *aigos* (genitive) – *aiks* (nominative) (1974, p. 102). Lass (1984, p. 69) locates the principal domain of sandhi as the interface between phonology and syntax; it is concerned with processes at the margins of words in syntactic configurations or at the margins of morphemes in syntactically motivated contexts. Sandhi rules form an important part of morphophonemic description. Andersen (1986) contains accounts of sandhi phenomena in European languages.

Over the years, much debate has taken place on the overall status of morphophonology in linguistic description. Chomsky's (1951) thesis on modern Hebrew sees the morphophonological statements of a language as the third stage in the generation of sentences from the basic syntactic statements to the final sequence of phones (Chomsky, 1979, pp. 3–4) (see TRANS-FORMATIONAL-GENERATIVE GRAMMAR), and Hockett (1958, pp. 135–42) makes morphophonemics centrally important but not independent; it is, rather, an interlevel between grammar and phonology. The changing emphases on the status of morphophonology in later years, including developments in Chomsky's position, are given full coverage in Kilbury (1976); Chomsky and Halle (1968, p. 11) reject the term 'morphophonology' altogether and deal with matters such as alternation under the umbrella of phonology (ibid., pp. 178ff.). The debate has resurfaced within modular approaches to linguistics and is best represented in Dressler (1985), whose view is that morphophonology mediates between morphology and phonology without being a basic level in itself.

MORPHOLOGY: SCHOOLS AND TRENDS

Three general approaches may be discerned within morphology; these are usually known as **word and paradigm**, **item and process**, and **item and arrangement**. In addition, the debates on morphology within the general framework of generative grammar must be mentioned.

WORD AND PARADIGM

This is the approach to morphology many will be familiar with from school-book descriptions of Latin grammar and the grammar of some modern European languages. Word and paradigm (WP) has a long-established history, going back to ancient classical grammars. In this approach, the word is central, and is the fundamental unit in grammar. WP retains a basic distinction between morphology and syntax: morphology is concerned with the formation of words and syntax with the structure of sentences. Central, therefore, to WP is the establishment of the word as an independent, stable unit. Robins (1959) offers convincing criteria for words and argues that WP is an extremely useful model in the description of languages. Word-forms sharing a common root or base are grouped into one or more paradigms (e.g. the conjugations of the different tenses of the Latin verb *amo*). Paradigm categories include such things as number in English, or case in Latin, or gender in French. Paradigms are primarily used for inflectional morphemes; derivational ones can be set out in this way but they tend to be less regular and symmetrical (see p. 318 above).

WP is particularly useful in describing fusional features in languages; using the word as the central unit avoids the problems of 'locating' individual morphosyntactic categories in particular morphs, especially where several may be simultaneously fused in one word-element (e.g. Latin *amabis*, where tense, mood, voice, number, and person cannot be separated sequentially). Matthews (1974, p. 226) points out that exponents of morphosyntactic categories may extend throughout a word-form, overlapping each other where necessary. He also illustrates, with reference to Spanish verbs, how identical forms appear in different paradigms and can only be meaningfully understood in relation to the other members of their paradigm. Thus the systematic reversal of inflectional endings to indicate mood in *-ar* and *-er* verbs in Spanish, e.g *compra* (indicative) – *compre* (subjunctive), compared with *come* (indicative) – *coma* (subjunctive) can only be captured fully within the paradigm (1974, pp. 137ff.; see also Molino, 1985).

WP avoids the morphophonological problems that beset other approaches and can also dispense with the ∅ morph, since morphosyntactic features are exhibited in the word-form as a whole. In general, WP may be seen to be a model which has great usefulness in linguistic description, although it may be of less use in describing certain types of language.

ITEM AND PROCESS

The item and process (IP) model, as its name suggests, relates items to one another by refer-ence to morphological processes. Thus *took* is related to *take* by a process of vowel change. IP considers the morpheme, not the word, to be the basic unit of grammar, and, therefore, the morphology/syntax division is negated. In IP, each morpheme has an underlying form, to which processes are applied. This underlying form will sometimes be the most widely distributed allomorph; thus in Latin *rex, regis, regi, regem*, etc., [ks] occurs only in nominative singular, suggesting *reg-* as the underlying form (Lass, 1984, p. 64; see also Allerton, 1979, p. 223).

In IP, labels such as 'plural' become an operation rather than a form (Molino, 1985). Processes include affixation, alternation of consonants and/or vowels (e.g. *sing/sang*), reduplication (e.g. Malay plurals: *guru-guru* 'teachers'), compounding, and stress differences (e.g. *récord/recórd*) (Robins, 1959). Matthews (1974, p. 226) exemplifies how generative grammarians have included processes in descriptions of lexical entries, to activate features such as vowel change when certain morphemes are present (e.g. English *goose* + plural → *geese*). IP, like WP, has great value as a model of analysis; it can do much to explain word-forms but, as with WP, it cannot account for all features of all languages.

ITEM AND ARRANGEMENT

Hockett (1954) contrasts IP and IA (item and arrangement) sharply, and Robins (1959) suggests that WP should be considered as something separate, not opposed to IP and IA in the way that IP and IA are opposed to one another. IA sees the word as a linear sequence of morphs which can be segmented. Thus a sentence such as *the wheel/s turn/ed rapid/ly* would be straightforwardly segmented as shown. Again, the morpheme is the fundamental unit. IA talks simply of items and 'the arrangements in which they occur relative to each other in utterances – appending statements to cover phonemic shapes which appear in any occurrent combination' (Hockett, 1954).

IA is associated with structural formalism and the systematization that followed from

Bloomfield. In his comparison of IA and IP, Hockett illustrates the contrast in the two approaches to linguistic forms: for IP, forms are either **simple** or **derived**; a **simple form** is a root, a **derived form** is an 'underlying form to which a process has been applied'. In IA, a form is either **simple** or **composite**; a **simple form** is a morpheme and a **composite form** 'consists of two or more immediate constituents standing in a construction'. IA encountered many problems in description, not least how to handle alternation, but its value lay in its rigorous, synchronic approach to unknown languages and its formalism. Its goal was to describe the totality of attested and possible sequences of the language using discrete minimal units established by distributional criteria (Molino, 1985).

WP, IP, and IA have different domains of usefulness and no one model can serve all purposes. All three leave certain areas unresolved, and the best features of each are undoubtedly essential in any full description of a language.

MORPHOLOGY AND GENERATIVE GRAMMAR

The place of morphology within a generative framework has been the subject of much debate since the late 1950s. Early transformational grammarians continued the structuralist tradition of blurring the morphology/syntax division. Chomsky (1957, p. 32) viewed syntax as the grammatical sequences of morphemes of a language. In general, morphology was not held to be a separate field of study (see Aronoff, 1976, p. 4; Scalise, 1984, p. ix). Phonology and syntax were the central components of grammatical description. Lees 1960 is a key document of the approach that attempts to explain word-formation processes in terms of syntactic transformations. A compound such as *manservant* was seen to incorporate the sentence *The servant is a man*; this sentence by transformation generates the compound (Lees, 1960, p. 119). Such a description is naturally highly problematic, especially when confronted with the idiosyncrasies of derived and compound words.

Chomsky (1970a) saw an opposition between this **transformationalist view** and the **lexicalist view**, which transferred to the lexicon proper the rules of derivation and compounding. In the **lexicalist view**, the rules of word-formation are rules for generating words which may be stored in the dictionary. Halle (1973) sees the dictionary as a set of morphemes plus a set of word-formation mechanisms; word-formation occurs entirely within the lexicon. The growing importance of the lexicon and the debate on the status of word-formation meant the steady re-emergence of morphology as a separate area of study. In the 1970s and 1980s, important works on morphology have been produced within the generative framework and accepting the lexicalist position (e.g. Jackendoff, 1975). Williams (1981) goes further, and attempts to break down the inflection/derivation distinction with regard to word-formation as does Selkirk (1982), who clearly places derivation, compounding and inflection within a morphological component of the grammar (but see also Anderson, 1982).

Most recently, interest has grown in natural morphology and in lexical phonology and morphology, lexical phonology for short. **Natural morphology** is an approach which looks for natural universals over a wide range of languages with regard to **morphotactic** (the way morphemes are joined) and morphosyntactic tendencies. The trend began in the mid-1970s and is summarized by Dressler (1986). **Lexical phonology** regards the lexicon as the central component of grammar, which contains rules of word-formation and phonology as well as the idiosyncratic properties of words and morphemes. The word-formation rules of the morphology are paired with phonological rules at various levels or **strata**, and the output of each set of word-formation rules is submitted to the phonological rules on the same stratum to produce a word. The lexicon is therefore the output of the morphological and phonological rules of the different strata put together (see further Pulleyblank, 1986; Katamba, 1989, Ch. 12).

M.J.McC.

SUGGESTIONS FOR FURTHER READING

Bauer, L. (1983), *English Word-Formation*, Cambridge, Cambridge University Press.

Matthews, P.H. (1974), *Morphology*, Cambridge, Cambridge University Press.

Origin of language

The question of the origin of language is approached with caution by many modern linguists, because they feel that it is not possible to provide any reliable evidence on the matter. Indeed, the Société Linguistique de Paris has as one of its foundation rules the exclusion from its meetings of any papers on the origin of language. However, the question of the origin of language is obviously of interest from an evolutionary point of view, and some fossil evidence exists from which the constitution of the vocal tract of earlier hominids and other factors which may have a bearing on the question can be deduced.

Lieberman (1984) argues that human language is built on a biological base that is present in other primates, and that both humans and animals have innate neural mechanisms which are matched to their respective sound-producing mechanisms (ibid., p. 324). Yet most linguists will readily agree that only humans have language proper, and that the possession of language puts humans at considerable advantage compared with other species: human language is virtually unconstrained in its communicative range, requires little expenditure of energy, hardly interferes with other physical activities, and allows for highly sophisticated collaboration among its users.

The relationship between thought and language is of considerable interest, and it seems clear that natural human language differs from all other communication systems, both those of other animals and those with which even the most sophisticated computers are able to operate (see ARTIFICIAL INTELLIGENCE): human language

is more diverse, represents reality in more detail, and allows its users to report not only on facts but to create fictions, poetry, and scientific hypotheses, which are generally assumed to be out of the range of any non-human individual, whether animal or machine. It is therefore not surprising that the question of the origin of this apparently unparalleled phenomenon has exercised and continues to exercise both the popular and the more academic imaginations.

In the past, in addition to the assumption made within most religions that the deity gave speech to humankind, speculation has centred around: (1) communicative noise-making, which gradually evolved into fully fledged language; (2) imitation of natural sounds (onomatopoeia), later conventionalized; (3) initially involuntary expressions of strong emotion, later conventionalized and made to include, for instance, calls for help; (4) analogizing with child language acquisition; and (5) analogizing with so-called primitive languages. Direct evidence bearing on the first three of these theses is unobtainable, but counterspeculation can easily be provided.

The first three theses are usually presented as if a group of individuals using communicative noises/imitation of natural sounds/expressions of strong emotion made a conscious decision to develop these systems, and this seems implausible (see PHILOSOPHY OF LANGUAGE, p. 330): (1) many animals make apparently communicative noises, but these have not developed into fully fledged human-like languages (see ANIMALS AND LANGUAGE); (2) onomatopoeia plays a part in all languages, but only a small part, and it is difficult to see how the imitation of natural sounds could have been developed into language as we know it; (3) even the leap from, say, a spontaneous scream of pure pain to the English expression *ouch* is great indeed; *ouch* is already part of a language, it is an English word which has different counter-parts in other languages.

Other types of difficulty beset the last two accounts: (4) it is clear that the analogy with child language acquisition can only hold in the most remote manner: as Robins (1989, p. 15) points out, the situation of a child growing up in an environment in which language is already fully established is very different from that of a whole group of people among whom there is no language; (5) although communities of people may be primitive in the anthropological sense, i.e. they may not engage in highly organized exploitation of natural resources, the languages used among such groups are in no sense primitive: phonetically and grammatically all languages are equally orderly and systematic and the vocabulary of any language adequately serves the needs of its speech community (ibid., p. 16).

It is, in fact, unlikely that the evolution of human language can profitably be considered in isolation from the evolution of humans as such, and it is probable that any stage of prelinguistic sounds (communicative, imitative, emotional, or whatever) is separated from our present stage of language proper, as we consider it, by countless generations of extinct humanlike, hominid species (Lieberman, 1984, p. 2). Lieberman argues that human linguistic ability is based on general neural mechanisms that structure both human and non-human animals' cognitive be-haviour, plus a set of species-specific mechanisms that structure the particular form of human speech (ibid., p. 256):

> Whereas the enhanced cognitive ability of modern *Homo Sapiens* involves the gradual elaboration of neural mechanisms that can be found in other living animals, the species-specific aspects of human speech are unique and follow from anatomical specializations and matching neural mechanisms that are not present in other living animals.

Lieberman presents an essentially Darwinian model of the origin of human language. According to a modern version of Darwin's theory, all evolution is subject to natural selection which operates on variations between individuals within a species. The individuals within a species differ genetically from one another to some degree, a low estimate for humans being 6.7 per cent (Ayala, 1978). Such genetic variation allows a species as such, if not every individual belonging to it, to adapt to a variety of changing circumstances (Lieberman, 1984, p. 6). Some variation may gradually diffuse through an entire species, if that variation is such that those young who have it stand a better chance of survival than those who do not. However, since the process of evolution is governed by the **mosaic** principle (ibid.): 'we are put together in bits and pieces that evolved separately', a small, peripheral change is more likely to be advantageous than a major change.

Lieberman gives the example of a creature born with two hearts – a major alteration. Such a creature typically does not survive the foetal stage because the viability of two hearts is subject to changes in the circulatory system of veins and arteries and the mechanisms that regulate the flow of blood through the body. But these are governed by separate genes, so that the requisite changes in the blood-flow system do not occur automatically in an individual with two hearts. A small, peripheral mutation which does not depend for its functionality on other major changes in the organism is therefore more useful to the organism, which is why (Darwin, 1859, Ch. 14): 'the more complex organs and instincts . . . have been perfected, not by means superior to, thought analogous with, human reason, but by the accumulation of innumerable slight variations'. Nevertheless, a series of small, gradual changes in the structure of individuals can open up the possibility of abrupt change in behaviour (Lieberman, 1984, p. 9), so that while it may, for example, have taken millions of years for the human vocal apparatus (each element of which has separate, non-linguistic, primary functions: see ARTICULATORY PHONETICS) to evolve – the larynx, for instance, has evolved over a period of 300 million years to facilitate the production of sound at the expense of respiratory efficiency (Negus, 1949; Lieberman, 1984, p. 213; and see below) – speech behaviour may have evolved comparative quickly once the structural apparatus was in place.

However, human speech behaviour is, of course, dependent on cognitive as well as physical characteristics of humans. According to Lieberman (1984, pp. 16–17) the biological basis of cognition, the brain, has evolved through gradual elaboration of the central nervous system. It seems to be built up of the same neural components as the brains of other animals, and, in contrast to Chomsky, Lieberman does not believe that any species- and language-specific neural devices determine the possible form of human language. Rather, he thinks that what is species- and language-specific is a set of peripheral neural mechanisms which are comparatively recent add-ons to the basic cognitive computer and which are interposed between it and the mechanisms that humans have available to transmit and receive information, 'the motor "output" systems that control the vocal apparatus, gestures, and facial expressions, and the visual and auditory "input" systems' (ibid., p. 17). The specialized input–output functions are localized, but feed into the central, general-purpose distributed computer.

Lieberman (ibid., p. 169) proposes that the species-specific anatomical and neural speech-production and -perception mechanisms which humans now possess have evolved through natural selection from a base of sound producing ability similar to that of present-day apes and auditory mechanisms which can be found in these and other living animals.

Lieberman (1984, pp. 256ff.) explains the evolution of the human supralaryngeal vocal tract in terms of a **functional branch-point** theory for natural selection, according to which 'a process of *gradual anatomical* change can at certain points yield *"sudden" functional* advantages that will lead to qualitatively different patterns of behavior in a species'. The evolution of the human supralaryngeal vocal tract begins with the functional branch-point in evolution

when a larynx appeared in ancient air-breathing fish. This first larynx was a valve, positioned in the floor of the pharynx, which had the function of preventing water from entering the lung (Negus, 1949, pp. 2–8). The next stage in its evolution was the development of fibres which pulled the larynx open to allow more air into the lung during breathing, and a further stage yielded cartilages which facilitated the opening movements of the larynx.

A second functional branch-point in the evolution of the larynx occurred when gradual alterations of the cartilages of the larynx had reached a point at which the larynx could take on a sound-producing function in addition to, though at the expense of, such vegetative functions as respiration, swallowing, and chewing (Lieberman, 1984, pp. 264–5). Different species 'solved' the conflict between sound-making and breathing ability in different ways, so that animals that use the strategy of running for long distances to escape from predators (e.g. horses) have retained wide-opening larynxes which do not impede the flow of air to their lungs during breathing, while animals, including dogs and humans, which are social and rely on vocal communication have developed shorter arytenoid cartilages which restrict the opening of the larynx, but which have a functional advantage for phonation (ibid., p. 270).

While the larynxes of all primates are adapted for phonation at the expense of respiratory efficiency (Lieberman, 1984, p. 324), the human vocal tract displays certain differences from that of any other animal. Some of these are very much to our disadvantage; for instance (Darwin, 1859, p. 191), 'every particle of food and drink which we swallow has to pass over the orifice of the trachea, with some risk of falling into the lungs'. Newborn humans, however, do not share this disadvantage. Until a baby is around three months old, it is able to breathe and drink at the same time, because its airway for breathing runs from the nose through the larynx and trachea into the lungs. The larynx is elevated in such a way that fluids can pass either side of it and enter the pharynx and oesophagus behind the larynx, but cannot fall into the larynx and trachea to choke the baby. The vocal tract of a newborn human baby is virtually identical to that of an adult chimpanzee. In fact, the ability to elevate the larynx to form an airway through the nose to the lungs that is sealed from the mouth is one which the human newborn shares with all other mammals, young and old, and Lieberman (1984, pp. 274–9) proposes that these animals have retained the **standard-plan supralaryngeal airway** from which the supralaryngeal vocal tract of modern humans has evolved. The standard-plan tract is also straighter than the adult human's and the lower jaw is relatively long compared with its height. There is more room for teeth, and the tongue is long and thin and lies wholly inside the mouth.

The process of evolution from such a tract to that of modern adult humans involves a recession of the jaws. As this took place without a reduction in tongue size, the tongue became curved and pushed the larynx down to lie opposite the fourth, fifth, and sixth vertebrae in the neck (these are numbered from the top down). The curved 'fat' human tongue can move upwards and towards the lips to produce the vowel [i], and down and back towards the vertebral column to produce the vowel [a]. The production of these vowels and the vowel [u], which are present in all human languages, depends on area-function variations in the vocal tract which cannot be created in the standard-plan tracts of chimpanzees and new-born humans. The vowels [i], [a], and [u] serve as the 'anchor points' for the normalization of formant frequencies which allows human beings to hear the essentially different versions of the 'same' speech signal produced by different humans as just that, a version, or token, of a particular type of signal.

The skulls of modern human newborns and of the classic Neanderthal La Chapelle-aux-Saints fossil show such striking similarities in structure that we can be almost certain that Neanderthal people's supralaryngeal airway was quite similar in form to that of modern human newborns and that the Neanderthal skull could not support a vocal tract similar to that of a modern adult human (ibid., p. 317): the tongue would have been located entirely within the oral cavity, the pharynx behind the larynx and the larynx close to the base of the skull. Computer reconstructions of such a tract show that it could produce neither the universal human vowels [i], [u], and [a], nor velar stops like [k] and [g].

Yet Neanderthal culture used tools and fire, had burial rites, and the fact that fossils with arthritis and healed bone fractures have been found indicates that Neanderthal hominids cared for the old, infirm, and injured. This has the advantage for a culture that the old can impart their knowledge to the young, but only if the culture has an adequate means for imparting this knowledge. It is therefore likely that Neanderthal hominids had a fairly well developed language of some kind, although their speech ability must have been inferior to ours, and it is likely that the extinction of Neanderthal hominids was caused by competition from anatomically modern human beings who were better adapted for speech and language, although they were inferior in terms of strength and agility (ibid., p. 329). So Neanderthal hominids appear to have been closely related to our more immediate ancestors (Skul V, Predmosti 4, Cro Magnon, Afalou, Ain Dokhara), with whom they coexisted for a time, in so far as they had similar general cognitive and linguistic abilities. Both Neanderthal and the direct ancestors of modern humans were descended from *Homo Erectus*. However, Neanderthal seems to have lacked the special characteristics of human speech, being specialized for chewing and muscular strength at the expense of speech communication.

In particular, Neanderthal hominids probably lacked complex syntax, because the rate at which they could communicate is likely to have been much slower than that of modern humans. Human language depends on (ibid., p. 35):

Innate specialized neural mechanisms that also play a part in structuring other aspects of behavior, such as the motor control involved in locomotion . . . the neural mechanisms that first evolved to facilitate motor control now also structure language and cognition. The rules of syntax, for example, may reflect a generalization of the automatized schema that first evolved in animals for motor control in tasks like respiration and walking. In other words ... the formal rules of Chomsky's 'fixed nucleus' are ultimately related to the way that lizards wiggle their tails.

The connection between the wriggling tails of lizards and human syntax lies in the notion of automatization; both motor activity and the use of syntax are rule-governed behaviour, and automatization ensures that rule-governed behaviour takes place precisely and quickly (ibid., pp. 57–9). Lieberman proposes that neural mechanisms which gradually evolved to facilitate the automatization of motor activity were gradually generalized and channelled towards a new evolving function, namely human syntactic ability (ibid., p. 67). This suggestion is consistent with evidence that children's linguistic ability develops in tandem with their sensory-motor development (Piaget, 1980), with Kimura's (1979) finding that motoric speech deficit in aphasics always occurs together with other motoric deficits, and with Bradshaw and Nettleton's (1981) suggestion that the functional asymmetry of the human brain (see LANGUAGE PATHOLOGY AND NEUROLINGUISTICS) follows from adaptations for the neural control of precise, sequential patterns of motor control in humans (Lieberman, 1984, pp. 68–9). Complex syntactic organization, however, depends on a fairly speedy delivery rate (Lieberman, 1984, pp. 325–6):

> You can easily perform the experiment of reading sentences to someone at a rate that is one-tenth of the normal rate. Your listener, and you, will forget the words that occurred at the start of anything other than a short, syntactically simple sentence. Rapid speech would thus, in itself, be an element that would provide a selective advantage for complex syntactic ability.

It is interesting to note that chimpanzees and other apes who seem to lack the neural substrate necessary for the production of human speech also seem unable to progress beyond the two- or three-word stage of human language (see ANIMALS AND LANGUAGE). Evidence that hominid cultural change has taken place unusually rapidly during the last 40,000 years, a period beginning around the time of the extinction of the Neanderthals, leads Leiberman (ibid., p. 328) to propose that the rapid rate of speech which is typical of modern humans became general throughout a hominid population with large, cognitively powerful brains at around that time; obviously, rapid speech and the attendant possibility of increasingly complex syntactic construction would greatly enhance the possibility of cultural development, since this depends to a great degree on the assimilation, retention, and dissemination of information.

Saban (1983), in a paper which unfortunately demands a more detailed knowledge of the anatomy of the brain than readers of this article can be expected to possess, suggests that the impressions left on the insides of fossil skulls show that the modifications of the brain's middle meningeal vein system required to achieve the vascularization necessary for human speech was still incomplete in Cro Magnon, but had reached its maximum in neolithic man. He therefore dates the appearance of speech to the neolithic period, 10,000 years ago.

Lieberman (1984, p. 328) is more cautious:

> Precisely when the full system of human speech evolved is not clear. The evidence of the evolution of the human supralaryngeal vocal tract indicates that it probably occurred sometime in the last 250,000 years or so. However, it is impossible to know just when the neural mechanisms involved in 'decoding' human speech were fully evolved. Even if we had a preserved fossil brain, it would not be possible to resolve this question, given our present knowledge of the brain.

He thinks that Saban's methods, which involve tracing the patterns of blood supply to the regions of the dominant hemisphere that are usually involved in speech perception in living humans and comparing the results with the above-mentioned impressions of veins on skulls, must be tested further on more living humans and more fossil skulls before any definite conclusions can be drawn.

K.M.

SUGGESTIONS FOR FURTHER READING

de Grolier, E. (ed.) (1983), *Glossogenetics: The Origin and Evolution of Language*, London and New York, Harwood Academic.

Lieberman, P. (1984), *The Biology and Evolution of Language*, Cambridge, MA, and London, Harvard University Press.

Philosophy of language

INTRODUCTION

Grayling (1982, pp. 173–5) distinguishes between the **linguistic philosophers**, whose interest is in solving complex philosophical problems by examining the use of certain terms in the language, and **philosophers of language**, whose interest is in the connection between the linguistic and the non-linguistic – between language and the world. This connection is held by philosphers of language to be crucial to the development of a **theory of meaning**, and this is their central concern. The philosophy of language is also known as philosophical **semantics** (compare SEMANTICS). To a philosopher of language, this entry will seem oversimplistic; but my aim is to make accessible to linguists some of the concepts and issues which have been central in the development of the discipline and which have influenced linguistics in more or less direct ways, or which linguistics could usefully draw on, but which are often ignored because they seem wrapped in complexities which are difficult to take on board by non-philosophers.

THE IDEATIONAL THEORY OF MEANING

Let us begin by examining a very early theory of meaning, one which assumes that meaning is attached to, but separable from words, because it originates elsewhere, namely in the mind in the form of ideas. This theory was developed by the British empiricist philosopher John Locke (1632–1704), and is commonly known as the **ideational theory of meaning**. Locke (1977, Book 3, ch. 2) writes:

1. *Words are sensible Signs, necessary for Communication.* Man, though he have great variety of thoughts, and such from which others as well as himself might receive profit and delight; yet they are all within his own breast, invisible and hidden from others, nor can of themselves be made to appear. The comfort and advantage of society not being to be had without communication of thoughts, it was necessary that man should find some external sensible signs, whereof those invisible ideas, which his thoughts are made up of, might be known to others. For this purpose nothing was so fit, either for plenty of quickness, as those articulate sounds, which with so much ease and variety he found himself able to make. Thus we may conceive how *words*, which were by nature so well adapted to that purpose, came to be made use of by men as the signs of their ideas; not by any natural connexion that there is between particular sounds and certain ideas, for then there would be but one language amongst all men; but by a voluntary imposition, whereby such a word is made arbitrarily the mark of such an idea. The use, then, of words, is to be sensible marks of ideas; and the ideas they stand for are their proper and immediate signification.

The theory underpinning Locke's view is, then, that language is an instrument for reporting thought, and that thought consists of successions of ideas in consciousness. As these ideas are private, we need a system of intersubjectively available sounds and marks, so connected to ideas that the proper use of them by one person will arouse the appropriate idea in another person's mind.

A major problem with this theory is that it does not explain how we can discover what the proper use of a word is. Ideas are private, so how can I know that when I use a word to stand for an idea of mine, the idea that that word evokes in your mind is like my idea? I cannot have your idea, and you cannot have mine, so how is it possible for us to check that our theory of meaning is correct? This problem is not solved by trying to clarify the notion of 'idea', or by reformulating the theory in such a way that 'idea' is replaced with the term, 'concept'; *any* referent posited in speakers' minds is going to be affected by the problem. In Locke's theory, God acts as guarantor of sameness of meaning (see Locke, 1977, Book 3, ch. 1); but as Peirce (1868) among others has pointed out, to say that 'God makes it so' is not the type of explanation we typically seek in the sciences, whether natural or human.

A further difficulty with Locke's view is that it assumes that meaning pre-exists its linguistic expression in the form of thoughts in the mind. But, as Grayling puts it (1982, pp. 186–7):

> It is arguable whether thought and language are independent of one another. How could thought above a rudimentary level be possible without language? This is not an easy issue to unravel, but certain observations would appear to be pertinent. For one thing, it is somewhat implausible to think that prelinguistic man may have enjoyed a fairly rich thought-life, and invented language to report and communicate it only when the social demand for language became pressing. Philosophical speculation either way on this matter would constitute *a priori* anthropology at its worst, of course, but it seems clear that anything like systematic thought requires linguistic ability to make it possible. A caveman's ability to mull over features of his environment and his experience of it, in some

way which was fruitful of his having opinions about it, seems incredible unless a means of thinking 'articulately' is imputed to him. The net effect of the 'private language' debate, instigated by some of Wittgenstein's remarks in the *Philosophical Investigations*, strongly suggests that language (this 'articulateness') could not be an enterprise wholly private to some individual, but must be, and therefore must have started out as, a shared and public enterprise.

Moreover, it appears on reflection plausible to say that the richer the language, the greater the possibility its users have for thinking discriminatively about the world. An heuristic set of considerations in support of this thought might go as follows. Consider two men walking through a wood, one of whom is an expert botanist with the name of every tree and shrub at his fingertips, and a command of much floral knowledge. The other man, by contrast, enjoys as much ignorance of botany as his companion enjoys knowledge, so that his experience of the wood is, on the whole, one of a barely differentiated mass of wood and leaf. Plainly, possession of the botanical language, and all that went into learning it, makes the first man's experience of the wood a great deal richer, more finely differentiated, and significant, *qua* experience of the wood as a wood, than is the second man's experience of it. Of course the second man, despite his botanical ignorance, might have poetic, or, more generally, aesthetic experiences arising from his woodland walk, which leave the first man's scientific experience in, as we say, the shade; but the point at issue here is the relevance of their relative commands of the language specific to making their experience of the wood *qua* wood more and less finely discriminative respectively.

So much is merely speculative. It does however show that the question whether language and thought are independent is more likely to merit a negative than an affirmative answer, in whatever way one is to spell out the reasons for giving the negative answer.

The argument from Wittgenstein's *Philo-*

sophical Investigations (1953/68), the **private-language argument**, merits further comment. By a **private language**, Wittgenstein means 'sounds which no one else understands, but which I "appear to understand"' (ibid., p. 169), and his argument is directed against the view according to which such a language is private in the sense that no one else could learn it because of the private nature of its referents. So when he says 'private language' he means a language which is necessarily unteachable – as Locke's ideational language would be because one person could not teach it to another by showing that other person the idea that a word stood for.

Any such private, necessarily unteachable language would have to be about sense data, entities very like Locke's ideas in many respects, and it could have no links with physical objects, since it would then be possible to use these links as **teaching links** – it would be possible to use them to teach the language to others. So a word in a private language would have to get its meaning by being correlated with a private sensation – otherwise the language would not be private. Because of the private nature of the sensation which was the meaning of the word, the meaning of the word could not be taught to somebody else.

Pears presents Wittgenstein's argument against the idea that such a language could exist as follows (1971, p. 159): Suppose you were trying to use such a language. Then

> there would be for any given statement that you might make only two possibilities: either you would be under the impression that it was true, or you would be under the impression that it was false. Neither of these two possibilities would subdivide into two further cases, the case in which your impression was correct, and the case in which your impression was incorrect. For since your statements would have been cut off from their teaching links, there would be no possible check on the correctness of your impressions. But it is an essential feature of any language that there should be effective rules which a person using the language can follow and know that he is following. Yet in the circumstances described

there would be no difference between your being under the correct impression that you were following a rule and your being under the incorrect impression that you were following a rule, or, at least, there would be no detectable difference even for you. So there would be no effective rules in this so-called 'language'. Anything you said would do. Therefore, it would not really be a language, and what prevented it from being a language would be the thing that prevented it, indeed the only thing that could prevent it from being teachable. Therefore, there cannot be a necessarily unteachable language.

Most present-day philosophy of language could be seen to be concerned in some way or other with the nature of what might serve as 'teaching links', and, obviously, reference to things in the world, which appear to be there for the sharing, seems a very useful teaching aid. We shall now turn to theories of meaning which are concerned with the nature of reference from language to items in the world.

SENSE AND REFERENCE

Let us assume that words mean by referring to objects and states in the world. Until the end of the nineteenth century, it was generally thought that the relationship of words to things was one of what might be called **primitive reference**, as expressed by Russell (1903, p. 47): 'Words have meaning, in the simple sense that they are symbols that stand for something other than themselves.' The meaning of a word *is* the object it stands for – words are labels we put on things, and the things are the meanings of the words. Then names and definite descriptions will stand for objects, while verbs, adjectives, adverbs, and prepositions will stand for properties of and relationships between objects. In addition, there would be **syncategorematic** words, function words, which get their meaning 'in context', there being, for instance, no ifs and buts in the world for *if* and *but* to refer to.

In the case of general terms, we can say that they refer to classes of things; so whereas *that cow* and *the cow over there* will refer to a particular cow, *cows* and *the cow*, as in *The cow is a mammal* will refer to the class of all cows; this class is the **extension** of the term *cow*. Exactly how a speaker is supposed to be able to refer to the class of all the cows there are, ever have been, and ever will be, when using the general term is one of the problems involved in the theory of primitive reference.

Some semanticists prefer to reserve the term **reference** for what speakers do: by their use of words, speakers **refer** to things, but the thing referred to is the **denotation** of a word. So words denote, speakers refer. I shall not draw this distinction in the following.

According to the theory of primitive reference, then, the sentence *Socrates flies* gets its meaning in the following way: *Socrates* means by referring to Socrates; *flies* means by referring to the action of flying; *Socrates flies* says of the man Socrates that he has the property of flying – that is, it says of Socrates that he **satisfies** the predicate *flies*. So the sentence names a state of affairs in the world, or refers to a state of affairs in the world, which is handy, since we can then check up on the accuracy of the sentence by seeing whether the state of affairs referred to in it actually obtains in the world: we can identify the referent of *Socrates* and check to see whether he is flying.

There are three insoluble problems inherent in this theory:

1 How can true identity statements be informative?
2 How can statements whose parts lack reference be meaningful?
3 How can there be negative existential statements?

These questions cannot be answered from the standpoint of a theory of primitive reference; and since there are true, informative identity statements, such as *The morning star is the evening star*, and since there are meaningful statements whose parts lack reference such as *The present king of France is bald*, and since there are negative existential statements such as *Unicorns do not exist*, the theory of primitive reference cannot be correct. This was demonstrated by Gottlob Frege, who showed how the first two questions

could be answered in his article, 'On sense and reference' (1892/1977a); he dealt with the third question in two articles, 'On concept and object' (1892/1977b), and 'Function and concept' (1891/ 1977).

The first problem is this: if the meaning of a word is its reference, then understanding meaning can amount to no more than knowing the reference. Therefore, it should not be possible for any true identity statements to convey new information; a = b should be as immediately obvious to anyone who understood it as a = a is, because understanding 'a' and understanding 'b' would simply amount to knowing their references. If we knew their references, we would know that the reference of a was the same as the reference of b, so that no new information would be being conveyed to us in a sentence like a = b.

However, many such true identity statements do, in fact, convey new information; for instance, that the morning star is the evening star was an astronomical discovery, and by no means a truism. Consequently, there must be more to understanding the meaning of a term than knowing what it refers to, and Frege suggested that in addition to that for which a sign stood, 'the reference of the sign', there was also connected with the sign 'a sense of the sign, wherein the mode of representation is contained'. Then (1892/1977a, p. 57): 'the reference of "evening star" would be the same as that of "morning star" but not the sense'.

Sense is the identifying sound or sign by means of which an object is picked out – it is a kind of verbal pointing; and understanding meaning amounts to knowing that this particular object is at this particular time being picked out by this particular sense. So (ibid., p. 61): 'A proper name (word, sign, sign combination, expression) *expresses* its sense, *stands for* or *designates* its reference.'

The new information in a true statement of identity amounts, then, to the information that one and the same referent can be picked out by means of the different senses. The circumstance that *the morning star* stands for the same as that for which *the evening star* stands, is not just a fact concerning relationships within language, but is also a fact about the relationship between language and the world, and the identity relation does not hold between the senses, but between objects referred to by the senses. Things are not the meanings of words; meaning amounts, rather, to the knowledge that a particular sense stands for a particular reference.

It is now also possible to solve the second question, concerning expressions that have no reference. These need not now be taken as meaningless for lack of reference; instead their meaning will reside in their sense alone: *The present king of France* is not meaningless just because it lacks reference, since it still has sense. Frege thought that it was a fault of natural language that it allowed a place for reference-lacking expressions – in a logically perfect language, every expression would have a sense – and he posited the fall-back reference 0 for reference-lacking natural-language expressions. Such lack of confidence in natural language is not likely to endear a philosopher to linguists.

While it may seem fairly obvious that objects are going to serve as references for names and definite descriptions, it is less obvious what should serve this function for whole sentences. What is the reference for *I am going home now*? Is it, perhaps, the fact in the world consisting of me going home now? If so, then the reference of *You are going home in two hours* would have to be the fact in the world consisting of you going home in two hours. Facts of this kind are clearly not such nice referents as objects are, and the world would be rather crowded with them. But worst of all, adopting this type of strategy could tell us nothing of the way in which word meaning contributes to sentence meaning, that is, it could not account for sentence structure.

In fact, Frege extended his theory to take in whole sentences in the following manner: we know that keeping the references of the parts of a sentence stable, we can refer to them by means of different senses. What, now, is to count as the sense of a whole sentence? Take the two sentences:

(1) The morning star is a body illuminated by the sun
(2) The evening star is a body illuminated by the sun

Here, the senses expressed by the nominal groups that are the grammatical subjects in the sentences differ from each other while their references remain the same. Because the senses differ, one person might believe one of the sentences, but not the other (ibid., p. 62): 'anybody who did not know that the evening star is the morning star might hold the one to be true, the other false'. This indicates that the two sentences express different *thoughts*; the **sense** of a whole sentence, then, is the thought expressed in the sentence. We now need something which will serve as the *reference* for whole sentences.

Frege points out that, in the case of declarative sentences, we are never satisfied with just knowing which thought they express; we want to know, in addition, whether the sentences are *true*. He says (ibid., p. 63):

> it is the striving for truth that drives us always to advance from the sense to the reference. . . . We are therefore driven into accepting the *truth value* of a sentence as constituting its reference. By the truth value of a sentence I understand the circumstance that it is true or false.

And, indeed, we can see that this circumstance remains stable in sentences (1) and (2) above when their senses are different; if (1) is true, so is (2).

Frege's full picture of linguistic meaning so far is, then, that the **sense** of a sentence is the thought it expresses, and this depends on the senses of its parts. The **reference** of a whole sentence is its truth value, and this, again, depends on the references of the parts of the sentences – for if we were to replace *the morning star* or *the evening star* in the two sentences with senses which picked out a different reference, then the sentence which resulted might well have a different truth value. Frege is thus the first philosopher of language to provide an account of semantic *structure*. The account is **truth functional**, in that it says how the truth value of a whole sentence is a **function** of – is dependent on – the references of its parts.

Consequently, there are going to be sentences which have no truth value because some of their parts fail to refer. The sentence

The present king of France is bald

will have no truth value, because part of it, *the present king of France*, has no reference. But the sentence is not therefore meaningless – it still has its sense (and the fall-back reference 0).

We have now seen how Frege deals with the first two problems which a theory of primitive reference was incapable of solving. His solution to the third problem, of how there can be negative existential statements, is more difficult to understand, but it is interesting in that it involves an **ontology**, a theory of what there is in the world – of the fundamental nature of reality. The world, according to Frege, consists of complete entities, **objects**, and incomplete, or unsaturated, entities, **concepts**. To this distinction in the realm of the non-linguistic, the realm of reference, corresponds another in the realm of the linguistic, the realm of sense, namely the distinction between **names**, including definite descriptions, and **predicates**. Objects exist in the realm of reference as the references for names, and concepts exist in the realm of reference as the references for predicates. The concepts, although they are incomplete entities, *do exist*; their existence, their being, consists in having some objects falling under them and others not falling under them.

They can be compared to mathematical functions: the function of squaring, for instance, exists – it is a function we can recognize as the same again every time we apply it, although we will apply it to different arguments. And every time we apply it to an argument, we obtain a **value**. The square on two, for instance, is the value four. We can represent the function of squaring: $(\ )^2$, and we can represent the number two with the numeral, 2. We can see that the sign for the function is incomplete or unsaturated, but that we can complete it by inserting *2*, the sign for the number in the empty brackets giving $(2)^2$. The value for this is four, represented by the numeral *4*, and we can write $(2)^2 = 4$. In other words, $(2)^2$ has the same referent as 4 does – they appear to be different senses by means of which the referent, four, can be picked out; and just as *the morning star is the evening star* has a truth value, namely true, so does $(2)^2 = 4$; and, again, if we change one

of the senses in the mathematical expression for another with a different sense, we may get a different truth value; while keeping the references stable and changing the senses will not produce such an alteration of truth value.

The comparison with mathematical functions is important, because in his argument Frege needs to show that just as it is possible to apply one mathematical function to another – we can, say, work out the square root of the square on four – there are linguistic expressions which are **second-order predicates**, and Frege insists that existence is one of them. The problem now concerning Frege is that there can be true negative existential statements like *Unicorns do not exist*. According to the primitive theory of reference, this statement ought to be a contradiction, because having said *Unicorns*, unicorns would have been labelled, so they must exist.

But quite apart from this problem, existence had puzzled philosophers for a long time. Consider the sentences (following Moore, 1936):

(3) Some tame tigers growl and some do not
(4) Some tame tigers exist and some do not.

While (3) seems perfectly acceptable, (4) is very odd indeed, and it looks as if existence is not a predicate that functions like other predicates in the language. On Frege's theory, we can say that the oddity resides in the fact that sentence (4) looks as if it is saying of some objects that they do not exist, while it is not, in fact, possible for objects not to exist. If they are objects, then they exist. However, recall that it is possible for *concepts* not to be realized – indeed, their very being consists in being or not being realized by having objects falling under them. So if there are second-order concepts, which have other concepts, rather than objects, falling under them, and if existence is one of these, then *exists* can still count as a predicate.

But a problem remains. For in sentences like

(5) Homer did not exist
(6) Unicorns do not exist

Homer and *Unicorns* are names, and names stand for objects. But we have just decided that existence ought to be predicated, not of objects, but of other concepts. So Frege is forced, once again, to say that natural language is somehow defective: it obscures the fact that existence is a second-order concept taking other concepts as arguments. In (5) and (6) above, *did/does not exist* is completed with names. But Frege says that this surface structure hides an underlying logical structure something like:

Predicate	Predicate
(7) There was not	a man called Homer
(8) There are not	things called unicorns

In these cases, the second predicates are first-order predicates, and the first ones represent the second-order predicate, existence, whose being is assured by having some first-order predicates falling under it and others not falling under it. So existential statements, although they look like statements about objects, are in fact statements about concepts, and they say that a particular concept is or is not realized.

Once again, though, Frege has alienated himself from a good section of the linguistic community by judging natural language defective. Nevertheless, his influence on linguistic semantics has been enormous; the whole enterprise of studying sense relations (see SEMANTICS) derives from his distinction between sense and reference, and he was instrumental in the development of propositional calculus, on which linguistic semanticists also draw; it was Frege who succeeded in taming terms such as *all*, *every*, *some*, and *no*, which the theory of primitive reference had had great difficulties with. A sentence like *All men are mortal* was seen as a simple proposition about men, which was, however, conceptually complex, the complexity having to do with our inability to conceive, in using it, of all the men there are, ever have been, and ever will be. On Frege's theory, this sentence hides a complex proposition: *For all x, if x is a man, then x is mortal*, and this simply means that the proposition *If x is a man, then x is mortal* holds universally. There is therefore no longer any problem about the way in which *all* modifies the way in which *men* refers to the class of men. The **logical constants**, *all*, *some*, *any*, and *no* are simply part of the metalanguage we use for talking about propositions.

Frege also made what Dummett (1973) has called the most important philosophical statement ever made, namely that it is only as they occur in sentences that words have meaning. And, as Davidson (1967/84, p. 22) adds, he might well have continued 'that only in the context of the language does a sentence (and therefore a word) have meaning'. Many linguists would be prepared to embrace him for this statement alone.

LOGICAL POSITIVISM

In spite of his great achievements, however, problems were soon perceived in the Fregean picture of linguistic meaning. Logicians found it difficult to accept that there could be statements that did not have truth values, because it is one of the founding principles of logical systems that a proposition is either true or false. Furthermore, Frege's theory proved inconsistent with the logician's truth table for *or*, '$\vee$' (see FORMAL LOGIC AND MODAL LOGIC):

P	Q	$P \vee Q$
T	T	T
T	F	T
F	T	T
F	F	F

According to Frege's theory, any sentence some of whose parts fail to refer is going to lack truth value. So the sentence

Either she does not have a cat *or* her cat eats mice

will lack a truth value if she has no cat – because the sentence part *her cat* will fail to refer. But according to the truth table, the sentence is true, because, as she has no cat, the first disjunct is true.

Finally, Davidson (1967/84, p. 20) indicates a further weakness. Frege says that a sentence whose parts lack reference is not therefore meaningless, because it will still have its sense. But if we are enquiring after the meaning of the reference lacking *the present king of France*, it is singularly unhelpful to be told that it is *the present king of France*, the sense. Yet, since there is no reference, this is all the answer we could be given.

Faced with such problems, a group of philosophers known as the logical positivists of the Vienna Circle tried to amend Frege's theory in such a way as to retain its strengths while removing its weaknesses. They began by trying to provide a consistent and satisfactory theory of meaning for at least a limited number of natural-language sentences. Which set is specified in Alfred Ayer's (1936/71, p. 48) **criterion of meaningfulness**, known as **the verification principle**:

A sentence is factually significant to any given person, if, and only if, he knows how to verify the proposition which it purports to express – that is, if he knows what observations would lead him, under certain conditions, to accept the proposition as being true, or reject it as being false.

Unverifiable sentences were said to be concerned with 'metaphysics', and not to be factually significant. Thus *God exists* is not a factually significant sentence, and nor is *God does not exist*; factually insignificant sentences may well be of great importance to some people, of course, but the logical positivists did not see them as falling within that part of the language that their philosophy should centre on.

Unfortunately, it soon became clear that very few sentences would, in fact, qualify as factually significant, so the relevant set of sentences for logical positivism to concern itself with became disappearingly small. For instance, the general laws of science, which are of the form 'All . . . ' are not factually significant, since they are in principle unverifiable: you can never be sure you have examined all instances of something. History also falls by the wayside, because present observation cannot be used to verify statements about the past. And what of the verification principle itself? How can that be verified? If it cannot be verified, it itself seems factually insignificant.

For a time, it seemed that the verification principle could be verified through Moritz Schlick's (1936) **verification theory of meaning**.

This is a theory of what meaning *is*, while Ayer's principle is a statement about what it is for someone to understand meaning. According to the verification theory of meaning, *the meaning of a proposition is its method of verification*. If this is true, then the verification principle is also true; for if the meaning of a proposition *is* the way in which it is verified, then to know that meaning one must know how to go about verifying it.

Schlick's theory is interesting in that it makes meaning into a *method*, rather than taking it to be an entity of some kind which attaches to words or sentences. He spells out the method: 'Stating the meaning of a sentence amounts to stating the rules according to which it is to be used, and this is the same as stating the way in which it can be verified (or falsified).' He thought that there were certain sentences called **protocol sentences** which consist in incorrigible reports of direct observation, and which therefore do not need to be further verified. These would provide 'unshakable points of contact between knowledge and reality' and all other factually significant sentences could be derived from them. Since protocol sentences are immediately observably true or false, it is possible to specify exactly the circumstances under which they are true, and these circumstances constitute the **truth conditions** for the sentences. Schlick's protocol sentences are essentially similar to Carnap's (1928) **meaning postulates** and Wittgenstein's (1921/74) **elementary sentences**.

Such proposals are open to the challenge that we do not have direct access to the basic stuff of the universe because all observation is theory laden. We bring our already formed theories about what we are observing to our observations which are therefore never objective. This objection is made forcefully by Quine (1960, ch. 2) (see pp. 337–8 below). Austin's speech-act theory was developed in reaction to the lack of progress in the philosophy of language caused by the problems involved in logical positivism (see SPEECH-ACT THEORY). The notion of truth conditions has, however, remained with many philosophers of language (see below), linguistic semanticists and pragmaticists.

THE INDETERMINACY OF TRANSLATION

Quine's (1960, ch. 2) objection to projects like that of the logical positivists is, briefly, that statements are never verifiable or falsifiable in isolation, and that it is impossible to find the truth conditions for individual sentences, because the totality of our beliefs about how the world is gets in the way. It is not possible to separate belief from linguistic meaning, because we do not have any access to the world independent of our beliefs about what the world is like. He argues as follows:

Imagine a linguist who is trying to interpret the language of a hitherto unknown people of a culture very different to the linguist's own. It is a friendly people, and they do their best (as far as we can tell) to assist the linguist in her or his endeavour. The linguist has chosen a native informant.

The linguist sees a rabbit running by, and the informant points to it saying 'Gavagai'. The linguist writes in her or his notebook, 'Gavagai means Rabbit/Lo! A rabbit'. S/he will test this hypothesis against the possibility that Gavagai might, instead, mean White, or Animal, or Furry creature, by checking the informant's reaction to a suggested 'Gavagai' in the presence of other white things, other animals, and other furry creatures – it being assumed that the linguist has been able to ascertain what counts as assent and dissent in the culture. If assent is only obtained in the presence of rabbits, then the linguist will take the hypothesis as confirmed, and assume that Gavagai does, indeed, mean Rabbit.

Although this example is supposed to illustrate a philosophical argument, the method presented is in fact a fair outline of that used by linguists engaged in field study, except that Quine's example is meant to deal with **radical translation** – with the case of a completely unknown language spoken by a people which has not previously been in contact with any other – whereas most linguists are now fortunate enough to be able to rely on informants with whom they share at least a working knowledge of some language, either that of the linguist, or a third language (see FIELD METHODS).

Quine calls every possible event or state of affairs in the world which will prompt the informant to assent to Gavagai the term's **positive stimulus meaning**, and he calls every event or state of affairs in the world which will prompt the informant to dissent from Gavagai the term's **negative stimulus meaning**. The two sets of events and states of affairs together make up the term's **stimulus meaning**. Since the stimulus meaning for any term covers all events and states of affairs, the stimulus meaning of each linguistic term is related to every other in a Saussurean manner (see STRUCTURALIST LINGUISTICS), except that reference to concepts has been replaced with reference to situation.

But Quine now puts a serious objection in the way of the linguist's project, and in the way of any verification/falsification theory of meaning. He points out that even when apparent stimulus synonymy has been established between two terms such as Gavagai and Rabbit, there is no guarantee that assent or dissent to their use is in fact prompted by the same experience (1960, pp. 51–2):

> For, consider 'gavagai'. Who knows but that the objects to which this term applies are not rabbits after all, but mere stages, or brief temporal segments, of rabbits. In either event, the stimulus situations that prompt assent to 'Gavagai' would be the same as for 'Rabbit'. Or perhaps the objects to which 'gavagai' applies are all and sundry undetached parts of rabbits; again the stimulus meaning would register no difference. When from the sameness of stimulus meanings of 'Gavagai' and 'Rabbit' the linguist leaps to the conclusion that a gavagai is a whole enduring rabbit, he is just taking for granted that the native is enough like us to have a brief general term for rabbits and no brief general term for rabbit stages or parts.

Our theory of nature, then, is always and inevitably underdetermined by all possible 'evidence' – indeed, there is no real evidence of what somebody else's theory of nature is. This argument can equally well be used for speakers of the 'same' language: I do not have access to your experience of what we both call rabbits any more than I have to the experience of the informant in Quine's story. But this means that truth conditions are not available, so no theory of meaning can be set up in reliance on them, and interpretation of the speech of another is always radically indeterminate. What is, in my opinion, the most important development in modern philosophy of language, still in the Fregean tradition, has developed in an attempt to show that Quine's pessimism is unwarranted.

RADICAL INTERPRETATION

Quine's argument shows that it is probable that any theory of meaning which begins by looking for truth conditions for individual terms or sentences will fail; such truth conditions are simply not evidence which is plausibly available to an interpreter. But suppose now that we give up the search for those bits of the world which provide stimulus for speakers to assent to or dissent from sentences and that, instead of beginning our account with truth conditions for individual terms or sentences, we begin by seeing truth as (Davidson, 1973/84, p. 134): 'a single property which attaches, or fails to attach, to utterances, while each utterance has its own interpretation'. That is, we could, perhaps, try initially to keep truth independent of the interpretation of individual utterances; we could see truth, not as a property of sentences, but as an attitude, the attitude of **holding an utterance true**, which is attached to speakers, rather than to their words. It is an attitude, furthermore, which it is not unreasonable to suppose that speakers adopt towards their own utterances a good deal of the time, even if we have not the faintest idea what truths they see themselves as expressing.

We are then no longer concerned to find some criterion for checking whether a sentence is true or not – which would depend on our already knowing what its truth conditions might be. Rather, we are assuming that a speaker whose words we do not understand sees her or himself as expressing some truth or other. The question is how this evidence can be used to support a theory of meaning. Perhaps we could proceed as

follows: we observe that a speaker, Kurt, who belongs to a speech community which we call German, has a tendency to utter *es regnet* when it is raining near him. We could take this as evidence for the statement (ibid., p. 135): ' "Es regnet" is true-in-German when spoken by *x* at time *t* if and only if it is raining near *x* at *t*.'

We have now used the case of Kurt to make a statement which is supposed to hold for every member of the German speech community, so we must gather more evidence, by observing other speakers and trying out *es regnet* on them in various circumstances, rather like Quine's linguist did in the case of the rabbit. Of course, we are assuming that German speakers are sufficiently like ourselves to hold true that it is raining if and only if it is in fact raining, and Quine's suggestion was that this assumption was unjustified. But perhaps it is not (ibid., p. 137):

> The methodological advice to interpret in a way that optimizes agreement should not be conceived as resting on a charitable assumption about human intelligence that might turn out to be false. If we cannot find a way to interpret the utterances and other behaviour of a creature as revealing a set of beliefs largely consistent and true by our own standards, we have no reason to count that creature as rational, as having beliefs or as saying anything.

Davidson is sometimes accused of arrogant Eurocentricity because of statements such as the above. But the theory is, of course, meant to work both ways – a person from the most remote culture compared to ours is supposed to be able to make use of the theory to make sense of us, just as we are supposed to be able to make sense of him or her.

The statement suggests that the moment one person tries to interpret the utterances of another, the assumption of sameness – at least at a very basic level – has already been made. If no such assumption is made, no attempt at interpretation will be made either, but any attempt at interpretation carries with it the sameness assumption. This contention is borne out by the facts: we do tend to ascribe more meaningful behaviour to things according to their similarity to ourselves – we are more likely to suggest that our neighbour is making meaningful noises than we are to suggest that our dog is doing so; but we are more likely to suggest that the dog is making meaningful noises than we are to suggest that our apple tree is signalling intentionally to us.

The theory of meaning which Davidson advocates, known as the theory of **radical interpretation**, provides a method and a conception of what meaning is which allows us to make sense of the linguistic and other behaviour of other persons, and to see how their use of certain utterances relates to their use of certain other utterances. It is important to be aware that the notion of truth with which Davidson operates is not a **correspondence theory of truth**: sentences are not made true or false because their parts correspond to bits of the world. Rather, stretches of language are taken by speakers to be appropriate to the ongoing situation. References for parts of utterances are worked out on the

basis, in principle, of an understanding of the language as a whole, and the theory can accommodate variance in reference with variance in situation (see Davidson, 1986). Reference is not a concept we need to set up the theory in the first place: it is not the place at which there is direct contact between linguistic theory and events, actions and objects. On this account, meaning is not an entity or property of an entity; it is a relation between (at least) a speaker, a time, a state of affairs, and an utterance. We have, therefore, a theory of meaning compatible with many empirically based twentieth-century linguistic research projects in areas like, for instance, sociolinguistics, functional grammar, intonation, discourse analysis and text linguistics, and critical linguistics.

K.M.

SUGGESTIONS FOR FURTHER READING

Grayling, A.C. (1982), *An Introduction to Philosophical Logic*, Brighton, Sussex, Harvester Press.

Phonemics

Phonemics is the study of phonemes in their various aspects, i.e. their establishment, description, occurrence, arrangement, etc. Phonemes fall under two categories, **segmental** or **linear** phonemes and **suprasegmental** or **non-linear** phonemes; they will be explained below. The term 'phonemics', with the above-mentioned sense attached to it, was widely used in the heyday of post-Bloomfieldian linguistics in America, in particular from the 1930s to the 1950s, and continues to be used by present-day post-Bloomfieldians. Note in this connection that Leonard Bloomfield (1887–1949) himself used the term 'phonology', not 'phonemics', and talked about **primary phonemes** and **secondary**

phonemes whilst using the adjectival form 'phonemic' elsewhere. The term 'phonology', not 'phonemics', is generally used by contemporary linguists of other schools.

It should nevertheless be noted that to take phonology simplistically as a synonym of phonemics may not be appropriate for at least two reasons. On the one hand, there exists a group of scholars who talk about phonology without recognizing, still less operating with, phonemes, be they segmental or suprasegmental; these are **prosodists** (see PROSODIC PHONOLOGY) and **generativists** (see GENERATIVE PHONOLOGY and DISTINCTIVE FEATURES). On the other hand, an English phonetician, Daniel Jones (1881–

1967), developed a theory of phonemes wherein he talked about phonemes *tout court* but neither 'segmental' or 'primary' phonemes nor 'suprasegmental' or 'secondary' phonemes. He did not recognize and practically never mentioned either phonemics or phonology.

Jones manifested an ambivalent attitude towards post-Bloomfieldian suprasegmental phonemes in that, on the one hand, he disagreed with the American practice of referring to suprasegmentals in terms of 'phonemes' but, on the other hand, he talked about **chronemes, stronemes**, and **tonemes** conceived along the same line as phonemes. Jones' followers largely did not and do not subscribe to his chronemes and stronemes. Jones insisted that what post-Bloomfieldians called phonemics formed part of phonetics and refused to recognize a separate discipline called phonemics. Given this rather complex situation, we shall look, in what follows, mainly at post-Bloomfieldian phonemics and Daniel Jones' phoneme theory.

The first and most important task in phonemics, both for post-Bloomfieldians and Jones, is to establish the phonemes of a given language. To do this, they analyse phonetic data according to certain well-defined procedures.

Post-Bloomfieldians operate with the notions of **contrastive** and **non-contrastive** which originally stem from the concept of **distribution** but are ultimately coloured by semantic implications. Sounds which occur in an identical context are said to be in **contrastive distribution**, or to be contrastive with respect to each other, or to contrast with each other. Such sounds are said to be **allophones** of different phonemes. For example [pʰ] and [m], which occur in an identical context in the English words *pit* and *mitt*, are allophones of two different phonemes, /p/ and /m/. (It is customary to enclose symbols for phonemes by diagonal lines and symbols for allophones in square brackets.)

However, this analytical principle does not work in all cases. For example [p⁼] (unaspirated), [p˺] (unreleased), [ʔp] (preglottalized), etc., which occur in an identical context in, say, the English word *sip* and which are therefore in contrastive distribution are nevertheless not allophones of

different phonemes, i.e. /p⁼/, /p˺/, /ʔp/, etc., but allophones of one and the same phoneme /p/ in English. The allophones in this example are said to be in **free variation** and therefore to be **free variants**.

But how can one conclude that in the one case the sounds in question belong to different phonemes and in the other case the sounds in question belong to one and the same phoneme? The explanation commonly proffered is that, in English, while exchanging [p] for [m] in the context /-ɪt/ produces a change in the meaning of the word, exchanging the above-mentioned allophones of /p/ for each other in the same context does not alter the meaning of the word, but are merely variant pronunciations of the word-final phoneme /p/.

Notice that, in this explanation, recourse is had to semantic considerations or meaning despite the fact that some post-Bloomfieldians, including Bernard Bloch (1907–65), Charles Francis Hockett (1916–), and Zellig Sabbetai Harris (1909–), avowedly refuse to operate with meaning in phonemic analysis. These post-Bloomfieldians have gone beyond their master who, while warning about the difficulty of dealing with meaning, did not exclude the possibility of recourse to meaning in either phonemics, which he called phonology, or in linguistics in general. They have therefore attempted to devise, if not always successfully or altogether consistently, such a series of analytical procedures in phonemic analysis as are primarily founded on distributional criteria. Their avoidance, at least in principle, if not always in practice, of meaning in phonemic analysis relates to their insistence that analysis at one linguistic level should be conducted independently of analysis at any other level; semantic considerations should therefore only operate in analysis at the morphemic and semantic levels of a language.

However, a few post-Bloomfieldians, most notably Kenneth Lee Pike (1912–), strongly claim that it is not only desirable but necessary to take meaning into account in phonemic analysis. It is not surprising in view of these facts that one should find in much post-Bloomfieldian phonemic literature that, apart from its original distributional implications, 'contrastiveness' is presented as almost equal to **distinctiveness**, i.e., capable of differentiating words. This has given rise to post-Bloomfieldians' general use of the term 'contrast' as a synonym of the functionalists' term **opposition** (see FUNCTIONAL PHONOLOGY); functionalists distinguish between opposition which relates to paradigmatic relation, and **contrast** which relates to syntagmatic relation (see PROSODIC PHONOLOGY).

Sounds which do not occur in an identical context are said to be in **non-contrastive distribution**. There are two subtypes. The first subtype is the following. If one of two or more sounds occurs in a context to the exclusion of other sound(s), i.e. in a context in which the other sound(s) never occur(s), they are said to be in **complementary distribution** or in **mutual exclusiveness**. For example, [h] and [ŋ] in English, as in *hat* and *ring*, are not only in non-contrastive distribution but also in complementary distribution since [h] never occurs in English in word-final position and [ŋ] never in word-initial position. Although, to post-Bloomfieldians, the occurrence of sounds in complementary distribution is a prerequisite to these sounds being allophones of one and the same phoneme, this is not the sole condition. The other necessary condition to be met is the **criterion of phonetic similarity**, that is to say that the sounds in complementary distribution must be phonetically similar to each other for them to be regarded as allophones of one and the same phoneme. This latter condition is not met in the example of [h] and [ŋ], which are consequently considered to belong to separate phonemes. One example in which both conditions are met is that of [b] in, for example, *robin* and [b̥] in, for example, *hub*, which are not only in complementary distribution but phonetically similar to each other (the diacritic mark ˳ in [b̥] signifies devoicing).

The second subtype of non-contrastive distribution is the following. The sounds in question occur in **partial complementation**, i.e. they occur in contrastive distribution in some contexts where they are allophones of different phonemes, but occur elsewhere in non-contrastive distribution or, more precisely, in complementary

distribution. The reference to this type of non-contrastive distribution within an explanation of the second subtype of non-contrastive distribution may be somewhat confusing but is inevitable, given the analytical procedures which are importantly, if not exclusively, based on the criterion of distribution adopted by the majority of post-Bloomfieldians. For want of an appropriate example in English, let us consider the occurrence of [ɾ], the alveolar tap, and [r], the alveolar trill (see ARTICULATORY PHONETICS), in Spanish, which are in partial complementation. [ɾ] and [r] occur in contrastive distribution in intervocalic position, i.e. between two vowels, cf. *caro* ['kaɾo], *carro* ['karo], but in non-contrastive distribution *cum* complementary distribution in, say, word-initial position and word-final position, cf. *rojo* ['roxo], *hablar* [a'blaɾ]. In the context where [r] and [ɾ] occur in contrastive distribution, they are considered as an allophone of /r/ and an allophone of /ɾ/, respectively; notice that this analysis involves recourse to meaning. In the contexts where they occur in non-contrastive distribution *cum* complementary distribution, [r] and [ɾ] are not considered as allophones of one and the same phoneme but an allophone of /ɾ/ and an allophone of /r/, respectively, on the strength of the post-Bloomfieldian axiomatic principle of 'once a phoneme, always a phoneme' (see further below). In such a case, different analyses are given by functionalists or prosodists. Thus, so far as post-Bloomfieldians are concerned, the fact of sounds occurring in complementary distribution does not in itself necessarily lead to the conclusion that they are allophones of the same phoneme. (Compare this conclusion with the one shown in the case of the first subtype.)

The analytical procedures whereby post-Bloomfieldians establish phonemes will be seen to be compatible with their concept of the phoneme as a class of phonetically similar and complementarily distributed sounds, i.e. the criteria of phonetic similarity and complementary distribution, these sounds being generally referred to as allophones of a phoneme. Further criteria are mentioned by post-Bloomfieldians, but the above-mentioned two are of crucial importance. This concept of the phoneme is, as we shall see further below, strikingly comparable to Jones's. Note that this concept does not accommodate those allophones which occur in free variation. Some post-Bloomfieldians, however, do accommodate such allophones in their definition of the phoneme, in which case recourse to meaning is inevitably involved.

Through the analytical procedures mentioned above, post-Bloomfieldians will establish for the phonemic system of English, for example, /k/ as a class of allophones which occur in complementary distribution, these allophones being: [kʰ], which is aspirated, as in *key*; [k⁼], which is unaspirated, as in *pucker*; [k̚], which is unreleased, as in *luck*, [k̟], which is fronted, as in *keel*; [k̠], which is backed, as in *cool*; [k], which is neutral, as in *cur*; etc. These allophones are considered to be phonetically similar to each other. Likewise, post-Bloomfieldians establish the other consonantal phonemes and the vowel phonemes of English, or of any other language they analyse.

There is no uniform descriptive designation for each of these phonemes in the practice of post-Bloomfieldians, who variously use articulatory features to describe them, so that /p/ may be described as the voiceless bilabial plosive, and /k/ as the voiceless velar plosive, /i/, as in *feet*, as the front high, /ɒ/, as in *hot*, as the central low, etc. (see ARTICULATORY PHONETICS for keys to these descriptions).

To post-Bloomfieldians, and also to Jones, whose theory will be explained further below, a **phoneme** is the minimum phonemic unit that is not further analysable into smaller units susceptible of concomitant occurrence; in other words, a phoneme is a block that cannot be broken down into smaller parts: it *is* the smallest element relevant to phonemic analysis. Therefore, the above-cited articulatory terms should be taken not as referring to subcomponents of a phoneme, but rather as convenient mnemonic tags derived from the study of how the sounds are produced by the speech organs.

Where there appear to be two alternative phonemic analyses according to which, for example, the phonetically complex consonants in *church* and *judge* may be considered as either **complex phonemes**, i.e. /tʃ/ and /dʒ/, respectively, or **simple phonemes**, i.e. /t͡ʃ/ and /d͡ʒ/, respectively, post-Bloomfieldians tend to be guided by the principle of establishing as economic an inventory of phonemes as possible and therefore opt for the latter analysis.

Post-Bloomfieldians conduct their phonemic analysis with an axiomatic principle often dubbed 'once a phoneme, always a phoneme', by which is meant that once a given sound has been identified in a context as an allophone of a phoneme, the same sound occurring in any other context must also be considered as an allophone of this same phoneme and not of any other phoneme. To use the Spanish example mentioned above, [r] has been identified as an allophone of /r/, cf. *carro*, as this sound is in contrast with [ɾ] which has been identified as an allophone of /ɾ/, cf. *caro*. It so happens that [r] occurs in a different context, cf. *rojo*, and [ɾ] in a still different context, cf. *hablar*. Post-Bloomfieldians do not hesitate to consider the first as an allophone of /r/ and the second as an allophone of /ɾ/ by invoking the principle of 'once a phoneme, always a phoneme'.

At first sight, there appears to be an exception to this principle. For example, [ɾ] is considered an allophone of /t/ that occurs in, say, intervocalic position, e.g. *Betty* /'beti/ ['beɾi], but may also occur as an allophone of /r/ after [θ], cf. *three* [θɾiː]. However, the two [ɾ]s are regarded as allophones of two different phonemes, /t/, /r/, without violating the axiomatic principle, because they are said to occur in 'separate' phonetic contexts – one intervocalic, the other not – and consequently to occur in **partial overlapping** when one takes into account other contexts in which they both occur, i.e. in contrastive distribution.

Investigation into the occurrence and arrangement of phonemes is of distributional concern to post-Bloomfieldians. The phonemes of a language are specified with regard to their occurrence or non-occurrence in specific contexts such as **syllable-initial, -medial,** or **-final position,** or **word-initial, -medial,** or **-final position,** etc. For example, in English, /p/ occurs in all the positions just mentioned, cf. *pea, apt, cap, packet, upper,* *ketchup*, while /ʒ/ occurs mainly in word-medial position, cf. *measure*, but rarely occurs in word-initial position, cf. *genre*, or in word-final position, cf. *garage*. /iː/, as in *see*, occurs in all the above-mentioned positions, cf. *eat, feet, tree*, whereas /æ/, as in *rat*, occurs syllable- or word-initially, cf. *at*, and syllable- or word-medially, cf. *mat*, but never syllable- or word-finally.

Post-Bloomfieldians say that, in the contexts where a given phoneme does not occur, the phoneme is defectively distributed, hence the term **defective distribution**. It is important for post-Bloomfieldians to determine which phoneme, /p/ or /b/, in English is considered to occur after /s/ in, for example, *spit* – /spit/ or /sbit/? – since this has implications for the distributional statement about /p/ or /b/. For a different analysis on the part of functionalists, see FUNCTIONAL PHONOLOGY. The study of the distribution of phonemes can be extended to cases of clusters of phonemes; for example, in English, the cluster /mp/ is disallowed and therefore defectively distributed in syllable- or word-initial position, but is allowed in syllable- or word-final position as in *hamp*, or across morpheme boundaries, as in *impossible*.

Related to the study of the distribution of phonemes is **phonotactics**, which is the study of the permitted or non-permitted arrangements or sequences of phonemes in a given language. For example, among the permitted consonant clusters in English are the following: /spl-/, as in *spleen*; /skl-/, as in *sclerotic*; /spr-/, as in *spring*; /skr-/, as in *screw*. Note that these clusters are permitted in word-initial position only, and that /stl/ is disallowed. Further examples are /pl-/, as in *play*, /-pl-/, as in *steeply*, and /-pl/, as in *apple*; /kl-/, as in *clear*, /-kl-/, as in *anklet*, and /-kl/, as in *knuckle*; /-tl-/, as in *atlas*, and /-tl/, as in *little*. Note that /tl-/ is disallowed. Many other permitted clusters of consonant phonemes could be cited. It will have been noted that some of the permitted clusters are occurrent in certain contexts only. And it goes without saying that many theoretically possible consonant clusters are non-occurrent in English; for example, no English word begins with /zv-/.

The kind of phonemes we have seen above are referred to as **segmental** or **linear phonemes**, simply because they occur sequentially. A speech chain can be segmented into a series of such phonemes; for example, *box* /bɒks/, is a sequence of four segmental phonemes, /b/, /ɒ/, /k/, and /s/. Post-Bloomfieldians operate with what they call **suprasegmental phonemes** as well, such as:

(a) **stress phonemes**, of which there are four: **strong** = ´, **reduced strong** = ˆ, **medium** = ˋ, **weak** = ∅, i.e. **zero**, hence no diacritic mark: all four are illustrated in *élevàtor-ôperàtor*;

(b) **pitch phonemes**, of which there are also four: **low** (1), **mid** (2), **high** (3), **extra-high** (4), illustrated in:

> *He killed a rat but George killed a bird*;
> 1   3   2–4 1   4   1   4–1

(c) **juncture phonemes**, of which there are at least three: **external open**, **internal close**, **internal open**, illustrated in *nitrate*, which has external open junctures before /n/ and after the second /t/ and internal close junctures between /n/, /ai/, /t/, /r/, /ei/, and /t/, and in *night-rate*, which has external open junctures and internal close junctures as in *nitrate* except that it has an internal open juncture between the first /t/ and /r/ instead of an internal close juncture. An internal open juncture is customarily indicated as /+/, hence an alternative name **plus juncture**.

Some, not all, post-Bloomfieldians operate with three additional junctures, i.e. /‖/, called **double bar**, /#/, **double cross**, and /|/, **single bar**. These are used in reference to intonational directions, i.e. **upturn**, **downturn**, and **level** (= neither upturn nor downturn), respectively. Suprasegmental phonemes are said not to be **linearly placed** but to occur **spread over**, or **superimposed on**, a segmental phoneme or phonemes, but this is obviously not the case with juncture phonemes though their effects themselves are phonetically manifested over segmental phonemes adjacent to the juncture phonemes.

Daniel Jones maintained that the phoneme is a phonetic conception, and rejected the separation of phonemics from phonetics, asserting that the two are part and parcel of a single science called phonetics. His use of the term 'phonemic', as in 'phonemic grouping' and other expressions, pertains to the phoneme, not to phonemics, a term which he does not use for his own phoneme theory. It is neither clear nor certain how much the latter benefited from the former. Jones' phoneme theory was intended for various practical purposes including foreign pronunciation teaching and devising of orthographies, not for theoretical purposes. He excluded any reference to meaning in his so-called **physical definition** of a phoneme as a family of phonetically similar and complementarily distributed sounds – which he called **members** or **allophones** of phonemes – within a word in an idiolect. Jones meant by an **idiolect** here 'the speech of one individual pronouncing in a definite and consistent style'.

This concept of the phoneme is strikingly similar, if not identical in detail, to that entertained by post-Bloomfieldians, who apply other criteria as well. Like post-Bloomfieldians, Jones admitted recourse to meaning as an expedient to establishing the phonemes of a language. He said that sounds occurring in an identical context belong necessarily to different phonemes and that it is phonemes which distinguish different words, not allophones of the same phoneme. He opined that a phoneme is what is stated in his definition of it and what a phoneme does is to distinguish words. Note, as Jones himself stressed, that it is a necessary corollary of his definition of the phoneme that different sounds occurring in an identical context must be members of different phonemes. A pair of words which are distinguished from each other through a difference between two phonemes, and through that difference alone, are known as a minimal pair. For example, *met* and *net* in English constitute a minimal pair since they are distinguished from each other only through the difference between /m/ in *met* and /n/ in *net*.

Unlike post-Bloomfieldians, Jones neither talked about nor operated with 'contrastive (distribution)' or 'non-contrastive (distribution)'. Jones's concept of the phoneme fails, like many post-Bloomfieldians', to accommodate those allophones that occur in free variation; such allophones are presumably accounted for by Jones through recourse to the concept of the

variphone, i.e. a sound susceptible of being pronounced differently and erratically in an identical context without the speaker being aware of it, which Jones proposed in 1932 at an early stage in the development of his phoneme theory (Jones, 1932, p. 23). For the concept of variphone, see Jones (1950).

Like post-Bloomfieldians, Jones took it as axiomatic that a given sound cannot be assigned to more than one phoneme, although, unlike post-Bloomfieldians, he admitted a few exceptions. Thus, for example, Jones considered [ŋ] in, say, *ink* as a member of /ŋ/ which will have been established in, say, *rung* /rʌŋ/. He therefore rejected any analysis which considered [ŋ] as being a member of /n/ occurring before /k/, as in *ink*, or before /g/, as in *hunger*. Post-Bloomfieldians will agree with Jones' analysis here.

Jones worked on **suprasegmentals**, which he called **sound attributes**, with the same analytical principle that he applied to segmentals considered in terms of phonemes and allophones, and talked about **tonemes**, a term which he coined in 1921 (see Jones, 1957, pp. 12–13; Fudge, 1973, p. 26) – Pike in America independently invented it in the early 1940s (Pike, 1948) – and **allotones**, and **chronemes** and **allochrones**, though he showed considerable reservations about **stronemes** and **allostrones**. Yet he was ultimately against considering suprasegmental phonemes *à la* post-Bloomfieldianism and even preferred the term **signeme**, proposed by Dennis Ward (1924–) (see Jones, 1957, p. 20, or Fudge, 1973, p. 32) to designate any phonetic feature, segmental or otherwise, that contributes to meaning difference, cf. the concept of significance = distinctiveness: thus, **signemes of phone** (= phonemes), **signemes of length, signemes of stress, signemes of pitch**, and **signemes of juncture**. The term 'signeme' has not caught on, however.

Jones's study of **intonation** is vastly different from that of post-Bloomfieldians. Unlike post-Bloomfieldians, he does not operate with a fixed number of pitches or pitch phonemes. This is obvious by merely looking at his representation of intonation, which uses a graphic transcription which has a stave of three horizontal lines; the top and bottom lines represent the upper and lower limits of the speaker's voice range, and the middle an intermediate pitch level. Unstressed syllables are indicated with small dots placed at appropriate pitch levels, while stressed syllables are indicated with large dots which are placed at appropriate pitch levels and which are accompanied with curves if the stressed syllables have either a rising, a falling, a rising–falling, or a falling–rising intonation. A specimen of his intonation transcription is shown below.

We did what we were told.

Jones himself and his followers frequently omit the middle line.

In the matter of transcription, it should be noted that Jones adopted from Henry Sweet (1845–1912) and used two different types of transcription, i.e. **broad transcription**, in which the symbols stand for phonemes – though Sweet himself did not use the term 'phoneme' – and **narrow transcription**, in which the symbols stand for allophones or members of phonemes. Jones used the expressions **phonemic transcription** and **allophonic transcription** as well.

Jones' followers continue to work on the phoneme theory inherited from him with no major modifications.

T.A.

SUGGESTIONS FOR FURTHER READING

Bloch, B. and G.L. Trager (1942), *Outline of Linguistic Analysis*, Baltimore, Linguistic Society of America, ch. 3.

Hill, A.A. (1958), *Introduction to Linguistic Structures: From Sound to Sentence in English*, New York, Harcourt Brace Jovanovich, chs 2, 3, 4, 5, and 6.

Jones, D. (1950), *The Phoneme: Its Nature and Use*, Cambridge, Heffer, (2nd edn, 1962; 3rd edn, 1967).

Port-Royal grammar

THE EDITIONS OF THE TEXT

The real title of what has become popularly known as **Port-Royal grammar** is *A general and reasoned Grammar containing the foundations of the art of speaking explained in a clear and natural way, the reasons for what is common to all languages and the main differences that can be found between them etc.*

After its first publication in Paris in 1660, it was published again with successive additions in 1664, 1676, 1679, and 1709. In 1754, the French grammarian Duclos added to the text of 1676 'Remarks' that were regularly reprinted in later editions (1768, 1783 etc). Moreover, the 1803 edition is preceded by an 'Essay on the origin and progress of the French language' by Petitot. In the editions of 1830 (Delalain, Paris) and 1845 (Loquin, Paris), the *Logic or the Art of Thinking* by Arnauld and Nicole (1662) is published together with the grammar. The grammar also represents volume 41 of the *Works of Antoine Arnaud gent* (Paris, 1780). More recently, H.E. Brekle has published a critical edition (Stuttgart, 1966); the edition of 1845 has been reprinted with an historical introduction by A. Bailly (Slatkine, Geneva, 1968) and the 1830 edition with an introduction by M. Foucault (Paulet, Paris, 1969).

THE AUTHORS

The authors, Antoine Arnauld (1612–94) and Claude Lancelot (1628–95) are both linked to the Jansenist movement whose devotees lived at the Abbey of Port-Royal des Champs, near Paris. Antoine Arnauld, a theologian and logician, was one of the leaders of the movement, and, with Nicole, wrote the logic. Lancelot, a scholar and teacher, master of several languages, and author of handbooks for learners of Latin (1644), Greek (1655), Italian and Spanish (1660), was the chief architect of the transformations in teaching carried out over a twenty-year period in Port-Royal's renowned 'Petites Ecoles'. Although it is impossible to determine exactly the contribution of each author, it seems reasonable to assume that the knowledge of former doctrines and grammatical studies and mastery of languages came from Lancelot, and that Arnauld contributed his powerful intellect and his capacity for marshalling a mass of data.

THE GRAMMAR AND THE LOGIC

The grammar belongs to the rationalist current of thought already visible in the works of Scaliger (*De Causis linguae latinae*, 1540), Ramus (about 1560), Sanctius (*Minerva*, 1587), and Scioppius (*Grammatica philosophica*, 1628). It is deeply influenced by René Descartes (1596–1650). In its second edition, the grammar includes an address to the readers informing them of the publication of *The Logic or the Art of Thinking* by Arnauld and P. Nicole, a work 'based on the same principles' which 'can be extremely useful to explain and demonstrate several of the questions raised in the Grammar'. The logic, which underwent several successive changes until 1683, includes several chapters (II, 1 and 2) reproduced almost literally from the grammar. Other chapters study in detail problems that had been dealt with cursorily or simply alluded to in the grammar. It is necessary to compare the two works – the second one often casts further light on the ideas on language in the first work – bearing in mind, however, that the successive emendations may have altered the unity of the doctrine on certain questions.

The difference in purposes of the two works must also be taken into account. The grammar deals with only three of the four 'operations of the mind' considered as essential at the time: to conceive, to judge, to reason, and to order, stating that 'All philosophers teach that there are three operations of the mind: to conceive, to judge, to reason' (II, 1). Although the authors acknowledge that 'exercising our will can be considered as one mode of thinking' distinct from simple affirmation, they study it only in connection with the different ways of expressing it – optative, potential, imperative forms – in the chapter on verbal modes (II, 6). The logic shows even more reticence as it avoids any allusion to the expression of the will. Out of the three remaining operations, the grammar leaves out the third one, reasoning, as being only 'an extension of the second one' : 'To reason is to make use of two judgements to form a third' (II, 1). Therefore, reasoning is studied in the logic, which returns to the ideas developed in the grammar merely to deal, in the third and fourth parts, with different ways of reasoning and the methods that enable one to judge correctly and to reach the truth. The chapters of the logic that deal, more exhaustively, with compound propositions are not a mere complement to the grammar, even though they seem to be so, but a study of reasoning, whose aim, as the examples analysed show, is apologetic and which should be situated in the context of the doctrinal conflicts and the metaphysical controversies in which the 'Messieurs' of Port-Royal were involved. As many commentators have pointed out (see for instance Chevalier, 1968; Donzé, 1971), the grammar, limiting its study to the problems of conceiving and judging, is a grammar of the single proposition. It lays down very firmly the simple sentence as the central linguistic unit of discourse. This idea influenced grammarians for more than two centuries.

CONTENTS

The grammar is composed of two parts. The first part, comprising six chapters, deals with words as sounds and with the graphic signs that serve to describe them. The second, which is more developed, deals, in twenty-four chapters, with 'the principles and reasons on which the diverse forms of the meaning of words are based'. The general plan follows the traditional pattern in studying successively spelling (I, 1–2), prosody (I, 3–4), analogy (II, 2–23), and syntax (II, 24). The original feature of the grammar is a new distribution of the parts of speech and a justification of the procedure in a central chapter (II, 1) which expounds the underlying principles of the plan followed. The second part studies in succession 'nouns, substantives and adjectives', including numbers, genders, and cases (chs. 2–6), articles (7), pronouns (8), especially relatives (9–10), prepositions (11), adverbs (12), verbs (13), together with the problems of person and number (14), tense (15), mood (16), infinitive (17), 'adjectival verbs' (18), impersonal verbs (19), participles (20), gerunds and supines (21), the auxiliary verbs in non-classical languages (22). Chapter 23 deals with conjunctions and interjections; the last chapter (24) deals with syntax from the double point of view of agreement and word order.

This plan, which may surprise the modern reader, is very coherent when we consider its underlying principles, which illuminate the authors' methods and their claim to have written a general and reasoned grammar. It seems that this was the first time a grammar had put forward such a claim. Unlike the grammars written by the Renaissance humanists, whose painstaking efforts to forge the description of modern languages from that of Latin remained for the main part centred on a morphological description, the grammar of Port-Royal was explicitly presented as applicable to all languages since it was based on an analysis of mental processes. Even though the authors started from an analysis of languages familiar to them – most of the examples being taken from Latin and French – their analysis was not based on morphology, but on the relationships between ideas and conceptual patterns on the one hand, and the words and discursive forms that serve to express them on the other. Beyond the diversity apparent in individual languages, they tried to find out 'the reasons for what all languages have in common, and for the main differences that can be found between them'. Their aim was to explain the fundamental and universal principles which formed 'the basis of the art of speech': 'The diversity of the words making up discourse' depends on 'what goes on in our minds . . . we cannot understand correctly the different kinds of meaning contained in words unless we have first a clear notion of what goes on in our thoughts, since words were invented only in order to express thoughts' (II, 1).

THE THEORY OF THE SIGN

Thus the grammar stated again explicitly the theory of the word defined as a sign: 'one can define words as distinct articulated sounds that man has turned into signs in order to signify his thoughts' (II, 1). Yet the concept of the sign, however fundamental, was not developed in the grammar; it was in the logic, and this only in 1684, that a general theory of the sign was sketched out (Log. I, 4):

> When we consider a certain object as a mere representation of another, the idea we form of this object is that of a sign, and this first object is called a sign. This is how we usually consider maps and pictures. Thus the sign contains two ideas, first the idea of the thing which represents, second the idea of the thing represented; and its nature consists in giving rise to the second idea through the first one.

What makes up the 'nature' of the sign is therefore as much the very representation involved in it as the power of representation that it possesses. It operates on the mind not only as a symbolic representation, but also as directly endowed with the power of representing. 'Between the sign and its content, there is no intermediate element, nor any opacity' (Foucault, 1966, p. 80). Hence, the question of the meaning of the linguistic sign does not arise, and the grammar includes no theory of meaning or of the word as a meaningful unit. Sounds are used by human beings as symbols of the representations of things as given by the mind. On the other hand, they are the creation of human beings – institutional signs as opposed to natural signs (see SEMIOTICS). As such, even though their capacity of representation is due to the Almighty's power at work in human minds, they have no inherent compulsory characteristics. In this respect, the theory foreshadows Saussure's theory of the arbitrary relationship between signified and signifier (see STRUCTURALIST LINGUISTICS).

THE TWO KINDS OF SIGNS

The original feature of the grammar is that it makes a distinction between two sorts of linguistic signs according to whether they signify the 'objects' of our thoughts or their 'form and manner'. The first sort included nouns, articles, pronouns, participles, prepositions, and adverbs. The second sort corresponds to verbs, 'conjunctions' and interjections. 'Conjunctions' include the particles that serve to express 'conjunctions, disjunctions and other similar operations', that is to say co-ordinating conjunctions, *and*, *or*, *therefore*, the subordinating conjunction *if*, the Latin interrogative particle *ne* and the negative particle *non*. These two kinds of words correspond to the universal mental patterns underlying the production of discourse and made apparent in the two operations studied by the grammar: the conception of ideas and the bringing together of two conceived terms.

Conception is 'simply the way our minds look at things in a purely intellectual and abstract manner, as when I consider existence, duration, thought, or God, or with concrete images, as when I picture a square, a circle, a dog, a horse' (II, 1), or it may be 'simply the view we have of the things that come across our minds' (Log. Foreword). Notice that the grammar gives no definition of ideas, although this concept was at the heart of the controversies aroused by Descartes' philosophy, in which Arnauld took part. According to the logic, ideas are 'all that is present in our minds when we can say with certainty that we conceive a thing' (Log. I, 1). Like Descartes, Arnauld identifies thought and conscience, as well as will and thought. Ideas must be understood as 'all that is conceived immediately by one's mind': notions, concepts, feelings: 'all the operations of will, understanding, imagination and the senses' (Descartes; see Dominicy, 1984, p. 36).

To judge is 'to state that a thing that we conceive is thus, or is not thus: for instance, once I have conceived what the earth is and what roundness is, I state that the earth is round' (Gram. II, 1). Here again Arnauld was borrowing from Descartes who said that in judgement we should distinguish 'matter' and 'form' and therefore judgement should be seen as resulting from a joint operation of understanding and will. While the authors placed particular emphasis on judgement, they did not neglect the other forms or manners of thinking: 'one must also include conjunctions, disjunctions and other similar operations of our minds and all other movements of our souls like desires, commands, questions etc.' (II, 1). However, judgement is the fundamental operation by which thinking usually takes place, for 'men seldom speak merely to express what they conceive, but nearly always to express the judgements they form about the things they conceive' (ibid.).

The example given above became the canon of affirmation and proposition. For if the underlying structure of 'what goes on in our thinking' seems to be outside the field of grammar, the transition to the grammatical domain is achieved through an equation, presented as absolutely obvious, between judgement, i.e. affirmation, and the proposition (II, 1):

> the judgement that we form of things, as for instance when I say, the earth is round, is a proposition; therefore, any proposition is necessarily made up of two terms: one is called the subject about which we make an affirmation: the earth; and the other called the attribute which is what we affirm: round, and in addition the link between the two terms: is.

The significance of the example chosen to illustrate the identification of judgement with its spoken or written expression must be clarified. It is an inclusive judgement whose enunciation entails non-explicit features, all of which are not equally important. It is not obligatory for the proposition to include only simple terms and a single affirmation, which would make it comparable to the basic sentence of generative grammar (see GENERATIVE GRAMMAR), as can be seen in chapter I, 9 of the logic that deals with the relative pronoun and 'incidental' clauses that we shall study below. The presence of the subject-attribute and, as a corollary, of the linking copula 'is' is, however, imperative. It is linked with the theory of the verb (II, 13).

THE VERB

The grammar rejects the definition given by Aristotle, according to whom the verb signifies actions and passions – and this is no more than an interpretation of the attribute – and by Scaliger, according to whom the verb signifies what is passing as opposed to the noun which signifies what is permanent. Instead, the grammar defined the verb as

a word whose main use is to signify affirmation, that is to say, to point out that the discourse in which this word is used is the discourse of a man who does not only conceive things, but also judges and affirms them.

The phrase 'main use' helps to distinguish affirmation from 'other movements of the soul, like wishes, requests, commands, etc.' that can also be expressed by the verb, but only through a change of inflection and mode, that is to say, by introduction of supplementary marks. The verb can also include the idea of subject, for instance in the Latin utterance *sum homo, 'I am human'*, where *sum* does not only contain the affirmation, but also contains the meaning of the *ego*, 'I' pronoun. The idea of subject itself can be combined with that of attribute: *vivo = I am alive*. Moreover, the verb can include an 'indication of time'. But the person, number, and time are only the 'principal incidentals' which are added to the verb's essential meaning.

There are two categories of verbs. The one archetypal verb, which marks affirmation and nothing else, is the verb *to be*: 'Only the verb to be, which is called substantival, has preserved this simple character', and even then 'it has preserved it only in the third person of the present tense, and in certain occurrences' (II, 13). The other verbs, called 'adjectival verbs', contain, in addition to affirmation, the meaning of an attribute. *Petrus vivit, Peter lives* are equivalent to *Peter is alive*. Every verb can thus be reduced to a paraphrase which equates its participle to the adjectival attribute.

The idea of this paraphrase, presented as universally applicable, belonged to an old tradition in grammar. The paraphrase is not purely grammatical and very often it cannot be used in real discourse. It is half way between logic and grammar, and it represents a form of logical relationship which can be formalized through a procedure of theoretical grammatical transformation. Thus, the notion of affirmation is organically linked with the verb which embodies at the same time 'the relationship that our minds set up between the two terms of a proposition', that is to say, the inclusion of the idea of attribute within the idea of subject. Inclusion belongs to the logic of ideas. It is connected with the axiomatic conditions of categorical propositions and can be expounded in terms of comprehension and extension (Pariente, 1985, p. 265). It appears that setting up a relationship also entails the acceptance of inclusion, 'the relationship that we set up in our minds', and this gives it an illocutionary (see SPEECH-ACT THEORY) character. It is in this respect that the verb differs

from those few nouns that also signify affirmation such as *affirmans, affirmatio*, because they signify it only in so far as it has become the object of our thinking, through a mental reflection, and thus they do not indicate that the person who makes use of these words is affirming, but only that he conceives an affirmation. (II, 13)

SIMPLE AND COMPLEX PROPOSITIONS

However, the definition of the proposition raises a number of problems when it comes to analysing more complex utterances than the minimal sentence used to illustrate it in the grammar. It is on this question that we find the most important changes in the successive editions of the grammar and the logic. Nowhere does the grammar really expound the concept of grammatical subordination and it deals with complex sentences only with reference to the relative pronoun (II, 9), to the interpretation of the Latin *quod*, the French conjunction *que*, which is in fact connected with the relative, of the Latin infinitive proposition and indirect interrogative propositions introduced by *si* in French and *an* in Latin (II, 17). The chapter devoted to the relative pronoun refers the reader back to the logic which deals with 'complex sentences'.

The 'simple proposition' includes only one judgement, and therefore only one subject and only one attribute: 'God is good'. When the utterance contains several subjects to which is applied a single attribute, or several attributes applied to one subject, the proposition is said to be 'compound' (Log. II, 5) for it contains several judgements: 'Life and death are within the power of language', 'Alexander was the most generous of Kings and the conqueror of Darius.' But the single subject or attribute can be expressed by a complex term – and in this case the proposition may itself be either simple or complex, depending on the logical interpretation of the term used. According to the grammar, when complexity is manifested by the 'union of two terms' one of which is governed by the other – as for instance when two substantives are linked by the preposition *of*, or, in English, the possessive case – 'this union of several terms in the subject and the attribute is such that the proposition may nevertheless be considered as simple, as it contains only one judgement or affirmation': 'Achilles' valour was the cause of the fall of Troy.'

Complexity on the other hand can occur in the linking of a single subject or attribute with a term or syntagm which can be interpreted from a logical point of view as expressing a first judgement distinct from the global one expressed by the subject and attribute and, so to speak, included within the latter. This is what happens with propositions introduced by a relative pronoun (Log. II, 5):

There are several propositions which have properly speaking only one subject and one attribute, but whose subject or attribute is a complex term, containing other propositions which we may call 'incidental' and which are only parts of the subject or the attribute, as they are linked by the relative pronoun who, which, whose function is to join several propositions, so that they together form one single proposition.

The grammar emphasized the innovative nature of its interpretation of the relative, according to which 'the proposition in which it appears (which may be called incidental) can belong to the subject or to the attribute of another proposition which may be called the main proposition' (II, 9). It will be noticed that the term 'main' is applied to the whole, whereas subsequent practice applied the term differently. But the authors considered an adjectival term directly related to the noun as equivalent to an incidental proposition, so that the complex proposition may very well contain no incidental proposition expressed grammatically: 'these types of propositions whose subject or attribute are composed of several terms contain, in our minds at least, several judgements which can be turned into as many propositions'. Thus 'Invisible God created the visible world' is the equivalent of 'God, who is invisible, created the world, which is visible.'

It is this passage, among others, that Chomsky (1966, p. 34) interprets in terms of deep structure and surface structure to present the Port-Royal Grammar as a forerunner of transformational-generative grammar (see TRANSFORMATIONAL-GENERATIVE GRAMMAR), a presentation which has been severely criticized by other writers (see, for instance, Percival, 1972; Pariente, 1985, Chs 1 and 2). Therefore, it is the logical interpretation of the complex term which tells us whether it contains a judgement distinct from – and included in – the global judgement, and whether one can find several propositions in the 'main' proposition, which is also called 'whole' (Gr. II, 9) or 'total' (Log. II, 6). But the effect of the assimilation of judgement with proposition: 'this judgement is also called proposition' (Log. II, 3), is that the two terms are used sometimes to mean different things and sometimes to mean the same thing. The result is to produce some terminological uncertainty : 'When I say invisible God created the visible world, three judgements are formed in my mind, which are contained in this proposition . . . ' 'Now these propositions are often present in my mind, without being expressed in words' (Gram. II, 9). The logic (II, 5) points out that incidental propositions 'are propositions only very imperfectly . . . or are not so much propositions that are made at the time as propositions that have been made before; as a consequence, all one does is to conceive them, as if they were merely ideas'.

THE INFLUENCE OF THE GRAMMAR

The theory of the sign, of the proposition and of the verb have been presented here as the most important parts in the grammar because of their decisive influence in the development of grammar and of the philosophy of language. In returning to a mentalistic viewpoint presented as universal and using theoretical tools at once powerful and simple, the Port-Royal Grammar was the starting-point of the current of thought in general grammar which was to prevail, with some changes, until the middle of the nineteenth century. The theoreticians of the eighteenth century developed their ideas in reference to it, very often to refute or modify particular aspects of it. But the grammar had a powerful influence in establishing the proposition as the central unit of grammatical study.

The fact that it was written in French, twenty-three years after Descartes' *Discours de la méthode*, also contributed to French being considered as a language to be studied in the same way as classical languages were studied, and as a language which could carry the weight of philosophical speculation, and whose clarity is derived from the 'natural order'. Finally, it was through its influence that the idea that a reasoned knowledge may facilitate language-learning became widespread.

J.B.

SUGGESTIONS FOR FURTHER READING

Dominicy, M. (1984), *La Naissance de la grammaire moderne*, Brussels, Márdaga.

Donzé, R. (1971), *La Grammaire générale et raisonnée de Port Royal*, 2nd edn, Berne, Francke.

Pariente, J.C. (1985), *L'Analyse du langage à Port-Royal*, Paris, Edition Minuit.

(Post-)Bloomfieldian American structural grammar

The body of work published in the USA mainly in the 1940s and 1950s by, among others, Bernard Bloch, Zellig Harris, Charles Hockett, Georges Trager, Henry Lee Smith, Archibald Hill, and Robert Hall, and which was heavily influenced by Leonard Bloomfield's book, *Language* (1933), is variably referred to in the literature as **Bloomfieldian**, **Post-Bloomfieldian**, **taxonomic**, **descriptivist** and **structural**. In this entry, the term **post-Bloomfieldian American structural** is preferred in order to distinguish the work to be referred to from other American descriptive structural work such as that of Sapir and Whorf (see MENTALIST LINGUISTICS) and Pike (see TAGMEMICS), and from European structuralism (see STRUCTURALIST LINGUISTICS).

Language is characterized by a strict **empiricism**; if linguistics was to be scientific, then it must confine itself to statements about observables, and this empiricism characterizes all post-

Bloomfieldian American structural linguistics. Therefore, a post-Bloomfieldian grammar arises out of direct observation: it is 'discovered' through the performing of certain operations on a corpus of data – through **discovery procedures**. The corpus consists of speech, so the first operation the grammarian will need to perform has to be a phonological analysis of the stream of sound into phonemes (see PHONEMICS).

The analysis is structural in the sense that the language is simply thought to consist of a string of phonemes, which will form a variety of types of structures. These types will be revealed during the next stage of observation; the phonemes can be grouped into minimal recurrent sequences, or **morphs**, and those morphs which are phonemically similar and which are in **complementary distribution**, i.e. have no contexts in common, are members of the same **morphemes** (see MORPHOLOGY). So when we look at language at this level, it consists of strings of morphemes. But morphemic information, since it can only be gained *after* phonemic information has been discovered, cannot be drawn on in the discovery of phonemic information, since then the account would be circular. This consideration gives rise to the principle that the levels of linguistics description must not be mixed and to a strict 'bottom-up' one way ordering of linguistic descriptions (compare IMMEDIATE CONSTITUENT ANALYSIS).

Having discovered the morphemes of a language, the task of the linguist is to discover how the morphemes may be combined, that is, to write the grammar. According to Bloomfield (1933/35, p. 184) words can occur as larger forms, arranged by **modulation, phonetic modification, selection**, and **order**, and any such arrangement which is meaningful and recurrent is a **syntactic construction**. By **modulation**, Bloomfield means intonation and stress, and by **phonetic modification** he means the kind of phenomenon by which *do not* becomes *don't*, and *run* becomes *ran*. The problems with these concepts are discussed in Palmer (1971, pp. 119–23), and see also MORPHOLOGY. Here I shall only discuss the two really structural ways of making syntactic constructions, namely selection and order.

Basically, what is at issue here is that in uttering a syntactic structure we select morphemes and place them in order. This ordering is clearly very important – it matters a great deal whether I say *Brutus killed Caesar* or *Caesar killed Brutus*. In Latin it would not matter, because the names would be inflected for **case**, that is, they would be given special endings showing whether they functioned as subject or object in the clause. So it looks as if, in English, word ordering performs the same kind of function which the morphemes that are used to give the Latin case endings perform in Latin.

Selection of morphemes, and combinations of selections is equally important, since when the same form is selected in combination with a variety of forms which differ from one another, the resultant forms are also different from one another. For instance, when a noun, *milk*, is combined with an adjective, *fresh*, the resultant combination, *fresh milk*, is different from the result of combining *milk* with the verb *drink*, *drink milk*. In the first case, we have a noun phrase, in the second a sentence in the imperative mood. So by combining a selected morpheme or group of morphemes with other, different morphemes the linguist is able to discover different **form classes** (Palmer, 1971, p. 123): '*drink milk* is different from *fresh milk*, and as a result of this difference we can identify *drink* as a verb and *fresh* as an adjective'. Thus the principle of complementary distribution influences discovery procedures in syntactic analysis too, albeit in a different way, as here morphemes are said to be of the same syntactic type if they are *not* in complementary distribution, that is, if they display **distributional equivalence**, i.e., if they occur in the same range of contexts. For instance, any morpheme that can occur before the plural {-s} morpheme is a noun (Newmeyer, 1986, p. 9).

The notion of the form class was developed by Fries (1952/7), who described English as having four major **form-classes** defined according to the kinds of **frames** words of a class could enter into, as follows (from Allen and Widdowson, 1975, pp. 53–4):

Class 1 words fit into such frames as
    (The) _____ was good
    (The) _____s were good
    (The) _____ remembered the _____
    (The) _____ went there

Class 2 words fit the frames:
    (The) 1 _____ good
    (The) 1 _____ (the) 1
    (The) 1 _____ there

Class 3 words fit the frames:
    (The) 1 is/was _____
    (The) _____ 1 is/was _____

Class 4 words fit the frames:
    (The) 3 1 is/was _____
    (The) 1 2 (the) 1 _____
    (The) 1 2 there _____

The numerals in the examples above refer to words of the respective classes.

Although the correspondence is not complete, it is clear that there is a large amount of overlap between Fries' classes and nouns, verbs, adjectives, and adverbs respectively; similarly, Fries recognized fifteen groups of **function words**, corresponding roughly to articles, auxiliaries, prepositions, and so on. However, the perceived advantage of Fries' classification was its distributional character. Because of the emphasis on classes, this kind of grammar is often labelled **taxonomic**.

There are, unfortunately, very few actual descriptive syntactic studies available from the post-Bloomfieldians, largely because the processes of arriving at them are lengthy; and what there is has, in any case, largely had to bypass its own prescribed procedures, since no complete morphemic analysis was ever worked out for English (or for any other language). Wells' (1947)

'top-down' immediate constituent analysis has, however, been widely applied (see IMMEDIATE CONSTITUENT ANALYSIS).

Post-Bloomfieldians also began to take an interest in a final linguistic level, the **discourse level**, as Harris (1952, 1957, 1965) attempted to develop discovery procedures for structure above the sentence level. This task was hindered by the infinite variety in the form of sentences which made it very difficult to use substitutional criteria to demonstrate sentence relatedness. Harris hoped that it would be possible to develop a set of procedures for relating complex sentences, like passives, to simple or **kernel** sentences, like actives, and he called the procedures by which they were related **transformations**. It is important to be aware that for Harris the transformation is a relationship between sentences; it is not the intrasentential phenomenon of the transformational-generative grammarian (see TRANSFORMATIONAL-GENERATIVE GRAMMAR). With the upsurge in transformational-generative grammar in the late 1950s and 1960s, Harris' work was widely ignored until interest in the analysis of discourse was rekindled in Britain in the 1970s (see DISCOURSE AND CONVERSATIONAL ANALYSIS).

K.M.

SUGGESTIONS FOR FURTHER READING

Dinneen, F.P. (1967), *An Introduction to General Linguistics*, New York, Holt, Rinehart & Winston.

Newmeyer, F.J. (1986), *Linguistic Theory in America*, 2nd edn, New York and London, Academic Press.

Palmer, F.R. (1971), *Grammar*, Harmondsworth, Penguin.

Pragmatics

Pragmatics may be defined as the study of the rules and principles which govern language in use, as opposed to the abstract, idealized rules of, for instance, grammar, and of the relationships between the abstract systems of language on the one hand, and language in use on the other (but see Levinson, 1983, ch. 1.2, who discusses and dismisses a large number of definitions more or less similar to that just given; see also Leech, 1983).

Basic to all research in pragmatics is, first, the so-called **natural-language philosophy**, or speech-act theory developed by Austin and Searle (see SPEECH-ACT THEORY), and secondly Grice's (1975, 1978) theory of conversational implicature. I shall begin by outlining the considerations which led Grice to develop this theory of how conversation works, and the theory itself.

The theory of conversational implicature was first presented by Grice in a series of William James lectures at Harvard University in 1967. Its overriding aim is to show that there are no divergences between the meanings of the formal logical devices, ¬, &, ∨, →, ∀, ∃, and ʃ, on the one hand, and their natural-language counterparts, *not, and, or, if–then, all, some,* and *the* on the other hand. Divergences may appear to exist as follows (see also FORMAL LOGIC AND MODAL LOGIC):

NOT

In logic, the negator works in such a way that if ¬ *p* is true, then *p* is false and *vice versa*; but in natural language, there seem to be many cases in which this is not so. For instance, it may not be true that James is not happy, but this does not guarantee the truth of the statement *James is happy*; James could simply be in a mental state somewhere in between happy and not happy.

AND

In logic, $P \& Q$ is true in exactly the same circumstances as $Q \& P$. But in natural language, *Jane got up and fell down* is not necessarily true in the same circumstances as *Jane fell down and got up*.

OR

Natural-language users of *or* appear, at the very least, to have a different type of interest when using the word from that of logicians. In logic, *The book is in the library or the book is in the book shop* is true, and is legitimately confirmable, if one of the disjuncts is true. But if someone asked me whether the book was in the bookshop or in the library, and I replied *yes*, thus confirming the truth of the whole disjunction, it is likely that my interlocutor would get annoyed, because in natural language, what is normally at issue is *which* of the disjuncts is true.

IF–THEN

In logic, $P \rightarrow Q$ does not imply that Q is true as a consequence of P being true; indeed, even if P is false, the conditional as a whole will be true as long as Q is true. But in natural language, if I say *If Charles is English then he is brave*, people will take me to mean that Charles' bravery is a consequence of his being English.

ALL AND SOME

In logic, the truth of $\exists x(Fx)$ need not in any way conflict with the truth of $\forall x(Fx)$. But in natural language, if I say *Some students pass their exams*, I will normally be understood to mean that not all students pass their exams.

THE

Many logicians hold that if *the* appears in a definite description, then the phenomenon being referred to by whatever *the* modifies must exist and be unique. So, in logic, *The restaurant on the Bristol Road is excellent* would be taken to mean that there is one and only one restaurant on the Bristol Road, and that it is excellent. This is not the case in natural language, and anyone to whom I made the statement in question might well ask *Which restaurant do you mean?*

So in all these cases, it is tempting to suggest that the formal logical devices do not, in fact, have natural-language counterparts at all – that their meaning is radically different from the meaning of those natural-language items which just happen to look like translations of the formal logical items.

To show that this suggestion is unwarranted, Grice draws a distinction between what is **said** and what is *conventionally implicated*. A logician and a natural-language user *say* exactly the same, but it is a convention of natural language not shared by logic that the use of the words we are concerned with has certain implications in addition to what they say: *and* normally implicates one particular order of succesion, *or* normally implicates exclusion of one of the disjuncts; *if–then* normally implicates consequentiality between antecedent and consequent, and so on. We can see that implicature cannot be part of what is being *said*, by considering the fact that it can be cancelled out. I can say *A happened and B happened, but not in that order*, where *but not in that order* obviously cancels out the implication of succession of *and*.

To illustrate what is meant by implicature, and to show that it is quite distinct from what is said, Grice introduces a third notion, namely **non-conventional implicature**. This differs from conventional implicature in that it is very obviously distinct from what is being said. Grice (1975, p. 43) gives an example:

A and B are talking about a mutual friend, C, who is now working in a bank. A asks B how C is getting on in his job, and B replies, *Oh quite*

well I think; he likes his colleagues, and he hasn't been to prison yet.

Whatever is implicated here obviously depends on many fact about A, B, C, and their life histories, and is thus in no sense *conventionally* implicated.

There is, however, a subclass of non-conventional implicature which has aspects of conventionality in it, and it is this class of implicature which has been so influential in pragmatic theory – it is what Grice calls **conversational implicature**. Conversational implicature is *essentially connected* with certain *general features of discourse*, and these general features of discourse arise from the fact that if our talk exchanges are to be rational, they must consist of utterances which are in some way connected to each other. What guarantees this connection is called the **co-operative principle**: make your contribution such as is required, at the stage at which it occurs, by the accepted purpose or direction of the talk exchange in which you are engaged.

In order to comply with this principle, speakers need to follow a number of subprinciples, which fall into four categories, of quantity, quality, relation, and manner:

I **Maxims of quantity** (which relate to the amount of information to be provided):

1 Make your contribution as informative as is required for the current purposes of the exchange.
2 Do not make your contribution more informative than is required.

II **Maxims of quality**
Supermaxim: Try to make your contribution one that is true.

More specifically:

1 Do not say what you believe to be false.
2 Do not say that for which you lack adequate evidence.

III **Maxim of relation**: be relevant. (Grice is, of course, aware of the difficulty of deciding what is relevant when. Smith and Wilson (1979, p. 177), suggest that one remark is relevant to another if the two remarks together, along with background knowledge, provide new information which could not have been derived from either of the remarks alone, along with background knowledge. See also Sperber and Wilson (1986), and *Behavioral and Brain Sciences* (1987, 10, pp. 697–754).

IV **Maxims of manner** (which concern not so much *what* is said, but *how* it is said):

Supermaxim: Be perspicuous.

More specifically:

1 Avoid obscurity.
2 Avoid ambiguity.
3 Be brief (avoid unnecessary prolixity).
4 Be orderly.

And there may be others.

A participant in a talk exchange may fail to fulfil a maxim in a number of ways:

1 S/he may **violate** it, in which case s/he will be likely to mislead.
2 S/he may **opt out** of observing the principle by saying things like *I don't want to talk about it*.
3 There may be a **conflict of maxims**: you cannot be as informative as is required if you do not have adequate evidence.
4 S/he may blatantly **flout** a maxim.

When a maxim is being flouted while it is still clear that the co-operative principle is being observed, the hearer will supply whatever implicature is necessary to reinstate the maxim, and when conversational implicature is generated in this way, Grice says that a maxim is being **exploited**.

The data the hearer relies on to work out the implicature include:

1 The conventional meaning of the words used, and the referents of referring expressions (see PHILOSOPHY OF LANGUAGE).
2 The co-operative principle and its maxims.
3 The co-text and context.
4 Background knowledge.
5 The supposition that all participants suppose that all relevant items falling under 1–4 are available to them all.

Conversational implicature must possess five features:

1 It can be **cancelled**, since it depends on the co-operative principle being observed, and it is possible to opt out of observing it. You can simply add *I don't mean to imply . . .*
2 It is **non-detachable** from what is being said. If the same thing is being said in a different way, then the same implicature will attach to both manners of expression: the same implicature of 'having failed to achieve something' which attaches to the expression, *I tried to do it*, will also attach to the paraphrases, *I attempted to do it* and *I endeavoured to do it*.
3 It is not part of the meaning of the expression, since if it were, it could not be cancelled, but is, rather, dependent on the prior knowledge of that meaning.
4 It is not carried by what is said – the meaning – but by the saying of what is said – by the **speech act**, not by the propositional content (see SPEECH-ACT THEORY).
5 It is **indeterminate**: there are often several possible implicatures – though the types of data mentioned above will, of course, help hearers determine the most likely implicature.

Although Grice states his maxims as if the purpose of talk exchanges was always simply the effective exchange of information, he is, naturally, aware that there are many other reasons for engaging in conversation, and that other maxims, principles, and concerns may influence the ways in which people conduct themselves in conversation, and we shall see below how later research in pragmatics has added to the basis provided by Grice. His schema works well for cases of information exchange. To give an example, if A has sent B out to buy milk and bread, and, on B's return, A enquires, *Did you get the shopping?*, then, if B replies, *Well, I got the milk*, B will either have been too informative (if one assumes that all that might have been required would have been *yes* or *no*), or not informative enough (if one assumes that a full statement of exactly what was bought was required). Since a maxim of quantity has thus been flouted, A will supply the implicature that no bread was obtained by B, and the maxim will be reinstated.

The major theoretical problem with Grice's theory, as with Austin's and Searle's (see SPEECH-ACT THEORY), and carried over into later research in pragmatics, is that the theory of meaning from which Grice and Searle derive the prior meaning on the basis of which the non-literal speech act in Searle's case and the implicature in Grice's case are in turn derived, arises from a traditional correspondence theory of truth (see Grice, 1978, p. 126). Austin was aware that this might be a problem, saying (1962, p. 142):

> We may well suspect that the theory of 'meaning' as equivalent to 'sense and reference' will certainly require some weeding-out and reformulating in terms of the distinction between locutionary and illocutionary acts (*if these notions are sound*: they are only adumbrated here). I admit that not enough has been done here: I have taken the old 'sense and reference' on the strength of current views.

The problem is that the 'current views' Austin mentions predate Quine's (1960) critique of truth-conditional semantics, and Davidson's (see Davidson, 1984) and others' subsequent moves to rescue it. These moves involve taking on board circumstances of utterance (see PHILOSOPHY OF LANGUAGE), as, indeed, pragmatics does. But they also amply demonstrate the impossibility of operating with a context-free semantics as a basis on which to build a pragmatics; this neo-Fregean truth-conditional semantics is such that there cannot be any dividing line between it and pragmatics. This is worth bearing in mind when studying pragmatics, not because it invalidates any of the very important insights provided by that discipline into general discourse behaviour, but, rather, because it will make the reader aware that some of the theoretical statements produced by pragmaticists may not stand up to scrutiny in the light of the state of the art of post-Quine semantics.

Leech (1983, p. 80) points out that

> The CP [Co-operative principle] in itself cannot explain (i) *why* people are often so

indirect in conveying what they mean; and (ii) what is the relation between sense and force when non-declarative types of sentence are being considered.

He suggests that a further, complementary, principle, the **Politeness Principle** (PP) is needed to complement the CP. The PP has two formulations, one negative: 'Minimize (other things being equal) the expression of impolite beliefs'; and the other positive: 'Maximize (other things being equal) the expression of polite beliefs' (ibid., p. 81). It works as follows (ibid., pp. 80–1):

[1] *A*: We'll all miss Bill and Agatha, won't we?
     B: Well, we'll all miss BILL.

In [1], B apparently fails to observe the Maxim of Quantity: when A asks B to confirm A's opinion, B merely confirms part of it, and pointedly ignores the rest. From this we derive the implicature: 'B is of the opinion that we will not miss Agatha'. But on what grounds is this implicature arrived at? Not solely on the basis of the CP, for B could have added ' . . . but not Agatha' without being untruthful, irrelevant, or unclear. Our conclusion is that B *could* have been more informative, but only at the cost of being more impolite to a third party: that B therefore suppressed the desired information in order to uphold the PP.

Politeness is gradable, an utterance tending to be more polite in proportion to the indirectness of its force (see SPEECH-ACT THEORY). This is because an increase in indirectness seems to allow the hearer more choice in how s/he responds – compare the options for response offered by *Answer the phone* and *Could you possibly answer the phone* respectively – and because indirectness decreases an utterance's force anyway (ibid., p. 108). Leech (ibid., in particular ch. 6) outlines a number of maxims covering politeness, and points out that different societies differ in the weight they attach to different maxims. The opportunities offered by pragmatics for comparative studies of the rules for linguistic behaviour in different societies and in different sub groups within one society constitute one of

the discipline's most fruitful and important applications. Studies of this kind tend to reveal that
the stereotypes we have of members of cultures
other than our own as being, for instance, more
polite/rude than ourselves arise largely because
we have insufficient understanding of the pragmatic rules by which these other peoples live.

In addition to implicature, which may be
viewed as one type of pragmatic inference
(Levinson, 1983, p. 167), much pragmatic
literature is concerned with another type, namely
presupposition (ibid.). However, there is not any

adequate theory of presupposition available,
according to Levinson, to whom readers are
referred for criticism of proposed theories.

                                                    K.M.

SUGGESTIONS FOR FURTHER READING

Leech, G.N. (1983), *Principles of Pragmatics*,
    London and New York, Longman.
Levinson, S.C. (1983), *Pragmatics*, Cambridge,
    Cambridge University Press.

Prosodic phonology

Prosodic phonology, alternatively referred to as
prosodic analysis, arose as a reaction against
what proponents of prosodic phonology sometimes dub **phonemic phonology**, i.e. **phonemics**
(see PHONEMICS), which operates with phonemes.
In this sense as well as in certain other senses,
prosodists' negative attitude extends also to
functional phonology (see FUNCTIONAL
PHONOLOGY). Prosodic phonologists reject the
notion of the phoneme altogether, asserting that
the phoneme has no existence in a language itself
and is merely one of the convenient categories to
which some linguists resort in order to present
the linguistic data they analyse. Prosodists'
objection to the phoneme arises out of their belief
that it has been developed for transcriptional
purposes so that phoneme theory is closely
associated with phonetic transcription and
the devising of orthographies, rather than with
serious phonological analysis.

Instead of operating with the phoneme, prosodic phonology operates with the **phonematic
unit** – not to be confused with phonemes of any
kind – and with **prosody**, terms which will be
explained below. Prosodic analysis is also some-

times referred to as **Firthian phonology** or **London
School phonology** because it originated with John
Rupert Firth (1890–1960), Britain's first professor of linguistics, who taught at the University
of London, especially at the School of Oriental
and African Studies. Prosodic phonology was
conceived by Firth in the mid-1930s and
subsequently developed by him. Firth's followers
have put his prosodic theory into practice in
their phonological analyses of, mainly, South-
East Asian and African languages (see Palmer,
1970).

Prosodic phonology is best characterized in
terms of the concepts and entities which
prosodists entertain and work with in their
attempt to distinguish themselves as far as
possible from 'phonemicists'.

Prosodists operate with the notions of **system**
and **structure**. The former relates to the concept of **paradigmatic relation** and the latter
to the concept of **syntagmatic relation**, two
concepts commonly ascribed to the Swiss linguist
Ferdinand de Saussure (1857–1913). Prosodists
often use the following diagram to indicate the
concepts of system and structure:

S
Y
S
S T R U C T U R E
E
M

Linguistic units function in terms of the inter-action between system and structure. In so far as linguistic units follow and precede one another, they form sequential syntagmatic structural relations with each other. Simultaneously, they form paradigmatic relations with each other, since a linguistic unit is significantly, i.e. differ-entially, replaceable with another or others at that specific place in the structure, where all of the mutually replaceable linguistic units form a system (see also STRUCTURALIST LINGUISTICS). Prosodic phonology attaches primary impor-tance to syntagmatic relation and secondary importance to paradigmatic relation and con-sequently highlights those phonetic features which are relevant to structure, i.e. prosody, which is a non-segmental unit. Prosodists are of the view that phonemicists attach excessive im-portance to paradigmatic relation at the expense of syntagmatic relation and are preoccupied with segmentation, which is consistent with their operating with phonemes.

Prosodists operate with different kinds of prosody. Firstly, a prosody may be a phonetic feature specifiable by dint of its occurrence over a certain stretch of structure and consequently characterizing the whole of such a structure. A sentence prosody, such as **intonation**, is one which occurs over the whole of a spoken sen-tence. The phonetic feature (**lip-)unroundedness** which occurs over the whole of, for example, the English word *teeth*, and the phonetic feature (**lip-)roundedness** which occurs over the whole of, for example, the English word *tooth* are both **word prosodies**. A **tone** (see TONE LANGUAGES), which is a prosody that occurs over a single syllable, e.g. in the Mandarin Chinese word for 'mother', ˉ*ma*, is a **syllable prosody**.

Secondly, a prosody may be a phonetic feature occurring at a particular place in a structure, rather than over a certain stretch of a structure, but which has ultimate relevance to a certain stretch of the structure. For example, the pho-netic feature **aspiration** (= a puff of air) in the pronunciation of a Tamil voiceless plosive con-sonant, e.g. [pʰ], occurs in word-initial position only – the focus of relevance – never in word-medial or word-final position. Ultimately, how-ever, its **domain of relevance** is the whole word in the sense that the aspiration characterizes the pertinent word as a whole. In Czech, the accent falls on the initial syllable of a polysyllabic word, at least in principle, and characterizes the whole word, though its incidence is localized on the initial syllable.

Thirdly, a prosody may be a phonetic feature which shows the demarcation between consecu-tive structures. Such a prosody is often referred to as a **junction prosody**. For example, aspiration accompanying a voiceless plosive consonant in Tamil or the accent on the initial syllable in Czech mentioned above have additionally the function of indicating the demarcation between words. To give yet another example, the glottal plosive [ʔ] in German is a prosody which reveals the demarcation between morphemes in cases where morphemes begin with accented vowels, e.g. *wir haben ein Auto* [. . . ʔain 'ʔauto . . .]; *ich verachte ihm* [. . . fɛr'ʔ axtə . . .].

Fourthly, a prosody may be a phonetic feature which is linked to, and which is therefore an exponent of, a grammatical or lexical category. Such a prosody is often referred to as a **diagnostic prosody**. For example, [z] in *rows* as in *rows of chairs* is a phonetic exponent of the grammatical category of number, plural in this case; this is not the case with [z] in *rose*. [ð] is a phonetic exponent of the lexical category of deixis which encompasses that group of deictic or demon-strative words whose referents are things, persons, places, times, etc., including *this, those, there, then*, etc; this is not the case with [ð] in *gather* or *either*. This last-mentioned type of prosody is obviously different from the others in that, for one thing, it does not characterize any particular stretch of structure, and for another, it involves a non-phonological factor, namely grammar or lexis in these examples. Note, however, that the involvement of non-phono-logical levels is not only admitted but recom-mended in prosodic analysis because of its principles of polysystemicness and context, which will be explained below.

In prosodic phonology, prosodists first ab-stract all the prosodies, starting with that prosody whose domain of relevance is the most extensive, i.e., intonation. However, it would seem perfectly valid to start with a prosody whose domain is even more extensive, that is, a prosody which characterizes a whole speech; for example, nasality may characterize some people's speech throughout, while, in the case of speakers of a foreign language, elements from their own language may pervade their pro-nunciation of the foreign language. Abstraction of prosodies is carried on until there are no more phonetic features which characterize structures.

What remains when all the prosodies have been abstracted are the phonological units which prosodists call **phonematic units**. These are – unlike prosodies – **segmental**, hence linear, units, which are considered as being placed at par-ticular points in the structure. A phonematic unit may be simply V (= vowel) or C (= consonant), or a phonetic feature like 'open' or 'close', if the phonematic unit happens to be vocalic.

To demonstrate how prosodic analysis is performed, we shall look at a few examples. Given the English word *tooth* [tuːθ], the prosodist abstracts the phonetic feature (lip-)roundedness which is manifested over the whole word: note that not only [uː] but also [t] and [θ] are rounded through assimilation (see ARTICULATORY PHO-NETICS) and this is precisely what the prosodist first wishes to abstract as a prosody. This pro-sody may be presented as **w prosody**, where 'w' refers to (lip-)roundedness. What remains are the phonematic units which the prosodist will present as **CVC** (consonant vowel consonant). The actual specification of a phonematic unit in terms of its phonetic components is neither important nor obligatory in prosodic phonology, so that it is not considered necessary to state which CVC are in question. Given the English word *teeth* [tiːθ], the prosodist abstracts as a prosody the phonetic feature (lip-)unroundedness which runs through-

out this word, and presents this prosody as **y prosody**. What remains of this word after y prosody has been abstracted are the same phonematic units as we have seen above, i.e. CVC.

The prosodic analysis of the two English words, *tooth* and *teeth* will be notationally presented as ᵂCVC and ʸCVC, or ᵂC̄V̄C̄ and ʸC̄V̄C̄. Note that the analysis did not start with segmentation, i.e. paradigmatically, into a series of phonemes, but with the abstraction of certain prosodies together with the identification of a structure, in this case a whole word, explicitly indicated by superimposed horizontal lines in one of the types of notation given above, the domain of relevance being words in these cases. Thus the two words in question, *tooth* and *teeth*, possess identical phonematic units, i.e. CVC, and differ from each other in that one of the words has w prosody and the other y prosody.

Another example of prosodic analysis that is frequently cited by prosodists is the following: Turkish possesses eight vowels which may be presented as: [i y e ø ɯ u a o]. These vowels may be re-presented in the following fashion:

$$[i\ y\ ɯ\ u]$$
$$e\ ø\ a\ o]$$

Four prosodies, i.e. **front (f)**, **back (b)**, **rounded (r)**, and **unrounded (u)**, can be appropriately abstracted from these eight vowels. This leaves two phonematic units, i.e. a relatively high, i.e. close, vowel (**H**) and a relatively low, i.e. open, vowel (**L**). The result of the analysis can be shown as follows:

$$[i] = ^{fu}H \quad [y] = ^{fr}H \quad [ɯ] = ^{bu}H \quad [u] = ^{br}H$$
$$[e] = ^{fu}L \quad [ø] = ^{fr}L \quad [a] = ^{bu}L \quad [o] = ^{br}L$$

Given a few Turkish words as examples, e.g. *el* ('hand'), *göz* ('eye'), *bas* ('head'), and *kol* ('arm'), prosodic phonology will yield the following analysis (the corresponding phonemic analysis is added for comparison):

$$^{fu}Ll \quad ^{fr}gLz \quad ^{bu}bLs \quad ^{br}kLl$$
$$(/el/ \quad /gøz/ \quad /bas/ \quad /kol/)$$

It so happens that there occurs in Turkish what is called **vowel harmony**, whereby a given prosody which occurs in the initial syllable of a poly-syllabic word prevails throughout the rest of the syllable(s), so that, for example, *elim* ('my hand') begins with [e] which, as has been seen above, possesses the prosodies of front (f) and unrounded (u), which prosodies also also occur in [i] in the other syllable of this word. We shall see how *elim* ('my hand'), *gözüm* ('my eye'), *basim* ('my head'), and *kolum* ('my arm') are analysed in prosodic phonology (the corresponding phonemic analysis will again be added for comparison):

$$^{fu}\text{LlHm} \quad ^{fr}\text{gLzHm} \quad ^{bu}\text{bLsHm} \quad ^{br}\text{kLlHm}$$
$$(\text{/elim/} \quad \text{/gøzym/} \quad \text{/basɯm/} \quad \text{/kolum/})$$

It will be seen that, in prosodic analysis, the Turkish morpheme denoting 'first person singular possessive', corresponding to *my* in English, is expressed in terms of an identical form, i.e. Hm, throughout, even though the initial vowel sounds in the above-cited Turkish words are different, i.e. [e ø a o], as reflected in the corresponding different vowel phonemes yielded in the phonemic analysis (/e ø a o/), hence the mutually different forms (/im ym ɯm um/) for the Turkish morpheme corresponding to the English word *my* in phonemic analysis.

Another characteristic of prosodic phonology is the **principle of polysystemicness**. This principle is intimately connected with the **principle of context**, as we shall see below. By **polysystemicness** – as opposed to **monosystemicness** which prosodists attribute to phonemic phonology – is meant that units operating at a given place in a structure are independent of those operating at another given place in the structure; in other words, the sets of units operating in different places in the structure should not be identified with each other. This applies, prosodists emphasize, even to cases where a physically identical sound is found in different places in the structure. For example, in English, [m] occurring in word-initial position where there exists what Firth called an **alternance** between [m] and [n], e.g. *mice, nice*, cannot be identified with [m] occurring in word-final position where there exists an alternance between [m], [n] and [ŋ], e.g. *rum, run, rung*. Furthermore, [m] occurring in word-medial position where there is also an alternance between [m], [n] and [ŋ], e.g. *simmer, sinner, singer*, is not to be identified with [m] in word-final position any more than with [m] in word-initial position. It is evident that the contexts involved are different in terms of different places in the structure.

Actually, the principle of polysystemicness is further linked to that of context which, according to prosodists, operates at every linguistic level, including the phonological. This means that, to return to an example earlier adduced, [z] in, e.g., *rows*, which is an exponent of the grammatical category of number – plural, in this case – is considered to be a separate unit from [z] in, e.g., *rose*, which is not an exponent of this grammatical category. The two [z]s in question belong ultimately to different contexts in this sense, and should therefore not be identified with each other, though their phonetic context, word-final position, is the same. Moreover, [z] of *rows*, the verb, as in *he rows a boat*, which denotes third person singular present indicative, is not to be identified with [z] of *rows*, the noun. [ð] in *this* and [ð] in *father* are similarly non-identical. To give yet another example, none of the sounds in *display*, the noun, are to be identified with any of the sounds in *display*, the verb, even if a given sound in the former is physically identical with its corresponding sound in the latter: the two words are associated with different grammatical categories, i.e. noun and verb, and are consequently considered to occur in different contexts and should not be identified with each other.

It follows that the concept of **place** in prosodic phonology should be understood not narrowly in the sense of a place in a physically, i.e. phonetically, identifiable structure, but broadly in the sense that a place is associated with a particular system, the structure in question being phonetic or grammatical or syntactic or morphological or lexical or whatever, as the case may be. The implication of all this is that prosodists are first and foremost interested in seeking out meanings which they believe permeate through all domains of a language. In prosodic phonology, an attempt is made to identify meanings ascribable to sounds in a speech chain: this, in prosodists' view, justifies ascribing a meaning directly to a sound itself, cf. [z] in *rows* as a noun or as a verb.

The principle of polysystemicness and that of context inevitably multiply the units identified in different places in structures, or contexts, without, however, alarming prosodists. They believe that this multiplication is justified in prosodic phonology so long as phonological analysis is carried out according to principles compatible with prosodic phonology. The oft-quoted dictum, attributable to Antoine Meillet (1866–1936), a disciple of Saussure, that 'une langue est un système où tout se tient' ('a language is a system in which everything holds together'), is irrelevant and unacceptable to prosodists because this conception of a language would be associated with the principle of mono-systemicness to which prosodists are opposed.

To prosodists, a language is a group of disparate and isolated subsystems which do not come together in a single global system.

T.A.

SUGGESTIONS FOR FURTHER READING

Palmer, F.R. (ed.) (1970), *Prosodic Analysis*, London, Oxford University Press.
Robins, R.H. (1964), *General Linguistics: An Introductory Survey*, London, Longmans, Section 4.4, 'Prosodic Phonology'.

Psycholinguistics

INTRODUCTION

Psycholinguistics is a discipline in which the insights of linguistics and psychology are brought to bear on the study of the cognitive aspects of language understanding and production. One of the earliest psychological accounts of language was Wundt's *Die Sprache* (1900), which is essentially a psychological interpretation of the linguistic work of the Junggrammatiker (see HISTORICAL LINGUISTICS, p. 194). However, the strongly empiricist and anti-mentalist attitude to science which dominated both linguistics and psychology during the first half of the twentieth century (see BEHAVIOURIST LINGUISTICS) inhibited theorizing about mental processes involved in linguistic behaviour, and it was not until the late 1950s and early 1960s that the work of Noam Chomsky (see RATIONALIST LINGUISTICS and TRANSFORMATIONAL-GENERATIVE GRAMMAR) provided a climate of thought in which the discipline could flourish.

The main impetus for psycholinguistic research in the 1960s was the wish to explore the **psychological reality** of grammars produced by linguists, that is, to try to show that these in some

way mirrored what went on in speakers' and hearers' minds. The two most famous controversies within this framework were produced by the **derivational theory of complexity** (DTC), according to which a sentence would be more difficult to process the further removed its surface structure was from its deep structure, and the theory of the **autonomy of syntactic processing**, according to which the syntactic analysis of sentences constitutes an independent stage in their perception. There is now general agreement that DTC is false, and the grammars which produced it have, in any case, been super-seded (see TRANSFORMATIONAL-GENERATIVE GRAMMAR).

There has also been a general shift within psycholinguistics during the 1970s and 1980s away from models which take grammar as their starting point towards more psychologically based models. The question of whether syntactic processing is carried out independently of, or is interrelated with, other processes has not been decisively answered. It is an aspect of a more general disagreement about whether language is processed in a series of autonomous stages by autonomous components unaffected by each other, or whether there is interaction between levels of processing. The latter view became the more popular during the 1980s (Flores d'Arcais and Jarvella, 1983, Introduction; Flores d'Arcais and Schreuder, 1983; Ellis, 1985; Altmann, 1989).

According to Clark and Clark (1977), psycholinguistics includes the study of children's acquisition of language. Many linguists would agree that both first and other language learning and also linguistic disabilities are the province of psycholinguistics (though see Garnham, 1985, Preface, according to whom they are specialist areas, rather than central topics for psycholinguistics). In this volume, language acquisition and linguistic disabilities are treated in entries of their own (see LANGUAGE ACQUISITION, APHASIA, and LANGUAGE PATHOLOGY AND NEUROLINGUISTICS). According to Lyons (1981), artificial intelligence is also an area of psycholinguistics, but this, again, has its own entry in this volume (see ARTIFICIAL INTELLIGENCE).

LANGUAGE PRODUCTION

Language production includes speaking and writing, but research on speaking predominates. Speaking is one of our most complex cognitive, linguistic and motor skills. We make around fifteen speech sounds per second, producing two or three words (Levelt, 1989, Preface and p. 22) and involving the co-ordinated use of around a hundred muscles (ibid., p. 413); but in most speech encounters, we are far less conscious of the flow of sound than we are of the meaning we hope to be producing by means of the sounds; that is, we are more conscious of what we want to say than we are of the mechanisms involved in saying it.

Planning an utterance involves selecting the information one wishes to share with the interlocutor (for whatever purpose) and arranging the information in such a way that its topic and focus are clear to the interlocutor, and so that it will attract their attention (ibid., p. 5).

Levelt suggests that in planning an utterance, speakers rely on two types of knowledge, procedural and declarative knowledge. **Procedural knowledge** takes the form of **condition/actions pairs** of the form *if X then Y* (where X is the condition and Y the action); for instance, 'if the utterance is to express a commitment to the truth of a proposition *p* then assert *p*'. **Declarative knowledge** includes all the knowledge about the world that the speaker has gathered throughout their life, called **propositional** or **encyclopedic knowledge**, plus knowledge about the immediate situation in which the speech exchange is taking place, **situational knowledge**.

There are probably at least two dominant modes of declarative knowledge, spatial and propositional representations. In **spatial representation**, a state of affairs is known, remembered or construed as a spatial image. In **propositional representation**, states of affairs are known, remembered or construed as sets of relations holding between phenomena. It is possible to switch between modes of representation: if someone asks me what kind of desk I have in my room, I may recall a spatial image of it and then translate it into the propositional information that the desk is rectangular with three drawers on the right hand side; on the other hand, in listening to conversation, we often construct **mental models** (Johnson-Laird, 1983), spatial images which help us make sense of and build on the propositions we are being presented with. Levelt (1989, p. 72) gives the following example:

> If I am given the propositional information that Arnold is taller than Betty, and also that Betty is taller than Christian, then I can evaluate the truth of Arnold's being taller than Christian by imagining three people – Arnold, Betty and Christian – such that Arnold stands head and shoulders above Betty, and similarly for Betty and Christian.

According to Levelt (ibid.), we use a system of procedures akin to logic (see FORMAL LOGIC AND MODAL LOGIC) to evaluate the truth and falsity of propositions on the basis of the truth or falsity of other propositions: 'If a person believes the proposition "All city centres are dangerous" and also the proposition "Manhattan is a city centre", he will be able to evaluate the truth of the proposition "Manhattan is dangerous."'

The procedural knowledge can obviously be applied to the propositions of propositional and situational knowledge. Finally, a co-operative speaker (see PRAGMATICS) will have kept track of the course of a conversation and constructed a **discourse record**, an internal representation of the evolution of the discourse in which s/he is engaged, which ensures that utterances will be appropriate to the ongoing conversation (ibid., pp. 110–11). There is also evidence (Schenkein, 1980; Levelt and Kelter, 1982; Harley, 1984) that the wording of the previous utterance by another speaker can affect the present speaker's wording (Levelt, 1989, p. 122).

It is envisaged that all of these elements enter into the **conceptualization** of a **preverbal** message, a conceptual structure which is the output of the speaker's **conceptualizer** and the input to their formulator (ibid., pp. 9–11, p. 17, and p. 72).

The **formulator** translates a conceptual structure into a linguistic structure. A first step in this process involves retrieving appropriate words from the speaker's **mental lexicon**, their store of declarative knowledge about the words and idioms in their language. For each item, the mental lexicon contains its **lemma information**, **lemma** for short, that is, declarative knowledge about the word's meaning, and information about its syntax and morphology which is necessary for constructing the word's syntactic environment. For instance, the lemma *she* requires the word to be used of a female (disregarding ships, cars, countries, etc., which may also be referred to as 'she' by some speakers) and that any following present-tense main verb must have the suffix -*s* attached to it; the lemma *know* requires a subject that expresses the role of experiencer, an object that expresses what is known, and that these elements appear in a particular order. The lemma also contains information about the word's composition in terms of phonological segments and its syllable and accent structure, and it may contain information about the word's **register**, the kind of discourse it typically enters into (see further FUNCTIONALIST LINGUISTICS), and about its pragmatics, stylistics, and affect (ibid., pp. 182–3) (see PRAGMATICS and STYLISTICS).

The process of retrieving and ordering lemmas is called **grammatical encoding**. A lemma will be activated if its meaning matches part of the preverbal message, and this activation will make its syntax available. This in turn will activate syntactic building procedures. For instance, when the lemma *know* is activated, its syntactic classification as V (verb) will activate verb-phrase-building procedures for constructing verb phrases like *knew the town*. Given access to all relevant lemmas and building procedures, the grammatical encoder produces a **surface structure**, an ordered string of lemmas grouped in phrases and subphrases, which is the input to phonological encoding. **Phonological encoding** is the process of retrieving the phonological form for each lemma and for the utterance as a whole; once phonological encoding has taken place, the speaker can construct a **phonetic** or **articulatory plan** for the utterance, that is, they can decide how such features as pitch, loudness, and stress should be distributed over the utterance. The phonetic plan is a rhythmic (re-)syllabification of a string of segments, because whereas each lemma contains information about an item's phonological segments and its basic rhythm, these will rarely be retained in the flow of speech (Levelt, 1989, p. 284) (see INTONATION). The phonetic plan is the output of the formulator and the input to the articulator (ibid., pp. 6–7 and pp. 11–12).

The **articulator** is responsible for the execution of the phonetic plan by the vocal apparatus. The formulator probably works faster than the articulator, which has to await activation of the muscles in the speaker's vocal tract, so a storage device, an **articulatory buffer**, is proposed, from which the articulator retrieves successive chunks of the plan for execution in **overt speech** (ibid., pp. 12–13). The minimum the buffer has to contain before articulation can begin is probably a phonological word: when isolated words or digits are read aloud, the length of time between the presentation to the subject of the word and the point at which reading begins, the **voice onset time** (**VOT**), increases with the number of syllables in the word (Eriksen, Pollack, and Montague, 1970), and this **syllable latency effect** is due, not to an increase in the duration of the visual process involved, but to the preparation of the articulatory process: Klapp *et al.*, (1973) show that VOT is an average of 14 milliseconds longer for words with two syllables than it is for words with the same number of letters, but of only one syllable (e.g. *camel* versus *clock*). This is the case both when subjects are presented with pictures and when they are presented with written words, and it cannot be due to a difference in word-perception time, because when subjects are asked to classify the same words as animal names or not animal names, by saying *yes* or *no* (both of which replies are one-syllable words), their VOTs do not differ between the words of one and two syllables which they are reading.

Klapp (1974) obtains the same results for the naming of digits: VOT is longer for four-syllable numbers (e.g. twenty-seven) than for three-syllable numbers (e.g. twenty-six). However, when speakers are given time to prepare for their response, e.g., the word to be read aloud appears on a computer screen, but the speaker is told not to articulate it until the signal GO appears, the difference in VOT between one- and two-syllable words disappears. In this case, the speaker has time to program a response and keep it ready in the buffer. Therefore it is likely that the number of syllables in a word affects programming before the word is delivered to the buffer rather than its retrieval from the buffer. This suggests that syllables are programmed serially and that only whole words are delivered to the articulator (Levelt, 1989, p. 417):

> In the phonetic spellout of a phonological word, syllable programmes are addressed one by one, in serial order. Hence, the number of syllables in a phonological word will determine the duration of phonetic spellout. If only plans for whole words are delivered to the Articulator, monosyllabic words will become available for articulation earlier than multisyllabic ones.

Speakers monitor their own utterances; they notice many of their own errors and correct them, but this process, during which a speaker is his or her own listener, is essentially an aspect of speech comprehension, rather than production. Speech errors are, however, important evidence for a model of production such as that outlined above (Levelt, 1989, p. 7 and pp. 13–17). For example, Garrett (1975, 1980) uses three general features of speech errors as evidence in developing a model of the structure of the speech-production system, its components, and the units involved at each production stage (Garnham, 1985, pp. 216–17). For example, Garrett postulates two syntactic subprocessors, one functional, the other positional. The **functional** subprocessor selects the syntactic and semantic properties of the main lexical items and determines the syntactic relations between them. The **positional processor** structures the sentence, adds appropriate inflectional morphemes (see MORPHOLOGY) and provides the sentence's intonational contour. These operations produce a **planning frame** into which phonetic forms and content words will later be inserted.

The three features of speech errors which support this model are the following:

1 Content words tend to exchange with other words of the same syntactic category across constituent boundaries whereas sounds exchange between categories and within constituents; this can be explained by assuming that word exchanges arise at the functional level – the words maintain their function, but are inserted into a representation of the wrong phrase or clause – while sound exchanges take place later in the production process.

2 When words exchange, they **accommodate** to their new environment by adjusting their inflectional endings and sentential stress so that *eating a marathon* becomes *meating an arathon* (Fromkin, 1971) and *It makes the AIR warmer to breathe* becomes *It makes the WARM breather to air*. This can be explained by assuming that inflections take a form appropriate to the phonetic representations of the content words in the planning frame but that they take on this form at a later stage in production.

3 While an inflectional morpheme may shift onto an adjacent word if a lexical item is

inserted in the wrong place in the planning frame, exchanges between inflectional morphemes do not occur. This finding is consistent with Garrett's assumption that items in the planning frame are always in the right order.

Levelt refers to the model he outlines as a **stage model**, while Garnham speaks of **serial models**. 'Stage' and 'serial' should not, however, be taken to imply that the speaker first generates a complete conception of what is to be said, then a complete surface structure, and then a complete phonetic plan, before beginning to articulate; the fluency of discourse belies such serialization. Rather, the processing involved is **incremental**: the next processor can start working on incomplete output of the current processor, and all components can work in parallel on different parts of the utterance to be produced.

The assumption of incremental processing hinges on automaticity. A speaker could not consciously attend to the separate but simultaneous workings of each processor. Conceptualizing and monitoring are conscious processes over which a speaker has executive control. Conceptualizing and monitoring rely on **working memory**, a limited-capacity resource in which a few concepts and aspects of plans can be held in a state of high activation, that is, available for processing. Formulating and articulatory procedures, however, are largely automatic (Levelt, 1989, p. 21 and p. 27).

Speakers monitor their own speech for a number of features which are relatable to the stage model of production outlined above. At the conceptual level, they monitor to ensure that what they are saying is likely to produce their intended meaning, and that the utterance is ordered appropriately for its stage in the ongoing discourse.

At the level of lexical selection, speakers ensure that their words are appropriate to the register of the discourse (Motley *et al.*, 1982), and monitor for **lexical errors**, that is, for inappropriate matchings between the phenomenon they want to mention and the chosen word. Levelt (1989, p. 461) gives the following example:

(1) 'Left to pink – er straight to pink'

in which the speaker probably meant to mention the phenomenon 'straight', but initially selected a word which does not match this phenomenon, namely *left*. Such a **word-substitution** error usually reflects an associative relation between the two lemmas involved which can result in the activation of the wrong lemma (ibid., pp. 218–21). *Left* and *straight* are associated lemmas in so far as they are both directional, and in this case, the speaker was engaged in the task of describing a configuration of coloured nodes in order that someone else would be able to reproduce the configuration, so the instructions 'left', 'right', and 'straight' would all have been in focus.

At the level of grammatical encoding, speakers monitor to ensure that the utterance's syntax and morphology are correct. Levelt and Cutler (1983) (reproduced in Levelt, 1989, p. 462) provide the following example:

(2) 'What things are this kid – is this kid going to say incorrectly?'

At the phonological encoding level, speakers monitor to ensure that their utterances are correct both segmentally and suprasegmentally. Levelt (ibid.) gives the following examples, the first of a segmental, the second of a suprasegmental corrected error:

(3) 'A unut – unit from the yellow dot' (from Levelt, 1983)
(4) '. . . from my prOsodic – prosOdic colleagues' (from Cutler, 1983).

However, speakers only correct around 75 per cent of their phonological errors and around 53 per cent of their lexical errors (Nooteboom, 1980), probably because they fail to detect the rest: the correction rate does not increase even when speakers know that correct lexical selection is particularly important (Levelt, 1989, p. 463).

There are two main classes of theory of monitoring, editor theories and connectionist theories. The **editor** involved in **editor theories** of monitoring is conceived of as external to the system of speech production. According to some editing theories (Laver, 1973, 1980; De Smedt and Kempen, 1987; van Wijk and Kempen,

1987), the editor is **distributed** in the sense that it can monitor at different levels of production. This implies that the editor possesses the same knowledge as each of the components it monitors (since otherwise it could not monitor and correct them), so that there is duplication of knowledge. According to others (Motley *et al.*, 1982), editing can only take place after phonological encoding, either before or after articulation.

Examples of self-correction such as those described above show post-articulatory editing. Evidence for pre-articulatory monitoring comes from Motley *et al.*'s, (1982) study of **induced errors**. Errors can be induced by presenting subjects with one pair of words which they are asked to repeat silently, and then with another pair of words which they are asked to read aloud. If the second pair of words have word-initial phonemes which are the same as those of the first pair, but in reverse order, the first pair can bias the utterance of the second pair in such a way that the speaker retains the order of the first pair's word-initial phonemes. Thus, if the first pair is *ball dome* and the second is *darn bore*, subjects may articulate the latter pair as *barn door* (Motley, 1980). If, however, the induced error would be an expression in which the second word would be a taboo word, speakers tend to produce only partial errors, that is, they will err on the first word but apparently edit the second before it is articulated.

However, the problem of reduplication of knowledge is not solved by restricting editing to the post-phonological encoding stage, because the editor must still be able to evaluate semantic, syntactic, and phonological aspects of speech. If, however, the editor is identified with the language-understanding system, as proposed by Levelt (1983), who identifies the monitor with the conceptualizer, then no duplication of knowledge is involved. According to Levelt's proposal, both the phonetic plan and overt speech may enter the speech-comprehension system, the output of which, parsed speech, is the input to the conceptualizer/monitor. The only difference is that the speaker's own, as well as other people's overt speech reaches the comprehension system via the auditory system, while the speaker's own

pre-articulated phonetic plan obviously does not (Levelt, 1989, pp. 464–74).

According to **connectionist theories** of monitoring (Dell, 1986; MacKay, 1987), no external editor is needed to monitor the production system's output, because the inherent feedback which operates in speech generation provides the system's self-control as well. A layered network of mental nodes, a **node structure**, is responsible for both language production and comprehension. The network includes layers of propositional nodes, conceptual nodes, lexical nodes, syllable nodes, phonological nodes, and feature nodes. Any activated node primes all nodes connected to it, and these, to a lesser degree prime their own connected nodes, and so on. The most highly primed node at each level becomes **activated** or **current** when it is needed. So if a speaker wants to say *green (traffic) light*, the mental nodes for the notions of greenness and traffic light are activated and prime nodes connected to them, such as the node for colour (from greenness) and perhaps the node for red (from traffic light). At the lexical level, the node for *green* is primed by 'green' and by 'colour'. The node for *red* is primed by 'red' and by 'colour'. At the exact moment when an adjective is needed by the speaker, it may happen that *red* is more highly primed than *green*, in which case it will be activated and the speaker will be in danger of making an error, saying *red light* instead of *green light*. However, the activation of *red* will spread activation back to the conceptual node for the phenomenon of redness, so that its priming increases and is perceived, in time for corrective action to be taken before articulation has begun (ibid., pp. 474–7).

The connectionist account is attractive in the economy it achieves by equating the mental networks for the production and comprehension of language, but it fails to account for **delayed error detection**. Obviously, as speech errors occur, they are not all detected before they are articulated.

The relationship between speech and writing is the subject of some controversy. According to Luria (1970, pp. 323–4), the writing process begins with a breaking down of the spoken word into its individual sounds, whose phonemic significance is then identified, whereupon the phonemes are represented by letters which are integrated to produce a written word. However, in many languages (English, French), there is no isomorphism between phonemes and letters, so the simple mapping of phonemes onto letters would produce uncharacteristically inaccurate spelling; normal, correct spelling in such languages cannot be absolutely dependent on spoken-word production (Coltheart, 1987, p. 17).

It is, however, possible that spelling may be assisted by speech. According to **dual-route models of writing**, writing words involves the activation of an abstract, orthographic entry in a **graphemic output lexicon (GOL)**. The activated graphemic representation is placed in a **graphemic output buffer (GOB)** where it awaits further allographic and motoric processing (Ellis, 1982). The writing of non-words, however, involves a **phoneme-to-grapheme conversion (PGC)** system which maps phonological segments onto graphemic forms which enter the GOB and are further processed in the normal way.

It has been proposed (Nolan and Caramazza, 1983) that the graphemic information in GOB decays rapidly and has to be refreshed by phonological information, held in a **phonological output buffer (POB)** and activated at the same time as the information in GOL. So the two routes to writing are not independent (Miceli *et al.*, 1987, p. 238): 'to write words both the "direct route" (through which lexical entries are placed in the GOB) and the "indirect" route (through which the same entries are refreshed) are needed'. If the language is opaque (has more than one possible grapheme per phoneme), the remaining, non-decayed information in GOB can help the choice of grapheme (Coltheart, 1987, p. 18). However, evidence for spelling without phonology also exists (Shallice, 1981; Bub and Kertesz, 1982; Patterson and Shewell, 1987).

LANGUAGE COMPREHENSION

Work on language comprehension includes studies of word recognition, sentence understanding, and discourse interpretation with a predominance of research in the first two areas. Since the mid-1970s, interest has been predominantly in the understanding of language in real time and in context, rather than in the comprehension of isolated words and sentences (Flores d'Arcais and Schreuder, 1983, pp. 1–2).

Language understanding involves two kinds of process: **perceptual processes**, which register written or spoken language (see AUDITORY PHONETICS for the physiological mechanisms involved in the latter); and **comprehension processes**, which interpret language; but perception and comprehension operate together (Just and Carpenter, 1987, pp. 4–5). According to Marslen-Wilson and Tyler (1980), lexical, syntactic, and interpretive knowledge all interact with perceptual input, and listeners begin to interpret even before they have heard a complete word (ibid., p. 28).

The recognition of words is an essential stage in comprehension; it involves both perceptual and contextual information, which allow **lexical access**, the retrieval of a word from the mental lexicon, to take place. An accessed word is a word that may be identical with the current input. When identity is achieved, **word recognition** has occurred (Garnham, 1985, p. 43). There are two general types of model of lexical access: search models and activation models (Flores d'Arcais and Schreuder, 1983, p. 26).

According to a search model such as Forster's (1976) **autonomous search model**, the perceptual attributes of a word call up a phonetic or orthographic **access file**, from which a set of lexical items are selected for comparison with the input word. The items are then examined in the order of their frequency of occurrence in the language, so the general sentence context in which the input word occurred has no influence on word recognition in this model. This means that the model fares badly in the face of evidence that sentence context does have a faciliatory effect, and while Forster (1981) finds no such effect, many other researchers do (Morton and Long, 1976; Schubert and Eimas, 1977; Underwood, 1977; Fischler and Bloom, 1979; Stanovich and West, 1981). However, semantically related lexical entries have cross-references, so once the lexical entry for one word has been selected, access to semantically related entries can bypass the access files. A previous word may therefore facilitate lexical access for a following word (Flores d'Arcais and Schreuder, 1983, pp. 26–8).

Examples of activation models include Morton's (1969; 1970) logogen model, Marslen-Wilson and Welsh's (1978) cohort model, and McClelland and Rumelhart's (1981; see also Rumelhart and McClelland, 1982) interactive activation model.

In logogen theory, each entry in the mental lexicon is a **logogen**, a device which detects features of input words. Each logogen is sensitive to different features and has a firing threshold. If a logogen detects a sufficient number of features in an input word to match its firing threshold, it makes the corresponding word available as a response. The output of the logogen system is passed to a separate cognitive system which constructs and updates a representation of context. This representation primes relevant logogens so that they will respond faster to words relevant in the context (Flores d'Arcais and Schreuder, 1983, p. 27; Garnham, 1985, pp. 46–8).

The cohort model does not assign a threshold to lexical units. A **cohort** is a class of word candidates which have all been activated in parallel by a few features of the input word and each of which will continue to monitor the input word. As mismatch increases, a word candidate will drop out of the cohort, although it will remain activated, until only one remains and the word is recognized (Flores d'Arcais and Schreuder, ibid.).

Both of these models are able to account for the effect of context on lexical access. However, Swinney (1979) finds that the presence of context does not suppress the context-inappropriate meaning of ambiguous words, a finding which must somehow be reconciled with the context-dependence of access for non-ambiguous words. Swinney's study suggests that all meanings of ambiguous words are accessed no matter what the context, and the inappropriate meanings discarded when the context is taken into account

later. Clearly this suggestion is at odds with Marslen-Wilson and Tyler's (1980) suggestion, referred to above, that context enables word interpretation to begin before a full word has been perceived.

Flores d'Arcais and Schreuder (1983, pp. 31–2) suggest that the conflict can be resolved if a distinction is drawn between activation of lexical units and activation of conceptual units. Context activates only one of the different conceptual domains corresponding to an ambiguous word, while activation of the lexical unit carries with it the automatic activation of all its meanings which are therefore all available and may be retrieved in particular experimental tasks. However, only the context-appropriate meaning will be used in interpretation.

Another explanation of Swinney's findings is provided by the **interactive activation model** of processing developed by McClelland and Rumelhart (1981; Rumelhart and McClelland, 1982). In this model, representations at the various levels of processing are taken to be patterns of activation over an ensemble of simple processing units. Activation within levels is **competitive**, that is, the activation of one pattern inhibits activation of alternative patterns at the same level. A representation at one level can influence and be influenced by representations at adjacent levels of processing. Processing interactions of this kind are always reciprocal, i.e. bidirectional, and **excitatory**. That is, a pattern of activation at one level will excite activation of compatible patterns at adjacent levels, but will not inhibit incompatible patterns. The competitive nature of within-level activation, however, ensures the inhibition of incompatible patterns. This allows alternative representations to accumulate support from various sources and the one with the most support to come to dominate all the others, so that the network can implement a **best-match strategy** for choosing representations (McClelland, 1987, pp. 5–8). In the case of an ambiguous word, then, both meanings can be accumulating support simultaneously, that is, they can be activated, until enough support is provided by the context for the choice of the representation which the context supports most strongly.

The immediate linguistic context in which a word occurs is a clause or sentence, and the central issue in research into sentence comprehension is the relationship between the **parsing** of a sentence, the assignment to it of grammatical categories and structural relations, on the one hand, and its interpretation on the other.

Most research into sentence processing since 1970 has focused on the garden-path phenomenon and on the processing and the choice of interpretation of ambiguous sentences, the subject of a seminal paper by Bever (1970). A **garden path** is a sentence like *The horse raced past the barn fell*, in which *the horse raced past the barn* is usually interpreted similarly to 'the horse ran fast past the barn', until *fell* occurs, at which point it is clear that the interpretation must be like that which would be given to 'the horse which was made to run fast past the barn fell'. There are two main accounts of the parsing strategies employed for this and a variety of other sentence types (see list below), namely the garden-path theory and the incremental–interactive theory.

According to the **garden-path theory** (Clifton and Ferreira, 1989, p. 78), a sentence-processing mechanism, the **parser**, has grammatical knowledge which is isolated from world knowledge and other information. It uses a portion of this grammatical knowledge initially to identify the phrases of a sentence and the relationships between them. If the parser is confronted with uncertainty about how to relate a new phrase to the existing structure, it initially commits itself to that structure which becomes available first. Which structure that is, is determined by strategies employed by the parser, namely **Minimal Attachment**, 'use the smallest possible number of phrase structure rule applications to attach each incoming word into the structure currently being built' (see Frazier, 1979, p. 76), and **Late Closure** or **Right Association**, 'if consistent with the rules of the grammar, attach each incoming word into the phrase currently being analyzed' (see Kimball, 1973a, p. 24). Clifton and Ferreira

(1989, p. 79) produce a useful list of some of the types of sentence whose difficulty or ease of comprehension can be explained by Minimal Attachment and Late Closure/Right Association. In each pair of examples below, the (a) form is disambiguated by world knowledge or by syntax towards the preferred Minimal Attachment or Late Closure reading, while the (b) form is disambiguated away from the preferred reading:

1 NP vs S complement (Minimal Attachment)
    (a) I knew the answer very well
    (b) I knew the answer was right
2 S complement vs relative clause (Minimal Attachment)
    (a) Tom told the man that he had fired him
    (b) Tom told the man that he had fired
3 VP vs NP attachment of prepositional phrase (Minimal Attachment)
    (a) The cop saw the man with the binoculars
    (b) The cop saw the man with the revolver
4 Main clause vs reduced relative clause (Minimal Attachment)
    (a) The horse raced past the barn and fell
    (b) The horse raced past the barn fell
5 NP vs S conjunction (Minimal Attachment and Late Closure)
    (a) I saw the girl and her sister
    (b) I saw the girl and her sister laughed
6 NP complement vs main clause subject (Late Closure)
    (a) Because Maria knitted her sweater it kept her warm
    (b) Because Maria knitted her sweater kept her warm
7 Low vs high attachment of relative clause (Late Closure)
    (a) The doctor called in the son of the pretty nurse who hurt herself
    (b) The doctor called in the son of the pretty nurse who hurt himself
8 Low vs high attachment of adverbials (Late Closure)
    (a) Martha will say that it rained yesterday
    (b) Martha said that it will rain yesterday

Frazier and Fodor (1978) claim that the parser's decision preferences are automatic consequences of its own internal structure. They propose a two-stage model of the parser. The first-stage parser, called the **Preliminary Phrase Packager (PPP)** or **Sausage Machine**, has a fairly limited 'viewing window' shifting continuously through the sentence and accommodating around six words at a time, to which it assigns lexical and phrasal nodes. The second-stage parser, the **Sentence-Structure Supervisor (SSS)**, adds the higher nodes which link the output of the first stage parser together in a complete phrase marker.

Because the nodes that have been established in the PPP are shunted to the SSS, the PPP will only be able to recognize a limited number of possibilities of attachment for the items it is processing; in particular, Late Closure/Right Association appears to be a principle which it must necessarily employ. If the initial decision turns out to be wrong, Rayner *et al.*, (1983) suggest that a **thematic processor** guides the parser to the correct analysis (Altmann, 1989, p. 9). So in a sentence fragment like *the spy saw the cop with*, the preferred analysis would be to attach the (at this point incomplete) propositional phrase to the main verb. If the sentence is completed by the word *binoculars*, the preferred analysis is compatible with the thematic frame ⟨experiencer, theme, instrument⟩ associated with the main verb, *see*. But if the sentence is completed with *a revolver*, then, as *a revolver* is unsuitable as an instrument for *see*, that verb's second thematic frame, ⟨experiencer, theme⟩, is provided by the thematic processor, and the sentence is reanalysed accordingly.

Note that the thematic processor assesses plausibility after the initial construction of the constituents, so that the model is non-interactive (Altmann, 1989, p. 16). As Altmann points out (ibid, p. 9), it would seem more economical to have the thematic processor involved from the beginning in order that the inappropriate analysis could have been avoided in the first place. According to Taraban and McClelland (1988), apparently structural preferences are in fact guided from the start by thematic expectations associated with the verb.

The alternative to the garden-path theory of sentence processing is Altmann and Steedman's (1988) **Incremental–Interactive Theory** (see also Crain and Steedman, 1985; Altmann, 1987, 1988, 1989). They point out that any information conveyed by a restrictive modifier (PP or relative clause) is assumed to be 'given' information, that is, information which speaker and hearer are presumed to share. But in the absence of context, no information can be assumed to be given. Therefore, an analysis of NP as unmodified will be preferred over an analysis of NP as restrictively modified (Altmann, 1989, p. 11).

The simple NP is thus not preferred for syntactic, structural reasons, but for referential reasons: the modification of NP is not licensed by the discourse context (Clifton and Ferreira, 1989, p. 81). Altmann and Steedman (1988, p. 201) express this in the **Principle of Referential Support**: 'An NP analysis which is referentially supported will be favoured over one that is not.' An NP is referentially supported when all its referential presuppositions are satisfied by the context. A simple NP expresses its user's presupposition that there is a unique item to which it refers, while a modified NP expresses the additional presupposition that this unique item is one of a set of items but is distinguished from the rest of the set by the information expressed in the modifier. So if there is more than one item in the preceding context, the complex NP analysis should be preferred, while if there is only a single item to which NP can refer, the simple NP analysis should be preferred. But the analysis of an NP is carried out in the same way whether or not it is simple or complex. The simple/complex distinction is not manifest until after the initial NP has been processed. If it fails to refer, then the subsequent input will be interpreted as a restrictive modifier (Altmann, 1989, pp. 11–12).

Clearly, this theory assumes that listeners use their internal representations of the discourse which is in progress during parsing, and that the referential information they rely on is made available to the processor early on, before it arrives at the post-nominal modifier (ibid., pp. 14–15).

Evidence exists to support both the garden-path theory and the incremental–interactive theory, and discussion is becoming increasingly focused on the experimental techniques by means of which the evidence is procured, and on what conclusions can be drawn from this evidence (see, for instance, the debate between Clifton and Ferreira, 1989, and Steedman and Altmann, 1989).

Although it is, of course, necessary to parse a sentence in order to comprehend it, the syntax of a sentence is not generally what is recalled, particularly not after some time has elapsed since the sentence was heard or read (Bartlett, 1932; Dooling and Christiaansen, 1977), although syntax recall is somewhat better for written than for spoken sentences (Flagg and Reynolds, 1977). What people usually remember is the state of affairs that a sentence represents, a representation of what the world would be like if the sentence were true (Garnham, 1985, p. 141). Thus, if subjects hear a passage which includes the sentence (Johnson-Laird and Stevenson, 1970):

(5) John liked the painting and he bought it from the duchess

they are unable, less than a minute later, to recall whether the sentence they heard was the one above or one of the following three:

(6) John liked the painting and the duchess sold it to him
(7) The painting pleased John and he bought it from the duchess
(8) The painting pleased John and the duchess sold it to him

They do not, however, confuse the state of affairs presented by all four sentences in which the duchess sells the picture to John, with the state of affairs in which John sells the picture to the duchess.

There is good experimental evidence that people's representations of states of affairs in the world are stored as sets of interrelated propositions. People either recall a simple proposition completely or not at all (Goetz *et al.*, 1981), and they are better at remembering that a word in a list occurred in a series of previously presented sentences when the word in question is preceded by another word from the

same sentence (Ratcliffe and McKoon, 1978). This can be taken to suggest that propositions form units in memory, but might also be explained by reference to grouping of information in, for example, a situational model (Garnham, 1985, p. 146).

It is customary to depict representations of states of affairs as networks of nodes and links between nodes, commonly referred to as **semantic networks** (Anderson and Bower, 1973; Rumelhart *et al.*, 1972; Schank, 1972). If one believes that knowledge of states of affairs is propositional, then the nodes in the network will be held to be propositional nodes which represent the meanings of simple sentences. Networks which share nodes are combined, so that all the information one has about a person, place, object, event, etc. is linked to the node representing it. As Garnham (1985, p. 143) points out, however, although this explains how information may be represented in memory, it casts no light on how we process long stretches of text: how, for example, we know when two expressions like *the man* and *he* should be taken to refer to the same individual.

To comprehend a text, a reader must constantly modify his or her opinion about the 'world' the text represents, as more and more information is provided. Usually, new information is related to information already presented, and coreferring terms are particularly good indications of these relationships. They must, however, be distinguished from references to new entities, and Just and Carpenter (1987, p. 206) propose that the cues about co-reference include (1) language-based cues provided by the text, such as word meaning, syntax, and text structure, and (2) knowledge-based cues such as schemata and scripts.

Language-based cues to pronoun reference include the gender, number and case of the pronouns in question. In the case of definite descriptions, coreference is often established by repetition, either exact repetition:

(9) Meredyth enjoyed her outing to *the movie* yesterday. *The movie* was about an opera star

or repetition using synonym substitution:

(10) Meredyth enjoyed her visit to *the movie* yesterday. *The film* was about an opera star

Reading time for the second sentence in the pairs above is about the same for exact repetition as for the synonym case (Yekovich and Walker, 1978). The occurrence in a text of definite and indefinite articles also helps to determine coreference; usually, *the* + *N* indicates that the referent of *N* has already been introduced in the text, while *a* + *N* suggests that the referent of *N* is being introduced for the first time. Finally, elements of the discourse which have recently been focused have privileged status in the reader's/hearer's search for a referent (Carpenter and Just, 1977). See TEXT LINGUISTICS, DISCOURSE AND CONVERSATIONAL ANALYSIS, GENRE ANALYSIS, and STYLISTICS, for further information about linguistic cues to text and discourse comprehension, and Just and Carpenter (1987, pp. 208ff.).

As Just and Carpenter (ibid., p. 207) point out, most research on the comprehension of text has focused on the linguistic cues involved. However, they list a number of findings from experiments designed to reveal some of the performance features characteristic of the cognitive processes associated with the assignment of pronominal reference (ibid., pp. 207–8):

1. Computations are often executed when a reader first encounters a personal pronoun, rather than later in the sentence. Eye-fixation studies indicate that the computation of the coreference, as indicated by a pause in the eye fixation, occurs while the pronoun is being fixated (Carpenter & Just, 1977; Ehrlich & Rayner, 1983; Just & Carpenter, 1978).
2. The duration of the computation . . . is longer if the antecedent occurred much earlier than if it occurred only recently (Ehrlich & Rayner, 1983).
3. If it is not possible to assign a pronoun to a referent at the time the pronoun is read, then there is sometimes another attempt to assign the pronoun at the end of the sentence, as indicated by a longer pause on

the final word of the sentence (Carpenter & Just, 1977; Just & Carpenter, 1978).
4. During the search for the antecedent of a pronoun, nonantecedents of the appropriate gender are activated to some degree (Corbett & Chang, 1983).

A hearer's or reader's knowledge of familiar events, the **non-linguistic cues** to text comprehension, also helps to establish a referential representation, or **mental model** (Johnson-Laird, 1983), as the text unfolds. Such knowledge is often known as a **script** (Schank and Abelson, 1977) or a **scenario** (Sanford and Garrod, 1981). Scripts or scenarios allow readers to infer the presence in the 'world' created by the discourse of characters, entities, and events not explicitly mentioned; for instance, if the action takes place in a restaurant, a reader can infer the presence of a kitchen even though the kitchen is not explicitly mentioned. In some texts, such inferred knowledge can be crucial to comprehension.

Inferencing raises two major questions: (1) which inferences are made **on-line**, that is, as the text is read, and are these encoded into a representation of its content? (2) how is knowledge organized in long-term memory, and how do textual cues access that knowledge? (Garnham, 1985, p. 157).

The technique most widely used to establish on-line inferencing is **self-** or **subject-paced reading** (SPR). In such experiments, subjects read passages on a **visual display unit** (VDU), that is, an apparatus similar to a television, linked to a computer. The passage is displayed one section at a time, and subjects press a button when they are ready for the next section. The computer can then measure the time it takes subjects to read each section. Haviland and Clark (1974) show that it takes subjects longer to read sentences such as *The beer was warm* when an inference has to be made in order to make the sentence cohere with previous discourse, than in cases where the connection to previous discourse is made obvious, as in the following:

(11) We got *some beer* out of the trunk. *The beer* was warm.

As it takes longer to read *The beer was warm* in

both of the following contexts, than it does to read it in the context just presented, it cannot be simply the repetition of *beer* which makes the difference:

(12) We checked the picnic supplies. The beer was warm.

(13) Andrew was especially fond of beer. The beer was warm.

The difference in reading time must be caused by the making of an inference which will connect *The beer was warm* to the preceding discourse in a plausible manner, so this type of inference, through which the discourse is made coherent, must be made on-line (Garnham, 1985, p. 158). However, readers' knowledge of the world allows them also to make vast numbers of **elaborative inferences**, inferences which are not necessary for the text to cohere. For instance, not every text about a restaurant visit requires readers to make explicit use of their knowledge that the restaurant has a kitchen. Such inferences are not made at the time of reading, but they can be used later, if required. Thus, when reading *Peter cut the steak* it is not necessary to explicitly infer that Peter was using a knife, but if asked later, *Did Peter use a knife?*, most readers would be able to make a **deferred inference** and answer *yes* (Garnham, 1985, pp. 157–61).

Experiments showing that elaborative inferences are not made on-line but only later, if required, include Corbett and Dosher (1978) and Singer (1979, 1980, 1981). For example Singer (1979) shows that verification of

(14) The sailor used the broom to sweep the floor

is faster after *The sailor swept the floor with the broom* than after *The sailor swept the floor in the cabin*. If *broom* had been inferred in the sentence where it was not mentioned, there should be no difference in reading time (Garnham, 1985, pp. 160–1).

Current ideas about the organization of memory for text comprehension derive from Bartlett's (1932) notion of the **schema**, 'an active organization of past reactions, or past experiences' (ibid., p. 201; Garnham, 1985, p.

166), but neither Bartlett's theory, nor those which have taken up the idea of schemata more recently (Minsky, 1975; Schank and Abelson, 1977; Rumelhart and Ortony, 1977) 'say much more than that information in memory has some structure' (Garnham, 1985, p. 167).

Scripts/scenarios can, however, be used in explanations about how knowledge in memory is accessed during comprehension. A particular script, say the restaurant script, may be activated by certain pertinent words, for instance, *waiter* or *menu*. Sanford and Garrod (1981, p. 114) report that people reading *John was on his way to school. He was terribly worried about the maths lesson* usually imagine that John is a schoolboy, but change their mind when reading *He thought he might not be able to control the class again today*. At this point, people imagine that John is a teacher. They are invariably surprised to read *It was not a normal part of a janitor's duty*. Sanford and Garrod suggest that the change-of-mind phenomenon and the surprise follow because readers set up the entire school scenario with all its associated roles from the start, a suggestion supported by reading-time experiments. In the case referred to, it is probable that it is the fact that the character, John, is only referred to by his first name which induces the reader to assume that he is a schoolboy. When the following sentence suggests otherwise, the reader calls up another role associated with the school scenario more likely to fit the text. The scenario–metaphor of knowledge accessibility thus complements the theory of deferred inferencing.

However, knowledge is often activated not so much by a single word or words, as by the way in which certain words co-occur in an expression. For instance, it cannot be any one particular word in the expression *the five-hour journey from London to New York* which activates a plane flight schema, because no word in the expression would, by itself, suggest a plane journey (Garnham, 1985, p. 167). Rather, we need to employ our knowledge about the distance between New York and London, and about the relative speed of different modes of transport to work out that only a plane could get from London to New York in five hours, and the type of knowledge employed here may be more helpfully referred to by the metaphor of mental models.

There can be no doubt that background knowledge is vitally important for text comprehension. It often plays a part in distinguishing deep from shallow comprehension, where by **shallow comprehension** is meant the type of reading in which the reader understands all the words and sentences but fails to grasp the gist of the text (Just and Carpenter, 1987, p. 218). Bransford and Johnson (1973) show how lack of background information can induce shallow, as opposed to deep, comprehension by otherwise competent readers in the case of a passage such as (ibid., p. 400):

The procedure is actually quite simple. First you arrange things into different groups. Of course, one pile may be sufficient depending on how much there is to do. If you have to go somewhere else, due to lack of facilities that is the next step, otherwise you are pretty well set. It is important not to overdo things. That is, it is better to do a few things at once than too many.

The impact of backgound information becomes clear to anyone who has experienced difficulty understanding what is going on in this passage when they are told that its title is 'Washing Clothes'.

K.M.

SUGGESTIONS FOR FURTHER READING

Balota, D.A., Flores d'Arcais, G.B., and Rayner, K. (eds) (1990), *Comprehension Processes in Reading*, Hillsdale, NJ, Lawrence Erlbaum Associates.

Brown, G. and Yule, G. (1983), *Discourse Analysis*, Cambridge, Cambridge University Press.

Garnham, A. (1985), *Psycholinguistics: Central Topics*, London and New York, Methuen.

Levelt, W.J.M. (1989), *Speaking: From Intention to Articulation*, Cambridge, MA, and London, MIT Press.

Rationalist linguistics

One of the reasons why the linguistic theory of Avram Noam Chomsky (1928–) has been considered revolutionary is that it represented a return to rationalism in linguistics at a time when the prevailing scientific opinion strongly favoured the mode of thought which is traditionally seen as its opposite, namely empiricism.

Rationalism is a philosophical theory according to which true knowledge is obtained through the exercise of pure reason, rather than through experience, since our senses, through which experience reaches us, may often deceive us. But the exercise of pure reason without reliance on the senses requires that there is something available for us to reason from – some starting point other than sense experience. This is provided by certain clear and distinct ideas which are **innate** in humans, ideas which we are born with. These innate ideas constitute a form of knowledge, though theorists vary in opinion about how relatively conscious or unconscious this knowledge may be. Of the great seventeenth-century rationalist philosophers, Descartes, Spinoza, and Leibniz, Descartes is probably the best known, and it is from him that Chomsky's *Cartesian Linguistics: a Chapter in the History of Rationalist Thought* (1966) derives its title. It is also in reaction against Descartes' philosophy that classical British empiricism developed as represented, first, by Locke's *An Essay Concerning Human Understanding* (1690) and in the writings of Berkeley and Hume.

According to **empiricism**, human minds are blank at birth, and all ideas and knowledge subsequently developed in them are initially derived from experience obtained through the senses. Empiricism had a profound influence on science from the late seventeenth century onwards, and in linguistic theory of the early parts of the twentieth century any statements about unobservables, such as mental phenomena, were actively discouraged (see BEHAVIOURIST LINGUISTICS) until Chomsky had the audacity to refer to his theory as 'a specific hypothesis . . . as to the nature of mental structures and processes' (1965, p. 53). Instead of reducing statements about mental phenomena to statements about physical phenomena, Chomsky proposed to infer conclusions about mental phenomena from observations of physical data – language. The process of inference from observation to hypothesis is, of course, commonplace in modern science, and the controversy surrounding Chomsky's theory has centred around the explicit claim for innateness to be discussed below, the claim which places Chomsky firmly in the rationalist tradition.

Chomsky considers the main task of linguistics to be the development of an account of **linguistic universals** (see LANGUAGE UNIVERSALS). He suggests that these universals, the **universal grammar**, reflect an innate schema of initial assumptions which all humans bring to language learning, and on the basis of which they construct the grammar of the one language among the many which is to become their mother tongue (1965, p. 27):

A theory of linguistic structure that aims for explanatory adequacy incorporates an account of linguistic universals, and it attributes tacit knowledge of these universals to the child. It proposes, then, that the child approaches the data with the presumption that they are drawn from a language of a certain antecedently well-defined type, his problem being to determine which of the (humanly) possible languages is that of the

community in which he is placed. Language learning would be impossible unless this were the case.

At the very least, such a view requires that there be evidence that language shares certain features with other innate capacities or faculties: we have to show that language is in some respect like those other innate faculties. It is important to be aware, when considering this question, that the distinction between what is genetically determined and what is purposeful, socially learnt behaviour, is not the same as the distinction between behaviour that depends on environmental stimulation and behaviour that does not; it is quite possible that an innate form of behaviour is dependent on environmental stimulation to trigger it off. Lenneberg (1964, p. 582) uses the following example to illustrate this point:

The maternal behavior of primiparous female rats reared in isolation is indistinguishable from that of multiparous individuals. Animals with no maternal experience build nests before the first litter is born. However, pregnant rats that have been reared in cages containing nothing that can be picked up and transported do not build nests when material is made available. They simply heap their young in a pile in a corner of the cage.

So, although, on the one hand, rats are not dependent on learning their nest-building behaviour – since rats that are pregnant for the first time and which have not had the opportunity to observe other rats still build nests – they are still dependent on the environmental stimulation constituted by transportable material having been available for some time before the nest is needed. They need environmental stimuli to trigger off the nest-building *sequence*, which begins with carrying material around randomly and ends with nest building proper. If the first stage is not completed as the sequence demands, no further stages will be completed by the rat.

Similarly, there is evidence that birds build nests sequentially in such a way that the stages of the sequence must be followed in the preordained way; that is, the bird is completing a series of mini tasks, each triggered off by the previous one. No amount of evidence for the need for external stimulus for a certain type of behaviour can, therefore, show that the behaviour in question is *not* innately determined. Language may therefore be an innate faculty even though it is obvious that a child is dependent to some degree on environmental stimulation in developing it.

Lenneberg (1969) mentions four criteria that biologists use to establish whether something is or is not innate:

1 Is there intraspecies variation, i.e., do different groups within the species carry out the activity in question in different ways?
2 Has the phenomenon a history within the species, i.e., can we trace its development from a more primitive stage to a more advanced one?
3 Is there evidence for inherited predispositions, i.e. can it be shown that someone who has not inherited a predisposition for the activity cannot be taught to engage in it habitually?
4 Is there an assumption of organic correlates, i.e., is it probable that a specific organ must be possessed by a creature if that creature is to be able to engage in the behaviour in question?

If the answer to 1 and 2 is 'no' and if it is 'yes' to 3 and 4, then the phenomenon is innate. If it is the other way around, then the phenomenon is one that a species has consciously invented and developed as part of its social history. Lenneberg provides illustrations from, on the one hand, the case of walking, and, on the other, the case of writing.

For walking, the answer to 1 and 2 are clearly 'no' and to 3 and 4 it is clearly 'yes':

1 The species has only this type of locomotion; it is universal to all humans.
2 We cannot trace the development of bipedal gait from a primitive to a complex stage through human cultures; that is, you cannot look at a culture and say that here is a case of primitive walking. Nor is there any geographical focus from which the trait seems to have diffused at earlier times. All human races have the same skeletal foot pattern, and for significant variation in gait we have to go back to fossil forms that represent predecessors of modern humanity.
3 Walking seems to be inherited, because no amount of training of an animal will induce that animal to adopt permanent and customary two-legged gait if it does not walk like that normally, as birds and humans do.
4 It is obvious that bipedal gait has organic correlates – to walk on two legs you have to have them, and they have to be in a certain relation to the rest of the body.

For writing, however, the opposite seems to be the case (see WRITING SYSTEMS):

1 There is plenty of variation in writing systems within the species. A number of successful systems exist side by side and have done so in the past too. The geographical distribution of these systems follows cultural and social lines of demarcation.
2 Writing has a history that can be traced within the species. There have been cultures that had no writing systems, and the history of any system can be traced. We have some knowledge of areas of invention and development, and writing is a relatively recent event in our history.
3 To argue that having a writing system requires inherited predispositions, we should have to show that cultures which did not have them differed genetically from those that did. This is not the case, and nor are there any problems about introducing a writing system into a culture.
4 So there was no organ missing in members of cultures which did not write.

Lenneberg now goes on to argue that language displays six characteristics which place it firmly under the innate rubric along with walking. He makes the following statements about language.

1 Language is a form of behaviour present in all cultures in the world.

2 The onset of language correlates with motor age.

3 The broad stages of language acquisition are the same in all cultures.

4 All languages, regardless of their outward form are based on the same operating principles.

5 These operating principles have remained unchanged throughout the history of human-ity.

6 Language is a form of behaviour which can be impaired by brain lesions which may leave other mental and motor skills relatively unaffected – so there is a clear organic correlation.

There is not much doubt that claims 1, 2, 3, and 6 are broadly true. And depending on one's definition of 'operating principle', claims 4 and 5 may well be true also. But Lenneberg is relying on Chomsky's notion of universal grammar here; he means, that the deep structure of all languages is the same, and that if we were now to write a transformational grammar for an ancient lan-guage, its deep structure would be the same as the deep structure of a modern language. That is, Lenneberg derived claims 4 and 5 from Chomsky's claims, which they cannot, therefore, be used to defend without circularity.

Nevertheless, it seems likely that all languages are, in fact, similar in some very broad respects, that they share some kind of underlying logic, simply because, at ground level, they are all connected to the same kind of world and used by the same kind of creature (see further PHILOSOPHY OF LANGUAGE). However, it is not clear that this kind of vague assent to Chomsky's innateness claim would please him, because he appears to be saying that the innate schema which children bring to language is far more specific than the vague assent allows. Besides, assent to innateness of this vague type does not bestow on the innateness hypothesis the kind of explanatory force with which Chomsky wishes it to be endowed. He is claiming that unless the child had a very specific innate knowledge of a specific universal grammar, language learning would be impossible.

It is possible to list various types of evidence in support of this claim, such as: (1) Language learning must take place before an individual reaches maturity, because it must take place along with the brain-lateralization process; this supports the claim that the development of language can be regarded as similar to the development of a bodily organ; studies such as Curtiss (1977) tend to support this claim, known as **critical-period theory**, as do studies of children of various ages, and of adults, with brain abnormalities. (2) Errors made in child speech are rule revealing; a child may have learnt to use a linguistic form correctly, say, *went*, but will subsequently start saying *goed*; this is held to be because the child has now become conscious of the rule of past formation in English – a grammatical rule – and this type of learning overrides other types. (3) A grammar is a very complicated mechanism; yet a very young child learns it, at a time when its general cognitive development should not, in fact, be capable of coping with such complexity. The fact that the child learns grammar nevertheless can only be explained by the presence of the innate faculty, the **language-acquisition device**, which is more highly developed – because innately complete – than the child's other faculties.

This last claim has been disputed by a number of child psychologists. For instance, Macnamara (1972) finds it just as likely that the reason children can learn language is that they possess certain other cognitive skills – they may, for example, have a more general but very extensive capacity for making sense of situations involving any type of direct human interaction. Donaldson (1978) questions whether the assumption, which Chomsky seems to make, that the child's task is substantially similar to that of a linguist developing a grammar for a language, is justified (p. 38 and p. 61):

> To Western adults, and especially to Western adult linguists, languages are formal systems. A formal system can be manipulated in a formal way. It is an easy but dangerous move from this to the conclusion that it is also learned in a formal way.

Chomsky obviously thinks of the child's task

as that of learning the sort of thing which language is for Chomsky himself. And so indeed it is – in the long run. But in the shorter run, during the early years of life, it may be something very different.

Ultimately, there can be no clear answer to the debate around innateness. Chomsky's hope is that (1976, pp. 4–5): 'by studying the properties of natural languages, their structure, organization, and use, we may hope to gain some understanding of the specific characteristics of human intelligence. We may hope to learn something about human nature. His preference for the innateness hypothesis of rationalism is given an explanation which is less frequently quoted in the linguistic literature, since it is not a linguistic argument (1970b, p. 22):

A vision of a future social order is in turn based on a concept of human nature. If, in fact, man is an indefinitely malleable, completely plastic being, with no innate structures of mind and no intrinsic needs for a cultural or social character, then he is a fit subject for the 'shaping of behavior' by the State authority, the corporate manager, the technocrat, or the central committee. Those with some confidence in the human species will hope that this is not so and will try to determine the intrinsic human characteristics that provide the framework for intellectual development, the growth of moral consciousness, cultural achievement, and participation in a free community.

One cannot help but feel much sympathy for this position; but, on the other hand, if humans were *completely* prestructured beings, then it would be very difficult to explain the existence of the tyrant in the first place; and prestructured humans would be suitable for manipulation in the form of genetic engineering, selective breeding, and so on, prospects at least as sinister as experience-determined shaping of behaviour. All in all, the preferable position is probably somewhere between extreme rationalism and extreme empiricism. What is certain is that Chomsky did much to free linguistics from its rather sterile preoccupation with pure description, and his suggestions inspired a great deal of research aimed at discovering what languages have in common, and in the area of child language acquisition.

K.M.

SUGGESTIONS FOR FURTHER READING

Chomsky, N. (1966), *Cartesian Linguistics: A Chapter in the History of Rationalist Thought*, New York and London, Harper & Row.
Lyons, J. (1977a), *Chomsky*, revised edn, Glasgow, Fontana/Collins, chs. 9 and 10.

Rhetoric

INTRODUCTION

An ancient Greek **rhetor** was a speaker skilled in addressing the law courts and large gatherings of people in order to persuade, and **rhetoric** originates from the theory or study of how, by means of what linguistic devices, a speaker or writer (since speeches are typically written) might best achieve this aim. Rhetoric is still studied as a subject in its own right in American universities, although the emphasis on persuasion occasionally gives way to one on appropriate expression in and organization of composition (though the two are, of course, not mutually exclusive). For instance,

Baker, (1973), provides chapters on Thesis, Structure, Paragraphs, Evidence, Writing Good Sentences, Correcting Bad Sentences, Punctuation, Words, The Research Paper, and appendices on A Writer's Grammar, Spelling and Capitalization, and A Glossary of Usage. On the other hand, Skwire (1985, p. 1) advises his intended student readers: *'Whenever possible, think of your writing as a form of persuasion'* (italics original).

Rhetoric does not figure as a named course on British universities' curricula, but students are, of course, still taught how to produce the type of essay appropriate to their subject. In addition, there are aspects of all discourse studies, such as stylistics, conversational analysis, discourse analysis, text linguistics, contrastive rhetoric (see below), and critical linguistics, which might be seen as falling under rhetoric; certainly, all these subject areas have their roots in it. Finally, rhetoric has remained a technical term in literary critical theory in the twentieth century, with Richards (1936, p. 23) defining it as the 'study of verbal understanding and misunderstanding' and Booth (1961, Preface) as the study of 'the author's means of controlling his readers'.

BACKGROUND AND DEVELOPMENT

The best-known ancient rhetorician is probably Aristotle (384–322 BC), who developed his theory of prose style in the *Rhetoric* and of poetic style in the *Poetics*. However, Aristotle built on a fairly long tradition of interest in effective language use. The earliest surviving formalized manifestation of this interest is the Sicilian Corax's handbook of rhetoric. Together with Tisias, Corax drew up a teachable system and set of rules for dealing with questions arising during civil law suits which Sicilian citizens returning to Sicily after the expulsion of the Tyrants (467 BC) instigated in order to reclaim their property. Corax's handbook deals chiefly with the **structure** of a speech, which he saw as divisible into three or five parts. A three-part speech would contain the **exordium**, in which the situation would be described, the **arguments** – both constructive and refutative – and an **epilogue**, summing up what

had gone before and drawing conclusions. A five-part speech would contain in addition a **narrative** after the exordium, and **auxiliaries** which were subsidiary aids to the speech.

Tisias taught Gorgias of Leontini (c. 483–375 BC), whose main interest was in style rather than subject matter of a speech, and whose emphasis was therefore on ornamental, poetic diction, using unusual compounds, figures of speech, and symmetrical patterns of clauses and longer stretches of speech which give a metre-like quality to his prose.

It is fairly obvious that it is possible to speak effectively and persuasively without speaking truthfully, and the sophist Protagoras (c. 485–415 BC) explicitly taught his pupils, who were fee-paying, to argue cases from opposing points of view, and how to make a weak case appear stronger. Some of the Platonic dialogues, in particular the *Gorgias,* criticize this activity for providing merely a means to instil in an audience certain **beliefs**, which may be true or false, rather than a way to **knowledge** of the truth. Aristotle, however, points out (*Rhetoric*, I.I.13) that all good and useful things, with the exception of virtue itself, may be abused; the fault lies not in the thing itself, but in those who abuse it. The Platonic objection to rhetoric survives in the popular definition of rhetoric as unnecessarily flowery language, employed to mislead or to avoid answering a question straightforwardly.

Aristotle's *Rhetoric* was written about 330 BC and is divided into three books. The first deals with the nature of rhetorical proofs, the second with the nature of psychological proofs, and the third with style and arrangement. I shall only deal with the latter in detail here, since it is questions of style and arrangement which chiefly occupy present-day linguists; all references to the *Rhetoric* are to the J.H. Freese translation in the Loeb Classical Library series (London, William Heinemann, 1926).

In Book I (I.2), rhetoric is defined as 'the faculty of discovering the possible means of persuasion in reference to any subject whatever'. It falls within the province of dialectic, since it is concerned with matters of common knowledge rather than with any particular science, and since a rhetorical proof is a type of syllogism, the **enthymeme**. It differs from dialectic, however, in that an enthymeme deals with the uncertain domain of human actions and events in the real world, whereas a logical syllogism deals with certainties. Nevertheless, since the form of enthymeme and syllogism are identical, skill in syllogistic reasoning is invaluable for a rhetorician. In addition to enthymeme, a rhetorician may use **examples** drawn either from things that have actually taken place, or from his or her own imagination.

In Book III (I.1), Aristotle points out that 'it is not sufficient to know what one ought to say, but one must also know how to say it'. He is of the opinion that a distinction must be drawn between poetic style (which he deals with in the *Poetics*) and prose style. Poetic style, such as that of Gorgias, is inappropriate to prose because it is artificial and 'that which is natural persuades, but the artificial does not' (III.II.4). Prose should be clear and should not differ too much from everyday talk: 'if a speaker manages well, there will be something "foreign" about his speech, while possibly the art may not be detected, and his meaning will be clear' (III.II.6). Metaphor and simile are the chief means of achieving foreignness and clarity, but they must not be too far-fetched, and they should be 'derived from what is beautiful either in sound, or in signification, or to sight, or to some other sense' (III.II.13). In addition, a prose writer or speaker may use epithets (adjectives) and diminutives (e.g. *cloaklet* for *cloak*), but again, 'one must be careful to observe the due mean in their use' (III.II.25).

The due mean lies between poetic style and what Aristotle calls frigidity of style. Frigidity of style arises from four causes: the use of compounds, strange words, too many or overlong or unnecessary epithets, and metaphors and similes that are inappropriate because they are ridiculous, too dignified, or too far-fetched.

According to Aristotle, 'that which is written should be easy to read or easy to utter' (III.V.6). This ease will depend on what Aristotle terms **purity**. Purity, he says, is the foundation of style, and it depends on five rules. The first is to make proper use of connecting particles; the second is to employ special, not generic terms; the third is to avoid using ambiguous terms; the fourth is to keep the genders (masculine, feminine, and neuter) distinct; the fifth is to observe the number system. Obviously, the fourth rule would not apply to English which does not have grammatical gender, but the fifth would, since English has a distinction between singular and plural.

The style of prose should not be **continuous**, by which is meant 'that which has no end in itself and only stops when the sense is complete. It is unpleasant, because it is endless, for all wish to have the end in sight' (III.IX.2). Rather, the style should be **periodic**, where by period is meant 'a sentence that has a beginning and end in itself and a magnitude that can be easily grasped' (III.IX.3). Much of what Aristotle has to say about style is not directly relevant to modern English, since it is based on the sound patterns and grammatical structure of ancient Greek, and since the contexts and subject matters which largely determine appropriateness of style are no longer applicable. Interestingly, however, the **arrangement** of the speech is not so far removed from the conventions of many genres of modern English writing – in particular polemical academic articles (see GENRE ANALYSIS) and political speeches.

Aristotle points out that a speech must have two parts, because 'it is necessary to state the subject, and then to prove it' (III.XIII.1). The first part is therefore called the **statement of the case** and the second the **proof**. In addition to these, he allows that there may be an **exordium** at the beginning and an **epilogue** at the end, both of which are merely aids to memory. Any refutation of an opponent that there may be is part of the proof, and so is comparison for the purpose of amplifying one's own argument.

In the exordium, 'the speaker should say at once whatever he likes, give the key-note and then attach the main subject' (III.XIV.1) which is to be approached in the statement of the case, or **narrative**. The statements of the case may consist of clearing oneself of disagreeable suspicion; contesting disputed points; excusing oneself by 'saying that it was a case of error, misfortune, or necessity' (III.XV.3); counterattacking the accuser; appealing to previous cases; attacking slander; and many more. Proofs concern four types of disputed points, namely facts, harm done, degree of harm done, and justification. Proofs are most effective if they are refutative of an opponent's position rather then merely demonstrative of one's own position. After all an opponent's or opponents' positions have been refuted, one can state one's own case. Finally, in the epilogue, one does four things in each of its four parts (1) dispose the hearer favourably towards oneself and unfavourably towards the adversary; (2) amplify and depreciate; (3) excite the emotions of the hearer; (4) recapitulate.

The Greek and Roman tradition of rhetoric influences our views of writing and speaking (see **contrastive rhetoric** below) via its place as one of the seven liberal arts on the medieval school curriculum, and readers may consult Howes (1961) and Bailey (1965) for examples of the writings on rhetoric from Aristotle to Joos, and Love and Payne (1969) for a number of influential articles on rhetoric written during the 1950s and 1960s. In particular, it is interesting to note a persistent interest in defining different styles appropriate for different purposes, as this relates directly to modern theories of non-regionally defined (non-dialectal) linguistic variation.

Thus Quintilian (c. 35–100) in *Institutio oratoria* differentiates, with subdivisions possible in finer and finer detail, three correct styles of speaking, namely, plain, grand or forcible, and intermediate or florid. **Plain style** is for purposes of instruction. **Intermediate style** is for charming or conciliating an audience, it will make more use of metaphor and digressions and will 'be neat in rhythm and pleasing in its reflexions; its flow, however, will be gentle, like that of a river whose waters are clear, but overshadowed by the green banks on either side'. **Grand style** is for moving an audience, and is likened to 'some great torrent that rolls down rocks ... and carves out its banks for itself'. It is exalted by amplification and rises 'even to hyperbole' (overstatement) (Bailey, 1965, pp. 102–3).

According to Joos (see Joos, 1961), writing much later, there are five styles: (1) **Frozen**, which is 'a style for print and for declamation ... defined by the absence of authoritative intonation ... as also by the fact that the reader or hearer is not permitted to cross-question the author'. It is a style 'for people who are to remain social strangers' (Bailey, 1965, pp. 297–8). (2) **Formal style** which is 'designed to inform' (Bailey, 1965, p. 296) and which is characterized by detachment and cohesion. It differs from consultative style in disallowing audience participation. (3) **Consultative style**, the two defining features of which are (a) that the speaker supplies background information (b) while the hearer participates continuously. 'Because of these two features, consultative style is our norm for coming to terms with strangers – people who speak our language but whose personal stock of information may be different' (Bailey, 1965, p. 290). (4) **Casual style**, which is used with friends and acquaintances, when background information does not need to be supplied since it is already shared. Its two defining features are ellipsis and slang. (5) **Intimate style** which excludes public information.

The interest in features of situational context as a major stylistic variable which is evident in Joos was present from the beginning of rhetorical study; Aristotle emphasizes that a speaker must be aware of which type of audience he is addressing, and that his style must vary accordingly. When, in the 1950s and 1960s the term **stylistics** began to gain currency (see STYLISTICS), the term 'rhetoric' tended to be retained by writers concentrating mainly on structural features of texts, excluding situational context. There are two major trends which retain the term rhetoric in their designations, and which will therefore be dealt with briefly in this entry. One of these trends is known as **generative rhetoric** and the other as **contrastive rhetoric**.

GENERATIVE RHETORIC

Generative rhetoric developed under the influence of Noam Chomsky's transformational-generative grammar (see TRANSFORMATIONAL-GENERATIVE GRAMMAR) in the late 1950s and

1960s. It stands in opposition to what Ohmann (1959, p. 1) calls the **organicist position**, according to which a difference in form always entails a difference in meaning. Chomsky had insisted that one common underlying deep structure was shared by, for instance, a sentence in the active voice, like *The cat ate the mouse*, and another sentence in the passive voice, *The mouse was eaten by the cat*. And since it seemed to generative rhetoricians that the concept of style could only make sense on the assumption that the same thing could be said in different forms, i.e., that one meaning could be expressed using different styles of expression, the new grammar appeared to them to offer the first valid theoretical foundation for stylistic analysis. Generative rhetoric took over the transformationalists' framework for dealing with sentences. Thus Katz and Foder (1963) claim that

> except for a few types of cases, discourse can be treated as a single sentence in isolation by regarding sentence boundaries as sentential connectives. As a matter of fact, this is the natural treatment. In the great majority of cases, the sentence break in discourse is simply *and*-conjunction. (In others, it is *but*, *for*, *or*, and so on.)

In addition, it is possible to see the agents and states and processes of the agents of whole texts (whether or not it is seen as a single sentence) as surface realizations of deep-structure nouns and verbs. The framework for sentences of TG is displayed in the following way by Fowler (1977, p. 28):

> a **sentence** has a **surface structure**
> formed by **transformations** of a
> **semantic deep structure** consisting of a
> **modality** component plus a **propositional** component
> the latter based on a
> **predicate** attended by one or more **nouns**
> in different **roles**

As Fowler points out, a theory that narrative plot can be reduced to a series of stock nouns and verbs – easily interpreted as constituting a deep structure of the narrative – had already been developed by the French structuralists, largely based on Propp's analyses of Russian folk tales.

According to Propp (1958), the nouns are realized as characters such as **hero**, **dispatcher**, **villain**, **helper**, **donor**, **sought-for person**, **false hero**, and the verbs as functions of these, such as **absentation**, **reconnaissance**, **trickery**, **departure**, **provision** or **receipt of a magical agent**, **pursuit** (see Fowler 1977, p. 29). Although these categories are probably specific to the folk tale, it is not difficult to see how texts in general may be reduced to sequences of verbs and nouns representing agents and states and actions of them. When we summarize a text, we report the sequences of events (verbs) undergone by the agents (nouns). In moving to looking at the structure of whole texts, generative rhetoric has developed into what is often known as **text linguistics** (see TEXT LINGUISTICS). It should, however, be noted that TG has also been employed for the purpose of carrying out stylistic analysis, and its methods are discussed in more detail in the entry in this volume on STYLISTICS (and see also CRITICAL LINGUISTICS).

CONTRASTIVE RHETORIC

The discipline of **contrastive rhetoric** is based on the notion propounded by Sapir and Whorf in the first half of the twentieth century that the different grammars of different languages reflect differences in the habitual patterns of thought of their speakers (see MENTALIST LINGUISTICS). Linguists working on contrastive rhetoric, such as Diane Houghton in Britain and Robert Kaplan in the USA, employ a modified version of this hypothesis, according to which each culture at any particular time adheres to certain 'canons of taste' (Kaplan, 1966, p. 2) which determine a popular notion of how argument ought to be structured. This popular notion is called a **discourse rhetoric**. Thus, for instance,

> the English language and its related thought patterns derive from the Greco-Roman tradition, modified by medieval European and later western thinkers. At the macro-discourse level this produces what Kaplan calls a dominant linear paragraph organization which, in an expository paragraph,

typically begins with a topic statement followed by a series of subdivisions of the topic statement, each supported by example and illustration. A central idea thus developed is related to every other idea in the essay and used as a proof or argument. . . . Conversely, other languages show a different, less linear or non-linear organization at the macro-level, and Kaplan attempts to prove this by a mixture of analysis of texts from other languages, and by identification of non-linear patterns in the work of non-native speakers writing formal essays in English. He concludes that such students need specific help in learning to write appropriately in English, and gives examples of specimen materials designed for this purpose.

(Houghton and Hoey, 1982, p. 9)

The notion of intercultural rhetorical differences and the problems associated with it are discussed by Houghton (1980) who also gives an account of a variety of studies in the area.

K.M.

SUGGESTIONS FOR FURTHER READING

Bailey, D. (ed.) (1965), *Essays on Rhetoric*, New York, Oxford University Press.

Howes, R.F. (ed.) (1961), *Historical Studies of Rhetoric and Rhetoricians*, Ithaca, NY, Cornell University Press.

Love, G. and Payne, M. (1969), *Contemporary Essays on Style: Rhetoric, Linguistics, and Criticism*, Glenville, IL, Scott, Foresman.

Scale and Category Grammar

Scale and Category Grammar is a model of linguistic description developed in the late 1950s and early 1960s by Michael Alexander Kirkwood Halliday (1925–). It constitutes an attempt at building insights derived from J.R. Firth (1890–1960) into an overall theory of what language is and how it works. While Halliday's ultimate aim of providing an overall theory of language and its functions has not altered, his post-1965 work has tended to move away from the scale and category model towards systemic and functional grammar (see SYSTEMIC GRAMMAR and FUNCTIONAL GRAMMAR); the model has, however, been modified by Fawcett (1974, 1975, 1976) for use as a basis for his version of systemic grammar (see SYSTEMIC GRAMMAR).

Halliday graduated in Chinese studies from the University of London, where Firth had been appointed to the first chair of General Linguistics in Britain in 1941. Firth viewed meaning as the

function of a linguistic item in its context of use (Butler, 1985, p. 5):

> Context of situation, though of central importance, was just one kind of context in which linguistic units could function. Other contexts were provided by the 'levels' postulated to account for various types of linguistic patterning. Thus grammatical items could be seen as functioning in grammatical contexts, lexical items in lexical contexts, phonological items in phonological contexts, and so on.

He considered the context of situation to be of the same abstract nature as grammatical categories, and insisted that all such abstract constructs should be relatable back to textual data, a concern which has remained with Halliday.

Within each of the levels, Firth saw language as organized along two axes, the **syntagmatic** (horizontal) and the **paradigmatic** (vertical) (see STRUCTURALIST LINGUISTICS). Along the syntagmatic axis, elements formed **structures**, while on the paradigmatic axis, elements were arranged in **systems**. Firth differs from Saussure (see STRUCTURALIST LINGUISTICS) in that whereas the latter saw language as one huge system, Firth thought that a large number of systems must be set up to account for the diversity of linguistic phenomena. In addition, he believed that it would not be possible to account in one fell swoop for all of language, but that linguistic descriptions should be applied, at least in the first instance, to so-called **restricted languages**, examples of which would be (Butler, 1985, p. 5) 'the specialist languages of science, sport, narrative, political propaganda, personal reference and address, the writings of a single author, or even a single text'.

Firth's work has been criticized for lack of explicitness and for incoherence (Langendoen, 1968, pp. 37–8). This criticism is largely justified, but in Halliday's work, Firth's categories and the relationships between them are made explicit (Butler, 1985, p. 13).

Halliday (1956/Kress 1976, pp. 36–51; all references are to the Kress reprint) began by providing a framework within which the relationships between linguistic units could be handled in a consistent manner (Butler, 1985, p. 14). He discusses three types of grammatical category to be established in the description, unit, element, and class.

The **unit** is 'that category to which corresponds a segment of the linguistic material about which statements are to be made', and five units are proposed at the level of grammar: **sentence, clause, group, word, character** (p. 36). Here, Halliday aims to provide an account of categories in modern Chinese; in later papers, dealing with English, the fifth unit, character, appears as **morpheme**. Each unit, except character, can be **simple**, composed of a single element, or **compound**, composed of two or more elements; the character is always simple.

The units are arranged hierarchically, in what is now known as a **rank scale**, the principle of the arrangement being that a unit at any rank other than character is composed of one or more elements of the classes of units at the rank below it. A **class** is defined according to its operation at a given place in the unit next above; thus the classes of groups are defined according to the structural positions they can occupy in the clause. Classes may be either **primary** 'when it is the unique term operating at a particular place in structure', or **secondary**, 'integral subdivisions of the primary classes and systems in other dimensions cutting across the primary classes'. The former are called **direct secondary classes**, the latter **indirect secondary classes** (p. 37).

The different classes of element operating at each rank form **systems**. For instance, at sentence rank, two classes of clause, **free** and **subordinate**, or **bound**, may be elements of structure (Butler, 1985, p. 15):

> These two classes of clause form a two-term *system* of clause classes in sentence structure. We can also recognize secondary classes of clause within the primary classes 'free' and 'subordinate': 'free' clauses are either 'disjunctive' or 'conjunctive' . . . 'subordinate' clauses are either 'conditional' or 'adjectival'.

The **sentence** is defined as 'the largest unit about which grammatical statements are to be made' (p. 37). Any statements made about the context in which the sentence occurs would be at another level, to which we would now refer as the level of discourse or text. Halliday symbolizes the structural elements of the sentence as O and X, with free clauses operating at O and subordinate clauses operating at X. The clause classes are thus defined in terms of their occurrence in the structure of the sentence, and the definitions of all other units and the structures set up for them proceed systematically downwards through the rank scale; thus there are two basic elements of clause structure, V and N. The verbal group operates at V, the nominal group at N. A basic structure will contain one V only, while subsidiary structures may contain two V elements; in addition, subsidiary structures may contain an element A at which adverbial groups will operate.

The 1956 paper set up the basic framework for

Scale and Category Grammar, although the most comprehensive account is to be found in Halliday (1961) (Butler, 1985, p. 15). In this paper, Halliday lists a number of different levels at which linguistic events should be accounted for (Halliday, 1961, pp. 243–4):

> The primary levels are 'form,' 'substance' and 'context.' The substance is the material of language: 'phonic' (audible noises) or 'graphic' (visible marks). The form is the organization of the substance into meaningful events. . . . The context is the relation of the form to non-linguistic features of the situation in which language operates, and to linguistic features other than those of the item under attention: these being together the 'extra-textual' features.

Form is further said to be, in fact, two related levels, namely **grammar** and **lexis**, while **context** is actually an **interlevel** which relates form to extratextual features. The meaning of a linguistic event derives from a combination of its **formal meaning** and its **contextual meaning**. 'The formal meaning of an item is its operation in the network of formal relations', while (ibid., p. 245):

> the contextual meaning of an item is its relation to extratextual features; but this is not a direct relation of the item as such, but of the item in its place in linguistic form: contextual meaning is therefore logically dependent on formal meaning.

For this reason 'the statement of formal meaning logically precedes the statement of contextual meaning'; in other words, before we can relate language to situation as Firth desired, it is necessary to provide a systematic description of the linguistic systems – the systems being the networks of formal relations of which language is composed.

The systems which operate at the level of grammar are **closed systems**, that is, systems which have the following three characteristics (ibid., p. 247):

(a) the number of terms is finite: they can be listed as A B C D, and all other items E . . . are outside the system.

(b) each term is exclusive of all the others: a given term A cannot be identical with B or C or D.

(c) if a new term is added to the system this changes the meaning of all the others.

System, class, structure, and unit are the fundamental, primary categories of the theory of grammar necessary for accounting for the data. All four are mutually defining, logically derivable from each other.

Unit is now defined as 'the category set up to account for the stretches that carry grammatical patterns' (ibid., p. 251), and, as in the earlier paper, the units are arranged in a rank scale in such a way that 'going from top (largest) to bottom (smallest) each "consists of" one, or more than one, of the unit next below (next smaller)' (ibid.). The scale is the same as that set up in the 1956 paper, except that, since Halliday is now concerned with describing English, the lowest rank is morpheme, rather than character.

Halliday has to allow for one type of instance in which the principle of arrangement of the rank scale appears not to apply. We can analyse a sentence like *I saw the house* quite un-problematically as consisting of one clause, consisting of three groups *I, saw* and *the house*; each of these groups consists of words – in the case of the third group, the words *the* and *house*. However, a sentence like *I saw the house on the corner* appears to present a problem: the third group here, *the house on the corner*, seems itself to be composed of two groups, namely *the house* and *on the corner*. But groups are supposed to be composed of words, since word is the unit next below group. To deal with this kind of problem, Halliday allows for a phenomenon to which he refers as **downward rankshift**, 'the transfer of a (formal realization of a) given unit to a lower rank' (ibid.), in this case the transfer of a group to the rank of word. So *on the corner*, a group, functions, in this clause, as a word.

The pattern carried by the unit is a **structure**, the category set up to account for likeness between events in succession; it is 'an arrangement of elements ordered in "places" ' (ibid., p. 255) and (p. 256):

Each place and each element in the structure of a given unit is defined with reference to the unit next below. Each place is the place of operation of one member of the unit next below, considered as one occurrence. Each element represents the potentiality of operation of a member of one *grouping* of members of the unit next below, considered as one item-grouping. It follows from this that the lowest unit has no structure; if it carried structure, there would be another unit below it.

Any account of the structure of the morpheme, therefore, would have to be given in phonology, not in the grammar.

According to Halliday (1961), four elements are needed to describe the structure of the English clause, namely **subject (S)**, **predicator (P)**, **complement (C)**, and **adjunct (A)**; Berry (1975) also only operates with these four, while others, for instance Sinclair (1972), introduce a further two, namely **object direct (O^D)** and **object indirect (O^I)**. To account for the structure of the group called **nominal group**, Halliday (1961, p. 257) uses the names **modifier (M)**, head **(H)**, and **qualifier (Q)**. However, a structure described as, for instance, MHQ, cannot account in very fine detail for the structure of a nominal group, like, for instance *the house on the corner*; it accounts only for its **primary structure**, the structure which distinguishes 'the minimum number of elements necessary to account comprehensively for the operation in the structure of the given unit of members of the unit next below; necessary, that is, for the identification of every item at all ranks' (ibid., p. 258) thus:

> *The house on the corner*
> M   H   Q

If we want to be more specific, we need to employ another type of scale of grammatical description, to which Halliday refers as a scale of **delicacy**, or depth of detail. This would, in this case, enable us to specify, for instance, that M is realized by a **deictic**, H by a **headword**, and Q by an **adverbial group**, rankshifted downward and consisting of a preposition and a nominal group, the nominal group, in turn, having the structure MH, M being a deictic and H a headword, and so on.

Such subsequent more delicate differentiations are stated as **secondary structures**; at finer and finer degrees of delicacy, structural statements become more and more probabilistic.

Classes are defined, as in the 1956 paper, by their operation in the structure of the unit next above. **Primary classes** stand in one-to-one relations to elements of primary structures, while **secondary classes** are derived from secondary structures. The primary classes form the link between elements of structure and more delicate classes.

System is the category set up to account for 'the occurrence of one rather than another from among a number of like events' (ibid., p. 264). At the ultimate level of delicacy of grammatical description, the grammar will be linked directly to the data, because the last statement made will specify which item from a given system (subsystem of a system) actually appears in the text. The notion of 'appearing in the text' is explicated in terms of a scale of **exponence** 'which relates the categories of the theory . . . to the data' (ibid., p. 270), although, in most cases, grammar must hand over to **lexis**, for the final statement of exponence.

The theory of the 1961 paper, and its differences from the 1956 paper may then be summed up as follows (Butler, 1985, p. 16):

> Four categories (unit, structure, class and system) and three scales relating them (rank, exponence and delicacy) are proposed. Several differences from the 1956 version of the theory are immediately apparent: system is now one of the fundamental categories, rather than secondary to class; the concept of structure, hitherto subsidiary to that of element, is now given full recognition; and the relationships between the categories, and between these and the data, are more explicitly accounted for in terms of the three scales, which were merely implicit in the earlier work.

Halliday's scale and category model has been extensively modified by Fawcett (1974) (see Butler, 1985, ch. 6). While the categories of unit and element of structure remain essentially unaltered, the notion of delicacy loses its importance. Fawcett removes the category of system to the semantics and provides a treatment of class, rank and exponence which differs from Halliday's.

The scale of exponence is split into three parts, **exponence**, **componence**, and **filling** (Butler, 1985, p. 95):

> Componence is the relation between a unit and the elements of structure of which it is composed. For example, a clause may be composed of the elements S, P, C and A. Each of these elements of structure may be . . . filled by groups. In the specification of a syntactic structure, componence and filling alternate until . . . the smallest elements of structure are not filled by any units. It is at this point that we need the concept of exponence, as used by Fawcett: the lowest elements of structure are expounded by 'items' which . . . are more or less equivalent to 'words' and 'morphemes' in Halliday's model. Exponence thus takes us out of syntax, as viewed by Fawcett.

It takes us out of syntax because Fawcett's rank scale for grammar only contains clause, group, and **cluster**, a new syntactic unit Fawcett needs to handle possessive constructions, proper names and premodifiers of adjectives and adverbs, because he gives up word and morpheme.

In giving up the sentence, Fawcett is following Huddleston's (1965) suggestion (see SYSTEMIC GRAMMAR); he justifies giving up word and morpheme by pointing out (1976, p. 50) that (Butler, 1985, p. 97):

> some elements of group structure are typically *not* filled by 'words': for instance, qualifiers in nominal groups are almost always rank shifted groups or clauses. Furthermore, when an element of group structure *can* be filled by a single word, it can equally well, in many cases, be filled by a higher unit: for example, the completive to a preposition can be a single word (as in 'in cities'), but this can be expanded into a nominal group with more

than one element of structure (as in 'in all the largest cities'). Another problem is that some elements of group structure can be filled by items which are not obviously 'words' in any meaningful sense, and yet have to be treated as 'functioning as a word' in a Hallidayan model. Examples include complex prepositions such as 'in spite of', 'because of', and complex conjunctions such as 'in order that'.

In order to resolve these problems, Fawcett removes from the theory any expectation that elements of group structure will be filled by a particular kind of unit, or indeed by any kind of unit at all. Some elements of group structure are indeed filled by units, but others may be expounded directly by items (for instance, the element p could be expounded directly by the item 'in spite of').

Fawcett's use of the notion of filling allows him to use the internal structure, or **constituency**, of units in his definition of class, instead of Halliday's criterion of function in the next highest unit of the rank scale. He points out (Fawcett, 1974, p. 10) that there is no one-to-one relationship between unit and element of structure (Butler, 1985, p. 96):

> Thus, for example, the Adjunct element of clause structure can be filled by adverbial groups such as 'very quickly', prepositional groups (or, as Fawcett calls them, 'prepend groups') such as 'for a month', or nominal groups such as 'last week'. Fawcett also allows the A element (as well as the S and C elements) to be filled by a clause.

K.M.

SUGGESTIONS FOR FURTHER READING

Butler, C.S. (1985), *Systemic Linguistics: Theory and Applications*, London, Batsford Academic and Educational, chs 1, 2, and 6.

Halliday, M.A.K. (1961), 'Categories of the theory of grammar', *Word*, 17: 241–92.

Semantics

INTRODUCTION

Semantics is the study of linguistic meaning, and is arguably the area of linguistics which is closest to the philosophy of language. The main difference between the linguist's and the philosopher's way of dealing with the question of meaning is that the linguist tends to concentrate on the way in which meaning operates in language, while the philosopher is more interested in the nature of meaning itself. However, it is a mistake to think that these two pursuits can, in fact, be undertaken independently of each other. Nevertheless, in this entry, I shall concentrate on those aspects of semantics on which most linguists focus most attention, namely sense relations and componential analysis.

Unfortunately, it is not easy to endow the term 'meaning' with the type of precise definition we may feel that the term for the grammarian's topic of investigation, 'structure', is capable of. We are fairly clear about what structure is – it is the way in which various pieces of something are put together – and every time, in whatever connection, the term 'structure' is used in English, we know that it has this same type of meaning – it has to do with how something is put together to form a whole: a body has structure; a car's engine has structure; a molecule has structure. But the term 'meaning' and its associates, 'mean', 'means', etc. are used in a variety of ways in naturally occurring English. We can say:

(1) I didn't mean to drop the brick on your foot
(2) She meant to become a solicitor
(3) He means well, but he always makes a mess of things

and in each of these cases, what seems to be at issue is a person's intentions to do something; cases like these are not examples of the sense of 'meaning' we are interested in as semanticists. Nor are cases like

(4) Her life lost all meaning with the disappearance of the cat
(5) Money means nothing to a true sportsman

where the topic seems to be what is of importance to someone. In neither type of case is the term 'meaning' being used with reference to any linguistic aspect of the situation.

Compare these to the following:

(6) Those black clouds mean rain
(7) Those spots mean chicken-pox

Again, no linguistic aspects are essentially involved in the relationships set up between features of the two situations. But they differ from the previous five situations in that it is possible here to perceive a relationship of **signification** between black clouds, on the one hand, and rain on the other, and between spots and chicken-pox. Cases like these, therefore, fall under **semiotics**, the study of signs and signification (see SEMIOTICS), but they are too general to be studied in semantics, where it is *linguistic* meaning in particular which is of interest.

Now compare these cases with

(8) The red light means 'stop'

Here we are beginning to approach more closely what we want, because in this case a linguistic expression, the quoted word 'stop' is part of the subject matter of the utterance. In addition, there is no natural connection between a red light and the word 'stop', as there is between clouds and rain and spots and chicken-pox. The red light gets its meaning purely by convention among humans, and is a case of **non-natural meaning** (Grice, 1957). Linguists (and philosophers of language) are interested only in non-natural meaning.

The traffic light case is very like cases of dictionary definition, where the meaning of one term is given by other terms. In such cases, the terms 'meaning' and 'means' are used to say things like

(9) What is the meaning of 'semantics'?
(10) *Bachelor* means 'unmarried man'.
(11) *Ungkarl* means 'bachelor'.
(12) *Rot* means 'rød'.

The study of this type of meaning falls clearly within semantics, and some linguists would prefer to limit their study to it. As we shall see, however, although it is possible to concentrate on the relations between words alone, such a study is ultimately reliant on assumptions about relationships between words and what they refer to, and many linguists, and all philosophers of language, would require that their subject matter include this dimension too. For example, consider case (12), and, by implication, cases (11) and (10). To a monolingual English speaker inquiring after the meaning of the German word *rot*, a reply like (12) would be of no use at all. To such a speaker inquiring after the meaning of the Danish word *ungkarl*, a reply like (11) would be useful only if s/he already knew what *bachelor* meant. And (10) is illuminating only to someone who already knows the meaning of one of the terms given.

In other words, dictionary definitions are circular – all the terms in a dictionary are defined by other terms in the dictionary (unless illustrations are used). Definitions like these say what terms *mean the same as*. Semanticists in general wish to break out of the definition circularity, they want, so to speak, to be able to remove the quotation marks from one of the terms in the definition, to gain an extralinguistic foothold – something which can function as the semantic coin.

There is one further usage of 'meaning' in English which ought to be mentioned here:

(13) He never means what he says
(14) She never says what she means

In these cases, an opposition is set up between what a speaker means and what his or her words mean. Cases of this kind are covered in detail in the entry on SPEECH-ACT THEORY, but it is worth mentioning here that if it is true that speakers can mean something other than their words seem to suggest, and if we are able to discover this, then we must, first, have a reasonably good grasp of the meaning of the words; otherwise we could hardly come to feel that their meaning was inappropriate in some cases.

SENSE RELATIONS

Let us begin by seeing how far it is possible to get in semantics by concentrating on relationships between words. Several such relationships can be set up, and we can, in addition, discover relationships between sentences. Such relationships are commonly known as **sense relations**.

On the assumption that we understand how negation works, it will seem obvious to anybody that if a proposition, P, is true, then its negation, *it is not the case that P*, which we shall symbolize as ⌐P, must be false. When two propositions stand in this relationship to each other, we say that the sentences expressing them **contradict** each other. We can also apply this knowledge of how negation works to a study of predicates. It is possible to produce two sentences that are contradictions of each other by simply negating the predicate of a sentence. For instance, if *Thomas is a tank engine* is true, then *Thomas is not a tank engine* is false. Of course, the opposite holds as well – if an unnegated sentence is false, then its negation will be true. Any predicate will behave in this way when negated in one of two otherwise identical simple sentences, a fact which is, in itself, not terribly exciting.

However, it seems that there are pairs of terms in natural language which behave in just the same way as predicates and their negations with respect to the ways in which they affect the truth and falsity of sentences in which they are used. Consider:

male – female
dead – alive
true – untrue
true – false
married – unmarried

It seems that if *Thomas is male* is true, then *Thomas is female* is as definitely and obviously false as *Thomas is not male* would be; but, of course, the predicates *is male* and *is female* can only operate in this way if the individual of whom they are predicated is one of which it makes sense to say that it is male or female. If Thomas is a tank engine, then it is only within a fictional context that maleness can be predicated of him.

Real tank engines, as well as stones, houses, tables, and so on do not fall within the **semantic field** of gendered things. Within specific semantic fields, we can call predicate pairs like those above **binary** or **complementary antonyms**. These produce sentences which are contradictions of each other when one of the pair is substituted for the other in a sentence. Linguistically, we can distinguish two ways in which the contrast between two antonyms may be realized, as the list above shows: either the graphological (and phonological) form of each member of the pair is distinct from that of the other, or they share a form, but one member has a prefix such as *un-*. When there are distinct forms we call the contrast **equipollent contrast**; when the basic form is shared and a prefix added to one member of the pair, we talk of **privative contrast**.

True binary antonyms such as the ones I have listed are, in principle, ungradable: something is either alive or dead, either male or female, either married or unmarried. One thing cannot be more dead than another, more male than another, more married than another, and so on. So when these terms appear in a simple subject–predicate sentence, the sentence has a very special relationship with a restricted set of other sentences. If

Socrates is dead

is true, then

Socrates is alive

is false,

Socrates is not alive

is true, and

Socrates is not dead

is false. From the truth or falsity of any one of the sentences in the set, we can **infer** the truth or falsity of each of the other three; the truth or falsity of any one of them is **entailed** by the truth or falsity of any one of the others. **Entailment** is another relation between sentences.

Some sentences are true and false in a special way:

Anyone dead is dead
Anyone alive is alive

are **tautologies, tautologically true, necessarily true, logically true, true in all possible worlds, true *a priori*, truths of reason**; we can see immediately that they are true. Correspondingly

Anyone dead is not dead
Anyone alive is not alive

are **contradictions, necessarily false, logically false, false in all possible worlds, false *a priori***; we can see immediately that they are false. In contrast,

Anyone alive is not dead
Anyone dead is not alive

are true by virtue of the sense relations between the predicates in them and

Anyone dead is alive
Anyone alive is dead

are false by virtue of the sense relations between the predicates in them. These are called **analytic truths** and **analytic falsehoods**.

Most sentences, of course, are dependent on the state of the world for their truth and falsehood; for instance,

Socrates is dead

is true because of how things are in the world, and

Socrates is alive

is false because of the way things are in the world. Such sentences are true or false **contingently, synthetically, *a posteriori***. There is now an obvious temptation to reduce – or elevate – all contingent sentences to analytic ones; if we could assign to *Socrates* the meaning 'the Greek philosopher who . . . and who is dead', then

Socrates is dead, which appears contingent, would be translatable as *The Greek philosopher who . . . and who is dead is dead*, which is logically true. If we could reduce all the terms in the language to predicates in logical relations to each other, we should be able to show that the whole language consisted of sentences that were true in virtue of the relations between the predicates in them. However, unless the language had direct purchase on reality at some point, it would be useless; and the obvious point at which to connect the language with reality would, of course, be at the time of renaming Socrates as *the Greek philosopher who . . . .* It would then, in principle, be possible to go into the world and check the truth of the statement, *Socrates is the Greek philospher who . . . .* Of course, we would need some criteria for having all the properties we were going to claim for Socrates; if, for instance, we wanted to claim that he was bald as well as dead, we would need to specify that *bald* means 'having no hair'. We'd then check to see if Socrates had hair or not – once we had discovered some way of identifying hair correctly, etc. We shall examine problems of this type of procedure on pages 395–8 below.

So far, the binary antonyms we have dealt with have been ungradable. Other pairs, such as

fast – slow
high – low
sweet – sour

are applicable to things in a more-or-less manner. These are called **gradable binary antonyms**, and we can recognize them by the fact that they can be modified by *very* and *how*. It is quite co-incidental that there are no linguistic realizations of the stages intermediate between the pairs of terms. In some cases, indeed, some of the inter-mediate stages are realized, as in the case of

hot – warm – cool – cold

These, and the gradable binary antonyms can be modelled as being situated at opposite ends of a continuum. As far as their effect on sentences in which they occur in predicates is concerned, they behave like the members of sets of **mutually exclusive** or **incompatible** terms, terms from

semantic fields like 'days of the week', 'months of the year', 'animals', and so on. They differ in their effects on sentences from binary antonyms in that we cannot infer from the falsehood of a sentence containing one of the predicates from a field the truth of another sentence differing from the first only in containing one of the other predicates. We cannot infer from the fact that *It is Monday* is false the truth of any particular one of the other possibilities – though we will, of course, know that one of them must be true; the point is that we do not know *which* one. We can, of course, infer from the truth of any one of the sentences, say, *It is Sunday*, the falsehood of all the others.

So far, we have confined discussion to one-place predicates (see SET THEORY), and thus to sentences containing one predicate and one referring term. When we start looking at two-place predicates, we shall be dealing with sen-tences containing one predicate and two referring terms. It is then possible to identify some properties that such predicates have, by looking at the forms of relationship between the referring terms that are set up by means of the predicate which links them. Some two-place predicates, for example, are **symmetric**; we know that if

a is married to b

then

b is married to a

We shall say of any predicate, R, which satisfies the formulation (see FORMAL LOGIC AND MODAL LOGIC),

$\forall x \forall y \, (xRy \rightarrow yRx)$

that is, 'for all x and for all y if x stands in relation R to y, then y stands in relation R to x', that it is symmetric.

Other predicates are **transitive**. We know that if

a is in front of b

and

b is in front of c

then

a is in front of c

We shall say of any predicate that satisfies the formulation

$$\forall x \forall y \forall z ((xRy \ \& \ yRz) \rightarrow (xRz))$$

that is, 'for all x and for all y and for all z, if x stands in relation R to y, and y stands in relation R to z, then x stands in relation R to z', that it is transitive.

Some two-place predicates are such that the relation they set up between the individuals in the sentence indicates that another, **converse** relation also holds between those individuals. Thus, we know that if

a is a parent of b

then

b is a child of a

We shall say of any pair of predicates which satisfy the formulation

$$\forall x \forall y (xRy \rightarrow yR'x)$$

that is, 'for all x and for all y, if x stands in relation R to y, then y stands in relation R' to x', that they are converse or **relational opposites** of each other.

Two predicates are said to be **synonymous** when it is logically impossible for a simple sentence, Rx, to be true while a simple sentence containing a predicate synonymous with R is false. We have seen that *is not alive* is synonymous with *is dead*, and that we can get from an analytic truth to a logical truth by synonym substitution; that is, we can get from *Anyone who is not alive is dead* to *Anyone who is dead is dead*, by substituting for *is not alive* in the first sentence its synonym *is dead*. The relation of synonymy has quite a complex logical form, in so far as specifying it involves saying not only that 'all Fs are Gs' but also that 'all Gs are Fs'; not only are all bachelors unmarried men, in addition, all unmarried men are bachelors. So two predicates, P and R, are synonymous if they satisfy the formulation

$$\forall x ((Px \rightarrow Rx) \ \& \ (Rx \rightarrow Px))$$

that is, 'for all x, if x is P then x is R, and if x is R then x is P'.

If only one of the conjuncts in the proposition above holds, then we have a relationship of **hyponymy** between the two predicates. If a particular semantic field has a name, then that name is a **superordinate term** with respect to all the terms for the items that are contained in the field in question, and these terms will all be hyponyms of the superordinate term. In relation to each other, they are **co-hyponyms**. So *animal* is the superordinate term for terms like *lion, tiger, horse, dog, cat* and so on, and all of these are co-hyponyms of each other. There are hierarchies of hyponyms; for instance, *plant* is a superordinate term having as hyponyms, at one level, *tree, flower, bush, vegetable*. These terms are themselves superordinate with respect to other terms. For instance, *flower* is a superordinate term having as its own hyponyms *tulip, rose, violet*, etc.; but these are also hyponyms of *plant*. Generally speaking, when the relationship of hyponomy holds between two English nouns, it is possible to state the relationship in terms of the formulation

x is a kind of y

There is an interesting link with syntax here, in so far as a noun modifier + noun construction always produces a term that is a hyponym of the unmodified noun; thus a rose bush is a type of bush. The logical form of the hyponymy relationship is

$$\forall x(Fx \rightarrow Gx)$$

If we are trying to set up a systematic theory of meaning for a language, then the hyponymy relationship is clearly going to be one of the most useful sense relations. If we could start with some very basic term, B, and place it in a universally quantified proposition:

$$\forall x (Bx \rightarrow Cx)$$

where C is either an equally basic or slightly more complex term, and if we could then place C in a similar proposition with another term, D, etc., then we could eventually build up a systematic account of the meanings of a large number of the terms in our language. Alternatively, we could start with the most general term we can think of, and then work our way down to the most particular terms in our language, terms which we might think of as being in direct contact with the world. In either case, the problem is going to lie in establishing what the most simple, particular terms are, how they are connected to the world, and what aspects of the world they are connected to. The componential theory of meaning tries to do just this, and will be examined on pages 395–8 below.

Some predicates in the language can be used to express more than one proposition. These are known as **ambiguous** predicates. Ambiguity is a property of predicates which will affect sentences in which they occur by making them capable of more than one interpretation. A word or phrase is ambiguous if it has more than one **referent**, that is, if it can be used to name more than one kind of thing. In such cases, usually, those referents will each be capable of being picked out by means of different terms also, thus (Palmer, 1981):

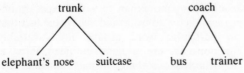

In cases like these two, where the referents of the ambiguous term are in no way similar, the ambiguous term is said to have different **homonyms**: *trunk* in the sense 'elephant's nose' is homonymous with *trunk* in the sense 'suitcase'. If the ambiguity is present in the spoken form only, we say of the form that it has different **homophones**; *site–sight*, *rite–right*, *there–their* are homophonous pairs. If, on the other hand, the ambiguity is present in the written form only, we talk of different **homographs**, such as (*a dog's*) *lead* and (*the metal*) *lead*.

When an ambiguous word has different referents which are nevertheles clearly perceptibly similar in some respect, we say that the word is **polysemic**. Thus *flight* in *I saw the flight* is polysemic between the senses 'unit of the air force' and 'a bird's movement through the air'. Similarly, *bottle neck* may refer to either the upper part of a bottle or to a narrowing part of a stretch of road tending to become jammed with

traffic. The cases mentioned so far seem fairly clear cut; but consider the sentence

She has good legs

This can mean that she has healthy legs, beautiful legs, athletic legs, or plain legs – if plain legs are considered morally superior to legs that are not plain. Is *good* therefore polysemic, and the sentence therefore ambiguous? If so, then there will be a vast number of polysemic terms in the language, and it may therefore be preferable to treat terms like this as **vague**, rather than ambiguous (see Kempson, 1977, ch. 8).

If so, then it is possible to distinguish two types of phenomenon which are apt to cause vagueness of linguistic expressions (Kempson defines four types of vagueness):

1 **Vagueness of the referent itself**: because things in the world do not come in clear, distinct categories, it is sometimes difficult to decide whether something is, for example, a wood or a forest, a stream or a river, and so on. So even when we know, in principle, what a term should be used to refer to, it is often difficult, in practice, to be certain about which things in the world are of the type in question.

2 **Referential indeterminacy**: sometimes it is impossible, out of context, to decide what the referent of an expression is. *John's book* can be used to describe the book John wrote, is reading, has been told to read, and so on.

Kempson proposes to test an expression for vagueness versus ambiguity by what she calls the **to do so too test**. For example, the sentence *John hit Bill and Jason did so too* implies only that Jason also hit Bill in some way – it does not matter whether he hit him with his fist, with the flat of his hand, with a stick, or however. *Hit* is therefore vague, but not polysemous, and the sentence is not ambiguous. In contrast, if a word in a sentence is ambiguous and the sentence is therefore also ambiguous, then it will matter which meaning is implied when we apply the test. For instance, *I saw the flight and June did so too*, is not acceptable if I saw a bird flying and June saw a unit of the air force.

The cases of sentence ambiguity we have looked at so far have all been dependent for their ambiguity on one word in the sentence. Such cases are called cases of **lexical** ambiguity. Some sentences, however, are **syntactically** ambiguous, and these are not dependent for their ambiguity on any one word in them. Rather, it is their grammatical structure which causes the ambiguity. Examples include *The chicken is ready to eat*; *Flying planes can be dangerous*; and *The police were ordered to stop drinking after midnight*.

Semantic theories of sense relations are sometimes criticized as inadequate by linguists on the grounds that their claims are not borne out by studies of naturally occurring discourse. In particular, the notion of synonymy has come under attack, because although it is often true to say that a true sentence containing one of a pair of synonyms does not become false if that member of the pair is exchanged for the other member, much language in use is not primarily concerned with stating truths, and frequently only one member of the pair is appropriate in a particular context. In fact, even the truth criterion is questionable. For instance, *husband* is often said to be synonymous with *married man*. Yet, in some contexts, the two sentences

(15) This is my husband
(16) This is my married man

may not both be true (I owe this example to Charles Owen). A researcher may, for instance, utter (16) with reference to one of his or her research subjects, in which case to utter (15) might well have constituted an untruth.

Clearly questions of reference and indexicality are at issue here, and the example is philosophically controversial. More obviously, it is unlikely that a woman, wishing to refer to the man to whom she is married, would do so using the term *my married man*: **My married man is an accountant* is highly unlikely to occur. Similarly, Sinclair (1984) points out that while *Prince Charles is now a husband* is not grammatically ill formed – and nor is it untrue – it is not natural. Yet *Prince Charles is now a married man* seems

perfectly acceptable. So pairs of words which are traditionally viewed as synonymous are often not interchangeable in context, so synonymy, if it has any value at all, has it only to philosophers of language. On the other hand, many pairs of words which would not traditionally be considered synonymous can in fact be used as such in discourse. For instance, the word *thing* seems capable of taking the place of vast numbers of other terms (I am indebted here to Michael McCarthy) as in *Will you have a look at the car? – I can't get the thing to go*.

Similar arguments could be extended to the other sense relations we have looked at in this section. In some cases of naturally occurring discourse, the words used by semanticists to illustrate sense relations do not behave in the stated manner. However, as I have pointed out elsewhere (Mason, 1986, pp. 175–6), the fact that pairs of words do not always and invariably instantiate certain sense relations should not be taken as an invalidation of the theory of sense relations any more than we would expect grammatical theory to be invalidated by the fact that no particular word always and invariably functions as, say, a noun modifier. What is important is our ability to make sense of discourse by means of our awareness of the possibility that (almost any pairs of) words may at various points in the discourse be placed in the types of sense relations discussed in linguistic semantics. Research into both spoken and written discourse clearly shows that we have this ability and that we use it to make sense of the discourse. As long as it is not assumed by semanticists that sense relations are stable relations between particular words, their pursuit is justifiable and valuable to linguistics in general.

COMPONENTIAL ANALYSIS

The interest in the hyponymy relationship dates back to Aristotle, and has always been related to an interest in linking the linguistic to the non-linguistic. According to Aristotle, to define a concept such as 'human' means, first, to state a more general concept, a **genus**, of which the concept to be defined is a type or **species**. Thus we might say that a human (species) is a type or species of animal (the genus). Secondly, it would be necessary to say which quality, which **differentia,** distinguishes a species from other species of the same genus. Aristotle thought that in the case of humans the differentia was the quality of being rational, so he defined a human as a rational animal. *Animal* is a superordinate term of which *human* is a hyponym. 'Animal' is, in turn, itself a species of a higher genus, and we could proceed in this way until we came to the highest or most general genus of all, *summum genus,* which, according to Aristotle, was substance. If we could specify precisely for each entity how it differs from those which bear cohyponyms of it and work our way down the hierarchy till we get to the most basic terms, then our language would have direct purchase on the world, it would be true, systematic, and useful. The problem lies in discovering what the basic terms are and in justifying the assumption, inherent in the theory, that when I say *lemon* I *mean* something more basic, such as the chromosome structure of lemons, which must be what the basic ultimate terms are going to stand for (Putnam, 1970).

The notion that there are some basic **meaning components** which make up the meanings of more complex terms is meant to offer a framework for handling sense relations when these are, in fact, interpreted as stable relations between particular words. Recall that we were forced on page 391 above to import a notion of semantic fields before we could begin to suggest that natural-language terms were capable of realizing logical relations and forms. Clearly, we must then give some justification for setting up these semantic fields in the way that we do: there must be something that all those things that we call animals have in common, something which all those things that we call tigers have in common, etc., and it is these features which would be named by the terms that are the meaning components of **componential analysis**.

If we have these basic components, we can also avoid the problems caused by the fact that not all languages cut up the world into the same semantic fields. English, for instance, has a field of birds, one of modes of transport, and one of occupations. Birds, obviously, belong in the first of these fields, aeroplanes in the second, and pilots in the third. Hopi Indians, however, would place all of these, birds, planes, and pilots, together in the same field, the field of fliers, on the grounds that they all fly. The whole system of Hopi would, in fact, be likely to be different from English, and it would therefore appear that each language, although systematically organized internally, is, in fact, arbitrarily related to the world, which could not, therefore, guarantee the appropriateness of any language.

In addition, many of the relationships named by natural-language terms, even biological relationships, are differently realized in different languages. For instance, the relationship between cousins, biological as it may be, is not realizable by one predicate only in Danish as it is in English. In Danish it is necessary to specify the biological gender of the cousin too: a male cousin is a *fætter*, while a female cousin is a *kusine*. So the predicate *is a cousin of* does not exist in Danish in a form that covers both male and female cousins. Of course, the relationship itself exists among Danes as well as among English speaking people, and Danes are aware of its existence. However, it is conceivable that some cultures might have no notion of, say, fatherhood – improbable, if not inconceivable; but there are cultures in which the distinctions between fathers and uncles, and between mothers and aunts are not considered important.

Terms like *cousin, father, mother, uncle, aunt* are therefore not basic enough to define the relationships that obtain between people, even though these relationships are universal because biological. What we require to define these terms is a set of **language-independent terms** which can be used to define the terms that are actually used in natural languages. In most English-language books on semantics, these language-independent terms are, in fact, stated in English, but it is important to note that they could, in principle, be given any names whatsoever, such as numbers, letters, or any kind of mark at all. They are supposed to function as labels attached to real-world phenomena, be they physical or non-physical, and the use of English terms is merely mnemonic.

For cases like those under consideration at present, four biological relationships in which people stand to each other suggest themselves: **generation, gender, lineage, related through** (compare Palmer, 1981, who does not include the fourth relationship which is, however, necessary to cope with some terms of Danish). We shall symbolize generation with the letter G, and specify which generation we are talking about by means of numbers. If 'ego' is generation 0, G0, then 'father' would be generation G1, 'grandfather' G2, 'child' $G-1$, etc. The gender would be two 'male' and 'female', M and F, or, in principle, any number, provided it was possible to specify the exact physiological characteristics in terms of which one could recognize an individual as falling in one category rather than another. Lineage is of three kinds: direct (son in relation to father), D; ablineal (cousin in relation to cousin), A; colineal (sibling in relation to sibling), C. Related through is either mother or

Table 1

Natural-language term	Generation	Sex	Lineage	Related through
mother	1	F	D	
father	1	M	D	
daughter	-1	F	D	
son	-1	M	D	
uncle	1	M	A	
aunt	1	F	A	
cousin	0	M/F	A	
kusine	0	F	A	
fætter	0	M	A	
brother	0	M	C	
sister	0	F	C	
sibling	0	M/F	C	
grandmother	2	F	D	
grandfather	2	M	D	
grandparent	2	M/F	D	
bedstemor	2	F	D	
bedstefar	2	M	D	
morfar	2	M	D	mother
mormor	2	F	D	mother
farfar	2	M	D	father
farmor	2	F	D	father

father – which must therefore be defined before this third category can be employed. We can now define precisely every term for a family relationship in any language by drawing up a grid (Table 1; I may have left out categories necessary to cope with some terms in some languages with which I am not familiar). Outside grids, components are usually listed thus: *man*: + HUMAN + ADULT + MALE.

An interesting application of componential analysis is that which uses it as a tool for disambiguation and for explication of the different meanings possessed by ambiguous lexical items, as proposed by Katz and Fodor (1963). They classify each item syntactically with **syntactic markers**, and semantically with **semantic markers** and **distinguishers**. The semantic markers are meant to reflect **systematic** relations between an item and the rest of the vocabulary of a language, while distinguishers reflect what is **idiosyncratic** about the meaning of the term in question. Note the similarity with Aristotle. A definition of the different meanings of *bachelor* would look like Figure 1 (syntactic markers are not bracketed; semantic markers are in round brackets; distinguishers are in square brackets).

Katz and Fodor are very specific about what they are doing here, saying, 'the semantic markers and distinguishers are used as the means by which we can decompose the meaning of a lexical item into its atomic concepts' (see Bolinger, 1965b, for a critique of this programme). The lines in the diagram are called **paths**; any lexical item whose entry in the dictionary (containing figures like that above) contains polyadic paths is ambiguous. Synonyms, on the other hand, will have identical paths. A sentence containing an ambiguous term may be ambiguous, but need not be. Thus, *The bill is large* is ambiguous, but *The bill is large but need not be paid* is not. As we hear the sentence, the part, *but need not be paid*, and the word *paid* in particular, will determine that we select one of the paths for *bill*, rather than another in our 'mental lexicon' (for further information on Katz and Fodor's work, see INTERPRETIVE SEMANTICS and LEXIS AND LEXICOLOGY).

Many objections can be raised to componential

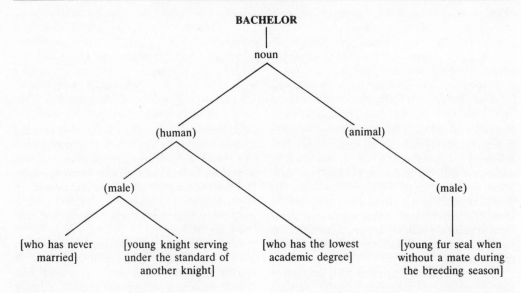

Figure 1

analysis as a theory of meaning. For instance, *human* may not be specific enough to function as a basic term; certainly, when we get down to items like lemons and oranges, then, as mentioned above, it seems that we should have to start defining them in terms of chromosome structure, and it is doubtful whether people in fact *mean* a specific chromosome structure when they say *lemon* or *orange*. Similarly, if there are cultures which have no conception of father-hood, or which do not make any practical distinctions between fathers and uncles, and mothers and aunts, then is not their whole notion of blood relationships so alien from ours that it seems senseless to suggest that a grid such as that set out above says anything about what the various family terms in that culture *mean*? Of course, there may be value in setting out the grid

as a way of showing how the culture conceives itself as being organized as compared to our own, that is, componential analysis may function quite well as a theory of the different taxonomic systems with which cultures operate. But as a theory of what meaning is, componential analysis does not seem a strong candidate (see further PHILOSOPHY OF LANGUAGE).

K.M.

SUGGESTIONS FOR FURTHER READING

Leech, G.N. (1981), *Semantics: The Study of Meaning, 2nd edn, Harmondsworth, Penguin.*
Lyons, J. (1977b), *Semantics,* 2 vols, Cambridge, Cambridge University Press.
Palmer, F.R. (1981), *Semantics,* 2nd edn, Cambridge, Cambridge University Press.

Semiotics

Semiotics or **semiotic** is the study of signs in general; so linguistics can be seen as that sub-discipline of semiotics which is particularly concerned with the nature of the *linguistic* sign. What is of relevance to linguistics from the discipline of semiotics, on the other hand, will be those of its conclusions and considerations about signs in general which are applicable to linguistic signs. The process of making and using signs is called **semiosis**.

The term semiotic originates with the American pragmatist philosopher Charles Sanders Peirce (1839–1914), and the discipline owes most to him, although in Europe Saussure's contribution was better known for a considerable time. Saussure called the study of the life of the sign in society **semiology**, and considered the sign relation **dyadic**, consisting in the relation between a concept and a sound (see STRUCTURALIST LINGUISTICS), while according to Peirce the relation is **irreducibly triadic**. He defines a sign as (1931–58, 2.228): 'something which stands to somebody for something in some respect or capacity'; and **semiosis** as (ibid., 5.484): 'an action, or influence, which is, or involves, an operation of *three* subjects, such as a sign, its object, and its interpretant, this trirelative influence not being in any way resolvable into an action between pairs'. The process is, furthermore, potentially infinite, because the **interpretant**, the interpreting

thought, is itself a sign and will therefore stand in its own triadic relation to a further interpretant (see Hookway, 1985, p. 121) – in other, simpler, terms, one thought leads to another *ad infinitum*. It is this third dimension, preventing **closure**, an end to interpretation, which has endeared Peirce to poststructuralist and deconstructivist thinkers.

Eco (1984, pp. 4–7) distinguishes between specific semiotics and general semiotics. A **specific semiotics** deals with a particular sign system, while **general semiotics** presents a theory of, or search for, that which is shared by all sign systems. Peirce's writings on signs is an example of general semiotics, while Halliday's (1978) work on language as social semiotic (see FUNCTIONALIST LINGUISTICS) is an example of a specific semiotics of particular interest to linguists.

As mentioned above, a sign stands for something, which we shall call its **object** ('object' does not mean 'thing' in this context – it is not confined to physical entities). Signs may stand for something *to* somebody, who will be called the **interpreter**. But a sign only functions as such to the interpreter in virtue of the interpreter's understanding that it does so function, and this understanding is called the **interpretant**. An example is given in the figure below (see Hookway, 1985, pp. 122–4).

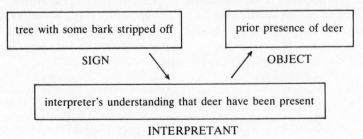

The stripped bark of the tree, which is all that the interpreter can see, gives her or him further knowledge, namely knowledge that deer have been present, because s/he understands it as a sign of this prior presence. The sign thus brings the interpreter into cognitive contact with the deer.

Signs can be placed into three classes according to their relationship to their object (see Peirce, 1931–58, 2.249; Eco, 1984, p. 136; Hookway, 1985, pp. 125–7):

1 An **icon** is 'a sign which refers to the Object that it denotes merely by virtue of characters of its own'. Thus, because of its shape, it is conceivable that a balloon could signify a cloud; because of the configuration of the lines in it, a floorplan can signify a room; because of its colour, a colour sample can signify the colour of paint in a tin. But the balloon has its shape independently of the cloud; the floorplan has its properties independently of the room; the paint sample has its colour in and for itself. They would each be as they are even if the cloud, room, and paint in the tin did not exist. The cloud, room, and paint have not actively caused the balloon, plan, and colour sample to come into existence. They function as signs only because an **isomorphism**, a correspondence of properties, between them and their objects allows us to decide that they shall so function. In order to be able to use icons, we need to know the conventions for interpreting them, as is particularly clearly seen in the case of the floorplan, where we must know the conventions of scale, of the representation of doors and windows, and so on.

2 An **index** is 'a sign which refers to the Object that it denotes by virtue of being really affected by that Object'. There is a real relation of dependency between the sign and its object, as in the case of the stripped bark and the prior presence of deer mentioned on page 399 above, and in the case of illnesses and their symptoms. Less obviously, perhaps, proper names, pointing fingers, and road signs are all indices – proper names because they are actively given to their bearers, pointing fingers because the placing of

what they point to determine where they point, and road signs for the same reason.

3 A **symbol** is 'a sign which refers to the Object that it denotes by virtue of a Law, usually an association of general ideas. . . . It is thus itself a general type.' A symbol stands in a signifying relationship with its object *only* because there exists a convention that it will be interpreted in that particular way. A flag at the beach may signify that swimming is safe; but there is neither any resemblance between the flag and the state of the tide, nor any direct causation from the tide to the flag. The only thing that qualifies the flag for signifying that swimming is safe is the general practice of using flags in this way.

Symbols are **tokens** of **types** (see Wollheim, 1968, pp. 91–3). The type itself is never encountered; only its tokens. But the type is thought of as having those properties which its tokens have *necessarily* (they may have other properties incidentally), that is, in virtue of being tokens of that type. For instance, we have never encountered the Stars and Stripes, the type, itself, only tokens of it. These may have been made of paper, linen, painted glass, etc., and these properties would have been incidental rather than necessary for us to class the flags in question as tokens of the type Stars and Stripes. But anything that is classifiable as a token of the Stars and Stripes must necessarily have a certain set of properties: it must be red, white, and blue and must have a certain number of stripes and stars in the right spatial and colour configuration. These are the properties that we think of the type as having, and they are physical properties just as much as the tokens' incidental properties *even though the type itself is not thought of as a physical entity*.

It is useful to see linguistic items as tokens of types. Consider the linguistic item 'Friday'. One of its tokens may look like the example just given, another may look like this: FRIDAY, yet another like this: *Friday*. Or consider phonemes; we have never encountered the bilabial voiced plosive, only instances of it; yet we can say that it exists, even that it has physical properties, namely that it is bilabial, voiced and plosive. The type/token distinction is very high in explanatory value from a linguist's point of view.

Language used purposefully for communication, for **telling** (see Grice, 1957), is always symbolic; but it is important to be aware that aspects of a person's language use can signify much that we would not say that he or she is actively telling others when speaking: for instance, I may become aware while listening to someone speaking that s/he is from Scotland, when all s/he is *telling* me is that s/he is heartily sick of linguistics. In such a case, the person's language seems to function indexically. But language also displays what appears to be iconicity: there are conventions whereby certain kinds of language are seen as appropriate to certain situations: convention plays a very large part in Halliday's theory of register, for example (see FUNCTIONALIST LINGUISTICS).

K.M.

SUGGESTIONS FOR FURTHER READING

Eco, U. (1984), *Semiotics and the Philosophy of Language*, London and Basingstoke, MacMillan.
Hookway, C. (1985), *Peirce*, London, Routledge & Kegan Paul.

Set theory

SETS

Set theory is a branch of mathematics which studies the properties of sets. A **set** is any collection of objects, which are described as its **members**. We can specify a set by reference to a property which all members share: for example, we can speak of the set of British towns with a population over 1 million, or of the set of English sentences. Alternatively, a set can be specified by listing its members: for example, there is a three-membered set whose members are Margaret Thatcher, the number 7, and the city of San Francisco. As this example indicates, the members of a set need not 'belong together' in any natural fashion.

We can describe a set by listing its members within curly brackets:

{Margaret Thatcher, 7, San Francisco}

The membership relation is expressed by the lower-case epsilon. Thus:

Margaret Thatcher $\in$ {Margaret Thatcher, 7, San Francisco}

This says that Margaret Thatcher is a member of the set whose members are Margaret Thatcher, the number 7, and the city of San Francisco. It is common to express the fact that some object does not belong to a set as follows:

London $\notin$ {Margaret Thatcher, 7, San Francisco}

i.e., London does not belong to the set whose members are Margaret Thatcher, the number 7 and the city of San Francisco. The notation for specifying a set by reference to a shared property is as follows:

{x: Fx} e.g. {x: x is an English sentence}

Hence:

'Snow is white' $\in$ {x: x is an English sentence}

says that 'Snow is white' belongs to the set of English sentences.

The notion of a set is **extensional**: there cannot be distinct sets with exactly the same members. For example: although ' . . . is red' and ' . . . is the same colour as a London bus' differ in meaning,

$$\{x: x \text{ is red}\} = \{x: x \text{ is the same colour as a London bus}\}$$

Although the property of being a three-sided plane figure is distinct from the property of being a three-angled plane figure, each property determines the same set.

Two special sets should be mentioned here. These are the empty set or null set and the universal set. The **null set, 0**, has no members; everything that exists has the property of not belonging to the null set. Given the fact that set membership is extensional, it follows that there is only one null set. The **universal set**, often denoted by '**1**', contains everything: there is nothing which does not belong to the universal set. The **cardinality** of a set is the number of members it has: the cardinality of the set of letters of the English alphabet is twenty-six, for example, and the cardinality of the null set is zero. A set with just one member is referred to as a **unit set**, and it is worth making clear that an object (say, my typewriter) is distinct from the unit set to which it belongs. They are different objects. My typewriter is a concrete object – I can touch it; the unit set containing my typewriter is, like all sets, an abstract object – it cannot be touched or manipulated.

PROPERTIES OF SETS AND OPERATIONS UPON SETS

Set theory studies the fundamental truths about sets and various operations upon sets which, for example, construct complex sets out of others. It was developed in the late nineteenth century and the twentieth century chiefly in order to provide rigorous foundations for number theory and other branches of mathematics. Gottlob Frege, Bertrand Russell, and others hoped to explain the truths of arithmetic by identifying numbers with certain sets and establishing that the whole of arithmetic could then be derived from the fundamental properties of sets and their relations.

Some of the main notions used in set theory are as follows. One set is included in another, is a **subset** of it, when all members of the first are also members of the second. Thus, the set of odd numbers is a subset of the set of natural numbers; and the set of three-word English sentences is a subset of the set of English sentences. 'S is a subset of T' is written as follows:

$$S \subseteq T.$$

S is a **proper subset** of T when every member of S is a member of T, and T contains things not in S. Our two examples of the subset relation also exemplify what is involved in the relation of being a proper subset. S is a proper subset of T is written thus:

$$S \subset T.$$

It will be apparent that if S is a subset of T and T is a subset of S, then S and T are the same set:

$$\text{If } S \subseteq T \text{ and } T \subseteq S \text{ then } S = T.$$

The **power set** of a set S is a set which contains as a member every subset of S. For example, consider a set T which contains just three objects, a, b, and c. The power set of T is

$$\{ \{a,b,c\}, \{a,b\}, \{a,c\}, \{a\}, \{b\}, \{c\}, 0\}$$

Note that every set is a subset of itself, and that the null set is a subset of every set.

Union and **intersection** are the two principal means by which sets can be constructed out of other sets. The union of S and T is a set which contains all objects which are in S and all objects which are in T. For example, the set of positive integers is the union of the set of positive odd numbers and the set of positive even numbers; the set of students in the university is the union of the set of undergraduates and of graduates; etc. The union of S and T (S ∪ T) can thus be defined:

$$(\forall x)\,(x \in S \lor x \in T \leftrightarrow x \in S \cup T)$$

The intersection of S and T (S ∩ T) contains only those objects which belong both to S and T. Thus:

$$(\forall x)\,(x \in S \cap T \leftrightarrow x \in S \,\&\, x \in T)$$

For example, the set of third-year philosophy students in the university is the intersection of the set of third-year students and the set of philosophy students; the set of brown horses is the intersection of the set of horses and the set of brown things; etc.

Here are some other set-theoretic notions. The **difference** of S and T (S – T) contains all those objects which are in S which are not in T. If A is the set of students at the university and B is the set of physics students, then A – B is the set of students at the university who do not study physics. The **complement** of a set is the set of objects which do not belong to it: thus, the complement of the set S is 1 – S.

SETS, SEQUENCES AND FUNCTIONS

Just as sets are to be distinguished from properties, they are to be distinguished from **sequences**. The expressions below specify the same sets:

{Margaret Thatcher, 7, San Francisco}
{7, San Francisco, Margaret Thatcher}

The members of a set are not placed in any particular order. In a sequence, the order matters: the sequences below being different:

(1) <1,2,3>
(2) <3,1,2>

Two- and three-membered sequences are referred to as **ordered pairs** and **ordered triples** respectively. '<' and '>' are employed when describing sequences.

Sequences can be defined in terms of the more fundamental notions of set theory. This can be done in several ways. For example, if we replace each member of the sequence by a set containing that member together with its predecessors, we ensure that the nth member of the sequence is distinguished by itself being an n-membered set. Thus, our two sequences above could be expressed set-theoretically as follows:

(3) { {1}, {{1} 2}, {{1} {{1} 2} 3} }
(4) { {3}, {{3} 1}, {{3} {{3} 1} 2} }

(3) is a three-membered set, all three members themselves being sets. The number three occurs as a member of just one of the members of (3), and this member is itself a three-membered set. The only member of (4) of which the number three is a member is a one-membered set. Hence, its different positions in the sequences (1) and (2) are reflected in the set-theoretic presentation.

Sequences are useful in studying the properties of **functions** and **relations**. Some examples will introduce the notion of a function:

4 = the square of 2
81 = the square of 9
London = the capital of the United Kingdom
Paris = the capital of France.

The squaring function determines a unique number as value when applied to any number as argument: the capital function determines a unique city as value when applied to a nation as an argument, and so on. The square function yields a value when applied again to the results of an earlier application; the capital function is undefined for arguments which are not nations. Hence, while

16 = the square of the square of 2

there is not a value assigned by the capital function to

the capital of the capital of France,

or, of course, to

the capital of Paris

We express that a is a function of b thus:

$$a = f(b)$$

The arguments of a function are drawn from a set which is called its **domain**. The domain of the squaring relation is the set of positive integers. The domain of the capital function is the set of nations. The values of the function for its different arguments belong to its **range** or **codomain**: the range of the squaring function may also be the set of positive integers; that of the capital function will be a set containing cities but no nations. When the domain and range of a function are the same set, the function is called an **operation**.

Functions can have two or more arguments: for example, the addition function yields a unique value for two arguments:

$$7 = + (3, 4)$$

A function can be understood as a, possibly infinite, set of sequences. For example, the capital function is a finite set of pairs, the second member of which is the capital of the first; and the addition function is an infinite set of triples, the third member of which is the sum of the first two:

> { <France, Paris>, <United Kingdom, London>, <Italy, Rome> ...}
> { <1,1,2>, <1,2,3>, <2,1,3>, <2,2,4>, <2,3,5>, <3,2,5> ...}

RELATIONS AND THE PROPERTIES OF RELATIONS

Set theory has many applications in formal semantics (see FORMAL SEMANTICS). Corresponding to a predicate expression such as 'red' or 'horse' is the set of things to which it applies: this is described as its **extension**. Thus, the set of horses is the extension of 'horse', the set of red things is the extension of 'red', and so on. This can be extended to the study of relations. Corresponding to a dyadic relational expression such as '... kills ...' is a set of ordered pairs of objects such that the first kills the second:

> {<Brutus, Caesar>, <St George, the dragon> ....}

This serves as the extension of the relational expression. Logicians often speak as if this set of pairs *is* the relation. In the same fashion, triadic relational expressions like '... gives ... to ...' have extensions which are sets of ordered triples, and so on. For discussion of the application of these ideas in semantics, see FORMAL SEMANTICS.

The attempt to use these ideas in explaining semantic properties of expressions from a natural language has led some cognitive scientists to a generalization of standard set theory: **fuzzy set theory**, due, primarily, to L.A. Zadeh and his followers. Since a word like *red* is vague, the suggestion that it has a definite extension is implausible. Some objects do not obviously belong within the extension of the term, but nor do they obviously belong outside it. Fuzzy set theory exploits the idea that there can be degrees of membership of a set. A bright scarlet flower belongs to the extension of 'red' to a higher degree than a flower that is approaching pink or orange does. Zadeh and his followers have developed fuzzy set theory in some detail (see Zadeh, 1975).

Logicians have developed some useful terminology for describing the properties of relations, and this is an appropriate place to present this vocabulary. A relation is **reflexive** if every object bears it to itself. For example, everything *is the same thing as* itself. If we are talking only of concrete objects, the relations of being the same size as, and being the same weight as, are reflexive. By contrast, an **irreflexive** relation is one that *nothing* bears to itself: for example, nothing is taller than itself, or the father of itself; no natural number is the result of adding 1 to itself, etc. Of course, most relations are neither reflexive nor irreflexive. For example, although there are many people who do not love themselves, it is plain that there are some who do, and so on.

In view of the claims made about relations in this section, these points can be put slightly differently:

> A relation R is reflexive if, for every object x, $<x,x> \in R$
> A relation R is irreflexive if, for every object x, $<x,x> \notin R$

A relation is **symmetrical** when it meets the condition that: if an object a bears the relation to b, then b bears the relation to a. For example:

> If John is the same height as Mary then Mary is the same height as John

A relation like 'is taller than' is **asymmetrical**: if one object is taller then another, the second cannot be taller than the first. Hence:

> A relation R is symmetrical if, whenever $<a,b> \in R$, then $<b,a> \in R$
> A relation R is asymmetrical if, whenever $<a,b> \in R$, then $<b,a> \notin R$

Finally, a relation is **transitive** if, whenever one object bears it to a second which, in turn, bears it to a third, then the first bears it to the third. If John is taller than Jane, and Jane is taller than Peter, it follows that John is taller than Peter. Hence the relation of being taller than is transitive.

On the other hand, the relation of being father of is **intransitive**: if John is father of Peter, and Peter is father of Jane, it follows that John is not father of Jane.

A relation R is transitive if, whenever $<a,b> \in R$ and $<b,c> \in R$, then $<a,c> \in R$

A relation R is intransitive if, whenever $<a,b> \in R$ and $<b,c> \in R$, $<a,c> \notin R$

If a relation is reflexive, symmetrical, and transitive, then it is called an **equivalence relation**. 'Is the same object as' is an equivalence relation, as is 'is the same height as'.

C.H.

SUGGESTIONS FOR FURTHER READING

Halmos, P. (1960), *Naive Set Theory*, Princeton, NJ, Van Nostrand.
Suppes, P. (1960), *Axiomatic Set Theory*, Princeton, NJ, Van Nostrand.

Sign language

INTRODUCTION

By **sign language** is usually meant a visual-gestural, non-vocal language used primarily by the deaf and not based on the language of the surrounding hearing community. Sign language is thus not to be identified with signed versions of spoken languages and cannot be translated sign-for-word into speech any more than two spoken languages are word-for-word intertranslatable. Sign language is not international; most signs used in different countries are no more alike than the words used in different countries, although it may be the case that adaptation to a different country's sign language is easier than adaptation to a foreign spoken language, and that it is easier to develop a sign-pidgin than a speech-pidgin (see CREOLES AND PIDGINS) (Miles, 1988, pp. 47–50).

A sign language almost always develops among groups of deaf-born people, even groups who are being taught to communicate orally (Wright, 1969). Not all deaf people have the opportunity to acquire sign language from birth, because many of them are born to hearing parents who do not know sign language, and because the use of sign language has been discouraged in the past (see below, pp. 405–10).

However, in those cases where sign language is acquired from birth, the stages of acquisition appear to be similar to those for spoken language (see LANGUAGE ACQUISITION), although the process seems to begin earlier in the case of sign language (Deuchar, 1984, p. 161). There is no evidence to suggest that the acquisition of sign language hampers acquisition of oral language; in fact, the reverse is probably the case (see below, p. 407).

The first school for the deaf to receive public support taught a sign language which its founder, Abbé de l'Epée, had developed by adding French grammar to the indigenous sign language of the poor deaf of Paris. L'Epée's school was established in 1755. He taught his pupils to read and write by associating signs with pictures and written words, so that they could write down what was said to them with the help of an interpreter and thus acquire a formal education. By the time of l'Epée's death in 1789 teachers trained by him had established twenty-one schools for the deaf in France, and by 1791 l'Epée's own school had become the National Institute for Deaf-Mutes in Paris led by the grammarian Sicard. His pupil, Roch-Ambroise Bébian, removed the imposition of the grammar of French from the indigenous sign language of the deaf, realizing that the latter had its own grammar (Sacks, 1989, pp. 16–20).

Sign language exists wherever groups of deaf people exist. Van Cleve (1987) contains descriptions of over fifty native sign languages, but in this entry, I shall concentrate on American Sign Language (ASL) and British Sign Language (BSL). Like all sign languages, these have their own syntactic rules. However, when they are used to accompany speech, the order of signs may reflect the word order of the spoken language, and incorporate special signs for English inflectional morphology. For example, the English words *sits* and *sitting* can be representend by the sign for SIT followed by separate sign markers invented for the English third person present indicative and the English progressive inflections (Klima and Bellugi, 1979, p. 244). In such circumstances the signed language is referred to as **Signed English**.

Neither Signed English, nor the Paget Gorman Sign System, nor Cued Speech are to be identified with ASL or BSL. The **Paget Gorman Sign System (PGSS)** was developed by Sir Richard Paget and Pierre Gorman between 1934 and 1971. Its signs are largely iconic representations combined with signs for affixes, and it was intended as an aid to the teaching of English, to be phased out as competence in English grew. **Cued Speech** is designed to assist the process of lipreading by providing disambiguating signs for sounds which look identical on the lips (Deuchar, 1984, p. 37; see further Griffiths, 1980, for details of PGSS and Cornett, 1967, for further details of Cued Speech).

AMERICAN SIGN LANGUAGE

The history of ASL begins with the establishment, in 1817, of the American Asylum for the Deaf in Hartford by Laurent Clerc, the Reverend Thomas Gallaudet and Mason Cogswell. Cogswell was a surgeon whose daughter was deaf. No special educational provision was made for the deaf in America at that time, and Cogswell and Gallaudet wanted to establish a school for the deaf in Hartford. Gallaudet went

to Europe to seek expert assistance. Having been turned away by the Braidwoods in Britain because they kept their methods secret (see pp. 410–11), he recruited Clerc, a deaf-mute French teacher of the deaf trained in the Sicard tradition.

The Hartford Asylum was successful, and other schools for the deaf were established as teachers were trained at Hartford. The French sign language used by Clerc amalgamated with indigenous sign languages used in America, in particular the language used by the deaf of Martha's Vineyard where a substantial proportion of the population was subject to hereditary deafness, to become ASL. Possibly because of the early influence on ASL by French Sign Language, ASL appears to be more similar to French Sign Language than to BSL (Deuchar, 1984, p. 2). In 1864, the Columbia Institution for the Deaf and the Blind in Washington became the first college for the deaf, under the leadership of Edward Gallaudet, Thomas Gallaudet's son. The institution was renamed Gallaudet College and is now **Gallaudet University**, still the only liberal arts college for the deaf in the world.

After its initial success, however, ASL came under attack from members of the **oralist school**, including Alexander Graham Bell, whose influence was so great that oralism prevailed, and the use of signs in schools was proscribed at the International Congress of Educators of the Deaf held in Milan in 1880. Since this resolution necessitated that teachers of the deaf be able to speak, the proportion of deaf teachers of the deaf fell from nearly 50 per cent in 1850 to 25 per cent by the turn of the century and further to 12 per cent by 1960.

The rationale for oralism is reasonable enough, in so far as deaf people who can only use sign language are excluded from spontaneous communication with hearing people, very few of whom know how to sign. Bell thought that just as sign language held the deaf community together, it kept deaf people from integrating with the rest of society, and that the teaching of speech and lipreading was essential if deaf people were to achieve full integration. Unfortunately, however, the price most deaf people have to pay for speech to the exclusion of sign language seems to be a dramatic reduction in their general educational achievements. Whereas pupils who had been to the Hartford Asylum and similar schools in the 1850s reached standards similar to those of their hearing counterparts, and had, effectively, achieved social integration through education, a study carried out by Gallaudet College in 1972 shows an average reading level for eighteen-year-old deaf high-school graduates comparable to that of fourth-grade pupils. Conrad (1979) shows a similar situation for deaf British students, with 18-year-olds having a reading age of nine (Sacks, 1990, pp. 21–9).

Because deaf people cannot hear the sounds made by other speakers, or by themselves, they cannot compare their own efforts at accompanying lipshapes with sounds to the sounds produced by hearing people. Hence, they are left to try to work out the system of speech from visual clues which are far less specific and detailed than the signs of sign language, and from instructions on how to use their vocal apparatus. But such instructions cannot make up for a deaf person's inability to monitor the sound itself: one has only to listen briefly to someone wearing headphones trying to sing along to music s/he hears through them to realize how important the ability to monitor one's own sounds is. Visual signing, on the other hand, seems to be a natural way of communicating for deaf people. As mentioned above, sign language appears naturally among groups of deaf people, for whom it provides everything that speech provides for people who can hear (including poetry, song, and humour produced by play on signs: see Klima and Bellugi, 1979, Ch. 4). Since such sign languages are now standardized within the communities which use them, they could profitably be viewed as natural first languages which should be firmly established in an individual required to learn another language, particularly a language which employs a medium, sound, which is alien to that individual (compare Skutnabb-Kangas and Toukomaa, 1976, discussed in the entry on BILINGUALISM AND MULTILINGUALISM). As Deuchar (1984, p. 175) points out, the recognition and use of sign language in schools would probably increase deaf people's confidence and their desire and ability to learn English, 'and would ultimately aid their integration as bilingual, bicultural adults, into both the deaf and the hearing communities'.

ASL was the first of the world's sign languages to be studied by linguists. It is the subject of what is probably still the most widely known work on sign language, Klima and Bellugi's (1979) *The Signs of Language*, in which description is strongly supported by psycholinguistic experiments. Although ASL and BSL are different languages, they share a number of characteristics and descriptive categories since they employ the same medium, so to avoid duplication a certain amount of cross-reference will be made between this and the following section.

Each sign of ASL is describable in terms of three parameters on which significant contrasts are set up between signs, namely **location, handshape**, and **movement**, and a limited number of combinations are permitted within each parameter. Stokoe (1960) describes 19 handshapes, 12 locations and 24 types of movement and provides a notation for ASL comparable to phonetic notation for speech. Location is called **tab** in the notation system, the part that acts, say, the index finger, is called **dez**, and the action performed is called **sig** (Deuchar, 1984, p. 54).

Stokoe *et al.*'s *Dictionary* (1976) lists 3,000 root signs arranged according to their parts and organization and the principles of the language. The following notation is used for tab (Deuchar, 1984, pp. 59–60):

Ø	neutral space in front of body
◯	whole face
⌒	upper face
⊔	nose
⌣	lower face
ʒ	cheek
⊓	neck
[ ]	central trunk
⋀	shoulder and upper arm

✓   forearm/elbow

Ɔ   back of wrist

A one-handed finger-spelling system can be used in conjunction with ASL for spelling out names or words for which no sign exists, and is also used as a notation for dez (Deuchar, 1984, pp. 61–4):

A: closed fist; Á: thumb extended from closed fist; B: flat hand, fingers together, thumb may or may not be extended; B̆: as for B, but hand bent; 5: same as for B, but fingers spread; 5̆: bent 5, 'clawed hand'; C: fingers and thumb bent to form curve as in letter 'c'; G: index finger extended from fist; O: fingers bent and all touching thumb; F: index finger and thumb touching, all other fingers extended; H: index finger and middle fingers extended from closed fist and held together; I: little finger extended from closed fist; L: index finger and thumb extended from closed fist; R: index and middle fingers extended and crossed, as in crossing one's fingers for good luck; V: index and middle finger extended from fist and held apart; V̆: as V, but with fingers bent; W: the middle three fingers extended from fist, may or may not be spread; X: index finger extended and bent; Y: thumb and little finger extended from fist; 8: middle finger bent, rest of fingers open.

The notations for sig can be divided into three categories; as shown in Table 1 (Deuchar, 1984,

pp. 69, roughly following the categories set up by Brennan *et al.*, 1980).

As mentioned above, a number of constraints operate on the combinations of formal elements into ASL sign forms. For example, Battison (1974) observes that two-handed signs (see below, p. 412) are constrained by the Symmetry Constraint and the Dominance Constraint. The **Symmetry Constraint** operates in such a way that in the vast majority of cases of signs in which both hands are used, both assume the same shape, location and movement. The **Dominance Constraint** restrains the shape of the non-leading hand in two-handed signs of type 3 (in which the leading hand contacts the other but the hand-shapes are different: see below, p. 412) to one of six, A, B, 5, G, C, and ø. These seem to be the most basic handshapes: they account for 70 per cent of all signs and are among the first acquired by deaf children of deaf parents (Boyes-Braem, 1973; Klima and Bellugi, 1989, pp. 63–4).

As mentioned above, ASL can employ a fingerspelling system to sign concepts or phenomena for which no sign exists. However, sign language exhibits the same facility as spoken language for creating new lexical items by compounding. Klima and Bellugi (1979, pp. 198–9) mention the phenomenon STREAKER, new to the 1970s, for which a sign compounded of the signs for NUDE and ZOOM OFF was invented which

Table 1

	Direction		Manner		Interaction
∧	up	ɑ	supinating rotation	)(	approach
∨	down	ʊ	pronating rotation	✕	contact
∿	up and down	ɯ	twisting	⧆	link or grasp
>	right	@	circular	+	cross
<	left	ɳ	nodding or bending	÷	separate
⋛	side by side	□	opening	⸲⸴	interchange
⊤	towards signer	#	closing	∼	alternation
⊥	away from signer	◊	wiggling		
⊥	to and fro				

became conventional throughout the deaf communities of the USA.

A compound is distinguished from the phrase consisting of the two words (BED SOFT meaning 'pillow' from BED SOFT meaning 'soft bed') by temporal compression, particularly of the first sign in the compound, by loss of repetition of movement in the second sign, by overlap between a first sign made by one hand and a second sign made by the other, and by smoothing of the transition between the two signs, for example by bringing the two signs closer together in the signing space (see below, p. 411). Finally, compression may integrate the movements of the two signs into one smooth flow (ibid., pp. 202–21). Newly coined signs are constrained in the same way as established signs.

Existing signs may also be extended in meaning, but such extensions are usually accompanied by a change in the sign, so that there are very few ambiguous signs. For example, the ASL sign for QUIET, which is made by moving both hands from a position in front of the lips downwards and outwards, is modified in the derived sign for TO ACQUIESCE so that the hands move down only, but until they 'hang down' from the wrists (ibid., pp. 200–1). Nouns are derived from verbs, for example ACQUISITION from GET, by diminishing and repeating the movement of the verb (ibid., pp. 199–201).

A number of specific changes in the form of signs, called **modulations**, correspond to specific changes in the signs' meaning. These include, among others, the **Circular Modulation**, which appears in citation signing (see below, p. 412) as a superimposed circular path of movement described by the hands. The Circular Modulation adds to the meaning of the sign the notion 'is prone to be' or 'has a predisposition to be' or 'tends to be'. It is the archetypical modulation on adjectival predicates like SICK, and Klima and Bellugi (1979, p. 249) refer to it as **Modulation for Predispositional Aspect**. Only signs which refer to incidental or temporary states, such as ANGRY, DIRTY, and SICK can undergo this modulation, and when they do, they refer to characteristics which are natural to the person, item, or phenomenon of which they are predicated, for

instance SICKLY. When such signs undergo a different modulation, the **Thrust Modulation**, a single thrustlike movement combining a brief tense motion with a lax handshape, they refer to a readiness for the state, quality, or characteristic to develop, or to a sudden change to that state, so Klima and Bellugi (1979, p. 255) call this the Thrust Modulation for **Susceptative Aspect**. When the sign for SICK is modulated in this way it means 'get sick easily'. Signs which stand for characteristics which are by nature inherent or long-lasting, such as PRETTY, INTELLIGENT, HARD, TALL, and YOUNG cannot undergo Circular or Thrust Modulation.

Transitory state adjectival predicates and durative verbs can accept the **Elliptical Modulation for Continuative Aspect**, a slow reduplication, which adds to the sign the meaning 'for a long time'; the **Tremolo Modulation for Incessant Aspect**, a tiny, tense, uneven movement made rapidly and repeatedly, which adds to the sign the meaning 'incessantly'; and the **Marcato Modulation for Frequentative Aspect**, which has a tense movement, well-marked initial and final positions, and a regular beat of four to six reduplications and which means 'often occurring' (ibid., pp. 256–8).

The meanings 'very' and 'sort of' can be added to a sign by the **Tense and Lax Modulations for Intensive and Approximate Aspects** respectively. The change in movement for the former is tension in the muscles of hand and arm, a long tense hold at the beginning of the sign, a very rapid single performance, and a final hold. The change in movement for the latter is a lax hand shape and an extreme reduction in size and duration of each iteration of the sign (ibid., pp. 258–260).

The meaning 'to become' is conveyed by the **Accelerando Modulation for Resultative Aspect**. In this aspect, the sign for RED, which is made by a soft downward brushing motion made twice, is made only once and with a tense motion which starts slowly before accelerating to a long final hold (ibid., pp. 260–1).

Klima and Bellugi (ibid., pp. 269–70) point out that the many forms displayed by modulations are realizations of grammatical processes: they

Table 2

Pairs of modulations	Reduplicated	Even	Tense	End-marked	Fast	Elongated	
Predispositional 'be characteristically sick'	+	+	−	−	+	+	transitory state
Susceptative/ frequentative 'easily get sick often'	+	+	−	+	+	+	change to state
Continuative 'be sick for a long time'	+	−	+	−	−	+	transitory state
Iterative 'keep on getting sick again and again'	+	−	+	+	−	+	change to state
Protractive 'be sick uninterruptedly'	−		+			−	transitory state
Incessant 'seem to get sick incessantly'	+	−	+	+	+	−	change to state
Intensive 'be very sick'	−	+	+	+	+	+	transitory state
Resultative 'get sick'	−	−	+	+	−	+	change to state

differ systematically on a limited number of dimensions and the differences in dimensions correlate with a network of basic semantic distinctions. They display this as in Table 2. In general, sign language morphology tends to resist sequential segmentation at the lexical level and to favour superimposed spatial and temporal contrasts in sign movement (ibid., p. 274). For syntactic use of the signing space, see pages 413–14 below.

BRITISH SIGN LANGUAGE

The first school for the deaf in Britain was established by Thomas Braidwood in Edinburgh in 1760. Braidwood kept his methods of in-struction secret, but he seems likely to have employed a combination of speech, lip-reading, and signs (McLoughlin, 1980). In this and similar schools which were opened in other parts of the country, deaf people could come together and the sign language they used among themselves could begin to become standardized. The Braidwood Academy, which was fee-paying, was moved from Edinburgh to London in 1783, and in 1792 a society was formed to provide free education for the deaf in 'asylums', the first of which, in London, was run by Braidwood's nephew Joseph Watson. After Braidwood's death in 1806 Watson published *Instruction for the Deaf and Dumb* (1809), from which it is apparent that he knew sign language and that he thought that all teachers of the deaf should learn it and use it to introduce the deaf to speech (Deuchar, 1984, pp. 31–2).

When the last of the Braidwoods, Thomas (the younger), died in 1825, he was replaced by a Swiss, Louis du Puget, (Hodgson, 1953, p. 163). Du Puget introduced Epée's silent method (see pp. 405–6 above). But from the 1860s onward BSL experienced a period of declining status similar to, and for the same reasons as, those described on pp. 406–7 above for ASL. But the system of education for the deaf was kept entirely segregated from the rest of the education system until 1944 so that although the aim of the system was to teach the deaf to use oral language, the schools provided a meeting ground for the deaf where they could sign between themselves.

Signing was also used in the 'missions' often attached to the schools. Missions were charitable organizations concerned with the spiritual welfare of the deaf, often established on the initiative of local deaf people themselves, and they also provided space for recreational and other social activities. The missions have developed into centres for the deaf which are to be found in most large British towns, but have become largely detached from schools for the deaf, most of which are residential. Therefore most children do not become fully integrated into their local deaf community until they leave school, and the school community and the adult community tend to use different variants of sign language. This situation bears some similarity to that which pertains to accent and dialect in spoken language; adult signers can usually tell where other signers come from and where they went to school (see further below) (Deuchar, 1984, pp. 32–5).

It was not until the 1980s that, largely as a result of action by the British Deaf Association and the National Union of the Deaf, BSL began to be perceived as a proper language, to gain a degree of official status and to find its way into some classrooms and onto the nation's television screens (Miles, 1988, pp. 19–40). BSL has therefore developed through its use in the deaf communities around Britain and it displays some regional and other types of variation, just as spoken language does.

Sign-language use necessitates a certain amount of space in front of and to the sides of the body in which to sign. This space, plus the front and sides of the body from the head to just below the waist, is known as the **signing space**. However, the signer's face remains the focus of gaze during signing, and movement of the hands is perceived by area vision (Miles, 1988, p. 53). Signs which are supported by the face, head, and the body from the waist up are called **multichannel signs**.

A forward tilt of the body indicates astonishment, interest, or curiosity, while a backward tilt indicates defiance or suspicion. Hunched shoulders imply effort, rising chest pride and falling chest discouragement. In addition, shifts in body direction and mime-like movements can aid story telling and the reporting of events (Miles, 1988, pp. 64–5).

Nodding and shaking the head are used to reply 'yes' and 'no' as in speech, but also to affirm and negate propositions. Thus rubbing the clenched leading hand (see below) with the thumb pointing upwards up and down on the stomach means 'I am hungry' when accompanied by nodding and 'I am not hungry' when accompanied by a headshake. Nods and tilts of the head also act as punctuation between and within sentences, and head movement can be used to indicate location (Miles, 1988, pp. 63–4).

Facial expressions include standardized versions of expressions used by everyone to express emotion, such as positive and negative face. Similarly, an open mouth with clenched teeth indicates stress or effort, while a loose pout with slightly puffed cheeks suggests ease; a loose or open mouth, possibly with the tongue showing, suggests carelessness, lack of attention, or ignorance. Lips pulled tight as in saying *ee* with the teeth just showing suggests intensity or nearness or exactness. In descriptions of sizes, volumes, etc. fully puffed cheeks mean 'a great amount' while pursed lips and sucked in cheeks mean 'a small amount'. The lip movements of words can also be used to disambiguate signs. For example, the sign for a married person can be accompanied by the lip shape for *hu-sp* to indicate that the married person in question is male (Miles, 1988, pp. 59–62).

The eyes are used to show surprise (wide eyes) and doubt (narrow eyes). Narrow eyes can also show intensity of judgements, making the difference between the signs for 'far' and 'very far', 'good' and 'very good', and so on. The direction of the signer's gaze can be used like pointing to indicate the location and movement of things. Raised eyebrows accompany questions (Miles, 1988, pp. 62–3).

Just as speech makes some limited use of imitation of natural sounds, **onomatopoeia**, some manual signs imitate actions, shapes, sizes, directions, and so on. Some signs, like that for 'drink', in which the hand imitates the shape and movement involved in holding a glass and putting it to one's lips, are **transparent**, that is, they would probably be understood even by people who do not know sign language. Other signs, in which the link between meaning and form only becomes apparent when it is explained are called **translucent**. The sign for 'cheap', for example, involves a downward movement which may suggest that something is being reduced. Signs which give no visual clues to their meaning are called **encoded**. **Iconic** or pictorial signs can be made by the fingers or the hand outlining the shape, size, or action of an object. For example, the sign for 'scissors' is made by the middle and index fingers performing movements similar to those of the blades of a pair of scissors. If the hand simultaneously moves across in front of the body, the sign means 'cut' (see further Miles, 1988, pp. 66–76).

There are three kinds of manual sign, one-handed, two-handed, and mixed, each having different types. One-handed signs are made by the right hand if the signer is right-handed and by the left if s/he is left-handed. The hand used for one-handed signs is called the **leading hand**. One-handed signs are either made in space (type 1) or by touching a body-part (though not the other hand) (type 2).

Two-handed signs are of three types. Signs of type 1 are made with both hands moving either in space or touching each other or the body. Signs of type 2 involve the leading hand contacting the other while both handshapes are the same. In signs of type 3, the leading hand contacts the other, but the handshapes are different.

A **mixed sign** is a sign which begins as one-handed and becomes two-handed, or vice versa, as in the sign for 'believe' in which the signer first touches his or her forehead just above the eye with the index finger of the leading hand and then brings that hand down in front of the chest, with the palm facing it, to make contact with the horizontal, upward facing palm of the other hand (Miles, 1988, pp. 54–5).

Each sign of sign language can be described in isolation, but just as words in sentences do not sound the same as their **citation forms**, that is the way they sound when pronounced one at a time out of context, signs adapt to context as the hands rapidly change from one shape to another. There are more than fifty handshapes in BSL and around twenty-five identifiable places in the signing space. The signs are described in terms of place, movement, and the direction in which the palm and fingers face (Miles, 1988, pp. 56–7), and Stokoe's 'tab', 'dez' and 'sig', developed for ASL (see above, pp. 407–8) can be applied to BSL signs too, as Deuchar (1984, p. 54) demonstrates: the sign for I in BSL is made by the index finger pointing to and touching the chest, and can thus be described as:

tab: chest
dez: index finger extended from closed fist
sig: contact with tab

The sign for THINK in BSL is made by the index finger pointing to the forehead, so it can be described as:

tab: forehead
dez: index finger extended from closed fist
sig: contact with tab

This shows the signs I and THINK to be **minimal pairs**: they differ only on one parameter, tab. Similarly, THINK and KNOW are minimal pairs differing only in dez, and KNOW and CLEVER are minimal pairs which contrast in sig (ibid., p. 55):

	KNOW	CLEVER
tab:	forehead	forehead
dez:	thumb extended from closed fist	thumb extended from closed fist
sig:	contact with tab	movement from right to left in contact with tab

For BSL, the following symbols for tab, dez and sig have been added to Stokoe *et al.*'s (1976) (see above, pp. 407–8):

Tab

⌒	top of head	⊐⊏	eyes
ᵕ	mouth/lips	⊃	ear
⌐⌐	upper trunk	∪	lower trunk

(Deuchar, 1984, p. 604)

Dez

⅃ middle finger extended from fist

(ibid., p. 64)

Sig

☒ crumbling action   ∅ no movement

(ibid., pp. 69–70)

The signing space forms an arena in which aspects of the syntax of sign language can be displayed through spatial relations between the signs and the type and frequency of their movements. For instance, the information encapsulated in the sentence *The house is on a hill, with a path winding up to it* can be provided in sign language by (1) establishing a hill by moving the arms with the hands flat and palms down sideways upwards, then forming the top of the hill; (2) next making the sign for house by touching the tips of the fingers of each hand to each other, arms still stretched upward where the hill is; (3) bringing down the arms and forming a path leading up the hill with the index and middle finger of both hands tracing the path; (4) then tracing a road below the hill with both hands flat, palms facing each other, and moving together across below where the hill has been established.

Anaphora, backward reference, can be made to items already placed in the signing space by pointing to them (Miles, 1988, pp. 88–9). This means that in many cases there is no need to employ the third person pronoun. However, sign-language grammar is not dependent on linearity, since more than one sign can be made simultaneously. For example, whereas in speech the words in a sentence must follow one another linearly as in *a small boy who was born deaf*, in BSL the left hand can sign BOY while the right is signing SMALL; the left hand can sign BORN while the right is signing DEAF (Woll, 1990, p. 775). In addition, signs made with the hands can be accompanied by non-manual behaviour: clause connectors are made with the head and eyebrows; for example, in an *if–then* construction, the *if*-part is signed with raised brows and the head tilted slightly back, and the brows and head drop to introduce the *then*-part. The topic of a sentence is introduced first, often with raised brows and a backward headtilt, followed by the comment, often accompanied by a nod.

A sign moves from the direction of the subject of the sentence towards the object, so that there may be no need to mark subject and object by pronouns. When pronoun signs are used, they are usually made at the beginning of a sentence and repeated at the end. In reporting the speech of others, the signer can adopt their different roles by body shift and eye gaze, and portray the different emotions of the interactants through facial expressions. As mentioned above, mood and modality can be indicated with the face, head, eyes, and eyebrows.

Tense can be marked by using the signs for 'will' (future), 'now' (present) and 'finish' (past). Tense and aspect are also marked by the use of four **time lines**, A, B, C, and D:

A, past to future, runs from just behind the signer's shoulder to a foot or two in front of him or her. Signs made just above or behind the shoulder indicate past time. Distant past is indicated by circling both hands backward alternately, and increasing the size, number, and speed of the circles in tandem with the length of time being described. To show the passing of time, the hands circle forward.

B, short time units, runs along the arm and hand that is not a signer's leading arm and hand. It is used to show calendar time, succession and duration.

C, continuing time, crosses in front of the signer; the sign for 'now' or 'today' is made here, but timeline C generally represents continuous aspect, particularly if the sign moves from left to right.

D, growing time, which is indicated by moving the flat hand with palm pointing down, from the position it would take to indicate the height of a hip-high child, upwards to shoulder height. The signs for 'small', 'tall', 'child(ren)', and 'adult' are made at points on this line, while for 'grew up' and 'all my life' the hand moves upward (Miles, 1988, pp. 90–105).

Plural number can be indicated by repetition of a sign. For example, the sign for CHILDREN is made by repeating the sign for CHILD. However, signs which involve the use of extended fingers can also be modified to include reference to plural number. For example, the two-finger handshape of the sign for DEAF PERSON can be replaced by one involving three fingers to indicate THREE DEAF PEOPLE, and the sign for GIRL, which involves the use of the index finger can be made to mean THREE GIRLS by the use of three fingers (Deuchar, 1984, pp. 87–8). Some one-handed signs (AEROPLANE, CUP) can be pluralized by making the sign with both hands (Woll, 1990, p. 762).

A two-handed fingerspelling system, the **British manual alphabet**, is used with BSL for spelling names and words for which no sign exists. The hands form the shapes of the letters, and some signs, for instance, 'father', 'daughter', 'bible', 'kitchen' and 'government', are made by repetition of the fingerspelled initial letter of the corresponding word (Miles, 1988, pp. 84–5).

There are several number systems used in BSL in different areas of Britain. They all involve a complex use of the fingers and various hand shapes. For example, in the system used in the south of England, the sign for 3 is made with the palm towards the body and the index, middle, and ring fingers of the hand pointing upwards while the thumb and little finger are folded into the palm; the sign for 8 is made with the palm towards the body, the thumb pointing upwards, and the index and middle finger pointing across the front of the body. Each region has its own

way of using the number system for indicating the time. A number sign starting near the mouth indicates that the number is a number of pounds (£); if it moves out from the nose, it indicates age (Miles, 1988, pp. 79–81).

BSL has its own discourse rules (Miles, 1988, pp. 51–3). For instance, it is considered bad manners to get someone's attention by turning their face towards you, as a child might do, to wave your hand in front of their face, or to flick the light on and off, *unless* you want to address all of a large group. Tapping a person on the arm or shoulder, and not anywhere else, is the polite means of getting their attention, but the tapping must not be too hard or too persistent. Taps can be relayed by bystanders, if one is out of physical reach of the person one wants to communicate with.

To show attention, a person is expected to keep looking at the person who is signing and s/he may nod to show comprehension, agreement, or just general interest. Looking away is interpreted as an interruption of the signer.

Bidding for a turn is done by catching the eye of the other person, or by bringing one's hands up ready for signing. A person finishing a turn will drop his or her hands from the signing space and look at another participant in the conversation.

K.M.

SUGGESTIONS FOR FURTHER READING

Deuchar, M. (1984), *British Sign Language*, London, Routledge & Kegan Paul.

Klima, E.S. and Bellugi, U. (1979), *The Signs of Language*, Cambridge, MA, and London, Harvard University Press.

Kyle, J.G. and Woll, B. (1985), *Sign Language: The Study of Deaf People and their Language*, Cambridge, Cambridge University Press.

Miles, D. (1988), *British Sign Language: A Beginner's Guide*, London, BBC Books.

Sacks, O. (1989), *Seeing Voices: A Journey into the World of the Deaf*, Berkeley and Los Angeles, The University of California Press; London, Pan, 1990.

Sociolinguistics

Sociolinguistics is the study of language in relation to society, and it draws on insights from sociology, anthropology, and social psychology as well as insights from other areas of linguistic study. It feeds insights back into these other disciplines and areas. In particular, studies in sociolinguistics have demonstrated the importance of the social function of language and shown that it is often possible to find social explanations for aspects of linguistic structure (see, LANGUAGE AND GENDER and CRITICAL LINGUISTICS).

Although there is a long tradition within linguistics of dialect study (see DIALECTOLOGY and LANGUAGE SURVEYS) and of the relationship between language and culture (see MENTALIST LINGUISTICS), it was not until the 1960s that interest in sociolinguistics became widespread, largely as a result of William Labov's work in the United States and Peter Trudgill's work in Britain (see DIALECTOLOGY and LANGUAGE SURVEYS).

Many sociolinguistic studies are concerned with the way in which language varies according to the social context in which it is used and according to the social group to which a user belongs. It aims to describe this variation and to show how it reflects social structure. Those linguistic units which vary fairly systematically in relation to social variables such as the user's region, class, ethnic group, age, and gender are called **sociolinguistic variables**, and their different forms are called **variants**. Since any linguistic unit may be seen as subject to such variation, it may be useful to think of sociolinguistics as a point of view from which language can be described.

Studies which are concerned with the relations between societies and languages as wholes may be described as falling under the **anthropology and sociology of language**. These include studies in the Sapir–Whorf tradition (the anthropology of language) (see MENTALIST LINGUISTICS), and studies of issues such as the effects of multilingualism on economic development and the possible language-planning policies a government may adopt (the sociology of language). However, there is much overlap between the areas, and any difference resides largely in the overall aim of an investigation, which may be primarily concerned either with language or with society and culture (Hudson, 1980, Introduction; Trudgill, 1974a, Introduction). For example, studies in the Sapir–Whorf tradition can be seen as using the outcome of the study of a people's language as evidence for claims about their general world view, that is, as a means towards understanding the culture.

A number of entries in this encyclopedia deal with topics which can be seen as falling within the province of sociolinguistics. See in particular BILINGUALISM AND MULTILINGUALISM; CREOLES AND PIDGINS; CRITICAL LINGUISTICS; DIALECTOLOGY; DIGLOSSIA; THE ENGLISH DIALECT SOCIETY; FIELD METHODS; FUNCTIONALIST LINGUISTICS; LANGUAGE AND EDUCATION; LANGUAGE AND GENDER; LANGUAGE SURVEYS; MENTALIST LINGUISTICS.

K.M.

SUGGESTIONS FOR FURTHER READING

Downes, W. (1984), *Language and Society*, London, Fontana.

Hudson, R.A. (1980), *Sociolinguistics*, Cambridge, Cambridge University Press.

Trudgill, P. (1974), *Sociolinguistics: An Introduction*, Harmondsworth, Penguin.

Speech-act theory

Speech-act theory was developed by the Oxford philosopher J.L. Austin in the 1930s, and expounded in a series of William James lectures which Austin gave at Harvard University in 1955. These lectures, twelve in all, were subsequently published under the title *How To Do Things With Words* in 1962. The theory arises in reaction to what Austin (1962 p. 3) calls the **descriptive fallacy**, the view that a declarative sentence is always used to describe some state of affairs, some fact, which it must do truly or falsely.

Austin points out that there are many declarative sentences which do not describe, report, or state anything, and of which it makes no sense to ask whether they are true or false. The utterance of such sentences is, or is part of, the doing of some action – an action which would not normally be described as simply saying something. Austin (ibid., p. 5) gives a number of examples: *I do*, as uttered as part of a marriage ceremony; *I name this ship the Queen Elizabeth*, as uttered by the appropriate person while smashing a bottle against the stem of the ship in question; *I give and bequeath my watch to my brother*, as written in a will; *I bet you sixpence it will rain tomorrow*.

To utter such sentences in the appropriate circumstances is not to describe what you are doing: it *is* doing it, or part of doing it, and Austin calls such utterances **performatives** or **performative utterances**, distinguishing them from **constatives** or **constative utterances** which are used to state a fact or describe a state of affairs. Only constatives can be true or false; performatives are **happy** or **unhappy**. Austin also expresses this by saying that the two types of utterance seem to have value on different dimensions; the constatives have value on the truth/falsity dimension; performatives have value on the happiness/unhappiness dimension.

The criterion for a happy, or **felicitous**, performative is that the circumstances in which it is uttered should be **appropriate**: certain **felicity conditions** must obtain. If a performative is unhappy, or **infelicitous**, something has gone wrong in the connection between the utterance and the circumstances in which it is uttered.

There are four main types of condition for the happy functioning of a performative (ibid., pp. 14–15):

1 It must be a commonly accepted convention that the uttering of particular words by particular people in particular circumstances will produce a particular effect.
2 All participants in this conventional procedure must carry out the procedure correctly and completely.
3 If the convention is that the participants in the procedure must have certain thoughts, feelings, and intentions, then the participants must in fact have those thoughts, feeling, and intentions.
4 If the convention is that any participant in the procedure binds her/himself to behave subsequently in a certain way, then s/he must in fact behave subsequently in that way.

If any of these criteria is unfulfilled, the performative will be unhappy in one of two ways, depending on which of the criteria is not fulfilled.

If we sin against either 1 or 2, the conventional act is *not* achieved: a person who is already married may go through another marriage ceremony, but this second marriage will be null and void because its circumstances were faulty (1). Or, a couple may go through all of the marriage ceremony except signing the register; the marriage will then be null and void because the ceremony was not carried out completely (2). Cases like these, in which the act is *not* achieved are called **misfires**.

If we sin against 3 and 4, then the conventional act *is* achieved, but the procedure will have been abused. A person may say *I congratulate you* or *I condole with you* without having the appropriate feelings of joy/sadness for the addressee; or s/he may say *I promise to be there* without having any intention of being there. In such cases, the act will be insincere (3). Or, a person may say *I welcome you* and then proceed to treat the addressee as an unwelcome intruder, in which case s/he will have breached the commitment inherent in the greeting to subsequently behave in a certain manner (4). Both types of case are called **abuses**: the act *is* achieved, but the procedure has been abused.

So the connection between performatives and constatives is that for a performance to be happy, certain constatives must be true (ibid., p. 45): for *I congratulate you* to be happy, *I feel pleased for you* must be true.

However, Austin soon begins to question whether the distinction between the truth/falsity dimension and the happiness/unhappiness dimension is really as clear as it first seemed to be (his argument in this connection is clearest in Austin, 1971); for it seems that not only performatives are subject to unhappiness: surely *All John's children are bald* as uttered when John has no children is just as unhappy as *I give and bequeath my watch to my brother* as written in the will of a person who does not possess a watch.

In each case, certain things are **presupposed** by the utterance, namely, in the first case, that John has children, and in the second case that the will writer owns a watch. These presuppositions fail, they are void for lack of reference. Similarly, *The cat is on the mat* as uttered by somebody who does not believe that the cat is on the mat seems to be just as much abused as *I promise to be there* as uttered by someone who has no intention of being there. Both are unhappy because their **implications** are unfulfilled: the utterance of *The cat is on the mat* has the implication that the speaker believes that the cat is on the mat just as *I promise to be there* has the implication that the speaker intends to be there. So constatives can be

as unhappy as performatives, and the unhappinesses arise for the same types of reason in the case of both types of utterance.

Furthermore, performatives seem to be able to be untrue just as constatives. *I advise you to do it* could be considered false in the sense of *conflicting with the facts* if my belief about what is best for you is mistaken. Similarly, *I declare you guilty* conflicts with the facts if you are innocent (at the time, a **correspondence theory of truth** was popular: a sentence was true if and only if it corresponded to the facts; see PHILOSOPHY OF LANGUAGE, pp. 336–8, and – for a different conception of truth – pp. 338–9). Austin also points out that it is often difficult to decide whether a statement is strictly true or false, because the facts are vague; and if facts are vague, so is the notion of truth which depends on them. He therefore reformulates the concept of truth as a **dimension of criticism**, including, even for declarative sentences, the situation of the speaker, the purpose of speaking, the hearers, the precision of reference, etc., and it is already beginning to look as if, as Austin indeed concludes (see below), all utterances may be performative in some sense (1962, p. 52):

In order to explain what can go wrong with statements we cannot just concentrate on the proposition involved (whatever that is) as has been done traditionally. We must consider the total situation in which the utterance is issued – the total speech-act – if we are to see the parallel between statements and performative utterances, and how each can go wrong. So the total speech-act in the total speech-situation is emerging from logic piecemeal as important in special cases: and thus we are assimilating the supposed constative utterance to the performative.

However, it might still be possible to save the distinction Austin set out with; instead of concentrating on the truth/falsity–happiness/ unhappiness distinction which is beginning to look unsound, perhaps we can decide whether something is or is not a performative by testing whether 'saying so makes it so'. If I say *I promise*, I thereby promise, whereas if I say *I walk*, I do not thereby walk. A possible test for performatives is therefore the **hereby-test**. In the case of performatives it is always possible to insert *hereby*: *I bequeath – I hereby bequeath; passengers are warned – passengers are hereby warned*. In a constative, it is not appropriate to insert *hereby*: *I walk – *I hereby walk*; *I am being watched – *I am hereby being watched*. This distinction is, however, about to be broken down too.

So far, the performatives mentioned have been clearly marked as performatives by containing within them a verb which stands for the action being performed; thus in saying *I promise*, I am promising (*I do* looks like an exception, but Austin assumes it is short for *I do take this woman/man to be my lawful wedded wife/husband*). However, there are many performatives which do not contain these so-called **speech-act verbs** or **performative verbs**, and which are not even declarative sentences; in many cases, uttering words such as *dog, bull*, or *fire* constitutes an action of warning just as much as uttering *I warn you that there is a dog/bull/fire*, so we would want to say that these utterances, too, are performatives.

A distinction is therefore drawn between **explicit performatives** and **implicit** or **primary** performatives. Austin believed that the explicit performatives had developed from the implicit performatives as language and society became more sophisticated. Any primary peformative is expandable into a sentence with a verb in the first-person singular indicative or the second- or third-person indicative passive, a verb which also names the action carried out by the performative. Austin estimated that a good dictionary would contain between 1000 and 9.999 of these performative or speech-act verbs, *and one of them will be 'state'*. Consequently, any constative is expandable into a performative: any utterance, *p*, can be encased in an utterance of the form *I hereby state that p*, and the distinction originally drawn between constatives and performatives has now been effectively deconstructed. *Any* utterance is part of or all of the doing of some action, and the only distinction that now remains is between performative and non-performative *verbs*. Performative verbs name actions that are performed, wholly or partly, by saying something (*state, promise*); non-performative verbs name other types of action, types of action which are independent of speech (*walk, sleep*). Because performative verbs are so numerous, Austin hoped that it might be possible to arrive at some broad classes of speech act under which large numbers of more delicately distinguished speech acts might fall. To arrive at these broad classes, he distinguished among a number of **illocutionary forces** that a speech act might have.

The illocutionary force of an utterance is distinguished from its locution and from its perlocutionary effect as follows.

Every time we direct language at some audience, we perform three simultaneous acts: a locutionary act, an illocutionary act, and a perlocutionary act.

To perform a **locutionary act** is to say something in what Austin (1962, p. 94) calls 'the full normal sense'. It includes:

1 The **phonic** act: uttering noises, **phones**.
2 The **phatic** act: uttering noises *as belonging to a certain vocabulary and conforming to a certain grammar*, that is, as being part of a certain language. The noises seen from this perspective are called **phemes**.
3 The **rhetic** act: using these noises with a certain sense and reference (see PHILOSOPHY OF LANGUAGE, pp. 332–3). The noises seen from this perspective are called **rhemes**.

These three simultaneous acts make up the locutionary act. However, each time one performs a locutionary act, one is also thereby performing some **illocutionary act**, such as stating, promising, warning, betting, etc. If a hearer, through his or her knowledge of the conventions of the language, grasps what one is doing, there is **uptake** on his or her part of the **illocutionary force** of the utterance. The effect the illocutionary act has on the hearer is called the **perlocutionary act**, such as persuading, deterring, surprising, misleading, or convincing. Perlocutionary acts are performed *by* saying something rather than *in* saying it.

Austin (1962, Lecture 12) suggests that it is possible to distinguish a number of broad classes or families of speech acts, classified according to their illocutionary force. He suggests the following classes:

1 **Verdictives** typified by the giving of a verdict, estimate, reckoning or appraisal; giving a finding.
2 **Excersitives**: the exercising of powers, rights or influence, exemplified by voting, ordering, urging, advising, warning, etc.
3 **Commissives**, typified by promising or otherwise undertaking (ibid., pp. 151–2): 'they *commit* you to doing something, but include also declarations or announcements of intention, which are not promises, and also rather vague things which we might call espousals, as for example, siding with'.
4 **Behavitives**, which have to do with social behaviour and attitudes, for example apologizing, congratulating, commending, condoling, cursing, and challenging.
5 **Expositives**, which make it clear how our utterances fit into the course of an argument or conversation – how we are using words. In a way, these might be classed as **metalinguistic**, as part of the language we are using about language. Examples are *I reply*; *I argue*; *I concede*; *I illustrate*; *I assume*; *I postulate*.

Austin is quite clear that there are many marginal cases, and many instances of overlap, and a very large body of research exists as a result of people's efforts to arrive at more precise classifications both of the broad classes and of the subclasses (see, for instance, Wierzbicka, 1987). Here, however, we shall follow up only Searle's (1969) development of Austin's theory.

Searle (1969) describes utterances slightly differently from Austin's triad of locution, illocution, and perlocution. According to Searle, a speaker typically does *four* things when saying something; this is because, as Searle rightly points out, not all utterances involve referring and predicating – Austin's rheme, which was part of the locutionary act. For example, *ouch* and *hurrah* do not involve rhemes. So the first of Searle's four possible elements of uttering only contains Austin's phone and pheme, that is, it only includes two of the elements of Austin's locutionary act. Searle calls this act the

1 **Utterance act**: uttering words (morphemes, sentences).

Austin's rheme, the third aspect of the locutionary act, constitutes an element of its own in Searle's scheme, the

2 **Propositional act**: referring and predicating.

In saying

(a) Will Peter leave the room?
(b) Peter will leave the room
(c) Peter, leave the room
(d) Would that Peter left the room

a speaker will **express** the same **proposition** (symbolized as Rp, where R stands for the action of leaving the room and p stands for Peter), her or his propositional act will be the same, but s/he will be doing other radically different things too in each case. S/he will perform one of a number of possible

3 **Illocutionary acts**: questioning, stating, ordering, wishing.

Many utterances contain **indicators of illocutionary force**, including word order, stress, punctuation, the mood of the verb, and Austin's performative verbs. Finally, speaking typically involves a

4 **Perlocutionary act**: persuading, getting someone to do something, etc.

Having isolated the acts from each other, in particular having made it possible to separate the propositional act from the illocutionary act, Searle is able to home in on the illocutionary act. To perform illocutionary acts, he says, is to engage in rule-governed behaviour, and he draws up the rules which govern this behaviour on the basis of sets of necessary and sufficient conditions for the performance of the various illocutionary acts.

A **necessary condition** for x is a condition which must be fulfilled before x is achieved, but which cannot, by itself, necessarily guarantee the achievement of x. For example, being human is a necessary condition for becoming a lecturer at Birmingham University, but it is not a sufficient condition; other conditions must be fulfilled too.

A **sufficient condition** for x is a condition which will guarantee its achievement, but which need not be a necessary condition. For instance, the entry requirements for a course of study might state that candidates must *either* have taught English for fifteen years in Papua New Guinea, *or* have green hair. Either quality would be sufficient for admittance to the course, but neither would be necessary.

The sum of all the necessary conditions for x constitutes the necessary and sufficient conditions for it.

Searle (1969, pp. 57–61) lists the necessary and sufficient conditions for the speech act of **promising** as follows:

1 Normal input and output conditions obtain (speaker and hearer both know the language, are conscious of what they are doing, are not acting under duress, have no physical impairments, are not acting, telling jokes, etc.).
2 The speaker, S, expresses that p (proposition) in making the utterance, U. This isolates the propositional content from the rest of the speech act on which we can then concentrate.
3 In expressing that p, S predicates a *future* act, A, of S. Clearly it is not possible to promise to have done something in the past; promises proper always concern the future.
4 The hearer, H, would prefer S's doing A to his or her not doing A, and S believes that H would prefer his or her doing A to not doing it. This distinguishes promises from threats.
5 It is not obvious to both S and H that S will do A in the normal course of events. If it were obvious, no promise would be necessary, of course.
6 S intends that the utterance of U will make him or her responsible for doing A.
7 S intends that the utterance of U will place him or her under an obligation to do A.
8 S intends that the utterance of U will produce in H a belief that conditions 6 and 7

obtain by means of H's recognition of S's intention to produce that belief in H; and S intends this recognition to be achieved by means of the recognition of the utterance as one conventionally used to produce such beliefs. Elucidation of this rather complexly formulated condition can be obtained through a study of Grice (1957), in which Grice sets out the necessary conditions for **telling** as opposed to **getting someone to believe**. There are many ways of getting someone to believe something; but to actually tell someone something depends on that person recognizing that you intend to get him or her to believe what you are telling him or her by your utterance.

9 The semantical rules of the dialect spoken by S and H are such that U is correctly and sincerely uttered if and only if conditions 1 to 8 obtain.

Conditions 1, 8 and 9 apply generally to all illocutionary acts, and only conditions 2–7 are peculiar to the act of promising. Conditions 2 and 3 are called the **propositional-content conditions** for promising; 4 and 5 are called the **preparatory conditions** for promising; 6 is called the **sincerity condition**; 7 is called the **essential condition**. Condition 6 can be altered to

6a S intends that the utterance of U will make him or her responsible for intending to do A

in order to allow for insincere promises.

From this list of conditions for promising, Searle now extracts a set of rules for the use of any illocutionary force indicating device for promising. Searle believes that the semantics of a language can be regarded as a series of systems of constitutive rules and that illocutionary acts are performed in accordance with these sets of constitutive rules, so that the study of semantics boils down to the study of illocutionary acts. In discussing the question of linguistic rules, Searle mentions two positions philosophers have taken with regard to them: (1) that knowing the meaning of any expression is simply to know the rules for its employment (see PHILOSOPHY OF LANGUAGE, p. 336); this position seems untenable, since no philosopher has apparently been able to say exactly what the rules are; and this has led to philosophers adopting the second position: (2) that there are no rules at all. Searle thinks that the failure of the first group of philosophers and the consequent pessimism of the second group are both consequences of a failure on the philosophers' part to distinguish between two types of rule – of thinking that there is only one kind.

In fact, Searle insists, there are two distinct kinds of rule: regulative rules and constitutive rules. But philosophers have tended to think of rules only in terms of regulative rules while, in reality, the rules for speech acts are much more like the constitutive rules.

A **regulative rule** is a rule which governs some activity which, however, exists independently of the rule in question. For instance, the rules of etiquette regulate the way in which we eat, dress, and generally conduct our interpersonal relationships. However, the activities of eating and dressing exist independently of the rules: even if I shovel food into my mouth with my knife, thus breaking one of the regulative rules for eating, I am, none the less, eating.

A **constitutive rule**, on the other hand, is a rule which both regulates and *constitutes* an activity. The activity could not exist if the rule were not being followed. These are things like rules for various games such as football and chess. If you do not play football according to the rules, you are simply not playing football; if you move your king more than one square at a time, you are simply not playing chess. Similarly, if you do not use the illocutionary force indicating devices for promising according to the rules, you are simply not promising: thus, in saying *I promise that I did it*, using the past tense, you are not, in fact, promising (you may be assuring).

The rules for the use of any illocutionary force indicator for promising, derived from conditions 2–7 above are:

1 Any illocutionary force indicating device, P, for promising is to be uttered only in the context of an utterance or larger stretch of discourse which predicates some future act, A, of the speaker, S.

2 P is to be uttered only if the hearer, H, would prefer S's doing A to his or her not doing A.

3 P is to be uttered only if it is not obvious to both S and H that S will do A in the normal course of events.

4 P is to be uttered only if S intends to do A.

5 The utterance of P counts as an undertaking of an obligation to do A.

Rule 1 is called the **propositional-content rule**; it is derived from the propositional-content conditions 2 and 3. Rules 2 and 3 are **preparatory rules** derived from the preparatory conditions 4 and 5. Rule 4 is the **sincerity rule** derived from the sincerity condition 6. Rule 5 is the **essential rule**, derived from the essential condition 7, and it is *constitutive* of P. Searle (1969, pp. 66–7) also sets out the rules for the use of illocutionary force indicating devices for the speech acts **request**, **assert**, **question**, **thank**, **advise**, **warn**, **greet** and **congratulate**. In a subsequent article, 'Indirect speech acts' (1975), he goes on to make a distinction which has been of tremendous influence in the study of pragmatics (see PRAGMATICS), between speaker meaning and sentence meaning. The distinction is drawn as part of the solution Searle offers to one of the great traditional problems in linguistic theory: how is it that speakers know when an utterance having a particular mood, say interrogative, functions as a question, and when it does not?

Normally, we expect utterances in the declarative mood to be statements, utterances in the interrogative mood to be questions, utterances in the imperative mood to be commands, and moodless utterances to be responses or announcements. Mood is an aspect of grammar, and can be read off sentences in a straightforward way:

I am studying
S   P   (S before P: mood declarative)

Is that your coat on the floor?
P   S

Am I studying?
⌈S⌉   (P before S or S within P:
⌊P⌋   mood interrogative)

Go away

P   (no S: mood imperative)

No

(No P: moodless)

But it is obvious, that sentence mood does not stand in a one-to-one correspondence to what might be called sentence **function**. Although in many cases *I am studying* may function as a simple statement of fact, in many other cases it might function as a command or request for someone who is disturbing to go away. Although in many cases *Is that your coat on the floor?* might function as a straightforward question, in many other cases it might function as a request or command for the coat to be picked up, etc. So how do speakers know which function utterances have on various occasions?

Searle begins by drawing a distinction between the **speaker's utterance meaning** or **speaker meaning**, on the one hand, and **sentence meaning** on the other hand. In hints, insinuations, irony, metaphor, and what Searle calls indirect speech acts, these two types of meaning 'come apart' in a variety of ways (Searle 1979, p. 122).

- In a literal utterance, a speaker means exactly the same as the sentence means, so speaker meaning and sentence meaning coincide.
- In a simple metaphorical utterance, a speaker says that S is P but means metaphorically that S is R. This utterance meaning is worked out on the basis of the sentence meaning.
- In an open-ended metaphorical utterance, a speaker says that S is P, but means metaphorically an infinite range of meanings, $R_1–R_n$, and again, these meanings can be worked out on the basis of the sentence meaning.
- In a dead metaphor, the original sentence meaning is bypassed and the utterance has the meaning that used to be its metaphorical meaning.
- In an ironical utterance, a speaker means the opposite of what the sentence means. So the utterance meaning is worked out by deciding what the sentence meaning is and what its opposite is.

In an **indirect speech act**, which is what concerns us here, a speaker means what s/he says *but means something else as well*, so that the utterance meaning *includes the sentence meaning but extends beyond it*. So in the case of an indirect speech act, the speaker means what the sentence means but something else as well. So a sentence containing an illocutionary force indicator for one particular type of illocutionary act can be used to perform that act and simultaneously, in addition, another act of a different type. Such speech acts have two illocutionary forces.

For a hearer to grasp both these forces at once, s/he must (1) know the rules for performing speech acts; (2) share some background information with the speaker; (3) exercise her or his powers of rationality and inference in general; (4) have knowledge of certain general principles of cooperative conversation (see PRAGMATICS and Grice, 1975).

Searle provides an example of how speakers cope with indirect speech acts:

(1) Student X: *Let's go to the movies tonight*
(2) Student Y: *I have to study for an exam*

Let's in (1) indicates that a speech act which we might call a **proposal** is being made. Example (2) is a **statement**, but in this context it is clear that it functions as the speech act **rejection of the proposal**. Searle calls the rejection of the proposal the **primary illocutionary act** performed by Y, and says that Y performs it *by way of* the **secondary illocutionary act**, namely the statement. The secondary illocutionary act conforms to the literal meaning of the utterance, so it is a **literal act**; but the primary illocutionary act is **non-literal**. Given that X only actually hears the literal act, but recognizes the non-literal, primary illocutionary act, how does s/he arrive at this latter recognition on the basis of the recognition of the literal, secondary illocutionary act?

Searle proposes that X goes through the following ten steps of reasoning:

Step 1:   I have made a proposal to Y, and in response he has made a statement to

Step 2: I assume that Y is cooperating in the conversation and that therefore his remark is intended to be relevant.

Step 3: A relevant response would be one of acceptance, rejection, counterproposal, further discussion, etc.

Step 4: But his literal utterance was not one of these, and so was not a relevant response.

Step 5: Therefore, he probably means more than he says. Assuming that his remark is relevant, his primary illocutionary point must differ from his literal one.

Step 6: I know that studying for an exam normally takes a large amount of time relative to a single evening, and I know that going to the movies normally takes a large amount of time relative to a single evening.

Step 7: Therefore, he probably cannot both go to the movies and study for an exam in one evening.

Step 8: A preparatory condition on the acceptance of a proposal, or any other commissive, is the ability to perform the act predicated in the propositional content condition.

Step 9: Therefore, I know that he has said something that has the consequence that he probably cannot accept the proposal.

Step 10: Therefore his primary illocutionary point is probably to reject the proposal.

As step 8 indicates, knowing the rules for speech acts enables one to recognize that a literal, secondary illocutionary act somehow contains reference within it to a condition for another speech act; and this will be the speech act which is the primary, non-literal illocutionary act performed by the speaker.

For instance, the rules (derived from conditions) for the speech act **request** are (1969, p. 66):

Propositional content	Future act A of H.

Preparatory 1. H is able to do A. S believes H is able to do A.
2. It is not obvious to both S and H that H will do A in the normal course of events of his own accord.

Sincerity   S wants H to do A.

Essential   Counts as an attempt to get H to do A.

Comment: *Order* and *command* have the additional preparatory rule that S must be in a position of authority over H . . .

Consequently, there is a set of groups of sentences that correspond to these rules, 'that could quite standardly be used to make indirect requests and other directives such as orders' (1969, p. 64). The groups are (I am leaving out many of Searle's example sentences; see ibid., pp. 65–7):

Group 1: Sentences concerning H's ability to perform A: *Can you pass/reach the salt*.

Group 2: Sentences concerning S's wish or want that H will do A: *I would like you to go now; I wish you wouldn't do that*.

Group 3: Sentences concerning H's doing A: *Officers will henceforth wear ties at dinner; Aren't you going to eat your cereal?*

Group 4: Sentences concerning H's desire or willingness to do A: *Would you be willing to write a letter of recommendation for me?; Do you want to hand me that hammer over there on the table?*

Group 5: Sentences concerning reasons for doing A: *It would be a good idea if you left town; Why don't you try it just once?*

Group 6: Sentences embedding one of these elements inside another; also sentences embedding an explicit directive illocutionary verb inside one of these contexts: *Would you mind awfully if I asked you if you could write me a letter of recommendation?*

That anyone should want to use an indirect rather than a direct speech act is due to considerations of politeness: by prefacing an utterance with, for example, *can you*, as in the case of indirect requests, the speaker is not making presumptions about the hearer's capabilities, and is also clearly offering the hearer the option of refusing the request, since a yes/no question like *Can you pass the salt?* allows for *no* as an answer. Politeness is one of the topics studied in pragmatics (see PRAGMATICS), a discipline that has drawn heavily on insights provided by speech-act theorists like Searle and Austin.

K.M.

SUGGESTIONS FOR FURTHER READING

Austin, J.L. (1971), 'Performative–Constative', in J.R. Searle (ed.), *The Philosophy of Language*, Oxford, Oxford University Press, pp. 13–23.
Searle, J.R. (1971), 'What is a speech act', in J.R. Searle (ed.), *The Philosophy of Language*, Oxford, Oxford University Press, pp. 39–54.

Speech therapy

DEFINITION

Speech therapy is the British label for the activities of an independent profession whose members are concerned with the diagnosis, assessment, treatment, and management of a wide range of disorders of communication which affect people from infancy to senescence. The prime interest is with disorders of spoken language, but the profession is also concerned with disorders of written language, especially in adults. Written language in children is usually seen as the responsibility of the teaching profession, but there is often an overlap of interests.

Speech therapy is a comparatively young profession, developed in the twentieth century. Similar professions exist in a number of countries, although there are some differences in their spheres of responsibilities as reflected in their different titles: for example **speech pathologists** in the USA, Australia, New Zealand, and the Republic of South Africa; **logopedists**, **phoniatrists**, and **orthophonists** in various European countries. Elsewhere in the world, e.g. Hong Kong, professions are developing where previously the country had relied on speech therapists trained abroad. Reciprocal recognition of professional qualifications is limited between countries, although there is a growing exchange of research and therapeutic techniques internationally between practitioners. The profession's international society, the **International Association of Logopedics and Phoniatrics**, was founded in 1924.

HISTORICAL BACKGROUND

At the turn of the century there was an increase in the study, interest, and knowledge of human behaviour, including speech, and a paralleled expansion of knowledge in the medical sciences. For example work by neuroanatomists such as Broca and Wernicke in Europe and Jackson in the United Kingdom, confirmed the relationship between cortical damage and acquired language disorders (see APHASIA and LANGUAGE PATHOLOGY AND NEUROLINGUISTICS). The original theories of speech therapy were based on such contemporary studies of neurology and the developing disciplines of phonetics, psychology, and a tradition of education (Quirk, 1972). In the early years of the twentieth century, increased sophistication in neurological studies had established a relationship between areas of cortical damage and aphasia. A framework for describing some of the components of such disorders evolved, but at that time the physicians and neurologists who were interested in speech disorders felt unable to explore methods of remediation and turned to the teachers of voice, elocution, and singing for help. These early interventionists, realizing their lack of scientific knowledge, sought help from eminent members of the medical and allied professions, and accumulated a relevant body of information which they were able to pass on to their own personal students.

Parallel to this development in medicine there was a growing interest in speech disorders in children which arose from educationalists specializing in remedial education. The first speech-therapy clinic for children was established in Manchester in 1906 and offered training for stammerers. This was followed by similar clinics elsewhere; in 1911 the first clinic for adults was established at St Bartholomew's Hospital, London, and in 1913 a second clinic opened at St Thomas's Hospital, London. In 1919 the Central School of Speech and Drama, London, in association with the clinic at St Thomas's, started a course for training speech therapists. Other courses were started in Scotland and in London.

During the 1930s there were two professional associations of speech therapists, one which represented the medical background, and one which was associated with the teachers of voice and elocution. These two associations, which reflected the two main roots of the profession, were amalgamated in 1945 to form the **College of Speech Therapists**. Speech therapy continues to be closely associated with medicine and education both in terms of employment and in the two main approaches to categorizing the range of disorders which are assessed and treated (See LANGUAGE PATHOLOGY AND NEUROLINGUISTICS).

Since 1975 the profession has been unified under the National Health Service. This followed the recommendations of the **Report of the Committee of Enquiry into the Speech Therapy Services** which, under the chairmanship of Randolph Quirk, was published in 1972. Prior to this time, speech therapists had been employed both by educational and health authorities.

TRAINING AND PROFESSIONAL BODY

Since 1985, entry into the profession in the United Kingdom is through a three- or four-year degree course at university or polytechnic college. All degree courses leading to a qualification in speech therapy are accredited by the College of Speech Therapists, which is responsible to the Secretary of State for Health and Social Services and to the Secretary of State for Scotland for ensuring that every graduate who is certified to practise as a speech therapist has reached the required levels of knowledge, expertise, and competence. The components of each degree course vary in emphasis, but all courses will contain the following subjects: neurology, anatomy and physiology, psychology, education, linguistics, phonetics, audiology, speech and language pathology (see LANGUAGE PATHOLOGY AND NEUROLINGUISTICS). All degree courses also contain a large component of clinical practice. The study of the disorders of communication is based on the study of normal speech and language from development in childhood to decay in the elderly.

PLACES OF WORK

In 1986 there was the equivalent of approximately two and a half to three thousand full-time speech therapists in posts in England and Wales, the large majority of whom are women. In the USA there are currently 41,000 members of the **American Speech, Language and Hearing Association (ASHA)** of whom approximately 70 per cent are practising clinicians. As in the United Kingdom, most American speech therapists are women. Most speech therapists practise in local-authority health clinics, schools, or hospitals. Some are employed by charitable bodies concerned with handicapped children and an increasing number work in specialized units, for example with physically or mentally impaired adults and children, or with those with hearing impairments. There are also units offering intensive rehabilitation to injured adults, mentally handicapped, and disturbed children.

Speech therapists work closely with a number of other professions, including medical specialists, nurses, other medical therapists, psychologists, teachers, social workers, and linguists. They are often part of a rehabilitation team. In all positions, the speech therapist remains ultimately responsible for the assessment, treatment, and management of the disorder of communication, although in cases which are secondary to disease or injury, a doctor will usually retain overall responsibility for patient care.

RANGE OF INTEREST

Communicative disorders may result from abnormalities of the production or resonance of voice, the fluency of language, language production, including the articulation of speech sounds, or they may arise from defects of the monitoring system at any level of production. Disorders at any of these levels can have a number of causes; they may be secondary to trauma, illness, or degenerative processes, for example acquired disorders of language such as aphasia and dysarthria; associated with structural abnormalities such as cleft palate; associated with abnormal developmental patterns, for example delayed language or phonological development; secondary to or associated with other defects, for example hearing loss or gross mental retardation; arise from environmental damage, for example aphonia, loss of voice, or dysphonia, abnormal voice; or they may be idiopathic, as in stuttering.

A significant number of people in the United Kingdom suffer from some type of communicative disorder. It has been estimated that approximately 800,000 people suffer from communication disorders where little or no spontaneous speech is possible and a further 1.5 million have speech or language which is noticeably disordered (Enderby and Philip, 1986). Some of these disorders can be alleviated and require remediation, others are chronic and require management and perhaps counselling. The speech therapist is responsible for assessing all those with communication disorders and selecting the appropriate treatment and/or management programme.

RANGE OF DISORDERS

DISORDERS OF VOICE

Disorders of voice such as **aphonia**, total absence of sound, or **dysphonia**, abnormal sound, may arise from organic causes such as growths on, or thickening of, the vocal folds, hormonal imbalance, damage to the laryngeal nerves, or vocal abuse, or they may arise from idiopathic, unknown, causes. Cases of unknown origin are often referred to as **functional** and may be associated with stress. All cases are referred to therapy through ear, nose, and throat specialists and close contact is maintained between the speech therapist and the surgeon. Assessment of the voice quality and assumptions about the functioning of the vocal folds are made after listening to the voice and, depending on availability, instrumental investigations. Such investigations may include **electroglottography**, which provides information on vocal-fold activity, airflow, and pressure measurements, and the use of visual displays of such information. Therapy is aimed at improving the quality of the voice through increasing the patient's awareness of the processes involved in voice production, encouraging optimal use of the voice, and increasing the patient's ability to monitor his or her own voice. Where stress is associated with the disorder, counselling techniques are added to the programme. Progress depends on the individual's physical and personal characteristics. In certain cases, additional assistance may be offered such as amplification of the voice, or systems to augment speech.

DISORDERS OF FLUENCY

Disorders of fluency include **disfluency**, which is associated with neurological damage, as well as those with no known cause, termed **stammering** or **stuttering**. Stammering is characterized by one or more of the following: involuntary repetition of sounds, syllables, words, and phrases; prolongation of sounds, often involving the closure phase of plosives (see ARTICULATORY PHONETICS) and associated with tension; an increase in the number of filled and unfilled pauses; and a relatively higher number of false starts, incomplete utterances, and revisions than normal. The position of each disfluency can be described in terms of the phoneme (see PHONEMICS) involved and its position within the word, tone unit, phrase, or clause. The speaker may also exhibit embarrassment or anxiety and fear certain words or communicative situations. The severity of disfluency can range from affecting more than 90 per cent of the utterances to less than 1 per cent.

Certain relationships have been observed between the occurrence of disfluency and the unit of speech involved. For example, there is some evidence that disfluency is more likely to be associated with open-class words and with stress and initial position in both words and clauses, but the exact relationship is far from clear. The complexity of the unit of language involved is also thought to exert an influence. There is a large amount of individual variation, and it may be that several different disorders with varying characteristics and arising from different causes are all being referred to as stammering; however, there is no agreement on where causal or symptomatic boundaries might be drawn. Many stammerers experience fluctuating periods of fluency or have fluency behaviour associated with specific situations or environments.

Most stammerers are able to increase their fluency with techniques taught by speech therapists, although the maintenance of fluency is often difficult. Discussion of the stammerer's perception of him or herself and his or her speech forms an important component of most programmes. The main influence on approaches to treatment are from psychology (see, for example, Ingham, 1984). There has been a limited influence from linguistics, although the discipline of phonetics is becoming increasingly influential with the expanding availability of instrumental measurement of speech production.

DISORDERS OF LANGUAGE

Disorders of language may be acquired as the result of disease or injury; associated with other major deficits in, e.g., hearing or cognition; or, as in developmental disorders, occur when the child fails to develop language according to expectations, notwithstanding normal development in other areas. The term **language disorder** is used as a broad category to include failure to develop, impairment, or loss of any level of language production and includes understanding of language (see also LANGUAGE PATHOLOGY AND NEUROLINGUISTICS). Developmental language disorders in children will be considered first.

Children may fail to develop age-appropriate syntax, phonology, lexicon, or pragmatics or may fail to develop the expected understanding of language while demonstrating other nonverbal cognitive skills. The extent of delay varies. For some children the delay may be slight and quickly resolved, for others the delay may also affect written language and problems with reading and/or spelling may persist for many years, while for yet other children the gap between their expected and actual linguistic abilities is so severe as to prevent them from benefitting from mainstream education. There is limited special educational provision for this small group of handicapped children in the United Kingdom, but in the USA these children are more likely to be integrated into mainstream education.

From time to time efforts are made to distinguish 'delayed' speech from 'deviant' speech. In practice, speech may resemble that of a younger child in terms of grammatical structures and the repertoire of sounds used, but there are very often differences that arise from the child's greater experience of the world and the influence of other aspects of development. There may also be differences in language use. Certain categories of handicapped children may produce characteristic speech that is both qualitatively and quantitatively different, for example psychiatrically disturbed children, but there seems to be little evidence that this is common for other categories of handicap, e.g. mental handicap.

Although the various levels of language are interdependent and the boundaries between, for example, syntax and phonology are fuzzy, the production of speech sounds is often considered separately. Some children are slower than their peers to develop a complete repertoire of phonemes and some of this group seem to have difficulty in controlling accurate movement and timing of the supraglottal (see ARTICULATORY PHONETICS) musculature despite the lack of frank neurological impairment. Errors may be at the phonetic level and fluency and vocal quality might also be impaired, although these factors are more usually considered to be characteristic of dysarthria (see below). For this particular group of children, therapy is directed at increasing the child's muscular control and ability to sequence sounds, rather than explaining or expanding the rule-governed behaviour of phonology and syntax. These disorders are known either as **articulation disorders** or as **articulatory dyspraxia**. The choice of terms seems to be related to the perceived severity of the disorder, as well as to success in therapy, the first term applying to less severe disorders.

Children with frank neurological impairments involving the central nervous system, frequently have disorders of speech arising from impaired muscle movement and control. These speech disorders are known as **dysarthrias** and are traditionally subdivided according to the site of the neurological lesion. Such children often have language disorders as well, either arising from damage to the cortical area (see APHASIA) or from a reduction in normal developmental stimulus and experience. Abnormal vocal quality and poor control of fluency are frequent in these conditions. In addition, because the neurological and anatomical structures used in speech are the same structures involved in feeding, these children often have disordered feeding patterns. Because of the close relationship between speech and feeding and because the speech therapist often has a uniquely detailed knowledge of the anatomy and neurology of this region, he or she

is often involved in programmes to improve feeding skills.

The speech therapist's assessment of language disorders is based on his or her knowledge of the major subjects of the qualifying degree course, including knowledge of normal development. Medical, sociological, and educational factors are considered as well as a characterization of the child's linguistic abilities. Studies in linguistics, including child language acquisition (see LAN-GUAGE ACQUISITION), as well as psycholinguistics (see PSYCHOLINGUISTICS) have contributed to the range of assessment procedures available and to the subsequent treatment programme that will be formulated. Two examples of assessment are **LARSP** (Crystal *et al.*, 1976), which offers a description of the child's surface grammar, and **TROG** (Bishop, 1982), which enables the speech therapist to examine the child's understanding of certain grammatical structures.

Having characterized the child's speech, the speech therapist strives to teach or encourage or enhance development, often in conjunction with parents and teachers. For the child to reach age-appropriate levels of language, it is necessary for accelerated development to take place. Progress is often slow, intervention taking place over months rather than weeks.

Following the Education Act 1981, speech therapists have an increasing involvement with mentally handicapped children, many of whom have a language delay over and above the delay that would be predicted from their mental age. The process of characterizing their language is the same as that for normally developing children. For these children, however, it is more appropriate to aim for language that is commensurate with mental rather than chronological age.

Disorders of language in adults arise from diseases or injury (see APHASIA) although the developmental disorders described above can persist into adulthood. Acquired disorders of language are usually considered under the two main categories of **aphasia** and **dysarthria**: **dys-** or **apraxia** nearly always occurs with aphasia. Aphasia or dysphasia (see APHASIA) is a disorder of language arising from damage to the cortex of the brain. Dysarthria is a disorder of sound production which arises from damage to the central nervous system and which can affect production at all levels: air supply, vocal-fold activity, supraglottal musculature including control of resonance. In addition, suprasegmental features of timing, stress, and prosody are often involved.

The distinction between these two levels of language is justified in terms of focus of treatment, although theoretically, and clinically in some cases, the boundaries are less clear.

Treatment of dysarthria is aimed at helping the patient make optimal use of residual skills, increasing self-monitoring of speech, teaching strategies to enhance intelligibility, and advising and providing augmentive or alternative means of communication. Aphasia therapy is aimed at other levels of language – phonology, syntax, semantics, and pragmatics – and aims to increase the patient's production and understanding of both written and spoken language. As in all speech therapy, intervention starts with an assessment of the patient's medical and social background as well as a full description of the language problem. Most of the dysarthric and aphasic patients seen by the speech therapist will have other medical problems, which, with the language problem, are secondary to the injury or disease. Thus the speech therapist working with these patients is usually part of a medical team and collaborates with other medical personnel.

Aphasia therapy reflects the major strands of aphasiology, neurology, psychology and, to a much lesser extent, linguistics. Approaches also reflect the underlying theories concerned with aphasia. For example, a **unitary** view of aphasia is associated with therapy which aims to stimulate language activity but does not select any level or process for particular attention. A more systematic approach which focuses on components of language behaviour arises from the detailed psychoneurological approach initiated in the USSR by A.R. Luria (see, for instance, Luria, 1970). A more recent detailed approach has been pioneered in the United Kingdom following investigations by psychologists and speech therapists who, by series of individually designed tasks, seek to pinpoint which levels, using models of dynamic speech production, are most impaired by the aphasia (Newman and Epstein, 1985). In all approaches both written and spoken language will be used. The prime concern of the therapist will be the individual's present and future need for language and it is also appropriate to consider the patient's social and emotional needs as well as those of his or her carers.

Dyspraxia of speech is often interpreted as a disorder which lies between the planning processes of language and the execution of speech production (Miller, 1986). In most cases it is concomitant with aphasia, which makes the extent of the linguistic influences on this disorder difficult to define. Clinically, exercises aimed at improving muscle strength and co-ordination often seem inappropriate despite the characteristic phonetic distortions which may resemble certain dysarthrias. Treatment strategies include a detailed approach to forming individual sounds; focusing on sequencing sounds within words; using context and linguistic contrast; and supplementing spoken with written language.

A third category of language disorders in adults is that associated with dementia. The speech therapist is most often asked to help in the differential diagnosis of aphasia and dementia in the elderly and to advise in the subsequent management of such cases, but in a population which has an increasing number of elderly and old citizens, this category is likely to make increasingly heavy demands on speech therapy.

S.E.

SUGGESTIONS FOR FURTHER READING

Crystal, D. (1980), *Introduction to Language Pathology*, London, Edward Arnold.

Davis, A.C. (1983), *A Survey of Adult Aphasia*, Englewood Cliff, NJ, Prentice Hall.

Stratificational syntax

STRATIFICATIONAL THEORY

Understood in its broadest sense, the term **stratificational linguistics** can be applied to any view of the structure of language which apportions such structure into two or more layers of organization, the strata. In practice, however, the term has commonly been applied to the outgrowth of ideas originated in the late 1950s and early 1960s by Sydney M. Lamb and H.A. Gleason, Jr.

Lamb's version originated as an elaboration of the theory of levels in neo-Bloomfieldian linguistics. Its first appearance was in Lamb's dissertation, a grammar of the California Amerindian language Monachi, presented at the University of California, Berkeley, in 1957. The initial idea was refined during subsequent years when Lamb was directing a project on machine translation at Berkeley.

By 1964, when Lamb joined the faculty of Yale University, he had become aware that Gleason, then at the Hartford Seminary Foundation, had been developing a broadly similar model. As a result of a degree of collaboration and interchange, the views of the two came to converge in their rough outlines, though they were never completely unified.

At about the time of his move to Yale, Lamb began to develop a unified notation as an adjunct to his theory. From this work there emerged a view that linguistic structure consists entirely of configurations of a few basic relationships. One of these was named the **AND** – the syntagmatic relation occurring, for instance, when an idiom such as *kick the bucket*, 'die', is seen as being made up of smaller elements *kick*, *the*, and *bucket* in combination. Another was named the **OR** – the paradigmatic relation evident, for example, when we enumerate the set of alternative suffixes compatible with such a verb stem as *walk*,

including *-s*, *-ed*, and *-ing*. Lamb soon began to use a notation depicting such basic relations for all of linguistic structure. At the same time, he came to accept the idea that linguistic structure consists not of items with relationships between them, as he once believed, but of relationships alone, interconnecting in a network. Since a similar idea had been asserted in the glossematic theory of Louis Hjelmslev (see GLOSSEMATICS), Lamb came to see Hjelmslev's work as a precursor of his own.

Soon afterwards, Lamb came to consider the relational-network structure of language as more essential to his view than the idea of stratification, which he treated as deriving from a confrontation of the relational view with linguistic data. This notion was not shared by Gleason, however, nor by all of those who had based their work on Lamb's model. Since about 1965 the term **Relational Network Grammar** has been applicable to the work of Lamb and some of his followers, particularly Peter A. Reich, who especially favoured this term, but also William J. Sullivan, David G. Lockwood, and others. The separate term **stratificational** is still needed, however, to apply to the work of Gleason and his students, and others such as Ilah Fleming, who has drawn from both Lamb and Gleason, as well as from other sources.

Unless otherwise indicated, the present discussion deals with the 'standard' model of stratificational theory. This view, based on Lamb's ideas of the 1970–1 period, was incorporated in Lockwood 1972. This model treats language as a relational network organized into four primary **stratal systems** and two peripheral, and probably extralinguistic, systems.

Each of the primary stratal systems has a **tactic pattern** specifying the arrangements of its units and a **realizational portion** relating these units to adjacent systems. The four systems are (1) the **sememic stratal system**, dealing essentially with the linguistic organization of meanings; (2) the **lexemic stratal system**, dealing with the internal relations of phrases, clauses, and sentences; (3) the **morphemic stratal system**, dealing with the internal structure of grammatical words; and (4) the **phonemic stratal system**, treating classical morphophonemic relations, but with a componential representation comparable to classical phonemics at its lowest level (see MORPHOLOGY and PHONEMICS).

Like the primary systems, the peripheral systems are seen as relational networks, but the organization of tactic and realizational portions appears not to be as strictly defined in these systems as in the primary ones. These systems serve as a bridge between language proper and the extralinguistic world. Bordering on the sememic system is the **gnostemic** or **conceptual** system, representing the organization of general knowledge. Some more recent views, probably more correctly, allow this system to connect to any of the primary systems, not just to semology, in order to handle various kinds of stylistically conditioned alternations. The other peripheral system is the **phonetic**, which correlates minimal phonological units with phonetic realizations of the classically subphonemic type. This system has the ultimate task of relating to both articulatory movements and auditory impressions.

SYNTAX IN A STRATIFICATIONAL CONTEXT

Strictly speaking, the stratificational model outlined above does not have a subportion called 'syntax'. In its etymological meaning 'the study of arrangements', however, syntax corresponds to the **tactics**, and each of the primary stratal systems contains such a tactics, or tactic pattern, as part of its organization. So each of the **semotactics**, **lexotactics**, **morphotactics**, and **phonotactics** is a kind of syntax treating the arrangements of basic units of its subsystem.

The more common meaning of 'syntax' in contemporary usage, however, refers to the study of internal structure of phrases, clauses, and

sentences in terms of words. Corresponding to syntax in this sense, the standard stratificational model has the lexemic stratal system, also termed the **lexology**, and more particularly the lexotactics. The present exposition therefore focuses on the lexology.

According to some contemporary views based on other theories, however, particularly in the Chomskyan tradition (see TRANSFORMATIONAL-GENERATIVE GRAMMAR), syntax is taken to cover much of what the standard stratificational model places in the stratal systems adjacent to the lexology: the sememic stratal system or **semology** and the morphemic stratal system or **morphology**. In order to facilitate comparisons, the discussion of lexology is followed by a survey of the relation of the lexology to these surrounding subsystems.

THE TASKS OF LEXOLOGY

The most important task of the lexology in any language, specifically of the lexotactics, is to specify the arrangements of words into larger units: phrases, clauses, and sentences. In order to illustrate how this is accomplished, we may consider the following formula, which expresses, in a somewhat simplified form, the structure of the English Nominal Phrase (NP):

$$\text{NP/[PreD] Det [Enum] [M] H}_n \text{ [Q]}$$

This states that a nominal phrase consists of an optional Predeterminer ([PreD]), an obligatory Determiner (Det), an optional Enumerator ([Enum]), an optional Modifier ([M]), an obligatory Nominal Head (H_n), and an optional Qualifier ([Q]), in that order. The symbol '/' can be read here as 'may consist of', though more generally it means 'leads down to'. An optional constituent is enclosed in square brackets, while the space between symbols on the right-hand side of the formula indicates a linear order between the constituents involved.

A sample phrase containing each of the six possible constituents is *all the ten large banks in the city*. Here each position is filled by a single word except for the final Qualifier, which is manifested by a phrase, *in the city*. The example

all my Uncle John's twenty-five large books here
shows the determiner position manifested by the
possessive phrase *my Uncle John's*, the
Enumerator by a numeral phrase *twenty-five*, and
the qualifier by the simple adverb *here*.

Figure 1 helps to illustrate the latter point: its
unboxed portion represents the same information as the NP formula, translated into the
relational-network notation. The fact that the

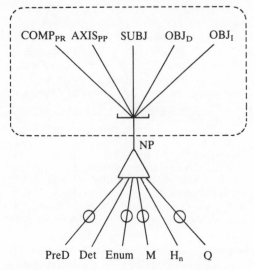

Figure 1

NP relates to the functions at the bottom is
represented by the triangular ORDERED AND
node below the NP symbol. The optionality of
four of these functions is shown by the small
circle on the line involved. In such a case, one
may either take that line or omit it. The boxed
upper portion shows some further connections of
the English NP: **Predicate Complement**
(COMP$_{PR}$), as in *These are **the three men I told
you about***; **Axis of a Prepositional Phrase**, the
traditional 'object of a preposition', (AXIS$_{PP}$), as
in *They were in **the woods***; **Subject** (SUBJ) as in
***Some dogs** were there*; **Direct Object** (OBJ$_D$) as in
*She gave them **some new books***; and **Indirect
Object** (OBJ$_I$), as in *They gave **all those boys** some
money*. The bracket-like node is an
UNORDERED OR, indicating alternatives. A
given NP may be *either* a subject *or* a direct

object, etc. – not more than one at the same time.

The point of showing this additional structure
is to emphasize that the internal label NP is just
an abbreviation for further structure and is not
independently meaningful in a relational system.
To some extent, we can show this even with
algebraic formulae. We could show the boxed
information by the additional formula:

$$COMP_{PR}, AXIS_{PP}, SUBJ, OBJ_D, OBJ_I / NP$$

where the comma represents the OR
relationship. The symbol NP then connects this
formula to the original one, and the two together
represent all the information in the diagram.
Alternatively, we can use a single formula for the
entire diagram:

$$COMP_{PR}, AXIS_{PP}, SUBJ, OBJ_D, OBJ_I / [PreD]$$
$$Det [Enum] [M] H_n [Q].$$

This latter formula represents all the information
of the diagram without actually using the NP
symbol. The choice between the alternative
formulations is a purely practical matter without
any theoretical significance.

In addition to specifying phrase, clause, and
sentence constructions in the manner of the
above example, the lexotactics is also responsible
for showing relevant subclassifications of its
units, the lexemes. In large part, such a
classification resembles a relatively finely grained
part-of-speech system, but it differs from a
traditional system (see TRADITIONAL GRAMMAR)
in providing classifications for syntactically
relevant affixes. Also, it details the interaction of
phrasal classes with lexeme classes. In the
example of the English nominal phrase, for
instance, the determiner position can be
manifested by a single lexeme like *the* or *any*, by
an inflected deictic word such as *this* (plural *these*)
or *that* (plural *those*), or by a possessive phrase
such as *Aunt Betty's*.

The latter type is best treated as a postpositional phrase with *'s* as an enclitic post-
position. This construction would be in the same
determiner class as the inflected deictics and
various uninflected words. These facts can be
shown graphically in Figure 2. This diagram,
expanding the determiner position from Figure

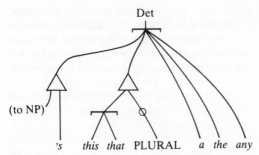

Figure 2

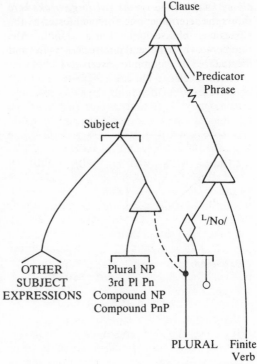

Figure 3

1, begins with a **DOWNWARD UNORDERED OR** node symbolizing the relation between the class (Det) and its members. Three of the members listed are simple elements, the lexemes *a, the, any*; another is the postpositional possessive phrase referred to above; the remaining one, covering the deictics, introduces an UNORDERED variety of AND node. This node conveys the notion that the relative order of the **plural** lexeme and its associated root is of no lexotactic consequence. Details of such ordering are left to the morphotactics. The line labelled 'to NP' loops to the nominal phrase construction via the upward OR node of Figure 1.

Beyond specifying the classes and constructions involved in phrase, clause, and sentence structures, a stratificational lexology must also deal with various sorts of congruence relations within such constructions. Such relations play a relatively minor part in modern English grammar, but are of greater importance in other languages. A fairly simple example is the concord occurring between the subject and the predicator phrase in an English clause. Essentially, a singular subject demands a singular predicator phrase, while a plural subject, such as *the rabbits* or *the cat and the dog*, demands a plural predicator phrase. A relational network treatment of these facts is sketched in Figure 3.

This diagram begins with an ordered AND for the clause. The two branches filled out represent the subject and the predicator phrase. Other parts of the clause not specified are implied by additional branches of the AND. The subject expressions are divided into those requiring plural concord – plural nominal phrases, the third-person plural pronoun, and compound nominal and pronominal phrases – and others. The occurrence of any member of the former class then leads to a dashed **conditioning line** which calls forth a plural marker on the verb.

The predicator phrase is not completely detailed – as is implied by the discontinuity in the line leading to the verb, which indicates omitted structure. Its essential part, however, is the finite verb with an accompanying number marker. These two constituents are shown under an unordered AND, the details of their order being left to the morphology. The line for the number constituent leads to a **diamond node**, a special type of node marking the intersection between the tactics and the realizational portion of a description. The upper line leads into the tactics, while the lower right one leads into the realizational portion. This diamond is labelled ^{L}/No/

for 'number lexeme'. In the realizational portion, this lexeme is shown to connect to either a plural element or to nothing via an ORDERED OR node. The latter node shows a choice, like the UNORDERED ORs shown previously, but here a choice further to the left has precedence over one further to the right when both are possible. In the present case the choice of the plural element is controlled by an **enabler node**, represented by a small shaded semicircle on the side of the line involved. This node connects to the tactics via the conditioning line mentioned above. When this conditioning line is made active by the occurrence of any kind of plural subject, the left-hand path to the plural element may be taken; otherwise only the path to the zero element, representing the unmarked singular, is possible. In this example, the precedence of the ordered OR requires one to take the plural when possible, and allows the zero alternative only when plural conditioning is not available.

This small illustration shows how a stratificational lexology handles concord and other types of syntactically conditioned alternation. This treatment, together with the specification of classes and constructions as previously illustrated, constitutes the major tasks of a lexological system.

LEXOLOGY IN RELATION TO SURROUNDING STRATAL SYSTEMS

Since the lexology does not handle all phenomena treated under 'syntax' in other models of language, a brief consideration is given here to the relation between lexology and the systems on either side of it: the morphology below it and the semology above.

The morphology deals principally with the internal properties of grammatical words, abstracting out those matters which can be handled still more generally by the phonology, including most of what is traditionally termed 'morphophonemics' (see MORPHOLOGY). In particular, there is a greater amount of linear order in the output of the morphology than in the corresponding lexological output, because inflectional elements are treated as simultaneous with their stems in the lexology, their ordering relations being irrelevant there. The morphology, on the other hand, distinguishes prefixes, suffixes, and simulfixes, and specifies linear orders among affixes where relevant. So in English the plural lexeme is shown as simultaneous with its stem, whether this be a suffix as with *trees* and *oxen* or a simultaneous element affecting the quality of a syllable nucleus, as in *feet, mice*, or *men*. The morphotactics, however, distinguishes these types tactically as well as providing conditions necessary to distinguish the regular suffixation found in *trees* from the irregular type found in *oxen*. The differences among *feet, mice*, and *men*, however, are connected to the details of the vowel nuclei of their respective singulars, and can be handled in the phonology. In short, the presence of a morphology and a phonology allows syntactically irrelevant details such as those just mentioned to be abstracted out of the syntax.

Similarly, the presence of a semology allows certain relations which might otherwise be treated as syntactic to be omitted from a lexological description. For example, it is not necessary to distinguish such apparent clause types as intransitive, transitive, and bitransitive because the event sememes involved with them must be distinguished in the semotactics according to the participant roles they can take. As a result, the three putative clause types can be collapsed into a single lexological type with optional direct object and optional indirect object. The more specific subclassification of event sememes – typically the realizates of verbs – and types of accompanying participant roles is specified by the semology and need not be repeated for the verbal and nominal phrases involved in the lexology.

Some alternative views of syntax, furthermore, include in their purview the relation of classes of verbs to various classes of nominals capable of serving as subjects and/or objects in the same clause with them, these classes involving such distinctions as concrete/abstract, animate/inanimate, and human/non-human. Such distinctions are not, on the other hand, within the domain of a stratificational lexology. They are treated in the semology, and even there provision must be made to treat them essentially as norms, capable of being violated in such contexts as fantasy stories, and not as absolutes.

Essentially, those 'syntactic' matters more easily handled in the semology of a language are treated there, while others, such as the linear order of phrasal constituents, are treated in the lexology.

RELATIONSHIP TO OTHER THEORIES

One dimension on which some views of language have been classified is based on the distinction between item-and-process (IP) and item-and-arrangement (IA) models, as discussed by Hockett (1954). From the beginning, stratificationalists have strongly rejected the IP view found in much traditional grammar and early anthropological description, which has seen its fullest elaboration in versions of the Chomskyan approach. In view of this rejection of IP, it might be thought that stratificational theory is an IA view. While this might justly be said of the earliest versions of stratificationalism, and of the continuing practice of some stratificationalists, it has not been true of Lamb's views since the mid 1960s. Lamb has pointed out that items are not essential in his theory, so it cannot be either IA or IP.

In holding a relational view, according to which such linguistic units as lexemes, sememes, and morphemes are not substantive items, but merely points in a network of relationships comprising the linguistic system, Lamb allies himself with a relational tradition in linguistic theory which, through Hjelmslev's glossematics, ultimately traces back to the views of Ferdinand de Saussure.

So the IA/IP distinction, as is indeed indicated in Hockett's discussion of it, is only a part of the picture. A more fundamental dichotomy separates relational systems from item-based ones, and the IA/IP distinction applies only within the latter group.

Lamb's refusal to use process in linguistic description is not meant to deny totally the relevance of processes in the domain of language.

It involves, rather, a recognition that true processes are undeniably relevant in certain aspects of language, but not for the description of the structure of the linguistic system. It is obviously essential to speak of processes, for instance, in the study of language change, both in a single individual (ontogeny) and for a whole speech community (phylogeny). Language use also involves processes of encoding and decoding. The linguistic system which develops as a result of processes of the second sort, is itself a relational system. The invention of pseudo-processes to describe the structure of such a system merely makes it harder to deal with the real processes when one's attention is on the aspects of language which involve them.

In more recent years, considerable attention has been focused on the distinction between formal and functional approaches to language. The formalists are those, like the Chomskyans, who rely on the supposed power of formalization to provide explanations for the facts of language, with the supposition that such formalization captures innate properties of the human brain. On the other hand, the functionalists seek to explain the facts of language by considering the way language functions in actual use, and many of them tend to neglect formalization.

The stratificational approach resembles that of the formalists in insisting on the value of a complete and explicit formalization of linguistic structure. In line with the functionalists, however, stratificationalists tend to seek explanations for language universals more in function, and function-related diachronic aspects, and less in formalism, which they treat as a foundation for explanation much more than as a source of it. Outlines of the standard stratificational models are generally non-committal on this matter, but in practice, their advocates are inclined to look predominantly to functional factors for explanations.

As already mentioned, Lamb's stratificational model evolved out of neo-Bloomfieldian structuralism with a strong influence from glossematics. It stands apart from the IA/IP dichotomy, since items are not essential for it, though it does oppose the use of processes in synchronic description. It is both a formal and a functional model, insisting on formalization of structures while still emphasizing the great importance of functional factors as sources of explanations. In its overall outlook, stratificationalism has a great deal in common with two other contemporary approaches: tagmemics and systemic grammar (see TAGMEMICS and SYSTEMIC GRAMMAR).

D.G.L.

SUGGESTIONS FOR FURTHER READING

Probably the most thorough introduction to stratificational syntax, emphasizing its interrelation to semology, is Sullivan (1980). Lockwood (1972) is an important source for the entire approach, with Chapters 4 and 5 treating

grammar and semology. Other valuable sources are Newell (1966) and various papers in Makkai and Lockwood (1973) and Copeland and Davis (1980).

The number of dissertations using the stratificational model is not large, and not all of them deal with syntax. Among those which do treat syntax and related semology in various languages are Ikegami (1970), D.C. Bennett (1975), and Coleman (1982) – all treating English – and also Vijchulata (1978) which is on Thai, and M.E. Bennett (1986) on Malagasy.

Articles on various aspects of stratificational theory are most often published in the journal *Forum Linguisticum*, published by Jupiter Press in Lake Bluff, IL and in the annual *Forum* volumes published for the Linguistic Association of Canada and the United States (LACUS) since 1974 by Hornbeam Press in Columbia, SC.

Structuralist linguistics

This article deals only with the tradition in linguistics founded by the Swiss linguist Ferdinand de Saussure (1857–1913). For information on the American tradition of structuralist linguistics, see (POST)-BLOOMFIELDIAN AMERICAN STRUCTURAL GRAMMAR.

Saussure is often described as the founder of modern linguistics, because it was he who first turned European linguistics away from its exclusive occupation with historical explanations of linguistic phenomena towards descriptions of the structure of language at a particular point in time. His famous *Course in General Linguistics* (1916) was not, in fact, published during his lifetime, but was put together by two of his colleagues, Charles Bally and Albert Sechehaye, from the lecture notes of students who followed the three courses in general linguistics that Saussure taught at the University

of Geneva between 1906 and 1911.

The nineteenth century is renowned for its occupation with historical explanation, its **historicism**. In linguistics, historicism was evident in the view shared by most researchers that the only valid explanation in the field was historical; languages are as they are because, over time, they have been subject to various internal and external causal factors affecting sound, syntax, and lexis. Therefore, linguists saw their task as consisting mainly of the comparison of Indo-European languages and, on the basis of such comparison, of discovering the principles guiding the changes undergone by the languages (see HISTORICAL LINGUISTICS).

Saussure does not claim that such historical, or **diachronic**, studies of the evolution of languages are worthless; he merely maintains that they should be kept apart from, and should not preclude, **synchronic** language studies aimed at describing a language as a whole at a particular point in time. Mixing the two is bound to mislead: the fact that the French for 'step', *pas*, and the French negative adverb, also *pas*, have the same origin is of no importance whatsoever to present-day users of French; the historical relationship between the two terms is of no consequence for the way in which each functions in the system now. Similarly, the fact that *ought* is an old past-tense form of *owe* in English should not be used as an explanatory feature in any account of how *ought* is used in present-day English. The distinction between synchronic and diachronic language study is the first of the four famous Saussurean dichotomies.

The language as it exists at a particular time is described as a system, which Saussure calls **la langue**. Langue is the underlying system on the basis of which speakers are able to understand and produce speech, and it forms a second dichotomy with **parole**, the actual utterances speakers produce. However, no speaker has complete command of langue, which only exists fully as a shared, social phenomenon. It is thus not the same notion as Chomsky's competence – although had Saussure wished to posit an ideal speaker, as Chomsky does, then that speaker would presumably have had a complete command of langue. Parole, on the other hand, is always an individual realization of the system. The distinction between langue and parole is a second dichotomy, although actually, langue and parole form a trichotomy with **langage**, which is the faculty of speech which all humans are endowed with.

The language system is seen as a system of signs. By **sign**, Saussure means *the relationship between* a concept, the **signified**, and some acoustic noise or graphic form which stands for the concept, namely the **signifier**. The bond between the signified and the signifier is absolutely arbitrary, as is shown by the existence of more than one language in the world: the concept 'tree' is signified in English by *tree*, in German by *Baum*, and so on, and no signifier is any more appropriate than any other (of course, once a signifier for a particular concept has been established within a community, speakers have to abide by it; the sign relation is only arbitrary in principle; speakers cannot go around renaming concepts at will – at least not if they want to be understood by other speakers; there is, as Saussure puts it, a type of contract in operation in a society by virtue of which langue exists, and which binds speakers to rely on it when engaging in parole). The signs in the language system are interdependent. Each sign has a **value**, by which Saussure means something very like meaning, and each sign has the value it has just because this is the value that all of the other signs have not got.

The signs in the language system are related to each other in two ways: there are rules for their combination, and there are contrasts and similarities between them. These two dimensions of language, combination and contrast/similarity, are commonly illustrated diagrammatically as two axes, the **syntagmatic** and the **paradigmatic**:

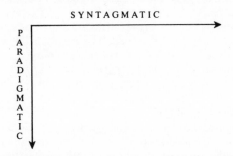

On the syntagmatic axis, words are linked, or chained, together according to grammatical rules, but we make choices about which words to link together on the paradigmatic axis, the axis of choice. The relationship a given sign has with those with which it is combined on the syntagmatic axis is evident in any given sentence, any instance of parole. But it is, at the same time, related to all those other signs in the system that is langue which *could* have taken its place but did not. It might now appear open to the linguist to concentrate either on parole, deriving statistical statements about frequency of occurrence, or to concentrate on the underlying system; however, it is fairly obvious that the two studies must be interdependent. It is not possible to make any important claims about a linguistic item derived from a frequency study without considering its place within the system, because the frequency of one item's occurrence can only have any significance when compared to the frequency of others in the system. And the system itself is only accessible through the study of instances of its realization, through parole.

Saussure's linguistic theory had a profound influence on the linguists of the Prague School (see FUNCTIONALIST LINGUISTICS), the Copenhagen School (see GLOSSEMATICS), and the London School (see SCALE AND CATEGORY GRAMMAR, SYSTEMIC GRAMMAR and FUNCTIONAL GRAMMAR), and the emphasis on the structure of the language system has remained a powerful influence on most linguistic theories after Saussure. In addition, structuralism in general and Saussure's insights about language in particular have profoundly influenced twentieth-century literary and social criticism. Both of these disciplines have taken very seriously the structuralist position that sign systems are shared, social phenomena, not provided, but constructed by a community, and the concomitant notion that they might have been otherwise than they are – and that not every system is structured like every other system. It is evident that the signs of different languages do not correspond to each other in a one-to-one relationship; but if every sign in a system derives its values from its difference from the other signs in that system, then it follows that the values of the signs in one system cannot correspond to those of the signs in another system. And since sign systems do change over time, it follows, for example, that the significance of works of literature must be reassessed – will inevitably be reinterpreted – with each successive generation, or even with each successive reading. Considerations of this nature have influenced, for instance, critics who have reacted against the realist critical tradition, including writers such as Barthes, Lacan, Althusser, and Derrida (see further Belsey, 1980).

K.M.

SUGGESTIONS FOR FURTHER READING

Lepschy, G.C. (1982), *A Survey of Structural Linguistics*, London, André Deutsch.
Saussure, F. de (1916/74), *Cours de linguistique générale*, Lausanne; translated as *Course in General Linguistics*, Glasgow, Fontana/Collin.

Stylistics

Stylistics is the study of style in spoken and written text. By **style** is meant a consistent occurrence in the text of certain items and structures, or types of items and structures, among those offered by the language as a whole.

A full stylistic analysis of a given spoken or written text would describe the text at all the traditional levels of linguistic description, i.e. sound, form, structure, and meaning, but it will not typically look at patterns created by long stretches of text (see DISCOURSE AND CONVERSATIONAL ANALYSIS and TEXT LINGUISTICS). In stylistic analysis, items and structures are isolated and described using terminology and descriptive frameworks drawn from whatever school of descriptive linguistics the stylistician subscribes to or finds most useful for a given purpose. The overall purpose, of course, will also vary according to the linguistic affiliations of the stylistician. For instance, to linguists of the

London School (see FUNCTIONALIST LINGUIST-ICS), the immediate goal of stylistic analysis 'is to show why and how the text means what it does' (Halliday, 1983, p. x).

The texts studied may be those produced in a certain period of time (texts in medieval English), or by a certain group of language users (people who write newspaper editorials), or by individuals (Wordsworth), and the purposes of the analyses range from the purely descriptive ('the verbal groups in scientific texts tend to be in the passive voice') through the explanatory ('scientists use the passive because they are describing universal processes which are independent of the individual scientist') to the interpretive ('by using the passive, scientists absolve themselves from any responsibility for their actions').

Stylistic analysis can be used as supporting evidence in law courts ('this cannot be a verbatim report of what the accused said; it conflicts with the person's normal patterns of language use'), and as an aid to deciding authorship of unascribed manuscripts. It is an important component of sociolinguistic surveys and it can be an important teaching aid (see, for instance, Widdowson, 1975; Carter and Burton, 1982; Davies and Greene, 1984); people who need to learn to write or speak in a particular style will benefit from becoming conscious of which linguistic devices realize the style in question. For instance, in the teaching of English for Specific Purposes, one of the things that are useful to do is to show people that particular types of texts have particular structures and conventions, and that stages of argument and evaluation as opposed to statement of fact, for example, tend to be fairly subtly signalled by linguistic devices of various sorts (see also GENRE ANALYSIS and TEXT LINGUISTICS). Knowledge of this kind can enhance understanding of the text and aid composition. Similarly, actors can benefit from becoming aware of the linguistic characteristics of those accents, dialects, and styles which they may have to adopt in order to represent characters.

Stylisticians may be also be interested in discovering the defining features of different genres of spoken and written texts (though see also GENRE ANALYSIS), and the major distinction drawn here is traditionally between literary and non-literary texts. There is a consequent major traditional division between literary and non-literary stylistics, although as Halliday (1983, p. viii) among others points out, there is no feature found in a literary text which is not also found in non-literary texts. The distinction between what is literary and what is not is often questioned (see, for instance, Eagleton, 1983), but it is possible to maintain it in purely practical terms: there are some texts that become literature by being attended to in the special way which involves among other things their inclusion in courses on literature and subsequent special treatment, including special attention to their language. It can then be argued that non-literary stylistics differs from literary stylistics simply in that in the case of the former, the texts which are being given the type of attention typically given only to literary texts are not, in fact, normally classed as literary texts. But basically, any text is open to stylistic analysis.

The methods and aims of the non-literary stylistician are the same as those of the literary stylistician, but non-literary stylistics may be seen as derivative, in so far as modern stylistics as a whole has developed from an interest in what is special about the way language is used in literary texts and from a belief that literary language does differ from non-literary language, at least in terms of its function. For example, Sebeok 1960, is a record of an *interdisciplinary* conference on style held at Indiana University, Bloomington, USA, in 1958 in the hope that 'a clearer perception of what *literature* is and what the constituent elements of style are' might result (foreword by John W. Ashton, p. v; italics added); Chatman 1971 arises from a symposium on literary style which was originally intended as a follow-up to the Indiana conference, but which, in the end, concentrated on literary style alone (see further the discussion of **foregrounding** below).

Textual genres studied in non-literary stylistics include advertisements (Leech, 1966; Vestergaard and Schrøder, 1986), political speeches and writings (Carter, 1963; Chilton, 1982), and other texts related to a particular sector of the social organization. Aspects of this type of stylistic analysis also enter into what Swales (1981) dubbed genre analysis, although here, as in discourse and conversational analysis and text linguistics the emphasis tends to be on supra-sentential structural features (see GENRE ANALYSIS).

Typically, writers on critical linguistics (see CRITICAL LINGUISTICS) make extensive references to stylistic features of the texts they are working with. For instance, a critical linguist may make a stylistic analysis of a political pamphlet which would reveal large numbers of occurrences of questions of the form 'Why do we need x'; this much constitutes pure stylistic analysis. He or she will then bring into the analysis an explanatory element by suggesting that the choice of this question form is motivated by the writer's desire to convince readers that our need for x is a foregone conclusion. The final step which turns the work into critical linguistics might be a claim that this wish on the writer's part reflects his or her ideology (see Chilton, 1982).

Claims about the relative frequency of elements in, on the one hand, the language as a whole and, on the other hand, a particular text or groups of texts, clearly imply that both have been subjected to some form of statistical analysis, and the tradition of using statistical analysis in the study of text has been with us for a long time:

> The beginning of the statistical study of style in modern times is commonly dated to 1851 when Augustus de Morgan suggested that disputes about the authenticity of some of the writings of St Paul might be settled by the measurement of the length, measured in letters, of the words used in the various Epistles. The first person actually to test the hypothesis that word-length might be a distinguishing char-acteristic of writers was an American geophysicist called T.C. Mendenhall, who expounded his idea in a popular journal, *Science*, in 1887. . . . Mendenhall took several authors and constructed their . . . frequency distributions of word-length.
>
> (Kenny, 1982, p. 1)

With the development of computer technology and the collection of large corpora of text (see CORPORA), statements about relative frequency of various linguistic items have become relatively accurate, and are used for a variety of purposes, including EFL text-book writing as well as the establishment of authorship and interpretive stylistics.

The interpretive element which tends to turn non-literary stylistic analysis into critical lin-guistics is a major component of much literary stylistics. For, although it is clearly possible to direct the stylistic study of a literary text solely towards the establishment of those linguistic features which characterize a writer, literary genre, or period, it is far more common to view literary stylistics as 'an extension of practical criticism' (Cluysenaar, 1976, p. 7) – as an interface between literary studies and linguistics.

An interesting debate about the value of linguistics to literary study was conducted between Roger Fowler (1967, 1968) and F.W. Bateson (1967); it is reprinted in Fowler (1971). The point of view generally adopted by people favourably disposed towards stylistics is that from the literary theorist's or critic's point of view, literary stylistics is valuable in that it affords a vocabulary for talking about those intersubjectively observable linguistic features of the text which prompt individual responses, thus providing a degree of objectivity which literary criticism sometimes lacks (see Richards, 1960; Burton, 1982b). From a linguist's point of view, literary stylistics is of interest because it allows the linguist to analyse texts in which language is used to create what the culture classes as art. However, the purpose of writing literature is obviously less easily defined than the purpose of writing advertising material or political pamphlets, and the fact that some features occur relatively frequently in a literary text does not by itself guarantee that they are of particular importance.

The typical way of dealing with this problem is by reference to the notion of **foregrounding** (see Van Peer, 1986, pp. 1–14). Foregrounding is Garvin's (1964) translation from the Czech term *aktualisace* used by the Prague School linguists, and its application to literature derives from an analogy with what is thought to be 'a fundamental characteristic of human perception' (Van Peer, 1986, p. 21), namely the ability to distinguish 'a *figure* against a ground' (ibid.).

The notion of foregrounding derives in the first place from the work of the Russian Formalists, notably Viktor Shklovsky (or Šklovskij) (1917), according to whom the main function of art was to make people see the world in a new way through **defamiliarization** or **making strange** (Russian *ostranenie*). The way to make the world strange through text is by **foregrounding** certain aspects or features of it, the idea being that certain aspects of a work can be made to stand out, be foregrounded, that a form of linguistic highlighting can be achieved through breaking the norms of the standard language.

The **formalists** were so called because they tended to concentrate on certain formal aspects of literary texts, say a rhyme scheme, in isolation from other aspects. The **structuralists**, in contrast, stressed the interdependence of the various elements of the text, and according to the Prague Scholar, Jan Mukarovsky (1932), although violation of the norms of the standard language is the essence of poetic language and the device whereby foregrounding is achieved, the literary work is a unified aesthetic structure 'defined by the interrelationships between those items that are foregrounded and those elements in the work that remain in the background' (Van Peer, 1986, p. 7). This view of foregrounding as relational paves the way for Roman Jakobson's (1960) notion of **parallelism**.

Literary language, and the language of poetry in particular, tends to differ from the standard language by being highly patterned – this independently of whether it also violates rules of grammar and lexis. This patterning is what Jakobson calls parallelism, which he takes to be the defining feature of poetic language.

Jakobson sees language as having six basic functions defined in terms of the language user's **set** towards, or emphasis on, one of the six factors involved in any successful act of communication. These factors are the **code** through which **contact** is established between the participants, **addresser**

and **addressee**, in such a way that a **message** will refer to a **context**. A given set relates to a given dominant function as follows:

Set	*Dominant function*
addresser	emotive
addressee	conative
context	referential
contact	phatic
code	metalingual
message	**poetic**

According to Jakobson (1960, p. 358) 'the empirical linguistic criterion of the poetic function', 'the indispensable feature inherent in any piece of poetry' is that '*the poetic function projects the principle of equivalence from the axis of selection into the axis of combination.* Equivalence is promoted to the constitutive device of the sequence'.

Jakobson thinks, with Saussure, that any piece of language is mappable on two dimensions represented schematically as two axes:

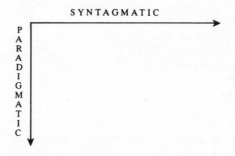

(see also STRUCTURALIST LINGUISTICS). Normally, one axis, the syntagmatic, is solely concerned with structure, while equivalences are mappable downwards on the paradigmatic axis. However, in writing poetry, the syntagmatic axis comes to contain equivalences too; in fact, a poem is constructed in terms of linearly sequenced equivalences of parallel structures at all levels (see below). To give an example; a language user may wish to report the fact that the cat was sitting on a rug. If the set is on the context so that the referential function of language dominates, the language user may simply use the words *The cat was sitting on the rug*. If, however, the set is on the message itself so that the poetic function predominates, the user will allow the principle of parallelism to predominate also and influence the word choice which may become *The cat sat on the mat*, where there is phonological parallelism (rhyme) between the words *cat*, *sat*, and *mat*. So while normal language consists of combinations of different kinds of elements, poetic language consists of combinations of the same kinds of element, and this device of parallelism both organizes the literary work and pervades all aspects of it. In this way, parallelism is foregrounded in, and defining of, literary language.

Parallelisms may be of many types at each linguistic level of description. It is possible to provide a full linguistic description of all the levels of a text, and this would show up the parallelisms. At the level of phonemic transcription, for instance, there might be alliteration, rhyme, and metre (see below). At the syntactic level, there might be parallel structures, and at the lexical level there might be various types of verbal repetition. At the level of larger stretches of text than the clause, parallelisms may operate in the structure of a whole work – some works, for example, are organized into chapters, sections, or books.

But clearly, the notion of foregrounding needs a finer definition than this before it can be used in a truly explanatory sense. For 'even a thorough scanning of all instances of parallelism [in a literary work] . . . does not provide a framework for a justifiable interpretation of the patterns that are described, which in themselves are only neutral with regard to interpreting the text' (Van Peer, 1986, p. 11). As Halliday (1971) points out, it is necessary to distinguish between 'mere linguistic regularity, which in itself is of no interest to literary studies, and regularity which is significant for the poem or prose work in which we find it' (p. 330).

As an illustration of the point at issue, compare the significance of a large number of references to the weather in, on the one hand, a weather report and, on the other hand, Hemingway's novel *A Farewell to Arms* (1929). In the case of the weather report, we would not want to claim that an unusually large number of references to the weather as compared with the language as a whole was foregrounded in the defamiliarization sense. The weather forecaster does not want to make the weather strange for us – he or she just wants to tell us about it. But if we are reading Hemingway's novel about an American in the Italian army during a war and find large numbers of references to the weather, then we might begin to think that there is some particular reason for this; that it is meant to be somehow meaningful; to add to the overall meaning of the book; that the passages about the weather have some sort of thematic importance in the work. That, in other words, Hemingway has a motive or reason for mentioning the weather so often.

Halliday (1971) defines **foregrounding** as 'prominence that is motivated' (p. 339). He discusses Golding's use of language in *The Inheritors* (1955), a novel about a group of Neanderthal people whose world is invaded by a tribe of more advanced people. He shows that the two groups have different grammars: in the part of the book that is about the Neanderthal people, most verbal groups are intransitive, and a large proportion of the grammatical subjects are realized by words which do not refer to people, but to plants and inanimate objects and parts of the body; where the subjects are people, frequently the clauses are not clauses of action. This creates a picture of a world 'in which people act, but they do not act on things; they move, but they move only themselves . . . the scene is one of constant movement, but movement which is as much in-animate as human and in which only the mover is affected – nothing else changes' (pp. 349–50). It is a world in which no cause and effect is perceived by its inhabitants, and this reflects their limited cognitive capacity. The pre-dominance of the kinds of structures and grammatical categories which Halliday describes in this part of the book, constitutes a breaking of the norms of the standard language, statistically speaking. Halliday shows that this is a motivated phenomenon: it constitutes part of the meaning of the novel. In the case of the language of the new people, on the other hand, there is no norm breaking – the language in the part of the book which deals with them is quite normal, reflecting their far greater similarity to people as they are now; their wider horizons and more complex perceptions compared to the Neanderthal people. The fact that the language here is normal while the language earlier in the book is not, illustrates the important point that norms broken need not be just the norms of the idealized standard language. A norm may be set up within a work itself, and then be internally broken as is often the case in poetry (see below).

In similar vein to Halliday (1971), Burton (1982b) shows how, in *The Bell Jar*, Sylvia Plath uses transitivity patterns to write her main character into inactivity and helplessness. Both writers arrive at their conclusions through a thorough grammatical analysis of their texts. As mentioned above, the analysis of choices of lexical items, such as references to the weather, is also an important aspect of a full stylistic analysis, and, in poetry in particular, much attention will normally be focused on the level of phonology.

A distinction may be drawn between **tropes**, which are stylistic effects created by choices in grammar and vocabulary, and **schemes**, which are segmental phonemic effects (Wellek and Warren, 1949, 1956, 1963) (see list at the end of this entry). Sound patterns within syllables include alliteration, assonance, consonance, reverse rhyme, pararhyme, and rhyme, all of which would be described in a full stylistic analysis of a poem. Normally, however, most attention is focused on 'the rhythmic measure, i.e., the unit of rhythmic patterning, which extends from the onset of one stressed syllable to the onset of the next' (Leech, 1969, p. 91). In English, there may be up to about four unstressed syllables between two stressed syllables, and when the pattern is regular, stylisticians talk of it in terms of **metrical** feet. A **foot** is 'the unit or span of stressed and unstressed syllables which is repeated to form a metrical pattern' (Leech, 1969, p. 112).

There are four kinds of metre usually employed to describe English poetry, namely

Iamb x/; Anapest xx/; Trochee /x; Dactyl /xx.
(Leech, 1969, p.112)
(x = an unstressed syllable, / = a stressed syllable)

As we can see, the metrical foot does not coincide with the unit of measure, since a foot may begin with an unstressed syllable. There are a number of problems involved in applying the classical foot to English (see Leech, 1969, pp. 112–14); however, it can be instructive to use it in the case of some types of poetry, and I shall do so at this point, in order to illustrate the importance a stylistician may attach to instances in which a norm set up within a text is broken. Compared to the language as a whole, the internal norm consisting of the regular iambic metre of Byron's 'She Walks in Beauty' (*Hebrew Melodies*, 1815) is deviant. But within the poem itself, the regularity is the norm:

She walks in beauty, like the night,
  x /   x / x / x   /
   Of cloudless climes and starry skies;
    x /   x   /   x   / x /
And all that's best of dark and bright
x   / x   / x   / x   /
   Meet in her aspect and her eyes:
    x / x   / x   /   x   /
Thus mellowed to that tender light
x   / x   / x   / x   /
Which heaven to gaudy day denies.
  x   /   x / x   / x   /

The metre here consists of four iambic feet per line; it is possible to read this poem aloud in strict iambs (provided that *heaven* is read as *heav'n*). A natural reading, that is, a reading of this text as if it were prose, would probably follow this pattern fairly closely for the first three lines – although, in line one, *like* is unlikely to receive a stress. If it does not, then the stressed *night* will gain extra emphasis by being preceded by three unstressed syllables. For the next two lines, the iambic pattern is likely to be followed, chiefly because the stresses at the level of sound coincide, at the lexico-syntactic level, with content words as opposed to the grammatical connectives, *and*, *of*, and *that's*, which are unstressed. However, in line four, a natural reading would stress *meet*, thus breaking the iambic pattern much more starkly than in the first line; in the first line, *like*, which is stressed in the metrical reading, is made unstressed in the natural reading; here, *meet*, which is unstressed in the metrical reading, will be stressed in the natural reading. We therefore have two consecutive stressed syllables, and this may make a reader, lulled by the regularity of the previous two lines, stop and catch his or her breath in surprise. *Meet* thus becomes very strongly emphasized. We can now add to this quite obvious internal norm-breaking prominence some literary-historical knowledge which will tend to indicate that this prominence is motivated, and is consequently real foregrounding.

We know that Byron was a Romantic poet, and that the Romantics objected to the rigid opposition traditionally claimed to exist between the heavenly, good, bright regions above the moon on the one hand, and the dark, evil, earthly regions beneath it on the other hand. And that they objected to all the oppositions that this opposition itself was used to symbolize. Byron lets beauty, night, dark, and bright **meet** in the woman he is describing, and the breaking of the regular metre on the very word *meet* emphasizes this meeting. The rhyme scheme gives further emphasis to the meeting of the phenomena in question: *night* rhymes with *bright* and *light* (see Cummings and Simmons, 1983, pp. 39–40).

Much more could be said about this poem by a stylistician; I have hinted at the interplay of analysis at the different levels of the poem, and Van Peer (1986, p. 16) adds to the notion of meaningful prominence the notion of a **nexus** of foregrounding. This is a nodal point in a text where foregrounding devices occur at several linguistic levels of a text. Fairly rigorously grounded in tests of reader reactions and text interpretations, his study is the first to show conclusively the influence of foregrounding as defined by textual analysis on these phenomena.

Sinclair (1982b, p. 172) provides an outline of the separate stages of a stylistic analysis, emphasizing that the text must already be in some sense understood before benefit can be gained from analysing it:

First . . . there is the reading and full critical understanding of the text. . . . Analysis must be interpreted through the impressions created by the work as a whole . . . .

The second stage . . . is the analysis of one area, perhaps sentence structure, rhyme or antonomy. In practice, the larger grammatical units offer the more fruitful starting-point, but there is no restriction . . .

The third stage is called *scan*. The analytical data are examined for patterns to see whether any aspects of the symbols in the display is worth following up. A decision is made: namely, a return to further analysis if no likely lead arises from the analysis, or a description of some aspect of patterning . . . .

At this point the nature of the patterning under attention should be described exactly. The next step is to consider how it relates to the unanalysed 'total meaning'.

In the analysis of the poem above, Sinclair's first step was assumed to have taken place already; an assumed analysis of rhyme and metre was drawn on; the patterning found there was followed up (though its exact description is not included here); and a beginning was made to relate this to the total meaning of the full text (there are more verses).

The type of stylistic analysis dealt with so far in this entry has been surface-structure orientated. The approach of stylisticians using the theoretical framework and terminology of transformational-generative grammar adds further dimensions to the stylistic analysis of text with the notion that both the deep structure itself, and the relationships between it and the surface structure are significant to a text (Closs Traugott and Pratt, 1980, p. 167):

On the one hand, there are texts in which deep structure matches surface structure very closely. In others, there is considerable difference between the two. In this latter case, we may find that deep structures are relatively diverse, while surface structures are relatively uniform and deceptively simple. Or we may find that surface structures are relatively diverse, whereas the deep structures are relatively uniform.

Traugott and Pratt illustrate the method employed through analyses of extracts from four texts, Donald Barthelme's short story 'Edward and Pia' (1967), Ernest Hemingway's *For Whom the Bell Tolls* (1940), Henry James' *The Portrait of a Lady* (1908), and Carl Sandburg's poem 'The Harbor' (1970); I shall quote extensively from their treatment of the first two texts, to give an indication of what is involved.

The Barthelme text consists mainly of simple sentences with few connectives between them and no subordination (Closs Traugott and Pratt, 1980, p. 169):

> One of the few exceptions is found in lines 14–15: '*What are you thinking about?*' *Edward asked Pia and she said she was thinking about Willie's hand*. The whole paragraph in which this occurs is coherent, and, significantly, this paragraph is about a person and events external to Edward and Pia. Others live connected lives; not so our hero and heroine except when thinking about others. This is reflected by the use of the embedded complement in *she said she was thinking about Willie's hand*, where *that* is deleted and the complement is thus more tightly related to the main clause *she said* than if it were not deleted.... Place expressions such as *in the mailbox, in London, at the train station* are moved out of their normal position at the end of the sentence to the beginning. This transformation takes on a significance it would not have in ordinary discourse, since place expressions are the only expressions that undergo an optional movement transformation in this passage. (Questions require movement, and therefore movement is stylistically irrelevant in such a question as *What are you thinking about?*)

The analysis of the Hemingway text contrasts two adjoining passages from Chapter 13 of the novel. In the first passage, both deep and surface structures are simple and therefore match quite closely; the passage describes a character's several actions, and an uncommonly large proportion of the sentences begin with *he*, in spite of an option to delete it. This 'has the special effect of drawing attention to the person.... In other words, nonuse of an optional transformation may foreground and make special the scene being presented' (ibid., p. 170). The second passage, a love scene, which precedes the first in the novel, contrasts with the first in several ways. The language is simple on the surface, but the deep structure is complex 'and contributes to the total orgasmic effect of the scene' (ibid., p. 172). However, (ibid., p. 174):

> What is striking again is that certain transformations have not been used, specifically not subject deletion. However, a subject deletion is used to great effect in one instance: *he held the length of her body tight to him and felt her breasts against his chest*. This allows an interpretation of simultaneity to the holding and the feeling which *and he felt her breasts* would not.

In contrast to Hemingway's simplicity of style, James' is known for its syntactic complexity – 'his surface structures are very diverse even when his underlying structures are similar. Furthermore, he will, at times, not use a transformation where use of one would aid comprehension' (ibid., pp. 174–5).

LIST OF TERMS WHICH MAY BE ENCOUNTERED IN STYLISTIC ANALYSES

(From Chatman, 1960; Leech, 1969; Chapman 1973.) C = consonant or consonant cluster; V = vowel or diphthong.

accent: stress on a spoken syllable

alliteration: (consonant alliteration): CVC *mellow moments*, *flags flying*; (vowel alliteration): VC *every effort employed*

allusion: allusion may be made to religion, history, ideals, etc.

ambiguity: double or multiple meaning of a word or longer stretch of text

anacoluthon: changed or incomplete grammatical sequence: *could you just . . ., oh, it's OK, I've done it*

anadiplosis: the last part of one unit is repeated at the beginning of the next: *The children were playing on the beach. The beach was a* *silvery white*

anaphora: initial repetition (but see also the section on **cohesion** in the entry on TEXT LINGUISTICS)

antistrophe (inverted clause or sentence): the repetition of items in reverse order: *I love you – you love me*

antithesis: definition of something by elimination; *or* parallelism of form combined with contrast in meaning

aphaeresis: an initial V is lost so that the C which follows it clusters with the initial sound of the next word: *it is – 'tis*

apocope: a word-final V is left out to allow the preceding C to cluster with the initial C or V of the next word: *the army – th'army*

appeal: appeal may be made to emotion

archaism: using the language of the past in a text of the present; often the result of a wish to emulate a writer or school of writers of the past, and often considered to provide poetic **heightening** (see below)

assonance: CVC *fame late*

augmentation: CC becoming CVC: *slowly and soulfully*

chiasmus: Reversed phoneme sequence /u/:/i/ ::/i/:/u/: *dupes of a deep delusion*

connotations: ideas or emotions which tend to be aroused by a linguistic item

consonance: CVC: *first and last*

dialectism: the use of features of dialect

diminution: CVC becoming CC: *silent and slow*

epanalepsis: the final part of each unit of the pattern repeats the initial part

epistrophe: final repetition

epizeuxis: repetition of a word or phrase without any break; free immediate repetition

euphuism: an artificial and ornate style of writing or speaking ('flowery' language)

eye rhyme: (written text only) identical letters representing different sounds: *blood mood*

free repetition: irregularly occurring exact repetitions of previous parts of a text

homeoteleuton: repetition of whole final unstressed syllables with preceding consonant stressed syllables: *fusion motion*

homoioteleuton: the repetition of the same derivational or inflectional ending on different words

hyperbaton: arranging syntactic elements in an unusual order: *pillows soft* instead of *soft pillows*

hyperbole: overstatement

litotes: understatement using a negation of a term with negative connotations to highlight the positive connotations of the opposite, unused term: *not bad*

meiosis: understatement

metaphor: implicit comparison (but see also METAPHOR): *You are my sunshine*

metonomy: the use of a feature closely associated with a referent to stand for it: *the crown* for *the monarch*

monosyllabification or **synechphonesis** or **synizesis**: very common in everyday speech – the reduction of several syllables to a single nucleus: *be-ing* /biŋ/

neologism: an item newly introduced into the lexicon of a language

nonce-formation: a neologism used on just one occasion, that is, one which will not become a regularly used linguistic item (Lewis Carroll uses these frequently in the poem Jabberwocky from *Through the Looking-Glass*, 1872)

onomatopoeia: the use of words which sound like 'natural' sounds: *buzzing bees*

pararhyme: CVC *tick tock*

ploce /plousi/: free intermittent repetition

poetic heightening: using language in a way which is perceived as particularly dignified; archaisms were often in the past considered to have this dignifying effect

polypton: the repetition of a word with varying grammatical inflections

pseudo-elision: might more logically be called syllabic expansion – 'the assumption of elision between two consonants that cannot be clustered without one of them becoming syllabic (for example, words ending in "-ism," "rhythm," etc.)' (Chatman, 1960, p. 163)

reverse rhyme: CVC: *mope and moan*

rhyme: CVC *cat mat*. A distinction is

sometimes drawn between **masculine** rhyme – repetition of final stressed V and final C if there are any (as above and *be agree*) – and **feminine** rhyme, which is as masculine but including also any additional unstressed identical syllables *taker maker* (Chatman 1960, p. 152)

simili: explicit comparison: *You are like sunshine*

stress: relative force of breath in uttering a syllable

syllepsis: one verb governing two or more nouns with at least one of which it is literally incongruous: *I bought the milk and the idea of going shopping*

symploce: initial combined with final repetition

synaeresis: 'the consonantizing of a vowel (usually into /y-/ or /w-/), or the loss of syllabicity of a syllabic consonant, such that it clusters with a following vowel rather then standing alone as a syllable (for example "many a" becomes /menyə/, "jollier" becomes /jalyər/, "title of" becomes /taytləv/)' (Chatman, 1960, pp. 162–3). This is a phenomenon which occurs constantly in normal speech

syncope: (consonant) the loss of a C and consequent fusion of the syllables on either side of it often involving loss of the second V: *by his* – *by's*; (vowel) the loss of a V which has the effect that a syllable is lost without affecting syllables on either side of it: *medicine* – *med'cine*

synecdoche: use of part of a referent to stand for the whole: *all **hands** on deck*

zeugma: one verb governing two or more nouns: *I saw the horses and sheep* (see also syllepsis)

K.M.

SUGGESTIONS FOR FURTHER READING

Cummings, M. and R. Simmons (1983) *The Language of Literature: A Stylistic Introduction to the Study of Literature*, Oxford, Pergamon Press.

Closs Traugott, E. and M. Pratt (1980), *Linguistics for Students of Literature*, New York, Harcourt Brace Jovanovich.

Turner, G. (1973), *Stylistics*, Harmondsworth, Penguin.

Systemic grammar

This article is best read in conjunction with the article on SCALE AND CATEGORY GRAMMAR. In **systemic grammar**, the notion of the **system**, as used in M.A.K. Halliday's earlier model, is no longer seen as a single set of choices available at a particular place in structure; now (Butler, 1985, p. 40):

we find the paradigmatic patterning of language described in terms of sets of systems, or system 'networks', operating with a particular rank of unit, and sometimes a particular class of a given rank, as their 'point of origin'.

Certain system networks are selected from a clause rank, others operate at the nominal class of the unit group, and so on.

The notion of the **network** of systems obviously indicates that there are interrelations between the various systems. So choices from within one system may co-occur with choices from within other systems, in one of two ways: either the choices made are independent of each other, in which case the systems are **simultaneous** and **unordered** with respect to each other; or a choice made from within one system implies certain choices from within other systems, in which case the systems are **dependent** on each other, and **hierarchically ordered** (Halliday, 1966a/Kress, 1976, p. 92):

> So for example the system whose terms are declarative/interrogative would be hierarchically ordered with respect to the system indicative/imperative, in that selection of either of the features declarative and interrogative implies selection of indicative.

A simplified system network for the English clause might look like Figure 1 (from Halliday, 1966a/Kress 1976, p. 93). The change from system of structure to paradigmatic system network is made possible in this model because the systemic relations, as well as the structural relations, are now described in terms of delicacy. A more delicate description of an indicative clause will show that it is of the type interrogative; a more delicate statement about the interrogative clause is that it is of the yes/no type; and so on.

The description of paradigmatic patterns in terms of system networks allows Halliday to deal, in his own way, with deep grammar (ibid., pp. 93–4):

Systemic description may be thought of as complementary to structural description, the one concerned with paradigmatic and the other with syntagmatic relations. On the other hand it might be useful to consider some possible consequences of regarding systemic description as the underlying form of representation, if it turned out that the structural description could be shown to be derivable from it. In that case structure would be fully predictable, and the form of a structural representation could be considered in the light of this. It goes without saying that the concept of an explicit grammar implied by this formulation derives primarily from the work of Chomsky, and that steps taken in this direction on the basis of any grammatical notions are made possible by his fundamental contribution.

According to Halliday, the paradigmatic relations between linguistic items are more fundamental than the syntagmatic relations, the underlying grammar is 'semantically significant' grammar – the part of grammar which is 'closest to' the semantics (ibid.). As Butler points out (1985, p. 46):

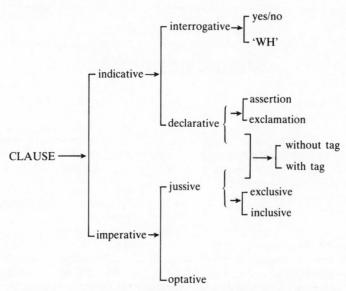

Figure 1 A simplified system network for the clause in English

This is an extremely important statement. Halliday's work had, from the beginning, always insisted on the meaningfulness of linguistic elements, building as it did on the work of Firth; but here we have an explicit claim that grammars can be written so as to reflect, at least in part, the specifically semantic meaning (to use a Firthian distinction) of formal choices, and that such a grammar can and should take the system as its most fundamental category.

This semantically significant grammar, to which Halliday often (for instance, 1970, p. 142) refers as the **meaning potential** of language, is, according to Halliday (for instance, 1968, 1970) functionally organized. The notion of **language function** is used to answer the question 'Why is language as it is' (1970, p. 141). A general answer is that 'the nature of language is closely related to the demands that we make on it, the functions it has to serve' (ibid.). But these functions are very diverse; 'we cannot explain language by simply listing its uses, and such a list could in any case be prolonged indefinitely' (ibid.). Generalizations such as Malinowski's distinction between pragmatic and magical functions, and Bühler's division into representational, expressive, and conative functions (see FUNCTIONALIST LINGUISTICS) 'are directed towards sociological or psychological inquiries' (ibid.). Halliday wants an account of linguistic functions which is related to an account of linguistic structure (ibid., p. 142):

It is fairly obvious that language is used to serve a variety of different needs, but until we examine its grammar there is no clear reason for classifying its uses in a particular way. However, when we examine the meaning potential of language itself, we find that the vast numbers of options embodied in it combine into a very few relatively independent 'networks'; and these networks of options correspond to certain basic functions of language. This enables us to give an account of the different functions of language that is relevant to the general understanding of linguistic structure rather than to any particular psychological or sociological investigation.

The basic functions of language listed are (1) the **ideational** function which (ibid., p. 143): 'serves for the expression of "content": that is, of the speaker's experience of the real world, including the inner world of his own consciousness'. (2) The **interpersonal** function, the function language has of establishing and maintaining social relations. Language serves (ibid.)

for the expression of social roles, which include the communication roles created by language itself – for example the roles of questioner or respondent, which we take on by asking or answering a question; and also for getting things done, by means of the interaction between one person and another.

(3) The **textual** function, the function language has of providing links with itself and with features of the situation in which it is used (ibid.):

this is what enables the speaker or writer to construct 'texts', or connected passages of discourse that is situationally relevant; and enables the listener or reader to distinguish a text from a random set of sentences.

Halliday now shows how these functions are reflected in the structure of the English clause; the functions, however, are supposed to be relevant for all cultures (ibid., p. 141). From the basic functions derive **structural roles**, 'functional elements such as "process" and "actor" (ibid., p. 144). These functional elements express certain very general meanings or semantic options which are realized in the clause. Each functional component contributes to structure through the functional roles (ibid., p. 144):

Since normally every speech act serves each of the basic functions of language, the speaker is selecting among all the types of options simultaneously. Hence the various sets of structural 'roles' are mapped onto one another, so that the actual structure-forming element in language is a complex of roles, like a chord in a fugue.

The ideational function is reflected in the expression of processes in the clause: 'the system of clause types is a general framework for the representation of processes in the grammar' (ibid., pp. 155–6). The clause in English serves to express **processes** of two kinds, **transitive** and **intransitive**, and 'associated with each type of process are a small number of functions or 'roles', each representing the parts that the various persons, objects or other classes of phenomena may play in the process concerned' (ibid., p. 146). The process itself is usually represented by a **verb**, for instance *built*, in the clause *Sir Christopher Wren built this gazebo*. The specific roles taken on by persons and objects involved in the process are referred to as **participant functions**, and there may also be **circumstantial functions**, 'the associated conditions and constraints such as those of time, place and manner' (ibid., pp. 146–7). The main types of transitivity role, process, participant, and circumstance, correspond more or less to the word classes verb, noun and adverb.

The participant roles are listed as (ibid., p. 148–9):

(a) actor ('logical subject'): prepositionally *by*
(b) goal ('logical direct object')
(c) beneficiary ('logical indirect object'): prepositionally *to/for*
(d) instrument: prepositionally *with/by*

with the possibility of further subdivisions. For different types of clause, the roles are either **inherent**, 'always associated with a given clause type even if it is not necessarily expressed in the structure of all clauses of that type', or **optional**. Any clause which is concerned with actions or events have an actor as inherent role; these are called **action clauses**, and may be of two types: if there is only the one inherent participant, agent, the clause is called a **middle** clause. If there are two participants, actor and goal, one of which may not be expressed in the structure, the clause is called a **non-middle** clause. Non-middle clauses may be either in the **active** or **passive voice**; it is thus the function of the voice system to align participants in various ways, and Table 1 shows the possibilities of voices in action clauses, and the roles associated with them; roles which are inherent but not

Table 1 Voice in action clauses in English

Voice (clause)	Roles	Voice (verb)	Example
middle	actor	active	the gazebo has collapsed
'active'	actor, goal	active	the Council are selling the gazebo
'active'	actor (goal)	active	the Council won't sell
'passive'	goal	active	the gazebo won't sell
'passive'	goal, actor	passive	the gazebo has been sold by the Council
'passive'	goal (actor)	passive	the gazebo has been sold

non-middle (bracket spanning the 'active' through 'passive' rows)

expressed are in parentheses (from Halliday, 1970, p. 152).

In addition to action clauses, English has two further types of clause corresponding to two types of process recognized by English, namely **mental** processes and **relations**. The roles inherent in mental process clauses, such as *I like your hairstyle*, are called **processer** and **phenomenon**. Relational clauses are of two types, **attributive**, such as *Marguerite is a poet* and *Marguerite looks desperate*, where Marguerite is being given membership of a class, the class of poets and the class of desperate-looking people respectively, and **equative**, such as *Templecombe is the treasurer*. Attributive clauses are **irreversible**: we cannot say **A poet is Marguerite*. The inherent role is **attribute**. Equative clauses are reversible, and have the inherent role **identifier**.

The interpersonal function of language is manifest in the structure of the clause through the system of **mood**, which defines the grammatical subject (as opposed to the logical subject which is defined by the transitivity system). The options in the mood system are **declarative**, **interrogative** and **imperative**, and the system is carried by the finite element of the verb plus one nominal, which is the grammatical subject. The fact that something is a grammatical subject contributes to the meaning of the clause through the interpersonal function (ibid., p. 160):

> The function of the 'grammatical subject' is thus a meaningful function in the clause, since it defines the communication role adopted by the speaker. It is present in clauses of all moods, but its significance can perhaps be seen most clearly in the imperative, where the meaning is 'I request you to . . .'; here the speaker is requiring some action on the part of the person addressed, but it is the latter who has the power to make this meaning 'come true'.

The textual function of language is manifest in the clause structure in the **thematic structure**, that is, the organization of the clause as message (ibid., p. 161):

> The English clause consists of a 'theme' and a 'rheme'. The theme is another component in the complex notion of subject, namely the 'psychological subject'; it is as it were the peg on which the message is hung, the theme being the body of the message. The theme of a clause is the element which, in English, is put in first position.

Normally, theme, actor, and modal subject are identical, as in *Sir Christopher Wren built this gazebo*. In the passive, however, the actor is dissociated from theme and modal subject, either b, being placed at the end of the clause: *This gazebo was built by Sir Christopher Wren*, or by being left out completely: *This gazebo is being restored*. In interrogative structures whose theme is a request for information, the questioning element is put first so that the theme is dissociated from actor and modal subject. A final option in thematic structure is the use of nominalization to split the clause into two parts as in *The one who built this gazebo was Sir Christopher Wren*.

Often the organization of a clause as message through the theme/rheme distinction corresponds with its information structure in terms of the notions of **given** and **new**. Information structure in English is expressed by intonation (see INTONATION). The theme will typically be associated with the given, the rheme with the new.

The functional model described above formed the basis for Halliday's later work in functional grammar (see FUNCTIONAL GRAMMAR). Other linguists, however, although operating within a general Hallidayan framework, have developed systemic grammar in other directions, which I shall discuss briefly here.

Fawcett's proposals for modification of Halliday's scale and category model are discussed in the article in this volume on SCALE AND CATEGORY GRAMMAR. In this entry, I shall concentrate on the models of systemic grammar proposed and developed by Hudson (1971, 1974, 1976). Two fundamental assumptions underlie each of these models. The first is that syntax and semantics are to be treated as separate linguistic levels, since otherwise it is difficult to be specific about the relationships between them.

Secondly, Hudson believes that the grammar should be generative, 'should consist of rules that can be used in a completely mechanical way to decide whether or not any given object is well-formed' (1971, p. 7). He differs radically from Halliday in believing that it is the goal of grammatical description to lay bare precisely what a native speaker of a language *knows*; for Halliday, the major question is always what a native speaker *can do* with language. However, Hudson's grammar is not transformational, because each one of his structural descriptions includes information which transformationalists would present in two separate representations, one for the surface and one for the deep structure, linked by transformations, Hudson, obviously, does not need transformations, since he only operates with one description.

This, according to Butler (1985, pp. 104–5), gives Hudson's grammar a large number of advantages over Chomsky's (1970a) 'Extended Standard Theory' (see TRANSFORMATIONAL-GENERATIVE GRAMMAR): (1) as there is only one representation, 'the difficulties of deciding whether deep sequence should differ from surface sequence are avoided'; (2) there is only one representation which needs to be referred to in a semantic interpretation; (3) the single structure provides all the information needed to map syntax onto phonology; (4) there is no need to carry out lexical insertion in stages – it can simply take place at the end of a syntactic derivation; (5) the question as to which structure has psychological validity will not be raised in a one-structure grammar; (6) it is easier to test the model by computer, since only a single structure has to be generated; in fact, Davey's (1978) computer program for producing discourse is directly based on Hudson's (1971) model of systemic grammar, and, in general, systemic grammar seems better suited for computer application than transformational-generative grammar (see Winograd, 1983).

Hudson's grammar accounts, like all systemic grammars, for two types of patterning, syntagmatic and paradigmatic (see STRUCTURALIST LINGUISTICS) (Butler, 1985, p. 105):

> Syntagmatic relations can be broken down into three components: constituency, sequence and dependency relations (1971, pp. 29ff.). Constituency and sequence relations are shown by the tree diagrams used for structural representation. By dependency, Hudson means relations of the type exemplified by subject-verb concord, concord between demonstrative determiners and head nouns ('this plate'/'these plates'), the relationship between 'have' and the '-en' form of the succeeding verb in the English perfect construction, and so on. The discussion of such relations is one of Hudson's major contributions to systemic theory (it is not entirely clear how Halliday would handle, for instance, subject–verb concord). . . .
>
> Paradigmatic relations are shown by means of systems.

The terms in the systems are classes of syntactic item, and the classes are defined by distribution and those internal constituency properties relevant to distribution. Since Halliday's units, clause, phrase (group), word, and morpheme are defined in this way, Hudson treats them all as classes, which means, in turn, that they are seen as being in paradigmatic relation; and all the classes have places in one supernetwork of systems, so that Firth's and Halliday's insistence on the multiplicity of systems in grammatical description (see SCALE AND CATEGORY GRAMMAR) is abandoned.

K.M.

SUGGESTIONS FOR FURTHER READING

Butler, C.S. (1985), *Systemic Linguistics: Theory and Applications*, London, Batsford Academic and Educational, chs 3, 6, and 9.
Halliday, M.A.K. (1970), 'Language structure and language function', in J. Lyons (ed.), *New Horizons in Linguistics*, Harmondsworth, Penguin, pp. 140–65.

Tagmemics

The term **tagmeme** was used by Bloomfield (1933/5) to stand for the smallest unit of grammatical form which has meaning. A tagmeme could consist of one or more **taxemes**, 'the smallest unit [of grammar] which distinguishes meanings, but which has no meaning itself' (Dinneen, 1967, p. 264). The notion of the tagmeme was developed largely by Kenneth Lee Pike (1912–) (1967, 1982; but see also Longacre 1964, 1970, 1976, 1983) into a fullblown grammatical theory, called **tagmemics**, although the assumptions on which the theory is based are such that language cannot be viewed as a self-contained system and that linguistics, therefore, cannot be self-contained either, but must draw on insights from psychology, sociology, anthropology, and so on (Jones, 1980, p. 78).

Tagmemics is based on four major assumptions (Waterhouse, 1974, p. 5):

(1) Language is ... a type of human behavior;

(2) as such, it must be looked at in the context of and in relation to human behavior as a whole;

(3) an adequate theory of language is applicable to other types of behavior as well, and to combinations of verbal and nonverbal behavior; thus, it is a unified theory;

(4) human behavior is structured, not random;

and on four postulates which are universals claimed to hold for all human behaviour (Jones, 1980, pp. 79–80):

(1) All purposive behaviour, including language, is divided into units.

(2) Units occur in context.

(3) Units are hierarchically arranged.

(4) Any item may be viewed from different perspectives.

A **unit** may have various physical forms. It may be distinguished from other units by its distinctive features and by its relationships with other units in a class, sequence or system. The distinctive unit of any behaviour is called the **behavioreme**, and the verbal behavioreme is the sentence (Waterhouse, 1974, p. 27).

The **context** in which a unit occurs often conditions its form, and any unit must be analysed in its context. So in the grammar, sentences must be analysed in the context of the discourse in which they occur, because the choice of a particular discourse type (narrative, scientific, etc.) affects the choice of the linguistic units of which the discourse is composed.

The notion of the **hierarchy** is a cornerstone of tagmemic theory. By hierarchy is meant a part–whole relationship in which smaller units occur as parts of larger ones. Language is viewed as

having a trimodal structuring: phonology, grammar, and reference. Reference includes pragmatics and much of speech-act theory, while semantics is found among the meaning features of phonology and grammar, and in various aspects of reference (Jones, 1980, p. 89). The modes and their levels interlock because units at each level may either be composed of smaller units of the same level, or units from another level; and they may enter larger units at the same level, or units at another level. The structurally significant levels of the **grammatical hierarchy** include morpheme (root), morpheme cluster (stem), word, phrase, clause, sentence, paragraph, monologue discourse, dialogue exchange, and dialogue conversation (ibid., p. 80).

The **perspectives** from which items may be viewed are the static perspective, the dynamic perspective and the relational perspective. From a **static** point of view, an item is a discrete, individual item or **particle**. A **dynamic** point of view focuses on the dynamics of items: the ways in which they overlap, blend, and merge with each other, forming **waves**. The **relational** perspective focuses on the relationships between units in a system. A total set of relationships and of units in these relationships is called a **field**. Language may be described from each of these perspectives, and descriptions adopting the different perspectives complement but do not replace each other (Jones, 1980, pp. 79–80; Pike, 1982, pp. 19–30).

Tagmemics is sometimes called **slot and filler grammar**. The unit of grammar is the **tagmeme**. The tagmeme is the correlation of a specific grammatical function with the class of items which performs that function (Waterhouse, 1974, p. 5). In other words, a tagmeme occurs in a particular place, or **slot**, in a sentence where it fulfils a **function**, such as Subject, Predicate, Head, Modifier, which items of its **class** (Noun, Noun Phrase, Verb, Verb Phrase, Adjective) are capable of fulfilling. Both slot and class must be represented in a tagmeme, because they represent different types of information, neither of which can be derived from the other: it is not possible to know from the fact that *student* is a noun which function it fulfils in any one of its possible occurrences. Thus, *student* is Modifier in *the student employees* (Jones, 1980, p. 81), but Subject in *The student went to bed early*. It is simultaneously Noun in both cases. Instead of providing two independent statements about a sentence, one dividing the sentence into minimal classified units such as noun phrases and verb phrases, and the other assigning grammatical functions like subject and predicator to these units, tagmemics offers an analysis into a sequence of tagmemes, each of which simultaneously provides information about an item's function in a larger structure, and about its class, which can fulfill that function (Crystal, 1971/81, p. 213).

The view of the tagmeme as a correlation between class and function also reflects Pike's objection to the extreme distributionalism of mainstream post-Bloomfieldians, which he refers to as an **etic**, or exterior view of language (Waterhouse, 1974, p. 6): 'The etic view has to do with universals, with typology, with observation from outside a system, as well as with the nature of initial field data, and with variant forms of an emic unit.' Such a view, he thinks, 'can provide no more than a point of departure for description', and needs to be supplemented with an **emic** view consisting in 'interpreting events according to their particular function in the particular cultural world to which they belong' (Ducrot and Todorov, 1981, p. 36; and Waterhouse, 1974, p. 6): 'The emic view is concerned with the contrastive, patterned system of a specific language or culture or universe of discourse, with the way a participant in a system sees that system, as well as with distinctions between contrastive units'.

The method of analysing data in terms of positions in stretches of text and the linguistic units which can be placed in these positions – a basic technique in code-breaking – is useful for describing hitherto unknown languages, and according to de Beaugrande and Dressler (1981, p. 19), 'the integration of anthropology and linguistics in the tagmemic approach has provided invaluable documentation of many rapidly disappearing languages in remote regions'. This has been one of the main aims of the **Summer Institute of Linguistics** which Pike founded. Waterhouse (1974) contains a comprehensive survey of the languages to which tagmemic analysis has been applied; see also Pike (1970).

While Longacre continues to employ a two-feature tagmeme, Pike adopts a four-feature view of the tagmeme in his later writings. He adds to slot and class the features role and cohesion. Jones (1980, p. 81) symbolizes the four features as a four-cell array:

slot	class
role	cohesion

Role may be, for example, actor, undergoer (patient), benefactee, and scope, which includes inner locative, goal and some experiencer. **Cohesion** here is grammatical cohesion, cases in which 'the form or occurrence of one grammatical unit is affected by another grammatical unit in the language' (ibid.). It includes such agreement features as number agreement in English and gender agreement in many Romance languages.

Tagmemes are the constituents of **syntagmemes**, also known as **patterns** or **constructions**. Some tagmemes are obligatory and are marked +, while optional tagmemes are marked −. In the four-cell notation, the intransitive clause *the farmer walks* would have two tagmemes, the first representing *the farmer*, the second *walks* (Jones, 1980, p. 82):

Intransitive = Clause	+	Subject	Noun Phrase
		Actor	Subject Number 〉

	+	Predicate	Verb
		Statement	〉 Subject Number 〉 Intransitive 〉

The arrowlike symbols in the cohesion cells above indicate cohesion rules such as (Jones, 1980, p. 83):

Subject Number: the number of the subject governs the number of the predicate.

Intransitive: mutual requirement of subject (as actor) and predicate tagmeme.

If the arrow is to the right, the tagmeme is the governing source; if the arrow is to the left, the tagmeme is the governed target.

The analysis can be summarized in a string such as IndeDecITClRt= +S:NP +ITPred: ITVP, which can be read as 'Independent Declarative Intransitive Clause Root consisting of obligatory subject slot filled by a noun phrase, followed by an intransitive predicate slot filled by an obligatory intransitive verb phrase (compare Waterhouse, 1974, p. 11; Pike, 1982, p. 82). There are a limited number of construction types at each of the grammatical **ranks** of sentence, clause, phrase, word, and morpheme (Allen and Widdowson, 1975, p. 57), and in this respect tagmemics bears a close resemblance to scale and category grammar (see SCALE AND CATEGORY GRAMMAR).

Tagmemes are the essential units of tagmemic analysis. But just as phonemes can be analysed into smaller units, which are classifiable as allophones of the phonemes, tagmemes can be analysed into smaller, etic, units called **tagmas** which are **allotagmas** of the tagmeme (Crystal, 1985, p. 304).

The ultimate aim of tagmemics is to provide a theory which integrates lexical, grammatical, and phonological information. This information is presented in terms of **matrices**, networks of intersecting dimensions of contrastive features (Waterhouse, 1974, p. 40). However, the view of language as part of human behaviour necessitates a recognition that language cannot be strictly formalized. No representational system could accommodate all the relevant facts of language, and tagmemics seeks a balance between the need for generalizations about language, and the particularities and variations found in it. Therefore, tagmemics accepts various different modes of representation for different purposes, and does not insist that there must be only one correct grammar or linguistic theory (Jones, 1980, pp. 78–9).

Tagmemics differed from most of the grammars of the period during which it was developed in looking beyond the sentence to the total structure of a text, and Longacre's work in this area is particularly well known. Longacre (1983, pp. 3–6) claims that all monologue discourse can be classified according to four parameters: (1) contingent temporal succession; (2) agent orientation; (3) projection; and (4) tension.

1 **Contingent temporal succession** refers to a framework of temporal succession in which some, usually most, of the event in the discourse are contingent on previous events.

2 **Agent orientation** refers to orientation towards agents with at least a partial identity of agent reference through the discourse.

3 **Projection** refers to a situation or action which is contemplated, enjoined or anticipated, but not realized.

4 **Tension** refers to the reflection in a discourse of a struggle or polarization of some sort. Most discourse types can realize tension, so this parameter is not used to distinguish types of discourse from each other.

The parameters of contingent temporal succession and agent orientation provide a four-way classification of discourse types, with projection providing a two-way subclassification within each, as shown in the following matrix (from Longacre, 1983, p. 4).

	+ Ag-orientation	− Ag-orientation	
+ Contingent temporal succession	Narrative	Procedural	
	Prophecy	How-to-do-it	+ Proj
	Story	How-it-was-done	− Proj
− Contingent temporal succession	Behavioural	Expository	
	Hortatory Promissory	Budget proposal Futuristic essay	+ Proj
	Eulogy	Scientific paper	− Proj

Narrative discourse tells a type of story which involves contingent temporal succession and agent orientation. But the story may present its event as having already taken place, as in story and history, or as projected, as in prophecy.

Procedural discourse, which is about how to do or make something, also has contingent temporal succession, but it does not have agent orientation because it focuses on the actions involved in doing something rather than on the doer of the actions. Again, the projection parameter distinguishes two types of procedural discourse, after-the-fact accounts of how something was done, and before-the-fact accounts of how to do something.

Behavioural discourse, which deals with appropriate behaviour, has agent orientation, but does not have contingent temporal succession. There are two types, one which deals with behaviour which has already taken place, as in eulogy, and one which prescribes/proscribes future behaviour as in hortatory discourse and a campaign speech-making promises about future actions.

Expository discourse, which expounds a subject, has neither agent orientation nor contingent temporal succession. It may, however, concern something which already pertains, as in the case of a scientific paper, or it may deal with something projected, as in the case of a futuristic essay.

Each type of discourse may be embedded within examples of the other types, and each type contains **main line** material, in which the main line of development takes place, and **supportive** material, which includes everything else.

The characteristic types of linkage of units displayed by each type of discourse are reflections of their classification on the contingent temporal succession parameter. Thus narrative and procedural discourse are characterized by **chronological linkage** (*and then*; *after that*; etc.), while behavioural and expository discourse have logical linkage (*if–then, because*, etc.). The presence or absence in different text types of lines of **participant reference** reflect their classification on the agent orientation parameter. Lines of participant reference are present in narrative and behavioural discourse, but absent in procedural and expository discourse. The projection parameter is reflected in tense, aspect, and voice characteristics (ibid., pp. 6–7). For example, past tense characterizes the main line of narrative discourse; present or future characterize the main line of procedural discourse (ibid., p. 14). Longacre also claims that different types of monologue discourse display characteristic initiating, closing and nuclear tagmemes and that each tends towards a particular paragraph and sentence type (see Waterhouse, 1974, pp. 45–8; and compare TEXT LINGUISTICS), but the most widely known aspect of his work on discourse is probably his view that narrative is structured in terms of Peak, Pre-peak and Post-peak episodes.

Peak may be marked by change in tense and/or aspect; sudden absence of particles which have marked the event-line of the story; disturbance of routine participant reference; **rhetorical underlining**, such as parallelism, paraphrase and tautologies (see STYLISTICS); concentration of participants (stage crowding); and a number of other stylistic effects (see Longacre, 1983).

The Summer Institute of Linguistics trains translators and field linguists in tagmemics.

K.M.

SUGGESTIONS FOR FURTHER READING

Longacre, R.E. (1983), *The Grammar of Discourse*, New York and London, Plenum Press.
Pike, K.L. (1982), *Linguistic Concepts: An Introduction to Tagmemics*, Lincoln, NE, and London, University of Nebraska Press.
Waterhouse, V.G. (1974), *The History and Development of Tagmemics*, The Hague and Paris, Mouton.

Teaching English as a Foreign Language (TEFL)

TEFL is the term used to refer to the activity of teaching English to non-native speakers of the language. This activity is also referred to as **Teaching English as a Second Language** (TESL). In the USA, the latter seems to be the preferred term, whereas in Britain TESL is used more specifically to refer to the teaching of English in those countries where English has an official role in the educational or political system, e.g. in former British or American colonies such as India or the Philippines where English is still used as a medium of education and is recognized as an official language alongside the national language. TESL thus contrasts with TEFL which refers to those situations where English is not used as a medium of instruction and has no official status. In Britain itself, TESL is often used to refer to the teaching of English to immigrants or non-native speakers born in Britain. Because of the possible confusion between TEFL and TESL, the more general terms **English Language Teaching** (ELT) and **English for Speakers of Other Languages** (ESOL) are often used, the former in Britain and the latter in the USA. Henceforth in this entry the term ELT will be used.

ELT can be traced back to the late sixteenth century, when large numbers of French Huguenot refugees needed to learn English and the first textbooks were written (Howatt, 1984). English has been taught in Europe and countries that were part of the British Empire since then, but it is undoubtedly the case that there has been a huge growth in English Language Teaching in the twentieth century and particularly since 1945. This is largely due to the growth in use of English as the international language of science, technology, diplomacy, and business. Baldauf and Jernudd (1983) and Swales (1985) have shown that the proportion of academic articles written in the areas of science, technology, and economics has been increasing rapidly, and it is estimated that of the several million articles published every year at least half are published in English (Swales, 1987). No corresponding figures about the proportion of business correspondence and negotiation exist, but it is reasonable to assume that growth in these areas is similar to that in the academic world.

These trends have led to the development of the teaching of **English for Specific Purposes** (ESP) which aims to teach specific language and skills related to different activities in academic or business life (see below for a fuller description of ESP). But the teaching of **General-Purpose English** has also grown considerably and the British Council and the American Information Services both run very successful institutes in many countries of the world. The British

Council, for example, stated in its annual report for 1987/8 that it was running fifty Direct Teaching Centres in thirty-one countries and was planning further centres in three more countries. It also reported that over 40 per cent of its revenue was derived from English language services.

The development of ELT has been dominated by issues of syllabus design and methodology. Howatt (1984) describes how the **grammar-translation method** developed at the end of the eighteenth century in Germany and spread throughout Europe. The method involved grammatical explanation of key structures, the teaching of selected areas of vocabulary, and exercises involving the translation of disconnected sentences into the mother tongue. The emphasis was on written text.

The **Reform Movement** developed in the late eighteenth century and was based on three fundamental points:

1 the primacy of speech;
2 the use of connected text as opposed to disconnected sentences;
3 the use of an oral methodology.

The syllabuses that arose from the Reform Movement still involved a graded, step-by-step approach. They thus contrasted with a parallel development in ELT, the rise of what Howatt (ibid.) refers to as 'natural methods of language teaching'. These have gone under the names of the **Natural Method,** the **Conversation Method** and most notably the **Direct Method**. The methodology of these approaches is less structured than that of the Reform Movement and is based on a theory according to which language learning is an 'intuitive process for which human beings have a natural capacity provided only that the proper conditions exist' (ibid. p. 192). These conditions are 'someone to talk to, something to talk about and a desire to understand and make yourself understood' (ibid.).

The early part of the twentieth century saw the fusion of these philosophies, particularly in the work of H.E. Palmer and his **Oral Method**. Palmer and Palmer's *English through Actions*

(1925) uses the question–answer techniques of the Direct Method but has a more systematic approach to the selection of vocabulary and the presentation of grammatical points than that favoured by the Direct Method. Subsequent courses in ELT, e.g. Eckersley's *Essential English for Foreign Students* (1938–42) and Hornby's *Oxford Progressive English for Adult Learners* (1954–6), have followed the approach used by Palmer, combining some Direct Method exercises with **pattern practice**, teaching the main structures of English. Even courses from the 1960s such as L.G. Alexander's *First Things First* (1967) with its extensive use of situations presented in pictures, and the courses that arose from the **Audiolingual Method** developed in the United States by Fries (see for example Fries, 1952) that used very controlled pattern practice, are really refinements of the basic Palmer/Hornby approach. The main emphasis is on teaching the form and vocabulary of the language, and the ways in which these forms are used in natural language are largely neglected.

In the 1970s, however, a very considerable change in emphasis arose, largely as a result of the writings of various British applied linguists, notably Widdowson (see for example Widdowson, 1978). Widdowson argued that language courses should concentrate on the **use** of language rather than **usage**. He defines **usage** as 'that aspect which makes evident the extent to which the language user demonstrates his knowledge of linguistic rules'; **use** is 'another aspect of performance: that which makes evident the extent to which the language user demonstrates his ability to use his knowledge of linguistic rules for effective communication' (ibid., p.3).

Widdowson's ideas have had a profound influence on ELT, particularly on ESP. The striking development has been the rise of a **Communicative Approach** which emphasizes language use rather than language form. The Communicative Approach aims to teach **communicative competence** (Hymes, 1972) which is the ability to apply the rules of grammar appropriately in the correct situation.

The actual syllabuses that have arisen from attempts to put the Communicative Approach into practice have varied considerably. Many courses have followed a **functional/notional** syllabus, putting into practice the ideas expressed in Wilkins' *Notional Syllabuses* (1976). The aim of such syllabuses is to base teaching on what people do with language, such as requesting, inviting, informing, apologizing, ordering, etc. These are **communicative functions. Notions** or **semantico-grammatical categories**, as Wilkins calls them, are more difficult to define; they are the basic 'building blocks' that constitute meaning, such as **location, time, duration, space**. The most general notions, such as **time**, are clearly too abstract to form the basis of teaching materials, but others that are more concrete, such as **quantity, location** or **cause and effect**, may be used. Most coursebooks following a functional/notional syllabus, e.g. *Strategies* (Abbs and Freebairn, 1975), have concentrated on functions rather than notions, even though the very full syllabus worked out by Van Ek (1975) in *The Threshhold Level in European Unit/Credit Systems for Modern Language Learning for Adults* does integrate both functions and notions.

Many have argued (notably Brumfit, 1980) that functional/notional syllabuses have done little more than reorganize and reorder the grammatical syllabus and have failed to address the question of methodology. The basic aim of a **communicative syllabus** should be the creation of tasks in which learners have to communicate in English in order to complete them. A typical **communicative task** would be the labelling of a diagram using information from a written or spoken text. The most interesting experiment in this regard is the project directed by Prabhu in Bangalore, south India. This project arose from dissatisfaction with the previous grammatical syllabus rather than with a functional/notional syllabus, and its underlying philosophy is that grammatical form is best learnt when the learner's attention is on meaning. The syllabus is thus based on a series of graded tasks for which the teacher provides necessary input and learners show their comprehension by carrying out an activity such as labelling a diagram. Grammatical points are not taught, but results of the project indicate that learners have in fact performed better on tests of grammar than learners following a traditional grammatical syllabus (Prabhu, 1987).

Since the late 1980s, both applied linguists and course designers have seemed to favour an **Eclectic Approach**, which selects features from grammatical syllabuses, functional/notional syllabuses, and task-based approaches. *The Cambridge English Course*, the most widely used coursebook in Britain in the late 1980s, is a good example of this eclecticism. An interesting development, however, is the reawakening of interest in the teaching of vocabulary and the emergence of the idea of a **lexical syllabus**. *The Cobuild English Course, Level 1* (Willis and Willis, 1988) is designed for **false beginners** (people who have had some experience of the foreign language, and usually some tuition, but who, for one reason or another, have not progressed beyond elementary level, or have forgotten what they had once learnt) and aims to teach the 700 commonest words in English. The list is derived from the 20 million word corpus built up at the University of Birmingham by the Cobuild Dictionary Project (see CORPORA).

The **English for Specific Purposes** movement has played an important and influential role in ELT since the 1960s. In ESP, the aims of the course are determined by the particular needs of the learners, and the growth of the use of English in science, technology, and business has led to both research into the nature of learners' needs (**needs analysis**) and the preparation of teaching materials to meet those needs. In ESP, as in ELT in general, there have been considerable changes in approach. Early courses, such as Herbert's *The Structure of Technical English* (1965) and Ewer and Latorre's *Course in Basic Scientific English* (1969), adopted a grammatical approach concentrating largely on those structures, such as the Present Simple – both active and passive – and the Present Perfect, that **register analysis** has shown to be important in scientific and technical English.

The functional/notional syllabus probably worked more effectively in ESP courses than in General English courses. Allen and Widdowson's *English in Focus* series (1974 onwards), based largely on functions, and, more particularly, Bates and Dudley-Evans' *Nucleus* series (1976), based on scientific notions or concepts, have both been influential courses. Subsequent courses, e.g *Reading and Thinking in English* edited by Moore and Widdowson (1980) and *Skills for Learning* which developed from a project at the University of Malaya directed by Sinclair (Sinclair, 1980), have concentrated on particular study skills, particularly reading. Task-based approaches have also been very appropriate for ESP work; a course called *Interface*, written by Hutchinson and Waters (1984) and developed originally for a group of technical students preparing to study in Britain, is a good example of such an approach.

It has become common to make a distinction between two main branches of ESP: **English for Academic Purposes** (EAP) and **English for Occupational Purposes** (EOP). In the United States, English for Occupational Purposes is usually referred to as **English for Vocational Purposes** (EVP). EAP began as the dominant branch, but with the increased interest in Business English, EOP has become increasingly important. Most EOP courses, except for early courses, have been strongly influenced by task-based syllabuses. The results of genre analysis (see GENRE ANALYSIS) are likely to have an increasing influence on both branches of ESP.

The relationship between ELT and linguistics or applied linguistics has always been interesting. At certain times, research carried out by either descriptive or applied linguists has had a strong influence on ELT materials and methodology. At other times, pioneering work done in the classroom has been ahead of applied linguistics, which has subsequently provided a theoretical framework to explain what has already been discovered in the classroom. The pattern seems to be that most new developments in ELT have been prompted by new work in linguistics or applied linguistics; the work in ELT then expands in a number of directions and leads to discoveries which feed back into applied linguistics.

Howatt (1984) describes how the Reform Movement of the late nineteenth century was closely associated with the development of phonetics and the formation of associations such as the International Phonetics Association (see THE INTERNATIONAL PHONETIC ALPHABET). Similarly, the professionalization of ELT in the first half of the twentieth century begins with the work of Daniel Jones in phonetics (see PHONEMICS) but was developed by the more practically orientated work of Palmer, West, and Hornby. Their work in developing teaching materials and ideas for using those materials culminated in a number of books on teaching methodology published in the late 1950s and early 1960s, notably West's *Teaching English in Difficult Circumstances* (1960) and Billows' *Techniques of Language Teaching* (1962). Abercrombie's *Problems and Principles* (1956) was also influential. As noted earlier, Widdowson had a considerable influence on the emergence of the Communicative Approach to language teaching and he in turn drew on the tradition of relating language and social context that begins with Firth and continues with Halliday (see FUNCTIONALIST LINGUISTICS). But the various interpretations of a Communicative Approach in the actual classroom and discussion of the claimed successes of these approaches have played an important part in the applied linguistics literature, both in journals such as *English Language Teaching Journal* (*ELTJ*) and books such as Johnson's *Communicative Syllabus Design and Methodology* (1982).

It is interesting to note that in the USA the influence of both descriptive and applied linguistics has been more direct. Howatt (1984) reports Fries as stating that the relationship should be hierarchical, with the descriptive linguist providing the description of the target language, the applied linguist selecting and grading the structures from this description and also providing a contrastive analysis of the source and target languages. The applied linguist then prepares the materials which the teacher uses in the classroom. It is perhaps noteworthy that the main American journal concerned with ELT, *TESOL Quarterly* has always published many more data-based empirical studies related to classroom methodology than the British *ELTJ*. It is likely that with the increased numbers of

ELT teachers following postgraduate courses in applied linguistics, the gap between the two professions will diminish and that more systematic approaches to the development and validation of teaching materials and methodology will emerge.

T.D.-E.

SUGGESTIONS FOR FURTHER READING

Howatt, A.T.R. (1984), *A History of English Language Teaching*, Oxford, Oxford University Press.

White, R. (1988), *The ELT Curriculum*, Oxford, Basil Blackwell.

Widdowson, H.G. (1983), *Learning Purpose and Language Use*, Oxford, Oxford University Press.

Text linguistics

BACKGROUND

As Hoey points out (1983–4, p. 1),

> there is a tendency . . . to make a hard-and-fast distinction between discourse (spoken) and text (written). This is reflected even in two of the names of the discipline(s) we study – discourse analysis and text linguistics. But, though the distinction is a necessary one to maintain for some purposes . . . it may at times obscure similarities in the organisation of the spoken and written word.

The distinction Hoey mentions is made in this volume on practical, not theoretical grounds, and the overlap between text linguistics and discourse and conversational analysis should be borne in mind.

Early modern linguistics, with its emphasis on discovering and describing the minimal units of each of the linguistic levels of sound, form, syntax, and semantics, made no provision for the study of long stretches of text as such; traditional grammatical analysis stops at sentence length. It is even possible to argue that 'the extraction of tiny components diverts consideration away from the important unities which bind a text together' (de Beaugrande and Dressler, 1981, p. 21), and although Zellig Harris (1952) had

proposed to analyse whole discourses on distributional principles (see DISCOURSE AND CONVERSATIONAL ANALYSIS), employing the notion of transformations between stretches of text, this emergent interest in text and discourse study was lost at the time in Chomsky's modification of the notion of transformation to an intrasentential phenomenon (see TRANSFORMATIONAL-GENERATIVE GRAMMAR).

Early large-scale inquiries into text organization remained essentially descriptive and structurally based (Pike, 1967; Koch, 1971; Heger, 1976), with occasional expansion of the framework to include text sequences or situations of occurrence (Coseriu, 1955–6; Pike, 1967; Harweg, 1968; Koch, 1971). **Text** was defined as a unit larger than the sentence, and the research was orientated towards discovering and classifying types of text structure; these were assumed to be something given, rather than something partly construed by the reader, and dependent on context. 'We end up having classifications with various numbers of categories and degrees of elaboration, but no clear picture of how texts are utilized in social activity' (de Beaugrande and Dressler, 1981, p. 23).

The descriptive method, however, tends to break down because the language is too complex with too many and diverse constituents to be captured. Ironically, it was the concept of transformations, lost by Harris to Chomsky, which allowed a new outlook on text that encouraged the upsurge in text linguistics during the 1970s. In transformational grammar, the infinite set of possible sentences of a language are seen as derivable from a small set of underlying deep patterns plus a set of rules for transforming these into the more elaborate actual surface structures. It was argued, first, (Katz and Fodor, 1963 – see also RHETORIC, p. 383) that a whole text could be treated as a single sentence by seeing full stops as substitutes for conjunctions like *and*. This approach, however, deliberately leaves out reference to speakers' motives and knowledge. In addition, it ignores the fact that 'factors of accent, intonation, and word-order within a sentence depend on the organization of other sentences in the vicinity' (de Beaugrande and Dressler, 1981, p. 24). This was noted by Heidolph (1966), who suggests 'that a feature of "mentioned" vs. "not mentioned" could be inserted in the grammar to regulate these factors' (de Beaugrande and Dressler, 1981, p. 24). Isenberg (1968, 1971) lists other factors which could be dealt with within a single sentence, such as pronouns, articles, and tense sequences. 'He adds features intended to capture the status of noun phrases . . . [and] appeals to coherence relations like cause, purpose, specification, and temporal proximity' (de Beaugrande and Dressler, 1981, p. 24).

This type of argument led to the **Konstanz project**, set up at the University of Konstanz, Germany. A group of researchers including Hannes Rieser, Peter Hartmann, János Petöfi, Teun van Dijk, Jens Ihwe, Wolfram Köck, and others, attempted to construct a grammar and lexicon which would generate a Brecht text; some of the results of this project are presented by van Dijk *et al.* (1972). The project highlighted more problems than it solved, though (de Beaugrande and Dressler, 1981, p. 24): 'Despite a huge apparatus of rules, there emerged no criteria for judging the text "grammatical" or "well-formed". . . . The problem of common reference was not solved', and the basic assumption of the

undertaking was questioned by Kummer (1972), who points out that 'the "generating" of the text is presupposed by the investigators rather than performed by the grammar' (de Beaugrande and Dressler, 1981, p. 25).

In contrast to the grammatical method employed by the Konstanz group, Petöfi's (1971, 1974, 1978, 1980) **text-structure/world-structure theory (TeSWeST)** operates with factors relating to text users rather than to the text as an isolated artefact, and with representational devices drawn from formal logic. His project is extremely complex (de Beaugrande and Dressler, 1981, pp. 25–6):

In the 1980 version, components are offered for representing a text from nearly every perspective. To meet the demands of the logical basis, a 'canonic' mode (a regularized, idealized correlate) is set up alongside the 'natural language' mode in which the text is in fact expressed. Rules and algorithms are provided for such operations as 'formation', 'composition', 'construction', 'description', 'interpretation', and 'translation'. The reference of the text to objects or situations in the world is handled by a 'world-semantics' component; at least some correspondence is postulated between text-structure and world structure.

Retaining the idea of a text grammar designed to cope with features of text which a sentence grammar cannot handle, van Dijk (1972) introduces the notion of the **macrostructure**, a large-scale statement of the text's context (de Beaugrande and Dressler, 1981, p. 27 – compare van Dijk, 1977, ch. 5):

Van Dijk reasoned that the generating of a text must begin with a main **idea** which gradually evolves into the detailed meanings that enter individual sentence-length stretches. . . . When a text is presented, there must be operations which work in the other direction to extract the main idea back out again, such as *deletion* (direct removal of material), *generalization* (recasting material in a more general way), and *construction* (creating new material to subsume the presentation). . . . Accordingly, van Dijk turned to cognitive psychology for a *process-oriented* model of the text. In collaboration with Walter Kintsch, he investigated the operations people use to summarize texts . . . (cf. Kintsch & van Dijk 1978; van Dijk & Kintsch 1978). The typical summary for a text ought to be based on its macro-structure. . . . However, research showed that the actual outcome involves both the macro-structure of the text and previously stored macro-structures based on knowledge of the events and situations in the real world.

De Beaugrande and Dressler (1981) view their own **procedural** approach to text linguistics as evolved out of these other views, and most text linguists make some reference to both micro- and macrostructural features of the text, and to speakers' world knowledge (see GENRE ANALYSIS and PSYCHOLINGUISTICS. By a **procedural approach**, de Beaugrande and Dressler (1981, p. 31) mean an approach in which 'all the levels of language are to be described in terms of their utilization'. They (ibid., p. 3) define **text** as a communicative occurrence which meets seven standards of **textuality**, namely **cohesion** and **coherence**, which are both text-centred, and **intentionality**, **acceptability**, **informativity**, **situationality**, and **intertextuality**, which are all user-centred. These seven standards, described below, function as the **constitutive principles** which define and create communication. In addition, at least three **regulative principles**, also described below, control textual communication (for the distinction between constitutive and regulatory rules and principles, see SPEECH-ACT THEORY). These are **efficiency**, **effectiveness**, and **appropriateness**.

THE CONSTITUTIVE PRINCIPLES OF COMMUNICATION

COHESION

The major work on cohesion in English is Halliday and Hasan (1976), but Jakobson's (1960) stress on textual parallelism created by patterning and repetition in text (see STYLISTICS)

is the earliest detailed development of the idea of cohesion (see Closs Traugott and Pratt, 1980, p. 21).

Cohesion concerns the way in which the linguistic items of which a text is composed are meaningfully connected to each other in a sequence on the basis of the grammatical rules of the language. In English, cohesion is created in four ways (Halliday, 1985, ch. 9): by **reference**, **ellipsis** (including **substitution**), **conjunction**, and **lexical organization**.

Reference may be of two types: (1) **exophoric**, referring out of the text to an item in the world (*look at that*); (2) **endophoric**, referring to textual items either by **cataphora**, forward reference (as in *the house that Jack built*, where *the* refers forward to the specifying *that Jack built*); or **anaphora**, backward reference, (as in *Jack built a house. It . . .*, where *it* refers back to *house*); **homophora**, self-specifying reference to an item of which there can only be one, or only one that makes sense in the context (*the sun was shining* or *She fed the cat*). Devices that refer are the personal pronouns and demonstratives, which corefer, and comparatives, which contrast.

Ellipsis works anaphorically by leaving out something mentioned earlier, as in *Help yourself* (for instance to some apples mentioned earlier). **Substitution** works by substituting a 'holding device' in the place of a lexical item *Help yourself to one*.

Devices which create **conjunction** constitute cohesive bonds between sections of text. There are three types, according to Halliday (ibid.):

1 **Elaboration** by **apposition**, either **expository** (*in other words*), or **exemplifying** (*for example*); or by **clarification**: **corrective** (*or rather*), **distractive** (*incidentally*), **dismissive** (*in any case*), **particularizing** (*in particular*), **resumptive** (*as I was saying*), **summative** (*in short*), and **verifactive** (*actually*).

2 **Extension**, which is either **additive** (*and, nor*), **adversative** (*but*), or a **variation** type, of which there are three, **replacive** (*instead, on the contrary*), **subtractive** (*apart/except from/for that*), and **alternative** (*alternatively*).

3 **Enhancement**, either **spatio-temporal** (*here,*

there, nearby, behind, in the first place) or **manner** (comparison, reference to means), or **causal-conditional** (*so, therefore*) or **matter** (*in this respect, in other respects*).

De Beaugrande and Dressler (1981, pp. 71–3) call these relationships **junctions**, and the devices signalling them **junctive expressions**; they distinguish four major types:

1 **Conjunction**, which is an additive relation linking things which have the same status, e.g., both true in the textual world (see below, under **coherence**). Their signals are *and, moreover, also, in addition, besides, furthermore*.

2 **Disjunction**, which links things that have alternative status, e.g., two things which cannot both be true in the textual world. Their signals are *or, either/or, whether or not*.

3 **Contrajunction**, which links things having the same status but appearing incongruous or incompatible in the textual world, i.e., a cause and an unanticipated effect. Their signals are *but, however, yet, nevertheless*.

4 **Subordination**, which links things when the status of one depends on that of the other, e.g., things true under certain conditions or for certain motives (precondition/event, cause/ effect, etc.). Their signals are *because, since, as, thus, while, therefore, on the grounds that, then, next, before, after, since, whenever, while, during, if*.

Lexical cohesion is created by **repetition**, **synonymy**, and **collocation**. While reference, ellipsis, and conjunction tend to link clauses which are near each other in the text, lexical cohesion tends to link much larger parts of the text (but see the discussion of patterns under **coherence** below).

One of the most thoughtful and prolific writers on the subject of relations between clauses is Eugene Winter (Hoey, 1983, p. 17):

His work on clause relations can for the most part be divided into two major strands. On the one hand, he is concerned to place a sentence in the context of its adjoining sentences and show how its grammar and meaning can only be fully explained if its larger context is taken into account . . . On the other, he is concerned to reveal the clause organisation of a passage as a whole without focussing on any one sentence in particular within it.

In similar vein, de Beaugrande and Dressler (1981, p. 79) distinguish between **short-range** and **long-range** stretches of surface text structures, the former set up as closely knit patterns of grammatical dependencies, the latter constituted by the reutilization of previous elements or patterns (see also van Dijk, 1977. p. 93).

However, as Hoey (1983, p. 18) points out, Winter's (1971) definition of the clause relation as 'the cognitive process whereby we interpret the meaning of a sentence or group of sentences in the text in the light of its adjoining sentence or group of sentences', has the implication that 'uninterpreted grammatical cohesion is not a relation'. Most writers on cohesion (see, for instance, Halliday and Hasan, 1976) stress that it is created by the reader on the basis of the signalling devices. None the less, in view of the force with which this is stressed by Winter, and also by Hoey, and in view of their emphasis on the larger, macrostructural patterns the reader is able to construct, only partly on the basis of cohesive devices, their work is discussed under **coherence** below.

De Beaugrande and Dressler (1981, p. 80) include as long-range cohesive devices (compare Halliday's lexical-cohesion devices listed above):

Recurrence: the exact repetition of material.

Partial recurrence: different uses of the same basic language items (word stems).

Parallelism: reuse of structures with different material in them.

Paraphrase: approximate conceptual equivalence among outwardly different material.

Proforms: brief, empty elements used to keep the content of fuller elements current and to reuse basic syntactic structures.

Ellipsis: allows the omission of some structural component, provided a complete version is recoverable from elsewhere in the text.

COHERENCE

Coherence concerns the way in which the things that the text is about, called the **textual world**, are mutually accessible and relevant. The textual world is considered to consist of concepts and relations. A **concept** is defined as 'a configuration of knowledge (cognitive content) which can be recovered or activated with more or less unity and consistency in the mind', and **relations** as the links between the concepts 'which appear together in a textual world' (de Beaugrande and Dressler, 1981, p. 4). Some of the most common relations can be classified in terms of two major notions, namely causality relations and time relations.

1 **Causality** relations 'concern the ways in which one situation or event affects the conditions for some other one' (ibid.), and are of four major types:

(a) **Cause**: *David hit the ball so hard that it flew over the hedge*; here the event of 'hitting the ball hard' has created the **necessary conditions** for the event of 'the ball flying over the hedge'.

(b) **Enablement**: *Tabitha lay quietly in the sun and Tomas crept over and pulled her tail*; here a weaker relation obtains between the event consisting of Tabitha lying quietly in the sun, and the event consisting of Tomas creeping over and pulling her tail; the former event is a **sufficient**, but not a **necessary**, condition for the latter.

(c) **Reason**: *Because I've been writing about text linguistics all day I deserve a rest this evening*; in this case, the second event follows as a rational response to the first, but is not actually caused or enabled by it.

(d) **Purpose**: *You are reading this to find out about text linguistics*; in this case, although the first event enables the second, there is an added dimension, in so far as the second event is the **planned outcome** of the first.

2 **Time** relations concern the arrangement of events in time. In the case of cause, enable-ment, and reason, an earlier event causes, enables, or provides the reason for a later one, so that we might say that **forward directionality** is involved. Purpose, however, has **backward directionality**, since a later event is the purpose for an earlier event.

Winter, for his part, divides clause relations into the two broad classes of **Logical Sequence** relations and **Matching** relations, where the most basic form of Logical Sequence relation is the time sequence (see Hoey, 1983, p. 19). Both of these types are, however, governed by 'a still more fundamental relation, that of Situation-Evaluation, representing the two facets of world-perception "knowing" and "thinking". Indeed . . . all relations are reducible to these basic elements' (ibid., p. 20). De Beaugrande and Dressler (1981) do not display such an overtly reductive tendency.

1 **Logical Sequence relations** 'are relations between successive events or ideas, whether actual or potential' (Hoey, 1983, p. 19). They include:

4 (a) **Condition–Consequence**, signalled by, e.g., *if (then)*;

(b) **Instrument–Achievement**, signalled by, e.g., *by (means of)*;

(c) **Cause–Consequence**, signalled by, e.g., *because, so*.

2 **Matching relations** 'are relations where statements are "matched" against each other in terms of identicality of description' (ibid., p. 20). They include:

(a) **Contrast**, signalled by, e.g., *however*;

(b) **Compatibility**, signalled by, e.g., *(and)*, *(similarly)*.

One of the most valuable aspects of Winter's work – and one which powerfully suggests that his (and Hoey's) work should be seen as a contribution to our understanding of coherence rather than only of cohesion – is his insistence that a clause relation cannot simply be read off from one textual surface signal. This must, of course, be obvious to anyone who peruses the various lists writers produce of signalling devices, since the same item is often listed as a signal for several relations (see, for instance, Halliday and Hasan, 1976, pp. 242–3).

What Winter importantly stresses, however, is that *other* lexical items, in addition to junctive expressions, help readers to determine which relation a given junctive expression signals. He divides junctive expressions proper into two traditional types, namely **subordinators**, which he calls **Vocabulary 1**, and **conjuncts**, which he calls **Vocabulary 2**. But he adds to these the class of **lexical signals**, which he calls **Vocabulary 3**. The *same* clause relation may be signalled by an item from any one of these three classes, as Hoey (1983, p. 23), drawing on Winter (1977) demonstrates. The **Instrument–Achievement** relation is signalled in each of the following three near-paraphrases (signals in italics):

(1) *By* appealing to scientists and technologists to support his party, Mr Wilson won many middle-class votes.
(2) Mr Wilson appealed to scientists and technologists to support his party. He *thereby* won many middle-class votes.
(3) Mr Wilson's appeals to scientists and technologists to support his party *were instrumental* in winning many middle-class votes.

In (1) the relation is signalled with a Vocabulary 1 item, in (2) by a Vocabulary 2 item, and in (3) by a Vocabulary 3 item. Furthermore (Hoey, 1983, p. 24),

Vocabulary 3 items not only help signal the relations that hold between the sentences of a paragraph. They also signal the organisation of longer passages and whole discourses. Winter (1977) [and see also Winter (1986)] draws attention, for example, to what he terms 'items of the metastructure'; these are lexical signals which serve a larger function.

Hoey's own work is mostly concerned with this metastructural organization of the text. He discusses **Matching patterns**, **General–Particular patterns**, and, in particular, the **Problem–Solution pattern**, where by **pattern** he means 'combination of relations organising (part of) a discourse' (Hoey, 1983, p. 31).

Both Hoey and Winter show that the stylistic device of **repetition** (see also STYLISTICS) both connects sentences and contributes to sentence and text interpretation, 'because where two sentences have material in common, it is what is changed that receives attention by the reader, while the repeated material acts as a framework for the interpretation of the new material' (ibid., p. 25).

Repetition typically signals Matching relations and General–Particular relations. It may take the form of **simple repetition** 'of a lexical item that has appeared earlier in a discourse, with no more alteration than is explicable by reference to grammatical paradigms' (ibid., p. 108), e.g., *they dance – she dances*. Or it may take the form of **complex repetition**, in which a morpheme is shared by items of different word classes: *she danced* (verb) – *the dance* (noun) – *the dancing shoes* (adjective). Repetition may, however, also take the form of **substitution** in Hoey's system (in contrast with Halliday and Hasan (1976), who treat substitution as a subclass of ellipsis – see above, p. 463). His signals of this type of repetition are the same as those listed by Halliday and Hasan (1976) (see above, pp. 463–4). Finally, **paraphrase** is also classed as repetition.

Repetition is the clearest signal of the **Matching** relation (Hoey, 1983, p. 113):

Matching is what happens when two parts of a discourse are compared in respect of their detail. Sometimes they are matched for similarity, in which case we call the resulting relation Matching Compatibility, and sometimes for difference, in which case we call the resulting relation Matching Contrast.

The only types of text that are occasionally organized solely in terms of Matching relations are letters and poems. Normally, the Matching relation is used together with one of the General–Particular relations (see below). This is because it is usual when matching pieces of information first to provide a generalization which will make sense of the matching. In the case of letters, the reader's background knowledge may, however, supply the generalization, and in the case of poetry, supplying it may be part of the process of interpretation.

Hoey (ibid., ch. 7) discusses two types of **General–Particular** pattern, namely the **Generalization–Example** relation, and the **Preview–Detail** relation, both of which, in combination with the Matching relation, may organize whole texts, or long passages of them. He shows, for instance, how two Matching example sentences (ibid., p. 113):

> (2) For example, a map will only contain those features which are of interest to the person using the map. (3) Similarly, architects' models will be limited to include only those features which are of interest to the person considering employing the architect.

are prefaced with the generalization for which they serve as examples:

> (1) It is interesting to note that iconic models only represent certain features of that portion of the real world which they simulate.

(The sentences are from Alan Jenkin, 'Simulation under focus', *Computer Management*, March 1971, p. 38).

In the case of a **Preview–Detail** relation, the Detail member of the relation supplies information about the Preview member, or about a part of it, and the details may be Matched. The most typical Detail member is definition. In the following example, sentence (1) is the Preview, and sentences (2) and (3) Matched Details:

> (1) The Danish word 'hyggelig' is interesting, but difficult to master for foreign learners of the language. (2) On the one hand, it can be used of situations in which one is comfortable, in a warm, snug, feeling-at-home sort of way. (3) On the other hand, it can be used about a person who makes one feel comfortable and at home.

One can test for the Preview–Detail relation by seeing whether, if one asks after sentence (1) 'Can you give me more detail?', the following clauses do so.

The most typical discourse pattern is, however, the Problem–Solution pattern. Many texts can be treated as conforming to the pattern **Situation – Problem – Response – Evaluation/Result** with recursion on Response – that is, a Response may itself cause a new problem, requiring a new Response, etc. Hoey gives the example shown in Figure 1 (from Hoey, 1983, p. 53). The pattern can be revealed by questioning. After each of the sentences in Figure 1, a reader might ask a question like, e.g., 'What happened then?', 'What did you do then?'. Or the pattern may be revealed by paraphrase using lexical signals (ibid.):

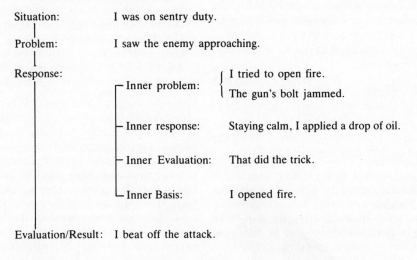

Situation: I was on sentry duty.

Problem: I saw the enemy approaching.

Response:
              ⎰ Inner problem: { I tried to open fire.
                                    { The gun's bolt jammed.

              – Inner response: Staying calm, I applied a drop of oil.

              – Inner Evaluation: That did the trick.

              – Inner Basis: I opened fire.

Evaluation/Result: I beat off the attack.

Figure 1

The *means* whereby I beat off the attack was by opening fire. The *cause* of my opening fire was that I saw the enemy approaching. The *circumstances* of my seeing the enemy approaching was that I was on sentry duty.

The lexical signals used in the paraphrase may be the terms used in the pattern itself (ibid.):
'My *situation* was that I was on sentry duty. I saw the enemy approaching. I *solved* this *problem* by opening fire. This *achieved* the *desired result* of beating off the attack.'

Hoey (ibid., pp. 57–8) draws up four sets of mapping conditions which show the relationship between the Problem–Solution *pattern* and the *relations* between clauses:

(1) We will assume two parts of a discourse, *a* and b, in a Cause–Consequence relation. *If (i) a* has been independently established as Problem *and (ii) b* contains the role of agent, then *b* is Response.

(2) We will assume three parts of a discourse, *a, b* and *c*, of which *a* and *b* are in an Instrument–Achievement or Instrument–Purpose relation (Purpose being more or less equivalent to hoped-for achievement), and of which *a* has not been independently established as a Problem.

Given these circumstances, *if (i) b* contains the role of agent *and (ii) c* prevents, reverses, avoids, avoids harm to, or seeks help in preventing, etc., some crucial aspect of *a*, then *a* is Problem and *b* is Response.

(3) We will assume two parts of a discourse, *a* and *b*, in a Cause–Consequence relation and that *a* has not been independently established as Problem.

If (i) b contains the role of agent *and (ii) b* also prevents, reverses, avoids, or avoids harm to some crucial aspects of *a*, then *a* is Problem and *b* Response.

(4) We will assume the same as for mapping condition 3.

If (i) b contains the role of agent *and* (ii) b also can have attached to it a Purpose clause, *c*, which spells out a layman's understanding of what *b* means, and if

(iii) the newly formed trio conforms to the conditions of mapping condition 2, then *a* is Problem and *b* Response.

Hoey's and Winter's approaches differ from that of de Beaugrande and Dressler (1981) and Van Dijk and Kintsch (1978) in remaining fairly strictly on the surface of discourse (although making reference to such 'deep' roles as 'agent', as in the above), and in not emphasizing the psychological processes of understanding and perceiving macrostructure (Hoey, 1983, p. 33):

> Instead, the emphasis is laid on the ways in which the surface of the discourse (not necessarily to be contrasted with hidden depths) contains sufficient clues for the reader/listener to perceive accurately the discourse's organisation.

This has the advantage that the phenomena described are fairly directly observable, while the reference to concepts and relations of the textual world and to schemata remains of a hypothetical nature. However, the two approaches are best seen as complementary; surface-structure linguists have provided valuable detailed work on cohesion and coherence; nevertheless, it would be naive to think that readers' cognitive processes and knowledge of various aspects of the world is not important in text comprehension. It might even be arguable that the reason why the Problem–Solution pattern is so fruitful for text analysis is that it closely matches those cognitive writer and reader processes which de Beaugrande and Dressler (1981) refer to in discussing the remaining five conditions of textuality.

INTENTIONALITY

Intentionality concerns the text producer's intention to produce a cohesive and coherent text that will attain whatever goal s/he has planned that it should attain. Text producers and receivers both rely on Grice's Principle of Co-operation (see PRAGMATICS) in managing discourse, but in text linguistics, the notion of conversational implicature is supplemented with the notion that language users *plan* towards a *goal* (de Beaugrande and Dressler, 1981, p. 123, and pp. 132–3):

> Planning in discourse involves interactive **problem-solving** on the part of both producer and receiver, since successful communication clearly demands the ability to detect or infer other participants' goals on the basis of what they say. . . . By the same token, text producers must be able to anticipate the receiver's responses as supportive of or contrary to a plan, for example, by building an *internal model* of the receivers and their beliefs and knowledge.

ACCEPTABILITY

Acceptability concerns the *receiver's* wish that the text should be cohesive and coherent and be of relevance to him or her (de Beaugrande and Dressler, 1981, p. 7): 'This attitude is responsive to such factors as text type, social or cultural setting, and the desirability of goals'. The receiver will be *tolerant* of things, such as false starts, which interfere with coherence and cohesion and will use *inferencing*, based on his or her own general knowledge, to bring the textual world together.

INFORMATIVITY

Informativity 'concerns the extent to which the occurrences of the presented text are expected vs. unexpected or known vs. unknown/certain' (de Beaugrande and Dressler, 1981, pp. 8–9). Hence it needs reference to the notion of **probability** (ibid., p. 140) – the more probable in any particular context will be more expected than the less probable. When something very unexpected occurs (ibid., p. 144),

> the text receiver must do a MOTIVATION SEARCH – a special case of **problem-solving** – to find out what these occurrences signify, why they were selected, and how they can be integrated back into the CONTINUITY that is the basis of communication.

If no solution is forthcoming, the text will appear as nonsensical.

A receiver's expectations of what will appear in a text are powerfully affected by her or his perception of what text type s/he is currently encountering. What is unexpected in a technical report may be less unexpected in a poem, and it is interesting to observe how people faced with apparent nonsense will normally be able to give it a meaning if they are told that the text is a poem.

SITUATIONALITY

Situationality 'concerns the factors which make a text RELEVANT to a SITUATION of occurrence' (de Beaugrande and Dressler, 1981, p. 9). Again, a text-receiver will typically try hard to solve any problem arising from the occurrence of apparently irrelevant items in text, i.e., s/he will engage in Problem-Solution in order to make such items appear relevant.

INTERTEXTUALITY

Intertextuality concerns the way in which the use of a certain text depends on knowledge of other texts. For instance, a traffic sign saying 'resume speed' only makes sense on the basis of a previous sign telling a driver to slow down. The interdependence of texts covered by the notion of intertextuality is responsible for the evolution of *text types*, which are groups of texts displaying characteristic features and patterns (see GENRE ANALYSIS). Parodies, critical reviews, reports, and responses to the arguments of others are highly and obviously reliant on intertextuality. In other cases, we are less aware of intertextuality. For instance, a novel we are reading may appear as an independent text; however, it relies on the tradition of novel writing, and we bring our knowledge of what a novel is to the reading of it.

REGULATIVE PRINCIPLES OF TEXTUAL COMMUNICATION

EFFICIENCY

Efficiency depends on the text being used in communicating with minimum effort by the participants; that is, it 'contributes to *processing ease* ... the running of operations with a light load on resources of attention and access' (de Beaugrande and Dressler, 1981, p. 34).

Effectiveness depends on the text leaving a strong impression and creating favourable conditions for attaining a goal. 'It elicits *processing depth*, that is, intense use of resources of attention and access on materials removed from the explicit surface representation' (de Beaugrande and Dressler, 1981, p. 34).

Appropriateness is the agreement between the setting of a text and the ways in which the standards of textuality are upheld. It determines 'the correlations between the current occasion and the standards of textuality such that reliable estimates can be made regarding ease or depth of participants' processing' (de Beaugrande and Dressler, 1981, p. 34). It mediates between efficiency and effectiveness which (ibid.)

> tend to work against each other. Plain language and trite content [efficiency] are very easy to produce and receive, but cause boredom and leave little impression behind. In contrast, creative language and bizarre content [effectiveness] can elicit a powerful effect, but may become unduly difficult to produce and receive.

In **Text Linguistics**, then, the links between clauses are observed across sentence boundaries, and these links can be seen to form larger patterns of text organization. In addition, however, reference to the text surrounding a given sentence may be seen to cast light on the **naturalness** of the sentence in question.

Naturalness is Sinclair's term for 'the concept of well-formedness of sentences *in text*' (1984, p. 203), and it is contrasted with what is normally thought of as sentence well-formedness, which is

a property sentences may or may not have when seen in isolation. Sinclair argues that many well-formed sentences do not appear natural to a native speaker, and that, since these appear odd in spite of being well formed, they 'must violate some restrictions which are not among the criteria for well-formedness' (ibid.), so that well-formedness and naturalness are independent variables.

Some of the determinants for the fulfilment of the criteria for naturalness are situated in the surrounding discourse, while those for well-formedness are all within the sentence itself. Thus *If you like* is not well formed by the traditional grammatical criteria, but is a natural response to a type of request. It contains what Sinclair calls a **rangefinder**, an indication that an item in the **co-text** (the rest of the text) or **context** (the situation in which the text is being used) will render it unproblematic, the item being, in this case, the request preceding it.

The degree to which a sentence depends for its naturalness on its cotext and/or context is called its **isolation**, and **isolation** is one of three parameters in terms of which statements about sentence naturalness can be made. Isolation also depends on **allowables**, so called because they are features of the sentence which, although dependent on co-text or context for their specification, do not interfere with its well-formedness. Allowables include pronouns, as displayed in the sentence *I wouldn't have bought **it** if **he** hadn't been **there*** (ibid. p. 204; allowables in bold; bold and italics added). The allowables in this sentence do not render it ill formed, but they do indicate its dependence on the surrounding discourse, since that is where we would expect to be able to discover their referents, i.e., what *it, he,* and *there* refer to.

In contrast, *Prince Charles is now a husband* is well formed by traditional grammatical criteria, but is not a natural sentence, chiefly because 'there is a conflict between the mutual expectations of the equative structure, the indefinite article, and the word *husband*. Words denoting occupations (e.g. *sailor*) would not cause this conflict.' The sentence violates the second parameter in terms of which naturalness statements are made, namely **idiomaticity**.

Had the item *husband* been preceded by the item *good*, however, the sentence would have been far more natural than it is. An item which has this effect on naturalness is called a **supporter**. The notion of support rests on the notion of collocation, the tendency which linguistic items have to occur with certain other items. When expectations about collocation are fulfilled in a sentence, it will display **neutrality**, a further parameter for statements about naturalness. Supporters also affect idiomaticity, so that in the sentence *I'm trying to rack my brains* (Sinclair, 1984, pp. 203ff.) the very low expectation of collocation between *trying* and *rack my brains* contributes considerably to its low status on the scale of idiomaticity and to its consequent non-naturalness.

Sinclair hopes that an extended study of text will establish the precise conditions for sentence naturalness (ibid., p. 210):

> The study of allowables will lead to the specification of an abstract text framework for any sentence. The study of rangefinders will
>
> a. show how each sentence is integrated into its text
>
> b. establish the range of individual features.
>
> The study of supporters will tell us a lot about the resolution of textual ambiguity, and will lead to a precise specification of
>
> a. complex items, eg phrases
> b. permitted range of variation.

The three scales of neutrality, isolation and idiomaticity will allow sentences to be compared with each other and might lead to a modern rhetoric at the rank of sentence.

It thus appears that while a grammatical approach was found to be unhelpful to text linguistics, further study in the field of naturalness may be able to provide illumination not just of the nature of text, but also of the traditional domain of grammar, the sentence.

K.M.

SUGGESTIONS FOR FURTHER READING

de Beaugrande, R. and Dressler, W.V. (1981), *Introduction to Text Linguistics*, London and New York, Longman.

Hoey, M. (1983), *On the Surface of Discourse*, London, George Allen & Unwin.

Tone languages

All the languages in the world use consonants and vowels to build morphemes, which in turn join together to form words. Thus the English word *me* is made up of a nasal consonant followed by a high vowel. If we change the consonant to a /b/ we would get a different word, *be*, and if we change the vowel to a low vowel, we would also get a different word, *ma*.

We may pronounce the word *ma* with various pitch patterns, depending on the occasion. We may pronounce it with a high pitch if we are emphatic; we may say it with a rising pitch in a question, etc. But these different pitch patterns do not alter the word in the way that changing a consonant or changing a vowel does. These different pitch patterns that do not change, but merely add to the basic meaning of words are called **intonations** (see INTONATION).

Yet there are some languages in the world which use pitch patterns to build morphemes in the same way consonants and vowels are used. The best-known such language is Chinese, as

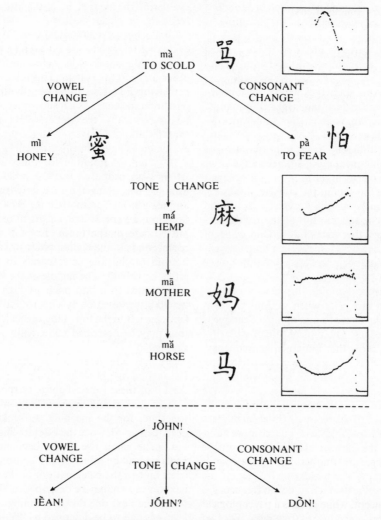

Figure 1 The four tones of Putonghua Chinese (from Wang, 1982, p. 58)

TONES are used to alter the meaning of Chinese words. Standard Chinese has only four tones: falling (as in *mà*), rising (as in *má*), level (*mā*), and dipping, or falling and then rising, (*mǎ*). The oscillograph traces at the right show the fundamental frequency of the authors voice as he spoke the words. In English, on the other hand, variation in tone is used to convey different moods; the meaning of the words being spoken does not change. In Chinese, changing tone has the same kind of effect on the meaning of a word as changing a vowel or a consonant.

illustrated in Figure 1 (Wang, 1973). As the figure shows, the syllable *ma*, when pronounced with a falling pitch pattern, means 'to scold' in the **Putonghua** dialect of Chinese. (Putonghua, which literally means 'common speech', is the speech form sponsored by the People's Republic of China. It is a variety of Mandarin.) When pronounced with a rising pattern, the meaning is 'hemp'; when pronounced with a high level pattern, the meaning is 'mother', as in some dialects of English; and lastly, when pronounced with a low dipping pattern, the meaning is 'horse'.

When pitch patterns are used in this lexical capacity, i.e., to build words and morphemes much as consonants and vowels do, they are called **tones**. And languages which use tones in this way are called **tone languages**. Putonghua, then, is a tone language. It has four tones, as illustrated in Figure 1.

Tones are different from consonants and vowels in a fundamental way. Whereas the latter are formed primarily in the mouth, by movement of the tongue, the velum, the jaw, etc., tones are formed primarily at the larynx – a box of cartilages situated at the top of the windpipe – which contains the vocal folds. One cycle of vibration of the vocal folds is the phonetic basis of sound in speech (see also ARTICULATORY PHONETICS).

During speech, the folds vibrate very rapidly. So rapidly, in fact, that when we look at them with the aid of a dentist's mirror, all we can see is a blur at the edges. The typical rate of vibration of the vocal folds, the fundamental frequency, abbreviated **F0**, is around 100 cycles per second (**cps**) for men and around 180 cps for women and children.

Variation in F0 is controlled by pulling the vocal folds toward the rear with different degrees of tension. As the folds are pulled more taut, somewhat in the manner of stretching a rubber band, they become thinner and vibrate at a higher frequency. The higher the frequency, the higher we perceive its pitch to be. So **frequency** is a physical concept, while **pitch** is a psychological one, i.e., the ear's response to frequency. The two scales are not identical. But they are sufficiently similar for our purposes here, so that we may interchange them for convenience.

We automatically normalize pitch for each speaker according to the pitch range we expect. When a man says 'hello', his average F0 may be around 100 cps. When a woman says 'hello', her average F0 may be around 180 cps. Yet we understand them to be saying the same linguistic thing, in spite of the great difference in the physical signal. We are able to do this by evaluating the average F0 of the utterance relative to the F0 of the speaker.

Similarly, in a tone language the F0 of a tone is evaluated relative to the F0 average and the F0 range of the speaker, as well as relative to the other tones in the system. This relative mode of perceiving F0 allows us constantly to adjust the baseline and range. As a result, different F0s may be linguistically the same, as in the 'hello' example above. Conversely, the same F0 may be evaluated as linguistically different.

A system of notation for tones, called **tone letters**, was proposed in 1930, which is widely used for describing the tone languages of East and South-East Asia (Chao, 1930). In this notation, a vertical line is used to represent the pitch range of the tones. The top of the line corresponds to the highest pitch, or value 5. The bottom of the line corresponds to the lowest pitch, or value 1. The middle of the vertical line corresponds to a mid pitch. A high level tone would be represented by a horizontal line drawn from the left to the top of the vertical line. Such a tone may be described numerically as '5–5', or simply '55'.

We may now refer back to the four tones of Putonghua, as shown in Figure 1. There we see the F0 of these four syllables, as spoken by the present author and analysed by computer. The top tone, for the meaning 'to scold', may be described as '51' since the F0 starts high and falls low. (The small rise at the beginning may be explained as an effect of the consonant and is irrelevant to the basic pattern of the tone.) The next one down may be described as '35', a rising tone. The next one down, meaning 'mother', is level enough to be described as '55'. And lastly, the bottom one may be described as a dipping tone, '424'.

There are many different linguistic systems which use more than four tones. The dialect of Chinese spoken in Guangzhou and Hong Kong, popularly called **Cantonese**, has nine tones (Wang and Cheng, 1987). In Figure 2 we see again the computer tracings of the F0 of the speaker's voice. For the six long tones in the left columns and the middle column, the syllable pronounced is /si/, as in the English word *see*.

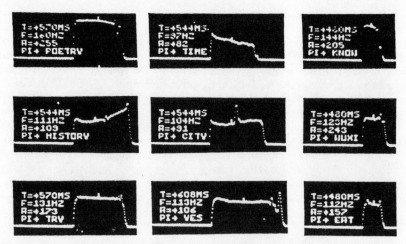

Figure 2 The nine tones of Cantonese (from Wang and Cheng, 1987, p. 515)

So we see in the upper left corner the F0 pattern for a high level tone, shown on the computer screen as 160 cps. (The 'HZ' in the figure is the abbreviation for 'hertz', which is equivalent to cps.) The meaning is 'poetry'. Compare this with the mid level tone in the lower left corner, at 131 cps, where the meaning is 'to try'. The other four long tones in these two columns have the meanings 'history', 'time', 'city' and 'yes'.

In Cantonese, the short tones occur only on syllables that end in plosive consonants, i.e. /p/, /t/, or /k/. These tones are short because they are stopped by these consonants; notice that they are less than half in duration when compared with the long tones. Strictly speaking, then, the short tones are never in minimal contrast with the long tones, because the long tones never occur on syllables that end in stop consonants. The syllable illustrated in the column to the right in Figure 2 is /sik/. Pronounced with a high tone it means 'to know', with a low tone it means 'to eat'. Pronounced with a mid tone it occurs in the name of a Chinese city, Wuxi.

The question naturally arises as to what is the maximum number of tones a language can have. Is there an upper limit? A theory of tones has been proposed to answer this question (Wang 1967). This is shown in Figure 3. The theory

states that the maximum number is thirteen, as shown by the tone letters in the figure. Furthermore, the theory states a maximum for each of the five categories of tones. The maximum for level tones is five. And the maximum is two for each of the other four categories: rising, falling, concave, and convex.

It is interesting to note that for the Putonghua system discussed earlier, there is one level tone (55), one rising tone (35), one falling tone (51) and one concave tone (424). This is a rather typical distribution. It is as though the language selects from as many categories as possible, rather than fill up its inventory with just one or two categories. In this respect, tones behave much like consonants and vowels in their selection process (Lindblom, 1989).

Consonants, too, tend to be selected a few from many categories, rather than many from a few categories. Notice that in English, plosives, affricates, fricatives, nasals, and liquids are all represented, but only a few from any one category. We can make the same observation about vowel systems. This similarity in the selection process suggests that tones too may be factored into a smaller set of phonological features, as has been done for consonants and vowels. This is the plan shown in Figure 3. The maximum set of thirteen tones can be analysed

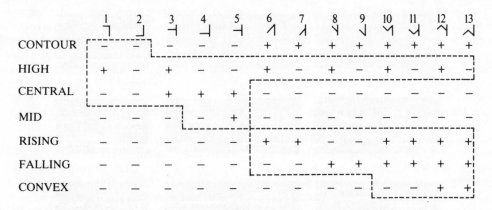

Figure 3 Phonological features of tone (from Wang, 1967, p. 103)

into seven binary features.

The Cantonese system illustrated in Figure 2 is an unusually complex one in terms of its tone inventory. There are tone languages all over the world; most of them have a simpler inventory of tones. In part, this is due to the fact that the majority of morphemes in these languages are polysyllabic, as opposed to Chinese, where most morphemes are monosyllabic. A language with two tones can have eight distinct tone sequences over three syllables, i.e. 2 × 2 × 2.

Below is a set of examples from **Kikuyu**, a Bantu language spoken in Kenya, where seven out of the eight possible sequences of high (H) and low (L) are actually used to build morphemes (McCawley, 1978, p. 127). The only sequence not used is HLL. (The phonetic notation has been simplified here.)

HHH	hengere	'slab'
HHL	ngauro	'person with shaved head'
HLH	tingori	'large boy not circumcised with his age-mates'
LHH	remere	'way of cultivating'
LHL	bariti	'anger'
LLH	boboto	'downpour'
LLL	beredi	'leaf-shaped spear'

Tones as a linguistic topic were discussed in China as early as 1,500 years ago, by the scholar Shen Yue (441–513). It is now well known that most of the languages of China and South-East Asia are tone languages, perhaps due to extensive mutual influence through the millennia. In western scholarship, an early study of this topic is by Beach (1924) on the Bantu languages of East Africa. Kikuyu, exemplified above, is one such language. Another Bantu language whose tone system has been studied extensively recently is **Makua**, spoken in southern Tanzania and in Mozambique (Cheng and Kisseberth, 1979–81). Numerous languages of West Africa are tone languages as well. Furthermore, these languages offer much important data for linguistic theory, as discussed by Hyman and Schuh (1974).

Among the languages of native America, many are tonal. A classic work on the study of tone languages is that by Pike (1948), which gives in-depth analyses of two Amerindian languages of Mexico, **Mazatec** and **Mixtec**. An especially intriguing phenomenon of the tone system of one of the Mixtec dialects, that of the town of Acatlan in central Mexico, is the presence of a **step-up tone**. (This phenomenon was discovered after the publication of Pike's book.)

The effect of the step-up is to raise the pitch of the syllable one step higher than the pitch of the preceding syllable, if the preceding syllable carries a high tone or a step-up tone. When a sequence of step-up tones occurs one after another in a sentence, it sounds a bit as if the person is singing a musical scale rather than speaking (Wang, 1972).

This phenomenon is all the more intriguing when we consider the so-called **terrace-level** tone languages of West Africa. In these languages, there is a **step-down tone**, which has the opposite effect of the step-up in Mixtec. Due to a complex interaction between these tones and the intonation of the sentence, the auditory effect is like going down a terrace, a step at a time.

Tone languages occur widely in Africa, Asia, and native America. They occur also in Europe. Among Germanic languages, Norwegian and Swedish are tonal in that a word can be classified according to two 'accents' differing primarily in their F0 pattern (Garding, 1973). Among Slavic languages, Serbo-Croatian and Slovenian are similar in this respect. Similar observations have also been made for **Lithuanian**, a Baltic language.

There is in fact a wide spectrum of criteria for what constitutes a tone language. The criteria may rest with the tone features used in the system (e.g., does it have contour tones?), with the lexical versus morphological function of the tones, and with the degree to which the various tones may be predicted on the basis of grammatical information. Some efforts have been made to construct a typology of tone languages, e.g. Wang (1972) and McCawley (1978). However, no comprehensive framework has been worked out as yet which has gained general usage.

Earlier in this article, I indicated that, unlike consonants and vowels, tones are produced primarily at the larynx. However, the activities of the articulators above the larynx frequently have a significant influence on the F0. This influence may be manifested physiologically and acoustically. Physiologically, different consonants and vowels are produced with different degrees of pull on laryngeal structures. This means that, everything else being equal, consonants and vowels may have distinct F0 patterns associated with them.

Acoustically, different sounds produce different degrees of opening within the mouth, which in turn influences the pattern of airflow through the larynx. Thus, a consonant may be voiced, aspirated, or glottalized; this has a clear effect on the F0 of the following vowel. Such effects have been extensively documented in the phonetic literature, sometimes under the term **intrinsic variation**, to suggest that the variation in F0 is due to the mode of production of the sound itself (Mohr, 1971). As a result of these physiological and acoustic factors, certain tones are favoured over others. For example, Cheng (1973), in a quantitative study of over 700 tone systems, found that high tones are used more often than low tones, and falling tones more often than rising tones.

How does a language acquire a tone system? The answer to this question may be sought in these intrinsic variations. Take, for example, the English words *bin* and *pin*. As suggested in the spelling, we consider the main distinction between them to be due to the initial consonant, i.e., /b/ versus /p/. But a careful analysis will show that the F0s of the two words are also quite different. The F0 of *bin* starts much lower and has a lower average value as well. Suppose that at some future point in time, the distinction between /b/ and /p/ is lost. That is, suppose that /b/ changes into /p/, a rather common sound change in the languages of the world. At that point, English will become a tone language, since the two words will then be distinguished exclusively by the two F0 patterns, i.e., the two tones.

Such a scenario is a very plausible one. In fact, many scholars feel that this is how Chinese became a tone language several thousand years ago. Presumably, this came about precisely through the loss of consonantal distinctions. It is a two-step process: first the consonants cause the F0 to vary, then the distinction shifts over to the F0 when the consonants merge or become lost (Wang and Cheng, 1987).

A tone language may also lose its tone system. This is probably the case with Swahili, a widely used language of the Bantu family. Almost all of the Bantu languages have tones, such as the Kikuyu example discussed earlier. However, because Swahili was used for a long time as a trade language in East Africa, it imported a large number of non-Bantu words, especially from Arabic languages. This importation was presumably implemented through the medium of many bilingual speakers of Arabic and Swahili. These speakers probably stopped using tonal distinctions on more and more Swahili words as they switched back and forth between the two languages, since Arabic is not a tone language. Through the decades, the tone system in Swahili was eroded until it became lost completely.

In conclusion, a few general remarks on the nature of tone languages. Because such systems are so dependent on F0, the questions naturally arise as to what happens to intelligibility (1) when F0 is absent, as during whispering, and (2) when the speaker has to follow a melody line, as in singing. The answer is that intelligibility is largely preserved in both cases. Briefly put, this is because there are a number of secondary cues in the signal which accompany these tones, such as duration, loudness, contour, vowel quality, etc. These cues take on increased perceptual importance when F0 is not fully available.

Finally, the question is often raised of the relation between linguistic tones and music. It appears that speakers of tone languages have no special advantage in learning music. In fact, they may be quite tone deaf musically, and yet use tones with normal facility. At the same time, neither is there any evidence that people who are exceptionally gifted in music have any special advantage in learning tone languages.

These observations are not surprising when we note that the resemblance between music and linguistic tone is really quite a superficial one: they share only some of the raw materials that each is made of. Tones can be decomposed into phonological features, as we have seen in Figure 3. In addition, tones are perceived in terms of linguistic categories (Wang, 1976), as is the case with consonants and vowels. Furthermore, tones appear to be processed more in the left hemisphere, together with consonants and vowels, rather than in the right hemisphere, with music (Van Lancker and Fromkin, 1973).

The evidence is quite strong, therefore, considered both from the viewpoint of internal phonological organization and from laboratory experimentation, that tones behave much like consonants and vowels in their contribution to building words. Through the happenstance of historical development, we find today that some languages make use of tones while other languages do not. But the pattern is a changing one, since historical development makes it possible for a tone language to lose its tones, and for a non-tone language to become one.

W.S.-Y.W.

SUGGESTIONS FOR FURTHER READING

Fromkin, V.A. (ed.) (1978), *Tone: A Linguistic Survey*, New York, Academic Press.

Pike, K.L. (1948), *Tone Languages*, Ann Arbor, University of Michigan Press.

Wang, W. S-Y. (1973), 'The Chinese language', *Scientific American*, 50 (March), reprinted in W. S-Y. Wang (ed.) (1982), *Human Communication*, New York, W.H. Freeman.

Traditional grammar

By **traditional grammar** is usually meant the grammars written by classical Greek scholars, the Roman grammars largely derived from the Greek, the speculative work of the medievals, and the prescriptive approach of eighteenth-century grammarians (Dinneen, 1967, p. 166; Allen and Widdowson, 1975, p. 47). Also, because many grammars used in schools for both native- and foreign-language teaching take their terminology from this tradition, the term also tends to be used to refer to the grammar that people who have been taught grammar at school have learnt (Allan and Widdowson, 1975, p. 47). Dinneen (1967, p. 170) therefore lists as one of the possible virtues of traditional grammar the fact that it is 'the most wide-spread, influential, and best-understood method of discussing Indo-European languages in the Western world'. Palmer (1971, p. 41), however, is less optimistic, suggesting that many of the terms used in traditional grammar are unintelligible to most people 'though they may have some dim recollection of them from their schooldays'.

Linguists tend to criticize traditional grammar for being based largely on intuitions about grammatical meaning, for being atomistic and not backed by an overall theory or model of grammar, for overemphasizing detail at the expense of attention to larger patterns (Chomsky, 1964b, p. 918), and for being internally inconsistent yet prescriptive or normative in nature, ignoring or classing as ungrammatical actual linguistic usage in favour of prescriptive rules derived largely from Latin and Greek and the linguistic categories appropriate to these languages – rules and categories which may not be suitable to even all Indo-European languages, and certainly not to most non-Indo-European Languages (Dinneen, 1967, pp. 170–1; Allen and Widdowson, 1975, pp. 50–55).

However, while much of this criticism is well founded, it should not be forgotten that a great deal of the grammatical terminology and many of the concepts used in linguistic theory derive from traditional grammar, and that, ultimately, western linguistics derives from the Greek preoccupation with language (see HISTORICAL LINGUISTICS for information about other ancient analyses of language), although traditional school grammar derives most directly from the adaptation of Greek grammar to Latin by Priscian (sixth century).

Priscian's work is divided into eighteen books. The first sixteen, which the medievals called *Priscianus major*, deal with morphology, and the last two, *Priscianus minor*, deal with syntax. Here, Priscian defined eight **parts of speech**:

1. The **noun** is a part of speech that assigns to each of its subjects, bodies, or things a common or proper quality.
2. The **verb** is a part of speech with tenses and moods, but without case [the noun is inflected for case], that signifies acting or being acted upon . . .
3. The **participles** are not explicitly defined, but it is stated that they should come in third place rightfully, since they share case with the noun and voice and tense with the verbs.
4. The **pronoun** is a part of speech that can substitute for the proper name of anyone and that indicates a definite person . . .
5. A **preposition** is an indeclinable part of speech that is put before others, either next to them or forming a composite with them. (This would include what we would distinguish as 'prepositions' and 'prefixes.')
6. The **adverb** is an indeclinable part of speech whose meaning is added to the verb.
7. The **interjection** is not explicitly defined, but is distinguished from an adverb, with which the Greeks identified it, by reason of the *syntactic independence it shows and because of its emotive meaning*.
8. The **conjunction** is an indeclinable part of speech that links other parts of speech, in company with which it has significance, by clarifying their meaning or relations.

(Dinneen, 1967, pp. 114–5)

It is easy to see that a variety of bases for classification are in operation here: for instance, the noun is defined on the basis of what it refers to, a semantic type of classification, and also on formal grounds – it is conjugated for case; similarly, the verb is formally defined as that class of item which is conjugated for tense and mood, but also in terms of what it signifies. Considering the grammar as a whole, Dinneen (1967, pp. 118–123) demonstrates that it was in fact an insufficient and often incorrect description even of Latin, largely because Priscian underemphasizes formal features while overemphasizing meaning in the process of classification.

Priscian's grammar was, however, 'the most respected grammar of the medieval period' (ibid.,

p. 128). It was adjusted in the twelfth century by Peter Helias, a teacher at the University of Paris, to take account of changes which the Latin language had undergone since Priscian's time, and also to take account of the new interest in Aristotelean logic of the period (ibid.). The only formal advance made in Helias' commentary was a development of Priscian's original distinction between **substantival nouns** and **adjectival nouns**, which became the now familiar distinction between nouns and adjectives (ibid., p. 132).

In addition to the notion of parts of speech, the Greeks developed most of the grammatical concepts we are familiar with today, such as gender, inflection, voice, case, number, tense, and mood, and the Romans retained them. Since Latin was of the utmost importance in the medieval period in Europe, as the language of diplomacy, scholarship, and religion (Lyons, 1968, p. 14), it is unsurprising that Latin grammar should have become a fundamental ingredient of the school system, and that the later grammars of the different vernacular languages should be modelled on Latin grammars. The earliest non-Latin grammars include a seventh-century grammar of Irish; a twelfth-century grammar of Icelandic; and a thirteenth-century grammar of Provençal; but it was during the Renaissance that interest in the vernacular became really widespread, and the writing of grammars of the vernacular truly common (ibid., p. 17). One of the most famous Renaissance grammars is the *Grammaire générale et raisonnée* published in 1660 by the scholars of Port Royal (see PORT-ROYAL GRAMMAR).

Grammars of English became common in the eighteenth century. The most famous of these are Bishop Robert Lowth's *A Short Introduction to English Grammar* (1762), and Lindlay Murray's *English Grammar* (1795). These early English grammars were written by scholars steeped in the Latin tradition, who felt that a grammar should provide a set of rules for correct language use, where 'correct' meant according to the rules of the grammar of Latin. Such grammars are known as **prescriptive** or **normative**, and are often compared unfavourably with the **descriptive** grammars produced by linguists, whose main concern is with how a language *is* used, rather than with how some people think it *ought* to be used. Thus Palmer (1971, pp. 14–26) shows that many of the rules of prescriptive grammars, derived from Latin, are unsuitable to English, and that the reasons commonly given for observing the rules are unsound:

Take the rule which says that *It is I* is correct and that *It is me* is incorrect. The sentence consists of a subject *It*, a predicator, *is*, which is a form of the verb BE, and a complement, *I/me*. In the case of Latin sentences containing the Latin verb ESSE ('be'), there is a rule according to which the complement must be in the same case as the subject. So if the subject is in the nominative, *ego* ('I'), say, or *tu* ('you'), then the complement must also be in the nominative, and we get in a play by Plautus *Ego sum tu, tu es ego* ('I am you, you are I/me'). The Latin case system and the rules for using it are then imposed on English – it is said that *I* is nominative and *me* accusative. But then, following the Latin rule, we clearly cannot allow *It is me*, since *it* is nominative and *me* accusative; *ergo It is me* is ungrammatical. Palmer argues that this proof suffers from two defects, one being the virtual absence in modern English of a case system, and the other being the unjustified assumption that Latin should be a model for English; had a case language other than Latin been chosen as a model (French, *c'est moi*: 'it is me'), the rule for BE might have been different; in other words, even among case languages the conventions governing the use of the various cases differ (as do the cases available in different languages), but English is not a case language anyway.

According to Palmer (1971, p. 26) the 'most notorious example' of a normative grammar within the last century is J.C. Nesfield's *Manual of English Grammar and Composition*, 'first published in 1898 and reprinted almost yearly after that and sold in huge quantities at home and abroad'. Palmer (1971, pp. 41–106) draws on this grammar as he deals in detail with the terminology of traditional grammar, showing, also, how these terms have been used in modern linguistics. The terminology refers to grammatical **units**, such as words, phrases, clauses, and sentences, on the one hand, and to **categories**, such as gender, number, person, tense, mood, voice, and case, on the other hand.

In traditional grammars, the **word**, although important in so far as other linguistic items are defined in terms of it, is in fact rarely given any definition. It is simply assumed that everyone knows what a word is (see MORPHOLOGY for difficulties involved in defining words), so that one can conveniently go on to define the **sentence** as a combination of words, and the **parts of speech** as **classes** of words. As we have already seen above, the parts of speech can then be defined according to the kind of reference they have, and also according to how the words of the various classes take on various forms according to rules of **inflection**, and combine in various ways, according to the rules of **syntax**.

According to most traditional grammars, there are eight parts of speech, namely noun, pronoun, adjective, verb, preposition, conjunction, adverb, and interjection. Nesfield defines the **noun** as (from Palmer, 1971, p. 39): 'A word used for naming anything', where 'anything' may be a person, quality, action, feeling, collection, etc. The **pronoun** is a word used instead of a noun; an **adjective** qualifies a noun; a **verb** is a word used for saying something about something else (Palmer, 1971, p. 59). The **preposition** is often

said to be used to indicate directionality or place, and the **adverb** to say something about the time, place, and manner of that about which something is said by the verb. The **conjunction** links sentences or parts of them together, and the **interjection** is a word or group of words used as an exclamation.

The **sentence**, as well as being a combination of words, is also often defined by traditional grammarians as the expression of a complete thought, which it can only do if it contains both a subject and a predicate. In the most basic subject–predicate sentence, the **subject** is that which the sentence is about, and the **predicate** is what says something about the subject; an example would be *John laughed*, where *John* is subject and *laughed* is predicate. Dividing sentences into their parts like this is called **parsing** in traditional grammar. Subject and predicate need not, however, consist of single words, but may consist of several words (Palmer, 1971, pp. 80–1):

In Nesfield, for instance, we are instructed to divide a sentence first into subject and predicate, then to divide the subject into nominative and its enlargement and finally its predicate into finite verb, completion and extension, the completion being either object or complement or both. For the [sentence] *The new master soon put the class into good order . . .* the analysis is [see the table below]:

1. Subject			2. Predicate			
Nominative or Equivalent	Enlargement	Finite verb	Completion			Extension
			Object	Complement		
master	(1) The (2) new	put	the class	into good order		soon

If what looks like a complete sentence appears as a part of something larger which also looks like a complete sentence, a traditional grammar will call the former a **clause**. Clauses are combined in two different ways to form sentences; they may either be **co-ordinated**, as when a number of clauses of equal standing or importance are joined together by and (*I wore a blue shirt* and *you wore a green dress*), or one clause may be **subordinate** to another, which is known as the **main clause**. Thus in *I wore a blue shirt while you wore a green dress*, *I wore a blue shirt* is the main clause to which the rest is subordinate. If the subordinate clause does not have a **finite verb**, that is, a verb which gives a time reference, in it, traditional grammars call it a **phrase**. In *I don't like you wearing that*, therefore, *you wearing that* is a phrase, not a clause, because *wearing* does not contain a time reference (as we can see if we try to change the time reference of the whole sentence from present to past; the change will occur in the main clause, *I didn't like*, while no change will occur in the phrase, *you wearing that*).

Of the grammatical categories of traditional grammar, some are thought to be categories applicable to the noun, others to the verb, and the inflections which affect the forms of the words derive from the categories. The traditional categories and their definitions are (adapted from Palmer, 1971, pp. 83–4):

GENDER, masculine, feminine, and **neuter**; a feature of nouns, associated with male, female, and sexless things.

NUMBER, singular and **plural**; a feature of nouns and verbs, associated with one thing and more than one thing respectively.

PERSON, first, second, and **third**; classifies the pronouns and is a feature of verbs.

TENSE, present, past and **future**; a feature of verbs, giving them a time reference.

MOOD, indicative and **subjunctive**; a feature of the verb associated with statements of fact versus possibility, supposition, etc.

VOICE, active and **passive**; a feature of the verb, indicating whether the subject is the doer of the action or the recipient of it.

CASE, nominative, vocative, accusative, genitive, dative and **ablative**; a feature of the noun, largely functionally definable (nominative for mentioning the subject, vocative for exclaiming or calling, accusative for mentioning the object, genitive for indicating ownership, dative for indicating benefit, ablative for indicating direction or agenthood; these definitions are not watertight and there are variations within languages) and translatable as *boy* (subject), *O boy, boy* (object), *of a boy, to* or *for a boy, from* or *by a boy*.

Other categories are applicable to languages other than English, and it is doubtful whether all of those listed are, in fact, applicable to English. They are, however, the ones often retained in traditional grammars. The definitions are not obviously helpful, as Palmer (1971, pp. 84–97) convincingly demonstrates. For instance, in most languages grammatical gender has little connection with biological sex; in French, the moon, which we must assume is sexless, is grammatically feminine, and in German, a girl is grammatically neuter. However, the terms for the categories recur in descriptive linguistics.

The grammatical categories restrict the forms of words through **concord** or **agreement** and through **government**. A verb has to agree with the noun which is its subject in person and number. In English this only affects the verb when the subject is the third person singular, except for the case of the verb TO BE. The concept of government is necessary in languages like Latin and German to account for the way in which certain prepositions and verbs determine the case of the noun. In English, however, the 'cases' are at most three, **genitive**, or **possessive**, which is indicated by *'s* or by the *of* construction (but where *of* does not alter the form of the noun following it), and, in the case of the pronouns only, **nominative** and **accusative**, *I/me, he/him, we/us*. These are not governed by verbs or prepositions, but by the grammatical function of the word in the clause, i.e. whether it is subject or object.

K.M.

SUGGESTIONS FOR FURTHER READING

Dinneen, F.P. (1967), *An Introduction to General Linguistics*, New York, Holt, Rinehart & Winston.

Palmer, F.R. (1971), *Grammar*, Harmondsworth, Penguin.

Transformational-generative grammar

This article is about the body of work which owes its inspiration to the insights of **Noam Chomsky** in the mid-1950s and which has become one of the most influential syntactic theories of the twentieth century. Although by no means all practising linguists adhere to its principles and results, none can ignore them. Since its inception there have been huge developments in the theory and reactions to it have often been violent. In the mid-1960s work on the developing theory of transformational grammar (TG) was perhaps coherent enough for one to be able to talk of a school of transformational linguistics. This is not possible today. Many who grew up within the model have gone on to develop theories of their own, often in reaction to the current work of Chomsky, and even among those who would describe themselves as transformational linguists there is considerable divergence. That having been said, many linguists adhere to some version of a grammar they would describe as transformational and that owes its intellectual genesis to one or other of the continually developing models offered by Chomsky. As for Chomsky himself, his ideas continue to develop and in this article I will concentrate discussion round three of Chomsky's most influential books: *Syntactic Structures* (1957), *Aspects of the Theory of Syntax* (1965), and *Lectures on Government and Binding* (1981).

When *Syntactic Structures* was published in 1957 the position it took on the nature of linguistic activity was sufficiently at odds with that of the prevailing orthodoxy that it seems quite legitimate to talk of it as revolutionary. The first chapter declared that grammar was an autonomous system, independent of semantics and of the study of the use of language in situations, and furthermore that it should be formalized as a system of rules which generate an infinite set of sentences.

This approach contrasted sharply with the then fashionable orthodoxy that believed that the application of appropriate procedures to a corpus of data would yield a grammatical description. Chomsky rejected the use of a corpus, proposing instead that the empirical adequacy of a grammar should not be judged by whether it accounted for some finite body of observable data but by whether it could generate an infinite number of grammatical sentences and in doing so account for certain types of intuitive judgements that native speakers have about their language. Among these judgements are: that a string of words, particularly a novel string, is or is not a well-formed sentence; that certain sentences are **ambiguous**, i.e. that a single sentence can have more than one interpretation; that distinct sentences can **paraphrase** each other, i.e. that distinct sentences can, in particular respects, have identical interpretations; that certain sentence types (affirmative and negative, declarative and interrogative, etc.) can be systematically related to each other, and so forth. Judgements of this kind, it is claimed, constitute what speakers know about their language, and in addition to accounting for the well-formedness of the sentences of the language a grammar should also account for this knowledge.

It was mentioned above that Chomsky proposed that grammar should be considered as an autonomous system, independent of semantic or phonological systems, though, of course, bearing a relation to them. Furthermore, he proposed that the syntax itself should consist of a number of distinct but related levels, each of which is characterized by distinct rule types and each of which bears a particular part of the descriptive burden. We shall look briefly at the two most important: the phrase-structure and transformational components.

The **phrase-structure** component consists of a set of **phrase-structure (PS)** rules which formalize some of the traditional insights of **constituent-structure** analysis. Consider, for example, the following set of rules (adapted from Chomsky, 1957, p. 26 and p. 111):

Sentence → NP + VP
NP → T + N + Number
Number → {sing, pl}
VP → Verb + NP
Verb → Aux + V
Aux → Tense
Tense → {pres, past}
T → the
N → man, ball, etc.
V → hit, took, etc.

(NP (Noun Phrase); T (Articles etc.); VP (Verb Phrase); Aux (Auxiliary verb: for ease of exposition the structure of Aux is radically simplified to cover only a marker of Tense); items

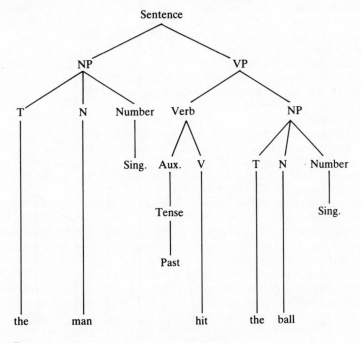

Figure 1

in curly brackets { } are alternatives, i.e., Number is either sing(ular) or p(lura)l, Tense is either pres(ent) or past.)

Each rule is an instruction to rewrite the symbol on the left of the arrow as the symbol or symbols on the right: informally, it can be construed as 'the category on the left of the arrow has the constituent(s) specified on the right of the arrow'. A derivation from this grammar can then be represented by the **tree** shown in Figure 1 (adapted from Chomsky, 1957, p. 27).

We will refer to structures generated by the PS rules as **underlying structures**. One small reason should be immediately apparent: the postulated underlying structure shown in Figure 1 is characterized by a degree of abstraction. The NPs are analysed as containing a marker of number, and the analysis of the verb form *hit* as a past-tense form is shown by postulating an element, 'Tense',

preceding the verb itself. None of these items has an overt realization in the actually occurring form of the sentence. We will see the reason for these analyses below.

PS rules of this kind can be elaborated to capture certain basic facts about the grammar of English, or indeed other languages: facts about **constituency**, that strings like *the man* are and those like *man hit* are not **proper constituents** of the sentence; facts about the **subcategorization** of lexical items, e.g., a **transitive verb** like *hit* requires to be followed by an NP; facts about **functional relations** like subject, object, and main verb, where the **subject** can be identified as the NP **daughter** of the Sentence **node**, the **object** as the NP daughter of the VP and **sister** of the main verb, and the **main verb** is a daughter of the VP which is itself a sister of the subject. A node is the **daughter** of the node immediately above it which

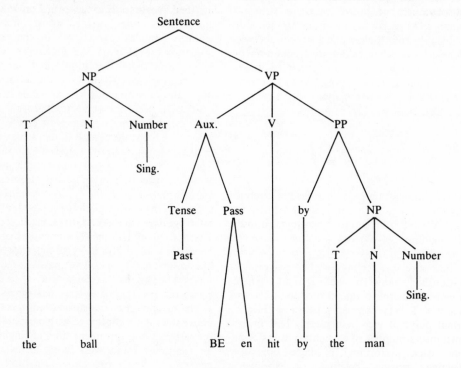

Figure 2

dominates it, as shown by the 'branches' of the tree. **Sister** nodes share a dominating node.

The **transformational component** consists of rules which perform a variety of functions. We will be interested in three: first, rules which relate particular sentence types to each other, as active sentences to their passive counterparts; second, a set of rules that account for morphological operations of various kinds, like number agreement between subject and verb; finally, those rules that are responsible for generating complex sentences.

A **transformational rule** is a rule which maps one syntactic-analysis tree into another. If PS rules can be informally thought of as instructions to build up structures like those in Figure 1, then a transformational rule can be informally thought of as an instruction to change one structure into another. A rule that takes one structure as input and outputs another structure, will obviously need two parts: a **structural analysis (SA)** specifying the input, the structure to which the rule applies, and a **structural change (SC)** specifying what the output structure will be: a double-shafted arrow is often used to signify a transformational rather than a PS rule. A version of the **Passive transformation** (modified from Chomsky, 1957, p. 112) is:

Passive (optional)
SA: NP – Aux – V – NP
SC: $X1 - X2 - X3 - X4 \Rightarrow$
$\quad X4 - X2 +_{Pass} (BE + en) - X3 -(_{PP}by - X1)$

The structure in Figure 1 can indeed be analysed as the SA stipulates: it contains the string NP – Aux – V – NP, so it can thus be subjected to the rule yielding the derived structure shown in Figure 2.

The native speaker may well conceive of the relationship between active and passive sentences as a unitary operation; but if this is so, then it is a very complex operation. From a formal point of view it is clearly best broken down into a number of elementary transformations, each performing a single operation, **adjoining, moving, deleting,** or **copying** a constituent. Several of these operations can be exemplified in the passive transformation: *by* is

adjoined to the subject NP *the man* to create a new piece of structure, a PP (Prepositional Phrase), which is then moved to the VP; the object NP is moved to the front of the sentence and adjoined as a daughter of the topmost Sentence node; a new passive auxiliary is introduced, and so forth. Perhaps the most compelling reason for considering passive to be a series of small operations rather than one complex one is that while it may be possible to specify exactly the structural change for each of the component operations, it is far from clear how to do this for a very complex operation. Given the version of the rule above, just how the derived structure shown in Figure 2 was constructed is actually a mystery, yet a formal grammar should be very precise on matters of this kind.

At this point there is a conflict between an intuition that 'construction types' should be matched as wholes, and the formal operation of grammatical rules, which would prefer to atomize complex operations. In the earliest transformational work the preference was to follow traditional intuitions and to relate construction types as wholes to one another, but this leads to prodigious formal difficulties and later work takes the opposite approach, as we shall see, and in more recent work construction types have been atomized. It should also be noted that the transformation is marked as 'optional'. This is for the obvious reason that not all sentences are passive sentences. Comparable transformations, often also complex and invariably also optional, were proposed to derive interrogatives from declaratives, negatives from affirmatives, and so on. Combinations of these operations will derive more complex structures like interrogative, negative passives, and so forth. The insight that operations of this kind encapsulates is that of **sentence relatedness**.

The second set of transformations mentioned above were those concerned with morphological operations – the agreement rules of English are an example – and with word formation in general, of which past-tense formation is an example. The traditional account of **number agreement** is that subject and main verb must

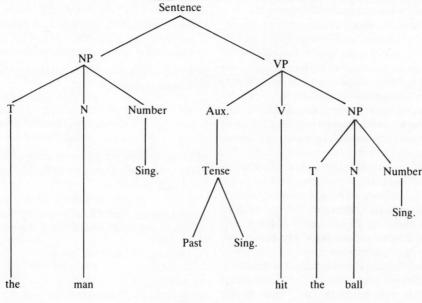

Figure 3

agree in number, an insight that can be captured very straightforwardly by a transformation. Given that subject and main verb can be identified in structural terms in the kind of way noted above, we need a rule that uses this structural information to copy a marker of number from the subject NP into the verb group. There is, however, a little bit more to it than that, since we need to be sure that the number marker on the verb group occurs in the right place, which is the tensed element within the verb group, whether this is an auxiliary verb (*is/are walking, has/have walked*) or the main verb itself (*walk/walks*). This can be ensured by copying the number marker into the tense constituent itself. The effect of such an operation is shown in Figure 3.

Before pursuing this matter further we should briefly consider how tense is marked. In English, the marker of past tense in verbs is most frequently a suffix, *-ed*, on the verb stem: *walk-s* (pres.) versus *walk-ed* (past). In this respect our example, *hit*, is an **irregular** past-tense formation, and we will come to that in due course. However,

in our grammar and in the analysis displayed in Figure 1 the fact that *hit* is analysed as a 'past-tense verb' is shown by a constituent labelled 'tense' positioned before rather than after the verb stem.

This apparently curious analysis is in fact rather ingenious, since it captures several important regularities in the formation rules for tensed verb groups in English. Firstly, tense is invariably realized on the initial constituent of the verb group, irrespective of whether this is an auxiliary (*is/was walking; has/had walked*, etc.) or the main verb itself (*walks/walked*). Secondly, whereas the auxiliaries are optional constituents of the verb group, all finite sentences must be tensed. Making tense obligatory at the beginning of the verb group captures this fact. The correct surface position of the actual tense marker can be ensured by proposing a rule that positions the tense marker as a suffix on whatever immediately follows it in the final derivation, and indeed such a transformation, later called **affix hopping**, was proposed in *Syntactic Structures*. It should be clear that this rule will also account for the position of the marker of number agreement: if it is copied into the tense marker, then where the tense marker goes so does the number marker. The reader can easily imagine the effect of affix hopping on the structure in Figure 3.

Consider finally the analysis of the passive. This introduces a passive auxiliary, 'BE + *en*', as the final constituent in the string of auxiliaries: 'Aux' in the SA will include whatever auxiliaries there are in the active sentence, so the stipulation 'Aux + pass' will get the ordering right; BE recognizes the fact that the passive auxiliary is indeed a form of BE; *en* recognizes the fact that the verb that follows the passive auxiliary always does so as a passive participle. Now, if *en*, like tense, is defined as an affix, affix hopping will ensure the correct surface facts. The reader can see that if the number-agreement rule and affix hopping are applied to the structure in Figure 2, the resultant sentence will be *The ball was hit by the man*. It will be clear that, whereas the sentence-relating rules, like Passive, are optional, the morphological rules will generally need to be obligatory.

We have only examined a part of the extremely complex formation rules for the English verb group, but it must be clear that a few simple but powerful rules can both generate the correct sequence of forms, and exclude ungrammatical ones, while at the same time capturing important generalizations about the structure of the language. It is worth mentioning that the elegance and insightfulness of this account was instantly recognized, and this was an important factor in ensuring the initial success of the transformational way of looking at syntax.

The structure that emerges after the operation of all the transformations is known as the **syntactic surface structure**. This will then need to go off to the morphophonemic and phonological components to receive its final phonological form. The rules in these components need not detain us, but it is perhaps worth noting that a complete description will clearly need a set of morphophonemic rules to specify the shapes of word forms. So, for example, there will need to be rules of the kind:

hit + past → *hit* (the past-tense form of *hit*)

hit + en → *hit* (the passive participle of *hit*)

man + pl → *men* (the plural form of *man*)

to accommodate irregular morphology; followed by others of the kind:

walk   → *walk*

past   → *-ed* (the past marker for regular verbs)

to accommodate regular morphology. The kinds of rules that are at issue should be clear and need not detain us further.

It will probably be helpful at this point to summarize the overall structure of the model as it applies to simple sentences: this is done below.

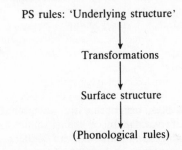

PS rules: 'Underlying structure'

Transformations

Surface structure

(Phonological rules)

Within this model all sentences will have at least two levels of description: an underlying structure created by the PS rules and a surface structure resulting from the operation of the transformations. Several things follow from this.

Perhaps most significant is that it draws particular attention to the fact that language is a complex structural organization. All the rules we have looked at work on structures, or subparts of structures, either developing them or modifying them. This **structure dependence** of the rules of language is held by all models of transformational grammar to be one of the characterizing features of human language.

Another is that the relationship between underlying and surface structure enables us to capture many of the generalizations mentioned in the opening paragraphs. Thus, a paraphrase relation between superficially distinct sentences, as, for example, an active sentence and the corresponding passive, arises from the fact that both derive from the same underlying structure. By contrast, an ambiguous sentence arises when a transformational derivation collapses distinct underlying structures onto a single surface structure.

Finally we may mention that this description allows us to identify a special class of sentences, **kernel sentences**, that have traditionally been recognized as of particular interest: simple active, declarative, affirmative sentences. The distinguishing feature of kernel sentences is that they are those sentences derived with the absolute minimum of transformational machinery, the obligatory transformations alone. As we have seen, the obligatory transformations are in essence those that account for number agreement, the surface ordering of markers of tense, and similar 'housekeeping' operations. Other sentences – questions, negatives, and the like – will undergo, in addition, one or more of the optional structure-changing operations.

The third group of transformations mentioned was those responsible for the generation of **complex sentences**, sentences which themselves contain sentences, or sentence-like structures as constituents: for example *($_{S1}$ Kim said ($_{S2}$ that his mother expected him ($_{S3}$ to tell John ($_{S4}$ that . . . ,* where the various embedded sentences are identified as S1, S2, and so forth. This process is clearly very productive. In *Syntactic Structures* the embedding operation is performed by a distinct set of transformations called **generalized transformations** that take as input two sentence structures, and yield as output a single structure with one sentence embedded into the other. The problem in general is obviously an important one, but the particular solution adopted in *Syntactic Structures* was extraordinarily complicated, led to considerable formal difficulties, and was soon abandoned so we will not pursue the matter here. It will be clear that the outline offered above says nothing about the generation of complex sentences.

There are two final remarks to be made about this model. The first has to do with the relationship between syntax and semantics. In *Syntactic*

Structures Chomsky is at pains to stress the autonomy of syntax, in particular with regard to semantics. He does, however, draw attention to the fact that a description of a language must have the means to discuss the relation between syntax and semantics and points out that in this respect kernel sentences have a privileged part to play since, if kernel sentences are in some sense 'basic' sentences, an understanding of how they are understood is the key to understanding how sentences in general are understood. How later versions of the theory come to terms with this insight, again a rather traditional insight, we will see.

The second remark has to do with Chomsky's interest in language as a formal system of rules and the fact that this led him to explore the mathematical properties of various kinds of formal grammar. The immediate spur to this investigation was the claim that PS rules alone were inadequate to describe the range of structures found in a natural language. It was claimed, for example, that some structures found in natural language are literally impossible to generate with PS rules; this is particularly the case where potentially infinite nested dependencies are at issue (e.g. if$_1$, if$_2$ . . . then$_2$, then$_1$). There are some kinds of structures that can be generated using PS rules, but the description is clumsy and lacks generality (e.g. the rules for number agreement or the formation rules for auxiliary verbs in English).

While it may be possible to generate particular sentence types, it is not possible to relate them to each other formally in the grammar, which means that certain of the kinds of insight (especially those about sentence relatedness etc.) mentioned above, cannot be captured in PS grammar alone. Furthermore, it is impossible to generate certain occurring structures without also generating certain non-occurring structures. Many of these alleged inadequacies of PS rules have subsequently turned out not to be sustainable. Chomsky's work on formal grammar, however, remains of importance since the investigation of the mathematical properties of grammars provoked by *Syntactic Structures* remains an important field of investigation both in linguistics and in related disciplines, notably computer science, artificial intelligence, and cognitive science. Chomsky's answer to the inadequacies of PS rules was to supplement a phrase-structure grammar with another, more powerful, kind of rule, the transformation. Interestingly, considering the amount of attention paid to the formal properties of PS rules, *Syntactic Structures* contains no discussion of the mathematical properties of transformational rules. This, as we shall see, was soon a source of trouble.

Syntactic Structures triggered an intensive research programme: we only have space to look at a few aspects of this. Of the new syntactic machinery the powerful tool of different levels of structure related by transformations was particularly beguiling since transformations appeared to offer a means of explaining the often amazingly complex relationships between the form of sentences and their understanding. An early and influential contribution was Lees' (1963) transformational account of the formation and understanding of nominal forms. For example, the superficially similar *talking machine, eating apple,* or *washing machine* differ in the kinds of relationships between the various parts: subject–verb as in *the machine talks,* verb–object as in *NP eats the apple,* and verb–object of preposition as in *NP washes NP in a machine.* Data of this kind seemed cut out for a transformational account: the various forms must be derived from different underlying structures (this accounts for the different interpretations) by transformational routes that have destroyed that structure (this accounts for the identical surface structures). A superficially appealing conclusion.

In syntax, intensive work on the structure of complex sentences eventually showed that it was possible to discard the unwieldy machinery of generalized transformations. A straightforward example will show the kind of thing that was at issue: in a *Syntactic Structures* type of grammar, the generation of relative clauses involved taking two sentences, say, *The cat died* and *We loved the cat* and embedding one in the other with whatever consequent changes were necessary to yield *The cat that we loved died.* Instead of taking

two sentences, it was suggested that the NP could be developed by a rule of the kind NP → Art N S, and permitting the S node to recycle through the rules. In this way an underlying structure could contain within itself a series of embedded sentences requiring only transformational machinery to tidy up the surface forms. Given this approach, the old optional generalized transformations responsible for the various embedding operations now become obligatory, being triggered by an appropriate underlying structure.

Another line of research looked at the derivation of different simple sentence types: for example, in *Syntactic Structures*, negative sentences would have been derived by an optional transformation inserting a negative element into an affirmative kernel. It was proposed that instead the underlying structure could contain an optional abstract negative **marker**, S → (neg) NP + VP. Now the transformational rule can be triggered by this marker to produce the appropriate negative sentence structure. A similar move is open to interrogative sentences: S → (Qu) NP + VP, and once again the abstract interrogative marker triggers the interrogative transformation. As before, what was formerly an optional operation now becomes obligatory, conditional on the presence of the abstract marker.

As proposals of this kind increased, they began to have profound implications for the structure of the grammar. A small consequence was the demise of the notion of the kernel sentence: kernel sentences, it will be recalled, were active, affirmative, declarative simple sentences derived by the application of obligatory transformations alone: the disappearance of a significant distinction between obligatory and optional transformations described above sounded the death knell for the kernel sentence. A more profound result was that the incorporation into underlying structures of more and more markers, like the negative and interrogative markers mentioned above, led to underlying structures becoming increasingly abstract. This in turn led to a requirement for ever more substantial transformational machinery to relate it to surface structures. And the explosion in the number of transformations created problems of controlling the way they operate and interact with each other; the formal implications of this are largely a 'theory-internal' problem. An interesting consequence was the exploration of an increasingly wide variety of syntactic facts, and the discovery of a range of syntactic problems that still defy proper description.

Perhaps the most profound consequence, however, was that the new ideas opened up the possibility of an interesting rapprochement between semantics and grammar. Consider, for example, the interpretation of a negative sentence. One way of thinking of this is to suppose that understanding a negative sentence depends on the application of negation to the understanding of the corresponding affirmative sentence. In a *Syntactic Structures* model, formalizing this procedure would require access to the underlying structure, to acquire an understanding of the kernel, and also a history of the transformational derivation of the sentence, to know whether the optional negative transformation has applied. However, if we suppose that there is a negative marker in the underlying structure itself and that this triggers off the application of the negative transformation, then all that is necessary for the semantic interpretation is already in the underlying structure, and can be read directly off it. The transformation would have no effect on the meaning, but be simply an automatic operation serving only to trigger off operations which will make the necessary surface adjustments. Katz and Postal (1964) proposed just this.

These and other modifications were incorporated into Chomsky's *Aspects of the Theory of Syntax* (1965). In its day this was an enormously important model of syntax, the basis of a wide variety of student textbooks, so much so that it became known as the **Standard Theory**. As before, the theory is modular. The components it recognized and the relations between them are set out in Figure 4.

The kind of research programme associated with the model is a natural development of that inaugurated by *Syntactic Structures*: an interest in the explanatory power of the grammar in so

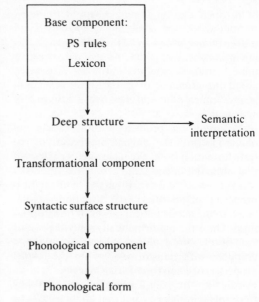

Figure 4

far as it bears on a set of questions related to the way grammar might reveal general properties of the human mind. What, if any, are the universal properties of language? What is the possible range of variation within human languages? What is the nature of the innate knowledge a child must bring to bear on the acquisition of language? How is grammar involved in adult language processing? In the *Aspects* model, the answer to all these questions seemed to lie in transformations, and more and more were proposed. So much so that within a few years the transformation itself became a major souce of difficulty.

As the number of proposed transformations rose, they began to raise a number of technical problems. A typical dilemma, for example, was the question of whether transformations should be ordered, and if so by what principles; a question that would also have interesting universal implications. At the time, the matter spawned miles of print, but it eventually proved to be an internal difficulty created by the theory itself rather than anything to do with the nature of language. The technical literature is now only of historical interest. It should be said, however, that although this eventually proved to be an unfruitful line of research, the investigation was not in vain, because in the course of the research a quite extraordinary amount was discovered about the grammar of English and other languages, much of it still awaiting a satisfactory explanation.

A more serious problem, and this time a real one, concerned the explanatory power of the transformation itself. We have already observed that although in *Syntactic Structures* Chomsky was very concerned to explore the mathematical properties of PS rules, little attention was devoted to the mathematical power of transformations. Once the mathematical properties of this kind of rule were explored, it became clear that a grammar with transformations has the formal properties of a **universal Turing machine**: in other words, they are such a powerful tool that they can explain nothing except that language can be described in terms of some set of rules. An obvious effect of this unwelcome result was to see whether the power of the transformational component could be constrained so that it could, after all, do some useful explanatory work. An early, and still influential line of research was inaugurated by Ross (1967).

To illustrate what was at issue, consider the formation rules for questions. From the earliest days, transformational grammarians postulated that a ***wh* interrogative sentence** is derived by a **movement rule** from a deep structure resembling that of the corresponding declarative. So, for example, and disregarding the inversion and the appearance of a form of *do*, a sentence like *What did Bertie give – to Catherine?*, would be derived from a deep structure of the form *Bertie gave 'wh' to Catherine* (the dash in the derived sentence indicates the site from which the *wh* word has been extracted). ***Wh* movement** can also extract *wh* words from within embedded sentences, and apparently from an unlimited depth: *What did Albert say Bertie gave – to Catherine?, What did Zeno declare that Albert had said that Bertie gave – to Catherine?*, and so forth. The rule is, however, not entirely unconstrained. For example, if the constituent sentence is itself interrogative, then extraction cannot take place: *Albert asked whether Bertie gave a book to Catherine*, but not **What did Albert ask whether Bertie gave – to Catherine?* In Ross' terms, certain constructions form **islands** (the example shows a *wh* island) and the transformational rule must be restricted from extracting constituents from islands. **Island constraints** turn out both to be quite general and to occur in many languages. An obvious question is, then, are island constraints a property of universal grammar and if so how are they to be formulated? Investigations to discover the properties of islands gradually focused on the notion of **bounding**: an attempt to identify what configurations of constituents constitute a **barrier** to movement.

Another line of research suggested that a movement transformation should leave a **trace** of the moved constituent in the **extraction site**: in these terms our example above would be: *What did Albert say Bertie gave 't' to Catherine?* The full implications of this proposal will become apparent below. Immediately, we will observe that the proposal offers an alternative way of constraining transformations. We can after all allow the rule to apply freely and then filter out ill-formed structures, which will be those which contain illegal traces. In other words, instead of constraining the operation of the transformation itself, we can scan the output of the operation to check its legality.

Yet another approach to restricting the power of transformations suggested that the range of operations they could perform should be severely limited. Emonds (1976) proposed a **structure-preserving constraint**. In essence, the proposal was that a transformation should be able neither to create nor destroy structure (structure preserving), but only to move lexical material around within already established structures. This entailed several radical innovations. First, no structure created by a transformation can be different from a structure that the PS rules themselves might create. Second, if lexical material is to move, there must be somewhere to move it to. Between them these constraints ensure that the deep structure must have some lexicalized nodes (to provide the material to move) and some empty nodes (to provide places for the lexical material to move to).

Consider the effect on the passive. The deep structure will have to look like this: *NP(empty) – was – hit – the ball (by – the man)*, and a rule of **NP movement** will move the object NP, *the ball* into the empty subject position. The surface structure will then be: *The ball – was – hit – 't' – (by the man)*. At first blush this may all seem a little odd, but we shall see that the proposal has some interesting consequences.

A consequence of all this is a move away from highly abstract deep structures. In fact, deep and surface structures become almost mirrors of each other, differing substantially only in the distribution of lexical items. Indeed, given a structure-preserving constraint and traced movement rules, the deep structure can always be reconstructed from the surface structure: this was by no means the case in the early days after *Aspects*. A further consequence of this development was to force attention once more on to the nature of PS rules. A consequence of this was the development of a more restrictive theory of phrase structure known as **X-bar syntax**, which I mention briefly below.

We have seen that one way of restricting the power of transformations is to constrain them. A more drastic way is, of course, to abolish them altogether. This was indeed the fate of many. A natural question follows: what happens to the generalizations that the transformation purported to capture? The answer was that many transformational operations transferred themselves from the grammar to the lexicon. In both *Syntactic Structures* and *Aspects*, the lexicon was more or less a word list, and a repository of exceptions. Gradually it came to have a more central role. It came to be seen that the kinds of operation that Lees (1963) had proposed for nominalizations were ill sorted as syntactic operations and more appropriately considered as lexical rules, hence appropriately situated in the lexicon itself. Furthermore, rules involving the redistribution of the arguments of the verb within a simple sentence also came to be seen as lexical rather than syntactic rules.

Consider for example the rule of **Dative**

movement: this was supposed to relate pairs of sentences like *John gave a book to Mary* and *John gave Mary a book*: the transformation deleting *to* and moving the NP following it to a position immediately after the verb. The problem for this as a general transformation is that it is in fact heavily constrained: there are some verbs which permit the first form but not the second (**They transmitted the enemy propaganda*) and others that permit the second but not the first (**John asked a question to Mary*). The constraints appear to be lexical rather than grammatical and hence perhaps better situated in the lexicon than in the grammar. The appropriate lexical rule would state that for appropriate verbs, if they occur in the environment 'NP1 – NP2 to NP3', they can also occur in the environment 'NP – NP3 NP2'.

Note that this line of argument can be extended to the passive: there are some verbs, like *resemble*, that do not typically occur in the passive, and others, like *rumour*, that hardly occur in the active. A lexical derivation for the passive would say in effect that appropriate verbs that occur in the environment 'NP1 – NP2' can also occur in the passive participle form in the environment 'NP was – NP2 (by NP1)'. This, of course, is the very structure I discussed above.

We have seen that in the years following *Aspects* the various modules of the grammar have developed into specialist components, each with a particular kind of rule and each dealing with a part of the derivation of a sentence: the phrase-structure component looks after particular basic syntactic relations and the distribution of lexical items in deep structure; the lexicon looks after word-formation rules; the transformational component is reduced so that the only substantial transformations left are very general movement operations, themselves heavily constrained.

The theory that emerges from these various changes is pulled together in Chomsky (1981) *Lectures on Government and Binding*. This version is more modular than any of the previous versions, a sentence being assigned a description simultaneously at four levels of description and according to a set of principles that regulate the different levels and the relations between them. Each level, and each theory contributing a bit to the total account. The same interest in Universal Grammar, in child language acquisition, and in language understanding still motivate the investigation, and indeed the machinery is now more subtly adapted to the task since there are now many interacting components, each of which can be fine-tuned. Thus, for example, whereas once transformational linguists might have been interested in whether all languages have a passive transformation, the question thus formulated no longer makes sense, since the notion of construction type has quite disappeared, being atomized into the various subtheories. Now each of the various modules and subtheories is concerned with a particular aspect of the description of a sentence; each module will stipulate the degrees of variation permitted for that particular module.

The levels of structure the theory recognizes are laid out below. In some respects they are rather similar to those proposed in *Aspects* though the relations between the levels are rather different.

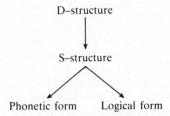

It will be seen that the principal difference is that **logical form (LF)**, the component of the grammar most concerned with semantic interpretation, is now interpreted off S- rather than D-structure: some of the reasons for this will have become apparent in the preceding discussion.

As before, the levels are related to each other by transformation. This is now the extremely general transformation **move alpha**, movement rules being practically all that is left of the plethora of rules spawned by *Aspects*. Move alpha means in essence 'move anything'. This may seem to be an extraordinarily relaxed approach to movement, but, as we shall see, it

will in reality be severely controlled by the various subtheories of the grammar. In effect, movement will be restricted to lexical material moving from one node to another, empty, node leaving an empty category behind marked with a trace. Movement will also be **chained**, so that we can see not only where a given item came from, but we can see all its intermediate stopping places.

The structures generated at the various levels are constrained by a set of theories which define the kinds of relationships possible within a grammar:

X-bar theory
Theta theory
Government theory
Binding theory
Bounding theory
Control theory

D-structures are formulated as the familiar syntactic trees. The possible configurations in a tree are defined by **X-bar theory**, a theory of phrase-structure grammar. It defines the nature and type of syntactic categories available to any language, defines the notion of a well-formed syntax tree, and lays down the degrees of variation that can be found from language to language: i.e., it defines possible phrase-structure configurations in language in general. The central notion is that each of the major lexical categories (Noun, Verb, Preposition, Adjective), is the head of a structure dominated by a phrasal node of the same category (Noun: Noun Phrase; Verb: Verb Phrase; etc.). The phrasal category is the maximal

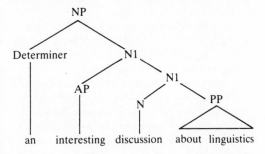

Figure 5

projection, though there may be **intermediate categories**. For example in English NPs we have structures like that shown in Figure 5.

The theory itself does not determine the number and type of intermediate categories, nor does it determine the relative order of the categories in any single tree. It does, however, set down the degree of variation permitted along each of these **parameters**. The way the parameter is to be set for any language is then an empirical matter for the language learner and may well differ from language to language. So, for example, in English the order of constituents in the VP is verb followed by its complements, since English is a SVO language; in Japanese the order is the opposite since Japanese is a SOV language (see LANGUAGE TYPOLOGY). This theory, as others to come, sets down the range of permissible variation in language, and a particular language chooses some position in the **syntactic space** thus defined.

Theta theory deals with the functional relationships between a predicate and its arguments: a predicate is said to **assign** a **theta role** to each of its arguments. Part of theta theory is the **theta criterion**, a requirement that each argument of the verb receives one and only one theta role and each theta role is assigned to one and only one argument. Taken together, these principles ensure that a verb will be associated with just the right number of lexical arguments. So, for example, a normal transitive verb like *catch* is associated with two lexical arguments, and the theta criterion will ensure that it occurs with two lexical NPs. In a sentence like *The cat caught the mouse*, *catch* will assign the roles **agent** and **theme** to its subject and object expressions. In this example subject and object correspond to agent and theme, but it should be noted that the thematic argument of a verb need not necessarily correspond to subject and object.

Suppose, for example, that we derive the passive, as suggested above, from a deep structure of the form 'NP1 – was – Passive Participle – NP2 (by NP3)'. We must ensure, as noted above, that NP1 is empty, that NP2 has a lexical NP, and that NP3, if chosen, also has a lexical NP. Theta theory will do this by ensuring that the verb assigns the theta role, agent, to NP3, if it is chosen, and the role of theme necessarily to NP2. NP1 will receive no theta role. By the theta criterion, the verb is associated with the right number of arguments and the subject slot is empty: just what we wanted!

As a further example, consider a verb like *seem*. *Seem* is associated with no lexical arguments, and hence will assign no theta roles. In a sentence like *It seems that the cat caught the mouse* the lexical NPs (*cat* and *mouse*) bear functional (theta) relationships to the verb *catch* in the subordinate clause, and receive their theta roles from that verb. What then of *it*? The traditional description would have it as a **pleonastic** or **dummy** subject, with no argument relation to the verb, but supplied because English sentences require tensed verbs to have grammatical subjects. The deep structure will then have the general form: NP (empty) seems (the cat chased the dog): a later rule will ensure that an empty NP with no theta role will be supplied with *it*.

A further principle of theta theory is the **Projection principle**. This ensures that the theta-marking properties of each lexical item are represented, or projected, at each syntactic level: D-structure; S-structure and logical form. In the case of *seem* this means that the D-structure subject of *seems* cannot be a lexical NP argument, but that the subject and object of *like* must be lexical NP arguments. *It* will be supplied between D- and S-structure and hence will be the S-structure subject of *seem*, but at no point is it an argument. In the schematic representation below a form of predicate calculus, which should be self-explanatory (but see FORMAL LOGIC AND MODAL LOGIC), is used to represent the logical form. The fact that both the verbs are tensed finite verbs is shown by the marking '+ tns' followed by the base form of the verb – some reasons for this will be seen later.

D-structure: ($_s$ e + tns seem ($_s$ the cat + tns catch the mouse)) (pleonastic *it* inserted)

S-structure: ($_s$ it + tns seem ($_s$ the cat + tns catch the mouse))

LF: (seem, (catch (the cat, the mouse))

PF: It seemed that the cat caught the mouse

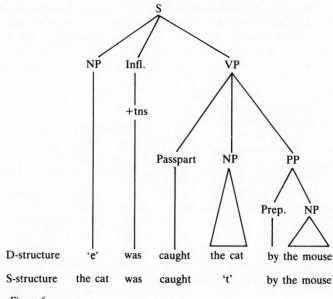

Figure 6

I will discuss another example involving *seem* below. It should be clear that the general principles of theta theory are universal, though the way in which they will be worked out will differ from language to language.

Government theory deals in essence with the relationship between a head and its complements, and defines relationships in other subtheories. To explain the intricacies of government theory would take us too far out of our way, so let us simply note that government is a configurationally defined notion, which we can illustrate by the configuration shown in outline in Figure 6, a simplified and schematic representation of the structure proposed for a passive sentence. Two structures are shown at the foot of the tree, one is the proposed D-structure and the other the proposed S-structure, with lexical material distributed at each level as discussed above. The sentence is a finite tensed sentence: indicated in the diagram by the labelling 'Infl(ection); ' + tns(tense)'. In this configuration, Infl(+ tns) governs the subject NP, V governs the object NP, and the NP in the PP is governed by the preposition. The relation of government

plays an important part in various subtheories, as we shall see.

Case theory regulates the distribution of phonetically realized NPs by assigning **abstract case** to them. **Case** is assigned by a set of **case assigners** to the constituents they govern. If we assume that V, Prep, and Infl(+ tns) are case assigners, then, given the definitions of government above, we can say that Infl(+ tns) assigns nominative case to the NP it governs (the subject, reflecting the fact that tensed sentences require subject expressions); the V assigns oblique case to the NP it governs (the object) and Prep also assigns oblique case to the NP it governs. In Figure 6, subject position will be assigned nominative case by Infl(+ tns), and the NP in PP will be assigned oblique case by Prep. The NP after the passive participle will receive no case since it is not governed by a case assigner according to our definition.

These definitions can now be associated with a **Case filter**, a checking device that will declare a sentence to be ungrammatical if it contains an NP containing phonetic material but assigned no case, or, vice versa, an empty NP which is assigned case but contains no phonetic material. In effect, case theory will require the positions of grammatical subject and object to be filled with phonetic material. The phrasing **phonetic material** is used to cover not only lexical NPs but also items like the dummy *it* associated with *seems*. The reader is invited to check this with the derivations shown in outline on page 494.

We are now in a position to sharpen up our notions of D-structure, S-structure, and the relationship between them: **D-structure** is the level at which theta positions must be filled by lexical material. At this level verbs must be associated with the correct number of arguments: if active *catch* is associated with less than two NPs, or if *seem* NP is associated with any NP then the theta criterion will rule the structure as ill formed. Transformations may then move material into empty nodes, and in appropriate cases a dummy *it* will be supplied. Case theory will then check the final distribution of lexical items, both moved and unmoved, and if material is found where it ought not to be, or if there is no material where some should be, the sentence will be marked as ill formed.

The matter can be illustrated by another example involving *seem*: Consider the sentence *The cat seemed to catch the mouse*. If we are to be consistent with our own account of theta theory, the distribution of lexical material in the D-structure and the logical form assigned to the sentence must be the same as that assigned to *It seemed that the cat caught the mouse* shown on page 494. These similarities are recorded in the derivation shown below. The differences between the two sentences are due to the fact that the constituent sentence in our first example is finite and tensed (*that the cat caught the mouse*) whereas in the second sentence it is non-finite, and hence untensed (*to catch the mouse*): this difference is recorded in the D-structure below by the notation + tns (finite, tensed) or − tns (non-finite, untensed). We saw above that + tns was a governing category and governed an NP in the nominative case: suppose now that − tns is not a governor; as such, it will not assign case: this reflects the traditional view that infinitives cannot have subjects. Now, according to the theory,

lexical material must be given case: this it can only acquire by moving into the position of subject of *seem* where, being governed by + tns, it will, as required, acquire case. Move alpha produces a situation where the chain created

D-structure: ($_S$ e + tns seem ($_S$ the cat − tns caught the mouse) (move alpha − for NP the cat)

S-structure: ($_S$ the cat$_1$ + tns seem ($_S$ 'e$_1$' − tns catch the mouse)

LF: (seems (catch (the cat, the mouse))

PF: The cat seemed 'e' to catch the mouse

by movement will, as required, ensure that the chain with the lexical NP *the cat* has one theta role (*the cat* is assigned agent as subject of *catch*: the subject of *seem* has no theta role) and one case (*the cat* acquires nom case from + tns in the main clause, but no case from − tns in the constituent clause). Similarly, the lexical NP *the mouse* gets oblique case as object of *catch* and is assigned the theta role of theme. The reader is invited to work out why strings like **It seemed the cat to catch the dog*; **The cat seemed caught the dog*, etc. are ill formed.

Binding theory is concerned with the syntactic domains in which NPs can or cannot be construed as **coreferential**. If we suppose that all NPs are assigned a **referential index**, then coreference can be shown by marking NPs with the same index and **non-coreference** by marking them with different indices. An NP with an index distinct from all other NPs is said to be **free**; an NP which has the same index as another is said to be **bound**. An NP must be either free or bound within a particular **domain**. Thus, for example, in *John$_1$ likes himself$_1$*, the reflexive pronoun, *himself*, must be bound by some other NP within its domain, in this case the subject NP *John*; this is shown in the subscripting. In *John$_1$ likes Mary$_2$* the full lexical NPs *John* and *Mary* cannot be coreferential, and this is shown by assigning them different indices. The relevant domain for the binding of reflexive pronouns in English is, informally speaking, the simple sentence, but different languages are able to select domains differently. Binding theory is concerned with the categories that must be bound and free and with defining the domain in which binding takes place: another area of grammar in which languages differ, or in terms of government and binding (GB) theory, set their **parameters** differentially.

I will pass over the final two theories rapidly. **Bounding theory** is concerned with the way the movement rule, move alpha, can be constrained. The problem is to find general principles that restrict movement: the issues have already been discussed briefly. In this respect too, languages seem to set the parameters for movement differently. **Control theory** is concerned with the way in which subjectless infinitive structures like *John wants to go* are construed.

We appear to have come a long way from *Syntactic Structures*, and in some senses this is indeed the case. In others, however, the thirty-four years since its publication have shown a remarkably consistent purpose. Details of grammatical organization have clearly changed and developed and the general architecture of the theory has changed. But in many ways the goals set out in the first sentences of the Introduction to *Syntactic*

Structures remain (Chomsky, 1957, p. 11):

> Syntax is the study of the principles and processes by which sentences are constructed in particular languages. . . . Linguists must be concerned with the problem of determining the fundamental underlying properties of successful grammars.

E.K.B.

SUGGESTIONS FOR FURTHER READING

Newmeyer, F.J. (1980), *Linguistic Theory in America: The First Quarter Century of Transformational Generative Grammar*, New York, Academic Press.

Radford, A. (1988), *Transformational Grammar: A First Course*, Cambridge, Cambridge University Press.

Van Riemsdijk, H. and Williams, E. (1986), *Introduction to the Theory of Grammar*, Cambridge, MA, MIT Press.

Writing systems

A **writing system** (script, orthography) may be defined as a given set of written marks together with a particular set of conventions for their use (Sampson, 1985, p. 19). The units of a writing system are known as **graphs**, and in citation (mention) of one or more graphs, angle brackets, <   >, are standardly used.

While speech may not be a logically necessary prerequisite for writing, it is a historical fact that any culture which has writing has speech, and that it had speech before it had a writing system. Therefore it is common to see a writing system as a means of representing the spoken language; but this does **not** mean that a writing system needs to be representative of the **sounds** of a language.

Those, such as alphabetic systems, which are designed with sound representation in view are known as **phonographic** systems, and they are of three types: **syllabic**, **segmental** and **featural** (see below). Systems, such as the Chinese (see below), which are not based on sound representation but rather on representation of the meaningful units of the language – words or morphemes – are known as **logographic** writing systems.

Early writing systems tend to be logographic, possibly because, as Sampson (1985, p. 36) suggests, the obvious thing to do if one wants to represent meaning in writing is to make a picture of the meaning unit one wants to represent. The terms **pictographic** and **ideographic** are frequently used to describe writing systems displaying varying degrees of iconicity (similarity to the entity referred to), but Sampson lists two good reasons for discarding these as technical terms for talking about writing systems: (1) their history of use is such as to make it unclear exactly what is meant by them; and (2) they tend to make it difficult to distinguish writing systems from **semasiographic** systems like road signs, which, although they clearly signify and are systems of visible communication, are not **glottographic**, i.e., visible representations of utterances; as Sampson (1985, p. 30) puts it, 'messages in the semasiographic system could be *translated* more or less faithfully into the spoken language, but it would make no sense to talk of *reading* them aloud word by word'. Semasiographic systems are forerunners of true writing, and are, according to Gelb (1963, p. 29) best represented among the American Indians (see ibid., pp. 29–32 for examples).

The oldest known writing system is that of the Sumer culture which existed from approximately 4500 to 1750 BC in lower Mesopotamia, now southern Iraq. The earliest Sumerian writing is believed to date from 3000 or 4000 BC, and consists of marks drawn onto clay tablets with a pointed reed stylus. Some of its graphs are:

< 𓁹 > meaning 'head',

< ≈ > meaning 'water', and

< 𓁹// > meaning 'drink'.

The subject of these tablets appears to be administrative matters like tax payments and distribution of rations, and the inscriptions were brief and context-bound, like entries in a note book. At this stage, many words of the language had no written form, and some graphs stood for two or more words. Early in the history of this writing system, the graphs were turned 90° anticlockwise, thus :

< ☞ >, < || >, < 𒄑 >.

Drawing onto clay, however, tends to cause clotting of the lines by small balls of clay accumulating in front of the stylus; and by around 2500 BC the pointed stylus had been replaced with a blunt one with which wedge-shaped impressions were made on the clay; most rounded lines were thus replaced with straight lines, although some graphs still required the stylus to be dragged through the clay:

< 𒀭 >, < 𒐊 >, < 𒈾 >.

This script is known as **Cuneiform** from the Latin term for 'wedge-shaped'. It was now being used for writing down myths and other types of literature, and legal judgements; it was linear, and 'capable of recording all lexical and grammatical elements of the spoken Sumerian language (Sampson, 1985, p. 50). By 1800 BC, there were no rounded lines left at all, and the direction of the wedges had been standardized for ease of writing:

< 𒀭 >, < 𒐊 >, < 𒈾 >.

The Sumerian writing system presents an interesting case of how an initially wholly logographic system may become increasingly phonographic. For example, the Sumerian word for 'water' was pronounced /a/; it so happened that the pronunciation of the word for 'in' was the same, so the graph for 'water' was used to stand for this word too, thus solving the problem of how in-ness might be depicted. Gradually, all grammatical morphemes and affixes came to be represented by graphs chosen chiefly on phonological grounds, and this **phonographic principle** was also employed to deal with proper names. Nevertheless, the Sumerian script remains primarily logographic, since signs were only used phonographically in cases where a logograph could not be readily created.

A writing system is not normally associated with any one language, and the Cuneiform script was adopted by the Akkadians around 2500 BC. The Akkadians were neighbours of the Sumerians, but they spoke an unrelated Semitic language. Whereas in Sumerian most root forms of words were monosyllabic so that individual graphs could easily be used to stand for syllables, Akkadian was inflecting, which meant that 'the chain of spoken sounds could not be neatly divided up into morphemic meaning-units (compare the way that English *men* collapses the idea of "man" and "plurality" into a single sound-shape)' (Sampson, 1985, p. 56). The Akkadians were therefore forced to develop the phonographic aspects of Cuneiform. Most of the Cuneiform writing available is, in fact, Akkadian, because the Akkadians, later known as Babylonians and Assyrians, gradually became the dominant cultural group in Mesopotamia 'eventually extinguishing Sumer as a political entity and Sumerian as a language' (Sampson, 1985, p. 56).

It is thought that the invention of Egyptian Hieroglyphic soon after the Sumerian writing system was influenced by the latter. It developed in a similar way to the Akkadian version of Cuneiform, though the shape of the graphs was different. The Egyptian Hieroglyphic script was mainly phonographic, although it is often mistakenly thought of as logographic (or even semasiographic) because of its obvious iconicity, retained throughtout the history of Egyptian civilization. It existed side by side with two non-iconic versions, Hieratic and Demotic, which were used for informal purposes. The Egyptian Hieroglyphic writing system largely followed what is known as the **acrophonic** principle, in that many Hieroglyphic graphs were iconic with some entity whose name began with the sound for which the graph stood. 'Thus the Hieroglyphic sign 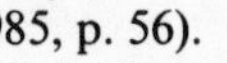, representing the rippled appearance of water, stood for /n/, the first sound of the Egyptian word for "water"' (Sampson, 1985, p. 78). However, there were also many Hieroglyphic graphs which stood for groups of sounds, rather than for single consonants.

It is believed that the inventors of the Semitic alphabet, from which all segmental writing systems probably descend, took the very idea of writing and the agrophonic principle from the Egyptians. However, the Semitic alphabet, created sometime in the 2nd millennium BC 'somewhere in the Palestine/Syria region' (Sampson, 1985, p. 78), probably by the Phoenicians, 'was clearly an independent creation: many of the graph-shapes are not similar to any Hieroglyphic graphs, and (more important) the relationships between objects pictured and graph-value hold for Semitic languages but not for Egyptian' (ibid.). Thus the Semitic letter < > /m/ looks as if it is adapted from the Hieroglyphic graph for /n/ referred to above. However, it is 'used by the Semites for /m/ because their own word for "water" [majim] began with that sound' (ibid.).

The original Semitic alphabet had no graphs for vowel sounds and is therefore often called **consonantal**, as are those of its descendant systems which still do not have letters for vowels, such as the modern Hebrew writing system and the modern Arabic writing system. However, it is wrong to think of consonantal writing systems and alphabetic writing systems as belonging to different categories. A consonantal system is alphabetic even though it does not have vowel letters. I therefore follow Sampson (1985, p. 77ff.) in referring to both the original alphabet and to those of its modern descendants which have no vowel letters as Semitic *writing systems*. But please bear in mind that not all Semitic *languages* (see HISTORICAL LINGUISTICS, pp. 214–15) are written in the Semitic writing system – Maltese is not – and that not every language written in a Semitic script is a Semitic language – Persian is an Indo-European language, but it is written in Arabic script.

The term **alphabet** derives from the names of the first two graphs of the Greek adaptation of the Semitic alphabet, alpha and beta. The first two Semitic graphs <> and <> are called ʔālep and bēt, and there are clear similarities between the ordering of the Semitic, Greek, and Roman alphabets; it is not known why this ordering was chosen. The reason why Semitic does not contain vowel letters is simply that they are unnecessary, since vowels play a very limited role as distinctive elements in the lexis of Semitic languages:

> A high proportion of the vocabulary of a Semitic language . . . consists of words derived from a root (having a verbal or adjectival meaning) which is made up purely of consonants (usually three consonants), between which different patterns of vowels, representing different grammatical inflexions, are interdigitated.
>
> (Sampson, 1985, p. 85)

Nevertheless, it is possible to indicate vowel value in two ways: (1) some consonant letters can be used also to indicate vowels, and these are referred to as **matres lectionis**, 'mothers of reading'; (2) tiny dots and dashes above, below, or within the consonant letters can be used to indicate pronunciation very precisely. This is known as **pointing**, and is used in modern Israel, for instance, to assist learner readers. The Arabic version of Semitic script, which, unlike modern Hebrew, has a **cursive** form, i.e. the letter shapes have been adapted so that whole words can be written without taking the pen from the paper, can be written down almost as quickly as short-hand because of the absence of letters for vowels. Semitic scripts are written from right to left.

The Arabic and modern Hebrew alphabets descend from one of two traditions of forming Semitic letter shapes, namely the eastern or Aramaic tradition. The other is known as the western or Canaanite tradition, and this was used by the Phoenicians. It is almost certain that it was this version of the Semitic alphabet which gave rise to the Greek, since the Phoenicians were the only Semitic people who traded and hence travelled overseas, and since the Greeks, who had colonies in ancient Phoenicia, called their alphabet Phoenician letters.

The Greeks used six of the Semitic letters, < ʔ h w ħ j ʕ >, to stand for vowels. It was important for the Greeks to be able to indicate vowels, because Greek is a European language and so vowels are used to indicate lexical contrasts. In addition, some Greek words begin with vowels and some contain sequences of two or more vowels. Of the five Semitic letters mentioned above, only one, <w>, had a value, /w/, which also existed as a phoneme in Greek. From <w>, the two Greek letters <FY> were developed to stand for /w/ and /u/ respectively. Of these, /w/ was lost in later spoken Greek so that the letter /F/ became obsolete. The Greeks used <ʔ> for /a/, <h> for /e/, <ħ> for /h/, <j> for /i/ and <ʕ> for /o/ (Sampson, 1985, pp. 100–101).

The Greeks very soon stopped writing every line from right to left; instead, they would use **boustrophedon** (ox-turning) style, writing the first line from right to left, the second from left to

right, and so on, as if ploughing a field. The direction of the letters varied with the direction of the writing, so that when a convention of writing only from left to right was finally adopted, the shapes of the Greek letters became mirror images of their original Semitic counterparts (allowing for other shape-changing developments, of course). Thus Semitic < 𐤁 >, < 𐤂 >, < 𐤄 > became Greek < B >, < Γ >, < E > (ibid., p. 103).

The Etruscans, who lived in Etruria, north of Rome, borrowed the Greek alphabet, and the Romans acquired it from them in about 650 BC. It is from the Roman adaptation of the Greek alphabet that the various modern European writing styles and typefaces descend. It is also believed that the runic **futharks**, named, like the alphabet, on the basis of the sounds represented by its initial graphs (f u th a r k), descended from the Roman alphabet, because they resemble several alphabetic inscriptions, dated from between the fourth and first centuries BC, found in the North Italic Alps. However, some runic figures which predate the Alpine inscription have also been found carved into stones and rocks, so it is possible that an earlier runic script blended with the Alpine. In any case, it is certain that the Roman alphabet influenced some of the graphs of the standard Scandinavian dotted (pointed) runic futhark (see Page, 1987, pp. 8–22).

As in the case of the Hebrew version of Semitic, each graph of the Roman alphabet was written separately, but all were simplified in various ways and could be written with a single pen-stroke. When the Roman Empire dissolved, different 'national hands' (Sampson, 1985, p. 111) developed in various parts of Europe. By the fifteenth century, there were two main rival styles, the 'Humanist' script used primarily in northern Italy in an attempt at reconstructing classical Roman handwriting, and the 'Gothic' or 'black-letter' script of France and Germany. Early printers emulated the handwritten scripts of the day, which thereby obtained a degree of permanence, although Gothic script was largely eliminated in Britain in the seventeenth century and in Germany in 1941.

Modern Hebrew, Arabic, Roman, and the

Russian 'Cyrillic' alphabets are all representatives of the Semitic alphabet, 'one of the two great systems of writing which between them provide the media of most of the world's written language' (Sampson, 1985, p. 145) and which also exemplify 'the two main typological categories of script' (ibid.), phonographic and logographic.

The other of the two is the Chinese logographic writing system, in which a graph does not stand for a unit of pronunciation, but for a morpheme, a minimal meaningful unit of the Chinese language. For this reason, and because written Chinese is not simply the written version of a particular dialect of Chinese, any Chinese speaker, of whichever version of Chinese – and some of these differ to such a degree that they are not mutually intelligible – is able to use virtually the same written form of the language. So two Chinese speakers who are unable to communicate with each other through speech will, nevertheless, be able to understand each other almost perfectly in writing.

There are several reasons why it is possible for the Chinese writing system to operate in this manner. First, Chinese morphemes always correspond to syllables, and the syllables are clearly demarcated from each other in speech. Secondly, Chinese is an isolating language, that is, 'its grammar works exclusively by stringing separate words together' (Sampson, 1985, p. 147). If English had this characteristic, we would have to say something like *I go already* instead of *I went*, and we would not have to observe rules of agreement such as the one which demands that *go* + third-person singular becomes *goes*. Finally, there is no clear distinction between compounds and collocates (see MORPHOLOGY and LEXIS AND LEXICOLOGY). For all these reasons, each Chinese word tends to correspond straightforwardly to what we would call a morpheme, and a graph of the writing system can straightforwardly represent such a meaning unit.

Since this is the case, and since Chinese, as any other language, contains thousands of meaning units, its writing system contains thousands of graphs. Of these, about 1,000 are so-called 'simple' graphs of relatively easily depicted

objects and concepts; for instance

< 日 > 'sun'

(derived from < ☉ >) and

< 東 > 'east' ('sun behind tree')

(derived from < ⊕ >).

In addition, Chinese contains complex graphs in the case of which a simple, iconic graph has been adapted to stand for a word whose pronunciation resembled it in the Old Chinese language of around 2000 to 1000 BC, when the script was developing. To distinguish among graphs which would thus otherwise be ambiguous, a further element is added, called a **signific**. This shows the semantic category of the word, while the element which has been adapted to stand for an item for reasons of pronunciation similarities is called the **phonetic**.

Since Chinese pronunciation has changed and diversified greatly since the writing system was stabilized, the relationship between morphemes and graphs is by no means transparent, and 'from the point of view of a modern speaker, the most important benefit of the phonetic/signific structure is that graphs involving many brushstrokes can be seen as groupings of familiar visual units, rather than having to be remembered stroke by stroke (Sampson, 1985, p. 157). The graphs are composed of a number of distinct elements in various configurations, and there is no evidence whatever to support claims that Chinese is more difficult to learn to read and write than any other system (see Sampson, 1985, pp. 160–5). Each graph occupies an imaginary square, and graphs were traditionally written downwards in columns, beginning at the right. In the People's Republic of China writing now begins at the left and it is common to write horizontally. Typing and word processing are relatively slow processes using the Chinese system; since there are too many graphs to be contained on a keyboard, typewriters have a single arm which picks up separate pieces of type, while word-processor keyboards invite users to select properties of the graph they want; several graphs with the selected properties will then appear on the screen, and the user can choose the relevant one.

The Japanese became familiar with the Chinese civilization in the first millennium AD, at which point they had no writing system of their own, and the modern Japanese writing system, which began to be developed in the seventh century AD, is wholly, though by no means straightforwardly, derived from Chinese. Some Chinese graphs are used in Japanese to stand for words whose meanings are the same, or nearly the same, as their Chinese counterparts. These graphs are said to have **kun** (instruction) reading. However, Japanese in not an isolating language, but is heavily derivational and inflectional, so that individual morphemes cannot be simply represented by individual graphs. To deal with this problem, graphs with *kun* readings were interspersed, in early Japanese writing, with graphs whose Chinese pronunciation resembled the Japanese pronunciation of the relevant grammatical item. This method of writing is known as **man'yogana**. Nor do Japanese words normally consist of one syllable only; however, the syllable structure is very simple, having either a single vowel or a single consonant followed by a single vowel. Therefore, a single Japanese word in this period, about 1,000 years ago, would be represent.d by at least one, but mostly by more than one Chinese graph, and a reader would simply have to work out from the context which graphs were supposed to have *kun* reading, and which to have *man'yogana* reading. To complicate matters further, Japanese also borrowed many Chinese words, and these would continue to be written with their Chinese graphs. Such graphs are said to have **on** readings.

Gradually, the *man'yogana* system developed in two ways. First, the graphs used for *man'yogana* were standardized so that the same graph or a small set of graphs was always used for a particular Japanese syllable. Second, the forms of the graphs were simplified so that they could be written faster, and so that it became possible to tell at a glance whether a given graph was in fact *man'yogana*, or *kun* or *on*. Ultimately, two syllabaries evolved of which one, **hirigana** (plain *kana* (script)) consists of simplified cursive outlines of complete Chinese graphs, while the other, **katakana** (partial *kana*) consists of small

distinctive elements of the original Chinese graph. Chinese graphs in their full form are called **kanji**. In modern Japanese, *kanji* are used for lexical morphemes, *hiragana* for grammatical morphemes and inflections, and *katakana* for foreign names. The Japanese writing system is **mixed**; it is partly logographic, partly phonographic (Sampson, 1985, ch. 9).

In order to provide examples of a purely syllabic writing system and a featural writing system, it is necessary to look at systems which have no connection with either Semitic or Chinese. A good example of a purely **syllabic** writing system is the system known as **Linear B**, adapted in about the sixteenth century BC by the Mycenaean civilization to write an early form of Greek, from **Linear A**, which was used to write the unknown language of the Minoan civilization of the second millennium BC. The Mycenaean civil service used Linear B for record keeping purposes until about 1250 BC, when the Minoan cities were destroyed, but a distant relative of Linear B was used to write Greek in Cyprus in the classical period. Linear B consists of at least eighty-nine graphs of which seventy-three have known values, and it is **genuinely** syllabic, in so far as each separate written mark stands arbitrarily for a distinct syllable, thus

< Ḻ > /ta/, < ≢ > /te/, < Λ > /ti/,
< Ŧ > /to/, < ⩗ > /tu/.

(Sampson, 1985, p. 65). This script was lost after the collapse of Mycenean civilization in the thirteenth century BC and was unknown to the later Greeks who adapted the Semitic alphabet used by the Phoenicians (see above).

Other scripts, often referred to as syllabic, are, in fact, **segmentally** based in so far as the shape of the graphs is relatable to sound segments of the syllable, so that syllables beginning with the same consonantal sound are of similar shape, as in the following examples taken from the Ethiopian writing system:

< ✝ > /ta/, < ✚ > /tû/,
< ℃ > /tî/, < ℃ > /tê/.

(Sampson, 1985, p. 66). Almost all Linear B

graphs stood for simple syllables consisting of one consonant followed by one vowel, while the spoken language used many other types of syllable. Consequently, the writing system did not reflect the pronunciation particularly accurately, and a reader relied on contextual clues to the meaning of any inscription. However, it is unlikely that this created many problems, given the restricted uses to which Linear B was put (Sampson, 1985, ch. 4).

More recent syllabic systems include the Cherokee script invented by the Indian Sikwayi in the early 1820s. Having given up the idea of devising a word-based script as too cumbersome, he divided the words of the spoken language into around 200 syllables with a sign for each. Subsequently, he was able to reduce the number of signs to a more manageable eighty-five, by disregarding unimportant distinctions and by introducing a separate sign for the sound /s/ which could be prefixed to signs for syllables beginning with other consonants. Thus it would no longer be necessary to have one sign for a particular CV syllable and a separate sign for a syllable beginning with /s/, but otherwise consisting of the same CV. The sign for /s/ represents an aspec' of alphabeticality in the Cherokee writing system. Otherwise it is, however, properly syllabic (Jensen, 1970, pp. 241–2). The Cree system, on the other hand, is segmentally based (see ibid., p. 244, for illustration), as is the system used for Inuktitut (Eskimo) in the Canadian Arctic (see Mallon, 1985).

For an example of a featural writing system, let us look at the Korean **Han'gul**, a phonographic script invented by King Sejong, who ruled Korea from 1418 to 1450, and a team of scholars he had assembled. This system is **featural** in that its graphs systematically represent the distinctive phonemic features of the spoken Korean language. Vowels are represented by graphs consisting of long horizontal and vertical lines combined with small distinguishing marks, for instance, < ㅣ > stands for /i/, < ㅔ > for /e/, and < ㅐ > for /æ/. Consonants are represented by more compact, two-dimensional graphs, divided into five families according to their places of articulation (see ARTICULATORY PHONETICS). Members of each family share a basic shape, for instance, < ㅁ > stands for the bilabial /m/, < ㅂ > for /b/, and < ㅍ > for /pʰ/ (Sampson, 1985, p. 124). In written text, the graphs are grouped into syllables, so that each group looks like a Chinese character; Han'gul thereby 'succeeds in reconciling two contradictory desiderata for a writing-system: the fewness of the basic graphic elements makes Han'gul easy to learn, while the large size of the perceptually-salient units makes it efficient to read' (Sampson, 1985, p. 132).

K.M.

SUGGESTIONS FOR FURTHER READING

Diringer, D. (1968), *The Alphabet: A Key to the History of Mankind*, 3rd edn, in 2 Vols, London, Hutchinson.

Gelb, I.J. (1963), *A Study of Writing:* revised edn, Chicago and London, University of Chicago Press.

Jensen, H. (1970), *Sign, Symbol and Script: An Account of Man's Efforts to Write*, London, George Allen & Unwin.

Sampson, G. (1985), *Writing Systems*, London, Hutchinson.

Bibliography

Aarts, J. and Meijs, W. (eds) (1984), *Corpus Linguistics: Recent Developments in the Use of Computer Corpora in English Language Research*, Amsterdam, Rodopi.

Abbs, B. and Freebairn, I. (1975), *Strategies*, London, Longman.

Abercrombie, D. (1956), *Problems and Principles*, London, Longman.

Abercrombie, D. (1967), *Elements of General Phonetics*, Edinburgh, Edinburgh University Press.

Abercrombie, D. (1968), 'Paralanguage', *British Journal of Disorders of Communication*, 3: 55–9.

Aboud, F. and Mead, R.D. (eds) (1974), *Cultural Factors in Learning*, Bellington, Washington State College.

Adams, V. (1973), *An Introduction to Modern English Word Formation*, London, Longman.

Adams Smith, D.E. (1986), 'Aspects of register variation in seven popular science articles and the research papers from which they were derived', unpublished M.A. dissertation, University of Birmingham.

Adams Smith, D.E. (1987), 'Variation in field-related genres', *ELR Journal*: 10–32.

Agar, M. (1980), *The Professional Stranger*, New York, Academic Press.

Aitchison, J. (1987), *Words in the Mind: An Introduction to the Mental Lexicon*, Oxford, Basil Blackwell.

Ajdukiewicz, K. (1935), 'Die syntaktische Konnexität', *Studia Philosophica*, 1: 1–28.

Akamatsu, T. (1972), 'The functional level of archiphoneme', in A. Rigault and R. Charbonneau (eds), *Proceedings of the Seventh International Congress of Phonetic Sciences*, The Hague, Mouton, pp. 1067–75.

Akamatsu, T. (1976), 'Peut-on dissocier "neutralisation" et "archiphonème"?', *La Linguistique*, 11 (2): 35–8.

Akamatsu, T. (1988), *The Theory of Neutralization and the Archiphoneme in Functional Phonology*, (Amsterdam Studies in the Theory and History of Linguistic Science, Series V: Current Issues in Linguistic Theory (CILT), no. 43), Amsterdam and Philadelphia, John Benjamins.

Alarcos Llorach, E. (1951), *Gramática estructural según la Escuela de Copenhague y con especial atención a la lengua española*, Biblioteca Románica Hispánica, Madrid, Editorial Gredos.

Albert, M.L., Goodglass, H., Helm, N.A., Rubens, A.B. and Alexander, M.P. (1981), *Clinical Aspects of Dysphasia*, Vienna, Springer.

Alexander, L.G. (1967), *First Things First*, London, Longman.

Allen, H.B. (1973–6), *The Linguistic Atlas of the Upper Midwest*, 3 vols, Minneapolis, University of Minnesota Press.

Allen, J.F. and Perrault, C.R. (1980), 'Analysing intention in utterances', *Artificial Intelligence*, 15 (3): 143–78.

Allen, J.P.B. and Widdowson, H.G. (1974 onward), *English in Focus*, Oxford, Oxford University Press.

Allen, J.P.B. and Widdowson, H.G. (1975), 'Grammar and language teaching', in J.P.B. Allen and S. Pit Corder (eds), *The Edinburgh Course in Applied Linguistics*, vol. 2: *Papers in Applied Linguistics*, London, Oxford University Press, pp. 45–97.

Allen, W.S. (1962), *Sandhi: The Theoretical, Phonetic, and Historical Bases of Word-Junction in Sanskrit*, The Hague, Mouton.

Allerton, D.J. (1979), *Essentials of Grammar Theory: A Consensus View of Syntax and Morphology*, London, Routledge & Kegan Paul.

Allwood, J., Andersson, L-G. and Dahl, Ö. (1977), *Logic in Linguistics*, Cambridge, Cambridge University Press.

Altenberg, B. (1987), *Prosodic Patterns in Spoken English* (Lund Studies in English, no. 76), Lund, Lund University Press.

Altmann, G.T.M. (1987), 'Modularity and interaction in sentence processing', in G. Garfield (ed.), *Modularity in Knowledge Representation and Natural Language Understanding*, Cambridge, MA, MIT Press, pp. 249–57.

Altmann, G.T.M. (1988), 'Ambiguity, parsing strategies, and computational models', *Language and Cognitive Processes*, 3: 73–98.

Altmann, G.T.M. (1989), 'Parsing and interpretation: an introduction', *Language and Cognitive Processes*, 4: 1–19.

Altmann, G.T.M. and Steedman, M. (1988), 'Interaction with context during human sentence processing', *Cognition*, 30: 191–238.

Ammon, R.P. (1968), 'The perception of grammatical relations in sentences: a methodological exploration', *Journal of Verbal Learning and Verbal Behavior*, 7: 869–75.

Andersen, B. (1959), *Rønnemaalet, en strukturallingvistisk analyse af udtryksplanet i en bornholmsk dialekt*, Copenhagen, Udvalg for folkemaals publikationer A 18.

Andersen, H. (ed.) (1986), *Sandhi Phenomenon in the*

Languages of Europe, Amsterdam, Mouton de Gruyter.

Anderson, J.M. (1973), *Structural Aspects of Language Change*, London, Longman.

Anderson, J.R. and Bower, G.H. (1973), *Human Associative Memory*, Washington, DC, Winston.

Anderson, S.R. (1971), 'On the role of deep structure in semantic interpretation, *Foundations of Language*, 6: 197–219.

Anderson, S.R. (1982), 'Where's morphology?', *Linguistic Inquiry*, 13: 571–612.

Anttila, R. (1972), *An Introduction to Historical and Comparative Linguistics*, New York, Macmillan.

Appelt, D. (1985), *Planning English Sentences*, Cambridge, Cambridge University Press.

Aristotle (*c*.330 BC), *Rhetoric*, trans. J.H. Fries (1926), London, William Heinemann.

Arlotto, A. (1972), *Introduction to Historical Linguistics*, Boston, MA, University Press of America.

Arnberg, L. (1979), MA, 'Language strategies in mixed nationality families', *Scandinavian Journal of Psychology*, 20: 105–12.

Aronoff, M. (1976), *Word Formation in Generative Grammar*, Cambridge, MA, MIT Press.

Ascoli, G.I. (1870), *Corsi di Glottologia: Lezioni di Fonologia Comparata*, Turin and Florence, Ermanno Loescher.

Austin, J.L. (1962), *How To Do Things With Words*, Oxford, Oxford University Press.

Austin, J.L. (1971), 'Performative–Constative', in J.R. Searle (ed.), *The Philosophy of Language*, Oxford, Oxford University Press, pp. 13–23.

Ayala, F.J. (1978), 'The mechanisms of evolution', *Scientific American*, 239: 56–69.

Ayer, A. (1971), *Language, Truth and Logic*, Harmondsworth, Penguin; 1st edn 1936, London, Victor Gollancz.

Babb, H.S. (ed.) (1972), *Essays in Stylistic Analysis*, New York, Harcourt Brace Jovanovich.

Bach, E. (1970), 'Pronominalization', *Linguistic Inquiry*, 1: 121–2.

Bach, E. (1988), 'Categorial Grammars as Theories of Language', in R.T. Oehrle, E. Bach, and D. Wheeler (eds), *Categorial Grammars and Natural Language Structures*, Dordrecht, D. Reidel, pp. 17–34.

Bach, E. and Harms, R.T. (eds) (1968), *Universals in Linguistic Theory*, New York, Holt, Rinehart & Winston.

Baetens Beardsmore, H. (ed.) (1981), *Elements of Bilingual Theory*, Brussels, Vrije Universiteit Brussel.

Baetens Beardsmore, H. (1986), *Bilingualism: Basic Principles*, 2nd edn, Avon, England, Multilingual Matters.

Bahl, L.R., Jelinek, F. and Mercer, R.L. (1983), 'A maximum likelihood approach to continuous speech recognition', *IEEE Transactions on Pattern Analysis and Machine Intelligence*, vol. PAM1-5 (March), pp. 179–90.

Bailey, C.-J.N. (1973), *Variation and Linguistic Theory*, Arlington, MA, Center for Applied Linguistics.

Bailey, D. (ed.) (1965), *Essays on Rhetoric*, New York, Oxford University Press.

Bailey, R.W. and Görlach, M. (eds) (1982), *English as a World Language*, Cambridge, Cambridge University Press.

Bain, B. and Yu, A. (1980), 'Cognitive consequences of raising children bilingually: one parent, one language', *Canadian Journal of Psychology*, 34: 304–13.

Baker, S. (1973), *The Practical Stylist*, 3rd edn, New York, Crowell.

Baldauf, R.B. and Jernudd, J.H. (1983), 'Language use patterns in the fisheries periodical literature', *Scientometrics*, 5: 245–55.

Ballmer, T. and Kindt, W. (eds.) (1980), *Zum Thema 'Sprache und Logik': Ergebnisse einer interdisziplinären Diskussion*, Hamburg, Buske.

Balota, D.A., Flores d'Arcais, G.B. and Rayner, K. (eds) (1990), *Comprehension Processes in Reading*, Hillsdale, NJ, Lawrence Erlbaum Associates.

Baltaxe, C.A.M. (1978), *Foundations of Distinctive Feature Theory*, Baltimore, University Park Press.

Bánhidi, Z., Jókay, Z. and Szabó, D. (1965), *Learn Hungarian*, Budapest, Tankönyvkiado.

Bar-Hillel, Y. (1970), *Aspects of Language*, Jerusalem, Magna Press.

Barley, N. (1983), *The Innocent Anthropologist: Notes from a Mud Hut*, Harmondsworth, Penguin.

Bartlett, F.C. (1932), *Remembering: A Study in Experimental and Social Psychology*, Cambridge, Cambridge University Press.

Bates, M. (1978), 'The theory and practice of augmented transition network grammars', in L. Bolc (ed.), *Natural Language Communication with Computers*, (Lecture Notes in Computer Science, no. 63), Berlin, Springer.

Bates, M. and Dudley-Evans, A. (1976), *Nucleus*, London, Longman.

Bateson, F.W. (1967), 'Literature and linguistics', *Essays in Criticism*, 17: 322–47.

Battison, R. (1974), 'Phonological deletion in American sign language', *Sign Language Studies*, 5: 1–19.

Bauer, L. (1983), *English Word-Formation*, Cambridge, Cambridge University Press.

Baugh, A.C. and Cable, T. (1978), *A History of the English Language*, 3rd edn, London, Routledge & Kegan Paul; Englewood Cliffs, NJ, Prentice Hall.

Bazell, C.E. (1949), 'On the problem of the morpheme', *Archivum Linguisticum*, 1: 1–15.

Bazerman, C. (1984), 'Modern evolution of the experimental report in physics: spectroscopic articles in *Physical Review*, 1893-1980', *Social Studies of Science*, 14: 163–96.

Beach, D. (1924), 'The science of tonetics and its application to Bantu languages', *Bantu Studies*, 2: 75–106.

Beale, A. (1987), 'Towards a distributional lexicon', in R. Garside, G. Leech, and G. Sampson, *The Computational Analysis of English: A Corpus-based Approach*, London, Longman, pp. 149–62.

Beardsley, M.C. (1967), 'Metaphor', in P. Edwards (ed.), *Encyclopedia of Philosophy*, vol. 5, New York, Macmillan.

Beaugrande, R. de (1978), *Factors in a Theory of Poetic Translating*, Amsterdam and Assen, Van Gorcum.

Beaugrande, R. de and Dressler, W.V. (1981), *Introduction to Text Linguistics*, London and New York, Longman.

Békésy, G. von (1960), *Experiments in Hearing*, New York, McGraw-Hill.

Bell, A. (1978), 'Language samples', in J.H. Greenberg, C.A. Ferguson, and E.A. Moravcsik (eds), *Universals of Human Language*, 4 vols, Stanford, CA, Stanford University Press, pp. 123–56.

Bellack, A.A., Kliebard, H.M., Hyman, R.T. and Smith, F.L. (1966), *The Language of the Classroom*, New York, Teachers' College Press, Columbia University.

Belsey, C. (1980), *Critical Practice*, London, Methuen.

Benedict, H. (1979), 'Early lexical development: comprehension and production', *Journal of Child Language* 6: 183–200.

Bennett, D.C. (1975), *Spatial and Temporal Uses of English Prepositions: An Essay in Stratificational Semantics*, London, Longman.

Bennett, M.E. (1986), 'Aspects of the simple clause in Malagasy: a stratificational approach', unpublished Ph.D. dissertation, Michigan State University.

Benson, D. F. (1979), *Aphasia, Alexia, and Agraphia*, New York, Churchill Livingstone.

Benson, M., Benson, E. and Ilson, R.F. (1986), *Lexicographic Description of English*, Amsterdam and Philadelphia, John Benjamins.

Bergman, C. (1976), 'Interference vs. independent development in infant bilingualism', in G. Keller, R. Teschner and S. Viera (eds), *Bilingualism in the Bicentennial and Beyond*, New York, Bilingual Press.

Berko, J. (1958), 'The child's learning of English morphology', *Word*, 14: 150–77.

Berlin, B. and Kay, P. (1969), *Basic Color Terms*, Berkeley, University of California Press.

Berlin, R. (1887), *Eine besondere Art der Wortblindheit (Dyslexie)*, Wiesbaden, Bergmann.

Bernard, J. (1972), *The Sex Game*, New York, Atheneum.

Bernstein, B. (ed.) (1971), *Class, Codes and Control*, vol. 1: *Theoretical Studies Towards a Sociology of Language* (Primary Socialization, Language and Education) London, Routledge & Kegan Paul, revised edn 1973, London, Paladin.

Bernstein, B. (1972), 'Social class, language and socialization', in P.P. Giglioli (ed.), *Language and Social Context*, Harmondsworth, Penguin, pp. 157–78.

Bernstein, B. (ed.) (1973), *Class, Codes and Control*, vol. 2: *Applied Studies Towards a Sociology of Language*, London, Routledge & Kegan Paul.

Berry, M. (1975), *Introduction to Systemic Linguistics*, vol. 1: *Structures and Systems*, London, Batsford.

Berry, M. (1981), 'Systemic linguistics and discourse analysis: a multi-layered approach to exchange structure', in M. Coulthard and M. Montgomery (eds), *Studies in Discourse Analysis*, London, Routledge & Kegan Paul, pp. 120–45.

Bever, T.G. (1970), 'The cognitive basis for linguistic structures', in J.R. Hayes (ed.), *Cognition and the Development of Language*, New York, John Wiley, pp. 279–352.

Beynon, J. *et al.* (1983), 'The politics of discrimination', *English in Education*, 17 (3).

Bhatia, V. (1981), 'Defining legal scope in statutory writing', paper given at the BAAL Annual Conference, Brighton.

Biber, D. and Finnegan, E. (1986), 'Uncovering dimensions of linguistic variation in English: a research report', *ICAME News* (Bergen), 10: 49–52.

Bickerton, D. (1971), 'Inherent variability and variable rules', *Foundations of Language*, 7 (4): 457–92.

Bickerton, D. (1974), 'Creolization, linguistic universals, natural semantax and the brain', *Working Papers in Linguistics* (University of Hawaii), 6 (3): 124–41.

Bickerton, D. (1977), 'Pidginization and creolization: language acquisition and language universals', in A. Valdman (ed.), *Pidgin and Creole Linguistics*, Bloomington, Indiana University Press, pp. 49–69.

Bickerton, D. (1979), 'Beginnings', in K.C. Hill (ed.), *The Genesis of Language*, Ann Arbor, MI, Karoma, pp. 1–22.

Bickerton, D. (1981), *Roots of Language*, Ann Arbor, MI, Karoma.

Bickerton, D. (1984a), 'The language bioprogram hypothesis', *Behavioral and Brain Sciences*, 7 (2): 173–88.

Bickerton, D. (1984b), 'Author's response', *Behavioral and Brain Sciences*, 7 (2): 212–18.

Billows, L. (1962), *Techniques of Language Teaching*, London, Longman.

Birch, H.G. (1962), 'Dyslexia and the maturation of visual function', in D. Money (ed.), *Reading Disability. Progress and Research Needs in Dyslexia*, New York, Johns Hopkins Press.

Birdwhistle, R.L. (1970), *Kinesics and Context: Essays on Body Motion Communication*, Philadelphia, University of Pennsylvania Press.

Bishop, D. (1982), *Test for the Reception of Grammar*, Medical Research Council.

Black, M. (1979), 'More about metaphor', in A. Ortony (ed.), *Metaphor and Thought*, Cambridge, Cambridge University Press, pp. 19–45.

Bley-Vroman, R. and Selinker, L. (1984), 'Research design in rhetorical/grammatical studies: a proposed optimal research strategy, part 2', *English for Specific Purposes*, Oregon State University, 84.

Bloch, B. (1953), 'Linguistic structure and linguistic analysis', in A.A. Hill (ed.), *Report of the Fourth Annual Round Table Meeting on Linguistics and Language Study* (Monograph Series on Language and Linguistics, IV), Washington, DC, pp. 40–4.

Bloch, B. and Trager, G.L. (1942), *Outline of Linguistic Analysis*, Baltimore, Linguistic Society of America.

Bloom, L.M. (1970), *Language Development: Form and Function in Emerging Grammars*, Cambridge, MA, MIT Press.

Bloomfield, L. (1926), 'A set of postulates for a science of language', *Language*, 2: 153–64.

Bloomfield, L. (1933/5), *Language*, New York, Holt, Rinehart & Winston (1933); London, George Allen & Unwin (revised, 1935).

Blumstein, S. and Cooper, W.E. (1974), 'Hemispheric processing of intonation contours', *Cortex*, 10: 146–58.

Boas, F. (1911), *Handbook of American Indian Languages*, Washington, DC, Smithsonian Institution, Bureau of American Ethnology, Bulletin 40.

Bobrow, D.G. (1968), 'Natural language input for a computer problem-solving system', in M. Minsky (ed.), *Semantic Information Processing*, Cambridge, MA, MIT Press, pp. 146–226.

Bolinger, D.L. (1948), 'On defining the morpheme', *Word*, 4 (1): 18–23.

Bolinger, D.L. (1961), *Generality, Gradience, and the All-or-None*, The Hague, Mouton.

Bolinger, D.L. (1965a), *Forms of English: Accent, Morpheme, Order*, Cambridge, MA, Harvard University Press.

Bolinger, D.L. (1965b), 'The atomization of meaning', *Language*, 41 (4): 555–73.

Bolinger, D.L. (1976), 'Meaning and memory', *Forum Linguisticum*, 1 (1): 1–14.

Bolinger, D.L. (1985), *Intonation and its Parts: Melody in Spoken English*, London, Edward Arnold.

Bolinger, D.L. and Sears, D.A. (1981), *Aspects of Language*, New York, Harcourt Brace Jovanovich.

Booij, G.E. (1986), 'Form and meaning in morphology: the case of Dutch "agent nouns"', *Linguistics*, 24: 503–17.

Boole, G. (1854), *The Laws of Thought*, London, Walton.

Boomer, D.S. and Laver, J.D.M. (1968), 'Slips of the tongue', *British Journal of Disorders of Communication*, 3: 1–12.

Booth, W. (1961), *The Rhetoric of Fiction*, Chicago, University of Chicago Press.

Bopp, F. (1816), *Über das Conjugationssystem der Sanskritsprache in Vergleichung mit jenem der griechischen, lateinischen, persischen und germanischen Sprache*, Frankfurt-am-Main, in der Andreaischen Buchhandlung.

Bowen, E. (1964), *Return to Laughter*, New York, Doubleday.

Bower, G.H. (ed.) (1975), *The Psychology of Learning and Motivation*, vol. 9, New York, Academic Press.

Bowerman, M. (1973), 'Structural relationships in children's utterances: syntax or semantics?', in T. Moore (ed.), *Cognitive Development and the Acquisition of Meaning*, New York, Academic Press, pp. 197–213.

Boyd, R. (1979), 'Metaphor and theory change: what is "metaphor" a metaphor for?', in A. Ortony (ed.), *Metaphor and Thought*, Cambridge, Cambridge University Press, pp. 356–408.

Boyes-Braem, P. (1973), 'The acquisition of handshape in American Sign Language', manuscript, Salk Institute for Biological Studies, La Jolla, CA.

Bradshaw, J.L. and Nettleton, N.C. (1981), 'The nature of hemispheric specialization in man', *Behavioral and Brain Sciences*, 4: 51–92.

Braine, M.D.S. (1963), 'The ontogeny of English phrase structure: the first phase', *Language*, 39: 1–13.

Braine, M.D.S. (1976), *Children's First Word Combinations (Monographs of the Society for Research in Child Development)*, no. 41 (1, serial no. 164)).

Brame, M. (1976), *Conjectures and Refutations in Syntax and Semantics*, New York, North-Holland.

Bransford, J.D. and Johnson, M.K. (1973), 'Considerations of some problems of comprehension', in W.G. Chase (ed.), *Visual Information Processing*, New York, Academic Press, pp. 383–438.

Braunwald, S. (1978), 'Context, word and meaning: toward a communicational analysis of lexical acquisition', in A. Lock (ed.), *Action, Gesture and Symbol: The Emergence of Language*, London, Academic Press, pp. 485–527.

Brazil, D.C. (1985), *The Communicative Value of Intonation in English*, Birmingham (Discourse Analysis Monograph, no. 8), English Language Research, University of Birmingham.

Bredsdorff, J.H. (1821), 'Om aarsagerne til sprogenes forandringer' ('On the causes of change in languages'), *Programme of the Roskilde Catholic School*, republished 1886, Copenhagen, Vilhelm Thomsen.

Brennan, M., Colvill, M.D. and Lawson, L. (1980), *Words in Hand*, Moray House College of Education, Edinburgh, British Sign Language Research Project.

Bresnan, J.W. (1978), 'A realistic transformational grammar', in M. Halle, J. Bresnan, and G.A. Miller (eds), *Linguistic Theory and Psychological Reality*, Cambridge, MA, MIT Press, pp. 1–59.

Bresnan, J.W. (ed.) (1982), *The Mental Representation of Grammatical Relations*, Cambridge, MA, and London, MIT Press.

Bresnan, J.W. and Kanerva, J.M. (1989), 'Locative inversion in Chichewa: a case study of factorization in grammar', *Linguistic Inquiry*, 20 (1): 1–50.

Bresnan, J.W. and Kaplan, R.M. (1982), 'Introduction: grammars as mental representations of language', in J.W. Bresnan (ed.), *The Mental Representation of Grammatical Relations*, Cambridge, MA, and London, MIT Press, pp. xvii–lii.

Bridge, J. (1977), *Beginning Model Theory*, Oxford, Oxford University Press.

Broca, P. (1865), 'Sur la faculté du langage articulé', *Bulletin de la Société d'Anthropologie*, 4: 493–4.

Brook, G.L. (1965), *English Dialects*, London, Deutsch.

Brown, E.K. and Miller, J. (1980), *Syntax: A Linguistic Introduction to Sentence Structure*, London, Hutchinson.

Brown, G. and Yule, G. (1983), *Discourse Analysis*, Cambridge, Cambridge University Press.

Brown, P., Cocke, S., della Pietra, V., Jelinek, F., Mercer, R. and Roossin, P. (1988), 'A statistical approximation to French/English translation', paper delivered at the RIAO 88 Conference on User-Oriented Context-Based Text and Image Handling. MIT Press, March.

Brown, R. (1973), *A First Language: The Early Stages*, Cambridge, MA, Harvard University press.

Brown, R. and Fraser, C. (1963), 'The acquisition of syntax', in C. Cofer and B. Musgrave (eds), *Verbal Behavior and Learning: Problems and Processes*, New York, McGraw-Hill, pp. 158–201.

Brown, R. and Gilman, A. (1960), 'The pronouns of power and solidarity', in T.A. Sebeok (ed.), *Style in Language*, Cambridge, MA, MIT Press, pp. 253–76.

Bruce, B. (1975), 'Case systems for natural language', *Artificial Intelligence*, 6: 327–60.

Brumfit, C. (1980), 'Problems and principles in English teaching', Oxford, Pergamon.

Bub, D. and Kertesz, A. (1982), 'Evidence for lexicographic processing in a patient with preserved written over oral single word naming', *Brain*, 105: 697–774.

Bulletin du Cercle Linguistique de Copenhague 1941–65 (1970), Copenhagen, Akademisk Forlag.

Burling, R. (1978), 'Language development of a Garo and English speaking child', in E. Hatch (ed.), *Second Language Acquisition*, Rowley, MA, Newbury House.

Burton, D. (1980), *Dialogue and Discourse*, London, Routledge & Kegan Paul.

Burton, D. (1981), 'Analysing spoken discourse', in M. Coulthard and M. Montgomery (eds), *Studies in Discourse Analysis*, London, Routledge & Kegan Paul, pp. 61–81.

Burton, D. (1982a), 'Conversation pieces', in R. Carter and D. Burton (eds), *Literary Text and Language Study*, London, Edward Arnold, pp. 86–115.

Burton, D. (1982b), 'Through glass darkly: through dark glasses', in R. Carter (ed.), *Language and Literature: An Introductory Reader in Stylistics*, London, Allen & Unwin, pp. 194–214.

Butler, C.S. (1985), *Systemic Linguistics: Theory and Applications*, London, Batsford Academic and Educational.

Butterworth, B. (ed.) (1980), *Language Production*, 2 vols, London, Academic Press.

Buyssens, E. (1967), *La Communication et l'articulation linguistique*, Paris, Presses Universitaires de France; Brussels, Presses Universitaires de Bruxelles.

Buyssens, E. (1972a), 'Intervention', in R. Rigault and R. Charbonneau (eds), *Proceedings of the Seventh International Congress of Phonetic Sciences*, The Hague, Mouton, pp. 1970–1.

Buyssens, E. (1972b), 'Phonème, archiphonème et pertinence', *La Linguistique*, 8 (2): 39–58.

Buyssens, E, (1974), 'Contre la notion d'archiphonème', in L. Heilman (ed.), *Proceedings of the Eleventh International Congress of Linguists*, Bologna and Florence, Il Mulino, pp. 765–8.

Buyssens, E. (1975), 'A propos de l'archiphonème', *La Linguistique*, 11 (2): pp. 35–8.

Buyssens, E. (1977), 'A propos de l'archiphonème', *La Linguistique*, 13 (2): 51–4.

Bybee, J.L. (1985), *Morphology: A Study of the Relation between Meaning and Form*, Amsterdam, Benjamins.

Bynon, T. (1977), *Historical Linguistics*, Cambridge, Cambridge University Press.

Campbell, R. and Wales, R. (1970), 'The study of language acquisition', in J. Lyons (ed.), *New Horizons in Linguistics*, Harmondsworth, Penguin, pp. 242–60.

Candlin, C.N., Leather, J.H. and Bruton, C.J. (1978), *Doctor Patient Communication Skills*, Chelmsford, Graves Audio-Visual Medical Foundation.

Canger, U. (1969), 'Analysis in outline of Mam, a Mayan language', unpublished Ph.D. thesis, Berkeley, CA.

Cannon, G. (1986), 'Blends in English word formation', *Linguistics*, 24: 725–53.

Capella, J.N. and Street, R.L. Jr (1985), 'Introduction: a functional approach to the structure of communicative behaviour', in R.L. Street Jr and J.N. Capella (eds), *Sequence and Pattern in Communicative Behaviour*, London, Edward Arnold, pp. 1–29.

Caputo, C. (1986), *Il segno di Giano, Studi su Louis Hjelmslev. Testi i Studi 54*, Milano, Edizioni Unicopli.

Caramazza, A., Yeni-Komshian, G.H., Zurif, E.B. and Carbone, E. (1973), 'The acquisition of a new phonological contrast: the case of stop consonants in French–English bilinguals', *Journal of the Acoustical Society of America*, 54: 421–28.

Carnap, R. (1928), *Der logische Aufbau der Welt*, Berlin-Schlactensee, Weltkreis.

Carpenter, P.A. and Just, M.A. (1977), 'Reading comprehension as eyes see it', in M.A. Just and P.A. Carpenter (eds), *Cognitive Processes in Comprehension*, Hillsdale, NJ, Lawrence Erlbaum Associates.

Carradine, J. (1968), 'Some notes on the differences between eight science reports from *The Times* and eight scientific papers on which they were based', unpublished M.A. thesis, University of Leeds.

Carroll, J.B. (ed.) (1956), *Language, Thought and Reality: Selected Writings of Benjamin Lee Whorf*, Cambridge, MA, MIT Press.

Carroll, J.B. (1971), 'Statistical analysis of the corpus', in J.B. Carroll, P. Davies, and B. Richman (eds), *Word Frequency Book*, New York, American Heritage, pp. xxi–xl.

Carter, B. Jr (1963), 'President Kennedy's inaugural address', *College Composition and Communication*, 14, (February): 36–40. Reprinted in G.A. Love and M. Payne, (eds) (1969), *Contemporary Essays on Style: Rhetoric, Linguistics and Criticism*, Glenview, IL, Scott, Foresman & Co., pp. 246–51 and 199–301.

Carter, R. and Burton, D. (1982), *Literary Text and Language Study*, London, Edward Arnold.

Carter, R.A. (1987), 'Is there a core vocabulary? Some implications for language teaching', *Applied Linguistics*, 8 (2): 178–93.

Catford, J.C. (1957), 'The linguistic survey of Scotland', *Orbis*, 6 (1): 105–21.

Cauldwell, G. (1982), 'Anglo-Quebec on the verge of its history', *Language and Society* (Ottawa, Office of the Commissioner of Official Language), 8: 3–6.

Cedergren, H.J. and Sankoff, D. (1974), 'Variable rules: performance as a statistical reflection of competence', *Language*, 50 (2): 333–55.

Chambers, J.K. and Trudgill, P.J. (1980), *Dialectology*, Cambridge, Cambridge University Press.

Chao, Y.R. (1930), 'A system of tone letters', *Le Maître phonetique*, 30: 24–7.

Chapman, R. (1973), *Linguistics and Literature: An Introduction to Literary Stylistics*, London, Edward Arnold.

Charniak, E. and McDermott, D.V. (1985), *An Introduction to Artificial Intelligence*, Reading, MA, Addison Wesley.

Chatman, S. (1960), 'Comparing metrical styles', in T.A. Sebeok (ed.), *Style in Language*, Cambridge, MA, MIT Press, pp. 149–72.

Chatman, S. (ed.) (1971), *Literary Style: A Symposium*, London and New York, Oxford University Press.

Chellas, B. (1980), *Modal Logic*, Cambridge, Cambridge University Press.

Cheng, C.C. (1973), 'A quantitative study of Chinese tones', *Journal of Chinese Linguistics*, 1: 93–110.

Cheng, C.C. and Kisseberth, C.W. (1979–81), Ikorovere Makua tonology. Parts 1, 2, 3 (*Studies in the Linguistic Sciences*, nos. 9, 10, 11).

Chevalier, J.C. (1968), *Histoire de la syntaxe – naissance de la notion de complément dans la langue française*, Geneva, Droz.

Chilton, P. (1982), 'Nukespeak: nuclear language, culture and propaganda', in C. Aubrey (ed.), *Nukespeak. The Media and the Bomb*, London, Comedia Press Group, pp. 94–112.

Chilton, P. (1984), 'Orwell, language and linguistics', *Language and Communication*, 4 (2): 29–46.

Chilton, P. (ed.) (1985), *Language and the Nuclear Arms Debate: Nukespeak Today*, London and Dover, NH, Frances Pinter.

Chomsky, C. (1969), *The Acquisition of Syntax in Children from 5 to 10*, Cambridge, MA, MIT Press.

Chomsky, N. (1957), *Syntactic Structures*, The Hague, Mouton.

Chomsky, N. (1959), 'A review of B.F. Skinner's *Verbal Behavior*', *Language*, 31 (1): 26–58, reprinted in J. Fodor and J. Katz (eds) (1964), *The Structure of Language: Readings in the Philosophy of Language*, Englewood Cliffs, NJ, New York, Prentice Hall, pp. 547–78.

Chomsky, N. (1962), 'The logical basis of linguistic theory', in H.G Lunt (ed.) (1964), *Proceedings of the Ninth International Congress of Linguists*, The Hague, Mouton, pp. 914–78.

Chomsky, N. (1964), *Current Issues in Linguistic Theory*, The Hague, Mouton; and in J.A. Fodor and J.J. Katz (eds), *The Structure of Language: Readings in the Philosophy of Language*, Englewood Cliffs, NJ, Prentice Hall, pp. 50–118.

Chomsky, N. (1965), *Aspects of the Theory of Syntax*, Cambridge, MA, MIT Press.

Chomsky, N. (1966), *Cartesian Linguistics; A Chapter in the History of Rationalist Thought*, New York, Harper & Row.

Chomsky, N. (1967), 'The formal nature of language', in E. Lenneberg (ed.), *Biological Foundations of Language*, New York, Wiley, pp. 397–442.

Chomsky, N. (1970a), 'Remarks on nominalization', in R. Jacobs and P. Rosenbaum (eds), *Readings in English Transformational Grammar*, Waltham, MA, Blaisdell, pp. 184–221.

Chomsky, N. (1970b), 'Language and freedom', *Abraxas*, 1 (1): 9–24.

Chomsky, N. (1971), 'Deep structure, surface structure, and semantic interpretation', in D. Steinberg and L. Jakobovits (eds), *Semantics*, Cambridge, Cambridge University Press, pp. 183–216.

Chomsky, N. (1972a), *Language and Mind*, New York, Harcourt Brace Jovanovich.

Chomsky, N. (1972b), 'Some empirical issues in the theory of transformational grammar', in S. Peters (ed.), *Goals of Linguistic Theory*, Englewood Cliffs, NJ, Prentice Hall, pp. 63–130.

Chomsky, N. (1972c), *Studies on Semantics in Generative Grammar*, The Hague, Mouton.

Chomsky, N. (1973), 'Conditions on transformations', in S. Anderson and P. Kiparsky (eds), *A Festschrift for Morris Halle*, New York, Holt, Rinehart & Winston, pp. 232–86.

Chomsky, N. (1975a), *Reflections on Language*, New York, Pantheon.

Chomsky, N. (1975b), *The Logical Structure of Linguistic Theory*, New York, Plenum Press.

Chomsky, N. (1976), 'On the biological basis of language capacities', in R. Rieber (ed.), *The Neuropsychology of Language*, New York, Plenum Press.

Chomsky, N. (1977a), 'On WH-movement', in P. Culicover, T. Wasow, and A. Akmajian (eds), *Formal Syntax*, New York, Academic Press, pp. 71–132.

Chomsky. N. (1977b), *Essays on Form and Interpretation*, New York, North Holland.

Chomsky, N. (1979), *Morphophonemics of Modern Hebrew*, New York, Garland (M.A. thesis, University of Pennsylvania, 1951).

Chomsky, N. (1981), *Lectures on Government and Binding*, Dordrecht, Foris.

Chomsky, N. (1982), *Some Concepts and Consequences of the Theory of Government and Binding*, Cambridge, MA, MIT Press.

Chomsky, N. and Halle, M. (1968), *The Sound Pattern of English*, New York, Harper & Row.

Chomsky, N., Halle, M. and Lukoff, F. (1956), 'On accent and juncture in English', in *For Roman Jakobson*, The Hague, Mouton, pp. 65–80.

Clark, E.V. (1973), 'What's in a word? On the child's acquisition of semantics in his first language', in T. Moore (ed.), *Cognitive Development and the Acquisition of Meaning*, New York, Academic Press, pp. 65–110.

Clark, H.E. and Clark, E.V. (1977), *Psychology and Language: An Introduction to Psycholinguistics*, New York, Harcourt Brace Jovanovich.

Clark, R. (1979), 'In search of Beach-la-mar: a history of Pacific Pidgin English', *Te Reo*, 22: 3–64.

Clements, G.N. (1976), 'The autosegmental treatment of vowel harmony', in W. Dressler and O.E. Pfeiffer (eds), *Phonologica, 1976*, Innsbruck, Institut für Sprachwissenschaft, pp. 111–19.

Clements, G.N. (1985), 'The geometry of phonological features', *Phonology Yearbook*, 2: 225–52.

Clements, G.N. and Keyser, S.J. (1983), *CV Phonology. A Generative Theory of the Syllable*, Cambridge, MA, MIT Press.

Clifton, C., Jr and Ferreira, F. (1989), 'Ambiguity in context', *Language and Cognitive Processes*, 4: 71–103.

Closs Traugott, E. and Pratt, M.L. (1980), *Linguistics for Students of Literature*, New York, Harcourt Brace Jovanovich.

Cluysenaar, A. (1976), *Introduction to Literary Stylistics: A Discussion of Dominant Structures in Verse and Prose*, London, Batsford.

Coates, J. (1983), *The Semantics of the Modal Auxiliaries*, London, Croom Helm.

Coates, J. (1986), *Women, Men and Language*, London and New York, Longman.

COBUILD (1987), *Collins COBUILD English Language Dictionary* (Editor-in-Chief, John Sinclair), London and Glasgow, Collins.

Cohen, J.L. (1979), 'The semantics of metaphor', in A. Ortony (ed.), *Metaphor and Thought*, Cambridge, Cambridge University Press, pp. 64–77.

Cohen, P.R. and Perrault, C.R. (1979), 'Elements of a plan-based theory of speech acts', *Cognitive Science*, 3: 177–212.

Coleman, D. W. (1982), 'Discourse functions of the active–passive dichotomy in English', unpublished Ph.D. dissertation, University of Florida (University Microfilms International order no. DA-8226378).

Collignon, L. and Glatigny, M. (eds) (1978), *Les Dictionnaires: Initiation á la lexicographie*, Paris, CEDIC (collection 'textes et non textes').

Collinson, C.W. (1929), *Cannibals and Coconuts*, London, George Philip.

Collinson, W.E. (1939), 'Comparative synonymics: some principles and illustrations', *Transactions of the Philological Society*, 11: 54–77.

Coltheart, M. (1987), 'Functional architecture of the language-processing system', in M. Coltheart, G. Sartori, and R. Job (eds), *The Cognitive Neuropsychology of Language*, London and Hillsdale, NJ, Lawrence Erlbaum Associates, pp. 1–25.

Comrie, B. (1981), *Language Universals and Linguistic Typology: Syntax and Morphology*, Oxford, Basil Blackwell.

Comrie, B. (1989), *Language Universals and Linguistic Typology: Syntax and Morphology*, 2nd edn, Oxford, Basil Blackwell.

Connerton, P. (ed.) (1976), *Critical Sociology*, Harmondsworth, Penguin.

Conrad, R. (1979), *The Deaf Schoolchild: Language and Cognitive Function*, London and New York, Harper & Row.

Cook, V.J. (1988), *Chomsky's Universal Grammar: An Introduction*, Oxford, Basil Blackwell.

Cooper, C. (1985), 'Aspects of article introduction in IEEE publications', unpublished M.Sc. dissertation, University of Aston in Birmingham.

Copeland, J.E. and Davis, P.W. (eds) (1980), *Papers in Cognitive–Stratificational Linguistics*, (Rice University Studies 66(2)), Houston, Rice University.

Corbett, A.T. and Chang, F.R. (1983), 'Pronoun disambiguation: accessing potential antecedents', *Memory and Cognition*, 2: 283–94.

Corbett, A.T. and Dosher, B.A. (1978), 'Instrument inferences in sentence encoding', *Journal of Verbal Learning and Verbal Behavior*, 17: 479–91.

Cornett, R.O. (1967), 'The method explained', *Hearing and Speech News*, 35(5): 7–9.

Coseriu, E. (1952), *Sistema, norma y habla*, Montevideo.

Coseriu, E. (1954), *Forma y substancia en los sonidos del lenguaje*, Montevideo, Universidad de la República.

Coseriu, E. (1955–6), 'Determinación y etorno', *Romanistische Jahrbuch*, 7: 29–54.

Coseriu, E. (1967), *Teoría del lenguaje y lingüística general*, Madrid, Greda.

Coulmas, F. (1979), 'Idiomaticity as a problem of pragmatics', in H. Parret, M. Sbisa, and J. Verschueren (eds), *Possibilities and Limitations of Pragmatics*, Amsterdam, John Benjamins, pp. 138–51.

Coulmas, F. (1981), *Conversational Routine*, The Hague, Mouton.

Coulthard, M. (1977), *Introduction to Discourse Analysis*, London, Longman.

Coulthard, M. (1985), *An Introduction to Discourse Analysis: New Edition*, London and New York, Longman.

Council for the Welsh Language/Cyngor yr Iaith Gymraeg (1978), *A Future for the Welsh Language/ Dyfodol i'r iaith Gymraeg*, Cardiff, HMSO.

Cowie, A.P. (1981), 'The treatment of collocations and idioms in learners' dictionaries', *Applied Linguistics*, 2(3): 223–35.

Crain, S. and Steedman, M. (1985), 'On not being led up the garden path: the use of context by the psychological syntax processor', in D.R. Dowty, L. Karttunen, and A.M. Zwicky (eds), *Natural Language Parsing*, Cambridge, Cambridge University Press, pp. 320–58.

Cresswell, M. (1973), *Logic and Languages*, London, Methuen.

Critchley, M. (1964), *Developmental Dyslexia*, London, William Heinemann Medical Books.

Critchley, M. (1970), *The Dyslexic Child*, Springfield, IL, Thomas.

Crookes, G. (1984), 'Towards a validated discourse analysis of scientific text', unpublished M.A. thesis, University of Hawaii.

Cruse, D.A. (1973), 'Some thoughts on agentivity', *Journal of Linguistics*, 9: 1–23.

Cruse, D.A. (1975), 'Hyponymy and lexical hierarchies', *Archivum Linguisticum*, 6: 26–31.

Cruse, D.A. (1986), *Lexical Semantics*, Cambridge, Cambridge University Press.

Crutenden, A. (1986), *Intonation*, Cambridge University Press.

Crystal, D. (1975), *Prosodic Systems and Intonation in English*, Cambridge, Cambridge University Press.

Crystal, D. (1980), *An Introduction to Language Pathology*, London, Edward Arnold.

Crystal, D. (1981), *Linguistics*, revised edn, Harmondsworth, Penguin.

Crystal, D. (1985), *A Dictionary of Linguistics and Phonetics*, 2nd edn updated and enlarged, Oxford, Basil Blackwell in association with André Deutsch.

Crystal, D. and Davy, D. (1969), *Investigating English Style*, London and Harlow, Longmans, Green & Co.

Crystal, D., Fletcher, P. and Garman, M. (1976), *The Grammatical Analysis of Language Disability*, London, Edward Arnold.

Cummings, M. and Simmons, R. (1983), *The Language of Literature: A stylistic Introduction to the Study of Literature*, Oxford, Pergamon Press.

Curtiss, S. (1977), *Genie: A Psycholinguistic Study of a Modern-Day 'Wild Child'*, London, Academic Press.

Cuyckens, H. (1982), 'Componential analysis in psycholinguistics', *ITL; Tijdschrift voor Toegepaste Linguistiek*, vol. 57, pp. 53–75.

Darwin, C. (1859/1964), *On the Origin of Species*, facsimile edn, Cambridge, MA, Harvard University Press.

Darwin, C. (1871), *The Descent of Man*, London, J. Murray.

Darwin, C. (1877), 'A biographical sketch of an infant', *Mind*, 2: 252–9.

Davey, A. (1978), *Discourse Production: A Computer Model of Some Aspects of a Speaker*, Edinburgh, Edinburgh University Press.

Davidsen-Nielsen, N. (1978), *Neutralization and Archiphoneme: Two Phonological Concepts and Their History*, Copenhagen, Akademisk Forlag.

Davidson, D. (1967), 'Truth and meaning', *Synthese*, 17: 304–23, reprinted in D. Davidson (1984), *Inquiries into Truth and Interpretation*, Oxford, Clarendon Press, pp. 17–36.

Davidson, D. (1973), 'Radical interpretation', *Dialectica*, pp. 313–28, reprinted in D. Davidson (1984), *Inquiries into Truth and Interpretation*, Oxford, Clarendon Press, pp. 125–39.

Davidson, D. (1986), 'A nice derangement of epitaphs', in E. LePore (ed.), *Truth and Interpretation: Perspectives on the Philosophy of Donald Davidson*, Oxford, Basil Blackwell, pp. 433–46.

Davies, C. (1981), 'Ysgolion Cymraig', *Education*, pp. 3–13.

Davies, F. and Greene, T. (1984), *Reading for Learning in the Sciences*, Edinburgh, Oliver and Boyd for Schools Council.

Davis, A.C. (1983), *A Survey of Adult Aphasia*, Englewood Cliff, NJ, Prentice Hall.

Davis, E. (1937), *The Development of Linguistic Skills in Twins, Singletons with Siblings, and Only Children from Age Five to Ten Years* (Institute of Child Welfare Monograph Series; no. 14), Minneapolis, University of Minnesota.

Day, E. (1932), 'The development of language in twins: 1. A comparison of twins and single children. 2. The development of twins: their resemblances and differences', *Child Development*, 3: 179–99.

Day, R. (ed.) (1980), *Issues in English Creoles*, Heidelberg, Julius Groos.

DeCamp, D. (1961), 'Social and geographical factors in Jamaican dialects', in R.B. Le Page (ed.), *Creole Language Studies II*, proceedings of the Conference on Creole Language Studies, University of the West Indies, March–April 1959, London, Macmillan, pp. 61–84

DeCamp, D. (1971a), 'The study of pidgins and creole languages', in D. Hymes (ed.), *Pidginization and Creolization of Languages*, proceedings of a conference, University of the West Indies, April 1968, Cambridge, Cambridge University Press, pp. 13–43.

DeCamp, D. (1971b), 'Towards a generative analysis of a post-creole continuum', in D. Hymes (ed.), *Pidginization and Creolization of Languages*, proceedings of a conference, University of West Indies, April 1968, Cambridge, Cambridge University Press, pp. 349–70.

de Grolier, E. (ed.) (1983), *Glossogenetics: The Origin and Evolution of Language*, London and New York, Harwood Academic.

Déjèrine, J. (1892), 'Contribution à l'étude anatomo-pathologique et clinique des différentes variétés de cécité verbale', in G. Masson (ed.), *Comptes rendus hebdomadaires des séances et mémoires de la Société de Biologie*, vol. IV (series no. 9), Paris, Librairie de l'académie de médicine, pp. 61–90.

Delgutte, B. and Kiang, N.Y.S. (1984), 'Speech coding in the auditory nerve: I. Vowel-like sounds', *Journal of the Acoustical Society of America*, 75: 866–78.

Dell, G.S. (1985), 'Positive feedback in hierarchical connectionist models: applications to language production', *Cognitive Science*, 9: 3–23.

Dell, G.S. (1986), 'A spreading activation theory of retrieval in sentence production', *Psychological Review*, 93: 283–321.

Denes, P.B. and Pinson, E.N. (1973), *Speech Chain*, New York, Anchor Books.

De Smedt, K. and Kempen, G. (1987), 'Incremental sentence production, self-correction and co-ordination', in G. Kempen (ed.), *Natural Language Generation: Recent Advances in Artificial Intelligence, Psychology and Linguistics*, Dordrecht, Kluwer.

Deuchar, M. (1984), *British Sign Language*, London, Routledge & Kegan Paul.

Dewar, H., Bratley, P. and Thorne, J.P. (1969), 'A program for the syntactic analysis of English sentences', *Communications of the ACM*, 12: 476–9.

Dijk, T.A. van (1972), *Some Aspects of Text Grammars*, The Hague, Mouton.

Dijk, T.A. van (1977), *Text and Context: Explorations in the Semantics and Pragmatics of Discourse*, London and New York.

Dijk, T.A. van, Ihwe, J., Petöfi, J. and Rieser, H. (1972), *Zur Bestimmung narrativer Structuren auf der Grundlage von Textgrammatiken*, Hamburg, Buske.

Dijk, T.A. van and Kintsch, W. (1978), 'Cognitive psychology and discourse: recalling and summarizing stories', in W.U. Dressler (ed.), *Trends in Textlinguistics*, Berlin and New York, Walter de Gruyter, pp. 61–80.

Dik, S.C. (1978), *Functional Grammar* (North Holland Linguistics Series, no. 37), Amsterdam, North Holland.

Dik, S.C. (1980), 'Seventeen sentences: basic principles and application of functional grammar', in E.A. Moravcsik and J.R. Wirth (eds), *Syntax and Semantics*, vol. 13: *Current Approaches to Syntax*, New York and London, Academic Press, pp. 45–75.

Dimond, S. and Beaumont, J. (1974), *Hemisphere Function in the Human Brain*, Elek, London.

Dinneen, F.P. (1967), *An Introduction to General Linguistics*, New York, Holt, Rinehart & Winston.

Dinnsen, D. (ed.) (1979), *Current Approaches to Phonological Theory*, Bloomington, Indiana University Press.

Diringer, D. (1968), *The Alphabet: A Key to the History of Mankind*, 3rd edn, in 2 vols, London, Hutchinson.

Dixon, P. (1971), *Rhetoric*, London, Methuen.

Dodson, S.J. (1981), 'A reappraisal of bilingual development and education: some theoretical and practical considerations', in H. Baetens Beardsmore (ed.), *Elements of Bilingual Theory*, Brussels, Vrije Universiteit Brussels.

Dominicy, M. (1984), *La Naissance de la grammaire moderne*, Brussels, Márdaga.

Donaldson, M. (1978), *Children's Minds*, London, Fontana.

Donegan, P. and Stampe, D. (1979), 'The study of natural phonology', in D. Dinnsen (ed.), *Current Approaches to Phonological Theory*, Bloomington, Indiana University Press.

Donzé, R. (1971), *La Grammaire générale et raisonnée de Port Royal*, 2nd edn, Berne, Francke.

Dooling, D.J. and Christiaansen, R.E. (1977), 'Levels of encoding and retention of prose', in G.H. Bower (ed.), *The Psychology of Learning and Motivation*, vol. 11, New York, Academic Press, pp. 1–39.

Dougherty, R. (1970), 'Recent studies on language universals', *Foundations of Language*, 6: pp. 505–61.

Downes, W. (1978), 'Language, belief and verbal action in an historical process', *UEA Papers in Linguistics*, 8: pp. 1–43.

Downes, W. (1984), *Language and Society*, London, Fontana.

Dowty, D.R., Wall, R.E, and Peters, S. (1981), *Introduction to Montague Semantics*, Dordrecht, Reidel.

Doyle, A., Champagne, M. and Segalowitz, N. (1978), 'Some issues in the assessment of linguistic consequences of early bilingualism', in M. Paradis (ed.), *Aspects of Bilingualism*, Columbia, SC, Hornbeam Press.

Dresher, E. (1981), 'On the learnability of abstract phonology', in C.L. Baker and J. McCarthy (eds), *The Logical Problem of Language Acquisition*, Cambridge, MA, MIT Press, pp. 188–210.

Dressler, W.U. (1985), 'On the predictiveness of natural morphology', *Journal of Linguistics*, 21: 321–37.

Dressler, W.U. (1986), 'Explanation in natural morphology, illustrated with comparative and agent–noun formation', *Linguistics*, 24: 519–48.

Dronkers, N.F., Koss, E., Friedland, R.P. and Wertz, R.T. (1986), '"Differential" language impairment and language mixing in a polyglot with probable Altzheimer's disease', paper presented at International Neuropsychological Society meetings.

Dubois, B.L. (1985), 'From NEJM and JAMA through the AP to local newspaper: scientific translation for the laity', in T. Bungarten (ed.), *Wissenschaft und Gesellschaft*, Bonn, Bouvier.

Dubois, J.W. (1974), 'Syntax in mid-sentence', in *Berkeley Studies in Syntax and Semantics*, vol. 1, Berkeley, Institute of Human Learning and Department of Linguistics, University of California, pp. III-1 – III-25.

Ducrot, O. and Todorov, T. (1981), *Encyclopedic Dictionary of the Sciences of Language*, Oxford, Basil Blackwell.

Dudley-Evans, T. (1986), 'Genre analysis: an investigation of the introduction and discussion section of M.Sc. dissertations', in M. Coulthard (ed.), *Talking about Text: Studies Presented to David Brazil on his Retirement* (Discourse Analysis Monograph, 13), English Language Research, University of Birmingham, pp. 128–45.

Dudley-Evans, T. (1987), 'Introduction', *ELR Journal*, 1: 1–9.

Dudley-Evans, T. and Henderson, W. 'Changes in the economics article', in progress.

Duffy, F.H. *et al.* (1980), 'Dyslexia: automated diagnosis by computerised classification of brain electrical activity', *Annals of Neurology*, 7(5): 421–8.

Dummett, M. (1973), *Frege. Philosophy of Language*, London, Duckworth.

Duncan, S.D. (1972), 'Some signals and rules for taking turns in conversations', *Journal of Personal and Social Psychology*, 23: 283–92.

Duncan, S.D. (1983), 'Speaking turns: studies of structures and individual differences', in J. Wiemann and R.P. Harrison (eds), *Nonverbal Interaction*, Beverley Hills, CA, Sage.

Duncan, S.D. and Fiske, D.W. (1977), *Face-to-Face Interaction*, Hillsdale, NJ, Lawrence Erlbaum Associates.

Dutton, T. (1985), *Police Motu: iena sivarai (its story)*, Port Moresby, University of Papua New Guinea Press.

Eagleton, T. (1983), *Literary Theory: An Introduction*, Oxford, Basil Blackwell.

Eakins, B.W. and Eakins, R.G. (1978), *Sex Differences in Human Communication*, Boston, M. Houghton Mifflin.

Earley, J. (1970), 'An efficient context-free parsing algorithm', *Communications ACM*, 6(8): 451–5.

Eckersley, C.E. (1938–42), *Essential English for Foreign Students*, London, Longman.

Eco, U. (1984), *Semiotics and the Philosophy of Language*, London and Basingstoke, Macmillan.

Edmundson, W. (1981), *Spoken Discourse: A Model for Analysis*, London and New York, Longman.

Education For All (1985), *The Report of the Committee of Inquiry into the Education of Children from Ethnic Minority Groups*, London, HMSO.

Edwards, J. (1985), *Language, Society and Identity*, Oxford, Basil Blackwell.

Edwards, V.K. (1984), 'Language Policy in multicultural Britain', in J. Edwards (ed.), *Linguistic Minorities, Policies and Pluralism*, London, Academic Press.

Ehrlich, K. and Rayner, K. (1983), 'Pronoun assignment and semantic integration during reading: eye movement and immediacy of processing', *Journal of Verbal Learning and Verbal Behavior*, 22: 75–87.

Eimas, P.D., Siqueland, E.R., Jusczyk, P. and Vigorito, J. (1971), 'Speech perception in infants', *Science*, 171: 303–6.

Ekman, P. and Friesen, W. (1969), 'The repertoire of non-verbal behavior: categories, origins, usage and coding', *Semiotica*, 1(1): 49–98.

Ellegård, A. (1978), *The Syntactic Structure of English Texts: A Computer-based Study of Four Kinds of Text in the Brown University Corpus* (Gothenburg Studies in English, no. 43), Göteburg, Acta Universitatis Gothoburgensis.

Ellis, A.J. (1889), *On Early English Pronunciation*, Part V: *The Existing Phonology of English Dialects*, London, Trübner.

Ellis, A.W. (1982), 'Spelling and writing (and reading and speaking)', in A.W. Ellis (ed.), *Normality and Pathology in Cognitive Functions*, London, Academic Press, pp. 113–46.

Ellis, A.W. (ed.), (1985), *Progress in the Psychology of Language*, Hillsdale, NJ, Lawrence Erlbaum Associates.

Elyan, O., Smith, P., Giles, H. and Bourhis, R. (1978), 'RP-accented female speech: the voice of perceived androgeny?' in P. Trudgill (ed.), *Sociolinguistic Patterns in British English*, London, Edward Arnold, pp. 122–31.

Emonds, J.E. (1976), *A Transformational Approach to English Syntax*, New York, Academic Press.

Enderby, P. and Philipp, R. (1986), 'Speech and language handicap: towards knowing the size of the problem', *British Journal of Disorders of Communication*, 21(2): 151–65.

Eriksen, C.W., Pollock, M.D. and Montague, W.E. (1970), 'Implicit speech: mechanisms in perceptual encoding?', *Journal of Experimental Psychology*, 84: 502–7.

Ervin-Tripp, S.M. (1969), 'Sociolinguistics', in L. Berkowitz (ed.), *Advances in Experimental Social Psychology*, vol. 4, pp. 91–165.

Espir, M.L.E. and Rose, F.C. (1983), *The Basic Neurology of Speech and Language*, 3rd edn, Oxford, Blackwell Scientific.

Ewer, J.R. and Latorre, C. (1969), *Course in Basic Scientific English*, London, Longman.

Fairclough, N. (1985), 'Critical and descriptive goals in discourse analysis', *Journal of Pragmatics*, 9: 739–63.

Farrar, F.W. (1870), *Families of Speech*, London, Longmans, Green.

Fasold, R. (1984), *The Sociolinguistics of Society*, Oxford, Basil Blackwell.

Fawcett, R.P. (1974), 'Some proposals for systemic syntax, Part 1', *MALS Journal*, 1: 1–15.

Fawcett, R.P. (1975), 'Some proposals for systemic syntax, Part 2', *MALS Journal*, 2(1): 43–68.

Fawcett, R.P. (1976), 'Some proposals for systemic syntax, Part 3', *MALS Journal*, 2(2): 35–68.

Ferguson, C.A. (1959), 'Diglossia', *Word*, 15: 325–40.

Ferguson, C.A. and DeBose, C. (1977) 'Simplified registers, broken language and pidginization', in A. Valdman and A. Highfield (eds), *Pidgin and Creole Linguistics*, Bloomington, Indiana University Press, pp. 99–125.

Ferguson, C.A. and Heath, S.B. (eds) (1981), *Language in the USA*, Cambridge, Cambridge University Press.

Ferreira, F. and Clifton, C., Jr (1986), 'The independence of syntactic processing', *Journal of Memory and Language*, 25: 348–68.

Fikes, R.E. and Nilsson, N. (1971), 'STRIPS: a new approach to the application of theorem proving to problem solving', *Artificial Intelligence*, 2: 189–208.

Fillenbaum, S. (1971), 'On coping with ordered and unordered conjunctive sentences', *Journal of Experimental Psychology*, 87: 93–8.

Fillenbaum, S. (1974a), 'Pragmatic normalization: further results for some conjunctive and disjunctive sentences', *Journal of Experimental Psychology*, 102: 574–8.

Fillenbaum, S. (1974b), 'Or: some uses', *Journal of Experimental Psychology*, 103: 913–21.

Fillmore, C.J. (1966), 'A proposal concerning English prepositions', *Monograph Series on Languages and Linguistics*, no. 19, pp. 19–34.

Fillmore, C.J. (1968), 'The case for case', in E. Bach and R.T. Harms (eds), *Universals in Linguistic Theory*, New York, Holt, Rinehart & Winston, pp. 1–90.

Fillmore, C.J. (1969), 'Toward a modern theory of case', in D. Reibel and S. Schane (eds), *Modern Studies in English*, Englewood Cliffs, NJ, Prentice Hall, pp. 361–75.

Fillmore, C.J. (1971a), 'Some problems for case grammar', *Monograph Series on Languages and Linguistics*, no. 24, pp. 35–56.

Fillmore, C.J. (1971b), 'Types of lexical information', in D. Steinberg and L. Jakobovits (eds), *Semantics: An Interdisciplinary Reader*, Cambridge, Cambridge University Press, pp. 370–92.

Fillmore, C.J. (1977), 'The case for case reopened', in P. Cole and J.M. Sadock (eds), *Syntax and Semantics*, vol. 8: *Grammatical Relations*, New York, Academic Press, pp. 59–81.

Finke, P. (1974), *Theoretische Probleme der Kasusgrammatik*, Kronberg, Scriptor.

Firth, J.R. (1930/64), *'The Tongues of Men' and 'Speech'*, London, Oxford University Press.

Firth, J.R. (1957a), *Papers in Linguistics 1934–1951*, London, Oxford University Press.

Firth, J.R. (1957b), *A Synopsis of Linguistic Theory 1930–55*, (Special Volume of the Philological Society), Oxford, Basil Blackwell.

Firth, J.R. (1968), *Selected Papers of J.R. Firth*, ed. F.R. Palmer, London, Longmans.

Firth, R. (1951), *Elements of Social Organization*, London, Watts.

Fischer-Jørgensen, E. (1967a), 'Form and substance in glossematics', *Acta Linguistica Hafniensia*, X: 1–33.

Fischer-Jørgensen, E. (1967b), 'Introduction' to H.J. Uldall, *Outline of Glossematics*, (Travaux du Cercle Linguistique de Copenhague, X₁), 2nd edn, Copenhagen, Nordisk Sprog- og Kulturforlag, pp. I–XXII.

Fischler, I. and Bloom, P.A. (1979), 'Automatic and attentional processes in the effects of sentence contexts on word recognition', *Journal of Verbal Learning and Verbal Behavior*, 18: 1–20.

Fisher, M. (1934), *Language Patterns of Preschool Children* (Child Development Monographs, no. 15), New York, Teachers' College Press, Columbia University.

Fishman, P. (1980), 'Conversational insecurity', in H. Giles, W.P. Robinson, and P.M. Smith (eds), *Language: Social Psychological Perspectives*, Oxford, Pergamon Press, pp. 127–32.

Flagg, P.W. and Reynolds, A.G. (1977), 'Modality of presentation and blocking in sentence recognition memory', *Memory and Cognition*, 5: 111–15.

Flege, J.E. and Hillenbrand, J. (1986), 'Differential use of temporal cues to the /s/–/z/ contrast by native and non-native speakers of English', *Journal of the Acoustical Society of America*, 79: 508–17.

Fletcher, P. and Garman, M. (1986), *Language Acquisition*, 2nd edn, Cambridge, Cambridge University Press.

Flores d'Arcais, G.B. and Jarvella, R.J. (eds) (1983), *The Process of Language Understanding*, New York, John Wiley.

Flores d'Arcais, G.B. and Schreuder, R. (1983), 'The process of language understanding: a few issues in contemporary psycholinguistics', in G.B. Flores d'Arcais and R.J. Jarvella (eds), *The Process of Languag Understanding*, New York, John Wiley, pp. 1–! .

Fodor, J.A. (1971), 'Recognition of syntactic structures', in D.L. Horton and J.J. Jenkins (eds), *The Perception of Language*, Columbus, OH, Charles E. Merrill, pp. 120–39.

Fodor, J.D. and Frazier, L. (1980), 'Is the human sentence parsing mechanism an ATN?', *Cognition*, 8: 417–59.

Fodor, J.A. and Garrett, M.F. (1967), 'Some syntactic determinants of sentential complexity', *Perception and Psychophysics*, 2: 289–96.

Fodor, J.A. and Katz, J. (eds) (1964), *The Structure of Language: Readings in the Philosophy of Language*, Englewood Cliffs, NJ, Prentice Hall.

Fodor, J.A., Bever, T.G. and Garrett, M.F. (1974), *The Psychology of Language: An Introduction to Psycholinguistics and Generative Grammar*, New York, McGraw-Hill.

Fodor, J.D., Fodor, J.A. and Garrett, M.F. (1975), 'The psychological unreality of semantic representations', *Linguistic Inquiry*, 6(4): 515–31.

Foley, W.A. (1988), 'Language birth: the processes of pidginization and creolization', in F.J. Newmeyer (ed.), *Linguistics: The Cambridge Survey*. vol. 4: *Language: The Socio-cultural Context*, Cambridge, Cambridge University Press, pp. 162–83.

Ford, M. (1982), 'Sentence planning units: implications for the speaker's representation of meaningful relations underlying sentences', in J.W. Bresnan (ed.), *The Mental Representation of Grammatical Relations*, Cambridge, MA, and London, MIT Press, ch. 12.

Ford, M., Bresnan, J.W. and Kaplan, R.M. (1982), 'A competence-based theory of syntactic closure', in J.W. Bresnan (ed.), *The Mental Representation of Grammatical Relations*, Cambridge, MA, and London, MIT Press, ch. 11.

Forster, K.I. (1976), 'Accessing the mental lexicon', in R.J. Wales and C.T. Walker (eds), *New Approaches to Language Mechanisms*, Amsterdam, North Holland, pp. 257–87.

Forster, K.I. (1981), 'Priming and the effects of sentence and lexical contexts on naming time: evidence for autonomous lexical processing', *Quarterly Journal of Experimental Psychology*, 33A: 465–95.

Foucault, M. (1966), *Les Mots et les choses*, Paris, Gallimard.

Foucault, M. (1972), *The Archaeology of Knowledge*, London, Tavistock.

Fouts, R. and Rigby, R. (1977), 'Man–chimpanzee communication', in T.A. Sebeok (ed.), *How Animals Communicate*, Bloomington and London, Indiana University Press, pp. 1034–54.

Fowler, C.A. (1986), 'An event approach to the study of speech perception from a direct-realist perspective', *Journal of Phonetics*, 14: 3–28.

Fowler, R. (1967), 'Literature and linguistics', *Essays in Criticism*, 17: 322–47.

Fowler, R. (1968), 'Language and literature', *Essays in Criticism*, 18: 164–82.

Fowler, R. (1971), *The Languages of Literature*, London, Routledge & Kegan Paul.

Fowler, R. (1977), *Linguistics and the Novel*, London, Methuen.

Fowler, R. (1986), *Linguistic Criticism*, Oxford and New York, Oxford University Press.

Fowler, R. (1987), 'Notes on critical linguistics', in R. Steele and T. Threadgold (eds), *Language Topics: Essays in Honour of Michael Halliday*, vol. II, Amsterdam and Philadelphia, John Benjamins, pp. 481–492.

Fowler, R., Hodge, R., Kress, G. and Trew, T. (1979), *Language and Control*, London, Routledge & Kegan Paul.

Fowler, R. and Marshall, T. (1985), 'The war against peacemongering: language and ideology', in P. Chilton (ed.), *Language and the Nuclear Arms Debate: Nukespeak Today*, London and Dover, NH, Frances Pinter, pp. 3–22.

Francis, W.N. (1958), *The Structure of American English*, New York, Ronald.

Francis, W.N. (1979), 'Problems of assembling and computerizing large corpora', in H. Bergenholtz and B. Schaeder (eds), *Empirische Textwissenschaft: Aufbau und Auswertung von Text-Corpora*, Königstein, Scriptor, pp. 110–23.

Francis, W.N. (1983), *Dialectology*, London, Longman.

Francis, W.N. and Kucera, H. (1964: revised edns 1971, 1979), *A Manual of Information to Accompany a Standard Sample of Present-day Edited American English, for Use with Digital Computers*, Providence, RI, Linguistics Department, Brown University.

Fraser, C., Bellugi, U. and Brown, R. (1963), 'Control of grammar in imitation, comprehension, and production', *Journal of Verbal Learning and Verbal Behavior*, 2: 121–35.

Frazier, L. (1979), 'On comprehending sentences: syntactic parsing strategies', unpublished Ph.D. thesis, University of Connecticut, Indiana University Linguistics Club.

Frazier, L. and Fodor, J.D. (1978), 'The sausage machine: a new two-stage parsing model', *Cognition*, 6: 291–325.

Frege, G. (1891/1977), 'Function and concept', address to the Jenaische Gesellschaft für Medicin und Naturwissenschaft, 9 January, 1891. English translation in P. Geach and M. Black (eds) (1977), *Translations from the Philosophical Writings of Gottlob Frege*, Oxford, Basil Blackwell, pp. 21–41.

Frege, G. (1892/1977a), 'On sense and reference', *Zeitschrift für Philosophie und philosophische Kritik*, 100, (1892), pp. 25–50. English translation in P. Geach and M. Black (eds) (1977), *Translations from the Philosophical Writings of Gottlob Frege*, Oxford, Basil Blackwell, pp. 56–78.

Frege, G. (1892/1977b), 'On concept and object', *Vierteljahrsschrift für wissenschaftliche Philosophie*, 16 (1892): 192–205, published in English in P. Geach and M. Black (eds) (1977), *Translations from the Philosophical Writings of Gottlob Frege*, Oxford, Basil Blackwell, pp. 42–55.

Freud, S. (1966), 'Slips of the tongue', in S. Freud, *Psychopathology of Everyday Life*, trans. A. Tyson (1960), London, Ernest Benn, pp. 53–105, first published in German in 1901.

Friedman, J. (1969), 'Directed random generation of sentences', *Communications ACM*, 12: 40–6.

Friedman, J. (1971), *A Computer Model of Transformational Grammar*, New York, American Elsevier.

Fries, C.C. (1952, 1957), *The Structure of English: An Introduction to the Construction of English Sentences*, New York, Harcourt Brace Jovanovich; London, Longman.

Frisch, K. von (1967), *The Dance Language and Orientation of Bees*, Cambridge, MA, Harvard University Press.

Fromkin, V.A. (1971), 'The non-anomalous nature of anomalous utterances', *Language*, 47: 27–52.

Fromkin, V.A. (ed.) (1973), *Speech Errors as Linguistic Evidence*, The Hague, Mouton.

Fromkin, V.A. (ed.) (1978), *Tone: A Linguistic Survey*, New York, Academic Press.

Fry, D.B. (1979), *The Physics of Speech*, Cambridge, Cambridge University Press.

Fry, D.B., Abramson, A.S., Eimas, P.D. and Lieberman, A.M. (1962), 'The identification and discrimination of synthetic vowels', *Language and Speech*, 5: 171–89.

Fudge, E. (ed.) 1973), *Phonology*, Harmondsworth, Penguin.

Gandour, J.T. (1978), 'The perception of tone', in V.A. Fromkin (ed.), *Tone: A Linguistic Survey*, New York, Academic Press, pp. 41–76.

Garding, E. (1973), *The Scandinavian Word Accents* (Lund University Working Papers, no. 8).

Gardner, B.T. (1981), 'Project Nim: who taught whom?', *Contemporary Psychology*, 26: 425–6.

Gardner, R.A. and Gardner, B.T. (1971), 'Two-way communication with an infant chimpanzee', in A.M. Schrier and F. Stollnitz (eds), *Behavior of Non-Human Primates*, New York, Academic Press.

Gardner, R.A. and Gardner, B.T. (1978), 'Comparative psychology and language acquisition', *Annals of the New York Academy of Sciences*, 309: 37–76.

Garfinkel, H. (1967), *Studies in Ethnomethodology*, New York, Prentice Hall.

Garnham, A. (1985), *Psycholinguistics: Central Topics*, London and New York, Methuen.

Garrett, M.F. (1975), 'The analysis of sentence production', in G.H. Bower (ed.), *The Psychology of Learning and Motivation*, vol. 9, New York, Academic Press, pp. 133–77.

Garrett, M.F. (1980), 'Levels of processing in sentence production', in B. Butterworth (ed.), *Language Production*, vol. 1: *Speech and Talk*, London, Academic Press, pp. 177–220.

Garside, R. and Leech, F. (1987), 'The UCREL probabilistic parsing system', in R. Garside, G. Leech and G. Sampson (eds), *The Computational Analysis of English: A Corpus-based Approach*, London, Longman, pp. 66–81.

Garside, R., Leech, G. and Sampson, G. (eds) (1987), *The Computational Analysis of English: A Corpus-based Approach*, London, Longman.

Garvin, P.L. (ed.) (1964), *A Prague School Reader on Esthetics, Literary Structure and Style*, Washington, DC, Georgetown University Press.

Gazdar, G. (1987), 'Generative grammar', in J. Lyons, R. Coates, M. Deuchar, and G. Gazdar (eds), *New Horizons in Linguistics*, vol. 2, Harmondsworth, Penguin, pp. 122–51.

Gazdar, G., Klein, E., Pullum, G. and Sag, I. (1985), *Generalised Phrase Structure Grammar*, Oxford, Basil Blackwell, and Cambridge, MA, Harvard University Press.

Gazzaniga, M.S. (1974), 'Cerebral dominance viewed as a decision-system', in S.J. Dimond and J.G. Beaumont (eds), *Hemisphere Function in the Human Brain*, London, Elek Science.

Geach, P. (1972), 'A program for syntax', in D. Davidson and G. Harman (eds), *Semantics of Natural Language*, Dordrecht, Reidel, pp. 483–97.

Geens, D., Engels, L.K. and Martin, W. (1975), *Leuven Drama Corpus and Frequency List*, Catholic University of Leuven, Institute for Applied Linguistics.

Gelb, I.J. (1963), *A Study of Writing*; revised edn, Chicago and London, University of Chicago Press.

Georges, R. and Jones, M. (1980), *People Studying People*, Berkeley, University of California Press.

Geschwind, N. (1982), 'Biological foundations of dyslexia', paper presented to BPS Cognitive Psychology Section Conference on Dyslexia, Manchester, England.

Giglioli, P.P. (1972), *Language and Social Context: Selected Readings*, Harmondsworth, Penguin.

Giles, H. and Powesland, P.F. (1975), *Speech Style and Social Evaluation*, London, Academic Press.

Gilliéron, J. and Edmont, E. (1902–10), *Atlas linguistique de la France*, Paris, Champion.

Gleitman, L., Newport, M. and Gleitman, H. (1984), 'The current status of the motherese hypothesis', *Journal of Child Language*, 11: 43–79.

Goetz, E.T., Anderson, R.C. and Schallert, D.L. (1981), 'The representation of sentences in memory', *Journal of Verbal Learning and Verbal Behavior*, 20: 369–81.

Goldstein, U. (1979), 'Modeling children's vocal tracts', paper presented at the 97th Meeting of the Acoustical Society of America, Cambridge, MA, June.

Goodman, M. (1984), 'Are creole structures innate?', *The Behavioral and Brain Sciences*, 7(2): 193–4.

Gordon, H. (1980), 'Cerebal organization in bilinguals. I. Lateralization', *Brain and Language*, 9: 255–68.

Gosling, J.N. (1981a), *Discourse Kinesics* (English Language Research Monograph, no. 10), University of Birmingham.

Gosling, J.N. (1981b), 'Kinesics in discourse', in M. Coulthard and M. Montgomery (eds), *Studies in Discourse Analysis*, London, Routledge & Kegan Paul, pp. 158–83.

Graf, R. and Torey, J.W. (1966), 'Perception of phrase structure in written language', *American Psychological Association Convention Proceedings*, pp. 83–4.

Graham, A. (1975), 'The making of a non-sexist dictionary', in B. Thorne and N. Henley (eds), *Language and Sex: Difference and Dominance*, Rowley, MA, Newbury House, pp. 57–63.

Grassmann, H. (1863), 'Über die Aspiranten und ihr gleichzeitiges Vorhandensein im An- und Auslaute der Wurzeln', *Zeitschrift für vergleichende Sprachforschung auf dem Gebiete des Deutschen, Griechischen und Lateinischen*, 12(2): 81–138.

Grayling, A.C. (1982), *An Introduction to Philosophical Logic*, Brighton, Sussex, Harvester Press.

Greenbaum, S. (1970), *Verb Intensifiers in English: An Experimental Approach*, The Hague, Mouton.

Greenberg, J.H. (1954), 'A quantitative approach to the morphological typology of language', in R.F. Spencer (ed.), *Method and Perspective in Anthropology*, Minneapolis, University of Minnesota Press, pp. 192–220, reprinted (1960) in *International Journal of American Linguistics*, 26: 178–94.

Greenberg, J.H. (1960), 'A quantitative approach to the morphological typology of language', *International Journal of American Linguistics*, 26(3): 178–94.

Greenberg, J.H. (ed.) (1966a), *Universals of Language*, 2nd edn, Cambridge, MA, and London, MIT Press.

Greenberg, J.H. (1966b), 'Some universals of grammar with particular reference to the order of meaningful elements', in J.H. Greenberg (ed.), *Universals of Language*, 2nd edn, Cambridge, MA, and London, MIT Press, pp. 73–113.

Greenberg, J.H. (1974), *Language Typology: A Historical and Analytic Overview* (Janua Linguarum, Series Minor, no. 184), The Hague, Mouton.

Greenberg, J.H., Osgood, C.E. and Jenkins, J.J. (1966), 'Memorandum concerning language universals: presented to the Conference on Language Universals, Gould House, Dobbs Ferry, NY, 13–15 April 1961', in J.H. Greenberg (ed.), *Universals of Language*, 2nd edn, Cambridge, MA, and London, MIT Press, pp. xv–xxvii.

Gregory, M. and Carroll, S. (1978), *Language Varieties and their Social Context*, London, Routledge & Kegan Paul.

Greimas, A.J. (1966), *Sémantique structurale*, Paris, Librairie Larousse.

Grice, H.P. (1957), 'Meaning', *Philosophical Review*, 66: 377–88.

Grice, H.P. (1975), 'Logic and conversation', in P. Cole and J.L. Morgan (eds), *Syntax and Semantics, 3: Speech Acts*, New York, Academic Press, pp. 41–58

Grice, H.P. (1978), 'Further notes on logic and conversation', in P. Cole (ed.), *Syntax and Semantics, 9: Pragmatics*, New York, Academic Press, pp. 113–28

Griffiths, P. (1980), 'Paget Gorman Sign System', *British Deaf News*, 12(8): 258–60.

Grimm, J. (1822/1893), *Deutsche Grammatik*, Göttingen (1822); Gütersloh, Bertelmann (1893).

Grimshaw, J. (1981), 'Form, function, and the language acquisition device', in C.L. Baker and J. McCarthy (eds), *The Logical Problem of Language Acquisition*, Cambridge, MA, MIT Press, pp. 165–82.

Grosjean, F. (1982), *Life with Two Languages: An Introduction to Bilingualism*, Cambridge, MA, and London, Harvard University Press.

Grosz, B.J. and Sidner, C.L. (1986), 'Attention, intentions and the structure of discourse', *Computational Linguistics*, 12 (3): pp. 175–205.

Grosz, B.J., Sparck Jones, K. and Webber, B.L. (eds) (1986), *Readings in Natural Language Processing*, Los Altos, Morgan Kaufman.

Gumperz, J. (1986), 'Introduction', in J. Gumperz and D. Hymes (eds), *Directions in Sociolinguistics: The Ethnography of Communication*, Oxford, Basil Blackwell, pp. 1–25.

Haas, W. (1960), 'Linguistic structures', *Word*, 16: 251–76.

Hall, R.A., Jr (1962), 'The life cycle of pidgin languages', *Lingua*, 11: 151–6.

Hall, R.A., Jr (1966), *Pidgin and Creole Languages*, Ithaca, Cornell University Press.

Hall, R.A., Jr (1972), 'Pidgins and creoles as standard languages', in J.B. Pride and J. Holmes (eds), *Sociolinguistics*, Harmondsworth, Penguin, pp. 142–53.

Halle, M. (1959), *The Sound Pattern of Russian*, The Hague, Mouton.

Halle, M. (1962), 'Phonology in generative grammar', *Word*, 18: 54–72.

Halle, M. (1973), 'Prolegomena to a theory of word formation', *Linguistic Inquiry*, 4: 3–16.

Halliday, M.A.K. (1956), 'Grammatical categories in modern Chinese', in *Transactions of the Philological Society*, pp. 177–224, reprinted in part in G. Kress (ed.) (1976), *Halliday: System and Function in Language*, Oxford, Oxford University Press, pp. 36–51.

Halliday, M.A.K. (1961), 'Categories of the theory of grammar', *Word*, 17: 241–92.

Halliday, M.A.K. (1966a), 'Some notes on "deep" grammar', *Journal of Linguistics*, 2: 56–67. Reprinted in part in G. Kress (ed.), (1976), *Halliday: System and Function in Language*, Oxford, Oxford University Press, pp. 88–98.

Halliday, M.A.K. (1966b), 'Lexis as a linguistic level', in C.E. Bazell, J.C. Catford, M.A.K. Halliday and H.R. Robins (eds), *In Memory of J.R. Firth*, London, Longman, pp. 148–62.

Halliday, M.A.K. (1967), *Intonation and Grammar in British English*, The Hague, Mouton.

Halliday, M.A.K. (1968), 'Notes on transitivity and theme in English, Part 3', *Journal of Linguistics*, 4: 179–215.

Halliday, M.A.K. (1970), 'Language structure and language function', in J. Lyons (ed.), *New Horizons in Linguistics*, Harmondsworth, Penguin, pp. 140–65.

Halliday, M.A.K. (1971), 'Linguistic function and literary style: an inquiry into the language of William Golding's *The Inheritors*', in S. Chatman (ed.), *Literary Style: A Symposium*, London and New York, Oxford University Press, pp. 330–65.

Halliday, M.A.K. (1973), 'Relevant models of language', in M.A.K. Halliday, *Explorations in the Functions of Language*, London, Edward Arnold, pp. 9–21.

Halliday, M.A.K. (1975), *Learning How To Mean: Explorations in the Development of Language*, London, Edward Arnold.

Halliday, M.A.K. (1978), *Language as Social Semiotic*, London, Edward Arnold.

Halliday, M.A.K. (1983), Foreword to M. Cummings and R. Simmons, *The Language of Literature: A Stylistic Introduction to the Study of Literature*, Oxford, Pergamon Press.

Halliday, M.A.K. (1985), *An Introduction to Functional Grammar*, London, Edward Arnold.

Halliday, M.A.K. and Hasan, R. (1976), *Cohesion in English*, London, Longman.

Halmos, P. (1960), *Naive Set Theory*, Princeton, NJ, Van Nostrand.

Hamers, J.F. and Blanc, M.H.A. (1989), *Bilinguality and Bilingualism*, revised edn, Cambridge, Cambridge University Press, originally published in French as *Bilingualité et bilinguisme*, Liège, Brussels, Márdaga.

Harding, E. and Riley, P. (1986), *The Bilingual Family: A Handbook for Parents*, Cambridge, Cambridge University Press.

Harley, T.A. (1984), 'A critique of top-down independent levels of speech production: evidence from non-plan-internal speech errors', *Cognitive Science*, 8: 191–219.

Harris, Z. (1942), 'Morpheme alternants in linguistic analysis', *Language*, 18: 169–80.

Harris, Z. (1946), 'From morpheme to utterance', *Language*, 22: 161–83.

Harris, Z. (1951), *Methods in Structural Linguistics*, Chicago, University of Chicago Press.

Harris, Z. (1952), 'Discourse analysis', *Language*, 28: 1–30 and 474–94.

Harris, Z. (1957), 'Co-occurrence and transformation in linguistic structure', *Language*, 33: 283–340.

Harris, Z. (1965), 'Transformational theory', *Language*, 41: 363–401.

Harrison, J.M. and Howe, M.E. (1974), 'Anatomy of the afferent auditory nervous system of mammals', in W.D. Keidel and W.D. Neff (eds), *Handbook of Sensory Physiology*, vol. V, New York, Springer.

Hartmann, R.R.K. (1985), *Data Base: Bibliography and Lexicography*, University of Exeter, Dictionary Research Centre.

Harweg, R. (1968), *Pronomina und Textkonstitution*, Munich, Fink.

Hasan R. (1984), 'Coherence and cohesive harmony', in J. Flood (ed.), *Understanding Reading Comprehension*, Newark, DE, International Reading Association, pp. 181–219.

Hausmann, F.J. (1977), *Einfürung in die Benutzung der neufranzösischen Wörterbücher*, Tübingen, Max Niemeyer.

Haviland, S.E. and Clark, H.H. (1974), 'What's new? Acquiring new information as a process in comprehension', *Journal of Verbal Learning and Verbal Behavior*, 13: 512–21

Hawkins, J.A. (ed.) (1988a), *Explaining Language Universals*, Oxford, Basil Blackwell.

Hawkins, J.A. (1988b), 'Explaining language universals', in J.A. Hawkins (ed.), *Explaining Language Universals*, Oxford, Basil Blackwell, pp. 3–28.

Hawkins, J.A. and Cutler, A. (1988), 'Psycholinguistic factors in morphological asymmetry', in J.A. Hawkins (ed.), *Explaining Language Universals*, Oxford, Basil Blackwell, pp. 280–317.

Hayes, K. and Hayes, C. (1952), 'Imitation in a home-raised chimpanzee', *Journal of Comparative and Physiological Psychology*, 45: 450–9.

Heger, K. (1976), *Monem, Wort, Satz, und Text*, Tübingen, Niemeyer.

Heidolph, K.-E. (1966), 'Kontextbeziehungen zwischen Sätzen in einer generativen Grammatik', *Kybernetika*, 2: 274–81.

Henderson, D. (1972), 'Contextual specificity, discretion and cognitive socialization', in J.B. Pride and J. Holmes (eds), *Sociolinguistics*, Harmondsworth, Penguin, pp. 314–35.

Herbert, A.J. (1965), *The Structure of Technical English*, London, Longman.

Hewings, A. and Henderson, W. (1987), 'A link between genre and schemata: a case study of economics text', *English Language Research Journal*, 1: 156–75.

Hewitt, C. (1971), 'PLANNER: a language for proving theorems in robots', *International Joint Conference on Artificial Ingelligence*, 2.

Hiatt, M.P. (1975), *Artful Balance: The Parallel Structures of Style*, New York and London, Teachers' College Press.

Hill, A.A. (1958), *Introduction to Linguistic Structures: From Sound to Sentence in English*, New York, Harcourt Brace Jovanovich, chs 2, 3, 4, 5, and 6.

Hinshelwood, J. (1917), *Congenital Dyslexia*, London, Levís.

Hjelmslev, L. (1928), *Principes de grammaire générale*, Det Kgl. Danske (Videnskabernes Selskab, Historist-filologisk Meddelelser XVI.1), Copenhagen, Høst.

Hjelmslev, L. (1935), *La Catégorie de cas I*, Aarhus, Universitetsforlaget.

Hjelmslev, L. (1938), 'Essai d'une théorie des morphèmes', *Actes du 4ème Congrés International des Linguistes*, pp. 140–51, reprinted in L. Hjelmslev (1959), *Essais linguistiques: Travaux du Cercle Linguistique de Copenhague*, vol. XII, Copenhagen, Nordisk Sprog- og Kulturforlag, pp. 152–64.

Hjelmslev, L. (1943a), *Omkring Sprogteoriens grundlæggelse, Festskrift udgivet af Københavns Universitet i anledning af Universitetets Aarsfest*, Copenhagen, University of Copenhagen, 2nd edn, 1966, Copenhagen, Akademisk Forlag, 1966.

Hjelmslev, L. (1943b), 'Langue et parole', *Cahiers Ferdinand de Saussure 2*, pp. 29–44, reprinted in L. Hjelmslev (1959), *Essais linguistiques: Travaux du Cercle Linguistique de Copenhague*, vol. XII, Copenhagen, Nordisk Sprog- og Kulturforlag, pp. 69–81.

Hjelmslev, L. (1947), 'Structural analysis of language', *Studia Linguistica*, pp. 69–78, reprinted in L. Hjelmslev (1959), *Essais linguistiques: Travaux du Cercle Linguistique de Copenhague*, vol. XII, Copenhagen, Nordisk Sprog- og Kulturforlag, pp. 27–35.

Hjelmslev, L. (1951), 'Grundtræk af det danske udtrykssystem med særligt henblik på stødet', in *Selskab for nordisk filologis årsberetning for 1948–49–50*, pp. 12–24, published in English as 'Outline of the Danish expression system with special reference to the stød', trans. F.J. Whitfield, in L. Hjelmslev (1973), *Essais linguistiques II: Travaux du Cercle Linguistique de Copenhague*, vol. XIV, Copenhagen, Nordisk Sprog- og Kulturforlag, pp. 247–66.

Hjelmslev, L. (1953), *Prolegomena to a Theory of Language*, trans. F.J. Whitfield, *International Journal of American Linguistics*, 1(1): Memoir no. 7, 2nd revised edn 1967, Madison, University of Wisconsin Press.

Hjelmslev, L. (1959a), 'La stratification du langage', *Word*, 10: 163–88, reprinted in L. Hjelmslev (1959), *Essais linguistiques: Travaux du Cercle Linguistique de Copenhague*, vol. XII, *Copenhagen, Nordisk Sprog- og Kulturforlag*, pp. 27–35.

Hjelmslev, L. (1959b), *Essais linguistiques: Travaux du Cercle Linguistique de Copenhague*, vol, XII, Copenhagen, Nordisk Sprog- og Kulturforlag, 2nd edn, 1970.

Hjelmslev, L. (1963), *Sproget, en introduktion*, Copenhagen, Museum Tusculanums Forlag, 2nd edn (1973), published in English as 'An Introduction to linguistics', trans. I. Nixon, in L. Hjelmslev (1959), *Essais Linguistiques: Travaux du Cercle Linguistique de Copenhague*, vol. XII, Copenhagen, Nordisk Sprog- og Kulturforlag, pp. 9–20.

Hjelmslev, L. (1973a), 'A causerie on linguistic theory', in L. Hjelmslev, *Essais linguistiques II: Travaux du Cercle Linguistique de Copenhague*, vol. XIV, trans. C. Hendriksen, Copenhagen, Nordisk Sprog- og Kulturforlag, pp. 101–17.

Hjelmslev, L. (1973b), *Essais linguistiques II: Travaux du Cercle Linguistique de Copenhague*, vol. XIV, Copenhagen, Nordisk Sprog- og Kulturforlag.

Hjelmslev, L. (1975), *Résumé of a Theory of Language. Travaux du Cercle Linguistique de Copenhague XVI*, Copenhagen, Nordisk Sprog- og Kulturforlag.

Hockett, C.F. (1947), 'Problems of morphemic analysis', *Language*, 23: 321–43.

Hockett, C.F. (1950), 'Peiping morphophonemics', *Language*, 26: 63–85.

Hockett, C.F. (1954), 'Two models of grammatical description', *Word*, 10: 210–34.

Hockett, C.F. (1955), 'A manual of phonology', *International Journal of American Linguistics*, 21(4): Memoir no. 11.

Hockett, C.F. (1958), *A Course in Modern Linguistics*, New York, Macmillan.

Hockett, C.F. (1960), 'Logical considerations in the study of animal communication', in W. Lanyon and W. Travolga (eds), *Animal Sounds and Communication*, pp. 392–430.

Hockett, C.F. and Altmann, S. (1968), 'A note on design features', in T. Sebeok (ed.), *Animal Communication*, Bloomington and London, Indiana University Press, pp. 61–72.

Hockey, S. and Marriott, I. (1980), *The Oxford Concordance Program, Version 1.0. User's Manual*, Oxford University Computing Service.

Hodges, W. (1977), *Logic*, Harmondsworth, Penguin.

Hodgson, K.W. (1953), *The Deaf and their Problems: A study in Special Education*, London, Watts.

Hoekstra, T. and Kooij, J.G. (1988), 'The innateness hypothesis', in J.A. Hawkins (ed.), *Explaining Language Universals*, Oxford, Basil Blackwell, pp. 31–55.

Hoey, M. (1983), *On the Surface of Discourse*, London, George Allen & Unwin.

Hoey, M. (1983–4), 'The place of clause relational analysis in linguistic description', *English Language Research Journal*, 4: 1–32.

Hofland, K. and Johansson, S. (1982), *Word Frequencies in British and American English*, Bergen, Norwegian Computing Centre for the Humanities; London, Longman.

Holm, J.A. (1988), *Pidgins and Creoles*, vol. 1: *Theory and Structure*, Cambridge, Cambridge University Press.

Holmes, J. (1984), 'Hedging your bets and sitting on the fence: some evidence for hedges as support structures', *Te Reo*, 27: 47–62.

Hookway, C. (1985), *Peirce*, London, Routledge & Kegan Paul.

Hooper, J.B. (1976), *An Introduction to Natural Generative Phonology*, New York, Academic Press.

Hopkins, A. (1985), 'An investigation into the organising and organisational features of published conference papers', unpublished M.A. dissertation, University of Birmingham.

Horgan, D. (1978), 'The development of the full passive', *Journal of Child Language*, 5: 56–80.

Hornby, A.S. (1954–6), *Oxford Progressive English for Adult Learners*, Oxford, Oxford University Press.

Horne, K.M. (1966), *Language Typology: 19th and 20th Century Views*, Washington, DC, Georgetown University Press.

Horrocks, G. (1987), *Generative Grammar*, London and New York, Longman.

Houghton, D, (1980), 'Contrastive rhetoric', *English Language Research Journal*, 1: 79–91.

Houghton, D. and Hoey, M. (1982), 'Linguistics and written discourse: contrastive rhetorics', *Annual Review of Applied Linguistics*, 3: 2–22.

Houston, S.H. (1972), 'Bilingualism: naturally acquired bilingualism', *A Survey of Psycholinguistics*, The Hague, Mouton, pp. 203–25.

Howatt, A.T.R. (1984), *A History of English Language Teaching*, Oxford, Oxford University Press.

Howe, C. (1976), 'The meaning of two-word utterances in the speech of young children', *Journal of Child Language*, 3: 29–47.

Howes, R.F. (ed.) (1961), *Historical Studies of Rhetoric and Rhetoricians*, Ithaca, NY, Cornell University Press.

Hubel, D.H. and Wiesel, T.N. (1968), 'Receptive fields and functional architecture of monkey striate cortex', *The Journal of Physiology*, 195: 215–44.

Huckin, T. (1982), 'A cognitive approach to readability', *Communication in English*, SELMOUS/UWIST Conference Report, University of Aston in Birmingham.

Huddleston, R.D. (1965), 'Rank and depth', *Language*, 41: 574–86.

Huddleston, R.D. (1970), 'Some remarks on case grammar', *Journal of Linguistics*, 1: 501–10.

Huddleston, R.D. (1976), *An Introduction to English Transformational Syntax*, Cambridge, MA, MIT Press.

Hudson, H.H. (1961), 'The field of rhetoric', in R.F. Howes (ed.), *Historical Studies of Rhetoric and Rhetoricians*, Ithaca, NY, Cornell University Press, pp. 3–15.

Hudson, R.A. (1971), *English Complex Sentences: An Introduction to Systemic Grammar*, Amsterdam, North Holland.

Hudson, R.A. (1974), 'Systemic generative grammar', *Linguistics*, 139: 5–42.

Hudson, R.A. (1976), *Arguments for a Non-Transformational Grammar*, Chicago and London, University of Chicago Press.

Hudson, R.A. (1980), *Sociolinguistics*, Cambridge, Cambridge University Press.

Hughes, G.E. and Cresswell, M.J. (1968), *An Introduction to Modal Logic*, London, Methuen.

Hulst, H. van der and Smith, N. (1982), 'An overview of autosegmental and metrical phonology', in H. van der Hulst and N. Smith (eds), *The Structure of Phonological Representations*, Dordrecht, Foris, pp. 1–45.

Husserl, E. (1913–21), *Logische Untersuchungen*, 3 vols, 2nd edn, Halle, Max Niemeyer, 1st edn 1900.

Hutchinson, T. (1978), 'The practical demonstration', *Practical Papers in English Language Education* (University of Lancaster), no. 1.

Hutchinson, T. and Waters, A. (1984), *Interface: English for Technical Communication*, London, Longman.

Hyltenstam, K. and Stroud, C. (1985), 'The psycholinguistics of language choice and code-switching in Altzheimer's dementia: some hypotheses', *Scandinavian Working Papers on Bilingualism*, 4: 26–44.

Hyltenstam, K. and Stroud, C. (1989), 'Bilingualism in Altzheimer's dementia: two case studies', in K. Hyltenstam and L.K. Obler (eds), *Bilingualism Across the Lifespan: Aspects of Acquisition, Maturity and Loss*, Cambridge, Cambridge University Press, pp. 202–26.

Hyman, L.M. (1975), *Phonology. Theory and Analysis*, New York, Holt, Rinehart & Winston.

Hyman, L.M. (1982), 'Nasality in Gokana', in H. van der Hulst and N. Smith (eds), *The Structure of Phonological Representations*, Dordrecht, Foris, pp. 111–30.

Hyman, L.M. and Schuh, R.G. (1974), 'Universals of tone rules: evidence from West Africa', *Linguistic Inquiry*, 5: 81–115.

Hymes, D. (1967), 'Models of the interaction of language and social setting', *Journal of Social Issues*, 23(2): 8–28. Revised and reprinted in J.J. Gupertz and D. Hymes (eds) (1986), *Directions in Sociolinguistics: the Ethnography of Communication*, Oxford, Basil Blackwell, pp. 35–71.

Hymes, D. (1971a), *On Communicative Competence*. Philadelphia, University of Pennsylvania Press. Extracts in J.B. Pride and J. Holmes (eds) (1972), *Sociolinguistics*, Harmondsworth, Penguin, pp. 269–93.

Hymes, D. (ed.) (1971b), *Pidginization and Creolization of Languages*, Cambridge, Cambridge University Press.

Hymes, D. (1972), *Towards Communicative Competence*, Philadelphia, University of Pennsylvania Press.

Ikegami, Y. (1970), *The Semological Structure of the English Verbs of Motion: A Stratificational Approach*, Tokyo, Sanseido.

Ilson, R.F. (ed.) (1985), *Dictionaries, Lexicography and Language Learning*, Oxford, Pergamon Press in association with the British Council.

Ingham, R. (1984), *Stuttering and Behavior Therapy: Current Status and Experimental Foundations*, San Diego, CA, College-Hill Press.

Ingram, D. (1985), 'The psychological reality of children's grammars and its relation to grammatical theory', *Lingua*, 66: 79–103.

Ingram, D. (1989), *First Language Acquisition: Methods, Description and Explanation*, Cambridge, Cambridge University Press.

Ingram, D. and Shaw, C. (1981), 'The comprehension of pronominal reference in children', unpublished paper, University of British Columbia. Revised version to appear in *The Canadian Journal of Linguistics*.

Inner London Education Authority (1979), *Report on the 1978 Census of Those ILEA Pupils for Whom English was Not a First Language*, London, ILEA.

Inner London Education Authority (1982), *1981 Language Census*, London, ILEA.

Ireland, J. (1989), 'Ideology, myth and the maintenance of cultural identity', *ELR Journal (new series)*, 3: 95–136.

Isenberg, H. (1968), 'Motivierung zur "Texttheorie"', *Replik*, 2: 13–17.

Isenberg, H. (1971), 'Uberlegungen zur Texttheorie', in J. Ihwe (ed.), *Litteraturwissenschaft und Linguistik: Ergebnisse und Perspektiven*, Frankfurt, Athenäum, pp. 150–73.

Jaberg, K. and Judd, J. (1928–40), *Sprach- und Sachatlas Haliers und der Südschweiz*, Zofingen, Ringier.

Jackendoff, R. (1969), 'An interpretive theory of negation', *Foundations of Language*, 5: 218–41.

Jackendoff, R. (1972), *Semantic Interpretation in Generative Grammar*, Cambridge, MA, MIT Press.

Jackendoff, R. (1975), 'Morphology and semantic regularities in the lexicon', *Language*, 51(3): 639–71.

Jacobsen, B. (1986), *Modern Transformational Grammar (with Particular Reference to the Theory of Government and Binding)*, Amsterdam, North Holland.

Jakobovits, L.A. and Miron, M.S. (eds) (1967), *Readings in the Psychology of Language*, Englewood Cliffs, NJ, Prentice Hall.

Jakobson, R. (1941), *Kindersprache, Aphasie, und allgemeine Lautgesetze*, Uppsala Universitetets Aarsskrift, published in English in R. Jakobson (1968), *Child Language, Aphasia and Phonologiocal Universals*, The Hague, Mouton, and in R. Jakobson (1962), *Selected Writings I*, The Hague, Mouton, pp. 329–96.

Jakobson, R. (1960), 'Closing statement: linguistics and poetics', in T.A. Sebeok (ed.), *Style in Language*, Cambridge, MA, MIT Press, pp. 350–77.

Jakobson, R. (1968), *Child Language, Aphasia and Phonological Universals*, The Hague, Mouton.

Jakobson, R. and Halle, M. (1956), *Fundamentals of Language*, The Hague, Mouton.

Jakobson, R., Fant, C.G.M. and Halle, M. (1951), *Preliminaries to Speech Analysis. The Distinctive Features and their Correlates*, Cambridge, MA, MIT Press.

Jakoby, S. (1987), 'References to other researchers in library research articles', *English Lanuage Research Journal*, 1: 33–78.

Jeffress, L.A. (ed.) (1951), *Cerebral Mechanisms in Behavior*, New York, John Wiley.

Jelinik, F. (1986), 'Self-organized language modeling for speech recognition', Continuous Speech Recognition Group, IBM Thomas J. Watson Research Center (unpublished).

Jensen, H. (1970), *Sign, Symbol and Script: An Account of Man's Efforts to Write*, London, George Allen & Unwin.

Jespersen, O. (1924), *The Philosophy of Grammar*, London, George Allen & Unwin.

Johansson, S., Leech, G., and Goodluck, H. (1978), *A Manual of Information to Accompany the Lancaster-Oslo/Bergen Corpus of British English, for Use with Digital Computers*, University of Oslo, Department of English.

Johns, T.F. (1986), 'Micro-concord: a language learner's research tool', *System*, 14(2): 151–62.

Johnson, K. (1982), *Communicative Syllabus Design and Methodology*, Oxford, Pergamon.

Johnson, R. (1983), 'Parsing with transition networks', in M. King (ed.), *Parsing Natural Language*, proceedings of the Second Lugano Tutorial, London and New York, Academic Press, pp. 59–72.

Johnson-Laird, P.N. (1983), *Mental Models*, Cambridge, Cambridge University Press.

Johnson-Laird, P.N. and Stevenson, R. (1970), 'Memory for syntax', *Nature*, 227: 412.

Jones, D. (1932), 'The theory of phonemes, and its importance in practical linguistics', in *Proceedings of the First International Congress of Phonetic Sciences*, Amsterdam, pp. 23–24.

Jones, D. (1950), *The Phoneme: Its Nature and Use*, Cambridge, Heffer, 2nd edn 1962, 3rd edn 1967.

Jones, D. (1957), 'The history and meaning of the term "phoneme"', supplement to *Le Maître phonétique*. Reprinted in E. Fudge (1973), *Phonology*, Harmondsworth, Penguin, pp. 9–32.

Jones, D. (1980), 'Gossip: notes on women's oral culture', in C. Kramarae (ed.), *The Voices and Words of Women and Men*, Oxford, Pergamon Press, pp. 193–8.

Jones, L.K. (1980), 'A synopsis of tagmemics', in E.A. Moravcsik and J.R. Wirth (eds), *Syntax and Semantics*, vol. 13: *Current Approaches to Syntax*, New York and London, Academic Press, pp.77–96.

Jones-Sargent, V. (1983), *Tyne Bytes: A Computerised Sociolinguistic Study of Tyneside*, Frankfurt, Peter Lang.

Joos, M. (1948), *Acoustic Phonetics* (Language Monograph, no.23), Baltimore, MD, Linguistic Society of America.

Joos, M. (1961), *The Five Clocks*, New York, Harcourt, Brace, & World.

Just, M.A. and Carpenter, P.A. (1978), 'Inference processes during reading: reflections from eye fixations', in J.W. Senders, D.F. Fisher, and R.A. Monty (eds), *Eye Movements and the Higher Psychological Functions*, Hillsdale, NJ, Lawrence Erlbaum Associates.

Just, M.A. and Carpenter, P.A. (1987), *The Psychology of Reading and Language Comprehension*, Boston, MA, Allyn & Bacon.

Kachru, B.B. (1978), 'Code-mixing as a communicative strategy', in J. Alatis (ed.), *International Dimensions of Bilingual Education*, Washington, DC, Georgetown University Press.

Kahn, D. (1976), 'Syllable-based generalisations in English phonology', unpublished Ph.D. thesis, distributed by Indiana University Linguistics Club.

Kaplan, R.D. (1966), 'Cultural thought patterns in intercultural education', *Language Learning*, 16: 1–20.

Kaplan, R.M. (1972), 'Augmented transition networks as psychological models of sentence comprehension', *Artificial Intelligence*, 3: 77–100.

Kaplan, R.M. (1973a), 'A general syntactic processor', in R. Rustin (ed.), *Natural Language Processing*, Englewood Cliffs, NJ, Prentice Hall.

Kaplan, R.M. (1973b), 'A multi-processing approach to natural language', in *Proceedings of the First National Computer Conference*, Montvale, NJ, AFIPS Press.

Kaplan, R.M. (1975), 'On process models for sentence analysis', in D.A. Norman, D.E. Rumelhart, and the LNR Research Group (eds), *Explorations in Cognition*, San Francisco, Freeman, pp. 117–135.

Kaplan, R.M. and Bresnan, J.W. (1982), 'Lexical-Functional Grammar: a formal system for grammatical representation', in J.W. Bresnan (ed.), *The Mental Representation of Grammatical Relations*, Cambridge, MA, and London, MIT Press, pp. 173–281.

Karmiloff-Smith, A. (1979), *A Functional Approach to Child Language*, Cambridge, Cambridge University Press.

Karmiloff-Smith, A. (1987), 'Some recent issues in the study of language acquisition', in J. Lyons, R. Coates, M. Deuchar, and G. Gazdar (eds), *New Horizons in Linguistics 2*, London and Harmondsworth, Penguin, pp. 367–86.

Karttunen, L. and Kay, M. (1985), 'Parsing in a free word order language', in D.R. Dowty, L.

Karttunen, and A.M. Zwicky (eds), *Natural Language Parsing: Psychological, Computational, and Theoretical Perspectives*, Cambridge, Cambridge University Press, pp. 279–306.

Karttunen, L. and Zwicky, A.M. (1985), 'Introduction', in D.R. Dowty, L. Karttunen, and A.M. Zwicky (eds), *Natural Language Parsing: Psychological, Computational, and Theoretical Perspectives*, Cambridge, Cambridge University Press, pp. 1–25.

Kastovsky, D. (1986), 'Diachronic word-formation in a functional perspective', D. Kastovsky and A. Szwedek (eds), *Linguistics Across Historical and Geographical Boundaries: In Honour of Jacek Fisiak on the Occasion of his Fiftieth Birthday*, Berlin and New York, Mouton de Gruyter, pp. 409–22.

Katamba, F. (1989), *An Introduction to Phonology*, London and New York, Longman.

Katz, J. (1972), *Semantic Theory*, New York, Harper & Row.

Katz, J. and Fodor, J. (1963), 'The structure of a semantic theory', *Language*, 39: 170–210.

Katz, J. and Postal, P. (1964), *An Integrated Theory of Linguistic Descriptions*, Cambridge, MA, MIT Press.

Kay, M. (1985), 'Parsing in functional unification grammar', in D.R. Dowty, L. Karttunen, and A.M. Zwicky (eds), *Natural Language Parsing: Psychological, Computational, and Theoretical Perspectives*, Cambridge, Cambridge University Press, pp. 251–78.

Kay, M. (1986), 'Algorithmic schemata and data structures in syntactic processing', in B.J. Grosz, K. Sparck-Jones, and B.L. Webber (eds), *Readings in Natural Language Processing*, Los Altos, Morgan Kaufman, pp. 35–70.

Kay, P. and McDaniel, C. (1978), 'The linguistic significance of the meanings of basic color terms', *Language*, 54: 610–46.

Kaye, K. (1980), 'Why don't we talk "baby talk" to babies', *Journal of Child Language*, 7: 489–507.

Keenan, E.L. (1979), 'On surface form and logical form', *Studies in the Linguistic Sciences* (Department of Linguistics, University of Illinois), 8(2). Reprinted in E.L. Keenan (1987), *Universal Grammar: 15 Essays*, London, Croom Helm, pp. 375–428.

Keenan, E.L. (1987), *Universal Grammar: 15 Essays*, London, Croom Helm.

Keenan, E.O. and Schieffelin, B.B. (1976), 'Topic as a discourse notion: a study of topic in the conversations of children and adults', in C.N. Li (ed.), *Subject and Topic*, New York, Academic Press, pp. 335–84.

Kellogg, W. and Kellogg, L. (1967), *The Ape and the Child: A Study of Environmental Influence on Early Behavior*, New York, Haffner.

Kempson, R. (1977), *Semantic Theory*, Cambridge, Cambridge University Press.

Kenny, A. (1982), *The Computation of Style: An Introduction to Statistics for Students of Literature and Humanities*, Oxford, Pergamon Press.

Kenstowicz, M. and Kisseberth, C. (1979), *Generative Phonology: Description and Theory*, Orlando, FL, Academic Press.

Kenyon, J.S. (1930), 'Flat a and broad A', *American Speech*, 5: 323–6.

Kershaw, J. (1974), 'People with dyslexia', *Rehab*, British Council for Rehabilitation of the Disabled.

Kertesz, A. (1979), *Aphasia and Associated Disorders*, New York, Grune & Stratton.

Kewley-Port, D. (1983), 'Time-varying features as correlates of place of articulation in stop consonants', *Journal of the Acoustical Society of America*, 73: 322–35.

Kiang, N.Y.S. (1980), 'Processing of speech by the auditory nervous system', *Journal of the Acoustical Society of America*, 69: 830–5.

Kiang, N.Y.S., Watanabe, T., Thomas, E.C. and Clark, L.F. (1965), *Discharge Patterns of Single Fibers in the Cat's Auditory Nerve* (MIT Research Monograph, no. 35), Cambridge, MA, MIT Press.

Kilbury, J. (1976), *The Development of Morphophonemic Theory*, Amsterdam, Benjamins.

Kimball, J.P. (1973a), 'Seven principles of surface structure parsing in natural language', *Cognition*, 2: 15–47.

Kimball, J.P. (1973b), *The Formal Theory of Grammar*, Englewood Cliffs, NJ, Prentice Hall.

Kimura, D. (1979), 'Neuromotor mechanisms in the evolution of human communication', in H.D. Steklis and M.J. Raleigh (eds), *Neurobiology of Social Communication in Primates*, New York, Academic Press, pp. 197–219.

Kintsch, W. and Dijk, T. van (1978), 'Toward a model of text comprehension and production', *Psychoanalytic Review*, 85: 363–94.

Kiparsky, P. (1982), 'From cyclic phonology to lexical phonology', in H. van der Hulst and N. Smith (eds), *The Structure of Phonological Representations*, Dordrecht, Foris, pp. 131–75.

Kipfer, B.A. (1984), *Workbook on Lexicography*, (Exeter Linguistic Studies Series, no.8) University of Exeter.

Kirp, D. (1983), 'Elusive equality: race, ethnicity, and education in the American experience', in N. Glazer and K. Young (eds), *Ethnic Pluralism and Public Policy*, London, Heinemann; Toronto, Lexington Books, reprinted 1986, Aldershot, England, Gower, pp. 85–107.

Klapp, S.T. (1974), 'Syllable-dependent pronunciation latencies in number naming, a replication', *Journal of Experimental Psychology*, 102: 1138–40.

Klapp, S.T., Anderson, W.G. and Berrian, R.W. (1973), 'Implicit speech in reading, reconsidered', *Journal of Experimental Psychology*, 100: 368–74.

Klatt, D.H. (1980), 'Speech perception: a model of acoustic-phonetic analysis and lexical access', in R.A. Cole (ed.), *Perception and Production of Fluent Speech*, Hillsdale, NJ, Lawrence Erlbaum Associates, pp. 243–88.

Klein, E. (1987), 'DRT in unification categorial grammar', in B.G.T. Lowden (ed.), *Proceedings of the Alvey Workshop on Formal Semantics*, University of Essex, pp. 8–23.

Klima, E.S. (1964), 'Negation in English', in J. Fodor and J. Katz (eds), *The Structure of Language*, Englewood Cliffs, NJ, Prentice-Hall, pp. 246–323.

Klima, E.S. and Bellugi, U. (1979), *The Signs of Language*, Cambridge, MA, and London, Harvard University Press.

Knowles, G. and Lawrence, L. (1987), 'Automatic intonation assignment', in R. Garside, G. Leech, and G. Sampson, *The Computational Analysis of English: A Corpus-Based Approach*, London, Longman, pp. 139–48.

Knowlton, E. (1967), 'Pidgin English and Portuguese', in F.S. Drake (ed.), *Proceedings of the Symposium on Historical, Archaeological and Linguistic Studies on Southern China, South-East Asia, and the Hong Kong Region*, Hong Kong, University of Hong Kong Press, pp. 228–37.

Koch, W. (1971), *Taxologie des Englischen*, Munich, Fink.

Kohts, N. (1935), 'Infant ape and human child', *Scientific Memoirs of the Museum Darwinian*, Moscow.

Koutsoudas, A., Sanders, G. and Knoll, C. (1974), 'On the application of phonological rules', *Language*, 50: 1–28.

Kress, G. (1985a), 'Discourses, texts, readers and the pro-nuclear arguments', in P. Chilton (ed.), *Language and the Nuclear Arms Debate: Nukespeak Today*, London, and Dover, NH, Frances Pinter, pp. 65–87.

Kress, G. (1985b), *Linguistic Processes in Sociocultural Practice*, Geelong, Australia, Deakin University Press, 2nd edn 1989, Oxford, Oxford University Press.

Kress, G. and Hodge, R. (1979), *Language as Ideology*, London, Routledge & Kegan Paul.

Kripke, S. (1963), 'Semantical considerations on modal logic', *Acta Philosophica Fennica*, pp. 83–94.

Kučera, H. and Nelson Francis, W. (1967), *Computational Analysis of Present-Day American English*, Providence, RI, Brown University Press.

Kuczaj, S.A. and Brannick, N. (1979), 'Children's use of the *wh* question modal auxiliary placement rule', *Journal of Experimental Child Psychology*, 28: 43–67.

Kuhl, P.K. (1979), 'Speech perception in early infancy: perceptual constancy for spectrally dissimilar vowel categories', *Journal of the Acoustical Society of America*, 66: 1668–79.

Kuhl, P.K. and Miller, J.D. (1975), 'Speech perception by the chinchilla: voiced–voiceless distinction in alveolar plosive consonants', *Science*, 190: 69–72.

Kummer, W. (1972), 'Versuch einer Exploration der neuentdeckten Formelwälder von der Insel Mainau', *Linguistische Berichte*, 18: 53–5.

Kurath, H. *et al.* (1939–43), *Linguistic Atlas of New England*, Providence, RI, Brown University Press.

Kurath, H. and McDavid, R.I. Jr (1961), *The Pronunciation of English in the Atlantic States*, Ann Arbor, University of Michigan Press.

Kussmaul, A. (1877), 'Disturbance of speech', *Ziemssens Encyclopedia of the Practice of Medicine*, London.

Kyle, J.G. and Woll, B. (1985), *Sign Language: The Study of Deaf People and Their Language*, Cambridge, Cambridge University Press.

Labov, W. (1963), 'The social motivation of a sound change', *Word*, 19: 273–309.

Labov, W. (1966), *The Social Stratification of English in New York City*, Arlington, MA, Center for Applied Linguistics.

Labov, W. (1969), 'The logic of non-standard English', *Georgetown Monographs on Language and Linguistics*, 22: 1–31.

Labov, W. (1970), 'The study of language in its social context', *Studium Generale*, 23: 66–84.

Labov, W. (1971a), 'Finding out about children's language', in D. Steinberg (ed.), *Working Papers in Communication*, Honolulu, Pacific Speech Association.

Labov, W. (1971b), 'Variation in language' in C.E. Reed (ed.), *The Learning of Language*, New York, National Council for Teachers of English.

Labov, W. (1972a), *Sociolinguistic Patterns*, Philadelphia, University of Pennsylvania Press.

Labov, W. (1972b), *Language in the Inner City*, Philadelphia, University of Pennsylvania Press, reprinted 1977, Oxford, Basil Blackwell.

Labov, W., Cohen, P., Robins, C. and Lewis, J. (1968), *A Study of the Non-Standard English of Negro and Puerto Rican Speakers in New York City* (Report on Cooperative Research Project no. 3288), 2 vols, Washington, DC, US Office of Education.

Labov, W. and Fanshel, D. (1977), *Therapeutic Discourse: Psychotherapy as Conversation*, New York, Academic Press.

Ladd, D.R. (1980), *The Structure of Intonational Meaning*, Bloomington, Indiana University Press.

Ladefoged, P. (1962), *Elements of Acoustic Phonetics*, Chicago, University of Chicago Press.

Ladefoged, P. (1971), *Preliminaries to Linguistic Phonetics*, Chicago, University of Chicago Press.

Ladefoged, P. (1975), *A Course in Phonetics*, New York, Harcourt Brace Jovanovich.

Ladefoged, P. (1982), *A Course in Phonetics*, 2nd edn, New York, Harcourt Brace Jovanovich.

Lakoff, G. (1970), 'Global rules', *Language*, 46: 627–39.

Lakoff, G. (1971a), 'On generative semantics', in D. Steinberg and L. Jakobovits (eds), *Semantics*, Cambridge, Cambridge University Press, pp. 232–96.

Lakoff, G. (1971b), 'Presupposition and relative well-formedness', in D. Steinberg and L. Jakobovits (eds), *Semantics*, Cambridge, Cambridge University Press, pp. 329–40.

Lakoff, G. (1971c), 'The role of deduction in grammar', in C. Fillmore and D.T. Langendoen (eds), *Studies in Linguistic Semantics*, New York, Holt, Rinehart & Winston, pp. 63–72.

Lakoff, G. (1973), 'Fuzzy grammar and the performance/competence terminology game', in C. Corum, T.C. Smith-Stark, and A. Weiser, *Papers from the Ninth Regional Meeting of the Chicago Linguistic Society*, Chicago, Chicago Linguistic Society, pp. 271–91.

Lakoff, G. (1974), 'Interview with H. Parret', in *Discussing Language*, The Hague, Mouton, pp. 151–78.

Lakoff, G. (1982), *Categories and Cognitive Models*, (Series A, Paper 96), Trier, Linguistic Agency, University of Trier.

Lakoff, G. and Johnson, M. (1980), *Metaphors We Live By*, Chicago and London, University of Chicago Press.

Lakoff, R. (1975), *Language and Woman's Place*, New York, Harper & Row.

Lamb, S.M. (1966), *Outline of Stratificational Grammar*, Washington, DC, Georgetown University Press.

Lambert, W.E. (1974), 'Culture and language as factors in learning and education', in F. Aboud and R.D. Mead (eds), *Cultural Factors in Learning*, Bellingham, Washington State College.

Landau, S.I. (1984), *The Art and Craft of Lexicography*, New York, Schribner's.

Langendoen, D.T. (1968), *The London School of Linguistics: A Study of the Linguistic Theories of B. Malinowski and J.R. Firth* (Research Monograph, no. 46), Cambridge, MA, MIT Press.

Large, A. (1985), *The Artificial Language Movement*, Oxford, Basil Blackwell.

Laskley, K.S. (1951), 'The problem of serial order in behavior', in L.A. Jeffress (ed.), *Cerebral Mechanisms in Behavior*, New York, John Wiley, pp. 112–36.

Lass, R. (1984), *Phonology*, Cambridge, Cambridge University Press.

Laver, J.D.M. (1973), 'The detection and correction of slips of the tongue', in V.A. Fromkin (ed.), *Speech Errors as Linguistic Evidence* (Janua Linguarum, Series Maior, no. 77), The Hague, Mouton, pp. 132–143.

Laver, J.D.M. (1980), 'Monitoring systems in the neurolinguistic control of speech production', in V.A. Fromkin (ed.), *Errors in Linguistic Performance: Slips of the Tongue, Ear, Pen, and Hand*, New York, Academic Press, pp. 287–305.

Laver, J.D.M. and Hutcheson, S. (1972), *Communication in Face to Face Interaction*, Harmondsworth, Penguin.

Lê, T. (1976), 'Syntax and semantics in Fillmorean theory: a study of Vietnamese case grammar', unpublished Ph.D. thesis, Monash University.

Le Page, R.B. (ed.) (1961), *Creole Language Studies II*, Proceedings of the Conference on Creole Language Studies, University of the West Indies, March–April 1959, London, Macmillan.

Leben, W. (1982), 'Metrical or autosegmental', in H. van der Hulst and N. Smith (eds), *The Structure of Phonological Representations*, Dordrecht, Foris, pp. 177–90.

Leech, G.N. (1966), *English in Advertising*, London, Longman.

Leech, G.N. (1967), *Towards a Semantic Description of English*, London, Longman.

Leech, G.N. (1969), *A Linguistic Guide to English Poetry*, London, Longman.

Leech, G.N. (1981), *Semantics: The Study of Meaning*, 2nd edn, Harmondsworth, Penguin.

Leech, G.N. (1983), *Principles of Pragmatics*, London and New York, Longman.

Lees, R.B. (1960), *The Grammar of English Nominalizations*, Bloomington, Indiana University Press; reprinted 1963, The Hague, Mouton.

Leguil, A. (1979), 'Neutralisation, alternance et complémentarité', *La Linguistique* (Paris, Presses Universitaires de France), 15(2), 23–39.

Lehmann, W.P. (1962), *Historical Linguistics: An Introduction*, New York, Holt, Rinehart & Winston.

Lehmann, W.P. (1967), *A Reader in Nineteenth Century Historical Indo-European Linguistics*, Bloomington and London, Indiana University Press.

Lehnert, W.C. (1978), *The Process of Question Answering: A Computer Simulation of Cognition*, Hillsdale, NJ, Lawrence Erlbaum Associates.

Lehrer, A. (1969), 'Semantic cuisine', *Journal of Linguistics*, 5: 39–56.

Lehrer, A. (1974), *Semantic Fields and Lexical Structure*, Amsterdam, North Holland.

Lehrer, A. (1978), 'Structures of the lexicon, and transfer of meaning', *Lingua*, 45: 95–123.

Leland, C.G. (1924), *Pidgin English Sing-Song or Songs and Stories in the China-English Dialect*, 10th edn, first published 1876, London, Trübner.

Lenneberg, E. (1964), 'The capacity for language acquisition', in J. Fodor and J. Katz (eds), *The*

Structure of Language: Readings in the Philosophy of Language, Englewood Cliffs, NJ, Prentice Hall, pp. 579–603.

Lenneberg, E. (1969), 'On explaining language', *Science*, 164(3880): 635–43.

Leopold, W. (1970), *Speech Development of a Bilingual Child*, vols 1–4, New York, AMS Press.

Leopold, W. (1978), 'A child's learning of two languages', in E. Hatch (ed.), *Second Language Acquisition*, Rowley, MA, Newbury House.

Le Page, R.B. (ed.) (1961), *Creole Language Studies II*, proceedings of the Conference on Creole Language Studies, University of the West Indies, March–April 1959, London, Macmillan.

Lepschy, G.E. (1982), *A Survey of Structural Linguistics*, London, André Deutsch.

Lesniewski, S. (1929), 'Grundzüge eines neuen Systems der Grundlagen der Mathematik', *Fundamenta Mathematicae*, 14: 1–81.

Lesser, R. (1978), *Linguistic Investigations of Aphasia*, London, Edward Arnold.

Levelt, W.J.M. (1970a), 'Hierarchical clustering algorithm in the psychology of grammar', in G.B Flores d'Arcais and W.J.M. Levelt (eds), *Advances in Psycholinguistics*, Amsterdam, North Holland, pp. 101–40.

Levelt, W.J.M. (1970b), 'Hierarchical chunking in sentence processing', *Perception and Psychophysics*, 8: 99–102.

Levelt, W.J.M. (1974), *Formal Grammars in Linguistics and Psycholinguistics*, vol. 3: *Psycholinguistic Applications*, The Hague, Mouton.

Levelt, W.J.M. (1983), 'Monitoring and self-repair in speech', *Cognition*, 14: 41–104.

Levelt, W.J.M. (1989), *Speaking: From Intention to Articulation*, Cambridge, MA, and London, MIT Press.

Levelt, W.J.M. and Cutler, A. (1983), 'Prosodic marking in speech repairs', *Journal of Semantics*, 2: 205–17.

Levelt, W.J.M. and Kelter, S. (1982), 'Surface form and memory in question answering', *Cognitive Psychology*, 14: 78–106.

Levinson, S.C. (1983), *Pragmatics*, Cambridge, Cambridge University Press.

Levy, Y. (1983), 'It's frogs all the way down', *Cognition*, 15: 75–93.

Lewis, C.I. (1918), *A Survey of Symbolic Logic*, Berkeley, CA, University of California Press.

Lewis, D.K. (1973), *Counterfactuals*, Oxford, Blackwell.

Lewis, D.K. (1983), 'General semantics', in *Philosophical Papers*, vol. 1, Oxford, Oxford University Press.

L'Hermitte, R., Hécaen, H., Dubois, J. and Tabouret-Keller, A. (1966), 'Le problème de l'aphasie des polyglottes: remarques sur quelques observations', *Neuropsychologia*, 4: 315–29.

Liberman, A.M., Cooper, F.S., Schankweiler, D.P. and Studdert-Kennedy, M. (1967), 'Perception of the speech code', *Psychological Review*, 74: 431–61.

Liberman, A.M., Delattre, P.C. and Cooper, F.S. (1952), 'The role of selected stimulus variables in the perception of the unvoiced stop consonants', *American Journal of Psychology*, 65: 497–516.

Liberman, M. (1975), 'The intonational system of English', unpublished Ph.D. thesis, distributed by Indiana University Linguistics Club.

Liberman, M. and Prince, A. (1977), 'On stress and linguistic rhythm', *Linguistic Inquiry*, 8: 249–336.

Lieberman, P. (1968), 'Primate vocalization and human linguistic ability', *Journal of the Acoustical Society of America*, 44: 1574–84.

Lieberman, P. (1975), *On the Origin of Language*, New York, Macmillan.

Lieberman, P. (1977a), 'The phylogeny of language', in T.A. Sebeok (ed.), *How Animals Communicate*, Bloomington and London, Indiana University Press, pp. 3–25.

Lieberman, P. (1977b), *Speech Physiology and Acoustic Phonetics*, New York, Macmillan.

Lieberman, P. (1984), *The Biology and Evolution of Language*, Cambridge, MA, and London, Harvard University Press.

Lieberman, P. and Blumstein, S.E. (1988), *Speech Physiology, Speech Perception, and Acoustic Phonetics*, Cambridge, Cambridge University Press.

Lieberson, S. (1970), *Language and Ethnic Relations in Canada*, New York, John Wiley.

Lightfoot, D.W. (1984), 'The relative richness of triggers and the bioprogram', *Behavioral and Brain Sciences*, 7(2): 198–9.

Lindblom, B. (1989), 'Models of phonetic variation and selection', *Proceedings of the International Conference on Language Change and Biological Evolution*, Turin.

Linden, E. (1976), *Apes, Men and Language*, Harmondsworth, Penguin.

Linguistic Minorities Project (1983), *Linguistic Minorities in England*, London, University of London Institute of Education.

Linguistic Minorities Project (1985), *The Other Languages of England*, London, Routledge & Kegan Paul.

Llorach, E. Alarcos (1951), *Gramática estructural según la Escuela de Copenhague y con especial atención a la lengua española*, Madrid, Biblioteca Hispánica, Editorial Gredos.

Lloyd, R.J. (1896), *Neuren Sprachen*, 3(10): 615–7.

Locke, J. (1977), *An Essay Concerning Human Understanding*, Glasgow, Fount, first published 1690.

Lockwood, D.G. (1972), *Introduction to Stratificational Linguistics*, New York, Harcourt Brace Jovanovich.

Lockwood, W.B. (1972), *A Panorama of Indo-European Languages*, London, Hutchinson.

Longacre, R.E. (1964), *Grammar Discovery Procedures*, The Hague, Mouton.

Longacre, R.E. (1968–9), *Discourse, Paragraph, and Sentence Structure in Selected Philippine Languages*, 3 vols, US Department of Health, Education and Welfare, Office of Education, Institute of International Studies, vols 1–2 reprinted 1970, *Philippine Languages: Discourse, Paragraph, and Sentence Structure*, Santa Ana, Summer Institute of Linguistics.

Longacre, R.E. (1976), *An Anatomy of Speech Notions*, Lisse, de Ridder.

Longacre, R.E. (1983), *The Grammar of Discourse*, New York and London, Plenum Press.

Love, G. and Payne, M. (eds) (1969), *Contemporary Essays on Style: Rhetoric, Linguistics, and Criticism*, Glenview, IL, Scott, Foresman & Co.

Luria, A.R. (1970), *Traumatic Aphasia: Its Syndromes, Psychology and Treatment*, London, Humanities Press.

Lyons, J. (1968), *Introduction to Theoretical Linguistics*, Cambridge, Cambridge University Press.

Lyons, J. (1970), 'Generative syntax', in J. Lyons (ed.), *New Horizons in Linguistics*, Harmondsworth, Penguin.

Lyons, J. (1977a), *Chomsky*, revised edn, Glasgow, Fontana Collins.

Lyons, J. (1977b), *Semantics*, 2 vols, Cambridge, Cambridge University Press.

Lyons, J. (1981), *Language and Linguistics: An Introduction*, Cambridge, Cambridge University Press.

McArthur, T. (1986), *World of Reference*, Cambridge, Cambridge University Press.

Macaulay, R.K.S. (1977), *Language, Social Class and Education*, Edinburgh, Edinburgh University Press.

Macaulay, R.K.S. (1978), 'Variation and consistency in Glaswegian English', in P. Trudgill (ed.), *Sociolinguistic Patterns in British English*, London, Edward Arnold, pp. 132–43.

McCall, S. (ed.) (1967), *Polish Logic 1920–1939. Papers by Adjukiewicz, Chwistek, Jaskowski, Jordan, Lesniewski, Lukasiewicicz, Slupecki, Sobocinski, and Wajsberg*, Oxford, Clarendon Press.

McCarthur, R. (1976), *Tense Logic*, Dordrecht, Reidel.

McCarthy, D.A. (1930), *The Language Development of the Preschool Child* (Institute of Child Welfare Monograph Series, no. 4), Minneapolis, University of Minnesota Press.

McCarthy, M.J. (1987), 'Interactive lexis: prominence and paradigms', in M. Coulthard (ed.), *Discussing Discourse* (Discourse Analysis Monograph, no. 14), English Language Research, University of Birmingham, pp. 236–48.

McCarthy, M.J. (1988), 'Some vocabulary patterns in conversation', in R.A. Carter and M.J. McCarthy *Vocabulary in Language Teaching*, Harlow, Longman, pp. 181–200.

McCawley, J.D. (1968), 'Lexical insertion in a transformational grammar without deep structure', in R.I. Binnick, A. Davison, G.M. Green, and J.L. Morgan (eds), *Papers from the Fifth Regional Meeting of the Chicago Linguistic Society*, Chicago, University of Chicago, pp. 71–80.

McCawley, J.D. (1978), 'What is a tone language', in V.A. Fromkin (ed.), *Tone: A Linguistic Survey*, New York, Academic Press, pp. 113–31.

McCawley, J.D. (1981), *Everything that Linguists have Always Wanted to Know about Logic . . . But were Ashamed to Ask*, Oxford, Basil Blackwell.

McCawley, J.D. (1988), *The Syntactic Phenomena of English*, 2 vols, Chicago and London, University of Chicago Press.

McClelland, J.L. (1987), 'The case of interactionism in language processing', in M. Coltheart (ed.), *Attention and Performance*, vol. XII: *The Psychology of Reading*, London, Earlbaum, pp. 3–36.

McClelland, J.L. and Rumelhart, D.E., (1981), 'An interactive model of context effects in letter perception. Part 1: An account of basic findings', *Psychological Review*, 88: 375–407.

McIntosh, A. (1961/6), 'Patterns and ranges', *Language*, 37(3): 325–37, reprinted in A. McIntosh and M.A.K. Halliday (eds), *Patterns of Language: Papers in General Descriptive and Applied Linguistics*, London, Longman, pp. 183–99.

Mack, M. (1983), 'Psycholinguistic consequences of early bilingualism: a comparative study of the performance of English monolinguals and French–English bilinguals in phonetics, syntax, and semantics experiments', unpublished Ph.D. thesis, Brown University.

Mack, M. and Blumstein, S.E. (1983), 'Further evidence of acoustic invariance in speech production: the stop–glide contrast', *Journal of the Acoustic Society of America*, 73: 1739–50.

MacKay, D. (1987), *The Organization of Perception and Action: A Theory for Language and Other Cognitive Skills*, New York, Springer.

McKeown, K. (1985), *Generating English Text*, Cambridge, Cambridge University Press.

McKeown, N. (1982), *Case Studies and Projects in Communication Studies*, London, Methuen.

McLaughlin, B. (1978), *Second-Language Acquisition in Childhood*, Hillsdale, NJ, Lawrence Erlbaum Associates.

Maclay, H. and C.E. Osgood (1959), 'Hesitation phenomena in spontaneous English speech', *Word*, 15: 19–44.

McLoughlin, M.G. (1980), 'History of the education of the deaf', *Teacher of the Deaf* (January), pp. 18–19.

MacMahon, M.K.C. (1986), 'The International Phonetic Association: the first 100 years', *Journal of the International Phonetic Association*, 16: 30–8.

Macnamara J. (1967), 'The bilingual's linguistic performance: a psychological overview', *Journal of Social Issues*, 23: 59–77.

Macnamara, J. (1972), 'Cognitive basis of language learning in infants', *Psychological Review*, 79: 1–13.

Macnamara, J. (1982), *Names for Things: A Study of Human Learning*, Cambridge, MA, MIT Press.

McNeill, D. (1970), 'The development of language', in P. Mussen (ed.), *Carmichael's Manual of Child Psychology*, vol. 1, pp. 1061–161.

Mahl, G.F. (1956), 'Disturbances and silences in the patient's speech in psychotherapy', *Journal of Abnormal and Social Psychology*, 53: 1–15.

Makkai, A. (1972), *Idiom Structure in English*, The Hague, Mouton.

Makkai, A. (1978), 'Idiomaticity as a language universal', in J. Greenberg, C.A. Ferguson, and E.A. Moravesik (eds), *Universals of Human Language*, vol. III, Stanford, Stanford University Press, pp. 401–48.

Makkai, A. and Lockwood, D.G. (eds) (1973), *Readings in Stratificational Linguistics*, Alabama, University of Alabama Press.

Malinowski, B. (1923), 'The problem of meaning in primitive languages', supplement to C.K. Ogden and I.A. Richards, *The Meaning of Meaning*, London, Kegan Paul, Trench, Trubner, pp. 451–511.

Malinowski, B. (1935), *Coral Gardens and their Magic*, vol. II, London, Allen & Unwin.

Malkiel, Y. (1959), 'Studies in irreversible binominals', *Lingua*, 8: 113–60.

Malkiel, Y. (1978), 'Derivational categories', in J. Greenberg (ed.), *Universals of Human Language*, vol. III: *Word Structure*, Stanford, Stanford University Press, pp. 125–49.

Mallinson, G. and Blake, B.J. (1981), *Language Typology: Cross-Linguistic Studies in Syntax* (North-Holland Linguistics Series, no. 46), Amsterdam, North Holland.

Mallon, S.T. (1985), 'Six years later: the ICI dual orthography for Inuktitut', in B. Burnaby (ed.), *Promoting Native Writing Systems in Canada*, Toronto, Ontario Institute for Studies in Education, pp. 137–58.

Malmberg, B. (1964), *New Trends in Linguistics* (Bibliotheca Linguistica, no. 1), Stockholm, Bibliotheca Linguistica.

Mandelbaum, D.G. (ed.) (1949), *Selected Writings of Edward Sapir in Language, Culture and Personality*, Berkeley and Los Angeles, University of California Press, and London, Cambridge University Press.

Maratsos, M. (1984), 'How degenerate is the input to Creoles and where do its biases come from?', *Behavioral and Brain Sciences*, 7(2): 200–1.

Marchand, H. (1969), *The Categories and Types of Present-Day English Word-Formation*, 2nd edn, Munich, C.H. Beck.

Marcus, M. (1980), *A Theory of Syntactic Recognition for Natural Language*, Cambridge, MA, MIT Press.

Marshall, H. (1987), 'Quarterly surveying reports', *ELR Journal*, 1: 117–55.

Marslen-Wilson, W.D. and Tyler, L.K. (1980), 'The temporal structure of spoken language understanding', *Cognition*, 8: 1–71.

Marslen-Wilson, W.D. and Welsh, A. (1978), 'Processing interactions and lexical access during word recognition in continuous speech', *Cognitive Psychology*, 10: 29–63.

Martin, E. (1970), 'Toward an analysis of subjective phase structure', *Psychological Bulletin*, 74: 153–66.

Martin, P. (1985), 'La Description phonologique', *La Linguistique*, 21: 159–75.

Martinet, A. (1946), 'Au Sujet des fondements de la théorie linguistique de Louis Hjelmslev, *Bulletin de la Société de Linguistique de Paris*, 42(1): 19–42.

Martinet, A. (1960), *Eléments de linguistique générale*, Paris, Armand Colin, published in English 1964 as *Elements of General Linguistics*, trans. E. Palmer, London, Faber & Faber.

Mason, M. (1988), *Illuminating English*, Wigan, Trace.

Mather, J.Y. and Speitel, H.H. (1975), *The Linguistic Atlas of Scotland*, London, Croom Helm.

Matthei, E. and Roeper, T. (1983), *Understanding and Producing Speech*, Bungay, Suffolk, Fontana.

Matthews, P.H. (1972), *Inflectional Morphology*, Cambridge, Cambridge University Press.

Matthews, P.H. (1974), *Morphology*, Cambridge, Cambridge University Press.

Matthews, P.H. (1984), 'Word formation and meaning', *Quaderni di Semantica*, 5(1): 85–92.

Mead, M. (1931), 'Talk-boy', *Asia*, 31: 141–51.

Mead, R. (1985), *Courtroom Discourse* (Discourse Analysis Monograph, No. 9), English Language Research, University of Birmingham.

Meisel, J.M. (1989), 'Early differentiation of language in bilingual children', in K. Hyltenstam and L.K. Obler (eds), *Bilingualism Across the Lifespan: Aspects of Acquisition, Maturity and Loss*, Cambridge, Cambridge University Press, pp. 13–40.

Mellema, P. (1974), 'A brief against case grammar', *Foundations of Language*, 11: 39–76.

Menn, L. (1976), 'Pattern, control, and contrast in beginning speech: a case study in the development of word form and word function', unpublished Ph.D. thesis, University of Illinois.

Meringer, R. (1908), *Aus dem Leben der Sprache*, Berlin, Behr.

Meringer, R. and Mayer, K. (1895), *Versprechen und Verlesen*, Stuttgart, Göschensche.

Miceli, G., Silveri, M.C. and Caramazza, A. (1987), 'The role of the phoneme-to-grapheme conversion system and of the graphemic output buffer in writing', in M. Coltheart, G. Sartori, and R. Job (eds), *The Cognitive Neuropsychology of Language*, London, and Hillsdale, NJ, Lawrence Erlbaum Associates, pp. 235–52.

Miles, D. (1988), *British Sign Language: a Beginner's Guide*, London, BBC Books.

Miles, T.R. (1983), *Dyslexia: the Pattern of Difficulties*, London, Granada.

Miller, C. and Swift, K. (1981), *The Handbook of Non-Sexist Writing for Writers, Editors and Speakers*, British edn revised by S. Dowrick, London, The Women's Press.

Miller, C.R. (1984), 'Genre as social action', *Quarterly Journal of Speech*, 70: 151–67.

Miller, N. (1986), *Dyspraxia and its Management*, London, Croom Helm.

Miller, W. and Ervin, S. (1964), 'The development of grammar in child language', in U. Bellugi and R. Brown (eds), *The Acquisition of Language* (Monographs of the Society for Research in Child Development, no. 29), pp. 9–34.

Milroy, J. (1984), 'The history of English in the British Isles', in P. Trudgill (ed.), *Language in the British Isles*, Cambridge, Cambridge University Press, pp. 5–31.

Milroy, L. (1980), *Language and Social Networks*, Oxford, Basil Blackwell.

Minkowski, M. (1927), 'Klinischer Beitrag zur Aphasie bei Polyglotten, speziell in Hinblick aufs Schweizerdeutsche', *Schweizer Archiv für Neurologie und Psychiatrie*, 21: 43–72.

Minkowski, M. (1928), 'Sur un cas d'aphasie chez un polyglotte', *Revue Neurologique*, 49: 361–6.

Minsky, M. (1975), 'A framework for representing knowledge', in P.H. Winston (ed.), *The Psychology of Computer Vision*, New York, McGraw-Hill.

Mitchell, T.F. (1958), 'Syntagmatic relations in linguistic analysis', *Transactions of the Philological Society*, pp. 101–18.

Mitchell, T.F. (1966), 'Some English phrasal types', in C.E. Bazell, M.A.K. Halliday, and R.H. Robins (eds), *In Memory of J.R. Firth*, London, Longman, pp. 335–58.

Mitchell, T.F. (1971), 'Linguistic "goings on": collocations and other lexical matters arising on the syntagmatic record', *Archivum Linguisticum*, 2: 35–69.

Mitchell, T.F. (1975), *Principles of Firthian Linguistics*, London, Longman.

Mitzka, W. and Schmidt, L.E. (1953–78), *Deutsche Wortatlas*, Giessen, Schmitz.

Mohanan, K.P. (1981), 'Lexical phonology', unpublished Ph.D. thesis, distributed by Indiana University Linguistics Club.

Mohanan, K.P. (1986), *The Theory of Lexical Phonology*, Dordrecht, Reidel.

Mohr, B. (1971), 'Intrinsic variation in the speech signal', *Phonetica*, 23: 65–93.

Molino, J. (1985), 'Où en est la morphologie?', *Langages*, 78: 5–40.

Money, J. (ed.) (1981), *Reading Disability*, Baltimore, John Hopkins Press.

Montague, R. (1974), *Formal Philosophy*, New Haven, Yale University Press.

Montgomery, M.M. (1977), 'The structure of lectures', unpublished M.A. thesis, University of Birmingham.

Montgomery, M.M. (1981), 'The structure of monologue', in M. Coulthard and M. Montgomery (eds), *Studies in Discourse Analysis*, London, Routledge & Kegan Paul, pp. 33–9.

Montgomery, M.M. (1986), *An Introduction to Language and Society*, London, Methuen.

Moore, B.C.J. (1982), *An Introduction to the Psychology of Hearing*, 2nd edn, London, Academic Press.

Moore, G.E. (1936), 'Is existence a predicate?', *Proceedings of the Aristotelean Society*, supplementary vol., pp. 175–88.

Moore, J. and Widdowson, H.G. (eds) (1980), *Reading and Thinking in English*, Oxford, Oxford University Press.

Moravcsik, E.A. (1980), 'Introduction: on syntactic approaches', in E.A. Moravcsik and J.R. Wirth (eds), *Syntax and Semantics*, vol. 13: *Current Approaches to Syntax*, New York and London, Academic Press, pp. 1–18.

Morgan, J. and Walton, P. (1986), *See What I Mean?*, London, Edward Arnold.

Morgan, J.L. (1979), 'Observations on the pragmatics of metaphor', in A. Ortony (ed.), *Metaphor and Thought*, Cambridge, Cambridge University Press, pp. 136–49.

Morse, P.A. (1972), 'The discrimination of speech and nonspeech stimuli in early infancy', *Journal of Experimental Child Psychology*, 14: 477–92.

Morton, J. (1969), 'The interaction of information in word recognition', *Psychological Review*, 76: 165–78.

Morton, J. (1970), 'A functional model of human memory', in D.A. Norman (ed.), *Models of Human Memory*, New York and London, Academic Press, pp. 203–54.

Morton, J. and Long, J. (1976), 'Effect of word transitional probability on phoneme identification', *Journal of Verbal Learning and Verbal Behavior*, 15: 43–51.

Motley, M.T. (1980), 'Verification of "Freudian Slips" and semantic prearticulatory editing via laboratory-induced spoonerisms', in V.A. Fromkin (ed.), *Errors in Linguistic Performance: Slips of the Tongue, Ear, Pen, and Hand*, New York, Academic Press, pp. 133–47.

Motley, M.T., Camden, C.T. and Baars, B.J. (1982), 'Covert formulation and editing of abnormalities in speech production: evidence from experimentally elicited slips of the tongue', *Journal of Verbal Learning and Verbal Behavior*, 21: 578–94.

Moulton, W.H. (1960), 'The short vowel systems of northern Switzerland: a study in structural dialectology', *Word*, 16: 155–82.

Mowrer, O.H. (1960), *Learning Theory and Symbolic Processes*, New York, John Wiley.

Mühlhäusler, P. (1980), 'Structural expansion and the process of creolization', in A. Valdman and A. Highfield (eds), *Theoretical Orientations in Creole Studies*, New York, Academic Press, pp. 19–56.

Mülhäusler, P. (1981), 'The development of the category of number in Tok Pisin', in P. Muysken (ed.), *Generative Studies in Creole Languages*, Dordrecht, Foris, pp. 35–85.

Mühlhäusler, P. (1986), *Pidgin and Creole Linguistics*, Oxford, Basil Blackwell.

Mukarovsky, J. (1932), 'Standard language and poetic language', in P.L. Garvin (ed.) (1964), *A Prague School Reader on Esthetics, Literary Structure and Style*, Washington, DC, Georgetown University Press, pp. 17–30.

Nauta, W.J.H. and Fiertag, M. (1979), 'The organization of the brain', in *The brain (A Scientific American book)*, San Francisco, W.H. Freeman, pp. 40–53.

Negus, V.E. (1949), *The Comparative Anatomy and Physiology of the Larynx*, New York, Hafner.

Neidle, C. (1988), *The Role of Case in Russian Syntax*, Dordrecht, Kluwer.

Newbrook, M. (1982), 'Sociolinguistic reflexes of dialect interference in West Wirral', unpublished Ph.D. thesis, Reading University.

Newell, L.E. (l966), 'Stratificational analysis of an English text', in S.M. Lamb, *Outline of Stratificational Grammar*, Washington, DC, Georgetown University Press, pp. 71–106.

Newman, S. and Epstein, R. (1985), *Current Perspectives in Dysphasia*, London, Churchill Livingstone.

Newmeyer, F.J. (1980), *Linguistic Theory in America: The First Quarter Century of Transformational Generative Grammar*, New York, Academic Press.

Newmeyer, F.J. (1986), *Linguistic Theory in America*, 2nd edn, New York and London, Academic Press.

Newton, B. (1972), *The Generative Interpretation of Dialect*, London, Cambridge University Press.

Newton, M.J. (1977), 'Dyslexia. The problem of recognition', *Medical Journal 'Update'*, (April).

Newton, M.J. (1984), *Specific Literacy Difficulties: Dyslexia*, Birmingham, Centre for Extension Education, University of Aston in Birmingham.

Newton, M.J., Thompson, M.E. and Richards, I.L. (1979), *Readings in Dyslexia* (Learning Development Aids Series), Wisbech, Cambs., Bemrose.

Newton M.J. *et al.* (1985), 'A positive approach to dyslexia: information processing and computer science', *Aston University Occasional Papers*, University of Aston in Birmingham.

Newton-Smith, W. (1985), *Logic*, London, Routledge & Kegan Paul.

Nice, M. (1925), 'Length of sentences as a criterion of child's progress in speech', *Journal of Educational Psychology*, 16: 370–9.

Nida, E.A. (1946), *Morphology: The Descriptive Analysis of Words*, Ann Arbor, University of Michigan Press.

Nida, E.A. (1968), *A Synopsis of English Syntax*, 2nd revised edn, The Hague, Mouton.

Nida, E.A. (1975), *Componential Analysis of Meaning*, The Hague, Mouton.

Nirenburg, S. (1987), *Machine Translation: Theoretical and Methodological Issues*, Cambridge, Cambridge University Press.

Nolan, K.A. and Caramazza, A. (1983), 'An analysis of writing in a case of deep dyslexia', *Brain and Language*, 20: 305–28.

Nooteboom, S.G. (1969), 'The tongue slips into patterns', in *Nomen, Leyden Studies in Linguistics and Phonetics*, The Hague, Mouton, pp. 114–32.

Nooteboom, S.G. (1980), 'Speaking and unspeaking: detection and correction of phonological and lexical errors in spontaneous speech', in V.A. Fromkin (ed.), *Errors in Linguistic Performance: Slips of the Tongue, Ear, Pen, and Hand*, New York, Academic Press, pp. 87–95.

Norman, D.E., Rumelhart, D.E. and the INR Research Group (1975), *Explorations in Cognition*, San Francisco, Freeman.

Obler, L. and Albert, M. (1978), 'A monitor system for bilingual language processing', in M. Paradis (ed.), *Aspects of Bilingualism*, Columbia, SC, Hornbeam Press.

O'Connor, J.D. (1973), *Phonetics*, Harmondsworth, Penguin.

O'Connor, J.D. and Arnold, G.F. (1961), *Intonation of Colloquial English*, London, Longman.

Oehrle, R.T., Bach, E. and Wheeler, D. (eds) (1988), *Categorial Grammars and Natural Language Structures*, Dordrecht, Reidel.

Ohmann, R. (1959), 'Prolegomena to the analysis of prose style', in H.C. Martin (ed.), *Style in Prose Fiction: English Institute Essays*, New York, Columbia University Press, pp. 1–24.

Oller, D.K., Wieman, L.A., Doyle, W.J. and Ross, C. (1976), 'Infant babbling and speech', *Journal of Child Language*, 3: 1–11.

Olu Tomori, S.H. (1977), *The Morphology and Syntax of Present-Day English: an Introduction*, London, Heinemann.

Orton, H. (1960), 'An English dialect survey: linguistic atlas of England', *Orbis*, 9: 331–48.

Orton, H. (1962), *Survey of English Dialects: Introduction*, Leeds, Arnold.

Orton, H. and Dien, E. (1962–71), *Survey of English Dialects: Basic Material*, 4 vols, Leeds, Arnold.

Orton, H., Sanderson, S. and Widdowson, J. (1978), *Linguistic Atlas of England*, London, Croom Helm.

Orton, S.T. (1937), *Reading, Writing and Speech Problems in Children*, London, Chapman & Hall.

Ortony, A. (ed.) (1979a), *Metaphor and Thought*, Cambridge, Cambridge University Press.

Ortony, A. (1979b), 'Metaphor: a multidimensional problem', in A. Ortony (ed.), *Metaphor and Thought*, Cambridge, Cambridge University Press, pp. 1–18.

Padilla, A. and Liebman, E. (1975), 'Language acquisition in the bilingual child', *Bilingual Review*, 4: 52–67.

Page, R.I. (1987), *Runes*, London, British Museum Publications for the Trustees of the British Museum.

Palmer, F.R. (ed.) (1970), *Prosodic Analysis*, London, Oxford University Press.

Palmer, F.R. (1971), *Grammar*, Harmondsworth, Penguin.

Palmer, F.R. (1981), *Semantics*, 2nd edn, Cambridge, Cambridge University Press.

Palmer, H.E. and Palmer, D. (1925), *English Through Actions*, Tokyo, IRET, reprinted 1959, London, Longman.

Paradis, M. (1977), 'Bilingualism and aphasia', in H. Whitaker and H.A. Whitaker (eds), *Studies in Neurolinguistics*, vol. 3 (Perspectives in Neurolinguistics and Psycholinguistics Series), New York, Academic Press, pp. 65–121.

Paradis, M. (1978), 'Bilingual linguistic memory: neurolinguistic considerations', paper presented to the Linguistic Society of America Annual Meeting, Boston, MA, December.

Paradis, M. (1980a), 'Language and thought in bilinguals', in H. Izzo and W. McCormack (eds), *The Sixth LACUS Forum*, Columbia, SC, Hornbeam Press, pp. 420–431.

Paradis, M. (1980b), 'Contributions of neurolinguistics to the theory of bilingualism', in R.K. Herbert (ed.), *Applications of Linguistic Theory in the Human Sciences*, East Lansing, Michigan University Press, pp. 180–211.

Paradis, M. (1980c), 'The language switch in bilinguals: psycholinguistic and neurolinguistic perspectives', in P.H. Nelde (ed.), *Languages in Contact and Conflict*, Wiesbaden, Franz Steiner, pp. 501–6.

Paradis, M. (1980d), 'Neurolinguistic organization of a bilingual's two languages', in J. Copeland (ed.), *The Seventh LACUS Forum*, Columbia, SC, Hornbeam Press, pp. 486–94.

Pariente, J.C. (1985), *L'Analyse du langage à Port-Royal*, Paris, Edition Minuit.

Pateman, T. (1981), 'Linguistics as a branch of critical theory', *UEA Papers in Linguistics*, 14–15, pp. 1–29.

Patterson, K. and Shewell, C. (1987), 'Speak and spell dissociations and word class effects', in M. Coltheart, G. Sartori, and R. Job (eds), *The Cognitive Neuropsychology of Language*, London, and Hillsdale, NJ, Lawrence Erlbaum Associates, pp. 273–94.

Pavlides, G.T. and Miles, T.R. (1981), *Dyslexia Research and its Application to Education*, Chichester, John Wiley.

Pears, D. (1971), *Wittgenstein*, Glasgow, Fontana Collins.

Peirce, C.S. (1868), 'Some consequences of four incapacities', *Journal of Speculative Philosophy*, 2: 140–57.

Peirce, C.S. (1931–58), *Collected Papers*, Cambridge, MA, Harvard University Press.

Pellowe, J. (1976), 'The Tyneside linguistic survey: aspects of developing methodology', in W. Viereck (ed.), *Sprachliche Handeln–Sociales Verhalten*, Munich, Falk.

Penfield, W.P. (1959), 'Epilogue – the learning of languages', in W.P. Penfield and L.R. Roberts (eds), *Speech and Brain-Mechanisms*, London, Oxford University Press, pp. 235–57.

Peng, J. (1987), 'Organisational features in chemical engineering research articles', *English Language Research Journal*, 1: 79–116.

Perecman, E. (1989), 'Language processing in the bilingual: evidence from language mixing', in K. Hyltenstam and L.K. Obler (eds), *Bilingualism Across the Lifespan: Aspects of Acquisition, Maturity and Loss*, Cambridge, Cambridge University Press, pp. 227–44.

Pereira, F.C.N. and Warren, D.H.D. (1980), 'Definite clause grammars for language analysis – a survey of the formalism and a comparison with augmented transition networks', *Artificial Intelligence*, 13(3): 231–78.

Perkins, W.H. and Kent, R.D. (1986), *Textbook of Functional Anatomy of Speech, Language, and Hearing*, San Diego, College-Hill.

Peterson, G.E. and Barney, H.L. (1952), 'Control methods used in a study of the vowels', *Journal of the Acoustical Society of America*, 73: 175–84.

Petöfi, J. (1971), *Transformationsgrammatiken und eine ko-textuelle Texttheorie*, Frankfurt, Athenäum.

Petöfi, J. (1974), 'Toward an empirically motivated grammatical theory of verbal texts', in J. Petöfi and H. Rieser (eds), *Studies in Text Grammar*, Dordrecht, Reidel, pp. 205–75.

Petöfi, J. (1978), 'A formal semiotic text theory as an integrated theory of natural languages', in W.U. Dressler (ed.), *Current Trends in Textlinguistics*, Berlin and New York, Walter de Gruyter, pp. 35–46.

Petöfi, J. (1980), 'Einige Grundfragen der pragmatisch–semantischen Interpretation von Texten', in T. Ballmer and W. Kindt (eds), *Zum Thema 'Sprache und Logik': Ergebnisse einer interdisziplinären Diskussion*, Hamburg, Buske, pp. 146–90.

Petrie, H. (1987), 'The psycholinguistics of speaking', in J. Lyons, R. Coates, M. Deuchar, and G. Gazdar (eds), *New Horizons in Linguistics 2*, London and Harmondsworth, Penguin, pp. 336–66.

Pettinari, C. (1981), 'The function of a grammatical alternation in 14 surgical reports', Mimeo, University of Michigan.

Petyt, K.M. (1980), *The Study of Dialect*, London, Deutsch.

Philips, S. (1972), 'Participant structures and communicative competence: Warm Springs children in community and classroom', in C. Cazden, V. John, and D. Hymes (eds), *Functions of Language in the Classroom*, New York, Teachers' College Press.

Piaget, J. (1980), in M. Piattelli-Palmarni (ed.), *Language and Learning: The Debate Between Jean Piaget and Noam Chomsky*, Cambridge, MA, Harvard University Press, pp. 23–34 and 55–64.

Pickford, G.R. (1956), 'American linguistic geography: a sociological appraisal', *Word*, 12: 211–33.

Pike, K.L. (1945), *The Intonation of American English*, Ann Arbor, University of Michigan Press.

Pike, K.L. (1948), *Tone Languages*, Ann Arbor, University of Michigan Press.

Pike, K.L. (1967), *Language in Relation to a Unified Theory of Human Behavior*, The Hague, Mouton.

Pike, K.L. (1970), *Tagmemics and Matrix Linguistics Applied to Selected African Languages*, Norman, Summer Institute of Linguistics of the University of Oklahoma.

Pike, K.L. (1982), *Linguistic Concepts: An Introduction to Tagmemics*, Lincoln, NE, and London, University of Nebraska Press.

Pinker, S. (1982), 'A theory of the acquisition of lexical interpretive grammars', in J.W. Bresnan (ed.), *The Mental Representation of Grammatical Relations*, Cambridge, MA; London, MIT Press, ch. 10.

Pinker, S. (1984), *Language Learnability and Language Development*, Cambridge, MA, Harvard University Press.

Pisona, D.B. (1973), 'Auditory and phonetic memory codes in the discrimination of consonants and vowels', *Perception and Psychophysics*, 13: 253–60.

Platt, J.T. (1971), *Grammatical Form and Grammatical Meaning: A Tagmemic View of Fillmore's Deep Structure Case Concepts*, Amsterdam and London, North Holland.

Pohl, J. (1965), 'Bilingualism', *Revue Roumaine de Linguistique*, 10: 343–9.

Poplack, S., Wheeler, S. and Westwood, A. (1989), 'Distinguishing language contact phenomena: evidence from Finnish–English bilingualism', In K. Hyltenstam and L.K. Obler (eds), *Bilingualism Across the Lifespan: Aspects of Acquisition, Maturity and Loss*, Cambridge, Cambridge University Press, pp. 132–54.

Postal, P. (1970), 'On the surface verb "remind"', *Linguistic Inquiry*, 1: 37–120.

Prabhu, N.S. (1987), *Second Language Pedagogy: A Perspective*, Oxford, Oxford University Press.

Premack, A. and Premack, D. (1972), 'Teaching language to an ape', *Scientific American*, 227: 92–9.

Preyer, W. (1882), *Die Seele des Kindes*, Leipzig, published in English 1880–90 as *The Mind of the Child*, trans. H.W. Brown, 2 vols, New York, Appleton.

Propp, V. (1928), *Morfologiya skazki*, Leningrad, published in English 1958 as *Morphology of the Folktale* (Indiana University Publications in Anthropology, Folklore and Linguistics, no. 10), Bloomington, IN.

Pulleyblank, D. (1986), *Tone in Lexical Phonology*, Dordrecht, Reidel.,

Putnam, H. (1970), 'Is semantics possible?', in H. Kiefer and M. Munitz (eds), *Languages, Belief and Metaphysics*, (Contemporary Philosophical Thought: The International Philosophy Year Conferences at Brockport, 1) New York, State University of New York Press.

Quine, W. van O. (1960), *Word and Object*, Cambridge, MA, MIT Press.

Quirk, R. (1960), 'Towards a description of English usage', *Transactions of the Philological Society*, pp. 40–61.

Quirk, R. and Svartvik, J. (1979), 'A corpus of modern English', in H. Bergenholtz and B. Schraeder (eds), *Empirische Textwissenschaft: Aufbau und Auswertung von Text-Corpora*, Königstein, Scriptor, pp. 204–18.

Quirk, R., Greenbaum, S., Leech, G. and Svartvik, J. (1985), *A Comprehensive Grammar of the English Language*, London, Longman.

Radford, A. (1981), *Transformational Syntax: a Student's Guide to Chomsky's Extended Standard Theory*, Cambridge, Cambridge University Press.

Radford, A. (1988), *Transformational Grammar: a First Course*, Cambridge, Cambridge University Press.

Rask, R. (1818), 'Undersøgelse om det gamle Nordiske eller Islandske Sprogs Oprindelse', Copenhagen, reprinted in R. Rask (1932), *Ausgewählte Abhandlungen*, ed. L. Hjelmslev, vol. I, Copenhagen, Levin & Munksgaard.

Rastier, F. (1985), 'L'oeuvre de Hjelmslev aujourd'hui', *Il Protagora XXV*, 4 (7–8): 109–25.

Ratcliff, R. and McKoon, G. (1978), 'Priming in item recognition: evidence for the propositional structure of sentences', *Journal of Verbal Learning and Verbal Behaviour*, 17: 403–18.

Rayner, K., Carlson, M. and Frazier, L. (1983), 'The interaction of syntax and semantics during sentence processing', *Journal of Verbal Learning and Verbal Behavior*, 22: 358–74.

Read, A.W. (1975), 'Dictionary', in *Encyclopaedia Britannica*, vol. 5, pp. 713–22.

Recherches structurales (1949), Travaux du Cercle Linguistique de Copenhague, *Interventions dans le débat glossematique, publiées à l'occasion du cinquantenaire de M. Louis Hjelmslev*, Copenhagen, Nordisk Sprog- og Kulturforlag.

Reddy, M.J. (1979), 'The conduit metaphor – a case of frame conflict in our language about language', in A. Ortony (ed.), *Metaphor and Thought*, Cambridge, Cambridge University Press, pp. 284–324.

Reddy, R. (1980), 'Machine models of speech perception', in R.A. Cole (ed.), *Perception and Production of Fluent Speech*, Hillsdale, NJ, Lawrence Erlbaum Associates, pp. 215–42.

Reichel, K. (1982), *Categorial Grammar and Word-Formation: The De-Adjectival Abstract Noun in English*, Tübingen, Max Niemeyer.

Renouf, A. (1984), 'Corpus development at Birmingham University', in J. Aarts and W. Meijs (eds), *Corpus Linguistics: Recent Developments in the Use of Computer Corpora in English Language Research*, Amsterdam, Rodopi, pp. 3–39.

Rescorla, L. (1980), 'Overextensions in early language development', *Journal of Child Language*, 7: 321–35.

Richards, I.A. (1936), 'Metaphor', in I.A. Richards, *The Philosophy of Rhetoric*, London, Oxford University Press.

Richards, I.A. (1960), 'Poetic process and literary analysis', in T.A. Sebeok (ed.), *Style in Language*, Cambridge, MA, MIT Press, pp. 9–23.

Riesbeck, C.K. (1978), 'An expectation-driven production system for natural language understanding', in D.A. Waterman and R. Hayes-Roth (eds), *Pattern Directed Inference Systems*, Amsterdam, North Holland, pp. 399–414.

Rischel, J. (1976), 'The contribution of Louis Hjelmslev', *Third International Conference of Nordic and General Linguistics*, Stockholm, Almqvist & Wiksell.

Robins, R.H. (1959), 'In defence of WP', *Transactions of the Philological Society*, pp. 116–44.

Robins, R.H. (1964), *General Linguistics: An Introductory Survey*, London, Longman.

Robins, R.H. (1967), *A Short History of Linguistics*, London, Longman.

Robins, R.H. (1980), *General Linguistics: An Introductory Survey*, 3rd edn, London, Longman.

Robins, R.H. (1989), *General Linguistics*, 4th edn, London, Longman.

Romaine, S. (1978), 'Postvocalic /r/ in Scottish English: sound change in progress?', in P. Trudgill (ed.), *Sociolinguistic Patterns in British English*, London, Edward Arnold, pp. 144–57.

Romaine, S. (1980), 'A critical overview of the methodology of urban British sociolinguistics', *English World-Wide*, 1(2): 163–98.

Romaine, S. (1988), *Pidgin and Creole Languages*, London and New York, Longman.

Ronjat, J. (1913), *Le Développement du langage observé chez un enfant bilingue*, Paris, Champion.

Rosch, E. (1973), 'Natural categories', *Cognitive Psychology*, 4: 328–50.

Rosch, E. (1977), 'Classification of real-world objects: origins and representations in cognition', in P.N. Johnson-Laird and P.C. Wason (eds), *Thinking: Readings in Cognitive Science*, Cambridge, Cambridge University Press, pp. 212–22.

Rosch, E. and Mervis, C.B. (1975), 'Family resemblances: studies in the internal structure of categories', *Cognitive Science*, 7: 573–605.

Rosch, E., Mervis, C.B., Gray, W.D., Johnson, D.M. and Boyes-Braem, O. (1976), 'Basic objects in natural categories', *Cognitive Psychology*, 8: 382–439.

Rosen, H. (1972), *Language and Class*, Bristol, Falling Wall Press.

Ross, J.R. (1968), *Constraints on Variables in Syntax*, Bloomington, Indiana University Linguistics Club.

Ross, J.R. (1970), 'On declarative sentences', in R. Jacobs and P. Rosenbaum (eds), *Readings in English Transformational Grammar*, Waltham, MA, Ginn.

Ross, J.R. (1973), 'Nouniness', in O. Fujimara (ed.), *Three Dimensions of Linguistic Theory*, Tokyo, TEC Corporation, pp. 137–258.

Ruhlen, M. (1975), *A Guide to the Languages of the World*, Language Universals Project, Stanford University.

Rumbaugh, D., Gill, T. and von Glasersfeld, E. (1973), 'Reading and sentence completion by a chimpanzee (Pan)', *Science*, 182: 731–3.

Rumelhart, D.E. (1975), 'Notes on a schema for stories', in D.G. Bobrow and A. Collins, *Representation and Understanding: Studies in Cognitive Science*, New York, Academic Press, pp. 211–36.

Rumelhart, D.E. (1979), 'Some problems with the notion of literal meaning', in A. Ortony (ed.), *Metaphor and Thought*, Cambridge, Cambridge University Press, pp. 78–91.

Rumelhart, D.E. (1984), 'Understanding understanding', in J. Flood (ed.), *Understanding Reading Comprehension*, Neward, DE, International Reading Association, pp. 1–20.

Rumelhart, D.E. and McClelland, J.L. (1982), 'An interactive model of context effects in letter perception. Part 2: the perceptual enhancement effect and some tests and extensions of the model', *Psychological Review*, 89: 60–94.

Rumelhart, D.E. and Ortony, A. (1977), 'The representation of knowledge in memory', in R.C. Anderson, R.J. Spiro, and W.E. Mongague (eds), *Schooling and the Acquisition of Knowledge*, Hillsdale, NJ, Lawrence Erlbaum Associates, pp. 99–135.

Rumelhart, D.E., Lindsay, P.H. and Norman, D.A. (1972), 'A process model for long-term memory', in E. Tulving and W. Donaldson (eds), *Organization of Memory*, New York, Academic Press.

Russell, B. (1903), *The Principles of Mathematics*, Cambridge, Cambridge University Press.

Saban, R. (1983), 'Asymmetry of the middle meningeal veins network in the fossil man and its possible significance', in E. de Grolier (ed.), *Glossogenetics: The Origin and Evolution of Language*, London, Harwood Academic, pp. 115–41.

Sachs, M. and Young, E. (1979), 'Encoding of steady state vowels in the auditory-nerve: representation in terms of discharge rate', *Journal of the Acoustical Society of America*, 66: 470–9.

Sacks, H. (1986), 'On the analyzability of stories by children', in J. Gumperz and D. Hymes (eds), *Directions in Sociolinguistics: The Ethnography of Communication*, Oxford, Basil Blackwell, pp. 329–45.

Sacks, H., Schegloff, E.A. and Jefferson, G.A. (1974), 'A simplest systematic for the organization of turn-taking for conversation', *Language*, 50: 696–735.

Sacks, O. (1989), *Seeing Voices: A Journey into the World of the Deaf*, Berkeley and Los Angeles, University of California Press; London, Pan, 1990.

Sadock, J.M. (1974), *Toward a Linguistic Theory of Speech Acts*, New York, Academic Press.

Sadock, J.M. (1979), 'Figurative speech and linguistics', in A. Ortony (ed.), *Metaphor and Thought*, Cambridge, Cambridge University Press, pp. 46–64.

Saifullah Kahn, V. (1980), 'The "mother-tongue" of linguistic minorities in multicultural England', *Journal of Multilingual and Multicultural Development*, 1(1): 71–88.

Samarin, W. (1967), *Field Linguistics*, New York, Holt, Rinehart & Winston.

Sampson, G. (1979), 'The indivisibility of words', *Journal of Linguistics*, 15: 39–47.

Sampson, G. (1980), *Schools of Linguistics: Competition and Evolution*, London, Hutchinson.

Sampson, G. (1985), *Writing Systems*, London, Hutchinson.

Sampson, G. (1987), 'Probabilistic models of analysis', in R. Garside, G. Leech, and G. Sampson (eds), *The Computational Analysis of English: A Corpus-Based Approach*, London, Longman, pp. 16–29.

Sanford, A.J. and Garrod, S.C. (1981), *Understanding Written Language: Explorations in Comprehension Beyond the Sentence*, New York, John Wiley.

Sankoff, G. (1977), 'Variability and explanation in language and culture: cliticization in New Guinea Tok Pisin', in M. Saville-Troike (ed.), *Linguistics and Anthropology*, Washington, DC, Georgetown University Press, pp. 59–75.

Sankoff, G. and S. Laberge (1973), 'On the acquisition of native speakers by a language', *Kivung*, 6: 32–47.

Sapir, E. (1921), *Language: An Introduction to the Study of Speech*, Oxford, Oxford University Press.

Sapir, E. (1927), 'The unconscious patterning of behaviour in society', in E.S. Dummer, *The Unconscious: A Symposium*, New York, Knopf, pp. 114–142, reprinted in D.G. Mandelbaum (ed.) (1949), *Selected Writings of Edward Sapir in Language, Culture and Personality*, Berkeley and Los Angeles, University of California Press, pp. 544–59.

Šaumjan, S.K. (1958), *Strukturnaja lingvistika kak immanentnaja teorija jazyka*, Akademija Nauk SSSR, Institut slavjanovedenija, revised edn 1971, *Principles of Structural Linguistics* (Janua Linguarum, Series Maior, no. 45), trans. J. Miller, The Hague, Mouton.

Šaumjan, S.K. (1962), *Problemy teoretičeskoj fonologii*, revised edn 1968, *Problems of Theoretical Phonology* (Janua Linguarum, Series Minor, no. 41), trans. A.L. Vaňek, The Hague and Paris, Mouton.

Saunders, G. (1982), *Bilingual Children: Guidance for the Family*, Philadelphia, Multilingual Matters.

Saunders, G. (1988), *Bilingual Children: From Birth to Teens*, Philadelphia, Multilingual Matters.

Saussure, F. de (1916/74, *Cours de linguistique générale*, Lausanne and Paris, Payot, reprinted as *Course in General Linguistics*, Glasgow, Fontana/Collins.

Scalise, A. (1984), *Generative Morphology*, Dordrecht, Foris.

Schane, S.A. (1968), *French Phonology and Morphology*, Cambridge, MA, MIT Press.

Schane, S.A. (1973), *Generative Phonology*, Englewood Cliffs, NJ, Prentice Hall.

Schank, R.C. (1972), 'Conceptual dependency: a theory of natural language understanding', *Cognitive Psychology*, 3: 552–631.

Schank, R.C. (1982), *Dynamic Memory: A Theory of Learning in Computers and People*, Cambridge, Cambridge University Press.

Schank, R.C. and Abelson, R.P. (1977), *Scripts, Plans, Goals and Understanding*, Hillsdale, NJ, Lawrence Erlbaum Associates.

Schegloff, E.A. (1968), 'Sequencing in conversational openings', *American Anthropologist*, 70(6): 1075–95, reprinted in H. Gumperz and D. Hymes (eds) (1986), *Directions in Sociolinguistics: The Ethnography of Communication*, Oxford, Basil Blackwell, pp. 364–80.

Schegloff, E.A. (1979), 'The relevance of repair to syntax-for-conversation', in T. Givon (ed.), *Syntax and Semantics*, vol. 12, New York, Academic Press, pp. 261–86.

Schegloff, E.A., Jefferson, G. and Sacks, H. (1977), 'The preference for self-correction in the organization of repair in conversation', *Language*, 53: 361–82.

Schenkein, J. (1980), 'A taxonomy for repeating action sequences in natural conversation', in B. Butterworth (ed.), *Language Production*, vol. 1: *Speech and Talk*, London, Academic Press, pp. 21–47.

Scherer, A. (1868), *Die Urheimat der Indogermanen*, Darmstadt, Wissenschaftliche Buchgesellschaft.

Schlegel, F. von (1808), *Über die Sprache und Weishelt der Inder: Ein Beitrag zur Begrundung der Alterthumskunde*, Heidelberg, Mohr Zimmer.

Schlick, M. (1936), 'Meaning and verification', *Philosophical Review*, 45: 339–82.

Schmidt-Mackey, I. (1977), 'Language strategies of the bilingual family', in W. Mackey and T. Andersson (eds), *Bilingualism in Early Childhood*, Rowley, MA, Newbury House.

Schön, D.A. (1979), 'Generative metaphor: a perspective on problem-setting in social policy', in A. Ortony (ed.), *Metaphor and Thought*, Cambridge, Cambridge University Press, pp. 254–83.

Schouten, J.F. (1940), 'The residue, a new component in subjective sound analysis', *K. Akademie van Wetenschappen, Amsterdam, Afdeeling Natuurkunde* (proceedings), 43: 356–65.

Schubert, R.D. and Eimas, P. (1977), 'Effects of context on the classification of words and nonwords', *Journal of Experimental Psychology: Human Perception and Performance*, 33: 27–36.

Schuchardt, H. (1882), 'Kreolische Studien II; über das Indoportugiesische von Cochim', Vienna, Akademie der Wissenschaften, Sitzungsberichte. Philosophisch-historische Klasse 102 (II), pp. 799–816.

Schuchardt, H. (1883), 'Kreolische Studien IV: über das Malaiospanische der Philippinen', Vienna, Akademie der Wissenschaften, Sitzungsberichte. Philosophisch-historische Klasse 105 (II), pp. 111–50.

Schuchardt, H. (1885), *Über die Lautgesetze; gegen die Junggrammatiker*, Berlin. Reprinted with English translation in Th. Vennemann and T.H. Wilbur (1972), *Schuchardt, the Neogrammarians and the Transformational Theory of Phonological Change*, Frankfurt, Atheneum, pp. 1–72.

Schuchardt, H. (1889), 'Beiträge zur Kenntnis des englischen Kreolisch II. Melaneso-englisches', *Englische Studien*, 13: 158–62; and in G. Gilbert (ed.) (1980), *Pidgin and Creole Languages: Selected Essays by Hugo Schuchardt*, Cambridge, Cambridge University Press, pp. 14–30.

Schuchardt, H. (1909), 'Die Lingua Franca', *Zeitschrift für Romanische Philologie*, 33: 441–61.

Schuchardt, H. (1914), *Die Sprache der Saramakkaneger in Surinam* (Verhandelingen der Koninklijke Akademie von Wetenschappen to Amsterdam, Afdeeling Letterkunde, Nieuwe Reeks, Deel XIV, no. 6), published in English in T.L. Markey (ed. and trans.) (1979), *Hugo Schuchardt. The Ethnography of Variation. Selected Writings on Pidgins and Creoles*, Ann Arbor, MI, Karoma Press, pp. 73–109.

Searle, J.R. (1969), *Speech Acts: An Essay in the Philosophy of Language*, Cambridge, Cambridge University Press.

Searle, J.R. (1971), 'What is a speech act?', in J.R. Searle (ed.), *The Philosophy of Language*, Oxford, Oxford University Press, pp. 39–54.

Searle, J.R. (1975), 'Indirect speech acts', in P. Cole and J. Morgan (eds), *Syntax and Semantics*, vol. 3: *Speech Acts*, New York, Academic Press, pp. 59–82.

Searle, J.R. (1979), 'Metaphor', in A. Ortony (ed.), *Metaphor and Thought*, Cambridge, Cambridge University Press, pp. 92–123.

Sebeok, T.A. (ed.) (1960), *Style in Language*, Cambridge, MA, MIT Press.

Sebeok, R.A. (ed.) (1977), *How Animals Communicate*, Bloomington and London, Indiana University Press.

Sebeok, T.A. and Umikev-Sebeok, J. (eds) (1980), *Speaking of Apes: A Critical Anthology of Two-way Communication with Man*, New York and London, Plenum Press.

Selkirk, E.O. (1980), 'The role of prosodic categories in English word stress', *Linguistic Inquiry*, 11: 563–605.

Selkirk, E.O. (1982), *The Syntax of Words*, Cambridge, MA, MIT Press.

Sells, P. (1985), *Lectures on Contemporary Syntactic Theories: An Introduction to Government–Binding Theory, Generalized Phrase Structure Grammar and*

Lexical-Functional Grammar, Center for the Study of Language and Information, Stanford University, University of Chicago Press.

Shallice, T. (1981), 'Phonological agraphia and the lexical route in writing', *Brain*, 104: 413–29.

Shamma, S.A. (1985), 'Speech processing in the auditory system, II: lateral inhibition and the central processing of speech evoked activity in the auditory nerve', *Journal of the Acoustical Society of America*, 78: 1622–32.

Shankweiler, D. and Studdert-Kennedy, M. (1967), 'Identification of consonants and vowels presented to left and right ears', *Quarterly Journal of Experimental Psychology*, 19: 59–63.

Shklovsky, V. (1917), 'Art as device', in L.T. Lemon and M.J. Reis (eds) (1965), *Russian Formalist Criticism: Four Essays*, Lincoln, Nebraska University Press.

Shuy, R.W., Wolfram, W.A. and Riley, W.K. (1968), *Linguistic Correlate of Social Stratification in Detroit Speech*, Michigan State University.

Siegman, A.W. and Pope, B. (1965), 'Effect of question specificity and anxiety producing messages on verbal fluency in the initial interview', *Journal of Personality and Social Psychology*, 2: 522–30.

Siertsema, B. (1954), *A Study of Glossematics: Critical Survey of its Fundamental Concepts*, The Hague, Martinus Nijhoff, 2nd edn 1965.

Sinclair, J.McH. (1966), 'Beginning the study of lexis', in C.E. Bazell, J.C. Catford, M.A.K. Halliday, and R.H. Robins (eds), *In Memory of J.R. Firth*, London, Longman, pp. 410–30.

Sinclair, J.McH. (1972), *A Course in Spoken English: Grammar*, London, Oxford University Press.

Sinclair, J.McH. (1973), 'Linguistics in colleges of education', *Dudley Educational Journal*, 1(3).

Sinclair, J.McH. (ed.) (1980), *Skills for Learning*, London, Nelson.

Sinclair, J.McH. (1982a), 'The integration of language and literature in the English curriculum', in R. Carter and D. Burton (eds), *Literary Text and Language Study*, London, Edward Arnold, pp. 9–27.

Sinclair, J.McH. (1982b), 'Lines about "Lines" ', in R. Carter (ed.), *Language and Literature: An Introductory Reader in Stylistics*, London, George Allen & Unwin, pp. 162–76.

Sinclair, J.McH. (1984), 'Naturalness in language', in J. Aarts and W. Meijs (eds), *Corpus Linguistics: Recent Developments in the Use of Computer Corpora in English Language Research*, Amsterdam, Rodopi, pp. 203–10.

Sinclair, J.McH. (1987a), 'The nature of the evidence', in J.McH. Sinclair (ed.), *Looking Up: An Account of the COBUILD Project in Lexical Computing*, London and Glasgow, Collins, pp. 150–9.

Sinclair, J.McH. (1987b), 'Collocation: a progress report', in R. Steele and T. Threadgold (eds),

Language Topics: Essays in Honour of Michael Halliday, vol. 3, Amsterdam, John Benjamins, pp. 319–31.

Sinclair, J.McH. (ed.) (1987c), *Looking Up: An Account of the COBUILD Project in Lexical Computing*, London and Glasgow, Collins.

Sinclair, J.McH. and Coulthard, M. (1975), *Towards an Analysis of Discourse: The English Used by Teachers and Pupils*, London, Oxford University Press.

Singer, M. (1979), 'The temporal locus of inference in the comprehension of brief passages: recognizing and verifying implications about instruments', *Perceptual and Motor Skills*, 49: 539–50.

Singer, M. (1980), 'The role of case-filling inferences in the comprehension of brief passages', *Discourse Processes*, 3: 185–201.

Singer, M. (1981), 'Verifying the assertions and implications of language', *Journal of Verbal Learning and Verbal Behavior*, 20: 46–60.

Singleton, D. (1983), *Age as a Factor in Second Language Acquisition*, CSLC, Trinity College, Dublin.

Skinner, B.F. (1957), *Verbal Behavior*, New York, Appleton Crofts.

Skutnabb-Kangas, T. and Toukamaa, P. (1976), 'Teaching migrant children's mother-tongue and learning the language of the host country in the context of the socio-cultural situation of the migrant family', (Tampere, Finland, UNESCO Report, Tutkimuksia Research Reports, no. 15), Department of Sociology and Social Psychology, University of Tampere.

Skwire, D. (1985), *Writing With a Thesis: A Rhetoric and Reader*, 4th edn, New York and London, Holt, Rinehart & Winston.

Skydgaard, H.B. (1942), *Den Konstituelle Dyslexi*, Copenhagen.

Skyrms, B. (1975), *Choice and Chance: An Introduction to Inductive Logic*, Enrico, CA, Dickenson.

Slobin, D.I. (1973), 'Cognitive prerequisites for the development of grammar', in C.A. Ferguson and D. Slobin (eds), *Studies of Child Language Development*, New York, Holt, Rinehart & Winston, pp. 175–208.

Slobin, D.I. (1977), 'Language change in childhood and history', in J. MacNamara (ed.), *Language Learning and Thought*, New York, Academic Press, pp. 185–214.

Slobin, D.I. (1982), 'Universal and particular in the acquisition of language', in E. Wanner and L. Gleitman (eds), *Language Acquisition: The State of the Art*, Cambridge, Cambridge University Press, pp. 128–70.

Slobin, D.I. (ed.) (1984a), *The Cross-Linguistic Study of Language Acquisition*, Hillsdale, NJ, Laurence Erlbaum Associates.

Slobin, D.I. (1984b), 'Cross-linguistic evidence for the language-making capacity', in D.I. Slobin (ed.), *The Cross-Linguistic Study of Language Acquisition*, Hillsdale, NJ, Laurence Erlbaum Associates, pp. 1157–257.

Smith, M. (1926), *An Investigation of the Development of the Sentence and the Extent of Vocabulary in Young Children*, (University of Iowa Studies in Child Welfare, vol. 3, no. 5), Iowa City.

Smith, N. and Wilson, D. (1979), *Modern Linguistics: The Results of Chomsky's Revolution*, Harmondsworth, Penguin.

Smith, P.M. (1985), *Language, the Sexes and Society*, Oxford, Basil Blackwell.

Soames, S. and Perlmutter, D. (1979), *Syntactic Argumentation and the Structure of English*, Berkeley, University of California Press.

Soares, C. and Grosjean, F. (1981), 'Left hemisphere language lateralization in bilinguals and monolinguals', *Perception and Psychophysics*, 29: 599–604.

Sommerstein, A.H. (1977), *Modern Phonology*, London, Edward Arnold.

Sparck Jones, K. and Wilks, Y. (1983), *Automatic Natural Language Parsing*, Chichester, Ellis Horwood.

Speech Therapy Service (1972), *Quirk Report*, London, HMSO.

Spender, D. (1980), *Man Made Language*, London, Routledge & Kegan Paul.

Sperber, D. and Wilson, D. (1986), *Relevance: Communication and Cognition*, Oxford, Basil Blackwell.

Springer, S.P. and Deutsch, G. (1985), *Left Brain, Right Brain*, New York, W.H. Freeman.

Springston, F.J. (1975), 'Some cognitive aspects of presupposed coreferential anaphora', unpublished Ph.D. dissertation, Stanford University.

Sridhar, S. and Sridhar, K. (1980), 'The syntax and psycholinguistics of bilingual code-mixing', *Canadian Journal of Psychology*, 34: 407–16.

Stabler, E.P. Jr (1987), 'Restricting logic grammars with government–binding theory', *Comparative Linguistics*, 13 (1–2): 1–10.

Stampe, D. (1969), 'The acquisition of phonetic representation', in R.I. Binnick, A. Davison, G.M. Green, and J.L. Morgan (eds), *Papers from the Fifth Regional Meeting of the Chicago Linguistic Society*, pp. 443–54.

Stampe, D. (1973), 'On chapter 9', in M. Kenstowicz and C. Kisseberth (eds), *Issues in Phonological Theory*, The Hague, Mouton, pp. 44–52.

Stanley, J.P. (1973), *Paradigmatic Woman: The Prostitute*, New York, Linguistic Society of America.

Stanley, J.P. (1977), 'Gender-marking in American English: usage and reference', in A.P. Nilsen, H.

Bosmajian, H.L. Gershuny, and J.P. Stanley (eds), *Sexism and Language*, Urbana, IL, National Council of Teachers of English.

Stanovich, K.E. and West, R.F. (1981), 'The effects of sentence processing on ongoing word recognition: tests of a two-process theory', *Journal of Experimental Psychology: Human Perception and Performance*, 7: 658–72.

Stati, S. (1985), 'Un ipotesi di semantica lessicale: forma-sostanza-materia', *Il Protagora XXV*, 4(7–8): 91–105.

Steedman, M. and Altmann, G. (1989), 'Ambiguity in context: a reply', *Language and Cognitive Processes*, 4(3–4) SI: 105–22.

Stemberger, J.P. (1985), 'An interactive activation model of language production', in A.W. Ellis (ed.), *Progress in the Psychology of Language*, Hillsdale, NJ, Laurence Erlbaum Associates, pp. 143–86.

Stern, C. and Stern, W. (1907), *Die Kindersprache*, Leipzig, Barth.

Stern, W. (1924), *Psychology of Early Childhood up to the Sixth Year of Age*, New York, Holt.

Sternberg, R.J., Tourangeau, R. and Nigro, G. (1979), 'Metaphor, induction, and social policy: the convergence of macroscopic and microscopic views', in A. Ortony (ed.), *Metaphor and Thought*, Cambridge, Cambridge University Press, pp. 325–55.

Sternberg, S., Monsell, S., Knoll, R.L. and Wright, C.E. (1978), 'The latency and duration of rapid movement sequences: comparisons of speech and typewriting', in G.E. Stelmach (ed.), *Information Processing in Motor Control and Learning*, New York, Academic Press.

Stevens, K.N. (1960), 'Towards a model for speech-recognition', *Journal of the Acoustical Society of America*, 32: 47–55.

Stevens, K.N. (1972), 'Segments, features and analysis by synthesis', in J.F. Kavanagh and I.G. Mattingly (eds), *Language by Ear and by Eye*, Cambridge, MA, MIT Press, pp. 47–52.

Stevens, K.N. (1981), 'Constraints imposed by the auditory system on the properties used to classify speech sounds: data from phonology, acoustics, and psychoacoustics', in T. Meyers, J. Laver, and J. Anderson (eds), *The Cognitive Representation of Speech*, New York, North-Holland, pp. 61–74.

Stevens, K.N. and Blumstein, S.E. (1978), 'Invariant cues for place of articulation in stop consonants', *Journal of the Acoustical Society of America*, 64: 358–68.

Stewart, W.A. (1962a), 'Creole languages in the Caribbean', in F.A. Rice (ed.), *Study of the Role of Second Languages in Asia, Africa and Latin America*, Washington, DC, Center for Applied Linguistics, pp. 34–53.

Stewart, W.A. (1962b), 'An outline of linguistic typology for describing multilingualism', *Study of the Role of Second Languages in Asia, Africa and Latin America*, Washington, DC, Center for Applied Linguistics, pp. 15–25.

Stokoe, W.C. (1960), *Sign Language Structure*, Silver Spring, MD, Linstok Press.

Stokoe, W.C., Casterline, D.C. and Croneberg, C.G. (1976), *A Dictionary of American Sign Language on Linguistic Principles*, revised edn, Silver Spring, MD, Linstok Press.

Strässler (1982), *Idioms in English: A Pragmatic Analysis*, Tübingen, Gunter Narr.

Streiff, A.A. (1985), 'New developments in TITUS 4', in V. Lawson (ed.), *Tools for the Trade: Translation and the Computer*, vol. 5, London, Aslib, pp. 195–92.

Stubbs, M. (1983), *Language, Schools and Classrooms*, 2nd edn, London and New York, Methuen.

Stubbs, M. (1986), *Educational Linguistics*, Oxford, Basil Blackwell.

Stubbs, M. and Hillier, H. (eds) (1983), *Readings on Language, Schools and Classrooms*, London and New York, Methuen.

Sullivan, W.J. (1980), 'Syntax and linguistic semantics in stratificational theory', in E.A. Moravcsik and J.R. Wirth (eds), *Syntax and Semantics*, vol. 13: *Current Approaches to Syntax*, New York and London, Academic Press, pp. 301–27.

Suppes, P. (1960), *Axiomatic Set Theory*, Princeton, NJ, Van Nostrand.

Sutcliffe, D. (1984), 'British Black English and West Indian Creoles', in P.J. Trudgill (ed.), *Language in the British Isles*, Cambridge, Cambridge University Press, pp. 219–37.

Svartvik, J. and Quirk, R. (1979), 'A corpus of modern English', in H. Bergenholtz and B. Schraeder (eds), *Empirische Textwissenschaft: Aufbau und Answertung von Text-Corpora*, Königstein, Scriptor, pp. 204–18.

Svartvik, J., Eeg-Olofsson, M., Forsheden, O., Örestrom, B. and Thavenius, C. (1982), *Survey of Spoken English: Report on Research 1975–81* (Lund Studies in English, no. 63), Lund, CWK Gleerup.

Swacker, M. (1975), 'The sex of the speaker as a sociolinguistic variable', in B. Thorne and N. Henley (eds), *Language and Sex: Difference and Dominance*, Rowley, MA, Newbury House, pp. 76–83.

Swadesh, M. (1934), 'The phonemic principle', *Language*, 10: 117–29.

Swales, J. (1981), *Aspects of Article Introductions* (Aston ESP Research Reports, no. 1), Language Studies Unit, University of Aston in Birmingham.

Swales, J. (1985), 'English language papers and authors' first language: preliminary explorations', *Scientometrics*, 8: 91–101.

Swales, J. (1987), 'Utilizing the literatures in teaching the research paper', *TESOL Quarterly*, 21: 41–68.

Swales, J. (1990), *Genre Analysis: English in Academic and Research Settings*, Cambridge, Cambridge University Press.

Swinney, D.A. (1979), 'Lexical access during sentence comprehension: (re)consideration of context effects', *Journal of Verbal Learning and Verbal Behavior*, 18: 654–9.

Taine, H. (1877), 'On the acquisition of language by children', *Mind*, 2: 252–9.

Taraban, R. and McClelland, J.L. (1988), 'Constituent attachment and thematic role assignment in sentence processing: influence of context-based expectations, *Journal of Memory and Language*, 27: 597–632.

Tarnapol, M. and Tarnapol, L. (1977), 'Dyslexia: the problem of recognition', *Update, Medical Journal*.

Taylor, D.R. (1959), 'On function words versus form in "non-traditional" languages', *Word*, 15: 485–589.

Taylor, D.R. (1960), 'Language shift or changing relationship?', *International Journal of American Linguistics*, 26: 155–61.

Taylor, I. (1976), *Introduction to Psycholinguistics*, New York, Holt, Rinehart & Winston.

Taylor Sarno, M., Newman, S. and Epstein, R. (1985), *Current Perspectives in Dysphasia*, Edinburgh, Churchill Livingstone.

Templin, M. (1957), *Certain Language Skills in Children* (University of Minnesota Institute of Child Welfare Monograph Series, no. 26), Minneapolis, University of Minnesota Press.

Terrace, H.S. (1979), *Nim: a Chimpanzee Who Learned Sign Language*, New York, Alfred Knopf.

Thernstrom, A. (1980), 'Language: issues and legislation', in S. Thernstrom, A. Orlov, and O. Handlin (eds), *Harvard Encyclopedia of American Ethnic Groups*, Cambridge, MA, Harvard University Press.

Thomas, C.K. (1958), *An Introduction to the Phonetics of American English*, 2nd edn, New York, Ronald Press.

Thompson, J.B. (1984), *Studies in the Theory of Ideology*, Cambridge, Polity Press.

Thompson, M.E. (1984), *Developmental Dyslexia*, London, Edward Arnold.

Thompson, R.W. (1961), 'A note on some possible affinities between the creole dialects of the Old World and those of the New', in R.B. Le Page (ed.), *Creole Language Studies II*, proceedings of the Conference on Creole Language Studies, University of the West Indies, March–April 1959, London, Macmillan, pp. 107–13.

Thomson, J.R. and Chapman, R. (1977), 'Who is 'Daddy' revisited: the status of two-year-olds' over-extended words in use and comprehension', *Journal of Child Language*, 4: 359–75.

Thorne, J., Bratley, P. and Dewar, H. (1968), 'The syntactic analysis of English by machine', in D.

Michie (ed.), *Machine Intelligence 3*, New York, Elsevier.

Threadgold, T. (1986), 'Semiotics – ideology – language', in T. Threadgold, E.A. Grosz, G. Kress, and M.A.K. Halliday (eds), *Semiotics, Ideology, Language* (Sydney Studies in Society and Culture, no. 3), Sydney, Sydney Association for Studies in Society and Culture, pp. 15–60.

Tiedemann, D. (1787), *Beobachtungen über die Entwicklung der Seelenfähigkeit bei Kindern*, Altenburg, published in English in F.L. Solden (1877), *Tiedemann's Record of Infant Life*, Syracuse, NY.

Tinbergen, N. (1972), *The Animal and Its World*, 2 vols, London, Allen & Unwin.

Todd, L. (1974), *Pidgins and Creoles*, London, Routledge & Kegan Paul.

Togeby, K. (1951), *Structure immanente de la langue française* (Travaux du Cercle Linguistique de Copenhague, VI); 2nd edn, Paris, Larousse, 1965.

Tomlin, R.S. (1986), *Basic Word Order: Functional Principles*, London, Croom Helm.

Tosi, A. (1982), 'Between the mother's dialect and English: the role of the standard language of the country of origin in a community of Southern Italian immigrants and its position in the linguistic education of their children', in A. Davies (ed.), *Language and Learning in Home and School*, London, Heinemann Educational Books, pp. 44–66.

Tottie, G. and Bäcklund, I. (eds) (1986), *English in Speech and Writing: A Symposium* (Studia Anglistica Uppsaliensia Series, no. 60), Uppsala, Acta Universitatis Upsaliensis.

Toukomaa, P. and Skutnabb-Kangas, T. (1977), *The Intensive Teaching of the Mother-Tongue to Migrant Children at Pre School Age* (Tutkimuksia Research Report, no. 26), Department of Sociology and Social Psychology, University of Tampere, Finland.

Trager, G.L. and Smith, H.L. Jr (1951), *An Outline of English Structure*, Studies in Linguistics, Occasional Papers no. 3, Norman, OK, Battenburg Press.

Trubetzkoy, N.S. (1929), 'Sur la "morphonologie" ', *Travaux du Cercle Linguistique de Prague*, 1, pp. 85–8.

Trubetzkoy, N.S. (1931), 'Gedanken über Morphonologie', *Travaux du Cercle Linguistique de Prague*, 4, pp. 160–3.

Trubetzkoy, N.S. (1939), *Grunzüge der Phonologie: Travaux du Cercle Linguistique de Prague*. Published in English (1969) as *Principles of Phonology*, trans. C.A.M. Baltaxe, Berkeley and Los Angeles, University of California Press.

Trubetzkoy, N.S. (1969), *Principles of Phonology*, Berkeley and Los Angeles, University of California Press.

Trudgill, P.J. (1972), 'Sex, covert prestige and linguistic change in the urban British English of Norwich', *Language in Society*, 1: 179–95.

Trudgill, P.J. (1974a), *Sociolinguistics: An Introduction*, Harmondsworth, Penguin, revised edn 1983.

Trudgill, P.J. (1974b), *The Social Differentiation of English in Norwich*, London, Cambridge University Press.

Trudgill, P.J. (1975), *Accent, Dialect and the School*, London, Edward Arnold.

Trudgill, P.J. (1979), 'Standard and nonstandard dialects of English in the UK: problems and policies', *International Journal of the Sociology of Language*, 21: 9–24, reprinted in M. Stubbs and H. Hillier (eds) (1983), *Readings on Language, Schools and Classrooms*, London and New York, Methuen, pp. 9–24.

Trudgill, P.J. (1983), *On Dialect: Social and Geographical Perspectives*, Oxford, Basil Blackwell.

Trudgill, P.J. (ed.) (1984), *Language in the British Isles*, Cambridge, Cambridge University Press.

Trudgill, P.J. and Hannah, J. (1984), *International English – a Guide to Varieties of Standard English*, London, Edward Arnold.

Tsui, A.B.-M. (in progress), *Utterances in Conversation*.

Tulving, E. (1972), 'Episodic and semantic memory', in E. Tulving and W. Donaldson (eds), *Organization of Memory*, New York, Academic Press, pp. 381–403.

Turner, G. (1973), *Stylistics*, Harmondsworth, Penguin.

Uldall, H.J. (1957), *Outline of Glossematics*, vol. 1: *General Theory* (Travaux du Cercle Linguistique de Copenhague X_1); 2nd edn 1967, Copenhagen, Nordisk Sprog- og Kulturforlag.

Ullman, S. (1962), *Semantics*, Oxford, Basil Blackwell, and New York, Barnes & Noble.

Underwood, G. (1977), 'Contextual facilitation from attended and unattended messages', *Journal of Verbal Learning and Verbal Behavior*, 16: 99–106.

UNESCO (1953), *The Use of Vernacular Languages in Education*, Paris, UNESCO.

Vachek, J. (1933), 'What is phonology?', *English Studies*, 15: 81–92.

Vachek, J. (ed.) (1964), *A Prague School Reader in Linguistics*, Bloomington, Indiana University Press.

Vachek, J. (1966), *The Linguistic School of Prague: an Introduction to its Theory and Practice*, Bloomington and London, Indiana University Press.

Valdman, A. (ed.) (1977), *Pidgin and Creole Linguistics*, Bloomington, Indiana University Press.

Valdman, A. and Highfield, A. (eds) (1980), *Theoretical Orientations in Creole Studies*, New York, Academic Press.

Van Cleve, J.V. (ed.) (1987), *Gallaudet Encyclopedia of Deaf People and Deafness*, New York, McGraw-Hill.

Van Ek, J.A. (1973), 'The "threshold level" in a unit/credit system', in *Systems*, Development in Adult Language Learning, Strasbourg, Council of Europe, pp. 89–128.

Van Lancker, D. and Fromkin, V.A. (1973), 'Hemispheric specialization for pitch and tone: evidence from Thai', *Journal of Phonetics*, 1: 101–9.

Van Peer, W. (1986), *Stylistics and Psychology: Investigations of Foregrounding*, London, Croom Helm.

Van Riemsdijk, H. and Williams, E. (1986), *Introduction to the Theory of Grammar*, Cambridge, MA, MIT Press.

Van Wijk, C. and Kempen, G. (1987), 'A dual system for producing self-repairs in spontaneous speech: evidence from experimentally elicited corrections', *Cognitive Psychology*, 19: 403–40.

Vellutino, F.R. (1979), *Dyslexia: Theory and Research*, London, MIT Press.

Verner, K. (1875) 'Eine Ausnahme der ersten Lautverschiebung', Zeitschrift für vergleichende Sprachforschung auf dem Gebiete der Indogermanische Sprachen, 23: 97–130.

Vestergaard, T. and Schröder, K. (1986), *The Language of Advertising*, Oxford, Basil Blackwell.

Vijchulata, B. (1978), 'The surface syntactic structure of the simple clause in Thai: a stratificational model with (deep) case hypothesis', unpublished Ph.D. dissertation, University of Florida (University Microfilms International Order no. 78–17464).

Vion, R. (1974), 'Les Notions de neutralisation et d'archiphonème', *La Linguistique*, 10(1): 33–52.

Volterra, V. and Taeschner, R. (1978), 'The acquisition and development of language by bilingual children', *Journal of Child Language*, 5: 311–26.

Voorhoeve, J. (1973), 'Historical and linguistic evidence in favor of the relexification theory in the formation of creoles', *Language in Society*, 2: 133–45.

Wakelin, M.F. (1972), *English Dialects: An Introduction*, London, Athlone Press.

Wall, R. (1972), *Introduction to Mathematical Linguistics*, Englewood Cliffs, NJ, Prentice Hall.

Walsh, K.W. (1978), *Neuropsychology: A Clinical Approach*, Edinburgh, Churchill Livingstone.

Wang, W.S-Y. (1967), 'Phonological features of tone', *International Journal of American Linguistics*, 33(2): 93–105.

Wang, W.S-Y. (1972), 'The many uses of FO', *Papers in Linguistics and Phonetics to the Memory of Pierre Delattre*, The Hague, Mouton, pp. 487–503.

Wang, W.S-Y. (1973), 'The Chinese language', *Scientific American* 50, reprinted in W.S-Y. Wang (ed.) (1982), *Human Communication*, New York, W.H. Freeman.

Wang, W.S-Y. (1976), 'Language change', *Annals of the N.Y. Academy of Science*, 280: 61–72.

Wang, W.S.-Y. and Cheng, C.C. (1987), 'Middle Chinese tones in modern dialects', in R. Channon and L. Shockey (eds), *In Honor of Ilse Lehiste*, Dordrecht, Foris, pp. 513–23.

Wanner, E. (1980), 'The ATN and the sausage machine: which one is baloney?', *Cognition*, 8: 209–25.

Wanner, E. and Maratsos, M. (1978), 'An ATN approach to comprehension', in M. Halle, J. Bresnan, and G.A. Miller (eds), *Linguistic Theory and Psychological Reality*, Cambridge, MA, and London, MIT Press, pp. 119–61.

Warren, D.H.D. and Pereira, F.C.N. (1982), 'An efficient easily adaptable system for interpreting natural language queries', *American Journal of Computational Linguistics*, 8(3–4): 110–22.

Warren, R.M. (1982), *Auditory Perception: A New Synthesis*, New York, Pergamon Press.

Wasow, T. (1983), 'Some remarks on developmental psycholinguistics', in Y. Otsu, H. van Reimsdijk, K. Inoue, A. Kamio, and N. Kawasaki (eds), *Studies in Generative Grammar and Language Acquisition*, Tokyo, Editorial Committee (available from N. Kawasaki, c/o Division of Languages, International Christian University, Tokyo).

Waterhouse, V.G. (1974), *The History and Development of Tagmemics*, The Hague and Paris, Mouton.

Watson, J. (1809), *Instruction for the Deaf and Dumb: Or, a Theoretical and Practical View of the Means by which They are Taught*, London, Darton & Harvey.

Watson, J.B. (1924), *Behaviorism*, Chicago and New York, University of Chicago Press.

Watson, J. and Hill, A. (1984), *A Dictionary of Communication Studies*, London, Edward Arnold.

Weaver, W. (1955), 'Translation', in W.N. Locke and A.D. Booth (eds), *Machine Translation of Language*, New York, John Wiley, pp. 15–23.

Webber, B.L. (1983), 'So what can we talk about now?', in R.C. Berwick and J.M. Brady (eds), *Computational Models of Discourse*, Cambridge, MA, MIT Press, pp. 331–71.

Weinreich, U. (1954), 'Is a structural dialectology possible?', *Word*, 10: 388–400.

Weinreich, U. (1968), *Languages in Contact*, The Hague, Mouton.

Weinreich, U. (1969), 'Problems in the analysis of idioms', in J. Puhvel (ed.), *Substance and Structure in Language*, Los Angeles, University of California Press, pp. 23–81.

Weizenbaum, J. (1966), 'ELIZA – a computer program for the study of natural language communication between man and machine', *Communications of the ACM*, 9: 36–45.

Wellek, R. (1960), 'Closing statement (retrospect and prospect from the viewpoint of literary criticism)', in T.A. Sebeok (ed.), *Style in Language*, Cambridge, MA, MIT Press, pp. 417–18.

Wellek, R. and Warren, A. (1949), *Theory of Literature*, Austin, TX, and (1956), New York, Harcourt Brace Jovanovich; 3rd edn 1963, Harmondsworth, Penguin.

Wellman, B.L., Case, I.M., Mengert, I.G. and Bradbury, D.E. (1931), *Speech Sounds of Young Children* (University of Iowa Studies in Child Welfare, vol. 5, no. 2).

Wells, J.C. (1982), *Accents of English*, 3 vols, London, Cambridge University Press.

Wells, R.S. (1947), 'Immediate constituents', *Language*, 23: 81–117.

Wells, R.S. (1949), 'Automatic alternation', *Language*, 25: 99–116.

West, M. (1960), *Teaching English in Difficult Circumstances*, London, Longman,

Wexler, K. and Culicover, P. (1980), *Formal Principles of Language Acquisition*, Cambridge, MA, MIT Press.

Whinnom, K. (1956), *Spanish Contact Vernaculars in the Philippine Islands*, Hong Kong, Hong Kong University Press.

Whinnom, K. (1965), 'Contacts de langues et emprunts lexicaux: the origin of the European-based creoles and pidgins', *Orbis*, 14: 509–27.

Whitaker, H. and Whitaker, H.A. (eds) (1976), *Studies in Neurolingustics*, vol. 1 (Perspectives in Neurolinguistics and Psycholinguistics Series), New York, Academic Press.

White, R. (1988), *The ELT Curriculum*, Oxford, Basil Blackwell.

Whitfield, F.J. (1954), 'Glossematics', in A. Martinet and U. Weinreich (eds), *Linguistics Today: Publication on the Occasion of Columbia University Bicentennial*, New York, Linguistic Circle of New York, pp. 250–8.

Whorf, B.L. (1939), 'The relation of habitual thought and behavior to language', in L. Spier (ed.) (1941), *Language, Culture and Personality*, Menasha, WI, Sapir Memorial Publication Fund.

Whorf, B.L. (1940), 'Science and linguistics', *Technological Review*, 42(6): 229–31 and 247–8.

Widdowson, H.G. (1975), *Stylistics and the Teaching of Literature*, London, Longman.

Widdowson, H.G. (1978), *Teaching Language as Communication*, Oxford, Oxford University Press.

Widdowson, H.G. (1983), *Learning Purpose and Language Use*, Oxford, Oxford University Press.

Wieman, J.M. (1985), 'Interpersonal control and regulation in conversation', in R.L. Street Jr and J.N. Capella (eds), *Sequence and Pattern in Communicative Behaviour*, London, Edward Arnold, pp. 85–102.

Wierzbilka, A. (1987), *English Speech Act Verbs: A Semantic Dictionary*, Sydney, Academic Press.

Wilensky, R. (1978), 'Why John married Mary: understanding stories involving recurring goals', *Cognitive Science*, 2: 235–66.

Wilkins, D.A. (1976), *Notional Syllabuses*, Oxford, Oxford University Press.

Wilks, Y. (1978), 'Making preferences more active', *FIArt.Int.*, 11: 197–223.

Williams, E. (1981), 'On the notions "lexically related" and "head of a word"', *Linguistic Inquiry*, 12(2): 245–74.

Willis, J. and Willis, D. (1988), *The COBUILD English Course*, Glasgow and London, Collins.

Winograd, T. (1972), *Understanding Natural Language*, New York, Academic Press.

Winograd, T. (1983), *Language as a Cognitive Process*, vol. 1: *Syntax*, Reading, MA, Addison-Wesley.

Winter, E.O. (1971), 'Connections in science material: a proposition about the semantics of clause relations', *Centre for Information on Language Teaching Papers and Reports*, no. 7, London, Centre for Information on Language Teaching and Research for British Association for Applied Linguistics, pp. 41–52.

Winter, E.O. (1977), 'A clause-relational approach to English texts: a study of some predictive lexical items in written discourse', *Instructional Science*, 6(1): 1–92.

Winter, E.O. (1986), 'Clause relations as information structure: two basic text structures in English', in M. Coulthard (ed.), *Talking about Text: Studies Presented to David Brazil on his Retirement* (Discourse Analysis Monograph, no. 13), English Language Research, University of Birmingham, pp. 88–108.

Witmer, L. (1909), 'A monkey with a mind', *Psychological Clinic*, 13(7): 189–205.

Wittgenstein, L. (1921), *Tractatus Logico-Philosophicus, Annalen der Naturphilosophie*, London and Henley, Routledge & Kegan Paul, reprinted 1974.

Wittgenstein, L. (1953), *Philosophical Investigations*, Oxford, Basil Blackwell. Reprint of 1953 English text with index, 1968.

Woll, B. (1990), 'Sign language', in N.E. Collinge (ed.), *An Encyclopaedia of Language*, London and New York, Routledge, pp. 740–83.

Wollheim, R. (1968), *Art and its Objects*, Harmondsworth, Penguin.

Woods, W.A. (1970), 'Transition network grammars for natural language analysis', *Communications of the ACM*, 13: 591–606.

Woods, W.A. (1973), 'An experimental parsing system for transition network grammars', in R. Rustin (ed.), *Natural Language Processing*, New York, Algorithmics Press, pp. 111–54.

Woolford, E. (1984), 'Why creoles won't reveal the properties of universal grammar', *Behavioral and Brain Sciences*, 7(2): 211–12.

Worden, F.G. (1971), 'Hearing and the neural detection of acoustic patterns', *Behavioral Science*, 16: 20–30.

Wrede, F. and Mitzka, W. (1926–56), *Deutsche Sprachatlas*, Marburg, Elwert.

Wright, D. (1969), *Deafness*, New York, Stein & Day.

Wright, J. (ed.) (1898–1905), *English Dialect Dictionary*, London, Frowde.

Wright, J. (1905), *The English Dialect Grammar*, London, Frowde.

Wundt, W.M. (1900), *Völkerpsychologie II. Die Sprache*, Leipzig, Engelmann.

Wyke, M.A. (1978), *Developmental Dysphasia*, London, Academic Press.

Yang, H. (1985), 'The use of computers in English teaching and research in China', in R. Quirk and H.G. Widdowson (eds), *English in the World*, Cambridge, Cambridge University Press, pp. 86–101.

Yekovich, F.R. and Walker, C.H. (1978), 'Identifying and using referents in sentence comprehension', *Journal of Verbal Learning and Verbal Behavior*, 17: 265–77.

York Papers in Linguistics II (1983), proceedings of the York Creole Conference, University of York.

Yost, W.A. and Nielsen, D.W. (1977), *Fundamentals of Hearing: An Introduction*, New York and London, Holt, Rinehart & Winston.

Young, E.D. and Sachs, M.B. (1979), 'Representation of steady-state vowels in the temporal aspects of the discharge patterns of populations of auditory-nerve fibers', *Journal of the Acoustical Society of America*, 66: 1381–403.

Young, F. (1941), 'An analysis of certain variables in a developmental study of language', *Genetic Psychology Monographs*, 23: 3–141.

Young, R.E., Becker, A.L. and Pike, K.L. (1970), *Rhetoric: Discovery and Change*, New York, Harcourt, Brace & World.

Yule, G. (1985), *The Study of Language: an Introduction*, Cambridge, Cambridge University Press.

Zadeh, L.A. (1975), 'Fuzzy logic and approximate reasoning', *Synthese*, 30(3–4): 407–28.

Zanguill, O.L. (1971), 'The neurology of language', in N. Minnis (ed.), *Linguistics at Large*, London, Victor Gollancz, pp. 209–26.

Zgusta, L. (1967), 'Multiword lexical units', *Word*, 23: 578–87.

Zgusta, L. (1971), *Manual of Lexicography*, Prague and The Hague, Mouton.

Zierer, E. (1977), 'Experiences in the bilingual education of a child of pre-school age', *International Review of Applied Linguistics*, 15: 144–9.

Zimmerman, D. and West, C. (1975), 'Sex roles, interruptions and silences in conversation', in B. Thorne and N. Henley (eds), *Language and Sex: Difference and Dominance*, Rowley, MA, Newbury House, pp. 105–29.

Index

Entries are in letter-by-letter order, in which spaces and hyphens between words are ignored; 'affixes' therefore precedes 'affix-hopping'.